THE SECRET WAR
FOR THE UNION

THE UNTOLD STORY

OF MILITARY INTELLIGENCE

IN THE CIVIL WAR

EDWIN C. FISHEL

HOUGHTON MIFFLIN COMPANY

BOSTON • NEW YORK

1996

For information about permission to reproduce selections from
this book, write to Permissions, Houghton Mifflin Company,
215 Park Avenue South, New York, New York 10003.

For information about this and other Houghton Mifflin trade
and reference books and multimedia products, visit
The Bookstore at Houghton Mifflin on the World Wide Web
at http://www.hmco.com/trade.

Library of Congress Cataloging-in-Publication Data
Fishel, Edwin C.
The secret war for the union : the untold story of
military intelligence in the Civil War / Edwin C. Fishel.
p.   cm.
Includes bibliographical references and index.
ISBN 0-395-74281-1
1. United States — History — Civil War, 1861–1865 —
Military intelligence. 2. Military intelligence — United
States — History — 19th century.   I. Title.
E608.F57   1996   96-12741
973.7'85 — dc 20   CIP

Printed in the United States of America

Book design by Robert Overholtzer

QUM 10 9 8 7 6 5 4 3 2 1

Thanks are due to Kent State University Press for
permission to reprint portions of the author's article
"Pinkerton and McClellan: Who Deceived Whom?"
Civil War History, 1988.

For Gladys, Reverdy, and Katie

Contents

List of Illustrations   ix

List of Maps   xi

Foreword by Stephen W. Sears   xiii

Introduction   1

1. Twenty Thousand Potential Spies   8

2. First Bull Run   29

3. "Known in Richmond in Twenty-Four Hours"   53

4. The Phony War of 1861   77

5. Mr. Pinkerton's Unique Arithmetic   102

6. "Outnumbered" on the Peninsula   130

7. Hard Lessons from Professor Jackson   165

8. Too Little and Too Soon   182

9. All the Plans of the Rebels   211

10. Luck Runs Out for Palmer and Stine   241

11. The Blind Campaign of Fredericksburg   250

12. A New Client for Attorney Sharpe   275

13. Ten Days of Southern Hospitality   298

14. Rebel Spies Are Now Second Best   311

15. The Gray Fox Swallows the Bait   340

16. Pinpoint Intelligence and Hairline Planning   360

17. Paralyzed by a Real Jackson and a Phantom
    Longstreet   387

18. Lee's Army Vanishes   412

19. Pursuit   433

20. Lost Intelligence, Lost Battle   444

21. Joe Hooker's Magnificent Error   454

22. Reaping the Pennsylvania Harvest   484

23. The Thirtieth of June   505

24. Decision and Victory   519

Epilogue   538

Appendixes

1. Successes and Failures of Federal and Confederate Intelligence   563
2. A Few Lessons from (and about) Civil War   569
   Intelligence
3. Two Strategic Surprises   572
4. Rose Greenhow's Reports   575
5. Strother's Rejected Warning of the Enemy's
   Stolen March   579
6. The McClellan-Pinkerton Estimates of Confederate Numbers   581
7. Pleasonton's Role in the Intelligence that
   Started Hooker in Pursuit of Lee   588
8. Lee's Crossing of the Potomac en Route to
   Pennsylvania   593

   Comment on Sources   595
   List of Abbreviations and Short Titles   600
   Notes   602
   Bibliography   690
   Sources and Acknowledgments   700
   Index   702

LIST OF ILLUSTRATIONS

Following page 368

Allan Pinkerton with William Moore, George H. Bangs, John Babcock, and Augustus K. Littlefield. *Miller's Photographic History*
General George B. McClellan. *National Archives*
Colonel Lafayette C. Baker. *National Archives*
Colonel George H. Sharpe, John Babcock, Lieutenant Frederick L. Manning, and Captain John McEntee. *Miller's Photographic History*
General Joseph Hooker. *Miller's Photographic History*
General Daniel Butterfield. *National Archives*
General Marsena R. Patrick. *National Archives*
Captain William J. Palmer. *Military History Institute*
William Wilson. *Miller's Photographic History*
General John Pope. *National Archives*
General Alfred Pleasonton. *National Archives*
David McConaughy. *Author's collection*
Belle Boyd. *National Archives*
Rose Greenhow and her daughter, Rose. *Miller's Photographic History*
Elizabeth Van Lew. *Author's collection*
Colonel Albert J. Myer. *Author's collection*
General George G. Meade. *National Archives*
Butterfield's draft of the hoax message that deceived Lee. *National Archives*
The Federals' intercept of the Confederate decode of the hoax message. *Hooker Papers*
John Babcock's report of the depleted condition of Lee's army at Gettysburg. *National Archives*
The signal officer's oath of secrecy given by Edward Porter Alexander. *Author's collection*
Order-of-battle chart of Lee's army. *Hooker Papers*

LIST OF MAPS

Region of First Bull Run Campaign	30
The Northern Virginia Theater	79
The Peninsula Campaign	145
Shenandoah Valley	166
Region of Second Bull Run Campaign	183
Region of the Antietam Campaign	212
Region of the Fredericksburg Campaign	252
Region of the Chancellorsville Campaign	299
A Section of the Chancellorsville Battlefield	317
Hooker's Advance to Chancellorsville	371
Situation, 5 P.M., May 2, 1863	398
Situation, Afternoon, May 4, 1863	408
Lee's Positions, May 27, 1863	418
Region of Captain McEntee's Operations	422
Situation, Morning of June 13, 1863	441
Ewell's Attack on Winchester	445
Situation, June 20, 1863	469
Ewell's Marches in Maryland and Pennsylvania	474
Lee's Advance into Maryland	476
Situation, P.M., June 24, 1863	482
Lee's Advance into Pennsylvania	485
Situation, P.M., June 28, 1863	500
Situation, Night of June 30, 1863	512
From Gettysburg to Appomattox	539

FOREWORD

BY STEPHEN W. SEARS

IN OCTOBER 1959, at the National Archives in Washington, Edwin C. Fishel made a discovery that was, in the context of Civil War historical research, sensational. In what he has described as "a half-roomful" of miscellaneous records of the Army of the Potomac were bundles of documents he had no idea still existed — the operational files of that army's Bureau of Military Information, arranged with bureaucratic thoroughness and neatly tied with red tapes. They had been undisturbed for nearly a century. Fishel had discovered the first building block for what would be — and is — the first authentic history of military intelligence in the Civil War.

It is truly remarkable that after all these decades, after the publication of more than 50,000 books and pamphlets, there could be a major gap in our knowledge and understanding of the Civil War. Certainly no period in our national history has been so minutely examined as the years 1861 to 1865. Yet until now we have known almost nothing — nothing authentic — of the critically important role of intelligence in Civil War campaigns. *The Secret War for the Union* is a truly groundbreaking story.

To be sure, in the vast Civil War library there is already a shelf devoted to "espionage" or "intelligence" titles. To the serious student of that war it is a sad array, the repository of (in publishing's apt slang) the potboiler. These books are descended from the memoirs of men and women who claimed, not all of them truthfully, to have been spies for the Union or the Confederacy. Later writers have added liberally to the numerous fictions and occasional facts in these books. The literature thus created tells mainly of spies' trials and tribulations; if it touches on the outcome of battles, it vastly exaggerates the spy's contribution and tells nothing that helps us understand the commander's decisions and actions. And it treats espionage as the be-all and end-all of intelligence, ignoring, for example, important information from balloonists and signalmen with their telescopes.

Edwin Fishel went on from that 1959 discovery to find intelligence records in other sources. He cast his net widely. General McClellan's papers, which had been available to researchers for nearly a century, contained, among much else of interest, more than a thousand pages of reports by his intelligence chief, detective Allan Pinkerton — a gold mine untouched by the potboiler writers. The privately held papers of General Hooker, originator of the Bureau of Military Information, yielded a trove of the bureau's reports. These, combined with the reports in the bureau's files, reveal that its officers integrated information from all types of sources — spies, scouts, cavalry, balloonists and Signal Corps observers, and interrogation of prisoners and deserters. This analytic operation is a milestone in the history of United States intelligence.

But putting previously unexploited sources to use does not make a definitive study. That goal required interpretation of the often disparate evidence in these documents, drawing on Fishel's thirty years of experience in the United States intelligence service. Thus we have a fully crafted "intelligence history" of each campaign examined, with intelligence's hits and misses, successes and failures. In these pages, for the first time, are answers to some of the most tantalizing "whys" of the war.

Walt Whitman, fresh from witnessing the effect of the Civil War on Americans of his time, offered an oft-quoted observation that "the real war will never get in the books." *The Secret War for the Union* takes us one very important step closer to that real war.

THE SECRET WAR
FOR THE UNION

INTRODUCTION

IN PRESIDENT LINCOLN'S VIEW, intelligence was the hardest nut to crack in the grand strategy that would defeat the Confederacy. Writing to his western generals early in 1862, Lincoln said that knowledge of enemy movements was "the most constantly present, and most difficult" of the problems to be solved if the Union was to maneuver its forces so that their superior numbers could be brought to bear to offset the Confederates' advantage in having "interior lines," which meant shorter marches to any point of concentration.

But intelligence — the business of acquiring that knowledge — has not been a favorite subject of those who study the Civil War. They find explanations of victory and defeat in the skill of commanders, the fighting qualities of troops, and resources in men and material. This book adds intelligence to those factors; it is the first one to examine at length the effect that information about the enemy had on those marches and battles.

In every case this "intelligence explanation" changes, sometimes radically, the known history of a campaign. For example, the standard depiction of the battle of Gettysburg as the accidental collision of two armies marching half blindly is found to be true only for the Confederates. Their 150-mile march from the Rappahannock River to Pennsylvania was penetrated by soldier-spies whose findings enabled the pursuing Federals to cross the Potomac simultaneously with the main body of the invaders, and unbeknown to them. The Confederates assumed dangerously dispersed positions across south-central Pennsylvania, their movements reported by fourteen locally organized groups of citizen-spies and scouts. Thus General Meade was able to foresee that the enemy would concentrate at or near Gettysburg. His forces seized commanding heights there and surprised the arriving Confederates, who never overcame the Federals' initial advantage of position.

Chancellorsville is another example. General Hooker's fifty-five-mile flank march to the Confederate rear, unopposed and effectively undetected, has been credited to good planning or good luck. Hooker did have an excellent plan — derived from an intelligence coup. A farmer-spy living near Hooker's objective reported a wide gap in the Confeder-ate lines, and a signal deception lured the Southern cavalry out of posi-tion for observing the march.

Not all of these revisions of history have to do with marches and battles. A notable case involves the excessive caution of General McClel-lan, which seriously delayed the prosecution of the war. McClellan's exag-gerated wariness has long been blamed on his being deceived by detec-tive Allan Pinkerton's vastly inflated estimates of Confederate numbers. McClellan was aware of this inflation; the two men had agreed that Pinkerton's estimates would be "made large." But the figures he pro-duced fell short of McClellan's preconceptions; it was the general's even more exaggerated estimates that he reported to Lincoln.

Why has Civil War history neglected a subject so important as intelli-gence? The main reason has been scarcity of documentary sources. The records of the intelligence bureau established by General Hooker, which continued in operation to the end of the war, serving Meade and Grant, were sequestered after the war and turned up somewhat by accident in 1959; this is the first book to avail itself of them. Untying the red tapes that bound the bureau's papers was a step one hesitated to take, lest they be found to consist of financial or other routine administrative papers, a type of record that stands a better chance of survival than "operational" material. But they turned out to consist of the bureau's intelligence reports and raw data that went into them, often including the experi-ences of the spies and scouts. And other bureau reports were found in the papers of General Hooker, one of the many officers from whom the War Department borrowed wartime papers for inclusion in the *Official Records of the War of the Rebellion*. Hooker had withheld nearly all the intelligence items in his possession; again, this is the first book to put these intelligence records to use.

Pinkerton's reports to McClellan, a huge body of intelligence material, have been available in the Library of Congress for a century but have been almost ignored by historians because of their all-trees-and-no-forest writing style, which produced many a twenty-page report of trivia from the interrogation of a refugee or a single enemy soldier. In fact Pinker-ton's wide reputation as the author of strength estimates that damaged the Union's war effort has cast a bad odor over the whole subject of Civil War intelligence.

Some readers will be aware of a subliterature on Federal and Confed-erate spies, consisting of two dozen spy memoirs and modern books descended from them. These writings are so heavily fictionalized that even the most believable parts are suspect. Some of the memoirists were not in intelligence work at all, a fact that modern writers are unaware of or choose to ignore. And even memoirists with experience in espionage, such as Allan Pinkerton, paid almost as little respect to factuality as did the authors of the complete fictions. Another severe shortcoming of these books is their avoidance of the relation, if any, between those alleged secret activities and the campaigns and battles. Still another shortcoming is their ignoring of types of intelligence other than espionage — scouting, cavalry reconnaissance, interrogation, visual observation (from balloons and elevated signal stations), and interception of enemy flag messages. The practitioners of those types, and important spies who left no memoirs, have been fugitives from history.

The campaigns covered here are those in the eastern theater from First Bull Run through Gettysburg. These form a progression in the development of intelligence capability, from an almost total lack of it at Bull Run to high effectiveness two years later in the Pennsylvania campaign. There was no guiding hand at Washington supervising or even keeping in touch with this development. The War Department itself did not have an intelligence unit. Each general in the succession of commanders in these campaigns was left to his own devices in arranging for intelligence. His only source of guidance was his predecessors' mistakes and successes, not all of which he would have known about. The maturing of intelligence capability came about by sheer force of necessity.

Pinkerton's intelligence bureau was the first one in any American army, but it was an incomplete intelligence service. McClellan charged it with performing only two types of intelligence, espionage and interrogation of prisoners, deserters, and refugees. Information from other sources went directly to McClellan, who also had Pinkerton's lengthy reports on his desk and was too busy to assimilate so much material. Even with his organized bureau, he was not as well informed about the enemy as his contemporary General Pope, who acquired intelligence simply by using his cavalry aggressively in reconnaissance and ordering subordinate generals to send out spies, who concentrated on penetrating the enemy army in the field rather than government circles in Richmond, the predominant "target" of Pinkerton's spies.

When Hooker set up his Bureau of Military Information early in 1863, its chief, a young lawyer-colonel named George Sharpe, took over Pinkerton's spying and interrogating functions (improving the performance of both) and merged their information with reports produced by the other types of intelligence activity. Now the army commander had, so far as the sources permitted, a comprehensive picture of the enemy situation. This young bureau, which performed so effectively in the Gettysburg campaign, was a sophisticated "all-source" operation, decades ahead of its time. It ranks alongside the war's well-known innovations, such as the control of distant armies by telegraph and the development of ironclad warships. Hooker and Sharpe would not have been consciously striving for innovation; the arrangements they set up simply came naturally to two intelligent men with a job to do. It is this unguided, almost unconceived development, spanning almost two years of war, that confers a unity on the story of intelligence in these eight eastern campaigns.

This book is not a straight-ahead tale of battles won by good intelligence and lost by wrong intelligence. A simple equation between intelligence success and battlefield success cannot be made. Victory did not always go to the better general, the troops of apparently superior fighting prowess, or the larger force — and it did not always follow from superior intelligence. Hooker's intelligence coup put his army in position to annihilate the enemy force, but it did not save him from battlefield misjudgments that brought defeat. In the Antietam campaign the Federals possessed intelligence — a copy of Lee's "Lost Order" — of an excellence rare in military history. It put McClellan in position to wipe out two or three of the five segments into which Lee's army was divided. But slavish attention to the terms of the order led him to ignore reports of deviations from it; he so maneuvered his army that the Confederates had time to reassemble and gain a drawn battle. And as good intelligence did not insure correct decisions, erroneous intelligence did not necessarily prevent them: the Federals' march that surprised Lee at Gettysburg had its origin in false reports of Confederate positions, spread by the Rebels, which had the unexpected effect of speeding the Federals on their way.

The reader will be introduced here to some unfamiliar types of intelligence. The Signal Corps practiced two of them, observation of the enemy by telescope and interception of enemy flag communications. These were made possible by the signal towers, rooftops, and hilltops that visual communication employed. Observation of enemy movements was so fruitful a source that some stations were established solely for watching the enemy; they were denied the use of their flags, which would betray their location. Interception was feasible in the none too frequent situations when the opposing army was visible in the signalmen's telescopes.

During the period examined here, codes and ciphers were either primitive or nonexistent. Federal commanders did not entrust sensitive messages to the flags except in emergencies. The Federal signalmen had the better of a contest of wits with the opposing Signal Corps: their successful deception of Lee in the Chancellorsville campaign consisted of a message sent in their usual signal alphabet, which they knew the Confederate signalmen could read. They correctly assumed that the enemy did not "know that they knew."

For long-distance communication the armies used commercial telegraph lines, extended as necessary by their own wires, and operated by a civilian telegraph corps. Popular history has it that enemy telegraph lines were frequently tapped by both armies, but the records of the campaigns examined here disclose only one brief tap, by the Confederates, with no indication that it yielded intelligence. Every phase of a tap was a risk — installing an undetectable and electrically successful connection, hiding and feeding the intercept operators, and getting their "take" back to headquarters.

The armies' balloons were another novelty. They were handicapped by fog, wind, and terrain that hid their targets; bulky gas-generating apparatus prevented them from accompanying the army except in the more static situations. With the departure of the Army of the Potomac in June 1863 on the march that terminated at Gettysburg, Civil War ballooning ended. The reason for the commanders' willingness to dispense with it may have been the availability of the Signal Corps observers; they could not see targets as distant as the balloons could, but they were free of logistical problems.

Reconnaissance was the cavalry's first duty, but army commanders sometimes indulged its penchant for raiding and fighting; the cavalry's effectiveness as an intelligence service varied according to its leaders' boldness and the commander's demands. Much scouting was done by individuals and small teams, including a detachment from Sharpe's bureau, whose forays into enemy territory took on the character of espionage, especially when they changed into civilian clothes or the Confederate uniform.

Espionage was not as steady or as big a producer as scouting, but when it had one of its fine hours, either it was an unduplicated source or its findings were superior to those from other sources.

Interrogation produced a volume of reports exceeding that of all other sources together. Deserters were more numerous than prisoners except during battles; they were usually better informed and more willing to talk. Both armies, especially the Confederates, employed pseudo-deserters to plant misinformation on the enemy. Refugees, looking for a welcome, were generous with their talk, but on average they had far less information than soldiers. A special class of refugee was the runaway slave, who might have a headful of information, especially if he had been an officer's servant.

The belief, widely held, that in intelligence and related matters the Rebels ran rings around the Yankees is a product of popular history's romanticizing of cavalier scouts and Southern lady spies. The findings reported in this book enable the intelligence prowess of the two armies at last to be compared on a factual basis. The Federals' intelligence service is found to have been considerably more productive than the Confederates'; in only one sector of the intelligence field, cavalry reconnaissance, did the Confederates outperform their enemy. In espionage the Federals appear to have had a decided edge, largely because of their spies' known successes in mingling with enemy troops in camp and on the march. Lee's surviving references to espionage indicate dissatisfaction with spies' attempts to penetrate Federal lines; when he employed spies it was usually for some specific purpose. The Federal Signal Corps, as already seen, had an upper hand in the game of intercepting flag messages. The Federal balloons had only insignificant competition from a Confederate balloon service that never got beyond its incipiency. All in all, the Federals produced more impressive intelligence successes than their enemy — but they also compiled a more grievous record of intelligence failures.*

Record-keeping was an important part of intelligence operations; beginning with Pinkerton's bureau the Army of the Potomac had detailed records of the composition and organization of the Army of Northern Virginia. Hooker's bureau developed these records to such a high state of usability that they assisted commanders' decision-making on the battlefield. Meanwhile Lee and his staff were unfamiliar with the enemy organization; when a staff officer at the corps level was captured, the element he belonged to could not be correctly placed on their mental enemy-organization chart (apparently they kept no other kind). Lee and his predecessor, Joseph Johnston, did not have even a single staff officer devoted to intelligence work; Stuart was the nearest they had to such a functionary, and he was the full-time commander of their cavalry. Merely by having a competent bureau, Hooker and his successors achieved an intelligence capability well in excess of Johnston's and Lee's.

The effect of intelligence on the decisions of commanding generals — the whole point of this study — is almost never stated for us by the generals or other participants. This avoidance of the intelligence background of their actions evidently was quite deliberate. Their after-action reports are almost devoid of references to the subject; such references would start gossip or leak into the press (many after-action reports were intentionally leaked). When there was overtly obtained intelligence, such as a captured dispatch, a commander could ascribe his action to that source even though he had secret intelligence that was more influential; but opportunities for a persuasive cover story were rare. Generals also tended to steer clear of references to intelligence in their postwar writings. Although the story of Americans' killing of one another could not be avoided, a recital of how they spied on each other would, in those years when the nation's wounds were healing, be unnecessarily painful. Northern commanders also had to keep in mind the inconvenient fact that many of their most important sources of information were people who lived in the South after the war, surrounded by former Confederate patriots.

But this severe shortage of illuminating statements by commanding generals of what they knew about the enemy is not as serious as it seems.

* For details see Appendix 1.

We would suspect any such statement of being self-serving and set about to show how the general's explanation was afflicted with second-guessing, rationalization, and error of memory. Such investigation would mean inquiring into what information was in his hands at each point where he made an important decision. And that is what is done in this book.

This may verge on mind-reading from historical record — doing the commander's thinking for him. History approaches fiction most closely when it presumes to tell what went on in someone's mind — and there is already too much fiction in print about Civil War intelligence. Still, whatever the historiographer may think of this mind-reading, we must either make the best estimate we can of the intelligence motivation of each major decision and action or throw up our hands and ignore such motivation.

Fortunately, in the campaigns treated here the intelligence-decision-action sequence is almost always clear. Thus our inferences at least are safer from error than they might otherwise be. The source notes will enable the validity of this sequence to be tested.

From what is revealed here about Federal commanders' knowledge of the enemy, a reexamination of their exercise of command would seem to be in order. There is a great deal to be done before we can have a really good understanding of how this much-written-about war was fought.

1

·········

TWENTY THOUSAND
POTENTIAL SPIES

January–July 1861

I T WOULD BE DIFFICULT to imagine a nation entering a war more unprepared to obtain information about its enemy than the United States of 1861. In the almost ludicrously small U.S. Army there was no intelligence staff, no corps of spies, trained or otherwise. There was not so much as a concept on which a plan for these services could be based. If, hidden away in some file of regulations, there was even one paragraph for the guidance of a commander with an intelligence problem to solve, it was for all practical purposes unknown in 1861, and its obscurity was preserved throughout the war.[1]

There was not even an official name for such activities. The word *intelligence* meant new information on any subject. Its nearest equivalent in the military lexicon of the 1860s was "secret service" — without initial capitals. However, "secret service" referred not only to the work now known as intelligence but often to nonmilitary detective work as well. And though it denoted this group of activities, it did not refer to any organization that conducted them, for there was none; the national Secret Service that has often been mentioned and even depicted by Civil War historians did not exist, from the beginning of the war to its end.

Yet there were reasons why the nation might have had a strong "secret service." Espionage directed by George Washington — who used the term *intelligence* in its modern military sense — had made a definite contribution to the winning of the Revolutionary War. So there might well have been a tradition of activity and adeptness in intelligence work strong enough to last until the next great test of national strength eighty-five years later. But it was forgotten by the time of the second war with Britain in 1812; then there was a total lack of organized intelligence work, with results such as the loss of Detroit and Washington, when British deception persuaded the Americans that they were outnumbered. In the Mexican War army engineers were drawn into the intelligence business as investigators of terrain features and the enemy's man-made defenses; Captain Robert E. Lee and Second Lieutenant George B. McClellan, engineer officers and future commanders of opposing armies, distinguished themselves as providers of intelligence. For coverage outside the engineers' reach, their commander, General Winfield Scott, had a company of Mexican banditti. The association of engineers with intelligence work was becoming a tradition, but it was an activity without a name or an identity.

European military writers, whom American officers could quote from memory, had strongly, almost vehemently, urged the importance of having good information about the enemy. Hundreds of the nation's career officers knew the dictum of Frederick the Great: "It is pardonable to be defeated, but not to be taken by surprise." Equally familiar was Marshal Saxe's injunction that "too much attention cannot be given to spies and guides. . . . they are as necessary to a general as the eyes are to the head"; and Jomini's question, "How can any man decide what he should do himself if he is ignorant of what his enemy is about?"[2]

Evidently the Europeans' urgings on the importance of intelligence were regarded as precepts to be taken into account only when the nation would go to war. But the neglect of the example set by General Washington is less easy to explain away. It is true that the records of his espionage service lay buried until the twentieth century, and that without history tradition has a hard existence. Yet the seeds of a strong intelligence organization had been planted in the nation's first army. That they withered away probably was due to the nation's isolation; a healthy wariness of foreign powers was lacking.

But the absence of intelligence organization or activity is no more strange than half a dozen other lacks that plagued the 1861 army. Although good weapons had been invented and were available, nearly all of those in use were badly antiquated. There was a dearth of officers trained in the higher arts of generalship; the septuagenarian Generals Winfield Scott and John E. Wool had commanded forces that were called armies in earlier wars but would not be large enough to merit the term in the 1860s. Younger officers' command experience was almost altogether limited to the companies, battalions, and regiments that had served on the western plains and the Pacific coast. The only way to acquaint these officers with the management of large forces was to send them to European armies as observers, and very few had that experience.

If some officers with ideas ahead of their time had set about to found an intelligence organization, the approaching division of the nation into warring halves would have stood in their way. Conducting, or even planning, espionage against foreign powers would have seemed a waste of money, when the only war likely to occur was an internal one. With all of the top positions in the army held by Southern officers, it would have been impossible to limit such preparations to officers certain to remain with the North when war came. And other factors discouraged intelligence planning. Overt sources of information — prisoners, deserters, refugees, enemy pickets — required only the application of interrogating skills. Cavalry reconnaissance, certain to be a major source, was already practiced against hostile Indians. Captured documents could be counted on as a source in any war that should develop, but how could a planning or training officer prepare for that? Enemy newspapers would be useful; they would be acquired as part of the contraband commerce that develops in a war.

Definite opportunities for intelligence planning were offered by two technological advances of recent times. Balloon reconnaissance was adopted early in the war, but only at the initiative of the balloonists. The other new technique was visual signaling by flag and torch; invented by Major Albert Myer, an army surgeon, in the late 1850s, it was the world's first successful system of alphabetic communication in forward areas. The inventor's assistants in his experiments were Southern officers; the certainty that the system would be adopted in the Confederate army at least meant that the Federals would have opportunities to intercept enemy signals. But on the Federal side the system was so poorly provided for in personnel and equipment that it was not available for battle when the war broke out. (The Confederates made decisive use of it at Bull Run while its inventor stood empty-handed on the same field.) The Federals, unable even to operate their own communication system, made no plans for the interception of the enemy's signals. Eventually intercept operations arose spontaneously when signal officers found enemy flag stations within view of their telescopes.

.. .. ..

When the war began, Winfield Scott, weighted down with years and obesity, a victim of dropsy and vertigo, had been head of the army for two decades. The old hero, a Virginian, had surrounded himself mainly with Southern officers. When he saw war coming and set about to equip himself with a "secret service," its operations had to be kept secret from the officers closest to him. The sharp-bearded quartermaster general, Joseph E. Johnston, would soon cast his fortunes with the South. Army routine called for him to pay spies along with all other civilian employees; instead Scott handled the funds for espionage himself. Adjutant General Samuel Cooper, though a Northerner, was Southern in his sympathies and also would soon join the Confederacy; his office, normally the army's information center, had to be short-circuited by Scott. So intimate a subordinate as the general-in-chief's military secretary was another who would soon go South. And the old general's son-in-law, Henry L. Scott, also an army officer, was believed in military circles to have been banished to Europe because of pro-Southern activities. Although the story qualifies as only an unproven rumor, it is an excellent example of the climate of suspicion that the country's troubles engendered. It was emphatically branded as a slander on Colonel Scott when General George McClellan denied having been the source of the report that the colonel had betrayed military documents to the enemy; he took occasion to label the story a slander. Even Attorney General Edwin M. Stanton, later Lincoln's secretary of war, had security problems; his office was so riddled with Southern sympathizers that he had to walk to its entryway to have a confidential conversation with a Republican senator.[3] Stanton, a newcomer to President Buchanan's cabinet, considered his position a vantage point for keeping an eye on Southern influence in the administration.

At this stage of oncoming war the government was standing by like a fond father while the professional soldiers chose up sides in the manner of boys organizing a baseball game. Its leniency extended to members of the diplomatic service and to career civilians in the military departments. Some who went South helped themselves to military documents before leaving.[4] And some obtained clerkships in Richmond. The situation offered the Federals an opening to plant their own men as spies in the Confederate bureaucracy, but this opportunity is not known to have been seized — though John B. Jones, writer of the well-known *Rebel War Clerk's Diary,* had "no doubt that there are many Federal spies in the departments. Too many clerks were imported from Washington."[5]

The story of one of the "secession clerks" shows the seemingly hopeless problem of preserving military secrets at that time. His name was John F. Callan, and he held at different times two important clerkships, one in the adjutant general's office and the other on Capitol Hill, where he served the Military Committee of the Senate. He owed his committee position, which dated from 1852, to Jefferson Davis, then a United States senator from Mississippi. Davis, later secretary of war, had something to do with the other appointment as well. On February 21, 1861, three days after his inauguration as president of the Confederate States, Davis began a telegraphic campaign to bring Callan to Montgomery as chief clerk of his new War Department. Callan kept Davis on the string for two months — until after the war began — before declining on the ground of family illness.[6] Neither the offer nor its final outcome need raise eyebrows, but the same cannot be said of the Confederate leaders' cheek in addressing their telegrams to Callan at the United States War Department. Equally conspicuous, or equally puzzling, is the generosity of Callan's Washington employers in retaining him in at least one if not both of his positions of high trust.

Since the telegraph wires were open to sedition, they were certain to be used by authorities of much greater puissance than John Callan. The capital harbored congressmen and even cabinet members who worked earnestly for the new nation forming in the South. By now the Confederate States of America had become a growing concern, and Southern elements in Washington had far less legitimacy in being there. One object that kept them hanging about was information on the doings of the Northern government; another was military recruitment. The channels of communication remained open regardless of how inimical to Northern interests was the content of what passed over them.

..   ..   ..

Lieutenant Colonel Robert E. Lee, on duty in Texas, was a special problem of divided loyalties. He was the favorite of both General Scott and the administration to take command of Northern armies in the field and eventually succeed Scott as general-in-chief. Such was the offer made to him in April, when he was home on leave at Arlington; he understood that it originated with the President. His answer was to resign his commission and offer his services to his beloved Virginia, which by now had joined the Confederacy. Before reaching this decision Lee had a three-hour talk with Scott in which the old generalissimo faced the problem of exercising persuasion on the younger man without confiding any "intelligence" secrets whose disclosure he would regret if Lee joined the Confederates.[7] In this interview the awkwardness of handling military secrets in the situation of divided loyalties reached its peak.

..   ..   ..

When in the closing days of 1860 President Buchanan finally obtained the resignation of his secessionist secretary of war, John B. Floyd, and Postmaster General Joseph Holt, a Unionist, moved over to take charge of the War Department, affairs were in a state of crisis because of events in Charleston Harbor. Major Robert Anderson had moved the tiny garrison of the defenseless Fort Moultrie into Fort Sumter, which was unfinished but incomparably more secure. The secessionist reaction in Washington was about as violent as in Charleston itself. Texas Senator Louis T. Wigfall on January 2 telegraphed the commander of the military forces of the now sovereign State of South Carolina: "Holt succeeds Floyd. It means war. Cut off supplies from Anderson and take Sumter soon as possible."[8] Wigfall proceeded later on to telegraph word — not very accurate — of plans for the provisioning and reinforcement of Fort Sumter.

Only 300 or 400 Marines and a small company of army ordnance men stationed at the Washington Arsenal stood in the way of an armed coup by the Southern element. Unionist leaders in the cabinet and Congress — such men as Attorney General Stanton, Secretary of War Holt, Senator William H. Seward — strongly believed that such a coup was in the making. Situated between two slave states, Washington was a Southern city in most ways. Its mayor and chief of police were secessionists; the part-time general who headed its militia organization was a Virginian, and the political complexion of his troops was uncertain.

Clearly the protection of the government rested with the army, and its Virginia-born general-in-chief moved quietly but effectively. His first step was to take army headquarters back to Washington from New York, where it had been for some years; Winfield Scott, the personification of the U.S. Army, had preferred to live at some distance from Jefferson Davis, secretary of war at the time Scott made the move. Upon returning to the capital he found President Buchanan fearful of inflaming Southern sentiment if he brought in more uniformed men. But Scott, declaring that he could not guarantee the safety of the capital for more than five days, reached out and moved in eight companies from widely scattered posts. He also asked for the loan of as many Marines as their commandant could spare.

The President's expectations in regard to Southern feeling proved correct; on February 11 the House of Representatives passed a resolution asking him to explain "the reasons that had induced him to assemble so large a number of troops in this city, . . . and whether he has any information of a conspiracy . . . to seize upon the capital and prevent the inauguration of the President-elect." Secretary Holt responded with a report assuring Buchanan that he believed such a conspiracy had been "in process of formation, if not fully matured," and that the presence of the troops caused it to be "suspended, if not altogether abandoned." But for this timely precaution, said Holt, the capital would have met the fate of the forts and arsenals in the South; it would be in the hands of "revolutionists, who have found this great Government weak only because, in the exhaustless beneficence of its spirit, it has refused to strike, even in its own defense, lest it should be the aggressor." Buchanan did not forward this impassioned communication to the House; presumably he considered their resolutions an impertinence.

For the task of dealing with the possible disloyalty in the local militia, Scott chose Charles P. Stone, an ex-officer of the army in his late thirties. Stone, a native of Massachusetts, had been out of the service for four years engaging in business in Mexico and the West. Now in Washington, he had been studying the sentiment of its people; when he made a courtesy call on Scott, the general asked his opinion on that subject. The younger man replied, "Two-thirds of the fighting-stock of this population would sustain the Government in defending itself." Scott announced, "These people have no rallying-point. Make yourself that rallying-point!" The next day Stone found himself a colonel and the inspector general of the District of Columbia.

Stone's estimate that two-thirds of Washington's 61,000 white citizens were pro-Union was comforting; still it meant that the government would have to worry about policing 20,000 people who would be glad to send the Confederacy information they might acquire by such easy means as observing new troops detraining or construction crews working on fortifications — or by deliberate spying. The loyalty of the local militia was the most critical problem, but at least it was identifiable and fairly manageable. There were four old-line militia units; a new one was forming. The captain commanding one company had stated its mission thus: to ". . . help to keep the Yankees from coming down to coerce the South." Whether Stone knew of this declaration is not certain, but he did find enough evidence of disloyalty to place detectives in that company and one other. They uncovered unmistakable secessionist connections; Stone came to believe there was a plot that extended to "seizing the public departments at the proper moment and obtaining possession of the seals of the Government." Against some reluctance on the part of Buchanan he organized and armed sixteen new companies; without these, Stone was convinced, "Mr. Lincoln would never have been inaugurated."[9]

It was in this atmosphere that Abraham Lincoln made his covert arrival at the capital. On his roundabout trip from Springfield he was scheduled to change trains in Baltimore, traveling a mile of downtown streets between the two railroad stations. Hearing rumors of assassination plots in Baltimore, Colonel Stone arranged for detectives to investigate; they confirmed the suspicion. Lincoln's friends also had employed detectives, who came to the same finding. Reluctantly Lincoln changed his rail route and timetable, passing through Baltimore incognito in the dead of night. He arrived at the Washington depot ahead of schedule, to be greeted only by one early-rising Illinois congressman. He regretted his furtive entry ever afterward, and scholars to this day disagree as to whether there was any real danger. But it is worth noting that the plot was reported by two different groups of detectives who were not only working independently but presumably were unaware of each other's presence in Baltimore. Even with allowance for an overly suspicious attitude on their part, the choice Lincoln made would have been immensely hard to reject.

Lincoln's tiny escort on the trip across Maryland included Allan Pinkerton, the Chicago detective-agency chief who had headed one of the Baltimore investigations. This was Pinkerton's introduction to a year and a half of "secret service."[10]

Public anxiety for the safety of the government focused not only on the approaching inauguration on March 4 but also on the Electoral College balloting on February 13. If the electors could be prevented from meeting, Lincoln's election would never become official. A visitor who voiced this fear to General Scott heard this choice bit of three-star rhetoric: "I have said that any man who attempted by force or unparliamentary disorder to obstruct or interfere with the lawful count of the electoral vote should be lashed to the muzzle of a twelve-pounder gun and fired out of a window of the Capitol. I would manure the hills of Arlington with fragments of his body, were he a Senator or a chief magistrate of my native state! It is my duty to suppress insurrection — *my duty!*"[11] Scott would have been offended if his auditor had interpreted this hyperbole as an attempt at humor.

An investigation paralleling Scott's and Stone's, aimed at discovering subversion within the government and in the city, was launched by a House of Representatives committee at the urging of Attorney General Stanton. On the day the Electoral College met, Washington was under arms, with soldiers and Marines on duty not only at the Capitol but at the White House, Treasury, General Post Office, Patent Office, and all the bridges. The precautions were not in vain, for an unorganized crowd did gather, though harmlessly, from within the city and from Virginia and Maryland. "Under the frowning gaze of artillery" the election of Lincoln was announced by one of the men he had outpolled in November — Vice President John C. Breckinridge, a future Confederate general and secretary of war.

Next day the congressional investigating committee reported finding no direct evidence of any organized effort to overthrow the government. Security measures for the inauguration went forward anyway. In the inaugural parade the presidential carriage had an escort of District of Columbia cavalry and infantry, with a regular Sappers and Miners company marching in front. As protection against snipers, riflemen were stationed atop houses along the parade route and in windows of the Capitol. Regular cavalry guarded the intersections of the side streets with Pennsylvania Avenue, and the inauguration site at the east front of the Capitol was under the protection of District of Columbia riflemen and a battery of horse artillery. One of Stone's detectives reported a plot to blow up the inaugural platform at the moment Lincoln took the oath of office; so the structure was guarded by a whole battalion of militia. Policemen in plain clothes mixed with the crowd. General Scott, although too infirm to mount a horse, and himself under threat of assassination, watched over the proceedings from his carriage. Lincoln was inaugurated without incident.[12]

· · ·· ··

South Carolina's secession in December, together with the presence of a Federal garrison in Charleston Harbor, created a situation capable of exploding into open hostilities. But the Federal government appears to have made no effort to find out by clandestine means what the Southerners were planning to do. Once the Carolinians had trained batteries on Fort Sumter from points three-quarters of the way around the compass, the position of Major Robert Anderson's little company would be hopeless whenever the Southerners chose to make it so. Reinforcing or simply reprovisioning the fort was considered for many weeks, both before and after the change of administration. Finally Lincoln came to realize, from unofficial reports as well as those of emissaries he sent to Anderson, that feeling in Charleston was too hot for even a supply ship to reach Sumter without drawing a barrage that would start a war.

Lincoln's information was obtained by these open dealings, but the blow that the Confederates finally struck was the result of their inability to content themselves with information openly acquired. After permitting mail to go in and out of the fort for many weeks, General P. G. T. Beauregard and Governor Francis Pickens, chief of state of the "Palmetto Republic," decided to put an end to this generosity. On April 8 they informed Anderson of this decision, at the same time opening a letter from him to the War Department. They were rewarded by the sight of three long paragraphs referring to a relief expedition that Anderson evidently was still expecting. The proposed help was to consist only of supplies, but the letter did not make that fact evident, and the Southern leaders would not have believed such a statement if it had been expressly made. They knew that Anderson's food was almost gone, and he formally stated to them that he intended to evacuate the fort on April 15 if not resupplied. But they feared that the expedition would arrive while he parleyed with them. So, at 4:30 A.M. on the 12th, they opened fire.[13]

Two days later the South had Fort Sumter and the North had a cause to fight for. In the long-drawn-out Sumter affair the Confederates held an "intelligence advantage," but the key piece of information, the intercepted letter, led them into a fateful miscalculation. For if Anderson had surrendered without firing a shot as he had planned, it would have had much less impact on Northern emotions than Beauregard's attack produced.

Fort Pickens in Florida, another bastion along the Southern coast that the Federals retained, was a different story. Although situated on Santa Rosa Island at a point that commanded the entrance to Pensacola Harbor and Navy Yard, it, unlike Fort Sumter, was not made a symbol of Federal "intrusion." Even the irresolute President Buchanan permitted its reinforcement — which, however, brought its strength only to two companies.

Florida authorities began putting pressure on the fort's commander, Lieutenant Adam J. Slemmer, even before the state seceded on January 10. He refused to surrender although he remained vulnerable to attack; the fort was anything but impregnable, and heavy Rebel forces glowered at him from across the bay. They never attacked, and Slemmer credited their failure to information supplied by a spy who was working for him on the mainland. His agent was Richard Wilcox, a watchman at the Navy Yard, who remained there after it was surrendered to the Confederates. Through Wilcox's reports, Slemmer wrote, he was "enabled to prevent the attacks on the fort designed by the rebels, and thus defeat their plans." Since the maneuverability of Slemmer's force was precisely zero, we may question how, even with perfect intelligence, he could have prevented an enemy attempt against his fort. But his statement, unelaborated as above, was accepted by so skeptical — and tight-fisted — an authority as Secretary of War Stanton when Wilcox sought $500 pay for his espionage services eighteen months later.[14]

The defenders of Fort Pickens were also blessed, or afflicted, with the services of a free-lance spy named Joseph O. Kerbey, a Pennsylvania telegrapher. Kerbey, a short, gray-eyed blond youth of nineteen, was having himself an adventure in Secessia, traveling about eavesdropping on conversations of Southerners and mailing reports of them North, sometimes to newspapers and sometimes to Washington authorities. Hearing of the expected excitement at Pensacola, he boarded a steamer for that place. Disguised as a fisherman, he got himself over to Fort Pickens, bearing, according to his own story, valuable information on Confederate plans against the fort. A letter that he tore up and cast into a spittoon was pieced together and proved to contain secessionist sentiments. They probably were no more than a part of the espionage game Kerbey fancied he was playing. Nevertheless, at the first opportunity he was put aboard a navy sloop and sent North.

Kerbey was not to be put down by one defeat. He continued his unwanted spying service for another sixteen months at various places before a short tour of duty in Old Capitol Prison at Washington persuaded him of the error of his unorthodoxy.[15] Fort Pickens, having survived the aid and succor provided by Kerbey, was amply reinforced in mid-April. Slemmer and his exhausted, underfed men were sent North, and the Union navy's blockading squadron took the fort under its wing. Eventually the Confederate forces abandoned the area. The fort that bore the same name as the head of the Palmetto Republic remained an island of Union might to the end of the war.[16]

· ·   · ·   · ·

For a week toward the end of April Washington itself was scarcely more able than Fort Pickens to communicate with the outside world. While recruits answering Lincoln's call for 75,000 men overwhelmed the states' facilities for inducting and organizing them, the capital of the nation stood alone and almost naked, cut off from the populace that was rising to support it. The handful of militia and regulars who had sustained the administration began to look pathetic when matched against the forces collecting in northern Virginia, some of them annoyingly close to the banks of the Potomac.

And when Lincoln's 75,000 began arriving, their movement through Maryland increased the isolation of the capital by inflaming the secessionist element of Baltimore to the point of bloody riot. The first reinforcement of regimental strength, the 6th Massachusetts Infantry, was attacked by an armed mob while changing trains in Baltimore on April 19. Brigadier General Benjamin F. Butler then avoided Baltimore by taking the rest of his command by ferryboat via Chesapeake Bay to Annapolis, which had a rail connection with Washington, thus establishing the route used by other arriving regiments until arrangements were made for safe passage through Baltimore. The rail route from Ohio and the West passed south of Baltimore, but it was now blocked by Virginia troops occupying Harper's Ferry. Even though Maryland Governor Thomas H. Hicks was pro-Union, Lincoln had to exercise considerable cajolery to persuade him and the officialdom of Baltimore that Washington could not be defended unless Federal soldiers were allowed to transit their territory.

One of the precautions the Maryland authorities took was to burn the bridges on the two railroads leading into Baltimore from the North. For reasons hard to perceive they also severed on April 21 the telegraph lines to the North, which carried all of Washington's telegraph traffic except purely local messages. Washington's line to Richmond, in enemy territory, was in working order but carrying no telegrams, while for a full week northbound traffic could travel only as far as Baltimore.

The War Department had installed a censor in the Washington telegraph office on April 19, fearing that the rioting in Baltimore was part of a plot. The censor inspected all incoming and outgoing telegrams and prohibited the operators from replying to conversational questions asked by their brethren in Richmond. He was not intelligence-minded enough to exploit the chattiness of telegraph operators to find out what was going on in Richmond. The Washington-Richmond wire was not severed until May 21 or 22, and then the action was taken not by the government but by the American Telegraph Company, whose officers held a conference on the Long Bridge leading from Washington into Virginia.[17]

On April 22, the first full day of the telegraphic outage, J. Henry Puleston, a reporter for the *Philadelphia North American,* was sent north from Washington with an accumulation of General Scott's unsent dispatches. Beyond Baltimore he had to go by carriage, paying fifty dollars to travel the forty-five miles to York, Pennsylvania. Among others who served Scott as couriers at this time were D. F. Williams and Charles Leib; they also performed secret-service work at the points they visited. A system of couriers was also worked out by the Washington correspondents of distant newspapers.[18]

The telegraphic hiatus was perhaps the most dangerous aspect of the government's weakness. It prevented Washington from exercising control over the meager forces that represented the national authority at distant points. The most seriously threatened of these was St. Louis, where another tiny detachment of regular troops, manning a United States arsenal, was surrounded by a small army of insurgent militiamen and hamstrung by a secession-minded United States Army general and an actively hostile state government. The Unionist element, led by Congressman Francis P. Blair, Jr., brother of Lincoln's postmaster general, set up a telegraph office across the Mississippi in East St. Louis because of the suspected disloyalty of operators in the St. Louis office. From their improvised telegraph station on the morning of April 21, Blair sent a warning that the insurgents were threatening to seize the arsenal and that General William S. Harney was refusing to allow Union volunteer regiments to receive arms or even to occupy the arsenal grounds.

The telegraph could not get this alarming news to Washington; it was held up at Harrisburg and Philadelphia. Into the breach stepped a regular-army officer, Major Fitz John Porter, who had just arrived at Harrisburg to hurry the mustering of volunteers and assist Pennsylvania authorities in protecting the railroads. Porter carried authority to use the names of Scott and Secretary of War Simon Cameron in these matters, but he was to be held responsible for his acts. Certainly his instructions did not contemplate his dealing with matters that did not directly concern Pennsylvania. But when Governor Andrew Curtin handed him the urgent message from Blair, Porter at once telegraphed orders in the name of General Scott instructing General Harney that Captain Nathaniel Lyon, a loyal officer in command of the arsenal, was to muster in and arm the 3500 Unionist volunteers and "use them for the protection of public property." Messages with the same import went from Porter to Lyon, Blair, and Harney's adjutant. The telegrams showed Harrisburg rather than Washington as their point of origin, but if that raised doubts as to Porter's authority, they did not prevent execution of the orders he gave. As for General Harney, he may never have learned that his pro-secession policy had been undercut by a major whose real authority, put to a legal test, would have been found to consist of the possession of a pen and a pad of telegram blanks.

Porter, whose boldness had achieved this bloodless rescue, became a general and months later himself fell under suspicion of disloyalty, not to his flag but to his commanding officer. A similar and even more lamentable fate met another officer with a record of bold action in the secession crisis — Colonel Stone. Their stories, which form two of the grimmest chapters in the history of the war, belong to later parts of this narrative.

St. Louis was the locale of probably the most elaborate and successful intelligence activity that the Union forces were able to set up outside Washington in those early weeks. The account of a one-man feat by Captain Lyon has hitherto dominated the history of this espionage. He is supposed to have toured the camps of the hostile militia disguised as a farm woman and wearing a veil, driving a horse and wagon and selling eggs. The story is implausible; such a mission by the commanding officer — Harney was removed and Captain Lyon became a brigadier general in one jump — was not very necessary anyway, for there is on record the performance of an unidentified spy who was covering a wide range of insurgent activities in and about the city. This man's secessionist contacts were as good as his literacy was poor. But lack of education was scarcely a handicap to the spy who could report:

> I have sean a consderabel nomber of Riffels at the [city] pollice offis standing in the back or rear of the large room thay are new I cannot tell wether thay ar U.S. or not one of the men told me that that was not all but that 700 more ware in the house there is a brass Cannon in the Cellar the Pollice are drill at loding and firing at least I saw them at it this morning. . . . 918 men all told at Camp Jackson, Davis of the [St. Louis] Democrat maid them 895. . . . thay have applied to the oald man [General Harney?] to fill hand grenauds for them

This agent uncovered several other secret armament projects about the city, pinpointed a huge shipment of powder to New Orleans, and identified Rebel spies who were moving among the Union camps. He was working for the Committee of Safety, a small group of Union men that included Congressman Blair. Approaching Federal authorities through Attorney General Edward Bates, a Missourian, the committee soon was receiving financial aid from the War Department despite its unofficial character.[19]

Blair felt a responsibility for the security of more than his city and state. With the approval of Secretary Cameron he employed a professional detective, Charles Noyes, and sent him to Utah "to watch the movements of United States officers in command" in that region. On Noyes's return from his expedition he remained in the secret service. Although old plainsmen who had scouted for the army in past years were available for such duty in the territories, they do not seem to have been used until later in the year. And when local talent was put to use the result was not always favorable. A company of twenty-four spies and guides was organized in New Mexico in August; six months later its captain, John G. Phillips, turned up as commanding officer of Confederate forces at Santa Fe. Indian scouts, available in profusion, were employed, among them Captain Fall Leaf, Ocque McMund, Flat Foot, General Jackson, Medicine

Armstrong, and Charles Youmeycake. They generally did their scouting in company with their sons, brothers, and cousins, with wives and daughters tagging close behind. Since their families found a home in the army, they were as much a headache to the quartermasters as a boon to the information service.

Compensation for spies was a major difficulty. The military forces gathering in Missouri found a successful agent in one J. L. Herzinger but could not pay him, so he was allowed to set up a mercantile sideline, selling sutler's goods and soft drinks to the troops. But Herzinger, the "Cherry Bounce Man," was soon indicted by civil authorities for selling without a license and was lost to the secret service.[20]

..   ..   ..

On April 18 Colonel Joseph K. F. Mansfield, a regular officer with nearly forty years' service behind him, assumed command of the newly organized Department of Washington, and with it much of the burden of directing espionage at the capital. Mansfield, soon made a brigadier general, put the secret-service business in the hands of William C. Parsons, a lawyer who had served in one of the local militia companies and was, like Mansfield, a native of Connecticut. From his law office Parsons directed a group of agents, all unpaid informers except one. Lawyerlike, he required them to put their reports in writing. He also employed a topographer and a varying number of clerks. Even the country about the capital was indifferently mapped; considerable effort was expended before the author of a published map was identified and his supply tapped.

For a few weeks the enemy forces to be reported on were close at hand: at Chain Bridge, which crossed the Potomac three miles above the city, and at Alexandria, eight miles downstream. Nevertheless, most of the work that came Parsons's way had to do with local security and counterespionage rather than information on the nearby enemy. His agents chased down arms concealed by secessionists in the vicinity of the capital. They investigated reports of "secession telegraphing by means of signal lights at night" — a communication system of improbable workability. Parsons himself was required to certify to the trustworthiness of anyone allowed to pass into Virginia. When he fell seriously ill in August his little group was disbanded; Allan Pinkerton was already setting up shop as the head of the principal secret-service activity in the capital. Parsons's connection with intelligence ceased, and he was paid off in November. Mansfield deducted a substantial amount from his bill, informing the War Department that Parsons "works for the cause & I doubt not will receive the amount I award without a word." But the authorities, displaying an uncommon generosity, gave him the full amount he claimed.

Only the informal nature and very short life of Parsons's group denies it the acclaim bestowed on Pinkerton's unit as the nation's first organized intelligence bureau. Later successes of intelligence chiefs drawn from the legal profession, as recently as the Second World War, and the short-comings of one with a detective background, that is, Pinkerton, tempt speculation as to how the course of the Civil War might have been affected if Parsons's little organization had survived beyond the embry-onic stage.

Mansfield also employed as a spy another Washingtonian, Abel Hun-tingdon Lee. Lee was active in uncovering routes of communication used by the insurgents between Washington and Virginia via the Potomac and the lower counties of Maryland. His employment antedated that of Par-sons; he may have been the unnamed paid agent in Parsons's organiza-tion. Late in July he went to work at the Navy Yard as a painter. This may have been a cover for his secret-service activities, but more probably he took the job because of the chronic shortage of funds for paying secret agents. In any case Lee continued his visits to the lower Potomac region and suffered the unusual experience of being arrested by the Confeder-ates in Maryland — Union territory. They took him across the river to Virginia and jailed him for sixteen months. "After returning home," Lee's wife informed the War Department, "he met with an injury which his shattered constitution could not sustain," and he died.[21]

Lower Maryland was also under the observation of an agent in the pay of Governor Hicks. He was George W. Howard, Jr., who according to Hicks was "the only man I have been able to engage that I had con-fidence in." Months later, when the governor's funds ran out, he recom-mended Howard to Secretary Cameron: "Mr. H. is perfectly reliable, and being a Democrat originally, now a good and loyal Union man, tho passing as a secessionist mixes with the Rebels' freely without suspicion, being a native of St. Marys [County]. He was an officer to the present miserable House of Delegates for Maryland."

Howard's position in the House had been abolished because the mem-bers did not like his Unionist politics. It is a mystery how he could have circulated freely among secessionists in much of Maryland while his Union sympathies were well known in Annapolis. Nevertheless Howard, who had begun spying in March, was credited by General Nathaniel P. Banks, commanding at Frederick, with having rendered "services that were of great value in breaking up the traffic with Virginia . . . and in detecting the passage of armed men to Va." He continued active through the early months of the Pinkerton period, entering the Rebel lines at Fredericksburg for General McClellan, Pinkerton's chief. Although he was more exposed to capture than the unfortunate Abel Lee, Howard escaped, but narrowly. When Stonewall Jackson drove Banks out of Win-chester in May 1862 he captured a trunk belonging to Banks that contained his correspondence with Howard. Word that the Confederates knew of Howard's activities leaked back to Baltimore, where it was picked up by Federal detectives in time to save him from capture. But his career as a spy was over.[22]

The upper Potomac presented a different sort of problem from the region where Lee and Howard were working. The river, relatively narrow there and fordable in many places, was no great barrier to organized bodies of troops. Spies who covered it would be looking for military activity as well as for contraband traffic and disloyal citizens. A large force of Virginia state troops began gathering at Harper's Ferry late in April. In May and June a New Yorker named Kirk R. Mason, acting under General Mansfield's orders, made three trips to investigate affairs at the Ferry. On his first attempt, about May 9, he entered the town with no difficulty but found himself hard put to get back out. The Confederates suspected his purpose and jailed him for several days; they failed, however, to obtain either a confession from him or evidence against him. Released, he departed on foot and boarded a Washington-bound train several miles away. The Confederates, having thought better of their leniency, boarded the same train in Maryland — another invasion of Union territory — and searched it. Mason wrote that "By a change of appearance, caused by shaving off my whiskers &c, which I had prudently adopted, I fortunately escaped identification and arrest."

Mason's is the earliest known purely military espionage mission in what was already becoming the main theater of the war in the East. The importance that was attached to his findings at the time is indicated by the fact that he delivered them personally to Secretary Cameron and the President. But the only report of his service that has come to light, written in December 1861 to support a claim for reimbursement, does not permit us to assess the accuracy of his findings. It states that he reported:

> (1st) The Evidences of Treason I discovered at Frederick, Maryland: (2) The number and position of the batteries established by the Enemy, both on the Maryland and Virginia side of the Potomac at and near Harper's Ferry, — and the range and strength (number and Calibre of the guns) of the said Batteries: (3) The Efforts making by the Enemy to obstruct the Rail Road & the passage of troops, on the Maryland side . . . (4) the Number of Cavalry under the command of Capt. Ashby: (5) The Extent of the Rebel pickets as then Established: (6) The Number and position of the Infantry and horse Artillery of the Rebels, and the States from which the different Regiments came: (7) The Preparations made by the Rebels to blow-up and destroy the R. R. Bridge across the Potomac at Harper's Ferry: (8) The state of the Fortifications on the Maryland heights [across the river from the Ferry], and the Number of Troops stationed there, — also the number and size of the cannon, &c. &c.

After a time spent touring the enemy positions at Arlington Heights and Alexandria and mounting counterespionage efforts about the capital, Mason was ordered back to Harper's Ferry. This visit he made prudently brief, starting back at midnight the same night he arrived. Coming suddenly upon two Confederate horsemen, he drew on the time-worn ruse of asking them for their countersign. His boldness paid well, for they gave it without asking for one in return. He had occasion to use it upon encountering more pickets farther on. On a third trip he did not even venture into Harper's Ferry, stationing himself at Knoxville, very near the Ferry but safely on the Maryland side of the Potomac.

Again only Mason's December statement of his findings is available. In this document he said that on his second trip to Harper's Ferry he discovered and reported that the Confederates were falling back to Winchester. They did not make that move until June 15, more than three weeks after the time given by Mason, so his discovery of it probably came on his later trip, to Knoxville. As this statement was made under oath and addressed to officials who had the means of knowing the facts, it is probable that this was an innocent error.

In thus being absolved of lying, however, Mason falls under a different charge, and one that suggests that he was a mediocre spy: evidently he had a poor memory, being unable at the time of his December statement to distinguish between his three trips, on the last of which he made a major finding. And his subsequent history indicates that his performance may have been considered deficient, for he seems to have been given little to do for a few weeks and then to have been dropped. Like many agents of the period, when he ended his service the government was deeply in his debt, and he received a settlement only after protracted efforts. In presenting his claim, he wrote, "I entered upon and performed these services, more from considerations of patriotism, and a desire to serve the Government & Country, than from any Expectation of reward, — knowing the risques which I must run, and the *pall of oblivion that would shroud my name and memory*, if it became my lot to fall in the service." Mason's superiors took him at his word and paid him only his expenses, some $300, although he broadly hinted that his services were worth far more.[23]

The service of these agents during the chaotic weeks when an army was being assembled at Washington and the existence of William Parsons's group of agents have hitherto been unknown. However, one agent who went into action in this period has been far from obscure. This was Lafayette C. Baker, a red-bearded, lean man of thirty-four years, a native of upstate New York, lately a San Francisco vigilante. Baker was to become famous, and infamous, as the government's chief detective. He entered the service in February, possibly as one of Colonel Stone's detectives; in July he performed one of his very few ventures in military espionage. This took place after the Confederates had pulled back from Washington's Potomac front and Union forces had occupied Arlington Heights and Alexandria. With newspapers conducting an "On to Richmond!" campaign and the same sentiments being thundered daily on Capitol Hill, the administration was under irresistible pressure to mount an offensive. A week before the army marched for Bull Run, Baker was sent South, not by Brigadier General Irvin McDowell, who was to command the field army, but by General Scott.

In the book in which Baker recounts, and grossly inflates, his Civil War activities, he says he left Washington in the character of an itinerant photographer — a pretense that a Confederate picket or provost marshal could easily have penetrated, for his camera box was empty and he had none of the photographer's usual cumbersome equipment. After losing a day through being arrested by the Federal commander at Alexandria (so his story goes), he reached Manassas, the Confederate field headquarters, there to be arrested again and questioned at length by the enemy commander, Brigadier General P. G. T. Beauregard, and forwarded to Richmond, by now the Confederate capital.

Again at Richmond, according to Baker, his presence commanded the attention of the highest authority, and President Davis himself was even more generous with his time than General Beauregard had been, giving Baker three extended interviews without penetrating his deception.

"In the mean time," Baker writes, "I had obtained information of military movements and plans, learned where the enemy had stationed troops, or were building fortifications, and what they were doing at the Tredegar [munitions] works." As Baker by his own account had been continuously confined or under guard since before his arrival at Manassas, such discoveries would have been a considerable feat.

Exploits of this degree of probability and believability appear repeatedly in the published reminiscences of Civil War spies. And Baker's book, one of the earliest of these, set the fashion in other ways. For example, he tells of being arrested immediately upon entering Confederate territory and of happening upon a "beer-house" (in a wooded and sparsely settled rural section) where his captors soon "were stupidly under the influence of the potations," whereupon Baker slipped away. Another alleged adventure of Baker's that became a cliché in the spies' memoirs was his manner of escape across the Potomac. He says that he obtained in Richmond a pass to Fredericksburg, halfway to Washington; that he hiked the ten miles from there to the Potomac by eluding a succession of pursuers and guards, and that he finally reached the Maryland shore by stealing a fisherman's boat and rowing across the wide river through a hail of bullets from the Virginia side.

But the tallest of Baker's tales concerns his meeting with a beautiful Southern girl in the stockade at Manassas. She was distributing religious tracts, and she employed her wiles with great skill in an attempt — which he easily saw through — to betray him into an admission of his Northern allegiance. She was no ordinary Southern girl; according to Baker this was none other than Belle Boyd, later the celebrated Confederate spy whose brushes with Federal authority involved Baker. Even Belle's fondest admirers have not credited her with the religious and patriotic services that Baker claimed.

Although this saga stretches credulity at every point, it cannot be entirely written off, for Baker did make a trip to Manassas and Richmond at about the time he claims. The record that supports his claim is sketchy but authoritative. It consists of his bill for $105 in expenses, naming Manassas and Richmond as the points visited, citing General Scott's orders as authority for the mission, and bearing endorsements by Secretary of State Seward and a disbursing officer of the War Department. These were the officials who customarily passed on expenditures for "secret service" at this period, and, as has already been noted, they were cautious about paying even the most obviously legitimate claims. That Baker was able to convince his chiefs that he had been to Manassas and Richmond is enough to compel acceptance of that much of his claim. Happily this can be done without also accepting either the thesis that the Confederate president personally questioned suspected spies at great length, or Baker's assertion that he brought back a substantial amount of intelligence. The other details of his story, even where they are circumstantially believable, come into question because of the general character of his book. What actually befell him on his trip to Richmond can only be guessed; the likeliest possibility is that while at Manassas and Richmond and en route between them he was under arrest as he claims, and that he did have interviews with Confederate officials of some importance, though not of the magnitude of General Beauregard and President Davis.[24]

On a later trip to Richmond, in September, Baker obtained a pass signed by Confederate Secretary of War Leroy P. Walker; again, his actual contacts probably were at a lower level.[25] His memoir does not mention this second Richmond trip; this omission is one more indication of the book's value as history, and there are other serious omissions in the Baker record, such as the lack of an official report on either of his Richmond visits.

In the case of the July mission, Baker's spying in the Confederacy would have been of more value if he had not made it to Richmond at all. Manassas, much handier to Washington, was where the Rebels had assembled an army to protect a railroad junction. That army was the Federals' chief intelligence target, and it was probably the target Scott had assigned to Baker, not the officialdom in Richmond, high or low. But field armies were much harder for spies to penetrate than cities; and, as has been seen, the commander of the field army at Manassas evidently did not care much for visitors. If Baker had been lucky enough to go from Manassas to Washington instead of to Richmond, he might have brought back some information that would have helped the Federals avoid their defeat and rout at Bull Run. The Richmond detour delayed his return to Washington until that battle was long over. Baker's account says that Richmond was his goal from the outset, and that he stopped at Manassas only because he stumbled into a patrol belonging to one of Beauregard's outposts. It is a reasonable guess that this is just one more of Baker's fabrications.

Baker had his work cut out for him, and it was not spying out military secrets in the Confederacy. With the loyalty of the Washington city police doubtful and an efficient military police system yet to be developed, the capital was an inviting intelligence target for the Confederates. Baker was to become chief of the longer-lasting of two organizations (the other was Pinkerton's) charged with limiting the damage that the friends of secession could do in and around the capital city. He formed a bureau that had as many as thirty employees during the war and a somewhat larger number during the investigation of the assassination of Lincoln. His wartime name for it, National Detective Police, probably lacked legal authorization; with the publication of his book in 1867 he became "Chief of the United States Secret Service," an even more imaginative concoction, which historians have eagerly accepted. Although his National Detective Police organization was much more local in character than national, Baker did have regular liaison with the New York City police, he sometimes had agents in Canada, and he had occasional dealings with headquarters of field armies and regional departments of the army, where there was usually a provost marshal general (a title Baker did not have) who outranked him.

At first Baker was a civilian employee, then a colonel, finally a brigadier general. Though working initially for General Scott, he was nominally subordinate to Secretary of State Seward. When Stanton became secretary of war he brought Baker into the War Department, where his status was first that of "Special Agent" and then "Special Provost-Marshal."[26] He reported to the "Special Judge Advocate," Major (later Lieutenant Colonel) Levi C. Turner, a lawyer associate of Stanton's who did not allow his inferior rank to soften the orders he gave Colonel (or General) Baker.

From his arrests of Copperheads and other pro-Confederate activists, Baker has acquired a reputation as a perpetrator of police-state tactics. His little detective bureau has even been imaginatively portrayed as "Lincoln's secret police." However, the standard treatment of even its most unmistakably guilty victims was release upon taking the oath of allegiance to the Union. More deserving of disrepute is his official lying and his spying on President Andrew Johnson, two parts of his history that lie outside the period under examination here. Civil War history has been content to leave Baker his bad name without making a close examination of his operations, especially his counterespionage activities, which appear to have been generally successful. He appears again in these pages on a few occasions when his policing of Washington and vicinity brought him into contact with provost marshals of the Federal armies, especially forces stationed in lower Maryland, a region known to have been traversed by Confederate couriers, whose traffic was one of Baker's principal concerns.[27]

2

....

FIRST BULL RUN

June–July 1861

IN THE FIRST MAJOR CAMPAIGN of the Civil War, which ended in humiliating defeat on Bull Run on that unforgettable Sunday, July 21, the Federals had little information that could be called intelligence. On one key question — how serious an obstacle was presented by Bull Run itself — they settled for an easy assurance that the stream was easily fordable, and they paid a heavy price for the lack of advance investigation. On another question — whether the Confederates were bringing their Shenandoah Valley army to add to the force on Bull Run — the Federals blundered away their opportunities to provide their Bull Run commander, Brigadier General Irvin McDowell, with timely warning of the oncoming enemy reinforcement. The result was that McDowell received word of it too late to change his plans or bring up his own reserves. The reinforcing brigades from the Valley turned a Federal advantage into a Confederate victory.

These failures were the predictable outgrowth of the lack of intelligence preparedness, combined with haste. The Bull Run campaign was the Lincoln administration's response to the now familiar "On to Richmond!" cry from Congress, the press, and the Northern public. The high command yielded to the pressure and ended up adding to it, overriding McDowell's warnings about the greenness and general unreadiness of his army.[1]

Beauregard's army on Bull Run, protecting a rail junction at Manassas, only thirty miles from Washington, was not the Federals' only concern in northern Virginia. There was also the Confederate army in the Shenandoah Valley, originally placed defiantly at its mouth on the Potomac, at Harper's Ferry, and moved in mid-June to Winchester. General McDowell assembled an army at Washington to oppose the Rebels at Manassas; another force of green Federals gathered in south-central Pennsylvania with a view to marching down into Virginia and reclaiming the Valley for

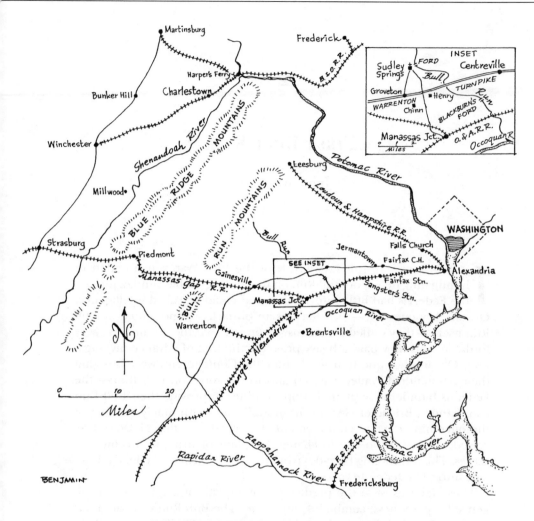

REGION OF FIRST BULL RUN CAMPAIGN

the Union. When that movement was about ready, McDowell was directed to work up a plan to assist the Valley campaign by marching northwest up the Virginia side of the Potomac. He answered with a studied paper showing that such a march would expose his left flank to the Confederates on Bull Run, and without any compensating military gain.[2] That argument reminded his superiors that the main target was Manassas.

It was certain that as soon as the Federals moved toward Manassas, the Confederates would hurry reinforcements there. They had units near and below Richmond, a brigade around Fredericksburg, and a regiment at Leesburg, but their biggest force available for strengthening Manassas was the one in the lower Valley, and its position at Winchester was fairly handy to a rail line to Manassas.

In a late June meeting at the White House, McDowell argued emphatically that he could not defeat both Beauregard's Manassas army and the Valley army, led by Joseph E. Johnston, former quartermaster general of the U.S. Army. McDowell won reassurance on that question. The Federals' army assembling in Pennsylvania, commanded by Major General Robert Patterson, a veteran of the War of 1812 and the Mexican War (when he was General Scott's second in command), was about to march for the Valley. That advance was expected to keep Johnston's Confederates well occupied; McDowell was assured that if Johnston should succeed in getting away to assist Beauregard, he would "have Patterson on his heels."[3]

July 8, the date set for McDowell's advance, turned out to be too hopeful, and the 13th was substituted, then the 15th. On that day, a Monday, regiments were still arriving, moving from Washington across to Arlington and Alexandria and joining McDowell's five divisions (one of which was a reserve division). The march began on the 16th, moving on four roads that converged at Centreville, a hilltop village four miles short of Bull Run and another four from Manassas Junction.[4]

The Confederates' brigade-size advance contingent at Fairfax Court House, halfway along the march route, retired hurriedly before the Federal advance on Wednesday, the 17th.[5] Arriving at Centreville the next day, McDowell planned to move his left across Bull Run, outflank the enemy, and cut the railroad southwest of the Junction.[6]

Beauregard was planning to attack in the same sector McDowell chose for crossing the run. One of McDowell's brigades spoiled both generals' plans by advancing too far down the Centreville-Manassas road and blundering into a fight. At Blackburn's Ford on Bull Run, instead of finding another Confederate outpost that was under advance orders to retire, the Federals met the army Beauregard had placed there in expectation of attacking. In this preliminary battle — it was no mere skirmish — the Yankees fared badly.[7]

Finding the enemy in his path and obviously in force, Beauregard suspended his attack plans. Still he retained the concentration on his right, though he was also concerned about his left, the direction from which Patterson might come, pursuing Johnston.[8] As his telegram to Richmond asking for reinforcements reflected a state of alarm,[9] it seems that Beauregard expected to have to fight on the defensive. Had that been his intention, he would have disposed his forces to cover various spots where the Federals might find a place to cross Bull Run. But his dispositions were for attacking, not defending.

Whereas Beauregard's action following the Blackburn's Ford battle has ever since been debated, McDowell's has been condemned. He stopped in his tracks for two days.[10] There were now two things wrong with advancing on the left. First, the brigade that had, only half mistakenly, exceeded his orders, had tipped his hand; it was clear that in that sector the Rebels were present in force. Second, the fords on that part of Bull Run were a poor choice. The roads McDowell had expected to find there were mere cart paths, too narrow and crooked to admit the passage of a large force.[11] He ordered his engineers to reconnoiter upstream, on the army's right. Meanwhile the troops had to cook rations.

Two days of reconnoitering and cooking gave the Confederates more time to bring Johnston's army to Manassas. Beauregard later credited his Washington spy, Rose Greenhow, with having given him on July 10 notice of the enemy's plan to advance, and on the 16th notice of the start of the march that day; but he had not telegraphed his plea for reinforcements until the enemy appeared in his front at Fairfax on Wednesday, the 17th. Richmond's order to Johnston was to move to Manassas "if practicable," allowing for the possibility that pressure from Patterson might hold the Valley army at Winchester. The order did not reach him at Winchester until about 1 A.M. Thursday.[12] Beauregard had also appealed for help directly to Johnston; this message did not arrive at Winchester until after the War Department order. Thus both armies were taking their time about launching into this first major battle, the one each side thought would end the war.[13]

Johnston was on the road within twelve hours of receiving his orders. He entrained most of his troops at Piedmont, east of the Blue Ridge. That route to Manassas amounted to twenty-three miles by foot and thirty-five by train; by entraining in the Valley he would have shortened the march by only a few miles while greatly lengthening the train ride. By early Friday the only troops left behind at Winchester were local militia and a large contingent of the sick. The last to leave were Colonel Jeb Stuart's men, who maintained a cavalry screen until darkness Thursday evening covered the army's movement.[14]

The trip started off with some smart marching, for the leading brigade was that of Thomas J. Jackson, about to be named Stonewall. Jackson's pace gave a foretaste of the 1862 marches that earned them the nickname "Foot Cavalry." But the Manassas Gap Railroad, although it made history by moving so many troops to such an important engagement, was painfully slow. A train loaded with soldiers averaged barely four jolting miles an hour. The train crews worked with what seemed treasonable sluggishness. (It later developed that at least a substantial part of the crews had no sympathy for the Southerners' war.) The rear elements of the army — more than a brigade — reached Manassas only on Monday, after the battle was over. That was the fifth day of the movement; a year later Jackson's force, more than twice as numerous as Johnston's whole

1861 army, would again move to Manassas, covering almost exactly the same distance in less than two days — and marching all the way.[15]

On Friday McDowell's engineers found the ford he wanted, over on the right at Sudley Church, more than two miles north of the Warrenton Turnpike, beyond the left of the Confederates' eight-mile line on Bull Run. According to Major John G. Barnard, the chief engineer, "Reliable information justified the belief that the ford was good; that it was unfortified; that it was defended by only one or two companies, and, moreover, that the run above it was almost everywhere passable for wheeled vehicles." But the roads — more cart paths — leading to the ford from the turnpike could not be reconnoitered without exposing to Confederate patrols the Federals' interest in that sector of the front. A second reconnaissance was attempted Friday night; the busybody Rebel patrollers would not get out of the way. Not until Saturday noon did Barnard find a route to the ford.[16]

When McDowell's two-division flanking movement set out on that route early on Sunday, a local guide insisted that it would expose them to the view of enemy batteries. He led them on a circuitous route which, Confederate reports show, was itself not fully protected from enemy observation. When the advance troops came in sight of Bull Run, also in their view was a column of Confederates, a mile or more away and marching to meet them. Sounds of a Federal march on the turnpike, from units that were to make a demonstration at the bridge over Bull Run, had been picked up by Confederate pickets as early as 3 A.M. Much later, well after sunrise, the flanking column had encountered cavalry pickets east of the ford and had been observed by a distant signal station. Thus McDowell's surprise was not as complete as he had planned; nevertheless his two divisions crossed the run unopposed. His original object of outflanking the enemy was accomplished.[17]

The flanking column pushed back the light forces on the Confederate left two miles before being temporarily stopped just short of the turnpike by lately arrived Confederate units, which reached the scene mainly through the initiative of their commanders, anticipating orders from army headquarters. For Johnston had concurred in maintaining Beauregard's concentration on the right. They had received reports of the Federals' appearance at the turnpike bridge as early as 5:30 A.M., and by midmorning they knew of the flanking column's march upstream. But its size was unknown; Beauregard still expected the principal enemy threat on his right, where the Federals' veterans of the Blackburn's Ford affair were demonstrating. Beauregard's after-action report says, "In my opinion the most effective method of relieving that flank was by a rapid, determined attack by my right wing and center." That attack never came off, chiefly because of a miscarriage of orders.[18] Although Beauregard's picketing and his observation facilities had partially penetrated McDowell's surprise, the Federals' mistaken action at Blackburn's Ford on Thursday had misled the enemy about as effectively as a well-planned deception scheme could have done.

The Federals steadily pushed their way across the turnpike; there the rest of the battle was fought. The story of the afternoon-long shootout on Henry House Hill and Chinn Ridge just south of the turnpike, ending in the rout of McDowell's army, has been told hundreds of times. One major point of general agreement is that the two armies were about evenly matched; the addition of Johnston's army, with smaller reinforcements from Richmond, Leesburg, and the Fredericksburg area, brought the Confederates' total strength up to about 35,000, the same as McDowell's, and about half of each army got into the fight.[19] A second point is that on the Confederate side, the half-army in the fight consisted mainly of lately arrived reinforcements. Johnston's Valley regiments did most of the fighting and were the decisive element. With the exception of the few regiments that had been guarding the Confederate left, and of the Hampton Legion from South Carolina, all of the units most heavily engaged belonged to the Valley brigades of Stonewall Jackson, Bernard Bee, and Francis Bartow. And a fourth Valley brigade, Edmund Kirby Smith's, which detrained after noon Sunday and quick-timed to the field to the sound of the guns, was one of two that delivered the telling blows late in the day. The other knockout blow was by Jubal Early's brigade, belatedly brought over from the right.[20] The Federals had the upper hand through much of the fight; the victors must have been much surprised by their victory. Those were *green* armies.

.. .. ..

In examining how McDowell's army could have got into so important a battle with information that was badly inadequate or just plain wrong, the first question is, what role did William C. Parsons and his agents play? Though inexperienced, they were the only intelligence game in town — and evidently they included several men from the numerous Unionist citizenry of northern Virginia. In the whole campaign, however, Parsons's men served only as guides, and even in that capacity they appear to have been little used, perhaps even ignored. For Parsons wrote of his men after the battle, "Had their advice been followed on the ground, it is probable the result would have been different."[21]

Parsons's remark could mean that his men had recommended the very route of attack that McDowell required two days to discover — that Parsons's men had known well in advance that the fords on the right were much more accessible and negotiable than those on the left but that their knowledge was discounted until McDowell's engineers had "eyeball evidence" confirming it. If that was what lay behind Parsons's remark, he was right — those two days did in all probability mean the difference between inglorious defeat and the victory the Union could have had by attacking on Friday or even Saturday.

But his complaint may have been mainly a product of an animus between McDowell's command and that of General Mansfield, who was Parsons's boss and who had been General Scott's preference over McDowell. Mansfield, commanding in the District of Columbia, had dragged his feet in supporting the buildup of McDowell's army across the river in Virginia.[22] If Mansfield was slow to release newly arriving regiments to join McDowell, as McDowell believed, it is not surprising that Parsons's men were turned over to McDowell only in time to serve as guides on the march when they could have been used to spy out Confederate positions at the planning stage. In the hurry-up-now-and-get-ready-later climate of those weeks, McDowell could not have taken the time or spared the energy to struggle with Mansfield over the services of a few would-be spies of untested ability, when what he needed most were those regiments on Mansfield's side of the Potomac.

In mid-June, when Patterson's scheduled advance in the Shenandoah Valley was the Federals' major concern and McDowell was being asked to support it, Scott's headquarters sent one William Johnston out on a spying trip for Patterson. The mission was well timed; it happened to coincide with the Confederates' withdrawal from Harper's Ferry to Winchester. Scott's adjutant informed Patterson on June 13, "The General has sent a man (William Johnston) to endeavor to pass through Harper's Ferry and then to join you and give you useful information. It is hoped the facilities he seemed to possess will make his mission successful."[23]

As William Johnston disappears from the records at that point, it is not known what information he provided Patterson, if indeed he succeeded in penetrating the Confederate lines, then in motion, and getting through to Pennsylvania. But a "Mr. J————n" turns up in the records just twelve days later with a long report of espionage against a different target, Beauregard's Manassas army. If Mr. J————n and William Johnston were the same man, Scott was correct in his generous estimate of Johnston's "facilities," for J————n had succeeded in spending three days, June 20–22, and possibly a fourth, in Beauregard's camps, and in getting away to report to McDowell at Arlington.

Only McDowell's summary of the spy's findings appears in the records. He omitted, probably for security reasons, any explanation of what cover — what "facilities" — J————n used. But he must have presented a good front, for Beauregard not only refrained from arresting him but issued him a pass that enabled him to move about among the camps in and between Manassas, Centreville, Jermantown, and Fairfax Court House.

His gleanings were recorded in a document that was no model of intelligence reporting. Apparently McDowell or a staff officer set them down as J———n uttered them, and apparently he spoke in scattershot fashion, with no effort to tell things in chronological or any other order. He had easily identified Beauregard's troops as being from Virginia, South Carolina, and Louisiana — and a few "guerillas" from Kentucky. The report, however, does not give the names of regiments or other units, an omission that seems odd in light of the spy's extensive sojourn. Evidently he felt that questions like "What is the name of your regiment, Soldier?" would have been risky.

J———n saw several units that were changing position; in fact it seemed that no part of Beauregard's army would hold still long enough for the Federal army to find it in the spot where the spy last saw it. But it was clear enough that Beauregard meant to keep considerable forces at Fairfax Court House, Fairfax Station, and Centreville — which would have told McDowell that he might have a fight on his hands well short of Bull Run.

The report also dealt with miscellaneous items such as types of weapons (highly varied), quality of horseflesh, troop morale (the South Carolinians were "spoiling for a fight"), food supplies ("chiefly ship biscuit and fresh beef"), the presence of measles in some camps, and even the fact that the South Carolinians had brought their slaves as camp servants.

J———n estimated Confederate strength at Manassas and its outposts at 20,000 — not a great exaggeration, for by this time Beauregard's army had grown almost to 15,000.[24] One obvious shortcoming in the report was the absence of information about the fortifications the Confederates must have been building. Since few of them, possibly none, were along Bull Run,[25] they played no part in the battle that McDowell was to fight; but they could have figured prominently in any fighting near the railroad — the objective he did not reach.

From the picture McDowell drew of the enemy situation in his march order three weeks after J———n's report, it appears that little new information reached him in those weeks.[26] As we have seen, Lafayette Baker's spying mission in the second week of July was well timed for updating J———n's information. But Baker, if he was actually under arrest at Manassas as he claimed, probably did not pick up much information while there. In any case, his Richmond excursion delayed his return North until some time after the battle.[27]

Still, McDowell's knowledge of the enemy was not as spotty as it might have been. In a day when estimates of enemy numbers normally doubled or even tripled the true count, he was not seriously wrong. Even with Beauregard's eleventh-hour moves to concentrate on his right, McDowell's general notion of where he would find the main enemy force — strung out along the south bank of Bull Run — was correct as far as it went. The one big gap in his pre-battle intelligence was the one already noted — how and where to get across the run. He had been given to understand that it was "fordable at almost any place."[28] Although it was a shallow stream and not very wide, its banks were wooded, steep, and rocky — and patrolled on both sides by alert Confederates in some force. However many fordable places there were, established fords accessible by road or cart path were few. McDowell's engineers had advance maps that showed, for example, Sudley Ford and another ford downstream from it, but "no known road communicated with them."[29]

Lacking such information, McDowell lost two days, the 19th and 20th, while the engineers pinpointed the excellent crossing place at Sudley Church. The second of those two days was critical. If he was to attack before the arrival of substantial reinforcements, he would have to do it with whatever information his guide could provide. In the end, it was the guide's choice of route that prevailed anyway.[30]

Those two days were the days when Johnston was bringing the bulk of his army to Manassas — Friday and Saturday, the 19th and 20th. If it is true that Johnston's reinforcements decided the battle, it is equally true that McDowell's intelligence failure — a piece of topographic misinformation of great importance that went unchallenged — made it possible for the Valley brigades to arrive in time to save the battle.

· · · · · · ·

The Federals' intelligence in advance of the battle was weak; on the battlefield it was virtually nonexistent. The Signal Corps consisted of one officer and no signalmen; there was no ground-based substitute for its observation and reporting facilities, and an eleventh-hour effort to arrange for aerial observation from balloons failed. There was nowhere near enough cavalry for the scouting needs of so ambitious a campaign.

The absence of the Signal Corps from the Bull Run campaign calls for explanation, for the United States Army on the eve of the Civil War had developed a system that advanced battlefield signaling a giant step beyond the point European armies had reached. But the tactical advantages of that system were not appreciated — nor would they be until several months later.

The inventor, Major Albert J. Myer, an army surgeon in his early thirties, had pursued an interest in communication for the deaf and blind until his experiments led him to develop, in the late 1850s, the aerial, or "wigwag," system for military use. In Myer's code, movements of flag (or torch) to right or left, like Morse's code of dots and dashes, served to form letters and numbers. This system became feasible when the telescope was invented in the early 1600s; why armies had not developed such a signaling system long before the United States came into being is hard to understand. Before Morse's invention of electric telegraphy in 1837, European nations had networks of semaphore towers capable of alphabetic signaling, but their immobility made them virtually useless by a marching and fighting army. In the 1850s England, France, Prussia, Spain, Italy, and Russia had all made military use of electric telegraphy, but Myer, who apparently was unaware of these European developments, devised a system much more adaptable to use at the tactical level.

Having with much effort persuaded a slow-moving War Department to give him the novel title of signal officer, Myer tried out his invention on an 1860–61 expedition against the Navajos. Not until June 1861 did he arrive back East, a signal officer without signal troops. He established a camp of instruction at Fort Monroe, in tidewater Virginia, where he had conducted some of his early experiments. Myer, some officer assistants, and their trainees were soon using their signals to direct artillery fire against Confederate positions across Hampton Roads.

But that history-making enterprise — the first use of the system in actual warfare — was short-lived. Myer, concerned about the incursion of a fledgling civilian organization, the United States Military Telegraph, into electrical telegraphy, made two trips to Washington to look after the army's signaling interests. It was no time to raise jurisdictional issues; McDowell's campaign against Manassas was being readied. Myer associated himself with the balloonists, who were in Washington offering the army their services. He had worked as a commercial telegrapher while in medical school in Buffalo, and he hoped to arrange for electrical or visual signaling between balloon and ground.

Unable to get his signal personnel and apparatus from Fort Monroe to Washington in time for McDowell's march, Myer started for the battlefield anyway, in command of the one balloon whose owner had won the honor of going with the army. Through a miscarriage of orders Myer did not learn of this assignment until Saturday, July 20. The balloon procession started from Washington around two o'clock on Sunday morning — the hour McDowell's troops were rising from their bivouacs and heading for the crossing of Bull Run. The balloon could not be inflated in the field; it was filled by connecting it to the Washington gas mains. And maneuvering the big bag around roadside trees while it was tethered to a wagon made for slow going. Near Fairfax it became wedged between trees. The teamsters sought to loosen it by driving "forward with a dash," a move that tore the bag. Myer ordered it back to Washington for repair and refilling. Hearing the sound of guns from the direction of Manassas, he rode forward alone, arriving on the battlefield in midafternoon, near the climax of the fight. He served as an aide to Brigadier General Daniel Tyler and then to McDowell, mostly during the retreat. When John Wise, the balloon owner, arrived back in Washington on Sunday, Thaddeus S. C. Lowe and his balloon had started for the battlefield, but they got only as far as Falls Church, where they encountered the retreating army.[31]

The absence from McDowell's army of both the balloon service and the signal service is that much more evidence of the hastiness of the Federals' preparation for the battle. The high command was wrong in believing that the Confederates would be just as unready as the Unionists. The Confederacy had 35,000 men under arms in March, well before Lincoln's first call for volunteers. And the Federals did some things wrong while the Confederates were doing them right. While Myer was occupied at Fort Monroe, Jefferson Davis — who knew about signaling from having been chairman of the U.S. Senate Military Affairs Committee during the years when Myer was seeking congressional support — was having flags and torches manufactured in Richmond and then sending an officer to Manassas to establish a signal service in Beauregard's army.[32] While the Federals' signal officer was engaged in training and minor operations, his Confederate counterpart was setting up a working shop on the battlefield-to-be.

Myer's move to Fort Monroe took place during the first week of McDowell's command. It is a safe assumption that the general, until recently only a major like Dr. Myer, had not given any thought to such matters as battlefield reconnaissance at the time when he could have intervened to keep Myer close at hand. And Myer may have been partly responsible for the army's failure to have a working group of signalmen on hand when it marched. Although he did make that eleventh-hour effort to get trained assistants to join him in Washington, he seems to have been more anxious about his Signal Corps' long-term role than its participation in the events immediately ahead.[33]

The usefulness of a signal service is suggested by the success that a Confederate organization, less than three weeks old, enjoyed in the Bull Run battle. The tiny corps put together at Manassas by Captain E. Porter Alexander, the officer sent by President Davis, employed the same system of flags and torches as Myer's system — and for good reason, for Alexander had served as Myer's assistant in most of his experiments.[34] In fact Myer had taken the precaution of having Alexander, a Georgian who was becoming his close friend, sign an oath not to "disclose, discover or use the plan for signals communicated to me, without the written consent of Dr. Meyer and the U.S. War Department."[35]

Alexander's central station — there were four outstations — was on a height a mile and a half east of Manassas Junction still known as Signal Hill.[36] It was from that vantage point that Alexander spotted the Federal turning movement. Many years later he recounted the incident:

> I was watching the flag of our station at Stone Bridge [where the Warrenton Turnpike crosses over Bull Run] when in the distant edge of the field of view of my glass, a gleam caught my eye. It was the reflection of the sun (which was low in the east behind me), from a polished brass

field piece. . . . Observing attentively, I discovered McDowell's column in the open field north of Sudley's Ford crossing Bull Run and turning our left flank.

The gun that brought that gleam of sunlight to Alexander's attention would have been seven or eight miles away. He signaled to Colonel Nathan G. Evans, commanding at Stone Bridge, "Look out for your left. You are turned." The message reached Evans at the same time news of the enemy's approach arrived from cavalry pickets who had been driven in by the Federals' cavalry advance guard. Of the reports from those two sources, Alexander's would have carried more weight, for he could see that a major flanking movement was in progress whereas the pickets could not have had a view of so large a part of the column. The two reports caused Evans to divert his attention from the Federals' demonstration at the turnpike bridge and send his small force to meet the enemy advancing from Sudley Ford.[37]

Of course Alexander also sent the alarm to Beauregard and Johnston, but their orders redisposing units to meet the attack, as we have already seen, had been anticipated by their subordinates — Bee, Jackson, and Wade Hampton — who moved to Evans's support.[38] Nevertheless, the two commanders' action in response to the enemy advance was more timely than it could have been in the absence of the signal service. It would be too much to say that Alexander's intelligence won the Bull Run battle, but it certainly helped save the Confederates from losing it. For that they had to thank an inventive young Yankee physician.

Before McDowell's arrival at Centreville, one of Alexander's outstations had been on the height at that place. It could not "see" over the trees hiding the Rebel camps several miles away across Bull Run, but at least it could see Alexander's central station on Signal Hill and probably also the station at the bridge. For the Centreville height is a commanding one; it looks at the Blue Ridge and two tiers of intervening foothills. After a visit to Centreville when the Federals reoccupied it months later, Myer wrote, "There is perhaps no country better formed by nature for the successful use of signal communication than on and near this battlefield."[39] This discovery would have heightened the frustration he suffered at the time of the battle.

. .   . .   . .

Officers' unfamiliarity with visual signaling and balloons contributed to the Federals' failure to have them at Bull Run. One kind of reconnaissance that generals understood was cavalry, but McDowell did not have much of that either. Nor did he use what cavalry he had — less than a full regiment — for the extensive reconnaissance he needed. He has been criticized for allowing that tiny force of horsemen to be assigned to one of his divisions instead of keeping at least some of it for his own use.[40]

That division (David Hunter's), however, was the one to which McDowell attached his own headquarters; the cavalry was handy enough if he had wanted it. Apparently he did not, for the cavalry commander's report of the battle describes combat activities but no reconnoitering. The one big reconnaissance target, as McDowell evidently saw it, was not enemy positions but the fords on Bull Run, and that kind of reconnoitering was a job for his engineers. Cavalry went along, but only as escort.[41] McDowell was giving information about the enemy a low priority, by necessity if not by choice.[42]

. .   . .   . .

Although McDowell was reasonably well served by "Mr. J———n," his advance intelligence was vastly inferior to Beauregard's. The Rebel leader owed his advantage to an unrestrained Northern press; newspapers had done such a thorough job of publishing Federal military secrets that the services of Confederate spies in Washington were almost redundant.

The smoke had hardly cleared over Fort Sumter when elaborately detailed reports of the buildup of the army about Washington began appearing in the local papers and all the others that could afford a Washington correspondent. On July 3 the *National Republican,* a Washington paper, came out with a carefully compiled recapitulation of "regiments in and around Washington" that had arrived since April 18, with names of commanding officers and estimated strengths. The *New York Herald* produced a less ambitious recap, listing nineteen recently arrived regiments. When movements from Washington over to Arlington Heights and Alexandria stepped up around July 10, in the initial stage of McDowell's advance on Manassas, that interesting development was duly published. His order of the 14th for the beginning of advance the next day (a deadline that was not met) reached all his units; its arrival in various regimental headquarters was promptly reported in the newspapers. The positions of many units in the four marching columns found their way into print. The *Herald* of the 16th carried a dispatch of the previous day saying the march had begun; that error was corrected the next day, in a report that said there was "little doubt" that Manassas Junction was the objective. The *Herald* put the advancing army's strength at 62 regiments; other papers gave troop totals of 50,000 or 55,000. The latter figure, a 60 percent overestimate, would appear in the reports of Beauregard's chief spy and in his own later writings.

The *Republican* of the 17th reported that on the previous night General McDowell had put in an appearance at Willard's Hotel, the capital's favorite watering place. As McDowell was a teetotaler, his visit to a popular bar may have been intended to create an impression that it was business as usual over at his Arlington headquarters. If that was the general's game, the *Republican* reporter spoiled it by writing that McDowell "did not seem to have much time to spare, as might be expected of a man having a column of fifty thousand men moving under him."

On that same day the *Republican* made a pretense of respect for military secrets by announcing, "We could mention now all about the battle to be fought over the river tomorrow or the next day, but 'we do not feel at liberty to state particulars,' as our buzzy little neighbor the *Star* properly remarks. We abstain for fear that we should 'jeopardize' the battle." But by Thursday, the 18th, what remained of journalistic discretion had been thrown to the winds with the publication of McDowell's general order, naming the regiments in each brigade and the brigades in each division, giving names of commanders down to brigade, and listing artillery and cavalry units and the division to which each was assigned. Some of the correspondents gave the routes of march for a number of regiments that first day and their bivouac locations that night.

When the correspondents were not sure enough of their facts to publish a military secret in plain terms, or when a secret seemed sensitive enough to deserve protection, they tried their hand at indirectness. An example is a dispatch filed by a *Herald* reporter on the night of the 16th: "The general impression in the city [Washington] tonight is, that the sudden disappearance of troops today from the other side of the river is in consequence of a desire to attend a big race about to come off." This was a piece of cuteness that the reader was expected to translate as follows: "General McDowell's forces, which (as this newspaper has so ably reported) have been crossing from Washington over to Arlington and Alexandria in great numbers in recent days, today marched away from those places, on their way, we confidently surmise, to engage the Rebels assembled at Manassas Junction. This movement will lead to a race to see which army can get to Richmond first — the Rebels' or ours."[43]

McDowell's army was not the only victim of this publicity. When Patterson's army, on its way to Harper's Ferry, stopped at Hagerstown, a local paper published the names of twenty-four regiments, a reliable indication of his total strength.

Midway in this orgy of giveaways the newsmen learned that their efforts were gratefully received in the South. Confederate papers published, and Northern papers copied and repeated, the following statement by Confederate Secretary of War Leroy P. Walker, addressed to Southern newspapermen: "You are aware of the great amount of valuable information obtained by us through the medium of the enterprising journals of the North, and we may derive profit from their example by unremitting and judicious reserve in communications for the Southern journals."[44] This could not have failed to give Northern editors a twinge of conscience, but it did not cut output of military secrets; it was immediately after Walker's statement that they published McDowell's general order, giving far more information about his forces than Beauregard and his staff would have had time to assimilate and put to use.

.. .. ..

At the time Johnston received orders from Richmond to go to Beauregard's aid, his army of about 11,000 was at Winchester and Patterson's Federals were at Charlestown, having just withdrawn about eight miles from their most advanced position, Bunker Hill, twelve miles from Winchester. After some preliminary backing and forthing that followed Johnston's retirement from Harper's Ferry to Winchester in June, Patterson had finally made the move to Bunker Hill, north of Winchester, which looked as if he really meant to press Johnston. But he stayed there less than two days, and when he moved it was sidewise and somewhat to the rear. He was now almost twenty miles from the enemy force he was supposed to be holding in the Valley, and the attitude he presented to the Confederates was not aggressive. General Johnston noted, "Although the Federal cavalry had greatly the advantage of the Confederate in arms and discipline, it was not in the habit, like ours, of leaving the protection of the infantry" — which enabled Jeb Stuart "to maintain his outposts near the enemy's camps, and his scouts near their columns, learning their movements quickly, and concealing our own." Three-quarters of Patterson's army — nineteen of his twenty-six regiments — consisted of three-month troops who were about to go home, but his unaggressive cavalry was not a troop of raw volunteers; it consisted mainly of four companies of regulars, brought from Pennsylvania by a regular cavalry officer, Colonel George H. Thomas, the future Rock of Chickamauga.[45]

Patterson moved from Bunker Hill to Charlestown on the 17th, the same day McDowell's advance appeared at Fairfax and Beauregard telegraphed Richmond for reinforcements. Johnston therefore reasoned that Patterson's shift of position, which was partly eastward — and which Johnston learned of quickly enough — might be a move to cut him off from Manassas. It was no such thing, but Johnston deferred action that Thursday morning until Stuart was able to inform him that the Federals had made no further move. Although Johnston probably did not realize it, the situation was made to order for a clean getaway, and he made one. Credit for it is traditionally given to Stuart for the cavalry screen he set up to keep the Federals from discovering the movement. But Stuart, according to Johnston's orders, pulled in his screen at dark on Thursday and started for Manassas. And Patterson remained ignorant (or unpersuaded) of the enemy's departure until some time on Saturday, which indicates that Patterson's scouting did not reach near Winchester even on Friday, after Stuart was long gone. So Stuart's screening on Thursday was conducted against an enemy that was too far away to appreciate the skill with which it presumably was performed.[46]

. . . . . .

It was not only unaggressive cavalry scouting that kept Patterson in the dark. He had a ready-made intelligence agent in his headquarters whose effort to serve in that capacity he rejected, and with it some critically important information. This man was David Hunter Strother, a writer and illustrator nationally known under the pen name Porte Crayon, now serving in Patterson's headquarters as a civilian topographer. Strother was a full-blooded Virginian, a native of the very locality where Patterson was operating, but thoroughly persuaded of the folly of secession. He had a wide acquaintance in the lower Valley; it included persons living within the Confederate lines who shared his Unionist sympathies. But after offering his services to Patterson, he spent two days waiting for an assignment, and when he got one it was at the urging of Captain Thomas H. Simpson, Patterson's topographical engineer.[47] There were no staff positions for "intelligence officer" in those days, so it is understandable that Patterson did not find the best use for Strother.

Yet Strother brought with him a good mental picture of the enemy, acquired when Johnston's little army drew back from Harper's Ferry to Winchester in mid-June. A short incursion into Virginia by a single Federal regiment based at Cumberland, Maryland, was mistaken by Johnston for an advance element of the Federal army that was then pushing the Rebels out of western Virginia. In that movement from Harper's Ferry Johnston's army had marched through Charlestown on a day when Strother, still unaffiliated with the Federals, was in the town. He watched the Southern troops with a journalist's practiced eye, noting their armament and other equipment, their appearance and demeanor, their regimental organization, and their numbers, as closely as a streetside observer could. Strother had *seen* the enemy, and at close range.[48]

It was in mid-July, nearly a month later, that he joined up with Patterson. By now he had become "satisfied . . . as to the true character of the contest which was opening. To my mind it represented the simple choice between a Government and Anarchy." He set out for Patterson's headquarters at Martinsburg, "taking an obscure road to prevent suspicion of my intentions." According to his postwar (1866) account, during the days he spent waiting for an assignment, he had an opportunity to discuss intelligence matters with Patterson's adjutant and chief of staff, Colonel Fitz John Porter, who as we have seen had lately been a bold actor during his one-man mission in Pennsylvania but was now evincing a quite different attitude. To Strother it seemed that Porter and Captain John

Newton, Patterson's chief engineer, received his estimate of Confederate strength in a cavalier manner. Strother thought he had been generous in allowing Johnston 15,000 effectives, but the most judicious estimate of the enemy that he could get from anyone around headquarters was 25,000 or 30,000, which would have been more than double the true numbers of Johnston's Army of the Shenandoah. "These men of war," Strother's account says, "seemed to be entirely satisfied with information obtained from other quarters, and I was equally well satisfied that this information had been furnished them by persons in the employ of the enemy."

A few days later, after interviewing two young and well-informed deserters, who told him that the Confederates had added more infantry and artillery units, Strother estimated the enemy's total strength at 17,000 and their effective strength considerably less. But when he presented these views at headquarters he was astonished "to find that they were totally discredited. They had satisfactory information that the enemy had a force of forty two thousand men and seventy guns. I was indignant and mortified that this 'invention of the enemy' should obtain credence." Without success Strother argued that the Confederates could not possibly mount such a force. But he "found the forty two thousand men and seventy guns the accepted belief, and no discussion permitted. . . . Being a stranger in camp, and without credit, . . . I returned to my tent, sketched a map and went to sleep with a contemptuous sense of security."[49] Colonel Porter had General Patterson's ear, and Strother, a civilian, did not. And Captain Simpson, who evidently had come to share Strother's views, obviously was not a member of the general's inner circle.

Months later, appearing before the congressional Joint Committee on the Conduct of the War, General Patterson explained how his headquarters had reached such unshakable conclusions about enemy strength. He proclaimed the Confederates' "immense superiority" over his own army, giving their strength as 35,000 to 40,000. Many statements had been taken "by different officers from different persons at different times and places," he explained, and those statements "agree[d] very much on the main facts," which were that Johnston "had at least three men and four guns to my one." Thus it evidently was the agreement between the reports of numerous and varied sources that impressed Patterson, and presumably his staff. But different sources, especially ones as disparate as Patterson claimed, are not likely to agree; in fact a marked disagreement is normal. In those remarkably consistent figures Patterson and his staff should have suspected the hand of some Southern deception artist. It does not matter that some of their sources, contrary to Strother's belief, were loyal Unionists; circulation of deceptive information would have reached them as well as secessionists masquerading as Unionists for the Federals' benefit.

Of course there is no proof that those reports of a huge Confederate Army of the Shenandoah amounted to a planted story. But numerous similar cases of misinformation evidently circulated by Confederate authorities will be found later in this history; taken together, these lend support to the suspicion of a plant in any given case. General Johnston's force of 35,000 or 40,000 men probably was the first creation of a not very imaginative but often successful Confederate deception effort.

The inquisitorial congressmen, hearing Patterson's testimony, rejected his figures outright and reported to the House and Senate that their best evidence gave Johnston 12,000 to 15,000 at the most. (The lower figure was only a little above the mark.) Although the committee listened to Patterson politely enough, their attitude was revealed when Patterson was asked what had been learned from a certain reconnaissance, and he began his reply with the words "The report . . . ." Congressman Daniel Gooch interrupted: "I did not ask what the report was, but what the facts were."[50]

. .   . .   . .

Strother had been in Patterson's service only nine days when the Valley campaign reached its climax with the departure of Johnston's army for Manassas. Before midnight that Thursday, July 18, according to his later account, word of the movement had reached him at Patterson's headquarters at Charlestown. This account does not say how the information was conveyed. It was corroborated next morning by word from a "loyal citizen, who was an eye-witness" of the troops' fording of the Shenandoah River; he had ridden to Charlestown during the night.[51]*

Strother passed the information to Captain Simpson, who hurried it to headquarters but returned shortly, saying, with irritation, that the report was "not credited." It seems odd that Strother did not then go to the staff and argue the case himself; although he was in a distinctly subordinate position, he must have possessed some force of address, for he was a successful journalist who one day would be a colonel himself (and after the war a brevet brigadier general).[52] He should have been able to gain the general's attention, arguing that the information demanded forwarding to Washington — qualified by as many maybes and perhaps as were necessary to satisfy the staff, but making clear that the originator had witnessed the Rebels' march. And Patterson, even while finding the report hard to believe, should have sent cavalry to Winchester to verify or disprove it.

Strother's story does not by itself explain the Union's inglorious defeat

* See Appendix 5, as well as note 51, for details regarding Strother's evidence.

of July 21, but it argues strongly that the battle was fought one day too late. That mistake, it turns out, was Patterson's fault more than it was McDowell's.

·· ·· ··

Patterson's staff evidently had complete confidence that Strother's information was wrong, for on the same day they rejected his report Patterson telegraphed Scott, "The enemy, from last information, are still at Winchester, and being re-enforced every night." The previous day, in answer to a nervous query from Scott on Johnston's whereabouts, Patterson had telegraphed, "The enemy has stolen no march upon me."[53] That was the very day the theft took place. What gave Patterson such confidence is not known; but his testimony to the congressional committee that his officers had been interviewing numbers of people "at different times and places" makes clear that rumor was the ultimate source of much of his information. Thus there was an ample opening for the entry of planted stories. Whatever the source, those two telegrams add up to an intelligence blunder of the most decisive kind.

By sometime Saturday, the 20th, Patterson accepted the fact that Johnston was gone — accepted it enough to confess that Johnston really had stolen a march. The War Department telegraph office was the focus of attention of anxious officials awaiting word from McDowell's army when this telegram arrived from Patterson: "With a portion of his force Johnston left Winchester by the road to Millwood on the afternoon of the 18th. His whole force was about thirty-five thousand two hundred."[54] Evidently Patterson and his staff were willing to believe Johnston was gone when the news came from a source whose calculation of enemy numbers matched their own estimates. The source was a "Mr. Lackland, brother of [Confederate] Colonel Lackland, residing a short distance from Charlestown, and just returned from Winchester" on Saturday. Lackland had given a state-by-state breakdown of the composition of Johnston's army that apparently just happened to add up to exactly 30,000 Confederate troops, with 5200 militia added on. He reported that all of the 30,000 had marched off, but Patterson telegraphed that only a "portion" of the army had left.[55] Presumably this editorial change was justified in someone's mind by the fact that 30,000 was, after all, only a portion of 35,200. The 30,000, however, would have represented Lackland's (and Patterson's) estimate of the sum total of Johnston's movable troops. The fact that he had left behind no usable forces was one of the few accurate details in Lackland's report, and it was the one major point that Patterson withheld from Scott. The general-in-chief was left to guess how big a fraction of the 35,200 was en route.

Since Patterson's news of the enemy's departure came from a walk-in source, it is evident that the Federal cavalry had not discovered John-

ston's absence even by Saturday. And the sources that had been feeding
Patterson strength estimates of 35,000 and 40,000 apparently were not
heard from.

Scott relayed Patterson's news to McDowell in these words: "It is known
that a strong re-enforcement left Winchester on the afternoon of the
18th, which you will also have to beat."[56] The literary license possessed
by a general-in-chief of twenty years' standing shows in Scott's translation of the "portion" of Johnston's army into a "strong re-enforcement."
It was not just the indefiniteness of the word "portion" that gave him
problems; it was also the difficulty of accepting the 35,200 figure. His
rewrite, on top of Patterson's omission of the report that Johnston's
whole movable force had gone, left McDowell with a much less clear
idea than he should have had of what Beauregard's reinforcements
amounted to. Still, the message McDowell received was less distorted
than it would have been if Patterson had telegraphed that 30,000 Confederate troops had marched for Manassas and Scott had swallowed that
figure and relayed it to McDowell. As it was, "strong re-enforcement" was
as good a phrase as could have been written, given Scott's two unknowns
— the true size of Johnston's army and how much of it had left for
Manassas.

Thus did McDowell learn that he was no longer assured of not having
to deal with Johnston's army. Scott had given up hope of Patterson's even
pursuing Johnston, much less holding him in the Valley.

Exactly when Scott's telegram reached McDowell is not known. It is
dated July 21, Sunday; although it is fair to assume that it went out very
early on that date — possibly immediately after midnight — McDowell
may not have received it very quickly, for he was eight or ten miles away
from his telegraph terminals at Fairfax Court House and Fairfax Station,[57] and his preoccupation with his march and battle could have made
him a hard target for a courier to find.[58] But any delay probably had no
effect on events. By whatever time the telegram could have reached him,
his troops were on the march or engaged with the enemy; even if at the
moment of receipt he had not been fully committed to battle, Scott's
ominous words "which you will also have to beat" would have forced him
to proceed with his attack. He could not delay it to bring up his distant
reserves without incurring unacceptable disadvantages: the impending
departure of many of his three-month regiments; the possibility that the
enemy could bring up reinforcements as fast as he could himself; the loss
of the initiative (which Beauregard was only too ready to assume); and
the likelihood that more delay would begin to look like an unwillingness
to do battle with the Southern cavaliers. Finally, there was the momentum that his campaign, from its planning stage to the arrival in the
enemy's front, had built up. That was having a strong psychological effect

on the high command back in Washington;[59] its effect on McDowell would have been even stronger. Everyone's mind was made up to do battle.[60]

.. .. ..

Patterson's rejection of Strother's report is one item on a long list of mistakes in his overcautious and bumbling Valley campaign. But there are substantial arguments in his defense. He argued that one of Scott's telegrams, reporting the Confederates' withdrawal of their Fairfax Court House outpost before McDowell's advance on the 17th, and predicting that "the Junction [Manassas] will probably be carried tomorrow," led him to think that McDowell's battle would be over on the 18th.[61] This supposition could account for his rejection of Strother's information. (Another excuse Patterson could have made for the rejection was that Strother's loyalty was not altogether certain at that point.) In any case, Patterson claimed that Scott's telegram on the 17th seemed to reduce the need for him to press Johnston. But a more substantial argument in his defense is that his mission, to hold Johnston at Winchester, was repeatedly muddled by discussion of pursuing a retreating Johnston to Manassas, which automatically reduced or negated the real mission. Scott's orders to Patterson were shifting and confusing; at one point, realizing he had given an inappropriate order, he followed it up by disingenuously misquoting it rather than admitting it was a mistake.[62] The approaching expiration of the three-month enlistments of the bulk of Patterson's army greatly hampered freedom of movement. At one point, in June, some of his best troops were called to Washington because of Scott's fears for its security. And Patterson had supply problems that he expected to alleviate by his move to Charlestown, which considerably shortened his line back to Pennsylvania.[63]

In hindsight it is evident that Patterson's army at the foot of the Valley could not have kept Johnston's away from Manassas, or even have seriously detained it. Even without the Manassas Gap Railroad, Johnston was favored by interior lines.[64] This basic infeasibility of Patterson's mission must have been the reason for Scott's difficulty in formulating clear and practicable orders. The old generalissimo was a Virginian who was persuaded to disregard part of the geography of Virginia — the Blue Ridge — and the restrictions it placed on the movements of armies.

McDowell, as well as Patterson, was ill served by Scott. When Patterson gave up his advance on Winchester on July 17, putting eighteen miles between his army and Johnston's, he informed Scott of his withdrawal to Charlestown.[65] It appears that Scott did not pass this important news to McDowell, even though the separation meant that Patterson could hardly be doing anything that would detain Johnston. If Scott did send such word to McDowell, it never got through, for on Saturday, three days after Patterson's arrival at Charlestown, we find *McDowell* informing *Scott* of Patterson's move. The news came from a visitor to McDowell's head-quarters.[66]

.. .. ..

The rejection of Strother's report of Johnston's departure cost the Federals dearly in the timing of McDowell's attack. Learning that Johnston's army had left Winchester on Thursday could have impelled McDowell to move up the attack from Sunday to Saturday. In the early hours of Saturday he would have met, of the Valley army, only Jackson's brigade — much less than half of the infantry reinforcements that fought on Sunday. The arrival of five more regiments at midmorning and noontime Saturday would still have left the Confederates well short of the infantry force they had on Sunday. And none of their artillery and cavalry reinforcements would have been on hand until quite late Saturday.[67] On Saturday the Valley troops' influence on the tide of battle would have been much less, probably decisively less, than it was on Sunday.

But whether McDowell would have attacked on Saturday is open to question. Although in his after-action report he claimed he could not have launched his army that day, his chief engineer, Major Barnard, reported that the reconnaissances on Friday ascertained the "perfect practicability" of the route of march that he re-reconnoitered on Saturday (Sunday's march started out on that route).[68] In McDowell's report ration cooking is given more blame than reconnaissance as a delaying factor, but the validity of his complaint about the arrival of rations is questionable.[69]

Some of McDowell's subordinates tried to persuade him that Johnston's army was being brought to Manassas or was already there on Saturday. Such rumors were rife, as were reports of train whistles and other railroad sounds reaching Centreville, McDowell's headquarters, from the direction of Manassas. General Tyler told McDowell, "I am as sure as there is a God in Heaven, you will have to fight Jo. Johnson's army at Manassas tomorrow." McDowell's attitude, as he expressed it later, was that of course the Confederates would be bringing up reinforcements — from wherever they could lay hands on them. At a conference with his division and brigade commanders Saturday night, he steered discussion away from the question of Johnston's presence or absence. Probably he shared his subordinates' suspicions that some or all of Johnston's army was present.[70]

McDowell's delay seems to have been a matter of irresolution and indecision more than of reconnaissance or ration cooking. Uncertainty as to Johnston's whereabouts was a major element of this psychological problem. A telegram announcing the Valley army's departure on Thursday from Winchester would have dispelled his indecision. McDowell's report implies that early on Saturday the possibility of forceful action that day was on his mind.[71] If the news from the Valley had come on Friday, or early enough on Saturday to be acted on that day, it probably would have shaken him out of his hesitancy. In the end he seems to have realized that he would in any case simply have to go ahead with the attack that was expected of him.

·· ·· ··

The Federals' lack of intelligence preparation being what it was, the wastage of vital intelligence reported by Strother is not surprising. That raises a question: How would information such as Strother's, from a distant command, have been handled when the Federals brought a competent intelligence service into being? One of the actions taken by the Army of the Potomac's intelligence bureau when it finally matured consisted of measures which, had they been in effect in 1861, would have prevented the suppression of Strother's information. A commander in McDowell's position would have had his own intelligence liaison officer at Patterson's headquarters.[72] The mere existence of such an arrangement would have impelled a prompt transmission of the report: Patterson would have been anxious to get the news to Washington before the visiting officer could. But an intelligence liaison arrangement was altogether unimaginable in 1861.

·· ·· ··

The tragic cost of the delayed discovery of Johnston's movement was not lost on President Lincoln. By the time six more months of war had passed, he had worked out a philosophy that stressed the need for good intelligence, and he had the Bull Run case in mind. His theory began by granting the Confederates their advantage in having interior lines, enabling them to concentrate "upon points of collision" more quickly than the Federals. But the Federals had the advantage of superior numbers, which they could use to threaten different points simultaneously. Outnumbering the enemy at each of those points, "we can," wrote Lincoln, "safely attack one, or both, if he makes no change; and if he weakens one to strengthen the other, forbear to attack the strengthened one, but seize, and hold, the weakened one." According to this scheme, Lincoln said, the Federals would have withheld their attack on Manassas and simply moved into Winchester. But he realized that that could not have been done unless Washington had learned of Johnston's departure from Winchester more promptly, for the next point in his strategy was this: "Every particular case will have its modifying circumstances, among which the most constantly present, and most difficult to meet, will be the want of perfect knowledge of the enemies' movements." (From Strother's story it appears that *acquiring* knowledge of the enemy's movements was somewhat less difficult than Lincoln assumed; the proper handling of it, once acquired, was more of a problem.) Lincoln noted that in the Bull Run case there was a difficulty more serious than the want of information about the enemy: the impending loss of the three-month regiments.[73]

.. .. ..

Irvin McDowell's path crossed David Hunter Strother's a year later, when both were serving under John Pope in the campaign that led to another inglorious Federal defeat on the same Bull Run. The two men talked for half an hour. Strother's diary does not say whether he asked if McDowell believed he would have won the battle if he had known of the Valley army's movement in good time.[74] The diary tells only that the two new friends had a good talk about McDowell's favorite sport — trout fishing.[75]

3

. . . .

"KNOWN IN RICHMOND
IN TWENTY-FOUR HOURS"

July 1861–March 1862

THE BULL RUN DEBACLE shocked the North out of its expectation of a short war. Lincoln immediately began the patient planning that should have preceded the advance on Manassas. He called to Washington the U.S. Army's ranking major general, George Brinton McClellan, the head of an Ohio-based army that by mid-July had driven the Confederates out of most of western Virginia.

Arriving in Washington five days after the battle, McClellan began reorganizing the forces around the capital on a grand scale. Only thirty-four, he possessed limitless ambition and was accustomed to seeing it gratified. After resigning from the army in 1857, he had soon become vice president of the Illinois Central Railroad, then superintendent of the Ohio and Mississippi. He returned to the service in 1861 as a major general of Ohio volunteers.[1] He was one of the few American officers who had observed European armies, but his record suggests that he learned more of grand conceptions than may have been good for him.

Part of the military capability McClellan brought to his Washington command was his personal intelligence service, Allan Pinkerton's nationally known detective agency, which had served McClellan during his railroading years. After escorting Lincoln to Washington, Pinkerton had returned to Chicago without waiting to see him inaugurated. Then, according to Pinkerton, he was called back to the capital and asked to take over the government's security problems, but such was the confusion in the administration that he despaired of being able to accomplish anything. Instead he went to work for McClellan, who had been placed in command of the Department of the Ohio and was making his headquarters at Cincinnati.

The detective chief, a Scotsman of forty-two years, now became an agent himself once again, making a sweep through Kentucky, Tennessee, and Mississippi to observe Confederate military preparations. We have only Pinkerton's own account, from his mainly fictitious memoirs: "It is needless to relate the valuable items of information which I was able to glean upon this journey — information which in later days was of vast importance to Union commanders, but which at this time would only burden a narrative of the events which they so ably assisted to successful results."[2] Pinkerton the memoirist took his cue from Lafayette Baker, who had set the style for Civil War espionage histories in claiming momentous discoveries that he would not trouble his readers to describe.

In his memoirs Pinkerton duplicated Baker's feat of self-promotion by naming himself "Chief of the United States Secret Service," a name his organization never possessed any more than Baker's did. Pinkerton's unit was nameless; its reports, which took the form of letters addressed to McClellan, were headed "Headquarters City Guard/Provost Marshal's Office," but neither half of that awkward combination was used elsewhere than in those letter headings. It was as near to anonymity as a letter heading could get, and thus was helpful to the maintenance of secrecy. To further that object Pinkerton adopted the nom de guerre "E. J. Allen" and retained it long after the identity of "Major Allen" (actually he remained a civilian) was well known.[3]

Pinkerton's organization was not a government bureau; he was a businessman under contract to the army. As for his employees, he would not tell anyone, even the War Department officer who paid him, who they were. On his monthly pay vouchers he gave the initials of each employee, but when in his absence an assistant listed them as "Operative D," "Operative F," and so on through the inevitable "Operative X," that was too much secrecy for Secretary of War Stanton, who had succeeded Cameron. Stanton tried to force the full names out of Pinkerton; the detective chief responded that keeping his agents' identity secret was vital to the future success of his detective business. Stanton rejected his argument, but Pinkerton continued to reveal only the initials of his people and still drew the full amount of pay claimed on his vouchers right up to the end of his service. Thus did Stanton suffer one of his very few defeats in his militant guardianship of Uncle Sam's bank account; for sixteen months the government paid the salaries and expenses of a sizable force of secret agents (twenty-eight at its peak) whose origins and probable loyalty it had no way of checking.[4]

Pinkerton's bureau was an innovation to the extent that earlier intelligence activities, in the Revolutionary and Mexican wars, were not conducted by a recognizable organizational entity. This was George McClellan's chief, or only, contribution to the nation's advancement of the military art. Although it engaged in both positive intelligence (gathering information about a potential or actual opponent) and counterintelligence, it was quite a limited intelligence operation. The counterintelligence mission was shared with Lafayette Baker (whose own organization, limited to counterespionage and military-police work, also was not a complete intelligence operation). And Pinkerton's positive-intelligence operation was incomplete in that the two functions the bureau performed, espionage and interrogation of prisoners, deserters, and refugees, were only a fraction of the total positive-intelligence mission; he had nothing to do with the other types of positive intelligence. Scouting, a function equally as important as spying, was left to the initiative of the division commanders; their findings, which were meager, went to McClellan, not Pinkerton. The chief duty of the cavalry, in theory at least, was reconnaissance; what little information the army's unaggressively led cavalry produced went to McClellan. The balloonists and the Signal Corps observation posts also bypassed Pinkerton, sending their reports to the nearest division headquarters or to McClellan. Southern newspapers, despite the probability of error and deliberate misinformation in their coverage of military matters, were an important source; although Pinkerton's agents would have participated in the contraband commerce that exchanged newspapers with Richmond, reporting on the contents of those papers was not part of his job. In a complete intelligence operation he would have received reports from the cavalry and the other sources not under his control and synthesized the information from all the sources into a comprehensive picture. But only General McClellan received the output of all the sources; he would be gone and the war would be half over before any commander thought of setting up an intelligence operation that would produce such a picture.

Even Pinkerton's well-known espionage operation was incomplete. With the exception of a few side trips by his ablest operative, Timothy Webster, and one or two others, Richmond was its dominant and in most respects its only target, probably because a city could be penetrated much more readily than a field army's headquarters. Pinkerton's spies were all transients, playing roles such as smuggler of contraband merchandise or courier to secession's friends in the North. Although there were thousands of Union sympathizers in Virginia, Pinkerton did not acquire a resident spy or informant there (or anywhere else); the Pinkerton agents planted permanently in Richmond are part of the Civil War's espionage mythology. When contact was finally established with a Unionist underground in the enemy capital, Pinkerton and his operatives were long gone from the scene.

.. .. ..

The coexistence of two spy-chasing services, Pinkerton's and Baker's, contained the potential for a secret-service war, but both found so much to do that they had no time to work up a rivalry. While Pinkerton was targeting suspected Confederate spies in Washington, Baker was directing his attention to the flow of contraband mail and merchandise. That problem drew him and his few employees to the lower counties of Maryland, where secessionist sentiment kept channels open to the Confederacy. Baker also tracked down disloyal businessmen in Baltimore, Philadelphia, and New York; before many weeks his investigations were ranging as far afield as Canada.[5] But it was inevitable that, lacking any common overseer (Baker worked for the War Department and Pinkerton for McClellan's army), their agents would cross paths and end up spying on each other. That happened when Baker, before Pinkerton's positive-intelligence mechanism gained momentum, ventured back into that field himself. One of his employees, J. T. Kerby, an Englishman from Niagara Falls, Canada, went on a mission to Richmond. In front of the Confederate provost marshal's office Kerby struck up a conversation with Pinkerton's first agent to visit Richmond, E. H. Stein. Both men, of course, were playing the role of arch Rebel. Months later, when both were back in Washington, Stein spotted Kerby in front of the office of the local provost marshal. He followed Kerby to New York, where he arranged an "accidental" meeting in which the two men continued the role-playing game begun in Richmond. Kerby, who had already seen the inside of Richmond's famed Castle Thunder prison on suspicion of being what he was, a Federal spy, proved so convincing a secessionist in New York that he was shadowed by Pinkerton men for several weeks and then treated to a stay in Old Capitol Prison in Washington. The comedy was brought to a close with his release, presumably through Baker's intervention. Evidently because of the attention that had been drawn to him, he was dropped from the payroll, but he kept in touch with Baker. Like J. O. Kerbey, J. T. Kerby had overplayed the Rebel role. Unlike his near-namesake, he may actually have had secessionist sympathies.[6]

There is no indication that the episode led anyone to suggest consolidating Pinkerton's and Baker's bureaus. Such a scheme would have come in conflict with the nation's traditional suspicion of concentration of police power.

. .   ..   ..

Even before Pinkerton moved his agency to Washington, action was under way on Capitol Hill to remove the greatest single threat to the secrecy of the government's plans. A congressional committee headed by Representative John F. Potter of Wisconsin had begun hearings aimed at discovering friends of secession who still held jobs in the government, continuing the investigation begun by the previous Congress. The new hearings began with a blunt notice in Washington newspapers asking for information "against every one now in . . . employ, not true to the Union." Later the investigators announced that care was being taken that "none shall be injured by mere malice or rumor."[7]

The Potter committee received some 550 charges, heard nearly that many witnesses under oath, and made determinations of Southern sympathies against more than 200 employees. Its published report named the witnesses and summarized their testimony. Coming on top of the widespread fears that the investigation had touched off, it caused turmoil and violent animosities in government circles. Yet the committee had no power to remove jobholders, and the number of dismissals and resignations by no means equaled the number of findings of disloyalty. In the War Department Secretary Cameron, presumably because Potter tended toward wild accusations, refused to listen to him. Then when Stanton came aboard, he made friends with Potter, read through the committee's bulky records of allegations, and gave the congressman four scalps: one officer and three clerks lost their jobs. So gratified was Potter that the pressure on Stanton's department ceased and with it the hysteria among its personnel.[8]

Whatever damage was wrought by disloyalty among the "secession clerks," it was not confined to those remaining in their jobs. Scarcely had the Confederate forces established themselves in northern Virginia in April and May than one J. D. Hutton, who had left a job in the War Department, arrived inside the Rebel lines with a document showing "the intention of the Federal Government as to Alexandria." That intention was to take the city by force; the Confederate commander, who had 380 poorly armed troops, almost all of them locals, on May 5 withdrew the entire command, against orders, rather than lose them all in a hopeless fight.[9] Another ex-clerk who assisted the Confederacy was James Taliaferro, who had worked in the Treasury Department. Early in July a party of Federal soldiers, seamen, and Marines found him, obviously en route South, at a hotel in lower Maryland. He was carrying $1700 in gold and letters indicating that he had sent "quite a lot of information to Virginia."[10] George Donellan, formerly an Interior Department clerk and more recently the manager of its land office in Nebraska Territory, carried to the Manassas headquarters the reports of the Confederates' leading spy in Washington, Rose Greenhow.[11] But one clerk who was potentially the most dangerous of all remained at his post. This was John Callan, who had been devoting full time to his position with the Senate Military Affairs Committee but in August moved back to the Adjutant General's Office, where he had worked earlier in the year. Committee activity apparently being light, the chairman, Senator Henry Wilson, recommended him for the army position.[12]

.. .. ..

A more obvious concern than the "secession clerks," though seemingly less dangerous, were the far more numerous Southern-sympathizing Washingtonians who did not hold government jobs. Among the most visible of these was Mrs. Greenhow, who drew attention by the number of visitors she received, many of them known secessionists. She was so careless as to offer to send a private letter through the army lines; the recipient of the offer was the wife of an assistant of Secretary Seward. The Federals' Bull Run defeat engendered a suspicion that information sent to Manassas from Washington had had something to do with the Confederate victory. (Mrs. Greenhow at this point was reporting to Manassas that the government was making "Every effort . . . to find out who gave the alarm.") One of the first actions taken was an order by Assistant Secretary of War Thomas A. Scott directing Pinkerton to watch Mrs. Greenhow. There would have been other suspects, but she evidently was singled out by the number of known contacts she had among two groups — Federal officials (or their wives) and local friends of secession.

One August night when Pinkerton had the Greenhow house under surveillance, an army officer was seen leaving. The detective chief and one of his men followed; the officer broke into a run; they kept up with him to his quarters, where he put them under arrest. Leaving them under guard, he disappeared upstairs for twenty minutes, during which time, Pinkerton assumed, he was destroying incriminating papers. The two prisoners spent the night in the guardhouse, "a most filthy and uncomfortable place," but in the morning they were discharged "by Mr. Secretary Scott in person." Pinkerton returned to Mrs. Greenhow's house the next day, August 23, and arrested her.[13]

Rose Greenhow is the most celebrated spy of the Civil War. Her espionage consisted of providing General Beauregard two warnings of the Federals' advance on Manassas. But her actual achievements have been exaggerated and other, grander ones fabricated. She may safely be credited with reporting that the Federals had finally and definitely determined to make the advance against the Confederates in northern Virginia that the whole country, North and South, was counting on. That was an extremely valuable nugget of information, but her admirers have been unwilling to let it go at that. They have had the field to themselves; her accomplishments have never been examined seriously enough to confirm or confound the claims made for her (and by her). How accurate, how complete, how timely was the information she sent to Manassas? How, and how much, did it contribute to the Confederate victory?

Reared in Washington and nearby Montgomery County, Maryland, Rose O'Neal Greenhow knew the great and near-great of capital society from girlhood. Her inbred Southern proclivities were strengthened by marriage to Robert Greenhow, a scholarly Virginian who made a career of service in the State Department. She was an aunt of Mrs. Stephen A. Douglas, a relative by marriage of James and Dolley Madison, and a longtime intimate friend of President James Buchanan. In the estimation of a man who was not her friend, Allan Pinkerton, she was a "very remarkable woman" whose social abilities and contacts together with her superior education conferred upon her "an almost superhuman power." Pinkerton also believed, without naming names, that she had used her "almost irresistible seductive powers" in the service of the enemy.[14]

In 1850 Robert Greenhow's work took him and his family to Mexico City and then San Francisco, where he was fatally injured in a fall in 1854. In 1852 or possibly 1851 his wife and three daughters had returned East, a trip that in those days was measured in weeks or months. Sometime in 1853 Mrs. Greenhow gave birth to a fourth daughter. This imprecision of dates introduces the possibility that the father of the child was someone other than Robert Greenhow. The point has some importance because, if Mrs. Greenhow maintained her high social position in the face of a rather public illegitimacy, we are that much better able to understand the brazen drive that made her the leader of a spy ring. But the records of the case, including the fourth daughter's birth certificate, are so vague that not even the writers of Civil War spy stories (published as history), ever on the lookout for romance, have undertaken to solve this puzzle.[15]

Although repelled by the unpolished Westerners and Northerners who were seen more and more prominently in Washington in the late fifties, Mrs. Greenhow maintained friendships on both sides of the House Divided. The arrival in 1861 of a Republican administration, headed by a President whose very appearance evoked angry sputterings from her, did not reduce her zeal to keep up her connections. She was plotting treason, of a kind that demanded friends in high places.

For the services she had in mind she found a client in Thomas Jordan, a Virginian who held his commission in the United States Army until late in May. Leaving Washington to join the Confederates, he arranged for her to send information South and provided her with a simple cipher. Apparently by prearrangement, he became General Beauregard's adjutant at Manassas.[16]

She is known to have sent Jordan two notes warning of McDowell's advance, the first on July 9 (arriving at Manassas on the 10th) and the other on the 16th, the day his army began the march. Neither message has survived. The existence of the July 9 report is known from an 1863 letter written by Beauregard and from the postwar recollections of former Brigadier General Milledge L. Bonham, who commanded Beauregard's advance post at Fairfax Court House and was the first to receive the dispatch. Of its contents, Beauregard said only that it reported "the intended positive advance of the enemy across the Potomac." Bonham was not privy to the contents of the message; he relayed it, unopened, to Beauregard. In a postwar letter he romanticized freely to Beauregard over the beauty of the courier, one Bettie Duval, and especially the luxuriant black hair from which she removed the message, sewed up in black silk. Beauregard wrote that it arrived "about the 10th of July"; that date has received indirect support in recent years from the discovery that on July 11 he issued orders for his two most advanced brigades, Bonham's at Fairfax and Ewell's on the far right flank, to withdraw at the first sign of the enemy's approach.[17]

As to timeliness, Mrs. Greenhow's report was seriously flawed, for (as we saw in chapter 2) the decision to advance on Manassas had been made late in June, about two weeks before she reported it. Her report was accurate in that it correctly stated the Federals' intention, but it was incomplete in that it missed the succession of dates McDowell set for the start of his march (from July 8 to the 13th, the 15th, and then the 16th). Each of these delays would have produced a highly interesting report if Mrs. Greenhow's contacts had really been close to the heart of Federal planning. Her July 9 report was enough, however, to cause Beauregard to commence immediately "making my preparations to receive [the] meditated attack."[18]

Her source could have been a highly placed official with a tongue loosened by Greenhow's charms, but it is more likely that the secret of McDowell's intended advance had leaked out to an inner, or perhaps even the outer, circle of Washington society. In any case, a Federal march on Manassas was so obvious a move, especially under the threat of the release, in late July and August, of the dozens of three-month regiments, that her warning could have been based on no more than a widely accepted rumor.

The episode is never recounted without crediting Mrs. Greenhow with predicting the timing, usually the exact date, of McDowell's planned advance, even though Beauregard's account, which originated the story, avoids that item almost pointedly. One version of the incident, often repeated, invents the exact words of the report: "McDowell has certainly been ordered to advance on the sixteenth."[19] It has even been possible to include in the same account two conflicting items — that Mrs. Greenhow's message written July 9 gave the July 16 date of march and that McDowell did not set that date until the 15th. Espionage miracles like this go beyond mere prescience.

According to Mrs. Greenhow's book, *My Imprisonment and the First Year of Abolition Rule at Washington* (published in London in 1863), the information for her second report was easily acquired: "On the morning of the 16th of July, the . . . papers at Washington announced that the 'grand army' was in motion, and I had heard from a reliable source (having received a copy of the order to McDowell) that the order for a forward movement had gone forth." But there was no order to McDowell on this occasion; he was setting his own timetable. And it may be doubted that Mrs. Greenhow first heard of the march from the newspapers; for two or three days regiments of infantry camped in and about Washington had been marching for the Potomac bridges, filling the streets in full view of the townspeople. At noon on the 16th, she says, "I despatched a messenger to Manassas," carrying a cipher message. The messenger, George Donellan, cut off from the direct route to Manassas by four columns of marching Federals, rode the byways of southern Maryland to a point on the Potomac forty-five miles below Washington and turned the sealed message over to a colonel commanding a small local force, whose facilities got it to Beauregard by 8 P.M.[20]

All that survives of Mrs. Greenhow's message is a short, rough summary that Beauregard wrote, presumably from memory, in his 1863 letter, an unofficial communication to a private citizen and therefore not an altogether reliable indication of the quality of the information she produced. The summary oversimplifies the four routes of McDowell's march, and it indicates that she reported his army's strength as 55,000, which would have been a good estimate for all the troops around Washington, but 20,000 of them did not belong to McDowell's army.[21]

Again Mrs. Greenhow's report rates poorly on the timeliness count. From July 9 to July 16 was a long time between reports, especially with an invasion of the Confederacy in the final stage of preparation. Some of her collaborators must have observed movements that preceded the army's departure on the 16th. The delay in her report may not have been her fault; for much of that time she probably was awaiting the arrival of Donellan or some other courier.

By the evening hours of July 16, when Beauregard had Mrs. Greenhow's report in hand, his most advanced pickets and scouts were within sight of, if not in contact with, McDowell's leading units.[22] Still he credited Mrs. Greenhow's message as the source of the information that caused him to reposition some of his troops that night. No information could have been of greater import, but not until the next day did he get around to telegraphing Richmond for reinforcements. His telegram was sent so late in the day (the 17th) that he was able to report that the Federals had arrived in Bonham's front at Fairfax; therefore it is clear that it was not Mrs. Greenhow's report of the previous day that moved him to send for reinforcements. McDowell's columns were converging from three different directions, and Bonham was retiring. As Joe Johnston's Valley army was to be the decisive element in the battle, Beauregard's delay in calling for reinforcements would have been disastrous if McDowell had not made his equally unaccountable delay upon reaching Centreville.[23]

Although Mrs. Greenhow's report that McDowell's army was on the march had little effect, the fact remains that her July 9 report made an important contribution to the Confederate victory by ending the state of suspense afflicting Beauregard and his army and energizing him to prepare for battle.

Beauregard summed up the case by stating that although he was "reliably informed of the enemy's main purpose" — to advance on Manassas — "nothing had been learned of his plans" for carrying out that purpose.[24]

. . . . . .

The Pinkerton detectives who arrested Mrs. Greenhow on August 23 were richly rewarded in a search of her house for incriminating papers. She had violated a first principle of espionage by retaining copies of her reports to Jordan. She had begun to destroy them and other papers, but the project was interrupted in an early stage. Some of the papers were found in her stove, unburned; others were elsewhere in the house. Some were torn up; the detectives assembled the fragments by the jigsaw method, not always into a readable state. The copies of her reports were partly in cipher, and she had done Pinkerton the favor of leaving the plain-language version of one cipher message among the papers he collected. By matching plain and cipher versions he could acquire a virtually complete reconstruction of the cipher without having to solve it analytically (though that would not have been difficult).

The detectives' find amounted to eight intelligence reports, totaling 1100 words and bearing dates between July 31 and August 21.* The collection reveals that her chief sources of information were collaborators whom she called scouts; they walked about picking up rumors and noting movements of troops, construction of fortifications, and other easily observable military developments. On August 9 she described her coverage as including observers at all of the city's inlets and outlets, and she informed Jordan that their findings verified the newspapers' reports. Later that day she rewrote this message, omitting the reassurance of the newspapers' reliability and the claim of eye-witness coverage at the approaches to the city. But her reports paid little attention to items reported in the press, an indication that she did not have the means of correcting its reports.

Apart from a street map of Alexandria, showing a fort and an encampment, Mrs. Greenhow had little or no coverage of the Virginia side of the Potomac, where most of the military activity was taking place. But the very fact that not much else went on in that rural setting robbed would-be observers of the casualness they could feign as they walked the streets of Washington. On the question of masked batteries that were to be expected in the Virginia countryside, she could only report that "[e]very reason is had to believe" that there were such batteries "throughout their whole line of fortifications from Alexandria to Chain Bridge."

Hoping that Beauregard would follow up his Bull Run victory by taking Washington, she announced, "At [the] proper time an effort will be

---

* For the texts of these reports, see Appendix 4.

made here to cut their telegraph wires and spike their guns wherever they are left unmanned." This scheme was an unreasoning product of the euphoria generated by the Bull Run victory, but its very existence indicates that the ring of collaborators centered on Mrs. Greenhow was more than a handful. Her faith in the feasibility of an attack by Beauregard was no more unreasonable than that held by a considerable body of Southern opinion — and by General McClellan, who feared himself outnumbered.

She disliked having to rely on her "untutored judgment" and repeatedly asked Jordan to send her instructions. This confession of imperfection in her coverage is at odds with history's standard picture of Rose Greenhow as an all-knowing, totally successful spy, and with a decidedly unhumble manner that she maintained before Federal authorities after her arrest.

Her reports were generally unemotional, although she once ventured to say that "You know that my soul is in the cause" and asked Jordan to "Tell Beauregard that in my imagination he takes the place of the Cid." At one point when she assured Jordan that "All I sent is reliable," she may have sensed a feeling among Confederate commanders that unreasoning patriotism so beclouded the judgment of their womenfolk as to disqualify them as spies.

Her reporting, however, was by no means as reliable as she claimed. Only the part of her scouts' reports that was based on visual observation rated a high degree of credibility. The recipients of her reports would have been assisted in evaluating them if she had shown the source of each item, but she withheld that information except in the case of the one item she obtained from an "inside" source, Senator Henry Wilson, her supposed lover. This lack of information on sources would have raised doubts in the minds of Jordan and Beauregard as to the competence of her whole operation. An example of reports that gave them this difficulty is one she sent, soon after the Bull Run battle, to the effect that the Federals feared a two-pronged attack on Washington by way of Leesburg and Baltimore — a scheme so far beyond the Confederates' capabilities that such a fear would not have been entertained even by McClellan. Another item presenting this problem was a report that McClellan expected to work a surprise on the Manassas army. Accompanied by information on its origin, this would have received serious attention; without such information, it had the flavor of mere gossip, and that is what it was.

The one item Mrs. Greenhow obtained from her prize source, Senator Wilson, was the number of heavy guns and other artillery in the Washington defenses. As the figures he gave are not known, there is no way of determining whether they were correct. But those figures were but a small fraction of the knowledge he possessed as chairman of the Senate's Military Affairs Committee; therefore the suspicion arises that he was deceiving Mrs. Greenhow by understating or overstating the true figures. However, she informed Jordan that the figures Wilson reported were confirmed by the observations of her scouts.

In regard to his own status, Wilson was not taking Mrs. Greenhow into his confidence. That is clear from a report to Jordan in which she wrote that he was joining McClellan's staff "as aid and adviser," at a time when he was arranging for himself the colonelcy of a Massachusetts infantry regiment, the 22nd — a fact she was unaware of or in any case did not report to Jordan. At first glance an association of Senator Wilson, an unwavering and vocal abolitionist, with General McClellan, an equally determined opponent of abolition, seems most unlikely; and nowhere in McClellan's papers does Wilson appear as a member of his staff. Although McClellan's intention to fight the war without disturbing the institution of slavery had not yet surfaced at this time, Wilson or McClellan, or both, could have discovered their ideological incompatibility before the senator performed any services on the staff. But months later we find a newspaper notice of his resignation from the position. As for Wilson's service with the 22nd Massachusetts Infantry, that appears to have come to very little.[25]

Thus we see that Wilson was no fountainhead of information for Mrs. Greenhow, but he evidently gave her correct figures on a key point regarding Washington defenses. The most probable meaning of this set of facts is that he took it on himself to tell her the truth about McClellan's formidable artillery, for the purpose of discouraging the Confederate attack on Washington that was genuinely feared at this time.[26]

· ·   · ·   · ·

The claims of Mrs. Greenhow's prowess most frequently seen are that she knew McClellan's plans as well as his own generals did and that she regularly obtained details of the meetings of Lincoln's cabinet. To the latter it is sometimes added that cabinet discussions were known in Richmond within twenty-four hours. The existence in archives of 1100 words of her reporting should have led to historians' evaluation of these claims many years ago. That would quickly have revealed Mrs. Greenhow as producing nothing at all about White House business; as to McClellan's plans, the only one she ever mentioned was for a flanking movement around Manassas to cut its rail communication — a movement favored by Lincoln, feared by General Johnston, but never planned by McClellan.

How then did these myths about Mrs. Greenhow's penetration of Lincoln's and McClellan's inner circles get into the books to begin with? They were originated by three people who all knew better: Rose Greenhow herself, Allan Pinkerton, and Lafayette Baker.

In her book, Mrs. Greenhow alternates for three hundred pages between diatribes against the hard-headed Yankees and accounts of how easily they succumbed to her cunning. She wrote: "I might almost be said to have assisted at Lincoln's Cabinet Councils, . . . having verbatim reports of them as well as of the Republican caucus. I was thoroughly competent to the task of giving a faithful synopsis of their deliberations."[27] Her claim of having acquired McClellan's plans is similarly generous: "McClellan did me the honour to say that I knew his plans better than President Lincoln or his Cabinet, and had caused him four times to change them." (If McClellan learned that the enemy knew his plans — learned it not only once but four times — he achieved quite a feat of counterintelligence.) Another claim was that she obtained "minutes of McClellan's private consultations, and often extracts from his notes."[28]

That these fictions would not be lost to history was assured when strikingly similar statements appeared in the memoirs of so good a pair of authorities as Baker and Pinkerton. According to Baker's *History of the United States Secret Service*, it was reports of the cabinet meetings that the Rebels acquired so efficiently;[29] that these reached Richmond within twenty-four hours was a claim made not by Mrs. Greenhow but by Baker. His improvement on her version is one plausible part of the story; early in the war Confederate couriers faced so little impedance from Federal policing that they probably could sometimes get to Richmond in a day's time. But that adds no believability to the claim that the couriers sometimes carried minutes of cabinet meetings.[30]

Pinkerton's contribution to the myth in his *Spy of the Rebellion* reads: "The rebel authorities were as fully conversant with the plans of the Union commanders as they were themselves. . . . they knew of the position of every regiment and brigade, and the contemplated movements of the commanders, and the time of proposed action, far in advance of any publicity being given to them." Pinkerton made a showing of authenticity by asserting that his information was from "reliable sources" and was "fully proven," but his source was Mrs. Greenhow's book; he happily accepted her inventions and expanded on them.[31]

Why would two counterespionage chiefs, writing self-serving books, go out of their way to credit the enemy with astoundingly successful espionage unless they believed that success to have been a fact? Pinkerton states explicitly that the Confederates' free-and-easy spying took place before he and his detectives came to town. Baker also places it in the early months of the war. Each man was telling his readers how bad things were until *he* took charge.

It is quite reasonable to accuse the two top-ranking secret-service officers of tampering with the facts. A challenge to Baker's veracity is completely in accord with his well-established reputation; his testimony to the House of Representatives in connection with the impeachment proceedings against President Andrew Johnson made him perhaps the most

celebrated liar in American history. The House record reads, "It is doubtful if he [Baker] has in any one thing told the truth, even by accident."[32]
As for Pinkerton, his book abounds in ludicrous stretchings of the facts
and outright fictions.[33]

If it had suited their purpose, Baker and Pinkerton could have deflated Mrs. Greenhow's claims by quoting the reports found in her house
and pointing out that they contained nothing like cabinet minutes or
McClellan's confidential documents. Instead, the two counterespionage
chiefs bequeathed to posterity a story of Confederate intelligence success
that has demonstrated great hardihood. Fragments of the language in
which they stated these claims survive in modern accounts by writers who
ignore the fact that Pinkerton and Baker were writing about the early
months of the war (and weren't even telling the truth about that period).
These stories, and others no better documented, have hardened into a
myth of Confederate superiority in spying, scouting, and related matters,
while the actual intelligence capabilities and accomplishments of both
North and South have remained for the most part uninvestigated.

· ·   · ·   · ·

Promptly upon her arrest, Mrs. Greenhow's home was made her prison;
other female suspects were soon brought there, with the result that it
came to be called Fort Greenhow. Historians have made much of her
cleverness and determination in sending messages to Jordan through
her household of military guards. It has not occurred to these admirers
— though it did to Mrs. Greenhow — that Pinkerton might have let
these messages pass in order to intercept them or follow their trail to her
accomplices. Her sources of information and her channels of transmission were limited to the visitors he permitted her to receive. Security in
Fort Greenhow was so tight that the first corporal of the guard was
"incarcerated in one of the dark and filthy cells of the 'Central Guard
House' . . . for merely allowing a bundle of unwashed linen to pass the
guard without the customary examination." We can safely assume that
Pinkerton carefully calculated the risk he took in admitting visitors who
could pass information to Mrs. Greenhow or depart with one of her
messages.

During this period Confederate authorities received several strong
warnings of impending Federal attacks. One of these messages definitely
known to have come from Mrs. Greenhow described a plan "to get
behind Manassas and cut off railroad and other communications with
our army while an attack is made in front." "For God's sake heed this. It is
positive," she urged. All of these alarms were false; this was a time when
McClellan's failure to mount an offensive or even plan one was Lincoln's
greatest worry.[34] The visitors Pinkerton allowed Mrs. Greenhow carried
as much misinformation to the Rebels as he could have wished for. But

Jordan did not trust information sent through channels subject to Pinkerton's control; he informed Richmond that "further correspondence with her [Mrs. Greenhow] is useless."

Fort Greenhow had been running smoothly for some time when a letter Mrs. Greenhow sent to Secretary Seward, complaining of her treatment and comparing herself to Marie Antoinette, found its way into a Richmond newspaper and was reprinted in the North. To the Northern public it appeared that if this leading traitor had freedom to communicate with Richmond, she was being coddled. So with her eight-year-old daughter, Rose, she was placed with the lesser lights of Washington Rebeldom in Old Capitol Prison.[35]

So many political prisoners had been taken by the early months of 1862 that a commission was appointed to interview them. The commissioners were two distinguished New York Democrats, Major General John A. Dix, a former senator and secretary of the Treasury, and Judge Edwards Pierrepont, a friend of Stanton's. They were empowered only to determine whether a prisoner should be discharged, retained in military custody, or remanded to the civil courts for trial.[36] Early in their hearings, in March, they examined the star prisoner, Mrs. Greenhow. Reading the transcript of the examination and observing the treatment the two gentlemen received at her hands, one admires their courage and patriotism in performing this service. She began the interview by complaining, "I have been waiting so long that my patience is nearly exhausted." They proceeded hesitantly, reminding her again and again, "You need not answer any questions which you do not want to." She turned on them with ". . . this kind of mimic court. . . . Now isn't this a farce! Isn't it solemn!" Her responses were a dizzying succession of qualified denials and similarly qualified admissions — for example, her answer to the charge of having sent the Confederates information in the Bull Run campaign: "I am not aware of that. It is certain that if I had the information, I should have given it. I should consider that I was performing a holy duty to my friends." Asked about her letter published in Richmond, she charged that Secretary Seward had sent it there; he was the perpetrator of this "outrage" on her privacy.

To Pierrepont's offer of release upon taking the oath of allegiance and giving parole of honor, she replied, "You would blush to do that." She made treason seem a civil right. Then she denied that she had exercised that right, but later she virtually admitted espionage, asking, "If Mr. Lincoln's friends will pour into my ear such important information, am I to be held responsible for all that?" The commissioners had in hand a number of her treasonable communications, yet they did not find the words to turn her numerous prevarications to her disadvantage, or even discomfiture. Her hauteur never lapsed. Confronted by a letter she had recently written that contained such expressions as "these Black Republican dogs," she announced that those were "my present feelings and sentiments." She scolded the government at every turn and closed by telling Dix and Pierrepont, "In these war times, you ought to be in some more important business than holding an inquisition for the examination of women."

By exhausting her examiners' patience Mrs. Greenhow confounded their charges more effectively than able lawyers could have done. Their decision — probably as much a relief to them as to her — was to deport her to the Confederacy. At Richmond she received a Presidential welcome and eventually was sent to England and France on a special diplomatic mission that sought to capitalize on her public-relations value. Returning on a British blockade runner that grounded in rough seas upon entering Cape Fear River, she insisted on being put ashore in a small boat. It capsized; weighted down by the English gold she was carrying, she sank quickly and drowned. The other five persons aboard survived.[37]

Rose Greenhow soon became a Confederate heroine. It would seem that the Southern gratitude she has received is more than she deserves. From the quality of her reports it is clear that she was no great success at garnering information. Whatever adulation she is entitled to must be for her tremendous courage and drive and her apparent ability to draw collaborators, some of them perhaps unwitting, into her net. A more serious failing was her irrational and arrogant underrating of the "Black Republican dogs." Such was her contempt for them that she became foolishly careless, as is shown by the evidence of espionage that she kept about her premises. With different emotional equipment she could have continued spying for a long time, perhaps as long as the war lasted.

That Rose Greenhow was a wrong choice for espionage was perceived by Judge Pierrepont. To him her activities did not rise to the level of treason; they amounted only to *mischief*.[38] We may doubt that that verdict pleased Rose Greenhow. It was the closest her distinguished examiners came to taking some of the wind out of her sails.

· · · · · ·

By retaining copies of her reports Mrs. Greenhow betrayed not only herself but also her friends, three of whom — George Donellan, Jordan's courier; Dr. Aaron Van Camp; and Colonel Michael Thompson, a lawyer — were named in the papers Pinkerton recovered.[39] Through them others were implicated. Her carelessness in allowing both the cipher text and the plain-language text (the latter untorn) of a dispatch to fall into Pinkerton's hands not only permitted easy solution of the cipher; it also placed the cipher in his hands for use in deceptive measures. Jordan some months later received a letter in that cipher. As he had issued it only to Mrs. Greenhow, whom he knew to be under arrest, he saw through this effort to draw him into a correspondence; he did not answer.[40]

Donellan, based with the Manassas army, was out of Pinkerton's reach. Although Van Camp and Thompson lived in Washington, he held off their arrest until December, presumably because he wanted more evidence against them or hoped, as the effort to correspond with Jordan indicates, to identify other links in the net. Matters came to a head in mid-December, when a navy brig cruising the Potomac stopped a schooner named *Lucretia* and took, among other contraband, fourteen letters from Thompson to Southern addresses. Either Pinkerton concluded that this occurrence forced his hand or he feared that Thompson would learn of the capture and slip away, for he arrested both Thompson and Van Camp within two days.[41] Half a dozen lesser figures already were in confinement; left at large, however, was a banker named William T. Smithson, who had already been identified as a collaborator with Thompson and who was found to be the writer of two cipher letters taken from the *Lucretia*. For reasons not apparent he was not arrested until January 8, 1862.[42]

One other principal agent found to be connected with the ring was arrested a month later. This was Mrs. Augusta Heath Morris, whom Pinkerton described as a Parisian lady married to one John Francis Mason of Frederick, Maryland, but living in style at Brown's Hotel in Washington under her maiden name. Confederate authorities had a somewhat different understanding of her situation; President Davis had approved her employment after being informed that "She claims to be married to an officer in our army, by whom she has two children whose legitimacy she wishes to establish, the father denying it and being about to marry another woman." In a cipher letter to Mrs. Morris that fell into Pinkerton's hands, "Thomas John Rayford," the alias Colonel Jordan had used with Mrs. Greenhow, expressed hope that she had not become involved through the arrest of "W.T.S." (Smithson). Mrs. Morris presumably was the woman agent whom Jordan had described to Richmond late in October as having the "capacity and wit to make an efficient emissary." He had overrated her; like Mrs. Greenhow, she attempted to carry on her secret correspondence from prison, and in doing so she demonstrated a fatuity that exceeded Mrs. Greenhow's. The letters she wrote after being arrested, easily acquired by Pinkerton, spelled out her culpability in terms far plainer than the evidence collected against her up to that time.[43]

Pinkerton made up for the cautiousness of his preliminary actions by recommending the confinement of these secessionist spies for the duration of the war. General Dix, Judge Pierrepont, and the higher authority they served (Lincoln and Stanton) felt otherwise. The penalty suffered by Mrs. Greenhow — nine months' confinement in her home and Old

Capitol, followed by deportation South — was the severest one meted out to any member of the ring.[44] One other woman, the wife of a former congressman from Alabama, who had made herself more a nuisance than a threat, also was banished to Richmond, after only a short stay in Fort Greenhow.[45] The others — Thompson, Smithson, Mrs. Morris, and several of their aides and accomplices — were released after short periods, none of them on terms more stringent than their taking the oath of allegiance or giving a parole of honor.[46] The disposition of Dr. Van Camp's case, though it does not appear in the records with the others, could scarcely have been very different from theirs. All the culprits escaped further difficulties with the Federal authorities except Smithson, who became so active as a financial agent for the Confederate government that he was arrested again in 1863. This time he was kept in prison for a long period, possibly for the rest of the war. Apparently feeling that he should have been let off with another slap on the wrist, he filed suit in 1866 against Secretary Stanton.[47]

· ·· ··

Ruling out Rose Greenhow's exaggerated claims of espionage success does not, of course, eliminate the possibility that someone, or several someones, performed some effective spying in Washington during these early months of the war. But hundreds of pages of Confederate records show that the Southern leaders possessed a very normal uncertainty about enemy movements and plans.

Of course there were exceptions, at least in this early stage of the war. Late in 1861 and again early in 1862 Confederates discovered the objectives of two Federal expeditions that were sailing under secret orders to invade the Southern coast. In one case Washington definitely was not the source of the Confederates' information, and in the other Washington agents are known to have been the source only of incorrect reports.

The first of these expeditions began assembling at Annapolis and Hampton Roads in October 1861, to move an army force down the coast and occupy some port that could serve as an auxiliary base for the North's blockading fleet. Selection of the objective was made the responsibility of Samuel F. Du Pont, commodore of the naval squadron, and Brigadier General Thomas W. Sherman, commander of the troops aboard the transports. They decided on Port Royal, between Charleston and Savannah.[48] According to one of Du Pont's subordinate captains, the two commanders were to insure secrecy by deferring the choice of destination until they were at sea. Instead, Du Pont gave his captains sealed orders revealing the objective, with instructions not to open them unless they became separated from the flagship.[49] But on November 1, three days after the fleet left Hampton Roads and another three before it appeared off the bar at Port Royal, Confederate chieftains in South Carolina received a telegram from Acting Secretary of War Judah P. Benjamin: "I have just received information, which I consider entirely reliable, that the enemy's expedition is intended for Port Royal."[50]

However, this strikingly correct and timely intelligence did not avail much, if anything. The forts guarding Port Royal's long, wide harbor were quickly overpowered by naval bombardment, with Sherman's shipborne troops as distant spectators.[51] Still, some anonymous Rebel had performed a noteworthy feat of espionage at Annapolis or Hampton Roads or Fort Monroe. Colonel Jordan at Centreville did receive two reports about the expedition from Washington sources. One was a new spy, a female, presumably Augusta Heath Morris, who reported that the Federals' expedition was destined for North Carolina — "Cape Fear River, Smithville, &c." The other source was Dr. Van Camp, who had managed to get through the lines to Centreville despite Pinkerton's awareness of his connection with the Greenhow ring. Van Camp also gave wrong information; his trip through the Federal lines may have been allowed as part of a deception scheme. Jordan wrote that Van Camp's information "is doubted here . . . but the army has been put in order for such an exigency" — thus indicating that the objective reported by Van Camp was within the area of the Manassas command, perhaps along the lower Potomac.[52]

Van Camp's informant, according to Jordan, was John Callan, still in his position of trust near the heart of the Federals' military affairs. But there is no way of knowing whether Callan had picked up and relayed a mistaken rumor or had been fed misinformation because of his known Confederate connection — or was consciously issuing misinformation.[53] He became an object of active suspicion late in November when he was mentioned in a letter found in a railroad car at an unnamed place and sent to Secretary Seward. It was dated at St. Catharines, Canada, and addressed in care of the Quebec post office; the names of the sender (Luke Marroney) and the addressee (F. Howlig) either were aliases or belonged to men not otherwise known to be working for the Confederacy. The text of the letter mentioned "JD" (Jefferson Davis) as involved in a correspondence of a nature that was not clear, and continued, "The letters [to Washington] are posted to an Irishman named Callen formerly a clerk to JD and put by him into the War Office under Floid — his brother is a lawyer so matters will be carried on by them properly and safe. They have promised a big thing."

It is tempting to speculate that someone who wanted to remain anonymous planted this letter in order to direct suspicion to Callan, or that Callan with the knowledge of his Federal superiors was cooperating with Confederate spies in order to penetrate their activities. The latter seems quite unlikely, though, for the "Luke Marroney letter" was promptly placed in the hands of George H. Bangs, Pinkerton's second in command, and Operative P.H.D. was assigned to investigate. There the known record of Callan's possible treason ends. As his Federal employment continued for two more years, it appears that Pinkerton either became satisfied that Callan was not communicating with the Confederates or continued watching him in the hope of obtaining better evidence or identifying accomplices. The fact that late in the war Callan went into business in Washington as a claim agent raises the possibility that the suspicion against him, even if unproven, led to his discharge or, perhaps, resignation on his own volition.[54] In any case, he evidently performed valuable service for the Union, having acquired a reputation as something of an authority on military legislation by publishing in 1862 a compilation of all United States laws on military matters.[55]

Well before the departure of the Federals' second coastal invasion it became widely known as the Burnside expedition; it was organized and led by newly appointed Brigadier General Ambrose E. Burnside. He took up headquarters at Annapolis in October and there began assembling a force, and then a fleet to transport it. Its objective was Cape Hatteras, where Federals under Major General Ben Butler had made a lodgment in August but without enough force to proceed beyond the inland waters. Not until January 9 did Burnside's troops set sail from Annapolis, proceeding to a rendezvous with supply ships at Fort Monroe. The troops numbered 15,000 and the fleet 80 vessels, whose captains each had sealed orders as to the objective.

"Not a man in the fleet knew his destination," Burnside wrote, "except the brigade commanders, and two or three staff-officers." But on January 5 Secretary Benjamin at Richmond had this telegram from North Carolina Governor Henry T. Clark: "We have reliable information that the Burnside expedition at Fort Monroe is destined for Pamlico Sound [between Cape Hatteras and the mainland] and New Berne. . . . Will you send us troops from Richmond or some of our own regiments from James River?"

Since it was Governor Clark who informed Benjamin of the approaching invasion instead of the reverse, it is evident that this intelligence originated in North Carolina. In all probability its source was some member of Butler's force who had assurance from Washington that reinforcements were on the way. Those troops, poorly fed, underequipped, and by now very tired of life on the outer banks, would have made friends with the locals, some of whom probably picked up from them the news of promised reinforcements and passed it to Confederate authorities. This discovery, then, was much less remarkable than the Confederates' acquisition of the Port Royal secret.

Burnside landed on the cape and advanced to Roanoke Island and the mainland. By the end of April, after a sharp fight near New Bern and a two-week siege of Beaufort, the Federal presence in North Carolina was firmly established. Governor Clark's warning had not gained him enough reinforcements.[56]

These two accomplishments of Southern intelligence have remained unheralded, while a myth of Confederate superiority, originating in the exaggerated successes of Rose Greenhow and other easily romanticized stories, has prospered. The lack of identifiable heroes — the discoverers of the enemy objectives — leaves these two feats without hope of gaining a place in Confederate intelligence tradition.

. . . . . .

Ranking next to the breakup of the Greenhow ring among Pinkerton's early successes was the arrest of a group of Maryland planters along the lower Potomac who were ferrying passengers and contraband (presumably including military information) across to Virginia. Also taking a hand in this operation were Lafayette Baker and a detachment from Brigadier General Joseph Hooker's division — three companies of the Third Indiana Cavalry.[57]

These planters were initially betrayed by relatives and other acquaintances who sympathized with the Union, and especially by their slaves, who ran away and eagerly joined the operation. The story of one of them, Thomas Washington, was transcribed by one of Hooker's officers: "I heard Massa say . . . 'I bought two kegs of powder and sent it over in Virginia. I'll assist them all I can, I'll assist 'em, . . . anything they want as far as I can.' . . . he use to say that when you soldiers came to his house, he would swear he . . . was a Union man — but after you would go he would be the same and said he would repent for that. A false oath was nothing under such circumstances." A son-in-law of "Massa" had been arrested on suspicion of espionage but was released; "when he returned to Massa's house he was talking to young Massa . . . and said 'Dick we can fool these Sons of B———' and then ripped out an oath and said he would be a secessionist as long as he lived and then laughed."

These families' secessionist activities were insultingly brazen. The Posey family, for example, whom Hooker arrested and sent to Washington, were released there and upon returning home were befriended by Hooker, only to be discovered again communicating across the river by mirror and lantern — right under the noses of Federal soldiery who swarmed over their property.

Although half a dozen Marylanders were arrested, their collaborators on the Virginia side were untouchable as long as Confederate forces remained around Fredericksburg. It is safe to assume that the ferrying was not interrupted for very long — although, once Pinkerton and Baker turned their attention to lower Maryland, the days of easy, regular communication from Washington to Richmond were over. Even when the forwarding of reports and newspapers came to be managed by the Confederate Secret Service Bureau (alter ego of the Confederate Signal Bureau), the Southern couriers had plenty of difficulties — bad roads, overworked horses, having to cross the Potomac where it is no mere river but an arm of Chesapeake Bay. Once the business of dodging Federal patrols was added to that list of problems, the couriers would have had to do much more traveling at night — often having to wait for a moonless night, which greatly lengthened their delivery time.[58]

A trans-Potomac communication project of a different kind ended with the arrest of two Maryland brothers, E. Pliny Bryan and William P. Bryan. They had an audacious scheme for signaling across the river from a high point in Washington or suburban Georgetown. By opening and closing window blinds or by changing the position of a coffee pot on a windowsill, they would "telegraph" to a Confederate post on a Virginia hill five or six miles away. Such an awkward system could carry only a very small amount of information, and the need for it is puzzling if Confederate couriers could move in and out of Washington with anywhere near the ease that has commonly been claimed. Before the system was in place, the Confederates' hilltop advance post was withdrawn too far for visual contact. The Bryans, still persuaded of the feasibility of their system, moved the project to the lower Potomac and there fell into the hands of Federal soldiers who were scouting the Virginia countryside between the lines of the two armies.

Pinkerton appears to have discovered a connection between the Bryans and "Mrs. Morris." He failed, however, to press for the treatment of Pliny Bryan as a military spy, although he had been taken in civilian clothes and admitted to being a member of the Confederate Signal Corps. He also admitted to having been one of the leaders of the secessionist element in the Maryland legislature. The Bryans, along with the planters arrested farther down the river, were evidently regarded as being more dangerous — or in any case more culpable in a legal sense — than the spies working in Washington, for they all were returned to prison by the Dix-Pierrepont Commission.[59]

One Southern agent was identified by a Pinkerton man in Richmond, an improbable place for such a discovery. The discoverer, Frank M. Ellis, a New Yorker, whose cover was selling bank-note paper to the Confederates, paid a call on Secretary of War Benjamin and overheard a conversation between Benjamin and a twenty-one-year-old Marylander named Henry A. Stewart, who was offering to smuggle arms into Virginia. Before Ellis's information could be used to effect Stewart's arrest, Stewart was captured by General Hooker's cavalry in lower Maryland and brought to Old Capitol. Ellis's information now came into play; the knowledge that Stewart was more than an ordinary prisoner caused him to be closely watched. To Pinkerton's hands came a letter from Stewart to a Miss Rose Grace in Baltimore, promising that he would soon escape and asking her to communicate with various accomplices who were to provide him with a boat and twenty men. The letter was copied and then sent on to Miss Grace. The evidence thus obtained led Dix and Pierrepont to send Stewart back to prison; he was fatally shot while making his promised escape attempt.[60]

. .　. .　. .

What part of the huge task of jailing or immobilizing Washington's thousands of potential promoters of secession did Pinkerton accomplish? His breakup of the Greenhow ring ends the known history of organized espionage by resident spies, and though the city was repeatedly a target of transient spies, their known successes are few. Contraband traffic across the lower Potomac was surely not totally quelled by Pinkerton and Baker; even Pinkerton's agents continued to use the Southern farmers' ferrying services in their travels to and from Richmond. The Confederates' courier route, the "Secret Line" to Richmond, continued to carry Northern newspapers; if some significant products of espionage also passed over it, they have escaped the known record, only partly because the files of the Confederate Secret Service Bureau did not, so far as is known, survive the war.

When we examine the correspondence of the Confederacy's military decision-makers it is clear that breaks in their uncertainty about Federal plans and movements were rare. In March 1862 General Robert E. Lee, returning to Richmond from duty in South Carolina, found that "secret correspondence with Washington had been almost cut off." During the Peninsula campaign the Confederate high command remained uncertain about McClellan's plans and actions even some weeks after his army had begun landing at Fort Monroe. And a year later Lee was complaining to President Davis of the lack of spies in Washington.[61] This tightening of security, though the visible part of it consisted only of the arrest of Rose Greenhow and a small number of her collaborators and some of their subagents, changed Washington into a place where Southern spies found military information quite hard to come by. Pinkerton — and Baker too, for there is no doubt that his organization made a substantial contribution to local security — could not watch Confederate sympathizers numbering in thousands, but it appears that they came close to neutralizing them. And this result was achieved in the face of a policy toward proven offenders so lenient that the two security chiefs must have wondered how any but the most timorous were deterred by the possibility of arrest.

One major service performed by the Greenhow ring was their engaging of the full-time attention of so many Federal secret-service people that they seriously held back the Federals' own intelligence collecting.

This is not to say that Pinkerton's counterespionage work was less important than the positive intelligence the same agents could have been
collecting instead. Of the two tasks, counterintelligence is the more difficult in one respect: the positive-intelligence officer knows what he is
getting and has a fair idea of what he is missing, but the counterintelligence officer can usually know only the first half of that pair.

4

....

THE PHONY WAR OF 1861–62

August 1861–January 1862

"ALL QUIET ON THE POTOMAC" was a condition that never lasted very long during General McClellan's first weeks in Washington. Rumors abounded of Confederate attacks in the making, and his intelligence arrangements, lacking both sufficient reconnaissance by cavalry and an organized scouting operation, could do nothing to verify or refute such reports. The victorious Confederates returned to some of the positions they had abandoned before the Bull Run battle, edging an outpost to a Virginia hilltop within eight miles of Washington. In such a situation, a little activity on the part of the Southern pickets and scouts was enough to send an alarm all the way to the top of the Federal command. The public's fears bordered on hysteria: an observation balloon brought to Washington in the hope that it would be used by the army evoked fears of the enemy "hovering over us." The alarm was scotched by twenty-eight-year-old Thaddeus Sobieski Constantine Lowe, who was to become the Federals' chief "aeronaut." Lowe wrote that he was personally acquainted with or knew of "all the experienced Aeronauts of the country" and knew that the South had no such capability.[1]

McClellan, now responsible for the safety of the capital, could not take these alarms lightly. On August 8, two weeks after arriving, he wrote General Scott that he had information from "spies, letters and telegrams" confirming his previous impression that "the enemy intend attacking our positions on the other side of the river, as well as to cross the Potomac north of us." He continued, "I am induced to believe that the enemy has at least 100,000 men in front of us. . . . I feel confident that our present army in this vicinity is entirely insufficient for the emergency. . . . I urge that nothing be left undone to bring up our force for the defense of this city to 100,000 men, before attending to any other point." The letter concluded, "A sense of duty which I cannot resist compels me to state that in my opinion military necessity demands that the Departments of Northeastern Virginia, Washington, the Shenandoah, Pennsylvania, including Baltimore, and the one including Fort Monroe, should be merged into one department, under the immediate control of the commander of the main army of operations" — General McClellan.

Relations between Scott and the young general had not been smooth. During his campaign in western Virginia McClellan had shown a tendency to impertinence and had received by telegraph a squelching in which Winfield Scott's three stars showed in every line. Once installed in Washington, he began going over Scott's head to the President and secretary of war. When he did take his business to Scott, the general-in-chief was scarcely more pleased than when he did not. Taken by surprise by McClellan's alarm at the capital's alleged defenselessness and his proposed cure for it, Scott gave himself twenty-four hours to digest the communication and then wrote to Secretary Cameron:

> Sir: I received yesterday from Major-General McClellan a letter of that date, to which I design this as my only reply.
>
> Had Major-General McClellan presented the same views in person, they would have been freely entertained and discussed. All my military views and opinions had been so presented to him, without eliciting much remark, in our few meetings, which I have in vain sought to multiply. He has stood on his guard, and now places himself on record. Let him make the most of his unenvied advantages.
>
> Major-General McClellan has propagated in high quarters the idea expressed in the letter before me, that Washington was not only "insecure," but in "imminent danger."
>
> Relying on our numbers, our forts, and the Potomac River, I am confident in the opposite opinion; and considering the stream of new regiments that is pouring in upon us (before this alarm could have reached their homes), I have not the slightest apprehension for the safety of the Government here.
>
> Having now been long unable to mount a horse, or to walk more than a few paces at a time, and consequently being unable to review troops, much less to direct them in battle — in short, being broken down by many particular hurts, besides the general infirmities of age — I feel that I have become an incumbrance to the Army as well as to myself, and that I ought, giving way to a younger commander, to seek the palliatives of physical pain and exhaustion.
>
> Accordingly, I must beg the President, at the earliest moment, to allow me to be placed upon the officers' retired list, and then quietly to lay myself up — probably forever — somewhere in or about New York. But, wherever I may spend my little remainder of life, my frequent and latest prayer will be, "God save the Union."

McClellan was persuaded to withdraw his letter, and Scott to remain in service. But one embarrassment did not cure McClellan; he could produce new effronteries much more frequently than Old Fuss and Feathers could threaten to retire. He was riding a wave of popular enthusiasm and seemed to have, along with a Napoleonic complex, the inspirational

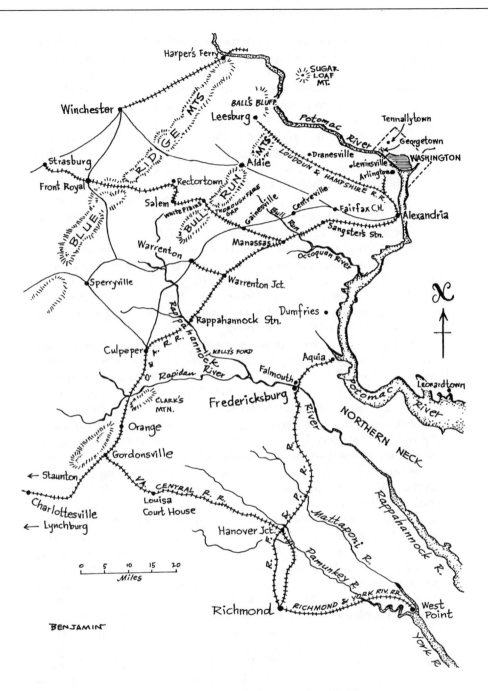

THE NORTHERN VIRGINIA THEATER

qualities that might justify it. The sense of urgency that impelled him to take his problems to Cameron and Lincoln instead of to Scott was honestly felt; and it seems that Scott was a hard man to see, even about such a matter as saving the Union. Finally, at the beginning of November, Scott's wish for retirement was granted. "Little Mac" became general-in-chief and retained command of the Army of the Potomac.[2]

McClellan's letter that so wounded General Scott was the second in a series of alarms that the young general sounded. Four days earlier he had alerted his division chiefs with these words: "Information has been received which goes to show that the enemy may attack us within the next forty eight hours. . . . Hold your command ready to move at the shortest notice." Two days later, with the alarm still in force, Brigadier General George A. McCall, whose division was posted northwest of the city, turned his field glasses on the Virginia fields and hills opposite his position. He reported that "what was supposed to be camps of the insurgents proved to be, under the scrutiny of the glass, only clusters of whitewashed houses, negro cabins, and fences." Presumably the report of enemy camps so close to the capital was at least partly responsible for the alarm that had alerted the whole army.

A third alarm came from downriver. Going outside his chain of command, McClellan wrote Navy Secretary Gideon Welles on August 12, "I have today received additional information which convinces me that it is more than probable that the enemy will within a very short time, attempt to throw a respectable force from the mouth of Aquia Creek [near Fredericksburg] into Maryland. . . . I must earnestly urge that the strongest possible naval force be concentrated . . . and that the most vigilant watch be maintained — day and night." A week later he was still expecting the advance from Aquia and at the same time crediting the enemy with the ability to mount a second crossing, upriver, from the vicinity of Leesburg and Harper's Ferry.

Charles P. Stone, whose performance in subduing the secessionist threat to Washington during the preceding winter had earned him promotion to brigadier general and command of a division stationed across the Potomac from Leesburg, reported on the 22nd that there were no signs that the Rebels were making preparations to cross in that part of the river. The next day McClellan's adjutant wired Stone, "[The Confederates] will probably change their plan of operation, as they see that we had divined their original plans." Evidently the threat of enemy aggression was causing McClellan so much anxiety that he drew this large conclusion from a very small development, information of withdrawal of a Confederate outpost a couple of miles from Vienna to Flint Hill, near Fairfax Court House — a good many miles from the expected crossings, but now ten miles from Washington instead of eight. But two days later came a report that the enemy was advancing in force; McClellan wrote his wife that night: "Started off Aides & put the wires at work — when fairly started alarm found false."[3]

At about the same time, on a nearby sector of the front, the Confederates put a sizable outpost on Munson's Hill, within four miles of the Potomac and in sight of the Capitol. That may have been the movement that touched off another "alert" on August 27, when McClellan ordered all units to be ready "to move at a moment's warning without packing up camp equipage." He claimed "that my movements had entirely disconcerted their plans."[4] The Confederates also kept up a program of annoyance near Chain Bridge, coming "in some force" within three-quarters of a mile of the pickets of General William F. Smith's division stationed there, scarcely four miles from the White House. After a few weeks, with Professor Lowe and other balloonists at work, the practice of making the whole army stand on tiptoe at each alarm ended, although the alarms did not.[5]

The army's state of nerves was indicated by frequent reports of enemy signal lights and other nighttime phenomena. Dr. Myer, the signal officer, who was called upon to defuse this type of alarm, once found that a reported "fire balloon" was actually the planet Venus hovering near the horizon.[6] Some commanders thought that the Confederates' game was insolence and intimidation; for example, a navy officer informed McClellan that a battery the Rebels were building on the lower Potomac "was intentionally exposed to our view before completion." On the other hand, when the Confederates gratuitously exposed their work on entrenchments at Leesburg, General Stone suspected that their defensive preparations were masking some offensive purpose.[7]

Experiencing this series of alarms that proved either false or greatly exaggerated did not save McClellan from completely swallowing one of the most frightening ones on September 13. He wrote Secretary Cameron, "The movement of the enemy so far as discovered by us and information reaching us from many directions and sources all indicated that the enemy intend at a very early date to advance; even that he has already commenced the movement." He thought it "more than probable" that the Confederates had concentrated all their force in his front and had been reinforced by troops from Missouri. Estimating the enemy's disposable force at twice the size of his own, he asked for the transfer from Missouri of 25,000 troops, half the number of Federals he understood General John Charles Frémont had in the vicinity of St. Louis.[8] McClellan gave no indication of the source or reliability of the reports that led to this panicky letter.

McClellan was not the only army commander taking stern measures against attacks that the enemy was not planning. During the early weeks of this period of Federal alarms, the Confederates were worrying about a second Union advance. On August 11 Beauregard repositioned his forces "in order to prevent a *coup de main* from McClellan." But this defensive turn of mind did not last; by the end of September the Confederates had a main line centering on Fairfax Court House, with eleven infantry regiments and all of Stuart's cavalry manning the advance posts whose activities were so annoying to the Yankees. Some of the movements into those positions were the probable cause of McClellan's September 13 alarm. There was more than insolence and intimidation in the Rebels' minds; the new line would afford more advantageous jumpoff positions for the advance that their generals had been criticized for not making immediately after routing the enemy on Bull Run.[9] Johnston and Beauregard pleaded for reinforcements to make such an advance possible, and at the end of September President Davis came to Centreville to confer with them. Until the uncertain time when a great influx of weapons should arrive from Europe, Davis could send only as many reinforcements, 2500, as he had weapons to arm them with. Crossing the Potomac with an army not greatly reinforced meant "almost certain destruction"; "it was felt that there was no other course left but to take a defensive position and await the enemy." The Flint Hill–Fairfax–Sangster's Station line was not suited to defensive purposes, and on October 17–19 the main line was drawn back to a base on Centreville with cavalry pickets as far forward as Fairfax.[10] For a month or more McClellan had been overrating the Confederates' capabilities but not their offensive dreams and schemes.

The Confederates' active scouting and picketing, combined with McClellan's slowness in readying his army, produced seven months of what eighty years later would be called a "Phony War." There were no major battles, but one minor one and many chance encounters, more visual than physical, involving scouting parties, pickets and patrols, woodgathering and foraging parties — almost any kind of small expedition except one looking for a fight. The Federals made a few sizable reconnaissances; the object of most of their activity was prevention of surprise, which involved discovering the enemy's positions, not only of his main line but more especially of his shifting outposts and picket lines. When General Smith made a reconnaissance in force to Lewinsville, five miles from Chain Bridge, on September 11, his column of 2000 naturally attracted resistance by Stuart's cavalry. Stuart reported that he drove the enemy away; Smith reported that he had made a successful reconnaissance and was en route back to base when Stuart attacked. Conceivably each general thought he was telling the truth. Smith paid another call at Lewinsville two weeks later, this time with a force of 5250. Again the Confederates reacted, but the action was limited to an exchange of artillery, the Federals' superior guns inducing the enemy to retire.[11]

When the Confederates withdrew their main line to Centreville October 17–19, the shift was not quickly understood by the Federals, even though large forces were seen at both Centreville and Manassas by John La Mountain, a balloonist who made a free flight over Confederate territory. His risky feat was made possible by wind conditions: a westward wind took him over the enemy lines, whereupon he jettisoned ballast and rose to a higher atmospheric stratum where a constant easterly wind returned him to friendly ground — or so he expected. But when he landed, near Alexandria, he received a welcome of gunfire and arrest from the Germans of General Louis Blenker's brigade, who assumed that the Confederacy now had gone in for aeronautics.[12]

La Mountain's report touched off a general reconnaissance of the Vienna-Dranesville area on October 19. McCall occupied Dranesville and sent out reconnoitering parties. McClellan asked General Stone to see if McCall's movements might induce a Confederate withdrawal from Leesburg, and on the 20th the Federal signal station on Sugar Loaf Mountain, in Maryland, correctly reported the Rebels' expected movement. But it must have been a reconnaissance in force, not a departure, for when Stone sent his own reconnoitering detachment across the river on the 21st, its overly aggressive moves encountered a strong enemy force between the river and Leesburg. The Federals escaped from this collision, known as the battle of Ball's Bluff, only with severe losses. Their excessive eagerness was the product of some fatally wrong information: scouts reported seeing, at some distance from the Potomac, a camp that appeared ripe for attack; thus the Federals were drawn dangerously far from the river, only to discover that the enemy camp was a row of trees "which presented, in the uncertain light, somewhat the appearance of a line of tents."[13] The victim of this error was a Massachusetts colonel named Charles Devens, Jr. It may have induced in Devens a skepticism toward scouts' reports that was to have tragic consequences in the Chancellorsville battle eighteen months later.

. .   . .   . .

Northern arms suffered another humiliation at the time of Ball's Bluff when the Confederates closed the Potomac to commercial navigation by installing batteries on the Virginia shore thirty miles below Washington. The city immediately felt the blockade; the burden of feeding its thousands of people and supplying the army fell on one thin rail line, whose normal freight deliveries had been eight carloads a day. McClellan, after sending Brigadier General Joseph Hooker's division to a position in lower Maryland opposite the batteries, would not order the movements that would silence them; he was sure they would disappear when his grand campaign against Richmond began. Hooker was scornful of the batteries; small boats were passing them safely, and he wrote McClellan's adjutant that "they are as likely to be struck by lightning as by the rebel shot." One of Hooker's colonels took 400 men across the river and back without orders, to show that it could be done. This was a reconnaissance, not an attack; it penetrated four miles inland without encountering opposition.

For the rest of the fall and winter Hooker kept urging aggressive action of one kind or another. At first he was frustrated by his inability to find out where the batteries' supporting force was positioned, or how numerous it was. When McClellan allotted him one of Professor Lowe's balloons, his lack of knowledge of the enemy's main positions was corrected in a single ascent. Then bad weather and a gas shortage grounded the balloon. Hooker became severely disenchanted with aerial observation and with the competence of Lowe's assistant aeronaut, William Paullin. Four weeks went by before a break in the weather and an excellent detailed map of enemy positions made from the balloon restored his faith.

The Potomac, two miles wide where Hooker commanded, provided a few diversions from the dullness of the blockade and stalemate. A schooner, defying the batteries and coming upriver under "easy sail," was suddenly stalled when the wind failed. A battery shelled her, the crew abandoned ship, the Rebels boarded and set fire to her, and a regiment and battery sent by Hooker to keep them from capturing her put out the fire. A month later Hooker's cavalry, the Third Indiana, captured a forty-ton ship loaded with contraband destined for Richmond. This exploit won the Hoosiers the nickname "Hooker's Horse Marines." Finding their horses not very effective against enemies who traveled by boat, they had retaliated by taking to the water themselves.[14] Another variety of small-scale expedition was the punitive one, a leading example being a December 20 visit to Dranesville, where "the enemy's pickets had advanced to within 4 or 5 miles of our lines and carried off two good Union men and plundered and threatened others." This brigade-size mission was stoutly resisted by Stuart, but this time Jeb, who had four infantry regiments with him in addition to his cavalry, was soundly defeated. He had been on a foraging expedition; the "punishment" the Federals had in mind was capturing a Confederate picket and collecting forage "from the farms of some of the rank secessionists in the vicinity."[15]

· · · · · ·

Pinkerton's intelligence bureau, numbering twenty-four people by the end of September,[16] is not known to have produced any intelligence on Confederate movements during the early weeks of McClellan's command. As we have seen, for its first several weeks it was preoccupied with a counterespionage mission, the pursuit of Rose Greenhow and her compatriots. The interrogation part of the positive-intelligence mission required no elaborate preparations, but launching the government's principal spy-running operation was a different matter. Finding suitable

agents and arranging cover for them was a slow business. But by mid-October Pinkerton had worked five agents into Richmond as transients. A
spy's operations also moved slowly; his trips going and coming could
each take a week, perhaps more. His business in Richmond occupied at
least a week, and a period of weeks in the North between trips was always
necessary. From October until March, when the army began moving to
the peninsula between the York and James Rivers, Pinkerton agents' trips
into the Confederacy totaled only fourteen, according to his well-main-
tained payroll records.[17]

The first agent in Richmond, E. H. Stein, was watched with so much
suspicion by the Confederates that he produced little information. Stein,
the one who engaged in the game of two-way deception with J. T. Kerby of
Lafayette Baker's force, was in Richmond during those August days when
Pinkerton was setting up shop in Washington. Starting from Cincinnati,
he entered the Confederacy by way of western Kentucky. That state's
insistence on neutral status invited spies to beat a path across its territory.
Mrs. Stein, who was also on Pinkerton's payroll, joined her husband at
Hickman, a Mississippi River town, where they entrained for Richmond.
En route they took few notes, for Pinkerton had instructed them to
concentrate on Richmond. For reasons unclear Mrs. Stein seems to have
made her base at Amelia, a rural county seat on the Virginia and Tennessee Railroad forty miles southwest of Richmond. Before the end of the
month her husband rejoined her there and sent her back North for
more expense money.

It is not known what cover Stein was using, but apparently it was not a
very convincing one, for he felt himself under such close surveillance
that he did not risk making a single note in his two or three weeks in
Richmond. At Amelia he wrote out from memory a dozen bits of information on tiny slips of paper that his wife secreted about her clothing for
her trip North. She arrived in Washington on August 31 with a gloomy
report to Pinkerton, and returned to Richmond by way of Nashville. Both
she and her husband were back in Washington by the end of September,
but no report of additional information appears in McClellan's or Pinkerton's papers.

Among the items from Mrs. Stein's August 31 report that Pinkerton
passed on to McClellan were the following: The adjutant of a Confederate regiment had figures showing 160,000 Rebel troops in Virginia,
including 40,000 with Lee in western Virginia; but "not over three regiments" were stationed at Richmond. Cannon "by the dozen" were arriving at Richmond and being rifled in a Richmond factory (this would
have been the well-known Tredegar works). There was much dissatisfaction because Beauregard had failed to "take possession of Washington"
after his Bull Run victory. The people of Richmond "are less 'rampant'
but more 'confident' than those of Tennessee." There was great con-

fidence that before winter "England will break the blockade." "The officers of the rebel army treat our prisoners well but the people, outside, would lynch them if they could." Southern troops considered themselves more than a match for Northerners and rated western men "better fighters than the Yankees" (New Englanders). Slaveholders maintained the loyalty of their Negroes by telling them the "Lincolnites" would kill them if the North won the war. "Direct information is obtained, daily, from the Head Quarters of the Federal Army in Washington, by the rebels in Richmond, respecting the movements of our troops and the plans of our army."[18]

Confederate troop totals for the months after the Bull Run battle are difficult to calculate; the 160,000 reported by Stein's source appears about double the true figure, as does the 40,000 estimated for western Virginia.[19] It is likely, however, that the source believed those figures himself; inflated figures for their own army were, and would continue to be, on the tongues of all true Southerners, and of almost everybody else.

Stein's report that Federal military secrets were sent daily to Richmond was either a serious exaggeration or a totally unfounded rumor, for Confederate records at this period reveal the usual uncertainty about Federal plans. Pinkerton may well have believed this claim, even though the reports he had acquired in Rose Greenhow's house fell far short of what Stein described.

The Confederates had similar suspicions that their military secrets were being leaked, suspicions often recorded in the diary of John B. Jones, a principal administrative figure in Davis's War Department.[20] The meagerness of Stein's findings during these weeks in Richmond indicates that these suspicions were unfounded. Stein was the only Federal agent in Richmond at this period.

· ·   · ·   · ·

The next agent to visit Richmond appears to have been Frank Lacy Buxton, who until now has been known to history as one of the *New York Tribune*'s corps of correspondents who managed to get their dispatches out of the South during the "secession winter" of 1860–61. Buxton, an Englishman, began his espionage services in September; he is the only Federal spy of the McClellan-Pinkerton period known to have worked for McClellan directly rather than through Pinkerton. He claimed to have enjoyed the trust of the Southerners to the extent that he was able to get General Johnston's pass to go to Richmond. But he seems to have spent little time there — as little as one day on one of his trips. His operations concentrated on the Manassas-Centreville-Leesburg area; thus they promised a welcome addition to Pinkerton's coverage of Richmond. Buxton's first reports, on September 27 and 28, gave the Johnston-Beauregard army 114,000 men, 27,000 of them at and near Leesburg.

Because he had passed through that place, the report carried some credibility; but it was about a tenfold exaggeration of the Confederate force stationed there and nearly a threefold overstatement of the whole army's strength. Buxton assured McClellan, "The Generals claim no more amongst themselves; perfectly reliable; correct beyond doubt, you may rest any calculation on these figures." The 27,000 figure was passed on, with no strings of doubt attached, by General Nathaniel P. Banks, the chief commander in the upriver area where Buxton made his base.

Early in October Buxton picked up word of the Manassas generals' recent council of war, though he failed to hear, or at least to report, that President Davis had been present. He reported that Beauregard considered the army too small to contend with McClellan's, "whilst Johnston prates of [his army's] invincibility." He predicted a small-scale attack by the Confederates in the upriver area but believed there was no intention to cross the Potomac elsewhere or in great force.

Buxton had acquired information on espionage against the Federals by a Baltimorean named Lamour, one Maddox, reportedly of Loudoun County, and a third man, unnamed. Because the latter two might have seen him in Washington in September, Buxton now feared to go there.

His next report, in mid-October, is lost. Then, after the battle of Ball's Bluff, he wrote to deplore the Federals' action in rushing "into the jaws of 7000 men." By now he had scaled down the size of the Confederates' Leesburg force but still estimated it at three times the true number. "It was only ten days ago," he wrote, "that General McClellan had positive information from me, via Fort Monroe, that there were 11,000 men still at Leesburg. It would therefore seem that [General Stone] must have acted without proper information."

Buxton turns up again in the records of the Shenandoah Valley campaign of 1862. On March 27, four days after the Federals defeated Stonewall Jackson in a small battle near Winchester, he reported information supposedly obtained inside the Confederate lines, again contributing little that was useful despite his apparently excellent opportunities. A few weeks later he was in Old Capitol Prison, charged with having "communicated valuable military information to the insurgents, and [being] in their employ as a spy." As he does not appear to have been furnishing the Rebels with anything of commercial value — he had no contraband merchandise as "cover" — it appears that he was playing the game of double spy, feeding information to both sides, and that McClellan or someone on his staff saw through this deception, perceiving that Buxton's information was so weak or so erroneous that the enemy must be getting the better of the bargain. Or this fact, or suspicion, may have been picked up by one of Pinkerton's agents in Richmond.

Once the War Department investigated Buxton's background, it was immediately clear that such dealing might have been expected of him. The chief of detectives in Philadelphia, Benjamin Franklin, found that Buxton's true name was William Saunders and that he was married and had two children "by his own proper wife — how many otherwise I cannot tell as many things are said about him." He had pilfered money and goods from merchants who employed him in New York and Philadelphia, then "ingratiated himself with the Republican party here, lectured politically for the party — & to save reputation, they got him out of his pilfering scrapes." "Long ago," Franklin wrote, "Mr. Seward was informed of him fully — his antecedents — character &c &c, who he was, and what dependence was to be placed in him. And one of the replies to the warnings was that he was well known and the [game?] was — to use him for the accomplishment of some purpose, design or end." But Seward probably did not learn that "Buxton" was in McClellan's employ until several months had gone by.

Again the War Department found itself dispensing leniency. After Buxton had been in Old Capitol for several weeks, Lord Lyons, the British minister, made the inquiry that was usual in cases of prisoners claiming British citizenship. The interest of Her Majesty's representative made the case a sticky one. Furthermore, presentation of hard evidence might expose its source, perhaps one of Pinkerton's operatives. Buxton won release on parole to remain north of New York City.[21]

.. .. ..

Meager and unreliable reports were not McClellan's only intelligence problem at this time. He was in possession of a purported Confederate document that he would have found difficult to evaluate. It was ostensibly a copy of a letter from Jefferson Davis to Governor Isham G. Harris of Tennessee. In three hundred words it touched on twelve subjects, three of which would have been of considerable interest to McClellan: Davis's reserved optimism about receiving British recognition of the Confederacy, his shortage of arms, and military intentions in the Virginia theater, expressed in the sentence "Genl Beauregard's defensive plan will be followed for the present." The style of the salutation and the signature stamps the letter as a forgery; the writer was not acquainted with Davis's letter-writing habits.[22] Those habits would have been unknowable by McClellan or Pinkerton, but they could easily have obtained samples of Davis's handwriting from War Department records of the years when he was secretary. The hop, skip, and jump over a dozen different subjects was an overdone attempt by the forger to make his text reflect an overview of events that would have a presidential flavor. The statement that Beauregard's intentions were defensive (which in fact they were,[23] much to that general's discomfort) was contrary to McClellan's belief; that was a reason for him to suspect that the letter was a Confederate plant, especially as so great an espionage "success" as the acquisition of such a letter was without precedent. The probable source of this forgery was someone on the Federal side of the lines who wanted to impress McClellan with his ability to penetrate to the highest level of the Confederate government. Among the people who are known to have been supplying McClellan and Pinkerton with intelligence, real or imagined, the likeliest nomination as possible author of this letter is Frank Buxton. The date fits the period of his known espionage activities, and the writing skill that made him a journalist could also have produced the imitation of a Victorian gentleman's letter-writing style. Another requirement was the brazenness necessary to perform a chancy bit of chicanery; Buxton was well endowed with that. However, these factors suffice only to stamp him as possibly the forger. McClellan left no record of his opinion in the matter.

. .   . .   . .

Timothy Webster, the star performer on Pinkerton's detective force, did not go into action in the Confederacy until mid-October. Webster, forty years old and, like Pinkerton, a native of Britain, had been one of the agents Pinkerton planted among the Baltimore secessionists early in the year. After moving to Washington in August he resumed contact with the Baltimoreans, thus developing a cover as courier between Richmond and secession's sympathizers in Baltimore, and using his true name. On his first trip he started from Baltimore October 15 and crossed the Chesapeake Bay on the 25th in a dugout canoe equipped with three sails, which plied a regular service between Cherrystone Lighthouse and Gloucester Point on the western shore — a thirty-mile run, always made on a dark night. This route to Richmond gave Webster a valuable but incomplete look at Confederate defenses on the north bank of the York River and on the peninsula that McClellan's army would occupy five months hence. The army led by "Prince John" Magruder on the peninsula was variously reported to Webster as containing 27 to 33 infantry regiments and 1200 cavalry — not unreasonably high numbers.

Calling at the office of Brigadier General John H. Winder, the local commander and provost marshal, for a pass that would authorize local travel, Webster requested a visit with Acting Secretary of War Benjamin but was told that the secretary was too occupied to see him, as an enemy attack was expected daily. The attack in question would have been the advance of the Federals' Port Royal expedition, whose destination was soon to be discovered by Confederate intelligence.

Webster's Richmond pass enabled him to take a ride about the city, where he saw seventeen "very superior earth work batteries" forming a semicircle with the two ends resting on the James. He was told that they were built to receive sixteen-pound and thirty-two-pound guns, not all of which had been installed. A visit to the ordnance department produced the information that a British ship had recently run the blockade with rifled cannon and cavalry swords.

From J. B. Jones, the civilian clerk who was sometimes called "General," Webster was able to get a pass to visit Manassas on what seems a slim pretext — delivering a letter to an express agent there, a Baltimorean who was sick with typhoid fever. Apparently Webster had entrée to General Winder's office through another Baltimorean, William Campbell, a contractor, who accompanied him to Manassas. Once there, they learned that the sick man had left that day for Richmond. Taking quarters south of the Junction, they had only a limited view of military installations, so Webster traveled twenty miles westward to Warrenton. There a provost marshal gave him a pass back east to Centreville, where Maryland troops for whom he had letters were stationed. On the way he added forty-nine regiments to the sixteen he had counted at and below Manassas. A Maryland captain told him that the cavalry with that army, scattered over a wide front, numbered ten or twelve regiments. The vaunted defenses of Centreville as observed by Webster turned out to be a dozen field batteries and two incomplete earthworks that would not accommodate more than four guns each; there were no breastworks for infantry, "nor were there any *certain* indications that they intended to make *that place* their battlefield; . . . everything indicated that they designed, if attacked, to fall back on Manassas."

Webster returned to Richmond by way of Warrenton, where he rejoined Campbell. En route a lieutenant from a regiment at Winchester told them the strength of the forces there and at Leesburg. Equally interesting information would have been the news of the appointment of the new Valley commander, Stonewall Jackson. Jackson had arrived at Winchester the previous day, November 4, but apparently the lieutenant was absent when the change of command became known.[24]

Webster had been promised a list of articles needed by the quartermaster general, but he found that officer too busy to compile a list and unable to think of anything the army needed in the North except emery cloth. As the quartermaster was privy to forthcoming army movements, Webster would have hoped to develop him as a frequent contact.

Webster was now ready to return North, but the pass issued him at Richmond took him only as far as the headquarters of General Holmes, commander of Johnston's right wing, near Aquia Creek on the Potomac northeast of Fredericksburg. But Holmes was absent and no one else could issue a pass to cross the Potomac to Maryland, so Webster returned to Richmond after getting a surgeon at Fredericksburg to issue him a pass for that trip. Having seen something of Holmes's command and learned its strength, fourteen regiments, Webster could forgo the Potomac crossing in favor of the trip via Chesapeake Bay and the Eastern Shore, the peninsula east of the bay. But he missed the regular boat by half an hour and had a two-day wait for the next run, made in a heavy sea. His troubles were not over; a Federal force was preparing to move down the Eastern Shore, Southern troops were assembling to offer resistance, and their commander had proclaimed that there would be no passes. Webster found a local physician who prevailed on the colonel to pass him to Baltimore, but he had been delayed three days — thus again having time to get a count on local troops, which he put at not over 2000, more than half of them militia. He was back in Pinkerton's office November 15, carrying no notes except those he could reduce to figures.

From the relative accuracy of the data Webster collected, it appears that he was a skillful interviewer, able to circumvent a good many of the obstacles presented by the resistance, mistaken knowledge, or gasconade of his various Southern subjects. Although he had not been within viewing distance of very many troops, the number of regiments he reported in Johnston's army, 104, compares favorably with the 87 listed in the Confederate return for the month preceding his visit. His figures for Magruder's Peninsula army and the Richmond garrison were less accurate, but the overage in his estimate for Johnston's army was only one-third the size of one previously made by Pinkerton. Pinkerton now took the view that every one of the enemy units reported by Webster must actually be present.[25]

. .   . .   . .

Another Pinkerton operative, Frank M. Ellis, was in Richmond at the same time as Webster; it is doubtful that either was aware of the other. Ellis, who has already appeared in this narrative as the traducer of Henry Stewart, was a twenty-eight-year-old native of upstate New York. He had been a literary and patent-rights agent before the war; he worked himself into Pinkerton's organization on the claim of having performed secret service for General Mansfield. He was one of the few employees accepted by Pinkerton from outside the ranks of the detective agency.

No report of Ellis's first visit to Richmond, in September, appears to survive. On October 17 he started out again, carrying 10,000 sheets of bank-note paper, merchandise that was an entrée to Confederate circles of authority. The paper was believed to be so scarce in the Confederacy that Pinkerton got the approval of the secretaries of both State and Treasury before allowing it to be carried South. Ellis crossed the Potomac to Leesburg, where, on the eve of the Ball's Bluff battle, he observed Confederate movements touched off by the Federals' reconnaissances from Dranesville. General Evans, the local Confederate commander, gave him directions for the rest of his Richmond trip, which was by rail from Warrenton. From traveling companions he learned of the Confederates' withdrawal from Fairfax to Centreville, which they described as so well fortified, with 150 to 200 "cannon," that a force of 10,000 could hold it against the whole Northern army. The artillery figures, if Ellis was reporting them honestly, were gasconade, and Pinkerton must have recognized them as such since Webster had observed a much smaller amount of artillery at Centreville. But Pinkerton's report on Webster's findings was another straight recital of the agent's statements, with no comment on their probable validity.

In light of the evident value to the Confederacy of bank-note paper, Ellis's claim that after delivering it he dined with Treasury Secretary Christopher G. Memminger, President Davis, Secretary of War Benjamin, and Assistant Secretary of State William H. Browne is believable enough. But his report of the talk he heard at their table raises questions. They would have been adjusting their conversation to the probability that Ellis would soon be telling Northern auditors about his Richmond experiences. They stated, he claimed, that their army on the Manassas front numbered 80,000, with another 20,000 under General Holmes at Aquia Creek and Evansport, and that "[t]heir whole design is to act on the defensive, for the present, as they wish us to attack them, if we will; but they do not think that we dare come out and fight them." The troop totals Ellis reported were excessive: the 80,000 figure was double the number Benjamin was even then preparing to build huts for at Manassas-Centreville, and the 20,000 reported in Holmes's command was an even greater overestimate. But Ellis's statement of the Confederate leaders' policy of remaining on the defensive was correct, as we have seen. That they would be willing for the Federals to learn of their basic military policy is unbelievable; so also is the idea that they would confide it to a mere visitor. Whether McClellan accepted or rejected that part of Ellis's report is not known, but he quickly adopted the 80,000 figure for Manassas-Centreville.

On his return trip Ellis crossed the Potomac at Harper's Ferry, which he reached after an interview with the Confederate militia commander at Winchester.

Pinkerton was so pleased with Ellis's report that in passing it on to McClellan he said that Ellis was "one of my most skillful operatives." He had hopes that Ellis would be able to penetrate "the most interior of their designs." Evidently Ellis had persuaded him that Davis and his ministers had not been doctoring their conversation for Northern ears.[26]

Setting out on his third Richmond trip on November 9, Ellis declined his consignment of bank-note paper, explaining that he was so well established in Richmond, many of whose business leaders and public men had entrusted letters to him on his last trip North, that he no longer needed a cover that was so helpful to the enemy. Passing through Winchester less than a week after Stonewall Jackson had been placed in command of the Shenandoah Valley, he was lucky enough to be in Jackson's presence when a Confederate officer asked the general how many troops he had. The ordinarily secretive Jackson replied, "Not over thirty-two hundred" — apparently an honest answer. Ellis had a pass bearing Secretary Benjamin's signature; it was standing him in good stead.

Fulfilling Pinkerton's hopes, Ellis had indeed greatly widened his contacts. He agreed with Richmond brokers to go to New York and arrange for a blockade-running vessel loaded with certain much-needed articles. A sewing-machine manufacturer engaged him to effect a transfer of investments held in Philadelphia. He was introduced to General Winder, who recited the usual story of huge armaments and invincible defenses at Centreville. Navy Secretary Stephen R. Mallory confided that the Confederates were successfully using light-draft boats to evade the coastal blockade over a ninety-mile span just above Wilmington; he gave Ellis a map of the Chesapeake and Albemarle Canal, which the agent forwarded to the intended addressee after Pinkerton had had it copied. The Confederate engineer office gave Ellis a number of northbound communications, which were similarly treated. Ellis arranged with Secretary Memminger for more bank-note shipments, totaling 100,000 sheets, after which, Memminger said, the Confederacy could manufacture its own supply. And Ellis persuaded an army captain named Quincy, who seemed to be well connected, to tell him the strength of Johnston's army. Quincy's answer added up to 115 regiments. (To this figure Pinkerton applied his averages of 700 per infantry and 600 per cavalry regiment, and came out with a total of 77,000.)

Ellis reported that Jackson's pass for his recrossing of the Potomac was readily given. At Harper's Ferry one of the Winchester officers introduced him to A. H. Herr, residing in that neighborhood, who entrusted to him $19,971 in drafts, coupons, and other paper, to be deposited in a Baltimore bank. As Ellis was carrying letters for Lord Lyons, the British minister in Washington, he was able to use a flag of truce to cross the river and put himself in Federal hands.

Ellis's rejection of the consignment of bank-note paper had planted uneasy thoughts in Pinkerton's mind, as he was allowing Ellis to retain his profits, which came to 100 percent. After Ellis's return to Washington he fulfilled Pinkerton's suspicions in handsome fashion. He visited his home town; word drifted back from there that "Frank Ellis, our great spy . . . had a mighty big yarn to spin" about the profits he had realized by duping his superiors in Washington. About the same time Mr. Herr came from Harper's Ferry in search of Ellis, found his way to Pinkerton, and complained that the $19,971 he had entrusted to Ellis, principally in nonnegotiable securities, had not been delivered to the addressee. Ellis, Herr said, had somehow converted securities worth several hundred dollars into cash. From a boatman who had ferried Ellis across the Potomac on his way South, Herr had learned that the spy's baggage included a trunk, "just as much as [he] could carry," filled with surgical instruments — a commodity that exceeded bank-note paper in value about as much as it did in weight. Pinkerton learned that apart from Herr's money Ellis had about $4000, which would have been his profit from the trunkload of surgical instruments.

Pinkerton's most alarming finding, however, was that Ellis had preceded two of his trips South with visits to the Federal camps around Washington, "which act of his," Pinkerton wrote, "was strictly and constantly forbidden to any and all of my operatives whose field of action was within the enemy's lines." The breach of so strict a rule meant that Ellis must have been spying for the South. Pinkerton knew Ellis had told Mr. Herr that he was going back to Richmond to accept a valuable position in the Confederate government, whose final success in the war he did not doubt. This no longer had the color of an idle boast.

These findings were more than enough to make Ellis a prison mate of his friend Henry Stewart. The agent who had exposed a Confederate agent was turning out to be one himself. Sent before General Dix and Judge Pierrepont, Ellis protested innocence, saying that he felt entitled to the cash he had realized from Mr. Herr's securities because "they belonged to a secessionist." His congressman, R. A. Sherman, attested to his good character. Even Sherman's statement, however, cast doubt on Ellis's fitness for the secret service. Naively the congressman wrote, "He showed me his private papers after his last return from Richmond which he had collected together in a scrap-book to preserve as a relic or trophy of his success. This he exhibited freely to his friends."

Once more the mighty Federal government found that it could not even slap the wrist of an obvious enemy agent. The formal charge against Ellis was communicating information to the enemy, but the evidence supporting that charge was not of the best, and he was discharged on taking the oath of allegiance and promising not to leave New York State for the duration of the war.[27]

If sheer brass were sufficient to make a successful spy, Frank Ellis would have made espionage history. In July 1863, long after Pinkerton's intelligence bureau had ceased to exist, Ellis applied for and received a position as a special agent of the War Department. He was discovered and discharged within two weeks, but not until he had drawn, and presumably spent, a $200 advance in pay.[28]

The two Franks, Ellis and Buxton, are not mentioned in Pinkerton's memoirs. They are significant for the same reason that led Pinkerton to ignore them: they are excellent examples of the many persons of doubtful character who found employment in the secret service, especially in the first year of the war. Some of them were mere brigands, as for example one George E. Tyler, a spy for General Fitz John Porter, who was sent to Washington under arrest after one of the most ambitious acts of individual pillaging on record — the theft of a piano from the home of a secessionist in Fairfax County. Others were employed on the strength of a thief's well-known ability to catch others of his kind. Such a case was that of Samuel Eakin, arrested in Philadelphia as a Confederate "commercial agent" (smuggler) and then hired by Lafayette Baker "to reside in Baltimore for the purpose of watching the movements of persons engaged in aiding and abetting the Confederate Government."[29]

. .   . .   . .

In mid-November Pinkerton tried another new operative from outside his agency, this one a "highly recommended . . . old-line Democrat Politician," who appears in the records only as "C.A.H." (probably his true initials). The only other clue to his identity is the fact that he had spent some years in the West, particularly Kansas and Nebraska; in Virginia he met several Confederates he had known in the West. Pinkerton thought C.A.H.'s political history would shield him from suspicion and "he might reach channels of information not yet opened to me." C.A.H.'s cover was a scheme for circumventing the coastal blockade by loading "a small vessel, say 150 tons," in New York with articles needed in both North and South, clearing it for Washington, and delivering it into the hands of the Rebels at Aquia Creek as it sailed up the Potomac. As this project does not appear to have been carried out, it may have been intended as no more than an empty proposition to cover one Richmond trip that would yield the agent a large number of contacts. And C.A.H.'s report on his return covered much more territory and many more topics than anything else appearing in Pinkerton's records.

Leaving Washington November 14, C.A.H. tried to cross the Potomac from lower Maryland and found that General Hooker's troops had halted traffic by breaking up the farmers' boats. He finally crossed lower down, but the delay lengthened his trip to eight days. His first contact was an assistant quartermaster from Centreville, ostensibly a good source, who said Johnston's army had 106 regiments, a reasonable figure, and that they averaged 700 men. The defenses at Centreville were reported so strong, with no less than 400 guns (including the field batteries) and nearly five miles of earthworks, that "the larger the force to come, the more [the Confederates] would bag." An officer from Evansport put General Holmes's strength at 40 regiments, about 25,000 men — radically exceeding both the true figures and Pinkerton's estimates. Pinkerton was careful to point out that the report of fortifications at Centreville was contradicted by "my own operatives who have been on the ground" (Webster is the only one of Pinkerton's men known to have visited Centreville). In comparing this report with information previously reported, Pinkerton was deviating from his practice of leaving such evaluative labors to McClellan, who was much too busy to perform them.

C.A.H. was allowed to see four rifled cannon, claimed to be 128- to 160-pounders, manufactured at the Tredegar works and supposedly destined for Centreville. He saw seven regiments en route to Johnston pass through Richmond, three of them from Texas under command of ex-Senator Wigfall. He made the tour of the Richmond defenses, reporting that each road leading into the city was fortified with medium-sized earthworks. Another useful piece of intelligence was that detectives visited every arriving steamboat and train and examined every hotel register. A naval authority, Matthew F. Maury, told him that only the upper decks of the *Merrimack* had burned when the Federal navy abandoned Norfolk; she now had been iron-plated throughout and given heavy armament. Rumor about the rebuilding of the ship, now the C.S.S. *Virginia,* was rife; Maury was surely the most authoritative source from which any of the considerable amount of talk about the ship originated. C.A.H. learned that the Rebels had experimented with steam rams — not very successfully, for the engines were disabled by collision with the intended victims. He heard the Confederate surgeon general say that the prevailing diseases in the army were pneumonia and typhoid fever. Friends in the army told him of a new ordnance works in Fayetteville, North Carolina, whose production of small arms would raise the Confederacy's manufacturing capacity to 4000 a week, a figure that contained more hope than fact.

A developing ill feeling between President Davis and General Beauregard reached C.A.H.'s ears. Beauregard's report on the Bull Run battle was suppressed by Davis because "it reflected upon his course in preventing Beauregard from following up their victory. . . . Davis admitted, what Beauregard claimed, that no doubt they could and might *take* Washington, but after doing so, they could not hold it."

In twelve days in Richmond C.A.H. managed to talk to visitors from several different distant command areas — Savannah and Charleston in the Southeast, western Virginia, General Albert Sidney Johnston's army in Kentucky — and he picked up news from most of the rest of the South, not much of which would have been likely to get into the Southern papers that reached Washington. Although his reports of troop strengths and other military information could not have been considered authoritative, they would have excited McClellan's interest, for as general-in-chief he was now directly concerned with those areas.

Leaving Richmond December 3, C.A.H. crossed the Potomac from Holmes's command area to Leonardtown, Maryland, learning that five small boats based there were the only dependable means of crossing the river. Pinkerton, receiving his report on December 9, thought that his information, except for the report on Centreville defenses, "may be considered reasonably reliable, making of course all proper allowance for the 'gasconading' quality of most Southern men."[30]

.. .. ..

Timothy Webster's second Richmond trip, from late November to mid-December, overlapped C.A.H.'s visit. His itinerary is unknown; although his report covered points as remote as Roanoke Island, on the North Carolina coast, it was probably compiled entirely from contacts in Richmond. An outstanding item was a collection of impressive details supplementary to C.A.H.'s report on the former U.S.S. *Merrimack*, making her seem an impregnable fortress, capable, it was said, of attacking Fort Monroe. The data on Roanoke Island, adjacent to Cape Hatteras, an objective of the forthcoming Burnside expedition, listed a defending force of 2100 and five batteries; Norfolk was reported to have seventeen regiments and twelve batteries. Several areas appeared to be very lightly defended: Petersburg, Suffolk, Weldon (a rail terminal in North Carolina), West Point (at the head of York River), and the lower Rappahannock and lower Potomac. Richmond was now reported to have 5000 to 6000 troops and seventeen fixed batteries, all still incomplete and not all armed with rifled guns. Defenses on the Peninsula were not mentioned, except for a reference to batteries at Yorktown which, along with others across the York at Gloucester, were said to be considered adequate to keep Yankee shipping out of that river.

Webster also reported identifying an apparent Confederate agent, the same Maddox who had been denounced by Frank Buxton in October. Webster gave the full name as Joseph H. Maddox and said Maddox had been on his way to an appointment in the Northern Neck of Virginia with Captain Alexander, the Confederacy's signal officer, to arrange for signaling across the lower Potomac. Maddox had solicited Webster's aid in this project and told Webster of having been imprisoned by the Federals, claiming that his release had been obtained late in November through the legal services of Maryland Senator Reverdy Johnson, whose fee was $1500. Maddox had given his parole and made bond in the amount of $10,000 not to go South but had lost no time in getting to Richmond. As Maddox's home was now known to be on the Maryland shore of the Potomac (Buxton had reported it as in Virginia), Pinkerton recommended that he be re-arrested; Maddox is known to have been in Old Capitol Prison in July 1862.[31] He makes a more extended appearance later in this book.

For more than a month, spanning two Richmond trips, Webster carried messages between General Winder and his son, William Winder, an artillery captain in the U.S. Army, who had returned from duty in California and was in Washington awaiting reassignment. William Winder did not want to draw his sword against the South, but he had a wife and child to support. According to Webster, "his father wished him to resign his commission if he could not find the means of certain escape by desertion, and come south; . . . his father had much rather that he should resign and, if it must be so, lay in jail until the close of the war, or if it should be demanded, that he would rather that his son should suffer death of the most ignominious character, than . . . be made to serve the United States in this war against the South." Reporting all this to McClellan, Pinkerton likened Captain Winder to Benedict Arnold and suggested that he be requested to swear allegiance to the United States, "not that I have much confidence in the saving power of such an oath, but for the purpose of testing whether Captain Winder will add perjury to the crime of Treason." That was not done; McClellan kept the captain out of the war by sending him back to California.[32]

Unaware of Webster's services for General Winder, J. B. Jones, who believed that couriers like Webster "render as much service to the enemy as to us," refused Webster a pass at one stage of these proceedings.

Webster's next trip extended from Christmas Day to January 30 and took him all the way to Nashville and the headquarters of the Confederates' western army at Bowling Green, Kentucky, an intelligence target that was part of McClellan's concern as general-in-chief. Webster was sick with inflammatory rheumatism throughout these travels and had to lay himself up in hotels for a day or two several times. He rode trains that dragged along at ten miles an hour, carrying reinforcements to the Confederates' western command. Bridges along the rail route were heavily guarded; the Unionists of East Tennessee had burned a number of them in November, and at one point the travelers had to make a detour of a mile and a half on foot. At Nashville he observed earthworks under construction along the Cumberland River, but only two regiments protecting the city. Near the railroad depot "15 to 20 houses of 'Ill Fame' [were operating] openly, day and night, in the most public manner" without interference from the civil or military authorities. The "almost universal drunkenness of the soldiers" was also going unnoticed. But the Nashville headquarters was strict about civilian travel, and only Webster's pass from Secretary Benjamin enabled him to continue to Bowling Green. Once there he had to get a further pass to visit the camps. En route from Nashville his train derailed; the cause was a thrown switch that the conductor attributed to sabotage.

Webster's cover story that won him Secretary Benjamin's pass to make his western trip is not indicated in his report. At Manassas and Centreville the delivery of letters to Maryland troops seems to have sufficed to win admittance to the camps; no such services to the Confederates in Kentucky are mentioned. Pinkerton's memoirs indicate that Benjamin rated Webster quite highly as a Southern agent, but that does not explain why he allowed him to travel to the western command.

Webster's friends at Bowling Green, one of whom was a brother of Tennessee's Governor Harris, told him there were eighty regiments there, but Webster concluded after examining the area that there were only sixty. He had counted thirty-eight en route from Nashville. Harris's regiment was the First Arkansas; in the report to McClellan, Pinkerton pointed out that one of the regiments on the Potomac also called itself the First Arkansas. Webster counted seven field batteries and three forts about Bowling Green; attempting to climb the hill where the largest of the forts stood, he was stopped by a sentry, but not until he had seen the muzzles of four very large guns.

Returning East, Webster learned at Nashville of the hanging of five of the bridge burners. Instead of returning to Richmond, he took an Orange and Alexandria train to Manassas and walked the eight miles to Centreville, only to learn that the First Maryland Regiment, the objective of his visit, had moved off another six or eight miles. His hiking gave him a look at the Centreville forts, now numbering three. Not all of their guns were yet mounted; some were lying on the ground and others had not arrived. The roads were too soft to haul eighty-four-pounders; a railroad from Manassas, under construction for some time, would be able to bring the guns when the ties were delivered, but the mud roads were so bad that the army's wagons had all they could do just to get the troops' food to them. Webster heard of defenses being built along the turnpike east and west of Centreville, but his poor health and the condition of the roads prevented him from inspecting them.

He counted ten regiments at Centreville and twenty-seven along the railroad and between Centreville and Manassas. The colonel of the First Maryland, George H. ("Maryland") Steuart, told him that the Johnston-Beauregard army numbered seventy-two regiments, including Jackson's force in the Valley but not including Holmes's troops along the lower Potomac. Steuart said that Southern men were wont to engage in a "game of Bluff" but "I am, and always was opposed to such a game," adding that at no time had there been "such an array of numbers" as had been claimed for the Southern army. Steuart was sincere; the figure he gave was four regiments under the number Johnston had on the rolls at that time. Steuart's own regiment claimed the usual 700 members — 707 to be exact — a partial explanation of its size being that it was "the most healthy of any in the rebel service."

Pinkerton reported that Webster had noted a strong change in the troops' attitude since his November visit. "Those who were 'bravest' to talk to" then were now "most eager to be released from service" — dispirited by inactivity and "the long talked-of and much expected advance of the Federal Army." Thus did Pinkerton pass the word to McClellan that even the enemy was impatient with his slowness.

Winder's force at Richmond amounted to only three regiments, Webster noted on returning there from Manassas. His pass for return North was obtained from Benjamin in person; J. B. Jones, now called "Colonel" (he was still a civilian), was now authorized to issue passes only to points within the Confederate lines. Webster learned that Jones and Winder were at odds over Jones's insistence that the general showed a "lack of stringency in regard to recommending persons to have passes." On his trip North Webster intended visiting the Rebels on the lower Potomac, but upon reaching Fredericksburg he encountered their commander, General Holmes, who spoiled the plan by countersigning his pass then and there. The best he could do was to pick up rumors current in Fredericksburg, which put Holmes's strength first at thirty regiments and again at fifty, both of which figures he probably had his doubts about. Crossing into Maryland, Webster found that the landowners, in order to prevent the escape of slaves, had destroyed all the boats at the mouths of creeks where there were no pickets.

Webster was the last of Pinkerton's agents to return from the Confederacy during the months of preparation for McClellan's campaign against Richmond. At the time of his January visit two other operatives were in Virginia. One was E. H. Stein, who had returned to Richmond by himself in December, having been unable to obtain transportation across the Potomac for his wife. The other was an agent listed in the records only as H.J.K., who apparently joined Pinkerton's force only a short time before leaving for Virginia. Stein's return North was being delayed again by close surveillance by Winder's detectives. H.J.K. disappears from the records after five months of payroll entries showing him in Virginia but indicating nothing about his movements or activities.[33]

Although Pinkerton agents are sometimes pictured as having obtained detailed information on Confederate forces from official sources,[34] in fact they produced disappointingly little information of military value. Neither Webster's business in the Confederate War Department (even with Benjamin) nor Frank Ellis's in the Treasury Department was of a kind to yield information on the Confederates' plans, strength in numbers, overall capabilities, or any other matters dealt with at the secretary level. Webster's reports on regiments and fortifications at Manassas-Centreville and Richmond were of unquestionable validity, but most of his findings dealt with the same questions as the interrogations of prisoners, deserters, and refugees that Pinkerton's Washington staff conducted. The worried "Colonel" Jones would have been much relieved if he could have learned how little information the enemy's much-feared spies were getting.

What Pinkerton really needed was agents in place, not only in Richmond but also in the other localities where Confederate forces were stationed. There were Richmonders who would have been willing to do more for the Union than take food and books to Federal soldiers in the city's prisons, but Pinkerton's operatives are not known to have made contact with any of them.[35] This may have been a case of deliberate neglect; Pinkerton's regard for his own operatives seems to have been accompanied by a distrust of any and all others — a policy now reinforced by his experience with Frank Ellis.

5

. . . .

Mr. Pinkerton's
Unique Arithmetic

August 1861–March 1862

CONSENSUS OF HISTORICAL BELIEF holds Allan Pinkerton's severe overestimating of Confederate numbers largely responsible for the extreme cautiousness that brought about General McClellan's failures — failures that delayed the successful prosecution of the war by a year or more. According to this view, Pinkerton, though a highly successful detective, was incompetent at the business of military intelligence, and McClellan, brilliant organizer and administrator though he was, was thoroughly deceived by Pinkerton's inflated estimates.[1]

Neither half of this widely shared judgment is correct. As already seen, Pinkerton was successful in spy-chasing (counterintelligence). In positive intelligence his early performance was weak, but before the end of his service he was keeping track of the composition of the opposing army with surprising accuracy. As for McClellan, he could not have been *deceived* by Pinkerton's overestimates, for he was a party to them — the dominant party, in fact.

The first of the famous exaggerations of Confederate strength was the 100,000 figure McClellan gave in his August 8 letter that General Scott branded a false alarm. Pinkerton probably did not contribute to that estimate, for on the day it was written he had just begun setting up shop, with only three of his detectives on hand.[2] And for some weeks or months he was preoccupied with tracking the activities of spies and would-be spies in the secessionist population of Washington.

The spies that McClellan said were among the sources of his 100,000 estimate could have been members of the short-lived bureau headed by William C. Parsons; but that group was disbanding at this time, and its positive-intelligence activity is not known to have extended beyond the vicinity of Washington and Alexandria. Thus it is more likely that the spies McClellan referred to were self-appointed amateurs. However, the likeliest single source was not a spy but a Confederate deserter, a Kentuckian named Edward B. McMurdy. McMurdy claimed that he had been impressed into the Confederate service at New Orleans, had been in the Bull Run battle, and had made his way to Washington, via Harper's Ferry, to seek an army commission. According to his later account, McClellan took him to see General Scott, whom they found with Lincoln and Secretary Seward. Those officials, McMurdy said, "thought my views of the resources of the Rebels to be extravagant." After the interview McMurdy was a guest in McClellan's house, where the general "told me I had saved Washington City and in all probability the very existence of the Government."[3] It may be that until McMurdy appeared McClellan's view of Confederate numbers had not reached so alarming a level.

McClellan kept the estimates flowing. In letters to his wife he gave the enemy "3 or 4 times my force"; then 150,000 to his own 55,000; after new troop arrivals at Washington, the enemy still had, he said, double his own strength. On September 8, in a letter to Secretary Cameron, he lowered the enemy's estimated total to 130,000, against which he could oppose only 70,000. Five days later, again writing to Cameron, he revised the 130,000 figure to 170,000 and his own total to 81,000. Although the Confederates' Manassas army during these weeks received a new brigade from Georgia and half a dozen regiments from other states, it still numbered only about 35,000. And though other substantial accretions were to follow, McClellan's estimate of enemy strength grew at an even faster rate.

McClellan claimed that in issuing these estimates he was giving figures below the "real strength" of the enemy, while taking "the reverse course as to our own [strength]." His superiors would have wondered why he did not give the figures he believed "real," instead of some other figures. Predicting an early advance by the enemy, he urged that the entire regular army except for artillerists, and all volunteer troops from other theaters of war, be placed in his own army.[4] So extreme a proposal indicates that he really believed, as McMurdy claimed, that "the very existence of the Government" was threatened.

With those communications McClellan's preoccupation with troop counts and presumed enemy advantages is in full view. The 100,000 estimate he gave Scott, after only two weeks in command, committed him to six-figure estimates for a Confederate army that in four years of war would never reach that level. When Scott pointed out that McClellan had thus placed himself on record, the old general was implying that that commitment might embarrass him in the future. But McClellan proved to be impervious to such embarrassment.

The proposal to strip other theaters for reinforcements, relying on the Federals' regular artillery to maintain a defensive stance there, indicates that McClellan was crediting the Confederates with having so many men in uniform that they could place a huge force in northern Virginia without seriously depleting their strength elsewhere. Although the South had scarcely a third of the white population of the North, it had mobilized a far greater proportion of its men of military age. This fact repeatedly came to McClellan's attention when Pinkerton reported on his interrogations of Northerners and foreigners who were in the South at the outbreak of war, had been forced into Rebel regiments, and deserted to the Federals.

How McClellan was deriving the estimates that appear in these letters is, except for the August 8 letter to Scott, unknown and unknowable. No strength reports traceable to Pinkerton appear in the records of these weeks; if bits and pieces of information about the Confederate armies were diverting his attention from the search for enemy spies, he may have delivered them to McClellan orally. Apparently McClellan already had begun the practice, quite evident in later months, of reporting intelligence from sources independent of Pinkerton. He did not identify these; he also avoided naming Pinkerton, and, so far as records reveal, he withheld Pinkerton's reports from Lincoln and his military superiors. Such was the obscurity with which he surrounded his estimating of enemy numbers that we are led to assume that some of his figures were inventions, made by guessing, on the basis of what the Confederates were believed to have had last week, how many they probably had this week.[5]

When Pinkerton finally accumulated enough enemy information to produce a strength estimate, it seriously overrated Confederate numbers, but not nearly enough to support the 170,000 that was McClellan's latest estimate. Pinkerton's report, written October 4, gave the opposing army 98,400, more than double its true strength, which was somewhere between 40,000 and 45,000 at that time.[6] Pinkerton made no reference to the fact that this estimate flew in the face of McClellan's much higher figures. He may have simply been avoiding an argument with his chief, but more probably he was unaware of what McClellan had been telling his superiors about enemy numbers.

Pinkerton also estimated 11,000 Confederates in western Virginia, 6800 at Richmond, and 10,400 in the Norfolk-Portsmouth area, for a statewide total of 126,600. He placed the total number of regiments at 184, only 33 more than the true number for the forces he covered, but his identification of these regiments was badly flawed.[7] For example, he listed 18 Alabama infantry regiments against a true figure of 10; 18 Georgia regiments against 24; 45 Virginia regiments against 75 (many of them militia). Of the 184 regiments, 143 were listed as in the Manassas army, a 64 percent overestimate. None of these flaws would have been detectable by McClellan, but others stood out glaringly. The report opened with the statement that it covered "what I deem to be the entire rebel force in Virginia," but it omitted "Prince John" Magruder's army on the Peninsula. As that army had exchanged blows with Federals, its existence was common knowledge; the oversight was a matter of careless writing. Another highly visible blunder was a tabulation repeatedly showing 700 as the average strength of infantry regiments, contrasted with a pointed statement that 700 was the highest number of *any* regiment. Pinkerton claimed that since the full-strength complement for every infantry regiment was 1000, the 700 figure was a conservative one.

Still another glaring blunder, not important for its effect on the totals for the various commands but significant for what it revealed about the statistical skills of the reporting office, involved the effective strength of the regiments and larger units. Owing to sickness and other causes, that strength was considered to be 15 percent less than the total number of troops present. But instead of subtracting 15 percent from each total, Pinkerton's clerk had subtracted one-fifteenth, which amounts to only $6\frac{2}{3}$ percent. This probably was only an ignorant error that got by unnoticed; but because it magnified the enemy's effective strength, it just might be the beginning of a pattern of shoddy arithmetic that in later occurrences seems intended to support the higher estimates Pinkerton could assume McClellan was issuing. But the error called attention to itself by producing columns of odd-looking figures. The number 15 does not divide evenly into most numbers ending in double zeros; thus most of the subtracted numbers ended in fractions, and the resulting totals likewise. Instead of rounding these off to whole numbers, the report writer produced a unit-by-unit tabulation loaded with numbers ending in $\frac{1}{3}$ and $\frac{2}{3}$. The 11,000-man army in western Virginia, for example, had $10,266\frac{2}{3}$ effectives and $733\frac{1}{3}$ ineffectives. In other words, the last man in many a unit was only one-third or two-thirds of a complete person.[8]

This curious document went to McClellan over the signature "E. J. Allen," Pinkerton's nom de guerre. Clearly, the abilities of Pinkerton's detectives did not include professional skill in presenting intelligence findings. And E. J. Allen's estimative reports were to get worse, not better.

Pinkerton's presentation of the October 4 report to McClellan was accompanied, or possibly preceded, by a discussion between the two men of the practice Pinkerton would follow in estimating enemy strength. All that is known of this discussion appears in a report Pinkerton wrote to McClellan six weeks later. Referring to his October 4 report, he said, "[That] estimate was founded upon all information then in my possession, derived from my own operatives, deserters from the Rebel service, 'Contrabands', &c, &c; and was made large, as intimated to you at the time, so as to be sure and cover the entire number of the Enemy that our army was to meet."[9]

Made large . . . so as to be sure and cover the entire number of the Enemy . . . In that half-sentence we have the explanation of Pinkerton's badly exaggerated estimates that historians have been ridiculing all these years, attributing them to Pinkerton's credulity and general incompetence.[10] Now it develops that the enemy numbers were deliberately "made large" and that McClellan was just as aware of that fact as Pinkerton. McClellan's reporting of six-figure estimates to his superiors in those early weeks, with little factual basis and before Pinkerton had had time to get his feet on the ground, made it necessary for the detective to produce some supporting data. And it was important that the information he provided would insure against their ever being surprised by enemy numbers they had failed to count.

McClellan spelled out this "worst-case" rationale in a paper prepared for but omitted from the final report of his command of the Army of the Potomac. He wrote, "The certainty that the enemy had . . . at ascertained places, other troops than those known in detail, in considerable numbers necessarily caused in my estimates additions to be made for the sake of safety, to the known quantities: which may have created the impression that the force of the enemy in front of Washington was exaggerated."[11] In McClellan's — and Pinkerton's — view thus expressed, estimating enemy numbers on the safe side was no more and no less than their patriotic duty. Even so, their two written statements raise the possibility that here was a collusion whose real purpose was to develop estimates that would justify McClellan's constant pleas for more men and more time, that this was a case of shady work in Intelligence's back room. Pinkerton's words, "as intimated to you at the time," do nothing to allay that suspicion. The question thus raised is whether McClellan and Pinkerton really believed those very generous estimates of the enemy. This question will be examined later in detail.

How this "safety allowance" was computed is not evident in Pinkerton's October 4 report. It may have consisted in using 700 as the regimental average in the face of the knowledge that it was a regimental maximum. It also could have consisted merely of a generosity in accepting the presence of regiments on weak evidence.

One reason McClellan did not forward Pinkerton's estimates to the President and the secretary of war may have been the reports' obvious flaws, their lack of professionalism. But a stronger reason for withholding, at least at this stage, was that Pinkerton's generous estimate still fell far short of the figures McClellan had been claiming. Pinkerton's 98,400 figure on October 4 should at least have reined McClellan in from his own hard-charging estimating, but it did not. He substituted his own considerably more liberal figure at the next opportunity. In a situation summary requested by Lincoln late in October he stated that "the enemy

have a force on the Potomac not less than 150,000 strong, well drilled
and equipped, ably commanded, and strongly entrenched." Against this
host he could oppose a maneuvering force of only 76,000, though he
had another 92,000 troops who were sick or otherwise absent, were still
unequipped, or were committed to stationary duty protecting Washington, Baltimore, Annapolis, and the Eastern Shore. The enemy would
have had to make similar subtractions from that 150,000 figure in order
to put an army in the field to fight the Federals' 76,000, but McClellan,
in reporting to his superiors then and thereafter, painted the worst possible picture by comparing his own maneuverable force with the enemy's
total force.

All his sources agreed on the 150,000 figure, he declared. In this case
we finally have a clue as to how he acquired his six-figure estimates. Frank
Ellis, at this stage not yet considered to be working for the Confederates,
had just come in from Richmond, reporting 80,000 at Manassas-Centreville and 20,000 on the lower Potomac. Ellis gave as his source Jefferson
Davis and the three cabinet members with whom he said he had dined.
(McClellan chose to ignore the certainty that the Confederate leaders
would not have entrusted Ellis with the truth about General Johnston's
numbers.) Another recent report, arriving at third hand from a Unionist
citizen of Fairfax County, gave Johnston 100,000 at Manassas-Centreville
and 30,000 at Leesburg. By taking the higher (but less reliable) of the
two Manassas-Centreville figures, the 20,000 from downriver, and the
grotesquely exaggerated 30,000 for Leesburg — thus straining to get
the highest possible total — McClellan could have produced that round
150,000. Another possibility of course is that the figure was simply a shot
in the dark.

Part of the draft of McClellan's paper is in the handwriting of Edwin M.
Stanton, the future secretary of war, who was at that time practicing law in
Washington and serving McClellan as a confidant. Stanton's professional
experience would have told him that McClellan's claim of unanimity
among a variety of sources was unlikely to be true; he also may have had
his doubts about the validity of the 150,000 total. But that figure satisfied
his lawyerlike proclivity for putting the client's case in the strongest
possible terms.[12]

The next episode in the Pinkerton-McClellan strength-estimating history followed Timothy Webster's first Richmond trip, ending in mid-
November. McClellan would be expecting a report of what Webster had
learned — and there were embarrassing discrepancies between his findings and Pinkerton's October 4 estimate.[13] For the two Confederate elements, Johnston's army and the Richmond garrison, that were covered
in both reports, Webster's figures were 29,600 lower than Pinkerton's,
and all but 2600 of this difference lay in the totals for Johnston, the one

force that was of more concern than all the others together. This much statistical disagreement could have been expected, but Pinkerton did his best to cover it by dwelling on the total for all Confederate forces in Virginia, 126,600, obscuring as far as possible the differences between the totals for individual components. As a result, what he produced was not a summary of Virginia forces, updated with Webster's information and nicely highlighted for quick reading by a busy army commander; it was instead a hard-to-understand reconciling effort, yielding a spurious near-agreement between the October 4 estimate and Webster's findings.

It was also a parade of errors, arithmetical and logical. There was error in the computation of the "safety allowance" and inconsistency in its application; figures for the two areas not covered by Webster, Norfolk-Portsmouth and western Virginia, were treated differently from those for the Peninsula, the one area missing from Pinkerton's October 4 estimate; and a sizable change in the October 4 total was introduced ex post facto. This last-named bit of doctoring consisted of fixing the amount of the safety allowance in that estimate at 6330, or 5 percent of the 126,600 total, bringing it that much closer to Webster's figure. But nowhere in the October 4 calculation can be found an addition of 5 percent or any other tangible amount. Pinkerton, aware that there was substantial surplusage in that 126,600 figure, could have felt justified in putting so modest a percentage figure on it. And some of the other flaws, even all of them, could have been honest errors; but the fact that they all had the effect of narrowing the gap between the two grand totals indicates that at least the largest ones were deliberate artifices.

Whatever their motivation, these "adjustments" reduced the 29,600 discrepancy to 10,170. Even if the introduction of the safety allowance, an obvious afterthought, is treated as legitimate, an erroneous doctoring amounting to 14,420 remains. It is hard to believe that so distinguished a detective would have allowed so obviously discreditable a piece of work to leave his office if he had seen it first. But as this was the report that contained Pinkerton's intimate reminder to McClellan that his estimates were "made large," it is quite unlikely that it was written and released by clerks without their chief's cognizance.[14]

Pinkerton pointed out that "in so extended a field, some encampments may have escaped [Webster's] observation; but when it is taken into consideration that a difference of only ten thousand exists between estimates taken under such different circumstances, and derived from entirely different sources, without any possibility of collusion, I submit that they both must approximate very nearly to accuracy." More than that, the near-agreement of the two totals demonstrated, he said, the "approximateness" of the October 4 figure. Webster was the standard against which the rest of Pinkerton's reporting was being compared. This was a correct view: Timothy Webster's performance is one of the few instances of professional competence in Pinkerton's bureau. However, before concluding that one acute spy is necessarily better than a team of desk-bound interrogators, we must recall that Pinkerton's office staffers were working under a "safety first" reporting policy that was guaranteed to produce inflated figures.

This was not the end of Pinkerton's arithmetical legerdemain aimed at bolstering his estimates for McClellan's benefit. In his report of Ellis's third and last Richmond visit he included a comparison of Ellis's troop counts with Webster's. Ellis's 77,000 figure for Johnston's army, he wrote, was 4400 above Webster's. That was a reasonably close agreement, but Pinkerton chose to improve on it by asserting, without showing any evidence, that six regiments, or 4200 men, had been added to Johnston's army in the two weeks between Webster's visit to Manassas-Centreville and Ellis's interview with his source, Captain Quincy, in Richmond. Now only 200 separated the two totals. Here was another dubious reconciliation attempt, which today has the effect of making Pinkerton's estimating seem less trustworthy instead of more so. Nevertheless Pinkerton "submitted" that the agreement of the two figures testified to the accuracy of both. But in less than a month Ellis was in Old Capitol Prison charged with spying for the enemy. The discovery of his disloyalty invalidated his 77,000 figure and threw serious doubt on Webster's closely agreeing one — a point that Pinkerton omitted from his report on the Ellis affair.[15]

If Pinkerton was aware of the huge gap between his estimates and the enemy numbers McClellan had been reporting to Lincoln (150,000) and Cameron (170,000), his clumsy efforts to persuade McClellan of the accuracy of his lower figures become forgivable. In any case, those figures may have induced a temporary caution in McClellan's reporting. Early in December Lincoln sent him a suggestion for a flank attack on the communications of the Manassas army via the line of the Occoquan River. McClellan rejected the proposal, saying that recent information "leads me to believe that the enemy could meet us in front with equal forces *nearly*."[16] This does not mean that he had so far changed his mind about troop strength as to give the enemy lower total numbers than his own. An attacker hopes to concentrate strength against a weak spot; McClellan appears to be saying here that so many of Johnston's troops were within easy marching distance of the Occoquan flank that he could deny McClellan the preponderance of numbers that an attack would need. McClellan's caution, if it truly *was* caution, lay in making his argument without the use of figures. The Confederates had only five or six brigades on or near the Occoquan line — far less strength than the numbers McClellan could put there. Lincoln's plan was the right one, the one most feared by General Johnston at Manassas; the only thing wrong with it was that it was Lincoln's and not McClellan's.

. . . . . .

By early December Pinkerton's agents on the Washington–Richmond circuit had brought in several hundred letters. Most of them were copied and forwarded to the addressees; a few were retained. The accumulation called forth a report on what Pinkerton and his staff had learned about public sentiment in the Confederate capital. "The general desire for correspondence, together with the confidence established by my operatives," he explained, "has lifted a curtain to southern public sentiment . . . and besides, has enabled my operatives to penetrate the very center of the motives and activity of public and private life." After summarizing the contents of the letters, he ventured some conclusions. "A general feeling of insecurity and want of stability in the Confederate Government pervades all monied men"; their preference for state bonds over Confederate stocks and bonds "shows at least a *remote* belief in the possible *re-union of the States.*" So great was the hope for British intervention that if England did not take decisive action "it would be impossible much longer, for the rebel leaders to keep their faith *with the people.*" The decline in the value of Confederate money and the extravagant prices of ordinary goods "argue a speedy crisis in commercial and money circles, which . . . must greatly accelerate if it does not complete the downfall of the pretended Government." And "the quietness of the Negro slaves, is owing to the . . . demonstration of power on the part of the Military Authorities" — shown by the carrying of slaves to the interior as Federal forces approach — and making them "believe that the 'Yankees' will sell them to Cuba to pay the expenses of the war."

Pinkerton extracted two points of military importance from the letters. One was that the "great body of the rebel troops have perfect confidence in Johnston and Beauregard. . . . a large degree of enthusiasm pervades the camps. . . . the troops seem to feel as if fighting for their homes and firesides." The second point was that the military information in the letters showed that his operatives' reports had been accurate as to the "numbers condition and feeling of the troops. . . . their arms, ammunition, clothing and location are very nearly as stated."[17] Timothy Webster would not have been flattered to learn that his reporting was rated according to how well it agreed with these miscellaneous, unofficial sources.

In mid-December Pinkerton stepped into a political situation and paid for his boldness by losing his cover. He investigated the condition of Negroes in the Washington city jail, over which he had no authority, military or otherwise. His findings, sympathetic to the black people in the jail, were aired in the Senate by Henry Wilson, whereupon the *Wash-*

ington Star undertook to educate "E. J. Allen," saying that the free Negro population of Washington was about 14,000, but the war had brought 50,000 more black people to the city, and if they all worked, the white men would be put out of work.

Pinkerton wrote Provost Marshal Andrew Porter that "the motives which prompted all our actions in this case were too sacred for attack by *any* man." Next day he had a more serious complaint: the *Star* had announced that "'E. J. Allen' means 'Pinkerton.' . . . Secrecy is the very basis of our action. . . . I deem it *absolutely necessary* for the safety of my operatives, *many of whom are at this moment periling their lives within the enemies lines,* that I should have the least public notoriety possible." (The statement that "many" of his agents were in the Confederacy was a flagrant exaggeration.) Pinkerton added that it was a local detective named A. R. Allen who had told the *Star* editor the true identity of E. J. Allen. Pinkerton's connection with the army, however, had not been perfectly guarded by Pinkerton himself; he had discussed military affairs with a *Chicago Tribune* correspondent, Henry M. Smith. Smith and his editor kept this discussion off the record. By now the *Star* was calling Pinkerton's force a "gang" employed in making reports for abolitionists, the "disturbers of the peace of the country."[18]

Correspondents of various papers had found that in their rambles among the camps they could get interesting news by interviewing people who were about to become sources for Pinkerton — refugees (including runaway slaves) and Confederate prisoners and deserters. In some cases correspondents were even able to find out what Federal spies were reporting, by quizzing Pinkerton's operatives and others engaged in spying (or amateurs who thought they were) as they passed through or near some field headquarters on their way back from their missions. Thus raw intelligence could find its way into print, to be read by the public before McClellan, or perhaps even Pinkerton, even knew it was on its way to them.

Pinkerton singled out the *Baltimore Sun* as a purveyor of these revelations. "The Public Press at the North, unlike that of the South," he wrote, "seems to care less for the country than for their own selfish interest." He attributed a recent tightening of Confederate security measures, especially in the issuance of passes, to the warning the Northern papers had thus given. Operative C.A.H. had brought some direct information on this point, having noted that the New York papers were received in Richmond in bundles of hundreds.

In mid-December McClellan sought to end this leakage of intelligence secrets by issuing an order, written by Pinkerton, requiring that people arriving from the enemy lines be questioned only by "the officer commanding the advance guard to elicit information regarding his particular post" and by the division commander himself or an officer deputized by

him. McClellan's widening circle of enemies in Washington could interpret these restrictions as an attempt to suppress the truth regarding
Confederate forces. If subordinate generals objected to it as interfering
with their legitimate need for information, they got no satisfaction from
a follow-up order that decreed that the division commander's examination must "only refer to such information as may affect the division and
those near it, especially those remote from general headquarters." But
the new order relaxed the earlier one by allowing provost marshals a role
in the interrogations. Another intelligent amendment was a requirement
that information affecting other divisions must be quickly communicated to them.[19]

One brigade commander had been especially energetic in pursuit of
enemy information. This was James S. Wadsworth, a brigadier from upstate New York who possessed legal training, wealth, and political standing, and did not fear to speak his mind on intelligence matters when
called before Congress's Joint Committee on the Conduct of the War. By
exercising congressional investigative authority, these senators and representatives were doing their bit to keep healthy the system of checks and
balances — healthier in fact than pleased many generals. The committee
was naturally disposed to investigate officers whose enthusiasm for the
war or for good Republican principles might be open to question. When
Wadsworth, a strong Republican, appeared before the committee, it was
McClellan and not Wadsworth who was actually being investigated. He
gave the inquisitive legislators a satisfying earful: "I think we are largely
superior to our enemy in numbers, and we have a vast superiority in
artillery." He backed up his assertions by describing his own aggressive
information-gathering effort. From the brigade's advanced position his
scouts had regularly been examining the country as far south as the Confederate outpost at Fairfax Court House, and maintaining contact with
Union sympathizers in that locality. He had also devoted careful attention to interviewing refugees, prisoners, and deserters who came his way.

Wadsworth's self-assigned intelligence operation may have been the
chief inspiration for McClellan's action restricting forward commanders'
prerogatives. But the energetic brigadier was not easily dissuaded by the
order. From his immediate chief, General McDowell, he obtained an
opinion that "it would not be a breach of the order to examine [these
persons] sufficiently for us to know whether the enemy were going to
attack us at once." With this much latitude he continued his efforts. He
became persuaded that the strength of the force about Manassas and
Centreville was between 40,000 and 50,000. Since Johnston's effective
force in December was 44,500 and his total present for duty was 55,000,
Wadsworth seems to have come nearer the truth about enemy numbers
than anyone else in the North. As he is unlikely to have had first-hand
sources on enemy units remote from his own location, this close estimate

may have been only a lucky hit. However that may be, he had enough confidence in his accumulated information to take it to McDowell, then McClellan, finally Stanton. Wadsworth's biographer states that "McClellan rejected it with a rudeness, so the story goes, surpassing his usual treatment of subordinates." But Stanton took favorable notice of the fifty-four-year-old soldier who stood before him, "so clear as to his facts and pressing them home with all the personal force of a man accustomed to make his ideas tell upon his auditors."[20]

Because of Wadsworth's arithmetical heresies, it could never have occurred to McClellan that here was the man who should be in the job held by Pinkerton. A year later, when a new commander of the Army of the Potomac was looking for an intelligence chief, Wadsworth was a division commander and would not have been considered. The job went to another lawyer-officer from the aristocracy of upstate New York, Colonel George H. Sharpe.

. .   . .   . .

At the end of 1861 Pinkerton's force still numbered twenty-four. The December payroll totaled $4486, with Pinkerton drawing $10 a day seven days a week and the others each $6, including George H. Bangs, Pinkerton's second in command. All operatives ran expense accounts, which totaled $1647 for the month.

Only five of the twenty-four would serve behind enemy lines; Pinkerton's principal source of intelligence was not espionage but interrogation of prisoners, deserters, and refugees, an activity that probably benefited considerably from McClellan's new orders on that subject. Interrogation was systematized into a routine: in addition to such obvious topics as the Confederates' numerical strength, their expectations of Federal action, and their fortifications and armament, informants were queried as to the Rebels' health, their food and forage (seldom reported adequate), clothing and shoes (likewise badly inadequate), condition of horses and harness, re-enlistment prospects (almost always reported poor), military and civilian morale, the condition of roads and railroads, and the state of the Southern economy (suffering badly from shortages as well as inflation). The Confederates' picketing routines, their strictness about passes, and other security questions — matters of concern to Pinkerton's operatives — were also topics of interrogation but not nearly so often as might be expected.

Many informants had something to say under almost all these headings; others knew little. A refugee who had had no contact with the military was likely to be put through much the same interrogatory drill as the Rebel soldier who had a headful of information. The resulting reports, drawn up by anonymous clerks who signed them with Pinkerton's nom de guerre, were ponderously wordy and formal, and as previously noted, were almost devoid of comparisons with earlier information that would make them more useful to McClellan. The report writers evidently were under instruction to give just the facts and not editorialize. So McClellan for some months received every week fifty or more closely written pages of information that was very hard for him to evaluate or put to use.[21]

These informants have received a large share of the blame for Pinkerton's overestimating of Confederate strength. Historians have too easily assumed that these people expected that high figures would please their interrogators, and that the latter credulously accepted their claims. Although nearly all deserters and refugees, and some of the prisoners, tried to impress their examiners with how much they knew, there is no reason to assume that they expected high figures to be more acceptable than low ones. Their high figures were based on rumors in general circulation, which gave them a chance to display their "knowledge." If Pinkerton's interrogators accepted high figures too readily, it was because Pinkerton had given them a "safety first" lecture.

.. .. ..

Although McClellan commanded all Federal armies from Scott's retirement on November 1 until his campaign on the Peninsula began in March, only the Virginia theater received the attention of Pinkerton's bureau, with two exceptions. One was Timothy Webster's January visit to the Confederates' western headquarters in Kentucky. The other was a long report that Pinkerton produced in February, covering the topography and defenses of the Mississippi River region between Columbus, Kentucky, and Memphis. It was based on operatives' visits made to that area in the summer of 1861, when McClellan's command was the widespread Department of the Ohio.[22]

As Pinkerton was nominally under Provost Marshal Andrew Porter, he was concerned not only with eliciting information from people reaching him from the South but with arranging for their disposition. The allegiance of Negroes was never doubted, but other refugees, along with Confederate prisoners and deserters, were treated with caution. If, for example, a deserter seemed to be telling the truth but only with reluctance, or if his Confederate service was understood to have been other than completely forced, Pinkerton recommended that he be held in custody for a time. The mildest restriction, placed on only the most cooperative deserters and refugees, was the requirement of a parole of honor not to go beyond the lines of the Union armies. Pinkerton's recommendations regarding the disposition of these people were made not to Porter but directly to McClellan, who routinely approved them, almost always without making any stipulations beyond those proposed by Pinkerton. After they had operated this way for several months, General

Randolph B. Marcy, McClellan's chief of staff (and also his father-in-law), gave Pinkerton authority to make final disposition of routine cases.[23]

The most fruitful informants were the deserters, especially Europeans or Northerners who had been impressed into Confederate service. Some of them claimed to have planned desertion from the moment they entered the army; they would have made mental notes about the Rebel army in order to improve their chances of a welcome from the Federals. Prisoners, much less numerous than deserters in these months without battles, were not likely to be as well informed or to give information willingly, and of course they were not unlikely to give misinformation, perhaps knowingly. Information from refugees was usually of poor quality, although some had had contact with the military. Refugees naturally tended to avoid Confederate soldiery and military posts on their way to the Federal lines. For Negro refugees, the most numerous and also the most cooperative class of informants, there was the further handicap of enslavement on the farms, which greatly limited their access to information.

Throughout the war, deserters were unequaled as sources of information on the enemy army's composition and organizational structure. But their contribution to military history is not limited to the information they provided; their reasons for desertion and methods of accomplishing it are a study in themselves. In the numerous Pinkerton reports on deserter interrogations, no two cases are alike; one searches in vain for the typical deserter. An example of a unique case was James F. Monroe, who in deserting was merely putting himself in the hands of his old service, the U.S. Army. He had received a disability discharge in 1859 and then joined the Winchester Rifles. When the Rifles were called up by the Confederate Army, he found himself fighting for a cause with which he had no sympathy. He deserted by swimming a horse across the Potomac near Harper's Ferry. Reaching Pinkerton's office, he asked to be released to go to Ohio, where he had friends. Pinkerton let him go.[24]

Three Northerners in a Tennessee regiment in Holmes's command reached Hooker's headquarters in lower Maryland, having crossed the two-mile-wide Potomac in a boat they had found. They reported that in escaping they had beaten a sentinel into insensibility and set out in their boat only to hear another sentinel give an alarm, too late to arrest their flight.

A Pennsylvanian in Jackson's cavalry arrived in the Union lines explaining that he had been drafted into the Virginia militia but had joined a regular cavalry unit because the cavalry's far-forward picketing improved his chances of getting away. Another Northerner, a native of Maine, claimed he had been arrested as a spy by a vigilance committee in Savannah; he joined a Georgia cavalry company, went to Manassas with it, and rode into the Federal lines while on courier duty.

An especially keen source of information was a native Virginian, G. L. Dulaney, said to be the inventor of a sewing machine. In January his militia company was in the advance of a march that Jackson's army made into western Virginia. A skirmish near the Potomac created enough confusion for Dulaney to escape into Maryland. Herman Pech, a French-born cavalryman from North Carolina, got away while sharing picket duty with a sergeant to whom he stated his desire to desert. Pinkerton's interrogator recorded, "The sergeant objected, both verbally and otherwise; . . . a scuffle ensued, but Pech having the advantage of the other man in regard to arms, induced the latter to let him go."

Numerous desertions were induced by the determination of General D. H. Hill, new commander at Leesburg, to improve the defenses there. Union-minded Virginians who had joined the militia in order to avoid more active service were called up to work on Hill's new forts and deserted in fear of being impressed further into volunteer regiments. Civilians, including a few slaves, found work on the forts unpleasant enough to leave for that reason alone. Escapees from Loudoun usually declared that most of that county was pro-Union.

An Irish native in a Louisiana regiment at Manassas deserted by walking sixty or eighty miles through woods and fields to cross the Potomac near Harper's Ferry. His hike consumed seventeen wintry days and nights. A widow named Margaret Stypes, living at the foot of Loudoun Heights, arranged for Federal pickets to take him over to Maryland in a skiff. Later deserters and numerous refugees had her assistance in making their escapes.[25]

A Pennsylvanian living with his Southern-born wife deep in the Shenandoah Valley chose service in the Confederate army because chances of escaping north were better there than in the militia. He feigned sickness during Jackson's January advance; the privations that Stonewall forced on his troops had loaded up the sick rolls. Like other deserters, this man declared he had been in the Bull Run battle without firing a shot and knew many others who also did not fire.

Another Irish native, Nugent T. Emmett, caught in New Orleans at the outbreak of war, bargained his way to Richmond by promising to enlist there; then, evading service, he was jailed and finally joined the First North Carolina Cavalry. He escaped while on picket duty.[26]

The most elaborate campaign of desertion recorded by Pinkerton was conducted by a twenty-two-year-old oysterman from Baltimore, James H. Maurice. He was working Florida waters when war came; with a view to returning home, he enlisted in a Pensacola company that was soon sent to the Virginia peninsula. Attempting desertion, he was caught, court-martialed, and given five days at hard labor. Months later he bought a sailboat, in which he escaped. Another boat pursued, but Maurice crossed the Chesapeake Bay and used his oysterman's knowledge of

Eastern Shore waters to sail onto some flats where the other boat could not follow. Two days after he told his story in Pinkerton's office, McClellan wanted more details about fortifications on the Peninsula, but Maurice was not to be found.[27]

Another double deserter was Joseph William Benson, a slave owner. After serving in a volunteer regiment in western Virginia, he deserted and worked as a driver on the Winchester–Strasburg stage line, where he was spotted by a member of his old company. He escaped punishment by enlisting in Jackson's cavalry. While on picket duty near the Potomac, he persuaded Union pickets to row across the river for him and his horse.

But the most resolute of these deserters was Spencer Harris, a Loudoun Countian and Bull Run veteran, who said he had escaped in October and remained at home — "most of the time under the floor" — until a Federal advance into the Shenandoah Valley in February improved the climate for Unionists in nearby Loudoun.[28]

Although Pinkerton's interrogators were sometimes skeptical of deserters' stories, they do not seem to have found any instances of the enemy's using planted deserters to deliver deceptive information or to spy on the Federals and then re-desert to the Confederates. Feigned desertion was often employed later in the war, when there were motives for deception that did not exist in these months of war without battles. And two-way desertion was not likely to be attempted by the Rebels, since the Union army was not short enough of manpower to accept the enlistment of a deserter. He would be sent North, away from the army.

Refugees from the Confederacy who had had contact with its army found a ready welcome across the Potomac. Jackson King, an ex-Marine residing in Georgetown, D.C., had gone to Centreville to look after the welfare of his sister. On her advice that "I had better be doing something or they would suspect me," he went to work as an army teamster. Deciding to return to the District of Columbia, he set out on foot and encountered gray-clad pickets. He had prepared a story for them, but they turned out to be Federals. He adapted his story for Northern ears; nevertheless he was sent to army headquarters in handcuffs. He was released after a lengthy and not very productive interrogation.[29]

A free Negro, W. H. Ringgold, sent from Baltimore by General Dix, reported gleanings from six months in Secessia. He had been a steward on a river steamer that was impressed with its crew into Rebel service by the accident of being at Fredericksburg at the time Virginia seceded. The Confederates set the boat to work transporting troops on the York River until it was put out of service by storm damage. The crew was sent home to Baltimore via the Eastern Shore, traveling on Confederate passes; evidently the authorities did not credit them with being able to disclose much military information. Thus black men enjoyed a freedom to travel that was denied to all but a few whites. Ringgold's report was one of the few detailed accounts of Confederate defenses on the Virginia peninsula that McClellan received before his army began landing there in March. But Ringgold's coverage of the north side of the York River was weak, and his report, unfortunately, was the only intelligence McClellan ever received on that region, which was of great concern to him as a more direct route to Richmond than the Peninsula approach he eventually chose.[30]

Early in March a sizable party of trainmen on the Manassas Gap Railroad decamped through the picket lines of the security-minded Jackson and sought Northern protection by claiming opposition to the rebellion. An advance up the Shenandoah Valley by General Banks, just begun, threatened the continued operation of the railroad, which had its shops at Woodstock in the Valley. These men faced, along with unemployment, the threat of being forced into the Confederate army. Their claim of Union sentiments is easy to accept when it is recalled that the train crews involved in the sluggish movement of Johnston's army to Manassas in July were suspected of having Union sympathies. Because of strong statements about Confederate numbers that these men made, on the basis of the contacts made on their trips to Manassas, Pinkerton obtained sworn depositions from three of them. One said a 100,000 figure for Manassas-Centreville was a "universally understood fact," and the other two gave 90,000 to 100,000 as a "generally understood fact." A fourth man's statement, estimating 70,000, was accepted without his oath. Johnston's return shows 30,900 men present at this time at the locations the four men reported on; but McClellan cited them in his final report as evidence of the reliability of a Pinkerton estimate of 80,000 for those locations.

These men came Pinkerton's way purely by accident. They and the other members of the party had taken an escape route through western Virginia; three or four days elapsed before they found their way to a Federal post on the Baltimore and Ohio Railroad. They were questioned on the spot, and one was interviewed by regional commanders at Cumberland. Although their information was recognized as important, apparently it was not telegraphed or even mailed to Washington, and they were given train tickets to the capital without so much as a polite suggestion that they drop in at army headquarters and report on affairs in the Valley and on the Manassas Gap line. Through a happenstance not described in the records, one of Pinkerton's detectives discovered their presence in Washington. As will be seen in chapter 6, they possessed information on enemy movements that was much more important than figures on Confederate strength.[31]

Refugees' civilian status enabled them to employ escape ruses not available to soldiers. Four Baltimoreans who had obtained work in Richmond shortly before the war represented that their families were living at Martinsburg and procured passes to that place; from there they hiked to the Potomac and signaled to Union pickets, who ferried them across.[32] Many refugees left young families behind, whom they intended to bring north whenever they could. Not a few were members of Virginia militia regiments whom Pinkerton chose to classify as refugees rather than as deserters; most of them had come directly from their homes rather than escaping while on military duty. These men almost always proclaimed strong Union sentiments on the part of fellow militiamen as well as themselves; often they professed a wish to enlist in the Federal army.[33] Other refugees' stories, including their reasons for leaving Virginia, were highly varied. They told of being detained for months in the Confederacy after going there to collect a debt or to aid a sick friend;[34] of not being able to collect their pay from the Orange and Alexandria Railroad without traveling to its Gordonsville shops, where they were forced to remain and work as machinists;[35] of being imprisoned for Union sentiments that came to light when they attempted to cross into Maryland — or of having allowed fear of such imprisonment to keep them at work in Virginia shops for many months;[36] of wanting to escape impressment into the army or construction crews at Leesburg.[37] Even free Negroes feared being forced into the Southern army; black men had been seen drilling under arms at Leesburg, and they were reported fully armed in the Peninsula army.[38] A few white refugees, not wanting to reveal their Union sentiments to secessionist neighbors, had had themselves apprehended at their homes by Federal troops and taken to Maryland.[39]

"Refugeeing" was a possible cover for Confederate spies, who could not use smuggling for that purpose since the North had no need of goods manufactured in the South. Two trainmen on the Orange and Alexandria were accepted as refugees and then were caught heading back South with goods evidently intended for sale.[40]

All through the winter refugees came in in such numbers that in February Pinkerton stationed two men at Hancock, Maryland, on the upper Potomac, to examine new arrivals on the spot.[41]

A physician, George Cross, Union-minded but not an activist, was willing to sit out the war treating his Fairfax County neighbors, but vigilance committees would not have it that way, and after repeated arrests he wound up in a Richmond prison. Upon being released he persuaded General Winder to get him a pass through army lines from Secretary Benjamin. He had to take oath not to bear arms against the Confederacy, but that did not prevent him from giving Pinkerton a detailed report of affairs at Richmond, Norfolk, Manassas, and Leesburg.

Another unusual refugee case was that of George Marshall, a Wisconsin soldier who had been taken prisoner in the Bull Run battle and claimed that he had escaped prison in Richmond by persuading a Union-minded guard to allow him and a fellow prisoner "to go and see some ladies" and that he had located an underground of pro-Union Richmond citizens whose contacts enabled him to be passed through the lines into western Virginia. He reported that he had been at large in Richmond for three weeks, had been within viewing distance of several forts, and had visited the Tredegar factory. His most sensational report was that Virginia Governor John Letcher "is claimed by the Unionists and trusted by them; . . . and is in communication with all the Union men in the city."[42] If Marshall's story was even half true, Pinkerton would have had some promising leads for obtaining resident spies in Richmond, but evidently he established no such contacts.

..   ..   ..

Under the laws of war the Southern planters' property could be seized as contraband. In the Civil War the word *contraband* became a synonym for escaped slave; it was quickly adopted by Pinkerton's staff. It was not a racial slur but a mockery of the fact that slavery made human beings a kind of property. *Contraband* in this sense was first used officially by contentious Ben Butler, the Massachusetts congressman-general.[43] Butler's purpose in applying the term to human property was as purely political as Butler himself, but the term lost its antislavery satirical force because it came in so handy as a label for a particular kind of refugee. For Pinkerton, contrabands were a problem because of their numbers. The few who had acquired military information by serving as servants or laborers in the Southern army or by living near Confederate posts were hidden among thousands of others. Fortunately some well-informed ones sought out Pinkerton's office, and others reached him through the army's provost marshals.

Some of the contrabands had motives that were not simply escape from slavery or from the threat of serving in slavocracy's army. Virginia Negroes feared being sent to the deep South for safekeeping. A Fairfax County slave, sold to a North Carolina officer for $1600, escaped from the cellar in which he had been locked up in preparation for removal to Carolina.[44] Another Fairfax Countian, one Charles Parker, escaped from his owner, Daniel B. Kincheloe, near Manassas, hours before he was to leave for Mississippi. Kincheloe had entrusted him with errands over a considerable area; thus he was able not only to identify four regiments stationed near the Kincheloe farm but to furnish elaborate details on artillery emplacements, forts, roads, and bridges throughout the Manassas area. Parker's unique knowledge of the daytime and nighttime limits of Confederate picketing enabled him to reach the Union lines in three days — or, more probably, three nights.

Equally determined to reach freedom was William Fisher, who came to Pinkerton with the story that he had escaped in Richmond, had been caught halfway on a journey to the Potomac, had been jailed, then bought and sold a couple of times, and had crossed the river from Harper's Ferry on a raft he built.[45]

. . . . . .

To Pinkerton's staff of interrogators, military prisoners were the least cooperative, least productive group in this period of static war. Information from only fifty-six captured Confederates appears in McClellan's and Pinkerton's papers for the seven months preceding the army's departure for the Peninsula in March. A disproportionate number of these were cavalrymen; mounted pickets suffered far greater exposure to the enemy than any other soldiers. The pickets of each army developed an acquaintance with the goings-on in the other's camps; for example, nine captive members of the First North Carolina Cavalry reported that a Federal deserter had informed them of the arrival in the Federal lines of Herman Pech and Nugent Emmett, two members of their regiment whose desertion to the Federals we have noted. The interrogator got little information out of these men and concluded that they had put their heads together and concocted a story that would discredit Pech and Emmett. Obviously those two had been interrogated at one of the Federals' forward headquarters, and the Federal soldier who became a deserter had learned some of the substance of statements they made there. McClellan and Pinkerton could see in this incident that observance of their order on the forwarding of prisoners and deserters to army headquarters was less than perfect.

The nine cavalrymen contradicted not only Pech and Emmett but also the dozens of deserters, refugees, and contrabands who had drawn pictures of destitution in the Southern army: bad food and little of it; shortage of uniforms, especially warm ones; worn-out shoes; starving horses in patchwork harness; farm wagons substituting for army wagons; broken-down railroads; roads so deep in mud that what food there was could not be hauled to the camps on time. Almost all militiamen predicted for the volunteer regiments a very low rate of re-enlistment, but according to the cavalrymen from Carolina, "nearly all of the twelve-month volunteers will re-enlist," the establishment of the Southern nation was a pretty sure thing, they had an "abundance of provisions, . . . a sufficiency of clothing [and] good shoes"; there was enough corn, although hay was scarce owing to the condition of the roads; their horses were in good condition. The interrogator noted that all but one of the nine came of families with "considerable interest in slave property."[46]

Three members of Virginia cavalry regiments, examined on the same day, evidently were interrogated individually, for their statements did not entirely agree. One said his entire company would refuse to re-enlist; "if they are pressed they will resist." However, none had any complaints

about shortages of food and clothing; the cavalry clearly was better supplied than the rest of the army.[47]

A third group of prisoners consisted of five men from the same First
North Carolina Cavalry and one from the First Virginia Cavalry who were
captured by a Federal scouting party. Pinkerton's examiner evaluated
them: "[F]our of the five North Carolina prisoners could neither read
nor write; . . . three of the five were not over 21 years of age; . . . all but
[one who was a sergeant] were ignorant as to the causes, or *any* cause,
about the war; . . . all but the sergeant were anxious to go home and not
back to their regiment; . . . four of the five North Carolinians were persuaded into enlistment, and *joined the Army because the crowd were going or
because they were intoxicated.*" All the North Carolina men appeared ignorant of any regiments except their own. Their statements about Centreville defenses were contradictory, and they were unable to confirm rumors of sizable troop movements from Manassas to the west or south.
However, their reluctance to give information was so obvious that their
negative response to this question did not serve to quiet the rumors. And
like their fellow cavalry prisoners, they had no complaints against the
army's food.[48]

The prisoners who received the most attention were two who had
every appearance of being Rebel spies. Hosea H. H. Williams, a twenty-
five-year-old British native, was wearing a Federal uniform when taken
near Fairfax Court House. He maintained that he had been impressed
into a South Carolina regiment at Charleston, that his regiment and
several others had been outfitted with new uniforms made for three-
month Federal troops, and that his presence in the Federal lines was
merely an effort to desert while on picket. His estimate of the strength of
the army at Manassas and Centreville — forty-five regiments, averaging
800 men — may well have been the most conservative one Pinkerton
had received. He gave elaborate details on Confederate artillery and
cavalry, infantry weapons and ammunition, fortifications, and camp life.
But Pinkerton found that in some important particulars, including Williams's report that troops had been moved from Manassas for the defense of Charleston, "he is flatly contradicted by every other source of
evidence which I have received." (When the subject was as important as
this probable spy, Pinkerton could make an exception to his practice of
avoiding comparison of a source's report with earlier information.) The
conclusion was that Williams was probably a spy who perhaps did intend
to desert. He was another who claimed that at Bull Run he had loaded his
gun only with powder, dropping the balls on the ground.

A somewhat similar case was that of William Fields, a cavalryman sixteen years old, arrested while wearing the Confederate uniform deep in
Federal territory. Fields was a native of the immediate locality where he
was taken, between Arlington Heights and Falls Church, and thus would

have been a logical selection to scout that neighborhood. He was believed to have been arrested in July and released. His estimate of troop strength about Centreville, 30,000, evidently excluding Manassas, was almost as conservative as the figures given by Williams. His information on certain transfers of units from Johnston's army contradicted Williams's, and he declared that none of Johnston's regiments had blue uniforms. Pinkerton recommended that Fields be held in custody because of his having returned within Rebel lines after taking the oath of allegiance. The disposition of Williams's case is not recorded, but he probably won quick release, the treatment normally accorded prisoners able to invoke foreign citizenship.[49]

· · · · · ·

Pinkerton's day-by-day reports left untouched the work of adding up his findings. To correct this lack, McClellan in mid-January found a couple of assistants who today would be called intelligence analysts. The task of boiling down those thousands of words into usable summaries fell to two young French aides-de-camp, Louis Philippe d'Orléans and his brother, Robert. Louis Philippe was the comte de Paris and pretender to the French throne; Robert was the duc de Chartres. The brothers were serving in the rank of captain but without pay; their uncle, the prince de Joinville, remained a civilian but accompanied McClellan's headquarters "as amateur and friend." The three princes' tent was the locus of much merriment. Having been living in exile in England, Louis Philippe and Robert were fluent in English; their prose, despite an occasional unidiomatic expression ("Here we sum up all the old and new informations"), is smoother than the labored language of the E. J. Allen reports. Although the brothers were competent summarizers of sometimes intricate data, their reports with minor exceptions fell considerably short of the sophisticated level of analysis and assessment later achieved by the intelligence bureau that succeeded Pinkerton's. As long as Pinkerton and McClellan remained in service, McClellan was his own assessor of the meaning of the reports.

This was doubtless the first time in the Civil War, and conceivably in any American war up to that time, that anyone was assigned analysis of intelligence as a full-time or principal duty; and the men McClellan found for that sensitive position, which today would require a security clearance not easily obtained, could not even take the oath of allegiance to the flag they were serving.[50] McClellan's movement to the Peninsula ended the brothers' report-writing career. Called home, they left in July immediately after the Seven Days battles.[51]

The January reports of the Orléans brothers reveal that they had not been able to get their hands on most of Pinkerton's output. Evidently McClellan, a glutton for paperwork, was sitting on Pinkerton reports that he had expected the brothers to be working from. On February 1, however, they came through with a richly detailed report on the Confederates' Potomac batteries and the positions of Holmes's troops in the Aquia–Quantico Creek area. That locality stood high on McClellan's list of intelligence priorities, not only because the Potomac batteries still dominated Federal shipping, but also because of General Hooker's persistent proposals to put them out of business. The elaborate details in the brothers' report were the product of legwork by the three Northerners in Holmes's command who overcame a sentinel and deserted from their Tennessee regiment to Hooker's command early in January. Additional information was provided by two fugitive slaves who had worked on the batteries. The Orléans brothers' summary synthesized all this information, but without comment as to its probable correctness. A troop total of 11,700 to 12,700 tallied well with the number of regiments Pinkerton listed at that location. Holmes's February return shows 7128.

New information soon enabled a similar detailing by Louis d'Orléans of the commands of W.H.C. Whiting, Robert E. Rodes, and Jubal Early, between Dumfries and lower Bull Run, along with five earthworks in the latter locality. But there still was haziness about some of the unit identifications; for example, the regiment-size Hampton Legion, a mixed command of infantry, cavalry, and artillery, was listed as a cavalry organization pure and simple. Its true nature was soon revealed to Pinkerton by none other than prisoner E. Pliny Bryan, who said he had camped with the legion while on signaling duty on the lower Potomac. Bryan was looser of tongue than might be expected of a Confederate secret agent.[52]

Information on Leesburg and vicinity was scanty or perhaps entirely missing from the materials the brothers were at first able to assemble; the blank spot was not filled until February. Robert d'Orléans found reports showing four regiments of infantry and, mistakenly, one of cavalry, plus eight guns and the artillerists to man them. The guns were at four different locations; the sources disagreed as to their distance from the town. By estimating regimental strengths between 530 and 900, he reached a total strength for Leesburg of 4580, almost double the present-for-duty number in the February return.[53]

The Orléans duo next turned their attention to the enemy's Shenandoah Valley force and received a lesson in the volatility of military information. In mid-February they produced a handsome report that had to be redone two weeks later when Pinkerton came through with information from three new sources. This was also a lesson in the ability of military action to turn up intelligence sources. One such action was Jackson's arduous winter campaign in western Virginia, with its stimulus to desertion. Another was the Federals' return to the Valley; Banks's army occupied Harper's Ferry on February 24, making it unnecessary for would-be deserters to risk crossing the Potomac. Other sources included a "scout" whom Banks, while still at Frederick, had had in the lower Valley, and a pair of Indiana privates who had gone off on a self-assigned scouting trip wearing civilian clothes and been jailed at Winchester, escaping apparently with the aid of Unionist citizens.

Joseph Benson, the slave-owning deserter from Jackson's cavalry, had information so persuasive that Robert d'Orléans went beyond his collating job and assumed an evaluative role; he wrote that Benson "designates so positively the location of each gun" in a certain fort that "we must believe" his information on the type, weight, and mounting of each.

New or corrective information on seven previously known Winchester fortifications led to a complete recapitulation in the second Valley report. An eighth work was added, and artillery data were refined to show a total of forty-one guns. The brothers cautioned that some guns had been moved from one fort to another and probably had been counted at both places. Making allowance for twelve such transfers, "we would have ... *29 guns* which number still appears exaggerated."

Confederate numbers in the Valley fluctuated widely during the winter. Jackson's brigades were joined by a force under Brigadier General W. W. Loring, estimated in the first Orléans report at 10,000 and then at 9000. Loring and Jackson picked a quarrel; when the War Department intervened in a way that Jackson thought ignored his authority over Loring, he resigned from the army. He was induced to withdraw the resignation, and Loring was disposed of by being made a major general and sent to General Benjamin Huger's army at Norfolk. His regiments went separate ways, to Manassas, Aquia, and Tennessee. Word of the Jackson-Loring feud reached Federal ears, but three weeks after the breakup was ordered, Pinkerton's records still carried Loring's force in the Valley. As a result, the second Orléans report showed 20,300 in Jackson's army at a time when his returns carried 6404 present.[54]

The Orléans brothers and Pinkerton were not the only ones suffering from inadequate information about the Valley army. Early in January General Johnston himself, asked by Secretary Benjamin for "a statement of your present organization, indicating the separate brigade commands with the designation of the regiments comprised in each," could not supply complete data for either the Valley or Holmes's Aquia District.[55] In fact the record of Confederate organization and command assignments in northern Virginia at this period is a tangle of changes, some of which were ordered but apparently not carried out.

Of Manassas-Centreville, locus of the enemy's main force, the Orléans brothers drew a picture much less formidable than the one McClellan is traditionally supposed to have had in his mind's eye. Even by allowing some regiments as many as 1100, and some brigades as many as 3500 when information on the regiments composing them was totally lacking, they found 50,600 to 53,100 from Centreville south through Manassas to the northern boundary of Holmes's district near Dumfries; the Confederates' February return shows 39,948 present. Numbers of fortifications and of guns in them were found much lower than McClellan probably was expecting. At and near Manassas Junction twelve defensive works had been reported; but the locations of some were uncertain, only one appeared to be a major fort, and although the total number of guns in them had been reported as high as fifty-five, only twenty-five could be counted in the reports that dealt with individual works. In the Centreville area, visited in November and January by Timothy Webster, only three fixed works and two or three field batteries were known; the exact location of all but one was uncertain. That one was a huge affair but was known to have only three guns, two of them not yet mounted. Another work, termed a "large bastion," was believed to mount twelve to fourteen heavy guns.[56] The small number of guns at Centreville, together with provision in some of the works for field batteries, confirmed Webster's opinion that the Confederates planned to defend the place but to be ready to fall back on heavier defenses at Manassas. The reports of guns numbering in three figures at the two places were shown to be a product of rumors, possibly originating (it would seem from Frank Ellis's experience) with the Jefferson Davis administration, no less.

For the Peninsula defenses the brothers' information was scanty; a report barely two hundred words long listed two brigades totaling 7000 troops, a considerable underestimate of Magruder's 11,000 — but McClellan was not likely to be misled by errors on the low side. The principal fort, believably enough, was reported at Yorktown on a bluff above the "Cornwallis Cave"; eight other defensive works, half of them extending toward Fort Monroe, were known, but less than a score of guns in fixed positions were listed. This information could have been regarded as seriously incomplete, and in fact it lacked the elaborate data furnished in December by the free Negro W. H. Ringgold, who identified and gave the positions of five regiments not listed by Orléans, reported on defenses on the north side of the York, and gave details on the Yorktown forts that do not appear in the Orléans summary. Ringgold had said there were no batteries or fortifications on the York above Gloucester Point and Yorktown, near the river's mouth; however, that statement left room for forts and batteries not only between Yorktown and Fort Monroe but also on the James River side of the Peninsula. From all of this it is clear that most of Pinkerton's information on the Peninsula was mislaid at the time Louis Philippe wrote his summary.[57] In any event, it is unlikely that this summary played more than an incidental role in McClellan's planning, which at this time was focused not on the Peninsula but on a route to Richmond by way of the lower Rappahannock.

The brothers' totals for the separate localities in Johnston's command add up to 87,180.[58] That figure, well above his February return showing 56,392 present, lay midway between 83,000 and 93,000, a rough estimate the brothers had made early in their reporting project.[59] At that time Louis Philippe recorded in his diary a "conclusion" that "we have in front of us much fewer troops than is generally believed."[60] The much higher numbers "generally believed" must have been headquarters opinion, independent of Pinkerton's reporting and dominated by McClellan's exaggerated view of the enemy.[61]

The Orléans duo finished their series of reports on March 3, near the end of McClellan's seven-month stalemate in front of Washington. Five days later Pinkerton issued an estimate considerably higher than the total the brothers had arrived at, using his own data. McClellan now had two competing estimates to choose from. Pinkerton's gave 115,500 (more than double the 56,392 in Johnston's February return) as a "medium estimate." This was the sum of a reported 80,000 at Manassas-Centreville, 18,000 on the lower Potomac, 13,000 in the Valley (evidently the departure of Loring's regiments had been discovered), and 4500 at Leesburg. Those were gross estimates, unrelated to numbers of regiments and other units known at each location. The 80,000 for Manassas-Centreville was a particularly damaging exaggeration; it was a total of rations being issued there, reported by "supposedly reliable persons."

The 115,500 figure bore the "medium estimate" label because Pinkerton had a still higher figure to offer, a "summary of general estimates." This was a gross figure for the whole of Johnston's army, created without reference to the totals for its individual components. Probably it was a rough average of a number of whole-army figures reported by various informants. Not surprisingly, this number turned out to be 150,000, topping by 34,500 the "medium estimate," which was itself composed of figures equally rough but pertaining instead to the respective components. The true total was a matter of high secrecy in the Confederate administration, so well guarded that, for example, Secretary Benjamin left the figure blank in writing to Johnston about the number of general officers his army was entitled to, a matter in which the total number of his troops was a crucial factor.[62] It was highly unlikely that any of Pinkerton's sources — soldiers, officers of low and medium rank, civilians white and black — would have reliable information on the total numbers of that army. Yet Pinkerton's interrogating staff faithfully collected rumors, or pure guesses, on that point, and a "summary" — a rough average — of those gross figures now shared top billing in his strength estimates.[63]

In limiting his estimate to these gross figures, Pinkerton abandoned the count of regiments as his estimating basis. He explained this change of method:

> It is unnecessary for me to say that in the nature of the case, guarded as the rebels have ever been against the encroachment of spies and vigilant as they have always been to prevent information of their forces, movements and designs from going beyond their lines, it has been impossible, even by the use of every resource at our command, to ascertain with certainty the specific number and character of their forces.

In other words, an accurate determination of the composition of the opposing army was more than could be expected of an intelligence bureau contending with so extensive a target. This complaint is difficult to understand, for Pinkerton had made good progress on that very problem. His count of regiments, 143 in his October estimate, had now been narrowed down to 105, a number that was close to the truth and possibly an underestimate.[64] The revision would have been brought about partly by new information but mainly by the adoption of more judicious standards of accepting reported regiments and other units as part of the army. As a result he had a fairly good comprehension of the forces arrayed against McClellan; but instead of recognizing that fact, he chose to view the reduced regimental count as signifying the fruitlessness of trying to get a complete list of the elements of so large an army.

His explanation continued, "It may, therefore, safely be assumed that in so large an army as our information shows them to possess very much of its composition and very many of its forces have not been specifically ascertained, which, added to those already known, would largely increase their numbers and considerably swell its proportions."[65] This was a dizzying piece of circular reasoning, and Pinkerton compounded the obfuscation by indulging in some shaky logic in his reference to the "very many" forces that had "not been specifically ascertained." If the gross estimates for Manassas-Centreville, the Valley, Leesburg, and the lower Potomac — the entire geographic spread of Johnston's command — totaled only 115,500 but the whole army had 150,000, where were the remaining 34,500 located? That was quite a large number of troops to have so ethereal an existence. Actually no locations of Confederate troops in significant numbers had remained hidden from Pinkerton.

Once again Pinkerton's explanation of his estimating method raises questions. He had replaced a fundamentally sound basis, his count of regiments and other units, with a method based on rumor and guesswork. With his overgenerous troops-per-regiment averages, the earlier method would have yielded an army total in the neighborhood of 80,000 — a serious overstatement but still one that would have given McClellan a much more nearly correct idea of the enemy force than had ever been available except in a few isolated reports by individual informants of unknown reliability.[66]

Pinkerton's purpose in adopting this strange estimating method, which he explained by resorting to sophistry, could only have been to produce figures more agreeable to McClellan's views. However, even the 150,000 "general estimate" failed to reach the figure the general was claiming. At a council of war he told Quartermaster General M. C. Meigs that the enemy had "not less than 175,000." But at a later council he unveiled a map showing enemy dispositions from Centreville south and east to Dumfries, giving their strength as 50,500.[67] That was scarcely half of the number Pinkerton's March 8 estimate gave those localities; obviously the mapmaker was not getting his strength figures from Pinkerton. The 50,500 would have been as big a surprise to McClellan as to his audience; how he explained it to them is not on record.

In this incident the business of estimating Confederate numbers descends to the level of low comedy. It warns us that we may be overanalyzing estimates that amounted to no more than unwitting nonsense.

6

. . . .

"OUTNUMBERED"
ON THE PENINSULA

February–August 1862

I N BOTH THE UNION and the Confederate armies it was an article of faith that the enemy's spies were everywhere, that no military secret was safe. In a war in which each side knew that within its borders were many, many people who sympathized with the enemy, this feeling came naturally; there was not necessarily an element of paranoia in it. Lafayette Baker's claim that detailed accounts of Lincoln's cabinet discussions reached Richmond (sometimes within a day's time) and Allan Pinkerton's statement that Rose Greenhow knew McClellan's plans as well as his own generals did were irresponsible exaggerations, but they were rooted in an actual belief in the prevalence of Confederate espionage in Washington early in the war. Similar beliefs on the part of a Confederate general appear in a letter D. H. Hill sent to Confederate Secretary of War George W. Randolph in March 1862: "There can be no doubt that the enemy has been fully apprised of our strength and movements through treachery in our own War Department."[1] Another Confederate who worried about enemy spies was J. B. Jones, a prominent figure in that very department, who as we have seen repeatedly assured his diary that Federal agents were finding Richmond an easy target.

The effect of this state of mind was nowhere greater than in the movements that broke up the two armies' seven-month stalemate in front of Washington and took them to a campaign on the peninsula east of Richmond. Neither General Johnston nor General McClellan had expected to fight there. Each had other plans, which he abandoned upon receiving information that he interpreted as indicating that the enemy had discovered them. But each general's plans were safe; both had greatly overrated enemy intelligence.

Johnston's involvement in this remarkable series of errors began February 19 with a visit to Richmond to discuss with President Davis and the cabinet the problem raised by his army's overextended positions at Manassas-Centreville and on the Potomac — a line nearly a hundred miles long. His principal fear was of a Federal movement against his right, below the Occoquan River. A second day of discussion covered problems such as the difficulties of moving heavy equipment, particularly guns, over roads too soggy to carry even light loads. Withdrawal would be so slow that the enemy could be expected to discover it in time to attack it at a vulnerable stage. But Johnston left the meeting with orders from Davis to draw back behind the Rappahannock River, thirty miles southwest of Manassas.

Although Davis had regarded the matter as so sensitive that his summons to Johnston had not even mentioned the purpose of the meeting, the general found that other participants did not share this concern with secrecy. Returning to his hotel after the second day's deliberations, he was greeted by one of his colonels, who had already heard that the cabinet had been discussing withdrawal. On the way back to Centreville the next day, he heard the same report from a fellow passenger who was "too deaf to hear conversation not intended for his ear." Two days later, from another officer who had been to Richmond, Johnston learned of the leak a third time.[2]

No indication that McClellan received so much as a hint of the Richmond leakage appears in his papers or Pinkerton's, although at least five and probably six Pinkerton operatives were in Richmond at this time. Timothy Webster was confined to the Monument Hotel with inflammatory rheumatism, the result of his three or four crossings of the Potomac in frigid or stormy weather. Operative Hattie Lawton, who had joined him in lower Maryland on his trip South, was posing as Mrs. Webster and was fully occupied in ministering to him. Newly arrived in the city were Pryce Lewis and John Scully, sent by Pinkerton to find Webster and ascertain the reason for his failure to return to Washington.[3] E. H. Stein, though not totally immobilized by the detectives' continued surveillance — he succeeded in visiting Petersburg and Suffolk — was unlikely to pick up anything better than gossip. He attended President Davis's second inauguration on February 22 and even succeeded in standing near Davis during the ceremony. But all he could hear were vague rumors that Manassas would have to be evacuated; "no one seemed to know anything about it," and he assumed that the rumor grew out of a statement in Davis's address that Stein quoted thus: "We have undertaken to govern more territory than we have the power to hold." That statement would have been gratefully received in Washington, and it might have made McClellan halfway alert for a Confederate withdrawal. But each operative was his own courier, and Stein did not succeed in getting out of the

Confederacy until April, when the armies were facing each other on the Peninsula. His travels in search of an escape route had taken him far to the west or northwest of Richmond.[4]

Davis's order forced Johnston to give up his hope of delaying the move until the roads dried. On February 22, immediately upon returning from Richmond, he began movement preparations on a scale that should have come to the attention of Union intelligence but did not. On March 1 he issued orders for evacuation by railroad — sick and wounded to go first, then ordnance and hospital equipment, then food and forage. The troops would move on foot. The process of assembling cars and engines collected from five different rail lines produced a state of confusion so visible that, although the terrain screened it from the Federal balloonists, it would have been observable by any would-be deserter or refugee who had been at Manassas (or by a resident spy, if Pinkerton had had one). Orders were given by railway managers and midway in their execution were countermanded by army officers. One especially noticeable development involved the army's new rail line from Manassas to Centreville: it had been carrying supplies to Centreville, and suddenly the shipments were in the opposite direction. The Orange and Alexandria road, which was to carry the shipments to safety behind the Rappahannock, soon had 332 cars and engines on its sixty-one miles of single track, with the result that the normal six-hour run between Manassas and Gordonsville now took a day and a half. Piles of boxes, crates, and baggage waiting to be loaded reached the height of the engines' smokestacks and extended along the track for half a mile. The concentration of rolling stock at Manassas created a severe lack of it at Thoroughfare Gap on the Manassas Gap line, where commissary authorities were operating a slaughterhouse in anticipation of supplying an invasion of Maryland and Pennsylvania that never reached a serious planning stage.[5]

This confusion was compounded into chaos by Federal movements in southern Maryland, some of which came under the eye of Confederate observers along the lower Potomac. McClellan was finally responding to the pressure to do something about the Confederate batteries that were still making the river useless to commercial shipping. Reasoning that such a move would meet strong resistance, he planned to use his whole army in the operation. Despite his penchant for careful organization and secrecy, some of the preparatory moves on March 5 were close enough to the river to come within view of Confederates in the neighborhood of the Occoquan. Their commander, Brigadier General W. H. C. Whiting, reported this unusual activity to Johnston. That section of the Potomac was the very one where Johnston believed the expected advance of the Federals was most likely to come; he had told Davis that they could outflank his position whenever they chose.

The action he now took may be described as based on a worst-case hypothesis: that the information on his plans that had leaked in Richmond had now been confirmed for the enemy by the highly visible accumulation of material along the tracks at Manassas; as he had feared, the well-informed Federals were readying pursuit of his retreat. Without waiting to see if McClellan's army was really taking the field and if so in what direction, Johnston suspended the orderly accumulation of material and ordered the army to depart on foot. The wings were to move on Friday, March 7, and the main body on the 8th; whatever properties could not be brought off were to be destroyed. Food and forage put to the torch at Thoroughfare Gap, Centreville, and Manassas amounted to over 3 million pounds. The heavy guns in the Potomac batteries were left behind. Even though evacuation of most of the army was delayed until the 9th, its departure was so hasty that the headquarters staff left, for discovery by Federals soon to arrive, a file of confidential papers that included Beauregard's July 20 order for the next day's battle, bearing Johnston's endorsement.[6] All this haste and waste was the price of the mistaken fear that the Federals were about to assail the orderly retreat that had been planned.

Not until March 12, a full week after issuing his order to evacuate, did Johnston inform President Davis of his action. If this neglect was deliberate, the reason for it would have been his experience with leakage in Richmond. In thus withholding vital information from the commander-in-chief, Johnston cost himself available reinforcements that could have significantly altered later events. For Davis, unaware that the army was already marching for the Rappahannock, on the 10th addressed Johnston at Centreville: "You shall be promptly and adequately re-enforced, so as to enable you to maintain your position and resume first policy when the roads will permit."[7] "First policy" was Davis's guarded reference to Johnston's original plan to postpone withdrawal until it could be done without severe loss of equipment and supplies. Although it is tempting to speculate that this news from Davis, received a few days sooner, would have enabled Johnston to hold his ground and move in his own good time, he probably would have gone ahead with the precipitate move in the belief that reinforcements from Richmond or points beyond could not arrive at Manassas and Centreville until McClellan's army was already there.

· ·   · ·   · ·

Why the enemy's withdrawal came as a surprise to McClellan calls for explanation. The inability of Pinkerton's Richmond operatives to pick up the gossip that Johnston abominated is understandable enough; in fact, even a fully active Timothy Webster might not have had the right contacts to tap into the leak. But we could reasonably expect some intelligence to flow from the withdrawal preparations at Manassas, which would have stimulated efforts at desertion and refugeeing. Yet the files of Pinkerton's interrogation reports show no deserters, prisoners, or refugees from the entire Aquia-Manassas-Centreville area during the two weeks those preparations were in progress.[8] Evidently Johnston, foreseeing that the accumulation of impedimenta at Manassas would become common knowledge, took action promptly upon his return from Richmond to tighten his picket lines against escapes and intrusions. The sudden absence of subjects for interrogation in Pinkerton's bureau was itself an indication of a forthcoming movement, but the records contain no evidence that its significance was noticed by Pinkerton or McClellan.

At Leesburg, however, no security measures sufficed to prevent escapes across the Potomac. These yielded several reports of General Hill's preparations to withdraw, and finally his departure, destination uncertain. One report said Manassas also was to be evacuated; but a Leesburg source, remote from first-hand information on Manassas, would not have claimed much attention. In the Federals' thinking, Hill's actions were associated not with plans that Johnston, his commander, might have but with a retreat that Stonewall Jackson's army was then making in the face of General Banks's invasion of the Valley. Leesburg was an incidental objective in Banks's program; one of his brigades entered the town on March 8, while Hill's rear guard was still visible in the distance.[9]

On the same day Leesburg was emptied of Confederate troops, Pinkerton was reporting the strength of its occupation force as 4500; he repeated this figure on the 17th.[10] The number was double Hill's actual strength, but that error is less significant than the revelation that Pinkerton was unaware of Hill's departure. McClellan's noteworthy innovation, an organized intelligence bureau, was isolated from what should have been a close-knit headquarters staff.

McClellan's best chance of learning of the enemy's imminent withdrawal lay with the Manassas Gap Railroad trainmen whose escape from their jobs has been noted. After the accumulation of transportables along the Orange and Alexandria tracks at Manassas had been in progress for more than a week, and shortly before their escape on March 4, three of these men had been at Manassas. They had witnessed those preparations for withdrawal and learned that "it was understood that the evacuation of Manassas and Centreville would take place in the course of a few days." But by the time they made their way into western Virginia, found a Federal military post, were interviewed by officers who apparently sat on the information they gave, traveled voluntarily to Washington, and were discovered by Pinkerton's operative, ten days had passed and Johnston's army had made a clean getaway.[11] By that time the only value of the railroaders' report of the withdrawal would have been in a post mortem on intelligence failures, an exercise unknown in McClellan's command. This episode was turning into an echo of the Bull Run fiasco in which Unionists in the Valley learned of Confederate movements, but their information, through the ineptitude of the local commander who received it, failed to prevent a stolen march by this same Johnston.

Thus McClellan was entirely dependent on the balloons for advance notice of the enemy's departure. From a balloon newly stationed at Pohick Church, three miles from the mouth of the Occoquan, came reports late on March 5 of heavy smokes along that river and at Fairfax Station. General Johnston, whose hurry-up withdrawal order had been issued only that day, would not have been pleased by the promptness of those telltale burnings. Next day the smokes extended south to Dumfries and west to Manassas. General Samuel P. Heintzelman, whose division occupied the Occoquan area, made three ascents; he saw enough to send Thaddeus Lowe to Washington to station a balloon near Fairfax Court House in the hope of getting a better look at what was going on at Manassas and Centreville. By the time Lowe succeeded in getting transportation for his equipment, no Rebels were left at those places. Meanwhile, back at Pohick, Colonel Hiram G. Berry, one of Heintzelman's brigade commanders, made several ascents on Friday, March 7, that revealed the enemy gone from the Occoquan.[12] The Confederates had opened a gap in their hundred-mile line.

However, McClellan was distracted by other serious problems that Friday. Called to an early-morning interview with Lincoln, he received the news, as he later remembered it, that his plan of shipping the army to the country east of Richmond — removing it from its position between Washington and the enemy — was raising suspicions of treasonable intent among his critics. After that disturbing session he proceeded to a meeting with his generals that he had called to outline his plans for moving against the enemy's Potomac batteries. But he turned that meeting into a council of war, surprising the generals with his "Urbanna plan" for advancing against Richmond. (That move would force the Rebels to abandon their Potomac batteries; the preparations for driving them away could be abandoned.) McClellan asked for a vote of approval or disapproval by each officer; a favorable vote would defeat this intrigue against him.

McClellan had been nursing the Urbanna plan for months without revealing it to anyone but Lincoln, Stanton, and a very small number of his confidants. Urbanna was a small tobacco port on the right bank of the lower Rappahannock, fifty miles east of Richmond. McClellan proposed to ship his army there by way of Annapolis and the Chesapeake Bay, and via the Potomac once the enemy's batteries were cleared out or abandoned. Eighteen miles inland from Urbanna was West Point, at the head of the York River, terminal of a railroad to Richmond that could carry the heavy guns needed in a siege. McClellan calculated that if this movement were well under way before the Confederates were aware of it, "we would fight them in front of Richmond before they could concentrate all their troops there."

He had won Lincoln's agreement to this plan, though the President had a strong preference for his own plan of advancing along the south bank of the Occoquan and striking not at the Confederates' fortified positions at Manassas and Centreville, much respected by McClellan, but at their rail communications southwest of Manassas. As noted above, this flanking movement was the one Johnston most feared.

McClellan assured his superiors that his plan promised "the most brilliant result" of any. He argued that Urbanna "is neither occupied nor observed by the enemy; it is but one [day's] march from West Point, the key of that region." Because of sandy (and therefore drier) roads in the York River area, and the more southerly climate, he said, the army's movements could be calculated "almost to a day," whereas under Lincoln's plan they would be "at the mercy of the weather." This argument was full of holes. How McClellan could expect Lincoln to believe that the weather would be appreciably milder on the York than on the Occoquan — they were separated by only seventy-five north-south miles — can only be imagined. Urbanna's port facilities were woefully insufficient for landing a large army; much of the country in rear of the port was swampy; two rivers had to be crossed before West Point would be reached; roads were poor and few in number, and none was a direct route. Slow disembarkation and slower marching would dissipate the effect of the surprise landing; thus the advance might find a sizable force in its path.[13]

McClellan's chief engineer, General Barnard, had warned him of most of these drawbacks.[14] Therefore the picture McClellan drew for Lincoln must have been consciously false. However, he may have regarded the reported defenselessness of Urbanna as outweighing all the disadvantages. How reliable, then, was McClellan's intelligence indicating that the landing and initial march would be unopposed? Apparently his information was from only one source, though a much better one than the single sources on which he based other important conclusions.[15] The Urbanna informant was W. H. Ringgold, the free Negro who had come from Baltimore in December to tell Pinkerton what he knew of defenses on the two sides of the York River. According to Pinkerton's report of the interview, Ringgold stated:

> That there are no batteries on the York River Railroad between Richmond and West Point, and no troops except Ordinary Guards at the bridges. That at West Point there is now no Battery at all, nor any troops, three heavy Columbiads having been removed from there to Gloucester Point, and about 500 troops having been transferred [elsewhere]; That there are no fortifications or batteries on York River above Yorktown or Gloucester Point; That the U.S. Gunboats have possession of the *Rappa-*

hannock River as far up as Urbanna; that there are no rebel fortifications or troops at Urbanna, or between there and West Point, a distance of 18 miles, the only communication being an ordinary stage road.[16]

The language of that report is firm; the source was of the most trustworthy class; he obviously was intelligent, and careful about particulars. But he made no claim of having been on any of the ground involved in the Urbanna plan except West Point, terminal of the York River boat line on which he had served. And there was no corroborating information, so far as Pinkerton's and McClellan's records reveal.[17] McClellan's Urbanna plan — it was an idea that never became a written plan — could have sprung from a two-minute study of a map that lacked enough detail to show swamps but did show Urbanna's accessibility by water and its proximity to a railroad to Richmond — attractions that would have been strengthened by Ringgold's unexpected report.

As no discussion preceded the generals' vote on the plan, it is probable that they were not even told of the intelligence (or the paucity of it) on the Urbanna area. Their vote, eight to four in favor, divided along lines of seniority and knowledge of the military situation. Barnard voted disapproval; so also did Heintzelman, whose balloon observations would have impressed him with the possibility that the Confederates were already on their way toward Richmond and West Point. Other negative votes came from Edwin V. Sumner and Irvin McDowell. Erasmus Keyes voted approval but with the proviso that the enemy batteries on the Potomac be cleared away as a prelude. After the meeting, with McClellan absent, the generals reported their approval to Lincoln.

McClellan regarded the generals' endorsement as sufficient answer to the suspicion of nefarious intent on his part. But now he had a new problem: on Saturday, the 8th, Lincoln went over his head and divided the Army of the Potomac into corps and, following lines of seniority, named McDowell, Heintzelman, Sumner, and Keyes as corps commanders. Thus the execution of the Urbanna plan was placed in the hands of three generals who had opposed it and a fourth who had reservations about it.[18]

That Saturday was also the day Lincoln issued a "war order" setting March 18 as the deadline for putting the approved plan into execution. It was a hectic day, and little or no attention seems to have been given to the possible meaning of the smokes from enemy camps and the evacuation of the Occoquan area.

Sunday brought even greater distractions. The telegraph line from Fort Monroe, which had been quieted by a broken connection, resumed operation with the startling news of a battle the day before in which the former U.S. ship *Merrimack*, now the Confederates' ironclad *Virginia*, had steamed into Hampton Roads, sunk one big Union frigate, and grounded two others, one of which surrendered. The Federals' new, untried ironclad *Monitor* had arrived from New York late Saturday, but before her ability to stop the *Merrimack* became known in Washington late Sunday, the high command had passed the day in consternation. McClellan had to take time to telegraph warnings of a possible *Merrimack* raid to army commanders in seaboard cities up the Atlantic coast and to initiate arrangements for blocking the Potomac with sunken scows.[19]

While tension mounted at the Washington end of the telegraph line, information arriving in bits and pieces finally provided some support of the balloonists' evidence of enemy withdrawal from the Manassas front. General Hooker telegraphed, doubtless with great pleasure, that the enemy had abandoned the noxious batteries on the river. "The rebels left in great haste," he wrote, "destroying everything," including a steamer and two sailing vessels that had been berthed near the batteries; those they burned. The guns were spiked and all but one of the magazines blown up. Another item of considerable interest was Pinkerton's report of the arrival of a runaway slave who had been jailed at Brentsville, south of Manassas, for two weeks, during which he ran errands for the jailer. Those contacts exposed him to bits of military news; for example, in taking a trunk to a local lady he learned that she was moving away because of the army's impending departure, which evidently was general knowledge in the Manassas area. Probably the most influential item was a short telegram from Heintzelman's headquarters reporting that a Negro had arrived at an outpost with information that the enemy was "leaving Manassas in haste. Cannon dismounted and being hurried to Gordonsville. Only five regiments remaining at Manassas."[20] Sketchy though this was, and from a source of unknown reliability, it was the only report McClellan had from anyone who had observed activity at Manassas during the fifteen days Johnston's army had been piling up highly visible physical evidence of its forthcoming departure.

These intelligence items, all bearing Sunday's date, show no times of transmission or receipt, but we have a clue to McClellan's state of knowledge at midday from a telegram he sent at 1 P.M. to General John E. Wool at Fort Monroe about measures to be taken against the threat the *Merrimack* posed to the safety of the troops on the Peninsula. He wrote, "From indications here I suspect an intention of the enemy to fall back nearer to Richmond that they may better concentrate their forces." This was intended as more than a bit of news: although the appearance of the *Merrimack* at the same time as Johnston's apparent withdrawal was completely accidental, to McClellan it suggested an enemy plan for a combined sea and land assault on Fort Monroe and Wool's force at Newport News.[21] Little Mac was thinking in broad terms appropriate to a general-in-chief, but at a time when he would have been better served by more quickly absorbing the fairly strong evidence that the enemy was pulling out of Manassas.

Later in the day he detached himself from the crisis atmosphere at the White House and rode over to General Fitz John Porter's headquarters near Falls Church. He may have expected to make a balloon ascent that would give him a look at some enemy positions or movements, but Porter did not have a balloon that McClellan evidently thought he had received. Before leaving Washington McClellan apparently gave at least tentative orders for the army to march the next morning, but he still was not sure what positions the enemy was abandoning, for we find him telegraphing General Marcy, back at headquarters, to instruct Banks to be cautious about advancing on Winchester "until we are sure about position of enemy at Centreville." One of McClellan's own brigades, led by General Philip Kearny, had an opportunity to practice similar caution Sunday morning when Kearny heard from contrabands of the evacuation of Manassas and set out to investigate. Moving carefully, Kearny's men encountered a picket, which they reported as 150 strong, between Fairfax Court House and Sangster's Station, just east of Bull Run, and drove it off, taking prisoners. Kearny reported in midafternoon, "The enemy evidently is disheartened and [is] retiring." McClellan seized the opportunity to report this success to Lincoln and Stanton, adding, "I am arranging to move forward to push the retreat of the rebels as far as possible." This was not a direct statement that the Confederates were retreating — his information was not firm enough for that — but he was finally committed to moving against them.[22]

All through these busy days he could not have failed to realize that if he waited too long to make sure the Confederates were preparing to leave, they would be gone when he finally moved.[23] Of course they *were* gone — long enough, in McClellan's judgment, for him to forget his promise to pursue them "as far as possible." But the retreaters had only a narrow head start. Because of delays in shipping off important public property, Johnston had revoked his order for a Saturday march and kept the troops at Manassas until Sunday evening. Colonel William W. Averell, at the head of two cavalry regiments that led McClellan's columns on Monday, rode through Centreville and all the way to Manassas without seeing any Rebels, but at the crossing of Bull Run he learned that a Confederate cavalry picket along that stream had been gone only two hours. Thus it appears that if McClellan had marched even as late as Saturday — basing that action on the intelligence available Friday — he would have been in time to trounce or capture a sizable portion of Johnston's army. In fact, General Whiting, whose camps were most exposed to balloon observation, thought that his withdrawal preparations over a period of days gave the balloonists and the country people so much information that "it was considered certain that the enemy would attack at once."[24]

The intelligence failure that permitted the Confederates to escape untouched was as damaging in its way as that other failure, McClellan's and Pinkerton's never-ending exaggeration of Confederate numbers. The same turn of mind that made Little Mac overrate enemy strength prevented him from seeing that the enemy probably feared his army as much as he did theirs. Thus he gave little or no thought to the possibility that the Confederate leaders considered their Potomac army overextended and sooner or later would draw it back to a safer and more manageable line.

The failure could be laid to an excessive skepticism regarding the significance of the balloon observations on Friday. Admittedly the balloonists' lack of military knowledge limited their ability to interpret what they observed, but Friday's observations, showing the Occoquan evacuated, were made not by a balloonist but by a highly regarded brigade commander. They should have elicited a probing action by even so cautious a commander as McClellan. The findings of Kearny's self-assigned probing of the lines Sunday morning show what probably could have been learned in the same way Friday or Saturday. The fact that deserters and refugees were not turning up was itself an indication that some kind of defensive or offensive action was in preparation. The remedy for that was to send out a raiding party and take prisoners for immediate interrogation.

Whether raids or mere probes were considered by McClellan cannot be known. The distractions engendered by his disturbing interview with Lincoln on Friday, his council of war, Lincoln's "war order," and the unwanted acquisition of a set of corps commanders were enough to cause him to put off a decision on what to do about those smokes.

If the fault did not lie in his preoccupation with other problems or in mistaken doubts of the reliability of the balloon observations, then it can be attributed to the inherent shortcomings in McClellan's arrangements for acquiring intelligence. Those arrangements did not contemplate the possibility of an enemy withdrawal. Such a discovery by itself would have made it worth while, many times over, for Pinkerton to employ resident spies. Another inadequacy lay in the weakness of the army's scouting efforts, an inevitable result of McClellan's policy of leaving scouting to the initiative of his subordinate commanders. Findings were few and seldom worth reporting to headquarters. Still another weakness was an unaggressiveness in the positioning of balloons. As has been seen, warning of Johnston's departure was dependent solely on them until the eleventh hour, and their unsupported findings were not persuasive enough to set in motion an army led by McClellan. Perhaps it was not feasible to station a balloon close enough to the enemy to observe their withdrawal preparations. An answer to that problem could have been to send John La Mountain on one of his free flights, but he had been dismissed from the service on February 19 after extended feuding with

Lowe,[25] who evidently regarded such flights as risking too much in manpower and balloons.

This blundering course of action was, however, not entirely a matter of intelligence failure. A conclusive factor was McClellan's stubbornness in preferring the unformed Urbanna plan to the advance up the Occoquan that Lincoln had advocated, which would have caught the Rebels in the midst of preparations to withdraw. But that opportunity could not be seized when McClellan, almost by his own choice, remained unaware of it.

.. .. ..

At Manassas Colonel Averell found "every combustible thing in flames. . . . Men women children horses present the most desolate appearance imaginable. You are never out of sight of a dead horse on the road." But he pronounced "splendid" the several enemy camps he had seen: "In one place there are about 2 acres of ovens." "From the extent of the camps," he wrote, "I conjecture that there must have been at least 80,000 men upon this line."

Newspaper correspondents roamed over the abandoned fortifications and camps and told the world about the "Quaker guns" (also known as "wooden ordnance") that the Rebels had left behind for Federal inspection; these were logs painted black and protruding from the embrasures on the forts. McClellan labeled these reports a delusion, citing the findings of his secret service as proof of their falsity and conveniently forgetting that Pinkerton in January had sent him the report of a deserter who had had a hand in putting the bogus artillery in place.[26]

The correspondents estimated the capacity of the huts the Rebels built at 60,000, but it appeared that "no more than 30,000 have occupied [them] within two months." The reporters were ungenerous in that last figure; Johnston's February return for Manassas-Centreville shows 42,860 present, of whom 36,267 were effective. Of course McClellan had a higher figure than any of these. On March 8 Pinkerton had estimated for Manassas-Centreville the same 80,000 that Averell would accidentally hit upon two days later. The detective's figures were never high enough to suit McClellan, who raised the estimate to 102,500: Pinkerton's 80,000 plus 22,500 for the forces that had been at Leesburg and on the lower Potomac. McClellan was correct in taking those units into account, but his addition of them made the 80,000 exaggeration even more glaring. The enemy's numbers in the new positions behind the Rappahannock were no more than 48,000.

McClellan's figures for enemy artillery were even more exaggerated. There were "about 300 field guns and from 26 to 30 siege guns . . . with the rebel army in front of Washington," he wrote. In canvassing Pinkerton's reports the Orléans brothers had found estimates for Manassas as high as fifty-five guns, but in adding up the guns reported in individual works they reached a total of only twenty-five. For Centreville they had reports of fifteen to seventeen guns. As McClellan would not use Pinkerton's individually reported figures, he also would reject the sum of a set of them computed by his two French aides. If he had reported that he was sending back to Washington three hundred guns that the Rebels left behind, we would have to believe they had had that many; but his report says nothing about *abandoned* guns.[27] It is doubtful that Johnston's real guns and Quaker guns together would have added up to three hundred.

On March 14 McClellan sent Brigadier General George Stoneman with ten squadrons of cavalry on the trail of the retreating Rebels. Lack of food and forage ended the pursuit, but not until it had confirmed numerous reports that the enemy was headed toward Culpeper. The rest of the Army of the Potomac remained about Manassas, Fairfax, and Alexandria while McClellan pondered his next move. Having taken the field, he was now relieved of his duties as general-in-chief. Lincoln left the position vacant.[28]

McClellan had "hoped to be able to throw at least a portion of the army on the [Urbanna] line of operations before the enemy evacuated Manassas." Now he reasoned that the Confederates' departure was in reponse to discovery by Johnston of his Urbanna plan; Johnston would now be in position to intercept, at full strength, an advance from Urbanna. McClellan fell back to a safer plan, a movement via the Potomac and Chesapeake Bay to Fort Monroe and the Peninsula. That would give him, now that the *Merrimack* threat was under control, an unopposed landing and a secure base. But it meant a fifty-mile separation from West Point instead of the eighteen miles from Urbanna to that objective. And John Magruder's 11,000-man Peninsula army, to be joined by 30,000 or 40,000 of Johnston's, would stand in its path. He called another meeting, this time with only General Barnard and the commanders of the four corps involved in the new plan. Only the four voted; they gave it unanimous approval.[29] Johnston's departure helped McClellan by shifting him into a plan that his immediate subordinates would support and away from the Urbanna plan that three of them had opposed. Some or all of them would have preferred Lincoln's Occoquan route.

McClellan was assuming that the Confederates' move had turned the time-and-distance factors of the Urbanna plan in their favor; but that was not necessarily the case. Their position behind the Rappahannock was scarcely fifty railroad miles closer to Richmond than Manassas was, and the bulk of their army was not significantly closer to West Point, the key to the plan, than McClellan would be at Alexandria, his port of embarkation. At this early stage of the war, army planners, it seems, had an exaggerated faith in the speed with which rails could move an army. McClellan, if he had been aware of the monumental traffic jam on the Orange and Alexandria during Johnston's withdrawal preparations, could have calculated that his steamships might well have an advantage over the trains. Perhaps it was fortunate that his intelligence service had not discovered the enemy's railroad problems; having that information, he might have gone ahead with his original plan, in which case there would have been a pileup at the Urbanna docks that would have dwarfed the earlier one along the tracks at Manassas. And the Urbanna mass would have consisted of men, not baggage and other impedimenta. A Confederate force could have crushed the invaders before most of them could disembark, form up, and fight.

.. .. ..

The response of McClellan's headquarters to the news of the enemy's departure is a prime example of his tendency to overestimate the enemy's prowess in espionage. The prince de Joinville, a member of Little Mac's official family, wrote that Johnston, "informed no doubt by one of those thousand female spies who keep up his communications into the domestic circles of the federal enemy," evacuated Manassas immediately after McClellan had been "forced to explain" the Urbanna plan to his generals. From this it appears that de Joinville did not know of or did not remember the unusual smokes that betrayed Johnston's preparations for withdrawal even before McClellan's meeting with the generals. Evidently balloonists' reports of real evidence enjoyed less regard in army headquarters than imaginary feats of female spies.

McClellan's statements, three of them, that the enemy knew his plans were indirectly worded but no less firm than de Joinville's. The first statement, made while he was in the process of changing to the Peninsula plan, gave the Confederates' discovery of the Urbanna plan and Banks's invasion of the Shenandoah Valley as twin causes of the evacuation of Manassas. He informed Stanton, "Most accounts substantially agree in this, & my information is very full." (No such information appears in the McClellan Papers or in the *Official Records*.) Two additional statements are in his final report, written months later: "When the enemy first learned of [the Urbanna] plan, they did thus evacuate Manassas"; and "their adoption of this course immediately on ascertaining that such a movement [to Urbanna] was intended . . . was unfortunate."

In none of these references to the leakage of his plan did McClellan suggest how it had occurred. John Nicolay and John Hay, Lincoln's secretaries and biographers, wrote that McClellan had named the administration as the source. Pinkerton had a different version, doubtful simply because of the loose character of his memoirs: the leak was a case of "direct treason, or, at least, criminal indiscretion" on the part of some one of the twelve generals who had voted on the plan on March 7.[30]

McClellan may really have believed that someone in the administration had disclosed his plan, but he was in no position to complain. He had committed a monstrous leak himself by divulging rather fully his plans for the western theater to a *New York Herald* correspondent, whose editors were patriotic enough to keep any hints of his revelations out of their paper, although they rewarded McClellan with continual puffs. His disclosures seem to have been rather general, perhaps even vague, but they were made specific after Johnston's retreat when Fitz John Porter, doubtless on McClellan's instruction, gave an hour's confidential briefing on the Peninsula plan to a reporter for the *New York World,* which was similarly discreet in withholding the information and similarly appreciative in its editorial approval of McClellan.[31]

With McClellan's decision to move the army to Fort Monroe and advance up the Peninsula, the Johnston-McClellan tragicomedy of errors came full circle. The eastern campaigns of 1862 took shape from the two commanders' misreadings of enemy movements — misreadings originating in badly mistaken fears of the effectiveness of their enemy's intelligence.

.. .. ..

Once decided upon, McClellan's movement to the Peninsula was begun promptly and executed handsomely. The assembly of a fleet of transports had been in progress since February 27, when its intended destination was Urbanna. On March 15, two days after the corps commanders' approval of the Peninsula plan, General Charles S. Hamilton's division of Heintzelman's Third Corps boarded ship for Fort Monroe. The grand army required 389 vessels — steamers, schooners, and barges. Two of the steamers, the *Constitution* and the *Ocean Queen,* together could carry 7000 men; nevertheless, the movement of 120,000 troops together with their equipment, horses, and vehicles took twenty days.[32]

This movement was a test of the effectiveness of the Confederate intelligence service. If General McClellan could have observed the performance of enemy scouts and spies and the qualms of doubt that their reports produced at Richmond, his faith in the potency of Confederate espionage would have been profoundly shaken. Clandestine coverage of the embarkations at Alexandria, a strongly pro-Southern city, seems to have been limited to observations by a volunteer civilian spy, A. M. White, who in delivering his information had to ride through fifty or sixty miles of Federal-held country to Jeb Stuart's headquarters on the upper Rappahannock. White reported the embarkation of only two of the army's four corps, and half of that information was wrong, for one of the two he included was McDowell's First Corps, which was held back by Lincoln for the protection of Washington. White's only information on the destination of the transports was that it was "some point down the river." He placed McClellan at Alexandria on a day when the general and his staff

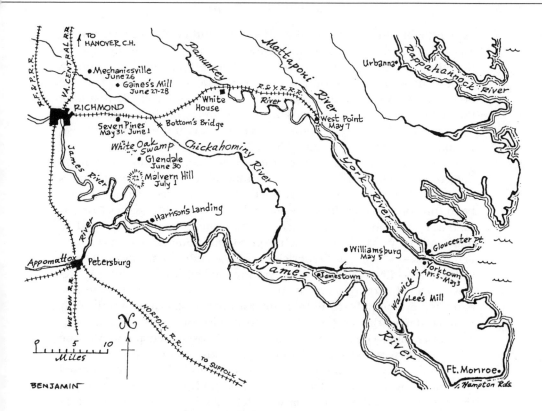

THE PENINSULA CAMPAIGN

were on their way. The Confederates' observation of the landings also was spotty, being largely dependent on irregular visits to the Peninsula by a scout or scouts from Norfolk. No intimation of the scale of the Federal operation was obtained until enough troops had arrived for their camps to overflow the immediate environs of Fort Monroe and spread out to Hampton and Newport News.

The Confederates suffered no lack of military brainpower for comprehending the meaning of this development. President Davis, himself a graduate of West Point, had brought General Robert E. Lee into the War Department. But uncertainty about Federal intentions plagued the Confederates during the entire three weeks of the movement. At first Lee was advised by informants that a fleet of transports that was departing the Peninsula to return to Alexandria probably was part of a movement to the Carolina coast. This view, which also occurred to Davis and Johnston, was owed to the fact that Hampton Roads had been a staging area for troop movements to the Carolinas. But by the time the influx to Fort Monroe was half complete, Lee realized that these invaders were not an expeditionary force assembled ad hoc from hither and yon; they were McClellan's Army of the Potomac. Then Lee's view shifted to an expectation that McClellan would make an elaborate feint on the Peninsula while striking in earnest on Norfolk, or vice versa. A few days later he believed Norfolk to be the more probable point of attack. By that time the Federals had been disembarking for two weeks but giving little or no sign of serious offensive purposes; thus the view that their Peninsula visit was only a demonstration gained favor.

When Johnston, from his positions on the Rappahannock and Rapidan, began feeling pressure from a cautious advance by Federal units not yet called to the Alexandria docks, he wrote Lee, "Perhaps I have been too confident of the slothful condition of our adversaries." But by March 27 he too was reporting that "the enemy seemed disposed to make a display." Meanwhile, each Confederate commander on the eastern fringe — Holmes at Fredericksburg, Magruder at Yorktown, Huger at Norfolk — firmly expected the visiting Yankees to come his way. Receiving calls for reinforcements from several directions, Davis and Lee extracted two brigades from Johnston's army, but Magruder was the only commander in the Virginia theater to receive one; the other went to North Carolina. Then on April 4 the Federals assembled at Fort Monroe took their first steps up the Peninsula; Lee lost no time in summoning Johnston's army to Richmond. But it was not until the invaders showed signs of laying siege to Yorktown that Davis and Lee completely made up their minds that the Peninsula was McClellan's choice for a route to Richmond.[33] This is the ultimate correction of the belief that the Confederates knew McClellan's plans in detail, well in advance.

. .   . .   . .

The invading Yankees were an army that had everything. The scope of its commander's preparations is indicated by his provisions for getting information. Professor Lowe was operating three balloons (a fourth was left at Washington to serve the local commander).[34] The civilian-operated U.S. Military Telegraph sent twenty-three operators to the Peninsula, enough to man stations at all major headquarters and provide twenty-four-hour service at many or all of them. Later the Signal Corps acquired an experimental wire telegraph printer system, but it found only limited use. Visual signaling was the Corps' forte; despite the Peninsula's flat, heavily wooded terrain, there was use for short-distance flag communication as the army inched its way over unfamiliar roads with few landmarks. The most prominent use of the flags was in communication with the ships of the navy's fleet assigned to cooperate with McClellan. As the navy had not adopted Major Myer's system, it was necessary to place Signal Corps officers on the ships.[35]

In February Fort Monroe had been provided with a direct telegraphic connection to Washington by installation of a twenty-five-mile cable across the mouth of Chesapeake Bay and a land wire up the coast connecting to commercial lines at Wilmington, Delaware. The cable used was a section of the first Atlantic cable, which had broken down after operating for a short time in 1858. The operators, though they knew their three-hundred-mile link to the War Department was a significant achievement in military communications, would complain that their Washington wire "always worked hard."[36] By this they meant that the electrical resistance on that long line reduced the responsiveness of their instruments to the dot-and-dash impulses.

The intelligence element of McClellan's Peninsula army consisted of Pinkerton, George H. Bangs, his second in command, and twelve other members of his bureau. William H. Scott and ten assistants remained in Washington to carry on the work of counterespionage.[37]

Aside from the improvements in observation and communication, prospects of fruitful intelligence work on the Peninsula were not good. The most remarkable fact about intelligence in McClellan's Peninsula campaign, his grand effort to win the war, is that during the last four months of the five-month campaign Pinkerton had not even one agent at work in Richmond or anywhere else behind Confederate lines. Nor, apparently, did any intelligence reach him from the Unionist underground in Richmond, though one of its members, F. W. E. Lohman, presented after the war a claim for services extending back to early 1862.[38] (Those early services could have consisted of nonintelligence activities such as aiding Federal prisoners.) So far as the record shows, only one of Pinkerton's agents, Timothy Webster, set foot on the Peninsula before the campaign, and his visit there was only in the course of his travels to and from Washington. Of course, McClellan had never planned to take the army to the Peninsula, but it does not appear that, once there, he looked to Pinkerton for the kind of intelligence that could be gained by penetrating the enemy lines. Scouting the country in the army's front had never been part of Pinkerton's mission, and it did not become one now. It was regarded as a task for the army's forward commands, but they seem to have been doing less scouting than a noncombat element, the Signal Corps. Major Myer, though chief signal officer of the whole U.S. Army, had joined McClellan's army for its grand campaign and was sending his officers as far forward as they could go without stumbling into enemy forces.[39] Although Myer's purpose was only to find sites for signal stations, this scouting reveals him as an officer alert to opportunities for getting information about the enemy for the commander's use as well as his own.

Pinkerton's lack of energy in intelligence collection may have been partly due to an illness that afflicted him during the campaign. Its nature and duration are not known.[40] He made one change in his operation: he discontinued written reports of routine interrogations. Presumably oral reports to McClellan took their place, though the general would have had little time for anything but the most important news. Thus we have a less full picture of intelligence activity in the campaign than for the quiet months when the army was at Washington and Alexandria.

. .   ..   ..

In the early weeks on the Peninsula Pinkerton's staff interrogated four prisoners who were members of an incipient flag-signaling organization serving the Confederates in the vicinity of Yorktown. This group used a signaling alphabet consisting of various arrangements of 1's and 2's, similar to Myer's and to the one Porter Alexander would have used at the first Bull Run battle; to this extent it was a descendant of Alexander's unit. But it was staffed with local militiamen rather than full-time soldiers. The group was headed by a Captain Robert Hogg and frequently visited by a "signal master," William Norris of Baltimore, soon to be named the Confederacy's chief signal officer. (Alexander had transferred to the artillery.) The four prisoners, all farmers, described their signaling system in detail, and three of them gave their alphabet. Myer wrote later that one of his officers, Lieutenant Henry Camp, "read [intercepted] messages before Richmond"; whether Camp received the farmers' alphabet via Pinkerton or solved it on his own is not known. As Myer's long report on the Peninsula campaign omits this episode, Camp's interceptions probably were few and had little intelligence value. Although the Confederate signalmen were continuously active during the campaign, the Peninsula's flat, heavily wooded land did not favor interception of enemy signals.[41]

. .   ..   ..

Agent E. H. Stein arrived at Pinkerton's tent April 20 with little information. Having been closely watched by Winder's detectives, he was not a candidate to test the enemy's lines again. Another reason for caution was the fact that at least four of the five Pinkerton agents remaining in the Confederacy were now in prison — Timothy Webster, Hattie Lawton, Pryce Lewis, and John Scully. The exact status of the fifth, H.J.K., is unknown, but no reports from him are in McClellan's or Pinkerton's papers; he may have been under detention by Confederate authorities.

The four arrests were the result of an unfortunate selection of agents to investigate Webster's situation. According to Pinkerton, he chose Lewis and Scully — who willingly accepted the assignment — because they were acquainted with some of the Baltimore secessionists who were now in Richmond and in contact with Webster. The cover story for the

Lewis-Scully mission was that they were in Richmond seeking to get into the smuggling business. They traced Webster to the Monument Hotel but never succeeded in finding him alone; his visitor on their second call was Samuel McCubbin, General Winder's chief detective, who advised them to call on the general. On returning from a long interview with Winder they were confronted by a detective accompanied by a citizen who had seen them in the street and recognized them as Pinkerton agents who had searched his home in Washington months before.

Pinkerton's book says that at first only Lewis and Scully were jailed; that both were tried and sentenced to death; that Scully confessed the nature of his mission to a priest, whereupon Lewis broke and confessed to the authorities. By implicating Webster they won reprieve from execution and were released in 1863. Pinkerton made excuses for their actions and wrote, "For myself, I have no judgment to utter." Webster was arrested, convicted of espionage, and condemned to hang.

Pinkerton describes a cabinet-level discussion of a proposal to intercede on Webster's behalf. It culminated, he says, in a trip by himself and Colonel Thomas M. Key of McClellan's staff, delivering to Confederate authorities via flag of truce a communication signed by General Wool at Fort Monroe, "representing that the course pursued by the Federal government toward rebel spies had heretofore been lenient and forbearing; that in many cases such persons had been released after a short confinement, and that in no case had anyone so charged been . . . sentenced to death."

The effort availed nothing. Webster climbed the gallows on the morning of April 29. When the trap was sprung, the knot slipped and he fell to the ground. From under the hood, as he was being borne back up the steps, he spoke: "I suffer a double death!" When someone said that the rope was too short, he complained, "Oh, you are going to choke me this time." Those were his last words.[42]

. .   . .   . .

When McClellan's troops began their advance up the Peninsula, they were promptly treated to theatrical General John Magruder's tableau designed to impress the Yankees with his numbers by marching the same troops time and again across the same clearing in full view of the invaders. The story invites suspicion that it is a myth, partly because generations of historians have passed it along with weak documentation or none at all, also because Prince John was perfectly capable of surrounding himself with a manufactured aura. It comes as something of a surprise, then, to discover that the story is true. Magruder spelled out the scheme in a training document he issued as a special order when it became clear that a major force of the enemy was arriving on his peninsula; this is known because a copy of the order wound up on

McClellan's field desk. And contemporary writings by two of Magruder's junior officers describe the backing and forthing that their imaginative general put them through.

It is not clear what effect, if any, Magruder's act had on McClellan's estimate of the enemy. As Prince John's instructions for it could scarcely have reached McClellan's hands until a month later, when he occupied Yorktown, where the Confederates had had their Peninsula headquarters, he would not have seen Magruder's written program until the show was over. In all probability Little Mac, if he witnessed the enemy's display or received reports of it, would have regarded it simply as confirming his habitual estimate that he was facing superior numbers. For an opponent like McClellan, Magruder did not need to work up an elaborate deception to magnify his numbers.[43]

.. .. ..

General Wool had prepared intelligence for McClellan by sending a soldier into the Confederate lines with instructions to assume the role of deserter, enlist in the Confederate service, learn whatever he could about Rebel forces and defenses, and desert back to the Federals. The Confederates accepted such enlistments because of their manpower shortage. They assigned this recruit to a unit in Magruder's advance line, barely a dozen miles in the Federals' front, thus easing his return to Fort Monroe. But this misjudgment did little harm: his information dealing with Confederate defenses at the foot of the Peninsula went for naught, for Magruder had no intention of defending his thin advance line. Its purpose had been only to deny the command at Fort Monroe an easy inspection of the Peninsula's topography and defenses, and it was abandoned as soon as McClellan's marching army appeared.

That denial was a complete success. The country between Fort Monroe and the Confederate base at Yorktown turned out to be, in the words of General Barnard, a *terra incognita*. The phrase was all too literally true; McClellan and his generals did not even know that their only feasible land route to Yorktown was blocked by the Warwick River. McClellan's map, drawn by Wool's staff, became the most famous map in Civil War history by showing the Warwick flowing parallel to, and close to, the James; its true course was across the Peninsula from headwaters near Yorktown. The Federals knew Yorktown itself was heavily fortified; since they did not know a Warwick River was in their path, they could not know that it too was fortified. Naturally marshy, the Warwick was made even more defensible by dams that transformed it into a succession of mill ponds. According to Barnard, this "was naturally a very strong line, and it was occupied throughout." It was a barrier to a flanking movement against Yorktown from the west, and the town's heavy fortifications stood in the way of a direct assault. Turning the position on the east by way of the upper waters of the York River, McClellan's original plan, was ruled out by the navy's judgment that its ships would be outgunned by the enemy's heavy batteries at the narrow passage between Yorktown and Gloucester Point.

How the Warwick and its defenses escaped discovery is a tale that exposes the catch-as-catch-can nature of McClellan's intelligence operation. During the many months when Pinkerton or McClellan himself could have sought out General Wool for information on the Peninsula and its defenses, no one had done so. Pinkerton's coverage came about only by happenstance and was almost completely limited to Yorktown and vicinity. W. H. Ringgold's observations had not extended far enough inland from the York to touch on the Warwick, and Timothy Webster's coverage was similarly limited. Although James Maurice, the former oysterman who deserted to the Federals, had worked on the Yorktown fortifications, his report contained no warning of the obstacles presented by the Warwick.

Thus McClellan was persuaded to take Yorktown by siege rather than attempt a bloody assault. He was also influenced by the withdrawal of McDowell's huge First Corps from its scheduled Peninsula trip, an action Lincoln took upon discovering that McClellan had left much less force to defend Washington than he had promised.

Joe Johnston's troops began arriving at Yorktown from the Rappahannock and the Rapidan in the first week of April. Hancock's brigade took a few prisoners; one of them, an Alabama private, told Pinkerton's interrogator that Johnston had 500 guns in position and that his force in a few days would number 100,000. McClellan, as usual, seized on this low-level, unsupported single-source report and informed Stanton, "It seems clear that I shall have the whole force of the enemy on my hands, probably not less than one hundred thousand . . . and possibly more." The estimate McClellan adopted so easily was almost double Johnston's actual numbers.[44]

Upon inspecting his defenses Johnston concluded that the Federal ships could outgun his heavies at Yorktown and Gloucester Point, enabling McClellan to turn the Yorktown position and proceed all the way to West Point. This view was not shared by McClellan or, as already seen, by his naval collaborators, whose respect for Johnston's guns matched Johnston's respect for theirs.

Johnston soon saw that McClellan was intent upon a siege. He regarded that too as certain death for the Yorktown fortress. Having stolen two marches on the Federals — from Winchester in July and from Manassas in March — he now decided on a third. His preparations repeated the story of the Manassas evacuation; he complained to D. H.

Hill, "I am continually finding something in the way never mentioned to me before." He conquered the delays by forcing evacuation on the night of May 3–4. But with the Federals sitting there almost in his face at many points, not all of the withdrawal actions could be hidden from their view, as they had been at Manassas. As early as May 2, Federal signal officers Charles Herzog and W. H. R. Neel reported the enemy's main works evacuated at Lee's Mill, halfway across the Peninsula, where a main road crossed the Warwick. On the morning of the 3rd, Lieutenant A. B. Jerome at a signal station opposite Yorktown observed Rebels destroying barracks. At some earlier point in these proceedings the removal of wagons to the rear, presumably to get them out of the way of a rapid retreat, was reported to Uriah H. Painter, of the *Philadelphia Inquirer,* by a contraband who had been an officer's servant. Painter evidently was scouting more aggressively than anyone in McClellan's service. When these indications of Confederate withdrawal persisted, he took his information to headquarters.

Thus Johnston's evacuation need not have been even a half-surprise to the Federals. But the signalmen's information from Lee's Mill was short-stopped at division or corps headquarters; it never reached McClellan. The report of barracks destruction was regarded as not necessarily indicating evacuation. According to Lowe's later report, no sign of the evacuation could be seen from his balloon opposite Yorktown as late as the afternoon of the 3rd. And General Marcy, to whom Painter had reported that "the rebels were all going away from there, . . . said that it was not so; that they had positive intelligence to the contrary; that [the Confederates] were going to make a desperate fight there."[45]

If Marcy actually had "positive intelligence," it was misinformation that had somehow gained belief in McClellan's circle, and the rejection of Painter's report is understandable. But the evidence of withdrawal preparations that is known to have reached army headquarters from Painter and the signal officers was at least as strong as the evidence of enemy evacuation of Manassas that was the basis of McClellan's belated pursuit order back in March.

The enemy's departure from Yorktown began at dark on the night of May 3, covered by a heavy, random bombardment that lasted until 2 A.M. Its very randomness signified that it was a cover for some action, probably evacuation.

The rivalry between the Signal Corps and the Military Telegraph was never closer than in their reporting of the Rebels' departure. The best information Myer could get was that a signal station in the center of the long line reported the evacuation at 4:30 A.M. His officers accompanied the troops that entered the enemy works and confirmed the absence of the enemy by flag message. The Military Telegraph's claim comes from a memoirist who wrote that at about 4 A.M. the station at army headquarters, "Mc," received a report of the evacuation obtained from a deserter who had arrived at a headquarters where an operator fortunately was on duty. By the time McClellan arrived, half dressed, at "Mc," operator Jesse Bunnell "was being frantically called by every one who could get in" with the news.[46]

McClellan's pursuit this time was prompt; it was in motion within a couple of hours and overtook the enemy's rear on the 5th at Williamsburg. There was fought a bloody but indecisive battle involving sizable fractions of both armies. But the Yorktown campaign ended with Johnston's army escaping to positions five miles in front of Richmond without suffering the devastation to which a retreating army may be exposed.

.. .. ..

With the occupation of Williamsburg McClellan was still fifty miles short of Richmond. He was not of a mind to rely on General Wool's mapmakers again. He wired Stanton, "We have absolutely no information in detail of the country to our front," and requested the loan of eight or ten officers from the staff of the Topographical Engineers section of the War Department. This was not a reasonable number to ask for; how many were sent, if any, is uncertain, but McClellan found mapmaking talent in Pinkerton's organization in the person of Private John C. Babcock, twenty-five years old, who had been an architect in Chicago. In March he had been added to Pinkerton's force to sketch enemy fortifications as described by prisoners, deserters, and returned spies.

In his new job as cartographer Babcock did his own scouting of the ground to be mapped; that made him much less dependent on second-hand information than other mapmakers had been. (It also made him the only member of Pinkerton's organization who ever did any scouting.) Because he obtained "the main points [by] my own reconnoissance," Babcock's maps were found to be "correct in almost every particular as we advance." This new standard in mapmaking was "commented upon on all sides," and Babcock wrote his aunt Jane that McClellan pronounced one of his maps "the finest piece of topographical work he has ever seen."

Babcock's method evidently was to map small areas in the army's front one at a time and consolidate the series on a map covering the whole front or, more probably, a sizable section of it. He added these findings to a published map of the Richmond area, which was then photographically reproduced and issued to commanders down to levels at least as low as brigade.

It was one of this series of larger maps, issued in nearly two hundred expensive copies, that won McClellan's praise. A copy was sent to Lin-

coln, probably by McClellan. The President also received one of Babcock's maps from Pinkerton, who had assumed the credit for this map
work by naming E. J. Allen as the cartographic authority, with Babcock
listed as an assistant.

Babcock continued adding to and correcting his maps as the army
advanced and until long after the fighting on the Peninsula was over. The
guaranteed slowness of McClellan's advance made this one-man mapmaking scheme acceptable, but it required Babcock to be repeatedly
exposed to the hazards of country occupied, patrolled, or scouted by the
enemy. He wrote, "I ofttimes had to run the gauntlet between a bullet
and a halter." In later years, when as an intelligence chief he sent men
out on hazardous missions, he would have the satisfaction of knowing he
was not asking more of them than he had risked himself many times.

His general mode of travel was his horse, Gimlet, but some of his
maneuvers, for example the pacing-off of distances, would have had to
be on foot. And occasionally his conveyance was one of Lowe's balloons,
which entailed direct arrangements between Private Babcock and General Marcy — an unusual pairing of ranks.

One of Babcock's associates was Alexander Gardner, a Mathew Brady
man who did document-copying work for Pinkerton. As a result of this
relationship, handsome John Babcock became the most publicized scout
of the Civil War. His picture appears three times in Francis Trevelyan
Miller's famous *Photographic History,* twice in company with intelligence
colleagues and once, in the frontispiece of Miller's volume on secret
service, in the company of Gimlet. But all this publicity missed the fact
that Babcock later became the assistant chief and then chief of a successful Army of the Potomac intelligence bureau.

He acknowledged that there probably was no military duty for which "I
am . . . so well qualified" as the mapmaking tasks that came his way on the
Peninsula. But the success of his maps naturally earned him the hostility
of the army's official topographers. He wrote that the topographical
engineers' maps, "prepared at an expense of $30,000, [were] thrown
away as worthless" by comparison with his products. And the officer
chiefly embarrassed by this development was the chief topographical
engineer, Brigadier General Andrew A. Humphreys, who in 1864 would
become Babcock's superior as chief of staff in the Army of the Potomac
headquarters.[47]

.. .. ..

Johnston's withdrawal to the Richmond front uncovered West Point, at
the head of the York River. McClellan was quick to put the port to use,
bringing in William B. Franklin's reinforcing division by water and, also
by water, a freight load consisting of five locomotives and eighty railroad
cars. Soon he had the Richmond and York River Railroad operating as far

as its crossing over the Chickahominy River, twelve miles east of Richmond. The road was ready to receive the army's siege guns.

The Confederates evacuated Norfolk May 10, and early next morning they blew up their unwieldy *Virginia* in the James River. With the James cleared, McClellan could move his base there and have the protection of the navy's gunboats in his final drive on Richmond.[48]

But he did not expect the Confederates to let him lay siege to their capital without first giving battle, and he expected to be badly outnumbered in that battle. To Stanton he telegraphed on May 10, "If I am not reinforced it is probable that I will be obliged to fight nearly double my numbers strongly intrenched." Four days later he repeated this exaggeration of enemy strength, complaining that he could not bring to battle more than 80,000 and must attack "perhaps double my numbers." Two-thirds of McDowell's First Corps was still being withheld by Lincoln.[49]

An immediate barrier to the execution of McClellan's plans was the Chickahominy, another marshy, easily flooded stream, running southeasterly and passing within six miles of Richmond at one point. Babcock's mapping would have located bridges, but pinpointing enemy forces called for a considerable scouting effort, and none appears to have been made until May 18, two weeks after the fight at Williamsburg left the roads cleared for the Federals. On that date a party of scouts found enemy in force near Bottom's Bridge, a principal crossing. Two days later Silas Casey's division of Keyes's corps found the bridge burned but forded without opposition; the absence of defenders puzzled McClellan. The rest of Keyes's corps and Heintzelman's two divisions next crossed. Now the Army of the Potomac was divided into two distinct parts, separated by an unpredictable river.[50]

The paltriness of the army's intelligence program is revealed in the next action. On the basis of no more than a report by a Southern civilian, one Dr. Pollock, that a force of 17,000 Rebels would appear next day on the army's right flank at Hanover Court House, McClellan sent Fitz John Porter with his newly created Fifth Corps against this supposed threat. Porter, with a three-to-one advantage in numbers (his opponent actually had about 4000), came away with 700 prisoners. McClellan labeled this a "glorious victory over superior numbers." The chief point of interest in this affair is an experiment conducted by Major Myer, who led a party of seven signal officers reporting information from the battlefield during the action. Their flags attracted too much enemy fire for the scheme to be rated workable.[51]

Pleased by Porter's success, McClellan went out on a limb, telling Stanton that Richmond newspapers were urging Johnston to attack; but "I think he is too able for that." At the same time Little Mac was complaining to Lincoln that "there is no doubt that the whole of the enemy is concentrating everything on Richmond." Lincoln, very much aware of a recent rampage in the Shenandoah Valley by Stonewall Jackson, countered this nonsense: "That the whole of the enemy is concentrating on Richmond, I think, cannot be known to you or me."[52]

The scene was now set for the attack Joe Johnston was "too able" to make. On May 31 he gathered his forces together and struck the corps of Keyes and Heintzelman, which were still isolated from the rest of the army. It was a badly mismanaged affair. The attack was five hours getting under way; divisions supposed to move on three parallel routes crowded onto a single road; more than 30,000 of Johnston's 51,000 did not fire a single shot. General Sumner, ordered to reinforce Keyes and Heintzelman, got his corps across the river on a rickety, flooded bridge that engineers insisted would wash away at the first footfall of his troops. (This order was McClellan's sole contribution to the battle; he was sick, confined to his tent.) Johnston had expected to overwhelm Keyes and Heintzelman with superior numbers; in the event, the Federals got more men into action than he did. The battle ended by simply dying out around noon of June 1. Johnston had been hit by a bullet in the shoulder and a shell fragment in the chest; his command devolved briefly on G. W. Smith and finally on R. E. Lee.

The battle of Seven Pines (or Fair Oaks) exposed again the weakness of McClellan's intelligence service. Johnston's attack, despite the five-hour delay and his subordinates' bungling, achieved as complete a surprise as could be hoped for against an enemy whose vulnerable position kept it constantly on semi-alert. But Keyes's scouting either was unaggressive or did not exist at all; the Rebels marched up to his doorstep undiscovered. The only warning he received, a late one, was the blundering arrival inside his lines of one of Johnston's aides who got lost in the course of the countermarches and stalls that delayed the attack. Fighting generals in McClellan's army did not feel the need for scouting as much as noncombatant Major Myer did in his quest for signal-station sites.[53]

The balloons gave no warning of the attack. Thaddeus Lowe's proudest claim in later years was that in this battle his observations of enemy movements saved the day by discovering the enemy's imminent attack, enabling McClellan to order Sumner across the river in time to prevent the Rebels from overwhelming Keyes's and Heintzelman's commands. Actually Lowe's balloons produced hardly a shred of useful information that day. Johnston struck at 1:00 P.M.; high winds prevented Lowe from ascending until 2:00.[54] In the historical report of his services, he wrote of this day, "I descended at 2 o'clock"; but an original copy of this dispatch in the McClellan Papers reads, "I ascended at 2 o'clock." Unless Lowe in writing his report a year later convinced himself that "ascended" in that May 31 dispatch had been a slip of the pen, his substituting of the word "descended" was a deliberate falsification. The rest of this message contains nothing to show that the terrain allowed him a view of any part of the battlefield.[55]

.. .. ..

General Lee found himself with the same intelligence problem as McClellan: there was plenty of enemy force out there, but where, specifically, were they? Exactly what units were they? And what activity, offensive or defensive, were they up to? Lee called on Jeb Stuart to explore the enemy's right flank; Stuart proposed a ride around McClellan's whole army, to which Lee gave an apparently silent assent. Stuart led 1200 troopers from picked regiments on a three-day ride that suffered only one casualty.[56] He kept a Jeb Stuart version of a safe distance between his column and major Yankee forces, but he captured enough prisoners to learn by interrogation the identity of the Federal units whose positions he passed.

Seeing that McClellan's plans for a siege would succeed if allowed to mature, Lee determined on the same course Johnston had taken — attack. As he would do on several later occasions, he sought to counteract the Federals' advantage in numbers by supplying them with a generous amount of false information. He had correctly sized up Little Mac's fighting qualities, but he credited McClellan the administrator with having an effective intelligence service. Like practically every other general in that war, Lee believed that "the country is full of spies, and our plans are immediately carried to the enemy."[57] As a result of his efforts at deception, the wire between Army of the Potomac headquarters and the War Department was soon humming with reports that Beauregard, who had been commanding in Mississippi, was on his way to Richmond with a huge reinforcement for Lee. This movement, reported in Southern newspapers, looked suspiciously like a planted story, but McClellan passed it on to Stanton without comment. The secretary had already assured him that Beauregard's signature was still carried on correspondence relating to prisoners of war received by General Halleck in Mississippi and that Halleck had noted no departures of enemy troops from his front.[58]

Meanwhile Lee had set about reinforcing his army from the south, though not from Beauregard. And he called Stonewall Jackson's army of 16,000 to Richmond from the Shenandoah Valley. This movement he surrounded with similar deceptive stories. He had the Richmond newspapers print reports that Jackson was being reinforced from Richmond, and he went the length of sending Whiting's division by rail from Richmond to the Valley. This was not so extravagant a ruse as it appears, for he intended to add Whiting to Jackson's command and to have the expanded force arrive as a unit on the Federals' right. At Staunton, Whiting's troops turned back toward Richmond and joined Jackson, whose movement in that direction had already started.[59]

Lee enlisted Jackson's aid in this elaborate hocus-pocus. He wrote, "In moving your troops you could let it be understood that [the purpose] was to pursue the enemy in your front."[60] This was a game that Stonewall well knew how to play. Generals Frémont and Banks, whose positions in the Valley were north of Jackson's, barraged the War Department with reports of enemy activity in their front.

Deserters informed McClellan of this reinforcement of Jackson; word of it also reached Washington from Fredericksburg. McClellan of course read it as one more indication of the enemy's wealth of numbers at Richmond, but Lincoln asked him, "Have not all been sent to deceive?"[61]

McClellan, after suffering through the campaign without anything approaching the intelligence coverage Stuart had just provided Lee, now was favored with some good information about Jackson's intentions. At dawn on June 24 a cavalry outpost of Porter's corps on the Federals' right was approached by a young man asking to be taken to headquarters. His name was Charles Rean; his age, seventeen. He impressed Porter with his brightness and his "confident . . . show of honesty," but Porter did not believe he was who he said he was and sent him to army headquarters, where Pinkerton took a 2300-word statement from him. Rean gave a history of residence in so many places, North and South, that his true allegiance may have been hard for him to know himself. He claimed Baltimore as his latest home and said he had been a member of the First Maryland Regiment (Federal) until taken prisoner in Jackson's capture of the Valley post at Front Royal in May. Here again anything was possible, for on that occasion the First Maryland (Federal) had fought with the First Maryland (Confederate).[62] Rean had, he said, escaped from his captors at Lynchburg and had gone to Richmond and then toward the Valley for the express purpose of discovering Jackson's whereabouts and movements in order to report them to the Federals. And Jackson's reinforced army, he had learned, was well to the east of the Valley and marching to attack McClellan on June 28, a date he inferred from hearing officers and privates say "Wish to God it was the 28th." He reported Jackson's strength as fifteen brigades; the actual number was nine.

When Rean was searched, in his drawers was found a slip of paper containing the name of Dr. Lumpkins, a local man Pinkerton happened to have identified as "an active rebel." Rean's claim of having toured much of Virginia on foot in search of information for McClellan instead of putting himself in Federal hands as fast as possible after escaping prison also must have raised doubts about his bona fides. The peculiar interest in the date June 28 was another unlikely story; Federal commanders could easily reason that whatever date was being bruited about in such a way, Jackson must be planning a surprise on some earlier date. In fact Lee had ordered him to attack Porter's right flank on the 26th as part of a general assault that Lee would direct from a position opposite Porter's center.

Under threat of being treated as a spy Rean broke down and admitted being a deserter from Jackson's army. But he held to his story of its advance toward Richmond, placing it forty miles away on June 21. This significantly overstated Jackson's progress, which was along the route of the Virginia Central Railroad. Pinkerton rated Rean "one of the most important persons that it has been my privilege to examine, being highly educated, shrewd, and thoroughly posted upon the names of all the leading generals in the rebel army, and in military matters thoroughly posted. . . . My own impression is that he has been sent within our lines for the purpose of conveying to us the precise information which he has thus conveyed."[63]

At midnight McClellan wired Stanton asking for "the most exact information you have as to the position and movements of Jackson, as well as the sources from which your information is derived, that I may better compare it with what I have." Stanton replied the next day, citing reports from several points that showed Jackson threatening western Virginia and also preparing to march down the Valley upon Washington and Baltimore. "Within the last two days," he said, "the evidence is strong that for some purpose the enemy is circulating rumors of Jackson's advance in various directions, with a view to conceal the real point of attack." Reasoning that Jackson's actual movement would be in a direction left unmentioned in planted rumors, Stanton suspected that Stonewall was headed for Richmond. Jackson's subordinates, baffled by their general's behavior and not a little disgusted by his secrecy toward them, thought he was overplaying his game of deception, and they were right, as Stanton's correct inference shows.[64]

McClellan decided to set the Jackson problem aside for the moment and go ahead on the 25th with a planned two-mile advance along the railroad toward Richmond, whose steeples and rooftops loomed ahead. This led to the engagement known as Oak Grove, the first of the Seven Days battles. The move gained less than half a mile; a disappointed McClellan was further dismayed by receipt of another Beauregard report, the most fantastic of all. This one told of a noisy Richmond reception for the Creole general on his arrival the previous day with strong reinforcements. The information was from a contraband arriving at Porter's headquarters. McClellan swallowed it whole without interrogating the man or having Pinkerton do it. He went into a state of despair and sent Stanton a long, hysterical telegram:

> The rebel force is stated at 200,000. . . . I regret my great inferiority in numbers, but feel that I am in no way responsible for it. . . . I will do all I can with the splendid army I have the honor to command, and if it is destroyed by overwhelming numbers, can at least die with it and share its fate. . . . if the result . . . is a disaster, the responsibility cannot be thrown on my shoulders; it must rest where it belongs.[65]

McClellan still had the habit formed back in Washington of issuing enemy strength estimates independently of Pinkerton. This is understandable, since hard information on Confederate numbers was not to be had from Pinkerton. The detective had not improved his sources or his estimating methods; he was still dealing in gross figures reported for the whole enemy army, with no indication of how they were derived. He had estimated Johnston's strength at Yorktown at 100,000 to 120,000; the true figure was about 56,500. Now, with McClellan's grand assault on Richmond about to start, he estimated Lee's numbers at 180,000, which included Jackson's addition of 30,000; the 180,000 figure was "probably considerably short of the real strength of their army," which he believed to contain 200 infantry regiments although he had identified only 91. In fact the number Lee was assembling, including Jackson, would come to 92,400, the largest army he would ever command — and still short, by 13,500, of the strength of McClellan's "outnumbered" army.[66]

Porter's corps was Lee's first and principal target because it was now isolated, the only Federal force still north of the Chickahominy, and it protected the army's communication with West Point and the supply base at White House on the Pamunkey River. Another important consideration was that the flank Porter covered lay in the path of Jackson's movement from the Valley. Lee's plans for coordinated attack, however, suffered the same fate as Johnston's at Seven Pines. With Jackson's arrival Lee would have an assault force of 55,800, enough to overwhelm Porter. But on the 26th Jackson was a no-show and was not even heard from all day; nothing could go according to plan. Lee got only 11,000 into the battle; Porter, using 14,000 of his big corps, suffered only a quarter as many casualties as Lee.

This, the battle of Mechanicsville, underlined the precariousness of Porter's position, and he began moving to cross the river to his south. He completed the move only after heavy losses in the largest and costliest engagement of the Seven Days, the battle of Gaines's Mill. It engaged almost 100,000 men in the two armies, cost Lee 8000 casualties and McClellan 6800, and ended in resounding defeat for Porter, who received only one division in reinforcements while 64,000 Yankees sat idle south of the river. Lee had left a long stretch of front on his right to be defended by his weakest elements, the commands of Magruder and Huger, numbering only 25,000, but their vulnerable situation attracted no notice from McClellan.

After Gaines's Mill McClellan, even more exhausted emotionally than after Oak Grove, announced that the army would now cross the Peninsula to a base at Harrison's Landing on the James, a position as far upriver as the navy could guarantee protection. Keyes's corps was already in motion.

These moves left Lee uncertain whether the enemy was pursuing the original plan leading to a siege, retreating toward Fort Monroe to make a new start, or heading for the James. For the Army of the Potomac the route to the James looked so much safer than the other two that McClellan had no difficulty in deciding which way to turn.

His units were, on average, a scant fifteen miles from the James, but it was a big army, and roads running north–south were scarce, bottlenecks were unavoidable, every mile of road had to be reconnoitered in advance or traversed blindly, there were bridges to be built or rebuilt and White Oak Swamp to be crossed. Intelligence bearing on this problem was negligible; Pinkerton's people, although they may have had a few opportunities to interrogate prisoners or deserters, were preoccupied with their own move. So were Thaddeus Lowe and his assistant aeronauts; they were seriously delayed in obtaining transportation for the gas generators.

There was little fighting on June 28, but a rear-guard action broke out at Savage's Station on the railroad on the 29th, by which time McClellan had ridden on ahead, abandoning the direction of battles to his subordinates. It would now have been clear to Lee that McClellan's march was heading for the James; confirming evidence came on the 30th from a balloon observation made by Major Porter Alexander. Led down the James with the balloon tethered to a steamer, he discovered a Federal camp on Malvern Hill, a prominent height. (The Confederate balloonists' short career ended a few days later when the towboat ran aground and had to be abandoned, the balloon with it.) At this point a favorable configuration of the roads presented Lee with his best if not his only opportunity to attack the Federal columns in flank or rear. At a crossroads named Glendale on the 30th his planned envelopment of the Army of the Potomac by overwhelming numbers degenerated into a series of frontal assaults by a mere third of his assembled force. They wreaked destruction on elements of Sumner's and Heintzelman's corps, but the Federals had already succeeded in taking a crucial position on Malvern Hill, which had an excellent field of fire. Porter and Keyes were assembling their troops there, having sent their trains on ahead. As McClellan came by en route to the river on the 30th he inspected the hill and designated it as a temporary position, too far upstream to receive the navy's protection but ideal for standing off the enemy while the army's trains were making their way to Harrison's Landing, the new base.

Again Porter was in general command of the battle; McClellan, still exhausted emotionally, spent most of June 30 and July 1, the last of the Seven Days, at his new headquarters and with Commander John Rodgers aboard the *Galena*. When he returned to Malvern Hill before the fighting began, he took station on the far right, two miles from the action. Lee made repeated attacks, again failing to get some of his best units into the fight, and sustained severe losses while making no headway whatever. He retired to Richmond, and the Federals to Harrison's Landing. His losses in the Seven Days were 20,000; McClellan's, 16,000.[67]

·· ·· ··

In the following weeks McClellan's estimates of enemy numbers changed with dizzying frequency. He began by estimating Lee's effective strength as reduced to 150,000 by battle casualties.[68] Then late in July, when visited by the new general-in-chief, Henry W. Halleck, he raised this figure to the familiar 200,000. Now Lee was believed to have lost 40,000 in casualties and to have sent another 40,000 under Jackson's command to oppose a threat in the Culpeper-Gordonsville area posed by General John Pope, who had organized the Federals' Army of Virginia by assembling the commands of Banks, McDowell, and Frémont, Jackson's opponents in his spring campaign. Thus McClellan was claiming that in a matter of a few weeks Lee had replaced losses of 80,000. Crediting him with reinforcements on such a scale, and with such immediacy, bordered on fantasy.

Having raised his own effective strength to 90,000, McClellan offered to resume his advance on Richmond if he could have 30,000 more. Halleck said only 20,000 could be raised, and McClellan agreed to go with that number. But when Halleck returned to the War Department he found a letter from McClellan that made a mockery of their agreement. Now McClellan was asking to be reinforced by troops that had gained extensive lodgments on the coast of North and South Carolina plus 15,000 or 20,000 from the West. The 20,000 requirement had grown to more than 50,000. The result, ten days later, was the administration's decision to withdraw the Army of the Potomac from the Peninsula.

Halleck does not seem to have challenged McClellan's statements about enemy strength, even though Little Mac at first was saying he would be willing to attack 200,000 well-entrenched troops with a force of 120,000, and even with 110,000. Halleck reported to Stanton that he had "had no time or opportunity to investigate the facts on which these estimates were based."[69]

With his campaign in collapse, McClellan suddenly changed his attitude about enemy strength. He gave ear to a report from one of his cavalry generals, Alfred Pleasonton, that the force in front of Richmond had been depleted, by casualties and by Jackson's detachment, to 36,000, an underestimate of perhaps 20 or 25 percent. He was claiming, in effect, that a Richmond army he had numbered at 200,000 late in July had now, in a little over two weeks, lost 164,000 of those men; this was the most irrational of all his numerical fantasies. He invited Halleck to change his orders so as to permit an advance on Richmond.

But the Blue Ridge region had become a major concern again, Jackson having just defeated a sizable portion of Pope's army at Cedar Mountain. If Jackson was being half as heavily reinforced as McClellan's new total for Lee indicated, Pope urgently needed McClellan's idle troops. His orders to withdraw from the Peninsula stood.[70]

At this same period, mid-August, Pinkerton had information pointing in the same direction as Pleasonton's. He reported Lee's forces reduced to 80,000, from a total of 200,000 reached during the Seven Days. He listed enemy casualties at 40,000, double the true number, and reported 80,000 troops added to Jackson's army. This tripled his previous estimate of Jackson's force, which itself had doubled the true number, 21,000.[71]

The 200,000 Pinkerton gave as Lee's total in the Seven Days was part of a retrospective report he delivered August 14 as McClellan's army was beginning its withdrawal. This report showed the Confederates with 46 brigades in those battles (against a true figure of 39); 226 regiments (true figure, 178); and 108 batteries and other smaller units. Despite its inclusion of numerous units that were not part of the Army of Northern Virginia, this was a striking improvement over Pinkerton's previous tabulation of units. It was the product of interrogations of hundreds of prisoners and deserters received during and after the battles. However, the 200,000 figure was based not on the number of regiments but on Pinkerton's ever handy "general estimates." He had eight of these in terms definite enough or inclusive enough to be used in getting an average for the whole army, and the average they yielded was 198,000. The records describe the sources of only two of these well enough for us to make a guess as to their reliability: an Englishman who had been a printer at a Richmond newspaper and a group of Federal officers who had escaped a Richmond prison and whose information was reported in only these words: "Rebel army estimated at 250,000 by the people of Richmond."[72]

In the ten months since Pinkerton had begun producing estimates of enemy strength, this August 14 report with its 200,000 Confederate troops was the only one to reach the enemy total McClellan was currently claiming. That Pinkerton finally succeeded in overtaking his chief's estimates invites the suspicion that he doctored this computation in order to echo McClellan. But he probably did not see copies of McClellan's reports to Washington, and the 198,000 average strongly suggests that he rounded off to 200,000 a figure that was only a rough average to begin with.

When he published his Civil War memoirs in 1883, Pinkerton included a nineteen-page appendix listing the "Rebel Forces Before Richmond," giving the brigade assignments of the regiments and the division assignments of the brigades. This tabulation gives every indication of being an unedited copy of a working record that had been in daily use by Pinkerton's staff during and after the Seven Days.[73] It reveals a respectably complete and accurate reconstruction of the Confederate organization. Of Lee's 39 infantry brigades, 36 were fully identified; 6 other brigades were listed, 3 of which, had their correct names been known, probably would have raised the 36 to a complete 39. And the 211 regiments that were listed included every one of the 178 regiments Lee had.[74] The most visible error in this array of data was the listing of 33 regiments that were not in the Army of Northern Virginia. While not misleading as to enemy organization, it fattened the apparent size of the army by nearly 20 percent. Still, 33 "wrong" regiments may be forgiven in a list that did not miss a single one of 178 "right" ones.

The conclusion Pinkerton drew from his remarkably complete list of enemy regiments eliminates any hope of finding some degree of rationality in his estimating method. He could not know that the regiments he had identified included every one that Lee had, but he could see that the enemy brigades were well filled out with identified regiments, and the divisions with identified brigades. However, instead of perceiving these facts as an indication of the completeness of his information on the composition of Lee's army, he contended that the large number of identifications meant that the Confederates must have an even larger army than had been supposed. To insist that there were large numbers of enemy units that he had no record of had always defied logic; now it was utterly irrational. What brigades and divisions did these unknown units belong to? He had received many, many reports about units in every one of the ten enemy divisions on his chart; could there be additional divisions from which he had never had a prisoner or a deserter, and about whose existence he had never received a breath of rumor?

Apparently the enemy had a phantom army on the field; Pinkerton cautioned that the 200,000 figure "must . . . be taken as below even a minimum estimate."[75] On this note Federal intelligence in the Peninsula campaign closed.

7

· · · · · · · · · · ·

HARD LESSONS FROM
PROFESSOR JACKSON

August 1861–June 1862

MARYLAND COUNTIES along the upper Potomac, a region of closely divided allegiances, came under McClellan's command with his arrival in Washington in midsummer of 1861. Across the Potomac from that region is the mouth of the Shenandoah Valley, whose occupation was one of the Federals' main objectives. The Valley was a shielded route by which a Southern army could cross the Potomac and get in rear of Washington, and keep its supplies coming from Richmond during a protracted invasion of the North. The presence of a Confederate army in the Valley compelled the Federals to keep a matching force in its path, thus reducing the size of the army they could send against Richmond. And if the Confederates' Valley troops should be needed at Richmond, they would have an inside track to get there well ahead of their erstwhile Valley opponents.

To these facts of geography was added a circumstance equally disadvantageous for the Union: in November 1861 the Valley came under the command of the Virginia Military Institute's eccentric former professor Stonewall Jackson, the one officer who needed watching more than any other in the Confederate service and at the same time was harder *to* watch.

Jackson's chief opponent was Major General Nathaniel Prentiss Banks, who had received command of Robert Patterson's Valley army and was stationed at Frederick, eighteen miles from Harper's Ferry. South of Banks were General Charles Stone's division, looking across the Potomac at the Confederate force occupying Leesburg, and, farther upriver, a division under the command of Brigadier General Frederick W. Lander. Like Stone, Lander had had a hand in the touch-and-go proceedings of the secession winter. Forty years old and a veteran surveyor of western lands marked out for railroad development, he had been sent to offer

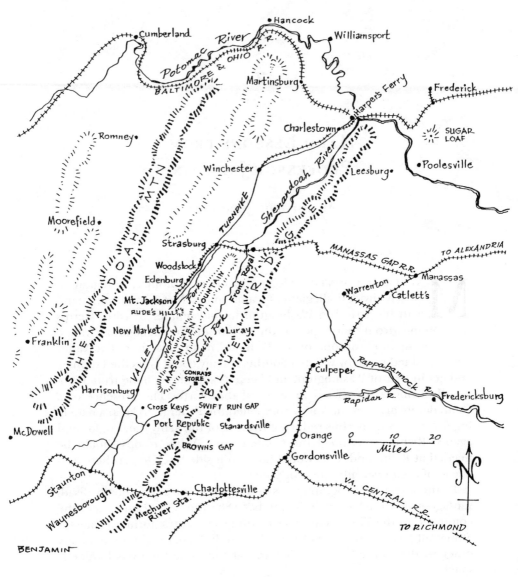

SHENANDOAH VALLEY

Sam Houston, the loyal governor of Texas, the support of United States troops. The offer was too late; the insurgents had taken over the state.[1]

Stone began by naming his command Corps of Observation. Upon arriving at Poolesville in mid-August he found that from nearby heights he could look in on enemy camps between the Potomac, five miles away, and Leesburg; thus the name turned out to be well chosen. Long-distance surveillance, later expanded by one of Professor Lowe's balloons, would be the chief element in Stone's intelligence program. He did not feel the need of spies; the Potomac River, his pickets, and his facilities for viewing the countryside protected him against surprise by the enemy. On one island in the river his pickets were within forty yards of the enemy's, a closeness that would have encouraged pickets' proclivity for exchanging military news. A Virginia militiaman who had served under the balloon's observation told the Federals that its occupants "must have had a full view of the fortifications" at Leesburg. Thus Stone could consider his sources of information adequate for defensive purposes, and it was unnecessary for him to seek intelligence for offensive operations since the Rebels' Leesburg post would be abandoned whenever the Federals began their expected occupation of the lower Valley.

Not only were Stone's intelligence needs quite simple; his intelligence activities were limited by McClellan's order restricting division commanders' questioning of prisoners, deserters, and refugees to matters of local concern. Comprehensive examination of such persons was to be performed by Pinkerton's bureau. A further limitation on Stone's coverage was the fact that routes used by some deserters and refugees to escape from Leesburg evaded his pickets by crossing the Potomac to points occupied by Banks's command.

One of the refugees whose route eluded Stone was an especially rich source, a young Ohioan named Jacob M. Shorb. He had come to Leesburg in April 1861 to collect a debt and had been prevented from leaving, though not forced into Confederate service. He supplied Pinkerton's interrogator with twelve pages of military data, including such minutiae as the names of farms where the Southerners were camped and details regarding General Hill's fortifications and their armament that could not have been obtained from the balloon. He described three routes by which, he believed, "an army can approach within a quarter of a mile of Leesburg before coming in range of their batteries."

The most useful fact yielded by balloon observation was that the force at Leesburg was small. It consisted of four Mississippi infantry regiments and a Virginia battery manning eight guns — 2490 men. Stone noted that Hill tried to put a better face on his numerical strength: "Officers bearing a flag of truce . . . took pains to boast that [Hill] had ten thousand Mississippi and Alabama troops." And Hill sent Stone a newspaper containing a statement, which Stone properly doubted but considered worth investigating, that a brigade led by General G. W. Smith was near by. But these little shams did not cost Hill any respect in Stone's eyes; he wrote, "It was the intention of the enemy to abandon Leesburg when Hill assumed command. He is a cool and good soldier and saw all the strong points of the position, and listening to influential men there, induced the chief of Rebellion to hold the position."[2]

Lander, as Stonewall Jackson's near neighbor, felt it necessary to provide himself with secret-service funds and an organization of citizen spies headed by one Charles Tull. No reports by Tull have been located, but Lander's correspondence indicates that he was not troubled by lack of information on the enemy. He stated confidently that he was opposed by half of Jackson's army, numbering 2500, on its winter expedition in western Virginia. That estimate was so accurate — Jackson's February return showed 5267 present for duty in the full army — that we conclude that unless Lander or Tull simply made a lucky guess, Tull had at least one very good source. Lander's closest brush with Stonewall occurred February 6, when he received a demand from Jackson that he evacuate Hancock, where he was headquartered, or face a shelling that would destroy private property. At the hour when he reported the incident to Banks, Lander's refusal of the demand stood unpunished. Jackson's half-army was not Lander's only concern; much of his energy was devoted to defending the Baltimore and Ohio tracks against demolition and pillage.[3]

Banks, who had been employing civilian spies, added to his intelligence capabilities by outbidding another general for the services of David Hunter Strother, newly commissioned as a captain and soon to be advanced to lieutenant colonel. Again Strother was needed for topographical duties, but now his knowledge of the Valley and its people would be applied to intelligence work uncensored by a Colonel Porter or a General Patterson.[4] At the same time, however, intelligence activity in Banks's command received a setback when his chief spy, George Rohr, was tricked by a false flag of truce into crossing the Potomac and received a fatal wound.[5]

.. .. ..

Lander, whose health was so frail that he had talked of resigning, died of pneumonia after sharing the midwinter exposures his troops suffered in tracking Jackson's expedition into western Virginia.[6] And Stone was lost to the army by incurring the wrath of the Joint Committee on the Conduct of the War. His troubles had begun in October when he was made a scapegoat for the defeat at Ball's Bluff. That debacle and the death of Colonel Edward Baker, leader of the attack, were caused by Baker's blundering in exceeding Stone's orders, but Baker's colleagues in Congress (he was a senator from Oregon) preferred to suspect that the misdirection of the battle grew out of a treasonable design on the part of General Stone. He had attracted suspicion by so rigorously enforcing the legal requirement for returning runaway slaves to their owners that it came to the attention of the Republican Radicals. Slaves, refugees, and deserters told Pinkerton's interrogators that Stone was rated a "nice man" and a "perfect gentleman" by the secessionist element of Loudoun County.

Secretary Stanton gave in to the Radicals and on January 28 ordered Stone arrested. McClellan pocketed the order for more than a week, but his hand was forced by the appearance of the most damning evidence against Stone yet received — a report that he had been maintaining a friendship with Confederate officers under flags of truce. The source of this claim was Jacob Shorb, Leesburg's unwilling visitor from Ohio. Stone, without being allowed to confront his accusers, hear the evidence against him, or receive a copy of charges, was arrested and confined in military prisons in New York harbor. Six months later he was released, but only after Congress passed a law prohibiting detention of a member of the armed forces for more than thirty days without formal charges. Finally allowed by the congressional committee to read the testimony against him, Stone demolished it point by point.

By including that hearing in its report on the Ball's Bluff affair, the committee exonerated Stone, indirectly but publicly. Their vindication came too late to save his military career. Both McClellan and, months later, Hooker applied for his services and were refused by Stanton. He did not obtain an assignment until General Banks, leading a campaign on the Red River in Louisiana in 1863, acquired his services. But Stanton in 1864 allowed, or caused, his demotion from volunteer brigadier general to regular army colonel. Again without an assignment, Charles Stone still felt the suspicion that had hung over him for two years, and he resigned from the army. Thus the man who had been a major figure in saving the government by purging Washington of disloyal militia in 1861 became one of the most tragic figures of the war by falling under a cloud of doubted loyalty himself a year later.[7]

. .   . .   . .

It was General Banks's lot to make the first move in McClellan's long-awaited campaign. In the last days of February his divisions crossed the Potomac, unopposed, to Harper's Ferry, which had been in a state of near-neglect by both sides. Banks, a former Speaker of the House of Representatives and governor of Massachusetts, possessed more military ability than most political generals, but the campaign he was undertaking against Stonewall Jackson was one that would tax the mettle of a general of much greater experience than Banks possessed.

The chief intelligence question of the moment was when and where the Federal advance up the Valley would begin to meet resistance. Jackson was at Winchester; Strother, believing he would not put up a fight to hold the place, sent a Negro acquaintance from Harper's Ferry to investigate. Later the same day, setting out for a walk with the general,

Strother heard his name called by a prisoner passing by under escort of a guard with fixed bayonets. The prisoner turned out to be his scout, who had just returned with confirmation of Strother's belief that Winchester was so weakly held that its occupation probably would not be opposed. That was correct; Jackson had been under instructions to "delay the enemy only as long as you can." When Banks's troops moved in on March 12, a citizen in a welcoming group warned Strother, "Well, Sir, they [the Rebels] have been longing to get you. Take care of yourself."[8]

Strother was kept busy at Harper's Ferry and Charlestown helping his friends and neighbors get relief from various difficulties raised by the presence of Federal soldiers, notably their fondness for pigs and chickens. One of the estates he saved from depredation belonged to a quartermaster in the Confederate army, Fred Briscoe. There Strother received another warning; Briscoe had sent one of his servants to tell the Virginia Yankee that he had been "denounced" among the locals for his service in Patterson's army, and now he would be wise to "keep out of the way."

Strother also crossed paths with another old friend now in the Confederate service, one Dick Staub, a lieutenant in Jackson's cavalry led by Colonel Turner Ashby. Taken prisoner and brought in for questioning, Staub enlightened Banks's officers by verifying a story previously told to them by one of their scouts who had been captured by the Rebels and had escaped, he claimed, by persuading his captors that his entire company wanted to desert to the Confederates; he had promised to go back to Banks's army and bring his fellows through the lines to the service of Dixie. In the Confederate ranks such trickery was known as "Yankeeing"; Staub claimed he was the only one of Ashby's officers who had not been Yankeed.[9]

· ·   · ·   · ·

The opening engagement in Jackson's Valley campaign, fought on March 23 at Kernstown, just south of Winchester on the Valley Pike, ended in victory for the Federals, the only one they would ever score on Stonewall Jackson. The battle grew out of intelligence mistakes on both sides, though they were much less complex than the comedy of errors that had removed the main armies from the Manassas front two weeks earlier. Banks's cavalry, unable to penetrate the screen maintained by Ashby, concluded somehow that there was no infantry behind the enemy cavalry, and so reported to Banks. Assuming that Jackson had left the Valley — a move that Federal generals would report hopefully time after time — or that in any case he was too weak to cause serious trouble, Banks began moving eastward to add his forces to McClellan's.

Banks's getaway meant to Jackson that he had failed in his mission. Anxious to settle for a lesser success if necessary, he now took his turn at receiving misinformation and acting on it. Ashby brought word from Winchester that only four regiments of Federal infantry remained there. In fact there was in the vicinity the whole of Lander's huge division of 9000 men, now commanded by Major General James Shields, a former U.S. senator and political associate of President Lincoln's at Springfield. On March 23 a hurried advance brought Jackson up with the enemy at Kernstown, close neighbor of Winchester. The day was Sunday, but such was the apparent opportunity to smite the enemy that Jackson put his piety in abeyance and attacked. He was soundly beaten — but his tactical defeat brought a strategic gain, for Banks now abandoned his move to join McClellan. Jackson's army of not over 5300 was holding enemy forces perhaps four times its own size in the Valley. He also caused Lincoln to look to the safety of Washington by holding McDowell's First Corps at Fredericksburg, disrupting McClellan's plans on the Peninsula. And that was not the limit of the Federals' strategic readjustments; one of McDowell's divisions, Louis Blenker's, was sent on a long march into western Virginia to reinforce the army of Major General John Charles Frémont, which stood behind the Alleghenies as a menace to Jackson's left flank.[10]

After the defeat at Kernstown Jackson withdrew up the Valley Pike for the second time in less than a month and settled in a naturally strong position on Rude's Hill, a ridge between Mount Jackson and New Market. Banks followed at an unthreatening distance to Strasburg, a convenient point for receiving supplies and troops via the Manassas Gap Railroad, which was now in Federal possession but required extensive rebuilding. He began entrenching at Strasburg, so that the place would "command absolutely the valley from mountain to mountain." Then he advanced to Woodstock and Edinburg, and by April 6 had pinpointed the enemy's position at Rude's Hill. He reported that Jackson's army was suffering from depression of spirit and was "not in condition to attack, neither to make strong resistance." But Banks made no move to take advantage of this supposed weakness.[11]

Banks's unusual precision in locating the Rebels' position and in reporting their condition mark the information as coming from an enemy soldier, probably a deserter. Intelligence-gathering by Banks's cavalry, led by Brigadier General John P. Hatch, was hampered by the cavalry screen and tight picketing certain to be found in an army led by Jackson. In the contest for intelligence Stonewall also enjoyed the advantage conferred by his penchant for deception and his habit of secrecy so extreme that even his immediate subordinates and nearly all of his staff were regularly kept in the dark as to his plans.

By April 15 Banks had detected a further withdrawal of the enemy. Four days later he reported that he believed Jackson had "left this valley yesterday." He was echoed by General Shields, who informed Stanton, "Jackson is flying from this department." Banks's misinformation came from a prisoner new to the Valley, a member of a detachment from General Richard S. Ewell's division, then being added to Jackson's army. In fact Stonewall had moved a considerable distance southward and had stopped on the western slope of the Blue Ridge, at a crossroads called Conrad's Store, near Swift Run Gap, where the road between Harrisonburg and Gordonsville crosses the ridge. His position there was discovered by Signal Corpsmen on the 24th, but Banks continued to believe he was east of the mountains until the 27th, when Hatch led the cavalry on an unaccustomed reconnaissance in force. He obtained "a complete and satisfactory view of the enemy's position." That dispelled the belief that Jackson was gone, but the next day the hope of his early departure was restored when Banks telegraphed Stanton, "A negro employed in Jackson's tent came in this morning, and reports preparation for retreat of Jackson to-day." This man's visit surely was a ploy intended by Jackson to disguise his next move, though at this point, April 28, he had not decided what that would be. By the 30th Banks had come again to the belief that Jackson's retreat was under way; in two telegrams to Stanton he insisted that "there is nothing more to be done by us in the valley" and "they are all concentrating for Richmond."[12]

Meanwhile Banks advanced along the Valley Pike, first to New Market and on April 26 to Harrisonburg, his forward element reaching within eight miles of Staunton, the most important town in the upper Valley. Other of his troops edged eastward to a point within six miles of Jackson's position. No clash of arms resulted, but Lincoln and Stanton stepped into the situation with a warning to Banks that he was getting too far from his supports and that he might lose Shields's division, needed by McDowell, whose occupation of the Fredericksburg area was being resisted by as much force as General Johnston could spare from his Peninsula defenses. On May 1 Lincoln ordered Banks to withdraw to Strasburg; Banks made a prolonged stop halfway, at New Market.[13]

Jackson on April 30 had begun a movement that simulated the Richmond move his opponents kept expecting; his real intentions lay in the opposite direction. His immediate concern was a threat to Staunton by General Robert Milroy's brigade of Frémont's small army. Milroy was posted twenty-two miles northwest of Staunton. Jackson, after an exchange of letters with General Lee in which they discussed resuming the offensive in the Valley, conceived a complex plan to combine with Staunton's defenders, a brigade led by General Edward Johnson, and drive Milroy back into the Alleghenies. The controlling feature of the plan was the need to prevent Banks from learning of the movement in time to interfere in operations around Staunton.

Leaving Ewell's division and Ashby's cavalry to hold Banks and Shields in check, Jackson headed toward Staunton, then turned southeast at Port Republic and crossed the Blue Ridge May 4 at Brown's Gap. Collected east of the mountains at the Mechum River railroad station were locomotives and cars; the sight of them confirmed for the troops the belief that they were headed for Richmond. But once the trains were well filled, they moved off not toward Richmond but westward, over the mountains, to Staunton. The rail movement took two days.

Stonewall had made his thirty-five-mile march over the Blue Ridge and to the railroad deliberately without concealment. At Staunton Jacksonian secrecy came back into force, with pickets and sentries posted on all the roads leading north and instructed to allow absolutely no one to pass.[14]

Banks failed to live up to Stonewall's expectations; perversely he remained unaware of the carefully arranged, unconcealed march over the mountains. By observing Jackson's march as far as Port Republic and missing the part that simulated a move to Richmond, he concluded that Jackson was heading for Staunton or neighboring Waynesborough; he perceived that Jackson's "march is possibly . . . to join Johnson and attack Milroy." Jackson's ruse was wasted because he had credited Banks with cavalry energetic enough to watch the gaps in the Blue Ridge. Probably he also hoped that Banks would learn of the assemblage of engines and cars at Mechum River. Stonewall had outsmarted himself; like many another commander, he overrated the enemy's intelligence prowess.

In addition to his basically correct understanding of the direction and purpose of Jackson's movement, Banks had a good idea of its size ("not over 8000"), and he had pinpointed Ewell's position. But serious errors beclouded his view. Somehow he had acquired the belief that Jackson's command was "greatly demoralized and broken." He reported as late as May 4 that Jackson was still at Port Republic. He learned of the crossing of the Blue Ridge in good time, May 5, but understood that Jackson was clinging to the east side of the ridge. On May 7, when Jackson completed his junction with Johnson west of Staunton, Banks believed he was at Harrisonburg. Two more days passed before Shields, who was moving with Banks, reported Jackson's rail trip to Staunton, and he understood Waynesborough, in the Valley, to have been the entraining point.[15]

Milroy, perceiving that his threat to Staunton was itself threatened by Jackson's move to Port Republic, on May 6 had sent Frémont a call for reinforcement. The plea brought, in two days, a small brigade headed by General Robert Schenck, who marched his troops thirty-four miles in less than a day and arrived before Jackson and Johnson could attack. Schenck immediately led his fatigued troops up a rocky hillside and assailed the enemy. In this engagement, fought on May 8 and known as the battle of McDowell, the Union forces gave a good account of themselves but were badly overmatched; unable to hold the field, they retired into western Virginia. Jackson had now relieved the upper Valley.[16]

.. .. ..

By this time McClellan had occupied Yorktown and fought the Williamsburg battle that speeded Johnston's retirement to the defenses of Richmond. Anxious to silence his pleading for reinforcements, Lincoln and Stanton had sent one of McDowell's divisions, Franklin's, to him from Washington. Now that Shields was about to move to McDowell's department, they made definite plans to join that general's entire command to the Peninsula army. Banks, thus reduced to 8600 troops, took station behind his entrenchments at Strasburg on May 13.[17] To guard his left flank he sent the First Maryland Infantry and a few other troops, totaling scarcely 1000, to Front Royal, ten miles to the east. This was a sensitive spot because his rail and telegraph lines entered the Shenandoah Valley there, and the town was open to attack from the south through the narrow Luray Valley, lying between the Blue Ridge and Massanutten Mountain, a ridge that runs for thirty-five miles down the Shenandoah Valley and divides it in half lengthwise.

Although he had been permitted to shift from an offensive to a defensive posture, Banks found his new situation far from comfortable. On May 21 he outlined his problem in a telegram, and the next day he set it out at length in a letter to Stanton, meanwhile sending Colonel John Clark to the War Department to ask for reinforcements. "I have no doubt," his letter said, "that Jackson's force is near Harrisonburg and that Ewell still remains at Swift Run Gap. Their united force is about 16,000," against which, with Shields gone to Fredericksburg, he could oppose only 6000. The estimate of Jackson's numbers was quite accurate, but the statement of his position was outdated, as Banks learned later in the day. Jackson had advanced to New Market. Of the report of his new position, Strother wrote, "If true, we are liable to attack at any moment."

Banks was now dissuaded of his hopeful belief that the Confederates had left the Valley. He now believed that "The persistent adherence of Jackson to the defense of the [Shenandoah] valley and his ... purpose to expel the Government troops from this country if in his power may be assumed as certain. There is probably no one more fixed and determined purpose in the whole circle of the enemy's plans. . . . I am compelled to believe that he meditates attack here."[18]

Before this gloomy prophecy could reach Stanton, it was fulfilled. Early in the afternoon of May 23 there burst upon Colonel John R. Kenly's little outpost at Front Royal the full force of what was to become a typical Jackson surprise attack. Forsaking the Valley Pike, the route to Banks's main front, Stonewall had crossed Massanutten Mountain from New Market to Luray; there he joined his division to Ewell's and turned north. Meanwhile Ashby's cavalry continued, as a feint, their march on the Valley Pike. Jackson's infantry fell on Front Royal without warning.[19]

He had the good fortune to arrive but an hour or two before two companies of cavalry — the warning facilities that Banks wanted Kenly to have — were to arrive from Strasburg. Thus Stonewall was able to achieve complete surprise.[20] Kenly, because he was altogether without cavalry, was not equipped to get word quickly from his more distant pickets.

While the magnitude of the assault was still unrealized by Banks, Jackson swept Kenly out of the way and was threatening the line of retreat of Banks's main force at Strasburg. But Banks, moving rapidly, gained the safety of Winchester on the 24th and elected to give battle there. Jackson drove him out the next day in an attack that was a model of perfection despite Stonewall's re-aroused misgivings about offensive action on the Sabbath. Banks, however, saved his command and much of his stores by retiring to Williamsport on the Maryland side of the Potomac. Although the retreat has sometimes been pictured as almost a rout, the unfortunate Banks was not panicked. Unlike many a general in his predicament, he gave an unexaggerated estimate of the enemy's strength and began immediately to prepare to recover the lost ground.[21]

· ·   · ·   · ·

The fighting at Front Royal left the Federals with a counterespionage problem complicated by a public-relations disaster. The press depicted Banks's army as the victim of espionage by an eighteen-year-old girl, Belle Boyd.

When Jackson's troops arrived at Front Royal's back door and the townspeople became aware of their presence, Belle, who was visiting kinfolk there, made her way to them across fields and over fences. "With the precision of a staff officer making a report" she told Brigadier General Richard Taylor what she knew of the defenders' numbers and positions, especially of artillery. (Jackson was too busy to talk to her.) As Taylor's brigade would lead the attack, and the close-mouthed Jackson had told him nothing about their objective, Taylor listened eagerly to Belle's breathless discourse.[22] His attack was an easy success.

Belle's audacious caper, which was witnessed by townspeople, was not long in coming to the attention of the press. On May 28 the *Philadelphia Inquirer* and the *New York Herald* printed identical accounts of the Valley action, describing Belle as an "accomplished prostitute." The highlight of the story was a Federal officer's statement that "An hour previous to the attack . . . Belle went out on a rise of ground south of the town, and was seen to wave her handkerchief toward the point from which the centre of the attack was made." It was "now known that she was the bearer of an extensive correspondence between the rebels inside and outside of our lines." This report was repeated in full in Washington's *Evening Star.* Belle, properly outraged, granted an interview to a *New York Tribune* correspondent, who corrected the other papers' assessment of her moral character but added that she was "certainly a provocator."[23]

Belle, finding life more interesting in Front Royal than back home in Martinsburg, remained there. By the time of Jackson's departure for Richmond in June, the Yankees had returned to the town and she was flirting flagrantly with their officers. Dr. Washington Duffee, a brigade surgeon, wrote to Secretary Stanton out of concern for his chief, a Dr. Rex. The "celebrated Belle Boyd the 'Rebel spy'" either had fallen in love with Rex or was "anxious to make a victim" of him. Duffee suggested that a skillful detective could easily trap "these rascals."

Pinkerton's Washington unit, headed by William H. Scott, was already at work on the case. Detective Alfred Cridge had interviewed Eugene Blockley of Alexandria, who apparently knew something of Belle's activities, and operatives B and E conducted an investigation at Front Royal. There was no action until July 18, when Cridge was ordered to Front Royal to arrest Belle Boyd and one William Dana. Twelve days passed before he returned to Washington with Belle in custody.

The cause of this delay may have been a need for evidence better than the newspaper reports. Such evidence is said to have been obtained by a Federal scout, C. W. D. Smitley, playing the role of a Confederate soldier headed homeward on parole, who agreed to deliver a letter Belle wrote to General Jackson. According to Smitley, that letter instead went to his chief, General Franz Sigel, stationed at Harper's Ferry. The story is entirely plausible, but neither the letter nor other incriminating papers Smitley is supposed to have seized in Belle's quarters are in the War Department's files on her.

No trial was held; this unrepentant female activist in the Rebel cause, if found guilty of espionage, would, like Rose Greenhow, be punished only by deportation to the Confederacy, and that could be done without trial. After a month in Old Capitol Prison Belle left for Richmond aboard a prisoner-exchange boat.[24]

The closest study Belle Boyd has ever received pronounced her "the Civil War's most over-rated spy," but the putdown was to no avail; eighteen years later the same authority found her "'The Pet of the Confederacy' still."[25] Skeptics argue, logically enough, that her celebrated scamper to aid Jackson was too public to qualify as espionage and that the reason Jackson attacked Front Royal was knowledge of its light defenses that he already had from his own sources; there was also the decisive fact that frontal attack on Strasburg would meet Banks's main force, protected by good fortifications. Jackson's information came from a spy named McVicar, whose skill and energy seem to have enabled him to cover considerable territory, working against the tight deadlines the general would have imposed. No skill or speed of movement, however, could assuredly have got the full details of Kenly's current positioning to Jackson at New Market by the time he decided to attack Front Royal.[26]

The Front Royal performance may have been the only significant feat in Belle Boyd's intelligence career. The stories of her other services are vague and undocumented. The leading one concerns her eavesdropping on a council of war held by General Shields. We can accept her story of having found a hole in the floor of a closet above the hotel room where the council met, but not her claim of taking down *in cipher* everything she heard. The whole story is lacking in particulars, especially the route of a very long midnight ride to locate Colonel Ashby and deliver her findings. And the rest of her history as spy and courier is even more barren of detail. Major Henry Kyd Douglas says that until the Front Royal affair, Jackson, who evidently dealt directly with his spies, had never heard of her.[27] One of her talents was the ability to get herself onto the front pages of the newspapers — not a very desirable quality in a spy. Had it not been for her public performance at Front Royal, the world would never have heard of Belle Boyd.

. .   . .   . .

The three-day clash at Front Royal and Winchester led to the most spectacular episode in the fast-moving Valley campaign, an attempt to trap Jackson, who had pursued Banks almost to the Potomac. Lincoln directed Frémont to cross the mountains from western Virginia to Harrisonburg and block the Confederates' line of retreat. He also halted McDowell's movement to the Peninsula and ordered him to move two divisions from Fredericksburg into the Valley. Banks's participation was a third possibility; one of his spies on May 31 had brought word of Jackson's unexpected tarrying at Winchester and Martinsburg.[28]

There was method in Stonewall's seemingly mad lingering near the Potomac. It posed a threat that he was going to cross onto Northern soil; he had no such intention, but the Federal troops assembled in anticipation of such a movement would be held in Maryland, reducing or even eliminating the chances of his entrapment. Word of the Federals' scheme reached his ears as early as the night of May 27–28, but he did not begin to leave his positions near the Potomac until the news became much more threatening on the 30th. By that time McDowell's leading elements, part of Shields's division, had swept into Front Royal. There was time for Shields to reach Strasburg ahead of the enemy, but his division had outrun the rest of McDowell's force and he could not risk sending his badly winded men against Jackson's whole army.[29]

Frémont, convinced that the state of his communications and supplies did not permit him to cross directly into the Valley, marched a considerable distance north before heading east. Thus he came into the Valley two days' march north of the point intended by Lincoln and Stanton. Instead of waiting for Jackson to appear from the north, Frémont now had to search for him. A Frémont army never lacked facilities for such purposes; he had brought from his command in Missouri an organization known as the Jessie Scouts, named for his wife, the daughter of Thomas Hart Benton, the leading figure in Missouri politics over several decades. The eastern armies' acquisition of this new intelligence capability was announced to the world by the *Wheeling Intelligencer*.[30] Captain John C. Hopper, Frémont's chief of scouts and spies, supplemented the Jessies by engaging a number of spies with experience in the Mountain Department, as Frémont's new command was called.

One of these men, John James Murphy, a propertied Virginian who had been recommended to Frémont by Governor Oliver Morton of Indiana, was selected to cross the mountains ahead of the army. He encountered enemy cavalry picketing the roads to the west of the Valley Pike. Passing them, he located their camp, secreted himself in a tree, and remained there eavesdropping until they withdrew a few hours later. Having detected the enemy's presence in the neighborhood, Murphy returned to his base, reported his discovery, then headed for Woodstock, where the pickets' conversation had indicated more details about Jackson's forces could be learned. The date was May 28 or 29, and Frémont, now within forty miles of his destination, Strasburg, was at least ten miles closer to that point than the bulk of Jackson's army, then positioned to maintain his pseudo-threat of an invasion of Maryland.

Murphy quickly found the Confederates at Woodstock, but with equal speed they spotted and arrested him. A Confederate officer told him that "Jackson would be certain to give me a collar of hemp for piloting the Yankees through the mountains, and acting as spy for them." Despite these suspicions Murphy after a few days was placed with Jackson's numerous ordinary military prisoners from Front Royal and Winchester and sent with them to Staunton. Weeks later he escaped by tricking his guards and obtained a pass from Jackson's provost marshal by representing himself as a refugee. Prudently he hastened to put distance between himself and Stonewall's army. Three months later he turned up at the Federal post at Gallipolis, Ohio, and reported to Frémont by letter.[31]

While McClellan and Johnston were fighting at Seven Pines on the last day of May, Jackson's "foot cavalry" was eating up many miles of the Valley Pike, heading south. On June 1 the Federals' trap closed on Strasburg from east and west, but Jackson was gone. The advance forces of both Frémont and Shields were fought off by the Confederate rear guard. Losing Murphy — who probably would have learned at Woodstock the whereabouts of Jackson's main force — had been costly: Frémont had given his army a full day's halt before entering the Valley, but with more

exact knowledge of enemy movements he would have resisted the impor-
tuning of his medical director, who had insisted that the men could go no
farther without rest.[32]

Murphy was not the only agent lost by Frémont in the effort to intercept Jackson. A spy named James J. Callahan went with a party of scouts
to learn the state of affairs at Strasburg as Frémont approached. They fell
in with Ashby's cavalry, and Callahan and one of the scouts were captured.[33]

Interception had failed, but Frémont pursued the Confederates up the
main Valley while Shields marched in parallel with them through the
Luray Valley. At Mount Jackson Frémont was overtaken by another civilian spy new to his service, Louis P. Stone, a Cincinnatian who, though
youthful-looking even for his nineteen years, was a veteran of several
months of espionage and scouting for Major General William S. Rosecrans, McClellan's successor in western Virginia.

Unlike the highly fictionalized memoirs that constitute the known
recollections of Civil War spies, a semi-official account of Stone's service
is in the records. It is mainly a report of a career as prisoner of several
Rebel commands. While working for Rosecrans he was sent in October
1861 on a trip to Wytheville, Virginia, 150 miles inside Confederate lines,
to locate possible routes to the Virginia and Tennessee Railroad. On his
return trip he was captured by a squad of Rebel cavalry belonging to the
army of Brigadier General John B. Floyd, who had been President Buchanan's secretary of war. Floyd sent Stone to Richmond, charged with
espionage. Five days before his trial was to begin he escaped, by means of
a deception that his report does not describe. Two months later, apparently confident that he could defeat the Confederates' security system a
second time, he wrote to Frémont asking employment "in the Secret
Service" of the "Path Finder." He was quickly hired.

From Mount Jackson Stone was started, along with several others,
toward the enemy's retreating lines. They accompanied the advance
of Frémont's column, which was exchanging shots with Jackson's rear
guard "every few moments." Soon a cavalry fight developed in which
the scouts were entirely surrounded by enemy but escaped by virtue of
wearing Confederate uniforms. They found that Jackson, upon reaching
the point where Massanutten Mountain ended — no longer separating
Frémont and Shields — had taken up a position at Cross Keys, where
several streams gave a measure of protection from both pursuing forces.
Stone's report claims that he was the one who discovered the enemy's
position.

Frémont attacked on June 8, but without success; the next day Stonewall went over to the offensive, assailing Shields's leading brigades at
nearby Port Republic and pushing them back on the rest of the division.[34] That action ended the Valley campaign of 1862.

Louis Stone's luck, after the scouting success at Cross Keys, was no better than that of Murphy and Callahan. As Frémont marched north-ward down the Valley, Stone undertook to scout along the left flank. "On the 11th of June," he wrote, "I started acrost from the mane Pike to a road running paralel with it about two miles back on the hills. I had got about half way over when I was serounded by Garrillas, taken prisoner with our Army on all sides of me." Although he was carrying a revolver and a Confederate cavalry saber, he told his captors that he was a phar-macist (which was true) and that he was wearing gray clothing because that color was the one least subject to staining by the chemicals pharma-cists handled. He was in the Valley, he claimed, because he had a brother in an Ohio regiment in Frémont's army who was sick and needed his assistance. This unlikely story seemed to be accepted, and Stone soon found other uses for it. "Not fifteen minutes after I was taken back [to Harrisonburg] a prisoner before the wohole town knew it and the Court houce was crowded . . . with people come to see one of Fremonts Scouts. They swore that I would be Hung as sure as hemp grew."

Again the inefficiency of Confederate provost marshals allowed Stone to lose himself among the Federal prisoners taken at Cross Keys. As a pharmacist he obtained a favored position as hospital steward in a huge prisoner-of-war camp at Lynchburg. There he inquired for his colleague James Callahan, and found him. They were soon transferred to Rich-mond, and Stone resumed the role of ordinary military prisoner. (As a hospital steward he would have had to work in the same building from which he had escaped months before while awaiting trial.) Callahan by now also had the status of prisoner of war; evidently the Confederates did not have enough evidence to try him as a spy. When a huge exchange of prisoners took place in September, Stone and Callahan were on the first boat that left Richmond. Transshipped to Annapolis, they obtained passes to Washington but were arrested there and jailed as deserters. Stone ended his report without explaining how the two men won release from this new set of provost marshals. He returned to Cincinnati, where he was sick for several months, and reported to Captain Hopper that he was detained at home for an indefinite time by the needs of his mother, his stepfather having died while serving as a navy officer.[35]

. . . . . .

After fighting off Frémont and Shields, Jackson placed his army at Brown's Gap in the Blue Ridge, from where it would be easy to withdraw to Richmond. His orders to join Lee soon came.[36] The Shenandoah Valley campaign is remembered for his successes in contending simul-taneously against three Federal forces — fighting when he could catch one of them at a disadvantage, outrunning them when he could not, and making everybody from Staunton to Washington wonder where he

would turn up next. These tactical successes, however, were merely incidental to two strategic objectives: in addition to impeding the reinforcement of McClellan, he staved off a planned campaign of Frémont's on
behalf of the strong Union element in East Tennessee.[37] Of the nine
Federal divisions in the Valley and at or near Fredericksburg, seven were
wanted on the Peninsula; only two ever got there — the same number
Jackson took to Lee, and Jackson's two divisions were equal in numbers
to four Federal divisions of normal size.[38]

Of the Union commanders who had the misfortune to oppose Jackson
in the Valley, only Banks confronted him long enough to show his mettle
in intelligence and related matters. His performance does not entirely
accord with the usual picture of him as an inept officer easily duped by
the Confederates. But the coolheadedness he manifested in defeat was
not evident in his handling of intelligence. The best example of this
deficiency is his several announcements that Jackson was leaving the
Valley; they were not supported by evidence that would have enabled
Lincoln and Stanton to believe that this time Banks had it right.

As a user of intelligence, Banks's main fault lay in not providing himself with enough of it. At no time did he have nearly enough spies and
scouts, though the Unionist population of the Valley was numerous
enough for him to have corrected this lack. He did not force aggressive
reconnaissance by his cavalry until late in April, and their increased
activity was only temporary. He believed that if he could have joined his
forces to Frémont's in the McDowell battle, "the valley would have been
cleared of the enemy from the Manassas Gap Railway to the Virginia
Central."[39] This was an impossibly big "if" when his scouting and spying
facilities were so limited and his cavalry was so poorly employed that
Jackson's crossing of the Blue Ridge went unobserved. In an army suffering inadequacies like these, only luck could have enabled Banks to discover Jackson's advance into the Luray Valley, a clear warning of his
attack via Front Royal. It gives Banks a left-handed compliment to say that
on May 22 he correctly predicted the attack and then to reveal that his
scouting up the main Valley was feeble and up the Luray Valley nonexistent. Evidently it was the writing of that prediction that produced in
him a full realization of his peril, for only after the letter was on its way to
Washington did he get around to sending cavalry to Front Royal.

Banks learned much during the campaign, for his instruction, coming
from Professor Jackson, was of the best. A bit of military knowledge he
could not have failed to pick up concerned the scope and intensity of
effort required in order to have an effective information service. But
even if he had known this at the outset, he might not have been able to
subdue a foe who marched so fast and who subordinated everything else
to the preservation of secrecy — and who would strike a blow for Southern liberty even on Sunday.

8

. . . .

TOO LITTLE AND TOO SOON

July–August 1862

T HERE WAS NO LACK of decisive intelligence findings when the armies returned to northern Virginia in midsummer. General Pope and General Lee each made a devastating discovery of the other's movements and purposes. The contest for information was about even, but the Federals' supply of it ran dry at a crucial time, and the Southern command remained the master of its adversary.

The Valley failures and McClellan's frustration on the Peninsula brought an important change in Washington. Abdicating as directors of field armies, Lincoln and Stanton brought Major General Henry Wager Halleck to Washington from his command in the Mississippi River theater and installed him as general-in-chief, which position had been vacant since McClellan was removed from it. In order to unify the three forces they had employed against Jackson, Lincoln and Stanton created the Army of Virginia, comprising three corps headed by Banks, Major General Sigel (who took over Frémont's divisions), and McDowell. In command of the new army they placed Major General John Pope, who had shared prominently in credit for the successes of the western armies.

Halleck was wanted for his technical knowledge as well as the administrative abilities he had shown. Author of a widely known book on military science, he would now add to his fame as a scholar, but at the expense of his reputation as an executive. His fondness for reflective pursuits soon resulted in an embarrassing incident. Seeking the solitude of wooded Lafayette Square, across Pennsylvania Avenue from the White House, he stayed too late one night and was locked in. The fence was too high for the climbing abilities of a major general of Halleck's proportions, but luckily the park contained a soldier in the same predicament. The younger man mounted Halleck's back, scaled the iron palings, and woke the keeper — and the general-in-chief was again a free man.[1]

Despite his knowledge and his impressive experience as a commander,

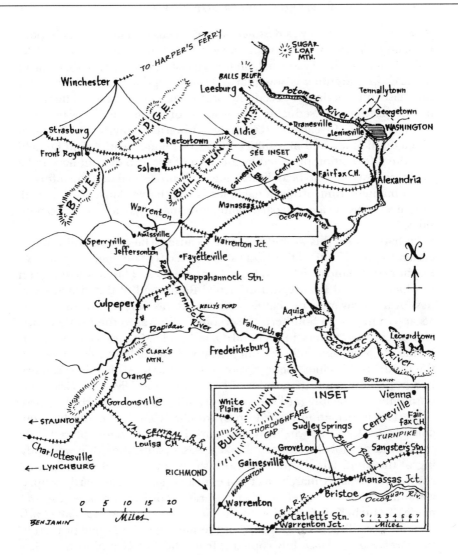

REGION OF SECOND BULL RUN CAMPAIGN

Halleck brought no new concepts of intelligence work. He did concern himself with such matters, personally serving the field armies — as did Lincoln and Stanton — as a clearinghouse for information on the enemy, and in the process applying his excellent intellect to its evaluation. But that was all; the War Department continued to do without an intelligence officer or bureau. In fact Halleck seems to have held views about espionage that would have made it awkward for him to organize such a bureau. He had published in 1861 a work entitled *International Law and the Laws of War,* which was destined to become as well known as his older book on military science. Late in the war he followed this with an article, published in a military journal, on the legal status of spies. In this, one of his principal arguments was that although a general could rightfully purchase information or accept the proffered services of a spy, he would not be justified in "seducing, by promise of reward, a fellow-being to commit an act of treachery [espionage] toward an enemy which makes him a felon at law and may subject him to a felon's death." And he held that the information provided by the kind of spy who did not have to be "seduced" was likely to be of little value: "It is proverbial that the information obtained from professional spies is unreliable. Moreover, they almost invariably act a *double* part, selling information, true or false, to both sides."[2]

Perhaps it was this attitude that had caused Halleck several months earlier to fumble one of the most valuable pieces of intelligence that ever fell into the hands of Federals or Confederates. This was a telegram in which General Beauregard informed Richmond of the dismal weakness of his army after the battle of Shiloh; it was obtained by the Federals apparently from Southern telegraphers disloyal to the Confederacy. Union cryptographers in General Ormsby M. Mitchel's command at Huntsville, Alabama, fully deciphered it, and Mitchel proudly forwarded the results to his chief, General Don Carlos Buell. At this time Halleck had in his command the armies of both Buell and Ulysses S. Grant, far outnumbering Beauregard's force twenty miles distant at Corinth, Mississippi. The information turned up by Mitchel's windfall could have enabled Halleck to overwhelm Beauregard, but he evidently placed little stock in it; possibly he suspected that it was a plant, though it was nothing of the kind. His advance on Corinth set a record for slowness that rivaled McClellan's march up the Peninsula, and Beauregard escaped without a scratch. Better — or at any rate more energetic — use was made of Mitchel's information by the Northern press. A *New York Herald* man at Nashville obtained a copy of the message, the *Herald* printed it, the *Richmond Examiner* duly copied it from the *Herald,* and within a few days Beauregard received a suggestion from General Lee that he change his cipher.[3]

In contrast with Halleck, Pope was a man of action, and he sailed vigorously into a host of problems.[4] They kept him from joining his army in the field for a full month, however; he was responsible for, among other things, the security of Washington, and he remained there, devoting part of the time to counseling with Lincoln and Stanton, until Halleck arrived late in July.

By that time the new Army of Virginia — Pope's army — had made considerable headway in an advance east of the Blue Ridge that was intended to draw off enemy strength from the Richmond front. The threat quickly attracted Jackson, who with his own division and Ewell's moved up the Virginia Central Railroad from Richmond and occupied the rail junction at Gordonsville on July 19, before Federal cavalry could get there.[5]

This time Jackson's movement was anything but secret, which suggests that his success in obscuring previous moves had depended on measures not available to him at Richmond, where word passed quickly from mouth to mouth and where he could not order affairs for miles around to suit his single object of secrecy. The Federals began picking up rumors of his detachment from the main army three days before he left the capital, and after he reached the vicinity of Gordonsville such reports were received daily. They came from a spy who had visited Richmond; from Banks's cavalry, operating in the vicinity of Gordonsville after being denied possession by the earlier arrival of the Confederates; from cavalry that had marched south from Fredericksburg to break up the Virginia Central; from McClellan's headquarters and from the local commander at remote Norfolk; from contrabands; and from a refugee Frenchman who made a nine-day trip from Richmond into the Federal lines by way of Gordonsville.[6]

Of all these sources, the one producing the best information was a cavalry detachment, the First (West) Virginia Regiment, sent by Banks toward Louisa Court House to break up the Virginia Central. Confederate forces blocked the raid, but the raiders made the expedition pay by ascertaining definitely that the enemy in the neighborhood was Jackson's army, that Stonewall had dined at the town that afternoon, the 19th, and that he had "left with 10,000 or 12,000 . . . for Gordonsville," placing a rear guard of 3500 at Louisa.[7]

The spy whose report was received at this time was Charles Whitlock, a native of Connecticut and a resident of the Shenandoah Valley. Sent out early in July by General John Geary, a brigade commander in McDowell's corps, Whitlock went to the enemy capital and remained there until the 17th. His return to the army at the very time of Jackson's movement should have meant a good yield of information, but it did not. Because the direct route from Richmond to Whitlock's announced destination (his home, near Staunton) was being used by Jackson's troops, he was forced to travel by way of Lynchburg and Charlottesville. En route he learned of Jackson's presence at Gordonsville and set out for that place. But before getting a look at any of the Southern troops in the vicinity, he encountered Union cavalry scouts and availed himself of their protection to proceed to headquarters with the information he then had. It was seriously inaccurate as to Jackson's strength, which Whitlock overstated at 30,000.[8]

This report conflicted with the preponderance of the Federals' information, which gave Jackson only his own division and Ewell's. As Jackson's force was thus seen to be essentially the same as he had had in the Valley during the spring, Pope believed Stonewall's true strength to be much lower than the figure given by Whitlock (Jackson in fact had about 12,000). So by July 21, two days after Jackson reached Gordonsville, Pope had a fairly accurate understanding of the force facing him and of its position. (Nevertheless, so expert a student of these campaigns as Freeman calls Jackson's move to Gordonsville "an admirable example of the manner in which rapid troop movements could be conducted secretly during the War between the States.")[9]

. .   . .   . .

The legalistic General Halleck may have thought planned espionage a doubtful policy, but in the days immediately preceding his arrival at Washington his subordinate John Pope thoroughly committed the Army of Virginia to that policy. Between July 20 and 23 there issued from Pope's headquarters a stream of telegrams instructing his subordinates to make the utmost effort to obtain information; he would rely, it was clear, on spies as much as on cavalry reconnaissance. "Spare no means through spies and others to inform yourself of the movements of the enemy's cavalry in the valley," he wired the commander at Winchester. "Send out some scouts and spies to ascertain if there is a considerable force of the enemy in the neighborhood of Staunton or east of Staunton" was his instruction to General Sigel. General McDowell at Warrenton was also told to employ scouts and spies: "I hope you will use every means and spare no money to get information." Even more explicit instructions in the same vein went to General Banks, whose corps, posted around Sperryville, was nearest the enemy.[10]

McDowell repeated these orders to his subordinates, then proceeded to act on them himself. He obtained the services of one Richard Montgomery, who until recently had had a "good situation" in Washington. The records show that in Montgomery's case Pope's instruction to "spare no money" was met with more enthusiasm than he may have wished. Montgomery claimed as much as three dollars' reimbursement for a single meal and proportionately generous amounts for lodging, stabling, forage, and horseshoeing. His ability to pay such prices in the relatively remote Piedmont country would have seemed suspect to its natives. But he managed to stay out of trouble except for one occasion, when he had the unusual experience of being arrested by order of a chaplain — whether Federal or Confederate he did not say.

Montgomery's later activities suggest that he would have been capable of compiling a highly imaginative expense account. In 1864 he became a double agent, acting as a courier between Jefferson Davis and the Confederate "commissioners" in Canada, stopping in Washington, going and coming, to allow his dispatches to be copied in the War Department. As one of the dispatches he carried, in October 1864, was very probably a plant, it appears that Davis had become aware of Montgomery's double dealing and was using it to work a deception on his Washington adversaries. That dispatch mentioned that General James Longstreet was leading a strong reinforcement to the aid of General Jubal A. Early, whose Shenandoah Valley army was heavily engaged with General Philip Sheridan's forces. But no reinforcements were planned for Early, and Longstreet was in Georgia nearing the end of a five-month convalescence from a battle wound. The same false information was planted on Sheridan in a flag-signal message sent by Early's signalmen and duly intercepted by the Federals.

Montgomery's doubtful character is further indicated by testimony he gave in the trial of John Wilkes Booth's accomplices in the Lincoln assassination. He told a story of the linkage between the Confederate commissioners in Canada and the plotters against Lincoln, thus aiding the prosecution's effort to implicate the Confederate government in the assassination. Montgomery's testimony stretched the facts, though not on the same grand scale as other witnesses did (the discovery of their perjury effectively destroyed the case against the Confederate leaders).[11]

Early in August Montgomery left Warrenton for Gordonsville. "From this trip," he later wrote, "I brought not only the number of Jackson's force at Mechanicsburg, but the number and exact disposition of the force under General Ewell at Liberty Mills — even the points at which pickets were stationed. I reached Genl. Pope with this information within 24 hours after I left Genl. Ewell's camp. A few days shewed that I had neither exaggerated the rebel strength, nor misrepresented his intentions." McDowell later said that Montgomery overrated the value of his information, but the general probably did not know that the locations the spy gave for both Ewell and Jackson were exactly right.[12] Thus it may be that the expense account, if it was a piece of fiction, was the only doubtful item yielded by Montgomery's trip. His records do not show whether he learned that A. P. Hill's big division had just come from Richmond and was also at Mechanicsburg. The 12,000 men Hill brought probably were covered, however, in the estimate of Jackson's total strength that Montgomery indicates he provided. That figure does not appear in his records; presumably he delivered it orally.

Another spy, unnamed in the records, was sent out by General Rufus King at Fredericksburg on July 31 and returned two days later, having passed through Louisa Court House to within a few miles of Gordonsville. This was the very time when Hill was arriving near Gordonsville, but King's agent, failing to mention Hill, put the total force with Jackson at 15,000. This man had the dubious distinction of underestimating the enemy force, which had been raised to 24,000 by Hill's arrival.[13]

Pope's intelligence mill lacked one kind of grist — men from the opposing army. On August 2 he set about to remedy this by sending a mixed column of infantry, cavalry, and artillery to Orange Court House. The result was a bag of some fifty prisoners, who yielded up the fact of Hill's arrival and estimated his strength at 10,000.[14]

If Pope's assiduous gathering of information could have been halted for a few days at that point, the state of his knowledge would have been good. But two more men were sent to Louisa Court House and returned on the 5th with the news that James Longstreet's divisions had passed through that point en route to Gordonsville; Longstreet "was seen by our scouts."[15] In fact "Old Pete" Longstreet was still in McClellan's front. (He was soon to receive the command of half of Lee's infantry, in which capacity he would constantly be the subject of reports, as already seen, of important movements that were never made.)

One other imaginary movement to Gordonsville, that of General John B. Hood's small division, had been reported to Pope, and he telegraphed Halleck that his sources were giving the enemy "full 50,000, though I think the number to be overestimated."[16]

Despite the quick buildup of Jackson's army — made more impressive than it really was by the false reports concerning Longstreet and Hood — and despite warnings of the speed with which Jackson was known to strike,[17] Pope not only maintained his aggressive posture but marched off on August 6 toward the enemy.[18] Banks's corps, which stopped at a point several miles south of Culpeper, was in a precarious position, for it was well in advance of the rest of the army. Its 8000 men were but a third the number of Jackson's force.[19]

Pope's movement went no further, for it soon became known that Jackson also was advancing. Montgomery apparently had uncovered signs of such a movement, corroborating evidence had come from refugees, and by the night of August 8 Banks's forward units had begun to feel the presence of the enemy north of the Rapidan.[20] Even if Banks had had none of this information, his experience at Jackson's hands would have led him to expect an attack. The situation was admirably suited to Jackson's game of assailing a superior force one fragment at a time, and such in fact was his object.

But Banks held his ground; then, discovering enemy infantry in his front at Cedar Mountain on the 9th, he surprised them by attacking first. His men threw themselves with great fury against their old enemies and had the better of the fight until Hill, leading Jackson's rearmost division, came onto the field. The Federals were driven back with considerable loss, but now it was their turn to be saved by late arrivals — the division of General James Ricketts, of McDowell's corps. Sigel's leading units were also nearing the battlefield, and when Jackson's cavalry brought in prisoners from them, Stonewall, realizing his scheme had failed, fell back on the 12th all the way to Gordonsville.[21] Pope followed as far as the Rapidan.[22]

.. .. ..

After Pope left Washington to join his army, General Halleck tackled the problem of what to do with the Army of the Potomac, inactive on the Peninsula. McClellan was still crediting Lee with 200,000 men, though even his own sources had discovered Jackson's departure from Richmond. And he was again asking for reinforcements, promising a new offensive if they were provided. Since McClellan wanted more than the high command felt could be spared, Halleck determined to join his army to Pope's. Also to be added to Pope's army was the small army of General Burnside, which had been brought up from the North Carolina coast.[23]

It was at this point that McClellan announced a drastic weakening of the enemy forces before Richmond, giving a figure that was well below Lee's actual strength.[24] For more than a week he protested Halleck's decision and parried the general-in-chief's daily telegrams urging him to get his regiments aboard ship with all possible speed. Despite Halleck's firmness, McClellan continued to stall; the withdrawal of his army from the Peninsula did not get fully under way until August 14.[25]

At the time McClellan suddenly concluded that Richmond was within his grasp, there had been no important dispersion of the Confederate forces there except for the three divisions with Jackson. On August 13, however, Lee ordered Longstreet with ten brigades to go to Jackson's support, since Stonewall, though victorious at Cedar Mountain, had not felt able to hold the field. Then from Federal deserters Lee learned of McClellan's withdrawal and also of Burnside's arrival at Fredericksburg. The report, as far as McClellan's movement was concerned, slightly anticipated the fact.[26] Thus it happened that August 14, the day when McClellan at last gave himself up to executing orders he had received on the 3rd, was a day of even greater bustle at Confederate headquarters. Lee arranged to draw further on his strength at Richmond, reducing it to three divisions, and, since McClellan was leaving the Peninsula, to go to Gordonsville himself. There he arrived on the 15th.[27] Other units followed him until within a short time little more than token forces remained to protect the Southern capital.[28]

Now began a race between two armies pulling out of the lines before Richmond and moving to "reinforce" the far smaller armies on the Rapidan. Having started in good time, with a much shorter distance to cover and with a railroad spanning the entire route, Lee was certain to complete his movement in time to meet Pope with considerably superior force.

The preparations he made after arriving at Gordonsville consumed but one day, the 16th. He planned to march to the Rapidan the next day, cross it on the 18th, and turn the Federals' left. Meanwhile Stuart's cavalry was to ford the river downstream, ride northward, and destroy the railroad bridge over the Rappahannock, Pope's main exit from the V formed by the confluence of the Rappahannock and the Rapidan.[29]

The chances of trapping the Union force between the two rivers were excellent. Pope had received but one of Burnside's divisions and none of McClellan's. The possibility that he would observe Lee's movements to the Rapidan was small: the presence of Jeb Stuart promised that the march would be shielded from Union scouts as completely as horseflesh and human skill would allow, and once the Confederates neared the river they would be hidden by a high ridge, known as Clark's Mountain, that ran along the south bank. Pope's spies were a threat; this was one occasion when the Confederates' automatic assumption that spies would be lingering near their movement stood a good chance of being correct. The best protection against them was to move fast enough to deny them time to work their way back to their own army. And speed was very much a part of Lee's plan.

Pope saw the danger he faced. That McClellan's departure from the Peninsula would induce Lee to attack the Army of Virginia he regarded as almost inevitable; he went beyond that to foresee with accuracy that the threat would come on his left, since the enemy by such a maneuver could interpose between him and the reinforcements coming from the Peninsula.[30] What he did not expect was the suddenness with which the blow was to fall. He declared afterward, "From the 12th to the 18th of August reports were constantly reaching me of large forces of the enemy re-enforcing Jackson from the direction of Richmond."[31] Although few such reports have come to light,[32] it can be inferred that the information in them did not give Pope a clear picture of the doom that was being prepared for him.

He was lulled into confidence on the morning of the 17th, when the Confederates were found to be withdrawing behind Gordonsville.[33] As Sigel's advanced positions gave a view all the way to that place,[34] the "withdrawal" must have been made for the purpose of deception; or it could have amounted to no more than putting the Southern troops on roads less exposed to view, some or all of them behind Clark's Mountain. For Lee had launched his strike, and by the close of the day his army stood on the Rapidan, almost as close to Pope's Rappahannock crossings as Pope himself was.

Then it turned out that Lee's plans had outrun his logistics. On the morning of the 18th a recently arrived infantry division was not yet in position, and Fitzhugh Lee's brigade, needed to carry the brunt of the cavalry's work, had not even come up. The attack was postponed to the 20th.[35]

And something else had gone amiss: a Union spy was marching with the Southern army. His presence proved to be a far greater blow to the Confederates than the absence of an infantry division and a cavalry brigade. The spy was Thomas O. Harter of the First Indiana Cavalry. Harter, whose company was part of General Sigel's escort, had been detailed by Sigel for espionage duty in July during the burst of zeal that Pope directed toward collecting information on the enemy. Twenty-eight years old and a railroad engineer by trade, Harter had entered the army at Terre Haute on July 4, 1861, and was now a sergeant.

Sigel provided him with civilian clothing and several hundred dollars in gold and started him on August 21 for Gordonsville, Charlottesville, and Staunton, the area that Pope had assigned Sigel's espionage to cover. Harter was to return in three weeks if possible. His cover was to be that of a refugee seeking railroad employment in the Confederacy. Before reaching Staunton he was arrested and sent to Harrisonburg, where, relieved of his pistol and money, he spent two weeks in jail. Moved to Staunton, he was put in irons for two days and then sent to Richmond, still being "detained." However, while at Staunton he had somehow obtained an interview with the general superintendent of the Virginia Central, who by a stroke of luck was well acquainted with the Terre Haute, Alton, and St. Louis Railroad, Harter's former employer. His new friend gave him a letter of introduction to the superintendent of the Richmond and Danville Railroad, then much in need of engineers. General Winder, still provost marshal at Richmond, set Harter free. Lee's forces were at that time departing for Gordonsville in great numbers, and presumably because of the heavy load with which the railroad to that point (the Virginia Central) was taxed, Harter was sent to work on that route. The pass he carried permitted him to go as far as Charlottesville.

Again luck was with him. Reaching Gordonsville on August 16, he abandoned his announced intentions and fell in with the army on its march the next day to the Rapidan. He did not record how he worked this bit of trickery, but undoubtedly a major ingredient of its success was the confusion produced by the descent on Gordonsville of the bulk of the Army of Northern Virginia and the haste with which it marched off to the Rapidan.

Harter did not risk a second day in the enemy ranks. On the morning of Monday, August 18 — the day of Lee's intended attack — he decamped, swam the river, and immediately found himself in the lines of his own army.

The nearest headquarters of importance was that of Major General Jesse L. Reno, commanding a small division of Burnside's force, near Raccoon Ford on the Rapidan. By still another piece of luck Harter found General Pope there, along with General McDowell and others. To them he reported that "the larger part of [Lee's army] was but a short distance from the river in our front, behind a mountain ridge [Clark's Mountain] running parallel with the river, that this army was on the point of marching, had their teams all ready to hitch up, and were evidently to move at an early moment to turn our left."

"The information," according to General McDowell, who gave an eye-witness account of this incident several weeks later, "induced Major General Pope to order his own army to retreat immediately behind the Rappahannock." In a personal letter to Harter written after the war, Pope wrote that "you were the first person to give the information" of Lee's impending attack.

Harter's critical piece of intelligence, without precedent in the Federals' warmaking experience, was brought to the attention of Judge Advocate Levi Turner in the War Department. It inspired Turner to suggest a policy for the rewarding of outstanding espionage services. He advised Secretary Stanton: "Such extra-hazardous service cannot be measured by a money valuation, but [Harter] should be compensated liberally, as a Government expression that such services are appreciated." Harter received a $500 award.

He also received a discharge from the army. As his former captors had a written description of him, further service as either spy or soldier entailed unacceptable risks in case of capture. He obtained employment as a detective under Provost Marshal James L. McPhail in Baltimore and, disregarding the risk of capture, assisted in scouting the Confederates' retreat from Gettysburg in July 1863. In November 1864 he was briefly on the payroll of the intelligence bureau of the Army of the Potomac. Presumably he was hired without full knowledge of his service under Pope and Sigel and was discharged upon telling the story of what had befallen him in July and August 1862.[36]

· ·   · ·   · ·

Pope had Harter's information by midmorning August 18.[37] Before his withdrawal could proceed far he had other information corroborating Harter's story. Richard Montgomery had left McDowell's headquarters on Sunday morning, the 17th, and "spent Sunday night and Monday with the rebels, returning . . . Monday evening. I learned this time, that the rebels had been reinforced by large bodies of troops from Richmond, and that they were advancing — that their pickets were then upon the banks of the Rapidan, and that it was their intention to cross the stream above us if possible and get to our rear."[38] Lee's threat upstream was only a feint.[39]

A further warning was a captured letter from Lee to Stuart, showing something of Lee's positions and intentions. Stuart had sent his adjutant, Major Norman R. Fitzhugh, on a ride to the east to hurry Fitz Lee's late-arriving brigade. Fitzhugh, who in the manner of a good cavalry headquarters officer kept his office in his haversack, neglected to divest himself of his papers. He was captured by troopers of a detachment consisting of the First Michigan and Fifth New York Cavalry, who had found Raccoon Ford unguarded and ventured deep into enemy territory. After taking Fitzhugh they surprised Stuart and his retinue resting at a farmhouse and nearly captured Jeb himself, settling instead for his briefly famous plumed hat, the gift of Northern friends from old army days, whom he had met during a truce following the battle of Cedar Mountain.

Repeatedly in histories of the Second Bull Run campaign the letter taken from Fitzhugh has been credited with saving Pope's army on the Rapidan. Meanwhile Harter's story and Montgomery's have remained unknown. The captured-letter version originates in no less authoritative a source than Pope's official report of his campaign. He wrote that among the papers taken from Fitzhugh was a letter in Robert E. Lee's own hand to Stuart, "which made manifest to me the position and force of the enemy and their determination to overwhelm the army under my command before it could be re-enforced by any portion of the Army of the Potomac."[40] Here Pope was using the capture of Lee's letter as a cover story (one that had the virtue of being basically true) to hide Harter's successful espionage. His resort to a cover story is of a piece with Union commanders' practice of keeping a tight lid on information about their spies. Their usual solution to this problem, in framing their after-action reports, was to remain silent. Pope's case was unusual in that he had, ready-made, an excellent cover; he would have been remiss if he had not availed himself of it. Possibly he overstated the revelations in Lee's letter in order to make its warning effect more plausible.[41] The letter could not have contributed anything to his escape from the Rapidan except as a belated corroboration of Harter's earlier report. The time Pope received the letter is unknown; it would have been sometime between the late hours of August 18, hours after Pope's decision to withdraw (Harter's arrival was early that day), and August 22, when Pope informed Halleck of the capture.[42]

This may be the clearest example Civil War history ever produces of a general's use of a cover story to protect a piece of espionage. And the Harter story is noteworthy in still another respect: his report to Pope may well be the timeliest single product of espionage received by any Union commander during the entire war. Espionage was not well adapted to situations in which armies were at close grips; the speed with which a spy could get his findings back to headquarters was the speed of a long horseback ride or, worse yet, a long trek afoot, with encumbrances such as enemy pickets and patrols that might limit travel to nighttime. In this case the spy, Harter, had been part of the movement he reported on, and it was army headquarters that did the traveling, meeting Harter, as it were, on the north bank of the Rapidan.

The rapidity of Lee's movement from Richmond had freed him from the usual risks of enemy espionage. But this haste produced a state of confusion that permitted Harter to penetrate his army in the most disadvantageous circumstance that could be imagined — the advance to an attack that bore great promise of surprise.

Harter's feat, though hidden from Northern eyes by Pope's cover story, did not escape the enemy's information net. A few days after the event Lee wrote President Davis that "the enemy, through the instrumentality of a spy, got information of our plans and concentration on his left flank while threatening his right, and commenced to retire." Lee's source for this information probably was Pope's quartermaster, who was captured by Stuart on August 22 and did some indiscreet talking.[43]

. .   . .   . .

For eight weeks General Pope had commanded the Army of Virginia, and for eight weeks it looked as if the administration had found in him a general who would provide himself with good intelligence, evaluate it correctly, and act decisively upon it. Pope has often been portrayed as a rash and uninformed blunderer; Freeman, for example, writes, "Pope's ignorance of Lee's movements had caused him incautiously to present his adversary as fair an opportunity as ever a soldier was offered."[44] Such estimates of Pope often seem to be a product of the common impression that Confederate leaders were invariably well informed and crafty and Federals ignorant and guileless — sometimes acting timidly, sometimes rashly, but always pretty much in the dark. This impression has been reinforced by the undoubted skill of two generals, Lee and Jackson, in reading the enemy's situation and finding the spot where a devastating blow could be struck. Pope was to receive one of the two harshest lessons in this art that the Southern chieftains ever administered; but up to the time of his departure from the Rapidan and for some days thereafter he maintained better than parity with them in his supply of intelligence and his interpretation of it. If his escape from the Rapidan was both narrow and lucky, it is also true that the active espionage that gave him his warning was the product of his own energetic direction of the army.

. .   . .   . .

Pope's divisions lost no time in gaining the left bank of the Rappahannock.[45] Lee followed to the opposite bank on the 20th,[46] and the armies sparred for five days, Lee seeking an opening that would allow him to cross the river and Pope skillfully parrying him. Although Pope believed his "true position, . . . should the enemy advance with his whole force, would be considerably in rear of the Rappahannock," he held to the river for three days, believing that by absorbing Lee's attention he would facilitate the movement of McClellan's troops marching from their disembarkation near Fredericksburg. Halleck endorsed his aggressiveness, telegraphing on the 21st, "Dispute every inch of ground, and fight like the devil till we can re-enforce you."[47] Soon, however, the threat of a flanking movement on his right caused Pope to draw back to Warrenton. The arrival on the 23rd of two divisions under Fitz John Porter brought his strength equal to or above that of the enemy, but he had not been given full authority over Porter's force; it still belonged to McClellan's command. Porter reached the Rappahannock in the region of Kelly's Ford to find Pope's army gone; he sent out scouts to locate it but was equally prepared to find the enemy instead.

Throughout these operations Pope kept his three brigades of cavalry hard at work reconnoitering along the Rappahannock, especially on the Confederates' side, tracking the enemy movements.[48] On the 21st John Buford reported that his cavalry brigade had engaged infantry belonging to Longstreet's and A. P. Hill's divisions. A contraband turned up with a report that partly corroborated Buford's.

Also involved in this search for intelligence was George S. Smith, a resident of Culpeper County, who had been serving with Pope's topographical engineers. The extent of Smith's contribution is uncertain; according to an account he gave months afterward, he had "passed through the whole rebel Army while they were in Culpepper Co [to] Pope at Rappahannock Station . . . , and told Pope what troops Lee had, and all about them."[49] But Pope's dispatches during these days do not display a detailed knowledge of the composition of the Southern army; evidently he rejected Smith's information as untrustworthy. Some weeks previously, while still in Washington, he had told David Strother, who was now a lieutenant colonel but still serving on the same topographical engineering staff, that Smith, "I am told, is a damned rascal. When you are done getting information from him, hand him over to the provost marshal." Strother was astonished; he wrote that he "had judged from the man's speech and demeanor that he was honest. I think so yet." Smith's claim of Northern allegiance appears sound; both he and his wife were natives of New England and had lived in the North until well into their thirties (Smith was now fifty years old). The 1860 census of Culpeper County lists his occupation as "gentleman," although it shows him owning only $4500 worth of real and personal property and a single slave.[50]

Whatever Pope's knowledge of the composition of Lee's army amounted to, he maintained an excellent grasp of its movements, actual and potential. Lee found each thrust blocked, sometimes to his own embarrassment. Now, however, it was the Confederates' turn to execute an intelligence coup that would change the course of the campaign. On the night of August 22, under cover of a cloudburst that raised the water level of the shallow upper Rappahannock by six feet, Jeb Stuart went off on a raid, intent on breaking Pope's supply line by burning a certain railroad bridge. The rainstorm defeated that project, but Stuart located a guide who knew that Pope's supply trains had been removed to Catlett's Station, twelve miles below Manassas. Stuart went for the supplies on these trains, but he found something of far greater value — the Army of Virginia's headquarters baggage. It included Pope's dispatch book and a generous file of correspondence. Stuart also found, and burned, the personal baggage of Pope's chief engineer, Colonel John N. Macomb, including a trunk containing $2500 in secret-service funds that the colonel had received from Washington that morning. On the day Pope's army fought the first of its battles on the old Bull Run fields, its chief engineer was at the War Department accounting for the loss of the Treasury notes.[51]

Stuart's troopers took Pope's letters as souvenirs, and they were painstakingly recovered over a period of days. By the 24th Lee had received one of them, dated the 20th, in which Pope detailed his total strength, 45,000, and dwelt upon his determination to hold the Rappahannock line until McClellan's divisions arrived. The conclusion to be drawn from this was that if Pope expected to hold his ground with so small an army, his reinforcements must have been getting near on the 20th, and by now might be arriving in great numbers. Once the two Federal armies were joined they would more than double Lee's force and would stand between him and Richmond. Here was the intelligence that governed Lee's actions for the rest of the campaign.[52]

. .   . .   . .

On the morning of August 25, from a Signal Corps station on a hill near Waterloo Bridge, at the Rappahannock crossing directly west of Warrenton, came reports that Confederate infantry, artillery, and cavalry were seen moving northwesterly. Pope concluded that the march was headed for the Shenandoah Valley. Even after the column was seen to turn northeast, he held to this view, believing that the troops seen turning were "covering the flank of the main body, which is moving toward Front Royal or Thornton's Gap, though of this I am not certain." The incident reveals a tendency on Pope's part to give intelligence evidence the meaning that pleased his wishes rather than a more probable interpretation. This tendency was to manifest itself repeatedly in the coming battle.

By 10:30 the Confederate column was seen to be fifteen miles long. The Signal Corpsmen and a visitor, Colonel John Clark of Banks's staff, counted guns, wagons, and regiments with great care; when they finally gave the strength of the marching force as 20,000, the precision they had demonstrated gave assurance that this was a major development in Lee's campaign.[53]

Before sundown the enemy's marching column was lost to view, and for more than twenty-four hours Pope was without information on where the enemy's huge movement had gone. He kept his spies busy, but he would not have their reports for several days. Richard Montgomery had started out on another trip that day, and he covered a great deal of ground on the enemy's side of the Rappahannock before discovering that the entire Southern army had moved off to the north. By the time he returned with these findings McDowell had made the same discovery in direct contact with the enemy. On the 24th, Pope had ordered Sigel to "send spies and scouts around by Front Royal to Thornton's Gap and into the valley of the Shenandoah, to ascertain whether any of the enemy's forces are moving in that direction." Scouts and spies also went from Winchester southward up the Valley.[54] As the enemy's objectives did not lie in that direction, these expeditions yielded nothing.

Spying was turning out to be either unproductive or untimely, and now Pope's other intelligence resource, his cavalry, the best instrument for tracking an enemy movement such as the one that appeared to be in progress, was going dry. Buford reported on the night of the 25th, "My command is almost disorganized," which evidently meant that not only his horses but also his men were wearing out. At about the same time Brigadier General George Bayard told McDowell, to whose corps his cavalry brigade was assigned, that "owing to the hard, unremitting services performed, [the brigade could] neither charge nor stand a charge." In Pope's third cavalry brigade, commanded by Colonel John Beardsley and assigned to Sigel's corps, the horses "had been taxed to the utmost of their strength" as early as August 18, the day they left the Rapidan. Pope reported that not over 500 of his total of 4000 cavalrymen were "capable of doing much service," and the horses were "completely broken down." What was left of the three brigades was kept busy following movements of the enemy close at hand. Pope had driven his cavalry so hard to obtain information that that excellent service was almost gone.[55]

Much of the infantry, especially in the corps of Sigel and Banks, was in little better condition. Pope ordered a probe along the whole front, but only McDowell was able to comply. A dispatch from Pope overtook him on the march, informing him that Sigel on his right and Reno on his left were unable to move and authorizing him to cancel his own march. But before he gave the countermand, one of his divisions got into a fight and discovered that the opposing troops were Richard Anderson's. As Anderson's division, so far as the Federals knew, had been the last to leave Richmond, McDowell concluded that they were the enemy's rear element. In other words, Lee's entire army, not merely the 20,000-man column, had moved off to the north from the region where the armies had been fencing for several days. This inference was correct, but information on the position of the Confederates' advance elements would have been incomparably more useful than what was learned about their rear.[56]

Sigel did succeed in sending scouts on the trail of the force whose northward march had been so minutely observed. One of them picked up word of its arrival at White Plains, east of Salem. If this was correct, Pope's apprehension that the enemy would attempt to turn his right was proving all too sound. Enough cavalry was assembled to pick up the trail; they found an enemy column between Salem and "the Plains." Meanwhile contrabands were making their way to Union headquarters with corroborating information on the enemy's movement. But none of these reports reached McDowell or Pope before the evening of the 26th.[57] Another misfortune was the failure of an attempt by Pope to have cavalry from Manassas or Alexandria watch Thoroughfare Gap, where the road eastward from Salem and White Plains comes through the Bull Run Mountains — an avenue of approach to Washington. To the end of the campaign Pope never learned what came of this project.[58] Hindsight makes clear that if he was to be so energetic in pursuit of information, he should have had much more cavalry.

About 8:20 in the evening of the 26th Pope's telegraph operators found they could not raise Washington; the wire had gone dead. Somewhat later it became evident that the railroad was cut above Catlett's. Writing to McDowell at midnight, Pope said, "Our communications have been interrupted by the enemy's cavalry near Manassas." But he was properly skeptical of the character of the raid: "Whether [the enemy's] whole force, or the larger part of it, has gone around [our right] is a question which we must settle instantly, and no portion of his force must march opposite to us to-night without our knowing it."[59]

By 10:00 the next morning, the 27th, he had learned that a large body of enemy was moving to gain his rear. Reports from Sigel's scouts, Buford, and the Negroes indicated a large concentration of enemy forces at White Plains, just west of the Bull Run Mountains, and Pope informed Halleck, "The enemy has massed his whole force at White Plains." This message had to be detoured via Burnside's headquarters near Fredericksburg. Pope now attributed the rupture of his communications to a "strong column" that "penetrated by way of Manassas Railroad last night to Manassas, . . . and I fear destroyed several bridges."[60] The contradiction between the statements of the "whole force" at White Plains and the "strong column" at Manassas was not explained.

Pope doubted strongly that Lee intended to attack him, but his position was still dangerous, and he ordered an immediate movement "to interpose in front of Manassas Junction." He had been strengthened by Heintzelman's as well as Porter's corps of the Army of the Potomac; his army numbered over 70,000, and more reinforcements were on the way.

With Hooker's division of Heintzelman's corps leading, the army pushed northeastward up the railroad and the Alexandria–Warrenton Turnpike on the 27th. At Bristoe Station late in the day Hooker encountered an enemy infantry force larger than his own. He attacked, and the Confederates fell back on Manassas. It was not much of a fight, but it uncovered the identity of the enemy force — a startling discovery. Hooker's opponent was Richard Ewell's division; in its rear were the divisions of Jackson and A. P. Hill. Jackson was in command of the three.[61] The mysterious disappearance of the long marching column was solved, but in a most ungratifying way.

The visit of this force to Manassas resulted from Stuart's capture of Federal correspondence at Catlett's. From it Lee had seen that the threatened junction of Pope's and McClellan's armies would force him to retire to Richmond, if indeed it did not cut him off on the way. Jackson's sweeping maneuver to the Federals' rear was born of the desperate situation that was rapidly developing. The object was only secondarily to attack Pope's supplies and communications. It was mainly to break the stalemate on the Rappahannock and trigger wide maneuvers in which there would be a greater chance that Pope would err. Only if he committed a serious error was Lee willing to risk a general engagement, since he expected to be outnumbered.[62]

Jackson, accompanied by Stuart's cavalry, had started from Jeffersonton, a scant four miles from the Union signal station across the Rappahannock that observed the movement. He bivouacked that night at Salem and on the 26th moved through Thoroughfare Gap to Bristoe. All day long his column, a third as large as Pope's army, marched on the Federals' right and rear, scarcely ten miles from their main body, without being detected.[63] Even dust clouds, the one clue to an army on the march that could not be suppressed by Jackson's fierce security measures or Stuart's adept cavalry screening, seem to have stayed close to the earth that day. On the 27th, while Pope was informing Halleck that the enemy was concentrated at White Plains, tons of good Yankee food from the big supply base at Manassas — twenty-odd miles from "the Plains" — were being gorged by some 20,000 ravenous Confederate soldiers. And the rest of Lee's army, under Longstreet, having on the 26th marched only a short distance from positions on the Rappahannock, was well short of the Plains.[64] The force that Sigel's scouts, Buford, and the Negroes had discovered there belonged to Jackson rather than to Lee's main body, but by the time the information reached Pope, Jackson had marched on to Manassas, his objective.

Far from being distressed by this news, Pope saw an opportunity to overwhelm the two halves of the Confederate army in turn — first Jackson, then Longstreet. He wrote McDowell, marching up the turnpike with Sigel, "If you will march promptly and rapidly at the earliest dawn of day upon Manassas Junction, we will bag the whole crowd."[65]

Now began the events that have earned Pope his reputation as a blunderer. The first is a measure merely of the degree to which luck had deserted him. Jackson, aware of his own precarious situation, began retiring to a defensive position north of the turnpike at Groveton, between Bull Run and Gainesville, there to await Lee and Longstreet. His subordinates took three different routes, Hill going as far east as Centreville.[66] Upon arriving at Manassas, Pope learned of Hill's move to Centreville; mistakenly assuming that this meant the whole enemy force was moving there, he changed his orders, sending all his units in that direction.

The three-way dispersion of Jackson's forces greatly multiplied the Confederates' chances of intercepting any Federal courier who strayed a little too far in seeking roads connecting Pope's forces on the railroad with those on the turnpike. Many Federal couriers were riding about with orders on the night of August 27 and the next day, and two of them fell into Confederate hands. The dispatches they were carrying told of Pope's intention to "bag the whole crowd" and displayed how he was going about it.[67]

The advantage that Pope's spies and cavalry had won for him at the start of the campaign had now been wiped out by the captures of his correspondence, beginning with Stuart's visit to Catlett's. His intelligence needs now amounted to an urgent need for cavalry — his own cavalry, not McDowell's or Sigel's or Banks's. He had had none at all throughout the maneuvers of recent days. Now he borrowed a regiment from McDowell,[68] but it is not known to have brought him any information, useful or otherwise.

Thus handicapped, Pope fell easily into errors that afflicted his interpretation of intelligence for the rest of his battle. The first of these errors was his assumption that all of Jackson's force had retired on Centreville; in sending all of his pursuing elements in that direction, he assured that most of his force would be out of position for the battle that was about to be fought at Groveton. Some of his later errors of interpretation would lead to similarly mistaken actions; others would end simply in inaction, with equally unfortunate results.

When one of McDowell's divisions, Rufus King's, came into Jackson's view late on the 28th, marching eastward on the turnpike, Stonewall knew from the captured dispatches that it was a force of a size he could risk attacking. Attack he did, having in mind that if the Federal columns were allowed to continue as far as Centreville, the heights at that place and its Confederate-built fortifications would give the enemy a well-nigh unassailable position. Although King's outnumbered force inflicted severe punishment on the attackers, the encounter had a favorable result for the Confederates by leading Pope to misconstrue Jackson's intentions; he thought King had struck an enemy column in retreat.[69]

When Pope learned that Hill had retired from Centreville and that Jackson had turned up giving battle to King six miles to the west, he naturally enough reasoned that Stonewall's Manassas adventure was over and he was retiring on the enemy's main body.[70] This error compounded another that Pope had made when, in issuing orders for his eastward march, he virtually ignored the possibility that Longstreet would move through Thoroughfare Gap to join Jackson.[71] So eager was Pope to make short work of Jackson that he made no provision for protecting the gap. The oversight is all the more strange when it is realized that his information on the 26th, which he accepted and relayed to Halleck, placed Lee's entire army on the western approach to Thoroughfare, a day ahead of Longstreet's actual arrival there. But Pope had his reason: now, on the 28th, with Jackson apparently retreating, there seemed less cause than ever for concern about Longstreet.

McDowell, having shared in all the information that had reached Pope, was mindful of the threat to Thoroughfare Gap. As he marched eastward up the turnpike on the 28th, he sent Ricketts's division to the eastern face of the gap along with as many cavalrymen as Buford and Bayard could collect. Their arrival was timely: Longstreet's advance came up in midafternoon. But by moving over mountain trails and through a neighboring gap, the advancing divisions outflanked the Federals, forcing them to retire. Buford made the effort pay by remaining near Gainesville until he had counted seventeen regiments passing through on the morning of the 29th — enough to establish that the enemy was bringing forward a major force, the half-army commanded by Longstreet.[72]

Here was information that could have corrected Pope's belief that only Jackson was to be dealt with. Partly responsible for that belief was misinformation about the timing of Longstreet's expected arrival. Pope had revised his earlier information, which placed Longstreet a day's march ahead of his actual position, only to replace it with a worse error. He now believed that Longstreet's force "is moving in this direction at a pace that will bring them here by to-morrow night or the next day." McDowell received that serious misestimate and also Buford's report that Longstreet was now only a few miles from the battlefield. Both items reached McDowell before noon of the 29th; he could not have been unaware of Pope's grievous misunderstanding, yet after he showed Buford's dispatch to Porter, he put it in his pocket. He did not forward Buford's intelligence to Pope until 7 P.M., by which time Longstreet's troops had entered the fray, on Jackson's right.[73] McDowell's egregious neglect was to have a disastrous result.

At 10 A.M. on the 29th, Pope issued a joint order to Porter and McDowell; he apparently intended for at least those two to be in position to attack Jackson's supposedly exposed right flank. But the order was confusing and contradictory. Porter, whose lately arrived corps was on the Federal left, then on the Manassas-Gainesville road, was to proceed to Gainesville. However, the order did not specifically demand aggressive action by Porter, and he soon was halted by a small force of Confederate cavalry that bluffed him by dragging branches down a dirt road, raising clouds of dust.[74] McDowell, joint order in hand, consulted with him. Buford's intelligence meant that Pope's order was unworkable; they decided to invoke a clause in the order that allowed them to ignore it under such a condition. But Pope was left in ignorance of this decision and of Buford's discovery of Longstreet's arrival.

Most of these errors of Pope's consisted of misinterpretation or ignoring of information provided by his own eyes and ears or those of subordinates. Around noon nineteen guns of Longstreet's artillery started firing with good effect from Groveton (Jackson's force was spread out from that point to Sudley Springs).[75] This amounted to an announcement to anyone within earshot that new forces were present, but Pope apparently took no notice of it. At midday he toured the battlefield north of the turnpike, but not south of it, where Longstreet was placing almost his entire force. Then Pope ordered General John F. Reynolds with his division to attack Jackson's right flank and rear, supposing that Reynolds's attack would augment the intended attack by Porter and McDowell. But Reynolds, having confronted Jackson's right that morning and then redeployed to the west to deal with Longstreet's newly arrived brigades, knew that the Rebel forces south of the turnpike would defeat this maneuver. He sent word of his concerns to Pope, who ignored them; Reynolds reluctantly ordered the attack, and it was stopped by infantry and artillery. He sent an officer to describe to Pope the huge number of regimental flags seen in the enemy force; Pope insisted that the flags would have been those of Porter's regiments going into position. He erred again by mistaking ambulances removing Confederate wounded along the turnpike for wagons whose movements would signify a retreat; he ordered a division-sized pursuit.[76]

The afternoon was now well advanced, and no sound had been heard of the attack on Jackson that McDowell and Porter had been ordered to make. Pope, still unaware of Longstreet's arrival, now issued his soon-to-be-famous "4:30 order" to Porter, directing him to attack Jackson's right flank. Porter, having received via McDowell Buford's report of Longstreet's movement through Gainesville, and having taken prisoners from some of Longstreet's units, knew that Longstreet was on the field, his troops holding two or three miles of the front across which Porter was ordered to march.[77] Porter sat still and did nothing — not even informing Pope of his intended inaction and the reason for it. Presumably he assumed that Pope by this time knew of the presence of Longstreet's troops but did not know they had taken position south of the turnpike, in Porter's front.

Even allowing for Pope's shortage of cavalry, it seems strange that so large a force as Longstreet's could have been so close at hand and still escaped Pope's observation; but that is what happened. However correct Porter's decision to sit tight may have been, his neglecting to inform Pope of his inaction was grossly insubordinate. For his failure to carry out the order Porter was court-martialed and cashiered. His story, so much like General Stone's in that both had supplied bold, forehanded action that did much to advance the safety of the government in the early months of secession, was different in that the charges against Porter came to trial. But the verdict, though it ruined Porter's career, did not stand. Twenty-four years later, largely on evidence supplied by Longstreet that Porter could not have complied with Pope's order, Porter was restored to his commission.[78]

Pope never believed what records available after the war clearly showed regarding Longstreet's arrival. Months after the battle he was still insisting that "at 5 o'clock in the afternoon of the 29th General Porter had in his front no considerable body of the enemy" and that "it was easily practicable for him to have turned the right flank of Jackson and to have fallen upon his rear; . . . if he had done so we should have gained a decisive victory over the army under Jackson before he could have been joined by any of the forces under Longstreet."[79] Pope's view remained unchanged even after Porter's exoneration.[80]

Although Longstreet was fully in position on Jackson's right by 1 P.M. on the 29th, Porter's corps in his front immobilized him. By sitting still, Porter, without knowing it, performed a useful function. Longstreet had to make a "forced reconnaissance" involving seven of his twelve brigades, which put him in a forward position for attack. At sunset this attack ran straight into the attack, by King's division, that Pope had ordered in pursuit of the supposedly fleeing Rebels. The good-sized clash that resulted was another warning to Pope concerning his left. McDowell had also accepted the retiring ambulances as meaning a general Confederate retreat, and when General John Hatch sent a message reporting heavy fighting and requesting permission to disengage, McDowell answered, "Tell him the enemy is in full retreat and to pursue him!"[81]

Pope had thrown brigade after brigade at Jackson's position all day, with heavy casualties, in the hope of attracting Stonewall's attention toward his front — away from the flank attack that was twice ordered by Pope but could never take place because Longstreet, unknown to Pope, stood in its path.

·· ·· ··

Richard Montgomery's tracking of Longstreet's march now had been the sum total of Pope's espionage efforts for over a week. In the evening of the 29th McDowell summoned Montgomery for a second hearing of the findings from that trip. It had taken him across the Rappahannock at Kelly's Ford and up the river until he encountered the Confederate rear, well to the north. Montgomery later said,

> Of their plans . . . it was reported amongst them, that they were going to fight us there [on the Rappahannock] — and . . . a rebel officer . . . told me that they expected to whip Genl. Pope, and start him running, and keep him running all the way to Washington, — which city (he said) they would not approach by the front, but that their forces was ready as soon as they beat Genl. Pope, to move at once up the valley, and cross the Potomac above us. That he *knew* it was the determination of his superior officers to carry the war north of the Potomac.

Here was one occasion when mess-table strategy coincided with Lee's actual thinking,[82] but McDowell did not rate the information important enough to pass it to Pope either upon Montgomery's return or after hearing him repeat it.

Another report of August 29, from General Julius White at Winchester, described a clever piece of espionage which, despite the serious gaps in Pope's information, added little or nothing to what he already had. White had conceived a way of introducing agents into the enemy's ranks: disguising them as Confederate guerrillas and pushing them through by force, supplemented by enough noise and excitement to dull Confederate suspicions. "On the 27th," he wrote, "I started 6 of my men across the Blue Ridge, through Ashby's Gap. Had them armed with shot-guns, and chased them into the enemy's line with a cavalry force from here." At the time of White's telegram, the pseudo-guerrillas had just returned. They reported that Jackson was at Manassas with 50,000 (by now Pope was able of course to correct both the location and the strength given for Jackson) and that Longstreet was at Salem on the 28th (Pope already knew of Longstreet's arrival at Salem and incorrectly believed him still in that vicinity). Concerning Elijah White's Confederate guerrillas, who roamed the area just east of the Blue Ridge, more detailed information was obtained; possibly it was their line into which the spies were chased.[83] General White's report was more interesting for his innovation in spying tactics than for the intelligence it contained.

·· ·· ··

In a dispatch to Halleck early on the 30th, Pope showed that his ignorance of Longstreet's presence was now corrected, but he believed that the new arrivals would only support Jackson's lines; he kept his army concentrated on Jackson's front, leaving Longstreet free to overlap his left south of the turnpike. He spent the day weighing eye-witness evidence from generals who sought him out at his headquarters — against a variety of reports that he interpreted as indicating that the enemy was retreating. The first of these was an observation by one of McDowell's brigade commanders of a rearward movement by one of Longstreet's divisions; unfortunately the report failed to note that the move was very short, a mere adjustment of position. There were several reports from wounded or paroled Federal soldiers who made their way back to their own lines, each claiming to have overheard Confederates' conversations that indicated an early retreat; General Porter was certain that one of these men was unwittingly relaying planted information. But the most influential report was the account of a reconnaissance of the right wing by none other than Generals McDowell and Heintzelman. They were checking on General Ricketts's claim to have fought with a considerable force of enemy; finding no such force, they concluded it had retreated, but actually it was still present though well hidden in a woods they did not trouble themselves to enter.[84]

Against this body of reports that seemed to corroborate each other was the contrary testimony of Generals Reynolds, Porter, Ricketts, and Isaac Stevens. Reynolds had the most persuasive story of the enemy's proximity: he had himself attracted the fire of a line of skirmishers, who all missed him. He rode to Pope's headquarters on Buck Hill and excitedly reported that "the enemy is turning our left"; Pope replied, "Oh, I suppose not." When Sigel confirmed this view of affairs on the left, Pope decided to reinforce Reynolds but sent him only a single brigade, which left him at a considerable disadvantage.[85] The enemy movements on the left would have been Longstreet's adjustments of position for an attack he was planning.

According to Colonel Strother, an observer of these doings, Pope and McDowell spent much of the morning under a tree waiting for the Confederates to retreat. It would have been more accurate to say that Pope, confused by the conflicting evidence, was awaiting developments. His own generals' observations presumably were fully reliable, but among those generals were McDowell and Heintzelman, whose evidence was on the side of the theory that the enemy was retreating. Seeking to resolve the conflict, Pope at noon ordered an attack by Ricketts on the right and Porter on the left; both were handily stopped, forcing him to abandon the retreat theory. But he did not abandon the assault by Porter's entire corps or his fixation on the territory north of the turnpike.[86]

Richard Montgomery at this point was set to try his hand at scouting the battlefield. His trip was a very short one; as he set out from the Federal left he was met by Southern troops advancing from ground that Pope had supposed to be unoccupied. Lee and Longstreet had each seen the opportunity posed by Porter's leaving his position on the Federal left to make his attack and the confusion that resulted. Longstreet had already scheduled a diversionary attack for 4 P.M.; he easily changed this to a full-scale attack.[87]

Longstreet's troops, finally unleashed, swarmed out of the positions in which they had been waiting, some for more than twenty-four hours. For hundreds of yards there was nothing to stop them; they rolled up the Union left. As the tide began to threaten the center, McDowell and other generals organized a hurried retreat that took the whole army back to Chinn Ridge and then Henry House Hill; the fighting ended on the same ground where the first Bull Run battle was fought. After night fell the Federals succeeded in retiring to the Centreville defenses; on September 3 they drew back all the way to the fortifications of Washington.

That the army was saved from total destruction or capture was due mainly to slowness on Jackson's part. His troops were unready to comply promptly with orders for their share of the all-out battle that Longstreet's attack turned into; their participation was hours late. Another commander unready for the occasion was Pope; the full meaning of Longstreet's onslaught — a disaster in the making — did not dawn on him until McDowell on his own began sending brigades to Chinn Ridge. Then Pope rode to Henry House Hill and took charge of the last-ditch fight there.[88]

Pope's decision to stay on the field on August 30 was his greatest error. Had he gone to Centreville and linked up with McClellan's arriving divisions, his wide-open left flank would not have been exposed, and the combined Union forces on that fortified height would have been so safe from attack that Lee would have been the commander in the precarious position.

But Pope's mistakes, numerous and ruinous though they were, were not the only cause of his defeat. Equally damaging was McClellan's slowness in getting his divisions to his beleaguered fellow general. Only Porter's and Heintzelman's corps and Reynolds's small division got into the fight, although the corps of Sumner and Franklin, which might well have saved the day if they had arrived a little sooner, did participate in the retreat. McClellan suffered no regrets over this failure. His letters show him taking a pleasure in Pope's difficulties that seems almost treasonous. On August 21 he wrote his wife, "I believe I have triumphed!! Just received a telegram from Halleck stating that Pope and Burnside are very hard pressed." On the 29th he suggested to Lincoln that as an alternative to opening communication with the embattled army, Pope should be left "to get out of his scrape" while Washington was being made "perfectly safe." He had written his wife that upon Pope's defeat "they will be very glad to turn over the redemption of their affairs to me."[89]

. . .. ..

Whether Lee would next move against Washington or invade Maryland, the beaten but angry Federals had to be reformed to fight him off. Lincoln faced the problem of naming a single commander — choosing between Pope, who despite his defeat had demonstrated aggressiveness and soldiership to a degree that must have inclined his superiors to give him a second chance, and McClellan, who was still his old self, thin-skinned, quibbling, full of alarms and excuses. His supreme slowness in coming to Pope's aid raised new doubts about his fitness to command, and Pope's report immediately after the battle did nothing to alleviate them. "I think it my duty," he wrote Halleck on September 1, "to call your attention to the unsoldierly and dangerous conduct of many brigade and some division commanders of the forces sent here from the Peninsula. . . . You have hardly an idea of the demoralization among officers of high rank in the Potomac Army, arising in all instances from personal feeling in relation to changes of commander-in-chief." Corps commanders, with the exception of Sumner, he said, "had continued persistently to inform me that their commands . . . had no spirit and no disposition to fight."[90] Pope seems to have felt this opposition so keenly that he dared not risk a new attack even after the arrival of Sumner and Franklin gave him a decided numerical advantage.

However, this allegiance to McClellan was possessed by most of the divisions that would have to be sent to repel the enemy movement across the Potomac that was now in prospect. With great misgivings his chiefs allowed him to resume active command.[91] Pope was relegated to the duty of fighting Indians in the Department of the Northwest.[92]

. . .. ..

Pope is remembered mainly as the hapless victim of one of Lee's and Jackson's greatest coups. Although the view of him as a rash blunderer has been somewhat softened in later years, his reputation as a general who did not know his enemy persists. To what extent is that view to be modified by what has been shown here?

It would have to be completely rejected if the final week of the summer-long campaign could be ignored. Up to that time Pope distinguished himself as the first army-level Union commander in the East who showed a really good understanding of the enemy's situation. He accomplished this by his use of spies and cavalry. He demonstrated that spies could produce information of critical value to a marching and maneuvering army. Previously espionage seems to have been counted on only for information of long-term, strategic value; by contrast, Pope's agents several times brought findings of immediate application. Their main target was not Richmond, as it was for Pinkerton's men, but the Confederate forces within range of Pope's army. Another point of difference — probably more interesting than significant — is the fact that they were not professionals of the Pinkerton stripe but inexperienced young men such as Montgomery and Sergeant Harter.

Pope also demonstrated that Union cavalry, if firmly directed, could get close to the enemy and come away with many useful findings. Generals had been taught to believe this; Pope proved it. How much personal attention he gave to his cavalry is uncertain; his success in obtaining bold and determined reconnoitering may have derived from his repeated insistence that nothing less was acceptable. (He once rebuked a subordinate charged with such tasks, saying, "The idea of retreating . . . with only 2 men wounded is hardly up to the standard of soldiership.")[93] However, his situation forced him to overwork his cavalrymen and particularly their mounts, so that he was able to get very little out of them at the climax of the campaign. Many of his mistaken actions during the battle could have been avoided if he had had enough horsemen on the field to keep track of enemy positions and reinforcements.

Further, in all the preliminary marching and maneuvering Pope showed a cool, clear head in evaluating what came to him from spies and scouts. Missing both from his telegrams and from his after-action report were the assertions, so familiar to the Washington authorities, that the enemy had 100,000 or 150,000 or 200,000 in his front. When he erred in estimating the strength of the Confederates, it was usually only a small error, and it was on the low side. His reading of enemy intentions was generally correct.

But this was Pope on the Rapidan and the Rappahannock. The general who showed such aptitude for acquiring good information was caught with very little enemy information at all as he approached the battle. On every major question that arose about the Confederates after the 24th of August, his information or the conclusion he drew from it was wrong. First was his assumption that the long column seen marching north on the 25th was headed for the Shenandoah (later commanders were to share with Pope what might be called the Valley fixation). Next was his belief, born of an understandable failure to appreciate Lee's willingness to take improbable risks, that the enemy in his rear at Manassas was only a raiding force. Once that error was corrected and Jackson identified, Pope assumed that the invaders had gone to Centreville. Their August 28 retirement from that place and the attack on King's division several miles to the west set this impression to rights but replaced it with a new error — the conviction that the enemy was withdrawing.

Here was the fixed idea that controlled Pope's battle. In one form or another he retained it for nearly two days, except possibly for a few hours on the evening of the 29th. If he understood then that the rest of the Southern army had come up, he was nevertheless wrong as to the time of its arrival, for he thought then, and maintained to the end of his life, that if Porter had attacked as ordered, Jackson would have been "crushed" before Lee and Longstreet could have reached the field.[94]

When the belief that the enemy was withdrawing was reinforced (or renewed) on the morning of the 30th and was then shattered — first by the Confederates' appearance in new positions as well as in their old ones, and further by Longstreet's decisive onslaught late in the day — Pope still misunderstood what had been going on across the lines. He reported that Lee, upon arriving, had begun to "mass on his right for the purpose of crushing our left."[95] In fact there was no great enemy concentration, the Confederates having been distributed fairly evenly across their front.

Although Pope's information service was a great improvement over those of earlier commanders in the East, it obviously was not good enough. It was not, in reality, his own service but that of his subordinates. It was the creature merely of his pen; with great insistence he issued orders to his corps commanders to send out spies and reconnaissance parties, but his own contribution to the project ended there. The lack of cavalry under his own immediate control was matched by the failure to have spies working directly for army headquarters. It would have been better to have all the army's spies under a single control. The flaws in McClellan's information service were partly organizational in that Pinkerton's bureau was isolated from the rest of headquarters. Pope avoided this pitfall but fell into the opposite one of having no intelligence organization whatever, nor indeed any recognizable intelligence system. An intelligence "staff" consisting of a single sharp-eyed and critically minded officer could have saved him from his too-ready acceptance of erroneous information on the battlefield.

The second flaw, the exhaustion of his cavalry, was a matter mainly of inadequate numbers: three small brigades. In cavalry organization Pope had made an improvement by minimizing the practice of breaking cavalry up into small detachments assigned to a scattering of tasks. He had Bayard's and Buford's brigades operate as units; only Beardsley's brigade was broken up, but into only two detachments, the larger of which was attached to Buford's brigade. Later army commanders would adopt Pope's arrangements, but his innovation is eclipsed by the breakdown from overwork that the three brigades suffered.

It was a piece of extraordinarily bad luck that McDowell, Pope's closest associate, neglected to forward Buford's very important report of Longstreet's arrival near the battlefield and that Porter, the one other corps commander who knew of this development, was too disaffected or too lethargic to report the discovery that the enemy was in force on his front.

Still, one is reminded of the aphorism that a good general is a lucky general; perhaps Pope's luck would have been better if the responsibility for providing him with information had not rested solely on the commanders of subordinate units.

What was the difference between the Pope of the Rapidan and the Pope of Manassas? It is often said that during the battle he lost control, which implies that the heat of combat unnerved him. A more likely explanation is simply that as long as he had good information about the enemy, he parried the Confederates' thrusts; when his information turned sour, he could no longer appreciate accurately even the developments that his generals observed. A few commanders in the Civil War who were forced into battle with inadequate knowledge of the situation possessed intuitive abilities that made up in large measure for this lack. Pope was not one of them.

In short, Pope's information service was good enough to keep up with Jackson and Lee during six weeks of sparring and probing, but short of what was required once the Southern chieftains launched a bold and far-ranging maneuver. The Confederates outran Pope's spies and his cavalry; without the information they had provided him, he was lost. On this the campaign of Second Bull Run turned.

9

. . . .

ALL THE PLANS OF THE REBELS

September 1862

THIRTY MILES UPRIVER from Washington, a mountain called Sugar Loaf towers above the surrounding Potomac country; on a clear day it can be seen from the capital. Commanding a view of a long stretch of river country from the Maryland side, it was the first place Federal lookouts turned to in a situation such as the prospective crossing of the Potomac by the victorious Confederates. Signal Corpsmen occupied the mountaintop on September 3; meanwhile cavalry and infantry from Falls Church and Arlington anxiously probed the Virginia roads for signs of an enemy move.[1]

It was the Signal Corps telescope on Sugar Loaf that first turned up something definite. Lieutenant Brinkerhoff N. Miner signaled to a colleague at Poolesville at 4:00 P.M. September 4:

> To Maj. Gen. Banks. [in Washington]
> A large wagon train — judge 50 to 75 wagons, moving out from Leesburg, easterly, in direction of Edwards Ferry. Continuous clouds of dust seen on roads leading in & out of Leesburg. A large wagon park 4 to 6 miles southeast of Leesburg, near turnpike. The enemy are now shelling the aqueduct over Monocacy river, and I judge are attempting to cross, from the reports of musketry heard.[2]

General Lee was carrying the war to Northern soil.

The commander of a small Union force in Maryland opposite Leesburg, convinced that 30,000 Confederates had crossed the river, retired a few hours after the exchange of "musketry" that had reached Miner's ears. By the 6th, Miner and his flagman, A. H. Cook, found themselves alone in a sea of Rebels. After signaling the near approach of the enemy they were seen to furl their flags as if to leave the station. Much later their superiors learned what then happened. While making their way across country after abandoning the lookout station, they captured a courier bearing dispatches from President Davis to Lee. The intercepted letters

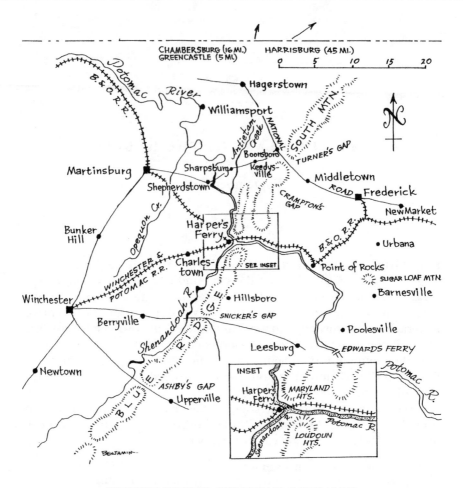

REGION OF THE ANTIETAM CAMPAIGN

never reached the Federal command, for Miner and Cook were captured and received a personal welcome from Jeb Stuart. Thenceforth for several days the invaders held the mountain, from which "the range of vision [was] unequaled by that from any other in Maryland." It was a serious loss to the information service, rendered more serious because Professor Lowe and his balloons, unable to make ascents for a moving army and again deprived of transportation, languished in Washington while Lee and McClellan were maneuvering and fighting in Maryland.[3]

Pope's defeat revived the fears of capture of Washington that the 1861 rout on Bull Run had raised. The government was slow to admit to the public that Lee's army had crossed the Potomac, as Uriah Painter, the *Philadelphia Inquirer* correspondent, learned on a visit to the War Department. Painter's habit of scouting in advance of the army had resulted in his capture by Stuart's cavalry; the Confederate officers' conversation revealed that they were preparing to enter Maryland, apparently as part of a general movement of Lee's army. They were so inattentive to their journalistic guest that he was able to slip away and get to Washington, but he found the War Department uninterested in his discovery. The official line was that Washington was in no danger from the Confederates; thus a visitor who could publish contrary information met a cool reception.[4]

Lee's decision to invade the North, though seemingly a sharp divergence from the Confederate policy of simply wanting to be let alone, was essentially defensive. Realizing that the Confederacy would never be let alone by the Army of the Potomac, he hoped to force that army into an all-out fight. The fruits of his victories over McClellan and Pope would be given up, his control over events would be lost, if he simply drew back to the Shenandoah Valley to feed his army, or to Richmond. A decisive victory on Northern soil might win European support; in any case it could be the basis of a Confederate offer of peace in exchange for independence. Even if rejected, such a proposal would win votes for opponents of the war in the upcoming Northern elections.

The decision to invade raised the question of whether to attack Washington. That was ruled out by the Confederates' shortages of munitions and supplies.[5]

. .   . .   . .

Forty-eight hours after Lieutenant Miner reported that the Rebels had crossed into Maryland, General McClellan, preceded by most of his army and what had been Pope's, marched out of Washington. He moved northwestward toward Frederick in a manner reminiscent of his unresisted but unhurried progress up the Peninsula. Allan Pinkerton was still with him, and so was his chronic respect for the enemy, whose position was unknown. Stuart maintained a tight cavalry screen, meanwhile scouting and threatening both of the Federals' flanks and spreading reports that had the invaders marching in several directions.[6]

Brigadier General Alfred Pleasonton, a short, cocksure regular officer of thirty-eight years, was now in command of McClellan's cavalry, moving in advance of the army and trying to locate the enemy. Although Pleasonton picketed the country from the Potomac to the Frederick-Baltimore highway, Stuart's screening kept him at a distance from infantry movements, and thus dependent on second-hand information from poorly informed local citizens. And Pleasonton was just as likely as McClellan to base important conclusions on information from a single source of unknown reliability.

On September 6 Pleasonton received a report that the march of "Lee's corps" and Jackson, though apparently directed on Frederick, was actually preliminary to an attack on Washington. This was misinformation calculated to inspire the most elaborate caution in McClellan. Next came a report of the interrogation of an Irishman who had escaped from Virginia to avoid conscription; he said that the enemy was headed for Baltimore. A spy whose name did not get into the records reached General Sumner, whose infantry corps was close in Pleasonton's rear, with the report that he had been at Poolesville and had seen the Confederate column marching unmistakably in the direction of Frederick. Finally came a telegram from a Baltimore and Ohio supervisor who had tried to run an engine toward Harper's Ferry and had been stopped a few miles from Frederick by the approach of Confederates in large force.[7] This was reliable information of the enemy's whereabouts, but it did not stand out sharply enough from the other reports to gain attention. On the 7th there was a convergence of reports, originating with deserters and with soldiers still in the enemy ranks, to the effect that Baltimore was the objective; such concurrence being abnormal, one suspects that the story was planted. Stonewall Jackson, who could be counted upon to spread a false story whenever opportunity arose, told a Frederick citizen that he "designed crossing [directly] into Pennsylvania, . . . to Philadelphia." On the same day Pleasonton correctly reported that the whole invading army was across the river.

All but a few sources gave conservative estimates of the invaders' strength — 30,000 was the usual figure, and only a very few times was the true number, 50,000 at that time, exceeded. A few of the reports were wildly off on one or two points, such as a dispatch from General Wool at Baltimore reporting that General Braxton Bragg's army from the Tennessee-Mississippi theater was approaching through the Shenandoah Valley, 40,000 strong. This drew an immediate challenge from President Lincoln, since Bragg was in fact then invading Kentucky, but the story died uncorrected.

September 8 closed with McClellan at Rockville — twelve miles on the way to Frederick — telling Halleck, "Our information is still entirely too indefinite to justify definite action. . . . As soon as I find out where to strike, I will be after them without an hour's delay." To Governor Andrew G. Curtin of Pennsylvania, who was calling for arms, men, and protection, he wired that he was ready to move, but "My information about the enemy comes from unreliable sources, and it is vague and conflicting."[8] McClellan probably overstated the case; there should have been little doubt by this time that the enemy was gathered around Frederick, and although planned Confederate movements in several directions had been reported, none had been observed.

The information suppliers that McClellan complained about were a great deal more numerous and more trustworthy than what he had been accustomed to in Virginia. He had, however, sustained a shrinkage in

Pinkerton's organization. With the detective were only George Bangs, John Babcock, and five others. This was half the number McClellan had had on the Peninsula and also half the number left in Washington to shadow suspicious persons and investigate claim agents. As in the Peninsula campaign, scouting had no place in Pinkerton's operation, despite the importance of locating the enemy's position. The number of deserters, stragglers, and other prisoners would have kept his small staff of interrogators and record-keepers more than busy.[9]

Some effort was put forth to enlist the services of local citizens. George W. Dawson, a tax collector for the district around Poolesville, brought information to Pleasonton on the 6th and was immediately put on Pinkerton's payroll, receiving fifty dollars for service within the Southern lines in ensuing days. Nine others were added as the army advanced, and still others served as guides or were paid small amounts for information obtained apparently outside enemy lines.[10]

Part of the intelligence activity was directed toward discovering the situation of the large Federal garrison at Harper's Ferry, now cut off by the enemy, and to getting orders through to it. Surrounded by commanding heights, the place was indefensible, but Halleck regarded it as important, since it stood at the entrance to the Shenandoah Valley, which the invaders would probably now begin using for their line of communication with Richmond. As events will show, Lee took the same view as Halleck. Both Halleck and McClellan attempted to get messengers through to Harper's Ferry. Atkins S. Lawrence and Edward Meagher, sent out by Halleck, both failed; Lawrence was captured but escaped the next day. Three couriers, provided by Pinkerton and sent out by McClellan with the same message, all failed to get through.[11]

Once Northern soil was threatened, even General Halleck had to relax his views about the propriety of officially encouraged espionage. He employed at this time W. J. Gaines and John A. Knight as spies; Gaines also performed messenger duty, beginning August 29, when Halleck was having to communicate with General Pope by courier. If Halleck's conscience was troubled by employing spies, his guilt may have been assuaged by their failure to achieve noticeable results. Gaines seems to have been an especially poor choice for the job; while the armies were fighting a major battle well to the north of the Potomac on September 14, he reported Longstreet and A. P. Hill at Leesburg. Halleck kept both men on the payroll for the rest of the month, however, and his object may have been more than obtaining information about the enemy. He was seriously worried about the possible enemy designs on Washington, a threat that concerned McClellan less than Halleck earnestly believed it should. Halleck may have maintained his own sources in the hope of checking McClellan's reports about the Confederates.[12]

By afternoon of September 9 there was no longer any doubt that the enemy was concentrated at and about Frederick, and McClellan asserted, "I am now in condition to watch him closely." This satisfied the requirement he had stipulated for going "after them without an hour's delay," but he had forgotten that promise; now he was awaiting findings from interrogation of captured enemy cavalrymen.

Earlier in the day he had informed Halleck that "Pleasonton's report of last night that there were 100,000 rebels on this side of the river was derived from the notorious [guerrilla] Captain White; it is not fully reliable." But at 7:30 P.M., again unmindful of what he had previously said, he topped White and Pleasonton by telegraphing Halleck, "From such information as can be obtained, Jackson and Longstreet have about 110,000 men of all arms near Frederick, with some cavalry this side." Now he was getting the feel of things; like the McClellan of old, he was giving the Confederates more than double their true strength. In fact the 50,000 with which the invasion began was rapidly being reduced by straggling.[13]

Stuart was now known to be based at Urbana, near Frederick, from where his horsemen were fanning out to screen the infantry. Jackson's force was in and immediately about Frederick, but McClellan, as if wishing to save Stonewall the future embarrassment of his legendary encounter there with Barbara Frietschie, put him at New Market, nine miles to the east. McClellan read this as an indication of an intended movement on Baltimore.[14]

President Lincoln probed gently for a hint of action by telegraphing McClellan on the morning of the 10th, "How does it look now?" He received in reply a long message showing that McClellan had corrected his error regarding Jackson's position but now believed him to be in command of the main Rebel force. "I have scouts and spies pushed forward in every direction," he wrote (a claim not substantiated in the records), "and shall soon be possessed of reliable and definite information." Early in the day he ordered his divisions to move up to a ridge within ten miles of Frederick, but he halted the right wing short of its destination when scouts with its advance units found "that the mass of the enemy was still at Frederick."[15]

Then came word that the enemy apparently was retiring. It was from a Unionist citizen who had been allowed to go from Frederick to Hagerstown that morning and had passed Jackson's command on the road, marching in the same direction. This report, telegraphed from Harrisburg by Governor Curtin, included one other interesting piece of news: "The sheriff of Hagerstown, a reliable Union man, . . . met a rebel scout, a personal friend, to-day, who advised him to leave Hagerstown immediately."[16] A short time later a telegraph operator at Hagerstown reported, "Jackson's advance within 3 miles of this place. He had only his own corps. I will retreat along the line of the railroad. . . ."[17] Before the end of the day fragments of information corroborating these reports were received from an unnamed spy whom General Julius White, at Martinsburg, had sent into Maryland two days before; from a party of cavalry that had been escorting a Union officer on a cross-country ride near Boonsboro; and even from Colonel Dixon S. Miles, commander at Harper's Ferry.[18]

Clearly the invaders were drawing back from Frederick, and the chief question was whether they were going into Pennsylvania or returning to Virginia by way of crossings farther up the Potomac. Now, on September 11, McClellan put his army in motion again; Burnside, commanding the right wing, was ordered to scout toward New Market, east of Frederick, and to go all the way to Frederick if he could do so without bringing on a general engagement.[19]

McClellan was "after them," but not without his familiar complaint of being outnumbered. (Confederate strength had been doubled simply by the replacing of Pope with McClellan.) Late in the day he wrote Halleck, "All the evidence that has been accumulated from various sources since we left Washington goes to prove most conclusively that almost the entire rebel army in Virginia, amounting to not less than 120,000 men, is in the vicinity of Frederick City. . . . Several brigades joined them yesterday, direct from Richmond, two deserters from which say that they saw no other troops between Richmond and Leesburg. . . . They are probably aware that their forces are numerically superior to ours by at least 25 per cent."[20]

If the Confederates had had 120,000, they would have outnumbered the Army of the Potomac by 35 percent. But the 120,000 figure, tripling the number to which Lee had been reduced by straggling, was a product of the same kind of intelligence work that had given the Confederates 200,000 in the Seven Days battles — rumors and guesses from sources with no access whatever to the facts — or the result of improvised plants by Stuart's men in contact with Maryland citizens. The record does not show that Pinkerton contributed to this estimate. The unusual amount of straggling would have enabled him to acquire fairly complete information on what divisions and brigades were present, but he had long since learned that his chief would not accept numbers estimated on so logical a basis as a list of the units composing the enemy army. McClellan adopted the 120,000 figure simply because it agreed with his thinking.

The invaders continued to spread the word that they were going to Pennsylvania.[21] If this was a planted story, it was easy to evaluate: the Rebels were either staying put or going almost anywhere *but* Pennsylvania. If it was a baseless rumor, however, Pennsylvania could not be ruled out. There was a third possibility — that Lee *was* planning to invade Pennsylvania and that word of his plan had leaked out to his troops. Confederate security had always seemed so tight that Federal headquarters officers could have been excused for rejecting this third interpretation out of hand, lest they be accused of naiveté.

Governor Curtin was calling out Pennsylvania's militia and asking for a general from McClellan's army to command it. He also urged that an army of 80,000 disciplined troops be sent to him. Citizen committees in Philadelphia were petitioning the Federal government for protection. To these pleas Washington yielded partway, ordering two regular officers to Harrisburg — General Andrew Porter, McClellan's provost marshal general, to supervise the mustering in and organizing of new volunteers, and General John F. Reynolds, a Pennsylvanian and a division commander, to take command of Curtin's militia.[22]

Reynolds's chief, Joe Hooker, now commanding the First Corps, was not an easy prey to alarms; he wrote headquarters urging, unsuccessfully, that the order be ignored. "A scared governor," declared the unscared Hooker, "ought not to be permitted to destroy the usefulness of an entire division of the army, on the eve of important operations. . . . It is satisfactory to my mind that the rebels have no more intention of going to Harrisburg than they have of going to heaven. It is only in the United States that atrocities like this are entertained."[23]

Curtin telegraphed on the 12th, gratefully accepting Reynolds in lieu of 80,000 troops, and adding a bit of information indicating that his tractability may have been derived from more than calming efforts that Lincoln had been making. "I have advices," the governor wrote, "that Jackson is crossing [back over] the river at Williamsport, and probably the whole rebel army will be drawn from Maryland."[24]

Jackson's crossing had been detected by an intelligence service improvised by the worried governor at McClellan's request. This group, headed by William J. Palmer, a twenty-five-year-old cavalry captain, was scouting the Hagerstown area, from the Maryland-Pennsylvania state line to the Potomac. Palmer reported to Alexander K. McClure, publisher and politico at Chambersburg, temporarily a major, who complained to Curtin that he had less than a hundred men, "not twenty of them within fifteen miles of me." When Curtin received this report, a visitor in his office, Congressman Thaddeus Stevens, told him, "Well, McClure will do something. If he can't do better, he'll instruct the toll keeper not to permit Lee's army to pass through."[25]

The only men Palmer had at hand were raw recruits. He was captain of the Anderson Cavalry, an elite troop of Pennsylvanians organized in 1861 to serve as headquarters cavalry under General Robert Anderson, the defender of Fort Sumter, during Anderson's brief command in Kentucky. General Buell, commanding the Department of the Ohio, inherited the Anderson Cavalry and now wanted more men of its caliber. In July 1862 Palmer returned to Pennsylvania to recruit his troop up to battalion strength. Business and professional men, eligible for commissions, flocked to his recruiting stations to enlist as privates in such numbers that he ended up with three battalions — a regiment, the 15th Pennsylvania Cavalry, with himself as its colonel. But only a handful of these men were available when the Army of Northern Virginia arrived on Pennsylvania's southern border.

Palmer, a native of Delaware and a Quaker, had been a personal assistant to the president of the Pennsylvania Central Railroad. This connection gave him a valuable partner in his scouting mission, William Bender Wilson, a Penn Central telegrapher who had served as a military telegraph operator at Harrisburg during the trying days of April 1861. And a small number of Palmer's recruits, as fast as they could be given arms and uniforms, were sent to him and Wilson at Greencastle, between Chambersburg and Hagerstown.

Palmer and Wilson moved to Hagerstown September 9; under instructions from Curtin to find the enemy and keep him in sight, they reported frequently to Chambersburg and Harrisburg. Wilson carried portable equipment so that he could communicate by tapping onto the wire that ran along the railroad northward from Hagerstown. In addition to his telegraphic duties he would assist Palmer in interrogating refugees and returned scouts, writing reports of the findings of their joint effort, and serving as a clearinghouse of information — activities so pressing that at one point he worked a full week on seven hours' sleep.[26] This arrangement, set up by a state government and a railroad, proved more effective than any intelligence-gathering system the Federal government had yet devised. Unfortunately, as will be seen, Palmer and Wilson were much more effective in gathering intelligence than McClure and Curtin were in communicating it to the army.

On September 10, Palmer's and Wilson's first full day in Maryland, several sources reported the enemy's withdrawal from Frederick toward Hagerstown, and the two men made contacts that confirmed the movement. Next they learned that Jackson had turned left off the Frederick-Hagerstown road, heading for the Potomac. This looked like a threat to Martinsburg and Harper's Ferry, and Wilson sent Thomas Noakes, a local spy, to inform General White, Noakes's chief, at Martinsburg.[27] Two days later White's command joined Colonel Miles at Harper's Ferry.

An enemy party consisting of about 250 cavalrymen came into Hagerstown the next morning. Palmer and Wilson decamped separately, arranging to meet again at the state line. From there Wilson got off a telegram reporting the cavalry's arrival; at 11 A.M. Curtin dispatched a one-sentence report of the incursion to Washington for relay to McClellan.

Palmer obtained temporary lodging at a farmhouse in the outskirts of Hagerstown; a few hours later the invading cavalry happened to establish their camp on the same farm. Although they did not learn the captain's identity or purpose (he had changed into civilian clothes), neither did he learn a great deal from them although he ate with their officers at the farmer's table. They restricted his movements so severely, however, that he was able that night to scout only the visiting cavalry and two regiments of infantry that had arrived by the same road and camped in town. But the appearance of even small numbers of infantry was a significant development, and in addition Palmer had some second-hand evidence, gleaned from townspeople and Confederate soldiers, that made interesting reading when telegraphed to Major McClure:

> My impression is that another infantry and cavalry force . . . people there say Longstreet's corps, came in [from the east]. . . . The rebel sentinels told me the main body of Jackson's cavalry, with Jackson himself, turned off at Boonsboro and went to Williamsport, probably to flank our men at Harper's Ferry. This was confirmed by the statement of another rebel cavalryman to my landlord, whom he knew and called [on] upon first reaching Hagerstown. . . . From the conciliatory manner toward the citizens in which the rebels behaved yesterday (they even went without grain for their horses, when plenty could have been seized), I think they imagine they will hold Maryland.

This was the earliest source of Curtin's "advices" on Jackson's recrossing of the Potomac. Although it was correct, at that moment it conflicted with an earlier report of Jackson's move in the opposite direction, toward Hagerstown. Also important, though still tentative, was the appearance of a major force at Hagerstown, Longstreet's "corps." It is more likely that the two infantry regiments Palmer had spotted were elements of a sizable force than that they were mere supports for a cavalry incursion.

Palmer's Confederate cavalry neighbors were under orders to march the next day (September 12) into Pennsylvania. Although aware that the movement might be merely a feint, he had neither enough men nor good enough horses to give them a fight, so he slipped through their lines and at 4 A.M. rejoined Wilson at Greencastle. The Confederates' intentions were still a mystery, but Palmer had learned enough to establish that they were not abruptly ending their expedition into the North.

Palmer soon left Greencastle for further reconnoitering; Wilson remained, sending out scouts, and at 12:30 P.M. he had more news:

> An enrolling officer of Washington County [Hagerstown], Maryland, left Williamsport at 9 o'clock this morning. He saw enemy crossing [the Potomac] yesterday at Williamsport. Says [the enemy] threw some fifteen thousand over the river and seventy-five pieces of artillery. This morning he saw the wagon train returning. . . . The main body of the troops that marched on Williamsport entered there at 11 A.M. yesterday under the command of Jackson in person, and immediately began to cross the river. . . . This gentleman's information is straight and reliable.

Within a few hours several more refugees corroborated the story of Jackson's crossing into Virginia, and General Darius Couch at Barnesville received a deserter from Brigadier General John G. Walker's division, who reported that Walker's troops had crossed into Virginia at Point of Rocks. These developments looked more and more like an encirclement of Harper's Ferry.

By now Palmer's pickets were retracing the steps of a retreat they had made that morning, and Wilson was telegraphing "I do not apprehend an invasion of Pennsylvania, but think a cavalry dash far more than probable, and that will be done out of impudence." Wilson's informants had given paroles at Hagerstown; he reported, "[They] are cautious about what information they give out and desire that their names be suppressed." And some of the people of Greencastle were showing another form of timidity. They wanted, Wilson said, "to haul down the flag this morning, but I told them I wanted it over me whilst I remained, and she still floats."[28]

Palmer's and Wilson's coverage of the Potomac crossings drew not only upon interviews with travelers from Williamsport but also upon interrogation of deserters from Jackson's command. Their dispatches included the kind of details a commanding general appreciates because it assures him of the reporter's intimacy with his subject matter. But in relaying their information to McClellan and the War Department McClure and Curtin severely abbreviated some of their reports and totally withheld the others. The only fractions of Palmer's and Wilson's output known to have survived this screening were shortened so radically in Curtin's dispatches that they lost most of their force. There were four of these, all transmitted from Harrisburg without mention of Palmer and with Wilson identified but once, as "our operator at the State line." The four were the September 11 report of the arrival of enemy cavalry in Hagerstown (with the significant appearance of infantry omitted); Curtin's September 12 telegram (quoted above), reporting that Jackson was recrossing the Potomac; a telegram of the 13th in which the governor with extreme overcaution reported the two-day-old news of Longstreet's arrival at Hagerstown (to be discussed later); and a very brief report derived from a spy's penetration of occupied Hagerstown on the 14th (discussed later).[29] Curtin's severe economizing in the transmission of information from his most reliable and by far most productive source is incongruous. On September 12 he devoted two hundred words to the report of a citizen who had been among a small force of Confederate cavalry northeast of Frederick and had come away thoroughly gulled. The enemy, he said, had 190,000 in Maryland and 250,000 in Virginia, and was seizing Harper's Ferry and Martinsburg merely in preparation for the influx of these hosts into Pennsylvania.[30]

Curtin's generosity with alarms was matched by Pleasonton, who relayed a citizen's report that Lee's maneuvers in Maryland were only a feint intended to cover a movement on Washington by Joe Johnston, now recovered from his Seven Pines injuries, who was in the Leesburg area waiting to cross into Maryland with an army of 150,000. Pleasonton was properly skeptical but felt compelled to pass on the report.[31]

. .   . .   . .

While Palmer and Wilson were at work thirty miles to the northwest of McClellan's army, General Burnside was advancing its right wing to find that the Confederates had indeed abandoned Frederick. The Federals entered the town on the 12th, and by the next morning McClellan had established headquarters there. Almost immediately he had an important message for the President:

> I have the whole rebel force in front of me, but am confident, and no time shall be lost. I have a difficult task to perform, but with God's blessing will accomplish it. I think Lee has made a gross mistake, and that he will be severely punished for it. The army is in motion as rapidly as possible. I hope for a great success if the plans of the rebels remain unchanged. We have possession of Catoctin. I have all the plans of the rebels, and will catch them in their own trap if my men are equal to the emergency.[32]

All the plans of the rebels. . . .

McClellan was referring to the greatest intelligence find of the war — a copy of Special Orders No. 191 of the Army of Northern Virginia. Wrapped around three cigars — surely the most famous cigars in American history — the order was found by Corporal Barton W. Mitchell, a soldier in his forties, when his regiment, the 27th Indiana Infantry, camped in a clover field at Frederick that morning, Saturday, September 13. Mitchell's regimental commander, recognizing the importance of the find, took it directly to Brigadier General Alpheus Williams, commanding the Twelfth Corps, who promptly sent his adjutant to army headquarters bearing the precious document.[33]

S.O. 191 revealed Lee's plans for troop movements over several days. McClellan immediately treated it as genuine; the censure he has sometimes received for this supposedly uncritical acceptance ignores the obvious fact that if the Confederates had wanted to place a false order in his hands, they would have chosen a much surer method than dropping it in a field that had only a remote chance of ever being occupied by Federal soldiers or anyone else who would put it in the right hands. General Williams's forwarding note had stated his opinion that the document was genuine; by mentioning that it was found in a field he invited McClellan to agree.

Although McClellan saw instantly the enormous value of this acquisition, he failed to insure that it would be treated as a military secret of the first rank. As a result, some officers who left Frederick early the next day told the story to a Washington correspondent of the *New York Herald,* which printed it on September 15. This was fast action even for the aggressive *Herald*.

This incident exposes a weakness in the Confederate secret service's coverage of the Northern press. Its headquarters failed to pick up the leak despite the supposed effectiveness of its "Secret Line" in providing Richmond authorities with newspapers collected at Washington. Lee did not learn of the loss of his order until some time early in 1863. The story appeared in the *New York Journal of Commerce* on January 1 and received wide publicity following McClellan's testimony to the congressional Joint Committee on the Conduct of the War the following March. Lee called the enemy's possession of the order "a great calamity."[34]

The copy of S.O. 191 that fell into Federal hands was intended for Major General D. H. Hill. Hill did not realize that army headquarters had made a copy for him; he had received a copy written out for him by Jackson, to whose corps his division belonged. Because headquarters records showed no receipt signed by Hill, the loss, once it became known through the publicity it received, was attributed to him. But he and his division had never been near the field where the paper was found. The only plausible explanation of the loss is that the order and the cigars were unknowingly dropped by a courier on his way to Hill's headquarters; the courier did not report the loss, and army headquarters' lack of a receipt from Hill escaped notice until the story became public.[35]

Lee's order, issued at Frederick on the 9th, prescribed specific missions for all the major elements of his army. Here was a detailed explanation of the mystery of the Confederates' sudden movement westward from Frederick: it was obviously intended to make their situation secure for protracted operations in the North. As Lee wanted the Shenandoah Valley for a reliable line of communication, his chief obstacle (aside from the Army of the Potomac) was the Federal force at Martinsburg and Harper's Ferry. His order directed Jackson's "command," its composition unstated, to cross back over the Potomac, "capture such of [the enemy] as may be at Martinsburg, and intercept such as may attempt to escape from Harper's Ferry." The divisions of Major Generals Lafayette McLaws and Richard H. Anderson, McLaws commanding, were temporarily separated from Longstreet's command and ordered to "endeavor to capture the enemy at Harper's Ferry and vicinity," approaching from Maryland Heights, on the north side of the Potomac opposite the Ferry. John G. Walker's division was to seize Loudoun Heights, across the Shenandoah River from the Ferry, and "co-operate with Generals McLaws and Jackson, and intercept the retreat of the enemy." Longstreet, also heading a "command" of unspecified composition, and accompanied by the army's trains, was to occupy Boonsboro, on the western slope of South Mountain, to await the return of the three detached forces, which were to rejoin the main body at Boonsboro or Hagerstown. D. H. Hill's division was to serve as rear guard.[36]

Lee's intention, not stated in his order, was to envelop Harper's Ferry on three sides, each with commanding heights — McLaws on the north, Walker on the east, Jackson on the west. The instruction to Walker to cooperate with McLaws and Jackson implied that there was likely to be joint action somewhere, in which case Jackson's seniority would confer on him the command of the merged forces. The likeliest locale for such action was Harper's Ferry, but the order seemed to make Martinsburg, thirteen miles distant, the focus of Jackson's operations. History has assumed, correctly, that Lee conceived the capture of Harper's Ferry as a Stonewall Jackson affair, since the three detached forces did unite there under his direction, but Special Orders No. 191 did not specify that he was to command a united force. It ordered the capture of the Federal troops at, or escaping from, Harper's Ferry and Martinsburg, but without explaining that the purpose was not simply to take prisoners but to seize those two places. S.O. 191 was not a well-written order.

McClellan did not telegraph the news of his good fortune to Halleck until 11 P.M., saying that the order had come into his hands that evening. That was an out-and-out misstatement: his "all the plans of the rebels" message to Lincoln was sent at noon; he forwarded a copy of S.O. 191 to Pleasonton at 3 P.M.; and at 6:20 he listed the enemy movements it projected in a dispatch to General William B. Franklin, whose posting with his Sixth Corps several miles to the south of Frederick would lead to operations separate from the rest of the army. To Halleck, McClellan said he had "good reasons for believing [the enemy force] amounts to 120,000 men or more," and he named eight of its components in a detailing of enemy organization so confusing that Halleck would not have had the time or the patience to unravel it by telegram.[37]

A more serious flaw in McClellan's message to his chief was a statement that the enemy columns "took the roads specified in the order." He had asked Pleasonton to "ascertain whether the order of march [prescribed in S.O. 191] has thus far been followed." As he must have known, Pleasonton could answer that question fully only by considerably expanding the area his troopers were reconnoitering. That would take a couple of days, and they would have to cope with Jeb Stuart's expert screening operations. Pleasonton chose to answer quickly and inconclusively: "As near as I can judge the order of march of the enemy that you sent me has been followed as closely as circumstances would permit."[38] That statement began with one strong qualifier and ended with another, but the words in between were words McClellan wanted to see. To Halleck he repeated Pleasonton's answer — minus qualifiers.

Thus McClellan adopted the view that the enemy's movements during the four days since the issuance of S.O. 191 were in strict accordance with its terms and that any intelligence reports of other movements were erroneous and could be ignored. This view would govern his actions for the next two days[39] — and it was grievously wrong; for three days important deviations from Lee's order had been in effect, governing actions of five infantry divisions — more than half of his army. Only as far as Boonsboro, fifteen miles northwest of Frederick, had Longstreet and Jackson, commanding the two principal segments of the army, followed the provisions of the order.

Longstreet's deviation was the move from Boonsboro to Hagerstown that we have seen. It involved his two infantry divisions, the cavalry unit that Captain Palmer had brushed against, and the army's trains. (As Lee's headquarters moved with him, these elements qualified as the army's main body, though their troop strength was less than that of one of the detachments, Jackson's.) By separating his command from D. H. Hill, who was based at Boonsboro, Longstreet formed a fifth segment of an already thoroughly segmented army. This shift was in response to an alarm concerning a Federal force advancing toward Hagerstown from the direction of Chambersburg. A Federal "force" actually was coming down from Pennsylvania; it was Captain Palmer's tiny collection of cavalry recruits.

Jackson's deviation from S.O. 191 was caused by a report that Federals still occupied Martinsburg, which was true at that time. That persuaded him to cross the Potomac at Williamsport instead of Sharpsburg, as called for in the order. Approaching from Sharpsburg, straight east of Martinsburg, he would not prevent the Federals from escaping westward back into the Alleghenies. Coming down on them from upriver, he could drive them down on Harper's Ferry, adding them to the force about to be enveloped. This change of route added at least a day's marching.[40] The delay in his return to Lee would have been fatal if the adversary in the upcoming battle had been anyone but McClellan.

These movements were promptly reflected in reports reaching McClellan — twenty-nine of them. They were clear on one point: there were movements beyond Boonsboro in a northwesterly direction, which did not accord with the terms of S.O. 191. On all other points they conflicted with each other so thoroughly that they made it impossible to draw detailed conclusions as to what was going on on the Rebels' side of the lines. In the four days Lee's troops had been on the road, September 10–13, seven reports had shown Confederate forces approaching Hagerstown or already there, but four of the seven showed Jackson in command, and only two named the actual commander of these forces, Longstreet. Jackson was four times correctly reported leading a force on or headed for the Potomac — and the same was incorrectly reported of Longstreet, also four times. Three reports had the invaders heading for Harrisburg and Philadelphia; as S.O. 191 clearly showed these to be dead wrong, they tended to harden McClellan's distrust of the whole accumulation of intelligence reports in which he could not distinguish the true from the false.[41]

These confused reports are the only visible reason McClellan decided to rely on S.O. 191 as his guide to the enemy's movements. But those reports were by no means a sufficient reason; that reliance required him to assume that four days after its issuance the order was still in effect down to the last detail — and that every one of twenty-nine reports to the contrary was wrong. So far as the records reveal, he had not one report of enemy movements to support his assumption that Lee's order was still being followed to the letter. His reliance on its exact terms insured that he would be acting on the basis of wrong information.

His most serious error was ignoring the seven reports of Confederates at or approaching Hagerstown. The conflicts as to who commanded that Rebel force could not logically be construed as nullifying the report that there were significant numbers of Confederates at that place. After all, S.O. 191 had made Hagerstown an alternative to Boonsboro as the place where the army would reassemble.

McClellan might have been spared his "Hagerstown error" if Palmer's and Wilson's reports had not been handled in such an inexplicably poor way at Chambersburg or Harrisburg or both. The McClure-Curtin team's worst mishandling occurred at the worst possible time — the day S.O. 191 was found, a crucial day in McClellan's decision-making. On that day Palmer interrogated the most impressive source he had found to date, a New Yorker who had deserted from Jackson's column. The captain's report to McClure emphasized the man's knowledge of Confederate organization, his intelligence, and his highly probable reliability, and stated that he "confirms the report that Longstreet's army corps [is] in Hagerstown." This was a report that would have shaken McClellan out of his fixation on the everlasting applicability of every detail of S.O. 191 if anything could. But it was condensed even more severely than the others; Palmer's firm language was watered down to this: "Longstreet's division is said to have reached Hagerstown last night."[42]

In fact, proper handling of the whole series of Palmer-Wilson reports could have saved McClellan from the hopeless problem of reconciling twenty-nine differing reports. The two men and their scouts were covering the entire area from the Mason-Dixon Line (the Maryland-Pennsylvania border) to the Potomac, and unlike the army's other sources they were not making any mistakes in reporting on enemy movements. Curtin's long-winded telegraphing of rumors and possible plants shows that he was not worrying about his telegraph bill. He should also have identified the source of each report; the name Palmer would have gotten McClellan's attention, since he had requested the captain's services, and

Wilson's partnership with him would have been evident. With the full reports in hand Little Mac would have realized that this was a trustworthy intelligence source, and one operating on the enemy's immediate flank. Those reports would have stood out so sharply that all the others could have been set aside. And at the time S.O. 191 was found, the earliest Palmer-Wilson reports had been in hand for two days at Chambersburg and presumably Harrisburg — long enough to establish their quality in McClellan's mind. That might have saved him from his obsession with the Lost Order.

A basic flaw in the Chambersburg-Harrisburg intelligence arrangements was the presence of amateurs, McClure and Curtin, in the reporting chain. The reason they screened out some of Palmer's and Wilson's reports and reduced others to weakly worded one-liners must have been that they did not recognize the quality of the intelligence and the investigative work that underlay it. Failing to appreciate that they had created a gem of a small intelligence service, they managed to quash its effectiveness.

. .   . .   . .

In the telegram that informed Lincoln of the acquisition of the enemy's plans, McClellan promised that "no time shall be lost" in seizing the opportunity that beckoned. Speed was of the essence, for the movements called for in S.O. 191 had been in progress for four days, possibly five as far as McClellan knew. Harper's Ferry's ammunition would hold out for only a few days; the enemy's detachments would soon be rejoining the main body. But neither that threat nor his promise to Lincoln deterred Little Mac from his habitual foot-dragging. He had had the Lost Order in hand for three hours when he asked Pleasonton whether the enemy's movements accorded with its terms. Three more hours went by before he informed Franklin of the contents of the order and directed him to enter Pleasant Valley via Crampton's Gap and attack the rear of the McLaws-Anderson detachment; it was then too late in the day for Franklin to do anything but plan an early start the next morning. And it was almost another three hours before McClellan began issuing orders to the elements of his main force — much too late to put any troops on the road from Frederick until the next day, though three divisions of one corps, the Ninth, were not far from Middletown, eight miles west of Frederick, at the time S.O. 191 was acquired.[43] By not setting his whole army in motion promptly upon receipt of the Lost Order, McClellan gave Lee an additional eighteen hours to reassemble his scattered forces. That extra three-quarters of a day was to prove crucial.

The delay was caused by McClellan's misjudgment of both the Confederates' numbers and their positions. His estimate of their strength,

120,000, called forth his usual caution. Of greatest concern was the un-counted "command" of Longstreet, normally the chief of a corps. A com-mand might be either smaller or larger than a corps; in Longstreet's case it was smaller, since he had given up McLaws and Anderson to their separate mission, but McClellan assumed it was larger. He also had to allow for D. H. Hill's division, the rear guard, to be available to Long-street as reinforcement. Accordingly, he placed nearly 70,000 in the force he would send against Longstreet and Hill, thus giving himself almost a five-to-one advantage over their three divisions. He spared only 19,500 men for Franklin to lead against McLaws's two divisions, but that would still give Franklin a two-to-one edge.

McClellan's initial objective when his army took the road on Sunday, September 14, would be Turner's Gap, the National Road's passageway over South Mountain and the principal entrance to the Cumberland Valley. Boonsboro, the supposed position of Longstreet and Hill, lay two miles beyond the gap. Hill as rear guard was virtually certain to defend the gap, and Longstreet's entire command, according to McClellan's calculations, would be in Hill's immediate rear.[44]

The orders that were so long in the writing were a product of McClel-lan's habit of planning for the worst case. A small mistake in the face of the awesome enemy numbers could be devastating; his army must func-tion with total efficiency. To assure clear lines of command, he arranged an order of march that ignored the need for speed. It happened that Hooker's First Corps, paired with Reno's Ninth in the right wing under Burnside, had the rearmost position at Frederick. But the Ninth, by now at and beyond Middletown, was perforce the army's advance element. McClellan joined Hooker's corps to Reno's by placing Hooker at the head of Sunday's march, which meant that two corps and an unattached division, occupying Frederick positions ahead of Hooker's, could not take the road until Hooker's troops had all passed. Reno and Hooker got into a fight with Hill's rear guard on South Mountain; as might have been expected, the units that had been held back to follow Hooker arrived too late to provide help that would have been decisive.

Although McClellan had warned Pleasonton of the danger probably lurking in Turner's Gap, the provision he made for clearing the way to Boonsboro, his all-important objective, consisted only of a cavalry force led by Pleasonton and a single brigade of infantry from Jacob Cox's division of the Ninth Corps. Warned en route that his brigade would meet stiff resistance at Turner's Gap, Cox summoned his whole division and took it on a flanking movement to nearby Fox's Gap, where it encountered Rebel infantry and artillery. Thus began the battle of South Mountain. Cox's brigades fought unsupported for four or five hours, until midafternoon. Burnside did not get his entire command into ac-tion until late in the day, when Hooker's corps arrived at their forward position. Meanwhile Hill had brought three more brigades into the fight and Longstreet had arrived from Hagerstown with David R. Jones's division and half of Hood's. Lee was only stalling for time; soon the sun would set and the battle would be over. The Ninth Corps, while losing its commander, Jesse Reno, to a sharpshooter's bullet, fought its way to within a half-mile of Turner's Gap, and Hooker's troops drove back a hard-fighting and outnumbered enemy force. But the battle dwindled down and ended under cover of darkness. Lee, after barely holding off a Yankee army that outnumbered him two to one (McClellan's slow movement had greatly reduced the odds), took his troops off the mountain during the night and withdrew westward toward the Potomac.[45]

Franklin's corps, six miles to the south, was halted in Crampton's Gap by a hastily assembled collection of Confederate cavalry and infantry. While he was pondering his next move, Henry W. Slocum's division made a head-on charge that took the gap and put the Sixth Corps in Pleasant Valley. A mile or two to the south the Rebels set up a defense line, and McLaws reinforced it from Maryland Heights, which he had taken on Saturday. Franklin, concluding that he was outnumbered, gave no further trouble.[46]

. .   . .   . .

McClellan had caught the enemy north of the Potomac with 25,000 men — the commands of Longstreet, Hill, and McLaws — to his own 87,000, and the only benefit he had thus far derived from this advantage was a slight edge in a battle whose main result was to alert Lee to his danger. McClellan expected that by advancing to Boonsboro he would bring on a general engagement with the Longstreet force that he evidently estimated at a third of the enemy's 120,000. But no straight-ahead movement such as McClellan organized would induce Lee with his present "main body" to give battle against the numbers he would count on the Federals to have. McClellan could force a general battle only by making a surprise attack via a flanking movement, and neither the geography nor McClellan's style favored such a maneuver.

One worthwhile objective was within reach, however — Hill's division, isolated at or near Boonsboro by Longstreet's departure to Hagerstown. There was enough time to engage Hill's brigades before Longstreet, now at least a half-day's march away, could bring reinforcements. That much McClellan probably could have accomplished if, without waiting for Hooker, he had sent the entire Ninth Corps to Turner's Gap at the time Cox led his division against its defenders. And by the time Longstreet could arrive, McClellan's three-plus corps from Frederick, which with Hooker in their rear would have had a much earlier start, could have been on the scene.

Thus McClellan could have had the general battle he sought if — this is a very big *if* — Lee saw fit to set his three divisions against such a huge army, and if McClellan in his march from Frederick gave priority to speed rather than organizational tidiness. But this course of action was beyond McClellan's ken; Governor Curtin's condensation of Palmer's report of Longstreet's move to Hagerstown was in language so weak that it could not begin to shake McClellan's faith in the captured order's placement of Longstreet at Boonsboro.

. .   ..   ..

On September 13, probably about the same time Lee's order came into McClellan's hands, Captain Palmer learned new details that added certainty to his findings. His pickets were then at the Maryland line, between Hagerstown and Greencastle, when a civilian approached them on a road leading from Williamsport. Taken to the captain, he identified himself as the Reverend I. J. Stine, of the Lutheran faith. Stine and Palmer rode to Greencastle, where in the home of John Rowe, a local political leader, they had an extended interview. Stine was a Pennsylvanian, thirty-two years old, a former schoolteacher; he had been temporarily filling a pulpit near Hagerstown. He said that on the 11th he had seen Jackson's rear guard cross the Potomac at Williamsport, that he had been in Hagerstown after the Confederates' arrival there, and that he had spent two days in the twelve-mile stretch of country between Hagerstown and Williamsport. He had learned much detail about Lee's various actions for taking Harper's Ferry and the positions of most of the force with Lee. Although his report of these moves came a day later than others, it was the most comprehensive of any, and much of it was eyewitness information.

Palmer promptly reported the acquisition of this promising new source to McClure. His message — written too hurriedly to show proper deference to McClure's military rank and political standing — reported: "Rev. Mr. Stine says they [the Confederates] told him in Hagerstown yesterday that all [their] scouts have returned reporting that the Yankees were as thick as grasshoppers at the State Line. It will be well to keep up this impression, & as Col. Campbell's force comes up to-night, it should come with considerable ostentation — the locomotives whistling, men cheering &c."[47] The deception that Palmer was hoping to effect with a reinforcement of about two hundred had already been accomplished by a "force" one-tenth that size. He did not learn that it was his own movement southward from Chambersburg that caused Lee to shift Longstreet to Hagerstown.

Hearing the cannonading from the battle at Turner's Gap and reasoning that troops might be pulling out of Hagerstown to join the fight, Palmer saw an opportunity to obtain more information from that locality.

Although he had information that the Rebels had pickets on all the local roads, with orders to shoot anyone attempting to pass, he sent Stine back to Hagerstown. The project was successful, and at 9 P.M. Palmer had more news:

> My scout reached Hagerstown at 3 P.M. to-day, at which time he says Longstreets corps excepting Toombs' Brigade was leaving Hagerstown. They commenced leaving about eleven A.M., and he saw rear of Longstreets column go over the hill near Funkstown, say two miles from Hagerstown on Boonsboro Road at 3:30 P.M. . . . He could not see any troops but cavalry and a few infantry sentinels in or about Hagerstown, but was informed that Toombs Brigade was still there encamped two miles this side of town on Green Castle Road. They also thought there was fighting to-day at Harpers Ferry from the direction of the cannonading.
> My scout also reports that the Division of rebel army which was encamped one and a half miles east of Hagerstown on Boonsboro Road . . . commenced leaving for Boonsboro this morning.

Stine's report gave better information than any yet received on the identity and positioning of the forces around Hagerstown; Longstreet's whole command was now firmly located. Palmer also had taken several enemy deserters; one of them, from the number of improbabilities in his story, may have been a plant, but another man gave a correct account of the composition of Jackson's "command," which had been omitted from S.O. 191. And "our intelligent deserter the New Yorker" had added to the information he supplied in his first examination. He estimated the enemy strength at and around Hagerstown at 40,000. Adding to this figure the 30,000 that had been given for Jackson's command and the estimates for other Confederate units in the locality that he had heard about, Palmer calculated 100,000 as the enemy's force in Maryland. He was too new to intelligence work to have acquired a professional's skepticism in regard to enemy numbers.

The product of all this information-gathering, including the findings of Stine's second visit to Hagerstown, was a 650-word telegram that Palmer sent to McClure late that day, September 14. This is the only piece of intelligence writing amounting to a "situation summary" to be found in the voluminous records of the months McClellan commanded the Army of the Potomac. (The Orléans brothers had only distantly approached such comprehensiveness in their analysis of data on fortifications and armament at the Confederate bases in Virginia.) Palmer detailed the movements involved in the enemy's occupation of Hagerstown and surveyed the situation in the entire area he and Wilson covered, up to the time Longstreet's troops departed for Sunday's battle. Despite the New Yorker's erroneous naming of two of the divisions normally in Longstreet's corps, which in any case would not have been detectable by

McClure or Curtin, this survey cried out for inclusion in McClellan's picture of the total situation. However, only one fragment of it, reporting Longstreet's departure from Hagerstown that day, survived the editorial pencils at Chambersburg and Harrisburg, and that was sent not by Curtin but by General Reynolds.[48]

. .   . .   . .

Lee had been aware of the Federals' advance since Saturday night, when Ninth Corps campfires dotted the landscape between Middletown and South Mountain. The Federals' impressive showing in Sunday's battle and the advance against McLaws's rear made clear to the Southern commander that his forces north of the Potomac were exposed to capture or a defeat approaching annihilation. He had sent word to Jackson and McLaws to hurry the seizure of Harper's Ferry and rejoin the army. When he began retiring westward he was already preparing to return to Virginia, but before reaching the Potomac he received Jackson's word of the imminent fall of Harper's Ferry. He halted his small army and placed it at Sharpsburg, south of Hagerstown in a pocket scarcely four miles wide between Antietam Creek and the river, as close to his detached forces as he could get without crossing into Virginia. His hope lay in the possibility that the fight at South Mountain had slowed the enemy's advance enough to enable him to concentrate his army in that pocket.[49]

After Sunday's battle McClellan reported a "glorious victory," a considerable overstatement. The next morning he said the Rebels had been "shockingly whipped." At the same time there was an ominous development in another direction; the booming of guns no longer came up the valley from Harper's Ferry. The garrison, its artillery ammunition exhausted, had surrendered, although its 2300 cavalrymen had escaped across the Potomac.[50] Lee's army, wherever it was heading, would soon be reunited.

McClellan's orders that put the army in motion Monday morning assumed that the enemy was in full retreat. He made no allowance for the possibility that a force left at Hagerstown could be lingering on his army's right rear; his assumption that S.O. 191 was still fully in effect meant that there had been no Confederate troops at Hagerstown in the first place. The force Lee and Longstreet had left behind in their march to the South Mountain battle was a brigade led by Robert Toombs, one of the Confederacy's political generals. McClellan was left unaware of its presence by the ruthless condensation of Palmer's reports, which mentioned it twice. But Toombs actually was no threat; he was marching to overtake the main body rather than attempting to harass the Federals.

Lincoln had urged that the invading army not be allowed to "get off without being hurt." Receiving the "glorious victory" report, the President raised his entreaty to "destroy the rebel army if possible." In an effort to comply, McClellan ordered Franklin to attempt to cut off Lee's retreat, a maneuver that could scarcely be made except by driving McLaws toward the objective Lee had assigned him, Harper's Ferry. By this time McLaws was already making his way across to the Ferry with no push from Franklin.[51]

As was his habit, McClellan issued no general order; his instructions went out one by one to individual commanders and had to be revised during the march in order to keep the different commands in their proper relative positions. Even then, it appears, there was neither concerted action nor rapid marching. Some of the slowness undoubtedly was the fault of the wing and corps commanders, particularly Burnside, who drew a reprimand from his good friend Mac. After an advance that was much slower than Lee's retirement, the Federals discovered the invaders' new position behind Antietam Creek. But by the time McClellan had his divisions sufficiently in hand to consider attacking, he judged the afternoon too far gone.[52]

That he had learned Lee's new position by midafternoon is shown by a 3:45 P.M. dispatch to Burnside: "The last news received is that the enemy is drawn up in line of battle about two miles beyond [Keedysville], which will bring them on the west and behind Antietam Creek. They are represented to be in considerable force under Longstreet." He verified his statement by personally inspecting the ground, drawing fire from an enemy battery. A few artillery shots directed against his person were enough to persuade McClellan that the Confederates actually could take a position not called for in S.O. 191.[53]

. .   . .   . .

The Federals' advance to the west side of South Mountain, together with the enemy's retirement almost to the Potomac, meant that Palmer's and Wilson's information, in order to reach McClellan, would no longer have to travel the long circuit through Chambersburg, Harrisburg, Washington, and Frederick, a loop of 200 miles encompassing almost 360 degrees, with two relay points where it was discarded or emasculated without their knowledge. Palmer now had a relatively unobstructed path into McClellan's lines. On the morning of September 15, even before he knew the Army of the Potomac had taken the gaps and was coming down into the Cumberland Valley, he led his Anderson Cavalry recruits into Hagerstown. He now had 200 troops and was able to capture many stragglers.

Leaving his command in Hagerstown, Palmer rode to McClellan's headquarters at Keedysville and reported to the general about midnight.

From his extensive scouting and the interrogation of deserters and stragglers, he and Wilson had a firm grasp of the situation in the Cumberland Valley. But his report fell on deaf ears; General McClellan had his own ideas about the enemy's situation. He told Palmer that Jackson that night had reinforced Lee at Sharpsburg.[54]

McClellan was crediting Jackson with a marching miracle that would have considerably surpassed Stonewall's earlier feats. Harper's Ferry had surrendered only that morning, as McClellan knew from the cessation of the very audible cannonading. It was seventeen road miles from there to Lee's new position at Sharpsburg; those were difficult miles on hilly and narrow roads, as even Jackson admitted. As commander of the combined investing forces, he had taken the surrender, and there was other business to transact before his divisions could set out to rejoin the army. Their start was much too late for so large a force to march that distance on those roads before darkness halted them. He actually reached Sharpsburg eighteen to twenty-four hours later than McClellan believed.[55] Of all the erroneous conclusions about enemy movements and positions that McClellan made after acquiring Lee's order, this one was the most damaging.

What persuaded the Young Napoleon that Jackson had overcome these restraints and rejoined Lee on the same day Harper's Ferry surrendered? The records reveal no erroneous report of Jackson's arrival. A likelier explanation is that McClellan heard cheering from the Rebel lines, inspired by news of the fall of Harper's Ferry, and interpreted that as indicating the return of one of Lee's detachments. Asking himself which one of the three detachments would most likely be the first to rejoin the main body, he would have picked Jackson's, clearly shown by S.O. 191 to be focusing attention on Martinsburg rather than Harper's Ferry. Of the three detachment commanders, only McLaws was specifically ordered to the Ferry; it could be assumed that he was expected to lead the assault and receive the surrender. Walker's orders to cooperate with the other detached forces made it unlikely that his division would return early to the main body. Jackson, however, under terms of the order could have started for Sharpsburg as soon as the Federals' capitulation was assured, without waiting for the formal surrender.

Although this explanation of McClellan's probable line of reasoning bears no resemblance to the facts of the taking of Harper's Ferry — its capture by all three of the detached forces, with Jackson directing McLaws and Walker (mainly by flag signal) and then accepting the surrender — it is consistent with his actions after he acquired S.O. 191, specifically his orders for the army's movements on both September 14 and 15, which ignored the numerous intelligence reports showing Jackson deviating from Lee's order. He was assuming that that order meant what it said, and that it contemplated for Jackson the earliest practicable time for rejoining Lee.[56] Thus we find McClellan's Lost Order fixation rational in this one case.

.. .. ..

Fog covered the ground along the Antietam on the morning of Tuesday, September 16. McClellan doubted that the Rebels were still there, but he telegraphed Halleck, "Will attack as soon as situation of enemy is developed." The promise was not kept; the fog lifted to reveal the enemy present, but McClellan took his time about placing troops in attack position, meanwhile issuing no attack orders. As much of this positioning went on before the eyes of the enemy, Lee was given a good deal of guidance as to where to place his own units. A move by Hooker's corps to the far right entailed a crossing of Antietam Creek that got him into a brief fight with Hood's division, but there was no other excitement that day. Since McClellan believed that Jackson's command was already on the field, he probably had persuaded himself that by now the other detached units had also rejoined; this would mean that the enemy was at full strength, so there was nothing to be gained by hurrying the attack. He seems to have made no attempt to reconnoiter, by cavalry or individual scouts, the routes the detachments returning from Harper's Ferry would use.

For half of the day only a third of Lee's troops, perhaps as many as 15,000, manned his lines. Walker's division and two of Jackson's divisions arrived during the afternoon, bringing the army up to two-thirds of full strength, but the divisions of A. P. Hill, McLaws, and Anderson were still absent. McClellan's army outnumbered Lee's at this point five to two; by the next morning, with McLaws's and Anderson's troops on the field, the Federal advantage would drop to two to one. McClellan always believed that the odds ran the other way. Apparently all this delay was needed to embolden him to issue, but only orally, orders to attack on the morrow, Wednesday, September 17.[57] This was the most costly of all the delays in his fourteen months in command; it reduced, probably decisively, the huge advantage in numbers he had on the morning of September 16.

.. .. ..

For the Army of Northern Virginia the battle of Antietam is a story of hopeless situations retrieved at the last minute. For the Army of the Potomac the battle is a continuation of our story of opportunities lost: it presented McClellan with several chances to redeem his costly deliberateness, but even during battle he continued to react too slowly.

His plan was to make the main attack on his right, north of Sharpsburg; then, "as soon as matters looked favorably there," to strike on the extreme left; and "whenever either of these flank movements should be successful, to advance our center with all the forces then disposable."

The sequence "right-left-center" became "right-center-left" once the battle began. It rolled from north to south as McClellan put in his units — or allowed them to go in — piecemeal: first Hooker's corps on the far right, then Mansfield's (formerly Banks's) on Hooker's left, then one of Sumner's divisions still farther down the line, finally the rest of Sumner's corps at about the center of the front. As the Federals' attack moved down his line, Lee shifted his forces to meet it; by midmorning he had thirteen of his twenty-four infantry brigades and most of his cavalry regiments defending about one mile of the four and a half miles of front. (A. P. Hill's brigades had not arrived from Harper's Ferry.) The first two Federal assaults nearly broke through, the third was punished severely, and the fourth resulted in frightful carnage in the "Bloody Lane," which the Federals took. After each of the first three attacks Lee was allowed a breathing spell in which to fill the gaping holes in his lines; after the fourth the Federal right was through for the day, even though General Franklin, whose Sixth Corps was fresh, pleaded with McClellan to be sent in. So badly used were the Confederates that if the first, second, or fourth of these attacks had been immediately followed up, the Southern army would have been crushed. The attacking forces were almost as exhausted as the defenders, and they were hurt by the wounding of Hooker and the mortal wounding of Mansfield, commanding the newly named Twelfth Corps, and of Major General Israel Richardson, a division commander in Sumner's Second Corps.

The attackers failed to wring a decision from their gallant efforts because McClellan was unable to judge the enemy's condition. He did not see how thin the Southern lines were, or discover that the same enemy units that stopped one onslaught were again in the thick of the fight when the next one struck farther down the line — for he did not witness the fighting at close enough range. He remained back at his field headquarters, well posted for a panoramic view of the battle, but more than a mile to the rear.

Burnside, who was to make the attack on the left, did not receive his order to advance until 10 A.M., by which time the fighting had begun to die down on the right and center. In his front the Confederate line came down to the creek, and he spent hours in taking a bridge at bayonet point because no ford usable by artillery was found in time for the flanking movement he had planned. (It was McClellan's habit to assign such reconnaissance tasks to engineers on his staff instead of officers with an experienced eye for getting men and artillery across a stream.) Burnside's lines were not formed for the assault on the bridge until midafternoon; then they swept forward and carried the defenders — four brigades of Jones's division — before them and into the village of Sharps-burg. An hour later Lee sent in the last of his available forces, some of them for the third time that day, but the Federal tide could not be stemmed.

Then, at the moment when the battle was all but lost, A. P. Hill's Light Division reached the field. Hill's men came up from Boteler's Ford directly in the Confederate rear and struck Burnside's forces on their flank, rolling them down the slope to the neighborhood of the bridge they had taken at such heavy cost. There the fight ended.

McClellan had shot his bolt. With four divisions that had not been used in the battle and two more arriving early the next day, he probably had about as many fresh troops as the entire remaining strength of the Army of Northern Virginia. The Confederates had had about 40,000, approximately half of the Federals' numbers, at the start of the battle, and lost 10,318 in killed, wounded, and missing — about 2000 less than the Federal losses. It was America's bloodiest day.[58]

Lee remained disdainfully in his positions around Sharpsburg throughout the 18th, and McClellan made no further moves. During the next night the Southern army, much too badly depleted to pursue its grand campaign in the North, quietly slipped across the Potomac by its one route of escape, Boteler's Ford. Porter gave chase on the 19th, but A. P. Hill's men beat him off more readily than they had Burnside. Instead of annihilating two or three of the five segments of Lee's army, as he could have at relatively little cost, McClellan was content with driving the reassembled army from Northern soil. It was a Federal victory only in the technical sense that the Army of the Potomac was left in possession of the field.

. .   . .   . .

After the battle Pinkerton called on the President and conveyed McClellan's assurance that Lee's army had numbered 140,000, giving him a five-to-three advantage over the number McClellan would acknowledge in his own army. Pinkerton's report of this visit indicates that Lincoln gave McClellan's not very reasonable claim a polite audience.[59]

In his final report, months later, McClellan revised the enemy total to 97,445, an estimate made by Colonel John Clark of Banks's staff in the Department of Washington, who interrogated 250 Confederates, from 228 regiments, in the Washington prisons after the Second Bull Run and Antietam battles. Even this figure was obviously inflated, for in the Maryland campaign Lee had only 181 regiments and about 10 irregularly named units such as legions and battalions. In the same report McClellan gave his own army's strength as 87,164.[60] That was more than double the Confederate numbers in the Antietam battle, but McClellan remained innocent of that fact; by staying back at headquarters he had deprived himself of the feeling for the enemy's numerical strength that a close-up view would have given.

.. .. ..

It is now clear that George McClellan was his own intelligence officer. Pinkerton never came close to filling that role; in the days when he was sending spies to Richmond, conducting the army's interrogation service, and turning out estimates of enemy numbers, the work of assimilating the information from the army's other sources was left to McClellan. The modern concept of an intelligence staff assembling information from all sources and integrating it into reports to the commanding general would be one of the innovations introduced by a later commander of the Potomac army, Joe Hooker. A real intelligence officer would not have ignored the incoming reports that conflicted with the terms of S.O. 191; in fact he would have been actively seeking to update that document. But at his first delivery to McClellan of a piece of integrated intelligence that corrected the Lost Order, he would have found himself assigned to new duties.

Up to this point the chief puzzle McClellan has given us has been the unreality of the estimates of enemy numbers that he made, independently of Pinkerton. They confounded reason: how could an educated man, a military professional at that, possibly think that the Southern states could put that many men and weapons on one front, even the one opposite Washington? Now we have a similar mystery: how could an experienced commander believe that every detail of an order as long and intricate as S.O. 191 would remain fully in force for four or five days, when an abundance of intelligence reports indicated movements by Jackson and Longstreet that were not called for in the order, and not a single report placed them in the positions the order specified?

At least this new puzzle makes the earlier one easier to accept; our impression that McClellan was eccentric, quite able to believe the unbelievable, is confirmed. We can give up trying to understand him. But we can make a judgment of how sincere he was in those unreasonable estimates of enemy strength: McClellan did not invent those figures in order to gain more men or more time or for any other purpose. He really believed them.

There are two reasons for this conclusion. One is the extreme caution with which he approached the enemy. The best example of this is the exasperating slowness of his response to the finding of Lee's S.O. 191. With the Southern army scattered over a wide area and its nearest segments vulnerable to crushing defeat or capture, McClellan spent most of a long day making plans and preparations to insure against the smallest mistake. Fairly successful in his first move, the attack on South Mountain, and fully aware of the Rebels' retreat, he then sat his army down for more planning and preparing. It took him two more days to nerve himself up to cross Antietam Creek and attack. Even on the second day, September 16, a general attack that preceded Jackson's and Walker's afternoon arrival could have quickly demolished Lee's main body, Longstreet's and D. H. Hill's three divisions, or driven them across (or into) the Potomac, with great loss. While McClellan was perfecting his plan, Lee was reassembling his army. McClellan could not have failed to realize that Lee could gain more from the delay than he could himself; he delayed anyway, and probably would have delayed longer if he could have found an excuse. Of all his displays of excessive caution in his months in command of the Army of the Potomac, this four-day delay in bringing Lee to battle in Maryland is the most egregious. Its most plausible explanation is that he was honestly convinced that he was outnumbered.

Another reason for believing McClellan was sincere in his claims of enemy numbers is found in his letters to his wife. He wrote to her nearly every day, even during the Seven Days battles and while pursuing the Rebels in Maryland. These letters make it hard to imagine that he was knowingly magnifying enemy strength. In them he bared his soul over a wide spectrum of subjects — his difficulties with Lincoln and Stanton and Scott, his disgust with Washington (that "sink of iniquity" and its "wretched politicians"), the constant adulation of his troops, his plans, and other military secrets. The President was "a well meaning baboon," the cabinet contained "some of the greatest geese . . . I have ever seen," and Stanton wished for his defeat so that the war would be prolonged until the abolitionists got their way. Repeatedly he saw divine purpose in his being called to Washington to save the country. At the same time he continually saw himself a victim of harassment. The personality revealed in all this is a mixture of complexes — persecution, messianic, Napoleonic. Irrational though he was, there is no reason to believe that he would have inserted, among these pages and pages of innermost thoughts, statements about enemy strength (or about anything else) that he did not believe. If he had thought that the Confederates did not outnumber his army, he would have taken pains to say so to his wife, as one of the reassurances about his safety that he occasionally gave her.[61]

Among Civil War generals McClellan had many companions in believing himself outnumbered. With no other army commander, however, did this belief so firmly condemn his campaigns to failure, as on the Peninsula, or deny him a decisive victory, as on the Antietam.

· ·   · ·   · ·

Possession of the Lost Order made McClellan one of the best-informed commanders in American history. Even among the thousands of highly accurate and informative pieces of communications intelligence with which Generals Eisenhower and MacArthur fought the Second World

War (to take an outstanding example), only a very few told as much about the enemy's totality of plans and intentions as Special Orders No. 191 did. It revealed, conclusively, Lee's intention to capture Harper's Ferry and Martinsburg and gave his plans for doing so. Despite the mishandling of Palmer's and Wilson's reports, McClellan was plentifully supplied with the means of knowing that S.O. 191 was no longer fully in effect. That information was fortified Monday night by Captain Palmer's visit, with his excellent understanding of the situation in the army's front. And still McClellan, by the force of his temperament, succeeded in transforming himself into a badly misinformed commander.

In the Maryland campaign, intelligence did not simply influence a battle; it caused one. Since S.O. 191 was the basis of McClellan's mistaken actions, it is tempting to ask whether he would not have been better off if the order had never been found. The encirclement of Harper's Ferry was unmistakable by September 13, and the presence of a large force at Hagerstown would soon become equally clear. But with only that much intelligence to go on, General McClellan would have been very slow in finding the incentive to attack. The Maryland campaign would have gone on for weeks. By that time Lee would have had a fully assembled army fattened on Northern food, with most of its numerous stragglers recovered. In any battle he succeeded in bringing about, he doubtless would have outgeneraled McClellan as he did on the Antietam, and with a result this time in the Southerners' favor. The most unfavorable outcome for Lee would have been having to return to Virginia without a battle, but after a sojourn in the North so protracted and so unresisted as to amount to a gross humiliation of the Union. The finding of Special Orders No. 191 did yield for the Federals a definitely better outcome of the Maryland campaign than they would otherwise have achieved.

10

. . . .

LUCK RUNS OUT
FOR PALMER AND STINE

September 1862–January 1863

OR CAPTAIN WILLIAM PALMER and his spy, the Reverend I. J. Stine, the battle of Antietam had an ugly aftermath. On the next day, September 18 — the captain's twenty-sixth birthday[1] — McClellan sent word that he urgently needed to know whether the Confederates were retiring and asked that a spy be sent across the Potomac to Shepherdstown. Evidently the general preferred Palmer's espionage services to Pinkerton's. Palmer undertook the mission himself, in company with Stine and a scout named Bardwell, in order to "procure this important information, on the possession of which I thought the complete destruction of the rebel army of Virginia might hinge." It was an unusual step for an officer, as the work of espionage in the Union army fell almost exclusively on enlisted men and civilians. The events that followed led Palmer to declare that his decision to go on the mission himself had been taken "in a fit of injudicious patriotism."[2]

About 2:00 A.M. on the 19th Stine came back into the Union lines alone. Returning to Hagerstown, he found General Andrew Porter and several members of Governor Curtin's staff. He reported to them that Palmer had probably been captured. The three men had gone, he said, to a house on the Virginia side of the Potomac; Palmer explained to the occupants — Union sympathizers, supposedly — that he was seeking information about the Rebel army, and asked the head of the house, a miller, to assist by making a scouting trip to Shepherdstown on the pretext of visiting a miller there. Already the trio had discovered signs that the invading army was preparing to cross the river. When Confederate cavalry in large numbers appeared, they concluded that it was the whole of Stuart's division. (Actually it was Wade Hampton's brigade, engaged in a movement intended to divert the Federals' attention from the main crossing at Shepherdstown.) Soon Confederate horsemen rode up and established a picket around the house, having heard of the trio's arrival from people in the nearby village. Stine went outside and talked to the Southerners at length — until, he said, they began to suspect him. He then returned inside and urged Palmer to join him in an attempt to escape. Meanwhile Bardwell assumed the pose of a feeble-minded rustic, which won his release.

Palmer, who was in uniform, decided against decamping, but Stine — who may have realized that his risk in event of capture was greater than Palmer's — left, evaded the pickets, found a boat, and rowed to the Maryland side. One of the pickets saw him when he was nearly across and ordered him to stop, but he paid no heed and the picket did not fire.[3]

Stine's story strengthened suspicions already held by his auditors that he was working for the Confederates. His admittedly long conversation with the soldiers in Hagerstown and his seemingly easy escape from them were too much for the Pennsylvanians to swallow. They had in fact been watching him closely for several days, their curiosity excited by the facility with which he entered and left the enemy lines. At the very least, they concluded, the Reverend Mr. Stine was an extremely talkative man. Robert M. Evans, one of Lafayette Baker's detectives,[4] had been warned by a Greencastle minister named Rebough that "the loyal people of Greencastle had to magnify every thing to Stine and make Stine believe we had a great maney moor troops than we had for fear of his leting the Rebels know the true conditions of afairs and they would cross the State line." William Wilson, Palmer's telegraph operator, had "left a dispatch so that Stine should see it making our force very large near the State line." During a visit by Stine and Evans to Hagerstown on the 16th, Stine hung about the telegraph office, and Evans left an order forbidding him from going behind the railing that separated the operators from the customers. Stine offered to take Evans to a house where the latter could procure a disguise, but Evans refused to accompany him further.[5]

Stine's claims of having worked with Captain Palmer were felt to be exaggerated; it is very unlikely that any of his auditors knew whether the information he had provided was substantial or, for that matter, correct. The one report about Confederate movements that he was generally known to have furnished related to Jackson's September 11 crossing of the Potomac into Virginia, but it had been received on the 13th, trailing by a full day the same information from other sources. Of course a few words from Palmer would have put all these suspicions to rest, but it was probable by now that he was a prisoner.

Evans then took Stine to Harrisburg, where Stine told his story to Thomas A. Scott, former assistant secretary of war, who had long ago returned to his position with the Pennsylvania Central Railroad. Scott told Evans to watch him. Stine then went to Shippensburg, Evans following, and after two days returned to Harrisburg, where he registered at a hotel as "I. J. Stine, U.S.A." Since the minister had no military position, this little pretension added to the belief that he was untrustworthy. He was taken to see Governor Curtin, who instructed him not to go near the lines of the army, but upon leaving the governor's office he proposed to Evans that they return to Shepherdstown to attempt to learn more about what had happened to Palmer — a project that stood more chance of damaging Palmer's hopes of escape or release than it did of improving them. Evans declined to participate.

Evans then wrote a long report on Stine's suspicious behavior, which General Andrew Porter (who was still on duty at Harrisburg) forwarded to Secretary Stanton, saying, "I am fully impressed with the belief that the man *Stine* betrayed Capt. Palmer — although I have but little more than the evidence contained within."[6]

There matters might have rested but for the reappearance of Confederate forces north of the Potomac. Between October 9 and 12 Jeb Stuart's horsemen repeated their Peninsula feat of riding completely around McClellan's army, Chambersburg receiving them for a brief but exciting visit. It was reported that Stine was there at the time and that his habitual garrulity was not inhibited by the fact that the visitors were enemy soldiers. He was said to have conversed openly with them. Promptly thereafter the War Department acted upon Porter's opinion as to Stine's treasonable activity. The minister, now occupied in selling books in central Pennsylvania, at a considerable distance from Chambersburg, was arrested by the United States marshal at Philadelphia and imprisoned there in Fort Delaware.[7]

Among his jailers Stine kept his own counsel.[8] Probably he feared that if he talked to anyone about his collaboration with Palmer, the story would leak to Federal authorities and then into the newspapers, thus providing the Confederates with enough evidence to convict Palmer of espionage. However, to a fellow minister in Baltimore, to whom he owed money for unsold books, he poured out his woes:

> Dear brother — I am here, as I have always been and everywhere, an undisguised Union man. I am a minister of the Gospel — I am a republican . . . opposed to secession — in favor of the most vigorous measures to put down the present most cruel and bloody rebellion that has ever disgraced our earth: and yet I am imprisoned as a rebel spy! "My God! why hast *thou* forsaken me?" . . .
>
> O my country! torn & bleeding, *must* thy wounds be healed in *this* manner? I would die willingly in my country's defense; but this treacherous, lingering cruel death — this wearing and pining away under worse than a felon's doom — who could endure it? My own conscious innocence of *any* treachery or treason is all that sustains me in this dark hour. . . .
>
> Dear bro. I was decoyed 23 miles from home to be arrested, without

the privilege of even bidding my little family good-bye. "Has God forgotten? Is Mercy clear gone forever?" Ah! "Vengeance is mine, I will repay, saith the Lord." "Father forgive them, for they know not what they do." . . .

I have no fault to find with any but the coward who had me arrested — I will not say whether through ignorance or envy. But it is, indeed, humiliating to be classed here with traitors and rebels as the meanest and most treacherous among them — without money — without clothing — the floor my bed with one U.S. blanket — and a crust of dry bread all of Uncle Sam's provisions that I can eat three times a day. . . .

Yours fraternally
I. J. Stine

P.S. A letter from my poor wife just received, states the death of our dear babe. God have mercy.[9]

Keeping the central facts of his story to himself must have been an added torment for the voluble Mr. Stine. His protection of Palmer accomplished nothing; almost as soon as he was behind the gates of Fort Delaware, the most sensitive details of his and Palmer's espionage and Palmer's capture were spread before the readers of Harrisburg and Philadelphia newspapers. The *Harrisburg Telegraph* added an account of Stine's actions during Stuart's visit to Chambersburg and stated that "it is confidently believed that the accused had perfected a plan to have Gov. Curtin captured" when the governor went to Hagerstown during Stuart's expedition.[10]

The *Greencastle Pilot* came to Stine's defense, thereby multiplying the quantity of incriminating evidence in print. The *Pilot* editor began by noting that at the beginning of the war, Stine had had a pulpit in Nova Scotia and had been forced to return to the United States because of his unpopular advocacy of the Northern cause. The editor pointed out that although Stine was not in Chambersburg at the time of Stuart's raid, his conversations with Stuart's men, had they taken place, would have been "nothing more than some of the citizens of the same place did." He disposed of the reported plot to capture Governor Curtin by showing that the governor was not in Hagerstown at any time when the Southern cavalry was in the vicinity. The *Pilot* then quoted a letter Stine wrote from Fort Delaware to a fellow minister in Pennsylvania, repeating many of the sentiments expressed to his Baltimore colleague and adding this: "At Captain Palmer's request, I was with him on that hazardous adventure which led to his continued absence; and at his own suggestion and solicitation left him in danger, and with great difficulty escaped a situation equivalent to more than captivity."[11] Stine, though he evidently feared publicity resulting from telling his story to the Federal authorities, did not hesitate to give its essential facts to a fellow clergyman. Through that channel it reached public print within a week.

A prominent Lutheran minister in Washington wrote to Secretary Stanton on Stine's behalf, as did a group of leading citizens of Perry County, Pennsylvania, where the unfortunate parson resided. These efforts availed nothing, but early in December Alexander McClure, whose prominence as a Republican was statewide, brought the matter to the attention of Major Levi Turner, who as judge advocate of the War Department was the ruling authority in most cases of alleged disloyalty. McClure forwarded the *Pilot* editor's article and wrote,

> Hon Jno Rowe, of Greencastle, who has investigated this matter very carefully, saw Mr. Bardwell recently, who is one of Palmers men & was captured with him, but effected his escape. He was astonished when he heard that Stine had been arrested, and declares that he acted at all times with entire fidelity. . . . When Chambersburg was threatened by Longstreet's command, Stine acted as a scout & spy for me . . . and his information was always entirely reliable.[12]

This won Stine's release, but he was placed on parole.[13] Although even Palmer could not claim to know what Stine had told the Confederates when he mixed with them, the captain could provide a fuller affirmation of Stine's loyalty than anyone else. It was hoped that the publicity regarding the two spies would escape the Confederates' notice and that Palmer might be released or exchanged.

After Stine had left him and eluded the pickets on the night of September 18, Palmer had again changed into civilian clothes, borrowing the Sunday suit of his host.[14] This action was unwise, for his uniform, although it meant certain arrest, would doubtless have caused his captors to treat him as a prisoner of war. Throughout the war the usage most generally followed in both the Union and Confederate armies followed the rule General Halleck would later publish, that "an enemy who comes within our lines, without disguise or false pretenses, and seeks information, no matter how secretly, is no spy. If captured he must be treated as a prisoner of war; he may be confined with rigor, as a dangerous person, and his exchange refused; but he cannot be hung as a spy. The terms 'in disguise' or 'under false pretenses,' are the essential requisites of the offense of military espionage; secrecy has nothing to do with it."[15] If the Confederates could acquire sufficient evidence that their captive in citizen's clothes was a Union officer, Palmer would get the noose. Evidently he was uninstructed in such matters.

Submitting readily to capture as soon as the Confederates entered the miller's house, Palmer told them that he was W. J. Peters of Baltimore, a mining engineer who had been to Cumberland, Maryland, to visit the mines of his company, and he was putting up at the miller's house because he could not get around the armies on his way back to Baltimore.[16]

The soldiers who arrested Palmer were artillerymen, and they turned him over to the army's chief of artillery, Brigadier General William N.

Pendleton. In addition to being an Episcopal clergyman, Pendleton was a former schoolmaster who knew enough about geology to test Palmer's story. The captain's formal education had stopped with high school, but he had worked one year for his uncle, a mine operator, and in a year spent abroad had visited many mines in Britain. He thought he passed the general's rather stiff examination, but his story was still not a likely one, and Pendleton wrote a very long report of his capture, stressing the probability that he was a Union spy. This accompanied Palmer to Castle Thunder, the former tobacco warehouse in Richmond used as a prison for officers and civilians. There the jailkeeper with a great show of irritation noted the bulkiness of Pendleton's report and deposited it in a desk, unread. Palmer, observing this, offered up a silent prayer of thanks for the ministerial habit of writing long sermons.[17]

Within a few weeks "W. J. Peters" had succeeded in communicating by mail with friends of W. J. Palmer. A letter received at Castle Thunder was addressed to Peters; the sender was one L. P. Cowgill of Wilmington, Delaware, who reported that he had been to see "Mr. Jackson" (this was Palmer's uncle, Frank H. Jackson). Cowgill wrote that Jackson had told him that Peters had been captured while visiting the mines; he asked Peters what condition they were in, as no one else knew anything about them.[18] This meant to Palmer that Union authorities, if not actually negotiating for his release under his assumed name, probably were at least aware of the identity he had adopted and were prepared to negotiate if the opportunity arose.

As weeks went by, the chances steadily grew that Pendleton's recommendations, which probably called for severe treatment of Palmer, had been permanently pigeonholed. But Palmer was not yet breathing easily, for he gradually concluded that at least twenty of his fellow occupants of Castle Thunder's "Citizens' Room" were professional spies — and here he was, evidently numbered among them.

Then an event occurred that seemed to spell the end of his hopes. The prisoners regularly managed to buy newspapers, a single copy making the rounds of the whole room. One day a fellow prisoner gave Palmer a circulating newspaper ahead of his turn, calling his attention to a certain item. There, reprinted from a Philadelphia paper, was the story of the September 18 mission from which he had failed to return. It gave his name and organization, named the exact spot at which his party had crossed the Potomac, and furnished other correct details by means of which anyone who had participated in his capture could easily identify him.

Palmer saw to it that the paper did not circulate further, but the odds that his captors would see that news item and connect him with W. J. Peters seemed great. However, they said nothing to him about the matter.[19]

Another hazard was meeting prisoners who recognized him and called him by name. This happened twice, the offenders being a Pennsylvania colonel and a man whom Palmer had arrested for thievery the previous year in Kentucky. Another indiscretion was threatened when he met a young Pennsylvania lieutenant named Izrael V. Hoag, Jr., whom he had unsuccessfully tried to rescue after a hard race with Hoag's captors a few weeks before; but Hoag was equal to the occasion and gave no sign of recognition.[20]

Palmer and two others shared a corner that was set off somewhat from the rest of the room by a tobacco press. Resolving to attempt to escape, they obtained a file from a Negro who delivered vegetables to the prison, used it to convert Palmer's jackknife into a small saw, and, working quietly at night, cut their way through the floor to an unoccupied basement room. The yard outside was so thick with sentries that there was no chance of getting across it unseen. They abandoned the project.

In November Palmer thought he was going to be released when William P. Wood, keeper of Old Capitol Prison, came to Richmond to carry out an exchange of prisoners. But Wood, Palmer wrote to a friend, returned to Washington without any civil prisoners, the War Department having "disavowed his [Wood's] acts" in relation to them. Then on December 11 Palmer wrote Cowgill that the Confederate authorities had agreed to exchange him for a Confederate citizen of "high importance." "Whether your efforts and those of my other friends can procure such a man is doubtful," he said, "but I pray that you will do what you can."[21]

At the Richmond end the exchange had been initiated by J. T. Kerby, Lafayette Baker's agent whom Pinkerton's men had shadowed so persistently. Kerby, although under Confederate arrest as a spy, had — according to a complaint made by Captain G. W. Alexander, commanding the prison — "the best room in the Castle, [had] a fire, good bed and [was] allowed to purchase anything from the outside that he may require."[22] He was in the habit of cursing Alexander and other officers in the hearing of the guards, he had succeeded in sending and receiving uncensored letters, and he had once refused release by flag of truce. When Kerby finally left Richmond, according to Palmer, it was only because he was removed forcibly at the order of General Winder. Kerby, Palmer said, took the case of his friend Peters "past Winder to higher authority."[23]

In January, after Thomas Scott had written Stanton asking that special efforts be made to obtain Palmer's release, Palmer was allowed to go North on parole to arrange his exchange for a Confederate citizen named White. When he reached Washington he found that no such person was being held. However, the Confederate authorities then released "W. J. Peters" from his parole.[24]

Palmer went home to Philadelphia to recuperate and within a few days turned his attention to the case of his collaborator, the Reverend Mr. Stine. He wrote to Stine,

> Nothing during my confinement in Confederate prisons caused me more regret than the report that you had been . . . imprisoned on charges of having betrayed me into Rebel captivity. . . . Allow me to add, that for the disinterestedness you manifested during your imprisonment, and since your release on parole, in not mentioning any of the particulars connected with my capture, preferring rather to suffer awhile longer under the imputation of being guilty . . . you have my profound gratitude.[25]

This overstated Stine's close-mouthedness; Palmer may never have learned of Stine's letter that was published in the Greencastle newspaper.

To Governor Curtin, Palmer wrote that the information provided by Stine "was of considerable importance to Genl McClellan — advising him of many movements which guided him in his pursuit & attack of the enemy at South Mountain." He urged that Stine be paid for his services, and in this plea he was joined by John Rowe. But Curtin had no fund for such a purpose; the papers were sent to Washington, and the only tangible result of the effort was Stine's release from his parole.[26]

Two years later Stine, whose fortunes had not improved, took up the effort to obtain reimbursement. This time he obtained a more detailed statement from Palmer as to the information he had provided. Palmer, now with his regiment in Alabama and about to become a brigadier general, repeated the story of Stine's observation of Jackson's crossing at Williamsport — which information had been received in Harrisburg a day earlier from another source — but he now revealed a greater accomplishment of Stine's. It was Stine, he wrote, who had penetrated the Confederate picket lines at Hagerstown on September 14 and obtained Palmer's important, detailed information about the composition and position of Longstreet's command, which were less well understood than in the case of Jackson's command.[27] Had Palmer's dispatch that evening named Stine instead of mentioning him only as "my scout," the men in Governor Curtin's entourage might have been less ready to suspect the minister of treason.

After an elaborate review of Stine's case by the War Department, Stine received $500 from the Secret Service fund, the same amount that had been given Sergeant Thomas Harter for his trip to Richmond and his report to Pope on the Rapidan.[28] Measured by the importance of the military action that could be based on it, Stine's information, like Harter's, was of course worth far more than that amount. Pope had saved an army by virtue of Harter's feat, but such was the mishandling of Palmer's reports and the sluggishness of McClellan's action based on what little he received of them, the Union may not have had $500 worth of benefit from the efforts of the itinerant parson who (in the words of

Captain Palmer) "although he might have been a saint, had the audacity of the devil."[29]

.. .. ..

Palmer was habitually uncomfortable when using what he termed the perpendicular pronoun; his subsequent career greatly added to his difficulties in avoiding it. In February 1863 he joined his regiment, which had gone on to Tennessee during his absence in the East. He found the supposedly elite organization in a deplorable condition. When the regiment late in December had been ordered into the battle of Stone's River, most of its members had mutinied, claiming that they were badly short of officers (which was true) and that if they were expected to do duty as ordinary cavalry, they had been enlisted under false pretenses. On Palmer's arrival hundreds of the men were in confinement, and morale and discipline among most of the others were in a hopeless state.[30] Colonel Palmer restored both, building in the process a regiment that more than lived up to the early promise of its talented membership. It did serve as "ordinary cavalry," and with such credit that it soon earned the scouting assignments its members craved. Major General George H. Thomas, in whose army it served longest, said he always felt safe when Palmer's men were guarding his lines; he called the youthful Palmer "the best cavalry officer in the service." Coming from Thomas, a most exacting general and a cavalryman himself, this was a great tribute. Thomas's rating would have been influential in Palmer's promotion to brigadier general in November 1864. But his attainments were not solely in administration and scouting; he was awarded the Medal of Honor for his display of courage in an engagement in Alabama in January 1865.[31]

Probably very few officers of his rank were so long and so steadily exposed to capture, and the threat was an extraordinarily grave one in his case, for the Confederates were known to have hanged at least one man, Spencer Kellogg Brown, who had performed espionage against them and was later taken as a military prisoner.[32] On all of Palmer's later scouting expeditions the "Citizens' Room" of Castle Thunder must have loomed in his mind, but we may doubt that he ever again knew the feeling that came over him when he saw enemy horsemen surround the miller's house on the Potomac on the night of September 18, 1862.

11

....

THE BLIND CAMPAIGN
OF FREDERICKSBURG

October 1862–January 1863

FROM LEESBURG, on October 29, in answer to a question from President Lincoln, General McClellan telegraphed, "I have the honor to state that the accounts I get of the enemy's position and movements are very conflicting."[1] The statement is a fitting theme for the aftermath of the battle of Antietam. For six weeks McClellan's army remained on Antietam Creek, while Lee, after stopping at Martinsburg for a week, drew back up the Valley toward Winchester. McClellan could have interposed between Lee and Richmond, but offensive designs were farthest from his mind. He was plagued with reports that had the enemy almost constantly on the march, sometimes for Culpeper or Richmond but more often for the Potomac and Maryland. The Federal command, though never badly misled, also was never quite sure just where the Confederates were or whether they really were on the move. It was almost as hard to locate them when their main force was sitting fairly still as when they were on the march and reported moving in two or three directions at the same time.

The cause of all this confusion was some adjustments of position, supplemented by rumor. The only noteworthy action of the entire six weeks was Stuart's ride around the Army of the Potomac between October 9 and 12. This was even more embarrassing to the Federals than his circuit around them on the Peninsula; now his ride was witnessed by thousands of Northerners. The raiders paid a visit to Chambersburg and returned without losing a single man, but without accomplishing one of their principal objects, the burning of a bridge on the Chambersburg-Hagerstown railroad, McClellan's supply line. The bridge turned out to be made of iron.[2]

In the end it was McClellan who ended the stalemate. When he telegraphed Lincoln on October 29, he had just crossed his army into Virginia, a full three weeks after the President had sternly ordered him to "move now" and "give battle to the enemy or drive him south."[3]

Even as McClellan's troops were crossing the river, a large reconnaissance force was probing the country between Harper's Ferry and Martinsburg, investigating a report that the Confederates were making threatening movements toward Maryland. On three previous occasions reconnaissance had proved the alarm false; this time the findings were less clear.[4] But the Federals' return to Virginia proceeded and no Rebel incursion across the Potomac developed. The Confederates took position on McClellan's front and right flank, a response Lincoln had expected.[5]

. .   . .   . .

During these weeks of inaction McClellan's intelligence service was at full strength. Pinkerton's field unit of six regular employees was supplemented, as before the battle, by short-timers, this time a group of six Virginians presumably familiar with the country the enemy was occupying. And immediately after the battle, during which McClellan had felt a strong need for the balloons, Professor Lowe returned to the army. By posting a balloon on Bolivar Heights at Harper's Ferry, an elevation of 1200 feet, he was able to look down at the enemy positions at Martinsburg, thirteen miles to the northwest. But the country was too hilly for dependable aerial observation; the Confederates' move toward Winchester hid them from Lowe's telescopes. With long marches in Virginia now in prospect, McClellan sent Lowe back to Washington; the balloons and their gas generators again would be unable to keep up with a marching army.[6]

The advance into Virginia was certain to set Lee's forces in motion. The task of tracking them fell to Alfred Pleasonton's cavalry brigade, soon to be joined by the brigade of Brigadier General George Bayard. Mindful of Pleasonton's haphazard reconnoitering in Maryland and recalling the bold scouting work done by Major Myer's signal officers on the Peninsula, McClellan attached a small party of signalmen to Pleasonton's force. Still the cavalry produced less information than was turned up by Virginia Unionist spies, two of them on the payroll of General Banks, now heading the local command at Washington. Banks also sent out reconnaissance parties, which turned up reports of the enemy's presence in unknown numbers in the vicinity of Manassas and extending toward the Blue Ridge and Culpeper. On October 7 General Halleck was certain that "the enemy are falling back toward Richmond."[7] A week went by before firmer information was turned up by a two-man team of Banks's spies, who correctly located the enemy concentration just north of Winchester. They reported Lee reinforced by 15,000, not an unrea-

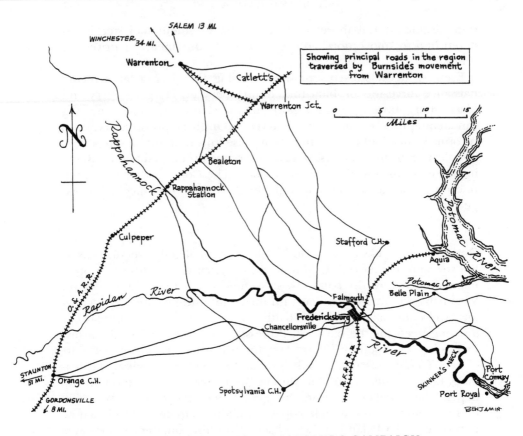

REGION OF THE FREDERICKSBURG CAMPAIGN

sonable estimate, but then gave his total strength as "not less than, and not over, 150,000." Both the high figure and the unreasonable precision should have rendered it suspect, but Banks commended the pair's findings as being "the opinions of intelligent people in the valley." Banks withheld the names of these spies; probably they were Charles Whitlock, who had visited Richmond in July while employed by one of General McDowell's brigade commanders, and Enos Richmond. In any case, those names are signed to another report from the same locality, fortuitously made on October 31, when the Confederates began moving. At that time, Whitlock and Richmond discovered Jackson at Berryville; moving southward from that point were unidentified forces.[8]

While the Army of the Potomac was engaged in a long-drawn-out crossing of the river, one of Pinkerton's Virginian spies, John Aiken, was thoroughly crisscrossing the twenty-three miles of country between Martinsburg and Winchester. In the last week of October Aiken made overnight visits with seven "Union men." He saw no assemblages of troops larger than 400 or 500 cavalry. His hosts, millers and farmers whose business often took them to Winchester, were not being allowed even a distant view of any large mass of troops. Such tight picketing was in itself a sign of movement, planned or in progress. Jackson's divisions, which were to remain in the Valley for several more weeks, were consistently reported at Bunker Hill, halfway between Martinsburg and Winchester. This was in sharp conflict with Whitlock and Richmond's placement of them at Berryville, and when Aiken reached Bunker Hill he found only 300 troops there. Longstreet was reported moving southward; the information on him was second- or third-hand, but it was consistent with the Whitlock-Richmond report of southward movement of unidentified forces.

The one solid finding that emerged from Aiken's mission consisted of several southward movements of troops and wagons that had been observed by his sources or persons they had talked to; the marching troops would have been elements of Longstreet's command. Missing from his report was one important movement east of the Valley by a Longstreet division; it was ordered by Lee after McClellan began crossing the Potomac on October 26 and probably did not begin until Aiken had ended his visit to the Valley.

Despite the meagerness of Aiken's findings, they were a useful supplement to Richmond and Whitlock's contemporaneous report. Cavalry was the instrument best suited to tracking the enemy in this situation, but reconnaissance by the brigades of Pleasonton and Bayard, judged on the basis of results, was tardy and feeble.[9]

A clue to Pinkerton's understanding of these developments appears not in one of his reports but in the diary of David Hunter Strother, who had joined McClellan's staff after Pope's departure. While Strother and McClellan were riding together on November 4, they were passed by two men on horseback traveling eastward. On the general's order Strother accosted them; they presented passes showing that they were agents of the "Secret Service" — presumably members of Pinkerton's bureau. "They assured me," Strother wrote, "that Longstreet was at Culpeper Court House, that Hill had marched this morning toward Manassas Gap [in the Blue Ridge], and that the whole Southern army was south of us, the troops in the Valley being left only as a blind." This report was correct as to Longstreet (who reached Culpeper about November 3) and believable enough as to either A. P. or D. H. Hill, but entirely wrong as to the "whole Southern army," since Jackson's command, which included the divisions of both Hills, was remaining in the Valley. How much of the two men's information had been reported to McClellan by Pinkerton at this time is unclear; McClellan's papers contain no such report.[10]

Another spy belonging to Banks's command, a woman named Frankie

Abells, made a successful visit to Leesburg in mid-September, when that town was on the Confederates' line of communication to Maryland. However, when she headed for the Southern lines again on October 4 she was captured by Virginia cavalry operating near the railroad below Manassas. When Mrs. Abells returned to Washington from Richmond in December (along with "Mrs. Timothy Webster"), it was in exchange for no less a personage than Belle Boyd; evidently the Federals placed a considerable value on her. Her later service, however, was less auspicious. After joining the detective force of the Middle Department at Baltimore, she was arrested in March 1863, along with a provost marshal and two other men, on charges brought by women who had been illegally permitted to pass North as refugees through a provost station on the upper Potomac. They complained that Frankie, packing two pistols, had forced them to undress, removed money from their clothing, and retained substantial amounts of gold coin. When Lafayette Baker's detectives from the War Department caught up with Mrs. Abells in Frederick, she was in bed with one of her male colleagues. All four miscreants were taken to Old Capitol Prison. A War Department officer who investigated the case reported that "by the proofs, as well as by personal appearance, [Mrs. Abells] is degraded and drunken." But Frankie, who was educated, apparently possessed more than the ability to make herself agreeable to her fellow detectives, for upon her release Baker put her on his own force. She served many more months as a detective, disguised at least part of the time as a male nurse and carrying, in addition to her pistols, a Spanish dirk.[11]

· · · · · ·

In the dispatch written on his arrival south of the Potomac, McClellan gave the President, along with his complaint that the information reaching him was conflicting, a set of recent reports that amply validated that claim. And the contradictions were not confined to reports about the enemy; there were serious inconsistencies in what McClellan had to say about his own army and his plans for using it. The resupply of his troops had become the subject of a long telegraphic controversy that ended with McClellan swallowing many heated words when they were challenged by the Washington authorities. Among the results of this exchange was the discovery that the equipage of many thousand soldiers had been left in storage at Alexandria upon McClellan's return from the Peninsula, and now, in answer to his complaints, had been replaced with new issues. Later McClellan's quartermaster would report that when the general's supposedly underequipped troops marched back into Virginia they left behind in Maryland 50,000 new, unissued uniforms. During this same period McClellan's request for a huge number of hospital tents raised doubt as to whether he really intended to move and keep moving.

He was evasive when Lincoln sought to pin him down about his intentions. Upon receipt of Lincoln's preliminary Emancipation Proclamation after the battle of Antietam, McClellan had issued an order commenting on it in a way seemingly calculated to call the attention of Northern conservatives to the political standard he himself would raise one day.[12]

Thus the President, already frustrated by McClellan's passive behavior after the battle, had new causes for complaint. And now McClellan was moving his army down the eastern side of the Blue Ridge apparently without any firm knowledge of whether the enemy was retiring before him or massing for an attack in his rear. (The reports that would bear on this question, from Richmond and Whitlock and from Aiken, were yet to be made.) Then it was learned that Longstreet's wing of the Southern army had crossed the Blue Ridge to Culpeper. According to John Hay, Lincoln's secretary, the President had made up his mind to remove McClellan if Lee succeeded in making such a move — interposing between the Federal army and Richmond. George McClellan, the innovator who gave the nation its first intelligence bureau, lost his command partly because of an intelligence failure; Pinkerton's celebrated organization was not designed to scout enemy movements.

That is one interpretation of McClellan's dismissal; another is that the President was only waiting for the congressional elections to be concluded; then he would unseat McClellan. In any event, on November 5, the day after the last of the elections and three days after the initial report of Longstreet's movement, Lincoln wrote the order that took the command of the Army of the Potomac from George McClellan and gave it to Major General Ambrose Everts Burnside.[13]

With McClellan went Allan Pinkerton, doubtless in a considerable huff over the ouster of his esteemed chief. Burnside apparently did not want Pinkerton to stay, and according to George Bangs, Pinkerton had "no confidence in the ability of General Burnside." Such was Pinkerton's attachment to McClellan that it is doubtful that any other general would have suited him. Unless Pinkerton changed his methods of estimating enemy numbers, a new commander would discover the flaws in his estimates, and perhaps even his collusion with McClellan. Later Pinkerton claimed that when he visited Washington in 1863, Stanton and Assistant Secretary Peter H. Watson urged him to return to service as the War Department's chief detective, the position held by Lafayette Baker. But for the rest of the war Pinkerton's government business would consist of investigating claims and civil crimes, prominent among them the frauds incident to the federally supervised cotton trade at New Orleans.[14]

Ambrose Burnside, whose spectacular muttonchop whiskers set a style that endeared him to a whole generation of barbers, was a big man of commanding presence, thirty-eight years old. After resigning from the army in 1853, he had settled in Rhode Island and had begun manufacturing a breech-loading carbine of his own invention. Failing in that venture during a panic in 1857, he moved to Chicago to take an executive position in the Illinois Central Railroad, bestowed on him by his West Point friend George McClellan. He commanded the First Rhode Island Volunteers at the first battle of Bull Run and during the following winter attained prominence by leading the successful Burnside expedition against the coast of North Carolina.

Not wanting the command that now came to him, Burnside exhibited a style much less imposing than that of his friend McClellan. He simplified the organization of the eight corps under him, forming three "grand divisions" of two corps each, with two other corps, the Eleventh and Twelfth, forming his rear. He rid himself of most of McClellan's large headquarters staff.

Burnside proposed to move on Richmond via Fredericksburg, using the intervening rivers to supply the army. The Fredericksburg move would put him twenty-five miles closer to Richmond than Longstreet's present position. Halleck demurred, but a few days later, on November 14, he telegraphed, "The President has just assented to your plan. He thinks it will succeed if you move rapidly; otherwise not."[15]

With that, Burnside was on his way, and with a speed that must have startled his chiefs. By the 17th his advance was at Falmouth, across the Rappahannock from Fredericksburg; two days later army headquarters arrived. Six corps of infantry began settling into camps they would occupy for the next seven months, except for two battles on the other side of the river.

Fredericksburg was known to be lightly held. Scouts from General Sigel's Eleventh Corps, headed by Captain Ulric Dahlgren, had visited the place on November 10 and captured a sizable fraction of its little garrison. So enjoyable did Sigel's men find this expedition that a new venture in the same direction had to be called off lest it unwittingly tip Burnside's hand.[16]

Although Lee received a wealth of reports relating to Burnside's movement, it succeeded in mystifying him. His first impression was that the move would be toward Fredericksburg; he was led to that inference by the Federals' placement of guards on the roads leading there from Warrenton. That interpretation soon gave way to scouts' reports that the Yankee troops were moving toward the Orange and Alexandria Railroad, which would mean either that they were resuming McClellan's march toward Gordonsville with a view to threatening Richmond from the west, or that they would entrain for Alexandria, there to embark for the James River and an approach to Richmond from the south. Lee was well served by scouts who quickly scotched the possibility of an overwater movement by ascertaining that there were no transports waiting at Alexandria, Washington, or Aquia Creek. But other sources, among them Jackson in the Valley, reported Federals in great force at all points from Harper's Ferry to Fredericksburg. A Northern critic notes that with all these reports in hand Lee "ended by accepting everything as equally credible and equally incredible."

Lee had started Longstreet's divisions for Fredericksburg almost as soon as Burnside's advance came in view of the Confederate garrison there, but it was not until a week later, November 25, that he concluded that Burnside must be intending to cross the entire Army of the Potomac over the Rappahannock in that vicinity. This prolonged uncertainty led him to allow Jackson to remain in the Valley several days beyond the time Stonewall should have been summoned to rejoin the army.[17]

At Fredericksburg Lee had a direct route from Richmond for his supplies, via the Richmond, Fredericksburg and Potomac Railroad. But the superintendent of that road was Northern-born Samuel Ruth, a member of Richmond's Unionist underground. Ruth succeeded in slowing down substantially the shipment of freight to Fredericksburg. Twice Lee sent written protests against the lack of "zeal and energy" in the management of the R. F. & P. Although the president of the company was a strong secessionist, Ruth had his support for these actions; private freight enjoyed priority over government freight (presumably because it was more profitable), and Lee's supply officers were neglecting to furnish proper requisitions for supplies that remained in Richmond awaiting shipment. This condition was never really corrected in the seven months the armies faced each other on the Rappahannock front.[18]

. . . . . .

Pinkerton's detectives left with him, leaving behind Private John C. Babcock, who seems to have been the only soldier in the Pinkerton bureau. Babcock had the private soldier's affection for Little Mac; he traveled with the McClellan party from Warrenton to Washington after the general's emotional farewell review. For thus absenting himself from a duty that no longer existed, Babcock was "ordered back to 'the ranks'" of his company, the Sturges Rifles, the elite Chicago outfit that had been officially designated as part of "McClellan's bodyguard." But soon there were no ranks for him to return to; McClellan ordered the entire company mustered out.

Back at Warrenton, Babcock was asked by Burnside to produce a report on the condition of the secret-service "department." It would not have been a very extensive report, for Pinkerton and McClellan had taken all their files on the Confederates. McClellan wanted the material for writing the report of his fifteen months in command; Pinkerton's justification for commandeering records would have been that he was a private contractor employed by McClellan, to whom he owed a final report.[19]

After finishing the report Burnside had requested, Babcock was preparing to leave for his home in Chicago when he was invited to take Pinkerton's position. Although he was only a young ex-private, Burnside knew him well. The two had become acquainted in Rhode Island, where Babcock was born, and had renewed their acquaintance during Burnside's years in Chicago, when he sought out Babcock's services as an architect. Babcock was working for one of the largest architectural firms in Chicago; he had contributed to the designs of numerous Athenian mansions on the millionaires' row along Michigan Avenue. With his parents he had moved from Rhode Island to Chicago in the mid-1850s.

He had been hoping to obtain a lieutenant's commission on the strength of his engineering skills. The prominence he had attained as a cartographer should have opened the way to an appointment, but it doubtless would have placed him in the army's topographical staff, an uncomfortable situation. General Humphreys had left that staff for a division command, but some or all of the topographers whose Peninsula maps had been judged so inferior to Babcock's would still have been there. Burnside could have made Babcock the commissioned head of a new bureau, but that process would have dragged on for months. Babcock accepted Burnside's offer of Pinkerton's job with the proviso that he be employed, like Pinkerton, as a civilian; that was agreeable to Burnside.

Babcock now wrote to his aunt in Rhode Island, "I am now a free man, . . . of as much importance in this bailiwick as though I had all the birds and stars in the heavens on my shoulders. My military ambition has settled into my pocket" — a reference to the $225 a month he had been drawing as a member of Pinkerton's force. His salary remained unchanged, as did his civilian status, though he eventually came to be called, unofficially, "Captain Babcock."

He was enjoying simply his freedom from military status when he could have been congratulating himself on his elevation to the chiefship of the army commander's secret service. As a member of the Sturges Rifles he had had only a very limited experience of life as a private soldier. While thirty of his fellows were posted to "Fort Greenhow" — curbing, he wrote, the secessionist proclivities of "many talented and accomplished women . . . including the celebrated Mrs. G." — Babcock along with most of the company was put on duty at the Central Guard House. Of this service he wrote, "No pen can describe such scenes of misery cruelty and degradation that it has been my lot here to witness." After three months he was transferred to the office of Provost Marshal General Andrew Porter as a pass examiner. Although the office was busy, issuing 400 to 500 passes a day, Babcock's workday was over in the early afternoon and he spent the rest of the day studying engineering books in the library of the Smithsonian Institution. He hoped to overcome his lack of a West Point education, supposedly a requisite to a Corps of Engineers commission. Burnside, then a frequent visitor to Washington, was encouraging this effort. Then on March 1, 1862, came Babcock's transfer to the Pinkerton organization. Of that he wrote, "I am more than gratified at this new change. . . . I am told by those who know . . . that I have got a big thing."

Babcock wrote that although he liked General Burnside "as a friend and a gentleman . . . I do say, and he will say so himself, that Gen. Geo. B. McClellan is his superior in military ability." Burnside's staff, with a few exceptions, was "worthless and inefficient," for which Babcock blamed political appointees foisted on Burnside by Rhode Island Governor William Sprague. Babcock's dislike of them came to a head when the chief of staff, General John G. Parke, made disparaging remarks about Pinkerton. Babcock spoke up in Pinkerton's defense and "had to suffer for it."

Of McClellan's removal Babcock commented that "the demands of the army were sacrificed to those of the people." His political opinions appear to have been more conservative than those of his New England kinfolk, but he sought to change the views of his Aunt Jane, whose Yankee abolitionism, possibly not very strong to begin with, was giving way to a desire for any compromise that would end the slaughter.

Despite his pride in his work, Babcock seems to have had a light-hearted attitude toward his position, setting him apart from Pinkerton and the type of men the detective tended to employ.[20]

Burnside placed Babcock under the supervision of Provost Marshal General Marsena R. Patrick, who had succeeded General Andrew Porter in October. This assignment was a continuation of Pinkerton's subordination to Porter and then to Patrick. Now the lack of the records that Pinkerton and McClellan had taken was a serious problem. Babcock found a partial solution by visiting the Department of Washington headquarters and copying a massive report compiled for the department commander, General Banks, from interviews with Confederate soldiers captured in the Second Bull Run and Antietam battles. That document listed 228 Rebel regiments.[21]

. .   . .   . .

Burnside planned to take Fredericksburg while it was too weakly held to resist. He needed pontoons to cross the Rappahannock at or below the town; upriver it was fordable, but highly subject to quick flooding that could trap an occupying force, separated from its supplies and support. Before leaving Warrenton he arranged with Halleck for a pontoon train to be sent to Falmouth from Washington. But the urgency of the shipment was not communicated down the line, with the result that Long-street's force began arriving November 21 ahead of any of the pontoons. The taking of Fredericksburg could no longer be a walkover; the whole history of the campaign turns on this one collective blunder, beginning with Halleck's failure to impress the engineer officers in charge of the pontoons with the gravity of the occasion.[22]

.   ..   ..

The story of Burnside's intelligence preparations for the campaign against General Lee is a list of things that were not done — for example, the recruitment of local Unionists as spies. One of the shortcomings of Pinkerton's operation was his reliance solely on his own employees, which meant that all of his espionage was conducted by visitors to the Confederacy, none by resident agents. In Burnside's move to Freder-icksburg there was an opportunity to correct this lack, for there was in that vicinity a circle, however small, of known Union sympathizers. But putting this resource to use turned out to be unexpectedly difficult.

The leader of an existing active group of Union agents was John Howard Skinker, a planter and slaveholder in Stafford County, across the Rappahannock from Fredericksburg.[23] Without assurance of compensa-tion, Skinker had done a great deal of information-gathering himself and had "employed friends to go where he could not." Even so, he had had some narrow escapes, with one horse killed and another disabled. At times of activity such as McDowell's movements in the Fredericksburg area during the Peninsula campaign and Burnside's occupation of the town during the Second Bull Run campaign, Skinker had furnished reports almost daily. General Reynolds, one of the succession of Freder-icksburg commanders, endorsed Skinker as "the truest, boldest and most deserving Union man I have ever known — always regarding property and even life itself as nothing compared to the duty he owed to the Constitution and the Union."

Skinker had been forced to take refuge in Washington in September when the armies moved into Maryland and the Confederates reoccupied Fredericksburg and its environs. The generals who gathered in the capi-tal after Pope's defeat included several who could attest to Skinker's services, and in November the War Department rewarded him with a check for $1107, nearly half of it for expenses he had incurred in his self-assigned labors for the Union. The endorsements supporting his claim attest to more than his loyalty and the value of his services; they reveal a strong bond of affection between the spy and his employers.[24]

But if Burnside counted on having Skinker reassemble his group of local spies, he was disappointed; Skinker remained in Washington. Evi-dently he thought his activities had become too well known among his secessionist neighbors for him to be of further use. If he feared reprisals the fear was justified, for Stafford County now became ground for the exercise of Jeb Stuart's penchant for raiding in the rear of the Federal army.

Swamped with work, Burnside did not have time to find a replacement for Skinker until his command of the Army of the Potomac was almost over. General Patrick, also well acquainted in the Fredericksburg neighborhood, likewise made no recruitment moves until that time. Thus the only visible information service in Burnside's army was in a rear element, Sigel's Eleventh Corps, where a group of scouts and spies had been assembled in response to Pope's demands for intelligence. The corps had remained in Virginia during the Maryland campaign; its intelligence party was still carrying out the mission of Pope's day, covering the country between the Washington environs and the Blue Ridge.

A second area of intelligence collection, observation by balloons, was now left uncovered. After leaving Harper's Ferry, Thaddeus Lowe sat in Washington awaiting developments. None came until two weeks after the change of command, when an impatient Lowe generated one himself by writing to General Parke asking for orders. He was soon at Falmouth, but still grounded; Burnside decided not to show the enemy his balloons until the moment his attack began.[25] Two explanations of this choice, not mutually exclusive, are possible. He could have reasoned that if the Confederates knew the balloons were now with the army they would position themselves so as to minimize their visibility from the air. Or he could have assumed that if he stationed the balloons where he most needed information on enemy positions, he would tip his hand as to his attack plans. Of course the latter problem could have been avoided by having the balloon — only one was used — cover all sections of the front equally. But Burnside evidently believed that even without the balloon he knew, or would learn, enough about the enemy's exact positions to direct his attack to advantage; thus he wanted those Rebels to stay put until his attacking troops were on top of them. The correctness of this strategy depended on the correctness of Burnside's faith in the intelligence he obtained independently of the balloon — or on his instinctual judgment unaided by information about the enemy.

Another neglected intelligence-gathering activity was cavalry reconnaissance. Unlike Pope, Burnside had cavalry aplenty, but it appears to have provided only meager intelligence, obtained by field glass from the north bank of the river. The cavalry is not known to have done any probing on the enemy's side of the river after Captain Dahlgren's visit to Fredericksburg, which took place before that town became the objective of Burnside's campaign. Stuart's performance shows that a small, fast-moving party could cross the Rappahannock, do some useful exploring, and get back across without a scratch. In Captain Dahlgren the Army of the Potomac had a cavalryman who would have been capable of such a feat, but he remained in obscurity as an aide-de-camp to General Sigel back at Fairfax.

Yet another item on the list of Burnside's misfeasances and nonfeasances is interrogation, which was performed by General Patrick and occasionally by Burnside himself. Very little use or no use at all was made of John Babcock's skills. He would turn out, under Burnside's successor, to be an expert in the art of getting facts, correct ones, out of unwilling or poorly informed enemy soldiers. Babcock had participated in the prisoner examinations on the Peninsula that identified 178 enemy regiments — all there were in Lee's army, although Pinkerton and Babcock were unaware of that fact.

Babcock's history as a Pinkerton operative now was only a drawback. Patrick had found no regular, responsible job for him; the one project he is known to have performed in these months was self-assigned. He noticed, hanging about near headquarters, a man going by the name of Johnson, whom he recognized as having "particularly distinguished himself" in some suspicious way during Stuart's October raid into Pennsylvania. Later "Johnson" was engaged to enter the Confederate lines in Virginia but had again behaved suspiciously. Now Babcock began watching him in the hope of learning his contacts. However, in another of Stuart's raids, this one directed ostensibly at sutlers' stores, the suspect was "captured" by the Southern cavalry and thus escaped from surveillance. Babcock learned later that "Johnson" had turned up at his home near Leesburg.[26] The Army of the Potomac's lines during Burnside's command were notoriously porous; the main effort to tighten up seems to have been Babcock's surveillance of "Johnson" — a counterintelligence project aimed at a one-man target by a single operative who had been hired to engage in positive intelligence.

Burnside's battle would produce prisoners by the hundreds; until then the cavalry's inaction meant a dearth of prisoners, and the river was an obstacle to all but a few would-be deserters. One who especially interested Patrick had been an officer's servant. He was intelligent and informative — qualities that pleased Patrick but would also have recommended the man for the pseudo-deserter role if his masters had regarded him as a true Southern loyalist. But this man probably was the source of an important finding, the construction of a road that now connected the Confederates' left wing on the heights in rear of Fredericksburg with the right wing, twelve to twenty miles downriver. Two Irish deserters impressed Patrick mainly by their story of having crossed the river well above the army's positions at Fredericksburg, but if he gained any useful information from them he did not record it. Even two officer prisoners, one of them a Signal Corps lieutenant taken in civilian clothes, did not excite Patrick's interest enough for him to record what he had learned from them.[27]

. . .. ..

While the Army of Northern Virginia was being strengthened by the arrival of thousands of new troops in the quiet days of October, Lee carried out a thorough reorganization. He divided his infantry into two corps, the First under Longstreet and the Second under Jackson. This merely formalized the arrangement that had existed de facto for three months, but numerous shifts were made at lower levels. The two corps commanders were made lieutenant generals, and many other promotions followed in train.[28]

The arrival of Longstreet's troops at Fredericksburg, beginning November 21, readily came under Federal observation. Again the Yankees' chief intelligence problem was the whereabouts and movements of the force under Stonewall Jackson. As usual, Jackson was seeing to it that he would be reported moving in several directions at the same time. A deserter had correctly placed him in the vicinity of Winchester on November 5,[29] but the effect of that report was soon erased. On the 9th Harper's Ferry reported him crossing westward into the Valley (he had never left it), and on the same day a contraband informed Sigel that one of the Hills was crossing in the opposite direction, heading for Culpeper. On the 10th various elements of Sigel's command reported a General Hill east of the Blue Ridge, and also west of it; as there were enough Hills to go around, both reports could be correct, but that was not the case. Two days later the Union forces on the upper Potomac heard that Jackson, with 40,000 men, was marching for Cumberland. Elsewhere this threat of another invasion of the North met with the skepticism it merited; nevertheless it served to cloud the picture for several days.[30] Then on the 13th Charles Whitlock came in from the Southern lines with a report that moved Stonewall equally erroneously in the opposite direction:

> General Lee's headquarters at Orange Court-House; Longstreet at Culpeper; D. H. Hill is at Culpeper; A. P. Hill and Jackson in the Valley of the Shenandoah, part at Newtown, at Staunton, and at Thornton's Gap. A small force at Snickersville Gap and at Ashby's Gap. Conscripts and recovered sick and wounded have arrived, and about made up the loss at Antietam. . . . No forces at Richmond; army in good condition; use carpets for blankets; have bread and meat enough for the present.[31]

As Whitlock said he had been all the way to Culpeper, the report commanded a high credibility rating, but in fact Lee had his headquarters at Culpeper, D. H. Hill was still in the Valley, and Jackson's and A. P. Hill's positions were much farther north than the ones given for them. And this report, like others at this time, reflected an unawareness of the reorganization that made the Hills' divisions part of a new element designated the Second Corps.

Substantially correct information, however, began to come in on the 14th. It was from Sigel's and Pleasonton's scouts and from a twelve-year-old boy who had escaped from Confederate captivity at Berryville, and it showed Jackson still lingering there and about Winchester.[32] When he finally began moving eastward — days in advance of Lee's summons — the discovery was made in good time, on November 23. The source was a Federal soldier who had been paroled in Richmond on the 16th and had been permitted to come north over a route that defies understanding — overland, by way of the region recently occupied by Longstreet. In addition to seeing large forces about Culpeper and Warrenton, he learned at Salem, well to the east of the Blue Ridge, that on the 22nd residents there were preparing to feed Jackson's men. Corroboration of this report came on the 24th, all the way from Cincinnati, headquarters of the department that included western Virginia. This report told of a hundred-man scouting expedition that had crossed the Alleghenies on the 22nd and reached eastward to within four miles of Winchester, learning that for three days Jackson's troops had been moving out to the southeast.[33] Sigel promptly reported Stonewall's crossing of the Blue Ridge on the 24th. But Union commanders on the upper Potomac, by insisting that Jackson was still in their neighborhood, partially thwarted this outbreak of correct information.[34]

Burnside's response to these uncertainties was to begin allowing for Jackson's presence at Fredericksburg at a time consistent with known performances of his "foot cavalry" but well ahead of his actual progress. The timing of this winter march was another matter, however; Burnside could not foresee that the movement would not be completed until November 30. By that date most or all of the pontoons, arriving in stages, had been at Falmouth for three or four days, perhaps longer. Burnside had enough time to launch an attack on a force consisting only of Longstreet's Corps and Stuart's cavalry, but his intelligence capability did not approach the level of competence that could have given him such assurance. Lee, facing attack in the absence of Jackson's corps, probably would have reverted to his original intention to make his stand twenty miles closer to Richmond, at the North Anna River, where the crossing places were more defensible than on the Rappahannock at Fredericksburg.[35] This failure to take advantage of the slowness of Lee's reassembling of his army was the Federals' highest cost to date of their inability to keep track of the whereabouts of General Jackson.

· ·   · ·   · ·

The Army of the Potomac now had a new potential source of intelligence, the enemy's visual signaling. The armies' positions — facing each other across the river — afforded the opposing signalmen a unique opportunity to train their telescopes on the other side's flags.

Intelligence from interception of enemy messages had not figured in any previous campaign. In the first Bull Run battle only the Confederates had a Signal Corps on the field. On the Peninsula, as already seen, there was occasional interception of Confederate signals, but it is not known to have produced any intelligence. The terrain was too flat and too wooded for intercept to become a regular source, if indeed the Rebels used the flags often enough to make it profitable. In the Second Bull Run and Antietam campaigns the geography was more favorable, but there was so much movement that the Federal signalmen would have had all they could do to maintain communication, leaving no time for watching the enemy flags, which were beyond their view most of the time anyway.

At Fredericksburg the two Signal Corps finally settled into a static situation with each other's flag stations in view. The Federals lost no time in reading the enemy's messages — for they were sent "in the clear" — unenciphered. In the long periods of minimal susceptibility to interception, the Confederate signal officers, or their commanders, had never felt the need of cryptography, with its inevitable delays and garbles produced by encipherment and decipherment. Furthermore, the use of a flag alphabet different from the Federals' gave the Confederate message traffic at least a thin layer of secrecy. The Federal and Confederate alphabets employed the same motions of the flag — two motions early in the war, now two additional ones — but the combinations of motions signifying each of the twenty-six letters and ten digits were altogether different in the two armies. (The Federals' signaling security also was limited to a secret alphabet.)

By November 25, four days after the arrival of Longstreet's troops at Fredericksburg, Federal signal officers had reconstructed the Confederate flag alphabet, according to a report Lieutenant James S. Hall sent to Captain Samuel T. Cushing, the Army of the Potomac's chief signal officer. Hall used the term *code* rather than *alphabet,* but the context of his report shows that the reconstructed code was only a flag-signaling equivalent of the Morse code, rather than a cryptographic code. Six of the twenty-six letters used the same flag motions as in the alphabet that had come into Pinkerton's possession on the Peninsula. But Hall and Lieutenant Peter A. Taylor apparently reconstructed the enemy's new alphabet from scratch, unaware of the Peninsula episode.

The texts of sixteen messages intercepted on November 25, 26, and 27 accompanied Hall's report to Cushing. Most of them dealt with the signalmen's own affairs — for example, "Is the line open for official messages?" (to which the reply was affirmative). The only valuable message had an unimportant text but a significant address: "Maj. Sorrel"; G. Moxley Sorrel was a prominent member of Longstreet's staff. Although the presence of Longstreet's corps was already known, this message indicated the location of his headquarters, which would have been near the signal station that received it. That information was worth having, but Hall's report failed to note the significance of the address; he and Taylor would not have known where Major Sorrel fit into the organizational scheme. If the message had been turned over to John Babcock, his knowledge of the Army of Northern Virginia would have enabled him to see its significance; it was his business to learn if possible whose staff a functionary such as Major Sorrel belonged to. But it is very unlikely that the signal officers were aware of Babcock's skills when even his own superior officers were ignorant of them.

One officer certain to be sensitive to prospects of signal intelligence was Major Myer in Washington. Receiving Hall's report, he instructed Cushing to treat their access to enemy information as a secret. But even Myer did not take note of the valuable inferences that could be drawn from merely the location of enemy signal stations.[36]

.. .. ..

On December 3 came the best piece of intelligence work of Burnside's weeks in command; unfortunately, most of the information it produced was of long-term significance when what was urgently needed was some down-to-earth information on the dispositions and fortifications of the enemy force in the army's immediate front. The source of this report was another of Sigel's agents, Joseph E. Snyder, a soldier, whom Sigel described as "one of the best scouts in this Corps . . . a close and accurate observer of objects and movements." Snyder had made an extensive compilation of data while a prisoner of the Confederates, much of the time in Richmond. His report does not explain how he was able to do this; either he was being treated as an ordinary prisoner of war by Confederate provost marshals, or their handling of prisoners possibly guilty of espionage was still as careless as in the case of Frémont's spies captured in the Valley. Presumably in uniform when captured, Snyder was treated as an ordinary military prisoner and luckily included in an early exchange.

After leaving Sigel's headquarters, then at Fairfax Court House, on October 27, Snyder had been captured by a squadron of cavalry, part of a Confederate force posted on the east side of the Blue Ridge — the very force that would have been his scouting target. Taken to Richmond by way of Winchester, Staunton, and Gordonsville, he kept his eyes and ears open and his tongue working. At Gordonsville, for example, observing that there were no fortifications, he made bold to ask the reason "among those I came in contact with, but being made to understand that I was not there to take notes, I failed to the best of my ability." Nevertheless the journal he somehow managed to compile runs to 3000 words and extends to the time of his exchange in late November. His information, surprisingly correct, covers events in the Valley up to November 14 and in Richmond to the 20th. On October 30 he noted, "Longstreet's army corps commenced passing through the streets of Winchester yesterday morning. . . . It consisted of mostly Inft. No less than 60 Field pieces and a small force of Cavalry — estimated at 50,000 men en route for Front Royal. Genl Lee having left for Richmond Genl Jackson was in chief command." Except for an overstatement of Longstreet's strength by about 35 percent, all this was correct.[37] Snyder's estimate of Lee's total strength less cavalry as 113,000 was over the mark by about the same proportion. He gave many details regarding the composition and strength of Jackson's units and of the Richmond defenses; but at the time Jackson left the Valley, Snyder was in Richmond. Thus his report, by bolstering Babcock's records, supplied much information of long-term value but did not touch Jackson's movements.[38] They could be learned only by scouting, as Pope had found. Snyder had performed a good piece of espionage while in custody of the provost marshals, the very officials whose business it was to prevent such impositions. It was easier to dupe them than it was to get a look at Stonewall Jackson's marching troops.

. .   ..   ..

While Jackson was still in the Valley, Burnside began planning to cross the Rappahannock at Skinker's Neck, twelve miles below Fredericksburg (and eight additional miles from Howard Skinker's farm). Still undefended by Lee, the Neck offered an easy crossing and also a position from which to sweep around Lee's right, attacking his flank or gaining the lead in a march for Richmond. As might have been expected, preparations for the crossing attracted the enemy's notice, with the result that when Jackson arrived, Lee placed one of his four divisions, Early's, on the Neck, D. H. Hill's five miles below at Port Royal, and Taliaferro's within supporting distance at Guiney's Station on the Richmond railroad. Jackson's fourth division, A. P. Hill's, was posted near Hamilton's Crossing, closer to Longstreet's five divisions at Fredericksburg than to Jackson's other positions.[39]

But Burnside acquired an exaggerated idea of the size of the force on the enemy's southern wing. To Halleck on December 9 he wrote, somewhat ambiguously, of concentrations at both Skinker's Neck and Port Royal. With six enemy divisions at and near Fredericksburg and only three at the lower positions, his understanding of the situation seriously deviated from the facts — and this misconception became a prominent feature of his attack plan; how he acquired it is a mystery.[40] Lowe's balloons were still grounded, the cavalry was still keeping to the north side of the river, and information from deserters and prisoners was scanty. Nevertheless, Burnside evidently was quite confident that his understanding of the situation was correct. In fact we have a postwar recollection to this effect from General William Smith, a corps commander, who wrote that while riding with Burnside along the heights on the Falmouth side of the river, he pointed out the obstacles presented by the hills on the other side, and Burnside responded, "I know where Lee's forces are, and I expect to surprise him."[41]

Now that Skinker's Neck had become a less attractive objective, Burnside turned his attention to Fredericksburg. Assuming that Lee would be surprised by an attack there, he decided to cross the river at and immediately below the town. In its rear was a fortified hill known as Marye's Heights, and beyond that a ridge that extended southward for six miles. Burnside's main attack, by Franklin's grand division reinforced by part of Hooker's, was to cross just below the town and push northward along the ridge, striking the defenders of Marye's Heights on their right flank. That height was the target of a second attack to be delivered frontally — from the east — by Sumner's grand division, also reinforced by troops borrowed from Hooker. If the Confederates had as large a portion of their force twelve or more miles down the river as Burnside believed, the force in Franklin's path would not be numerous enough to block a determined drive northward to Marye's Heights. He would have 60,000 men; the rest of the army, numbering 53,000 and consisting of Sumner's grand division and part of Hooker's, would be available for Sumner's attack. Lee's total force numbered about 78,000, less than half of which Burnside believed to be on the Fredericksburg end of the enemy's long line. Sumner's attack would have to be synchronized with Franklin's successful driving of the enemy; the telegraph lines needed for that, connecting the two grand divisions with Burnside's headquarters in rear of Falmouth, were in place.[42]

Not until December 10 were Burnside's preparations finished to his satisfaction, and by that time of course the Confederates' readiness was equally well advanced. Engineer troops, though protected by the Federals' excellent artillery and by picked regiments of infantry, required almost a full day, the 11th, to put five pontoon bridges down in the face of sharpshooters' persistent fire from houses on the riverbank. Late on that day and all day on the 12th Franklin's and Sumner's attacking forces marched across the bridges and took position on low ground around and below the town; the attack was set for the next morning.[43]

Two days had now elapsed since the bridge-laying showed the enemy where Burnside would attack. Whatever surprise his plan yielded was now dissipated; that was predictable, but this weakness does not appear to have been contemplated in his plan. Lee quickly moved A. P. Hill's and Taliaferro's divisions into position to meet the advance on the lower bridges, leaving Jackson's other divisions, Early's and D. H. Hill's, temporarily downriver as protection against a possible crossing at Skinker's

Neck, where the Federals were still making a show of activity for the purpose of deception. Seven of Lee's nine divisions were now on the Fredericksburg end of his line, and Early and D. H. Hill would arrive there after an overnight march in time for the battle on the 13th.[44]

As if to save Sumner's and Hooker's soldiers from their fate on Marye's Heights, there came to Burnside an eleventh-hour chance to correct his misunderstanding of the relative strength of the enemy's positions. On the morning of the 13th a prisoner gave him — according to Hooker, who along with Sumner was also present — "full information of the position and defenses of the enemy, stating that it was their desire that we should attack . . . in rear of Fredericksburg . . . that it was perfectly impossible for any troops to carry the position." The prisoner, a German, claimed he "had been impressed into their service, and wanted to quit it. His appearance and his story were such as to carry conviction to the mind of every one who heard him. He told us precisely the arrangements . . . they had made on the [Federal] right, but in regard to the left he knew less."

The German's account of the impregnability of the defenses on Marye's Heights was truthful. But with Franklin already on the march to an attack in coordination with the one on Marye's Heights, canceling the latter might prove disastrous. And Burnside could assume that with Franklin on their right flank the defenders of the hill would no longer be invincible. Over Hooker's objections he left his battle plan unchanged.[45]

Details of Franklin's attack had been worked out late on the 12th when Burnside conferred with him and his two corps commanders, Smith and Reynolds. But the next morning Franklin received written orders from Burnside that he interpreted as calling for actions much less ambitious than those agreed upon in their conference. Without asking for clarification, he sent George Meade's 4500-man division, one of the smallest in the left wing, with assistance from John Gibbon's division, to gain a position near Hamilton's Crossing at the south end of the ridge. Meade found an undefended opening in the enemy line and reached the objective, but in the process he became separated from Gibbon. They were overmatched and driven back by Jackson, thus losing the position from which Franklin was expected to drive toward Marye's Heights.[46]

Having met unexpectedly heavy resistance, Franklin reverted to an overcautiousness reminiscent of his action, or inaction, at Crampton's Gap on September 14. He allowed Smith's Sixth Corps, the largest in the army, to devote the entire day to protecting the bridgehead from enemy forces that never came near it. His limited attack plan assigned no role to Reynolds's third division, Abner Doubleday's. The only significant support given Meade and Gibbon was from elements of Daniel Sickles's and David Birney's divisions of Hooker's command; this help came belatedly but was vital in saving the attackers' broken ranks from rout. Although

Burnside had a staff officer, Brigadier General James Hardie, on liaison duty with Franklin, and although he twice sent other staff aides to urge Franklin forward, one of them carrying a direct order to advance, there was no advance. The only excuse Franklin ever gave for his inaction was a claim that both Burnside's original order and its follow-up received in midafternoon were obscurely worded. The first order, it is generally acknowledged, was poorly worded, but Reynolds, having in mind the agreement that had been reached in the conference with Burnside the previous evening, had no difficulty in perceiving the commanding general's wishes. The follow-up order, Franklin argued, was inapplicable to the changed situation in which he found himself. He had enough manpower for Burnside's plan to have worked even though it was based on the expectation of meeting much smaller numbers of Rebels; he should have realized that his failure probably meant failure for the whole army, but he remained unmoved, physically and mentally.

While Meade was still fighting his way to the ridge, Burnside received a telegram from General Hardie that gave him an unwarrantedly favorable impression of Franklin's progress. Even so, this was no indication that Franklin's advance had reached the point of threatening Marye's Heights. But with midday fast approaching, Burnside felt it was now or never; he ordered Sumner forward. Without Franklin's assistance Sumner's charges were hopeless; in just three hours Marye's Heights became a symbol of attack against murderous odds. Division after division — French's, Hancock's, Howard's, Humphreys's, finally Getty's — advanced up the slope to crumble before the fire of Confederates who stood several ranks deep, protected by stone fence and sunken road. Even Humphreys's charge, made with bayonet, fell short of the defenders' front rank.

Humphreys's division belonged to the command of Hooker, who midway in the attack made two attempts to persuade Burnside to call it off. At dusk Hooker ordered his men back. For this decision he had a characteristically caustic explanation: "Finding that I had lost as many men as my orders required me to lose, I suspended the attack." Burnside finally called an end to the debacle without learning until later that Franklin's assault on the ridge had been seriously delayed and had been "in such small force as to have . . . no permanent effect upon the enemy's line."

At the end of the day the Army of the Potomac had 10,200 killed and wounded, 6300 of them at Marye's Heights; Confederate casualties were only half as great.

On the following day, December 14, Burnside had to be dissuaded from leading in person his old command, the Ninth Corps, in a renewed attack on Marye's Heights. By the next day he was thinking clearly, and that night he and his staff and subordinate commanders executed, without the enemy's notice, a smooth withdrawal to the Falmouth side of the river.[47]

. .　. .　. .

While the armies settled into their old camps and Burnside began working out his next move, Stuart kept the pot boiling by raiding as far behind the lines as Fairfax Court House. When he captured Burke's Station on the Orange and Alexandria Railroad, a telegraph operator accompanying the raid took down a number of Federal messages concerning the raiders' depredations before identifying himself to Federal operators up and down the line and then decamping.[48] In reporting this caper, General Henry Slocum, commander of the nearby Twelfth Corps, commented, "I believe, from the fact that the [telegraph] line is not much more frequently broken by them, that they obtain much information [from it]."[49] This suspicion was shared by operators at the War Department and at Burnside's headquarters, who had spotted a strange "fist" (operator jargon for individual keying characteristics) on the circuit between Washington and Falmouth. After a few days the interloper revealed himself and then announced that "having learned all that he wanted to know, he was about to cut out and run." The episode occurred at a time when Burnside's cipher operator was away; the telegraphers were forced to improvise a crude scrambling of the words handed to them for transmission. The wiretapper's gleanings may not have matched his braggadocio, for the information he said he acquired has yet to show up in the records of the generals he would have delivered it to. His jolly openness with his Yankee brethren and his recklessness in coming on the line with his strange fist show this to have been a less than serious intelligence project. Yet it is one of the very few reasonably well established instances of a sustained wiretap in the entire war, and the only one that has come to light in the records of the eight campaigns examined in this book. Despite the severe barrenness of evidence, numerous historians have assumed that intelligence-producing wiretaps were a commonplace in Civil War telegraphy.[50]

. .　. .　. .

Late in December Burnside ordered another movement across the Rappahannock, this one to be made seven miles below Fredericksburg. The cavalry was already in motion when he received a message from the President reading, "I have good reasons for saying that you must not make a general movement without first letting me know of it." Countermanding the order, Burnside went to Washington and there learned that two of his subordinates had visited the White House to protest the wisdom of the proposed movement. The conference ended with Burnside's submitting a statement that he did not have the confidence of the army and that the same lack was true of General Halleck and Secretary Stanton. Lincoln refused to accept Burnside's statement and his offer to retire to private life.[51]

Although "convinced that the general officers of this command are almost unanimously opposed to another crossing of the river," Burnside persisted in a new attempt. This time the crossing was to be above Fredericksburg — the plan favored by the high command from the beginning of the campaign. Burnside's decision, however, was based not on the views of his chiefs but on newly acquired information indicating that the enemy was most vulnerable in the upriver sector. This information came from Ebenezer McGee, thirty-three, member of one of several McGee families living on the turnpike six to eight miles west of Fredericksburg, and Jackson Harding, who resided on the north side of the river between Banks's Ford and United States Mine Ford. McGee, who had been working for the army on the railroad between Falmouth and Aquia, visited his home by crossing the Rappahannock on a raft where the banks were steep and unguarded. Crossing on two consecutive nights, he brought a report written by one of his neighbors, Isaac Silver, revealing that the Confederates had placed a brigade at U.S. Ford. Patrick had Harding brought in to headquarters under arrest, obviously to give his neighbors the impression that he was suspected of secessionist activities. Burnside and Patrick interviewed him at length regarding roads on the enemy's side of the fords. Harding's name would become the first one on the secret-service payroll records maintained by Captain Henry P. Clinton, quartermaster of Patrick's brigade, the army's Provost Guard.[52]

The enemy brigade at U.S. Ford was in Burnside's path, but he did not regard it as enough of an obstacle to change his plan, which was to put his army on Lee's left flank. As the blue columns took to the roads on January 20, the skies opened, and soldiers, horses, and wagons soon found themselves in a vast slough. Return to camp was ordered on the 22nd. The "movement" went into official records under the name Mud March; it earned the derision of the entire army, including John Babcock. Receiving a letter in which his grandfather advised him to "be a good boy and don't get shot in the back," Babcock replied that "in order to make sure that such a calamity will never befall me, I will have to practice running backward, if I follow the Army of the Potomac much longer."[53]

The Mud March served to bring Burnside's disagreements with his subordinates to a head. On January 23 he asked the President to approve an order cashiering from the service General Hooker and three lower-ranking generals and relieving from duty with the Army of the Potomac Generals Franklin, Smith, and three others. The result, after the President called Secretary Stanton and General Halleck into the discussion, was quite different. Franklin and Sumner were relieved, the latter at his own request; Burnside, also at his own request, was also relieved; and Hooker, whose actions inimical to the good of the service had been dwelt upon at length in Burnside's proposed order, was given command of the Army of the Potomac.[54]

. . . . . .

The known history of intelligence leading up to the Fredericksburg battle consists of a mere handful of gleanings — all from interrogation. And even the few interrogations known to have been performed were not nearly as productive as they would have been if John Babcock had been the interrogator. His knowledge of the Army of Northern Virginia would have yielded productive questions, beyond the ken of anyone else, to ask of the Negro servant Patrick found so informative, the two Irish deserters, the two officer prisoners, the German prisoner who warned of the invulnerability of the defenses on Marye's Heights, and possibly a few others who did not get into the records. One or more of these might have turned out to have information that would have corrected Burnside's mistaken understanding of enemy positions. And if Babcock had been treated as a full-fledged intelligence officer, as he was later, he might have been able to urge Sigel's scouts into so effective a tracking of Jackson's approach as to persuade Burnside to cross the river during that brief period when the pontoons were on hand and an attack would have met, besides Stuart, only Longstreet's half of Lee's infantry.

Babcock did not rest easy in his obscurity. On the last day of 1862 he wrote a letter to General Parke describing in detail his counterespionage against "Johnson"; this was a thinly disguised way of pointing out that he had spent nearly two months not doing the positive-intelligence job he supposedly was hired to do. In going over General Patrick's head by addressing the chief of staff, he was committing an indiscretion; he struggled to find discreet language in which to do it. The result was a hopelessly equivocal letter, though he did manage one forthright statement, a request for "a greater license in making . . . examinations" — interrogating. If he had had any "license" at all, it does not show in the records, and his status remained unchanged.[55]

. . . . . .

In order to visualize the Burnside that might have been, it is necessary only to recall John Pope. A Pope in command at Falmouth would have kept cavalry parties busy across the river, their findings supplemented by individual scouts and spies; Ebenezer McGee, Isaac Silver, and Jackson Harding would have been discovered early on. Burnside's wherewithal for obtaining intelligence was far greater than Pope's: he had cavalry aplenty, his situation was suitable for ballooning, he was in a country where Unionist citizens were known from prolonged Federal occupation earlier in the year. And Burnside's later record, in his 1863 campaign in East Tennessee, shows imaginative and energetic use of spies and other kinds of agent.[56] How he expected to conduct a successful campaign against Robert E. Lee with whatever information drifted in of its own accord is one of the major puzzles in the study of the too-numerous commanders of the Army of the Potomac.

The Fredericksburg campaign is the low point of this story. Other defeats suffered by the Federals' eastern armies are also traceable to intelligence insufficiency or error, but none were so devastating.

12

. . . .

A NEW CLIENT FOR
ATTORNEY SHARPE

February 1863

PROVOST MARSHAL GENERAL Marsena Patrick combined the qualities of a regular army disciplinarian with those of an Old Testament prophet. Each morning he held solitary devotions in his tent, sometimes extending them to the length of the Presbyterian sermons he had listened to all his life. Then, looking like an artist's conception of Elijah, with his spare figure, stern countenance, bald head, and full beard, he emerged to practice all day long a different code, in which he believed as strongly as he did in his religion — the Army Regulations.

Patrick had taken over the brigade of James Wadsworth in March 1862 when that general became military governor of the District of Columbia. The soldiers saw their new brigadier for the first time when, unannounced and unidentified, he came walking through their camp with a Mexican blanket "hanging over his shoulders and enveloping his form, his head passing through a hole in the center," and evidently "spying out the barrenness of the camp." The next day, when Patrick formally assumed command — now resplendently uniformed and mounted on a magnificent horse — the soldiers scrutinized him minutely and concluded that no description fitted him so well as the time-honored line, "He could bite the head off a tenpenny nail." They decided that they were going to "miss Uncle Wadsworth for a while." But after they had been through a few battles — Second Bull Run, South Mountain, Antietam — with their regulation-minded general, they were persuaded of the wisdom of his ways, and they opened their hearts to him. And Patrick reciprocated their affection. The same men whom he had so often disciplined were surprised to find, after he became provost marshal general, that he wanted them to join him as provost troops. Patrick's explanation was, "It was absolutely indispensable that I should have troops around me on whom I could rely."[1]

While General Burnside was in Washington being relieved of the command of the army, General Patrick's hardest problem at Falmouth was getting some sleep. A perpetual insomniac, he now had more than the usual after-hours chattering of headquarters officers to contend with, for their camp buzzed day and night with gossip about the army's affairs. He had written to General Parke, Burnside's chief of staff, "The disorderly character of the Camp at Hd Qrs is not creditable to this Army. . . . I would suggest the propriety of Taps at 10:30 PM to mark the time beyond which unnecessary noise will not be regarded as a breach of propriety, but as a violation of orders."

On the night of January 26, while Patrick was still awaiting action on this recommendation, he retired at 11 o'clock "and had a good nap until about 1–1/2 or two o'clock, when I was routed out by Hunt [the army's chief of artillery], who commenced to sing & whistle, keeping it up for over half an hour." That was the end of his night's rest.[2] Next morning, feeling all the aches to which his fifty-two years entitled him, he had cause to wish for a happier state of health, for it was to be an important day in the army's history. The news of the change of command was now official; soon General Hooker arrived and Burnside gathered his generals in his tent to take leave of them. His brief speech, which is not recorded, somehow left the air charged with strife and resentment — not surprising in view of Burnside's having urged Lincoln to sack Hooker. It was Patrick who found his tongue and attempted to save the situation. He admitted to himself that his remarks "prevented anything unpleasant from taking place."[3]

.. .. ..

Hooker sailed immediately into his new job. How should the army have been run all these months? Joe Hooker knew; had known all along. Such in any case was his confident belief. His character is summed up in his biographer's statement that upon learning of his appointment as Burnside's successor, Hooker was the least surprised man in the army.[4] The quotations from his bitter pen that have appeared in these pages are only a few among many that challenged the competence and judgment of his superiors and civil authorities and indicated a conviction that he could manage the army better than anyone else.[5] It is not surprising that along with his appointment he received a written admonition from Lincoln in which the President said he was not blind to Hooker's agitation against Burnside and of the character that underlay that behavior. This was the occasion of Lincoln's often quoted advice to Hooker: "I have heard, in such a way as to believe it, of your recently saying that both the Army and the Government needed a dictator. . . . Only those generals who gain successes can set up dictators. What I now ask of you is military success, and I will risk the dictatorship."[6]

Hooker's estimation of his own abilities was not without foundation. He had made a good academic record at West Point (he was graduated in 1837), though demerits for conduct held down his class standing. He entered the Mexican War as a first lieutenant, and although continuously assigned to staff duties he gained prominence, coming out of Mexico a lieutenant colonel. But the unembellished record of his assignments and promotions fails to tell what the Mexican War did for Joe Hooker. He served as aide-de-camp, adjutant, or chief of staff to a succession of five political generals. Though men of ability, they frequently found themselves in tactical situations that were over their heads. It was Hooker, the young regular assigned to give headquarters professional brainpower, who was his commanders' salvation. He did not simply ride at his general's side and give advice; in a crisis Hooker took part of the command, or sometimes all of it, and charged the enemy. In Zachary Taylor's bloody storming of Monterey, Hooker led General Thomas Hamer's brigade; at Chapultepec he headed a mixed command of cavalry and infantry picked from the divisions of William Worth and Gideon Pillow. He also fought at the head of small units. All of his three brevets, in fact, were for gallantry in action. But he also acquired administrative experience in units as large as division; his standing orders from Pillow were: "When you see occasion for issuing an order, give it without reference to me. You understand these matters." Thus while most of the officers who would become generals fifteen years later were in command of nothing higher than a company or battery, Hooker was acquiring a much broader experience. His case modifies somewhat the oft-repeated statement that in 1861 only the North's septuagenarian generals had handled large bodies of troops. And it establishes that there was more than vanity in Hooker's boast to President Lincoln that he was "a damned sight better General" than any the Federals had on the field at First Bull Run.[7]

In 1853, deciding to try his abilities in the civilian world, Hooker took up farming in California. His success was less than mediocre, but he obtained civil offices that used his military training in engineering. He was later to regard his years in the West as unfortunate in that they brought him, he believed, the dislike of Henry Halleck, then practicing law and engineering in San Francisco. After the war Hooker would claim that he "only consented to take command . . . on the unequivocal assurance of the President that he would stand between me and Genl. Halleck." Halleck, however, disclaimed any animus against Hooker.[8]

Halleck was not the only obstacle Hooker might face in the army that he came East to join in 1861. If Winfield Scott kept a blacklist, near the top of it stood the name of Joseph Hooker. After having the good fortune to perform much of his Mexican War service under Scott's eye, Hooker immediately thereafter sided against him in a controversy between Scott and Pillow.

When Hooker spoke his mind to Lincoln about the quality of the generalship at Bull Run, he was making a last-ditch effort to obtain a commission, having been in Washington more than a month without making visible progress. The President took up the case and found that Hooker had friends in Congress who were already at work on it. Nominations for brigadier general were sent to the Senate at the end of July; Hooker's name was on the list along with that of Ulysses S. Grant and nine others. He was speedily confirmed.[9]

Under General McClellan, his first chief, Hooker was given command of a brigade in the northeast suburbs of Washington. It soon became a division, and near the end of October it moved into the position in lower Maryland where we previously saw it, thirty-five miles below Washington. The distance was enough to throw upon Hooker the responsibilities of separate command, including the gathering of information about the enemy. He was quick to respond, for he intended to lose no time in going after the Confederates whose batteries, across the river in Virginia, effectively blockaded commercial shipping on the broad Potomac. However, Hooker's sources of information speedily persuaded him that the enemy's strength was too great for him to undertake such an operation alone.[10] He had to shelve his aggressiveness for the time being: no help was to be expected from McClellan, who was keeping the entire army on a tight leash.[11] But Hooker never relaxed his quest for information about what was happening over in Virginia. It occupied all the time he could spare from his other chief concern — trying to curb the contraband activity in the region under his charge. That offered as great an intelligence challenge as did the Confederate army.

Against these two targets he employed spies. (Plain-spoken Joe Hooker called them spies; most commanders used the softer word *scouts* in referring to spies as well as to scouts.) He discovered that he had an unusually competent and well-disciplined cavalry force, consisting of eight companies of the Third Indiana. The Third, raised in the Ohio River counties just below Cincinnati, was an elite regiment, at least to the extent that its men commonly owned their horses. Hooker set them to work scouring the countryside for smugglers and enemy couriers.[12] And as we saw in chapter 4, his position opposite a substantial enemy force entitled him to the use of one of Professor Lowe's balloons.[13]

Still, Hooker's first weeks in lower Maryland left him nearly empty-handed of enemy information. He wrote McClellan in mid-November that "it has been necessary to form my opinion [of enemy positions and strength] almost wholly from their camp fires, for, strange to say, I have not . . . fallen in with any one able or willing to enlighten me on this subject."[14] At times the best he could do was to have his pickets on the river note the number of camps from which bugle calls could be heard —

when reveille or tattoo was sounded six times, he assumed the presence of six regiments.[15] Of course this method of counting meant that the Rebels' apparent strength went up or down every time the wind changed.

But the enemy's secrets could not resist discovery indefinitely; soon Hooker's fortunes improved. At first skeptical of the practicability of balloons, he began making ascents himself. The information brought down from aloft improved, and so did Hooker's confidence in Professor Lowe. Lafayette Baker, whose detectives apparently had been busy in the region, paid Hooker a visit, took a detachment of the Third Indiana with him, found what he was after ("four noted Traitors and one Rebel Spie," he wrote Hooker),[16] and in the process taught the soldiers a few tricks of his trade. Hooker, stimulated by Baker's praise for his cavalrymen, extended their picketing operations all the way to Point Lookout, where the Potomac reaches Chesapeake Bay. Their instructions were to "radiate in all directions and at all times" in search of contraband trade and correspondence. A week later came the unusual spectacle of the capture of a Rebel trading sloop by the Indiana cavalrymen (described in chapter 4).[17]

When Confederate soldiers or the servants of Southern officers came over to the Federals, they were examined in fine detail.[18] The navy's Potomac flotilla cooperating with Hooker's command came to have no fear of the Confederate batteries and supplied detailed information about them. Improved results came from the spies, some of whom were Negroes. Soon Hooker's dispatches to his chief showed a great deal more confidence in his information, although he occasionally complained about the balloon's failures and about the difficulty of getting agents through the enemy pickets. His statements about the Confederates' strength had a matter-of-fact tone and were uniformly conservative;[19] their Potomac artillery, although plentiful, he now considered no threat at all against distant targets.[20]

To Hooker the enemy's Potomac batteries were an opportunity for a movement independent of the rest of the army. In February he obtained McClellan's approval of such an attack, but it was suddenly ordered suspended when McClellan learned that transports to move the army for his campaign against Richmond would be assembled: the Confederates would have to abandon the batteries when McClellan's movement cut them off. When the Confederates drew back from their Manassas line in March and abandoned the batteries, Hooker's hopes shifted to an attack on Fredericksburg. Stepped-up activity by his spies across the river, plus what he could see from the balloon, convinced him that he could go at least as far as the Rappahannock River. But McClellan, believing he would meet too much opposition, halted him again.

Hooker would get his chance to fight on other ground; his division, one of the best trained at McClellan's disposal, was part of the army that was leaving for the Peninsula. It was in the Third Corps, commanded by General Samuel P. Heintzelman.[21]

Early in May the battle of Williamsburg, the first serious engagement of the campaign, produced accurate prophecy about Joe Hooker. His division carried the fight against superior numbers; from then on it was in the thick of most battles, its commander riding all day through a storm of bullets, "as cool and collected under fire as if directing a parade or a picnic."[22] His reputation for fearless and inspired leadership, established that day, was confirmed in many subsequent battles. (After the Seven Days battles one of his staff officers remarked, "Let Hooker go where he will, he invariably meets the enemy, and always in superior force.")[23] But Hooker felt he had been allowed to carry too much of the Williamsburg fight alone; his after-action report exposed his tendency toward acidulous utterance: "History will not be believed when it is told that the noble officers and men of my division were permitted to carry on this unequal struggle from morning until night unaided in the presence of more than 30,000 of their comrades . . . nevertheless it is true."[24]

But the same battle revealed, to one who knew him intimately, a disturbing lack of decisiveness and determination. His good friend General Philip Kearny, another hard fighter, who saw him in action that day, wrote, "Hooker has been beaten because he did not know his mind; I have full evidence by the field over which he fought; . . . he wanted to take the enemy's works but did not even think that he could do it."[25]

After McClellan's campaign stalled, Hooker's division was one of the first units of the Army of the Potomac sent to General Pope. His vigorous fighting at Second Bull Run made him one of the few generals of the Potomac army to receive praise from Pope, who wrote of "Fighting Joe": "As I saw him . . . on his white horse riding in rear of his line of battle, and close up to it, with the excitement of battle in his eyes, and that gallant and chivalric appearance which he always presented under fire, I was struck with admiration. As a corps commander, with his whole force operating under his own eye, it is much to be doubted whether Hooker had a superior in the army."[26]

McClellan, the recipient and target of Hooker's blistering report on Williamsburg,[27] nevertheless gave Hooker the command of the First Corps — in preference to McClellan's friend General Reno — in the reorganized army that set out in pursuit of Lee after the Second Bull Run battle.[28] And after Hooker received an incapacitating wound early in the action at Antietam, McClellan wrote him a letter warm with praise and recommended him for a brigadier generalcy in the regular army, which he soon received.[29] Burnside, although thoroughly aware of qualities that made Hooker a doubtful subordinate,[30] was another who could not afford to pass over such manifest ability; hence Hooker's selection in November to command one of Burnside's short-lived grand divisions.[31]

If appearances counted for anything, Hooker — tall, robust, ruddy, showing his forty-eight years and yet almost extravagantly handsome — was every inch a commanding general. And his personality was not what his conceit might suggest; he was genial and warm, altogether pleasant company.[32]

Soon it developed that Hooker *had* known all along how to run an army. That he was a great battlefield leader had come to be taken for granted; the administrative ability that he now demonstrated came as a surprise.[33] This was not simply a matter of correcting a list of Burnside's deficiencies, as might be concluded from accounts of the supposedly deplorable condition of the army when it passed into Hooker's hands. The personnel situation under Burnside was contradictory. The men had never fought more bravely, the machine they composed had never moved with greater efficiency; yet morale was low, and Hooker found that one man out of every ten was either a deserter or an absentee without leave.[34] He was irrevocably committed to making improvements, and everywhere he turned he found room for them. And his ideas worked.

He began with an organizational shakeup. The job of managing the defenses of Washington was a millstone to the commander of a field army; Hooker had the capital and its environs made into an independent department under his former chief, General Heintzelman. Likewise he disposed of Harper's Ferry and the Shenandoah Valley, which were added to the command of General Schenck at Baltimore.[35] His most significant change was the disbandment of Burnside's grand divisions. The return to the familiar corps arrangement allowed routine administrative matters to be handled more efficiently; however, the plan of campaign that he eventually conceived and executed called for the army to be widely separated into two wings. This required temporary groupings of two and more corps; the grand-division arrangement would have provided the necessary groupings under permanent commanders. (The campaign was to show the origin of Hooker's desire to have each corps directly under his own command; he found it difficult to direct operations beyond the range of his own vision.) One other organizational change within the army was, however, unquestionably for the better: the cavalry, hitherto assigned by brigades to infantry corps, was now constituted as a corps, though its divisions were distributed on a geographic basis.[36]

Brigadier General George Stoneman was moved from command of the Third Corps to head the Cavalry Corps; Brigadier General Daniel E. Sickles became acting commander of the Third Corps. There were two other new corps commanders, Major General George G. Meade of the Fifth Corps and Major General John Sedgwick of the Sixth. Major General John F. Reynolds continued in command of the First Corps, Major General Darius N. Couch of the Second, Major General Franz Sigel of the Eleventh, and Major General Henry W. Slocum of the Twelfth. Sigel would soon be replaced by Major General Oliver O. Howard.

Whoever became Hooker's chief of staff would join him and General Patrick in a triumvirate that would establish and oversee the intelligence activities of the army. For that position Hooker wanted General Charles P. Stone, but Stone was unacceptable at Washington even though he had exploded the charge of treasonable involvement in the defeat at Ball's Bluff.[37] The man Hooker settled upon as staff chief probably had had no experience at being second choice for anything. He was Major General Daniel Butterfield, thirty-one years old, son of a leading figure in the American Express Company. Although taken early into the family business (he managed the New York City office), Butterfield had traveled in the South and had long believed that the war was inevitable. Along with his easy pathway to prominence he had inherited a driving energy and a good deal of ability. Despite his business responsibilities he found time to enter the state militia; soon he was a colonel. Then came Fort Sumter. Even his own well-prepared regiment could not be mustered in fast enough to suit Dan Butterfield; within two days he was in Washington asking for any appointment that was available. The position given him was that of drill sergeant of the Clay Guard, a battalion composed of prominent citizens of the capital. After his regiment was finally called, he led it only briefly, being quickly summoned to brigade and then division command under Fitz John Porter. In November 1862, when Porter was cashiered, command of his corps, the Fifth, went to Butterfield.

During this period of rapid advancement the versatile and energetic Butterfield wrote and published *Camp and Outpost Duty for Infantry,* containing "standing orders, extracts from the revised regulations for the army, rules for health, maxims for soldiers, and duties of officers." The little book filled a gap in the everyday literature of soldiering for the volunteers in blue and was widely praised and promoted by their generals. Butterfield has long been credited as the composer of the bugle call Taps; although he was the principal or only sponsor of its adoption as the army's "lights out" call, recent research has established that he adapted taps from a disused cavalry call.

Bald, black-mustachioed Butterfield stood only as high as Hooker's shoulders, but he owned much the same reputation for battlefield gallantry as his chief. He also shared with Hooker the status of bachelor.[38]

Hooker's genius for administration was matched by Butterfield's gusto for the paperwork that would put his chief's flow of ideas into effect. A torrent of circulars and memoranda began pouring from army headquarters. They dealt with the entire spectrum of military subjects, including such small but important matters as company funds, certificates furnished to discharged soldiers, regulations governing sutlers and purveyors to officers' messes. The profusion of paper caused considerable annoyance, if General Patrick's reaction was typical; he complained that Butterfield singlehandedly was generating more business than a provost marshal could handle along with his other activities. "Too busy for thought," Patrick wrote. "Action — action seems to be all that is necessary around this establishment."[39]

Patrick's department dealt with the urgent task of rounding up the army's AWOLs and clamping down on desertions. He needed no prodding to devise and enforce the sternest measures within his reach. When Hooker directed that his own name and authority be used freely, Patrick confided to his diary, "My position is not an agreeable one and I hardly know how I am to manage"; but manage he did.[40] He called for each command to furnish him with descriptions of its deserters, to aid the civil authorities in apprehending them. When this mountain of paper was collected, he unloaded it on General Halleck, who set twelve clerks to work to pass it on to the draft authorities in the states.

Patrick also communicated directly with civil police departments; to the New York City superintendent of police, for example, he complained that a five-dollar reward offered the city's policemen for each arrest was resulting in the detention of many men who were rightfully in New York, on furlough or duty. He tempered his sternness in the case of a boatman arrested at Washington for allegedly ferrying deserters across the Potomac; Patrick wrote to the adjutant general that the case was well known to him and the suspect should be released. No disposition toward leniency was to be seen, however, in the orders and dispatches on desertion issuing from army headquarters. Assistance of the navy's Potomac flotilla was obtained to cut off the river as a route of escape; pickets were instructed not to permit any passage whatever in a northward direction; telegraph repairmen, who regularly traveled in the army's rear, were required to carry credentials so that deserters could not successfully impersonate them. Finally, it was ordered that anyone not answering the summons of a sentinel was to be shot.[41]

The effort to end desertion brought 467 men back to the fold in the first week of Hooker's command, even before the civilian agencies had received Patrick's requests for help. A prime source of the leakage was located: soldiers were getting civilian clothes from home through the army's own post office. Patrick had the mail service placed under his own control, authorized inspection of packages, and required the Adams Express Company to itemize the contents of each package sent to the army.[42] He put some of his officers to work as detectives to check the shipping entering and leaving the army's supply bases at Aquia Creek

Landing and nearby Belle Plain. Although few deserters were turned up, other interesting discoveries were made, as when a steamboat hand was found selling liquor to soldiers from a stock of forty-six bottles concealed in the coal pile on his ship.[43]

Patrick needed the cooperation and good will of provost marshals at Washington, and here he ran into trouble. Some of the difficulties were more amusing than otherwise, a case in point being the accidental inclusion of a member of the Marine Corps in a group of deserters sent from Washington prisons to the Army of the Potomac.[44] Such problems were solved easily when Patrick could deal with the new military governor of Washington, Brigadier General John H. Martindale, with whom he had soldiered in the old army.[45] All too often, however, he found that the Washington end of his affairs was being handled by Lafayette Baker, who now had an official name for his position as the government's chief detective: special provost marshal of the War Department. A feud of major proportions grew up between Patrick and Baker over the activities of Baker's detectives within the lines of the army, and especially on the supply ships plying between Aquia and Washington. Baker's men repeatedly ran afoul of Patrick's officers; one of the latter went so far as to arrest three Baker detectives, although he soon released them.[46] Patrick wrote Butterfield that the detectives "have systematically robbed the officers and men of this Army of Clothing, subsistence, mess & other stores and necessaries." And, he declared, "from my knowledge of their Chief, 'Baker' I believe him to be capable of making any statement however false, & of committing any act, however criminal and of damaging the Public Service to gratify his own Passions."[47] This accusation eventually reached the War Department, and Patrick found himself retracting the phrase "& of committing any act, however criminal." He explained that the words had been written "in the belief, then almost universal in this Army," that Baker was guilty of a certain homicide.[48]

On a visit to the War Department Patrick had a long talk with Assistant Secretary Peter H. Watson and succeeded in getting to the source of difficulties he was having at Washington. According to Watson, Baker's men had reported finding large quantities of salt in Richmond that had been sent there from the North bearing Patrick's printed permit. He was also accused of assisting in the shipment to the North of plunder taken from Fredericksburg and of other misdeeds. Baker charged General Rufus Ingalls, the army's able quartermaster, with a "vast amount of peculations in forage." "Baker swears hostility eternal against Ingalls and myself," Patrick wrote. Most astonishing of all was Watson's revelation to Patrick that "I was to have been dismissed, 2 or 3 times, but circumstances prevented it — I would have been dismissed now, within a few days past, but [for the fact] that such a storm was raised about [Watson's] ears that he became satisfied he must be in error, but could not see how."

Patrick too had friends at Washington, old army men who knew he was incapable of corruption. His diary reveals that even before becoming provost marshal general, he worried constantly about soldiers' proclivity for pillaging, stealing, and contraband activities — the very wrongs he now learned he was suspected of.

Burnside, like Hooker, had ordered that Baker's men be kept out of the lines of the army. Patrick now thought he knew why Burnside had not enforced the order. During his stay at Falmouth in the summer of 1862, Patrick wrote, "Burnside kept a woman, whom Baker passed down here to him & who was one of Baker's creatures. Watson told me that he had heard Burnside ask Baker to come & see him." He added, "So, too, Hooker is to some degree in [Baker's] clutches. He went up to Washington the other day, drew his pay in the middle of the month, went to a gambling house, staid all night, lost all his money, went . . . next day & drew his commutation for fuel & quarters. These be queer things, certainly." Patrick had heard that Baker had such a free hand that all hotel guests in Washington were subject to his surveillance. Baker, it was believed, was working pretty much as a henchman of Secretary Seward though nominally in the employ of the War Department. Patrick wrote, "Well! I come to the conclusion that where so much roguery exists, the country is hardly worth saving."[49]

The thinness of the ice he trod on at Washington put no fear in Patrick's heart. Nor was he held in check by the knowledge that Hooker might not have much elbow room to support him in his feud with Baker. Still less did he care for his family's fear, expressed in a letter, that he was to be arrested on Stanton's order. A few days after returning from Washington he sent Watson a letter so strongly worded that he would have done well to have Hooker's signature on it rather than his own. He wrote, "Should this principle be admitted, that these detectives may make arrests & seizures within the lines of this Army, without the sanction of its Commander, there can be no military responsibility or discipline." Patrick could not have failed to realize that his stubborn integrity might cost him his job. That was a sacrifice he was willing to make; he had not been pleased with his position at the time of Hooker's appointment, and now his thoughts turned to resigning or obtaining a command in the South or West.[50] But he remained in his job to the end of the war, at that time serving as General Grant's provost marshal general.

Although Patrick could not very well have known it, Baker's own stock was not so high at the War Department at this period. Fifteen hundred dollars had been stolen from the office of Major Turner, one of whose duties was supervising Colonel Baker, whom he treated as a subordinate despite the disparity in rank. The thief who robbed Turner was a veteran named Nicholas Johnson, who had come from Philadelphia to seek a pension for his loss of an arm; he somehow found his way to Turner, who directed him to a professional claim agent. Johnson disappeared while Turner was out of his office; after the theft was discovered he was traced by Pinkerton's men to a house in Philadelphia's red-light district. He admitted that he had been "sporting and spreeing around town" with two of the landlady's resident belles, providing them with clothing and furs, and wining and dining them; the money was gone. What this meant to Baker was that the case had been broken by his late opposite number, Pinkerton, while Baker was supposedly working on it himself; and Pinkerton's report showed that Johnson had abstracted the money while there was no one else in the room but Baker. If any office can be said to have been the sanctum sanctorum of the War Department at that time, it was Major Turner's; Confederate spies and Northern secessionists would have liked to penetrate that office and make off with some of its contents, but only one-armed ex-Private Johnson is known to have done so. He made history when he performed the feat in the presence of the government's chief detective.[51]

.. .. ..

In the policy code governing Union intelligence — unwritten but nevertheless visible in the records of a number of Northern spies — one article stands out prominently: We are in the enemy's country; he already knows just about everything about us that he can use; therefore we can afford to let him have some correct information about our own forces if we get a comparable amount of correct information about his. A Federal spy who pretended among Southerners to be spying for them fell quickly under their suspicion if he veered very far from the truth in his reports about Union forces. Moreover, an even trade in information seemed good business for an army operating in the enemy's country.

That being the case, two actions taken by General Hooker in the early weeks of his command appear puzzling. He ordered that his pickets stop exchanging newspapers with the Johnnies on the other side of the Rappahannock, and he stopped newspaper exchanges when flag-of-truce parties met between the lines.[52] But Hooker had a reason for this singular action: the Northern newspapers contained more military information than the Southern; an even trade in newspapers was not an even trade in facts. And there was another reason: Hooker now had an intelligence service. He had made up his mind that by applying proper talent and energy to the problem he could have information as good as General Lee's, despite the Southerners' advantage in being on their home ground. Unlike his fellow commanders, Hooker was not interested in a quid pro quo trade of information.

John Babcock, still at headquarters, was certain to emerge from his obscurity when the army acquired a commanding general as concerned about intelligence as Hooker was. On February 4 he began his service to the new commander by writing, as he had done for Burnside, a report describing the duties of the "secret service department." Hooker or Butterfield sent the paper to General Patrick, along with Hooker's instructions to "organize and perfect a system for collecting information as speedily as possible." To the new department, Patrick was told, would be sent "all deserters, contraband[s], prisoners &c . . . for examination."[53] The project was not an appetizing one, at least for Patrick. He recorded in his diary: "I am trying to make up a system of Secret Service, but find it hard to organize where there is so little good material. It seems probable that I shall take a few men into my employ at once. Several have offered, but as yet none have been employed. I do not fancy the class of men & think they do not fancy me."[54]

Already, however, Patrick had received a windfall that got him off to a good start. On the 5th, a day when headquarters was swimming in rain and mud, he was visited by a delegation of civilians from upstate New York, the region he called home, and upon their departure another New Yorker entered his tent. This was one Colonel John Morgan — not an officer of the army but the owner of the Eagle Gold Mine, situated in the army's lines near United States Mine Ford above Fredericksburg. Morgan was "obliged to be out of the way when his friends are not in power . . . and is not now, of course, able to carry on any business." Morgan gave him, Patrick wrote, "a good deal of information about men living around here, in this & the adjoining counties."[55] It was just such men, some or all of them Union sympathizers, whom Patrick needed to know about.

On February 10 he recorded, "I have made some arrangements about [the] Secret Service Department. Have had a long conversation with Col. Sharp of the 120' N.Y. as to the organization of the Dept. with him, a Lawyer, for its Chief. He appears well, & I think he would be a pleasant man to be associated with." Patrick in those days was wanting company, for he found headquarters society extremely distasteful. "I . . . am very much disgusted with [Butterfield's] manner and the view he takes of our affairs — his ex cathedra way of speaking, & the flippancy of the whole Head Quarters establishment. Hooker has gone to bed having just returned from Washington. O I am sick, sick, sick!" Next day his opinion of "Dan the Magnificent" was not improved. "If there is not more weight," he observed, "we shall go into the upper regions, thro' the agency of Gas!" He was also expecting to have difficulty with General Pleasonton, commander of the cavalry division stationed nearest to headquarters, but was pleased to learn that "Pleasonton stands no higher in the opinion of Hooker than he does in mine."[56]

By February 11 Colonel Sharpe (Patrick had learned that the name had a final "e") had decided to take the intelligence job and had reported for duty. The title given the new position was deputy provost marshal general.[57] Sharpe would occasionally substitute for Patrick as provost marshal general, but as chief intelligence officer he was directly subordinate to Hooker, while receiving most of his supervision from Butterfield. Thus he was a victim of triple subordination. Patrick, nominally Sharpe's immediate superior, would see little of the intelligence produced by the bureau; his concerns with it mainly had to do with personnel and compensation.

Sharpe owed his selection to Butterfield, who claimed that he simply called the colonel to headquarters and put him in charge of the new bureau. The two men may have had a prewar acquaintance in the New York state militia.[58] Butterfield probably realized that a lawyer's habits of mind were a strong qualification for intelligence work, but that fact would have had less to do with his choice of Sharpe than did the colonel's evident executive ability and force of character.[59]

In his thirty-five years George Henry Sharpe had acquired a good education, traveled widely, become a versatile linguist, and served as a diplomat. He was born in the Hudson River town of Kingston, of colonial stock, mainly German and French. His father, Henry, a wealthy merchant, who spelled the name Sharp, died at forty-eight, when George was two years old. His mother was a member of the numerous Hasbrouck family, the most prominent in Ulster County; so also was his wife, whom he married in 1855. Kingston knew him first as a slim boy who was passionately devoted to books. In manhood he was of medium height, perhaps less, and had lost the blondness of his youth. At nineteen he graduated from Rutgers, delivering the salutatory address in Latin. He went on to the Yale Law School and, barely of age, passed the New York bar in 1849 after an examination that he described as "anything but rigid after my experience at Yale." Before beginning law practice he went to Europe for several years, dividing his time between travel, language studies, and service at the United States legations in Vienna and Rome.[60]

In 1861 Sharpe, enjoying a successful practice and a rising reputation, resigned his captaincy in the militia. The news of the bombardment of Fort Sumter found him on business in a distant town; he hastened back to Kingston, hung out the Stars and Stripes at the local armory without taking time to inform the colonel of the regiment, and began enrolling additional soldiers. Apparently his resignation was conveniently lost, for when the 20th New York militia regiment, the Ulster Guard, left for New York and Annapolis two weeks later, Sharpe was with it as captain of Company B.[61] In June, while the regiment was guarding the rail line connecting Annapolis with Baltimore and Washington, its lieutenant colonel resigned. Sharpe was nominated as his successor but lost the election to Major Theodore B. Gates.

At First Bull Run the 20th's colonel was killed. Being in the three-month service, the regiment was mustered out soon after the battle. After reorganizing, it left for service a second time in October, now designated the 80th New York Volunteer Infantry (a name it disliked and never used except on payday).[62] But Captain Sharpe was no longer with it; his company had been so reduced that it was disbanded; his law business may have prevented him from raising another.

When Lincoln's call for 300,000 volunteers came in the summer of 1862, Sharpe was in New York City being treated for a bronchial illness. Receiving word that Secretary Seward had suggested to Governor Edwin Morgan that Sharpe raise a regiment, he left his bed, worked every day, and spoke every night for three weeks, and — with the liberal use of his family's influence and several thousand dollars of its money — had 900 men on the rolls at the end of that time. Sharpe then applied to the governor for a few days' leave to close up his law practice; Morgan's answer was that he "could not give me ten minutes." The regiment marched on August 24, the colonel's current business papers thrust, a jumbled mass, into his office safe.

The new regiment was named the 120th, Sharpe's choice, to signify its connection with the old 20th Militia. The 120th arrived at Washington the same day General Pope arrived at Manassas to find Stonewall Jackson in the near vicinity. During Pope's battle the regiment occupied a fort in the outer defenses of the capital, and it remained on picket duty near the city while the armies were fighting at South Mountain and on the Antietam. In the early days of September, when a Confederate attack was expected, Sharpe was in command of a demibrigade at Upton's Hill, a position south of the Potomac that he described as "the key to the whole front of Washington." The place, he said, "had been most insanely abandoned by a whole brigade of infantry, and several regiments of cavalry at once — and the rebels knew it as soon as we did."

The excitement of Antietam over, Sharpe suffered a recurrence of his bronchial ailment. "During two weeks," he wrote his uncle, Jansen Hasbrouck, "I could not get a particle of moisture from any part of my body." He repaired to Washington to receive the attention of the assistant surgeon general, who "seemed to know exactly what was the matter — broke the fever in two days." A few weeks later he described himself as "the heartiest man in the regiment."[63]

Late in November, after Burnside's arrival before Fredericksburg, the 120th was ordered there as a part of the Excelsior Brigade in Sickles's division of the Third Corps. The regiment was well to the rear in General Franklin's crossing of the Rappahannock, but once across the river it found itself within musket range of the enemy. The fighting it saw amounted only to heavy skirmishing, but the 120th acquitted itself well. Sharpe's report of the action concluded with the statement that "although the operations of this command were not of the most serious nature, the conduct of the officers and men . . . was marked with coolness and propriety." General Sickles concurred: "This regiment . . . had not before been under fire, and I had great pleasure in observing the steadiness and spirit which characterized all [its] movements."[64]

The 120th shared in the grisly struggle known as the Mud March; Sharpe observed afterward that "nothing but balloons can move us." Well along in this march his men were ordered out without arms to corduroy a road to a point within sight of the enemy. When they reached the Rappahannock they were greeted by a large sign erected by the Johnnies on the south bank: "Burnside and his pontoons stuck in the mud — move at 1 o'clock, 3 days' rations in haversacks."[65] As at Upton's Hill, the effectiveness of the enemy's intelligence was waved in the face of the 120th's young colonel. Perhaps the display had something to do with his difficult decision to accept Hooker's bid to put him in charge of collecting information for the Army of the Potomac.

For Sharpe was most unwilling to leave his regiment. He not only preferred line duty to a staff position; he preferred the command of his regiment to a higher position in the line. He had already refused a brigade command because the brigade offered him was not to include his beloved 120th.[66] Once separated from his regiment, he began looking for an opportunity to bring it into Patrick's provost command, but he never succeeded. However, it was only his position as colonel of the 120th Regiment that made Sharpe an officer in the Federal army, and no thought was given to his holding the intelligence job as a civilian, though that was the status of Pinkerton and now of Babcock. Thus the 120th's lieutenant colonel had to lead the regiment without hope of promotion. But Sharpe did not allow his debt to the regiment to go unpaid. He never relinquished his fatherly interest in it, he continued to be consulted often about its problems, and he even operated an unofficial system of pay allotment for it. After each payday the men brought him much or all of their money; Sharpe deposited it in the Riggs Bank in Washington and then wrote a check on his account there and sent it to his uncle Jansen, president of one of the Ulster County banks.[67] The soldiers' families then drew on these credits. A single check amounted to $5000 or $6000 — a sum the army's sutlers must have hated to see going to the farmers, shopkeepers, and factory hands up in Ulster. This might seem less a service to the regiment than a means of increasing business in "our bank" (the term Sharpe used in his letters). In fact, however, he regarded it as a case of the bank's assisting him "in the effort to care for the soldiers' families." He made loans out of his own pocket to men who were absent on payday; Uncle Jansen was equally generous, giving the families interest-free credit out of the bank's funds when Sharpe's liquid funds there were not sufficient. Sharpe's stock holdings gave his uncle security for these extensions of credit; nevertheless, the picture this gives of Jansen Hasbrouck is not that of the sharp-eyed small-town banker with no concerns beyond the debits and credits in his ledgers.[68]

Sharpe's ability to get away from headquarters to travel into Washington facilitated the banking scheme. His intelligence duties provided for these trips, and there was an additional reason for visiting the capital, for his wife, Carrie, and their three children resided there.[69] He also made good every chance to visit the Willard Hotel[70] and talk with Congressman John Steele, his law partner, who was more able than Sharpe to give some attention to their business. Sharpe and Steele were acquainted with Secretary Seward, and they once drew on their influence with Stanton in arranging emergency leave for Sharpe to transact legal business. Stanton approved two weeks' leave, but as Burnside was about to assail the heights of Fredericksburg, the effort was dropped.[71]

Such was George Sharpe — natural leader, a man who unthinkingly accepted responsibility and just as unthinkingly accepted the perquisites that went with it. His troop-raising feat attests to the magnetism of his personality. In one photograph — with hands in pockets, European-style mustaches curving down to the level of the clean-shaven chin, and eyes frowning imperiously from beneath garrison hat — he is the casting director's beau ideal, the personification of a swashbuckling nineteenth-century spymaster. Hatless in another picture, he is shown to be quite bald; now the mustaches droop but do not curve; the eyes are gentle, the mien subdued. Though the subject is a lawyer and a colonel, it is easier to believe that he is a chaplain recruited from some big-city rectorate.

During the week that preceded his decision to accept Hooker's offer, Sharpe performed an important errand for the general. Down at Fort Monroe, as adjutant to General Dix, now commanding on the Peninsula, was Colonel Daniel T. Van Buren, three years Sharpe's senior, a fellow member of the Kingston bar and a fellow ex-member of the New York militia. Only politics divided the two men; Sharpe was an active Republican, whereas Van Buren, as the name suggests, was a strong Democrat, and now a close military associate of General Dix, a Democratic leader of national importance for many years.[72] Sharpe sought Van Buren's help in solving a problem: how to put spies inside the Confederate lines. The two men met on February 6 in Baltimore. (They probably did not know that their place of meeting, Barnum's Hotel, had been considered by Allan Pinkerton to be "the Head Quarters of Secessionists from all parts of the country."[73]) They discussed casting agents in the role of deserters from the Federal service and sending them South as smugglers of contraband.

Dix, whose Peninsula command offered a likely entry into the Confederacy, would have much to say about the execution of the scheme. After talking to him, Van Buren wrote to Sharpe, "Dear George: The General will cooperate with you in any thing that can be done. He does not think favorably of the plan by deserters, at least from this place, as they would not be allowed to go anywhere near Fredericksburg. He thinks the plan by smuggling would result the best, taking such things as I mentioned to you — and are needed in camps."[74] Dix was familiar with the "plan by smuggling," for one of his own spies was already using it successfully.[75]

As the case of Frank Ellis, purveyor of surgical supplies to the Rebels, who turned out to be spying for them, was still active at the time Babcock joined Pinkerton's bureau, he would have made Sharpe aware of the risks in employing smuggler agents. Sharpe evidently was ready to accept this hazard as a fixture in the intelligence business, but in recruiting other types of agents he kept to a minimum the chance of taking on a possible traitor, profiteer, or blabbermouth.[76] But Lafayette Baker would continue to have jobs for known malefactors and presumably reformed Confederate agents.[77]

As in the Pinkerton period, a smuggler agent's target would be Richmond; unlike Pinkerton, Sharpe would send out spies to penetrate the enemy army, and he expected to use soldiers on these missions. A team of soldier scouts had been developed in "Hooker's Horse Marines," the elite Third Indiana Cavalry, during those months in lower Maryland. Sharpe arranged the transfer to his bureau of three of these men, Sergeant Milton W. Cline, Sergeant Daniel Cole, and Private Daniel Plew. Also transferred were Sergeant Mordecai P. Hunnicutt from an Ohio infantry regiment, who had experience as a detective, and another Ohioan, Private Henry W. Dodd, an artilleryman who had been serving as a scout.[78] General Sedgwick had a promising nomination, a New York cavalryman named D. G. Otto who had been a schoolmaster in the South and had been successful in scouting for Pleasonton's cavalry. Otto, however, could not at first be located; he remained on Pleasonton's rolls.

There was also a nucleus of civilian agents in the bureau. Already on duty when Sharpe took charge were Jackson Harding, a holdover from the Burnside period, and Joseph M. Humphreys, formerly a civilian telegraph operator in the western theater.[79] Soon Howard Skinker made his appearance, having ended his retreat to Washington, ready to risk his neighbors' suspicions or knowledge of his activities.[80] Ebenezer McGee, who had provided important volunteer service as a messenger during the last weeks of Burnside's command, would soon join the bureau and reactivate the contact with his source, Isaac Silver.[81] General Heintzelman, commander of the Washington defenses, responded to an inquiry by Butterfield by turning over to the Army of the Potomac his principal guide and scout, a German named Ernest Yager. With Yager came a letter from Heintzelman saying, "I can find a number of [other] persons who will undertake the services you name, but few of them are worthy of confidence." Unaware of Lafayette Baker's feud with General Patrick, Heintzelman suggested Baker as a source of recruits, but he admitted that they would be "professional" and added, "I have more confidence in such as I have tried."[82] Some weeks later George S. Smith, the Culpeper County "gentleman" who had worked for General Pope, although lacking his confidence, arrived from Washington and was assigned to work for Pleasonton's cavalry division. Evidently Patrick and Sharpe knew of Pope's suspicions of Smith and decided to use him in a way that would not compromise Sharpe's bureau if the suspicions were correct; he was on Sharpe's payroll, however. By mid-April the bureau's force numbered twenty-one.[83]

Sharpe and Patrick evidently shared Heintzelman's opinion about "professionals." A detective named Stanley who came down from New York City seeking employment[84] and a former Pinkerton agent, D. G. McKelvey, were not hired. McKelvey made a favorable impression on Patrick, but he proposed that he be hired without resigning his job as a detective in the Washington Police Department.[85]

As the bureau gathered men and momentum, Sharpe felt the need of a second assistant. One main duty for this man would be to lead information-gathering expeditions into or near the enemy's lines. For such assignments soldier-agents were much preferable to civilians, and it was necessary that the man in charge be an officer. With the Ulster Guard's manpower available in Patrick's command, it was easy for Sharpe to find one whose ability he could be sure of. He selected John McEntee, the tall, gaunt captain of the Guard's Company A, whom he knew well as a former merchant at Rondout, Kingston's next-door neighbor. When not occupied on a distant mission, McEntee would serve as a report writer and interrogator.

McEntee represented mainly the Irish element of Ulster County stock, although his lineage, like Sharpe's, ran back to several European nationalities. He had attended college at the Clinton Institute, then engaged in the flour and feed business with his father. He was a quartermaster sergeant in the reconstituted Ulster regiment that left Kingston in the fall of 1861. Late in the winter, when a second lieutenancy became available, he was appointed to it; by October 1862 he was a company commander. He was an old hand at Falmouth, having served there with General Patrick's brigade through the spring and summer of 1862. The brigade's hard service in the Second Bull Run, Antietam, and Fredericksburg campaigns created the casualties and resultant vacancies that led to McEntee's promotion to first lieutenant and then captain. Then came the exacting but less hazardous provost duty, followed by what probably was a welcome transfer to Sharpe's bureau. At that point McEntee, a bachelor, was nearing his twenty-eighth birthday.[86] He was welcomed into his new assignment in April and dubbed "McAnty," a nickname Babcock concocted, evidently by shifting the accent in his surname from first to second syllable.

The staffing of Sharpe's organization followed a Federal convention: officers could direct espionage activities but not perform them. Exceptions usually came about because a situation called for makeshift coverage — as when Captain William Palmer stepped into the intelligence vacuum on Lee's flanks and rear in the Maryland campaign. Even McEntee in his most dangerous expeditions would usually supervise and coordinate the work of his men rather than share directly in their adventures. The policy assured that an expedition would have a managerial hand constantly at work. But it did not make sense for the army to cut itself off from the espionage talent (as distinct from supervisory talent) in its officer ranks. Presumably it was thought that spying was a business suited to the lower ranks on the social scale. Fortunately for the army, its "lower ranks" were not wanting for men of wit and nerve.[87]

The new organization was first called the Secret Service Department. In this it set something of a precedent, for as we have already seen, the similar title United States Secret Service appeared only after the war, when Pinkerton and Baker each appropriated it as the name of his wartime organization. But before "Secret Service Department" could get firmly established, the name Bureau of Military Information began to appear in the heading of Sharpe's reports, and in a short time it replaced the earlier name. ("Bureau of Intelligence" would not have been considered, because of the meaning attached to the word *intelligence* at that time.) Charged with getting information about the enemy (positive intelligence) but not with detecting enemy agents (counterintelligence), the bureau was not a complete "secret service."[88]

Its members, soldiers and civilians alike, were listed as "guides" for pay purposes; otherwise they were commonly referred to as scouts, occasionally as agents. The avoidance of the word *spy* was not altogether a matter of bureaucratic squeamishness; most of the agents would spend much more of their time in scouting than in spying. In fact much of the territory they worked was a no-man's-land that belonged to neither army — or to both. Despite General Hooker's willingness to call a spy a spy, the habit of speech that made Sharpe's men scouts was undisturbed.

Ahead of all other details of setting up in business, Sharpe had to put that of paying his men. His own pay and McEntee's came of course whenever the paymasters visited the army; and Babcock's salary was not a problem, for all along his $7.50 a day had been paid from the War Department's Secret Service Fund. A separate civilian payroll had been set up by Patrick's quartermaster, Captain Clinton, for Jackson Harding, the only other locally paid secret-service employee of the Burnside period. As the bureau expanded, its new men were added one by one to this payroll. Soldiers as well as civilians were included; however, a soldier was more likely than a civilian to find that he was not to draw pay until he had performed his first mission or otherwise proved himself.

At first there was little distinction as to pay rates. Skinker and Smith at $5 a day and Humphreys at $4 were the only exceptions to a uniform $2-a-day rate that remained in effect for the first five months of the bureau's operations. Raises to $3 and $4 were in store for the more active and useful of the journeyman spies who were still on the rolls after the Pennsylvania campaign of June and July.

The bureau acquired its own mess, and three employees designated as "colored" went on the payroll, evidently as cooks or perhaps also as teamsters, at $1 a day. The fact that their rate was never raised drew a postwar protest from two of them, Dabney Walker and Louis Battail. The fact that they filed a protest suggests that they may have been used as agents, but they did not make any such claim.

All members of the bureau were paid for every day they were on the roll; there were no weekends off, no holidays, and no leaves. Sharpe's disbursements through Clinton for salaries, only $108 in February, rose to $522 in March, $1200 in April, and $1697 in May. The source of the money evidently was John Potts, chief clerk of the War Department and the custodian of its Secret Service Fund. Potts visited Patrick and Sharpe on occasion and in turn was visited by them at his home when they were in Washington.[89] He had supplied the funds for Pinkerton's organization when it served the Army of the Potomac and had also made disbursements to Andrew Porter, Patrick's predecessor as provost marshal general. It is evident that soon after Sharpe's bureau was formed, a change was made whereby its costs — which rose in 1864 to as much as $4000 a month in salaries alone — were met through quartermaster channels rather than passing from Potts to Clinton.[90]

. . .. ..

Except for users of the "plan by smuggling," the cover that gained Sharpe's soldier-spies entrée to enemy territory generally consisted of nothing more than the Confederate uniform. Confederate identification credentials such as a pass or furlough paper were taken from many prisoners and deserters, but little use was made of them; although a Southerner's credential would admit the spy to enemy territory, the identity he assumed in using it would compromise him if it forced him into the camp of the regiment to which its rightful owner belonged. Even the use of the enemy uniform was rather limited, though at times the soldier-agents seem to have gone out in their own blue uniforms one day and in gray ones the next. At other times they wore civilian clothes.

Sharpe's records, like Pinkerton's, do not indicate the extent to which his agents assumed false identity. Such usage probably was infrequent for the simple reason that it was easier to win acceptance of a counterfeit Southern allegiance than it was to devise a foolproof Southern identity.[91]

Expenses on visits to Secessia might run high, especially if bribes or gratuities to some of the agent's hosts were involved, as they not infrequently were. The smuggler-agent could be provided with gold coin, but an agent in almost any other guise would be suspect if he displayed any sizable amount of specie. Thus Sharpe's bureau was the point to which Confederate paper money reaching the Army of the Potomac was funneled.[92] Of course this was not the only theater where Federal espionage had need of Confederate currency; in fact, it might be said that although the Confederate government was unquestionably the biggest user of Confederate currency, the Federal government ranked high on the list — ahead, for example, of some important Southern business enterprises.

Rather than attempting to send reports through the lines, a smuggler-agent (or a courier-agent such as Timothy Webster) would report his findings only during his visits back North. The two-way deserter also staked his chances of reporting his findings on his ability to slip back through the lines. Similar communication practices were followed by agents who used other ruses to enter the Confederacy. Few agents risked carrying even brief memoranda of their gleanings.[93]

Resident spies, on the other hand, sent written reports by messenger. Although there is some truth in the common description of such reports being enciphered or written in a script so small as to fit into a watch case or a piece of jewelry, such precautions were less common than ordinary handwriting on small pieces of paper. Secret ink was on hand in the Bureau of Military Information, but it was probably so crude as to involve considerable risk, and would have been used but rarely. A story of uncertain authenticity says that Army of the Potomac spies carried papers bearing innocuous writing in ordinary ink and truthful credentials in invisible ink that became readable upon exposure to heat or light; the agent would use these credentials to obtain readmittance to his own lines on his return from an expedition.[94] This may explain an obscure reference to secret ink in Sharpe's files that shows it was used there but does not indicate for what purpose.

It was not always necessary to be on Confederate ground in order to obtain news of Confederate military forces. Many Southern officers and soldiers were from places held by the Federals or situated in the ambiguously held country between the armies or beyond their flanks. These members of the Southern forces sometimes made flying visits home; they were seldom very close-mouthed about what was going on in the army, and some of their news was likely to reach the ears of Union sympathizers, perhaps even at first hand. The lengths to which some Union-minded Southerners went in betraying the confidences, or even the persons, of their near kin on the Rebel side would have curled the toes of the Southern patriot.[95] But even when a Confederate soldier's relatives and home-town friends had no affection for the Union, army gossip could be pumped out of them by men of the stripe of Howard Skinker or George Smith — known friends of the North.

Union sentiment professed by Southerners was not always genuine.

Some of Dixie's loudest advocates of abolition and Unionism asked to have their property confiscated by Confederate forces in order to establish a Unionist character that was fraudulent.[96] This pitfall was one of the reasons it paid Sharpe to have men like Skinker, Yager, and Smith on hand, for they might know the true sentiments of professed Unionists far back enough in time to penetrate such subterfuge.

Deception of the same kind, but much more dangerous, was perpetrated by pseudo-deserters from the Confederate army. For this delicate business Lee, Jackson, Stuart, and other generals could always find a man with a smooth tongue, and it is clear that they gave him careful coaching. The story he brought into Federal lines was one that time would prove mistaken but would mislead the enemy or at least sow confusion for a few critical days. All of this had to be carefully worked out by the Southern chieftains, for even an ordinary Federal picket would scent fraud if a story had one or two improbabilities protruding around its edges. Sharpe, Babcock, and McEntee were constantly alert to this practice, though their files contain only indirect references to it. Despite the loss of effect that this device would suffer if used too much, Lee applied it liberally, and with increasing frequency as the odds piled up against him. He also employed variations on it: some of the Confederates' deceptive stories were planted with their pickets, and on at least one occasion with, apparently, an entire infantry corps. Lee gave little ground to his lieutenant Jackson when it came to willingness and ability to employ deception.[97]

13
....

TEN DAYS OF
SOUTHERN HOSPITALITY

February 1–March 8, 1863

THE BUREAU OF MILITARY INFORMATION was not to be simply a new intelligence organ on the Pinkerton model. To Pinkerton's collection mission, which consisted of espionage and interrogation, was added a third function, scouting of enemy positions, which Pinkerton's men had never performed though it was at least as important as espionage. And the bureau's reporting mission was an even greater expansion: Sharpe not only reported the findings of the three collection functions under his own control but also merged them with the products of six other types of collection — cavalry reconnaissance, balloons, Signal Corps observation stations, flag-signal interception, examination of Southern newspapers, and reports telegraphed by neighboring commands.

Pinkerton's reporting had covered only the findings of his own collection activities, espionage and interrogation; other reports had gone directly to McClellan. Reading raw intelligence items from any and all sources had been part of the daily workload of every army commander since the days of General Washington, but the new sources of information challenged the ability of a busy commander to assimilate it all. McClellan's ignoring of the balloonists' reports of telltale burnings on the Manassas front was an extreme, and especially unfortunate; case of the neglect that this volume of paperwork forced on him.

By having Sharpe's bureau sort out and synthesize this jumble of information, Hooker obtained a picture of the enemy's situation as coherent and complete as the supply of information permitted. This was an innovation: Hooker invented a process and a product now called all-source intelligence. Actually it was a re-invention, for General Washington had engaged in all-source intelligence by virtue of being his own spymaster

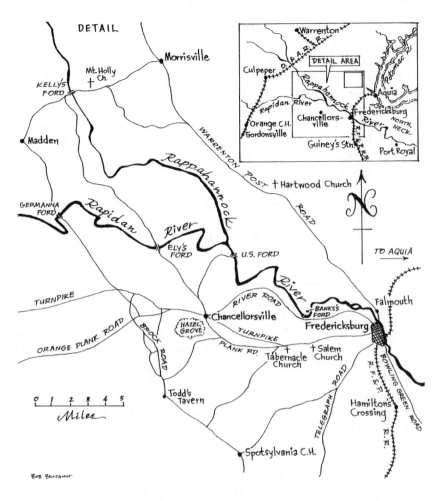

REGION OF THE CHANCELLORSVILLE CAMPAIGN

and also the one to whom the other sources, the cavalry and individual scouts, reported.[1]

Hooker's own view of this achievement would have been that here was an obvious problem, the wastage of intelligence, with a solution that was equally obvious. But in this simple action he made intelligence history.[2] His all-source intelligence operation was decades ahead of its time; it passed from the scene with the end of the Civil War,[3] not to be re-invented until the Second World War. It was legislated into permanence in the National Security Act of 1947, which established the Central Intelligence Agency.

The roots of Hooker's innovation can be seen in his Civil War experience; every assignment he had up to the command of the Army of the Potomac had made him conscious of the need for an intelligence program much more aggressive and comprehensive than Pinkerton's. His months of isolation in lower Maryland, opposite the enemy's Potomac batteries, created a need for intelligence and the necessity of developing it himself. The Peninsula campaign, beginning with the Yorktown–Warwick River fiasco and Hooker's prominent role in the battle of Williamsburg, exposed him continuously to the consequences of McClellan's neglect of scouting. The slowness in locating Lee's concentration in Maryland added weak cavalry reconnaissance to this list of deficiencies that taxed the patience of an intelligence-conscious corps commander like Hooker. And uppermost in his mind would have been Burnside's rejection of the prisoner's eleventh-hour report of the formidable defenses on Marye's Heights, which exposed to Hooker the lack of systematic intelligence effort that would have yielded at least a rough understanding of the relative strength of the Confederates' positions.

Sharpe's acquisition of the ingredients of his all-source reporting operation did not proceed smoothly; the new bureau did not enjoy the willing cooperation of the cavalry chief and his staff, who guarded jealously their prerogatives in intelligence reporting. The balloonists, however, welcomed anyone's attention, and the Signal Corps officers came forward in an attitude of across-the-board cooperation. Whether these contributors addressed their intelligence items to Hooker, Butterfield, or Sharpe, Butterfield saw to it that each one was properly circulated. Not all of them ended up in the bureau's files as they should have, but those that are now found in other files often bear notations in Sharpe's or Babcock's handwriting, showing that the superefficient Butterfield was taking care that the bureau was not overlooked. Further, the more comprehensive reports produced by the bureau consistently indicate, and sometimes expressly state, that information from all of the Army's sources went into them.[4]

.. .. ..

While Colonel Sharpe was meeting with Colonel Van Buren and slowly making up his mind to accept General Hooker's intelligence job, John Babcock was enjoying the prospect of an energetic intelligence operation. Having seen the service perform weakly under McClellan and not perform at all under Burnside, he could only welcome a new arrangement that promised the commanding general's active interest. He was to be the bureau's principal interrogator, on his way to becoming a walking encyclopedia of facts and figures on the Army of Northern Virginia. Babcock automatically became the bureau's assistant chief; Sharpe was quick to recognize the talent that Patrick had made no effort to discover.

Sharpe shared with Babcock the work of interrogation and reporting, but much of his time was given to directing his agents and running operations such as the one he was trying to arrange with Colonel Van Buren. The bureau's reports, including the signature "G. H. Sharpe, Colonel," began appearing in Babcock's handwriting. Thus Babcock is seen to have had authority to release reports that Sharpe had not yet read.

General Patrick, now more conscious of his role in the intelligence service, was assimilating useful odds and ends from the contacts a provost marshal general makes in the course of his daily activities in an occupied community. He regarded himself as an agent of good will to the male-less Confederate households, and was disposed to grant favors when that could be done without stretching the rules too far. "I do tease these rebel secesh ladies very much without doubt, but they take it very gracefully," he wrote in his diary one night after he had given one of them a pass out of the Federal lines. Leniency had its reward: the lady's officer escort brought back a bottle of Old Madeira, which Patrick was not too puritanical to appreciate, and another gift even more welcome — a paper (probably a safe-conduct pass) carrying the names of Lee, Longstreet, and McLaws. Longstreet's whereabouts had been a matter of some concern; Patrick was gratified to learn he was still at Fredericksburg.[5]

Patrick also fell into a piece of luck in having to play host to a Confederate chaplain, the Reverend John Landstreet, of Stuart's cavalry. Chaplains were supposed to be exchanged immediately, but the Confederates held up Landstreet's return for three days on a point of protocol. The delay was most agreeable to Patrick, for the chaplain turned out to be "very amusing and full of fun all day long," though Sharpe found him merely "argumentative." More interesting than the reverend gentleman's wit was the picture he drew of life in the Southern cavalry; he included in his stories many a point that the Bureau of Military Information could put to use. When Landstreet finally left, Patrick felt he was "deeply affected by our kindness and frank manners towards him" and would find it "rather hard . . . to look upon us as enemies again."[6]

Now, during the early days of February, the difficulty of finding someone to interrogate was a thing of the past. Hooker's active interest in intelligence amounted to a new broom that swept Confederate soldiers from eight regiments and batteries into Babcock's tent on February 1 alone. Bad weather slowed down the influx before long, but not until the divisions with Lee were firmly identified and their positions well established. Although information down to brigade and regiment level was much less complete and firm, a good start was made there too.[7]

Babcock's knowledge of the enemy, the bureau's main instrument for distinguishing truth from falsehood in the statements of those under interrogation, was supplemented by Sharpe with an ingenious method of getting the facts. The prisoner or deserter was told that upon making a full and correct statement of his knowledge of Confederate forces, he would be recommended for release to work as a civilian in the North. Experience showed, Sharpe would report late in 1863, that the offer was effective in eliciting truthful statements, "the state of our information [being] such as to form a standard of credibility by which these men were gauged, while each was adding to the general sum."[8]

.. .. ..

Hooker's young information service was scarcely open for business when its mettle was tested by a major movement of the enemy, touched off by a shifting of Federal forces. In the second week of February Hooker, in response to orders from Halleck, transferred the Ninth Corps to General Dix on the Peninsula. The Ninth, being Burnside's old command, was a potential source of trouble for Hooker. And he seized on its departure as an opportunity to solve a second problem. He gave it a new commander, General William F. Smith, a contentious officer who had sided with Franklin in his protest against Burnside and had narrowly escaped Franklin's fate, banishment from the Army of the Potomac.[9]

The Confederates learned promptly of this movement, which was made in broad daylight over the wide-open waters of the lower Potomac. But for the next several days Lee's expected countermove was hidden under a sky filled with rain, snow, and then rain again.[10] When the storm abated for a while on the 19th, a signal officer on the Union left, Lieutenant Peter Taylor, got a view of the fields and woods below Fredericksburg and perceived that numerous camps were gone. No troop movements of any size could be seen, but wagons were observed going toward the enemy's railroad terminal south of the town — "moving down heavily laden and coming up light." A battery of four guns also moved off; meanwhile the smoke of two locomotives was seen in the gray sky.[11]

On the evening of the 20th headquarters learned that a larger movement, also downriver, had been seen opposite Fredericksburg the previous day but had gone unreported. The observers were the pickets of the Second Corps; their commander, General Couch, informed Hooker that the enemy activity had been "seen by so many that nobody reported the fact . . . until twenty-four hours after the movement was observed — as stupid a thing as ever occurred in military history." Hooker agreed, terming Couch's communication "a most extraordinary report." The commanding general was especially displeased because, in addition to sixteen guns, the pickets claimed to have seen eleven pontoons, and it was too late to pursue the important question whether the Confederates now, for the first time, had pontoons.[12]

A fierce storm of snow and sleet began on the night of February 21. This time foul weather proved an aid to information-gathering, for at the height of the storm two Negro servants in a North Carolina regiment slipped through the Confederate pickets and crossed the Rappahannock. They were taken to Colonel Judson Kilpatrick, commanding a cavalry brigade down toward the Northern Neck — the long, narrow peninsula between the Rappahannock and the Potomac on which stood the birthplaces of George Washington, James Madison, James Monroe, and Robert E. Lee. Questioned separately by Kilpatrick, the two men said that their regiment, part of Early's division in the Second Corps, had been ordered that morning to move upriver to Hamilton's Crossing. This shift was news, but far more important was the reason for it: the division, the Negroes said, was to fill positions in the defenses formerly held by elements of Longstreet's corps, all of which had departed.[13] Presumably, then, the artillery and wagons seen going southward on the 19th belonged to Longstreet. That his entire corps had gone, however, was doubtful, for on the 20th and 21st prisoners and deserters came in from four brigades in McLaws's and Anderson's divisions, both of which belonged to Longstreet's corps.[14]

Kilpatrick had sent a scout down the river to test the truth of another Negro's statement that cavalry pickets had replaced Confederate infantry on the enemy's far right. He returned with corroborating evidence.[15]

Dawn of February 22 found the camps buried under snow. The day was given over to artillery, the two armies striving to outgun each other in salutes to the father of their common nationality.[16] The ensuing days of snow shoveling saw the arrival in camp of Ernest Yager, the German "scout" whom General Heintzelman had given up to Hooker a few weeks before. He had been in the information service since the March day in 1862 when McClellan occupied Manassas and had been back and forth in the country west of that point many times, usually working for local commanders and other lesser figures. He had a wider local reputation as a scout than would have pleased Sharpe. He seems to have been only a partly assimilated immigrant: even his written English had a strong German accent; for example, he spelled his name *Jager,* which confused headquarters clerks and telegraph operators. They rendered the name four different ways, to the owner's despair; sometimes when called upon for his signature he made an X instead. He was known more generally as Van Van, not an alias but a nickname.

Setting out to learn what Confederate forces lay in Hooker's rear and on the right, Yager left the army's lines at Dumfries on February 17. Wade Hampton's cavalry brigade had been picketing as deeply as Brentsville, directly in the Federals' rear; at a house where one of Hampton's officers had dined the previous day, Yager heard that Fitzhugh Lee's brigade was to relieve Hampton's. The report, although it amounted to little better than hearsay, was correct; Hampton retired far into the interior of Virginia to rehabilitate his starving horses.[17] Traveling the line of the Orange and Alexandria Railroad all the way to Culpeper, Yager spotted Fitz Lee's camps near a way station just beyond the Rappahannock.

At this point Yager had accomplished his assigned mission, but a new source suddenly presented itself. At the home of a Culpeper friend named Myers he met a German man and wife traveling to Philadelphia on a pass obtained through the Prussian consul at Richmond. It was made out to two men, but one had remained behind; Yager obligingly joined the travelers to fill the vacancy. They hired a conveyance and drove up the turnpike through Warrenton toward Washington, Yager meanwhile questioning his companions about Confederate troops they had seen in Richmond and along their route. A few days before leaving Richmond they had seen a force that they described as Longstreet's corps passing through the city. The soldiers had believed they were headed for two different points — Charleston, South Carolina, and Suffolk, a town in southeastern Virginia held as an advanced position by part of General Dix's army. And along the railroad between Gordonsville and Culpeper, the German couple said, they had passed an army of 20,000 under General Jackson. Other forces belonging to Jackson were over toward the Blue Ridge, "and the people of Culpeper are certain that a raid is to be made in Maryland." Stuart was reported in the neighborhood, bent on assisting in the raid. All this added up to indications of the absence of four-fifths or more of Lee's army from the Fredericksburg lines, a very unlikely development. Yager left his friends at Fairfax on February 24 and wired his findings to Hooker. His return trip was an easy one despite numerous encounters with small cavalry detachments scattered as far east as Centreville.[18]

There was more fiction than fact in Yager's report; information from prisoners, deserters, and contrabands showed not only two of Longstreet's divisions to be in the Fredericksburg lines but also the bulk of Jackson's corps.[19] The rest of the needed information came as the result of a three-week trip through Virginia by the wife of Michael Graham, a spy for General Milroy. She had left their Valley home in mid-January, having obtained a Confederate pass to join her husband in Washington. Expecting to travel North by water, she went to Richmond but was shunted back through Gordonsville and used the same rail and highway route later taken by Yager's friends. She gave the total Confederate strength about Gordonsville and Culpeper at 1500.[20] Evidently it was this force, possibly augmented somewhat, that the German couple had magnified to 20,000.

Comparing the information from all sources, Hooker on the 25th wired Halleck this opinion:

> That the enemy have decreased their forces in our front; that two or more divisions of Longstreet's corps have gone to Tennessee and South

Carolina; that the enemy are under the impression that we are evacuating from Aquia, leaving a sufficient force to keep Lee's army in front of us. . . . The general tenor of the statements received make[s] it appear that Jackson's corps is left to guard the passage of the river. Ransom's division, of Longstreet's corps, is one mentioned as gone to Tennessee or South Carolina. Pickett's division is one gone to Charleston, commencing their departure February 17.[21]

Later in the day a report from an unnamed source enabled Hooker to state confidently that "Jackson, with his whole command, was yesterday across the Rappahannock from me." Observations made that day by the balloonists strengthened this belief. Hooker also discredited, probably on the basis of common sense alone, the portion of Yager's story that concerned a prospective enemy raid into Maryland.[22]

The facts of the Confederate situation were these: Robert Ransom's small division had been sent to North Carolina early in January. Then General D. H. Hill left his division with Lee and assumed command of the Confederate forces in the Old North State. By the time Sharpe's bureau began operating, these changes had become intermingled with later movements in the Federals' information. Then, after the departure of the Federal Ninth Corps from Aquia, Lee sent off George Pickett's division on February 15, followed it with Hood's, and on the 18th ordered Longstreet to Richmond to command them. The movement halted south of Richmond until the destination of the Federal transports could be determined. (Before Longstreet came to grips with any of these forces, his primary occupation became the collection of food for the army from the largely untapped farms of southeastern Virginia.) Longstreet's other divisions, McLaws's and Anderson's, remained under Lee's direct command. Jackson's troops also remained in the Fredericksburg lines, as Hooker believed, and Stuart was where Yager reported him, near Culpeper. Neither Jackson nor Stuart was planning a Maryland expedition, though it would not have been unusual for either of them to have launched rumors of such a venture.[23]

Hooker had not yet noted Hood's departure, and he named the ultimate destination of Pickett's movement with more firmness than Lee himself could have done at the time. (Equally misinformed, it seems, was the entire population of the Confederacy: Federal spies in the western theater picked up reports that Longstreet's destination was central Tennessee.[24]) But Hooker's understanding of the forces in his front was substantially correct. He was also correct in saying that Lee (and Lee's superiors at Richmond) believed that the Federals were pulling out of their position opposite Fredericksburg — a movement that Hooker was not making or even planning.[25]

· · · · · ·

On February 24, the day Yager's trip ended, another wide-ranging spying expedition began, this one a penetration of enemy camps. The man Sharpe selected for this mission was Sergeant Milton W. Cline, one of his recruits from the Third Indiana Cavalry. Cline, a short, red-headed man with gray eyes, had an unusual background for a cavalryman, having been a sailor before joining the army. A native of the Lake Champlain country of New York, he was nearing his thirty-eighth birthday; thus he was older than all three of his superiors in the Bureau of Military Information.[26]

Like Yager, Cline headed first into a no-man's-land — in this case the Northern Neck. (Neither army could afford to station troops on that isolated peninsula, but the Confederates persisted in seeking food and other supplies there, and the Federals kept busy trying to defeat their efforts.) Again like Yager, he next worked his way onto the remote fringes of Lee's army; but there the similarity of the two expeditions ends. For Cline was not bent on scouting the enemy or picking up second-hand news; he entered their camps. In company with Confederate soldiers he crossed the Rappahannock three miles below Port Royal, seventeen miles below Fredericksburg, on the night of the 27th. Heading upriver, he passed numerous infantry regiments and conversed with soldiers and civilians as he went. Presently he encountered Captain John W. Hungerford, commanding a company of the 9th Virginia Cavalry, one of W. H. F. Lee's regiments, and accompanied the captain to his headquarters. Of this part of his mission Cline wrote, "On the way Below port royal saw a brigade of infantry in a ravine. Was told By the Capt No infantry Below that [point] But 3 regts of Cavalry in Essex County." Hungerford had correctly identified for him the outer limits of the infantry lines on the Confederate right. The brigade they had passed belonged to Jubal Early's division, a fact that the captain neglected in his otherwise excellent sightseeing lecture.[27]

In some fashion Cline managed to attach himself to Hungerford for an extended visit. His long report of these experiences gives no hint as to what kind of cover story he fed his hosts. The most common cover for missions such as Cline's was that of a Federal soldier wishing to desert to the Confederates, but he is known to have been in Confederate uniform, regular or irregular. Thus it is likely that he represented himself as a Confederate scout or partisan ranger who, in pursuit of some objective or in escaping capture, had become widely separated from his command and was trying to make his way back to it. If he had named a regiment in Lee's army as his home unit, he would have been sent off to that unit instead of being allowed to remain as a visitor in a cavalry camp. The likelihood that he claimed to belong to the ranger band of John S. Mosby or some other Confederate partisan leader operating west or north of Hooker's army is strengthened by the fact that he was allowed to ride far over on the Confederate left, toward the country where partisan bands held forth.[28]

The trip over to Lee's left was made in the company of Hungerford and twenty-five of his men. Cline's report does not indicate its purpose. They rode westward some fifty miles to Orange Court House, passing well to the rear of the main body of the Army of Northern Virginia. Several infantry regiments were seen, but Cline's companions named only a few of them correctly. The most significant sighting was that of a large camp near Bowling Green; that would have been the winter camp of the bulk of Jackson's artillery,[29] but Cline's view of it was not close enough to indicate its character. Near Spotsylvania Court House he saw a battery and a camp which (although he did not learn its identity) would have been part of Joseph Kershaw's brigade of McLaws's division.[30]

Orange Court House was occupied by two infantry regiments, Georgians and Louisianians, supported by "two batteries of light guns" and one large rifled gun. Hungerford left Cline for an hour or two with the Georgians, who told him of the fictitious "large force" at Gordonsville that Hooker had already heard about.

As if designed to suit Cline's purpose, the return trip was over a different route closer to the river — down the Plank Road through the desolate wooded country known as the Wilderness, past a crossroads with a large brick house, which with its outbuildings bore the imposing name of Chancellorsville. The Wilderness held numerous small camps, most of them deserted, and gun positions, mostly without guns; on the Plank Road there were only a few wagon trains. But around the pillared Chancellor mansion were rifle pits, a large wagon park, a battery of brass howitzers, and earthworks, some with guns in place. About the place, Cline wrote, there "seamed to be conciderabell force." And a mile or two to the west were occupied camps, one containing a number of light guns.

Over the last five or six miles of the road into Fredericksburg observations came thick and fast. In his report Cline poured them out without punctuation:

> To the left of the road Before Crossing the holow Betwene the First and second hills saw a Briggade of Infantry i think of Alabama troops turned to the left across the hollow on rising the hill Could see the Rear of the first and front of the second Lines of Earthworks No appearance of Large Force about the Front Line am sure some had no guns mounted passed Down Into a Creek Bottom Near an old mill Saw a waggon park som Cassons also a Camp on the oposite hill side Could not see it plain enough to Judg its Extent after Crossing the Creek passed a Camp Near a skirt of timber also som artillery Came out to the road saw som soldiers Encamped said to be provost Guard stoped five minets Crossed a stream Saw mile & Half to the right of Road saw an old Camp also Camp Fires in the woods farther up the stream.[31]

Sharpe's interrogation of the sergeant brought out several additional camps, gun sites, and fortifications. Cline had spotted all the major encampments on the left and center of Lee's line with the exception of the brigades of William Mahone and Carnot Posey, on the extreme left at United States Ford; these were too far off the road to be seen by him, though their presence was well known to the Federal pickets across the river. The Alabama brigade was that of Cadmus Wilcox, of Anderson's division, camped between Banks's Ford and the Plank Road. At Tabernacle Church (halfway from Chancellorsville to Fredericksburg), Cline reported, was a headquarters of some importance; this would have been Edward Perry's small Florida brigade. The camp that he "Could not see . . . plain enough" was probably that of the demibrigade of General Semmes of McLaws's division, a mile or two to the east of Perry. A brigade seen clearly on a height about two miles west of Fredericksburg (not referred to in Cline's written report but mentioned by him to Sharpe) would have been that of General Wofford, also of McLaws's division. And immediately behind Fredericksburg were massive clusters of artillery and fortifications, a wagon and ambulance park, and camps — the latter being the location of the brigade of General Barksdale, another of McLaws's units, which occupied Marye's Heights.[32]

Hungerford led his party through this mass and southward on the Bowling Green road, which passed between the railroad and the river. At Hamilton's Crossing they turned to the southwest and followed an interior route, stopping overnight a few miles from Hungerford's headquarters. This leg of the trip — from Fredericksburg southward — took them through the whole of Jackson's corps, Lee's right wing. (These units, though most were not named by Cline, would have been parts of the divisions of A. P. Hill, Trimble, and Rodes.[33]) Possibly because troop concentrations here were much thicker than on the center and left, Cline's report attempted very little detailing of these positions, and Sharpe's questioning added little more. Even for the left and center, which Cline described thoroughly in his report, Sharpe would have asked for further details. Since the report names only a few landmarks, Sharpe certainly would have called on Cline to point out the others on a map, together with unit locations, but no such map is in the records. Patrick's brigade had occupied the Fredericksburg area in the spring and summer of 1862,[34] and its officers could have identified for Sharpe many of the woods, streams, hills, ravines, and other features that could fix the locations of the enemy troops, guns, and fortifications that Cline had seen. The details thus collected could then be verified and elaborated in the interrogation of deserters and prisoners received during the weeks preceding Hooker's campaign.

Altogether, Cline's written report and Sharpe's notes mentioned, in terms definite enough for the locations to have been determined on a map,[35] a total of sixty-four major installations: twenty-four camps, twelve locations of batteries or heavy artillery, twenty-three fortifications, and five wagon and ambulance parks. Many of these observations were the result of Hungerford's choice, as the party drew near Fredericksburg, of a route between two lines of fortifications.

On the principal intelligence question of that period — what forces had gone south — Cline's report was similar to Yager's but with errors less serious. He said that all of Longstreet's corps and part of Ewell's division (now Early's) were gone. Sharpe could ascertain the facts about Longstreet from prisoners and deserters, but since none from Early were on hand,[36] the mistaken information about his division could not so easily have been rejected. Although the forces with Lee were scattered, Cline reported that the Confederates believed they could assemble 75,000 men in four to six hours.

One of Cline's best contributions to the store of knowledge of the enemy was his direct observation of the conditions in Lee's camps. For example, he learned that the infantry was getting a daily ration of a quart of flour and a pound of bacon per man.[37] Often this monotonous fare was not to be had; the troops were issued money in lieu of rations and told to purchase their own food. In some cases even officers were needing footwear.

A last, uneventful leg of his trip with Hungerford's party was completed on the morning of March 4. Upon returning to Port Royal, Cline had an opportunity to converse with a number of infantry officers; he obtained the names of four of them, thus adding to the bureau's collection of data that would be useful in conducting interrogations. However, one of these officers, Colonel William H. Richardson, advised him to go to Richmond, and another, a Colonel Ambler, asked him to pay a call the next day. These remarks revealed curiosity about Cline's status; clearly his sojourn among the enemy was going to be less comfortable the longer it lasted.

But his luck held. That night, back at the cavalry camp, Hungerford entertained visiting officers. A card game began and a bottle was produced. After the party was well under way, Cline took leave of it, ostensibly for only a moment. He picked out a good horse, rode ten miles downriver, found a skiff, and put himself on the left bank of the river with as much speed as he could muster. The nighttime stealing of another horse in strange country could not have been easy, but he was able to find one. He rode fifteen miles up the Northern Neck into the Union lines. At one point he was fired on; he did not say whether by friend or foe, and possibly he did not know. At daylight he came up to the Federal pickets, "was taken prisoner and sent to Genl Gregg & released on my pass." It appears that unless he had carried an ordinary Federal pass all this time — a most unlikely possibility — or had secreted one somewhere outside the lines, the story of Union spies using invisible-ink passes is true.

When Cline arrived at headquarters that day, March 5, he had covered 250 miles in the ten-day expedition.[38] His story might now be hard to believe but for the fact that Sharpe, an experienced examiner, accepted it after a thorough interrogation — and the fact that Cline's information is corroborated at a great many points by known data on Confederate positions. Much of the intelligence history of the Civil War still awaits critical investigation, but Cline's exploit is the deepest, most extended penetration of enemy lines, by either side, that has been documented.

. .   . .   . .

On the day Cline returned, Sharpe started several other men on expeditions. Some of them were arrested by pickets of Averell's cavalry division and sent back to headquarters even though they carried Patrick's pass. It was a great piece of "arrogance and stupidity combined," Patrick wrote, and it "caused Fighting Joe Hooker to swear very wickedly & send for Averell in a great hurry." One man at least got through, however — Cline's comrade, Daniel Cole, another recruit from the Third Indiana Cavalry, who was heading toward the Confederate right. Cole's success in "penetrating" his own lines may have been due to a note from Sharpe that he carried to the cavalry outpost commander, asking that his horse, which he owned, be returned to headquarters. Cole, twenty-eight years old, a blacksmith by trade and the father of three children, had enlisted from North Madison, Indiana, in July 1861. He had scouted for Hooker during the Third Indiana's service in lower Maryland. Like Cline, he had risen to the rank of sergeant, but his regiment relieved him of his stripes after he joined Sharpe's bureau.[39]

If Sharpe had known, at the time Cole left, that Cline had taken leave of the Confederates on the downriver flank in a way certain to arouse their suspicion, he would have sent Cole in a different direction. For Cole, after crossing the Rappahannock in a skiff on March 8, followed Cline's method by giving himself up to the pickets of the 9th Virginia Cavalry, but he was accorded quite different treatment. He was forwarded to W. H. F. Lee's headquarters, thence to Stuart's, and finally to Libby Prison in Richmond.[40]

14
. . . .

REBEL SPIES ARE
NOW SECOND BEST

February 24–April 11, 1863

GENERAL LONGSTREET'S MISSION in southeastern Virginia gave
him a lasting taste for the independence and prestige of separate
command. During the entire war Lee appeased this penchant
of the First Corps commander only twice. In the reports that Colonel
Sharpe had to sift, however, Lee was by no means so stingy with his special
missions for "Old Pete." One week Longstreet would be reported leading
a detached force into Tennessee; the next week an equally likely story
would put him and his men in South Carolina or Georgia. The First
Corps seemed to be as ubiquitous as Jeb Stuart's troops or even the phantom army created by Allan Pinkerton. The ambitious Longstreet may
have suggested such distant missions to Lee about as often as Sharpe's
sources suggested them to Sharpe. But it was much easier for Lee to keep
Longstreet in his place with the Army of Northern Virginia than it was for
Sharpe's men to keep him properly placed in their records of Confederate dispositions.

Longstreet's February trip terminated in southeastern Virginia for the
simple reason that it had begun as a pursuit of the Federals' Ninth Corps,
whose destination was in that region. But Longstreet's halt there became
clear to Sharpe's bureau only gradually. The stream of prisoners and
deserters from the enemy slowed to a trickle after February 25, the day of
Hooker's report to Halleck on the Confederates' recent movements.[1]
But at this juncture another source was heard from; a sizable batch of
Confederate mail, most of it intended for Maryland, was captured in the
Northern Neck. In one letter, dated February 19, a soldier stationed near
Fredericksburg said that his unit was to start for Richmond the next
morning. It was enclosed in another letter written by a Richmond resi-
dent on the 25th and reporting that 11,000 troops had passed through
the city four days before.

The capture also yielded a few valuable items about the force remaining at Fredericksburg. A soldier's letter of February 16 gave Moss Neck, a plantation near Skinker's Neck, as the position of Jackson's old division, which meant that Stonewall himself probably was near by (he was). It also announced, correctly, that the division had a new commander, General Isaac Trimble. Another writer offered the opinion that "if this good weather continues Mr. Hooker will have to come over and try his luck," and still another declared that "there is nothing but death and destruction to stare [the Yankees] in the face from Fredericksburg to Port Royal." (This was not a great exaggeration, compared with the observations of enemy fortifications that Hooker's signal officers were reporting day by day.) An officer convalescing at Richmond wrote, "We are fully posted as to the plans of the enemy and are prepared for them at every point." More reassuring to Hooker was another writer's belief that Lee was not going anywhere: "We is to stay here and picket the Rappahannock."

Some of the writers had been sending letters through the lines with considerable regularity; a Richmond woman acknowledged receipt of her correspondent's "No. 47." Of mild interest as military news was the report that General Ewell, in Richmond, was considering the purchase of a cork leg to replace the limb he lost at Second Bull Run. A Northern Virginia soldier's letter announcing that furloughs were being denied men whose homes were north of the Rappahannock meant to Sharpe that the relatives and friends of these men would have much less news of Lee's army to convey to agents such as Skinker, Smith, and Yager.[2]

Although Hooker's own sources left unanswered many questions about Longstreet's movement, the gaps soon began to be filled by dispatches from General Dix and his subordinates in southeastern Virginia. By March 1 they had learned that Hood's and Pickett's divisions, which had been reported back at Fredericksburg, were in their front. Butterfield queried Dix about the soundness of his information; Dix replied that General John J. Peck at Suffolk had just received deserters from Pickett's division, one of whom knew that Hood's was also with Longstreet. Having had the better of this exchange, Dix went on to obtain on the 5th, from a small force sent out by Peck seeking information, the news that Longstreet's force numbered 20,000 and that Jackson, contrary to a previous report, was not in the vicinity. Corroborating details were added the next day by three "very intelligent" noncommissioned officers who passed themselves as Confederates and "had the freedom of the house of a leading rebel" at Windsor, near the enemy lines. They added the unhappy news that "Their spies knew all about Suffolk; that we had 12,000, and two gunboats" on the Nansemond River. A few days later Peck obtained a two-week-old copy of a Charleston newspaper that reported Longstreet's movement in persuasive detail and scotched the reports that he was destined for South Carolina. Peck had already rejected the equally common reports that Longstreet had gone west. Then on March 13 Dix learned that Longstreet had assumed command over all Confederate forces in the Richmond area following the resignation of General G. W. Smith. Dix's sources also reported that the enemy was largely abandoning Fredericksburg; in relaying this information, however, he did not indicate that he placed any reliance on it. Thus Dix and Peck, urged on by the prospect of an attack on Peck's isolated command, had acquired a substantially correct understanding of the recent changes in the enemy forces in Virginia.[3] Hooker's "Longstreet problem" was solved when it became the urgent problem of his neighboring commander.

Attention focused occasionally on the Shenandoah Valley although it was no longer part of Hooker's command. Halleck wired him on the 6th that "General Milroy thinks a large cavalry force is collecting in front of Winchester." At this time Hooker had information from General Slocum's sources — one of them apparently was Charles Whitlock's brother at Aldie — indicating a movement of Fitzhugh Lee's brigade toward the Valley. It was hard to credit these reports, since they included a statement that Jackson also was in the Valley and approaching Milroy. Jackson had outworn his ability to alarm an Army of the Potomac commander with reports of his nonexistent movements. However, this apparent attempt at deception succeeded in a way not intended: Hooker was inclined to yawn over the whole matter, whereas the part of the reports that concerned Fitz Lee was essentially correct; he had been ordered to aid the Valley commander, General William E. Jones, against Milroy and was on his way, though currently tarrying near Culpeper. Hooker reminded Halleck of Milroy's reputation as a "stampeder," declaring that "if a large cavalry force is in his front, I am puzzled to know where it came from. Certainly not from the army in my front." This roused Halleck's spleen against Milroy (not a difficult feat), and he wired Schenck, "General Milroy seems to be a very unreliable man, and hardly fit for such a position." Although Hooker was technically correct, since Fitz Lee was still east of the Blue Ridge, this time Milroy was not stampeding.[4]

Hooker's assurance was founded not only on his sound information about Jackson but on detailed though not very accurate statements about Jones's Valley force, obtained from a deserter and a captured letter.[5] Jones's command included the famous Maryland Line, a mixed force of infantry, cavalry, and artillery. Its usual area of operation was the Valley; having originated north of the Potomac, it was a source of many of the letters to be found in the contraband mails.

Sharpe's prospects improved on March 8 with the return of Howard

Skinker from Washington. Even though his brother Thomas was home on sick leave from the Confederate army and lived near enough to get at least hearsay information on his movements,[6] Skinker went immediately to work. His first project was a short trip up the north bank of the Rappahannock, past his own farm on Poplar Road; he was back on the 11th with a report that focused on Rebel cavalry scouting in Hooker's immediate rear. Patrols from General Averell's headquarters, Skinker said, "neglect . . . a belt of Country, lying between Wood Cutting Road and Poplar Road." One of Hooker's aides who inspected the line at the same time reported that although the picket line was "thorough and well established," the officers and men were "generally very careless and unsoldierlike."[7]

Regarding Lee's dispositions and strength, Skinker's information was mostly erroneous. His estimate of Jackson's strength at 28,000 to 35,000 was reasonable enough, but he reported that all of Longstreet's corps was gone, even though Anderson's division, one of two remaining, was directly across the river from the region he covered; he confused W. H. F. Lee with Fitzhugh Lee, said Hampton's absent brigade was present, and placed Stuart in the Valley.[8] This important part of his information, or misinformation, came from his "relatives outside the lines (who sympathize entirely with the other side)."[9]

Babcock, who was temporarily in charge of the bureau (Sharpe was with Hooker in Washington), promptly sent Skinker out again, for there was evidence of threatening activity across the river.[10] A spy had been placed in Fredericksburg, from where she (there is evidence that it was a Negro woman) was to communicate across to Falmouth by means of a simple "clothesline code." Babcock described it to Butterfield:

> A cloth[e]sline with one piece denotes that the forces in the vicinity of Fredericksburg are on the move. An empty line denotes that they have all gone away. Two pieces shows that they are in force as they have been since the fight, three pieces that they are being reinforced.
>
> One piece has been displayed all day yesterday and today, till 4 P.M. when observer came away.

Butterfield wired Hooker in Washington that "Sharpe's signals" indicated an enemy move.[11]

Skinker's second trip, again upriver, produced no corroboration of the clothesline warning; if the Rebels were moving, their move was not toward the Valley.[12] However, the absence from Skinker's report of any noteworthy movements toward the Blue Ridge was in itself a useful indication. A small cavalry reconnaissance made concurrently with Skinker's trip apparently failed to discover any enemy movements of note.[13] An additional reason for discounting the possibility of significant moves was that the enemy had permitted one of Patrick's officers, Lieutenant John V. Bouvier, to escort a Southern woman into Fredericksburg.[14] So the clothesline alarm subsided, probably written off as originating from a routine change of camp sites.

Although Skinker was better able to uncover evidence of enemy scouting in the rear than the army's pickets, they were not entirely out of the running. An outpost commander at Stafford Court House reported: "Several suspicious persons have been seen in our neighborhood. One is supposed to be Western the noted rebel scout, formerly of 4th Virginia Cavalry who has lived many years in this vicinity. He has one of our blue overcoats and large broad brimmed hat — he is a tall man with long black hair and large bushy whiskers. A bright look out is necessary to keep him from passing through our lines."[15] One of the Confederates' haunts in Stafford was identified with the capture of a letter from a young woman residing there to her brother in the Southern army. She wrote that so many scouts were stopping at the family home — over which she apparently was now presiding — that "it looks something like old times." "One of them," she confided, "is the handsomest man I have seen for this many a day."[16]

Skinker also reported what he assumed to be the first casualty of Sharpe's bureau. Near Morrisville, in neighboring Fauquier County, on March 10, Skinker said, "one of your Scouts . . . came upon two of the B[lack] Horse cavalry . . . and ordered them to surrender, which they did." The scout paroled them and was mounting one of their horses when "two others came up and captured him and carried him across the river." Skinker's only clue to the identity of the "scout" was that he was dressed in brown clothing. Weeks later it developed that the victim was Private D. G. Otto, General Pleasonton's scout who had been recommended to Sharpe; this word came in the form of a letter to Pleasonton from Otto, brought by an exchanged prisoner from Richmond. Otto, in Castle Thunder, hinted that his capture had resulted from "foul play."[17]

The unventuresome nature of Skinker's trips suggests that he was by this time too widely known as a Union sympathizer to be used south of the Rappahannock. However, by now Sharpe had made contact with Isaac Silver, a farmer living inside the Confederate lines, previously seen as the source of the information that led to Burnside's January plans for a campaign upriver from Fredericksburg.

Silver, fifty-two years old, was born in New Jersey; his wife, Catherine, twenty-one years his junior, was a native of Scotland. His farm was on the Plank Road three miles east of Chancellorsville, an important crossroads, and seven miles west of Fredericksburg This put him at the eastern edge of the densely wooded and sparsely populated region known as the Wilderness. He was near the center of Lee's left wing.

Silver became known as "the Old Man," though this appears to have been a mere sobriquet rather than a term used for security purposes. His reports would continue to be brought by Ebenezer McGee, Burnside's spy in the January episode, who was now on Sharpe's payroll. His brother or cousin, Richard McGee, eighteen, was one of Silver's farm hands, living on his premises.

Although most occupants of this barren locality were lucky to scratch out a living, Silver was a man of better than average means, but not a slave owner; he employed a second farm hand in addition to Richard McGee and a mulatto house servant.[18] Silver's services as a spy would continue to the end of the war, aided by his business interests, probably the ownership of a farm, which provided cover for repeated visits he made to Orange County, where Lee's army was headquartered for most of a year in 1863–64. In view of Silver's Northern origin, the location of his home not far from Morgan's mine, and the fact that the older of his two sons was named Morgan, it is probable that Colonel Morgan had something to do with Silver's recruitment, and possibly Ebenezer McGee's as well.[19]

Either Ebenezer McGee was a most confident man or else he was extraordinarily adept in traveling at night the byways through the woods and fields and in arranging secure means of crossing the Rappahannock, for no effort was made to put Silver's reports into a form that would give them any security. Using a pencil, Silver scrawled them in a large, uneven script on long, heavy sheets of paper; McGee folded them, presumably fitting one end into a shirt pocket, and carried them that way across the river. Their language showed that the writer lived very near the Confederate camps and identified someone named McGee as the messenger. Silver's only precaution was leaving his reports unsigned.[20]

McGee brought in the first report on March 13. So proud was Silver of being selected to serve the Federals that he headed his communication "headquarters union army"; this was not an address but an imaginative statement of the office of origin of the report. Where Silver's information did not raise eyebrows, his spelling did:

> I feel glad to have the privelege of giveing all the information that I can to support a couse worthy of suport the preservation of the union.
>
> Jackson is down around or near hamilton crossing or below to wards the rappehanick river and A. P. hill Early And [Ewell] they are all below the crossing [with] perhaps 30 or 40 thousand men at [Banks's] ford thare is wilcoxes briggade they say about 3 or 5 thoussand [McLaws's][21] & andersons divisions is above salem church with 5 or 6 thouseand their is two divisions gone to Petersburg they still think their is over one hundred thoussand [Federals] hear yet it is true from last fall they ordered more men out from eightteen to forty five they have been cuming in all winter they have much larger army then I expected they have several batterreys fitchew Lee is stationd a little east of culpeper court house with his calverry it is said near 3 thoussand general Lee is on the telegraph rad near or within 3 or 4 miles of fredericksburg they have but little forage according to the best I can learn
>
> I cannot say but little more at presant try to let your messenger come

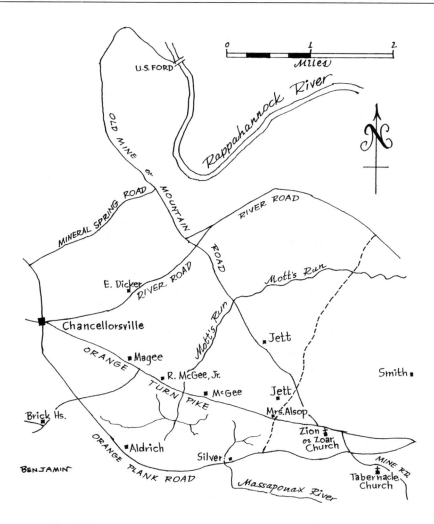

**A SECTION OF THE CHANCELLORSVILLE BATTLEFIELD
SHOWING SILVER AND McGEE FARMS (after Bigelow)**

onst more if possible before the battle I will try to be better posted about
the rebble armey

they are stealing your horses and saddles from forkear [Fauquier]
and the lower part of louden.

They have got inchrenchments dug at the bark mill and Ealeys ford
but no artilerry as I can learn I think it is certain that there is none....

the rebbles now say hear they only want one more battle and their
independence is sure.[22]

Except for Sergeant Cline's report, this was the most comprehensive
information on Lee's army from a single source to date. Hooker had a

clerk make a copy (correcting the interesting spellings but not the unconventional grammar), which he sent to Stanton. The War Department and Army of the Potomac headquarters did not trust each other's security enough to share such secrets routinely, but Hooker had too much pride in his new information bureau to keep this secret to himself. He took out insurance against Washington's reputation for leakage by asking Stanton to destroy the paper, a request that the secretary either forgot or chose to ignore.[23]

Because Silver's first-hand information was limited to the Rebels' left wing, where he lived, there were several points on which Sharpe would have wished for more information than the report gave. It omitted D. H. Hill's old division and represented Ewell and Early as commanding separate divisions, whereas Early was now in command of Ewell's; it did not indicate what troops held the six or seven miles of front from Hamilton's Crossing to Salem Church, which included the town of Fredericksburg (this was the area occupied mainly by McLaws). Silver's troop-strength figures were too high for Wilcox's and Fitz Lee's brigades and too low for McLaws's and Anderson's divisions.[24] Even on the left wing, the report, although placing Wilcox's brigade at Banks's Ford, failed to indicate the spread-out postings of Anderson's division, the farthest left of Lee's infantry. It would have been Mahone's or Posey's brigade, belonging to Anderson, that dug the entrenchments at "bark mill"; but the existence of those entrenchments, protecting United States Ford, was far more important than the brigade identifications that Silver missed. And other flaws in his report were correctable from other sources; this first report was easily good enough for Sharpe to have congratulated himself on acquiring the services of "the Old Man."

.. .. ..

Brigadier General Joseph W. Revere, whose brigade included the 120th New York, went over the heads of his division and corps commanders on March 14 to ask of Hooker's adjutant that Sharpe be returned to his regiment.[25] Revere would have had just as good a chance of being granted his request if he had asked that Sharpe be elevated directly to a major generalcy. The reason Sharpe could not be pried loose from headquarters was not that he was finding life there congenial, though it appears that he did (for example, Patrick complained to his diary that he had missed most of a night's sleep because "a set of the Butterfield clique of New York, were in Col. Sharpe's tent and talking all night").[26] What would hold Sharpe on the commanding general's staff was the substantial progress his bureau had already made. This pleasing development was very plain to Hooker in a long report Sharpe sent him through Butterfield on March 15, summarizing the findings made by the Bureau of Military Information in the first month of its existence. The bulk of the report is in Babcock's handwriting, but insertions by Sharpe show that its composition was the joint handiwork of the two men. It opened as follows:

> Prior to the middle of January the Rebel Army of the Potomac [*sic*] consisted of the two Corps of Lieut. Generals Longstreet and Jackson, the Cavalry Division of General Stuart, . . . and the artillery. . . .
> Lieut. General Longstreet had five divisions — viz:

Anderson's.	Pickett's.
McLaws'.	Ransom's.
	Hood's.

> Lieut. General Jackson had four divisions — viz:

A. P. Hill's	D. H. Hill's
Early's.	Trimble's.

> and thus with their Cavalry their Army consisted of *ten* divisions, which at their maximum ought to consist of five brigades each. This was not and is not now the case, as remarked below. . . .
> About the middle of January the enemy began moving forces south, and we now know that General Longstreet has gone south, and has taken with him, (or there have been sent south from his corps d'armee,) the divisions of Ransom, Pickett, and Hood.
> It is also known that General D. H. Hill has gone south, but it is not thought that any of his division has accompanied him.
> Generals Lee, Stuart, and Jackson are now opposite us: their H'd Q'rs being located in the annexed "Extracts," together with the following divisions of the rebel army:

of Jackson's Corps.	*of Longstreet's Corps.*
A. P. Hill's.	Anderson's
D. H. Hill's.	
Early's.	McLaws'.
Trimble's.	

> This is all that is believed to be opposite to us. (Infantry.)
> From the fact that most of our informants have seen little Artillery, we believe that a fair proportion of that arm has gone south with the divisions of Longstreet — but it should be remembered that the greater part of it was sent back some time ago to Hanover Junction, or near it,[27] to obtain forage along Pole Cat Creek, and from Louisa C. H.

The composition of Stuart's division was left to an annex, Sharpe explaining that "it is with difficulty that we locate Cavalry from one week to the next." The annex gave the regiments in the cavalry brigades of the two Lees with substantial correctness; these were the brigades that had been most exposed to Hooker's cavalry and pickets in the weeks the bureau had been in operation. The makeup of Hampton's brigade, however, was poorly understood, and Jones's brigade, although well known, was not listed as part of Stuart's division. Another error arose out of

the fact that two of Stuart's colonels had at times exercised independent command; they were mistakenly named as brigade commanders.[28]
Sharpe would soon improve on this analysis, although keeping track of
the constantly moving Confederate cavalry with frequent changes in
composition would remain a problem.

In estimating the enemy's total strength Sharpe and Babcock took
account of the old problems with Pinkerton's and McClellan's inflated
estimates. Carefully they went into the question of the average number of
brigades to the division, regiments to the brigade, and men to the regiment and to the brigade — making allowance for such irregularities as
battalions, which occupied regiments' places in brigade organizations
without contributing a corresponding number of men to the total. Then
they showed that Lee's infantry force must be much smaller than previously believed:

> We think the six [infantry] divisions before mentioned . . . have doubt-
> less twenty five brigades in all. And we have many evidences to show that
> 1700 men (for duty) is a liberal estimate of the average of their bri-
> gades. By this we should have $25 \times 1700 = 42,500$ men.
>
> Again, we have many evidences that 350 men is a liberal average of
> their regiments. And four and one-half regiments to a brigade is rather
> over than under the proportion. By this we should have $4-1/2 \times 350 =
> 1575 \times 25 = 39,375$ men.
>
> On account of the numerous battalions . . . we think these figures are
> too large, and believe that a calculation of our own, from several scat-
> tered regiments, is nearer the truth, viz — that the brigades will average
> about 1300 men for duty. By this we should have $1300 \times 25 = 32,500$
> men.[29]

Here was a straightforward, logical statement of the method of estimating enemy numbers by adding up assumed totals for individual components of Lee's army. Babcock wrote these paragraphs as if he had one eye
on the no-longer-available Pinkerton reports and was using them as an
example of estimating methods to be avoided. All three suggested totals
— 42,500, 39,375, 32,500 — were well short of Lee's true numbers,
which stood at about 49,000.[30] One cause of the shortage was an underes-
timation of the number of brigades; Lee had twenty-eight;[31] Sharpe and
Babcock estimated twenty-five, though they had identified only nineteen.[32] They also underestimated the numbers per brigade and per regiment. Winter weather was holding down the number of deserters, the
main source of organizational data; spring temperatures would bring a
correction of these figures to a remarkably accurate total. The main fault
in this first estimating effort was that in supporting their preferred total,
32,500, they cited Skinker, whose information was second-hand at best,
rather than Silver, a near neighbor of much of Lee's army. Skinker's
estimate was 28,000 to 35,000, whereas Silver's figures, for which he did
not give a total, could be added up to yield a total infantry force of

38,000 to 51,000. In any case, the Sharpe-Babcock "errors on the low side," and their avoidance of Pinkerton's arithmetical sleight of hand, were refreshing.

Regarding the placement of enemy divisions along the front, the report merely repeated the statements of different sources without evaluating them, even where there were conflicts. One source, unnamed, had given a fairly exact picture of Jackson's actual positions (A. P. Hill near Port Royal, Trimble above him and on the river, the division formerly led by D. H. Hill in rear of A. P. Hill, Early in rear of Trimble),[33] but equal credence was attached to another report that erroneously placed A. P. Hill in the interior and Early somewhat south of his actual position. Silver's distorted placement of McLaws (west of Salem Church) also was repeated.

The report gave Hooker some of the leading prospects for information in the future:

> . . . an attempt has been made to establish communication with the other side of the river [with Silver], which has been successful, and of which the General has been informed. Another has also been attempted which has not yet been fruitful, but from the short time which has elapsed since the departure of the agent [Cole] it is hoped it may be — and if successful it will probably be productive of the highest results.
>
>   The enemy's lines have been penetrated a number of times, notice given of . . . movements of the enemy — the number of persons employed and the expenditures very inconsiderable.
>
>   . . . If not otherwise reported to the General it should also be stated, although the credit thereof is not due to this department, that Captain Fisher (Chief Signal Officer) is in possession of the full code of signals used by the enemy's Signal Corps, with the exception of the numbers, and that their messages are read, daily, by his officers, whenever they can be observed from our stations.

The fact that Sharpe and Babcock included in their report the signalmen's ability to read the Confederate flag alphabet, which had been solved back in November, indicates that the availability of this source was not known at headquarters or in any case that it had never been exploited as a producer of intelligence. Evidently Captain Benjamin F. Fisher, who was only temporarily the chief signal officer of Hooker's army, gave promise of being a willing if not eager collaborator in the new all-source reporting system.

Although based on little more than a month's operation of the new bureau, the March 15 report was by far the most comprehensive piece of intelligence ever produced in the campaigns of the Army of the Potomac — surpassing to a considerable extent Captain William Palmer's modest "situation summary" written under the pressure of the enemy's presence in Maryland (and never relayed to the army). Babcock would have told Sharpe about the shortcomings of Pinkerton's reporting; avoidance of those faults was second nature to Sharpe and Babcock. Professionalism had taken over in General Hooker's intelligence service.

Babcock could not resist the opportunity to include a statement of the shortcomings of the previous regime:

> It is considered fair to add that . . . the rebel organization has never before been obtained in this army, until it was too late to use it; and that at no previous time has any attempt been made to locate the enemy's forces, that has proved [in] any way successful, or to estimate them within any reasonable number of men.

Babcock had participated in the excellent compilation produced by Pinkerton's staff using the greatly expanded fund of information on the composition of the Army of Northern Virginia that resulted from the large haul of prisoners taken in the Seven Pines and Seven Days battles — too late to be of use, as he noted, since McClellan's effort to take Richmond was over. The lack of "any attempt . . . to locate the enemy's forces, that has been in any way successful" refers to the absence of scouting from Pinkerton's mission and his lack of espionage in the Peninsula and Antietam campaigns. The neglect of scouting, the likeliest way of determining enemy positions, would have been galling to Babcock, since his mapmaking experience had shown that it was possible to cover quite a lot of ground without being captured.[34]

The constant use of the pronoun *we* in the report shows that Babcock had received the welcome from Sharpe that was denied him in the Burnside period. Sharpe made plain his pleasure in this collaboration by closing the report with the statement that it was "respectfully submitted in behalf of Mr. Babcock, and myself."[35]

. .   . .   . .

This long report must have caused Hooker to reflect that he had been right in deciding to put a stop to the quid pro quo trading of information with the enemy by way of newspapers and flags of truce. The Bureau of Military Information had now given promise that soon it would be producing intelligence as good as the exacting commanding general could expect. But Hooker was doing much more than this to improve his posture in the matter of information. He was devoting a great deal of attention to tightening the army's security. On his first full day in command he had written to Patrick, "The practice of permitting any person to move about through the lines of the Army, without scrutiny and examination, must be stopped."[36] Sutlers and other purveyors were a prominent target of new regulations; those not assigned to a specific regiment or other organization were likely to be trading with the enemy, a ready-made channel for military secrets. The crackdown caused repercussions that reached all the way to the White House, taking the form of complaints against Butterfield's prolific output of rules and regulations; because his promotion to major general was now before the Senate, Hooker defended him in a heatedly worded message to Lincoln that laid the complaints at the door of headquarters traders who were "tinctured with the McClellan and Burnside issue." Patrick seems to have escaped similar abuse, though he too was wielding a heavy broom. When an unauthorized trader died in the hospital at Aquia, his belongings were searched for contraband; Southern bank notes totaling $300 were found in the lining of his boots. Pseudo-sutlers from Washington, passed legally through General Heintzelman's lines ostensibly bound for the Army of the Potomac, were found to be heading southwest and making rendezvous with traders from the enemy, who bought their entire loads. Orders, stringent and in great detail, were issued by General Schenck at Baltimore to prevent leakage through the upper Potomac region and the Shenandoah Valley.[37] At Hooker's request the War Department published an order requiring that all passes to citizens wishing to visit the army be countersigned by a single officer assigned that function. Halleck assured Hooker that foreign officers would not be permitted to leave Washington without a request from their minister or diplomatic agent, approved by the War Department.[38]

Some of the other sources of leaks that Patrick went after were more obvious than the sutlers and visitors. He issued orders against cutting down timber within a mile and a half of army headquarters and within half a mile of the railroad to Aquia, "so that the enemy cannot from commanding hills look in upon our operations." When he learned that Confederate deserters paroled to go North were being released at Washington, he wrote to the commissary general of prisoners asserting that "the interest of the service requires [parolees] to be sent further north. I would respectfully . . . recommend that they be forwarded to New York to report at the headquarters of Major General Wool."[39] Confederate citizens already within the lines of the army could do nearly as much damage as enemy soldiers who feigned desertion in order to perform espionage; accordingly, Patrick's permit was required for any nonresident civilian to remain within the lines.

Next came the inevitable effort to stop picket communication with the enemy. One of the provost troops, a regular-army soldier, discovered volunteers in a Massachusetts regiment using a tiny boat to send newspapers across the Rappahannock several miles below headquarters. Hooker ordered a thorough investigation and a trial by military commission;[40] although his severity may have temporarily put a few of these front-line trading posts out of business, it was not long until Yankee coffee was going south and Rebel tobacco coming north in about the same quantities as before.

Drawing a lesson from the laxity of the Confederates in permitting

Sharpe's "clothesline" communication across the river, Hooker took steps to prevent the enemy from adopting this or some other nonalphabetic system of signaling. Cavalry pickets were made responsible for vigilance against "signal lights of different colors."[41] At the suggestion of a visiting member of Hooker's staff, a signal officer on the Federal left, six miles downriver from Fredericksburg, "made arrangements that the Seddon House shall undergo no change in its outward appearance from day to day — by opening or closing windows or blinds or by anything being exhibited upon the lawn in front of the house, that the inmates may not use these means for transmitting information to the enemy."[42] The owner of the house, Major John Seddon, brother of the Confederate secretary of war, was absent, and the family frequently received the solicitous attention of General Patrick. He amused himself by gently teasing the mistresses of important estates, but he was not so soft on Southern feminine charms as to put them above suspicion. And the suspicion may have been well founded in Mrs. Seddon's case; after the Chancellorsville battle, rumors circulating in the Army of Northern Virginia credited Southern ladies at that point on the river with conveying a timely warning of the Federals' advance, using hand signals.[43]

It was the monotony of picket duty that accounted for the pickets' avocation of communicating with the enemy. Almost the only excitement they ever enjoyed was an occasional shot at a fleeing Rebel — sometimes a scout but probably just as often an ordinary Johnny who had slipped through the lines to visit home for a few hours. The closest most of them ever came to bagging a Rebel was when a Southerner gave himself up as a deserter. One important capture was made by the pickets that spring when a civilian named E. M. Strange accidentally rode upon their lines; he had made the additional mistake of having on his person letters he had exchanged with the Confederate Navy Department relating to an invention that he claimed could destroy ironclad ships. Imprisoned at Aquia, Strange wrote to General Halleck, whom he had known in San Francisco, asserting that his status as an inventor proved him "above the character necessary to constitute a spy" — a defense that impressed the legal officers of the War Department as a perfect non sequitur.[44]

Hooker's restriction on flags of truce matched a similar action already taken by the War Department. In January Major Turner had put a stop to large-scale exchanges of civilians by flag-of-truce boats.[45] These exchanges had offered a way of slipping spies into Richmond and had been used for that purpose, though not with invariable success.[46] In shutting off this avenue of espionage, Turner and his superiors surely calculated that the Confederates had been paying them back in the same coin.

Newspapers were another certain target of the pursuit of security. While Patrick at Falmouth and Major Turner at Washington were working on the problem of soldiers' letters to the newspapers, Hooker himself tackled the larger one presented by the newspaper correspondents present with the army. The *New York Herald* on March 14 published a report of "unmistakable preparations now being made for a speedy movement of the army," which, no one doubted, "will come at the earliest possible moment." That the confidently worded prediction was altogether in error — and might help to unnerve the enemy — made no difference to Hooker. Butterfield ordered the offender jailed and ironed, but Patrick, who for some inexplicable reason looked upon the prisoner as "another poor correspondent," merely sent him off to the provost stockade at Aquia, free of irons. A military commission sentenced him to six months' hard labor, which Hooker commuted to transportation outside the lines.[47]

Other correspondents took warning from the *Herald* man's treatment and prepared codes by which innocent-looking telegrams to their editors could carry brief reports on the military situation. "Will send your twelve pages tonight," for example, meant "Hooker will fight tomorrow." One of these cryptographically inclined men was a *New York Tribune* reporter appropriately named J. R. Sypher.[48]

Hooker reserved the climactic move in his security campaign for the last week of March, when he wrote Halleck's adjutant:

> In view of the fact that when this army moves the sudden stoppage of all visitors to this camp would be a preliminary notice thereof . . . I would respectfully suggest that hereafter the permits to visit this army be restricted to absolute positive necessity, and that the permission heretofore granted to females [be] denied.
>
> It is advisable that these restrictions be gradually introduced within the next few days, and not upon the ground that anything is likely to occur here requiring such a course. It cannot be foreseen at what moment this army will move, and the action in respect to the stoppage of travel heretofore has invariably been such as to indicate to the country nearly the precise time of a movement.[49]

One last security measure was Hooker's holding the plans for his attack on Lee to a very small circle. This he declared to General Herman Haupt when he showed the plans to that officer, who had to know them in order to bring up rail transportation of supplies at the right times and places. In thus borrowing a page from Stonewall Jackson's book, Hooker was repeating the error McClellan and Burnside made in not issuing a general order for the army's advance. The object of those two officers in giving their orders piecemeal is not known to have been secrecy: that was Hooker's object, and a commendable one, but it remained to be seen whether he could handle his huge army effectively with his subordinate commanders kept in the dark as to one another's missions, especially their routes of march.

Hooker's tightening of security was not an immediate and unqualified success. The Confederate cavalry scouts still roamed in the rear, their visits usually undiscovered except by Skinker, days after they had come and gone. Even if Hooker could prevent further incursions within his lines, he would run into more enemy scouts as soon as he moved the army to the left or right. On the left was the Northern Neck, a nest of scouts and resident observers for the enemy; on the right was a country frequently visited by Stuart's patrols, and beyond that, General Heintzelman's Washington command, whose security Hooker could not control.

The officers on Heintzelman's front, at and around Fairfax Court House and Manassas, were full of warnings about leakage. General Alexander Hays complained to Heintzelman that newspapers were publishing information he had obtained from prisoners he had sent to the provost marshal at Alexandria. Young Brigadier General Edwin H. Stoughton believed that "there are those here who, by means known to themselves, keep the enemy informed of all our movements." He was especially suspicious of the "rampant secessionist" women of the neighborhood. One night when Stoughton was absent from his Fairfax Court House headquarters for only a short time, a man dressed as a Federal captain "interrogated all my servants minutely respecting the troops in the vicinity, asking if I kept my horse saddled in the night, and other suspicious questions." Stoughton was especially worried because neighboring commanders off to the northwest were leaving gaps of one or two miles in their picket lines. The opening had also been reported to Heintzelman by the telegraph operator at Centreville. For taking the trouble to send this warning the telegrapher was upbraided by a local cavalry officer, whereupon his superiors in the Military Telegraph instructed him to make such reports directly to Secretary Stanton in the future.[50]

Stoughton and the telegrapher were not raising an imaginary alarm. A few nights later John Mosby and thirty of his men came through the picket lines, rooted Stoughton and several of his staff out of their beds, and sent them off to Warrenton and Richmond. Included in the haul was a spy of Heintzelman's, an Austrian baron named Rudolph R. de Wardener. Mosby, who boasted that he had invaded Stoughton's bedroom and waked the general by slapping him on the posterior, failed to see through de Wardener's effort to pass himself off as a Federal private. The baron was exchanged four weeks later but, obviously not wishing to risk a second arrest, he collected $388 in overdue salary from the War Department and took his leave.[51]

Before these events transpired early in March Hooker was already trying his luck with security measures in the Northern Neck, the main route of enemy communication to the North.[52] Westmoreland Court House and Warsaw were visited on February 10 and 11 by a cavalry force looking for Confederate conscript officers. The conscription party had decamped, but the expedition broke up a "post-office in full blast." One of the letters captured was from a representative of a Baltimore mercantile house who was visiting the region, seeking payment on purchases made by a local storekeeper between April 1860 and March 1861. This indication that Northern business concerns in the area might be concerned only with cleaning up prewar debts was belied by the capture at Westmoreland of "smuggled tobacco, sugar, and coffee, some saltpeter, and nearly fifty barrels of villainous whisky." Another expedition two days later went farther down the Neck with similar results, capturing mail, seizing large quantities of stores and draft animals, and learning that Confederate conscript officers had paid the Neck a visit.

Regardless of how often the Federals visited the Neck, they never failed to make some kind of haul, usually a large one. However, the only really useful result of these raids was the capture of letters containing military information. The large variety of commercial goods showed the determination of the traders; few traders and no spies were taken.[53] The navy could not begin to patrol the Potomac closely enough to prevent nighttime crossings to the Neck from Maryland, and cooperation between the Potomac flotilla and the army was at a low state. The flotilla commander wrote to General H. H. Lockwood, commanding on the Maryland shore, complaining that army officers were unwilling to submit their boats to inspection. Lockwood forwarded the letter to his chief, General Schenck, asserting that the navy was a "nullity" as far as stopping the trade was concerned and that the flotilla commander was "affiliated with the 'Secesh.'"[54]

Finally Sharpe was put to work on the problem. Union cavalry already had several resident spies or informants in the Neck. The most active of these men signed his dispatches "Echo"; an entry on one of them indicates that he was the Reverend George Northam. "Echo" once tipped off the 8th Illinois Cavalry that a wooden bridge had been undermined in preparation for the regiment's next expedition. He asked that its officers when visiting his community "associate some heavy threats against my person as a rebel, or arrest me for effect." (He also asked them to burn his letter, but it was forwarded to Sharpe.)[55]

March 17 was a day of scant attention to business; the headquarters staff celebrated Saint Patrick's Day in the camp of the Irish Brigade. General Patrick was there, but only because Hooker had ordered him to be. He left early and that night recorded that his adjutant and Colonel Sharpe "came home at dusk, tight as bricks."[56] But Sharpe found time that day to dispatch Sergeant Cline to the Neck. The mission was tame in comparison with his visit to the enemy army in February, and it was over country that he may have scouted when Hooker's division occupied lower Maryland. But he made the visit as interesting as he could and topped it off with a report that made informative if unpleasant reading. Hidden under the portico of a house near King George Court House, he had seen and heard an officer of the 10th New York Cavalry, "addressed as such," treating with three officers of W. H. F. Lee's cavalry brigade and promising to return cattle taken from a secessionist farmer by Federal troops. Among other services of the 10th New York to the Confederates was the rejection of a party of eight or ten Negroes seeking to enter the regiment's lines. Another overheard conversation yielded the names and connections of five men who were prominent in transporting supplies from the Neck to Lee's army and were scheming for the capture of "another squad of our Cavalry."

Cline's principal findings, however, had to do with the value of the Neck to the Confederacy as a granary. He "met and conversed with many of those who are boastfully engaged in supplying the rebel army," Sharpe wrote. An earlier visitor had estimated that "there remain in those counties 200,000 bushels of corn and wheat of the best quality; his information being drawn from relatives, Union men, . . . who beg that it be seized by our forces, and are willing to lose their own for the good of all." It was Cline's belief, Sharpe said, that this estimate "is under the mark; that some of the barns contain the whole or a part of 3 years' stock; and that . . . the river is lively with scows and 'batteaux' carrying over their valuable supplies." Sharpe contrasted this condition of plenty with the low ration in Lee's army:

> From a mass of testimony, that, in a court of record, would authorize the judge to rule that no further evidence on that point would be received, we know that the ration of the army opposite us is . . . 1 pint flour and ¼ lb. bacon or pork per diem. Soldiers escaped thence remember the issue of a little sugar or rice in addition to the above amount about once in three weeks; but all other articles, including candles, have long since disappeared from their Commissary Stores.

Some prisoners, it was true, had

> boastfully asserted the endurance of their resources — they were well clad when they spoke — but the ragged and beggarly fellows who [form] their rank and file on the other side did not so understand the 'tea cup of flour and patch of bacon' which was daily issued them by those who are interested in the success of the rebellion.

Because the spring wheat crop had failed in the South, Sharpe continued, "There is . . . nothing to carry the Southern army through to the corn crop, if we exercise the greatest vigilance in closing against them *their outside granaries.* And one of the greatest of these, I am satisfied, is the *Northern Neck.*" But he regretfully concluded that although the small boats carrying the trade across the Rappahannock might be easily captured, "they would soon be replaced by men working for their bread, or enormous profits."[57]

A renewed effort followed close upon Sharpe's report, but all it accomplished was to underline the hopelessness of attempting to control the

Neck by occasional visits of small bodies of troops. This time the usual infantry expedition took along twenty cavalrymen belonging to Rush's Lancers, part of General Reynolds's headquarters escort. The cavalrymen struck out on their own under the command of Lieutenant Colonel John A. Kress. The colonel's report reads like the record of a pursuit of Robin Hood. In a region where every householder had draft animals, the people were quietly at work in the fields with scarcely a horse or mule in sight. Somehow they had learned of the Yankees' arrival in time to hide the livestock in their barns.

When the Lancers arrived at Rappahannock Ferry, a landing known to be constantly used by the boats plying the river trade, there were no boats to be seen, no people, not even a wharf. In the distance they saw a party of mounted Rebels watching them and gave chase; their quarry not only got away across the river but took along a drove of cattle. Next morning Kress learned the names of two officers in the Confederate party and heard that the Rebels had come back across the Rappahannock during the night and made off with three wagonloads of contraband. He heard of a large storehouse filled with grain, but only after he had passed by it; his party was too small to risk returning. Even a "large party of Jews" bound for Maryland had got away. Next he heard of five enemy soldiers who were in the neighborhood, but he could not find them. Two days later a Negro traveling with him told him that his troops had passed within a hundred yards of the five men. The Negro had kept quiet about the men in the bushes because he thought they were Federals, whose hiding place he did not want to expose to their commanding officer.

Finding that all their movements were anticipated, the Lancers had to keep constantly on the move and take circuitous routes to avoid ambuscades by parties of bushwhackers and furloughed enemy soldiers. After riding 180 miles in four days, they returned to camp with a total yield of thirty horses and eighteen mules.[58] General Wadsworth thought that the results of the expedition confirmed "the opinion I have hitherto expressed as to the expediency of occupying the Neck" with a permanent force of considerable size.[59] But Hooker ignored Wadsworth's advice; his experience in lower Maryland had shown him that occupying a rebellious region would not put an end to secessionist activities.

Of as much importance as stopping the shipment of supplies from the Northern Neck was preventing transmission of information through it. Hooker and his staff did not feel that even partial security had been achieved, on the army's flank toward the Neck or anywhere else. General Patrick had a security worry even more fundamental, he was convinced that the army's flanks were so weakly protected that "there is nothing to prevent [the enemy] from making a dash upon our Depot [at Aquia] and destroying it before we can get anything up there to defend it."[60]

The main source of Hooker's feeling of insecurity was a surprise suffered by his cavalry at the hands of Fitzhugh Lee, who led 400 troopers of his brigade on a deep penetration of the Federal lines in the last days of February. Crossing the Rappahannock at Kelly's Ford, twenty miles above Fredericksburg, the Southern horsemen, whose purpose was not raiding but reconnoitering, drove within four miles of Hooker's head-quarters at Falmouth and captured 150 prisoners before being turned back. Three quarters of Hooker's cavalry and 2600 of Heintzelman's were sent against them, with General Stoneman commanding, yet they escaped with light damage. So badly managed was the search for them that General Pleasonton, through no fault of his own, took his division north instead of west, putting himself fifteen miles away from any possi-ble action. When he wired Butterfield that he was at Aquia and Dumfries but could find no trace of the enemy, Butterfield forgot for a moment the demeanor incumbent on a chief of staff and wrote to Stoneman: "Pleasonton [reports himself] in position at Aquia Church!! . . . his bril-liant dash and rapid movements will undoubtedly immortalize him." The heavy sarcasm was unjust; Stoneman in his order to Pleasonton had mentioned Dumfries as a possible target of the invaders.[61]

After this embarrassment Hooker wrote to one of his cavalry generals:

> I know the South, and I know the North. In point of skill, of intelligence, and of pluck, the rebels will not compare with our men, if they are equally well led. . . . Now, with such soldiers, and such a cause as we have behind them — the best cause since the world began — we *ought* to be invincible, and by God, sir, we *shall* be! You have got to stop these dis-graceful cavalry "surprises." . . . I give you full power over your officers, to arrest, cashier, shoot — whatever you will — only you must stop these "surprises." And by God, sir, if you don't do it, I give you fair notice, I will relieve the whole of you and take command of the cavalry myself.[62]

Hooker translated this strong language into action by ordering Averell to take his cavalry division across the river and beat up Fitz Lee's trouble-makers. Strengthened by a battery from the artillery camp at Aquia, Averell on March 17 crossed at Kelly's Ford by using small groups of picked men to outmaneuver a strong picket consisting of sixty sharp-shooters. In this success Averell was luckier than he knew, for Stuart and Fitz Lee had had eighteen hours' advance warning that the enemy was heading their way. Their own scouts' coverage of the Federal side of the upper Rappahannock was the likeliest source of such a warning, but in fact this one came by telegraph from the headquarters of R. E. Lee. The source of the report could have been a spy — Lee is known to have been receiving "information from Falmouth" at this time — or it could have been a nonalphabetic visual-signaling system connecting Lee's head-quarters with the Federals' side of the river. Such a system had severe limitations; it could indicate the existence and direction — upriver or downriver — of a sizable movement, but it could scarcely distinguish between a cavalry march and a general advance. In any case, Lee's telegram made no such distinction; as far as he knew, this could be General Hooker's long-expected big move. Immediately he sent orders to Longstreet to put Hood's and Pickett's divisions on the road back to Fredericksburg. Hood's march was under way by the time Lee, learning on the day after the fight that no infantry had accompanied the attacking cavalry, countermanded his order.

In spite of the timely warning received by Stuart and Fitz Lee, Averell's advance achieved a limited surprise. The action that to him was an outmaneuvering of a strong picket was to his adversaries a case of "picket failure." Having several fords to look out for, the two generals had stationed themselves at Culpeper and did not receive word of Averell's crossing until it was complete.

In a day-long fight Averell gained the upper hand, but he fell victim to a combination of intelligence errors. He mistakenly believed that the Confederates had reached ground where they were protected by earthworks; he evidently accepted a report that Rebel infantry was advancing on his right and rear; and he fell for the enemy's hoary ruse of running trains back and forth on the nearby Orange and Alexandria tracks to simulate the arrival of reinforcements. With victory within his grasp, he retired across the Rappahannock. Hooker believed he should have routed Fitz Lee.[63]

To R. E. Lee the timely discovery of Averell's advance was an isolated success in a period of intelligence drought; he was having considerable difficulty in getting information about Hooker's army. Fitzhugh Lee's bold reconnaissance was his uncle's major effort to remedy this shortage, and in spite of its deep penetration it evidently produced little useful information. And these difficulties worsened as Patrick's security measures gradually took hold. (Even the impressively timely warning of Averell's advance revealed an embarrassing shortcoming in the Confederate intelligence service, since it led to Hood's departure for Fredericksburg and then his recall.) Late in March Lee informed President Davis that "Their pickets are placed within sight of each other, with dismounted men in the intervals." Another complaint had the Federal pickets "posted within 50 steps of each other."

At the same time, Lee was suffering a shortage of scouts and spies. (Scouts technically became spies at the point where they crossed into territory the Federals held, but Lee uniformly called them scouts regardless of their "legal" status, which in any case was often ambiguous.) He had lost one scout killed in a skirmish and others simply by their not being on station; a worse development was an order he received from Richmond transferring Captain Pliny Bryan to South Carolina. He had sent Bryan, undeterred by the captain's stay in Old Capitol on suspicion of espionage the year before, over to Maryland, where he was subject to capture, to observe Federal shipping on the lower Potomac. Lee had "scouts" north of the Rappahannock, but nothing is known of their number or their findings beyond the fact that one of them had a contact, a person from Alexandria, who reported on activity on the important docks at that city. For days or weeks the only significant reportage on Hooker's army came from a Stafford County citizen who had picked up some information while imprisoned at Aquia.[64]

Lee was forced to work out his estimates of enemy intentions in the face of this shortage of information. The first problem he encountered after Hooker's accession to command was a confusion that developed from the movement of the Federals' Ninth Corps to Dix's command. There were as many erroneous and conflicting reports from Confederate scouts on the Potomac as occurred later on the Federal side when Longstreet's divisions went in pursuit of the Ninth. And now, before Burnside's old Ninth had had time to get comfortably settled on the Peninsula, the War Department decided that those troops should follow him to a new assignment in Ohio and Kentucky. Two divisions traveled to Baltimore via Chesapeake Bay and had left there by rail by the time the movement came to Lee's attention — discovered not by his own sources on the Potomac but by General Jones out in the Shenandoah Valley. The movement was slow enough for a "scout" sent by Lee to overtake the trains in western Maryland. He talked with the troops and came away with the "fact" that there were five divisions in the movement. As it was too big a move to remain hidden permanently, the Federals' best result from the intelligence standpoint would be gained by covering it with such misinformation.

Through these weeks Lee changed his mind about enemy intentions as often as he had at the time the Federals' Fredericksburg campaign was developing. Now his thinking swung between two opposing theories: one, that Hooker was abandoning his position between the Potomac and the Rappahannock; the other, that reports of an advance by the Army of the Potomac were "propagated" to cover the removal of some of its forces, as much as three corps, to other theaters where offensives would take place while Hooker remained on the defensive at Falmouth. And Lee did not neglect other theories lying between those two.[65]

Comparison of these intelligence successes and failures in the two armies in this period reveals that for the first time in the two years of war in Virginia, the Federals knew more about their enemy than the Confederates knew about them. A reversal of the "intelligence advantage" had been achieved in the first two months of Hooker's regime. The contributions of Milton Cline and Isaac Silver were more than enough to make this difference; and there was also the fact that Hooker had an organized intelligence service headed by two talented men, while Lee had nothing of this kind.[66]

·· ·· ··

On March 16, when the forthcoming attack on Fitz Lee was uppermost in Hooker's mind, he received from Halleck a warning, "apparently more reliable" than previous ones, that a force of 10,000 was threatening Milroy in the Valley. Halleck wanted Hooker to hold Stuart in check so that no "large body" could menace Harper's Ferry. Knowing that Fitz Lee had never completed the movement toward the Valley reported earlier, Hooker queried Halleck in language very similar to his previous challenge on the same question: "Can no one tell where all the enemy's cavalry come from?" The reply was, "It was supposed you would know from your scouts whether or not there was good foundation for the report."[67] As the Army of Northern Virginia was only one of several commands from which Jones's Valley command could have been strengthened, Halleck seemed to be expecting a great deal of Hooker's new information service. It would have been like Hooker to point that out to his unloved chief in Washington, but he held back his pen.

Milroy was telling his "old story," as Halleck as well as Hooker suspected,[68] but his 10,000 figure was made to look miserly by a report that came in on the 18th, originated by a spy in General Dix's employ. "My man," as Dix called agent William Crawford, was just back from a two- or three-week excursion in Confederate-held Virginia. "He was at Staunton on the 7th," Dix reported. "General Jones was in command with 35,000 men." (This was ten times the number Jones was showing on his returns.) Two days later Crawford visited Fredericksburg, where, he reported, Lee had 85,000 (a mere 35 percent exaggeration).[69] He stated that Lee's army contained 107 regiments (this was close to the number Sharpe and Babcock were estimating but 30 or 40 under the true figure[70]). For the area around and below Richmond — which must have been more familiar to him than other parts of Virginia — he gave an estimate of 62,000 troops (Longstreet, now commanding those forces, was reporting 25,300 on his returns[71]). It appears that like Pinkerton, Crawford knew how to penetrate enemy territory, a skill exceeded only by his ability to multiply enemy numbers.[72] His information would have been much more useful to Sharpe if a list of regiments and the strength of each, which he was said to have compiled,[73] had been copied and sent to Hooker.

·· ·· ··

Not knowing of Sergeant Daniel Cole's capture upon his arrival in the Confederate lines, Sharpe and Babcock in their summary of the enemy situation on March 15 had expressed confidence that his mission would be highly productive. When, or if, Cole came back, his return could be expected to follow a route similar to Cline's up the Northern Neck. His chiefs must have been surprised when Cole presented himself at headquarters on March 22 and announced he had come from Washington. He had made an escape similar to those of Frémont's spies who had been caught by the Rebels the previous year and to Joseph Snyder's more recent experience as a guest of the enemy's provost marshals. Hearing that there was to be an exchange of prisoners, Cole had slipped himself into the stockade with ordinary Union prisoners of war. When the Federals lined up to sign their paroles, Cole's was readily issued. Soon he was aboard the exchange boat at City Point.

Sharpe would have been glad to get his man back with no new information whatever, but Cole had picked up a number of useful items. He had been taken to Richmond by rail from Hamilton's Crossing. Two sizable troop positions of Jackson's corps were visible from the cars, and pickets along the entire line of track. (This last point was very pertinent to the campaign plan Hooker was making.) Cole saw a few troops in Richmond, and on the way to Petersburg and City Point with his fellow prisoners he passed through parts of Longstreet's two divisions, which someone correctly identified for him. The reports that Longstreet had gone to South Carolina or Tennessee were pretty well exploded by this time, but knowledge of his exact position at any given time was very much worth having. It seemed to be the general belief in Richmond that the Confederate forces there and at Petersburg were much greater than those on the Rappahannock, though Cole did not try to assess the basis or the validity of this impression. Longstreet's troops were "not so far distant from the railroad, but that they can reinforce the Rappahannock army in 48 hours."

Cole also noted some of the heavy fortifications about Richmond, especially on its southern approaches. No earthworks or guns were within sight of the railroad between Hamilton's Crossing and Hanover Junction (a fact of special interest to Hooker). The report also covered enemy transportation: in Jackson's camps was the largest wagon park he had ever seen; on the railroads there were no large concentrations of locomotives and rolling stock except at Petersburg. No great quantities of rations and forage were in sight at the enemy depot at Hamilton's; Cole heard a quartermaster say that there were "rations for the whole army for 90 days in Richmond, but when that was gone, 'God knows when we shall get any more.'" The daily ration as reported to him was three quarters of a pound of flour and a quarter-pound of fresh meat. Food was bringing famine prices in Richmond.[74]

Cole's report, as far as Sharpe's records reveal, was the only important piece of information received in the second half of March from Northerners who had been behind the enemy lines. The influx of prisoners and deserters, mainly the latter, resumed during this time, however, and was enough to keep the bureau's pot simmering. They were from nine different regiments, well spaced along the Rappahannock front, and thus gave good coverage of Lee's army. There was also a deserter from Pickett's division with Longstreet.[75]

The lull in activity gave Sharpe time for the project he had begun with his meeting with Colonel Van Buren. His attention turned again to Baltimore, not for another rendezvous with his Kingston friend but simply because the Chesapeake Bay metropolis was known, in the words of an officer stationed there, as "the great thoroughfare of goods and travel as well as the very citadel of smugglers, mail carriers &c."[76] Sharpe had returned there late in February seeking an agent to go to Richmond in the guise of contrabandist, as recommended by General Dix. Now, a month later, he made another trip to complete arrangements for the services of a Richmond agent he was never to know except through an intermediary who would operate the Baltimore end of the "Richmond Line."

For the intermediary function Sharpe had singled out James L. McPhail, civilian provost marshal of Maryland.[77] The prescribed duty of McPhail's position, as in other states, was to head an organization of county provosts who enforced the conscription of soldiers and as a collateral duty sometimes assisted in apprehending and returning deserters. In the latter capacity McPhail had had communication with the Army of the Potomac and thus was known to Patrick.[78] But his connection with activities under Patrick's supervision went back to days long before the enactment of conscription. Although by trade he was a hatter and furrier, he had come to prominence as president of the First Baltimore Hose Company, which proclaimed itself "the oldest civic organization in the United States."[79] It was one of two "law and order companies" of the Baltimore Fire Department, and when the city was put under martial law early in the war McPhail, then forty-four years old, became assistant provost marshal, a civil office. His rooting out of secessionist activities, particularly by apprehending Southern agents, won the praise of Allan Pinkerton and General Dix (then commanding at Baltimore). He also attained notoriety, largely as a result of his role in the sensational arrest of a pro-Southern county judge on the Eastern Shore; McPhail ascended the bench and took the judge by force while court was in session.[80] Among the Confederate agents he caught was Mrs. Catherine V. Baxley, who owned a modest fame through having been sent South with Rose Greenhow.[81]

General Wool, one of the succession of officers who commanded at Baltimore, considered McPhail to be in league with the "Jacobin" element in the city and believed that he made some arrests on mere suspicion. But Dix, who preceded Wool, while praising the "great body" of Baltimoreans for their moral virtues, declared that the city "has always contained a mass of inflammable material which ignites on the slightest provocation" and urged the commissioners of police to retain McPhail when police powers were returned to civil authorities in March 1862.[82]

As the head of a detective force and the possessor of extensive knowledge of the channels by which contraband activities were carried on with the Confederacy, McPhail was Sharpe's obvious choice for setting up communication with Richmond. The local commander at Baltimore, now General Schenck, also maintained a force of detectives headed by his own provost marshal; Sharpe might have worked more effectively with Schenck's command because of its military character, but its provost marshal office was undermanned[83] and evidently did not match McPhail's acquaintance with contraband channels.[84]

By the time of Sharpe's visit toward the end of March, it appears, McPhail had made the desired arrangements for a Richmond listening post. The man he obtained to operate it would ever afterward be referred to in correspondence and reports as "our friend." Conclusive evidence in War Department files identifies him as Joseph H. Maddox, whom both Timothy Webster and Frank Buxton had denounced as a Confederate agent in the late months of 1861, and who had been imprisoned by the Federals earlier in that year and again in mid-1862.[85]

Maddox, a native of Georgetown in the District of Columbia, had been a captain of dragoons in the Mexican War, when he was in his early twenties. Well educated, he later became owner and "leading editor" of the *New Orleans Crescent* but left journalism in 1855, still a young man, to operate a plantation in upstate Louisiana. He moved from there to Lexington in the Shenandoah Valley, and in 1859 to St. Mary's, at the southern tip of Maryland. His wife owned property at Taneytown, Maryland, neighbor to the Pennsylvania town of Gettysburg, and it was Taneytown that Maddox now called home. His lawyer, Reverdy Johnson, was a United States senator from Maryland, and he claimed friendship with prominent Marylanders in the Confederate army, including Colonel Bradley T. Johnson of the Maryland Line. He also claimed that he had worked for General McClellan, had traveled on a pass signed by Secretary Seward, had succeeded in the task assigned him, and had worked with Timothy Webster. Frank Buxton had worked directly under McClellan rather than through Pinkerton, and Maddox could have had the same arrangement, but no evidence substantiating this claim has been found. The signaling project in which Maddox had tried to engage Webster would have been an ideal means of penetrating the Confederates' courier line to Washington and at the same time furnishing a cover for Federal espionage. Although that project did not come to fruition, Maddox seems to have moved back and forth between Maryland and Richmond through much of 1862. He engaged in large-scale smuggling enterprises and, according to his own statements at least, was acquainted with President Davis and his secretaries of war, Judah P. Benjamin and George W. Randolph.

Much of Maddox's history would have been known to McPhail, though he probably did not know the full extent of Maddox's involvement in pro-Southern actions. The status of Southern gentleman and slaveholder was not enough to establish bona fides in the eyes of the Confederate leaders; they could name many a gentleman who, despite a background more Southern than Maddox's, was strongly opposed to secession. Maddox had repeatedly proposed to Confederate authorities that he be commissioned to raise a regiment or battalion of cavalry in Maryland, and he claimed that during McClellan's stand in front of Richmond he had actually taken a unit of Marylanders into the city's defenses.

He also proposed schemes for spying against the North. Captain William Norris, a Baltimorean and chief of the Confederate Signal and Secret Service Bureau, was impressed with Maddox's abilities in this line and with his Southern patriotism as well. In September 1862 Norris proposed to Secretary Randolph that a second line of communication (one was already operating) employing eight couriers be established through southern Maryland to Washington and points north as far as Quebec, where an officer would be stationed to relay dispatches to and from the Confederate representatives in Europe. Norris wrote, "Mr. Maddox now raising a Regiment of Cavalry in Maryland has volunteered to execute this part of the duty" (all sections of the line north of the Potomac). "His means for obtaining intelligence from men of judgment and position in Washington are peculiarly great; also his facilities for forwarding dispatches."

Maddox's pro-Southern activities bore little fruit. Virginians began to notice that "he has never yet found it convenient" to complete the raising of the often projected cavalry organization. Maddox claimed that Davis failed to come through with a commission for him. It may or may not have been Davis who kept the cavalry unit from materializing, but he did block the communication project, on the ground that some of the dispatches would probably fall into enemy hands. Davis's language probably was deliberately intended to throw cold water on the project without giving Norris his true reason, which could have been distrust of Maddox.

Maddox also claimed important contributions as an intelligence agent for the South, but here again his performance is questionable. Norris does not cite any specific accomplishments of his friend, and the one intelligence report Maddox is known to have made to the Confederates is anything but impressive. On September 12, 1862, in the wake of the fears of attack on Washington by the victors at Second Bull Run, Maddox reported to Secretary Randolph that the Federal government was removing its stores from Washington. This he inferred from the fact that the Potomac "has been for several days, full of vessels going to Washington and returning. All go up empty and return *deeply loaded.*" Maddox's statements seem to exaggerate any shipments that actually took place.[86] Moreover, Maddox had claimed access to men of high position in Washington, but this report of shipments from Washington was derived from observation along the lower Potomac — a duty that was being performed for Davis and Lee by dozens of men in and out of the military service. The report probably was more misleading than helpful.

At a time when McPhail was looking for an agent to go to Richmond, Maddox came to him, proposing to provide military information in return for permission to trade with the South. Whatever reservations McPhail may have had about his visitor's ultimate loyalties, the proposal offered advantages to the Union. Even if Maddox intended to provide intelligence to the Confederates, the information he could obtain in the North would pertain to Baltimore and lower Maryland, where Federal forces were of little importance. From this standpoint Maddox was a desirable acquisition, but his history of pro-Southern activities was quite a drawback. Whether Sharpe knew of that history is uncertain; Babcock, his likeliest source, had not joined Pinkerton's bureau until after Timothy Webster, who knew of Maddox's collaboration with Rebels, had left on his last trip to Richmond. Even in the face of that history, Sharpe could have viewed Maddox's cooperation with Confederates as a price a smuggler-spy would have to pay.

McPhail accepted Maddox's proposal and provided him with an outfit of goods consisting of an assortment of groceries and dry goods and "five or ten" barrels of wet goods — whisky. In limiting him to this modest selection of merchandise, McPhail may have been seeking to insure that Maddox would have to make profit-taking secondary to information-gathering. Probably he was also testing the agent, intending to be more generous in the future if the first trip should be successful. But in making Maddox a purveyor of job-lot quantities of scarce goods McPhail would seem to have risked arousing suspicion on the part of Confederate authorities. Maddox had represented himself as a man of parts; a greater supply of goods would have been a more convincing cover.

But if Maddox's commercial activity was held to the level of a small-time operator, his mode of reaching Richmond was not. Rather than having him cross into the Northern Neck from St. Mary's County by skiff, as dozens of blockade-runners were wont to do, McPhail sent him down the Chesapeake Bay in a government-hired sloop. Since some residents of the Neck were suspicious of Maddox's loyalty to the South, the purpose of this mode of transportation was probably to put him on a land route to Richmond through country where he was not too well known.

After setting Maddox ashore, the sloop returned to Baltimore and the captain reported to McPhail that the landing had been accomplished. Then silence descended on the "line to Richmond." The date was April 11.[87] General Hooker was almost ready to begin a movement that would call for all possible assistance in the way of information from the Confederacy.[88]

15

· · · · · · · · · ·

THE GRAY FOX
SWALLOWS THE BAIT

April 1863

TROUBLES WERE BESETTING General Dix's "plan by smuggling," and they did not bode well for its offshoot, Colonel Sharpe's plan. William Crawford, Dix's agent, had extended his shopping from Baltimore, his home city, to Philadelphia, without giving notice to Benjamin Franklin, who as chief of detectives in that city was a friendly collaborator with Federal authorities. The purchases came to Franklin's attention anyway, for they were a clear case of smuggling. He learned that Crawford claimed to have been "two or three times South, and talked about 'the inexhaustible resources of the rebels,'" declaring that they could not be conquered. He was in possession of such incriminating articles as percussion caps, $1216 in Confederate notes, and $9000 in North Carolina state bonds. He carried passes from General Schenck, the Baltimore commander, and General Dix, and said he was a spy for Dix, though that claim did not impress Franklin enough for him to include it in his letter to Levi Turner in the War Department.

In a few days Crawford was brought to Old Capitol Prison, whereupon the case took on a different color. General Dix happened to be in Washington en route to New York for a short leave. He told Turner that Crawford was his "tried and trusted agent," who "swam rivers, waded swamps, at the risk of life to give . . . the most important information." Crawford's reports were always reliable; he was Dix's "my man" who had recently visited Richmond, Fredericksburg, and Staunton.[1]

Crawford was released and went on his way with $100 from the Secret Service Fund to fill his otherwise empty pockets. Turner wrote the U.S. attorney at Philadelphia that "all's well that ends well," a platitude that ignored the fact that Dix's "plan by smuggling" had been thoroughly compromised. Philadelphia newspapers, picking up the story that had originated with Crawford's loose talk as he made the rounds of his suppliers, did their best to put an end to his career as a spy by giving their readers the minutest facts of the case, and other points that did not qualify as facts. One account, for example, said that a photograph found on Crawford was that of a "young female" who had a white father and a colored mother. "The father . . . is said to be a wealthy resident of Richmond, and prominent in the rebel cause."[2]

The publicity accorded Crawford's troubles posed a threat to the Maddox mission in Richmond: if any of the Richmond papers copied the Philadelphia reports or if Confederate authorities noticed them, the appearance of this new supplier of scarce Northern goods would excite a suspicion that here was another Yankee spy. But the spying of Captain William Palmer and the Reverend I. J. Stine had been reported by Philadelphia papers without being noticed by Richmond officials; Confederate authorities' response to Maddox's approach would reveal whether this new leakage of military secrets by the same Philadelphia press had come to their attention.

Sharpe and McPhail were spared from concern about this threat by the fact that they too had no time for reading Philadelphia papers, and Major Turner, unaware of the Maddox project, would have had no reason to communicate with them about Crawford. As for General Dix, he may have learned of his agent's compromise, for the record of Crawford's spying career appears to end with the Philadelphia episode.

Despite the exaggeration of enemy numbers that afflicted his reports, Crawford evidently was a competent agent, as indicated by the wide range of his travels. His loss would have seriously crippled Dix's collection of intelligence at a time when it was urgently needed not only by Dix but also by Hooker, who had a constant problem in keeping track of Longstreet, then campaigning in Dix's theater. To Hooker it was important to move against Lee while Longstreet was still at a safe distance from Fredericksburg. His information on Longstreet was contradictory. On a single day, April 10, conflicting reports came from two sources, each of which commanded attention if not credibility. Babcock interrogated at great length a Scot named James Craige, a naturalized citizen, who had fled Richmond, having been a baker at a downtown location that gave him both access to military gossip and a post for observing troop movements through the city. He furnished substantially accurate details of Longstreet's southward movement in February and subsequent advance toward Petersburg and Suffolk. From him Babcock learned of the false start for Fredericksburg that Hood's division had made in March when Averell was advancing toward Kelly's Ford. Of Longstreet's current situation Babcock wrote, "Informant states, that he knows of no bodies or organizations of troops having returned to Fredericksburg, since the divisions of Hood and Pickett went away."[3]

An unqualified contrary assertion about Longstreet's movements came from George Smith, just returned from six weeks inside enemy lines. Reporting through General Pleasonton, under whose supervision he was still working, Smith stated, "Two divisions of Longstreet's Corps have returned to the Rappahannock." His claim to knowledge on that subject was a visit he made to Richmond while under arrest on suspicion of disloyalty to the Confederacy. He had been released because the authorities lacked proof; later he would claim that his release had cost him a considerable sum. He corroborated previous reports that the enemy was fortifying crossings of the Rapidan. (Pleasonton explained that this construction was to protect "supplies for two years subsistence" at Charlottesville, Lynchburg, and Danville.) "The rebels are under the impression, we shall cross above, or both above and below, Fredericksburg," Pleasonton wrote. As to Smith's loyalty, he wrote the War Department that the agent's "explanations are consistent, and appear satisfactory"; to Hooker, however, Pleasonton suggested that Smith be questioned by Butterfield.[4]

Another contradiction of Craige came from a furloughed Rebel soldier, interviewed by Skinker, who claimed to have been in a detachment of Longstreet's force that returned North on March 23. Skinker recorded this man's statement that "12 or 13 Regts belonging to Longstreet's Comd have returned from Petersburg & North Carolina and have taken the places — back of & above Fredericksburg — of troops that have gone up the River." This was a bald-faced lie; the man was not one of Longstreet's troops, for he misstated the locales where they were operating. He was hoping to mislead Hooker by deceiving Skinker;[5] Longstreet was not moving.

.. ..

For the first time since Longstreet's departure from Fredericksburg, a contest of major proportions was now developing in southeastern Virginia. It was precipitated by the departure (seen in chapter 14) from Dix's command of two divisions of the Ninth Corps to join their old chief, General Burnside, in Ohio and Kentucky.[6] Longstreet had started out from Petersburg on March 30 bent only on foraging, but his purpose grew aggressive when he learned of the depletion of Dix's army.[7] His resultant threat to Suffolk so alarmed the Federals that their reports had all of Longstreet's First Corps on that front, though Sharpe had a deserter from Anderson's division, which was prominently mentioned in the reports. General Dix cut short his leave to manage this crisis, then was surprised to learn that Longstreet was falling back. He had not appreciated the stoutness of the defense his men had put up.

This fighting made clear, for Hooker's benefit, that any report of Longstreet's return to Fredericksburg must be wrong; the Confederates could not possibly put forth so strong a pressure on Suffolk without both Hood's and Pickett's divisions.[8]

.. .. ..

While attention was focused on the Dix-Longstreet issue, Ebenezer McGee produced Isaac Silver's second report. Its chief point of interest was the announcement that the Rebels at Fredericksburg were sending off their baggage, an indication of offensive plans. Another development, equally offensive and defensive in nature, was the appearance of the army's artillery, which had been wintering twenty and more miles below Fredericksburg; Silver said it was now "quite handy." Other preparations suggested purposes strictly defensive: the Rebels were moving stores from Culpeper to points behind the Rapidan and, as also reported by George Smith, were fortifying at least one ford on that river. "Conscripts have been cuming in quite fast all winter," Silver wrote, and "it is thought that their force is stronger than it ever was befor," but "their horses many of them looks greatly worsted." Despite the apparent significance of the movement of baggage, Silver said, "They are making no preparations to move eneyware that I can learn. . . . I do not think they intend to move away soon."[9]

Silver's appraisal was correct; not much was happening on the other side of the river except in Lee's mind. He was, as Skinker had guessed, thinking that if Hooker did not move soon he would himself head for the Valley. He would "make a blow at Milroy" at Winchester as a way of drawing Hooker out and perhaps driving him across the Potomac. Later Lee's thinking turned to a Maryland move with a different purpose, to relieve pressure on Charleston and Vicksburg.[10] On the whole, Silver's report, although it was not as comprehensive or detailed as Hooker would have wished, gave the truest reflection available to Federal intelligence of the somewhat unsettled situation in the Army of Northern Virginia. Lee was getting ready for a spring campaign but was committing himself to neither the defensive nor the offensive.[11] On the one big problem, Longstreet's whereabouts, Silver's report did not disturb the status quo, but his silence on the subject was an indication that Hood and Pickett had not returned to Lee.

.. .. ..

Hooker and Lee, like the rest of the country, had an eye on a siege of Charleston by the Federal navy. It was coming to a head with an attempt to take the city by a fleet of monitors commanded by Admiral Samuel F. Du Pont, with the assistance of General David Hunter's army. When the monitors met a severe repulse on April 7, the news was flashed from Charleston to Richmond and thence to Fredericksburg, spread through

Lee's army by signal flag, intercepted by Federal signalmen, and read by Captain Benjamin F. Fisher. The anxiously awaited news of the outcome of this important campaign reached the North through a medium, communications intelligence (interception and decoding), that was too sensitive to permit its release to the public.[12]

. .   . .   . .

A visit from President Lincoln early in April helped to bring Hooker's preparations for attacking Lee to a head, even though so much of the President's time was taken up with reviews, receptions, and excursions among the troops that the event seemed almost altogether ceremonial. Of course General Patrick disapproved of the extended rituals. A festivity in honor of the President meant exactly as much to him as the one for Saint Patrick, and when headquarters officers held a reception Hooker again had to give Patrick an explicit order to attend. Immediately after being presented to the President, he "crawled out . . . the Back Way." Lincoln's eagerness to visit the front appalled the security-minded Patrick; one night he wrote, "The enemy have had us [the President's party] in plain sight all day & if they had desired, could have dropped a shell amongst us." He hoped that "the President will soon get off" so that the army could settle down to business.

Patrick may have been the only one in the vast encampment who was that eager for a battle. Lincoln enjoyed himself hugely, especially among the enlisted men. But he told a companion that despite the benefits of a week in the open away from his cares, "nothing touches the tired spot."[13]

Lincoln and Hooker seized the opportunity to talk over the coming campaign. Hooker's staff had been at work studying in great detail the problems connected with his various possible movements. Descriptions of the roads, railroads, fords, and terrain were presented to him on maps and in skillfully prepared briefs. Though honed down to essentials, they reflected painstaking work by a number of hands. Officers who had been in the Fredericksburg occupation force the previous spring (there were many in Patrick's command) could have supplied much of this information; more was available from prisoners and scouts, especially those whose homes were in the neighborhood; more still from the balloonists and signal officers, who were equipped to measure distances by triangulation.[14]

Much if not most of the collected information was put together by Hooker's talented chief engineer, First Lieutenant Cyrus B. Comstock. Early in February Comstock had produced a memorandum summarizing the advantages and disadvantages of the various places for crossing the Rappahannock, extending from Skinker's Neck, twelve miles below Fredericksburg, to United States Mine Ford, twelve river miles above the town.[15] (The ford got its name from its proximity to a federally operated gold mine, currently inoperative; it was familiarly known as U.S. Ford.) Comstock's findings pretty well ruled out all of the places studied except U.S. Ford and the two sites just below Fredericksburg where Franklin's grand division had crossed in December. The other crossings, presumably including even Banks's Ford five miles above the town, would involve an uphill attack against strong fortifications or were so placed that the trajectory of the Federals' artillery could not be raised enough to "see" the Confederate guns and so could not cover the advance of the infantry. Immediately after Lincoln's visit Comstock produced another study recommending that the river be crossed at Port Royal and also at Franklin's crossing and nearby Smithfield with only cavalry and a small force of infantry taking the upriver route and crossing at U.S. Ford. Placing the main attack on the Confederates' left, Comstock thought, would leave the army too far from their "central masses" to engage or capture them.[16] The downriver route also had in its favor the well-remembered penetration by Meade in the December battle.

By April 11 Hooker had sorted out the pros and cons of the various routes of attack and written Lincoln a letter on the subject. Butterfield, who carried it to the President, had to resist attempts by Stanton and others to worm its contents out of him.[17] The letter began, "After giving the subject my best reflection I have concluded that I will have more chance of inflicting a serious blow upon the Enemy by turning his position to my right."[18] This language shows that he had considered the leftward (downriver) route seriously enough to have discussed it with Lincoln during the President's visit. And, since he did not find it necessary to explain what he meant by "turning his position to my right," it appears that they had discussed the upriver crossings.

The bulk of the letter dealt with a plan to send the army's cavalry on a long, circuitous raid, via Culpeper and Gordonsville, to sever the Richmond-Fredericksburg railroad, the enemy's supply route. Hooker knew that Lee had only a very short reserve of rations and other supplies at Fredericksburg; not until 1864, however, would there be a channel of information through which a Federal commander could learn that the condition of Lee's commissariat was made especially serious by the inefficient operation of the railroad, whose superintendent, Samuel Ruth, was still running the line to the detriment of the Southern cause, as far as he dared.

Hooker expected the turning movement of his infantry to force the enemy to retreat toward Richmond, and he hoped the cavalry, in addition to its demolition chores, would be able to hold the retreat in check until the Federal infantry could fall on its rear. The letter said no more about the infantry's movements, but it is clear that they were not to begin until the cavalry was well on its way.

The earlier scheme, for the main attack below Fredericksburg, evidently had never matured as a formal plan. The new plan retained a movement via Franklin's crossing as a secondary attack, but this and other significant features were not mentioned in the letter; these plans evidently were incomplete at the time Hooker wrote.[19]

General Stoneman received the instructions for his raid in consultation with Hooker Sunday afternoon, April 12. Before the troops could move out the next morning, a driving rainstorm set in. The weather cleared sufficiently for the brigades to reach Rappahannock Station, but before they were in position to cross, the sky opened again and the river became a raging torrent, pushing far over its banks. Parties belonging to one division managed to cross and were warmly received by the Confederates; they got back to the north side only by swimming their horses. Here was the luck of Ambrose Burnside, closing in on Hooker. The rain did not abate long enough for the river to go down until almost two weeks had passed. Hooker's infantry, ordered to prepare eight days' rations, never left camp. Only by its remaining in place was a second Mud March averted.[20]

Hooker went to great lengths to keep even the broad outline of his plans from leaking beyond his own very small inner circle. His own staff was kept in the dark, though eventually one or more of them would have to write the orders that put the plan into effect. At least in the early stages Cyrus Comstock was not told what plans were evolving from the underlying studies he was still writing. Corps commanders were not informed of the roles designed for them; the commanders of the army's right and left wings, which were to be widely separated, each had orders with only the vaguest indication that another wing would be in action somewhere.

Stoneman's orders did not say how the cavalry's movements were to relate to those of the rest of the army. Regiments from the Fifth Corps (Meade) and the Eleventh (Howard) were ordered up the river to prevent communication across it during Stoneman's ride to his crossings; the underlying purpose of their march was not stated, even to Meade and Howard. (That infantry would be shifted about to protect the secrecy of the cavalry movement is difficult to understand in light of Hooker's instructions to Stoneman to spread the word that the cavalry was headed for the Valley.) Stoneman's movement, however, could not be kept from Sickles and Slocum, for the picket lines of their corps (the Third and Twelfth) connected with cavalry picket lines that were being withdrawn; their two corps would now have to cover all of the army's rear and flanks except in the region patrolled by the small force of cavalry that Stoneman was leaving behind. So a more elaborate instruction went to Sickles and Slocum over Butterfield's signature: "A large portion of General Stoneman's cavalry force have gone in the direction of the Shenandoah Valley, and will be absent some days. Your infantry pickets must be vigilant and strong." Although this statement was literally correct, Sickles and Slocum would soon learn that the cavalry was not going very far "in the direction of the Shenandoah Valley" and that its mission would have been more truthfully described as requiring two or three weeks. In thus misleading his corps commanders Hooker risked losing more in their confidence than he would gain in secrecy.[21]

. .   . .   . .

In the early days of April one of Hooker's signal officers learned, from a captured Confederate signal officer, that the Rebels had possession of the Federals' signal *code*. This was a term the Federals used for their flag alphabet. Evidently their messages were being sent in the clear (unenciphered), their only protection being the closely guarded secrecy of the alphabet.[22] Yankee signalmen, as we have seen, had months ago reconstructed the Confederate alphabet, also used without encipherment.

The Confederate signalmen were sure to return that compliment sooner or later. Even the ability to read the Federals' traffic, however, did not put them on the same capability level with their enemy, for they virtually eliminated the value of their accomplishment by revealing it in their own messages. The situation was this: the Federals knew the enemy code and also the fact that the enemy knew their (Federal) code; the Confederates knew the enemy code but did not know either that the enemy was aware of that fact or that the enemy could read their (Confederate) code.

Colonel Myer in Washington reacted to the news of the enemy's intrusion on his organization's secrets by quickly providing a cipher, in which letters were substituted for each other; the pairings changed daily and repeated weekly. This system was designed for field use: the necessary paraphernalia could be carried in a shirt pocket, and it was uncomplicated enough to be reproduced from memory if destroyed in an emergency. In effect, Army of the Potomac signalmen would now be using seven alphabets. The Confederates could reconstruct each one, using the same method by which they had recovered the Federals' original alphabet. This was a weakness that Myer was fully aware of; evidently he considered that weeks or months probably would pass before the enemy's cryptographers accumulated enough intercepts to recognize the weekly repeats and determine the letter-for-letter pairings in the individual alphabets. One consideration that led Myer to take this risk would have been the difficulty of putting a more complicated new system in operation on what might be the eve of a major battle. The event seems to have confirmed his judgment; no evidence has turned up that the Confederates ever penetrated his new system, which in any case was superseded in September by a cipher disc, a much more secure kind of cryptography than any the Federals had used up to that time.[23]

As not all messages were sensitive enough to require encipherment,

Myer directed that some should be sent according to the old system. He ordered that these include messages that would lead the enemy "to believe that we cannot get any clew to their signals" and that messages about "imaginary military movements" also be sent.

Captain Samuel T. Cushing, the Army of the Potomac's chief signal officer, sought General Butterfield's instruction before attempting deceptive transmissions. Myer's order presented a problem: as the enemy interceptors would now be seeing a good many enciphered (and therefore unreadable) messages, and would suddenly encounter one so important as a discussion of a troop movement that was sent unenciphered, they would easily suspect that message of being an attempted deception. Butterfield had the answer to this problem at the tip of his pencil; he devised a way to make the lack of encipherment unsuspicious. His text, sent at 4 P.M. April 13 from a station in front of headquarters and near the river, read:

> Our cavalry is going up to give Jones & guerillas in the Shenandoah a smash. They may give Fitz Lee a brush for cover. Keep watch of any movement of infantry that way that might cut them off & post Capt. C[ushing].

Butterfield hoped to escape the suspicion of trickery by avoiding the official message format — address, text, signature. His words simulated signalman-to-signalman conversation, drawing persuasiveness from the well-known chattiness of the Civil War soldier.

The ruse worked. On April 14 the signal officers on the army's left intercepted a Rebel message that began "Dispatch received from Yankee signal flag" and went on to repeat the planted message in full, though not without a couple of garbles. Next day the Federals again intercepted their own hoax message.[24]

The plant captured Lee's immediate attention. He wired Jones in the Valley:

> I learn enemy's cavalry are moving against you in Shenandoah Valley; will attack Fitz. Lee in passing. They have crossed at Rappahannock Station. General Stuart, with two brigades, will attend them. Collect your forces and be on your guard.

The reference to Fitz Lee shows that this warning was based on the signaling ruse rather than on the officially disseminated rumor of Stoneman's movement. Lee followed with corroborating evidence, not entirely correct: "The dispatch I sent you is confirmed; main body of enemy's cavalry is moving via Liberty toward Warrenton with the intention to march into Shenandoah Valley against you."[25]

Fitz Lee's brigade, which had been on a foraging mission well to the north, was called partway back to resist the Federal move in cooperation with W. H. F. Lee, most of whose brigade had already been moved to Culpeper from the lower Rappahannock. Stuart moved his own head-quarters from Fredericksburg to Culpeper. He did not credit the report that the Federals were headed for the Valley, but his reading of their intentions was equally wrong; he sized up the movement as "a feint to cover other operations," namely a return of the Army of the Potomac to the Richmond front. Lee at first derived a theory not far from Hooker's original downriver "plan": he agreed that Stoneman's movement was a feint but one "intended to draw us to the upper Rappahannock, that Fredericksburg might be seized, and the bridges across the river rebuilt." But this theory wore away; continuing to worry about Stoneman and the Valley, he kept Stuart in his upriver position. At one point he thought the enemy was "rather fearful of an attack from us than preparing to attack." As late as April 25 he was still discussing with Stuart the prospect of Stoneman's crossing the Blue Ridge.[26]

As the hoax message was Colonel Myer's idea to begin with, Butterfield probably wrote it without giving much thought to its consequences. He surely hoped it would cause Stuart to expect a cavalry strike westward rather than the southward one actually intended. Hooker, Butterfield, and Sharpe could know only that the fake message had been forwarded to Lee's headquarters. Stuart's position opposite the Federal cavalry could have been taken solely in response to Stoneman's move, with no regard to the message intercepted by the Rebel signalmen. But a week went by and he was still there. That was to have an effect on Hooker's plan not only for the cavalry but for his whole grand maneuver. For Stuart had left a gap twenty miles wide, facing Kelly's Ford.

The signalmen's ruse was not the final length to which Hooker went to surround his movements with secrecy. Another measure was his request to the city postmaster at Washington to hold up mail sent from the army for twenty-four hours. The reason was "very urgent . . . as you may readily imagine."[27]

· · · · · ·

On April 17, while these elaborate secrecy efforts were going on, a slip-up took place in Washington that made a laughingstock of the army's secu-rity: the composition and strength of the Army of the Potomac were disclosed for all the world to see in the pages of the *Washington Morning Chronicle*. A major in the office of the surgeon general had unthinkingly given a *Chronicle* reporter access to a report by Hooker's chief surgeon on the state of health in his army. It put the number of sick at 10,777 and stated that this represented a sickness rate of 67.64 men per thousand. From that the army's total strength could easily be computed at 159,329. Furthermore, the report went on to give the complete organization of the army, taking it down to regiments in the case of two corps. Hooker complained to Stanton: "The chief of my secret service department would have willingly paid $1,000 for such information in regard to the enemy at the commencement of his operations, and even now would give that sum . . . to verify the statements which he has been at great labor and trouble to collect and systemize."[28]

But the lapse in the surgeon general's office was matched by Confederate ineptness in the handling of this valuable information. It did not reach Richmond until nine days after its appearance in the *Chronicle,* a time lag very unlike the speed and efficiency usually credited to the Confederates' famed "Secret Line" to Washington. And when the information arrived, its authoritative source was completely obscured; Major William Norris, head of the Signal and Secret Service Bureau in the Confederate War Department, could only report it in this watery language: "A special scout of this corps arrived last night from Washington and reports the following: The effective strength of Hooker's army is confidently stated at from 150,000 to 160,000." From this it appears that the "special scout" was not in Washington at the time of the leak and was dependent on a word-of-mouth source; or perhaps he deliberately left the source unnamed in order to claim a more impressive feat of espionage. Receiving the information in that weakened form, Lee preferred an estimate of 120,000 based on his own sources. Not until after the battle of Chancellorsville did he learn that the figure he had rejected as "much exaggerated" was based on an official return for Hooker's entire army.[29] The "special scout" did not know of, or in any case his report did not indicate, the unusual reliability of this strength figure.

. .   . .   . .

Hooker's Jacksonian secrecy is easily understood when the full extent of his security problem is seen. Averell's effort to punish Fitz Lee had not made the enemy scouting in the army's rear any less frequent. Whenever Skinker learned what neighborhoods these men were visiting, they found new targets for their next scouting trip. But the intruders were not penetrating the area where they could learn what Lee most wanted to know — indications of preparations for an advance and of arrivals and departures of Federal regiments and larger units.

On one of Skinker's trips, shortly after the fight at Kelly's Ford, a citizen mistook him for his brother, who was still on sick leave from the Confederate cavalry, and told him that in recent days only three Rebel scouts had been seen in the vicinity. But Skinker found the tracks of eleven horses, undoubtedly belonging to Rebels, heading north. There were only nine sets of tracks returning south. Even so, it seemed to Skinker that the past week had seen a reduction in enemy scouting. He deplored the excitement caused by a recent rumor of an enemy raid, but added that "it has had the effect of putting the outposts on the alert, which was decidedly needed."

Skinker saw a party of fourteen riders of a unit known as the Black Horse Cavalry as they crossed in front of him, striking boldly in the direction of the picket lines of Generals Pleasonton and Howard. At the same time he discovered a threat not only to the security of the army but also to his own safety. He wrote:

> Wm. N. Thom, a conscript, who was hunted for months by the Rebel Cav and finally caught about three weeks since, is now at his home, in Fauquier, by permission.
> He is one of the best scouts they could have and has doubtless been sent over for the purpose.
> He is immediately in my path and I desire him taken care of.[30]

Skinker's anxiety over security rose sharply as the time for Hooker's movement approached. After his next trip he gave a few details about the enemy's strength and vigilance along the upper Rappahannock and filled the rest of a long report with warnings about information leakage and the inefficiency of the pickets. On leaving the Federal lines he had twice been stopped and brought back to cavalry posts, where he was forced to identify himself before being allowed to proceed. Apparently he felt that the Northern pickets' vigilance was satisfactory only against himself, for he wrote Sharpe, "In consideration of the fact, that no movement, not even of Pontoon wagons, can be made in this Army without being *immediately* reported to the enemy, I most earnestly recommend that an order be issued prohibiting *any one* — not connected with the Army — from being passed in or out, and that there shall be *no* exception."

Skinker named nine citizens living in the region of the rear and right flank whose arrest and confinement "until this Army shall have moved" was necessary. "They are," he declared, "all cooperating with the enemy and giving him information and a short time in the Old Capitol will decidedly benefit us, if it does not improve them." (If these men were obtaining any valuable information, it was not reaching General Lee.) The suspected Rebel scout, Thom, was "still at home — professes to belong to the 'Black Horse,'" and Skinker again — this time "respectfully" — suggested his arrest. One of Skinker's servants had warned him that other members of the Black Horse company "were in the neighborhood, with the purpose of capturing the horse I rode, having heard that it belonged to Genl Patrick." On receiving this news he "thought it prudent to lay by" for an afternoon but then set out again. Immediately he met a member of the 9th Virginia Cavalry who gave him the same warning, whereupon he gave the man a note to deliver to an acquaintance in the Black Horse party. He gave Sharpe a copy of the note:

Oakley April 8th 1863

Mr. Scott George
> Sir
> I have just learned, from what I deem a reliable source, that you and other members of the Black Horse Cavalry, are lurking about, in this neighborhood, for the purpose of taking the horse I ride, and me with it, if I put on any airs.
> I give you fair notice, that if the horse is taken, either from my stable or from me, I will immediately report the fact to Hd. Qrs. and make application for permission to bring out a Cav. Force sufficient to take *five* of the best horses I can find and arrest *five* citizens, both to be held until the horse is returned.
> Your threat to arrest me, I scorn.

> Respty
> Jno. H. Skinker[31]

Colonel Sharpe could have wished that Agent Skinker was not so ready to advertise his Northern sympathies.

.. .. ..

Hooker, possibly encouraged by the evidence that the story planted by his Signal Corps was being accepted, at least by the Confederate signalmen and possibly by Lee and Stuart, informed Lincoln on April 15 that "Up to late last night the enemy appeared to have no suspicions of our designs." Two days later he repeated this qualified assurance,[32] but then came a rude contradiction. A major commanding a section of General John Sedgwick's picket lines reported that the Rebels knew not only of the cavalry's march but of the infantry movement that was to follow:

> On April 14 it was reported to me that the enemy's picket called across the river that [our] paymaster had come. . . . This . . . was not over fifteen minutes after I heard from the camp that the paymaster had arrived. The same day . . . they called across that 'you need not be so still; we know all about it; you have got orders to move.' This was provoked by one of our officers breaking up a small boat sent across to us, and his arresting one of our men apparently about sending back one in return. . . . The same day, after some officers had ridden along the enemy's picket line, they called out that it was Stonewall Jackson and his assistant adjutant-general. On Monday, April 13, they called out that our cavalry had moved.

That was the day Stoneman's march started.

A surgeon in Sedgwick's corps was named as the one who had leaked word of the movement to a family residing near Sedgwick's camp, who in turn had spread the news to neighboring Union infantrymen. This part of the incident had already been investigated by General Patrick. The alleged culprits had been arrested and brought to him, but he wrote off the arrest as "a Butterfield display" and sent them away. The surgeon's written report, received from Sedgwick several days later, forced him to go into the matter more thoroughly. He began by calling on a few of his "rebel secesh ladies" but saw before long that loose Yankee tongues and subtle communications among the secesh were not needed to explain some of the enemy's discoveries. A day or more before the leak by the surgeon, the cavalry's departure had become known simply by the absence of its pickets from their usual posts. Many of these posts could be seen from the homes of secessionists, and others were visible from across the river.

This much was no surprise, of course, and the cavalry's departure was a fact that headquarters had gone to some trouble to put in the enemy's hands. But Patrick also found that communication between the Federal and Confederate pickets had been going on fairly regularly. This information came from citizens, servants, and soldiers belonging to Patrick's command whom he had posted as replacements of cavalry detachments that had been guarding the signal stations. These sources, he reported, "do not like to say much about it, for fear of the consequences to themselves from the parties of whom they speak." However, one of his soldiers, member of a regiment of regulars, had already intervened by breaking up a boat being used by a New York volunteer lieutenant to send sugar, coffee, and newspapers across the river; the lieutenant had been relieved. The soldier told Patrick of a conversation he had heard one night between pickets of a Pennsylvania infantry regiment and the Rebels:

> The first part of the conversation was about rations. Secesh then asked, "Any signs of a move?" Reply, "Yes, we have got eight days' rations, and expect to move in a few days. We have three days' rations in our haversacks and five in our knapsacks." Secesh then asked, "Where is the move to be"? Reply, "Up to the right."[33]

By the 18th the Johnnies all up and down the river were turning their knowledge of the Federal plans into derisive banter, which they heaped on their friends the Yanks.[34]

What was general knowledge in Lee's army was having little or no influence on its commander's thoughts about enemy intentions. On the 20th he wrote Stuart that although Federal pickets were being reinforced, he considered that there was "no evidence of a forward movement."[35] The intelligence acquired by his pickets had not given him any aid and comfort, and it led Hooker to introduce further security measures that proved to be a benefit, probably an immense one. By the 20th the policing of the pickets' conduct was no longer left to a scattering of Patrick's enlisted men; the pickets' own officers were posted on the lines with them, stopping any communication before it could get started.[36] And since Patrick's investigations had reminded everyone that there was no use in hoping that Confederate citizens would avert their gaze when a Federal march passed by their parlor windows, or that they would keep quiet about what they saw, precautions much more stringent than any previous ones were adopted for the marches that were about to begin. Burnside had used road guards to precede his march from Warrenton to Fredericksburg and seal it off from the enemy, leaving Lee in doubt as to whether the Federals were really taking the Fredericksburg roads, where the guards appeared, or were heading for Alexandria to board transports and leaving guards far to the south of their line of march to cut off the flow of information.[37] Even if Hooker had known how Burnside's scheme had frustrated Confederate intelligence, he would have opted for sterner measures. Instead of road guards he decided to use house guards. At Falmouth and along the march route of the right wing, at houses where the occupants' observations would pose a threat to the secrecy of the march, detachments of infantry were to be stationed to keep the members of these families at home.[38] The house guards would maintain these postings until the march appeared in force in front of Confederate defenders.

.. .. ..

Security worries took a surprising turn on April 21 with the circulation of a report that a Rebel-operated underwater telegraph line connecting Falmouth with Fredericksburg had been discovered and put out of operation. This was news to General Patrick, in whose jurisdiction such matters lay. Evidently he regarded the report as a fanciful elaboration of camp gossip or vague reports about nonalphabetic visual signals — suspicious-appearing lights or daytime activities on estates such as Mrs. John Seddon's, the object, back in March, of a prohibition against manipulation of window blinds or windows proper in a manner that could convey information. Patrick mounted his horse, Snowball, and rode off to call on his secesh lady friends, among them Mrs. Seddon, who might know something about that kind of signaling. It is not clear why he thought these loyal Confederate women might yield even a faint hint of the kind of information he sought. After one visit during which his hostesses "were very polite to me and said many very handsome things," the old warrior was in no condition to tax Southern womanhood with suspicious questions. Awkward language in his diary entry that night reflects his unease: he had asked the ladies "about matters in the way of signals and that sort of stuff." He learned nothing.[39]

The underwater telegraphy story was certain to reach the ears of newspaper correspondents with the army. It appeared in the *Philadelphia Inquirer* of April 25, the discovery credited to a guard who heard the clicking of a telegraph instrument emanating from a house near the river bank. According to the *Inquirer,* the guard, after getting instructions from his superior officers, entered the house and found four or five men, one of whom was operating a telegraph instrument. They were arrested, and their punishment, the *Inquirer* averred, would be "according to the laws of war, . . . death by hanging." A headline over the story called the men traitors, though the paragraphs that followed said nothing about their allegiance, actual or feigned.

The *New York Times* printed a strikingly different version of the story on April 28. According to the *Times,* the telegraphing was discovered by an unspecified person who saw the wire leading to the river, touched it, and received a slight shock; and only the operator, a Confederate, was arrested.

The *Inquirer,* and probably also the *Times,* falsified the place of origin of the story. The *Inquirer*'s account, datelined "Washington, April 24," actually was written in the paper's editorial office, and the *Times*'s version, bearing the impressive dateline "Headquarters, Army of the Potomac, April 26," almost certainly was originally a dispatch that was delivered to the Washington telegraph office on that date and was rejected by the censor. Evidently the writer then mailed it to his editor in New York. These fictitious datelines were intended to enhance the credibility of a story for which the newspapermen had no official or eye-witness source.

General Hooker learned of the *Times*'s rejected dispatch, and another addressed to the *Inquirer.* On April 27, the day his army marched against Lee's, he took time to fire off an angry telegram to Stanton, requesting that those papers' Washington agents be required to identify the correspondents who furnished the information. He also asked for the source of the information in the *Inquirer*'s published story of the 25th.

Uriah Painter, the *Inquirer*'s chief Washington correspondent, was in Ohio; the telegraph censor, A. A. Lovett, could learn only that the information in the rejected dispatches of the 26th came from an *Inquirer* correspondent at Falmouth, whose name he did not learn. Regarding the *Inquirer*'s story of the 25th, William W. Harding, variously identified as publisher or chief editor, telegraphed Lovett: "The matter in Saturday's [April 25] paper was obtained by one of our city editors from a sutler of a New York regiment while riding in a railway car in this city the evening previous to its publication." The believability of that explanation, small to begin with, is reduced almost to zero by a fact recorded in Patrick's diary: Harding was visiting Falmouth at the time the report of the underwater telegraph was circulating. He had called on Patrick on April 23 with a proposal for his paper and the *Baltimore American* to be represented by a single agent-correspondent stationed with the army. The April 25 version of the story would have made its way to Philadelphia in the form of data carried on Harding's person or, more probably, in his memory.[40]

Meanwhile reports of enemy signaling were spreading through the Falmouth camps. A captain of engineers picked up the cross-river telegraph story on April 21, and an enlisted man in an engineer battalion recorded in his diary that on the night of April 23 a fellow soldier on guard duty had observed light signals aimed at Fredericksburg from a house on the north bank directly across the river.

Patrick, continuing his investigation of visual signaling, wrote on April 27, "I have Robt Walker and Arthur Bernard here, prisoners, for signalling the enemy last night. It will be very strange if this should be proven on them."[41] These words leave us uncertain as to whether Patrick was simply dissatisfied with the evidence against his prisoners or was unsure that the signaling actually took place. The night of April 26, though, was a likely time for such signaling, for the advance of Hooker's right wing was to begin the next morning, and neighboring farmers might have observed regiments or larger units repositioning themselves in preparation for an early start.

On the 29th Patrick's concern with the two prisoners vanished, and with it his uncertainty about enemy signaling. He recorded, "I have been down to the Lacy House, to try and ascertain *how* communications get across the river. We need not look beyond the pickets for a solution to the question. They allow citizens & all others about & in front of the Lacy House, without any molestation whatever." Not only were the pickets fraternizing with the enemy across the river; they were also allowing citizens — potential spies — to frequent the very place where military news was most available.

The existence of such a source is suggested by a March 12 note from Lee to Stuart in which he referred to "information from Falmouth." The Lacy house, close to the river bank, was a satellite of army headquarters, used among other things as the base of the army's Officer of the Day, a one-day assignment that rotated among a large number of officers of medium rank. The duties of the "O.D." were to field alarms and other contingencies. This gave him cognizance over picketing along the army's entire front. The Lacy house was within headquarters' picket lines; the lax security that was tolerated there would have seemed to each successive O.D. to be beyond his power to correct in his twenty-four hours of army-level authority.[42]

Patrick's diary does not indicate that he took any corrective steps on the basis of his brief inspection at the Lacy house. Although he stopped worrying about visual signaling for the time being, his observations on that visit only strengthened his suspicion that the Rebels were acquiring Federal secrets by some means, such as eavesdropping by men whose presence at and near the Lacy house was going unchallenged by the pickets.

This story of clandestine telegraphy operating at the very heart of the Federal command has not entered the literature on Confederate intelligence successes, though the argument for its factuality is as strong as for many an achievement long acclaimed. This argument consists of Lee's impressively quick notice of Averell's advance to his attack on Fitz Lee; his warning, which reached Culpeper before noon on the day preceding the attackers' arrival at Kelly's Ford, obviously came from a source that could communicate with headquarters much more quickly than any scout could. Another impressive point is the fact that no such timeliness was achieved after the supposed underwater telegraph line was shut down.

However, the story meets a strong rebuttal in General Patrick's diary. April 21, when the report of the cross-river line was circulating, was the day he went calling on his secesh lady friends to inquire about visual signaling; this indicates that either no telegraph line had been found or, if it had, he had heard nothing of the matter, even though he was the officer having primary concern for the army's security. Although his anxiety about enemy signaling is revealed by three diary entries in a nine-day period during the last half of April, there is no mention of a telegraph line or even a suspicion of one. And no record of such an incident is found in headquarters files.[43]

The simple fact of Patrick's inspection at the Lacy house argues strongly against the reality of the reported telegraph line. If he had known of such a line, he would not have needed to "ascertain *how* communications get across the river."

Even the newspaper accounts betray the story as a fabrication. The *Inquirer* and the *Times* versions agreed only that there was an underwater telegraph line connecting Fredericksburg with Falmouth; they contradicted each other in their answers to the two basic questions, how the discovery of the clandestine operation came about and what arrests resulted. The writers' dependency on guesswork produced these discrepancies and led to some foolish errors. For example, the *Inquirer*'s claim that the sounds made by the telegraph instrument were detected by a passerby implies a carelessness on the part of the operator that is almost unbelievable; the instrument that his telegraph key activated was called a *sounder* precisely because its clattering was quite loud. Even more improbable is the *Inquirer*'s claim that the superior officers of the soldier who heard those sounds instructed him, an enlisted man, to enter the house and take appropriate action. That is glaringly inconsistent with the army's way of doing business; such a matter would have been placed promptly in the hands of no less an official than General Patrick.

The *Times* account raises the obvious question: how could a telegraph line carry a current under water when the section of wire strung on the bank at Falmouth was so poorly insulated that it was "live" to the touch? If Confederate installers had wire capable of underwater service, they would not have left a link on the ground so weak as to threaten the whole operation.

Although the Confederates' early discovery of Averell's movement against Fitz Lee was an impressive piece of intelligence work, its quick reporting is not necessarily to be credited to cross-river telegraphy. It could have been accomplished in the same way as the cross-river convey-ance of Isaac Silver's reports, the information having been obtained by the kind of spying Patrick suspected was going on at the Lacy house. Or it could have been based on nonalphabetic (visual) signals. Either of these possibilities is a plausible explanation of Lee's order to Longstreet, which evidently assumed that the force in motion might be Hooker's whole army. Lee's mistaken action could have been caused by a spy's picking up information that was only fragmentary, or by the inability of nonalpha-betic visual communication to convey more than the existence and direc-tion (upriver or downriver) of an enemy movement.

In fact, none of the intelligence we know Lee to have had could have reached him only by way of a telegraph line from Falmouth. For proof, this story of underwater telegraphy has only itself, as printed in two newspapers — each version disproving the other. All this leads to the conclusion that the underwater telegraph story was a mere rumor that two newspapers decided to take a chance on.

.. .. ..

Even his labors on behalf of the army's security did not provide enough activity to keep Patrick from being edgy. The campaign could not get into motion too soon to suit him — not because of any especial pugnacity but simply because he had had his fill of waiting. The cold, wet weather that was delaying the grand campaign set his mood to oscillating. One day he was thoroughly angry: while struggling with the problems of the security of the impending movement of an army, he had to take time for so nettlesome a matter as the case of an embalmer who was misrepresenting himself as doing business for the government; Patrick sent the man away "with a flea in his ear." Anger gave way to disgust when he had to hear a liquor-selling charge against the headquarters sutlers — one named Mar-cus Aurelius Cicero Stanley and the other identified simply as Gallagher. Although Patrick had his doubts about the truth of this particular charge, it caused him to reflect that there was unquestionably a great deal of corruption around headquarters.[44] The next day, Sunday, April 26, the thought that "May Day is close at hand and we *must* move" brought on a somber feeling. The war seemed to be standing still: exactly a year ago, he recalled, he had been preparing to move his brigade, then part of McDowell's corps, from Falmouth over to Fredericksburg. He recorded poignant recollections and spent hours looking over "the old familiar hymns and carry[ing] myself in imagination on back to my old Home. . . . I have thought a great deal about my family today and am deeply anxious about them all, especially about the little Boys."

Patrick was shaken out of this mood the next day when Hooker called

him in for a long talk in which he unfolded the campaign plan in detail
— thus making Patrick privy to secrets denied to the corps commanders.
But soon he had to see Butterfield about the protection of the Aquia base
while the army was away, and "the Great Mogul . . . concluded to tear
things up and talked very large." Then came the unimportant but annoying news that Lafayette Baker in Washington had relieved a Southern
woman of a parole granted by Patrick. He ended his diary entry on a
note of concern for the campaign: "There is a curious state of things now
in this Army. Confidence enough is felt in Hooker, I think, but not a
great deal in some of his corps commanders." He was especially dubious
about Sedgwick, "a good honest fellow and that is all," who was to have
the most important assignment of any of the corps generals, also about
"Sickles & the most of his crew, [who] are very poor concerns." Only
General Reynolds came in for praise; Patrick took comfort in the thought
that after the initial moves Hooker would be controlling the entire operation.[45]

Patrick's state of mind was shared throughout headquarters. The officers did not know what Hooker's plan was, but they knew he must have
had one ready on the 13th, and the strain of waiting made the coming
battle seem like a kind of relief. On the 24th one of the aides wrote
home, "Could you come into Headquarters at any time during the day
you would see that something was wrong; every one is moving around in
an aimless, nervous way, looking at the clouds and then at the ground,
and in knots trying to convince themselves that it is going to clear off and
they will be able to move day after to-morrow."[46]

16

. . . .

PINPOINT INTELLIGENCE
AND HAIRLINE PLANNING

April 15–30, 1863

W HILE STONEMAN and the headquarters staff were fretting over the weather and Patrick was busy with security problems, Sharpe and his men were putting the delay to use. On April 15, the day Stoneman reached the Rappahannock to find it becoming impassable for cavalry, Ebenezer McGee crossed the river with another report from Isaac Silver, his third. Possibly not realizing the significance of his information, Silver opened with an apology:

> General Hooker Sir I am glad to have the opertunity to let you no of what little I could find or learn of the rebble army at this time there is but or about twenty five hundred men at banks ford under General wilcox at the united states ford or bark mill there is only about the same number under General posey mahone is away for what reason I cannot tell they have two batterreys there but their horses is in low order one of the slodiers made the remark and said if the yankies was to come their horses was not able to move the canon I do not expect it is so bad as this but they are weaker thare by one half then they have bin enny thime before since they whent thare and they are very much scattered from a little below the ford [United States Ford] all the way round to ealeys ford [Ely's Ford, on the Rapidan] it will take them at least three or four ours to get to gether . . .
>   there is . . . under posey a little below the ford about ten or twelve hundred campt near gradeys your messenger will tell you ware that is
>   there is no other standing troops from poseys untill you get to the courthouse road leading from fredericksburg to spotsylvania court house . . . the whole boddey of their arme except Jacksons core lies camped round about in squads as they can find timber on or near the telgeraph road from four to six miles from fredericksburg
>   the soldiers say them selves there is nothing to hinder the yankeys from cutting them all to pieces with their shells . . . [1]

Here was a new and different picture of defenses in the enemy's rear. Six weeks had elapsed since Sergeant Cline had reported what seemed "a conciderabell force" at and about Chancellorsville, with numerous gun positions and earthworks, some with guns; a battery of howitzers; rifle pits; also a wagon park. Now there were no "standing troops" — infantry and artillery — in a span of country stretching southeastward five miles from Mahone's and Posey's brigades at United States Ford. The unprotected area included Chancellorsville itself, consisting of only a country mansion and its outbuildings but important because five roads, two of them from the upper fords, converged there. Farther downriver, however, were Wilcox's brigade at Banks's Ford and Perry's at Tabernacle Church; only Semmes's regiments had withdrawn, moving almost to Fredericksburg.[2] Silver's report did not mention Perry or Semmes, nor did he report anything about the upper fords of the Rappahannock and the cavalry in that locality. The recent transfer of the bulk of W. H. F. Lee's cavalry brigade to Culpeper County from its posting on the far right, below Fredericksburg,[3] also was not mentioned. But these lacks would have gone almost unnoticed in a report that revealed a five-mile span of country in the enemy's rear that was devoid of "standing troops." General Hooker would find use for that discovery.

Silver's estimate of troop numbers, 6000 to 6200 (2500 at each of the fords and 1000 to 1200 at the Grady farm), was fairly close to the mark.[4] His estimate of the recent decline in strength — one-half of the numbers formerly in the locality — was not excessive, for the arrival of spring weather would have brought a considerable shifting about of troops. Many or most of the units at and about Chancellorsville had not been there primarily to defend the place; like the rest of the army, they were simply wintering near a supply of timber.[5]

In several matters remote from Silver's direct observation he erred; however, as he was only one of several sources, no great reliance would have been placed on his statements. Hood and Pickett, for example, he placed in Culpeper County "with about ten thousand men"; but he stated flatly, and correctly, that Longstreet himself was below Richmond, "and I think quite a good many men with him." He said that Germanna Bridge, up the Rapidan from Ely's Ford, was being repaired by the Confederates; since the work was in fact going on,[6] he may have seen it himself, but he interpreted it as evidence that Lee was preparing to move into Culpeper. This was guesswork, but the guess was partly correct, in view of Lee's half-formed intention to make a move in the Valley if Hooker remained in place.[7]

Silver concluded with a demonstration that he was anxious for Hooker's campaign to start, even if it meant a major battle in his own neighborhood:

there is no stores of enny amount at hamilton crossing and in fact it appears their eating is near run out I do not think they are so strong in to forty thousand as they was four weeks ago

I do not think you would have a better time to make a rade on them at bankses ford . . . I think if you would cross about twenty thousand at the united states ford you could sweep your way down as far as the old mine road at the tabernicle church then agein at bankses ford about thirty thousand and you would sweep your way out

Look out for these cursed stewards and hamtons rades in time of battle

your bumshells at the battle at fredericksburg did not much more then one half or two thirds burst

I want to write more but can not for the want of time when you come across pleas let magee see me as soon as possible and I will try to be posted ware the boddeys of there armey is so you will no how to take them[8]

Silver's evidence of weakness on the enemy's left was corroborated by a deserter who came in the same day with an account showing that the concentration on the Confederate right had not been appreciably lessened. This man was a Virginian — his home was near Aquia Creek Landing, the Army of the Potomac's principal supply base — and he referred to his comrades from other states as "foreigners," but while looking down his nose at them he had learned enough of their positions to locate all of Jackson's divisions, which formed the enemy's center and right wing.[9] A Confederate flag message intercepted on the 14th had given Sharpe reason to question whether Jackson's corps was remaining in place, but the deserter's report, because of its completeness and consistency, erased the doubts raised by the intercept.[10]

· ·   · ·   · ·

On April 15 Butterfield told Stoneman that he seemed to be "maneuvering your whole force against the command of Fitz Lee, numbering not over 2,000 men." But three days later headquarters informed Stoneman that he was now opposed by no more than 4000 or 5000 men.[11] This sudden change in number was due to the somewhat belated discovery of the arrival of W. H. F. Lee's troops from below Port Royal to relieve Cousin Fitz at Culpeper so that the latter's troops could go foraging.[12] The discovery of this move was part of a busy day, the 18th, in Sharpe's bureau. Deserters and prisoners showed up from all the main elements of Lee's army — Jackson's corps, the two-division wing of Longstreet's corps remaining at Fredericksburg, the cavalry, and even Longstreet's force below Richmond. What Silver's information lacked in completeness and accuracy now was being supplied by Southern soldiers.[13]

The troops under W. H. F. Lee took position south of the Rappahannock, and Fitz Lee's regiments occupied the north side, facing Stoneman near Warrenton Junction and foraging as far north as Loudoun County.[14]

More information came from the *Richmond Enquirer,* which announced, "The cavalry pickets have all been withdrawn from Port Royal to a point up the river within 6 miles of town [Fredericksburg]."[15] Evidently the editor was assuming the Yankees had observed this withdrawal; he withheld its real significance, W. H. F. Lee's move to Culpeper. The fact that Federal intelligence understood Stuart's concentration upriver with some clarity was probably due to information obtained from one of W. H. F. Lee's men who was captured on the 18th.[16]

April 18 also brought a surprise, the return of Private D. G. Otto, the New York cavalryman-scout, from his imprisonment in Richmond. He had been exchanged without having to resort to any stratagems in the manner of Daniel Cole. Fitz Lee, whose Black Horse company had captured Otto, recommended that he not be exchanged, on the ground that he had been inside the Confederate lines a number of times; but General Winder, administrator of the Richmond prisons, ruled that there was no evidence that Otto was a spy. Winder's decree shows that Otto was in Federal uniform when captured.

Otto was the eighth Northern spy in the eastern theater to win release after being imprisoned in Richmond. The earlier cases were those of Joseph Snyder, George Smith, and Daniel Cole of the Army of the Potomac; Louis Stone, John Murphy, and James J. Callahan of Frémont's army; and Captain William Palmer. The Confederate security authorities are not known to have established the guilt of any agents sent against them except for the four Pinkerton operatives, Webster, Lewis, Scully, and Hattie Lawton.

Otto reported that before being sent to Richmond he had been closely questioned by R. E. Lee and Stuart, who wanted "to know if we were sending off troops from here," but he "gave them no satisfaction." His report to Sharpe consisted of the usual miscellany collected by an observant visitor to Richmond, but it included several points not covered by Cole and Smith, other recent guests of the Confederate authorities. Probably of most interest to Hooker was the observation Otto made on his rail trip to Richmond via Gordonsville, that large amounts of supplies were being shipped to Lee's army from the direction of Lynchburg.[17] Lee, he learned, had received substantial numbers of conscripts, hospital guards, provost troops, and the like from Richmond and the South. An English surgeon in the Confederate army had told him that Federal infantrymen habitually fired too high; "not 10 percent of the rebels are hit below the shoulders," he said, adding that the Southern troops were trained not to emulate the error. Otto had learned the names of several persons who were running the blockade from Baltimore and Washington via the Valley. The fortifications below Richmond, so far as he had been able to see on his way to the port of exchange, were devoid of guns. He had sampled the views of Confederate soldiers regarding the war and believed that while thousands were anxious to desert, the "general opinion [among them] was, that we could not conquer them by fighting, but that we could by starving them." On Longstreet's force below Richmond, Otto had little information, and what he had was wrong, for he placed Anderson's division there whereas Anderson was actually with Lee.[18]

The circumstances regarding Otto's capture turned out to have been as Skinker had reported. He brought back a paper, retained through his captivity, in which the captain of the Black Horse company, 4th Virginia Cavalry, certified that before being taken, Otto had captured and paroled two members of that company.[19]

By April 21 the bad weather, despite occasional short breaks, had become so oppressive that Hooker began to think of pulling in his horns. He wrote Lincoln that he was considering a less ambitious plan, which he did not describe beyond saying that although it could not promise as much as his original scheme, it would at least have the advantage of putting the whole army within range of his personal supervision. But later the same day he was more sanguine, writing Lincoln again to say he was keeping up threats at several points because only by stratagem could he hope to cross the river without great loss. He told Stoneman, who hitherto had been under orders to cross the river as soon as possible, "to remain in position for the present, as [your] presence [on the upper river] tends to deceive the enemy."[20] Those words indicate that Stoneman had not been made privy to the deception begun by the hoax message.

Stoneman was now to await a signal from headquarters. He was offered the assistance of "vigorous demonstrations . . . by the infantry and artillery at Kelly's Ford . . . which . . . will tend to draw the enemy in that direction."[21] Hooker may have viewed a demonstration at Kelly's as an aid to more than the cavalry; it might draw off enough Confederates from Banks's or United States Ford to permit a crossing there.

On the 22nd the picture of great strength on the enemy right, which except for W. H. F. Lee's departure had remained stable for several weeks, was briefly challenged. Lieutenant J. B. Brooks at the signal station at Seddon's picked up a signal message that read: "To Gen H—— all your command to us save your pickets [signed:] Gen Lee." It was evident that the missing word had been "move" or "march," for "Gen H" replied, "Message received. Will leave four regiments for picket duty. Will move at dark."[22] Thus it appeared that the division of "Gen H" — surely A. P. Hill — was being moved from the right to the center of the army. Immediately Butterfield scrawled on the signal officer's report a request for details. But no other reference to this interesting bit of intelligence appears in headquarters correspondence of this or succeeding days. Thus the messages appear to have been written off as an attempted deception, which they probably were.[23] Butterfield had reason to regard them with more suspicion than his own fake message had aroused in Lee.

One conspicuous feature was the direct communication between Lee and "Gen H"; since Hill was in Jackson's corps and there was no "Gen H" among Lee's immediate subordinates, such correspondence would have been irregular and would have brought an angry protest from Jackson (or a repeat of the resignation he submitted during the Loring affair). Another suspicious feature was the use of the signal line for messages that could have been delivered quickly enough by courier.

.. .. ..

While Hooker's hopes were being eroded by day after day of rain, a new blow came when one of his main sources of information was suddenly threatened from an unexpected quarter. Aeronaut Lowe was in trouble with the War Department's bookkeepers. So bearish was Secretary Stanton in any case of suspected invasion of the public till that he did not hesitate to draw Lowe off to Washington at so critical a time. Ebenezer Mason, Jr., of Philadelphia, who had superintended the construction of a gas generator and two of Lowe's balloons, had come to the department claiming that Lowe owed him money. Lowe, it was alleged, had not only withheld wages of Mason and two other employees but had extracted substantial kickbacks from wages he had paid; had shipped off a government balloon for his own use after the war; had shipped off captured tents too; and had kept on the payroll his elderly and infirm father, who spent most of the time in Philadelphia but was with the army long enough to sell forage and flour from the government supplies. Lowe, Mason contended, had drawn rations for double the number of men in his force and had used the surplus to feed newspapermen, who were constantly about his tent. The correspondents also drew liberally on Lowe for transportation by both horse and boat, "which services were generally repaid by puffing the Balloon [sic] and Prof Lowe in their papers." Stanton or Major Turner doubtless heard Lowe's standard complaint of having sustained considerable financial loss in order to serve the government. He was sent back to the army with instructions to submit a report "whenever the convenience of the service will permit it."

Hooker seems to have had his own problems with Lowe. Earlier in the month he had given the aeronaut an activist supervisor, Cyrus Comstock, now a captain. Comstock began by reducing Lowe's pay from ten dollars a day to six, forcing him to dispense with the services of his father and one other employee, and announcing a schedule of ascents that would surely keep the remaining crew busy. The battle of Chancellorsville brought only a temporary lull in the dissension that grew out of Comstock's supervision and Lowe's resistance to it.[24]

.. .. ..

While most of the army was battening down tents and trying to stay warm and dry, Hooker kept the troops on his far left busy with a series of raids and demonstrations toward Port Royal. Lee was more bored than amused, but Hooker received a few useful odds and ends of information as reward for his byplay. These forays began with orders on the 20th for a small detachment to march a pontoon train down the Northern Neck; while "apparently endeavoring to conceal their train," they were to "let just enough be seen to betray the movement." By the time this got under way the "small detachment" had grown to two brigades of Abner Doubleday's division of the First Corps, and its purpose had been enlarged to include a brief visit to Port Royal to investigate the contents of the post office. "The enemy's pickets," Doubleday reported, "offered us every facility for crossing quietly, watching our movements and actually fishing in the river while we were making our preparations. Crowds of females looked on from the other side as if it were a mere holyday performance." But Doubleday had to disappoint his audience: lacking rope to tie his pontoons together, he was forced to call off the attempted crossing. Before returning to camp his men started campfires and erected Quaker guns over a wide area. The enemy was not deceived by them, but messages intercepted by Doubleday's signal officers revealed that the Confederates had a serious misapprehension on another question: they "signalled all along their line that a fleet of [Federal] transports was on its way down the Potomac."

From the fact that his movement quickly attracted a large force to the lines behind Port Royal, Doubleday confirmed that the Confederates were well prepared on their right. This was probably the most useful of his findings.

On the morning of the 23rd two regiments from Wadsworth's division, also of the First Corps, crossed in boats to Port Royal, surprised the Confederates in the town, and returned unhurt with a quantity of army horses and some fresh impressions of enemy strength in the neighborhood. Two days later the commander of this expedition learned that one of his soldiers had also taken a Rebel mail. Forwarded to headquarters, the letters yielded in considerable detail the story of W. H. F. Lee's movement to Culpeper early in the month, and of the disposition of a regiment he had left behind.[25]

The raids down the Neck were kept up until after the army was in motion. Two demonstrations upriver, at Kelly's Ford and in Stoneman's front, were added for good measure. Discerning the true nature of all this activity, Lee as early as the 23rd wrote Jackson, "I think that if a real attempt is made to cross the river it will be above Fredericksburg." He viewed United States Ford as the limit "within which an attempt to cross . . . may be expected."[26]

At this time Hooker obtained a view of the enemy's theorizing about his plans from Ernest Yager, who had been on an expedition in the direction of Culpeper. Yager came in to Cavalry Corps headquarters on the 23rd with a report that the Confederates thought Stoneman's move a feint to cover a crossing below Fredericksburg.[27] Although that was a possibility that Lee allowed for at one point, Hooker could not have regarded such a report as reliable enough to figure seriously in his planning.

By now Stuart, like his chief, was not discounting the possibility that Hooker's move would be toward the Valley. On April 25 he endorsed a scheme of Major Mosby for a raid into Fairfax County, saying he was "extremely anxious to know . . . whether Hooker is moving any troops up in that vicinity." The next day he ordered Mosby to strike the Federals along the railroad near Warrenton Junction, keeping well away from Stoneman's main force, which was camped at the junction and halfway along the railroad to Warrenton. "Information of movements of large bodies is of the greatest importance to us just now," Stuart wrote. "The marching or transportation of divisions will often indicate the plan of a campaign."[28]

That order could not have been better designed to suit Hooker's purposes. Mosby's annoyingly inquisitive troops were a constant threat to the secrecy of any Federal movement within his reach. And Stuart had now sent Mosby and his band fifteen to twenty miles away from the roads Hooker's advancing army would travel. Such were the effects of the signal ruse of April 13 and subsequent positioning of Federal cavalry: at the height of the battle of Chancellorsville Mosby was occupied in surprising one of Stoneman's regiments at Warrenton Junction and taking a large quantity of arms.[29]

Lee's concern about an enemy invasion of the Valley did not prevent him from allowing part of his force there to depart on a raid deep into western Virginia. News of this movement was reported to Stoneman by a citizen of Maine, a fellow townsman of the cavalry's chief quartermaster. This man had traveled through the Valley en route from North Carolina; presumably he was in the South by permission, on personal business. He correctly named Jones's and Imboden's brigades as the raiding force. Receiving this report from Stoneman, Hooker answered with information showing an accurate understanding of the composition and strength of Jones's command but with no comment on his intentions, which were not relevant to Hooker's own plans.[30]

. .   .. ..

Saturday, April 25, the day of Stuart's orders to Mosby and of Lee's latest instructions to Stuart on action to be taken if Stoneman crossed the Blue Ridge, was a proper time for renewed apprehensions among the Confederates. The day had dawned "bright and springlike, with a good stiff breeze." Under sun and wind, the mud that had engulfed the armies rapidly dried up. Hooker called in his more remote infantry detachments to rejoin their parent units. With the smell of action in the air, all activity about the headquarters camp was now to a single purpose.

Rations were being cooked, but General Hooker was still working out his plan of campaign. Despite the impressive collection of staff studies that had been done for him, the ideas he had expressed to Lincoln on April 11, of "turning [the enemy's] positions to my right," apparently had never reached the stage of a finished plan. In midmorning of the 26th he wired Stoneman for information on routes southward from the upper Rappahannock, "leaving Culpeper and Gordonsville to the right, the best place of crossing the Rapidan, the best roads, &c."[31] That such information had not been collected much sooner indicates that the April 11 scheme had involved crossing the Rappahannock below its confluence with the Rapidan, presumably at U.S. Ford, which was Comstock's choice for any crossing above Fredericksburg (although he did not clearly rule out Banks's Ford). Hooker had now decided on a much less obvious place of crossing — Kelly's Ford, twenty-four road miles above Falmouth. Before Stoneman could reply to his inquiry, Hooker ordered the Eleventh and Twelfth Corps to Kelly's Ford; the Fifth Corps would receive the same orders. Although his movement beyond Kelly's would be eastward, toward the enemy's left wing, his query to Stoneman could also be interpreted as indicating a wider sweep, around Lee's whole army.

This was a wholly new plan, not merely a revision of the preceding one. As Hooker later explained to the Committee on the Conduct of the War, his object now was to "strike for the whole rebel army, instead of [merely] forcing it back on its line of retreat."[32] He meant to block that avenue of retreat by placing his army in the enemy's immediate rear.

Hooker's change of route at the eleventh hour has seldom been noted, and his reason for it has remained unexplained. There was more to it than a desire to reach the enemy's rear; Kelly's Ford, despite its remoteness, was now a surer and safer place of crossing the Rappahannock than any other. Hooker had never cared much for the routes by U.S. or Banks's Ford, which had unfavorable terrain features and were defended by infantry well dug in; Kelly's Ford was defended by cavalry and guarded only by pickets. Averell's crossing in March had earned Hooker's army valuable experience in overcoming a strong picket at Kelly's Ford. If there was now artillery at the ford, as Skinker had heard, the terrain would allow it to be brought under the fire of the Federals' guns. But the main reason Hooker chose Kelly's Ford was that the concentration of Fitz Lee's brigade far upriver and W. H. F. Lee's at Culpeper obviously must have left lightly covered the rest of the span of country that Stuart was

Allan Pinkerton, seated (right), with William Moore, secretary to Secretary of War Stanton. Standing, left to right, operatives George H. Bangs, Pinkerton's first-ranking assistant; John Babcock; and Augustus K. Littlefield.

Colonel Lafayette C. Baker, whose counterespionage work was somewhat less unsavory than the reputation it brought him.

General George B. McClellan's overestimates of enemy numbers deceived both himself and his intelligence officer, Allan Pinkerton.

The heads of the Bureau of Military Information. Left to right, Colonel George H. Sharpe, John Babcock, Lieutenant Frederick L. Manning, and Captain John McEntee.

General Joseph Hooker, who invented "all-source" intelligence.

General Daniel Butterfield, Hooker's chief of staff and author of the hoax message that deceived Lee.

General Marsena R. Patrick, provost marshal general and confidant of three commanders of the Army of the Potomac.

Captain William J. Palmer (right) and William Wilson (below), heads of the team that scouted Lee's army in the Maryland campaign (1862).

General John Pope, who demanded and received good intelligence but exhausted his facilities for obtaining it.

General Alfred Pleasonton, cavalry leader and erratic reporter of findings made by his troops' reconnoitering.

David McConaughy, head of the Gettysburg group of citizen scouts and spies.

Belle Boyd, "the Civil War's most overrated spy."

Rose Greenhow and her daughter, Rose, in Old Capitol Prison. Her overemotional Southern patriotism stood in the way of success as a spy.

Elizabeth Van Lew, co-leader of the Richmond Unionists' remarkable espionage successes in 1864–65.

Colonel Albert J. Myer, founder of the Federals' Signal Corps, whose suggestion led to the hoax-message deception.

General George G. Meade, who foresaw the Confederates' concentration at Gettysburg.

Butterfield's draft of the hoax message that deceived Lee.

The Federals' intercept of the Confederate flag message sent to the signal station at Lee's headquarters, carrying the hoax message as intercepted and decoded by Rebel signalmen.

July. 2. 1863.- 4½ P.M.

Major General Butterfield
Chief of Staff.

Prisoners have been taken to day, and last evening, from every brigade in Lee's Army excepting the four brigades of Pickett's Division.—

Every division and has been represented except Pickett's from which we have not had a prisoner.— They are from nearly onehundred different regiments—

Respectfully.
G. H. Sharpe
Col &c.

John Babcock's report of the depleted condition of Lee's army late in the second day's battle at Gettysburg — a principal factor in Meade's decision to hold his ground. Colonel Sharpe's signature is in Babcock's handwriting, a regular procedure in their bureau.

I will not disclose, discover or use the plan for signals communicated to me, without the written consent of Dr. Myer, & the consent of the U. S. War Department.

Edwd. P. Alexander
2d. Lt. of Engrs
&c. U. S. Army

The oath of secrecy given by Edward Porter Alexander, a U.S. Army officer assisting Albert Myer in the prewar development of the flag-signaling system. Alexander, a Georgian, joined the Confederate army in 1861 and installed the system in Beauregard's army at Manassas.

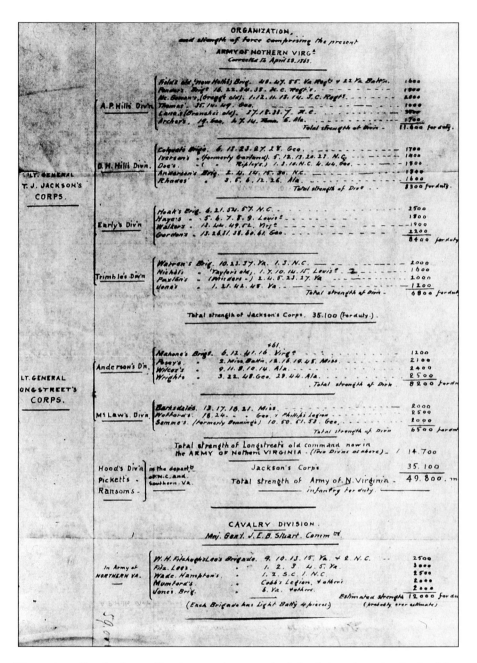

The order-of-battle chart of Lee's army drawn up by John Babcock on April 28, 1863, the day Hooker crossed the upper Rappahannock en route to Chancellorsville. Note the figures for infantry (49,800) and cavalry (12,000); the total, 61,800, was very close to the Confederates' actual numbers.

responsible for. And R. E. Lee's persistence in sparing so strong a force to watch Stoneman indicated to Hooker that the deception produced by Stoneman's position upriver was still in force or the signalmen's ruse of April 13 had not lost its deceptive effect. The weather had been bad enough to provide, for Lee, a sufficient explanation of Stoneman's long halt. As late as April 25, as we have seen, he was still taking into account the enemy's prospective expedition to the Valley. As a result, the disposition of the Southern cavalry could scarcely have been better suited to Hooker's purpose if he had written Fitz Lee's orders himself. Looked at in this light, the Kelly's Ford route was a compelling one for safety reasons alone.

The three corps ordered to Kelly's Ford would cross the Rappahannock, then the Rapidan, then turn eastward and march through Chancellorsville and the gap (reported by Silver) between the rearmost infantry units on the Confederate left. This route would flank the three brigades guarding U.S. and Banks's Fords. They were well protected by artillery and fortifications and could offer serious resistance to a column crossing in their face, but a Federal army crossing above them could easily push them aside if they offered resistance.

Only five miles east of Chancellorsville was high, open ground, and just beyond it, the main mass of the Army of Northern Virginia. His march would be a race against the forces Lee would bring from Fredericksburg and Stuart from Culpeper and upriver, once they learned of the flanking movement. The distance to his first objective, Chancellorsville, via Kelly's Ford would average fifty-five to sixty miles from the various starting points of the participating units. The odds in Hooker's race would be determined by how many of those miles he could cover before the enemy began arriving in force from Fredericksburg, Culpeper, and the upper Rappahannock.[33]

The march could not hope to escape discovery once it reached Kelly's Ford, but the great size of the strung-out advancing forces and their objective would not be immediately evident to the discoverers, Stuart's pickets. Stoneman's advance southwest, simultaneous with the infantry's crossing, would muddle the enemy's view, screening the infantry movements to some extent. In the country south of the rivers Confederate cavalry patrols might discover marching Yankees, but it would take more than a few observations to develop the magnitude of the advance.

If none of these factors worked to the Federals' advantage, there was still a good possibility that the Confederates would be held at Fredericksburg by diversionary movements to be made two and three miles below the town by a three-corps wing commanded by General John Sedgwick. Although the Confederates had improved their defenses in places where weaknesses had been revealed in the December battle and

Burnside's subsequent operations, the downriver sites where Franklin's forces had crossed in December were still practicable for bridging the river and crossing troops in large numbers. Sedgwick's crossing and the highly visible hugeness of his force would give the enemy a strong impression that this was Hooker's main effort. That would detain Lee at Fredericksburg for one or two days; by that time the force that crossed at Kelly's Ford would be ensconced at Chancellorsville and points east. What would happen after that could not be certain, but the plan bore strong promise of effecting a major surprise.

Butterfield's object in his wording of the hoax message had been only to deceive Lee as to the direction Stoneman's massive raid would take. Now the deception would serve a much greater purpose — clearing a path twenty miles wide for the main thrust of the army's infantry. It was, however, only half of the contribution intelligence made to that all-important maneuver. The other intelligence component in Hooker's master plan was Isaac Silver's discovery of a five-mile gap between infantry forces on that flank. Each of these components was a significant feat in itself; in combination they became the genesis of Hooker's whole plan. The connection between the two gaps (the one created by the signal deception and the gap reported by Silver), one leading into the other, was the key to the plan. Thus Hooker made himself the beneficiary of one of the most salutary performances by an intelligence service in the entire war.

. .   . .   . .

In making this change of plan Hooker had not had time to consult with Lincoln. He wrote the President about it on the 27th, after the march of the right wing was under way. The ever-patient Lincoln replied by imploring Hooker not to "waste a moment's thought on me, to your own hindrance, or discomfort."[34]

The march to Kelly's Ford of the Fifth Corps (Meade), Eleventh (Howard), and Twelfth (Slocum) was to occupy two days, ending in late afternoon of the 28th (Tuesday). If everything went as expected, they were to cross before the day (or night) was over. Once on the south bank, Slocum and Howard would take a southerly route and cross the Rapidan at Germanna Ford; Meade's course would be on their left, crossing at Ely's Ford. Roads leading southeast from Germanna and Ely's would bring the three corps together at Chancellorsville.[35] Whether or not the outflanked enemy forces offered resistance, they would have to abandon United States Ford, which would then be available for bringing up reinforcements from Falmouth and Sedgwick's front by a comparatively short march.

One day after the departure of Meade, Howard, and Slocum, Sedg-

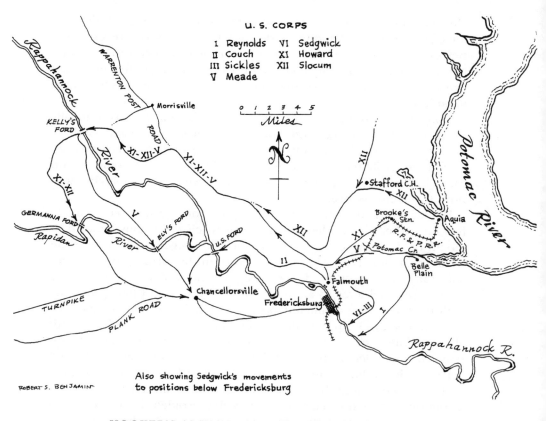

Also showing Sedgwick's movements
to positions below Fredericksburg

HOOKER'S ADVANCE TO CHANCELLORSVILLE

wick's wing would begin moving into position to cross the Rappahannock early on the 29th. On the basis of the Confederates' choice in the December battle, it was expected that they would not resist a crossing, preferring a fight on the heights back from the river to one on the flat ground along the shore. Sedgwick would have his own Sixth Corps and Reynolds's First, with Sickles's Third in reserve. If the Confederates remained in their lines at and below Fredericksburg, Sedgwick was to conduct a demonstration and holding action; but if Lee should detach a considerable force toward Chancellorsville or retreat southward, he was to attack with vigor.[36]

Midway between the two Federal wings was the Second Corps, under General Couch. Two of his divisions were to move to positions opposite Banks's and U.S. Fords, with a view — although it was not stated in

Hooker's order — to crossing as soon as the advance of the right wing forced the enemy to abandon the defenses there. To avoid a repetition of Burnside's error in removing the whole army from Lee's front at Culpeper,[37] Couch's third division, whose camps at Falmouth were more exposed to the enemy's view than any others in the army, was to remain in position.[38]

Stoneman's mission and his route of march remained as originally planned: he would make a wide sweep far to the southwest and south, to destroy Lee's communications and harry him or block the way if he should retreat. Three cavalry regiments under Pleasonton would remain with Hooker to lead and protect the right wing on its marches and provide reconnaissance.[39]

Hooker pursued to the very end his policy of extreme secrecy, modified only where it was desired that news reach the enemy by word of mouth or direct observation. There was still no general order for the various marches. The orders to each corps in the turning column were issued in two sections, the first sending it as far as Kelly's Ford and the second, released after its arrival there, directing it to Chancellorsville. Only the three corps commanders were told their destinations, and they were enjoined to keep the information "strictly confidential." Not until about the time when the second set of orders was issued was Slocum, the senior commander on the right, informed of the operations planned below Fredericksburg. Since Sedgwick had to know the circumstances under which he was to change his holding action to an attack, he was told of the operations upriver, but in a way that avoided disclosure of the turning movement via Kelly's Ford; his orders read: "In the event of the enemy detaching any considerable part of his force against the troops operating at the west of Fredericksburg, [you] will attack . . ." Couch was informed of the general plan at the start of the march, but this disclosure was unavoidable: as next in rank to Hooker he might have to take command in Hooker's place. Only at the very end of the preparations were most of the members of Hooker's own staff let in on the plan, though the aides and adjutants who wrote the orders must have discerned it somewhat sooner. But others of the staff knew nothing whatever of the plan until they saw it being carried into effect by the various movements of the corps.[40]

Not only were the columns marching upriver kept out of sight of the enemy; bugle calls, almost an indispensable part of company and regimental routine, were prohibited lest the wind carry a few stray notes across the river. Whether or not the report was correct that underwater barriers made Kelly's Ford unfordable, pontoons would be used for the crossing; that fact was hidden from the enemy, and from the marching force, by sending the pontoons by the rear, by rail from Alexandria to Bealeton, a station not far from Kelly's Ford.

Sedgwick's march was to be concealed up to the moment his advance troops, crossing in boats, were first seen — or heard — by the Confederate pickets along the river just before dawn on the 29th. This latter concealment, and other "ordinary" security measures, were intended to induce the impression that his was the main attack. In the orders for Couch's movement he was given advance instructions enjoining secrecy, but these were changed, apparently on the 28th, to call for him to throw up works that day at Banks's Ford, where they would be in view of the enemy. The next day, when he moved to U.S. Ford, he was pointedly told that secrecy was no object. The purpose of allowing the enemy some observation of activity at those two fords was to give it the color of a demonstration, an attempt to divert attention from Sedgwick's crossing. This would reinforce the enemy's impression that Sedgwick's was a main attack, or *the* main attack. At the same time it would threaten the enemy with a possible major crossing at one or both fords.

The cavalry, except for Pleasonton's small force, was already out of the way; no sudden disappearance of horsemen from the Fredericksburg lines would alert the enemy or Confederate citizens. Only around Falmouth and in the direction of the upper crossings, it appears, were guards placed on houses. Lee was welcome to information on Sedgwick's and Couch's movements, but he would reject it if it were too obviously placed in his hands.

At the time Hooker settled finally on his plan of campaign, he was confident that it was one his adversary was not expecting. One of his dispatches to Stoneman on the 26th said, "We know the strength of the enemy in front, and he is looking for us to advance in this vicinity." (This belief regarding enemy expectations may have come from Yager's report three days earlier.) The fact that Stuart's positions were no closer than Culpeper was a strong indication that Lee had not plugged the gap in his rear and that he was unaware of Hooker's designs.[41]

One great flaw in Hooker's plan was sending off the bulk of his cavalry on a distant raid. However successful Stoneman might be in cutting the Confederates off from their supplies, he was not going to be doing the cavalry's main jobs — reconnoitering and protecting the flanks of the army. Hooker, with only three regiments of horse on hand to cover the wide expanse of country embraced in the planned movements, was going to be almost without eyes. Like Burnside, he evidently relied heavily on the fact that once the movement started, the burden of finding out what was going on would be on Lee, not on himself.[42]

. . . .

"I beg you," Colonel Sharpe wrote his uncle on April 28, "to rest strong in the faith that we are now commanded by a man who means to fight to win — and that when the blow is struck, it will be one of the heaviest ever felt on this continent."[43]

The blow was already on its way; the right wing had been on the march for twenty-four hours, and everything was going well. General Patrick, despite his recent worries over information leaks, was confident that Hooker's big secret was safe. "So far," he wrote on the night of the 28th, ". . . the rebels have not the slightest idea what we are about. . . . Even the pickets know nothing of it."[44]

While these marches were in progress Hooker stationed himself at Morrisville, where a road from Kelly's Ford met the Fredericksburg-Warrenton Post Road. He was to direct the operations on the right while Butterfield remained at headquarters to provide liaison between the two wings. Sharpe was to join Hooker after the advance was well developed; Babcock would stay with Butterfield to handle the considerable flow of information that was expected from prisoners, deserters, signal stations, and balloons.[45]

Butterfield opened headquarters business on the 28th by calling in Sharpe, Professor Lowe, and the signal officers to read them a lecture on the need "to be vigilant and watchful; to get all information possible." Lowe was at first unable to ascend because of high wind, and once in the air he was baffled by the daily Rappahannock fog, which on this day of all days did not lift — nor, with over 100,000 Federal troops in motion, was a clear sky to be desired. What few camps Lowe and the signal officers could see seemed quiet. For all their technical ability and equipment, their combined efforts produced scarcely as much useful information as did a woman member of the Sanitary Commission, who reported that from her house directly opposite Fredericksburg she had heard regimental meetings held by the Confederates in town the previous evening. She heard them cheering and being addressed by their officers but "could not judge whether the addresses . . . were in contemplation of a departure or of a battle." From deserters it was learned that up to the night of the 26th the divisions of A. P. Hill, Rodes, and Trimble — three-quarters of Jackson's corps — had shown no sign of moving.[46]

Timed to coincide with the army's advance were expeditions by both Skinker and McGee, the former to the vicinity of Kelly's Ford and the latter to obtain last-minute information from Silver. Unlike some of his predecessors, Hooker intended to use espionage as one of his sources of information during active operations. Reports from both agents were received on the 28th. Skinker had accompanied or preceded the march of the right wing and had ridden all the way back to Falmouth with his findings, probably passing close to Hooker's Morrisville-bound party on his return. What he had to say contained a suggestion that the march might encounter serious interference: again he reported that there was artillery as well as cavalry on the south bank at Kelly's Ford. "The idea is current among the people on this side," he said, "that the rebel army has fallen back beyond the Rapidan river and intends to make that the line of defense." But Silver again pictured a bridge-building force at Germanna Ford on the Rapidan; no bridge would be under construction if the Confederates were preparing for defense in that locality. Silver's principal message was, "I think the armey otherwise lays about as it was when I last whrote." Apparently the five-mile gap in the Confederate rear was still there.

The two reports agreed that the enemy was unaware of the turning movement. Skinker's said, "They have no idea of an attack at Kellys." (Evidently this much of Hooker's plan had been confided to him, presumably only after his return from his trip.) Stoneman's movement, he reported, was regarded by the enemy as a feint; the Confederates believed that "the crossing will be made at U.S. Ford where they [are] still busily engaged in throwing up fortifications." Silver had different evidence of enemy unawareness: "wee have not herd your drums nor no movement scarcely at all." He reported further that "the cry is now among the rebbles no more fightting hear the yankeys is moveing away and wee will soon move. . . . I think your time is good to make a sucksessfull [attack] on the mad fanticks . . . god grant you suckssess."[47]

One of Hooker's fears had been that when he moved, the Confederates would cross the Rappahannock and make for his supply base at Aquia Creek. Now a bit of information suggested that the Confederates might be capable of such an attack. Silver reported that Lee had pontoons at Gordonsville and that Jackson had additional pontoons in his own corps. Only the first half of this was correct.[48]

. .   . .   . .

The most useful report headquarters received on the 28th was a compilation of previously existing data on the composition and organization of the Army of Northern Virginia and the numerical strength of its components.[49] Like Hooker's information on roads, his information about the enemy was assembled into a usable summary after the army was in motion. He wanted it for use by subordinate commanders in questioning prisoners.

This report was the work of John Babcock. He estimated the strength of Lee's infantry and cavalry units that would be involved in the coming battles at 55,300 — a percent less than the total in John Bigelow's authoritative Chancellorsville study (based of course on troop returns available after the war).[50] The accuracy of Babcock's figure is, however, largely accidental, for his subtotals for individual divisions in three cases contain substantial errors that cancel each other out. But for the remaining four divisions his deviation was remarkably low — 2 percent or less.

Army of Northern Virginia Infantry and Cavalry in the Chancellorsville Campaign

	As computed by Bigelow	As estimated by Babcock	Babcock's "error"
First Corps (Longstreet)			
Anderson's Division	8,050	8,200	+2%
McLaws's Division	8,345	6,500	−22%
Second Corps (Jackson)			
A. P. Hill's Division	11,351	11,600	+2%
Rodes's Division	9,663	8,300	−14%
Early's Division	8,276	8,400	+1%
Trimble's Division	6,669	6,800	+2%
Subtotal, infantry	52,354	49,800	−5%
Cavalry			
Stuart's Division	4,138	5,500	+33%
Grand total (less artillery)[51]	56,492	55,300	−2%

In one page of figures Babcock signaled the improvement Hooker had wrought in the army's information service. Although his estimates deviate from Bigelow's figures by 2554 for the infantry and 1192 for the grand total, such are the vagaries of Civil War troop returns that Babcock's totals could be as close to the true numbers as totals computed with official returns at hand are.[52] His identification of regiments and brigades, however, was less complete than Pinkerton's, since Pinkerton by the end of the Peninsula campaign had listed all 178 of Lee's regiments. Now Lee had 152 regiments and Babcock had identified 126, along with 30 of the enemy's 32 brigades.

Pinkerton's access to prisoners and deserters had extended over a full year and included the huge number of prisoners taken in the Peninsula battles. Babcock's April 28 compilation was produced without any significant number of prisoners, and from only three months of interrogating deserters, after the arrival on the scene of Hooker and Sharpe. Babcock's standards in accepting evidence of the presence of previously unreported regiments were much stricter than Pinkerton's, a fact revealed by his listing only seven regiments not belonging to Lee's army, a fifth as many erroneous listings as Pinkerton had carried. Of Babcock's 126 "correct" regiments, he placed 116 in the brigades to which they belonged, and all 30 brigades in the correct divisions. Of course he had no "phantom" divisions.

The fact that Babcock's estimate was within 2 percent of the "official" figure in the case of four of the six infantry divisions but missed by 14 and 22 percent in the other two cases is doubtless a reflection of the numbers of deserters from the various divisions. The even larger discrepancy in the total for the cavalry would have been due to its remote postings;[53] for any would-be deserter from the Confederate cavalry, the Federal lines for some months now had been quite a long ride, with a river to cross. The four remarkably close estimates — for the divisions of Anderson, Hill, Early, and Trimble — reflect an additional factor: an improved interrogating technique. As their knowledge of the makeup of Lee's army grew, Babcock, Sharpe, and McEntee were able to take an increasingly effective line of questioning. Much effort was devoted to refining their estimates of company and regimental strengths; the result was regimental averages mostly in the 400 to 500 range but some as low as 300, and even 280.[54]

This improvement in the information service was well understood by Hooker. One example of his confidence in Sharpe's bureau was the assurance he had given Stoneman on the 26th as to the reliability of his information on Lee's strength and expectations of Federal action. Another indication was the assured tone in an April 27 letter to Lincoln in which he detailed the new plan. There were no subjunctives in his statements about the enemy's situation or his own forces' routes and timetables; the only "if" he permitted himself had to do with the weather. In fact news of the competency and successes of Sharpe's bureau was coming to notice outside headquarters and even outside the army, possibly with a boost from Hooker himself. A visitor to the army at this period wrote, "We have a moral certainty of all that is necessary to know in regard to the enemy, every regiment and brigade, division, etc., all their latest arrivals and departures, etc., all collated, compared from many sources, and fully confirmed. The secret service of Gen. Hooker is far superior to anything that has ever been here before. . . . Nothing transpires in the enemy's camp that he is not speedily informed of."[55] This exaggeration of the bureau's effectiveness has the flavor of the boasts Hooker is known to have made at this stage of his campaign. He may not have been the source of the leak, but it is plain that he did not surround his intelligence bureau with the high secrecy in which he cloaked his campaign plans.

. . . .

The thick sky that frustrated Professor Lowe and the signal officers early on the 28th turned into rain in a few hours. The right wing, whose progress on its long march was already behind schedule, was further slowed. In midafternoon Hooker ordered Sedgwick to hold back because of the delay on the right. But once Kelly's Ford was reached, there were no more hitches and halts. About 6 P.M. 400 men of Adolphus Buschbeck's brigade crossed the river in boats downstream from the ford and in cooperation with engineer troops began laying down the pontoons.

According to Howard, to whose corps the brigade belonged, the defenders gave up after firing exactly one shot.

Stuart had been completely surprised. Kelly's Ford was in the Federals' possession by the time he learned they were attempting to cross. Hooker had marched 39,000 men an average distance of twenty-eight miles, most of it on the much traveled Fredericksburg–Warrenton Post Road, undetected by any Confederate force that could do so much about the movement as to send word of it to higher headquarters. If any citizen on the march route worked his way past the Federals' house guards, he did not get his news to any Confederate outpost. Mosby's rangers, ordinarily Stuart's best hope of receiving such a warning, were engaged, as we have seen, in a project well removed from the Federal infantry's line of march, and any other scouts Stuart had were busy watching Stoneman.

The surprise was produced by a deception within the cavalry's larger deception. Buschbeck's brigade, one of two infantry units that had accompanied Stoneman, had been in the vicinity of the ford for two weeks. This was one of several actions Hooker designed to amuse the enemy while he was waiting for good weather and searching his mind for the right plan. But two weeks was a much longer time than any demonstration could last without betraying itself as a feint. Buschbeck lapsed into inactivity, which further persuaded Stuart that the visit to the upriver country by these infantrymen was a sham. Thus Stuart and his men became accustomed to the presence of considerable numbers of Yankee infantry bent on no very aggressive purpose. Buschbeck effected a deception merely by sitting still; when the leading elements of Hooker's turning movement reached Kelly's on Tuesday, their appearance evidently caused no alarm until they began laying down pontoons. Stuart's after-action report opens with a discussion of Buschbeck's prolonged feint, by way of explaining why the enemy's crossing was so easy: the force he had posted to defend the ford was unable to reach the point of the enemy's crossing until their numbers (Buschbeck's 400) were so great that resistance would have been futile. Stuart did not try to explain why the long march from Falmouth and vicinity escaped the observation of his scouts.[56]

By 10:10 P.M. Slocum was able to telegraph Hooker that the bridge was complete; Hooker then rescinded the order holding Sedgwick back. First across the bridge was Howard's corps, then Slocum's, finally Meade's, leaving the bridge for Stoneman's immediate use. It was now 11 A.M. Wednesday, April 29.

Meade, taking the more easterly of the two roads to Chancellorsville, arrived at Ely's Ford on the Rapidan in late afternoon. Encountering no resistance from the few lookouts posted there, the troops immediately began fording the swift, hip-high stream. Slocum's corps led Howard's in the march to Germanna Ford, meeting there the Rebels' 125 bridge builders, who fired a few shots and then surrendered. The Yankees put the enemy materials to immediate use, hastily constructing a footbridge. The column finished crossing at dawn Thursday.

Hooker's second set of orders to the right wing, issued on the march, set forth his conviction that from the moment Chancellorsville was reached, "all will be ours." That objective now lay ten unobstructed miles ahead.[57]

The left wing, whose advance was delayed by rain until Wednesday afternoon, also surprised the enemy, without attempting to do so. No resistance was met, but an unexpected haul of prisoners was taken; they told Sharpe that the movement was not suspected until Sedgwick's pontoniers began laying his bridges.[58]

．．　．．　．．

From the beginning of the river-crossing operation at Kelly's Ford until General Lee became aware that the Federals had crossed, more than a half-day passed. It was almost another twelve hours before he learned that their march was directed at his army. So long a delay in enemy headquarters' discovery of his three-day turning movement and its objective was more than Hooker could have hoped for.

The first cavalry commander to learn of the action at Kelly's Ford was W. H. F. Lee, at Brandy Station. When the news reached Stuart at Culpeper, at "about 9 p.m.,"[59] it was too late for him to telegraph a report to R. E. Lee. His telegrams to Fredericksburg had to be relayed through Staunton and then Richmond, and it appears that on at least one of the three legs of that route there was no nighttime operation. His thirty-five-mile cross-country separation from Lee evidently was considered too great for a courier to traverse it at night. The result was that Sedgwick's Wednesday afternoon crossing below Fredericksburg became known to Lee before he learned of Tuesday evening's crossing upriver.[60]

And Stuart's telegram reporting that crossing mistakenly pointed to the rail junction at Gordonsville, twenty-seven miles southwest of Kelly's Ford, as the Federals' objective. Germanna Ford on the Rapidan, Slocum and Howard's objective, was straight south of Kelly's Ford, but the first leg of that march was south-southwest, in the general direction of Gordonsville, and Stuart too readily deduced that that was the enemy's objective. Receiving this report Wednesday morning, R. E. Lee assumed that Gordonsville would also be the objective of the Federal cavalry, which was then crossing. On Lee's recommendation the War Department began collecting an emergency defense force at Gordonsville, beginning with a detachment from Richmond, and notified Longstreet that his divisions were wanted back at Fredericksburg.[61]

Stuart had identified the advancing Yankees as belonging to Howard's corps by capturing a Belgian officer in General Carl Schurz's division of that corps. In telegraphing this development to Richmond, Lee, apparently unaware of Howard's advancement to command of a corps, referred to him as the head of a division. But Lee did not overlook the fact that this "division" contained six batteries — enough artillery for a corps. The captive officer said there were 20,000 in the Federal column; that was reduced to 14,000 in a later version. He did not know what units other than the Eleventh Corps were in the movement — an unawareness that casts a favorable light on Hooker's secretiveness.[62]

The supposed threat to Gordonsville was Lee's only news from upriver until 6:30 P.M. Wednesday, when couriers reached him with the news that Germanna and Ely's Fords were now in the enemy's possession. These reports evidently were from General Mahone, whose source for Ely's Ford was a pair of cavalry pickets who had escaped from the encounter at the ford. Enemy cavalry was reported at Ely's, and cavalry and infantry at Germanna; that was all that was known.[63]

Now, almost a full day after the Federals had set foot on the south bank of the Rappahannock, Lee could see, from the sketchy information the couriers brought combined with Stuart's discovery of a sizable infantry force (Howard's "division" with its corps-sized complement of artillery), that his own army was a target, or *the* target, of the enemy's upriver movements. However, with what appeared to be a full-scale advance by Sedgwick in his front, he spared only one brigade, Wright's, from Fredericksburg to reinforce the rear. He ordered General Anderson to assume command there, where four brigades of his division were already stationed. Early Thursday he telegraphed Davis reporting Stuart's captures and saying the enemy's object "evidently [is] to turn our left."[64]

By this time Stuart had intelligence that would confirm Lee's inference. On Wednesday afternoon, receiving picket reports of the continued presence of enemy infantry to the south of Kelly's Ford, he took cavalry from Culpeper to reinforce the small parties that all day had been harassing the head and rear of the Slocum-Howard column. The march of those two corps had turned from its south-southwesterly course and was now headed southeast, toward Germanna Ford. Stuart had brought enough force to pierce the column; he took prisoners not only from Slocum's and Howard's corps but also from Meade's. As Meade's march route was several miles away, these troops would have been members of a connecting patrol — a lucky find for Stuart.[65]

He had established that the Federals' objective was Lee's left flank rather than Gordonsville and that their force consisted of at least three infantry corps. Lee's receipt of the telegram containing these highly significant findings almost certainly was delayed until sometime Thursday morning.[66] By that time unaggressiveness on the part of Sedgwick's force was making it apparent that this was no more than a huge demonstration. But even this assessment, combined with the discovery of considerable enemy forces in his rear, did not immediately move Lee to start any more brigades in that direction.

When Anderson reached Mahone and Posey Wednesday midnight, they had responded to the news from Germanna and Ely's Fords by transferring their brigades from the U.S. Ford position to Chancellorsville, an obvious goal of the approaching enemy. Anderson soon moved them, and with them Wright's brigade, to a position three miles closer to Fredericksburg.[67]

That move increased to twenty miles the length of undefended roadway between Kelly's Ford and the rear of Lee's infantry.[68] At the eastern end of that twenty miles the Federals would be within six miles of Fredericksburg. Those mileages, particularly the latter, are a measure of the level of perfection of Hooker's plan. But there were other factors in this success. One was the element of luck. Even the most comprehensive system of house guards could not insure total secrecy for the long march to Kelly's Ford of 39,000 men. Hooker gambled that either no one would get through his security screen or, if someone did, the information he carried would be too scanty to betray the immensity of the movement. He also gambled that the scouts Lee or Stuart routinely had in the country beyond the Federals' right flank would be (as Mosby's whole command actually was) out of position for discovering the movement or for getting around the heads of the Slocum-Howard column and Meade's column to cross the Rappahannock with their findings. Hooker won that gamble — he had done his best to arrange the odds in his own favor — and with it a head start in his race against Lee's discovery of what was going on up the river.

Hooker's good luck was bolstered by Confederate errors. The mistaken assumption that the invading infantry was heading for Gordonsville delayed by a half-day Lee's learning of the threat to his left. Another error was a delay by the harassers of the Slocum-Howard column in getting the word to Stuart of the true direction of the invaders' march. Prompt reporting of that could have enabled Stuart to make the captures that revealed the size of the invading force, in time to get off a message before his roundabout telegraphic connection with Lee closed down for the night. But the greatest error was Lee's and Stuart's persistent concern with the threat posed by the Federal cavalry's position so far upriver; the deception that began with the signalmen's planted message was never penetrated.[69] The Federals' well-known "Valley fixation" now had a Confederate counterpart; so many cavalry regiments, and so much attention, had been diverted to that threat that when the expected general advance of the Federals finally came, Stuart did not have his men where they would do the most good — on Lee's left flank. So placed, even his two small brigades could have seriously delayed the invaders at Kelly's Ford or, if surprised there, at the unruly Rapidan. History might then record the Battle of Rapidan River instead of the Battle of Chancellorsville. But by the time the actual direction of the Federals' march was discovered, they were so far advanced that Lee and Stuart feared they would cut the Confederate cavalry off from the rest of the army.[70] The whole affair compels the conclusion that at both Lee's and Stuart's headquarters the wide expanse of country between Stuart's positions and the left of the Confederate infantry had been forgotten.

.. .. ..

Chancellorsville was now within the Federals' grasp at virtually no cost in lives or materials of war. Although enemy error and oversight had helped bring about this situation, the stunning success of Hooker's maneuver may fairly be regarded as an intelligence coup, conceivably the greatest one of the entire Civil War. In all the campaigns examined in this book, even Second Bull Run with its Sergeant Thomas Harter, there is no stronger indication that the successful action a Federal decision-maker took was based on some product of his intelligence service. Yet no statement by any of the participants — Hooker, Butterfield, Sharpe and Babcock (as Silver's managers), Colonel Myer, and the young signal officers on the Rappahannock line — ever revealed the intelligence role. If ever a battle gave a commanding general an intelligence story to tell, this was that battle. But Hooker filed no report of the campaign, published no memoirs or other postwar writings. His only written reference to this feat that has ever surfaced is an unilluminating paragraph in a letter he wrote in 1877 to Samuel P. Bates, who was then at work on *The Battle of Chancellorsville*. Hooker sought to save Bates from falling into an error he felt had been committed by an earlier writer, William Swinton, in *Campaigns of the Army of the Potomac* (1866). To Hooker, Swinton's account appeared to credit, as the chief point in his strategy, the deceptive effect of the diversionary operations of the left wing under Sedgwick. For Hooker's flanking movement by the upriver route Swinton had high praise — its "secrecy and celerity" made it "an achievement which has few parallels" — but he said nothing about any deception that might have played a part in its success.

This treatment of his brilliant maneuver so angered Hooker that his habitually strong command of the mother tongue deserted him. He wrote Bates that "this individual attempts to dissuade and disparage my successful ruse to throw my army across the Rapahannock and Rapidan rivers in [the] presence of a formidable adversary and obscurely . . . disparages the movement." In struggling to find words to denounce Swinton's error, Hooker himself erred: he forgot that the very essence of his ruse was crossing in the *absence* of a "formidable adversary." Also, Hooker could not justifiably have labeled anything in Swinton's account as dissuasion; and Swinton's omission of the ruse certainly did not amount to disparagement of it.[71]

Swinton must simply have been unaware of any ruse, a condition that has persisted among historians of the Chancellorsville campaign to this day.[72] Even Bates's account ignores the deception, although he had from Hooker (as Hooker reminded him in the 1877 letter) a paper on "the means I adopted for crossing the Rapahannock and Rapidan rivers," containing "an elaborate . . . statement of my plans and the reasons for them." Apparently that paper has not survived.

Hooker's rating of the ruse as successful would have been based on the visible results of his flank march, uncovering as it did the enemy's total unpreparedness. Of Butterfield's persuasively crafted fake message that was a key element in the deception, Hooker could have known only that Confederate signalmen had decoded it and forwarded it to headquarters. But the continued presence of Fitz Lee along the route to the Valley assured that deception had succeeded, even if it consisted of no more than Stoneman's threatening position on that route, as Hooker pointed out when he reminded the cavalry chief that while remaining stationary he was accomplishing something.

Bates's neglect of the deception is explained by the fact that Isaac Silver's contribution was a vital half of the coup; any mention of Silver's role that Hooker made to Bates would have been accompanied by a "Don't print that" warning. Hooker, like all other Northern generals, preserved after the war the secrecy of their former spies who were still living among Confederate patriots. Hooker undoubtedly told Bates about Silver; in 1876 he and Bates together made a visit to Fredericksburg and Chancellorsville, during which they would several times have passed very near the farm where Silver lived during the war years.

· · · · · ·

When the Rebels would shift troops from Fredericksburg to meet the force advancing on their rear turned out to be a perplexing question for Sharpe and Babcock. Because most of the Army of Northern Virginia was still in its widely dispersed winter camps, many units had to be moved to new positions for defense against Sedgwick. Many of those moves, as observed from the balloons and signal stations, would not be distinguishable from the initial marches of a general movement toward Chancellorsville. Particularly subject to misinterpretation would be the movement of McLaws's troops from camp sites at and around the town to the rifle pits on the heights to the west that they had occupied in the December battle. Jackson's corps, forming the bulk of the Fredericksburg army, was spread out down the river; movements to concentrate it for the defense of Fredericksburg also would present Federal observers with many ambiguities.

From earliest daylight on Wednesday, April 29, the balloonists and signalmen were at work with everything they had. One of Lowe's balloons, in the air over Banks's Ford, was towed up and down the bank, giving Hooker, who was briefly back at headquarters, something roughly describable as airborne mobile reconnaissance. Signal Corps teams were stationed at intervals down to Buckner's Neck, fifteen miles below Fredericksburg, and upriver as far as U.S. Ford. Fog and hidden roads combined to hinder the observers, but what they saw left no doubt that the enemy was in motion. Captain Joseph Gloskoski, at the south end of the signal line, spotted a marching column of brigade length at noonday. From Sedgwick's crossing a single Confederate column estimated at 8000 to 10,000 was visible in midafternoon, and shortly afterward a signal officer directly opposite the town tallied twelve regiments and sixty vehicles before he lost count in the haze. A large camp of wagons, forming southeast of U.S. Ford, was observed at 5:30 P.M.; this suggested a westward movement of considerable size, but because of malfunction of Signal Corps telegraph instruments and problems with the details of the information, the report was five hours old when it reached Butterfield. Although this was more important than most other reports, Butterfield, evidently worn down by a day of trying to interpret ambiguous intelligence, returned it to the signal officer with the remark that General Hooker had already gone to bed and his repose was "worth more than the commissions of a dozen signal officers."[73]

When Sedgwick and Reynolds began to collect prisoners, Sharpe rode from the right wing all the way around to the left to interrogate them. Butterfield had another high-priority question: Was Longstreet rejoining Lee? After taking a statement from each prisoner, Sharpe reported, "Their information shows that no troops have arrived from Richmond since the departure of Longstreet's Corps during the winter. . . . No movement of A. P. Hills, D. H. Hills [now Rodes's], or Trimbles divisions had taken place up to daylight." Most of the enemy's artillery was not in position, and no fortifications had been built along the railroad between Hamilton's Crossing and Fredericksburg since the December battle.[74]

By Wednesday evening it was clear from prisoner information alone that Jackson's whole corps was present in the lines opposite Sedgwick. Encouraging word was received by telegram from General Peck, who reported affairs unchanged on the Suffolk front; he thought he could "hold Longstreet here for some time."[75]

While at headquarters Hooker gave orders to be sent to Slocum, urging him to press on to Chancellorsville: "The map indicates that from

Chancellorsville to the Rappahannock is a very strong position. You must have that, and move to command the Plank road, which is the line of the enemy's retreat. As soon as you uncover United States Ford, you will be re-enforced by C[ouch] (two divisions) and then probably by S[ickles]'s entire command."[76] By omitting the plan to uncover Banks's Ford, five miles downriver from U.S. Ford but a much more practicable crossing place for reinforcements from the left and center, this order suggests a weakening in Hooker's intentions. His thinking was moving toward an eventual belief that all he had to do was erect strong earthworks at Chancellorsville; that Lee would be compelled to attack the position or retreat.

Before returning to the right wing at midday Thursday Hooker gave another sign of weakening resolve by ordering and then canceling a demonstration by Sedgwick to determine if the enemy opposite him was still at full strength; the demonstration was not to be made if Sedgwick was already certain that no forces had left his front. Sedgwick replied that Reynolds reported the Confederates in greater strength in that sector than in the December battle. But he said Reynolds's corps would make the demonstration. On the back of Sedgwick's letter Hooker wrote, "Let the demonstration be suspended until further orders." At an undetermined point in this exchange Sedgwick wired an addendum saying that Reynolds was "satisfied that the enemy have not weakened their force . . . and that a demonstration will bring on a general engagement."[77] Whether or not Hooker's decision was the right one, these exchanges may help to explain the unaggressive spirit that Sedgwick has been charged with.

Reynolds, whose crossing was a mile below Sedgwick's, reported Thursday morning that two trains had come into Hamilton's Crossing from the south. Butterfield asked if they could have carried pontoons, which apparently he was certain Jackson had. Reynolds could reply only that the trains consisted of passenger and platform cars. Later in the day Reynolds surmised that a force of 3000 to 5000, which had marched up from below Hamilton's Crossing, was from Richmond. Hooker, elated by the progress of his movements thus far, answered that he hoped "they are from Richmond, as the greater will be our success."[78]

Movements of large and small bodies of the enemy were seen during the morning by Reynolds and the signal stations on the left. These suggested no more than consolidation of the enemy's positions; the general tenor of the signal officers' reports supported Sedgwick's and Reynolds's contention that the Confederates in their front were at full strength.[79] But early in the afternoon Reynolds got the impression that the enemy was passing troops up to Fredericksburg and beyond. The same suggestion was conveyed in a message from General Gibbon, commanding the division holding at Falmouth, reporting that the force in his view was reduced. None of this, however, was considered significant by Butterfield, who wrote Hooker two or three hours after the latter's departure from headquarters that there was "no apparent diminution in enemy's strength in front of Sedgwick." And a later report by Lowe, who ascended at Sedgwick's headquarters and remained aloft until after dark, seemed to support Butterfield's view.[80]

Butterfield's rejection of Reynolds's and possibly Gibbon's reports seems arbitrary, but it produced a correct result. Although the Confederates for more than a day had been busy realigning their forces at and below Fredericksburg, the only unit leaving that front was the brigade Anderson had taken with him, out of sight of Federal observers, Wednesday night.[81] Two days had passed since the Federals first exposed their advancing columns to enemy view at Kelly's Ford, yet the only observable enemy movements were in reaction to Sedgwick's crossing. The secret that Hooker had guarded so carefully seemed to be still holding up. To General Patrick this success seemed too good to be true. Even after supervising the handling of some eighty prisoners taken by Sedgwick and Reynolds, and observing in his diary that the enemy had been "taken napping, undoubtedly," he remained uneasy. The same lack of firing that meant an absence of resistance on the right made a "stillness [that] has been painful."[82]

17

· · · · · · · · · · ·

PARALYZED BY A REAL JACKSON
AND A PHANTOM LONGSTREET

Thursday, April 30–Tuesday, May 5, 1863

T O REACH CHANCELLORSVILLE from their crossing of the Rapidan, Meade's troops had a march of only five miles, half as long as
Slocum's and Howard's. When he arrived there shortly before
noon Thursday, Meade found four ladies well turned out for the occasion, on an upper veranda of the Chancellor mansion. "Neither abashed
nor intimidated, [they] scolded audibly and criticized severely. They
urged a more expeditious movement, representing General Lee as just
ahead, and anxiously awaiting an opportunity to dispense 'the hospitality
of the country.'"[1] General Meade would have been too tactful to reply
that the ladies were better prepared to receive Yankee visitors than General Lee seemed to be.

Slocum arrived during the afternoon to find Meade in a spirit as
pugnacious as that of the Chancellor ladies. Meade had already sent a
brigade to scout well beyond Chancellorsville. He greeted Slocum with a
strong expression of pleasure at the success of Hooker's strategy and
urged that they keep moving, his own corps on the turnpike and Slocum's on the Plank Road. But Slocum showed him an order from Butterfield reading, "The general directs that no advance be made from
Chancellorsville until the columns are concentrated. He expects to be at
Chancellorsville to-night."[2] This meant that the three-corps right wing
was not to move until joined by Couch's two divisions, then en route from
Falmouth, and Sickles's corps, from Sedgwick's wing.

Before returning to the right wing Hooker issued a congratulatory
order:

> It is with heartfelt satisfaction the commanding general announces to
> the army that the operations of the last three days have determined that
> our enemy must either ingloriously fly, or come out from behind his

defenses and give us battle on our own ground, where certain destruction awaits him.

The operations of the Fifth, Eleventh, and Twelfth Corps have been a
succession of splendid achievements.[3]

These words are said to have generated wild enthusiasm throughout the army, but the soldiers did not have to read between the lines to
see that the enemy was unlikely to fly without a pitched battle in which
there would be many casualties. And the implication that any battle
would be a defensive one, on the Federals' "own ground," was misleading, for Hooker still intended to make the attack that everyone expected
as the culmination of the long march.[4]

He had planned to establish a crossing at Banks's Ford and take position on high, clear ground in that vicinity, as the initial move toward an
assault on Lee's Fredericksburg lines. That position was his true objective. Couch and Sickles were to have marched directly there from the
Banks's Ford crossing, but Hooker changed their orders and put them
on a less exposed route, via United States Ford, terminating at Chancellorsville. He was proceeding with attack plans in his own good time,
delaying movement until Friday; the position near Banks's Ford was to
be only a way point near the end of an advance starting from Chancellorsville.[5]

Hooker's order delaying advance beyond Chancellorsville until his
arrival there is sometimes seen as the beginning of a loss of confidence
that was to afflict his conduct of the whole battle. No such theory is
necessary to explain this order; it came naturally to Joe Hooker, who
strongly preferred to have his operations take place under his own eye.
But whatever the cause, it was a costly delay.

Back at Falmouth General Patrick continued to be both elated and
uneasy. After talking at length with both Hooker and Butterfield he
wrote, "So far as we can . . . judge, [the Confederates] still believe that we
are making all our arrangements for a ground attack in front of Sedgwick
& Reynolds. The body of their troops are there apparently and unless
they are playing us a deep game, we shall cut them sadly to pieces —
being on their flank & rear. We cannot understand how they are so
blinded and that is all that makes us afraid some deep plan is laid for us.
However, my belief is that they must skedaddle tonight, or get a terrible
licking, hereafter."[6]

Lee was holding still, but only until the late hours of Thursday. Sedgwick's own inactivity had continued; so quiet was his front that, in observance of a day of national humiliation declared by President Lincoln, the
chaplains in a few regiments had actually succeeded, "with the aid of
more or less coercion, in getting an audience."[7] To Lee "it was now apparent that the main attack would be made upon our flank and rear."
Leaving Early's division and Barksdale's brigade of McLaws's division —

11,000 men — to hold Fredericksburg and the heights downriver, he set out at midnight Thursday for Anderson's position east of Chancellorsville at Tabernacle Church. McLaws marched out first and Jackson followed at dawn on Friday, arriving at 8 A.M., ahead of his three divisions.[8]

At that time Hooker had information, sent by Butterfield at 5:30 A.M., from a deserter, probably bona fide, who could report only that at the time he decamped, Jackson's corps was still in its lines below Fredericksburg.[9] That was enough to encourage Hooker to proceed with his planned advance; but by the time he was ready to move, the enemy forces were only four miles away, headed toward him on the turnpike and the Plank Road, and he did not know it. Silver and McGee's operation was not geared to reporting on tactical situations, and in any case it was now suspended by the presence of throngs of Southern troops in Silver's immediate neighborhood. Now Hooker learned the price he had paid for stopping his advance Thursday at Chancellorsville — and for having held back from Stoneman only 1300 cavalrymen, less than a tenth of the Cavalry Corps. Possessing superior information, he had planned a campaign with the greatest precision of any commander of the Army of the Potomac (or, for that matter, of the Army of Northern Virginia). Without hindrance he had marched to an objective fifty-five road miles away. Now, arrived on the field he had chosen with such certitude, he had no cavalry reconnoitering for the approach of an enemy force from Fredericksburg — a foreseeable action, and one that would obstruct the consummation of his grand maneuver.[10]

The army's considerable observation facilities, centering on Falmouth and consisting of Lowe's balloons and the several Signal Corps stations, unavoidably missed much of the enemy's movement from Fredericksburg, made in darkness and then under cover of the daily Rappahannock fog, which made observers thankful for so much as an occasional glimpse of the reflection from a bayonet. Another obstacle to a successful intelligence operation was a telegraph breakdown; the line worked badly, and at one point Friday morning Butterfield was reduced to sending a message to Hooker via an orderly. Even when operating normally, the wire terminated at U.S. Ford, five road miles from Chancellorsville; Hooker's close hold on his planning secrets had made the Signal Corps officers unaware of the scope of the forthcoming operations, with the result that they had not laid in a sufficient supply of wire for their telegraph printers.[11]

After the fog lifted about 9:15, a series of observations of Jackson's column generated excitement among the signal officers. Lieutenant Peter Taylor at Falmouth spotted a column of infantry, artillery, and wagons that extended over the entire span of a long ridge south of Fredericksburg. Professor Lowe was able to distinguish several columns, "moving with great rapidity." From Banks's Ford the aeronaut in Lowe's second balloon, the *Eagle,* could see a force he estimated at 5000 — probably double the actual number — in a clearing a mile back from the river. At 11:30 Captain James Hall, on the left wing, estimated that troops equal in number to two corps had passed, headed toward Chancellorsville (he was thinking in terms of Federal corps, which were as little as a third the size of the enemy's).[12]

Butterfield, faced with a shortage of telegraph time, forwarded to Hooker only the two most impressive of these reports, the one that stressed the length of a single column and another, also from Taylor, mentioning an amount of artillery that indicated a major movement. In writing to Hooker at 12:30 he deflated Hall's estimate of a two-corps movement, stating that the enemy "cannot, I judge, have detached over 10,000 or 15,000 men from Sedgwick's front since the fog cleared."[13] Hooker would assume that many more than that had passed during the hours of darkness and then of fog, but the message arrived after his troops were on the road; whether it would have affected his determination to advance is uncertain.

Thus the army, Meade and Slocum in front, headed blindly into collision with Jackson, whose state of knowledge may have been no better. Slocum marched up the Plank Road and at about 1 P.M. met Posey's and Wright's brigades, which had been on the road for two hours and were within four miles of Chancellorsville. On the turnpike George Sykes's division of Meade's corps ran into McLaws's skirmishers at one of the McGee farms, drove them a half-mile, and seized an elevated clearing not far from Hooker's designated objective. On the River Road Charles Griffin's division, also one of Meade's, was unopposed and came within sight of Banks's Ford. But the columns were isolated from one another by the enemy and by the pine and oak thickets. Far from being able to deploy and form a front, as their orders provided, they could not even establish contact by messenger. Sykes paid for his aggressive advance by attracting enemy in force to both of his flanks. Jackson had much the shorter front and was near his division commanders, personally seeing to the cooperation of his two columns; the Federals did not have the advantage of a common superior on the scene, since Hooker had elected to remain at Chancellorsville, the terminus of his communications.[14]

As reports from the front reached him, they seemed to show that his beloved army was threading forward in narrow files into what would be one ambush after another. Two of his three advancing columns were not faring well: Slocum's had made little progress and Sykes's was in trouble. Hooker's hope of finding in his path only the two or three brigades that had constituted Lee's left wing had been thoroughly dashed. Nothing had been heard from Sedgwick, to whom he had sent orders to occupy Lee's attention with a vigorous demonstration. These problems were enough to remind him of the attractions of a defensive battle fought on his own terms, spoken of so glowingly in his congratulatory order. Now he received information to the effect that the enemy force in his front was more formidable than he had yet realized. He ordered the army, Couch and Sickles along with Meade and Slocum, back to the line they had occupied Thursday night.

Couch, who was with Sykes, sent a senior aide back to Hooker to protest the retreat with the argument that the position of the advance was valuable enough to be worth the fight it would take to hold it. Hooker sent the aide back with a peremptory order to retire; then he countermanded his order, but the withdrawal had proceeded too far for the ground given up to be retaken.

He telegraphed Butterfield, "From character of information have suspended attack. The enemy may attack me — I will try it." He followed with a fuller statement: "I suspended the attack on receipt of news from the other side of the river. Hope enemy will be emboldened to attack me. I did feel certain of success. If his communications are cut, he must attack me. I have a strong position." The information "from the other side of the river" that induced his withdrawal almost certainly was Lieutenant Taylor's two reports; Hooker was unaware that it was through Butterfield that they had reached him. They impressed him with the "character" of their information; the one that reported a column of considerable length also noted that the Confederates had evacuated the stone wall on Marye's Heights and reduced their force in the trenches south of Fredericksburg, moves that suggested a massive withdrawal from that front.[15]

Hooker's withdrawal is another action that has been attributed to loss of confidence; again there is another, better explanation. Whether or not his confidence had begun to weaken, he had sound reasons, both strategic and tactical, for his decision: a defensive battle was a better bet than an attack, and there was a strong indication that Lee was going to accommodate his wish for one. Lee's communications with Richmond were threatened by Sedgwick and Stoneman, and with Gordonsville by the right wing's five corps. And even without any such threat, Lee was fully capable of deciding to attack, as Hooker had reason to assume.

However justifiable Hooker's withdrawal to Chancellorsville was, it cost him his mastery of the tactical situation. When the action of May 1 closed, the initiative had passed to the enemy.

Lee had a problem to solve before he could even become aware of this changed situation. He was mystified by the light resistance his opponent offered in Friday's exchange of blows. Of the three Federal corps that had crossed the Rapidan, he could account for only Meade's; evidently he had made no captures from Slocum's force. The missing corps might be moving on Gordonsville or Richmond. He had not detected Griffin's division on the River Road, and he had no inkling that Couch and Sickles were at Chancellorsville. His misimpression had two profound results: it encouraged his habitual offensive spirit by leading him to think he might have the enemy outnumbered, and it caused him to raise questions with Jeb Stuart that started the cavalryman on an unusually vigorous search for the missing enemy, a search that uncovered a fatal weak spot in the Federals' dispositions.[16] The positions taken Thursday, to which Hooker ordered a return on Friday, had been only temporary.

. . . . . .

While Butterfield was keeping an eye on enemy movements on the Fredericksburg front and sending reports on them to Hooker, the question of Longstreet's expected return kept pressing itself on his attention. His 5:30 A.M. telegram carrying a deserter's report that Jackson's corps was still in the Fredericksburg lines had included a "camp rumor that Longstreet had gone to Culpeper." That seemed the kind of movement that camp gossip was uniquely capable of inventing, but Culpeper would turn out to be the terminus of Hood's and Pickett's eventual return to the army. In midafternoon two more deserters gave information on Longstreet's whereabouts much more definite than anything obtained up to that time. Like Butterfield, these men were natives of New York State; one of them made an especially favorable impression. While detached from their company to bake provisions, the New Yorkers had talked with troops marching away from a detraining point who said they belonged to Hood's division, then arriving from Richmond. Other deserters reported that A. P. Hill's division had marched off from Fredericksburg toward Chancellorsville.[17]

Butterfield sent one of the New York pair off to Sedgwick with a map and a copy of Babcock's April 28 "table of regiments" showing the organization of Lee's army. When Sedgwick sought Reynolds's opinion, he heard some skeptical comments: if A. P. Hill's was the only division Jackson had detached from the downriver wing, Stonewall was feigning weakness "with a view to . . . tempting us to make an attack on their fortified position."[18] But this view, if Sedgwick relayed it to Butterfield, is not likely to have changed his acceptance of the deserters' story. General Peck also had his doubts about the deserters' truthfulness, for he was still receiving deserters and contrabands from Hood's and Pickett's divisions, and both of those divisions were still picketing the roads in his front.[19] Reynolds and Peck were the only generals receiving the New York deserters' report who considered it a plant, which it almost certainly was.

. . . . . .

"You damned Yanks, reckon you've got us this time!" shouted a Southern voice across the picket line on Sedgwick's front on the morning of Saturday, May 2.[20]

This generous sentiment was not completely shared by General Sedg-wick. Johnny Reb's remark referred to the Federal right wing's success-ful march to the Confederate rear. But Sedgwick could not agree that the Confederates were in the palm of his hand unless he knew which units were on his own front; and the appearance of inactivity that they presented to him was a puzzle. Professor Lowe, who was contending against a wind so strong that he could scarcely use his glass, reported that "they do not show themselves quite so much this morning." He thought the enemy's positions were the same as the day before. A signal officer observed "much less display of force" on part of Sedgwick's front but pointed out that "their position enables them to conceal troops."[21] That there had been more departures for Chancellorsville was the natural inference to be drawn from this picture, but none had been observed and in fact none had taken place.

The division of the front into two halves had created a new intelligence problem, that of determining which enemy units were at Fredericksburg and which on the road to Chancellorsville. Babcock's April 28 organiza-tional breakdown now became a handy tool. A telegram Saturday morn-ing from Sharpe to Babcock gave a rough summary based on captures in Friday's action: "we have evidence that [the] Anderson, McLaws, Rhodes and Trimble [divisions] are in front of us. . . . I think only Early & A. P. Hill are left down there." Hill's position at Jackson's rear had saved his men from capture, with the result that Sharpe assumed that his division was still on the Fredericksburg front.

In midmorning Reynolds's First Corps began pulling out of Sedgwick's lines to cross the river and join Hooker. When the supposedly quiescent Confederates set up an artillery barrage that sank some of Reynolds's pontoons, Sedgwick telegraphed that this would delay the movement. Hooker wired Butterfield, "Sedgwick is all right — he has but Ewell's division [now Early's, as Hooker knew] in his front. The balance are here." Thus Hooker revealed that A. P. Hill's presence on his front was now known, and his (and Sharpe's and Babcock's) understanding of the enemy dispositions now lacked only the fact that one of McLaws's bri-gades, Barksdale's, was with Early.

Hooker acted on his improved state of knowledge by ordering Sedg-wick to attack "if an opportunity presents itself with a reasonable expecta-tion of success." Although in Hooker's view Sedgwick outnumbered Early about two to one, he evidently was mindful of the Federals' inability to hold the ground they won on the downriver front in the December battle.[22]

Sedgwick, thus authorized to use discretion, delayed attacking, puzzled now by enigmatic Confederate activity. An infantry column was seen in motion; the observer was about to report what direction it was taking when it suddenly halted and went into bivouac. Then a battery of six brass guns made a similar false start. The signal station in front of the Falmouth headquarters observed the departure of a battery, but at about the same time a line of gray-clad skirmishers advanced and occupied rifle pits in a far-forward position.[23]

Next came a series of reports of evacuation, beginning with the departure of the Confederate detachment at Banks's Ford, estimated at 1500 or 2000. At 2 P.M. Sedgwick learned from his own front that one battery and part of another had just been removed from their positions and were facing upriver. Lowe added to this picture: he reported a brigade-size movement headed upriver and also the evacuation of the enemy's downriver position. There were still other movements indicating withdrawal toward Chancellorsville whose details did not get into the record.[24]

While this information was going to Butterfield in bits and pieces, and from him to Hooker, an order came in from Hooker, timed at 4:10, indicating that he had seen enough. It told Sedgwick that "as soon as indications will permit" he was to "capture Fredericksburg and vigorously pursue the enemy."[25]

By 5:30 Sedgwick was persuaded that "Nearly all of the enemy's force have been withdrawn." But by the time Hooker's order reached him at 5:50 the picture had changed. After a flurry of withdrawal reports, the army headquarters signal station spotted fifteen guns in place and infantry going into position on Marye's Heights. Nevertheless, Sedgwick advanced and drove a Confederate force from a highway leading south from Fredericksburg. But the enemy stopped him there; clearly the Confederates were not abandoning Fredericksburg.[26]

The reason for this peculiar sequence of events was a march-up-the-road-and-march-back-down-again maneuver that Early's troops had been put through, a blunder certain to tax the vocabulary even of Jubal Early, an acknowledged master of profanity. At about 11 A.M. Colonel R. H. Chilton, Lee's chief of staff, had called on him and delivered, orally, orders to leave a brigade and some artillery at Fredericksburg and join the rest of his force to Lee. Early did not let Chilton leave until he had quizzed the colonel enough to assure himself that the order accurately represented Lee's intention. Then when he began carrying it out, he devoted considerable effort to masking it. He moved the brass guns, chosen for their eye-catching quality, in a way that indicated they were merely changing position on the Fredericksburg front. The movement of the infantrymen into the forward rifle pits had a similar deceptive effect. Many another strange-seeming movement would thus have been one designed by Early to amuse his audience across the river.

Early himself had scarcely left the main ridge behind and below Fredericksburg when he received a dispatch from Lee saying that the orders brought by Chilton should have been to withdraw from Fredericksburg only if he could do so in safety. At this he turned about and reoccupied the ridge, just in time to stop Sedgwick. That evening Signal Corps Lieutenant Peter Taylor reported, "We see distinctly men carrying fire-brands about, lighting them promiscuously"; the signalmen at first viewed this as a deception but then concluded that it must mean that the Rebels were burning goods preparatory to withdrawal. The Federals never clearly understood that the ridge had been very weakly held after Early marched away and had then been reoccupied. To that extent Early's deceptive efforts had accomplished something; they did not delay Sedgwick's advance, however, for the timing of that move was governed simply by the receipt of Hooker's order.[27]

. . .. ..

Saturday morning, from treetops at the edge of a clearing unaccountably named Hazel Grove, a mile southwest of Chancellorsville, Federal lookouts spotted Confederates marching across an opening in the woods to the south. The column was a mile or so away and at the point where it was visible it was headed south. Probably it was also seen from the Federal balloon at Banks's Ford; in any case, the Confederate marchers saw the balloon.[28] The march continued all through the morning.

When the enemy movement was first seen, General Hooker was inspecting his lines; this was necessary because the positions taken late Thursday had not been carefully chosen; the army would be moving out early Friday; but when he withdrew his forward units from their advanced positions Friday, they returned to those same temporary positions. Hooker, on completing his inspection trip at midmorning, found couriers waiting at headquarters with the news from Hazel Grove. He found he could see the same enemy column from his tent — infantry accompanied by artillery, ambulances, and ammunition trains — their southward movement taking them away from the Federal lines. He spread a map on his cot and studied it. Although the movement was in the direction of a retreat, it led him to a concern for the safety of his right flank.[29] He had just seen that it was "in the air" — separated from the Rapidan by a couple of miles of unoccupied woods and fields. On Friday he had directed the Eleventh and Twelfth Corps, on that flank, to pull in closer to the rest of the army, but Howard and Slocum had dissuaded him, arguing that the move would have a demoralizing effect and that the woods were so thick that no would-be attackers could get through. Hooker compromised by settling for the erection of breastworks and abatis in the positions the two corps then occupied. In the Eleventh Corps, the element farthest right, so strong was the belief in the impenetrability of the forest that only the sketchiest defenses were erected. A brigade and a battery that Hooker sent over from the Third Corps to reinforce the flank was refused by Howard as a reflection on his troops.[30]

The enemy movement induced Hooker to send Slocum and Howard a reminder that they were positioned to resist a frontal attack; he directed that they take specific measures to provide against attack on the exposed flank. "We have good reason to suppose that the enemy is moving to our right," reads a postscript in one of the surviving copies of this order.[31]

The enemy column soon came in view of Howard's troops, well to the north of Hazel Grove. Its leading elements had now reached the Plank Road a mile or more southwest of Howard's position. Its direction was now northwestward, but the reports that reached Howard said it was heading west, and Howard reported at 10:50 that he was "taking measures to resist an attack from the west." His "measures" seem to have been limited to bringing up his reserve artillery to face west, and to sending Signal Corps Captain Davis E. Castle out to the far right to watch the enemy.[32]

The marching column was not being neglected by the Federal element closest to it, General David Birney's division of the Third Corps, which was stationed about Hazel Grove, sharing with Slocum's corps the southern edge of the Federal front. Birney's artillery could reach the clearing where the marchers were still seen; he followed up barrages with an infantry attack that accomplished little more than to delay the enemy's rear elements. Still this affair engaged the attention of the Federal command all through the afternoon. Prisoners were taken; had they been adequately questioned, they would have yielded the information that the column's trains were limited to ammunition wagons and ambulances. The absence of all the other appurtenances of military life, even food, meant that the marching men were bent on fighting, not retreating.[33]

By early afternoon the men on Howard's farthest flank were becoming very much aware of an enemy presence. Colonel Leopold von Gilsa's brigade of Brigadier General Charles Devens's division held the extreme right; two of its regiments were facing northwest and the rest of the division faced south, with several regiments strung out along the Plank Road. Before noon there had been skirmishing between Nathaniel McLean's brigade on von Gilsa's left and a Confederate cavalry detachment. Enemy cavalry continued to show themselves; a contact with them by a small unit of cavalry that had been lent to Devens was reported to Howard. Aggressive behavior by Rebel cavalry was not unusual, but now the marching infantry began arriving in the neighborhood. Captain Castle promptly flagged a report of its appearance to Howard; he learned afterward that his report was not credited.[34] Colonel John C. Lee, commanding the 55th Ohio in the front line, had been watching the marching Confederates since 10 A.M. About 1 o'clock he went to Devens, taking with him a messenger from the division's picket line, with a report of enemy infantry and artillery moving toward the right flank. Devens replied that he had "no information to that effect from headquarters, and that if such was the fact he certainly would receive it from corps headquarters."[35] Colonel Lee made two later calls on Devens, bringing men who had seen the enemy massing in their front. On his third visit his persistence earned him an upbraiding from Devens, who said, "You are frightened, sir!" Another colonel, William P. Richardson of the 25th Ohio, came in with four of his scouts who had been well to the front and had seen an enemy mass assembling; Devens rejected the report and ordered Richardson and his men back to their regiment. A cavalry captain whose squadron had returned shortly after being sent out "said he could go but a little way, as he met a large body of infantry"; Devens's response was "'I wish I could get some one who would make a reconnaissance for me.' The captain firmly replied, 'General, I can go further, but I can't promise to return.'"[36]

When the division's Officer of the Day, a lieutenant colonel named Friend, brought in a report similar to the others, Devens treated him more respectfully, but his information met the same rejection, and when Friend took it to corps headquarters, he was accused of cowardice and warned not to bring on a panic. He had found Devens "not in a condition to realize the danger"; the general seems to have spent the afternoon lying down to favor a leg injury sustained in a riding accident. He behaved more circumspectly, however, when his pickets brought in two scouts belonging to one of the other divisions. They reported Southerners in great numbers moving on the corps' flank; Devens put a "trusty sergeant" in charge of the scouts and sent them to report to Howard and then to Hooker.[37]

By now word was spreading that the enemy movement was a retreat. This impression was reinforced in midafternoon when a circular order came from Hooker's headquarters directing that supplies of forage, food, and ammunition be replenished so that the army would be "ready to start at an early hour to-morrow"[38] — obviously in pursuit of the "retreating" Confederates. This order meant that it would now be even harder for warnings of Confederate massing on the army's flank to get an audience from Devens and Howard. As an indication of enemy retreat Howard had not only this order but also a visit from a captain on Hooker's staff requesting the services of a brigade to reinforce the attack on the Confederate column. Their rear guard, according to the visitor, was now being driven so effectively that there was every expectation of reaching the main Rebel force. Howard granted the request.[39]

The commander of the division on Devens's left, Major General Carl Schurz, was in a less exposed position but was more concerned about the corps' situation. He had urged Howard to face Devens's whole division west. Meeting refusal, Schurz refaced two of his own regiments westward and had Captain Hubert Dilger reposition his artillery to fire in that direction. Dilger, a German officer known as Leather Breeches, had heard the rumors of an enemy force on the western flank; he undertook

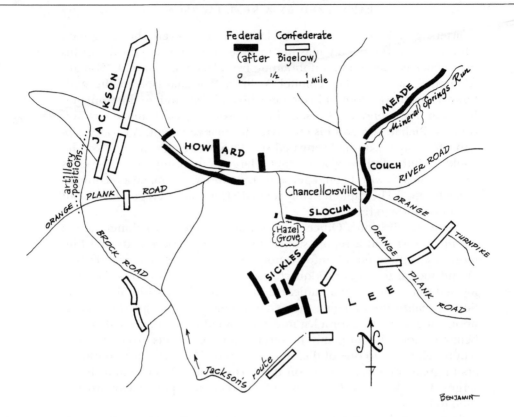

Federal ▬ Confederate ▭
(after Bigelow)
0 ½ 1 Mile

SITUATION, 5 P.M., MAY 2, 1863

a one-man reconnaissance. Riding out the Plank Road, he encountered von Gilsa, who urged him not to venture farther. Dilger ventured anyway, stumbled into enemy cavalry a mile or so farther out, outran them but got lost in doing so, and wound up late in the afternoon all the way back at Chancellorsville. Approaching a staff officer at Hooker's headquarters, he reported that a large enemy force was assembling in the army's rear. The officer advised him to return to the Eleventh Corps "and tell his yarn there." Dilger did so, in a great hurry. Howard's officers informed him that the general was absent, accompanying his reserve brigade, which was being lent to Birney to assist in the attack on the Confederate trains. Dilger, given to understand that scouting was none of his business, could only return to his battery and await events.[40]

Scouting was *some*body's business, though — the cavalry's; but its efforts were no better received. Horsemen attached to Howard's command rode out to clear the front and flank, were fired upon when they got beyond the pickets, and returned, unable to go farther. A captain on

Pleasonton's staff saw an enemy battery posted on the flank; calling on Howard with that information, he was received with courtesy — and with disbelief. But not all of the cavalry efforts were so noble; a reconnoitering party sent out late in the day, when the Rebel visitors would have been well massed, "returned after about ten minutes, [reported] that it was all right, and went quietly to rest."[41]

The most urgent alarm of all had come about 2:45, carried by von Gilsa to Devens and on to corps headquarters. It was a note written by a Pennsylvania major named Owen Rice, commanding von Gilsa's picket line. According to Rice's postwar version, he addressed his brigade chief as follows: "A large body of the enemy is massing in my front. For God's sake, make disposition to receive him!" This news was tauntingly rejected at corps headquarters.[42] Von Gilsa had reports on the enemy's presence not only from the pickets but from two groups of sharpshooters he had stationed a half-mile or more beyond his front. Around 4 o'clock Confederate cavalrymen showed themselves to the pickets, and soon afterward Captain Castle at his signal station also spotted them.[43] Presumably the report of this sighting reached Howard, for Castle was in direct communication with a station at corps headquarters; thus his warning could not be shortstopped by Devens. Howard's reaction is not recorded.

The scene in Howard's camps that Saturday afternoon, a standard part of accounts of the Chancellorsville battle, is a picture of tranquility — soldiers lounging, cooking supper, playing cards, chatting. But they were keeping their weapons handy. We have seen that some of their colonels knew what was going on in the woods to the west; and what the colonels knew the rest of their regiments would soon learn, for the alarm had originated in the rank and file — pickets, scouts, cavalrymen, signalmen.[44] This pastoral scene would be more believable if it had everybody cooking, not just a soldier here and there, all trying to get in a meal before the fight.

So when the cataclysm finally came, around 5:30 or 6:00, it was not a surprise to the men on whom it first fell. The two regiments of von Gilsa's that faced west, though nearest the enemy, fared better, by offering a brief resistance, than their comrades behind them, who were overwhelmed from flank and rear and in many cases could not get off a single shot. The attackers were three divisions of the corps commanded by Stonewall Jackson, leading the last and greatest of his famous turning movements. They numbered between 26,000 and 30,000, and their front, which somehow maintained order despite the thickets, was over two miles long, far more than enough to envelop the Federal wing.

Their movement had originated in the discovery by Stuart's cavalry of the Federals' exposed flank. Neither that discovery nor the envelopment it led to would have occurred if Hooker had had enough cavalry to cover his flanks.

The attack did not bring a halt to Colonel John Lee's effort to impress Devens with what was going on. In his last two calls on the general, Lee implored him to turn and face west, and twice Devens refused. The division crumbled and melted away. Schurz's 5000 next received the attack, stopped it briefly, then found themselves similarly flanked, enfiladed, and forced to retreat. About half of them joined a brigade of Adolph von Steinwehr's division in a last stand. Again the attackers overlapped the Union flanks. What had been a partial panic now became a general one. The Eleventh Corps, composed largely of German-Americans, became known in the army as the Flying Dutchmen. Some of them retreated so far that they passed clear through the Federals around Chancellorsville and became prisoners of the Confederates over on the east flank. One innocent German, hoping to get back over the Rappahannock, made the mistake of asking directions of General Hancock; according to Hancock's biographer, General Francis Walker, the answer this man received "has been handed down by tradition, but it is best not to put it into cold and unsympathetic type." Fear, however, need not have driven the beaten troops so far, for the attack had bogged down in darkness and the attendant confusion, one result of which was the fatal wounding of General Jackson by his own men. About 3000 of the Eleventh Corps were rallied before the night was over but saw little action. The next day, by now occupying a position on Hooker's left, they were out of the battle.[45]

. . . . . .

For many years after the Second World War the U.S. Army, newly conscious of the importance of intelligence, had an intelligence school, situated at Fort Devens, Massachusetts. It is ironic that soldiers received intelligence training at a post named for the general who operated on the principle that the only reliable intelligence was what came down from higher headquarters. That error lies at the root of Charles Devens's actions, or inaction, that led to the rout of the Eleventh Corps. As the officer who received the most numerous and most direct reports of the enemy threat, he seems the most culpable. Perhaps the pain from his leg injury was so severe as to cloud his judgment; perhaps he should have disqualified himself from command.

This was not the first intelligence error in Devens's history. It will be recalled that in October 1861 he had accepted a scout's report based on an optical illusion that in bright moonlight transformed an orchard near Leesburg into rows of tents forming an enemy camp, a mistake that led to the fiasco at Ball's Bluff.

General Howard of course made his share of mistakes: first, his weak response, almost a non-response, to Hooker's warning order about the vulnerability of his flank; second, his belief that no force could get through the undergrowth that gave the Wilderness its name; third, his refusal, like Devens's, to listen to the intelligence originating with his own troops. Hooker, unaware of the daylong struggle of Devens's officers to warn their general, placed the blame entirely on Howard, who, he said, could have stopped Jackson's column before it formed for attack if he had followed Hooker's orders and had heeded "the information furnished by Genl. Devens."[46]

Hooker's belief that Devens provided Howard information that would have saved the day reveals how badly misinformed he was about what had gone on in Devens's and Howard's headquarters. Those generals' belief that the enemy massing on Devens's flank was retreating does not excuse Howard's failure to notify Hooker of that mass, if only to confirm Hooker's impression that the enemy was retreating. If Howard had reported that fact, Hooker probably would have recognized the mass as indicating that the enemy action his order warned against had materialized.

This lack of information from Howard does not, however, explain Hooker's misjudgment that Lee was retreating. The only indication of retreat, aside from his own visual observation, that Hooker is known to have had in time for it to influence his thinking is a statement by Sickles, "I think it is a retreat." This was a mere opinion, weakly expressed and lacking supporting evidence or explanation; it could scarcely have produced the conviction Hooker developed. The part of Jackson's march that he observed was in a southerly direction, but that fact would not have had much influence on him, since his own successful turning movement had begun with a long march away from the enemy. A movement highly suggestive of retreat on the Fredericksburg front was observed, but too late to have influenced Hooker's thinking about the march seen on his right flank.[47] It is known that the rumor of Confederate retreat had reached the remotely posted Fifth Corps; if the news had spread that far, it could have been believed throughout the army, perhaps infecting its commander. Whatever the cause, Hooker somehow acquired a strong belief that the enemy was retreating, for at 4:10 he had informed Sedgwick that "we know that the enemy is flying, trying to save his trains. Two of Sickles' divisions are among them."[48]

Deception by a planted deserter is an unlikely explanation of Hooker's mistaken belief. Jackson's famed midnight cracker-box conference with Lee, at which they planned the flanking movement, seems to have lasted until almost the very hour the march began;[49] they probably did not have time to find a deserter-actor and instruct him. And no record of a deserter carrying a "retreat" story appears in the exchanges between Hooker's headquarters and Butterfield or Babcock. Those two were busy with deserters, though — all carrying the story that Lee was being reinforced by Longstreet. On that May 2 the Confederates were better served by having the enemy believe the retreat story than the reinforcement story, but it was the latter that they elected, or were able, to deliver.

Hooker's culpability is mitigated somewhat by the fact that his subordinates "protected" him from the unwelcome news that the enemy was massing on his flank. He would have been most unhappy to learn that some of his generals seemed to think that intelligence could travel downward through the chain of command but never upward. He had created a competent intelligence service, but evidently he had failed to impress on his subordinate commanders the basic point that they were all part of an intelligence *system.*

That Hooker put a share of the blame for the debacle on himself is indicated by the fact that he did not relieve Howard or Devens or bring charges against them although he did relieve General Averell for a less culpable malfeasance. Hooker believed that Averell had been guilty of near-inactivity for some days; but Hooker's wishes had not been properly conveyed to Averell by Stoneman.[50]

The Eleventh Corps' debacle has several rivals for the appellation "worst intelligence failure of the war," but it was surely the most avoidable one.

. .   . .   . .

While tactical intelligence was suffering a total breakdown on May 2, important strategic intelligence arrived: Joseph Maddox was back in Baltimore after two weeks in Richmond. McPhail availed himself of General Schenck's cipher facilities in the Middle Department headquarters office to send a telegram to Sharpe:

> Our friend just returned. The works around Richmond are most formidable at Meadow Bridge and Mechanicsville road, they are intended for field artillery, no guns in position. 59,000 rations issued to Lees army exclusive of cavalry. Not able to learn their number. Rumor put it down from 8 to 12 thousand. Troops at Richmond are the City Battalion and some artillery. 2700 rations issued to troops in Richmond in active service. Genl Wise has 5000 on the Peninsula. Longstreet has three divisions at Suffolk. When they left Lee they were each 8000 strong. Their effective force all told not over 15,000 men. D. H. Hill is ordered from Washington [North Carolina] to reinforce Longstreets Corps. He may however take Longstreets place at Suffolk and Lee may be reinforced by Longstreet.
> Imboden has twenty five hundred men at Staunton — if not sent to Jones may go to Lee. No other reinforcements can be brought to [Lee] in any reasonable time. Jones has forty five hundred men in Western Virginia. [51]

This report, though providing much good information, must have disappointed Sharpe's hopes by failing to deal more explicitly with his

Longstreet problem. Maddox (or McPhail) did not specify the date when Longstreet was last known to be at Suffolk; even the fact that Maddox had been four days en route to Baltimore was omitted, though that much travel time considerably increased the age of his information. The emphasis was on Longstreet's strength, a matter of much less concern than his whereabouts. Maddox's 15,000 figure was reasonable enough for Longstreet's two divisions from Lee's army, but his placement of a third division at Suffolk was an error.[52]

The 59,000 figure for Lee's army, less cavalry, would have been a remarkably accurate total for the same army *with* cavalry. Maddox's overstatement of 8000 to 12,000 cavalry, based on rumor, doubled and tripled the true figure. His estimates of the forces on the Peninsula and at Richmond were conservative and therefore believable, though not of immediate concern in the Army of the Potomac. The similarly conservative estimates of the Rebel forces in the Valley and in western Virginia were close to the mark[53] and would have attracted notice because of Maddox's statement about Imboden's possible reinforcement of Lee, which did take place a few weeks later when Lee marched for Pennsylvania.

In a letter expanding on his telegram, McPhail quoted Maddox as saying that "a fight at Fredericksburg would be a surprise to the Confederates," who were expecting a more direct Federal move on Richmond.[54] This wording reflects the newspaper blackout Hooker had enforced; by the date of the letter, May 2, leaks were beginning to develop, but McPhail was attempting to describe the attitude of Richmonders at the time Maddox was there.

From Maddox's report it is clear that McPhail had gotten Sharpe an able man and that whatever Maddox's deepest sentiments were, he was delivering honest information for the Union. How he acquired his information is not known. Confederate records reveal a War Department inquiry into his bona fides; that probably resulted from his effort to do business with government authorities, but it could have been induced by an awareness of the deception worked on them by William Crawford, General Dix's smuggler-spy, and exposed by the Philadelphia newspapers after Crawford's arrest.[55] In any case Maddox had made a favorable enough impression on Confederate authorities to gain some access to military information.

. .   . .   . .

Although Jackson's attack wrecked the Eleventh Corps, it left Hooker's forces in a better position than they had been in Saturday morning. Their lines were now more compact, they occupied a dominating height, Hazel Grove, and the ground they held separated the divisions with Lee from Jackson's attacking force, now led by Stuart. But only their physical position was stronger; casualties were heavy and morale was devastated.

General Hooker was not immune to demoralization; he now began a series of errors that are reminiscent of Pope's inability on the Bull Run fields to make a correct move once battle lines were drawn. On Sunday in a general engagement Hooker had Lee and Stuart badly outnumbered but did not use his numbers. The First and Fifth Corps, some of the Second, and the sizable remnant of the Eleventh saw little action; Hooker had forgotten Lincoln's admonition that he should put in all his men.[56] His most serious mistake was giving up Hazel Grove, a move that turned the tide of a hard-fought battle in the Confederates' favor.

Hooker's irresolution may have been partly due to an injury he received during the battle when a pillar of the Chancellor house that he was leaning against was struck by a shell; he was knocked to the ground and briefly rendered unable to exercise command. After the battle he contracted his lines further, giving up the road hub at Chancellorsville and drawing back toward the rivers, with U.S. Ford at his back. The new position between Chancellorsville and the Rappahannock was the one that at the end of the planning stage he had described to Slocum as very strong, one they "must have." His hope of fighting a defensive battle on ground of his own selection was at odds with the obvious advantage of holding a position like Hazel Grove and of interposing between Lee and the half-army now commanded by Stuart.

Hooker now bore down on Sedgwick, urging him westward to join forces. On Sunday morning Sedgwick carried Marye's Heights — this was the Second Battle of Fredericksburg — and struck out toward the rear of the forces with Lee. But Lee, now reunited with Stuart's divisions, about-faced the bulk of McLaws's and Anderson's divisions and stopped Sedgwick at Salem Church. Early, recovering after being driven from the heights, now came up in Sedgwick's rear. Sedgwick gave a good account of himself at Salem Church and in a battle next day nearer the river, but now he had been forced into such a position that his only way of joining the right wing was to cross at Banks's Ford and recross at U.S. Ford. By the time he began that move, it was a move to save his army; he remained on the north bank.[57]

For Hooker had abandoned him. Sedgwick had been given to understand that in advancing westward he would have the cooperation of Hooker's army; in uniting, the two Federal forces might crush the enemy between them — "use him up." Though Lee's removal of troops to meet Sedgwick left Hooker facing opposition lighter than ever — 25,000 to his own 75,000 — his attack never took place.[58]

Hooker may not have learned until too late how many enemy divisions were gone from his front. The number may be inferred from a cryptic telegram sent on Tuesday — after the fighting had stopped — from Babcock to Sharpe, who was still with Hooker. It read, "Early's, Anderson's, and McLaws'. Will send you the regiments by Manning" (a lieutenant in

Sharpe's bureau).[59] The three divisions Babcock named were the three Sedgwick had been fighting at Salem Church. Evidently Sharpe had wired him asking what Confederate units Sedgwick was known to have been engaged with. But Hooker had not been totally unaware of Lee's shift of troops to meet Sedgwick; signal officers back at Falmouth had counted seven regimental flags in a Rebel column heading eastward several miles away, and Butterfield had telegraphed the discovery to Hooker late Sunday afternoon.[60]

Cavalry reconnaissance would have been very useful at that point, but Pleasonton's three regiments were now thoroughly used up; they were being sent back across the Rappahannock. Averell's entire cavalry division was available in replacement; it was now at Ely's Ford, having been recalled by Hooker from Stoneman's march on Saturday. But on Monday Hooker, much displeased by what he described as Averell's failure to attack and rout Fitz Lee's brigade during Stoneman's ride through Culpeper County, now relieved Averell of command and sent his division across the Rappahannock to report to Pleasonton.[61] And this was a time when Hooker needed information about more than the forces in his immediate front; he also wanted to know whether there were any enemy units in position to attack him at U.S. Ford, his prospective route of retreat. He ordered this reconnaissance to be done by infantry, and also sent for one of Lowe's balloons, "inflated if possible." Withdrawal of his entire right wing across the river was very much on his mind; yet he still allowed Sedgwick to hope for a cooperating attack, though not until the next day, Tuesday.[62]

The ground on which Sedgwick was now fighting was the very position just west of Fredericksburg, near Banks's Ford, that had been the objective of Hooker's turning movement. General Doubleday, one of the historians of this campaign, pointed out that if Hooker together with Sedgwick could have driven the Confederates from that ground, the whole scheme of his campaign would have been achieved, though in a way vastly different from his original conception.[63]

. .   . .   . .

Through the last three days of the battle — Saturday, Sunday, and Monday — the question whether Longstreet's two divisions had been ordered back to Fredericksburg plagued Butterfield and Babcock. The Rebels' eager desire for their return and the Federals' fear of it produced a tangle of conflicting reports, of varying degrees of believability. Reports from Army of the Potomac sources, including captured Confederates, said Longstreet was on his way or already present; these were steadily contradicted by telegrams from General Peck. When Longstreet finally set out, his departure would be reported promptly enough by his Suffolk opponents.[64]

On Saturday Butterfield received another prize pair of Confederate deserters, these from Pickett's division, no less. They said Pickett had shown no signs of moving by the time they left the Suffolk front, on Thursday, the 30th. (Even if they had stolen horses, these men could not have traveled the 120 miles to Falmouth in two days. Thus it appears that the Confederate provost-marshal system was so loose that soldiers without furlough passes could ride the trains.) General Peck wired corroborating information, also from deserters from Pickett's division, that no brigades had left Longstreet's command.[65]

Butterfield's next source, on Sunday, was a captain in the enemy's Washington Artillery, who reported that Hood's and Pickett's divisions were "expected tonight." Butterfield reported to Hooker that the general impression among the many prisoners received that day "seems to be that we shall hear from Hood before long." He also pointed out that trains had been coming up from the direction of Richmond all through Saturday night and the early hours of Sunday, though a principal object of Stoneman's raid was wrecking the Richmond-Fredericksburg railroad. But in a separate message at about the same hour Butterfield sang a different tune: 824 prisoners had been received, and still there was "nothing definite or certain as to any reinforcements of the enemy."[66]

Butterfield's caution on the Longstreet question was induced by a report Babcock sent him after examining many of Sunday's prisoners, some of whom had been sent over from the right wing, where Sharpe had already examined them. Prisoners from Early's command had confidently expected 10,000 reinforcements that supposedly were only an hour away when Sedgwick's attack struck Marye's Heights. But in Babcock's questioning it developed that the expected reinforcements were to be from parts of Lee's army already on the field, not from Richmond or below. This elementary distinction had been eluding him and Butterfield. Other prisoners, however, did report Longstreet's arrival, saying he brought 20,000 troops who detrained Friday night at Hamilton's Crossing. For a single day's shipment this figure was highly improbable, and Babcock could "find none of them who had *seen* any of the reinforcements spoken of. [They] make the statement on mere rumor."

The conflicts in these reports introduced uncertainty as to whether the railroad had been put out of operation as Hooker had ordered. So Babcock put his own resources to work, sending scout William Chase to watch the trains at Guiney's Station, eighteen miles below Fredericksburg. Guiney's was Lee's transportation and supply depot; since many trains from points south would go no further, they would not come in view of the Federals' balloons or signal stations. Chase found a hiding place and remained eighteen hours, long enough to assure Babcock that there was not much activity at Guiney's. He saw two trains; each arrived twice and departed twice, bringing no troops or supplies and leaving with loads of tents and baggage. The fact that they had come up empty was good evidence that Stoneman had cut the railroad somewhere above Richmond. And Lee is known to have been cut off from the capital briefly in at least two places. An Illinois cavalry regiment, one of several parties detached from Stoneman's main body, broke the line Sunday at Ashland, fifteen miles above Richmond. More extensive destruction, including a long stretch of track nearer the city, was wreaked by Judson Kilpatrick's New York cavalry regiment on Monday. But the interruption of traffic lasted only two days or less; Chase's observation may have covered its entire duration. That was not long enough to deplete Lee's food supply. Although Hooker's orders had stressed the importance of cutting the railroad, Stoneman diverted some manpower to less important destruction. Hooker came to consider his raid a complete failure.[67]

Chase had done a good piece of intelligence work, producing information both important and reliable, but it came to nothing, for the battle was over by the time he returned. Again, as in the case of Richard Montgomery at Second Bull Run, a spy going deep into enemy territory during battle could not get back to base quickly enough for his information to be used.[68]

Daylight Monday found Butterfield in receipt of a two-day-old telegram from General Peck reporting that D. H. Hill had brought 4000 troops from North Carolina — a strong indication that Hood's and Pickett's divisions would soon return to Lee. They "are ready to go at a moment's warning," Peck wrote. Butterfield answered that there was "nothing positive on Hood and Pickett. All prisoners say they were due here last night." Evidently on the basis of Maddox's report, he added that the Confederates "had nothing at Richmond to send here." Peck responded with two messages refining the information in the delayed message. He reported that Hill's division was nearing Suffolk on Saturday; he knew this from a Hill-to-Longstreet "communication" that had come into his hands, by what means he did not say. And he had learned of two more brigades from North Carolina, James Kemper's and Henry Benning's, that had joined the enemy force facing Suffolk. He was expecting the new arrivals to replace Hood and Pickett.[69]

On Monday a Fredericksburg citizen named Bell told Butterfield that Hood's and Pickett's troops had reached Petersburg on their way north on Thursday; Hood was to move to Lee via Gordonsville and Pickett via Fredericksburg. A Southern citizen was a doubtful source, but Butterfield explained: "Circumstances connected with his statement convince me that it has good foundation." Butterfield's "circumstances" consisted of, or at least included, a similar report that had just come from a

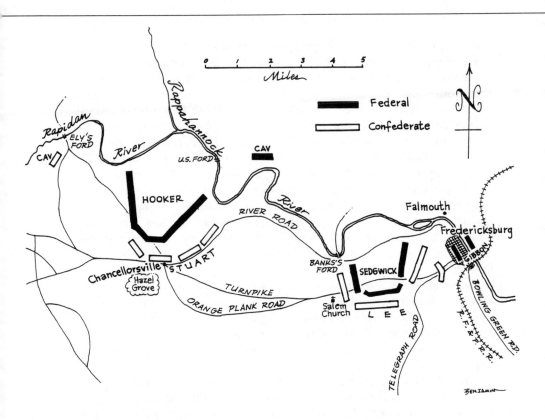

SITUATION, AFTERNOON, MAY 4, 1863

cavalry source, that 15,000 or 20,000 of Longstreet's force had detrained at Gordonsville.[70] (Troops arriving at this time would have been part of the small emergency force from Richmond or Staunton.)

Another report of enemy reinforcements resulted from a Confederate counterattack that retook the Fredericksburg heights Monday morning. Here was a new kind of error: the attackers were the same Confederates that Sedgwick had driven from the heights on Sunday, but because they came from the south, word spread that they were reinforcements from Richmond. Sedgwick put their number at 15,000. Bell, Butterfield's citizen-informant, said they were Pickett's division, which seemed to corroborate an earlier report from a deserter that had placed Longstreet's advance somewhere around Bowling Green. Still another variation in enemy threats was turned up by General Patrick, who was directing provost-marshal affairs from U.S. Ford; he examined a deserter who said the report was current among the Confederates that Longstreet had turned Hooker's right and would cross the river and attack from the rear.[71] This rumor was a derivative of the reports about the force at Gordonsville.

Even Babcock was now willing to believe that at least some of Longstreet's troops had arrived, though he still needed prisoners for confirmation. On Monday he wired Sharpe, "There is no doubt that reinforcements have arrived this morning in our front. I have information that it is Pickett's Division." So far as the records reveal, Babcock's "information that it is Pickett's Division" may have amounted to no more than the persuasive report of Bell, whom Babcock normally would have examined even though he was also interviewed by Butterfield. But the presence of Pickett's troops, or Hood's, was convincingly refuted in Babcock's interrogation Monday night of prisoners captured that day; he telegraphed Sharpe a retraction Tuesday morning.

In the meantime a telegram from General Dix at midday Monday announced that Longstreet was now in full retreat from Suffolk. Hood, the first to move, had begun his march Sunday night.[72]

There stood the troublesome Longstreet question at the close of business in the Falmouth headquarters Monday night. Of all the reports, the only ones that proved correct were Peck's several telegrams placing Hood and Pickett still in his front, Dix's report that Longstreet had finally begun to move out, and Babcock's correction on Tuesday of his erroneous telegram on Monday.

.. .. ..

Late Monday night Hooker brought his corps commanders together to consider whether the army should advance against the enemy or draw back across the Rappahannock. The discussion led to a vote in which Meade, Reynolds, and Howard favored advance and Couch and Sickles were for withdrawal. (Sedgwick was necessarily absent and Slocum arrived late.) Hooker responded to the majority opinion favoring advance by announcing that he was taking on himself the responsibility of ordering withdrawal. It had been clear from the beginning of the discussion that that was his preference; now it was clear that he had called the meeting only to get his generals to share the responsibility.[73] Another indication of his intention to obtain such a verdict is his omission from the options he gave them of fighting a defensive battle on the same ground they now occupied. More than once he had pictured such a battle as the ideal outcome of his whole campaign; now it was deliberately forgotten. In offering the generals the choice between attacking and withdrawing, he was hoping, probably expecting, that their preference would be "anything but an attack."

Information about the enemy is not mentioned in the records of the generals' discussion, but Hooker was clearly factoring it into his calculations, for at 10:45 Monday night, not long before the corps commanders assembled, his aide-de-camp sent the Falmouth headquarters a badly confused query for General Averell about a report he had made late Friday. From a mail he captured at Culpeper, Averell had obtained information that Jackson was leading a force of 25,000 at Gordonsville; rumor had magnified the tiny emergency force the War Department had sent there from Richmond and Staunton when the place was thought to be Hooker's objective. That report, evidently lost by Monday, was being confused with Monday's report of Hood's and Pickett's 15,000 or 20,000 men detraining at Gordonsville.[74]

The confusion regarding Gordonsville was not the only threat to a clear understanding of the status of Longstreet's return. Babcock's Monday statement of the arrival of troops belonging to Pickett's division was still in force at the time the generals met Monday night, though by that time Babcock's examination of prisoners had disproved his earlier conclusion. But this new finding did not reach Sharpe until too late for it to have influenced Hooker's decision. Whether Babcock attempted to telegraph this important change late Monday night is not known; the telegraph line had been extended from U.S. Ford to Chancellorsville, but the operators are not known to have maintained a twenty-four-hour schedule.

Hooker, even if he discounted all reports of Longstreet's return except General Dix's Monday announcement that the movement had started, could not safely assume that Hood and Pickett could not arrive in time to exert an effect on the battle. The fighting had been going on for four days without any sign of concluding; after another four, the advance elements of Longstreet's divisions could be getting off the trains at Fredericksburg and Culpeper. They would have had rail transportation for at least two thirds of the trip. Even Dix's telegram was not an ironclad assurance that no departures earlier than Sunday had escaped his notice. And the possibility of enemy reinforcements from Gordonsville could not be entirely ruled out.

Another problem for Hooker was the discovery that the position between Chancellorsville and the Rappahannock was no longer attractive now that his six corps were in place there. The land was flat and offered few if any commanding positions. Moreover, it was backed up to the river, noted for quick and unpredictable flooding. If 100,000 men were to get across, it was a case of the sooner the better.

It had become apparent to Hooker that his masterful plan, so successfully executed for its first four days, was no assurance of victory. It had not sufficed to prevent mistakes, especially Saturday's debacle at Jackson's hands. And Sedgwick's wing had not absorbed as much of Lee's energy and resources as Hooker had counted on.

These disappointments were so severe as to cause Hooker to lose confidence in himself and his army.[75] That was a development that lent force to all the visible reasons for retiring. Those reasons could have been surmounted by the confident Joe Hooker of an earlier day.

. . . .

General Hooker had placed an army of more than 70,000 in the Confederates' rear — unopposed, and undetected by their commander. Military theorists greatly admire such a feat; there is an entire literature devoted to the study of strategic surprise. To this history Hooker added a new chapter. His exploit has a textbook-perfect quality in several respects. It had a strong intelligence component, which greatly reduced the effect of chance. Much effort was spent on deception, and the various deceptive measures were successful, even including, up to a point, the left wing's demonstration. The security of the march, as judged by the easy passage of the rivers, was excellent. The whole plan had a beautiful simplicity in that no severe precision of timing was required of the main maneuvering force, since the telegraph facilitated synchronizing with the cooperating force, Sedgwick's left wing; thus the ancient problem of getting two widely separated forces to move in concert was eliminated.

The significance of Hooker's achievement was soon recognized by a European writer, who placed the maneuver on a par with river-crossing feats of Hannibal, Alexander, Napoleon, and Wellington. But almost no American historians of the Civil War have seen any more in it than a good plan for the infantry that was nullified by a bad one for the cavalry.[76] The prophet Joseph Hooker is unhonored in his own country for a reason: he lost the battle.

18

· · · · · · · · · ·

LEE'S ARMY VANISHES

May 5–June 10, 1863

HOOKER'S ARMY had reached Chancellorsville by way of a stolen march; it now returned to its camps north of the Rappahannock by the same means, though this time without deceptive intent. On Tuesday, May 5, after his midnight council of war, Hooker revealed his desire to end the battle in a note to Lee requesting "the privilege of sending a burial party . . . to bury the dead and care for the wounded officers and soldiers of my command." If Lee received this on the day it was written, he evidently saw it as an attempt to stall for time. The note went unanswered while he prepared an attack for Wednesday — the very attack Hooker had once hoped he would make. But when the Rebel skirmishers advanced at daybreak, the Federals were gone. They had stolen a retreat to U.S. Ford, where pontoon bridges awaited them. Their preparations for withdrawal, occupying all of Tuesday, consisted mainly of cutting miles of roads through the woods. The Confederates evidently assumed that the sounds of those hundreds of axes signified the construction of fortifications, for the withdrawal took them by surprise. The Federals' retirement was not completed until almost 9 A.M. Wednesday, when the rearmost brigade of Meade's corps, the army's rear guard, reached the bridges.[1]

After the crossing, when the burial of the Federals' dead and removal of their wounded was finally arranged, supervision of the task — a difficult one, for ambulances were few and the river was swollen — fell to Colonel Sharpe. He was instructed to go to U.S. Ford, arrange details with the Confederate commander there, and oversee the burials and the transfer of wounded. Although the assignment fit his nominal position as deputy provost marshal general, it would also allow him to pick up Confederate camp gossip and learn something about the postbattle positions of Lee's forces, including, of course, whatever was known about Hood and Pickett. The record, however, indicates that Sharpe gave his undivided energies to getting the suffering men across the river. After the war he often said that the one act from which he got the greatest satisfaction was the rescue of the Chancellorsville wounded, whose number he put at 4000.[2]

While the Army of the Potomac was settling into its old camps around Falmouth, additional information on the Longstreet question came to hand. It was from Richmond, obtained not from espionage but through Confederate carelessness in allowing Union prisoners who were being exchanged to pass within the view of a major movement of Southern troops. One prisoner, Brigadier General August Willich, was interviewed by President Lincoln on arriving in Washington May 8. The President informed Hooker that the brigadier had observed a column three miles long approaching Richmond from the south; Willich *thought* it was Longstreet. (Except for Lee's army, there were no forces in Virginia that could make a column of that size, and none so likely as Longstreet's to be marching northward.)

Lincoln's telegram said also that at the time of Willich's release "there was not a sound pair of legs in Richmond" and that Stoneman's troopers "could have safely gone in and burnt every thing & brought us Jeff Davis." Willich's news would not have made believers out of Hooker and Sharpe, who knew the Confederate capital to have a competent local defense force of respectable size. Concerning Longstreet's movement, however, Willich's statement was essentially correct; Hood's division was moving toward Richmond at the time the Union prisoners were embarking.[3]

More persuasive to Sharpe and Babcock, however, would have been the simple fact that no prisoners or deserters from Hood's division or Pickett's had turned up in Army of the Potomac stockades as a result of the Chancellorsville battle. By May 13, but probably several days before then, the earlier reports of Longstreet's arrival had been thoroughly discounted, although his whereabouts at that date were an open question.[4]

Lee's forces that had fought at Chancellorsville and Fredericksburg also gave Sharpe and Babcock a problem for several days. The first information received was a report in the *Richmond Examiner* of May 11, almost too unqualified to be true, that "Our army has resumed the position occupied by it previous to the advance of Hooker." Supporting evidence came from a spy named James Clifford, a member of the 9th New York Cavalry, whose reliability was probably unknown at army headquarters since his past service in espionage had been for General Sigel and he was now working for General Slocum. Clifford reported that the entire enemy force was near the heights of Fredericksburg. He had learned this from Confederate scouts he met twenty-five miles up the Rappahannock. He had passed himself off to the Rebels as a member of "Lige" White's band of Confederate rangers.[5]

One other unusual episode enlivens the secret-service record for this period. On May 14 a report of Confederate raiders caused an alarm in Hooker's rear. Scouts who could lead Union cavalry to that kind of prey were always scarce, but this time one was found — Bertram E. Trenis, a resident of Prince William County, aged ten years. A detachment comprising parts of seven cavalry regiments started out under the lad's guidance on the 16th and flushed a party of bushwhackers, capturing nine of them. Scout Trenis was twenty-four consecutive hours in the saddle on this expedition and won himself a job in the secret service of the Union. So unusual was this application for employment that it was brought to President Lincoln's attention. He wrote that if the troops "desire this boy to remain with them and if he can in any way be allowed to do so and receive pay, I shall be glad."[6]

. .   . .   . .

May 13 saw the first of a series of telegrams from Hooker to Lincoln in which Hooker pictured himself outnumbered by the enemy and advanced various excessive demands and impracticable schemes. These messages raise the question whether Colonel Sharpe was another Allan Pinkerton, seeing two or three Confederate soldiers where there was one, and whether he was reporting what he saw or what he thought his commander expected him to see. But Sharpe and Babcock had not produced any strength estimates since the Chancellorsville battle,[7] so it is clear that Hooker, when he sat down in a petulant or complaining mood to write to Lincoln, was doing his own estimating, or guessing, about enemy numbers. In his May 13 message, which is typical of these communications, he said that he was informed that "the bulk of Longstreet's force is in Richmond" and that if Longstreet should rejoin Lee the enemy army would be much his superior. He argued that if the Union army in southeastern Virginia could not hold Longstreet at Richmond, the Army of the Potomac ought to be reinforced to the tune of 25,000; where this many troops might come from he admitted he did not know. He also said, "I hope to be able to commence my movement tomorrow." Such a movement reached the planning stage — Babcock and McEntee drew up a long report on the condition of the fords across the Rappahannock and the Rapidan — but no movement orders appear to have been written.[8]

At the time Hooker wired Lincoln that most of Longstreet's detached force was at Richmond, Sharpe's sources had been silent as to Longstreet's position for several days. The profusion of conflicting reports had given way to an uncomfortable silence. One major hope for solving the mystery was Ernest Yager; although the country where he habitually worked lay well to the west of Lee's main body, the railroads in that region might carry part of a northward movement by Longstreet. But

Yager, shortly after the Chancellorsville battle, had set off on a self-assigned detective mission, arranging the arrest of some twenty Virginians whom he believed guilty of destroying railroad tracks and bridges that the Union forces had needed months before in Pope's campaign. On May 10 he telegraphed Sharpe from Washington, asking if there were any tasks for him. Sharpe told him to go to Culpeper and find out whether Lee had received reinforcements, and try to discover the position and strength of Stuart's cavalry. Four days later Yager responded with a report, put into standard English by an operator somewhere along the railroad:

> I crossed about 1 o'clock this a.m. at Rappahannock Station. No force at Culpeper except a few scouts of Stuart's cavalry. Longstreet's forces are guarding the Rapidan. The Bridge will be done by to-morrow. They expect Longstreet's division at Culpeper soon. The rumor in Culpeper is that General Beauregard is to re-enforce Lee as soon as the roads are repaired. The greater part of Stuart's cavalry went toward the Peninsula yesterday.[9]

Despite the mistaken reference to the no-longer-existent "Longstreet's division," this report was a useful indication, however tentative, that Hood or Pickett, or both, would not be returning to Fredericksburg. This in turn suggested that Lee had plans for his army beyond merely maintaining a defensive stance on the Rappahannock; such plans were soon to mature in a northward movement that would terminate in Pennsylvania. Yager's statement that "Longstreet's forces" were on the Rapidan was a rough approximation of the facts: Hood was well short of the Rapidan but clearly headed for Gordonsville (and presumably then Culpeper), and Pickett was a day's march in his rear. But the rest of Yager's report, concerning Stuart and Beauregard, was so hard to accept that it would have cast doubt on his fairly correct statements about Longstreet. And Sharpe had no other recent information on Hood and Pickett with which to compare Yager's shaky findings. In spite of these problems, however, Yager's report gave Sharpe a start in tracing the later stages of Longstreet's return to Lee's army.[10]

Two days later, on the 16th, Sharpe went to Baltimore on business, not specified in his travel orders, that probably included not only the management of McPhail's line to Richmond but also arrangements for spies to cover a possible enemy attempt to cross the Potomac.[11]

. . .. ..

In Lee's Pennsylvania campaign, a natural follow-on to his decisive victory at Chancellorsville, his army was the largest he ever commanded after the Seven Days. Eighteen thousand men were added to the Army of Northern Virginia between mid-May and mid-June.[12] While the buildup was in progress, Lee spent three days, May 15–17, at Richmond in planning sessions with his chiefs. His journey was not detected by Sharpe's men, so far as the record shows, but the failure was small loss, for Sharpe, in addition to learning of the successive additions to the enemy army, soon found out that it was about to embark on a major movement. The source of this information was a deserter, whose possession of it surprises anyone acquainted with security practices in the Army of Northern Virginia. He proved to be a native of Sharpe's own Hudson River country and a relatively recent migrant to the South. At a dress parade four or five days previous to his desertion on May 21, an order from General Lee had been read announcing that a movement would be made soon that would require stripping down personal baggage to the barest minimum — a clear indication of a long march.

Sharpe's spies soon brought in the same information. The corroboration was a timely one, for he might well have rejected the Confederate's statement because of the recent experience with deserters evidently chosen by Lee in the hope that Butterfield (or Patrick) would have a weakness for fellow New Yorkers. This latest deserter likewise may have been sent across the river with a planted story, but if so, he turned on his Southern employers and delivered the facts as he knew them.[13]

On the same day, May 22, one of Sharpe's men just in from the right of the line reported that a division of the enemy was now at Culpeper. The division in question could only have been Hood's, but Sharpe continued to carry Hood at stations on the Virginia Central. Longstreet in person had been reported at Fredericksburg by a New York chaplain who had remained there with Federal wounded after the battle of Chancellorsville and had just rejoined the army.

One of the Richmond newspapers now contributed in a small way to the steadily sharpening picture. Along with its gloomy dispatches from Mississippi, where Grant was closing in on Vicksburg, the *Examiner* printed an editorial that sought to arrest Southern despondency. "Whatever may be the result of the military operations about Vicksburg," it said, "their interest will soon be eclipsed by greater events elsewhere. Within the next fortnight the campaign of 1863 will be pretty well decided. The most important movement of the war will probably be made in that time." Even after making the usual discount for journalistic bluster, Sharpe saw fit to call this item to the attention of his chiefs.[14]

His information gradually solidified, and on May 27 he was able to send Hooker a summary of the enemy situation:

1. The enemy's line in front of us is much more contracted than during the winter. It extends from Banks' ford on a line parallel with the river to near Moss Neck. Anderson's division is on their left. McLaws' is next, and in rear of Fredericksburg. Early's is massed about Hamilton's Crossing, and Trimble's is directly in the rear of Early. Rhodes' (D. H. Hill's old Divn) is farther to the right, and back from the river, and A. P.

Hill's is the right of their line, resting nearly on Moss Neck. Each of these six divisions have five brigades.

2. Pickett's Division of 6 Brigades has come up from Suffolk and is at Taylorsville near Hanover Junction.

3. Hood's Division of 4 Brigades has also left from the front of Suffolk and is between Louisa C. H. and Gordonsville.

4. Ten days ago there was in Richmond only the City battalion, 2700 strong, commanded by General Elzey.

5. There are 3 brigades of cavalry 3 miles from Culpepper C. H. towards Kelly's ford. They can at present turn out only 4700 men for duty; but have many dismounted men, and the horses are being constantly and rapidly recruited by the spring growth of grass. These are Fitz Lee's, Wm. H. Fitzhugh Lee's & Wade Hampton's Brigades.

6. Genl. Jones is still in the Valley, near New Market with about 1400 cavalry & 12 pieces of light Artillery.

7. Mosby is above Warrenton with 200 men.

8. The Confed Army is under marching orders and an order from General Lee was very lately read to the troops announcing a campaign of long marches & hard fighting in a part of the country where they would have no railroad transportation.

9. All the deserters say that the idea is very prevalent in the ranks that they are about to move forward upon or above our right flank.

The most important item in this report, the strong indication of an impending advance by Lee's army, was relegated to the very end; it would already have been reported to Hooker orally, or perhaps in a separate note that is not in the records. But Hooker also buried this sensational news in sending the report to Halleck by writing, "Respectfully forwarded for the information of the General-in-Chief. *Note:* Colonel Sharpe is in charge of the Bureau of information at these Head Quarters."[15]

Hooker's telegram to Washington announcing that the report was on its way said that he placed "a good deal of confidence" in it. If he had had the means of fully knowing the enemy situation, he could have given the report a higher rating. Its only shortcoming of any importance was the absence of estimates of the numbers of troops in the army and in the individual divisions. The weeks since the Chancellorsville battle had seen constant organizational changes and influx of new regiments and brigades, to the point that the men in the Confederate ranks were not able to keep up with the positioning and subordination of Lee's brigades. Sharpe always made the most of the American fighting man's penchant for concerning himself almost as much with the "big picture" as with the affairs of his own company and regiment; but in the fluid situation of May 1863 the Confederate soldier's curiosity about affairs at the higher levels was largely frustrated. Still Sharpe was able to cover the organization of the Army of Northern Virginia with precision to a level of detail ample for Hooker's purpose.

Hooker told Stanton that the information was derived from deserters. That was an oversimplification; as has been shown, some of it came from

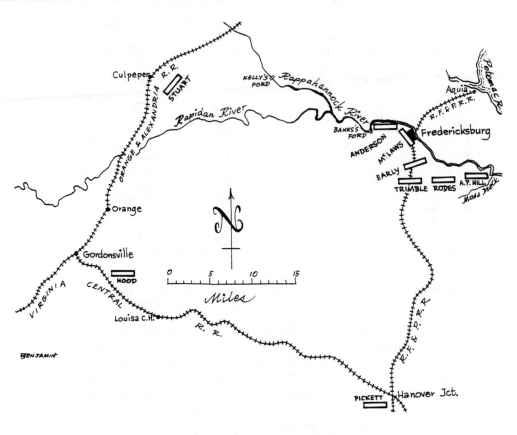

LEE'S POSITIONS, MAY 27, 1863

Sharpe's spies; other important contributors were the Signal Corps look-out stations and the balloons.[16] It was an example of the all-source report-ing that Hooker's intelligence system was designed for.

For the War Department, however, this virtue was wasted by a malfunc-tion of clerical machinery. From unknown causes the May 27 report was delayed in getting to Washington until June 8; by that time it had been outdated by an erroneous report on later developments. That misfor-tune would rob it, with disastrous results, of its impact as a warning of the enemy's "campaign of long marches & hard fighting."

· · · ·· ··

General Lee was worried at this time about the leakage of information to the Federals, but he partly misunderstood the nature of the sources they were exploiting. To Lieutenant Colonel John Critcher of the 15th Vir-ginia Cavalry, whose mission was to observe and report movements on the Federals' left flank, Lee issued an admonition regarding secrecy. He wrote, "The chief source of information to the enemy is through our Negroes. They are easily deceived by proper caution."[17] Lee was correct to the extent that contrabands, slaves, and officers' servants always were eagerly questioned by Union scouts and spies, but he failed to realize how much information the Federals were also getting from Southern citizens, deserters, prisoners, and occasionally men still in his own ranks. And his idea of trying to mislead the Negroes was impractical; too many were with the army or near it for any large percentage of them to be kept in a state of misinformation greater than that of the white people in the same region.

Lee was also having trouble with his own supply of information. On the day he wrote to Critcher, that officer was a prisoner. Union attention had been attracted to the area of his operations, the Northern Neck, on May 18, when Captain Benjamin Fisher, now Hooker's chief signal officer, read an intercepted message that showed that the Rebels were sending men across the Union-held part of the Neck. A letter from Critcher to Lee, intercepted by the Federals, showed that he was engaged in intelligence activities. During the same week, according to the story Critcher told when captured, he crossed into the Neck and went home "to receive the dying kiss of his child" and remained for the funeral; he was captured recrossing toward the Confederate lines. Although the Federals realized that they could not convict him of espionage, they were so certain of his secret-service activities that they resolved to hold him prisoner as long as possible.[18]

On May 30 Lee wrote to President Davis about the general failure of his intelligence-gathering efforts. He cited as an example the failure of a recent attempt by Longstreet to get a spy into Washington; the man had been unable to get closer than Baltimore.[19] Not only Hooker but also the nearby department commanders, Schenck and Heintzelman, had succeeded in tightening up. These improvements, together with the maturing of Sharpe's bureau, widened the advantage in information that Hooker had achieved over Lee two months before.

But it was an advantage the Federals would never believe they possessed. An example of the Yankee state of mind on the ever-present question of enemy prowess in intelligence matters is a complaint made by Captain Fisher shortly before he succeeded Samuel Cushing. He declared that the Signal Corps "is distrusted, and considered unsafe as a means of transmitting important messages." He was correct in diagnosing the technical weakness of the cipher Colonel Myer had provided in April, but he had no evidence, so far as his complaint shows, that the enemy had exploited Federal messages in the recent battle. It was during and immediately after the fighting that he learned of the general distrust of the Signal Corps that he alleged. He may even have been unaware of his own organization's contribution to the brilliant maneuver of Hooker's right wing — visible evidence of the upper hand Hooker's Signal Corps held over the enemy's.[20]

. .   . .   . .

On May 30 General Lee issued an order reorganizing his army. This was a thorough rearrangement, as it had to be with the great Jackson gone. Stonewall's successor in command of the Second Corps was the explosive but well-liked Richard S. Ewell, considerably tamed by his recent marriage, and back on duty for the first time since his loss of a leg at Second Bull Run. The corps, formerly comprising four divisions, now had three — those of Jubal A. Early, Robert E. Rodes, and Edward Johnson. Johnson's division previously was Trimble's, before that Jackson's own.

A Third Corps, with A. P. Hill its commander, was created from elements of the First and Second and new brigades brought up from southeastern Virginia and North Carolina. Richard Anderson's division moved over to Hill from the First Corps, and Hill's own division was transferred from the Second. Four of Hill's six brigades were kept together, forming a division under the command of Dorsey Pender, and the other two were combined with the two newly arrived brigades to compose a division under Henry Heth.

At the brigade level the reorganization was a nightmare for Babcock. Six enemy brigades had new commanders; six others had been left in charge of colonels, but most would still be called by the names of their former brigadiers. Three infantry brigades had come up from Richmond and farther south (besides the two in the Third Corps, there was one in the Second), but these were in exchange for three smaller brigades; the fact that the latter three had been left south of the James River would not become apparent for some weeks. Then there were maddening fillips such as the replacement of Brigadier General John R. Jones by Brigadier General John M. Jones in command of one of Johnson's brigades. Albert Jenkins's cavalry brigade from southwestern Virginia joined Lee's army, while Micah Jenkins's infantry brigade, long part of the army, was left in southeastern Virginia.

Albert Jenkins's brigade was one of three added to Stuart's cavalry. Still another Brigadier General Jones — this one William E., better known as "Grumble" — led his horsemen across the Blue Ridge to join Stuart, and Brigadier General Beverly H. Robertson came from North Carolina bringing two regiments of his brigade. In addition, the brigade of General John D. Imboden was made a part of the Army of Northern Virginia though it remained in the new state of West Virginia.

The army's fourteen artillery battalions were increased to fifteen, divided up five to a corps. There was no longer a general reserve of artillery.

An example of the thoroughness of the reorganization is the fact that of the seventeen general-officer positions in the Second Corps, only seven were held by men who had had assignments of the same rank at the battle of Chancellorsville.[21]

By June 9 the Bureau of Military Information had enough data on the enemy reorganization for Sharpe to summarize the changes in a report to Hooker. This report and others produced by Sharpe and his men in the succeeding days show that they had learned of Lee's new three-corps arrangement, had correctly identified the two new corps commanders, and had placed most if not all of the infantry divisions in their proper corps. They had also learned of the several additions to Stuart's cavalry.[22]

.. .. ..

A "campaign of long marches & hard fighting in a part of the country where they would have no railroad transportation" — this, added to the need to fill in the blanks in the enemy's organization chart, put Sharpe under pressure to deliver results quickly. A general forward movement by Lee would almost certainly begin with a shift to the northwest, to or toward the Valley. Sharpe took action to detect such a move by sending a six-man detachment in that direction. Brigadier General Alfred Pleasonton, now commanding Hooker's cavalry, had two divisions operating in the region around Warrenton Junction. Orders were written placing Captain McEntee and a party of soldier-scouts on detached service with Pleasonton; on May 29 McEntee and five men — Henry W. Dodd, Benjamin F. McCord, Ed Hopkins, Anson Carney, and a fifth who may have been Edward A. Carney — arrived at the advanced cavalry post at Bealeton Station.[23] McEntee's mission, not stated in his orders, was to penetrate enemy lines, using his men's skills that presumably exceeded those possessed by the cavalry. He was expected also to apply his own skill in interpreting evidence and thus supply reports more reliable and more informative than Pleasonton and his staff were producing.

McEntee quickly found that he was not to be allowed to proceed with his task unmolested. The train that had delivered him, on its return trip toward Alexandria, was attacked by Mosby's rangers. They created so much confusion that McEntee was delayed in setting up shop; he had to send off his personal and official impedimenta and operate out of his shirt pocket, moving back and forth every day or so between Bealeton and Warrenton Junction, the latter being somewhat safer. He wrote Sharpe, "I suppose you have heard how ungraciously Mr Moseby has acted towards us folks out here. The day I came . . . he hove a shot across the bows of the down train as a signal for the engineer to heave to, which

**REGION OF CAPTAIN McENTEE'S OPERATIONS
MAY 30-JUNE 14, 1863**

he did without any ceremony." An infantry company was escorting the train, but "as Mr. Moseby had the kindness to relieve them of such duty they took a double quick and soon arrived at their camp, leaving Moseby to the enjoyment of his fireworks." Having nearly lost his baggage "on the altar of freedom," McEntee decided it was time to load his pistol.

Under the pressure of a telegram from Sharpe, he proceeded immediately to try to get his men through Lee's lines, sending McCord and Hopkins across the Rappahannock well upriver. They returned the next day, the 31st, with word that Hampton's cavalry brigade was in that locality, a fact previously reported by the Union cavalry, and that this was the northernmost of Lee's units. Anson Carney and Dodd attempted to cross the river farther down, at Field's and Ellis's Fords, but they found the cordon of enemy pickets too tight. Carney talked with the pickets, who fed him the story that they belonged to the Sixth South Carolina Infantry, a regiment that was actually with General Micah Jenkins in southeastern Virginia. They encountered an enemy scout, whom they termed a bushwhacker, and Carney shot him dead when he tried to get away. He proved to be a member of the 4th Virginia Cavalry, a regiment belonging to Fitzhugh Lee's brigade.

McEntee was not pleased with his prospects. He wrote Sharpe that it would be difficult for his raw men to get over the river, but that they were all anxious to accomplish something and would go as far as possible. He asked that Babcock send him "a small phial of his S. S. fluid" — secret ink.[24]

Things were not going noticeably better back at Falmouth. Hooker complained to Washington about the difficulty of getting information on enemy movements; when several men failed to return from across the river, he assumed that they had been captured. But none of these disappearances is known to have marred the record of successful return from Confederate prisons set by Sharpe's man Daniel Cole, Sigel's Joseph Snyder, and Frémont's trio of spies who suffered arrest.[25]

The source of the activity that was worrying Hooker was an order from Lee that put the Army of Northern Virginia on the first leg of its advance to Pennsylvania. On June 3 Ewell's corps and McLaws's division began leaving Fredericksburg for Culpeper; then major elements of Hill's corps, which had been on the downriver wing, joined the newly arrived brigades in filling the vacancies left by the departing troops in the Fredericksburg lines. The need for secrecy in these movements caused the tight picketing that was preventing McEntee's men from penetrating Confederate lines. Apparently it was also preventing Ebenezer McGee from crossing the river, for Isaac Silver was not heard from during this period when thousands of enemy troops were passing his way, many of them probably marching past his farm.[26] Also forestalled for several days by the stringent picketing were escapes to the Federal lines by would-be deserters; this lapse in desertion was in itself a warning of Confederate movements. Babcock, who had been a member of Pinkerton's bureau when General Johnston scored a stolen march from Manassas at McClellan's expense, would now have recalled the lack of deserters at that time, though Pinkerton and his report writers had failed to recognize the warning it conveyed.

The number of observations of enemy movements was enough in itself to give Hooker cause for concern. In the seventeen days from May 27 to June 12, at least thirty-seven reports of observed movements were supplied by balloonists, Signal Corps observers, and pickets. Prominent among these were reports of abandoned camps; for example, signal officers at one observation post spotted the fires of six regimental camps in a single night; all were gone in the morning. Old battery positions were abandoned and new ones appeared. Even forces stationed near the fords, presumably as guards, disappeared. One report on a certain area said that nothing could be seen there but signal stations; a small corral of cattle was "all of the animal kingdom" that Captain Fisher could see at a point where there had been a cavalry detachment. A scout, evidently one of Sharpe's, went down the river bank for ten miles and told Fisher he did not see even a picket on the opposite side.

Another daily occurrence was observation of marching infantry and artillery; one artillery column took three quarters of an hour to pass a certain point. Other columns were detected only by clouds of dust, always portentous, or by rumblings of wagon trains heard at night by pickets. The pickets were a frequent source of these reports, for the appearance of a set of new faces on the Confederate picket lines across the river meant that one enemy unit had been replaced by another. Picketing was so fruitful a source of information that a few officers in Meade's corps went on picket dressed as privates; this subterfuge led to the discovery that A. P. Hill was now in command of the Fredericksburg forces. Much of the difficulty of determining what was going on in Lee's army was the movement of Hill's units into positions hitherto occupied by Ewell's and McLaws's troops. Until the discovery of Hill's new status, these moves could be interpreted as caused by the reorganization rather than by departure of large numbers of troops.[27]

No general trend was apparent in all these movements. The Rebels might be shifting upriver, but they continued to picket the right bank down to Port Royal, seventeen miles below Fredericksburg. On June 4 Hooker wired General Dix asking whether offensive actions Dix had been planning "might have caused the commotion . . . in the rebel camps opposite me." Dix's reply was negative.

June 5 saw the arrival of one of the strangest reports Sharpe ever had to evaluate. It was from an infantry captain up in Maryland who on May 30 had encountered, between Hagerstown and Frederick, a mulatto boy who claimed that until a few days before his arrest he had been a body servant of General Hill. He said he had heard Hill telling his officers of Lee's plans to invade Pennsylvania by a Culpeper-Luray-Romney-Cumberland route while Stuart rode through the Shenandoah Valley. The boy's story was not shaken by close questioning or by putting him under oath. But the invasion route he named was improbable, and even less probable was the route given for retreat should one be necessary — across all of West Virginia. Not the least peculiar feature of the report was its source; officers' servants were often received as deserters, but not a hundred miles away from the army. The youth said he was bound for Lancaster, Pennsylvania; presumably his questioners were to assume that his purpose was the usual one, escape.[28] But it was equally possible that he was telling a planted story or was on a spying trip for the Confederates. This was the kind of incident that Sharpe could only file away in his memory as a puzzle that might be solvable by later developments.

Seeking information on the activity around Fredericksburg, Hooker had pontoons thrown over the river below the town on the 5th and sent part of Sedgwick's corps across. The Confederates soon hemmed the visitors in so closely that the slightest attempt to reconnoiter threatened to bring on a general engagement. But the venture yielded fifty prisoners, who explained that the recent shifting about of Southern troops was due to the reorganization of their army.[29] This was probably the truth so far as Johnny Reb knew it.

After a few days of this uncertainty, an idea began to take hold that what was afoot was more than a reorganization but yet something quite different from a general movement of Lee's army. Pleasonton's scouts were busy in the same area as McEntee's men, and as early as May 27 they had begun reporting that the concentration of Confederate cavalry around Culpeper signified preparations for one of Jeb Stuart's raids. This information was soon supported by Sharpe's bureau. Howard Skinker left headquarters on the 29th and was back on June 3 with a long report that added nothing to Sharpe's information on the Confederate infantry but predicted an important move by Stuart. He had learned that Grumble Jones's cavalry brigade had crossed the Blue Ridge and was now in the Culpeper neighborhood with Stuart's main body. That was only one of the three substantial accretions to Stuart's division; these reinforcements were themselves enough to generate talk of a cavalry raid.

Like McEntee's green men, the veteran Skinker had been unable to penetrate Lee's lines on the upper Rappahannock, but he had persuaded another resident of the neighborhood to cross the river. The man, whose identity Skinker revealed only to General Patrick, had not returned after two days, whereupon Skinker came back to headquarters. His friend, Skinker said, might try to extricate himself from Rebel territory by turning himself in to Confederate authorities and asking to be sent to the Federals by flag of truce.

Skinker had had to return without any information obtained across the river, but his information on Jones's movement was from an interesting source — some of Jones's men who had taken advantage of his move east of the Blue Ridge to visit their homes. Skinker confidently forecast a cavalry raid "of magnitude."[30]

Two days later, on the 5th, the prediction was reinforced. At the headquarters of General Buford's cavalry division at Warrenton Junction arrived one J. Robinson, a refugee who had made his way from Madison County, below Culpeper. He informed Buford that Stuart's division had been augmented not only by Jones but by Robertson's demibrigade from North Carolina and Albert Jenkins's brigade from southwestern Virginia, also by 800 Texas infantrymen of Hood's division who had been mounted on horses shipped from Richmond. Robinson put Stuart's total force at 20,000 and thought a raid was in the offing.

Robinson's report won substantial acceptance at both Buford's and Hooker's headquarters. It was correct, however, only as to the arrival of Jones's and Robertson's troops. Jenkins, though technically part of Stuart's command, remained west of the Blue Ridge. Stuart's total strength was scarcely half of Robinson's estimate. The 800 newly mounted Texans existed only in rumor; horses capable of cavalry service were so scarce in the Confederacy that the fact that this report gained a serious hearing seems strange.[31]

Although Stuart was about to move, he was planning no raid. There is good evidence that the talk of a raid was a Confederate deception. Evidently the report was confidently believed throughout Stuart's division, if not the whole army. Probably it was launched by Lee's headquarters in the expectation that it would reach Federal ears. An indication that the Confederates were attempting a grand deception at this time is an interception made by Federal signalmen on the army's downriver wing. They had been amusing themselves daily by reading Confederate flag messages of minor interest. On June 5 their watchfulness was rewarded with a one-line message reading, "Have any of our troops crossed the Rappahannock?" The signer was "Capt. F" (Fraser, a signal officer).[32] As Lee had no plans to cross the Rappahannock, it is evident that this was a hoax; the Rebels were making an operationally important matter appear in mere operator "chat," the Butterfield trick that had proved so effective for the Federals back in April. The purpose of the ruse would have been to mislead any Federals who, undeceived by the cavalry-raid rumor, were correctly interpreting the observed infantry movements as a move aimed at the Valley. Whether the intercept received serious attention at Hooker's headquarters is unknown.

.. .. ..

Although Captain McEntee was located with General Buford at Warrenton Junction, he did not succeed in interviewing the refugee Robinson until Buford's report was in Falmouth and Washington. His report to Sharpe repeated Buford's information, but it put the strength of the North Carolina cavalry force at two brigades though it was actually two regiments. His acceptance of the refugee's story was to have a pronounced effect at headquarters.

McEntee was having his troubles. Not only was he in competition with a brigadier general who had prior access to choice pieces of information; he was having no success in getting men across the river, and he was being harried by questions from Sharpe that he could not answer. After enemy activity began to make a noticeable stir around Fredericksburg, Sharpe wired him on June 4, "There is a considerable movement of the enemy. Their camps are disappearing at some points. We shall rely on you to tell us whether they go your way or towards the Valley. You must be very active in the employment of everybody and everything. Telegraph 2 or 3 times a day if there is the least thing to say." McEntee took pen in hand to acquaint his chief with the realities of intelligence operations along the upper Rappahannock. "I am laboring under sundry disadvantages here which you do not seem to take into consideration," he began, and proceeded to call attention to the greenness of his men, the distance of about fifteen miles that separated him from "any scouting grounds," the complete absence of prisoners and contrabands, and the tightness of the enemy's security.

He informed Sharpe that George Smith, who had accompanied Stoneman's raid and more recently had been in Washington, had received orders there to return to the army and was now on the scene. Smith's home in Culpeper County was only two and a half miles beyond the Rappahannock opposite Field's Ford; Smith, however, was not sent across the river; possibly his service to the Union was known among his neighbors. Going down to the ford "to see how the land lies there," McEntee and Smith had found the banks strongly picketed on one side by infantry and on the other by cavalry. Smith had therefore sent a person, whom McEntee identified only as "the lady," across to the other side, carrying instructions to his family and taking them a quantity of fishing tackle. His children were to come down to the river to fish and were to meet him there several days hence, bringing information collected by the family.

McEntee and Smith visited several other places, hoping to find someone who could penetrate the enemy camps across the river. "But," McEntee wrote, "they have all left this country. The men I have here know nothing about the other side of the river and as far as I have traveled along the river almost every piece of woods has a cavalry reserve in it." McEntee was about to start Hopkins, whom he rated his best man, to try to get around the enemy left flank. "Please consider," he wrote, "that scouting is a business that must be worked slowly."

Still another source of anxiety to McEntee was his doubt as to Smith's loyalty. "He thinks," McEntee said, "that acting the spy is exceedingly despisable and dishonorable as his affections he says are with the Southern people, but still he knows they are wrong and he will do all in his power to thwart their purpose. . . . He seems more anxious to know the situation of our troops than of the enemy." Smith's ability to aid the Union cause was considerable, but he displayed little interest; his actions and the tone of his conversation were indifferent. Toward McEntee he was "exceedingly guarded and particular in his language." McEntee concluded that "he may be afraid of his neck, or he may be a spy for [the enemy]." Sharpe replied by wire, "It is well to watch Smith and give him no information, but use him."

Soon, however, a quite innocent explanation for much of Smith's peculiar behavior appeared. He unburdened himself to McEntee after learning that a woman neighbor, an avowed secessionist, had gone to Washington and, on a pass from Secretary Stanton, had returned with a trunkful of purchases. Meanwhile, said Smith, "people who had suffered much and made great sacrifices for the sake of the Union, were not allowed to enter our lines to purchase the necessaries of life." For his year of service, much of it very risky, Smith had received only one payment of $150, about a third of what it had cost him to obtain his freedom when he was arrested on suspicion of "being a Federal." Pope's army had destroyed his crops, and altogether his devotion to the Union had cost him fifteen or twenty thousand dollars. While at headquarters, said McEntee, Smith "lived in a tent with the guides, men with whom he would not have allowed his negroes to associate. . . . I think Mr Smith a gentleman — a man who has always enjoyed the comforts of life, and the best society of the neighbourhood in which he lived. He was well off at home and looked upon as sort of leader . . . and the rough treatment that a civilian is apt to receive in the army displeased him very much."[33]

. .   ..   ..

On Sunday, June 7, Sharpe summarized for Hooker the recent intelligence from the vicinity of Culpeper. He reviewed the reports of additions to Stuart's cavalry, beginning with the arrival of Grumble Jones. "Having procured his organization [a list of the cavalry and artillery units making up Jones's brigade]," Sharpe said, "we estimate his force at not less than 1600 men for duty." He also repeated McEntee's reports that the cavalry from North Carolina amounted to two brigades and that those 800 Texans of Hood's had been mounted. This hard-to-believe news about the Texans was continuing to win believers; it had come from two independent sources, and it evidently was widely accepted among Southern citizens and soldiers.

These supporting details out of the way, Sharpe proceeded to his theme: that Stuart was about to ride off on an immense raid. The evidence, he wrote,

> . . . would seem to show that the preparations for the expedition on which this force is to be sent, are nearly complete, and I respectfully suggest that a force of the enemy's cavalry, not less than 12000 and possibly 15000 men strong are on the eve of making the most important expedition ever attempted in this country. Upon [its] departure . . . there are strong indications that the enemy's entire Infantry will fall back upon Richmond and thence reinforce their armies in the West.[34]

The tone of these sentences contrasts sharply with Sharpe's usual style, half reportorial and half legal, and his estimate of the enemy's intentions goes beyond his habit of delivering the facts in their broadest perspective but leaving the main burden of their interpretation to his superiors. This practice often seems overly conservative, but in this one departure from it Sharpe erred mightily. The numerous postwar chronicles written by members of Stuart's cavalry make no mention of a projected raid. In fact, Lee's correspondence with Stuart in early June shows that Stuart had in mind a different kind of project — an attack on a Union infantry division that was supposedly in a vulnerable position. Lee vetoed this proposal; he had other plans for Stuart.[35] It is this background that leads us to conclude that the forecast of a cavalry raid was launched from Lee's headquarters to mask the preparations for the northward movement of his whole army; however, those preparations, especially the sharp increase in the size of Stuart's division, were enough to give birth to the cavalry-raid rumor, with no assistance from headquarters.

What "strong indications" Sharpe had that Lee would move his infantry to Richmond are not known, but they too probably were created for Hooker's benefit. Perhaps Lee's shifting about at Fredericksburg was a large element in this deceptive picture. (Lee thought, however, that his deception had failed.) Sharpe's acceptance of the "strong indications" is understandable, for Lee himself had been worried about the safety of Richmond, and in General Halleck's view a movement in that direction was one of the three most likely courses of action open to Lee at this time.[36]

As for Sharpe's statement that the Confederate armies in the western theater might be reinforced from the Army of Northern Virginia, it was, in the light of Grant's tightening hold on Vicksburg, a reasonable conjecture, but the western armies had already been reinforced from Beauregard's command in South Carolina and Georgia.[37]

Hooker started a courier to President Lincoln with Sharpe's report on the forthcoming raid, adding a note that it was his "great desire to 'bust it up' before it got fairly under way."[38] Arriving in Washington on the same day as Sharpe's delayed report of May 27, this newest estimate canceled the warning of a general movement of Lee's army contained in the earlier report.

While Sharpe was putting together his forecast of a cavalry raid, more than half of the Southern infantry was moving into Culpeper. Ewell's entire corps was now there, along with Hood's and McLaws's divisions. Longstreet's third division, led by Pickett, had been detained at Hanover Junction because of the Federals' recurrent threats against Richmond. Hill's Third Corps alone held the lines at Fredericksburg, guarding the approaches to Richmond and keeping up a bold front for Hooker's benefit. Sharpe's, and Hooker's, erroneous view of Confederate intentions was due to lack of information on Ewell's and McLaws's movement up the Rappahannock. In spite of the plethora of observations of enemy movements, the units involved had not been identified, nor had the absence from Fredericksburg of these major elements of Lee's army been detected. The discovery by Meade's officers masquerading as pick-

ets that Hill was in command at Fredericksburg did not reveal that Ewell
and McLaws were now at Culpeper. Hood had advanced from the Rapidan to Culpeper, but the only report of this short move indicated that it
had been in the direction of Fredericksburg.[39] If the Federals had been
aware of the state of affairs in Lee's infantry, they would not have been so
preoccupied with Stuart's impending operations.

Up in the Union cavalry's territory John McEntee was still trying to get
his men into or near the enemy camps around Culpeper. To his little
group had been added Ernest Yager, who left Warrenton Junction on
June 5 with instructions to make for Culpeper. Two days later George
Smith started out with one of the Carneys, hoping to "engineer himself
or [Carney] over to his house." All three men were back on the 8th, with
results that show how maddeningly unpredictable was the business that
McEntee was engaged in. Carney had got across the river and had quickly
found an "intelligent contraband" at the home of one of Smith's neighbors. The Negro, who had been to Culpeper, provided considerable detail concerning the buildup of Stuart's force there, but he said that there
was little infantry in the area and that Lee's brigades at Fredericksburg
had merely changed camps for sanitary reasons. Yager, on the other
hand, reported brief but definite information of the highest importance: infantry from Lee's army was being sent to the Shenandoah Valley.
McEntee, however, had reason to disbelieve Yager. He had been gone
nearly three days, but McEntee had good evidence from the Union
soldiers who now picketed the river — "a lot of Dutchmen," McEntee
said — that Yager had not been over the river half an hour in the entire
time. When Yager told McEntee that he had gone as far into Confederate
territory as Brandy Station, five miles from the river, McEntee in disgust
ordered him back to headquarters.

On going outside the Union lines Yager had destroyed his pass; upon
his return he was made prisoner and taken to General David Gregg, one
of Pleasonton's division commanders. He told his story to Gregg before McEntee saw him, and Gregg's report of the interview was telegraphed to Hooker. Three hours later a telegram from McEntee to
Sharpe branded Yager's story "false and worthless." Thus denounced by
the third-ranking member of Hooker's information bureau, Yager's report stood no chance of acceptance. But the shift of Confederate infantry toward the Valley was also reported the same morning from another
source. A reconnoitering detachment of cavalry from the Department of
Washington reached Winchester with a report that included news of the
arrival of Ewell's corps at Culpeper. Although this information clamored
for telegraphic transmission, the detachment commander's report was
sent by courier to Fairfax, from where only a summary of it, omitting the
news from Culpeper, was sent to Hooker.

The information about Yager's behavior given by his compatriots the

"Dutchmen" probably was not McEntee's only reason for rejecting Yager's report. It failed to mention Stuart's known additions from North Carolina and the Shenandoah Valley, and it placed most of Stuart's camps away from the positions where McEntee apparently knew them to be. But it seems entirely possible that Yager's stay "over the river" was long enough for him to make contact with someone who had recent gossip from Culpeper. The incident may be summed up as a case of intelligence correct in its most important particular, but provided by a questionable source.[40] Yager was a useful agent, but his status as an irregular member of Sharpe's organization freed him from the discipline that made Sharpe's regulars much more reliable.

. . .. ..

If Hooker had been aware of the enemy's overextended positions — from Fredericksburg to some point beyond Culpeper — he might have sized up the situation as an opportunity to attack Hill. Instead, he settled for a glorious but unproductive attack on Stuart. The flamboyant cavalryman had staged a grand review of his division on June 5, as McEntee's sources had reported. Because Lee had been unable to attend, Stuart repeated the performance for him on the 8th, by which time he had moved his headquarters to Culpeper. Stuart's indulgence of his fondness for pomp was rewarded at dawn on the 9th when his advance units were surprised in their bivouacs by Pleasonton. Thus began the battle of Brandy Station, the largest cavalry engagement of the war — waged to forestall a cavalry raid that never would have taken place anyway.

Not only was Pleasonton's attack touched off by erroneous intelligence, but it took place on ground where the attackers did not expect to find the defenders. Pleasonton put his divisions across the Rappahannock at Beverly and Kelly's Fords, which are six miles apart, intending to bring his two wings together at Brandy Station and move in unison on Culpeper. But Stuart, after his review on the 8th, had anticipated the army's northward march the next morning by encamping his brigades between Brandy Station and the river. The two halves of Pleasonton's force thus found the routes to their rendezvous occupied by the enemy.[41] That was not their only surprise; Stuart's horse artillery was parked on the road to Beverly Ford, in advance of everything except the pickets on the river — a most unorthodox position for artillery. Upon the Federals' approach Major R. F. Beckham sent most of his guns rearward but put enough of them into action near the path of the attackers to impede their advance most painfully. This looked to Pleasonton like an ambuscade, and he sent word to Hooker that his attack had been anticipated. It had not, but only because a *New York Times* report announcing it in advance had not yet reached the Confederates.[42] The battle of Brandy Station was a two-way surprise: Stuart's ready-to-march positioning of his units upset Pleasonton's attack plans as much as the Federals' arrival caught the Rebels off guard.

The fight that ensued was a confused one, full of charges and counter-charges, rapid deployments and regroupings. Part of Pleasonton's left wing and one of Stuart's brigades did not get into the fight or even manage to collide with each other though they marched all day in the same neighborhood. The Southern brigade took a wrong road and failed to intersect the route of the would-be attackers. (Of this phase of the action Major Mosby observed, "As parallel lines meet in infinity, there might have been a collision between [these two forces] if the fight had lasted long enough.") One division of Federals reached Brandy Station and took the hill on which Stuart was massing his brigades. But the attackers were driven off to the east, and Pleasonton, satisfied that the enemy was well prepared for him, broke off the fight and retired across the river.[43]

Stuart was soon under attack again, this time from journalistic quarters. Richmond newspapermen understood far better than did Pleasonton how successful his attempt at surprise had been, and they discussed the management of the Southern cavalry in scathing terms. The *Examiner* went so far as to use the word "tournament" in reference to Stuart's recent displays.[44] This humiliation of the proud cavalryman was to have a profound effect on later events.[45]

General Lee was close at hand during the fighting at Brandy Station. Sizing up the Federals' advance as a reconnaissance to determine his strength and position, he warily kept out of sight most of the huge force of infantry that he had within reach. In the Federal cavalry's aggressiveness he saw an important message. He had been plagued with doubt as to whether he could march north without exposing Richmond to attack; now he could see that if Hooker's forces were prepared to begin a general offensive, the Federal cavalry would be occupied at something other than riding around in quest of either information or a fight. Lee accordingly made no important change in his invasion timetable. On the morning of June 10 his army struck out for the North, Ewell's brigades marching smartly on two roads leading toward Chester Gap in the Blue Ridge. Five days were to elapse before Longstreet and Stuart set out from Culpeper; by this time Hill, whose force at Fredericksburg had for some days been recognized as merely a front for the rest of the army, had begun his march.[46] The army that had disappeared behind the Rappahannock was now placing a much more formidable barrier, the Blue Ridge, between itself and the prying eyes of Union intelligence.

19

....

PURSUIT

June 10–14, 1863

I F THERE IS A SPECIAL PLACE in Valhalla for generals who achieved marvels in the art of public relations, Alfred Pleasonton will be found there. Several generations of historians have credited him with making the momentous discovery, in his Brandy Station attack, that Lee's army was headed for Pennsylvania. This acclaim is a product not of Pleasonton's considerable military ability but of his bold storytelling.

His extension of the facts of the case took some time to develop. Immediately after the Brandy Station battle his claim was simply that he had broken up Stuart's long-expected cavalry raid.[1] When it became clear that Stuart was on the march but merely as part of a general advance of Lee's army, he diverted attention from his embarrassingly wrong claim by introducing a new one not so visibly erroneous: that at Brandy Station his men had "seized Stuart's headquarters with all its documents." This great intelligence prize was a complete fabrication; Stuart's headquarters baggage had been moved out of harm's way.[2] From a field desk that had bounced off a wagon in the hurried retreat of Beckham's horse artillery, the attackers did pick up three official papers, all of them unenlightening as to Lee's or Stuart's planned movements. In two personal letters that were also acquired, Rebel troopers confidently predicted a "grand" cavalry raid, their numbers raised to 12,000 (the same figure that had reached Sharpe). These letters were the only captured papers mentioning a cavalry raid; thus Pleasonton's information on the raid amounted to no more than camp gossip. But by omitting from all his stories any mention of what the captures actually amounted to, he led his audience and his readers to believe that they revealed official plans for the raid.

His most extravagant claims were delivered when he appeared months later before the Joint Committee on the Conduct of the War, by which time Hooker was in General William T. Sherman's command, too far away to critique these latest improvements in the story. Pleasonton now described his assigned mission at Brandy Station not as beating up Stuart's cavalry but as conducting a reconnaissance in force. He told the committee that the Brandy Station attack "proved conclusively that the bulk of Lee's army was then around Culpeper, and that [Stuart] was about to make a raid to destroy the Orange and Alexandria railroad, to prevent our army going by that way into Pennsylvania after them." Even this extravagance did not satisfy its author; he sent the committee a written account claiming that "very important information was obtained relative to [the] proposed invasion of Pennsylvania, on which General Hooker acted immediately, and moved his army towards Maryland."[3]

Hooker's action was not immediate; not until three days after the cavalry battle did he receive the information that led him to move his army. And as we are about to see, the principal contributor of that information was Captain McEntee, not General Pleasonton. The captain's reports have lain undiscovered in Sharpe's files all these years, while Pleasonton's letter to the congressional committee has been in print, providing a deceptive credibility to his extravagant claim.

The predictions of a Stuart raid that led to the Brandy Station battle had come from Confederate deserters, Pleasonton's scouts, Howard Skinker, and the refugee Robinson. Now the captured letters provided Pleasonton with the same information in written form; the original camp gossip was verified — by the same camp gossip. This faulty logic must have been noticed by Hooker, but he continued to regard the cavalry raid as a threat. It dominated his thinking for three days.*

Sharpe's acceptance of the reports of a forthcoming cavalry raid was a serious error. But its principal effect was a benefit to the Federals: it led to a battle in which Northern cavalrymen found they could match sabers on even terms with the proud horsemen of the Confederacy.

At Brandy Station Pleasonton's men had had a close look at Confederate infantry; the encounter was short and slight, but definite enough to correct Hooker's belief that cavalry was the only enemy force there. Now, on June 10 and 11, there were more sightings of infantry along the river bank and a confusing miscellany of reports of infantry from deserters and from prisoners and contrabands taken in the fight with Stuart. The best of these reports was from an officer's servant who placed Ewell and Longstreet at Culpeper and Hill at Fredericksburg. This was fully correct as to Hill and Ewell and substantially correct as to Longstreet, who was still completing the gathering-in of his forces that had been in southeastern Virginia. But Hooker's belief now was that Ewell was still at Fredericksburg, along with Hill, and Longstreet at Culpeper with Stuart.

* See Appendix 7 for a more detailed analysis of Pleasonton's claims and their survival in modern accounts.

Another Negro's statement to Pleasonton largely corroborated the first, but Hooker persisted in his mistaken opinion.

Deserters reported that the Confederates now had the startling number of 60,000 troops at Culpeper. The cavalry staff did not turn these men over to McEntee, whose examining skill might have brought out the fact that the 60,000 figure was a fair enough indication of what was going on out at Culpeper. The captain might also have shaken the deserters' report that placed Ewell still at Fredericksburg.[4]

While the fight at Brandy Station was in progress, word arrived that Lee had gathered in his forces between Richmond and Fredericksburg. This came from scouts, apparently some of Sharpe's best men, who had been as far south as Hanover Junction, twenty-five miles short of Richmond. They reported Pickett's brigades gone from that locality, where he had been stationed for some weeks. The country seemed to be nearly empty of Confederate troops, and Richmond too, the scouts reported, had been stripped to strengthen Lee. Since they named the Rapidan country as Pickett's destination, Pleasonton's discovery of infantry at Brandy Station took on added credibility. Another piece of news came from Signal Corps Captain Benjamin Fisher, who was in Port Royal on June 10 under a flag of truce; a Confederate signalman "acknowledged that Lee had moved." Still another source, a routine one that would have been watched with more than usual attention at this time, was the Richmond press; one of the capital's newspapers was stating confidently that Lee's army was on the march.[5]

Hooker's response to these reports was a heavy reinforcement of his right wing.[6] This would assist Pleasonton in preventing the enemy cavalry from crossing the Rappahannock; it was also a safeguard against envelopment of the wing by infantry.

.. .. ..

John McEntee was not enjoying the part of his job that entailed reporting the same information that Pleasonton also reported, often before McEntee could even learn of it, as in the case of prisoners, deserters, or refugees, whom the cavalrymen naturally turned over to their own headquarters rather than to McEntee. The captain probably was not even aware of the shifting accounts that Pleasonton put on the telegraph wires, although at times he would have suspected that his findings would shoot down one of the cavalryman's latest errors.

To McEntee these were days of discouragement; even the battle of Brandy Station, in which the cavalry learned that they could fight Stuart's men on even terms, had been only an unpleasant episode to him. After George Smith was selected to go on the expedition as Pleasonton's guide, McEntee offered his own services to General Buford, commanding Pleasonton's right wing, but he received a lukewarm response. He rode up to the battleground, however, and "came near loosing the top of my head." Afterward he was allowed to interrogate only a small number of the prisoners taken. Pleasonton's officers were polite to him, but usually the only prisoners or refugees he could see were those he heard about by happenstance. And the handling of prisoners by Pleasonton's command, he had observed, was slipshod. "They are generally allowed to pass to Washington without being searched and if they have any important papers on their person they have every opportunity to destroy them. Yesterday the prisoners were sent to Washington, many of them wearing spurs and carrying saddle bags, officers with memorandum books and pencils." General Stuart's officers were well schooled in prisoner-handling methods that were very unlike these, McEntee said, and he urged that General Hooker issue an order to correct these evils. He also wanted an order directing Pleasonton's provost marshals to cooperate with him. The root of his troubles, he thought, was the cavalry officers' resentment of his mission of reporting on the same matters they reported on.

A few successes, however, were about to come McEntee's way, beginning on the 11th, when he nailed down one elusive fact, the location of Albert Jenkins's cavalry brigade, a part of Stuart's command that was still west of the Blue Ridge. Some of the prisoners taken at Brandy Station were likely to know where Jenkins was, but these men, McEntee found, were very unlike infantry prisoners. They were gentlemen's sons, well educated, veterans of considerable scouting experience, and hence "familiar with all the different means of pumping." But one of them, a lieutenant in the 12th Virginia Cavalry, was "wise in his own conceit." The prisoner asked what the losses in the recent battle were; McEntee replied that Benjamin F. Davis, a well-known colonel in Pleasonton's command, had been killed (which was true) and that General Jenkins also was killed (a fabrication). Falling for this ancient ruse, the Virginian replied that "that was a damned lie, that Jenkins was in the Valley in command of all the forces there, infantry and cavalry."[7]

Another pleasing development for McEntee was the arrival from headquarters of a man who looked as if he could get into Lee's camps if anyone could. This was Martin E. Hogan, a twenty-five-year-old private in the First Indiana Cavalry. Hogan was a veteran of a year's scouting for General Sigel, during which time he had once been captured. He had been imprisoned by his own army the preceding December on suspicion of passing himself as a Federal officer. The fact that Hogan was now back in good graces suggests qualities that McEntee immediately noticed: "He has considerable Irish wit about him and would be likely to work his way out of a tight place." That suggested a project that McEntee proposed to Sharpe: "If you think it advisable [Hogan] will don the gray and turn their left, taking nearly the course the refugee Robinson came in."

Hogan was to contribute to McEntee's next stroke of good fortune. On

Friday, June 12, the captain heard that somewhere inside the Federal lines was a Negro who had come across the river after the cavalry battle and had been permitted to go his own way. In searching the cavalry camps for this man, McEntee chanced upon another Negro, a lad who had come from Culpeper and, without being interrogated, had been put to work as a quartermaster's servant. This boy, Charley Wright, would turn out to have an intimate knowledge of the Army of Northern Virginia. Meanwhile, Hogan had set out on his first espionage mission. He too encountered a contraband with important information; he returned quickly to McEntee with his find.[8]

Back at the Falmouth headquarters Sharpe was struggling to fit many new pieces of his huge puzzle — dozens of observations of enemy movements — into place. Five deserters from Pickett's division, all recent conscripts from Fauquier County, had come in; they brought no new information on Pickett's position, but in passing through the Confederate forces on the Rappahannock they had learned, some days previously, that Ewell was then near Chancellorsville and Hood was on the Rapidan moving toward Culpeper. Sharpe and Babcock by now had interrogated sixty cavalry prisoners taken at Brandy Station, who gave information on Hood similar to the deserters'. But they had nothing on Ewell and McLaws, who had been near enough to Stuart during the cavalry battle to lend him support. Theirs were the very units that had decamped from Fredericksburg. McEntee had other information that Hood was at Culpeper on the 8th and that "infantry was arriving in great force."

At midday of June 12 Hooker sent General Dix a situation summary:

All of Lee's army . . . is extended along the immediate banks of the Rappahannock from Hamilton's Crossing to Culpeper. A. P. Hill's corps is on his right, [extending] below Fredericksburg; Ewell's corps joins his left, reaching to the Rapidan; and beyond that river is Longstreet's corps, with not less than 10,000 cavalry, under Stuart. . . . For several days past Lee has been at Culpeper.

Except for Ewell's position and the fact that not all of Pickett's brigades had reached Culpeper, this was a fairly good understanding of the actual situation. But the meaning drawn from it was still afflicted with the misconception of an intended raid by Stuart, now regarded as confirmed by Pleasonton's report based on the papers captured at Brandy Station. Apparently the fact that the papers' information on the raid amounted only to camp gossip was still being ignored, at least by Hooker. Sharpe may have begun to doubt the cavalry-raid dogma by this time, however, for his reports are silent on the subject, and even Hooker had grown skeptical enough to issue, on the 11th, an alert for general movement of his whole army.[9]

It was Friday evening, June 12, when Sharpe received notice of McEntee's great find, Charley Wright and the other contraband turned up by

Hogan that day. Sent from cavalry headquarters at 5:20 P.M., McEntee's telegram read:

> A contraband captured last Tuesday [June 9] states that he had been living at Culpepper C. H. for some time past. [That he] saw Ewells (Jacksons) corps pass through that place destined for the Valley & Maryland. That Ewells corps had passed the day previous to the fight & that Longstreet was then coming up. A full division at Fredericksburg. Hogan saw another contraband who made a similar statement.[10]

Now the enemy was seen, much more clearly than before, to be embarked on a general movement, and rather well advanced on it at that. Hooker's cavalry-raid fixation dissolved quickly; at 6:20 he wired President Lincoln, who had been planning to visit him, that "if I am not very much mistaken," the army would soon be on the march.[11]

The two Negroes were quickly turned over to Pleasonton. At 7 P.M. he telegraphed, "A colored boy captured on the 9th states that Ewell's corps passed through Culpeper on Monday last [June 8], on their way to the Valley, and that part of Longstreet's has gone also. A second Negro just across the river confirms the statement. I send a reconnaissance to find out the truth."[12]

Duplicate reporting by Pleasonton and McEntee was usual whenever McEntee could get to see prisoners and refugees after Pleasonton and his staff had completed their questioning. In this case McEntee had had first chance at the information because the Negroes had been found not by the cavalry but by himself and Hogan. But now McEntee's information was coming in ahead of Pleasonton's; this was to raise questions at headquarters.[13]

Two hours later, at 9:00, another report from McEntee came across the wire. It read:

> Continuation of last statement. Gen. R. E. Lee Hd Qrs were at Culpepper C. H. on Tuesday last. Ewell arrived there with command night of 6th. Cooked 4 days rations. Marched morning of 7th. Column half day passing through town. Longstreet arrived night of 8th. Cooked rations & marched 9th. This boy knew many of the troops. I think statement reliable. Send Gen [Hooker's] order that I may see deserters. Two came in to-day, sent away before I knew of it. Scouts are all out.[14]

Pleasonton too had a follow-up report, although not until the next morning at 8:00:

> Mr. Smith reports this morning that Ewell left Culpeper last Sunday morning [June 7], and Longstreet Monday and Tuesday, for the Valley. Have parties over the river, and expect to know more to-day. Would it not be well for General Stahel to send out toward Valley and see?[15]

The information that Pleasonton attributed to George Smith, though it did not mention the two contrabands, was doubtless from the same source or sources as McEntee's reports. Possibly Smith had assisted him in the interrogation.

If McEntee's first message nearly brought Hooker to a decision to march, we might expect his second one to have settled the matter. Although it did not change the burden of the captain's story, it added persuasive detail, supplied the important fact that Charley Wright "knew many of the troops," and gave McEntee's favorable assessment of the boy's reliability. Pleasonton's reporting on Wright of course could not match McEntee's thoroughness, derived from his knowledge of the enemy, which enabled him to perceive that the boy possessed much of the same knowledge.

But Hooker remained undecided; it was still not known whether Ewell and Longstreet had gone beyond Culpeper. The two corps did pass through the town, as the Negroes said, but then they halted, Ewell until June 10, Longstreet until the 15th.[16] These delays complicated for more than a week Sharpe's task of tracking the enemy.

Headquarters queried Pleasonton on the morning of June 13 as to the route taken by the infantry that had passed through Culpeper. To this message Butterfield added a postscript asking whether the information in Pleasonton's first message was from the same source as McEntee's reports. It was important to know whether these singularly coincident reports could be regarded as corroborating each other; but Pleasonton's reply ignored the question. Of the enemy's route he reported that the Negroes said Ewell had taken the road toward Sperryville, which was on a fairly direct route to Chester Gap in the Blue Ridge. Ewell's columns actually had taken two roads toward the gap, one of them to the right of Sperryville.[17]

Hooker, and also General Reynolds, under whose command the cavalry was temporarily serving, now put considerable pressure on Pleasonton to widen his search, presumably for Longstreet as well as Ewell. At one point Hooker had Butterfield ask the cavalry commander "in what portion of the Valley your scouts have penetrated"; but Pleasonton does not seem to have been attempting such deep penetration as that. One of the localities to which the scouts were directed was Sperryville, but it should have been assumed that Ewell's rear had passed that point. The results of this extensive effort, on June 12 and 13, were negative; the fact that Ewell was now in the Valley and Longstreet had not yet left Culpeper was unknown.

Hooker reasoned that the enemy march might return east of the Blue Ridge through Manassas Gap, to threaten Washington. He also continued, despite the evidence pointing to the Valley route, to allow for the possibility that Lee, or Stuart, was heading for the upper Rappahannock, in the manner of Jackson's flank march to Manassas in August 1862. If the message intercepted on June 5 asking whether the Rebels had crossed the Rappahannock was a ruse, as it almost certainly was, such a crossing was quite unlikely; but Hooker was overlooking no possibilities. Even the cavalry-raid theory was still alive; Butterfield conjectured that Lee may have been intending to send Stuart on a raid to cover his infantry movements.

It was obvious that Hooker's army could not sit still at Falmouth until the Confederates made their intentions clear by appearing on the upper Potomac or on one of the routes to Washington. On Saturday morning, June 13, Butterfield wrote to Reynolds, now commanding the right wing, "It is probable that a movement is on foot to turn our right or go into Maryland"; but the information was "not of such a settled character as to warrant abandonment of this line."[18]

As late as 2 P.M. Hooker was still worrying his way toward a decision to move the army. Some time around 3:00 it came, possibly induced by a third communication from McEntee, this one a letter that spelled out Charley Wright's knowledge of the composition of Lee's army. Wright had given details about more than a dozen Confederate units, well spaced through Longstreet's and Ewell's corps, whose troops he knew; he had served with some of them.[19] No longer could there be any doubt that Wright knew, in detail, what he was talking about when he described the march of those two corps through Culpeper.

McEntee's letter was written that same June 13; the time of its delivery at Falmouth is not known. But Hooker, whether or not he had the information in the letter in hand that afternoon, owed his usable knowledge of the enemy situation almost entirely to Wright and his fellow contraband; as we have seen, the intelligence picture as drawn from all the other sources was one big muddle. Charley Wright, a walking "order of battle" chart, is entitled to the credit, until now bestowed on the cavalry, for the intelligence that set Hooker's army in motion. That would easily have earned him a place in Sharpe's bureau; one Negro "guide" (the term paymasters and quartermasters used for scouts and spies, white and black) was already on the payroll. Wright could have planted himself as servant to an officer in some major headquarters, thus making a sustained penetration where even a Milton Cline was necessarily limited to a short visit. But once Charley Wright was turned over to Pleasonton, he was out of McEntee's reach, and gone from the pages of history.[20]

. . . . . .

Hooker's march order was crafted to make almost irrelevant the uncertainties surrounding the direction and goals of the enemy movements. He sent Reynolds's wing straight north to Manassas Junction and put the remainder of the army on Reynolds's right, following a parallel route[21] — a movement that would serve equally well whether Lee was marching for

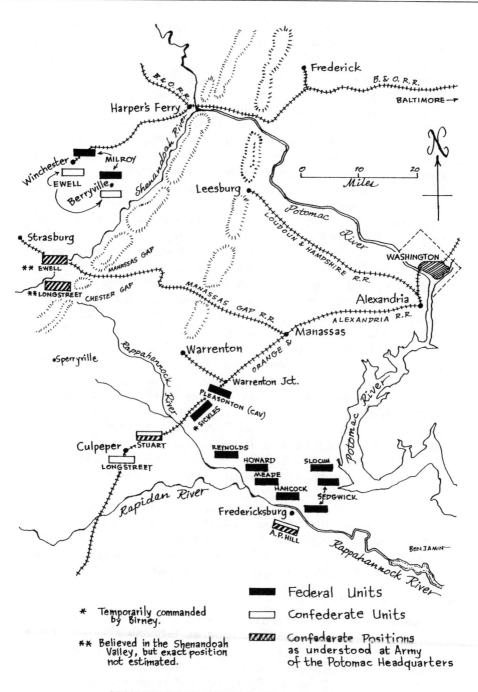

SITUATION, MORNING OF JUNE 13, 1863

Maryland or attempting to flank the Federal right. So complex an order must have been many hours in preparation; the writers might even have set to work before Hooker's decision was firm, and the order was issued as soon as its numerous provisions could be worked out and copies made. Some of the troops could have been started on their way while the details were being ironed out, of course, but instead Hooker used those hours to await a sharpening of the intelligence picture, which never came.

A thesis that Hooker tarried too long on the Rappahannock[22] arises out of the vacillation revealed in his dispatches and also out of the mistaken belief that Pleasonton's attack at Brandy Station had disclosed Lee's movement with considerable clarity. In fact the Army of the Potomac, in beginning its movement on June 13, was on the road more than a day ahead of Longstreet and Hill — all of Lee's infantry except Ewell's corps, which was then arriving before Winchester. Thus the Federals had a lead over Lee's main body in a race for advantage of position to the north, though they were not aware of this favorable situation.

Had Hooker known on the 13th that only Ewell's corps had moved north, his proper action would have been to send only enough of his own army northward to block a possible eastward strike, toward Washington, by Ewell. That is a counsel of perfection — too much to ask of Hooker, though one could wish that the cavalry's search on the 12th and 13th had been made a day or two earlier, when Ewell's march was within reach, and that it had uncovered Longstreet's tarrying near Culpeper. And the inability of Charley Wright and his fellow contraband to track Ewell's and Longstreet's movements beyond Culpeper was another inescapable fact of life. As has already been noted, Hooker's action contained safeguards against error in the estimates of enemy positions and intentions; and while insuring that Washington could not be threatened or his army hurt, he had put it in an excellent position for the further race into Pennsylvania.

The armies had looked at each other across the Rappahannock for seven months; now the river country was to be almost denuded of troops. "Our last night in this camp," General Patrick remarked in his diary — possibly out of sentiment but more probably out of irritation at an order of march that called for headquarters to move out at 3 A.M.[23]

. .   . .   . .

The balloons and balloonists did not accompany the army on its march; with the departure from the Rappahannock, ballooning in the Civil War ended. Thaddeus Lowe, relieved from duty (at his own request, he claimed) in a disagreement with Captain Comstock, had been in Washington for a month, writing the report that Stanton in April had instructed him to make. Ignoring problems that had caused his summons from Stanton, he turned out a 33,000-word history of his ballooning operations with the army. He also sent the secretary a detailed proposal for formal organization of the balloon corps, recommending that the chief aeronaut (presumably Professor Lowe) be directly subordinate to Stanton, the status enjoyed by Colonel Myer as chief of the Signal Corps. Stanton referred the proposal to Halleck; that was the end of it. Then Hooker, after leaving the Rappahannock, endorsed a proposal by Lowe, still in Washington, to have the balloon service placed in the Signal Corps. But Myer proved averse to enlarging his domain; he pleaded lack of money and men. After the battle of Gettysburg Lowe approached Myer directly, but without success.[24]

After Lowe's departure on May 7 the Allen brothers, James and Ezra, Lowe's long-time assistants, kept the service alive back at Falmouth. They operated two balloons, one near headquarters and the other downriver. The military supervision of the balloonists was now even more disagreeable than in Lowe's day. The service was still in charge of the army's chief engineer, but that position was now held by Brigadier General Gouverneur K. Warren. He had instituted a hands-on supervision by two young lieutenants, who showed their mettle by forcing an ascent, to nearly 1000 feet, in weather so stormy that it caused an accident that, as reported by the Allens, could have been fatal. The wind tore a hole in the balloon; they claimed that it descended safely "by the resistance of the atmosphere alone," a statement which, left unexplained, is hard to understand. Warren wrote that the relations "between the Messrs. Allen and the two lieutenants are of the most unfriendly character; their [the balloonists'] language . . . being a series of bitter recriminations and personal insults."[25]

The last balloon observation report on record tells a story typical of those June days: a new camp had appeared southwest of Fredericksburg early on the 12th; it was gone before the morning was over.[26] That was the kind of report the signal officers could produce in quantity; therein may be the underlying reason for the discontinuance of the balloons: although their advantage in altitude yielded observations the signal stations could not make, that may not have been enough to compensate for their logistical troubles.

For months after the return from Gettysburg the armies' relative positions, which changed constantly, did not invite the resumption of ballooning; but once Grant laid siege to Richmond and Petersburg — a year after the departure from the Rappahannock — his army was in positions where balloons would have a close and continuous view of the enemy lines. That was the Grant campaign that was not expected to last even through the summer — too short a time for such a project to be revived and brought to fruition. Nevertheless, the Union armies' willingness to fight the last year of the war without balloon reconnaissance is a riddle, an important unanswered question in the intelligence story.

20

. . . .

LOST INTELLIGENCE,
LOST BATTLE

May 27–June 15

O N MAY 29, Major General Robert Milroy, stationed at Winchester and commanding the Union forces in the Shenandoah Valley, received two brief and not altogether clear telegrams from Washington. "There are reasons why your force . . . should be on the alert and prepared for an attack," said a message from General Halleck. The other message, from Secretary Stanton, told Milroy that it was "necessary that a vigilant watch should be kept at all points. . . . Your position should enable you to have early information of any movement in the Shenandoah Valley or in that direction."[1]

Although the two chiefs at Washington may not have been showing each other their telegrams before sending them, there was no discrepancy in their instructions. But General Milroy, whose towering height, aquiline nose, black eyes, and long silver hair caused him to be known as the "Gray Eagle," was in a situation where any action he took was likely to run counter to the wishes of one or more of his superiors. His position was ambiguous because of a difference of opinion between General Halleck and Milroy's immediate commander, Major General Robert C. Schenck, at Baltimore. The disagreement involved the proper way of carrying out Milroy's mission, which was to protect the Baltimore and Ohio Railroad. Schenck, a former congressman, diplomat, and railroad president who dealt confidently with regular officers, believed that protection was best gained by having a cordon of sizable garrisons at Winchester and other key points well to the south of the railroad. Halleck insisted that the proper disposition of Milroy's 7000 troops was along the railroad with only small outposts at such places as Winchester, twenty-five miles to the southwest. This difference of view had never been resolved; Halleck and Schenck had often discussed it — pleasantly, as Schenck later recalled — but despite Halleck's belief that Winchester was danger-

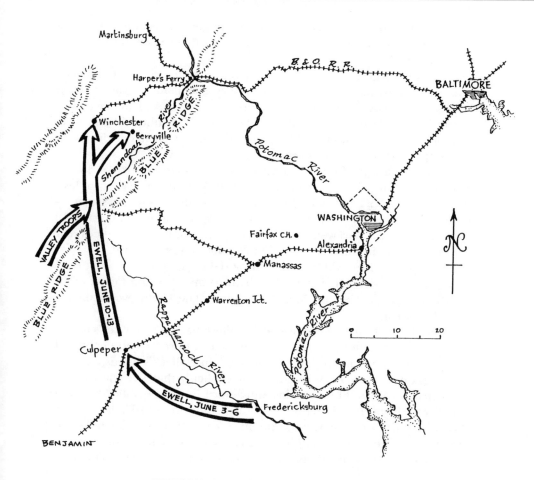

EWELL'S ATTACK ON WINCHESTER

ously exposed and despite his repeated and unmistakable instructions to treat it as an outpost, Schenck had never done so. As recently as May 8 he had promised compliance, but the month ended with Milroy's brigades still ensconced at Winchester and nearby Berryville.[2] Because the general-in-chief issued orders and did not enforce them, the situation of Milroy and some of Schenck's other subordinates contained a built-in hazard. For the day would come when an emergency order would be thwarted because of the way Halleck's standing orders had been habitually treated.

Stanton's and Halleck's concern that gave rise to their telegrams to Milroy was General Hooker's telegram of May 27, summarizing Sharpe's report of that date, which forecast the movement that became Lee's invasion of Pennsylvania. Hooker's telegram gave very little of the substance of the report, saying only that "it seems that the enemy will soon be in motion."[3]

Hooker's telegraphic gist of this all-important piece of intelligence omitted details that would have been very useful to his superiors in Washington. Worse than his excess of brevity, however, was an inaccuracy and inconsistency that he introduced. The report had unqualifiedly forecast an enemy movement; Hooker watered down this firm conclusion to a statement that the enemy *seemed* to be about to move.

To Hooker this perfunctory condensation appeared sufficient, for he assumed that the full report would reach Washington in half a day or less. But it did not arrive in General Halleck's office until twelve days later — June 8, the same day the report of Stuart's planned grand raid arrived.[4] How the May 27 report went astray is unknown. Stanton and Halleck had too much on their minds to query Hooker about its nonarrival.

This slip combined with Hooker's too-brief telegraphic gist amounted to a grand blunder, for it started a chain of mistakes and failures that sealed the fate of General Milroy's division. The chain eventually acquired twelve links.

From May 27 to June 8 Stanton and Halleck had only Hooker's inadequate telegram to use in directing preparations to receive the expected enemy movement. Had the full report been in Halleck's hands, his May 29 telegram would have warned Milroy explicitly that Lee's army or a major part of it would be coming northward down the Valley. Stanton had given Milroy an inkling of what was behind his and Halleck's telegrams by saying that there was "intelligence from General Hooker of movements by the rebels"; but his emphasis was on the need for information from Milroy rather than on preparations against attack. The message could be misread.

Milroy proceeded to misread it. He expected merely increased activity by the enemy's small Valley forces. He did not worry about Lee's army; Hooker would follow closely on any movements it made.[5] Halleck's message he apparently ignored, perhaps because it had been forwarded not over Schenck's signature but over that of Schenck's chief of staff, Lieutenant Colonel Donn Piatt, who paid more heed to Halleck's orders than Schenck did. Stanton and Halleck in their unavoidably inadequate instructions, and Milroy in his reading of them, had added link no. 2 to the chain that was beginning to encircle the garrison of Winchester.

Milroy was vigorous, however, in complying with Stanton's request for intelligence. On the same day the message from Washington reached him, he replied, through Schenck, that he had learned, from "a secret rebel source entitled to some credit," of a plan formed by Lee to outmaneuver Hooker and get between the Army of the Potomac and Washington. An elaboration of this report followed by mail the next day.

The report was from one of Milroy's secret agents, Michael Graham, a Virginian and a railroad builder by occupation. Graham, who claimed that his "secret rebel source" was a member of Lee's staff, explained at length how Lee would draw Hooker out of position and uncover Washington. Milroy praised Graham's reliability; Halleck forwarded the report to Hooker. But Graham or his informer had been misled; Lee's plans had not yet been worked out in detail, and what plans he had bore no resemblance to the scheme sketched by Graham.

Halleck may not have known that earlier in that same week Graham had sent two long letters to Stanton, letters that told the secretary in no uncertain terms exactly how the war should be conducted in northern Virginia — creating the impression that the writer was a crank. But Graham's forebodings were not all wrong; one of the letters warned, "General Milroy will be attacked in less than ten days unless he is re-enforced."[6] It was the erroneous intelligence on Lee's plans, however, that took root in Washington, reinforcing Milroy's supposition that if Lee came north, his route would be east of the Valley. Link no. 3 had been added to the chain.

On June 2 Milroy's sources reported that "the rebs have returned to the Valley with much increased force, and are about to attack this place"; the enemy's strength was put at 10,000. Schenck, to whom Milroy passed this information, sought to quiet him by suggesting, "It is very possible that the rebels may only be intending to hold the Valley for the harvest." Thus Milroy's tendency to expect only routine operations by the enemy received his superior's encouragement. This was link no. 4.

If Halleck and Stanton had seen Schenck's message to Milroy, they would have realized that the possibility of Lee's coming through the Valley was making an insufficient impression on Schenck and probably on Milroy as well. But nothing revealing the two field commanders' evaluation of the situation appears to have reached them.[7] Their unawareness of Schenck's and Milroy's thinking was link no. 5.

By June 8 Milroy's sources, independently of Colonel Sharpe, had persuaded him that Jeb Stuart was planning the same grand raid that had drawn Sharpe's and Hooker's attention away from the predicted general movement of Lee's army. Milroy joined General Pleasonton in accepting the reports that the enemy had acquired mounted infantry, enlarging on Pleasonton's version of that story by stating that Lee had mounted the whole of Hood's division, a feat well beyond the capabilities of the Confederate economy. He estimated that Stuart's cavalry division now numbered 24,000. But Stuart's strength even after strenuous efforts to build it up was still only about 10,000; he would have been glad to have Milroy's ideas as to where 14,000 more horses, or even 14, could be obtained.

Although Colonel Sharpe did not accept the most fanciful parts of

Milroy's report, he shared Milroy's expectation of a Stuart raid, as we have seen, and his report predicting it arrived in the War Department on June 8, the same day as the "lost" report of May 27.[8] It was the later of the two reports that won attention. Hooker, Halleck, and Milroy now shared a common erroneous belief — link no. 6.

Evidence of the true situation was available on June 8, but it escaped the notice of Hooker and the Washington authorities. On the 7th a cavalry detachment from the Department of Washington had made an east-to-west sweep of a forty-mile stretch of country between Manassas and the Blue Ridge looking for traces of the enemy. They encountered a few isolated detachments of Confederate forces, but their chief accomplishment was learning somehow that Ewell's corps was at Culpeper, well along the route from Fredericksburg, Lee's headquarters for many months past, to the Valley.

The blue-uniformed troopers rode into Winchester with this information early on June 8. Promptly their commander, Major Melvin Brewer of the First Michigan Cavalry Regiment, posted a report to his chief, Major General Julius Stahel, back at Fairfax Court House. The information about Ewell called for telegraphic transmission, but Brewer sent his dispatch by courier. Stahel had taken his cavalry division into the field and probably did not see the report for two or three days. When it came to his attention he passed it to General Pleasonton, giving Hooker, on June 12, only a summary that ignored Brewer's one big finding. In Hooker's hands that finding would have amounted to a warning that the enemy was engaged in more than a grand raid by Stuart.

Brewer must also have imparted his information to General Milroy, who, if he had seen any significance in it, would have risen to the occasion with a telegraphic report. But Milroy was by now less inclined than ever to feel himself threatened by Lee's infantry.[9] Thus link no. 7 was added to the chain by the flagrantly poor handling of Major Brewer's discovery.

Halleck, carried along by the portents of a raid by Stuart, sent a warning to Schenck on June 8, adding, "I can only repeat the recommendation . . . to mass your troops in more convenient places for rapid and concerted operations, . . . exposing no large force in advanced positions, where they are liable to be cut off." Colonel Piatt pointed out to Schenck that the general-in-chief was referring to Winchester, but Schenck declined to take any action other than to instruct Milroy to keep a sharp lookout.[10] Halleck, though motivated by incorrect intelligence of a Jeb Stuart raid, had taken an action that was proper in the light of both the true situation and the situation as he understood it. Link no. 8 was the handiwork of Schenck alone.

Schenck then sent Piatt to Winchester and the exposed positions along the Baltimore and Ohio to ascertain the condition of affairs. On

June 11 another message from Halleck, relayed to Piatt at Harper's Ferry, gave outright orders for the removal of the Winchester garrison. Piatt promptly wired Milroy, directing him to evacuate Winchester, and Milroy just as promptly wired Schenck, saying he could hold the town "against any force the rebels can afford to bring against me." Schenck countermanded Piatt's order and telegraphed Halleck, "Your instructions in regard to withdrawing troops from Winchester . . . have been received & I have given direction to be ready [to] carry them out."[11] Brazenly Schenck told the general-in-chief that his orders to withdraw had been translated into orders to be *ready* to withdraw. The significance of this change passed unnoticed by Halleck, who had other serious concerns at this time, chiefly General Grant's siege of Vicksburg. The Winchester matter stood where Schenck's telegram left it; another link, no. 9, had been added to the chain.

Milroy dug in and awaited developments. Strong reconnaissances on June 12 met heavy enemy forces on both of the principal roads leading southward up the Valley. Milroy concluded that he was facing both the regular Valley cavalry forces and Stuart's cavalry. In reality his opposition contained only a small cavalry force and consisted mainly of the infantry corps of Lieutenant General Ewell — one third of Lee's army.[12]

Next day, the fateful Saturday, June 13, the enemy mass closed in on Milroy, and he fought all through the morning without recognizing that his 7000 troops were struggling against more than 20,000. About noon the sounder at the Winchester telegraph office began clicking off a cipher telegram from Baltimore. It was a critical message, but Milroy never received it; transmission had just commenced when the Rebels tore down the wire. That was a momentous near-miss; the message was an order from Schenck that would have evacuated Milroy's force at the eleventh hour.[13] Its failure to arrive was link no. 10 — not the work of Northern hands but of Southern.

Meanwhile, at Army of the Potomac headquarters General Hooker was so occupied in deciding to move out and pursue the enemy, and then in organizing a march of more than 100,000 men, that he did not get around to informing Halleck and Stanton of the move until 7 P.M. By that time Halleck needed word from Hooker to answer an urgent query from Schenck: whether Lee's infantry had been reported in the Valley or moving in that direction. Halleck could only reply that scouts (necessarily Hooker's) probably would be reporting late information during the day.

Halleck could have answered that question affirmatively if he had had the information on Ewell's and Longstreet's departure from Culpeper that Captain McEntee had telegraphed to Hooker's headquarters Friday evening. For many weeks telegrams between Hooker and his cavalry's base at Warrenton Junction, where McEntee was stationed, had been relayed through the War Department telegraph office; copies of those telegrams were available to Halleck. But on Thursday, June 11, the telegraph service had strung a wire connecting the cavalry base and Hooker's headquarters; that ended the relay arrangement. This improvement in telegraph communication was the reason Halleck had no answer to Schenck's query.[14]

Sometime in the morning of the 13th Schenck received alarming intelligence from within his own command. Scouts from Harper's Ferry had learned from Rebel citizens in Loudoun County, Virginia, east of the Blue Ridge, that Lee's army was marching for Winchester. Civilians were the weakest source of information, and these were situated far from the route of the reported march. But Schenck, who was a recognized authority on draw poker, now listened to his gambling instincts. He wrote an order for Milroy to fall back to Harper's Ferry. This was the message that was being transmitted when Milroy's telegraph line went dead.[15]

Next morning, the 14th, a good twelve hours too late for it to be of any use, Schenck received from Halleck the intelligence that had originated with Captain McEntee late on the 12th.[16] It had not been improved upon during its twenty-six-hour delay at Hooker's headquarters and its fifteen hours in Washington. In Halleck's eyes the situation at Winchester was less than critical; he had ordered the place abandoned on the 11th, and Schenck had at least given assurance of being ready to withdraw in good time. But these reasons looked terribly weak when the next news came from Winchester. This delay added another link, no. 11.

Nor was that the end of the slippage. General Schenck, frustrated by the telegraph break, had not exhausted his means of getting the evacuation order to Milroy. He directed his Martinsburg outpost, twenty-three miles from Winchester, to put it through by courier. No orders of any kind, however, reached Milroy after the telegraph break; yet, as will be seen, courier communication was still possible at that time. One more link — twelve in all.

It was left for Milroy to learn for himself, and in a most painful way, the news Schenck had tried to send him. Late on the 13th his troops took a prisoner who said he belonged to a Louisiana brigade.[17] Louisianians! There were none in the Virginia theater except in Lee's army.

A brave officer (he was always conscious that his family claimed descent from the Scottish hero Robert Bruce), Milroy determined to make a fight of it. At 10 P.M. on the 13th he wrote a dispatch to General Schenck saying that he had been sharply engaged, that there were prospects of a general battle, and that he would "hold this place in spite of fate."

For the task of getting this message through the investing force there was an unrivaled candidate. In Milroy's command was Captain William H. Boyd, Sr., of the First New York Cavalry, who had been court-martialed on charges that included sharing his tent with a woman wearing masculine garb. The court had acquitted him, but with censure for having failed to ascertain "the truth or falsehood of the current camp report that the reputed boy George, his servant, was a female, which was, in the opinion of the Court fully proven." Boyd already had established a reputation as a scout; the court-martial only added to his celebrity as an officer of dash and nerve.

Boyd fulfilled Milroy's confidence by getting the message through to Martinsburg.[18] His success shows that Schenck's evacuation order to Milroy probably could have been pushed through that night had a sufficient effort been made at Martinsburg.

Without new orders from Schenck, Milroy lacked authority to abandon Winchester. He stood no chance against a siege, for he had been required to keep no more than five days' stores on hand at a time. By evening of the 14th his ammunition and provisions were almost gone. The enemy occupied commanding ground, including some of his fortifications. In consultation with his brigade commanders, one of whom had marched from Berryville to join forces with him, he decided to cut his way out to Harper's Ferry rather than surrender. He would leave his artillery behind in order to avoid a noisy march that would alert the enemy.[19]

The escape produced a series of improbabilities somewhat like the sequence that had led to Milroy's entrapment. The withdrawal started in the middle of the night and soon encountered Edward Johnson's division of Ewell's command. Johnson had just come into position across the Harper's Ferry road four miles northeast of Winchester. Northerners and Southerners both attacked; there followed a wildly confused melee involving nearly 10,000 men in pitch dark. Milroy's lack of artillery now put him at a severe disadvantage in the contest for a bridge that stood in his path. Soon his horse was shot from under him and he could not immediately get another; he was immobilized long enough to lose whatever hope he had of exercising control over his units. He could not find his Third Brigade, and neither could its commander, who was riding back and forth across the fields and hills trying to organize a flank attack by regiments that one by one lost their positions in the darkness and drifted away. A plan was improvised to save the Second Brigade by withdrawing it over a supposedly safe route while the First provided cover by continuing the fight; but most of the Second was captured and a sizable part of the First, despite its exposed position, was kept together and made a successful withdrawal.

When the affair was over, Milroy and perhaps 1500 of his command got through to Harper's Ferry and another large column wound up in Pennsylvania. The Third Brigade's wagon train did not find its way back to the command until it had set some kind of record for outdistancing the enemy by marching to Harrisburg and Philadelphia. Twenty-three excellent pieces of artillery and large quantities of other heavy property were in the hands of the enemy, and Milroy's command was a shambles, with 95 killed, 346 wounded, and 4000 reported captured or missing.[20]

The fall of Winchester, and with it Martinsburg, sent shock waves through the North. Authorities at Pittsburgh set about building fortifications; Philadelphia newspapers reflected a state of near-panic in that city. President Lincoln issued a call for 100,000 short-term militia to defend the threatened states, and Ohio's governor hopefully raised his 30,000 quota to 50,000.[21] All this took place before the Confederates' movements had revealed with certainty anything more than an intention to regain possession of the lower Shenandoah Valley.

Halleck blamed the Winchester debacle entirely on Milroy, wiring Schenck, "Do not give General Milroy any command at Harper's Ferry. We have had enough of that sort of military genius."[22] Late in the summer a court of inquiry took a position quite different from that blistering comment. Although it was Milroy whose conduct the court was investigating, the evidence brought out clearly the fact that he was acting in accordance with Schenck's orders and that Schenck had taken undue liberties with explicit instructions of General Halleck. President Lincoln endorsed the court's findings with the statement "Serious blame is not necessarily due to any serious disaster, and I cannot say that in this case any of the officers are deserving of serious blame."[23] Schenck's political prominence may have led the President to deal softly with his case, in the hope of retaining his political support. But Schenck returned to Congress later in the year, soon became chairman of the House Committee on Military Affairs and later of the Ways and Means Committee, and in both positions of power proved a strong Republican critic of the administration. Lincoln's indulgence in this case was only typical of his patience with military mistakes; and Halleck's leniency in forcing compliance with his orders was only an especially grievous instance of his and Lincoln's difficulties in dealing with political generals.

Milroy was less fortunate than his chief. He suffered through many months without an assignment before congressional friends arranged for him an obscure rear-echelon command in the western theater.[24]

. .   . .   . .

In the events that ended in the ruin of General Milroy's division, everything possible had gone wrong. Such a combination of misunderstandings, oversights, communication failures, laxity in the enforcement and execution of orders, and plain bad luck probably was not equaled in any other event of the Civil War, even in an army so dogged by failure as the Army of the Potomac had been up to that time.

This disaster occurred at a time when the Potomac army had finally developed a competent intelligence service, the one capability most vital in preventing the surprise that struck Milroy. Hooker's intelligence bureau had turned in an excellent performance in discovering Lee's plans more than two weeks before that surprise came. Proper handling of its May 27 forecast would have given us a very different history of the Confederates' advance to the Potomac. With Halleck's relay of the report in hand, Milroy would have been shaken out of his complacency and Schenck out of his insubordinate foot-dragging. If they persisted in their sluggishness, there would have been ample time for that to become evident to Halleck, who then would have laid on them a no-nonsense order for withdrawal.

This was a situation in which an intelligence element in the War Department — an innovation that apparently no one ever thought of — could have saved the day. So small an investment as a single staff officer, assigned as part of his duties to keep an eye on intelligence affairs, would have sufficed in the Winchester case. When the obviously important intelligence report that Hooker promised on May 27 failed to arrive in a day or two, that officer would have gone into action and got his hands on a copy. By then familiar with the work of Hooker's bureau, he would have impressed Schenck and Milroy with the probability of a threatening movement by the enemy. He would have urged Milroy to a vigorous probing of the Valley and kept a finger on the situation to assure that Schenck's and Milroy's response to the available intelligence was adequate.

The Winchester debacle was a failure of coordination and discipline at the highest levels of the army. It was also a case of critical intelligence going to waste.

21

. . . .

JOE HOOKER'S
MAGNIFICENT ERROR

June 14–26

EVEN THE OVERWHELMING of the division at Winchester did not make Lee's purpose plain at Hooker's headquarters. Although the fixation concerning Stuart's "raid" died away (Pleasonton relinquished it most unwillingly), a serious question remained whether the enemy's objective was Washington or Maryland and Pennsylvania. One reason for the uncertainty was that Ewell, after knocking out the garrisons at Winchester and Martinsburg, had advanced to the Potomac with most of his forces and set them down astride the river; he was giving no clear indication that he intended to send more than his cavalry farther north. In addition, Milroy's reputation as an alarmist cast doubt on his statement that it was Ewell's corps that had thrown him out of Winchester. The sketchy messages that his courier, Captain Boyd, carried to Martinsburg on the night of June 13 were also open to the interpretation that the investing army was not Ewell but a reconstituted Valley force under General Isaac Trimble, lately appointed to the command of that district.

To add to the confusion, prisoners and cavalry scouts were telling Pleasonton, who relayed their statements to Hooker, that Longstreet and Stuart were Lee's advance elements and Ewell was still south of the Rappahannock. The fact that this story could gain that much circulation suggests that it must have been conveyed to the Federals at Lee's or Stuart's direction. In any case Pleasonton, whether or not he was the victim of deception, sent so many contradictory telegrams that he exhausted the patience of General Halleck, who termed the cavalry chief's reporting "very unsatisfactory."[1]

The discouraged Captain McEntee, sent to Pleasonton partly because his knowledge would enable him to detect false or innocently incorrect statements by persons under examination, was still being circumvented by the Cavalry Corps staff. Now a new difficulty had arisen: his men were being arrested when reentering the Union lines, even though they carried credentials entitling them to admittance. McEntee and his whole party were uprooted from their bivouac in the middle of the night by a cavalry colonel, who next morning "condescended to examine my papers and gave me any quantity of apologies for satisfaction."

McEntee's success in being first with the news that started Hooker's army in pursuit of Lee was repeated when he supplied the first piece of hard fact that came the Federals' way as they moved northward over clogged roads. While Pleasonton's scouts were being stopped short by the enemy, Martin Hogan and Yaller Carney got across the river on June 13 at Field's Ford and penetrated far enough into enemy territory to observe dense clouds of dust over the Blue Ridge. McEntee got word of this movement (which was probably that of Ewell's wagon trains) to Sharpe the next day. He added that George Smith had gone to Washington, "thinking he could be of no use to me."[2]

The dust clouds' revelation of an enemy march in the Valley was followed on the 14th by discovery that Hill's corps was beginning to draw off from Fredericksburg. The source was another pair of Sharpe's men, unnamed in the records, who had crossed the river above the town. They reported Hill's strength as 20,000 with sixty guns, a conservative estimate on both counts, and said that 4000 of this force had moved off toward Culpeper on the afternoon of the 13th, before Hooker's march began.[3] Hill's prompt beginning of his march was a response to the withdrawal of Sedgwick's corps on the night of June 12 from its position on the Confederates' side of the river below Fredericksburg. And Hill wasted no time in discovering the Federals' departure northward, despite Hooker's familiar injunctions to his subordinates to maintain secrecy. This time the security measures included an elaborate effort at deception; beginning several days before the army moved, the Signal Corps kept up a steady traffic in flag messages intended to give interceptors the impression that the movement would be toward the Peninsula.[4] Hill, who was under orders to oppose any such movement, must not have been seriously impressed by these messages; moving westward rather than southward, he marched briskly enough to close in six days the thirty-five-mile gap between himself and Longstreet.

As Longstreet, accompanied by Lee, moved off from Culpeper on the 15th, the happenings in the region between Winchester and the Potomac monopolized Northern concern. Milroy's shattered remnants were coming in to Harper's Ferry; the reports from that area could finally be sorted out and the loss of Winchester and Martinsburg confirmed. Ewell had left Early's division at Winchester and taken the rest of his infantry to the Potomac in the vicinity of Williamsport, making a leisurely four-day crossing of the river. Jenkins's cavalry brigade, which had joined him south of Winchester, did not stay with the infantry but rode across the narrow belt of western Maryland directly to Chambersburg, Pennsylvania.

For a week these 1500 troopers were the only part of Ewell's force that was not hugging the river or remaining south of it, but their foray raised a near-panic in Pennsylvania, Maryland, and Washington. The alarm was magnified by the appearance of the Union wagon train from Martinsburg, which had retreated into Pennsylvania and was mistaken there for part of the invading army. Pittsburghers began fortifying; Philadelphians prepared to follow suit. Stanton wired Governor David Tod of Ohio that his state, along with Maryland and Pennsylvania, was a probable target of the invasion. General Butterfield observed in disgust that "[c]avalry enough is reported . . . to fill up the whole of Pennsylvania and leave no room for the inhabitants"; yet, he noted, nobody who had counted the invading force was able to credit it with more than 1500 men.[5]

Hooker pointed out to Lincoln that his information service was not equipped to cover country as far afield as that where the enemy was operating. This and other complaints inspired by wild reports from north of the Potomac drew a reply from Stanton: "You shall be kept posted upon all information received here . . . but must exercise your own judgment as to its credibility. The very demon of lying seems to be about these times, and generals will have to be broken for ignorance before they will take the trouble to find out the truth of reports." This scathing remark ill became the secretary who only a day earlier had foreseen Lee marching into Ohio, and it was especially gratuitous when directed to a general who had established an effective intelligence-gathering system. But at the moment Hooker was not covering himself with distinction in such matters; he had suggested that Stanton "have the newspapers announce that I am moving on to the James River line" — a deception that Lee would readily have penetrated.[6]

General Darius Couch, whose experience as second in command at Chancellorsville had given him a distaste for serving under Hooker, had been placed in command at Harrisburg; he was already arranging to supplement Sharpe's coverage. At Gettysburg, center of a highway network and a likely target of the invaders' attention, he established a group whose spying and scouting recall the successful espionage performed by an earlier generation of Pennsylvanians against the armies of Generals Sir William Howe and Sir Henry Clinton.[7] The head of the Gettysburg spies was David McConaughy, a leader in local politics and the founder of a cemetery that was to achieve lasting fame as a battleground. McConaughy, then in his fortieth year, was the descendant of Adams County pioneers; two of his great-grandfathers had served in the Continental Army and in the Pennsylvania legislature both before and after the Revolution. After graduating from Washington College at seventeen, David McConaughy taught high school in Maryland and entered the practice of law in his native Gettysburg in 1845. At first a Whig, he was a member of the Republican convention that nominated Lincoln in 1860. Under Couch he served as a temporary captain and aide-de-camp. The size of the organization he recruited is not known; of his assistants, the names of only R. G. McCreary and T. D. Carson have come to light.

The Gettysburg group displayed prowess as early as June 16. Within a day after Jenkins's cavalry had entered Pennsylvania at Greencastle, twenty-five miles across the mountains to the west of Gettysburg, McConaughy had pinpointed his movement. The next day scouts sent out by General Schenck at Baltimore had also caught up with Jenkins, and word was in from residents of Hagerstown and Chambersburg, towns he had visited, who had counted the invading force and reported its number between 1200 and 1500.[8]

The scare was over for the moment, but Jenkins's little command was the only part of Lee's whole army about which the Federals had exact information. On the 17th a *New York Tribune* correspondent in Washington wrote an off-the-record letter to his home office that he had heard "quite directly from the chief of Hooker's detectives that the whereabouts of Lee are absolutely unknown." The "chief of Hooker's detectives" meant John Babcock, who was in Washington that day. That Babcock would make such a statement to a newspaperman is surprising; his frankness could be a reflection of discouragement caused by the confusing and contradictory reports that he and Sharpe had been struggling with. There was that day, for example, a report to the effect that A. P. Hill was still at Fredericksburg and Longstreet was investing Harper's Ferry, with Ewell's position still undetermined. That was the situation as General Patrick recorded it in his diary; but since Sharpe's men three days previously had brought word of Hill's departure from Fredericksburg, it is unlikely that Sharpe and Babcock shared Patrick's view.[9]

Hooker, his army sprawled over the country between Fairfax, Leesburg, and the Potomac, brought the march to a near-halt "until the enemy develops his intention or force." Butterfield observed, "We cannot go boggling around until we know what we are going after." Sharpe called on all the means at his disposal to solve the quandary; he organized four separate espionage expeditions, whose targets were spread over a wide area from Fredericksburg in the rear to the country north of the Potomac. Hooker bore down on Pleasonton, telling him, "It is better to lose men than to be without knowledge of the enemy, as we now seem to be." He told the cavalry chief to make use of McEntee's knowledge and to see to it that the captain received prisoners, deserters, and contrabands after the cavalry officers had examined them.[10]

Pleasonton was already complying with his chief's orders to use lives if necessary. That same day, June 17, one of his brigades encountered Fitzhugh Lee's brigade at Aldie and drove it toward the Blue Ridge.

There were heavy losses on both sides. The Federals took seventy-five prisoners, whose statements mentioned one of the key pieces in Sharpe's puzzle, the position of Longstreet's corps, but their knowledge was so defective that their reports only worsened the problem. Longstreet had been marching along the east side of the Blue Ridge as support to Stuart, who was on his right, screening the entire movement. However, the prisoners said they had come through Thoroughfare Gap; that landmark was so far east of the Blue Ridge — thirty miles — that the statement could not be even a crude attempt at deception. It amounted to a mere puzzle, unsolvable except by reexamining the prisoners, who were now well out of McEntee's reach. He had already been told by his own men that there was no enemy infantry east of the Blue Ridge; Pleasonton passed that information to Hooker and then displayed a rare consistency by repeating it the next day. It was correct; after two days of marching on the mountain slopes, Longstreet's troops had crossed into the Valley. Stuart would need them again, however, and it was three days before they were able to settle down in the Valley.[11]

While McEntee was away on a brief visit to army headquarters, Pleasonton commandeered all of his men for duty as guides and couriers, leaving him without any means of operating. Now that the cavalry was on the march, he did not even have any way of getting his meals. To Sharpe he described an incident that he thought wrote finis to any hope of a successful intelligence mission at cavalry headquarters. When he asked Pleasonton's provost marshal to allow him to examine papers taken from the Confederate officers captured in the fight at Aldie, the provost replied that if anything of interest was found in them, it would be shown to him. "I then asked Gen. Pleasonton if he had any objection to my examining those papers. With a shrug of the shoulder he said No, *he* had no objection; I might ask the Pro Mar to let me see them." McEntee said no more about the matter, but later he observed that a group of Pleasonton's aides "gathered around the light and had a right jolly time reading over the letters." The next day McEntee picked up a paper that these officers had allowed to blow away. It proved to be a complete muster roll of Company B, Fifth Virginia Cavalry. Such a document was highly prized by the Bureau of Military Information; though it related to only one enemy company, its figures could be projected to give an indication of the strength of the regiment and even the brigade to which the company belonged. A dozen or so such projections, well spaced through the Army of Northern Virginia, would provide a more reliable strength estimate than the best spy could get in any way short of reading the strength returns in Lee's headquarters.

McEntee, unaware that Hooker's injunction about cooperating with him was en route to Pleasonton, asked Sharpe to bring him back to headquarters, to return to his regiment or to be given some other assignment "where I can act on my own responsibility or else be subject to some [one] man's orders." His main need, if he was to stay at Pleasonton's headquarters, was for an official definition of his status, but he also wanted something more tangible — an ambulance, a small wagon to be used for foraging, which would, he said, "leave me more independent and at the same time harden my cheek." But the wish to be relieved of his mission with Pleasonton could not be granted; as the army moved north, McEntee remained with the cavalry.

Pleasonton took a hand in headquarters' intelligence operations by assisting one of the groups of spies sent out on June 17 by Colonel Sharpe. The beneficiary of his aid was a party of men headed by Milton Cline. The sergeant and his men, instructed to make for the Warrenton area, found the direct route denied to them by Wade Hampton's cavalry brigade; they were deflected to their right, were again stopped by the enemy, and, turning still farther to the right, came up with the Federal cavalry. Riding forward to Pleasonton's headquarters, they consulted with him; whether they also saw McEntee is not known. They proceeded onward to General Gregg's division, part of which was engaged with the enemy. In the confusion of the fight they merged into the enemy's ranks. It is not clear whether they were in regular Confederate uniforms or were masquerading as partisan rangers driven away from customary haunts by advancing Yankees. Although they were no longer headed in the direction of Warrenton, they had achieved the long sought penetration of enemy lines; whether any of them would return remained to be seen.[12]

.. .. ..

On June 18 General Halleck, who had heard more than enough from Hooker about the lack of information on the enemy, telegraphed him, "They are asking me why does not General Hooker tell where Lee's army is; he is nearest to it."[13] Halleck's jibe touched a question about the Pennsylvania campaign that is still being asked: How could Lee's movement to the Potomac have been surrounded with so much mystery? It is puzzling that 55,000 men (Longstreet's, Hill's, and Stuart's) marching along the two sides of the Blue Ridge would not have created such a stir that some fairly accurate idea of their whereabouts would have permeated across the lines to the Federals. How did Lee defeat this probability? The chief answer to this question is his elaborate attention to security. His first line of defense against Union intelligence was planted information, but pseudo-deserters would have had a difficult time finding the Federals' headquarters, and he seems to have made little or no use of them at this time. Instead, his troops apparently were supplied with false information for use if they were taken prisoner and for distribution to civilians along the route of march. And the excitement induced by his advance could be counted on to expand the errors and exaggerations in rumors reaching the enemy.

Lee's second line of defense was Jeb Stuart, whose well-run organization simply outsmarted the men sent to penetrate the lines, until Cline's party got through. Hence, although many thousands of Southern infantrymen were marching on the eastern slopes of the Blue Ridge for much of the time, they were almost as well shielded from Northern eyes as those on the Valley route. Stuart simply sealed off the area.

Finally, Lee could still count on the Federals' inadequacies in intelligence-gathering. Sharpe's bureau, even after recent additions, had only eighteen men, plus the three chiefs (Sharpe, Babcock, McEntee); even eighteen Milton Clines would not have been enough. His operation had been geared to the relatively stable situation that had prevailed along the Rappahannock, but the territory to be covered was suddenly much expanded. And this was one of the times when intelligence in the Army of the Potomac was especially hampered by the lack of an intelligence element in the War Department. Among other things, officers from Washington could have seen to the prompt interrogation of those of Milroy's men who reached Harper's Ferry; their accounts would have immediately satisfied Hooker, Halleck, and Schenck as to the identity of the force that had driven Milroy out of Winchester. However, there was no one to quiz even Milroy. An enemy who shows himself sufficiently to engage in battle expects to be identified in the process; Ewell was spared this embarrassment for four days after his first attack at Winchester, although Milroy and his officers had accumulated a good many facts showing who their assailants had been. But the War Department's shortcomings in intelligence matters seemingly were never noticed, even by Lincoln.

Halleck's telegram with its indirect slap at the effectiveness of Sharpe's bureau was not the only unfair criticism the colonel was receiving. He was now sharing Hooker's and Butterfield's sleeping tent; yet, in the words of General Patrick, Hooker treated "our 'Secret Service Department,' which has furnished him with the most astonishingly correct information, with indifference at first, and now with insult."[14]

Affairs now took a slight turn for the better when a fog of uncertainty that had been hiding the enemy force in one area of concern, the Potomac country above Harper's Ferry, began to lift. Brigadier General Daniel Tyler, who had taken the Harper's Ferry garrison across the Potomac to safer ground on Maryland Heights, wired Hooker late on the 17th a correct appraisal of the situation in his area. The enemy infantry, he said, seemed to be holding still near Williamsport while the cavalry and light batteries pushed on into Pennsylvania. When Tyler followed this dispatch the next day with word that he had a prisoner, Butterfield was ready with numerous questions to be used in examining him. But-terfield pleaded, "Give us the name and locality certain at any time of any regiment of infantry." The request reflected his familiarity with Sharpe's method of operation: Babcock's records were so detailed that the iden-tification of a single regiment would indicate the presence of the bri-gade, the division, and the corps to which it belonged.

Tyler answered with reports showing he was convinced that the forces on the Potomac really were Ewell's corps, as Milroy had said. One of the smaller garrisons in the enemy's path had escaped after receiving a demand for surrender signed by General Rodes, who was known to command one of Ewell's divisions. But a brigadier general who had been in Milroy's command had given Tyler a statement about the investing force that named several general officers who belonged to Ewell's com-mand, and one, A. P. Hill, who most certainly did not. And Tyler con-fused matters further by insisting that one of Ewell's division command-ers was one of the two generals named John Jones who commanded brigades in Johnson's division. There was just enough error in Tyler's reports to cause Army of the Potomac headquarters to reserve judgment as to whether the force on the Potomac was in fact Ewell's corps.

Equally as important as the tentative placement of Ewell was Tyler's discovery that the enemy had bridged the Chesapeake and Ohio Canal near Williamsport. To Tyler the bridge meant that Ewell was intending to come no farther and was providing means for his cavalry to make a fast withdrawal southward.[15] Actually the bridge was soon to feel the tread of many thousands of Southern infantrymen, marching north.

. . . . . .

While the identity of the Confederates' advance elements was emerging from the mass of confused reports, information arrived revealing also the situation in Lee's rear. It came by telegram all the way from Charleston, West Virginia, and it covered developments in Richmond and vicinity up to June 9. It was from one of Sharpe's spies, Sergeant Mordecai P. Hunnicutt, who took a roundabout route from Richmond through western and southwestern Virginia; his trip occupied ten days. This mode of travel would have disappointed any hope Sharpe had that Hunnicutt could provide fresher information than Joseph Maddox could on his occasional trips to Baltimore. Hunnicutt's arrival at Charleston so surprised the local department commander, Brigadier General E. P. Scammon, that he wired Sharpe for instructions before even allowing the spy's report to be put on the telegraph wire.

Hunnicutt was no stranger to the Richmond area, having lived his early years in Prince George County, twenty miles south of the city. He had two kinds of valuable experience: he had led a life of danger and adventure for many years, and he had seen service as a detective. Descended from Quaker pioneers who settled in Dinwiddie County, Virginia, he had moved to southern Ohio some time before his twenty-first year, when he enlisted in a volunteer regiment and fought in the Mexican War. A decade later he joined one of William Walker's unhappy filibustering expeditions to Central America; captured along with most of his comrades, he ended this phase of his career in an odd but exotic job as pastry cook in the palace of the President of Costa Rica. He was back in the United States in time to take part in the Kansas hostilities that foreshadowed the Civil War. At some point he earned his living as a detective in Memphis. He did not get into the Civil War until November 1862, when he enlisted in the 73rd Ohio Infantry as a "high private in the rear rank." The enlistment record shows that he was a blue-eyed man of slightly less than medium height and credits him with having brown hair, although by his own statement he was completely bald as the result of privations suffered in Mexico.

Hunnicutt quickly found himself promoted to sergeant and just as quickly found he had lost his taste for soldiering. He sought a way out by volunteering for espionage and was soon assigned to duty with Colonel Sharpe. Never, he recalled, "was an order obeyed with more alacrity than *that* one."

The role assumed by Hunnicutt for his trip to Richmond was that of deserter from the Federal army. There is fairly good evidence in family papers that he established his bona fides by enlisting in a Tennessee regiment that he encountered in Virginia. He was able to remain in Richmond long enough to compile a long budget of information. He learned what Confederate units were stationed over a fifty-mile stretch from the Blackwater River below the city to the South Anna above, providing a wealth of detail. About the Army of Northern Virginia, however, his report was rather limited, as might have been expected. His sources of information on Hood's and Pickett's divisions were poorly informed. He learned of the addition of a large North Carolina brigade (this would have been Junius Daniel's) to Lee's command, but two other infantry brigades sent to Lee escaped his notice, apparently having left Richmond before he arrived. He ventured estimates on two difficult points — Lee's total strength, which he put at not over 85,000 (fairly close to the correct figure), and Lee's intention, which he said was "to divide our forces and dash into Washington." For this last statement he named as his source two officers, one a Mississippi colonel whose regiment was in one of the brigades going to Lee, the other an assistant adjutant general on A. P. Hill's staff. Colonel Sharpe would have diagnosed such an attempt at penetrating General Lee's thoughts as a case of mess-table masterminding; but when one of the sources was a member of a corps staff, the story could not be dismissed out of hand.

Hunnicutt's most important discovery was that there were no longer any bodies of troops in the Richmond area that were likely to be sent to Lee. The forces he reported there, although they included some regular brigades, were a bare minimum for the protection of the capital against General Dix's operations. The troops removed from commands farther to the south — from South Carolina and Georgia — Hunnicutt reported as having gone west, which was correct.[16]

.. .. ..

General Hooker, his army spread out from Fairfax to Manassas and Leesburg, was now, on June 20, fairly well posted on the two extremities of the area under Lee's command — Richmond in the south and the upper Potomac in the north. Although the whereabouts of A. P. Hill were uncertain, he very probably was marching to overtake the rest of the army. As for the cavalry, two of the five brigades that fought at Brandy Station had been located, and Stuart with them. The picture was nowhere complete, but a great deal had been filled in since Babcock's statement to the *Tribune* man that Lee's position was absolutely unknown. Approximate locations had been marked out for all the principal enemy commands save one: again the chief mystery was the force led by James Longstreet.

Longstreet's divisions could be sought on either or both slopes of the Blue Ridge, where Sergeant Cline's party was now headed. Meanwhile Ewell's corps could not be counted upon to remain on the Potomac. Fortunately Sharpe, as one of his projects undertaken on June 17, had set about to provide his own coverage of the neighboring part of Maryland. Hooker exercised no command north of the river, but the intelligence activity there was uncoordinated and its coverage was woefully incomplete; nothing short of his own information service would suffice. John Babcock, having been a member of Pinkerton's unit in the Antietam campaign, was the logical selection for an intelligence job that was begging to be done up in Maryland.

Frederick would be his operating base. En route he stopped at the War Department to provide himself with funds and at Provost Marshal McPhail's office in Baltimore to learn if McPhail could provide him with an assistant or two. Ex-Sergeant Thomas Harter, Pope's spy who had traveled with Lee's troops from Richmond to the Rapidan, was now one of McPhail's detectives, but one reason for his employment in Baltimore was that he was not known there; he could easily lose his anonymity among the invaders now approaching Frederick.

Babcock's arrival at Frederick early on the afternoon of June 19 coincided with Ewell's resumption of his advance. Two divisions had stirred out of their camps; Elijah White's partisans had raided at Point of Rocks, downriver from Tyler's position on Maryland Heights; Jenkins's cavalry had come down from Pennsylvania; and, Babcock heard, enemy horsemen were expected in Frederick at any moment. But he was full of fight. "Shall remain whether they come or not, and go to Hagarstown if possible," he wired Sharpe.[17] The indication of the nature of Babcock's mission that this message contained would not have been lost on the commercial telegraph operators at Frederick. He was not equipped with a cipher.[18]

Like McEntee on his mission in cavalry country, Babcock was to remain at his base, organizing espionage to be performed by others, evaluating their findings and sending the results to Sharpe. He began the task of assembling a group of assistants by telegraphing Sharpe asking that Cline be sent to him; he did not realize that at that moment the sergeant was hemmed in by several thousand Confederates. But he soon had two volunteer assistants who were veterans of spying or scouting in Lee's invasion of the preceding autumn. These were James W. Greenwood and Isaac E. Moore, residents of Martinsburg, who were in Maryland because they had not wanted to trust their lives to the Confederates who had swept into their town a few days before. Babcock also knew, probably from General Patrick, that H. Winchester, principal of the Frederick Female Academy, was likely to be well posted on Confederate movements. Winchester was not sure of the visitor's bona fides; Babcock's boyish face did not fit well with the responsibility he had been sent to discharge. But after considerable persuasion Winchester agreed to assist. With this much help Babcock began work.

Soon he had a telegram with a set of instructions bearing Hooker's signature. Besides suggesting espionage practices that were by now second nature to Babcock, the army commander urged him to "employ only such persons as can look upon a body of armed men without being frightened out of their senses. . . . Send me no information but that which you know to be authentic. Be vigilant and active. Use money, and it shall be returned to you." Doubtless with an unspoken fulmination on the commanding general's gratuitous advice, Babcock wired back a crisp statement that he had already made the desired arrangements. Greenwood and Moore were en route to South Mountain, which demanded coverage because an approach to any of its gaps would indicate an intention to march on Baltimore or Washington.[19]

By this time an important development had taken place back at headquarters. Early in the evening of the 19th — a day so wet that Sharpe's tent was full of water — a dispatch arrived from General Pleasonton transmitting a pass taken from an enemy soldier. The prisoner reported, correctly, that Richard Garnett's brigade of Pickett's division was in the region back of Warrenton — evidence of the enemy's deepest incursion into the country north of the Rappahannock and east of the Blue Ridge. Butterfield wrote, "We think the enemy are in the Shenandoah Valley, Longstreet and A. P. Hill, one portion, perhaps, this side of the Blue

Ridge. Ewell is reported in Maryland or Pennsylvania, but we cannot get any reliable or definite idea from there. The whole country, generals and all, seem struck with heavy stampede."

Since the pass carried by Pleasonton's prisoner had already expired, it was quite possible that the man had been visiting his family and was expecting to rejoin his unit as it marched toward him; in other words, Pickett might be marching eastward. This clue, considered in relation to the energy with which Stuart's forces were masking the country behind them, suggested to Pleasonton that Longstreet might be making for Thoroughfare Gap, an obvious route to Washington.[20]

Pleasonton's theory was shared by Colonel Sharpe. In a letter to his uncle on the 20th, the colonel said he wanted to write about the situation at length but did not have the heart to do so; besides, he was "too 'near the throne' to say much." Lee, he said, was "trying to get upon the old field of Manassas. He must whip us before he goes in force to Md. or Penna. If he don't, we propose to let him go, and when we get behind him we would like to know how many men he will take back."[21] The remark is significant as an indication that Hooker's staff was not in the bemused and irresolute state that is commonly attributed to the commanding general on the basis of his correspondence at this time with Washington. Sharpe's theory that Lee was seeking to reach the Manassas area had become more plausible than ever in the light of the prisoner's report to Pleasonton.

A disagreement over some intelligence matter seems to have taken place that day. Sharpe must have told his troubles to General Patrick, for that officer recorded in his diary, "We get accurate information, but Hooker will not use it and insults all who differ from him in opinion. He has declared that the enemy are over 100,000 strong. It is his only salvation to make it appear that the enemy's forces are stronger than his own, which is false & he knows it. He knows that Lee is his master & is afraid to meet him again in fair battle." Like many of Hooker's other subordinates, Patrick was in a state of mind that stood in the way of wholehearted cooperation with his commander. Two days before, he had described Hooker as a man without a plan: "Whatever he does is the result of impulse." Hooker was a "Mr. Micawber . . . waiting for something to turn up."[22]

The possibility of another battle near Washington, in addition to the capital's renowned summer heat, may have been in the back of Sharpe's mind, for he sent his wife and children home to Kingston. Also at this time he again made a formal request to be returned to his regiment. In telling his uncle of this he did not say why he was so unimpressed with his position "near the throne."[23] The army's great need for the services he was performing might be expected to have overridden any ordinary personal motive that opposed it. But hundreds of Sharpe's brother officers were learning that staff duty holds no satisfactions comparable to those of line duty. Added to that important fact of military psychology was Sharpe's attachment to the men of the 120th New York. To these factors must be added the ill treatment which, in General Patrick's view at least, Sharpe was receiving from Hooker, and the frustrations of dealing with the inconsistencies and outright discrepancies in the steady fire of reports from General Pleasonton, who as cavalry chief was the main source of information on a marching enemy. It comes as something of a surprise, nevertheless, to observe that George Sharpe, who gave the country its first modern military-intelligence service, would have preferred to serve as one of a thousand colonels of infantry.

Pleasonton's reports could not be set aside, for some of them turned out to be right, and his report of infantry east of the Blue Ridge was one of these. A succession of infantry prisoners on the 20th confirmed the belief that elements of Longstreet's corps were in his front, but reversed the previous indications as to the direction of their movements. Pleasonton now judged that "Longstreet has the covering of the gaps, and is moving up his force as the rebel army advances toward the Potomac." The infantry east of the Blue Ridge, he correctly reasoned, was there simply to assist Stuart. By the end of the day Pleasonton had information that Longstreet's entire corps had crossed westward over the Blue Ridge. That was correct, but the identification of the corps was still tenuous, resting as it did on the statements of prisoners from a small part of the command.[24]

While the dispatches about Longstreet were being digested, news arrived from Babcock that clarified the situation on the Potomac. On the 19th he had begun telegraphing short reports without waiting to accumulate enough information to produce a comprehensive account of affairs in the Frederick region. His first report, sent a few hours after getting off the train, mentioned the approach of a small detachment of enemy cavalry, a fact that was significant mainly for the threat such an incursion would offer to his own activities. "Very few individuals," he reported, "are permitted to leave the places occupied by the enemy, and those must give satisfactory assurance of secession proclivities."

Nevertheless he succeeded the next day in locating two refugees who were willing to talk. One of them, a physician, had left Williamsport on the evening of the 18th. Up to that time, according to his account, only Rodes's division of infantry and Jenkins's cavalry were across the Potomac; that information was correct but already somewhat outdated. The second refugee, from Martinsburg, gave later news: the number that had crossed at Williamsport was 6000, and more were crossing; there was a scattering of enemy infantry between Williamsport and Hagerstown. Intelligence on the Williamsport area was now satisfactory, and the identification of Ewell's corps was regarded as confirmed, but Babcock was able to write only vaguely of movements by Ewell's other two infantry divisions — Johnson's division crossing the Potomac at Shepherdstown, twenty miles downriver from Williamsport, and Early's advancing from Winchester to Shepherdstown. The strengthened identification of Ewell was less important than another finding of Babcock's: "The main body of Lee's army is not in the vicinity or within supporting distance of [Ewell's] force." In a separate communication to Sharpe, he confided, "I do not intend to waste any time by pretending to post you of Lee's plans."[25] Thus he assured his chief that he was not forgetting the policy of going after facts on what the enemy was doing and leaving theorizing to others.

Babcock, although operating in a locality much less exposed to the enemy than McEntee in his tour with the cavalry, was now in for some trouble more exciting than the captain's. It developed that the espionage activities of his man Greenwood in the 1862 Maryland campaign were known to the secessionist element in Frederick; Greenwood had traveled from Baltimore with Babcock, and the two had been observed in conversation. This fact, combined with the expected visit of enemy cavalry, caused Babcock to revise his announced determination to remain in Frederick whatever the risk. On the afternoon of the 20th he reported in a letter to Sharpe:

> [T]wenty-five of the 1st Maryland Cavalry made a dash into the city. I tried to get out but found all the approaches picketed and gave it up as dangerous. I had been dogged about all day as a suspicious character by several notorious rebels. . . . I had sundry papers about me stating in very strong terms my business here. Being at the time the rebel cavalry entered, in front of the Central House, a notorious rebel hole, I could not hide my papers and had to carefully destroy them by piece-meal and throw them away. A large crowd having collected I made my escape from the parties on my track and put up in a private house in a remote part of the town.

The risk of detection did not end with the destruction of his papers, for two of the messages he had sent from the Frederick telegraph office that day clearly identified him and the nature of his business. The privacy of his telegrams depended on the loyalty and discretion of operators who were not under military control. Even if he had come equipped with a cipher, he would have been no less suspicious a visitor to any Frederick secessionist who might hear of his telegrams. But this predicament did not keep "Bab" from having his little joke with Sharpe. In his letter he wrote, "I am not over-anxious to be ———" and in place of the last word in the sentence he sketched a gallows and its victim.

The raiders belonged to Major Harry Gilmor's battalion, which divided its time between guerrilla warfare and regular cavalry service. Next morning, finding that they had withdrawn to the outskirts of the town, Babcock got himself a handcar and ran the pickets, continuing for several miles along the railroad toward Baltimore. He hired two men to "grind me down" farther in search of a telegraph office. It was 6:15 P.M. before he got a message off to Sharpe reporting the raid and saying that his agents, Greenwood and Moore, might have been captured. His Frederick operation was at a standstill.[26]

. . . . . .

From developments of June 19 and 20 at Frederick and in Pleasonton's front, the positions of Longstreet and Ewell had been determined to a fair degree. By late afternoon of the 20th, A. P. Hill, five days out of Fredericksburg, had become the chief target of Hooker's reconnaissance operations. Orders went out to locate Hill.

Pleasonton turned up a clue when another prisoner from Longstreet's corps came in, "just from Culpeper"; very few troops were there, "the whole rebel army," presumably including Hill, "having marched up the Rappahannock, and gone to the mountains." But Pleasonton now weakened the effects of his recent good performance by concluding that once the Confederates were across the Potomac, they would turn toward Pittsburgh.[27]

It was Longstreet's recently discovered move into the Valley that now most interested Pleasonton. Confident that Stuart was east of the mountains without infantry support, he determined to attack the Southern cavalry again and "cripple it up." Supported by a division of infantry, he moved forward on the morning of June 21 and drove the enemy up the Blue Ridge and into the gaps.

Information, not damage to the enemy, was what headquarters wanted at this moment, and Pleasonton supplied the most sweeping report he had made in the entire campaign. He stated that the Confederate army was about Winchester and Martinsburg, with Lee and Longstreet in person at Winchester and Hill coming through the Valley to join them. This was grossly inaccurate: Ewell, except for small rear elements of his force, was well past Winchester and Martinsburg, and the rest of the army was considerably short of those places; Hill's leading division had already overtaken Longstreet; Lee was making his headquarters at Berryville.[28]

Pleasonton also reported that Ewell had gone toward Winchester. The fact that this was news to him shows that Hooker's headquarters organization, though notably superior to those of his predecessors, must not have provided for routine circulation of even the most important intelligence to corps commands. General Slocum also had picked up and reported the week-old news of Ewell's assault on Winchester. Slocum's Twelfth Corps was at Leesburg, almost as near the enemy as Pleasonton was; like Pleasonton, he was entitled to the best information headquarters could provide. Newspaper readers from Maine to California knew by this time that Winchester had fallen to Ewell, but Hooker's corps com-

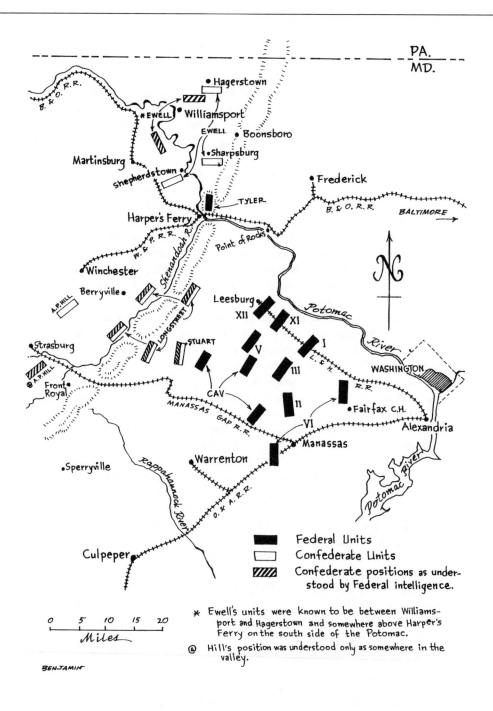

PA.
MD.

• Hagerstown

B. & O. R.R.

Williamsport

* EWELL •

EWELL • Boonsboro

Martinsburg

• Sharpsburg

shepherdstown

• Frederick

B. & O. R.R. →

BALTIMORE →

TYLER

Harper's Ferry

W. & P. R.R.

Point of Rocks

Shenandoah R.

• Winchester

Berryville •

A.P. HILL

LONGSTREET

Leesburg •

XII

Potomac

XI

River

STUART

V

I

III

L. & H.

WASHINGTON

• Strasburg

⊕ A.P. HILL

Front
Royal •

CAV

MANASSAS GAP R.R.

II

VI

R.R.

• Fairfax C.H.

Alexandria

Manassas

Potomac River

• Sperryville

Warrenton

Rappahannock River

O. & A. R.R.

• Culpeper

■	Federal Units
□	Confederate Units
▨	Confederate positions as understood by Federal intelligence.

* Ewell's units were known to be between Williamsport and Hagerstown and somewhere above Harper's Ferry on the south side of the Potomac.

⊕ Hill's position was understood only as somewhere in the valley.

BENJAMIN

SITUATION, JUNE 20, 1863

manders were just now being let in on the fact.[29] The oversight was Butterfield's.

June 21, the day of Pleasonton's assault on Stuart, was a Sunday, and Jeb wrote Lee that he had wanted to attack but had "recognized my obligation to do no duty other than what was absolutely necessary." More than Jeb's Sabbath piety was disturbed: Longstreet uprooted McLaws's division from its camp in the Valley and sent it hurrying back to support Stuart.[30]

It now developed that Pleasonton's attack accomplished more in the way of intelligence than the report he sent to Hooker. In driving the enemy into the mountains, his troopers shook loose a valuable prize — Sergeant Cline's party. Cline and his men, who must have been waiting for such an opportunity, filtered through the enemy skirmishers during the fighting. They were soon at the headquarters of General Gregg, whose advance had launched them into the Southern lines on the 17th. Late on the night of the 22nd they walked into the Bureau of Military Information tent at Fairfax.

For four days, passing themselves off as Confederate irregulars of some sort, they had mingled with Lee's troops in their camps, a feat that Sharpe's spies had been attempting with almost no success ever since Lee began preparing for his northward move. How deep their penetration of enemy-held ground reached is not clear, but their observations ended the uncertainty in regard to what Confederate infantry forces had been supporting Stuart and had then crossed over the Blue Ridge. Cline stated flatly, and correctly, that Hood and Pickett were posted in Snicker's Gap. "The rest of Longstreet's corps," which would have been McLaws, he placed between Front Royal and Winchester, with a small force behind Ashby's Gap; actually McLaws's division was concentrated near the gap. Cline sketched in some detail the line that the Southern infantry had occupied in Stuart's rear. He even had correct news from the Potomac, to the effect that Ewell had established a line for drawing supplies from Maryland and Pennsylvania. He also had a report on A. P. Hill; the spies had encountered a disabled Confederate soldier in a house and had heard from him that Hill was in the Valley.

Cline's error in regard to McLaws's position was corrected by information from other sources. A deserter, whose story was partly verifiable from Cline's report, had informed General Slocum of McLaws's position at Ashby's Gap. And a party of Pleasonton's scouts had reached the crest of the Blue Ridge and observed a large camp below the gap, which would have been McLaws's brigades. Sharpe now knew where Longstreet's troops were and where they had been.[31]

Federal intelligence had now scored its fourth penetration of Confederate camps or marches. The earlier ones were Sergeant Harter's feat of losing himself among Lee's troops massed for attack along the Rapidan in August 1862, the Reverend I. J. Stine's mingling with Jackson's troops along the Potomac and with Longstreet's at Hagerstown the following month, and Cline's own ten-day visit with Confederate cavalry along the Rappahannock in February.

·· ·· ··

"The result of my mission here has undoubtedly been as unsatisfactory to you, as unfortunate to me," Babcock wrote to Sharpe from Frederick on the evening of June 22. The incursion of Rebel cavalry, now ended, had cost him a valuable two days. "Had I not been known and a subject of suspicion," he said, "I might have mingled among them and learned the news. Most incredible rumors are afloat here as regards the strength of the enemy over the river and I cannot nor will not pretend to say anything about it until I know." Greenwood and Moore had still not been heard from, and Babcock had just located two men, well recommended, who would essay to get over South Mountain to Sharpsburg, in the locality where Ewell was operating. Two days or more would be required, Babcock said, "but I am bound to know what is there if I have to go myself." Again he asked for Cline, adding, "If my mission here is of any importance, for Gods sake send me one man who wont run when there is nobody after him and is not frightened when he sees a greyback." This time Cline was available and was put on the road for Frederick accompanied by several of his colleagues.[32]

·· ·· ··

By now thirteen information-gathering efforts, in addition to Babcock's operation and David McConaughy's group based at Gettysburg, were under way in the mountains and valleys between Harper's Ferry and the parts of Pennsylvania to which Lee might be moving. One of these operations was run by the Signal Corps; the War Department at Hooker's urging had sent out a dozen signal officers to heights on both sides of the river.[33] The other twelve groups were all engaged in espionage and scouting. Three worked out of Baltimore; one directed by Provost Marshal McPhail, one by General Schenck, and the third by the chiefs of the Baltimore and Ohio Railroad.[34] One operation was run from Washington by General Heintzelman's department headquarters. A second Washington group, under the War Department's chief detective, Lafayette Baker, now a colonel commanding a unit called the 1st District of Columbia Cavalry Battalion, would begin work a week later, after the appearance of Southern cavalry near the capital. It was one of Baker's rare opportunities to take a hand in obtaining information for the fighting forces, but the area where it operated is unknown and no productive results have come to light.[35]

The Pennsylvania Central and Northern Central Railroads ran separate scouting operations, directed from Altoona and Harrisburg. The former had one group under Alexander Lloyd working the area around Mount Union and another under William B. Wilson, Captain William Palmer's assistant and telegrapher of the preceding September. As might have been expected of Wilson, he had his men hovering close to Ewell from the time that general crossed the Potomac until he reached the Susquehanna.[36] General Couch at Harrisburg had the benefit of the railroad scouts' findings and also was operating his own information service, in which McConaughy's Gettysburg group seems to have been the most active unit.

Chambersburg's experiences in the Confederates' 1862 invasion had induced several members of the local town council and other leading citizens, urged on by Alexander McClure, to organize a scouting service before the new threat materialized; this foresight was to be richly rewarded. Some distance west of Chambersburg was General Milroy, who by now had joined the portion of his command that had retreated into Pennsylvania; some of his scouts covered country to the west of Hagerstown and Chambersburg. Still farther west, working out of Uniontown for General W. T. H. Brooks at Pittsburgh, was a group led by Samuel D. Oliphant.[37] Finally, General Benjamin Kelley at New Creek, West Virginia, and General Tyler on Maryland Heights, who were nearer to Lee's advance than any of the other Union forces, were getting a steady flow of information from their scouts and, in Tyler's case, from visual observation of the river country. In addition to all this organized coverage, freelance observers were at work everywhere, sending information to local commanders or sometimes to Washington.[38]

Secretary Stanton had urged upon General Couch his belief that "[t]he people being friendly, [it] would seem that with proper diligence and system accurate and full information might be had."[39] Halleck and Lincoln also were urging the field commands to greater information-gathering efforts. Now many citizens were rising to the occasion, though more of them remained behind shuttered windows and acted as if they feared that cooperating with their Federal defenders would bring reprisals from the invaders.

By their very nature these scattered scouting and spying activities were uncoordinated. Even two participants situated so close together as McPhail and Schenck appear to have operated independently of each other. Nor was all the information being brought together at any one place — although most of it seems to have found its way to Washington and from there to the army. The War Department was the logical place for the accumulation to be assimilated and put into usable form, but the Department's lack of an intelligence element meant that no such integration could take place except haphazardly, in the minds of Halleck, Stanton, and Lincoln.

The penalty for these casual arrangements was that although a surprising amount of the information being reported was substantially correct, no comprehensive picture of the enemy situation was emerging. Lee allowed his advance, Ewell's corps, to hold still while Hill was overtaking Longstreet in the lower Valley. From June 19 through the early hours of the 22nd Ewell's force was virtually stationary, with Rodes and Jenkins near Hagerstown, Johnson at Sharpsburg, and Early remaining south of the river.[10] Of Early, nothing appears to have been reported. The presence of an enemy force at Hagerstown was known, but only Babcock's source, the physician from Williamsport, had identified it as Rodes's division. McPhail estimated its size as low as 3000 and Milroy as high as 40,000. Somewhat detailed information was in hand concerning Johnson, since his crossing at Shepherdstown and his camps at Sharpsburg could not hide from the Signal Corps telescopes that were supplying intelligence to General Tyler on Maryland Heights. Tyler supplemented this information by sending out scouts who worked themselves close enough to the enemy to learn the names of some of the generals. But this good work was largely nullified by continued confusion in Tyler's reports; his successive estimates of the size of the invading force were inconclusive, and his faulty knowledge of the composition of Ewell's corps so muddled his telegrams that the core of correct information in them could not be discerned.[41]

It was not Tyler, however, who produced the wildest of these reports. Schenck, McPhail, and Couch all telegraphed in a tone of alarm that the enemy had advanced to Frederick or its vicinity. Since Hooker and Sharpe knew that Babcock had brushed against this supposedly threatening force — 25 of Gilmor's riders, later increased to 150 — the effect of the alarm at army headquarters could only have been annoyance. Perhaps because of this new demonstration of panicky reporting, Hooker remained skeptical in the face of the mounting evidence of a strong enemy force in the vicinity of Hagerstown, and on June 23 he had Sharpe wire Babcock, again directing that men be sent to South Mountain to observe the valley to the west. By now Hooker was puzzled at Ewell's stationary attitude along the river; this state of mind led to what General Howard described as "the singular multiplicity and sudden changes of orders" he was receiving.[42] Howard's unconscious oxymoron mocked the confusion issuing from army headquarters.

By morning of the 22nd, A. P. Hill had so nearly closed on Ewell's rear that Lee started Ewell for Pennsylvania. Southern infantry were across the Mason-Dixon Line by midday; Rodes camped at Greencastle, with Johnson behind him on the same route and Jenkins's cavalry ahead of him at Chambersburg. Early crossed the river at Shepherdstown and set out on a route to the right of the rest of the corps. Hill headed for the Shepherdstown crossing; of Lee's infantry forces, only Longstreet, who

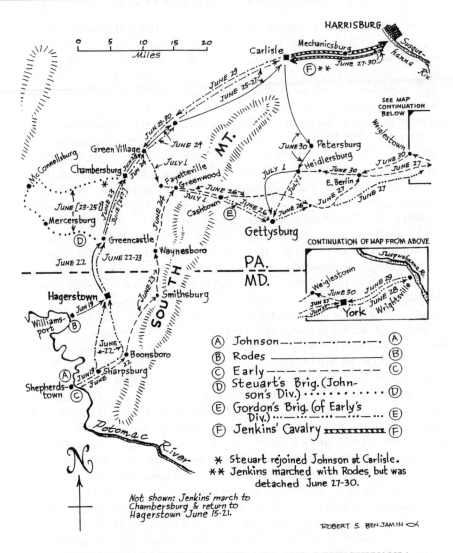

EWELL'S MARCHES IN MARYLAND AND PENNSYLVANIA

was to march last, remained in the vicinity of Berryville and the Blue Ridge. His crossing of the Potomac would be at Williamsport, twenty miles above Hill's.[43]

· ·   · ·   · ·

The haze that gives the Blue Ridge its name has inspired much poetry and song, but its praises were never sung by the armies' signalmen, who needed clear skies for the transaction of business, whether they were receiving flag messages or watching the enemy. June 23 was an unpoetically clear day on Maryland Heights, and it drew a grateful expression from Signal Corps Captain Nahum Daniels, who opened a dispatch to General Tyler with the report that "[t]he view this morning is very fine." He could see clearly down into Sharpsburg, eight miles away. The camps were gone and the rear of a marching column could be seen moving north toward Hagerstown. Another marching column, ten miles long and still several miles south of the Potomac, was visible on a road that led to the Shepherdstown crossing. The body of troops that had just left Sharpsburg was Early's division (which had been preceded by Johnson's) and the one approaching the river was Hill's corps, but Tyler had identified only Early's force when he reported Daniels's observations to Hooker. The number of troops that had marched through Sharpsburg he estimated at 30,000 to 40,000 — figures that would have been reasonable if divided in half. Tyler added the important point that "General Ewell, I am sure, passed through Sharpsburg yesterday in an ambulance."[44]

Tyler's numerous telegrams of the preceding days must have been a nightmare to Colonel Sharpe. Despite their discrepancies, they left no doubt that a large force of the enemy was marching for the Mason-Dixon Line, with a force probably equally large on its heels. But there was still no indication whether Lee's objective was Pennsylvania, Washington, or Baltimore.

Another unanswered question was whether the body of troops north of the Potomac was the whole of Ewell's corps. Meanwhile the advance element of his infantry was correctly identified and placed. General Couch had wired from Harrisburg the previous evening, "Rodes' division of infantry are reported as entering Greencastle at 12:30 P.M. this day. Their cavalry advancing upon Chambersburg." The source of this information probably was one or more of the scouts working out of Gettysburg, who had provided prompt reports of information on the Greencastle region a week earlier and who are known to have been covering the area again on June 24.[45] Couch was now getting accurate as well as fast reporting, at least from within his own department. Had he been as well provided with fighting forces as he was with scouts and spies, he

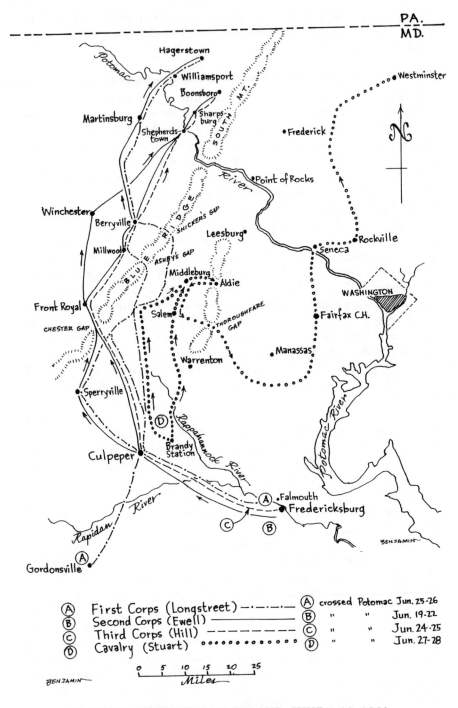

LEE'S ADVANCE INTO MARYLAND, JUNE 3-28, 1863

would not have had to allow Ewell's march through Pennsylvania to go uncontested.

On their maps Sharpe and his chiefs could now trace Southern columns stretching forty miles, from below the Shepherdstown crossing up into Pennsylvania. Their understanding of the enemy's positions was correct, if lacking in detail. Events now conspired, however, to lead them to a badly erroneous conclusion regarding the identity of the big force seen coming up to the river from the south. On that conclusion Hooker was to base his most important action of the long march from the Rappahannock.

This combination of events took place on June 24, a day when General Butterfield was on a trip to Washington and Baltimore to arrange for reinforcements and Sharpe was filling in for him as Hooker's right-hand man.[46] The colonel had a busy day in his double assignment, for the telegraphic traffic pertaining to his regular duties alone was probably the heaviest he had ever known, and the story it unfolded raised the pressure on him with every advancing hour.

Very early that morning headquarters had received a telegram from Tyler reporting the capture of a courier returning to Lee after carrying a dispatch into the area now occupied by Ewell. The prisoner placed Ewell at Hagerstown, Lee at Berryville, and Longstreet and his corps with Lee.[47] Couriers were better informed than other soldiers, and they often told their captors the truth. Sergeant Cline's party had reported Longstreet in the vicinity of the Blue Ridge gaps near Berryville; the new report indicated that he had advanced a short day's march closer to the Potomac.

At that point Hooker summarized his view of the situation for Halleck. Ewell, he had concluded, was now across the Potomac. "Of the troops that marched to the river at Shepherdstown yesterday," he wrote, "I cannot learn that any have crossed, and as soon as I do I shall commence moving." His army, except for recent additions, was ready. If the Confederates made no further crossings, Hooker said, he would — while making Washington secure — strike Lee's line of communication with Richmond. He hoped also to put one or two corps across the river, to join Tyler's force and attempt to "sever Ewell from the balance of the rebel army, in case he should make a protracted sojourn with his Pennsylvania neighbors."[48]

The telegram could scarcely have reached Halleck's desk when intelligence arrived that met Hooker's conditions for setting his army in motion. General Tyler telegraphed at 10 A.M. that already that morning the enemy had put 15,000 men across the river at the ford a mile below Shepherdstown. He identified this force as Longstreet's corps.

Corroborating information arrived at about the same time from Pennsylvania. General Couch reported that his outposts now had the first prisoners and deserters from the invading columns; they said that Long-street's and Hill's troops to the number of 40,000 were over the river.[49] Since Couch did not say what command these informants were from, it would be assumed that they were from one of Ewell's units and therefore would not know very much about movements of Longstreet and Hill. Still the report seemed to reinforce Tyler's information.

In less time than it would have taken for Hooker to issue marching orders based on these reports, information arrived to dispute them. General Slocum, whose corps now was nearest to the enemy hidden behind the Blue Ridge, reported in midmorning the alarming news that he was threatened by a sizable force that had advanced to within a few miles of his position at Leesburg. This could be the much feared move on Washington. Moreover, Slocum identified the force as Longstreet, al-though not with the same assurance as Tyler, who had placed this same enemy corps at a river crossing thirty miles away. Lacking cavalry to reconnoiter, Slocum would not discover until the next day that the size of the body of troops in his front had been grossly exaggerated.[50] For the time being Hooker, left with a head-on intelligence conflict, was im-mobilized.

This state of affairs was dangerous because, if Slocum was being misled by a feint, the enemy could greatly lengthen his lead in the northward race. But the impasse soon began to resolve itself with the arrival of a refugee from the Shenandoah Valley. He had traveled fifty miles of the Valley, crossing the Blue Ridge from Front Royal, and he said he had seen no wagon trains and only one small body of troops. Unless the man was carrying a planted story, his information was strong evidence that all of Lee's army was now closing upon or over the Potomac. This in fact was the situation, Longstreet having set out for the river early in the day.[51]

Early in the afternoon word came from General Tyler that he had two prisoners from Longstreet's corps. They said that they belonged to the 18th Georgia Infantry, McLaws's division, and that the corps was then crossing at Shepherdstown. Since the 18th Georgia was in McLaws's division and Sharpe's records showed it there, the report added strength to Tyler's previous unexplained statements that the force moving into Maryland that day was Longstreet's corps.[52]

Although telegrams had been pouring in from many sources north of the river, nothing had been received from John Babcock since his letter of the 22nd. Finally, in midafternoon of the 24th, he was heard from. He had been chafing at his frustrations; now at last he had some important information:

> I learn beyond a doubt that the last of Lees entire army has passed through Martinsburg towards the Potomac. The last of them passed Monday night [June 22]. The main body are crossing at Shepherds-town. Scouts report them building a pontoon bridge at Shepherdstown.

Can see them from the mountain —

9.000 men & 16 pieces of artillery passed through Greencastle yesterday p.m. Gen[s]. Ewell Walker Johnson Ex[tra] Billy Smith & Hays took up their Hd Qrs day before yesterday at house two miles from Shepherdstown on the Winchester pike. Large bodies of troops can be seen from South Mountain at Antietam furnace by aid of glasses. Cavalry & pickets were drawn in this morning beyond Boonsboro. All of which may be considered as reliable.

B[53]

This intelligence, if correct, meant that Hooker must cross the river. Ordinarily John Babcock's assertion that the last of Lee's army was "beyond a doubt" nearing the Potomac would have settled the question. But Hooker, as he had done in the case of equally conclusive evidence back on the Rappahannock, tarried over his decision. His reason this time probably was the alarm in Slocum's front. Another possible reason was that Babcock's telegram gave no information as to what elements constituted "the last of Lee's entire army." Hill, supposedly in rear of Longstreet, had been reported north of the Potomac by sources of doubtful validity, but their information was corroborated late in the afternoon when General Schenck telegraphed that students of an academy at Mercersburg, north of Hagerstown, had arrived near Frederick with word that Hill as well as Ewell had passed through Hagerstown the previous day.[54] And Tyler had two more reports: one said that Longstreet's corps had crossed the river and taken the Boonsboro road to Hagerstown; the other was from "an influential man from Hagerstown," an acquaintance of Tyler's, who had passed troops claiming to belong to Longstreet's corps as he made his way to Tyler's headquarters on Maryland Heights.[55]

Still Hooker delayed action. After 8 P.M. another telegram arrived from Babcock, now in Baltimore. This was not a sweeping story like his first message but a report of the interrogation of another group of student refugees, from St. James College at Hagerstown. It began with additional details of Ewell's march through that city. Of more concern at army headquarters was what it told on two other questions — whether Lee was seeking to come eastward through the South Mountain gaps toward Baltimore and Washington and what forces were crossing the river. This passage read:

[The students] report no force between Hagerstown and Frederick on the Boonsboro road except one cavalry camp 4 miles from Hagerstown where they passed the pickets. No force at Boonsboro to be seen at South Mountain. From reliable sources they say they learn that Longstreet and A. P. Hill are crossing rapidly.[56]

Now Hooker was satisfied. The assertive telegram from Babcock earlier in the day had not swayed him to the point of decision; that was left to this later and relatively cool message, reinforced perhaps by the two dispatches from Maryland Heights repeating Tyler's "Longstreet theme" that he had been singing all day. The conclusion to which this information led was that Hill and Longstreet were across the river and that the force in Slocum's front must be a phantom (which it was) or a feint. Accordingly, Hooker ordered his army to cross the river.

To General Howard's Eleventh Corps, already camped at Edwards Ferry near Leesburg, orders went at 11:35 P.M. to move into Maryland the next morning. The other elements of Reynolds's left wing, the First and Third Corps, followed the same day. By the evening of the 26th the other four infantry corps were over; the cavalry crossed on the 27th.[57]

It was forthright action and good marching, but it was based on wrong information. For the rear of Lee's army was two days' march short of where the persuasive accumulation of intelligence had placed it, and marching by a different route. Lee's rear corps was now Longstreet's, not Hill's. And everything that had been reported about Longstreet that day (the 24th) had been mistaken, with the possible exception of the information about his position on June 23 given by Lee's courier. Tyler's prisoners "from the 18th Georgia Regiment, McLaws' division," were not from that regiment, that division, or even Longstreet's corps; they could only have belonged to Hill. Their statement that Longstreet was crossing at Shepherdstown was untrue. The soldiers who told the Hagerstown citizen that they were part of Longstreet's corps were likewise putting out false information. Since that report turned up in two different places, it appears that some of Hill's troops, perhaps a large number or even the entire corps, had been coached to tell anyone they met, Yankee sympathizer or secessionist, that they belonged to Longstreet's corps. Babcock's sources had fallen into the same trap, probably from the same cause.

The deception was made easy by the fact that Longstreet had been for so long far in advance of Hill. In the absence of corrective information, the Federal command's only means of penetrating the ruse was the knowledge of Confederate organizations and their commanders possessed by Sharpe, Babcock, and McEntee. By interrogating just a few of the soldiers masquerading as members of a corps other than their own, they would have exposed the fraud; but none of its perpetrators came within their reach for a quizzing. Although Babcock was no longer in hiding, a trip to Maryland Heights to examine Tyler's prisoners would have been an infeasible interruption of his activities at Frederick.

As we have seen, Longstreet's troops were never near Shepherdstown, their reported crossing place. The deception, however, did not relate only to their route; it led Hooker to believe that Longstreet was crossing the river or was already in Maryland at a time when he actually was in Virginia. On June 22, when, according to Babcock's sources, the last of the invaders passed Martinsburg, Longstreet's brigades were lying in their camps around Berryville and Millwood, thirty miles south of Martinsburg and another fifteen miles from the point where they would cross the river. Not until the 24th, the day of the remarkable concurrence of erroneous reports and of Hooker's decision based on them, did Longstreet set his troops in motion for the Potomac and Williamsport — through country well hidden from the telescopes of Union signal stations. They crossed on the 25th and 26th. Twenty-four hours in advance of them were Hill's three divisions, which *had* crossed at Shepherdstown, and which in doing so had been mistaken for the whole of Lee's main body.[58]

In planting the story that the troops crossing at Shepherdstown were Longstreet's, the Confederates presumably hoped to deceive Hooker into believing that Longstreet was still marching in advance of Hill — that Hill was still in Virginia. This would diffuse and delay Hooker's pursuit. The deception produced an amount of false information that proved persuasive. But Hooker also had at least two reports that Hill had crossed into Maryland. The misinformation regarding Longstreet and the reports of Hill's presence in Maryland and Pennsylvania indicated that all of Lee's main body would soon be north of the Potomac.

The cavalry of each army was the last to cross; the Federal cavalry's crossing on the 27th was a half-day ahead of Stuart's crossing farther downriver. The Confederates' deception boomeranged: Hooker, supposedly the pursuer, actually had his whole army over the Potomac some hours ahead of Lee's. By having acted on an understanding of the position of the enemy's rear units that was in error by two days' march, Hooker was now abreast of Lee's main body and marching on an inside track toward the point of eventual collision.

However, in crossing the Potomac so promptly Hooker left open a path to Washington that Longstreet, as the rearmost of the invading forces, could have taken: down the right bank of the river and across at fords or ferries relatively near the capital. Even though Lee, unaware of the Federals' crossing, had no plans for such a move, Hooker's action can be interpreted as a violation of the standing order to keep his army interposed between the enemy and Washington. Had he known Longstreet's actual position, he would have kept a couple of infantry corps and a brigade or two of cavalry south of the river to block that downriver route. In dealing with an enemy force that straddled the Potomac, Hooker was entitled to a wide range of judgment in balancing probabilities as to Confederate moves. And once the threat to Slocum's position was exposed as a phantom, there was no evidence whatever to dispute the reports of Longstreet's presence in Maryland; the risks entailed in crossing the river were much less weighty than the disadvantages that would be incurred in letting Lee's army once again get out of his sight.

Hooker's action, then, was correct in light of the information he had.

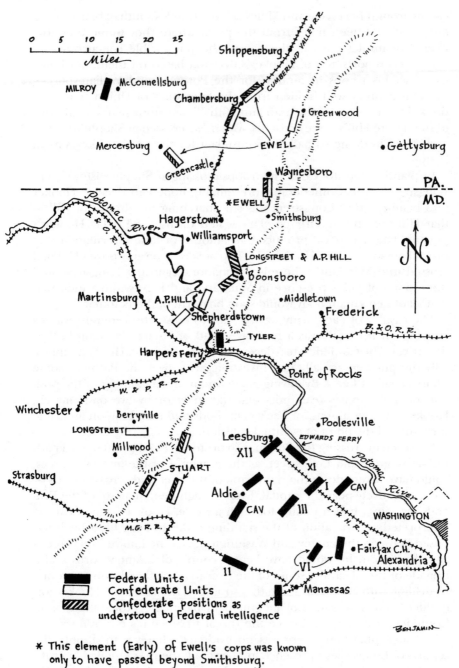

SITUATION, P.M., JUNE 24, 1863

He had erred, however, in not keeping himself better informed. Since the Confederates would not confine their movements to territory under the coverage of his Signal Corps telescopes, Pleasonton should have been close on their trail. The Federal troopers would have found that the enemy's cavalry screen was no longer the formidable barrier it had been for more than a week; Jeb Stuart was off on a project of his own, as we are about to see. It would not have taken a very deep penetration of the Valley to ascertain that on June 24 Longstreet was only leaving Berryville, not entering Maryland. Thus we see that Hooker's failure to keep up the pressure on Pleasonton was an intelligence error, one that led to a greater error, his acceptance of the enemy's crude deception.

A more serious intelligence error was the decision — probably Hill's but possibly Lee's — to plant the deceptive information. The chance was quite strong that it would combine with reports of Hill's crossing in exactly the way it did — failing to delay the Federals' pursuit and instead hastening them on their way.

To the thesis that good intelligence does not necessarily win battles, General Hooker here added the corollary that intelligence error does not always lose them. Chancellorsville, the battle engendered by a brilliant intelligence success, ended in inglorious defeat because of battlefield mistakes. Now intelligence error had a magnificent result: it put Hooker's army in the lead in what turned out to be a race for a crucial position on a fishhook-shaped ridge at Gettysburg.

22

. . . .

REAPING THE
PENNSYLVANIA HARVEST

June 16–29

HOOKER'S EXTRAORDINARILY TIMELY crossing of the Potomac had the effect of a stolen march, repaying Lee for his disappearing act at Fredericksburg. Not for two days would the Confederate commander learn that the pursuing Federals were no longer down in Virginia. During that time his army continued dispersing over a sixty-mile expanse of south-central Pennsylvania, Ewell's cavalry and one of his infantry divisions reaching the Susquehanna River.

Crossing the Potomac brought a radical change in Sharpe's quest for intelligence. Once the armies were on Northern soil — while the ill-fed Southerners were enjoying the plenitude of Pennsylvania crops — a harvest of intelligence was ready to be gathered in. In the eight days between the arrival of Lee's main body in Maryland on June 24 and the opening of the battle of Gettsyburg, there were well over a hundred substantial reports on the movements and strength of the invading army. The sources of these, in addition to Sharpe's own spies, were the numerous groups of citizen-scouts described in the preceding chapter. In the country where the Rebels were operating were scores or hundreds of men who were acting as if each had personally received a copy of Secretary Stanton's fervent telegram to General Couch urging that intelligence of the enemy be pursued with "diligence and system."

More impressive than the quantity of this reporting, however, is the fact that three quarters of it was substantially correct. Such accuracy was much better than Sharpe could have expected from the haphazardly organized groups of agents, and from the army's own agents operating in unfamiliar country.

As it developed, information 75 percent correct was sufficient for headquarters to produce results of a much higher order of correctness. In the last days preceding the battle, estimates of the enemy's situation

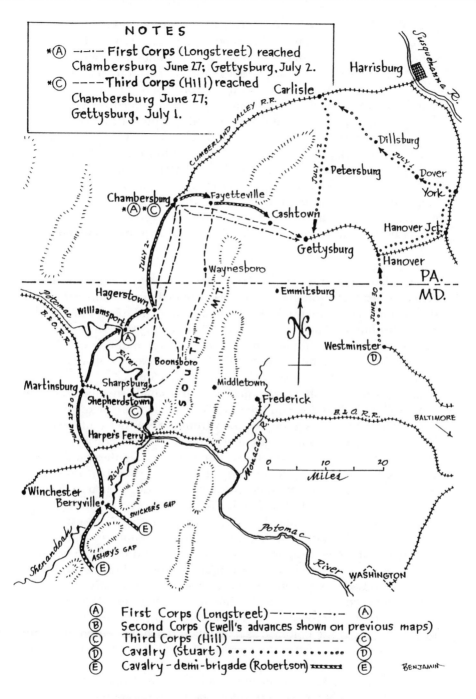

NOTES

*Ⓐ —··—··— First Corps (Longstreet) reached Chambersburg June 27; Gettysburg, July 2.

*Ⓒ ———— Third Corps (Hill) reached Chambersburg June 27; Gettysburg, July 1.

Ⓐ First Corps (Longstreet)—··—··—··— Ⓐ
Ⓑ Second Corps (Ewell's advances shown on previous maps)
Ⓒ Third Corps (Hill) ———————— Ⓒ
Ⓓ Cavalry (Stuart) •••••••••••••• Ⓓ
Ⓔ Cavalry — demi-brigade (Robertson) ⚊⚊⚊⚊ Ⓔ

BENJAMIN

LEE'S ADVANCE INTO PENNSYLVANIA

passed at short intervals from Army of the Potomac headquarters to subordinate elements and to Washington and Harrisburg. These were written with telling accuracy. Their few shortcomings were caused chiefly by the inevitable delays in the passage of the information over the considerable distances it had to travel. A few errors resulted from faulty information reported from the front, but they were rapidly corrected.

The analysis that went into these situation summaries was the work of Sharpe unaided by Babcock or McEntee. Before leaving Fairfax he had sent Babcock instructions to join General Reynolds's advance wing. Failing to receive acknowledgment, he sent McEntee to Reynolds, then learned that Babcock had received his instructions and complied.[1] Reynolds had good use for both men, for his wing was to take prisoners, the main source of intelligence in the battle now developing, for a half-day or longer before Sharpe, with army headquarters, arrived at Gettysburg.

. .   . .   . .

The Confederates' overextended positions facilitated the citizens' intelligence-gathering by forcing Lee to relax the elaborate security that had shielded his army from the view of Federal scouts and spies until near the end of his hundred-mile advance to the Potomac. In fact he appears to have almost thrown caution aside in allowing large numbers of refugees to pass through his lines; he lacked the manpower to maintain tight picketing. But what he lacked most of all was Jeb Stuart.

That marvelously able cavalryman, for all his embarrassment at Pleasonton's hands, had done on the whole an excellent job of keeping prying eyes and questioning tongues away from the Southern infantry. Stuart, however, was no longer marching with Lee. Jenkins's cavalry brigade and Gilmor's and White's battalions of rangers were far ahead with Ewell. Two other units, Grumble Jones's brigade and Beverly Robertson's demi-brigade, had been left behind guarding the Blue Ridge when Longstreet and Hill moved into Maryland. John Imboden's brigade, another new addition to Stuart's command, was operating in its familiar western Virginia and Maryland surroundings, tearing up Baltimore and Ohio Railroad tracks and collecting livestock. And Stuart with the three brigades he obviously considered most thoroughly his own, those of Hampton and the two Lees, was off on a long ride around the Federal army.

In a conference with Lee as the time for crossing into Maryland drew near, Stuart had proposed with considerable urgency that he operate near the Army of the Potomac as it marched north. Lee responded with instructions, poorly written, that provided that Stuart, if he should find the enemy moving northward, was to cross the Potomac and take position on Ewell's right. In a second letter Lee stated that if Hooker remained inactive, Stuart should follow the Confederate infantry by the Shepherdstown route. Nothing was said of his supposedly primary mission of furnishing information to Lee, although he was instructed to perform that service for Ewell. He was given secondary assignments such as collecting supplies and damaging the enemy as he went. These tasks, so suggestive of a pure cavalry raid, and the discretion that the orders accorded him, were a strong temptation to operate independently. The inducement was heightened by an instruction from Longstreet pointing out that unless the cavalry marched close upon the infantry, its route of advance would disclose Lee's intentions more fully by following the infantry than by marching east of the enemy.[2]

The result might have been predicted from Stuart's known proclivities and his manifest desire for a solo assignment. He rode eastward early on the 25th and quickly encountered Hancock's Second Corps, marching northward for the Potomac. This was quite an obstacle, but Stuart invoked the discretion given him to be his own judge as to whether he could pass around the enemy unhindered. Instead of seeking the quickest route to Maryland, he kept shifting to the south and east until finally, two days later, he gained the Federal right and rear twenty-five miles southwest of Washington. Crossing the Potomac fifteen miles above the capital on the night of June 27–28, he captured 125 wagons carrying supplies to the Army of the Potomac, disrupted communications, caused a great alarm in Washington, and, reaching Pennsylvania at last, found the enemy's entire army on his left, blocking his way to both Ewell and Lee. The battle of Gettysburg was half over before his fatigued troopers, still shepherding their 125 wagons, returned to the army.[3]

This performance cost the South dearly in intelligence that Stuart could have provided if he had stayed with Lee. The aspect of his fool's errand that is under examination at the moment, however, is what the absence of the cavalry meant to Lee's security against Union scouts and spies. Those one hundred and more reports, revealing the invaders' positions, the direction of their advance, and often their identity, came out of the country they traveled in the last eight days of June. Had Jeb Stuart been in his proper place alongside the Southern infantry, the men who obtained and forwarded information would have had incomparably greater difficulty in getting through the Confederate lines. And even those whose findings consisted merely of observations made as the invading army passed by their homes would have been seriously slowed down, if not blocked altogether, as they attempted to make their way to telegraph offices and Federal positions.

Stuart's madcap ride had its genesis in the Richmond newspapers' criticism of his surprise by the enemy's cavalry at Brandy Station. Hooker's uncertainty as to what was going on behind the Confederate lines was only deepened by Pleasonton's indecisive performance; still the affair helped to drive Stuart to this latest demonstration of his prowess. During the eight days it occupied, intelligence flowed freely into the Army of the

Potomac; here, more than a fortnight after the cavalry battle, was a real intelligence yield resulting indirectly from Pleasonton's apparently vain attack.

Stuart must not, however, be given all the blame for Lee's lack of cavalry. Back in western Virginia was Imboden, and back in Ashby's and Snicker's Gaps in the Blue Ridge were Robertson's regiments of horsemen, idly admiring a Loudoun Valley panorama empty of Federal troops. Robertson was under orders to watch the Federals, but their crossing of the Potomac twenty miles away appears to have escaped his notice for four days. Not until June 29 did he set out for Pennsylvania; at Martinsburg he met a courier bearing Lee's belated orders to rejoin the army. Had he moved promptly, his troopers could have been with Lee by the 27th or 28th, supplying some of the security and reconnoitering that Lee needed; but they reached the army barely in time to help guard its retreat. Major Mosby, one of Stuart's chief spokesmen in the postwar literary battles, ridiculed Robertson's slowness in leaving the mountains and his somewhat circuitous march, observing that "Stuart had ridden around General Hooker while Robertson was riding around General Lee." But Imboden was even slower; he rested his brigade along the Potomac so long that he drew one of Lee's rare demonstrations of anger.[4]

.. .. ..

While Stuart was picking his way around the Federals in Virginia, Ewell's columns toiled northward and eastward with scarcely a show of resistance from the green regiments of New York and Pennsylvania militia that had been hastily sent out from Harrisburg. Early, most southerly of Ewell's divisions, pushed through and around Gettysburg on June 26. Although the town was an obvious target, only a single regiment of militia held it. Showing commendable prudence, the militiamen withdrew.[5] There could not have been many exchanges of shots, but among the townspeople who got a taste of entertaining contending armies was the family of David McConaughy. On that rainy Friday the wife of the leader of the Gettysburg spies gave birth to their third son, Samuel. During her delivery three rifle balls came into the bedroom; a stoutly maintained family tradition says that all three struck the headboard of her bed.[6]

Early drove rapidly eastward, took the surrender of York on the 27th, and the next day had John Gordon's brigade on the west bank of the Susquehanna at Wrightsville, forcing the defenders to burn the bridge at that point. Ewell's other two divisions, with Jenkins's cavalry, moved through Chambersburg, Shippensburg, and Carlisle, and by the time Gordon reached the Susquehanna at Wrightsville, Jenkins was approaching the same river opposite Harrisburg. Meanwhile, Hill's main body came up to Chambersburg, turned right on the Gettysburg Pike, and camped between Chambersburg and Cashtown Gap in South Mountain.

Longstreet's divisions followed to Chambersburg the same day. It appears that Lee intended for Hill to follow Early toward York while Longstreet set out on Ewell's trail toward Harrisburg. But for the moment Longstreet's and Hill's corps remained quiet, awaiting the arrival of Stuart with intelligence of the enemy's whereabouts.[7]

. . .. ..

By June 24 Professor Winchester, the Frederick schoolmaster, was in action as an intelligence agent, having been persuaded by Babcock to communicate with the army via the War Department. In a telegram to General Halleck he revealed himself as a friend of Ward Hill Lamon, one of Lincoln's intimates at Springfield, and provided some excellent information on Ewell's forces. His investigations coincided neatly with Ewell's movements that initiated Lee's full-army advance beyond the Potomac. Winchester located a Federal soldier, member of a Maryland regiment, who had witnessed Rodes's and Johnson's march through Hagerstown, and he found two citizens who had seen Early pass through Smithsburg, eight miles east of Hagerstown. There also was further word in regard to the progress of Rodes and Johnson into Pennsylvania; this came via General Couch from the Gettysburg spies, who were still covering the valley twenty-five miles to the west of their town. Couch then learned that the enemy advance had passed Chambersburg.

Couch's sources gave Ewell a total strength of 30,000; Winchester's total, 19,000, was somewhat under the mark but seemed more reliable since it was obviously based on counting by eyewitnesses. His information was especially valuable in that it dealt individually with Ewell's three divisions, giving for each the route of march and the strength in men, artillery, and other equipment.[8]

Couch had now begun to hear from the Chambersburg citizen-spies as well as those based at Gettysburg. The Chambersburgers were led by Judge Francis M. Kimmel, who in 1862 had been secretly instructed by Governor Curtin to "exercise a general supervision" in the locality. The judge's fellow townsmen, although ignorant of this "appointment," sent him reports of their observations and other findings. Evidently because the visiting Rebels had taken care to cut Chambersburg's telegraph connections, Kimmel wrote these reports on tiny slips of paper or had them committed to memory by a messenger. Jacob Hoke, a Chambersburg merchant who published in 1887 an account of these doings, says that the messages contained only "the number of troops and guns that passed that day, and the route they took," but since other information, such as the identifications of the Confederate units, came out of Chambersburg, it appears that Hoke's memory overstated the simplicity of these messages.

The courier to whom one of these slips was entrusted would conceal it in a plug of tobacco or in his clothing or shoes and filter through the Confederate pickets north of the town, cross the mountains to the north and east, and make his way to a telegraph station, usually Newport, on the Susquehanna thirty miles above Harrisburg. Not all of the couriers went unmolested; some attracted pursuit, some drew fire from the pickets, some were caught and had to swallow their dispatches and assume previously prepared roles. One of them, J. R. Kinney, convinced his captors that he was a country schoolmaster traveling through the woods to get his clothes washed. The Confederates released him and his companion, Anthony Hollar, but he was not so persuasive when he fell into the hands of Federal troops farther along the way; he arrived at Harrisburg a prisoner but succeeded in delivering his message.

The news carried by these couriers was one or two days old when it reached Harrisburg. For example, Kimmel's dispatch of the 24th, the day Johnson's division arrived at Chambersburg to join Rodes, reached Washington via Harrisburg at 12:50 A.M. on the 26th. It correctly reported the Confederate advance to Shippensburg, which was then occupied by Daniel's infantry brigade and Jenkins's cavalry.[9]

General Milroy, back in the mountains to the west at a hamlet called Bloody Run, was in contact with Harrisburg by telegraph and was getting much more effective intelligence-gathering than he had been accustomed to during his days at Winchester. On the 25th he informed Couch, correctly, that Lee in person had ridden through Winchester the previous day. Milroy's telegraph operator had an opportunity for a little direct espionage on the same day when a Confederate detachment occupied McConnellsburg and an enemy operator named Scanlon appeared on his circuit. The Bloody Run operator reported to his colleague at Harrisburg, "The rebel opr. very abusive, damning all of us; said . . . that they were bound to have Milroys boys tomorrow or next day." Unlike many of his comrades in the Confederate telegraph service, however, Scanlon did not transmit a set of military secrets along with his insults. On the contrary, he attempted to make the man at the other end of the circuit believe that it was Jenkins's cavalry that was at McConnellsburg; actually it was George H. Steuart's infantry brigade of Johnson's division.[10]

June 27 brought Lee, Hill, and Longstreet together at Chambersburg,[11] and with them the opportunity for Judge Kimmel and company to perform some intelligence work of much greater importance than even their statistics on troops and guns. Hoke and his colleagues noted the significance of the fact that Heth's division, leading the two corps, had turned right on the Gettysburg Pike upon reaching the diamond at the center of the town. Somewhat later General Lee rode up and received Hill's salute; the townspeople began speculating whether he would make the same eastward turn. The two commanders detached themselves from their troops and the crowds of curious onlookers and held a whispered consultation. Standing beside Hoke in the crowd was one of Kimmel's couriers, a young man named Benjamin S. Huber, just back from Harrisburg. As Hoke recalled the incident years later, he said to Huber, "There, Ben, is perhaps the most important council in the history of this war, and the fate of the Government may depend upon it. If General Lee goes on down the valley, then Harrisburg and Philadelphia are threatened; if he turns east, Baltimore and Washington are in danger, and the Government ought to know which way he goes as soon as possible." Hoke's memory probably was not exaggerating the importance that Chambersburgers in 1863 had attached to their role in these events.

The two men watched as the consultation broke up. Hill drew back, Lee rode out in advance, and the column moved forward. As Lee neared the middle of the diamond, he drew on his right-hand rein and turned his horse onto the Gettysburg Pike. Huber waited only long enough to observe this fateful choice of direction, then began elbowing his way through the crowd and was off for Harrisburg.

Proceeding at first on foot, he had no difficulty with enemy pickets, but later, after procuring a horse, he suffered the usual threat of arrest by Federal troops as a Rebel spy. But he arrived at Newport at 3 A.M. on the 28th; instead of trying to awaken a telegraph operator, he boarded a train bound for Harrisburg that soon came along. On its arrival there he was taken to the Capitol and underwent a grilling in the presence of Governor Curtin and General Couch. When he had satisfied his questioners, "telegraphers in the room were hurriedly set to work." The significance that Curtin and Couch placed on the invaders' eastward turn at Chambersburg is unknown, but today we can see that the Chambersburgers read too much meaning into it, for Lee's plans were not yet firm, and upon reaching the town he halted the army to await developments. Longstreet's troops, like Hill's on an earlier day, did turn eastward, but they too went into bivouac.[12]

While Lee's main body marched for Chambersburg, Hooker's staff was busy moving through a drizzling rain and establishing headquarters at Poolesville, a Maryland village that General Patrick found "a most disgusting hole." The army's information producers were somewhat slow in beginning to function in the new circumstances; it appears that little of their news reached headquarters until the 27th.

The first report from Reynolds's leading element, General Howard's Eleventh Corps at Middletown, must have been disheartening to Sharpe. Fifteen horsemen of Howard's headquarters cavalry had crossed South Mountain on the 26th and driven a squad of Confederate riders out of Boonsboro. Questioning the townspeople, they obtained much correct information concerning Ewell's and Hill's forces that had moved through that place; they also reported with fair accuracy Lee's crossing of the Potomac in person the previous day, and they gave an estimate of the total enemy force that had crossed the river, 60,000 to 70,000, that was on the low side. Howard repeated the erroneous report, by now a commonplace, that Longstreet had crossed at Shepherdstown. That mistake would not yet have been detectable by Sharpe, but another one was: Howard placed Early's division in Hill's corps, a blunder so glaring that it must have cast doubt on the entire report.[13] This mixture of impressively correct information with obvious errors characterized most of Howard's numerous reports for the rest of the campaign.

Howard had had the telegraph wire at Middletown disconnected lest it be used by Southern sympathizers. He should have left a few cavalrymen at the station to police its use, instead of arranging this slowdown of the army's communications by placing complete reliance on flag signaling and couriers. Another maddeningly peculiar action was performed by General Stahel, whose cavalry division from the District of Washington had been added to Pleasonton's corps and was with Reynolds's advance wing. Stahel on the 26th compiled an excellent summary of the strength and movements of Ewell's corps and of the passage through Boonsboro of Anderson's division of Hill's corps. The report remained unsent for about twenty-four hours while Stahel tried to learn the position of Reynolds's headquarters, although he had been instructed that either Reynolds or Hooker would be at Poolesville.[14]

One of Hooker's first actions taken in light of the newest intelligence was to order cavalry pushed forward toward Emmitsburg and Gettysburg. The foresight reflected in this order was one of his proudest memories of the war.[15] Only Early's division was then to be expected in that area, but the cavalry division that went forward would discover, a few days later, most of Lee's army.

By the afternoon of the 27th headquarters knew the most essential fact of the situation: the entire infantry force of the invading army was now in Pennsylvania. The passes in South Mountain leading to Frederick had been occupied by Federal observation parties for several days without revealing any eastward moves by major Confederate elements. Now abundant information came from Hagerstown and vicinity showing that Lee's three corps of infantry had all passed that way marching north.

The source of much of this intelligence was two coachloads of refugees who left Hagerstown the morning of the 27th and came into Howard's lines at Middletown. Besides accounting for all of Lee's infantry, they reported the Southern commander's own passage through Hagerstown the previous day, and they correctly indicated that Early's column was headed toward Gettysburg. They placed Lee's strength at 90,000 to 100,000; this figure, although it exaggerated the numbers of the invading infantry by 20 or 25 percent, was a much closer estimate than was usual for such sources. One of the refugees was a woman who had left Richmond June 7; her statement of the number of troops stationed there tallied well with the report of Sharpe's spy Mordecai Hunnicutt, who was in Richmond at that time.[16] This much corroboration of Hunnicutt's report was very much worth having, for his principal finding was that there were no forces in the Richmond area that might turn up later as reinforcements for Lee.

If Lee's action in permitting so many refugees to pass their lines is surprising, what is more surprising is the fact that these people were so ready and willing to tell what they knew. It will be recalled that in his 1862 invasion of the same locality, refugees had been put on parole and had given information to the Federals only guardedly. The information now brought by the Hagerstown people was so extensive that one would assume that paroles had not been required of them, were there not definite evidence to the contrary from an officer who received many of the refugees.[17] Perhaps these Marylanders were now such old hands at playing host to Confederate armies that the threat of reprisal no longer disturbed them. The Pennsylvania farmers visited by the Federal advance a few days later were not similarly willing to give information on the Confederates; they were without experience in entertaining invasion. To them, however, reprisal was a less remote possibility than it was to the people who had fled Hagerstown and other places. The farmers of south-central Pennsylvania were staying put, and they could expect their Southern visitors to return, an expectation that no doubt was fulfilled in many cases.

The Hagerstown refugees had done well by Colonel Sharpe, but their contribution was soon outstripped by one of their fellow townsmen who made his way to the army on horseback to deliver information that he and other Union men had been collecting since the first appearance of Ewell's cavalry at Hagerstown eleven days before. This was Thomas McCammon, a blacksmith. He and his colleagues had counted troops by day and met at night to compare notes. He delivered a fairly detailed history of the marches through Hagerstown, now virtually completed with the passage of the rear of Longstreet's corps on June 27, the day McCammon set out. He described Jenkins's roundup of horses and cattle in Pennsylvania, Ewell's arrival and his attendance at the Catholic church, his departure with Rodes toward Greencastle, Hill's visit, and that of Lee and Longstreet traveling together.

The closest count of the invaders, it appears, was made by William Logan, a county official, and one William H. Protzman, who "could not make them over 80,000." Their count of the artillery came to 275 guns — very close to the figures history later accepted. The total of 80,000 men was accurate to almost the same degree, although McCammon mentioned that a local secessionist had said that Confederate officers were claiming 100,000. The strength of individual regiments ranged as low as 250 and as high as 700; he thought they averaged less than 400. He had mingled with some of the invading units and was able to give the names of numerous generals; it is likely that Sharpe obtained much more of this kind of information from McCammon than appears in the records. The report closed with some interesting miscellaneous observations: "Officers and men in good condition; say they are going to Philadelphia. Lots of Confederate money; carry it in flour barrels, and give $5 for cleaning a horse; $5 for two shoes on a horse rather than 50 cents United States money."[18]

.. .. ..

All of this intelligence from Hagerstown appears to have been in hand within a few hours after army headquarters arrived at Frederick on the 27th. By that time also, a fairly clear picture had emerged of Ewell's progress toward Carlisle and Early's toward York. There was reason for confidence: Lee's army, though as formidable as ever, was widely extended, probably overextended.

But the state of mind in the army command was such that no amount of intelligence and no advantage of position would have induced optimism or even resolution. Hooker's war of words with Halleck reached a climax in a dispute over the proper use of Tyler's 10,000-man Harper's Ferry garrison, now holed up across the river on Maryland Heights. Hooker, ignoring the fact that it was the force at Harper's Ferry that caused Lee to make the disastrous division of his army in September 1862, wanted this force put at his disposal; Halleck insisted that it remain at its station as a threat to Lee's communications. Hooker complained further about having to protect Washington and at the same time contend with an enemy army that was free to maneuver. And he returned to the assertion that his own force, which he put at 105,000, was outnumbered. The intelligence available to him at this time — which put Lee's strength as low as 60,000 and never above the doubtful 90,000 to 100,000 given by the Hagerstown refugees — reinforces the impression that Hooker was trying to get rid of the command of the army. If he was looking for a way out for General Hooker, he had in this a common purpose with Lincoln, Stanton, and Halleck.

While his headquarters train was en route from Poolesville to Frederick, Hooker took the opportunity to visit Tyler, then being replaced by Major General William French. He wired Halleck that Tyler's troops there were in condition to take the field and argued that behind their fortifications they were "of no earthly account." Hooker, however, did not wait for an answer to his renewed plea. Five minutes after his telegram was laid on General Halleck's desk, the general-in-chief had another in which Hooker said that he was unable to comply with the conditions placed on him and requested to be relieved from his position at once.[19]

Within a few hours a colonel of Halleck's staff was on a train to Frederick with orders appointing Major General George Gordon Meade, commander of the Fifth Corps, to the command of the Army of the Potomac. Hooker much later credited, or blamed, himself for Meade's selection, saying that he had once told Lincoln that Meade was his ablest corps commander, but that after the army reached Maryland John Reynolds's handling of a three-corps wing made him realize "I never had an officer under me acquit himself so handsomely."[20]

Joe Hooker, the general who had given the American army its most competent intelligence service since the days of spymaster George Washington, was gone. In his place was a general who had never been tried in command of independent operations; what use he would make of the intelligence organ inherited from Hooker was unknown. Although noted for his irascibility, Meade was likely to be fundamentally more considerate of subordinates than Hooker had been. The limited correspondence he had had with Sharpe up to this time shows him giving deferential and earnest attention to the colonel's problems.[21]

Meade's ability as an evaluator and user of intelligence was put to an immediate test. Hooker's practice of keeping corps commanders in the dark put the new commanding general in roughly the same position he would have been in if he had come from another theater to take command. Meade had to spend the better part of that Sunday, June 28, in getting his bearings as to both the enemy's situation and that of his own army.

He began his correspondence with Halleck at 7 A.M. by admitting his ignorance of the positions of the enemy.[22] Well before the close of the day, however, he was telling a different story. Probably the first intelligence to reach him was a report from Gettysburg, written on the 27th by McConaughy and his two colleagues, McCreary and Carson,[23] and forwarded by the advance brigade of Pleasonton's cavalry at Emmitsburg. This report, besides showing that McConaughy was probably attending to his voluntary duties as a spy even while his wife was giving birth, gave a correct account of the force — Gordon's brigade of Early's division — that had occupied their town on the 26th. It also supplied the first news that another column was marching a few miles north of Gordon (this was the main part of Early's command). McConaughy's report covered the advance of both columns in the direction of York and the presence of still another force (which would have been Rodes's and Johnson's divisions) moving on Carlisle. These facts were considerably elaborated on later in the day when this same Federal cavalry brigade rode into Gettysburg, but the additional information did not reach Sharpe until the next day.[24]

Details of the enemy's progress were telegraphed to Harrisburg from several Pennsylvania towns on the 28th; they included the report that York had surrendered to Gordon the previous evening, and the fact that the column now advancing from Carlisle toward Harrisburg was led by General Rodes. Jenkins had been identified by his signature on a demand for the surrender of Mechanicsburg, between Carlisle and Harrisburg. Couch seems to have omitted these items from his messages to Washington, but he did send a summary to the effect that the force in his front (Rodes and Johnson) numbered 15,000, and the more southerly column, 4000 to 8000. The figures reflect cool-headed observation by the citizens feeding the news to Harrisburg. Couch's summary of the situation was terse but gloomy: "By night the rebels will have possession up to my defenses on the river."[25]

The remainder of the reporting from all quarters on the 28th was confused, a mixture of fact and error that must have exhausted Sharpe's patience on that day of all days when the commanding general needed a firm, clear story on the enemy. There was, for example, a report from Lieutenant J. H. Carr of Howard's headquarters cavalry, who had made the rounds of the advance cavalry positions and had returned with a reasonable (and correct) report on Longstreet, a doubtful one on Hill, and a summary of Ewell's movements that put all three of his divisions in one column. Another confusing item came from the commander of one of Buford's cavalry brigades; he reported a visit from a Hagerstown railroad stationmaster who put Longstreet on the route that was actually being followed by Early. And Lieutenant Colonel Piatt, Schenck's chief of staff at Baltimore, wired Stanton that a refugee from the Shenandoah Valley had informed him that Hill and Longstreet were south of the Potomac and would remain there. Piatt added, "This . . . is a reliable man and I give you his story merely because it had been my belief all along."[26] Halleck could have winced at the thought that this message would have been included in the War Department telegraph office's routine retransmission to the Army of the Potomac of all messages of possible operational value.

The wildest reporting of all had to do with the activities of Jeb Stuart, who was raiding the countryside north of Washington in the best Confederate style. Halleck sent the first report of his incursion to Meade early in the afternoon; it identified the enemy force only as the brigade of Fitzhugh Lee, a third of the force traveling with Stuart. Halleck also said there was a considerable force of enemy cavalry on the southern front of Washington. Then Meade heard from a badly misinformed Howard that Stuart had crossed the Potomac at Williamsport, seventy miles above Washington, and was approaching Hagerstown. Finally, Quartermaster General Meigs, who had wired Meade's quartermaster that "[y]our communications are now in the hands of General Fitzhugh Lee's brigade," followed up with word that Stuart was with the raiders.[27] If half of the reports were true, Stuart was even more ubiquitous than his journalistic fame had made him. As for the raiders with Stuart, Meade's rearmost elements were feeling their nearness to such an extent that he soon realized they amounted to more than a brigade.

One of Halleck's early telegrams indicated that the Southern force reported south of Washington was not limited to cavalry; Meade challenged this statement, saying, "All our information here tends to show that Lee's entire army passed through Hagerstown, the rear passing yesterday a.m." The new commander was feeling considerable confidence in the intelligence that had been placed in his hands. Colonel Sharpe could scarcely have sorted out the day's receipts of confused information sufficiently to draw a firm line between the correct and the incorrect, but he had at least settled on the one leading fact, the passage of all of the enemy's infantry through Hagerstown, and was sticking to his guns. Meade was correct, and Halleck soon acknowledged that the force near Washington was thought to be no more than a few thousand cavalry.[28] Even that, however, is now seen to have been quite an exaggeration.

George Meade showed his mettle as an evaluator of intelligence by the firmness and accuracy of his reports to Halleck in the confusion of his hectic first day as army commander. Of course he had the acute and articulate Colonel Sharpe at his side, but the language of his telegrams to Washington reflects his own direct involvement in the interpreting of this mass of often contradictory material.

On the next day he put this knowledge of the enemy's positions to use in an order that sent his army fanning out on an angle of almost 60 degrees, its left headed for Emmitsburg and its right for Westminster. Emmitsburg was on a direct route that would cut across the probable line of march of the enemy's main body, the corps of Longstreet and Hill. The force directed to Westminster was aimed at Ewell's divisions, particularly Early's, on his right, and Meade hoped to fall upon "some portion of Lee's army in detail." His view was that despite the twenty-five-mile spread of his seven corps, the movement would enable him to "hold my force well together."[29] But the hope of intercepting an isolated enemy division was to be in vain, and the separation from the rest of the army of Sedgwick's big Sixth Corps, sent to Westminster, was to pose a severe problem when the armies came to blows.

. .   . .   . .

The information on Confederate positions that Meade and Sharpe had obtained up to the evening of June 28 was incomparably sharper than the picture Lee had of the Federals' situation. Only Major Mosby seems to have produced for the Southern commander any substantial intelligence during this fast-moving contest for information. On June 17, the day of the cavalry fight at Aldie, he captured two officers and an orderly who were on their way to Pleasonton with a message from Hooker. The trio had stopped to take dinner at the home of a Unionist family a quarter-mile outside the Federal picket lines. Upon leaving they were seized by Mosby and three of his men before they could reach the yard gate. The dispatch taken from them revealed a great deal about the operations of Hooker's cavalry and showed the Federal commander's alertness to the possibility of a Confederate advance toward Washington on the Virginia side of the Potomac. It may also have revealed the positions of some or all of Hooker's infantry.[30] And Mosby came through with more intelligence a few days later, after twice scouting Hooker's camps. The enemy army, he concluded, was so scattered that if it remained stationary, Stuart could probably make his proposed ride eastward.

As late as June 23 Lee's information on Hooker's movements led him to think they were preparatory to crossing the Potomac. He had heard also of the construction of the enemy's pontoon bridge at Edwards Ferry. At this point he was fairly well served with information, but the service suddenly stopped. While Lee himself was fording the river on the 25th, the advance units of more than 100,000 Federal troops were making a parallel movement less than twenty miles from his right wing. Their march to the river was through the heart of "Mosby's Confederacy," and Hooker must have taken it for granted that his crossing would be discovered by Mosby or by Stuart's regular troops. But the day Hooker marched north was the day Stuart separated from Lee and headed south to get on the Federals' right. Then came Stuart's contact with Hancock's corps, one of Hooker's rearmost elements, which he reported to Lee.[31] But this was only a small fraction of the information Lee should have had on that day.

Once Stuart found the Army of the Potomac separating him from his chief, complete silence descended on his reporting mechanism. By June 28 Lee had been advancing blindly for at least four days. That was his reason for keeping Hill and Longstreet at Chambersburg, though he did allow Ewell's advance toward the Susquehanna to continue. He asked repeatedly if there was any word of Stuart, perhaps unmindful of the fact that it was Ewell and not himself to whom the cavalry leader had been directed to furnish information. The stationary attitude of the army was beginning to puzzle the officers around the headquarters in Shetter's Woods just east of Chambersburg.

By June 28 Stuart knew that the Army of the Potomac was across the river and marching for Frederick. But he was busy that day appropriating and destroying Federal property in Maryland; he makes no mention of any attempt to send this news through the enemy lines to Lee or around them to Ewell.[32] Had he succeeded in doing so, the information of the

Federals' arrival north of the Potomac might have served only to confirm a report from another source — for that night Lee's intelligence drought was ended by the unexpected arrival of Henry T. Harrison, concluding one of the half-dozen most important one-man feats of espionage that have entered the literature of the war.

Harrison, long known to history by only his surname, was a Mississippian, thirty-one years old, of medium height and stoop-shouldered, with hazel eyes and a manner that bespoke a "man of great activity." He was an amateur actor, a skill that may explain his talent for espionage. He was not Lee's spy but Longstreet's, having been sent to the latter by Secretary Seddon during that general's recent Suffolk campaign. At first regarded with suspicion, Harrison soon convinced Longstreet and his chief of staff, Colonel Moxley Sorrel, that he was both an able spy and a man unlikely to gain information by trading away Confederate secrets. His employment did not last long, however, for the following September he turned up at Richmond in a performance of *Othello,* playing the difficult role of Iago with considerable competence and verve — and very much in his cups. His ability to control his speech while in liquor might have commended him to his employers, but Colonel Sorrel, who observed the performance, investigated and found that Harrison had been gambling as well as drinking, and he was dismissed. Sorrel sought him again for Longstreet's next independent campaign, in Tennessee, but he could not be found.

During the last few days on the Rappahannock Longstreet had supplied Harrison with gold coin and sent him off to Washington. His instructions were simply to return to the army when he could "bring information of importance." When he asked where he was to report, Longstreet replied that "the headquarters of the First Corps were large enough for any intelligent man to find." Longstreet was not simply being close-mouthed with a man who was expecting to spend weeks in frequent contact with the enemy; he was also conveying to Harrison the message that great reliance was placed on his initiative.

Unlike a previous attempt by Longstreet to get a spy into Washington, this one succeeded, and Harrison is believed to have mixed with Federal officers in the saloons and other gathering places of the capital for perhaps three weeks. The newspapers told him the general direction to take to reach Longstreet; en route he passed near enough to the Federals' camps at Frederick to realize that they would have represented the bulk of the Army of the Potomac. He arrived at Chambersburg late on June 28, after the Southerners had settled down to a night's rest. His gentleman's clothing was so travel-worn and dirty that he fell under suspicion; we again have an account of the spy returning to headquarters and being arrested by his own forces.

Longstreet, awakened to hear Harrison's report, quickly sent him to

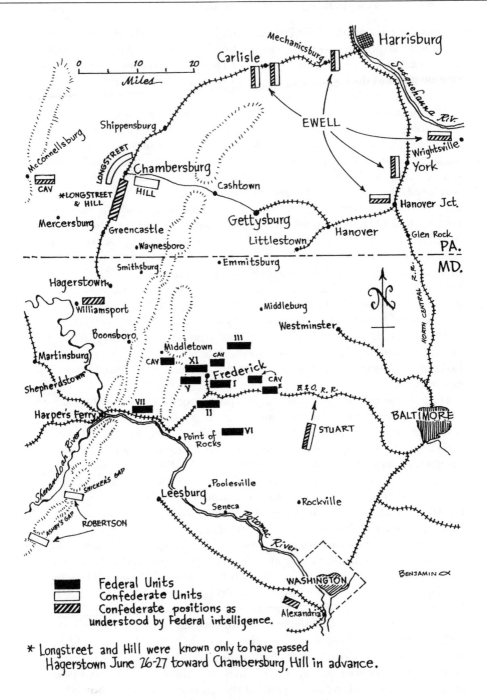

Harrisburg

Mechanicsburg

Carlisle

Susquehanna Riv.

EWELL

Shippensburg

Wrightsville

York

LONGSTREET

McConnellsburg

CAV

*LONGSTREET & HILL

Chambersburg

HILL

Cashtown

Hanover Jct.

Mercersburg

Greencastle

Gettysburg

Hanover

Glen Rock

Waynesboro

Littlestown

PA.

Smithsburg

Emmitsburg

MD.

Hagerstown

NORTH CENTRAL R.R.

Williamsport

Middleburg

N

Boonsboro

Westminster

III

Martinsburg

Middletown

CAV

X1

CAV

Shepherdstown

CAV

V

Frederick

I

CAV

B.& O. R.R.

BALTIMORE

VII

II

Harper's Ferry

Point of Rocks

VI

STUAR T

Shenandoah River

SNICKER'S GAP

Poolesville

ASHBY'S GAP

ROBERTSON

Leesburg

Seneca

Rockville

Potomac River

BENJAMIN

	Federal Units
	Confederate Units
	Confederate positions as understood by Federal intelligence.

WASHINGTON

Alexandria

Scale: 0 — 10 — 20 Miles

* Longstreet and Hill were known only to have passed
Hagerstown June 26-27 toward Chambersburg, Hill in advance.

SITUATION, P.M., JUNE 28, 1863

General Lee, who appears never to have heard of the man up to that moment. According to Longstreet's account and that of the staff officer who took the spy to Lee, the commanding general refused to see Harrison, but according to Sorrel, Lee received him and "heard him with great composure and minuteness." Lee's willingness to believe Harrison's story is likewise reported with considerable variation, but there is no doubt that he soon reached a decision based on it.

Some accounts say Harrison had learned of Hooker's replacement by Meade; that was possible, of course, but better evidence indicates that that discovery came two or three days later. He is also believed to have reported the positions occupied by five of the seven corps of Federal infantry on the night of the 27th, placing three at Frederick and two near South Mountain; of the missing two, one (the Sixth) was some distance to the rear of Frederick and the other (the Twelfth) was near Harper's Ferry. The evidence does not credit him with mingling with enemy troops in the manner of a Milton Cline, but Longstreet spoke truth when he said that a large force of cavalry might not have done as well as had his lone spy.[33]

Up to this time Lee had thought that the enemy was still in Virginia, for to him it was unthinkable that the Army of the Potomac could have crossed into Maryland without his receiving prompt notice of the movement from Stuart. It was almost equally hard for him to believe that Hooker would have moved so decisively and rapidly. But from knowing nothing of the enemy, Lee had suddenly come to know a great deal. It was less than the enemy knew about him, it was less than he would have known if he had also had the benefit of reconnoitering by Stuart or the idle cavalry brigades, but it was enough to dictate a complete change in the dispositions of the army.

Frederick was only forty miles away — two days' march. Harrison's report made the bulk of the Federal army seem rather closely grouped (it was, and Meade by that hour had brought his seven corps even closer together). The Army of Northern Virginia, on the other hand, was stretched over an expanse of sixty miles, with Ewell widely separated from the main body, and Early from the rest of Ewell's force.

Thus Lee was vulnerable to attack from the south against one of the isolated parts of his army. He seems to have concluded, however, that the principal threat was of another kind. Harrison's report of two Federal corps near South Mountain, or some other part of the story he told, suggested to Lee that the main body of the enemy was moving westward into the Cumberland Valley (the northern extension of the Shenandoah Valley) and would thereby shut off the only route for his ammunition supply. Since Ewell's advance to the Susquehanna had not attracted the Federals in that direction, Lee decided to move Longstreet and Hill eastward out of the Valley. That would pose a threat to Baltimore and

Washington and would surely hold the enemy east of the mountains. It might also bring on a general battle; Ewell would have to be drawn back to the main body. Lee lost no time in issuing orders for these moves.[34]

But the Federals' intentions were not as Lee pictured them. The two infantry corps near South Mountain — the First and the Eleventh, both under Reynolds — were not there for any offensive purpose; they had merely been watching the gaps, and they had been drawn in that day to Frederick, along with the Twelfth Corps from near Harper's Ferry.[35] And although the army under Hooker had been headed in a northerly direction, Meade was now planning to shift the bulk of it rather sharply northeastward,[36] thus making the move that Lee had at first expected. Hooker had known where Lee's main body was and had marched his army parallel to it; Meade also knew, but elected to move more than half of the army toward the area occupied by Ewell.

. .   . .   . .

As the Northern brigades stepped off according to the new plan of campaign on the morning of June 29, their commander's telegraphic connections were suddenly gone. Early in the day Stuart's men tore down the Baltimore-Frederick line; the Washington-Frederick line had fallen under his hand on the 28th. These were the only lines reaching the Army of the Potomac from Washington, Harrisburg, or anywhere else. Communication from Washington to Frederick was restored on the 30th at least as far as Point of Rocks, but by then Meade had advanced well beyond Frederick and was sending his telegrams eastward by courier to a station on the Harrisburg-Baltimore line.[37] There was no commercial line in the direction of his march, and he elected not to have a field wire constructed along the route.[38] This caused delay in his receipt of the reports from Harrisburg and Washington. He evidently counted on getting enough intelligence from the front of the army, and fortunately there was now a good amount of it. But Couch's reports, an important fraction of the whole, were delayed from four to about twenty-four hours in addition to the one or two days consumed in getting the information to Harrisburg.

Sharpe's sources were now his own men, the Gettysburg spies, and Pleasonton's cavalry corps, especially Buford's division, which was marching in advance of the left wing of the army. Meade ordered on the 29th that Sharpe's men be sent out in all directions — to Hanover on the east, Gettysburg to the north, and Greencastle and Chambersburg on the west. Cline had already stationed himself in Hagerstown and was mixing easily with the townspeople and with Confederates he found there, sending an agent to Williamsport and reporting through a citizen-courier to General Doubleday, commanding one of the divisions of Reynolds's advance. Cline found no enemy in force but learned of a large wagon train en route from the south.[39]

Gettysburg, at the time Meade ordered it covered, was already the focal point of the operations of Ed Hopkins, one of the men McEntee had left with Pleasonton during his visit to army headquarters back in Virginia. Hopkins was still with the cavalry, riding in advance of it, but his function, once he reached Gettysburg, seems to have been establishing rapid liaison between Colonel Sharpe and McConaughy's group of citizen-spies. On the 29th Hopkins rode twenty-five miles back to army headquarters at Middleburg, in Maryland, detouring to deliver an oral report to Reynolds at Emmitsburg that gave additional details of Ewell's operations.[40] The report as Reynolds hastily relayed it to Meade was limited in scope and confusing in several details, but as Hopkins delivered it to Sharpe it must have been otherwise, for the colonel replied to McConaughy that evening in a letter that shows that McConaughy's information pleased him greatly. The letter also reveals, more than anything else in the records, Sharpe's feeling for the mission he was performing. He addressed his fellow lawyer — not forgetting, despite his haste, to include an "Esq." in the salutation — in these words:

> The General directs me to thank you for yours of today. You have grasped the information so well in its directness & minuteness, that it is very valuable. I hope our friends understand that in the great game that is now being played, everything in the way of advantage depends upon which side gets the best information. The rebels are shortly in advance of us — but if thro' the districts they threaten our friends will organize & send us information with the precision you have done, they may rest secure in the result — and we hope a near one.[41]

Sharpe went on to suggest the need for agents in the region beyond Gettysburg and also stressed the importance of getting troop counts and names of generals. He expressed the hope of meeting McConaughy, but it was not to be fulfilled. McConaughy continued sending reports up to the hour of the opening of the battle, and after the fighting was over he called at army headquarters but failed to find Sharpe.[42]

Fate had laid an important task in McConaughy's hands. Of the various suppliers of intelligence serving the Army of the Potomac in the last days of June, he was the one whose reports, more than any others, drew the Union forces to Gettysburg. Yet the evidence of his performance is scanty. Aside from Couch's announcement of his appointment to head a group of spies at Gettysburg,[43] it consists of only the few excellent reports that have already been mentioned here. His June 27 report is in the records, carrying McConaughy's signature and those of his two colleagues;[44] the others appear only as Couch condensed them for transmission to Washington and the army. There is also a note from McConaughy to Sharpe, written after the battle and expressing thanks for a letter of appreciation sent to him by General Meade. In that note McConaughy asked Sharpe to send him copies of his reports.[45] As these documents are missing from Army of the Potomac records, it is possible that the original copies were sent to him; but they are not in the extensive collection of McConaughy's papers.

Acknowledging General Meade's expression of appreciation, McConaughy modestly promised Sharpe that he would "cherish it as an heirloom."[46] His important service to the Union seems to have evoked in him an attitude approaching humility; Colonel Sharpe, on the other hand, had a decidedly unhumble attitude. To McConaughy he had ventured a bold promise: Give us information and we will give you victory. He was about to see demonstrated the truth of his conviction that in the "great game" of saving the Union, "everything depends upon which side gets the best information."

23

. . . .

THE THIRTIETH OF JUNE

"I AM IN POSITION between Emmitsburg and Westminster, advancing upon the enemy," was Meade's summary of his situation in a dispatch to Couch on the morning of June 30. Although he realized that a collision was developing between his left wing near Emmitsburg and Confederates from Chambersburg, his Westminster position indicates that he still hoped to fall on an isolated element of Ewell's corps.

On the strength of Harrison's information, General Lee had ended his halt at Chambersburg. Hill, the first to move, had marched Heth's and Pender's divisions through Cashtown Pass, between Chambersburg and Gettysburg. Their campfires on the eastern slope of the mountain were visible in the valley to the east on the night of the 29th. By the next morning Meade knew that the advancing enemy force was part of Hill's corps.[1] Throughout the daylight hours of the 30th his attention focused westward on the gaps leading into the Cumberland Valley and northward on the town of Gettysburg. Although most of the resultant reports are missing, the several summaries issued from his headquarters during the day reveal that in addition to being aware of Hill's appearance in Cashtown Pass, he knew, though somewhat less exactly, of the position of Stuart and his three brigades, then arriving at Hanover, close on the Federals' right. But Ewell's withdrawal from the Susquehanna, ordered by Lee on the basis of Harrison's report, was now well under way and Meade had no information that he had moved. That lack must have been caused by the communications outage; Jeb Stuart had partly made up for his failure as an intelligence collector for Lee by severely impeding the transmission of intelligence to Meade.

Soon after the message to Couch, Meade wrote to Reynolds saying that he had not made up his mind "whether the holding of the Cashtown Gap is to prevent our entrance or is their advance against us." In the latter event, Reynolds, upon meeting an enemy advance in force, was to give up his position halfway between Emmitsburg and Gettysburg and retire on Emmitsburg. Meade even gave him permission to make such a withdrawal without having encountered the enemy. "Your present position," Meade explained, "was given more with a view to [our] advance on Gettysburg than [as] a defensive point."[2] This change in Reynolds's orders was a sign that Meade was beginning to lose his offensive turn of mind.

Caution was enjoined on Reynolds not only by the instructions from his chief but by a piece of oddly erroneous intelligence from the cavalry. Early that morning one of Buford's brigades had skirmished briefly with Southern infantry at Fairfield, seven miles southwest of Gettysburg. The enemy consisted of only a single company of North Carolina infantry from Heth's division, but the Federals somehow got the impression that their opposition consisted of two Mississippi regiments. For several hours the belief persisted at Reynolds's and Meade's headquarters that the enemy were present in force in the vicinity of Fairfield, close on Reynolds's left.[3]

Another erroneous report, around noon, put the enemy in strength at Gettysburg. This had a brief but significant influence on Meade's thinking; he issued a circular order that announced his intention "to hold this army pretty nearly in the position it now occupies until the plans of the enemy shall have been more fully developed." Corps commanders were directed, however, to be ready to march at a moment's notice.[4]

Thus Meade arrested his advance on the basis of incorrect information. But his mistaken belief that the enemy's move on Gettysburg was in great strength lasted only until the next dispatch arrived from General Buford. Having also heard of the massive enemy advance on Gettysburg, Buford determined to investigate the matter himself. He arrived there about 11 A.M. to find many excited Gettysburgers but no Confederates.

Pushing on a little to the west of the town, however, Buford encountered enemy infantry — a regiment, he thought, but in fact it was the brigade of General Johnston J. Pettigrew, making the famous march in search of supplies, "shoes especially." This risky project was undertaken in the face of the fact that the Gettysburg stores would have had in stock only the amount of men's shoes for a town of 2400; and that stock would have been reduced to zero by the recent visit of Early's division (though that detail of Ewell's advance may have been unknown to Hill and Heth).

The Southerners withdrew before Buford could identify them. He had the good luck, however, to locate a citizen for whom General Lee had signed a pass that morning at Chambersburg. This was, of course, excellent evidence of the location of Lee's headquarters, and another instance of Lee's passing out of his lines people who could and would give the Federals useful information. Buford also reported having established contact with "reliable men" in Gettysburg; this probably referred to David McConaughy's group. The first information he obtained from this source was a report that Anderson's division of Hill's corps had come through the mountains and was passing a few miles north of Gettysburg heading for York. This was mistaken — Anderson's advance had not yet begun — and Reynolds, the first to receive the report, appended an expression of doubt. His skepticism, however, did not prevent the error from receiving a degree of acceptance at army headquarters for a few hours.[5]

The army's vigorous pursuit of intelligence on that last day of June was being hampered by fear that the invasion had aroused among the villagers and country people, some of whom, fearing for their homes, would not even acknowledge that Confederate forces had passed by. On the night of the 29th, Buford said, he "encamped within 2 miles of . . . Reb forces — I heard nothing of them until I found them. Had the people a spark of enterprise, I could have captured the whole." But not everyone was cowed into silence; John Sigfouse, a rural mail carrier in the country east of Frederick, while making his rounds on the morning of the 29th, was taken prisoner by Stuart's cavalry, but after six hours he spotted an interval in their columns that gave him the chance to take leave of them. Stuart had cut a wide swath through central Maryland, but little exact information concerning his force was obtained until Sigfouse paid a visit to Colonel Sharpe on the 30th. Sharpe was able to report in some detail on the size of the enemy column; it had been six hours in passing him, Sigfouse said. He also corroborated the previous reports that Stuart and Fitzhugh Lee were with the column.[6]

One other important piece of intelligence also reached Meade about the same time, from Chambersburg by way of Harrisburg. On June 27, after Benjamin Huber had set out to report Lee's turn toward Cashtown and Gettysburg, two other members of Judge Kimmel's group started out with the most comprehensive report that is known to have come out of Chambersburg. These two men, who are unidentified, made slower progress than Huber, arriving at Harrisburg only in time for Couch, late on the 29th, to send Meade a summary of their information. The message said that Generals Lee, Longstreet, Hill, and Ewell in person were all in Chambersburg, although in fact Ewell had left a few days before. As the messengers were said to have furnished "very accurate" descriptions of the Southern commanders, it is hard to understand how they could have concluded that Ewell, with his wooden leg, was present. Despite this one flaw, the report was of considerable value in rounding out the picture of events west of the mountains. And the error regarding Ewell's personal whereabouts was largely nullified by the statement, substantially correct, that two of his divisions, Rodes's and Johnson's, were the only Confederate units that had gone toward Harrisburg. (Early's had taken the more southerly route to Gettysburg and York.) Also useful was the

Chambersburgers' latest count of Confederates who had marched by: 37,000, with part of Hill's corps (but none of Longstreet's) apparently included, along with Ewell's.

Scarcely an hour later Couch received still more information from Chambersburg. He sent a follow-up wire adding two points of importance: the count of the invaders' artillery had reached 162 pieces, and General D. H. Hill was reported among the visitors, although Couch had his doubts about that. He also questioned the validity of the report of Longstreet's presence.[7] (Union intelligence suppliers were almost as free with their reports of D. H. Hill's return to the Army of Northern Virginia as they were with reports of Longstreet's detachment from it.)

Summarizing the situation for Halleck and Couch late in the afternoon, Meade wrote that his information "seems" to place Ewell in the vicinity of York and Harrisburg, Longstreet at Chambersburg, and Hill moving between Chambersburg and York. Only his intelligence on Stuart lacked the qualifying word "seems"; he gave the cavalry's route accurately and placed its strength at 6000 to 8000, a quite reasonable estimate. Judson Kilpatrick, commanding Stahel's old cavalry division, had had a sharp fight with Stuart that morning at Hanover, but the result was not yet known.

In this dispatch Meade stated his intention to move his right the next day to Hanover and Hanover Junction, a decidedly northeastward movement that is hard to reconcile with the facts of the moment: the main body of the enemy was, as he knew, on his left, and Reynolds, whether or not he exercised Meade's permission to fall back, was to remain with three corps so close to the enemy's known position that he might bring on a general battle at any time.

This plan was motivated by Meade's interpretation of his requirement to cover Baltimore and Washington, and by a hope he still retained of falling upon a detached portion of the invading army. He explained these objectives to Pleasonton in a dispatch that also pointed out the desirability of finding out *if* Lee's army was divided. (Meade also lectured Pleasonton on his intelligence-gathering duties, saying that they must be given a higher priority than fighting cavalry battles.) That Meade knew beyond doubt of Ewell's wide separation from Lee's main body, and of Early's separation from the rest of Ewell's corps, is plainly shown in numerous other dispatches sent that day and previously.[8] He was looking for signs of the reuniting of Confederate forces that was then in progress, though the telegraph outage denied him that knowledge.

Not long after his dispatch to Halleck, Meade issued another order to the army, specifying movements for the next day. He had had time to digest the most recent intelligence, and again his intentions had changed: Hanover Junction, the farthest east of the targets he had named to Halleck, was not mentioned. Instead, the Sixth Corps, which would have drawn the assignment to march there, was to remain in its camp at Manchester. This ignored the very apparent fact that a meeting with the enemy was developing on the left; at Manchester the Sixth Corps, the largest in the army, was even farther from the probable place of a collision than it would have been at Hanover Junction. And two other corps, the Second and Fifth, were ordered to Taneytown and Hanover, destinations that looked more like continuation of Meade's advance on a broad front than a massing of the army toward the main body of the enemy. Meade was abandoning his hope of finding a vulnerable element of Ewell's forces, but he had not yet decided what to do with the Sixth Corps. He did, however, order four corps of infantry into a close grouping on the left — the First Corps to Gettysburg; the Eleventh to Gettysburg or within supporting distance of the First; the Third to Emmitsburg; and the Twelfth to Two Taverns, five miles southeast of Gettysburg. The Second Corps remained in the army's rear.

Meade at the same time gave this intelligence summary: "From present information, Longstreet and Hill are at Chambersburg, partly toward Gettysburg; Ewell at Carlisle and York. Movements indicate a disposition to advance from Chambersburg to Gettysburg." (Gone were the erroneous assumptions of Confederate movements south and north of Gettysburg.) Then he repeated a statement of his view, which was also General Couch's, that the Confederate advance to the Susquehanna was less offensive in intent than it was an attempt to prevent cooperation between their two forces. He concluded with the statement that he believed he had "relieved Harrisburg and Philadelphia" and now desired to look to his own army "and assume position for offensive or defensive, as occasion requires, or rest to the troops."[9]

Meade's actions on June 30 have been described as those of a "vacillating, disturbed officer, who could not add 2 and 2 and get 4."[10] If one considers only his grasp of the enemy's situation, this judgment must be reversed. As has been shown, he did change his announced intentions several times, but each change was supported by a statement of new intelligence about enemy positions or movements; he was not vacillating but simply responding to new information or to refinements in his interpretation of previous reports. Three times during the day, as we have seen, he received erroneous reports about Confederate forces that had come through the mountains. These errors did find their way into some of the numerous intelligence summaries that issued from his headquarters; the summaries were correct in the main, however, and errors were soon corrected. This quick discarding of faulty information is as impressive in its way as a completely errorless performance by the army's sources of information would have been. All errors had been purged by evening.

These statements about the enemy situation appear over the signatures of Meade, Butterfield, and General Seth Williams, the army's adjutant. Although Sharpe undoubtedly had a hand in conclusions reached by his chiefs, and some of the wording is probably his, the dispatches are so phrased as to leave no doubt that Meade himself was assimilating every shred of new information and was prominent in, perhaps dominating, its evaluation.[11]

.   .   ..   ..

Whereas Meade's several changes of orders were in response to arrivals of information about enemy movements, Lee's one change was based not on new intelligence (Harrison's report remained his latest information) but on his decision to concentrate east of the mountains. That not only relieved his anxiety about a Federal incursion into the Cumberland Valley; it also promised to shorten Ewell's move to the concentration point by at least a day's march.

Gettysburg appears in Lee's changed order to Ewell, not as a concentration point alternative to Cashtown but as a convenient place, along with nearby Heidlersburg, for Early to reunite with Ewell. There was no suggestion that Gettysburg might be worth seizing as an advantageous position for battle.[12]

The time had now passed when intelligence could influence the time and place of a collision of the armies, but there was still a great deal it could contribute to the outcome. The story of this last phase of the pursuit of information about the enemy begins on the Union left. From comfortable quarters with Jesuit fathers in Mount Saint Mary's College at Emmitsburg, General Howard was summoned on the evening of the 30th to General Reynolds's headquarters six miles away at Marsh Run on the road to Gettysburg. He found Reynolds occupying a sparsely furnished room of a roadside house. The two generals spent the evening discussing the intelligence that had reached them that day. "Reynolds seemed depressed, almost as if he had a presentiment of his death," Howard recalled, but he added that this mood might simply have been induced by anxiety about the scattered condition of the army. The dispatches of the day, according to Howard, "were abundant and conflicting. They came from headquarters at Taneytown, from Buford at Gettysburg, from scouts, from alarmed citizens, from all directions. They, however, forced the conclusion upon us that Lee's infantry and artillery in great force were in our neighborhood."

After returning to his quarters at the college, Howard had been asleep about an hour when an orderly wakened him. A dispatch had arrived from army headquarters, addressed to Reynolds as wing commander. It was Meade's order for the grouping of Reynolds's three corps, at and just below Gettysburg. Howard opened and read it before sending it on its way. When Reynolds was awakened about 4 A.M. to receive it, he had it read to him three times, for in the light of new information from Buford, its portent was grave.[13] Buford had discovered a further advance by Hill; that was ominous enough, but he also reported strong indications that Ewell was approaching Gettysburg from the north. Thus it was evident that Lee's columns were converging in front of Reynolds; the left wing, on its prescribed march of the next day, could expect to meet Ewell, Hill, and — probably not many hours in Hill's rear — Longstreet.

Buford's information about Ewell was the result of his scouting that day in the country north of Gettysburg. Near Heidlersburg, ten miles away, one of his parties captured a courier of Lee's. The prisoner was empty-handed but not empty of talk, and he correctly reported that Ewell was marching southward and that Rodes's division had reached Petersburg, halfway from Carlisle to Gettysburg. Buford had also heard that Early was approaching from York, but he was uncertain of the validity of this information. He had expanded the previous knowledge of Hill's positions by discovering that Pender's division was now east of the mountains (Heth's had preceded it). Longstreet, he said, "from all I can learn, is still behind Hill."

Buford wrote this excellent report at 10:30 P.M. and a similar dispatch ten minutes later to Pleasonton, who was at Taneytown with Meade. Doubtless Reynolds also forwarded Buford's information to the commander; Meade would recall that he received it, from whichever source, in midmorning of July 1.[14]

Exactly who acquired this information for Buford is an interesting question. When he wrote his report of the battle of Gettysburg two months later, he said, "No reliable information of value could be obtained [that night] from the inhabitants, and but for the untiring exertions of many different scouting parties, information of the enemy's whereabouts and movements could not have been gained in time to prevent him from getting the town before our army could get up."[15] Buford's scouts unquestionably are entitled to the credit for the capture of Lee's courier — the chief source of his information about Ewell — but the information concerning Heth's and Pender's advance appears to have been obtained by penetration or close-up observation, and the army's cavalry was not accustomed to that kind of intelligence activity. It may have been obtained by some or all of the several men McEntee had left with the cavalry when he returned to army headquarters back in Virginia. Another possibility is that McConaughy was the source; he is known to have continued his espionage and reporting work "up to the morning of the 1st July."[16] Buford's term "scouting parties" ordinarily would have meant cavalry scouting, but it was unspecific enough to include some of Sharpe's men or McConaughy and his civilians. Still another possibility is that McConaughy was working with Buford's scouts and at the same time sending reports to Sharpe. That would explain why reports about Confederate forces that were closer to Reynolds than to

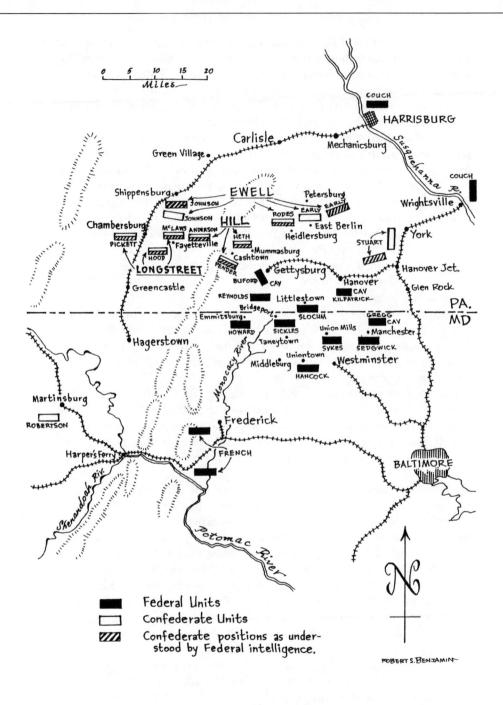

Federal Units
Confederate Units
Confederate positions as under-
stood by Federal intelligence.

ROBERT S. BENJAMIN

SITUATION, NIGHT OF JUNE 30, 1863

Meade were passed to Reynolds and Howard that day from army head-quarters.[17]

. . .. ..

Buford's report was not the only intelligence concerning Ewell received that night. Late on the 30th and on through the early hours of July 1 there was a rush of telegrams telling the story of the recent happenings on the Susquehanna front, reaching the army by courier from telegraph offices and railheads to the south and east.

Lee's order based on Harrison's report had reached Ewell at Carlisle on the 29th, perhaps by the hand of the courier Buford captured the next day. Now the general who had treasured his mission of taking Harrisburg was countermarching to join his corps to the rest of the army. The order gave Chambersburg as the point of concentration, and Johnson's division on the 29th was started on its way there. Then came still another order: March the corps to Gettysburg or Cashtown. Two changes in quick succession, plus uncertainty as to his objective point — all this irritated Ewell, who (like Early) was known for his volatile temper and the impressive articulation he gave it. But ambiguous orders could be carried out ambiguously: Ewell sent his troops to Gettysburg *and* Cashtown. Johnson's division headed for Cashtown by continuing its westward march and turning off to the left at Green Village, a few miles short of Chambersburg, and marching over to the Chambersburg-Cashtown pike. Ewell and Rodes took the latter's division south from Carlisle toward Gettysburg, stopping on the night of the 30th at Heidlersburg. Early's division rejoined Ewell by marching to Heidlersburg from its positions at York and at Wrightsville on the Susquehanna.[18]

The story of these movements arrived in fragments at Harrisburg, which was not only Couch's base but also the junction of the Pennsylvania Central and Northern Central railroads, both of which were running espionage and scouting operations. Private enterprise could never have a more intimate role in military events than it did that 30th of June.

The earliest of these reports was from S. S. Blair, superintendent of the Baltimore division of the Northern Central, who produced the first detailed information to come out of York after Early's arrival there. He brought it out on foot, leaving without hindrance in midday on the 29th and walking fifteen miles down the railroad to Glen Rock, where he put it on the wires to Harrisburg and Baltimore. In addition to his report on Early's visit, the telegram gave a full account of the advance of Gordon's brigade beyond York to the Susquehanna. Blair placed the total strength of the invaders at 10,000 or less, a good estimate under the circumstances; he could hardly have seen more than a rather small fraction of Early's force on the march. He reported that Early and his officers had favored the locals with some big talk as to their strength and forthcoming movements, but against this he observed that the troops seemed "very uneasy — their cavalrymen are in the saddles and infantry are resting on their arms."

Blair had left York several hours before Early received the order to countermarch. It was left for another Northern Central official, F. T. Scott, to report the enemy's withdrawal. Early marched on the morning of the 30th; in midafternoon Scott had the news at Hanover Junction, ten miles down the railroad. The two telegrams — Blair's of the 29th and Scott's a day later — arrived at Meade's headquarters together.[19]

Scott reported that Early's route was toward Carlisle.[20] The most probable meaning of this fact was that Ewell was consolidating his forces for an attempted crossing of the Susquehanna opposite Harrisburg, where Darius Couch was feverishly preparing the capital for the expected enemy advance. But Ewell, who in Couch's opinion could have forded the river, had remained puzzlingly out of sight of it; hence Couch had come to believe that Ewell had never intended a serious offensive against him. Somewhat later in the day he began to get a flow of dispatches that told him that Early's departure from York was only part of a general withdrawal by Ewell from the Susquehanna.

While York and its vicinity were being covered by Northern Central observers, Ewell's movements around Carlisle were being watched by the Pennsylvania Central spies headed by William B. Wilson, whose services with Captain William Palmer in the Antietam campaign were well remembered at Harrisburg. As one of the chief telegraphers of the Pennsylvania Central, Wilson was sometimes equipped with a locomotive to enable him to keep up, or catch up, with the enemy's marches — an interesting contrast with the conventional picture of the spy attempting to blend with his surroundings and moving about as inconspicuously as possible. But if Wilson's means of transport was a bit obvious, his method of conveying information gave him a tremendous advantage; again, as in 1862, he carried a portable telegraph instrument and tapped onto the railroad wires to send his reports to Harrisburg. When necessary he lowered the wire to give the impression that it had been torn down, while carefully protecting it against electrical contact with the ground. He connected his instrument to the circuit using a fine silk-covered wire, which he ran into a thicket or other hiding place. Despite these precautions, at times in this campaign the enemy came upon him "before I could arrange my toilet for leaving," compelling him to find a hiding place.

Wilson focused his efforts on Jenkins's cavalry, operating between Carlisle and the Susquehanna. Temporarily without his locomotive, he was traveling by handcar. Jenkins's troopers spotted him at Mechanicsburg and drove him out of the town, shooting at him as he "ground" his way down a stretch of track that paralleled the highway to Carlisle.[21]

Another spy at work in the Carlisle area at this time, probably as a member of Wilson's group, was John A. Seiders of Chambersburg. Seiders was in Ewell's camps in a Confederate uniform acquired during Jenkins's first visit to Chambersburg two weeks previously. With their bare hands Seiders and a fellow townsman had captured a Confederate lieutenant and taken his mount and arms. Seiders used the victim's pistol to divest another enemy officer of all his belongings. Thus equipped, he was present at the beginning of Ewell's withdrawal.

Both Alexander McClure and Jacob Hoke accepted this story; though it lacks verification in official documents, it qualifies as a fifth case of Federal spies mingling with Confederate troops, though probably less extensively than in the other four cases.[22]

The reports that the Union spies in the Carlisle area produced on June 30 can be praised more for the promptness of their dispatch from Harrisburg than for their abundance of detail, but they did give a compelling picture of the invaders' sudden withdrawal from the Susquehanna front. By midday of the 30th, Couch knew the countermarch had begun; a few hours later he wired that the first units to depart had passed Shippensburg "in great haste." He was so sure that Carlisle was or would soon be free of the enemy that he was preparing to occupy the town with part of his own motley force, which he would never have risked in an offensive move against Ewell. Late in the afternoon he knew of the withdrawal of the remaining Rebels, who did not march in the wake of the others but instead headed southward. The first departure was that of Johnson and the second was Rodes's; Couch, however, did not (and perhaps could not) name them.

Concerning Early's decamping from York, Couch had later information than had come from the Northern Central officials. Early, whom he did name, had employed a deceptive route, first heading northwest for Carlisle (as F. T. Scott of the Northern Central had reported) and then, after a march of eight or ten miles, turning to the left toward Heidlersburg. Couch's sources followed this twist well enough to report by the end of the day that Early had gone to the west or northwest. Buford at Gettysburg had begun, as we have seen, to pick up word of Early's approach, and Meade appears to have correctly chosen west over northwest as Early's true route.

The suddenness of the Rebels' new move had not escaped the spies' notice. Couch's last telegram of the day said, "Rebels at York and Carlisle yesterday a good deal agitated about some news they had received."

Couch's reports of these developments arrived in the War Department as early as 5:30 P.M.[23] But Buford's report of Ewell's movement, written five hours later and delivered to Meade in midmorning of July 1, probably was Meade's first news of this all-important development. The communication outage caused by Stuart's marauding probably was over by this time, but Meade was paying a price for the marching speed he gained by moving without his own telegraph line. His usual telegraph terminal, Frederick, still had no direct communication with Harrisburg; his messages to and from Couch traveled via the War Department.

Brigadier General Herman Haupt, the army's able director of railroads, arrived in Harrisburg that evening and began helping Couch sort out and interpret the information that was coming in.[24] Writing in an excited tone, Haupt produced the following telegram, sent at about 11 P.M.:

> Lee is falling back suddenly from the vicinity of Harrisburg, and concentrating all his forces. York has been evacuated. Carlisle is being evacuated. The concentration appears to be at or near Chambersburg. The object, apparently a sudden movement against Meade, of which he should be advised by courier immediately. This information comes from T. A. Scott, and I think it reliable.

Both the substance and the tone of this message ignored Couch's earlier reports, which were inconclusive as to Lee's place of concentration; Gettysburg would be as likely as Chambersburg. If Haupt had later information that invalidated Couch's statement that part of the force at Carlisle had gone south (toward Gettysburg) rather than west (toward Chambersburg), he should have said so. And this message was to exert considerable influence on Meade's eleventh-hour estimate of the enemy's intentions, for it probably was the last word from the Susquehanna region to reach the Army of the Potomac before the opening guns sounded at Gettysburg. Couch had provided excellent intelligence to his brother commander for several hours; it was partly nullified at the end of the eventful day by the earnest but superficial efforts of a visiting general.

Haupt's message was forwarded to Meade from two directions. Before midnight General Schenck at Baltimore sent it by courier to Westminster, a railhead twelve miles southeast of Meade's headquarters at Taneytown. This was in addition to the usual transmission to Frederick from the War Department, which was also keeping late hours. The responsibility of getting it from Frederick to Taneytown fell upon two young civilian telegraph operators, Ten Eyck H. Fonda and Luther A. Rose; Fonda said he started from Frederick in the middle of the night and made the thirty-mile ride over strange roads in four hours and fifteen minutes.[25]

The Chambersburgers were still at work; their next feat corrected both the serious error in Haupt's message and cleared up the confusion that had made Gettysburg and Chambersburg alternative possibilities for the enemy concentration. During the night of June 29–30, Jacob Hoke, who lived above his store on the town's square, was awakened by the clattering of a wagon train. Peering through the shutters, he saw wagons being driven hurriedly through the town, loaded so heavily that they made a grinding noise. They were coming in from the northeast on the Harrisburg road, turning left and leaving on the road to Gettysburg. They proved to be Ewell's. When Judge Kimmel called on Hoke early the next morning the two men had to exchange only a few words in order to agree on the tremendous significance of what they had witnessed: Lee was concentrating his army in the direction of Gettysburg.

The courier they started for Harrisburg this time was Stephen W. Pomeroy, son of another Franklin County judge and a recently discharged veteran of the Union army. The message went into the bucklestrap of Pomeroy's pantaloons. Spotted by enemy pickets on his way out of town, he was over a fence before they could fire at him. Along most of his route he was greeted with surprise by friends — including his future wife — who had heard that he had recently been killed in resisting the Confederate cavalry's incursion into the country north of Chambersburg. He did not reach Harrisburg; his trip terminated on the night of June 30 at Perryville (now Port Royal), forty miles northwest of the capital. It was on a railroad, which meant that it might well have a telegraph office. About midnight he found an operator; in a few minutes his important dispatch was in Harrisburg. It was unsigned, and Governor Curtin, the addressee, did not learn the identity of the sender until twenty years later, when he chanced to mention the incident to a group of Presbyterian ministers that included the Reverend Mr. Pomeroy.[26]

General Haupt hastened to put the latest findings on the wire to Baltimore and Washington.

> Information just received, 12:45 A.M., leads to the belief that the concentration of the forces of the enemy will be at Gettysburg rather than Chambersburg. The movement on their part is very rapid and hurried. They returned from Carlisle in the direction of Gettysburg by way of the Petersburg pike. Firing about Petersburg and Dillsburg this p.m. continued some hours. Meade should by all means be informed, and be prepared for a sudden attack from Lee's whole army.[27]

The telegram reflects the difficulties inherent in Pomeroy's travels. The firing Haupt mentioned had cut off the courier's direct route to Harrisburg, if it was not already barred by the mere presence of Confederate troops (Rodes's division) on the Carlisle-Gettysburg road (the "Petersburg pike"). The development that enabled Pomeroy to cross the Carlisle-Chambersburg road and detour to Perryville was the absence or near-absence of enemy troops on that road. Johnson's division, the one Ewell ordered to Chambersburg, had cleared the Carlisle area by the time Pomeroy arrived there. Thus Johnson's movement escaped Pomeroy's notice, and also Haupt's. Haupt also left unmentioned the passage of Ewell's wagons through Chambersburg, the movement that had touched off Pomeroy's mission.[28]

Although Haupt's second message reached the War Department at 1:35 A.M. July 1, and although operator Rose's journal indicates that the Frederick telegraph office had no shortage of extra operators who could have carried the obviously important message to Meade at Taneytown, the records indicate that it was not started from Frederick until 2 P.M., by which time Buford's news of Ewell's approach had been in Meade's hands for some hours. Whether General Schenck at Baltimore forwarded the telegram to Meade is unknown. In any case, as will be seen in the next chapter, no copy of it seems to have reached Meade by the time his army was engaged with the forces whose march toward Gettysburg it reported.[29]

Here was an outstanding example of good intelligence work nullified by poor communications. It was also an example of the need, in a headquarters dealing with an emergency as important as Couch's, of an intelligence officer, whose very presence would have forestalled the visiting officer's takeover of the reporting function, or at least would have assured that the visitor was properly informed of the situation before he started writing.

24

· · · · · · · · · · ·

DECISION AND VICTORY

July 1–3

I N THE NATURE OF THINGS, an army headquarters ordinarily has a better understanding of the enemy's total situation than any of its subordinate elements can have. That, however, was not the case in the Army of the Potomac on the morning of July 1. General Reynolds, in command of the left wing, left his position north of Emmitsburg and marched to Gettysburg, where he quickly learned that Confederate forces were arriving on the road from Carlisle. Until General Meade would receive this news from Reynolds, he had no information to correct General Haupt's first message, which reported enemy departures from Carlisle in the direction of Chambersburg. Reynolds, because of having made an early start for Gettysburg, probably never received the misinformation from Harrisburg that Meade would have relayed to him. Meanwhile, Meade's headquarters, still lacking Haupt's corrective message, produced for Reynolds an estimate that straddled the divergent views of the enemy's objectives. The various reports, this estimate said, "seem to indicate the concentration of the enemy either at Chambersburg or at a point situated somewhere on a line drawn between Chambersburg and York, through Mummasburg and to the north of Gettysburg."[1]

The information that greeted Reynolds at Gettysburg had been obtained by Buford from two prisoners. One said he belonged to Rodes's division,[2] thus corroborating the statement made by the captured courier the previous evening that Rodes was marching south from Carlisle. The other captive was an even more valuable acquisition, since he was another courier, bearing a dispatch dated June 30 to an unnamed colonel:

Get between Gettysburg and Heidlersburg, and picket at Mummasburg and Hunterstown. Send in the direction of Gettysburg, and see what is there, and report to General Ewell at Heidlersburg. A small body of Yankee cavalry has made its appearance between Gettysburg and Heidlersburg. See what it is.

The signature was especially interesting: "J. A. Early, Major-General." Early's approach was no longer a matter of rumor, and Ewell's proximity was now beyond doubt. The dispatch-bearer added that he had seen Early on the night of the 30th at East Berlin, fifteen miles northeast of Gettysburg.[3]

Until Buford's information (or Haupt's second message, pointing to Gettysburg rather than Chambersburg as the objective of the enemy's movements) could reach Meade, he would remain in doubt as to Lee's point of concentration. But headquarters' situation summary quoted above had weaknesses apart from its uncertainty on that question. It included an estimate of enemy strength that was less accurate than one Meade had accepted the day he took command. Then he had confidently endorsed the figure of 80,000 enemy infantry that Thomas McCammon had brought from Hagerstown. Now, three days later, that estimate was abandoned; the invaders' infantry strength was placed at 92,000, the cavalry at 6000 to 8000, and the artillery at 270 guns. The cavalry figures were a good estimate of the strength of Lee's mounted arm in Pennsylvania, and the number of guns was only two short of the total long accepted, but the 92,000 for the infantry was 15 or 20 percent too high, swollen by a 38,000 figure for Ewell and 30,000 for Longstreet. The figures were worked out at Harrisburg from counts of marching troops made at Chambersburg, Carlisle, York, and possibly other places.[4] Army headquarters accepted those estimates; as they were based on eye-witness counting, Sharpe would have preferred them to any estimates that could be made from his bureau's records. Lee's army had left Fredericksburg soon after its expansion into three corps, and contact between the armies had been so slight on the long march north that Babcock's enemy-organization chart had several gaps.

In this dispatch to Reynolds, Meade explained, "The movement of your corps to Gettysburg was ordered before the positive knowledge of the enemy's withdrawal from Harrisburg and concentration was received."[5] Only to that extent was Reynolds reminded that the orders to him of the previous night might be taking him closer to the enemy than Meade had intended. There was no instruction, as there had been in a previous order, as to what Reynolds should do if he encountered the enemy in force, no hint that Meade expected that he might have to send support. These omissions may, however, have been deliberate; Meade is known to have placed high trust in Reynolds's judgment and may have purposely refrained from giving him detailed guidance.

Since Reynolds at that hour possessed a clearer picture of the enemy's concentration than did his chief, it would have been no unsoldierly act if in sending Buford's new information to headquarters he had added a statement to this effect: "There is every reason to believe that the entire enemy army is concentrating in my front and on my left. From here

it appears that reinforcements should be hurried toward Gettysburg."
Many a general would have asked for reinforcements or permission to
fall back. Reynolds had been given such permission the previous day,
when the intelligence outlook was less grim, and new orders to the same
effect were even then being written, but at this time his orders contained
no such proviso. Still he did not request any support, indicated no doubt
as to whether Meade realized what the orders to the left wing were likely
to lead to. Reynolds's response to the alarming prospect raised by the
enemy's concentration was to march into the teeth of it. General Doubleday, his senior division commander, explained Reynolds's aggressiveness on two grounds — that he was incensed at the invasion of his native
Pennsylvania, and that he had great confidence in his men.[6] Probably he
was also confident of finding at Gettysburg favorable ground for a battle
— or had assured himself that Gettysburg was a position that must be
held whatever the cost.[7]

Two last-minute intelligence summaries sent by Meade show that the
latest information from Buford was in his hands as the morning hours
waned. To Couch he wrote, "The enemy are advancing on Gettysburg —
Hill, from Cashtown; Ewell, from Heidlersburg. . . ." At the same time he
wrote to Halleck, "Ewell is massing at Heidlersburg. A. P. Hill is massed
behind the mountains at Cashtown. Longstreet somewhere between
Chambersburg and the mountains." An hour later he added a postscript
(which brought the message into agreement with the one to Couch):
"The enemy are advancing in force on Gettysburg, and I expect the
battle will begin today."

The dispatch to Halleck contains a startling revelation: "The news [of
Ewell's withdrawal] proves my advance has answered its purpose. I shall
not advance any, but prepare to receive an attack in case Lee makes one."
To the army he announced in a circular, "[T]he object of the movement
. . . in this direction has been accomplished, viz, the relief of Harrisburg,
and the prevention of the enemy's intended invasion of Philadelphia,
&c., beyond the Susquehanna. It is no longer [the] intention to assume
the offensive until the enemy's movements or position should render
such an operation certain of success."[8] This was the order that directed
the army, in the event of a Confederate attack, to take up a defensive
position along Pipe Creek, fifteen miles south of Gettysburg; Meade was
to be plagued by the difficulty of explaining the "Pipe Creek Order" for
the rest of his life. Its "if the enemy attack" proviso was unrealistic since
the advance wing of the army was heading into a well-nigh unavoidable
collision with Lee's main body. The order had a further flaw, in a provision that allowed any corps commander on his own initiative to begin a
movement that would draw the entire army back to Pipe Creek. This instruction read, "Whenever such circumstances arise as would seem to indicate the necessity for falling back and assuming this general line indi-

cated, notice of such movement will be at once communicated to these headquarters and to all adjoining corps commanders." Thus Meade was offering the authority to move the whole army to any corps commander who might find himself in a tight spot.[9]

But the Pipe Creek Order had no effect other than the future embarrassment of General Meade. Before it left headquarters — in fact, before Meade wrote Couch that "The enemy are advancing on Gettysburg" — the battle had begun.

·· ·· ··

That the Federals' arrival in force at Gettysburg was a surprise to Lee is made plain in his after-action report: "The advance of the enemy to [Gettysburg] was unknown." But Lee and his generals had a very plain warning of the proximity of Northern forces in General Pettigrew's brush with Buford in his attempted visit to Gettysburg's shoe stores on the 30th. From the behavior of the cavalrymen he encountered, Pettigrew had good reason to believe they were not local militia. (His officers had a mistaken impression that Federal infantry were close behind the cavalry.) But his report met with complete disbelief by his division commander, General Heth, and by General Hill, to whom the matter was referred. According to Heth, Hill said, "The only force at Gettysburg is cavalry, probably a detachment of observation. I am just from General Lee, and the information he has from his scouts corroborates what I have received from mine — that is, the enemy are still at Middleburg [in Maryland, fifteen road miles north of Frederick], and have not struck their tents."[10] We may question whether Hill was accurately reporting what Lee had said, and whether Heth was accurately quoting the two of them, but this much is clear, that the Southern commanders had fixed ideas that made them unwilling to consider that the rendezvous at Gettysburg might be seriously opposed. The scouting effort that Hill attributed to Lee and to himself could not have amounted to very much — just enough to tell the generals what they were hoping to hear.[11]

So Heth, with Hill's concurrence, decided he could not let a few Federal horsemen stand between him and the badly needed shoes. On the morning of July 1 he set out from Cashtown with his entire division, followed by Pender's. About three miles from Gettysburg the Southern troops encountered Buford's cavalry patrols, which retired. Two miles farther on, a line of battle — dismounted cavalrymen — met the Confederates head-on. The Federals fought stubbornly as Buford, from the belfry of the Lutheran seminary west of the town, watched the battle and kept an anxious lookout for Reynolds, to whom he had reported the Confederates' advance.[12]

Reynolds was already nearing Gettysburg. About six o'clock that morning he had called in General Doubleday to say that he was going forward with James Wadsworth's division to join Buford. Of his three divisions, Wadsworth's was camped in the most advanced position. The other two ordinarily would have marched first, passing Wadsworth, but Reynolds upset the normal sequence in order to speed the march.

Riding out ahead of his advance, he was met by the sound of Buford's battle. A mile south of Gettysburg a courier reached him with word that the Confederates were coming down from Cashtown in great strength; his response was to send an aide to tell the people of Gettysburg to stay in their homes. He reached Buford as the latter climbed down from the belfry. The two generals' gaze took in not only the fight between William Gamble's brigade and the Confederate advance but also the numerous unoccupied ridges and hills to the north and beyond the town to the south and southeast.[13]

By now Reynolds's decision had hardened: he would give battle on that ground. Since he knew that the force approaching from the west must be the leading elements of Lee's main body, he could not expect to match it in numbers with his own force, but the high ground that he saw to both front and rear would give him the advantage of position if he seized it first. The position must be held; here was the place to fight the Army of Northern Virginia. Reynolds sent word to Meade that he would hold on "even if driven through Gettysburg from house to house." Then he rode back to Wadsworth's troops to lead them onto the field.

The position that was to give the Union the victory was not Seminary Ridge, on which Reynolds had stood with Buford, or any of the other elevations west or north of Gettysburg, but Cemetery Ridge and adjoining heights south of the town. These were, to one facing north and reading counterclockwise around an arc: Culp's Hill, three quarters of a mile southeast of Gettysburg; Cemetery Hill, a half-mile south of the town; and — extending south from Cemetery Hill — Cemetery Ridge, Little Round Top, and Round Top. These five together with a few less prominent heights formed a curving line (so often likened to a fish-hook) about four miles in length, capable of containing a huge army and providing all of its elements with high ground. Because the line bent back on itself, no two points on it were separated by much more than a mile — an advantage that Meade was to exploit heavily in moving troops back and forth to reinforce threatened spots. The Confederates' line would be much longer and their communications would have to be around a long arc rather than across a shorter one. Whether Reynolds saw these heights as the key position has been a matter of dispute; General Howard was favorably cited by Congress for his seizing of Cemetery Ridge although there is evidence that he did so on express orders from Reynolds.[14] The essential point in any case is that Reynolds elected to bring on a general engagement at Gettysburg, in the face of circumstances — namely, the concentration of Lee's whole army — that would have justified holding back.

Reynolds returned with Wadsworth's brigades about midmorning, and the field blazed forth in a small but fierce contest for McPherson's Heights to the west of Seminary Ridge. Before the battle he had marched into was fairly started, Reynolds fell dead, shot through the head as he was posting two of his regiments in the immediate front of the enemy.

Next in command was General Howard, who arrived about noon with the Eleventh Corps and placed two of his divisions to the north of the town, leaving the third on Cemetery Ridge. The remaining divisions of the First Corps were now on hand, but in midafternoon Ewell reached the field with Rodes's and Early's divisions, taking position in front of Howard, and the Federals were again outnumbered. They had had the better of the morning's fighting, shattering two of Heth's brigades, but Heth reformed and added his attacks to Ewell's. After breaking up a succession of these, the First and Eleventh Corps, much battered, found themselves outflanked on both right and left. With the aid of some excellent work by their rear guards, they made good a retreat through the town to Cemetery Ridge.[15]

General Hancock soon arrived, not with his corps but as Meade's personal representative, under orders to take command of the field and decide whether to continue the battle or order a movement back to Pipe Creek. Hancock is reported to have said that the position was the strongest he had ever seen, but his report to Meade said merely that the position was one that could not well be taken but could easily be turned. The work of digging in was already well along, and by the end of the day most of the Third and Twelfth Corps had marched up. Cemetery Ridge was now safe for the time being, but Longstreet, known to be in Hill's rear, was yet to be reckoned with.

Before receiving Hancock's message, Meade had tentatively concluded that "we have so concentrated that a battle at Gettysburg is now forced on us." But not until reports of the fighting had begun to come in did he begin hurrying forward the rear of the army, the Fifth and Sixth Corps.[16]

Meade and his staff rode the thirteen miles from Taneytown to Gettysburg after midnight. Dismounting at the cemetery gateway as a full moon reached its zenith, the commanding general was met by Howard, Slocum, and Sickles, who expressed unanimous satisfaction with the position. Meade answered, "I am glad to hear you say so, gentlemen, for it is too late to leave it."[17]

. .   . .   . .

The position that so pleased Meade's subordinates was to have a tremendous effect on the battle; to what extent was its possession the result of the Federals' intelligence successes? Conceivably Reynolds would have acted exactly as he did simply because Meade had ordered him to Gettysburg and upon reaching the place he came upon high ground that had to be seized in order to prevent the enemy from taking it. But there was more than that behind the Federals' prompt occupation of Cemetery Ridge. Reynolds, being so heavily engaged west of the town, would not have permitted Howard's entire corps to occupy quiet ground well to his rear if he had not known that that sector was likely to come under attack by Ewell from the east and north. At this stage of the battle, Cemetery Ridge was important primarily as Reynolds's insurance against an attack from the rear on his hard-pressed forces. General Adolph von Steinwehr, whose division of the Eleventh Corps was the one assigned to hold Cemetery Ridge, said in his report of the battle that he knew of Ewell's approach. General Schurz, commanding Howard's forces in the battle north of the town, also knew Ewell was approaching and ordered a reconnaissance to discover the enemy positions on the road from York.[18] Evidently Howard's Chancellorsville experience had raised his awareness of the need for full dissemination of intelligence.

At one point von Steinwehr had only one brigade and some artillery on Cemetery Ridge. But at the end of the day's battle, the ridge and adjacent Cemetery Hill were securely in Union possession because all the Federal forces that had been engaged, the First and Eleventh Corps, had been driven back behind the considerable fortifications that von Steinwehr had had time to erect. The success of the Confederates — Early's and Rodes's divisions of Ewell's corps and Heth's and Pender's divisions of Hill's — had the effect of planting their opponents on high ground, the most favorable position for miles around.

.. .. ..

The field was quiet except for occasional small outbreaks of gunfire as the morning of July 2 dawned. Over on Seminary Ridge Lee was organizing an attack against the Union left. It was to be led by Longstreet, using Hood's and McLaws's divisions; his third division, Pickett's, had been left at Chambersburg as a rear guard. Anderson's division of Hill's corps was to assist Longstreet, and Ewell was to demonstrate against the Federal right, turning his operation into a real attack if an opportunity developed. There were no plans for the Confederate cavalry, aside from the assignment of Imboden, a new arrival, to relieve Pickett at Chambersburg. The three brigades with Stuart were on the last leg of their long ride, having overshot Lee's and Ewell's positions by paying a fruitless visit to Carlisle the evening before, looking for Ewell. Robertson's regiments likewise had not yet arrived from their stations on the Blue Ridge.[19]

Although Lee did not know it, by now he was facing the entire Army of the Potomac except the Sixth Corps, which had been thirty-two miles away, down in Maryland, when Meade ordered it to Gettysburg; it would arrive in midafternoon after one of the stiffest marches of the war. Meade had placed his units skillfully and, after giving some thought to assuming the offensive, had decided to await the attack he believed the enemy would be forced to make.[20]

Sharpe, Babcock, and McEntee began their battlefield labors expecting that the face-to-face proximity of the enemy would enable them to fill in most or all of the gaps in their organizational records. Some of the recently added regiments were still unidentified; the brigades to which many regiments belonged were still unknown; and this dearth of information may have extended to the division assignments of a few brigades. These were not mere bookkeeping problems; as previously noted, the presence of a mere regiment would indicate the presence of an entire corps, provided its subordination to the larger units — brigade, division, corps — had been determined.

. .   . .   . .

Longstreet's attack was delayed until 3:00 or 4:00 in the afternoon for reasons that are still debated. The question has been whether the delay was necessitated by legitimate difficulties or was caused by Longstreet's foot-dragging arising out of a strong preference he had for a turning movement around the Union left. One serious difficulty is unquestioned — a time-consuming countermarch by two divisions to hide the movement from a Federal signal station on Little Round Top. The attack struck squarely at the sector held by the Third Corps, which General Sickles, acting on his own judgment, had moved into a salient half a mile or more in advance of the Second Corps on its right. Though delivered piecemeal, the blow fell with such fury that it wiped out the salient and much of Sickles's corps. The line of the Second Corps was penetrated briefly. Meade was forced to draw the Fifth Corps and most of the Twelfth from the right of his line; into supporting positions he also moved parts of the much battered First Corps and some of the Sixth Corps units, which had just arrived, badly fatigued. The attack was stopped, but it had gained valuable ground and had done a great deal of damage.

On the Union right, the point of the fishhook, Ewell's intended demonstration turned quickly into a real attack. Johnson moved into the entrenchments vacated by the withdrawn brigades of the Twelfth Corps, and Rodes and Early stormed Cemetery Hill, only to be driven off by a counterattack thrown against them in near-darkness.[21]

The day's fighting brought 1360 prisoners into the provost marshal's fenceless stockades. They gave Babcock something more valuable than neatly filled-in rows and columns on his chart. He wrote General Butterfield:

Prisoners have been taken today, and last evening, from every brigade in Lee's Army excepting the four brigades of Picketts Division.

Every division has been represented except Picketts from which we have not had a prisoner. They are from nearly one hundred different regiments.

Babcock had arrived at a fact of the greatest significance: Lee in the two-day battle had used almost his entire force of infantry; every brigade known to be on the field had been in enough action to suffer losses by capture. Pickett's division, known to have been bringing up the enemy's rear, was Lee's only remaining body of fresh troops; it was the smallest division in the army, although this fact was apparently not yet reflected in Sharpe's records.

It was the taking of hundreds upon hundreds of prisoners that made Babcock's important finding possible. This seems a strange time for such a tedious bookkeeping task, but his sweeping conclusion — "every brigade in Lee's Army excepting the four brigades of Picketts Division" — seemed justified by the huge numbers of Rebels in the provost marshal's stockades.

Babcock signed Sharpe's name to the note, as was his custom when writing for his chief, and dated it "4½ P.M." As Longstreet's battle was only well started by 4:30, it is evident that Babcock's watch was among the many that were badly off that day. The repetitiveness of his first two sentences shows that he wrote hurriedly, perhaps because of stress from an injury. Babcock, like Butterfield, his addressee, is known to have been injured sometime during the three days of the battle, but as he was a civilian, no record was made of the date or nature of the wound.

When night fell, the Army of the Potomac held substantially the same positions, except for the vacated entrenchments on the extreme right, that it had occupied that morning. Fighting their way through a succession of crises, inflicting tremendous casualties, the Northern troops had stood off an onslaught that in Longstreet's judgment was unsurpassed in ferocity. They had done so without tapping more than an insignificant part of the strength of the big Sixth Corps, and large parts of two other corps, the Fifth and Twelfth, had been only lightly used.[22]

But Meade was not sure that his army could weather another day like the one just ended. Sometime after 9:00 that night he gathered his subordinates at his headquarters in the tiny Leister house for a discussion that developed into a formal council of war. Before they were all assembled he sent for Sharpe. As the colonel entered he found General Meade seated at a little table and General Hancock sitting on a rough cot, on which General Slocum was stretched out. On the table was a plate of crackers and a half-pint of whiskey; the sight of the untouched repast puzzled Sharpe, as he knew Meade had not eaten a meal during the two days. Without preliminaries, Meade asked Sharpe for more details on the questions already rather well answered by Babcock's note to Butterfield — the number of units Lee had used and the number yet unused.

Sharpe, who was weak from hunger himself and felt his mission would be considerably furthered by a couple of the crackers and a swallow of whiskey, could not properly ask for a share in the commanding general's supper. He left, and quickly learned that little was needed to supplement the information in Babcock's report. Returning to the Leister house, he found the scene unchanged: Meade at his little table, Hancock and Slocum occupying the cot, the trio of generals not yet joined by other corps commanders, the crackers and whiskey still untouched.

As Sharpe remembered the incident years later, he began his report to Meade by modifying slightly the earlier indication that all the enemy brigades except Pickett's had been in action; there was also, he said, a small body of cavalry still unused (probably one of the three cavalry units that had marched with Ewell's corps). He added, "Pickett's division has come up and is now in bivouac, and will be ready to go into action fresh tomorrow morning."

At this Hancock rolled around to sit up straight without disturbing Slocum. Perched on the edge, he raised a hand and said, "General, we have got them nicked!"

The sentence stuck in Sharpe's memory because Hancock did not say "licked." Slocum sat up; a moment of quiet settled on the room, and the eyes of all four officers fell on the crackers and whiskey. Hancock broke the silence, saying, "General Meade, don't you think Sharpe deserves a cracker and a drink?" It dawned on Sharpe that the generals had been ignoring the repast because there was not enough to go around. By the time Meade's council assembled, the crackers and whiskey were gone and in their place stood a pail of water and a tin cup.[23]

Today it is easy to see, with Hancock, that Meade's army had the enemy "nicked," but that fact did not make enough of an impression on General Meade to overcome his liking for the Pipe Creek position. When the council's discussion opened, he asked his subordinates to consider whether the army should retire to a position nearer to its base of supplies. A formal vote was taken, and the decision of nine generals — Hancock and Slocum (wing commanders) and Newton, Gibbon, Birney, Sykes, Sedgwick, Howard, and Williams (corps commanders) — was unanimously against retirement. Three generals who favored adjusting or "correcting" the army's lines specified that no such move should amount to a retreat or a giving up of the field.

A second question was proposed — whether the army should attack or await the enemy's attack — and the opinion, again unanimous, was in favor of remaining on the defensive. A third question, how long an enemy attack should be awaited, produced an inconclusive result, though most of the generals opposed waiting more than one day.

Meade accepted the council's verdict "quietly but decidedly" with the words, as remembered by Gibbon, "Such then is the decision." As that decision upsets the axiom that "A council of war never fights," one looks for the reason for this council's verdict — especially noteworthy because it was unanimous. The likeliest explanation of the council's action is its knowledge of the Confederates' depleted condition. Two of the voters, Hancock and Slocum, had heard Sharpe's report to Meade, and Butterfield, though not voting, had received substantially the same information in Babcock's 4:30 note. Evidently in order to compare the enemy's condition with their own, the council members estimated the numbers of their fresh or lightly used troops, corps by corps, and arrived at a total of 58,000 for the army. By matching this against the probable number of effectives Lee could put on the field, they could see that on the morrow they would have a huge advantage in numbers (actually as great as four to one).

Another principal consideration that entered into the voting was the effect on morale that a retirement would have had. A statement attributed to Hancock, that the Army of the Potomac had retreated too often, called to mind the bitter effect of McDowell's and Pope's retreats to Washington and Burnside's and Hooker's recrossings of the Rappahannock to Falmouth. Still another major factor was of course the advantages of the Federals' dominating position on the battlefield, but not all of the generals were completely sold on this; General Newton, a respected engineer, although voting with the others, was concerned about the position's vulnerability to a turning movement. But neither of these two reasons would have carried any more weight than Hancock's unhesitating assessment that what was known about the enemy's condition meant that "we have got them nicked."[24]

All their lives Sharpe and Babcock believed it was their reports that brought the decision to remain at Gettysburg. Former intelligence officers would not have been as much given to telling "war stories" as other veterans, and neither man is known to have told relatives and friends a great deal about his intelligence service — the town of Kingston remembered Sharpe as a general of infantry — but neither man held back this one story.[25] They both seem to have regarded the night of July 2, 1863, as the high point of the secret war they fought.

Their contribution is to be judged, as always, not only by its effect but also by the accuracy of their information. When they said they had prisoners from all of Lee's brigades except those in Pickett's division, how near to 100 percent correct was that statement? One item in their files answers that question, though only for Ewell's corps. This document is Babcock's reply to a note sent by General Butterfield early the next morning asking, "Are you satisfied that there are only two Divisions of Ewell in front of Slocum and how strong do you think they are — If the General was pretty sure of this he would make an attack there. Write me soon —"

Babcock's reply named twelve brigades in Ewell's corps, four to a division. But Rodes's division, like only one other in Lee's army, had five brigades; the fifth was missing from the bureau's records. This was Junius Daniel's North Carolina brigade, 2200 strong, one of the three brigades Lee had added shortly before marching north. That Babcock had received no deserters from Daniel's ranks in those weeks of tightened picketing is not surprising, but the brigade also suffered no losses from captures in the two days' fighting; none of its members turned up on the lists of prisoners the provost marshal officers were turning over to Babcock.

Thus we see that Babcock's information on the composition of Lee's army was less than perfect. Nevertheless it was, by a comfortable margin, full enough to serve as a basis for the council's decision. And this one defect was not a misleading one; the brigade missing from the prisoner records had suffered in killed and wounded, thus sharing in the depletion of Lee's army.[26]

In his reply to Butterfield Babcock gave Johnson's and Early's divisions 7000 each and Rodes's 7200, making Ewell's total strength 21,200. But this total, computed from prisoners' estimates of the strengths of individual regiments and brigades, looked too large to Babcock and Sharpe, and they appended a note expressing conviction that the figures they had been given were exaggerated. Twenty-four hours earlier, 21,000 would have been a low but reasonable estimate for Ewell; in light of the enemy's losses since that time, however, their skepticism was well taken.[27]

. .   . .   . .

For over a century, when intelligence has been mentioned as a factor in holding the Army of the Potomac at Gettysburg, the intelligence thus credited has been a windfall, this one even more revealing than Special Orders 191. It consisted of dispatches to Lee from Jefferson Davis and his ranking general at Richmond, Samuel Cooper, describing the Confederacy's overall military situation. A scouting party headed by Captain Ulric Dahlgren captured these letters from a courier party at Greencastle on July 2; Dahlgren hastened to put them in General Meade's hands. Although they were loaded with strategically valuable information, it had only a remote bearing on the decision Meade had to make that night. But because of the effect on his decision that has been attributed to the captured letters, an examination of their contents, and of the feat that made Captain Dahlgren a colonel, is in order.[28]

He had been freelancing as a scout in between chores as a courier and aide-de-camp to General Hooker.[29] While the army was back in Virginia, Hooker received a letter from the captain's father, Rear Admiral John A. Dahlgren, chief of the navy's Bureau of Ordnance, requesting the transfer of twenty-year-old Ulric to the Navy Department. Hooker replied that he would interpose no objection but added that "justice to the merits and services of Captain Dahlgren requires me to state that I consent to his withdrawal from me at this time with very great reluctance."[30] Hooker had found the right words to persuade Admiral Dahlgren to drop the matter.

At Frederick on June 30 Captain Dahlgren received permission to take a party into the Cumberland Valley to scout the enemy's rear. This was an ideal project for Milton Cline, and he was assigned to it, possibly accompanied by members of McEntee's detachment, now reduced to courier duty with Pleasonton. Dahlgren's party, composed mainly of cavalry regulars, numbered less than twenty; on the march he added two recently discharged Maryland soldiers who were familiar with the roads in the lower Valley. While the party was at Greencastle on July 2, one of the Marylanders spotted Confederates approaching on the Williamsport road. Dahlgren's soldiers, heretofore disguised as civilians or Confederate cavalrymen, changed into their uniforms, surprised the Rebels at the Greencastle town square, captured all twenty-two of them, and took bags of mail intended for members of the Army of Northern Virginia.

Attached to the saddle of one of the captured officers was a valise containing a shirt in which were hidden Davis's and Cooper's letters.[31] They were in answer to a proposal by Lee that during the usual summer lull on the southern coast, troops be moved to Culpeper as if to threaten Washington, thus creating a diversion that would benefit both Lee's army and Richmond, then under pressure from General Dix. The threat presented by the small force to be assembled at Culpeper was to be greatly amplified by rumors, which Lee and Davis well knew how to plant. The Culpeper commander would be General Beauregard, a name much respected in the North.[32]

The response was a strong "No," which Davis spelled out in 800 words and Cooper in 400. The Confederate armies were hard pressed everywhere. Beauregard at Charleston and Bragg in Tennessee had sent all the troops they could spare to General Johnston, operating in rear of Grant's siege of Vicksburg, and Johnston was still pressing for more. North Carolina had been stripped to meet Dix's threat to Richmond. Davis had all he could do to protect his capital. One of the details he worried about was the railroads on Lee's supply line; Cooper suggested to Lee that he detach a portion of his army to guard his communication with Richmond — a sound idea, in view of Dahlgren's easy interruption of that communication.

After making a poor mouth at such length, Davis suggested somewhat ambiguously that he might part with a few brigades for Lee's army. He also hinted that he was considering taking forces from Richmond to "threaten if not capture" Washington.[33] Given the desperate manpower shortage that he had just described, those suggestions would have seemed a mere fantasy to the Federals, and to Lee if he had received the letters. Secretary Stanton, ignoring Davis's puzzling afterthoughts, pronounced the captured dispatches "the best view we have ever had of the rebels' condition, and it is desperate."[34] So valuable was Dahlgren's feat that he was made a colonel, a three-step promotion, after he had lost a leg in a cavalry fight during Lee's retreat from Pennsylvania.

This picture of the totality of the Confederacy's military situation, this gem of strategic intelligence, was the most valuable information an official in Stanton's position could hope to receive. Meade's need, on the other hand, was for *operational* intelligence — information (such as the contents of S.O. 191) immediately usable in making decisions as a field commander. One item in Davis's and Cooper's 1200 words that would have had operational value for Meade was the assurance that the enemy force he was engaged with was all he would have to reckon with in this campaign — a valuable updating and confirmation of Sergeant Hunnicutt's two-week-old report. That question was one of several Meade faced in deciding whether to remain at Gettysburg or move to Pipe Creek. That movement would take days, during which reinforcements from Richmond and below could reach Lee; the news that there was almost certainly no chance of such reinforcements erased one of the arguments against the Pipe Creek move. It is quite unlikely that the members of Meade's council were aware of the intelligence in the captured letters, but even if they did know of it, that roomful of generals who had been in a toe-to-toe slugging match for two days would not have had the patience to debate the imponderables involved in a move to Pipe Creek. They knew that by remaining at Gettysburg they could fight from a favorable position against an enemy force that was badly depleted — and get the business over with.

Another indication that the letters did not influence the council's action and Meade's decision is the fact that Dahlgren in his diary said nothing about the effect on events that his capture may have had. Still another is the probability that Dahlgren did not arrive at Gettysburg until some hours after Meade's council had broken up.[35]

. .   . .   . .

To Sharpe and his colleagues, the battle of July 3 must have seemed like the grisly playing out of a script written from what they knew of the enemy's condition. The Confederates' situation virtually compelled them to attack, yet they could scarcely mount an attack that would succeed against the excellent Federal position.

Lee's determination to make the attempt seems to have come from a stubborn confidence in the invincibility of his men. He had struck the Federal right on the first day, the left on the second; now he would try the center and, as a secondary effort, the extreme right, lightly held since Meade's withdrawal of most of the Twelfth Corps to assist in the second day's battle.

Any possibility of coordinating the two attacks was gone before the sun rose on July 3. At 3:45 A.M. a pistol shot rang out on Culp's Hill on the Federal right — the signal for an artillery bombardment in preparation for an assault by the Twelfth Corps to regain its former trenches. This took the initiative from General Johnson, whose division, reinforced by three brigades from Rodes and Early, was under orders to storm the hill. Johnson sent his regiments forward anyway. The situation has been likened to that of Marye's Heights, and the slaughter of the force driving uphill was as fearful, if on a smaller scale. At the end of seven bloody hours, Slocum's men held their old positions and the Confederate timetable had been wrecked.

Even without Slocum's attack, the Confederates' coordination would have been lost. Half an hour after Johnson began his part of the offensive, a courier reached his chief, General Ewell, with word from Lee that the main Confederate attack would be delayed several hours.[36]

Over on Seminary Ridge Longstreet was remonstrating with Lee, as he had done on the two previous days, arguing that the proper move was to swing around to the right and get south of Meade's army, forcing the Federals to attack. When this argument failed, Longstreet advanced another: that his own corps, assigned to the attack on the Union center, was not enough for the task. He asserted that "there never was a body of fifteen thousand men who could make that attack successfully."[37] Lee remained firm, and next Longstreet pointed out that to withdraw Hood's and McLaws's divisions from the positions they had taken the day before would dangerously expose the Confederate right. Lee's response to that argument was to leave Hood and McLaws in place and reconstitute the attacking force. To Pickett's division, which (as Sharpe had reported) was now on the field, he added Heth's division, half of Pender's, and two brigades of Anderson's — all from Hill's corps. These were as much weakened by fighting as Hood and McLaws (Heth and Pender themselves were among the numerous casualties), but they occupied less critical places in the Southern line.[38]

That Pickett would spearhead the charge was foreseeable from the Union side of the field, since his was known to be Lee's only fresh division. The point of the main attack was correctly predicted several hours in advance on the basis of enemy movements that were visible from the northern and southern extremities of the Union line. General Hancock's corps was the probable target; during the mighty cannonade that preceded Pickett's advance, Hancock, exposing himself heedlessly, rode the entire length of his line to nerve his men for the expected onslaught.[39]

One point that no one in the Union command could have foreseen, however, was that one badly injured enemy division and parts of two others would be all that would accompany Pickett in Lee's crowning effort. But if the attacking force does not look formidable on paper, it made an awesome impression on the men who waited for it on Cemetery Ridge. Its forty-two regiments moved almost with parade-ground precision across nearly a mile of open ground in full view of the defenders. When the Southern ranks came close, the Federal artillery raked one swath after another through them. The men still erect came on as if unmoved. But the attack, like that of the previous day, was poorly coordinated. Pickett's right was in the air; a brigade swung out of the Union line and poured a devastating fire on its flank. In the center, two brigades that were already reduced to remnants stormed over a stone fence behind which the defenders were massed. Federal reinforcements hurried to the scene of a hand-to-hand fight. The only attackers who survived it were captured; the two brigade commanders, Generals Lewis Armistead and Richard Garnett, were among those who gave up their lives. An attack by Pickett's left was made only after the one on the center was almost spent. It was crushed; likewise, another division-sized attack still farther left did not reach its objective until the attackers on its right had given way.[40]

The gray tide receded. Their organization lost, most of their officers killed or wounded, the Southerners streamed in disorder across the plain to their own lines. About a third of the force that had constituted the Army of Northern Virginia that morning had been shattered. The situation was one in which textbooks call for a counterattack. Lee expected one; so did his subordinates; so also did Meade's subordinates. But the Federal commander ventured no more than a reconnaissance by one brigade.[41] Meade had just seen an attack by 15,000 men broken up by a force of about two-thirds that number, dug in on a gentle slope. The situation, he reasoned, would be reversed if he assailed Seminary Ridge. He wrote, "I knew [Lee] was in a strong position, awaiting my attack, which I declined to make, in consequence of the bad example he had set me in ruining himself attacking a strong position."[42] This reasoning does not take into account the tremendous difference in the morale and state of organization of the two armies at that hour. It also ignores the very pertinent fact that after "Pickett's Charge" Meade still had a large number of fresh or lightly used troops, while Lee, as Meade could not have failed to realize, had now used all of his army, and nearly all of it to and beyond the limit. One is tempted to believe that if the lion-hearted Reynolds had survived, his passion would have nerved Meade to a crushing counterstroke.

Gettysburg went into the records as a decisive though not a war-ending victory for the Union. Vicksburg would fall the next day, the nation's birthday. Although the Confederacy still held most of the territory that it claimed, the course traveled by Southern arms from then on led only downward. The road back from Gettysburg ended at Appomattox.

.. .. ..

A dozen reasons have been adduced for the outcome of the battle of Gettysburg. It has become conventional to point to the Federals' unusually advantageous position and Lee's error in repeatedly attacking it. Equally common are the indictments of his subordinates — Stuart for blinding the army by his long absence, Longstreet for his slow if not sulking response to his chief's wishes, Ewell for failing to seize Cemetery Ridge after his defeat of the Eleventh Corps on July 1. The Confederates' poor liaison and lack of coordination in attack, their inefficiency in such routine administrative matters as ammunition supply have been cited as important factors in the result. Too infrequently is it noticed that the Army of the Potomac was well led and fought superbly.

Now comes Union intelligence to take its place beside these numerous other nominees for the credit for the victory. Its case is a strong one.

Intelligence started the army from the Rappahannock line in time to assure the safety of Washington. Concerted efforts had failed to establish that the week-long movements along the upper Rappahannock early in June amounted to a general advance by Lee's army. Then Captain McEntee on June 12 found two Negroes who had witnessed the march — one of them a boy, but old enough to carry the organization of the Army of Northern Virginia in his head.

Without Charley Wright's knowledge, the pursuit of Lee probably would have been delayed until the force that captured Winchester was firmly identified as a major element of Lee's army. That could scarcely have been done before the 17th, and a pursuit that began that late might not have been able to prevent the enemy from coming through the gaps leading to Manassas and Washington. Hooker's severest detractor would have to admit that his departure from the Rappahannock was in time to save the army from being off balance for the rest of the campaign and that Lee therefore had a much less free hand than he was striving for.

It gave the army a distinct advantage in the race for Pennsylvania. The useful life of the discovery that the Confederates were on their way north was short; within a few days Hooker and Sharpe were again in the dark as to the enemy's whereabouts. The action that restored the enemy positioning to their view was a feat of espionage, the four-day penetration of Longstreet's lines by Sergeant Cline's party.

The next decisive event in the intelligence story was the convergence of planted reports placing the Confederates' rear across the Potomac two days' march ahead of its actual crossing. The most remarkable aspect of this deception was the total absence of conflicting information. Hooker's mistaken acceptance of the misinformation was his good fortune; a much worse mistake was the Confederates' spreading of misinformation that hastened him on his way, marching abreast of the enemy and on an inside track. This certainly was no Federal intelligence success, but it was a Confederate intelligence failure, a resounding one.

Federal intelligence aided greatly in directing the army to the all-important high ground at Gettysburg. The advantage acquired by the Federals in their extraordinarily timely crossing of the Potomac was almost erased as Lee, learning tardily of the enemy's presence in Maryland, quickly reassembled his forces while Meade scattered his. *Almost* erased — for the head of Reynolds's infantry column arrived at Gettysburg perhaps as little as an hour before Lee's advance could have bowled over Buford's thin lines to reach the heights beyond the town. The information that guided Reynolds on the morning of July 1, provided by Buford, came from the interrogation of two captives, one of them a courier; from a dispatch taken from a second courier; and from the correct identification of the enemy forces approaching Gettysburg from the west and north. Reynolds knew, before Meade could have learned, that the two wings of Lee's army were concentrating near Gettysburg.

And intelligence was a major factor in keeping the army at Gettysburg until the victory was won. All the efforts and successes of Sharpe and his subordinates and collaborators might have availed nothing but for his and Babcock's reports of July 2, to the effect that Lee's army was badly depleted, while Meade had a decisive superiority in fresh troops. That intelligence virtually compelled the decision that the generals reached.

The Pennsylvania campaign would have had a far different result if Meade's decision that night had been for moving to Pipe Creek. In the course of the move the army might have been so severely damaged that it could not have won the victory it achieved on July 3. Even a completely successful move would not necessarily have produced a victory, for Lee, upon discovering the enemy in a position even more favorable to the defense than the ridges and hills at Gettysburg, would probably have headed for Virginia. That would have given the Federals another Antietam — settling for a drawn battle though victory was within reach.

. .   . .   . .

Intelligence had come a long way from its near-zero capabilities in the First Bull Run campaign, a condition repeated in the Fredericksburg campaign — and almost equally as long a way from the limited intelligence mission of the Pinkerton period. A measure of the progress from those primitive conditions was Babcock's accomplishment on July 2 — assimilating in the heat of battle a mass of new data and filling large gaps in his records, to develop a decisive picture of the enemy's situation. This was a fitting climax to the intelligence operations that had put the Army of the Potomac on the winning ground at Gettysburg. Previous successes, notably Sergeant Harter's rewarding penetration of Lee's army and the intelligence coup that opened the way to Chancellorsville, had not been followed by success on the battlefield. At Gettysburg intelligence's operatives were rewarded by victory.

Epilogue

I N THE FIRST HOURS of daylight on July 4 Lieutenants Henry Camp and John Wiggins, at a signal station on Cemetery Ridge, spotted a long train of wagons moving southwesterly from the position the beaten enemy had assumed after the battle. Lee's retreat from Gettysburg had begun.

General Meade observed the Fourth by issuing an order congratulating his troops on their victory and calling for "greater effort to drive from our soil every vestige of the presence of the invader." Those words, together with copies of dispatches sent by Meade's generals indicating that resistance to certain retrograde movements of the enemy was being deliberately avoided, left President Lincoln "a good deal dissatisfied. . . . These things all appear to me to be connected with a purpose to cover Baltimore and Washington, and to get the enemy across the river without a further collision, and they do not appear to be connected with a purpose to prevent his crossing and to destroy him." It was to be the story of Antietam all over again, a grievously damaged and depleted Confederate army escaping to Virginia — but this time starting from a position a half-week's march from the Potomac instead of a half-day's.

Meade's caution was partly due to uncertainty as to whether Lee was intending retreat to Virginia or maneuvering for favorable position to receive an attack he would expect Meade to make. Meanwhile Meade, while hoping to find the Rebels disposed to his own advantage, cautioned subordinates against bringing on a general engagement. Although the Confederates could not hide their march, it was not well covered by Meade's scouts or cavalry; the citizens' scouting and spying that had served so well before the battle were sorely missed. Cavalry reconnaissance was Meade's most promising source, but the supply of horses was being depleted so seriously as to threaten the movement of the whole army.

True to expectations, most or all enemy movements were westward, on the Cashtown and Fairfield roads. Sick and wounded had already been

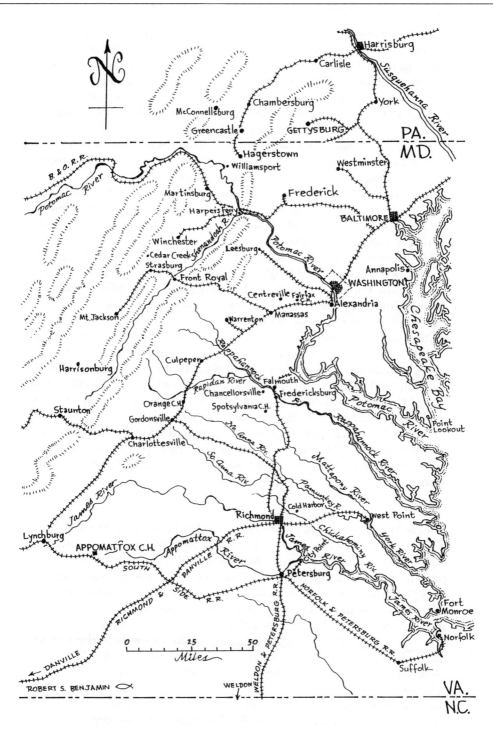

FROM GETTYSBURG TO APPOMATTOX

sent to Williamsport, and the army's trains began arriving there as early as July 6, when they were attacked by Buford's cavalry division, which was driven off by John Imboden's command, a miscellany of cavalry, mounted infantry, and partisan rangers. The rest of Lee's army assembled on the 7th near Hagerstown, awaiting a fall in the waters of the swollen Potomac. Lee fully expected to be attacked in his stationary posture by a superior force, but Meade had no such intention.

An infantry expedition from Frederick, anticipating the Confederates' retreat, destroyed a pontoon bridge at Falling Waters, near Williamsport, guarded by only fourteen men. Aware that this might divert the route of retreat from Williamsport to the Shepherdstown crossings, Sharpe sent a scout there, but he found no sign of Rebels. Another scout found them at a third crossing place, sending wounded across on flatboats, which returned bearing ammunition.

The enemy's concentration between Hagerstown and Williamsport finally drew Meade to that locality. On July 12 he called a council of war and proposed attack on the line of entrenchments the enemy had dug on that route; all but one of his corps commanders voted against it. Nevertheless, on the next day he mounted a reconnaissance in force, finding that the Confederates had used the time his unaggressiveness had given them by fortifying their positions so strongly that he would not attack without detailed examination and planning. Before that could be done, the Rebels were safe on the Virginia side of the river, Ewell's corps having forded at Williamsport while the other two crossed on pontoons improvised by razing buildings to obtain wood.

Lee had escaped pursuit while marching on the most obvious of withdrawal routes. On July 24 he established headquarters at Culpeper, from where he had launched his Pennsylvania campaign forty-four days before.

. .   . .   . .

George Meade's style was as different from Joe Hooker's as Hooker's had been from McClellan's. When Meade put his stamp on the conduct of intelligence affairs, the name "Bureau of Military Information" disappeared, and with it the bureau's all-source reporting. Sharpe's reports henceforth were to consist only of current intelligence from his own sources — espionage, scouting, and interrogation. There would be no more of the Sharpe-Babcock situation summaries that drew also on visual observation and cavalry reconnaissance. An example of the new organizational arrangements was an action by the Army of the Potomac's chief signal officer, Captain Benjamin F. Fisher; formerly a direct collaborator with Sharpe and Babcock, he now "went through channels" — army headquarters — with a tip on the identity of a certain division that turned up in one of his intercepts. But he suggested to headquarters that the matter be brought to the attention of the "secret service" — evidently Fisher's carefully chosen term.

The change was signified on Sharpe's reports by the heading "Head-quarters Army of the Potomac, Office of the Provost-Marshal-General"; although this implied that General Patrick was the authority releasing the report, he was no more a part of the reporting chain than he had been during Hooker's command. Sharpe continued for a time to receive some of the cavalry's and the signalmen's reports, but he no longer integrated them into his own reports. Meade took into his own hands the work of assimilating the information from the army's numerous sources. He would have the assistance of a chief of staff of his own selection, Brigadier General Andrew A. Humphreys.

There was sure to be an initial awkwardness in the relationship between John Babcock and General Humphreys, head of the staff of topographical engineers whose maps of Peninsula country were superseded by those drawn by Private Babcock. For a few weeks Sharpe suspended Babcock's high visibility in the reporting process. He drew on their clerk to write the final draft of reports formerly issued in Babcock's hand. This eliminated the free and easy procedure under which Babcock regularly speeded up the issuance of reports by signing Sharpe's name.

Meade was enough of a scholar to make the feat of assimilating so much information seem possible. One indication of a scholarly bent is his military vocabulary. He is the only one to appear in this narrative who used the word "intelligence" in the sense of information about the enemy rather than simply new information on any subject. Meade could have learned the information-about-the-enemy meaning from study of the Revolution. It was General Washington's usage, frequently occurring in his writings but abandoned in standard American English by the time of the Civil War.

. . . . . .

Lee soon drew back from Culpeper to a position on the south bank of the Rapidan that dominated the opposite bank. Meade, who had head-quartered his army at Warrenton, now placed a third of it between the Rappahannock and Culpeper. Repeatedly from then on, until winter set in, one army or the other had a force in motion as its commander maneuvered to gain an advantageous position or forestall the enemy's efforts to gain one.

Sharpe had scouting parties constantly on the move. One group ranged as far eastward as the Potomac, its members posing alternately as Confederate soldiers and as local civilians, and repeatedly encountering enemy picket lines. Fredericksburg was found defended by a small cavalry force. Scouts who visited Front Royal returned with prisoners. After a few weeks communication was established with Isaac Silver, who owned enough property in Orange County, now Lee's base, for him to make business in that locality a cover for visits that yielded enemy information. "The old man" evidently had been expecting to hear from Sharpe's men; he was ready with a report on the positions of Lee's right wing.

One pair of scouts whose travel took them to the vicinity of Chancellorsville somehow picked up word of the departure of Longstreet's corps, two divisions of which were sent to reinforce General Braxton Bragg in Tennessee, leaving the third, Pickett's, at Petersburg. Longstreet's arrival during the battle of Chickamauga turned the tide in the Rebels' favor and sent General Rosecrans's army back to Chattanooga, into a state of siege. The War Department then reinforced Rosecrans with the Eleventh and Twelfth Corps from the Army of the Potomac, under the command of Hooker, who had been rejoined by Butterfield. Hooker and Butterfield told Rosecrans of the capabilities of Sharpe's bureau, and Rosecrans telegraphed Meade a request for Sharpe to send him intelligence that might apply to his theater of operations. Meade had had reports of Longstreet's movement to Tennessee at least five days before the Chickamauga battle and had passed the information to Halleck, but apparently neither Meade nor Halleck sent it to Rosecrans. In a Hooker regime, Sharpe would have sent it himself or written it into a telegram for Butterfield's signature, but he may not even have been informed of Rosecrans's request.

. .   . .   . .

The Piedmont, where the opposing armies were now based, consists of a dozen counties of north-central Virginia lying between the Blue Ridge and the Potomac. It is dotted with tall hills, invariably called mountains, that provided both armies with elevations for visual signaling, intercepting enemy messages, and observing enemy movements. Meade's signalmen enjoyed a field day in the intercept business, for the Rebels, though they may have changed their flag alphabet by this time, evidently were still sending their messages without encipherment, while the Federals had Colonel Myer's newly issued cipher disk.

On October 7 a series of intercepts by Captain Davis Castle revealed meetings held by Lee's generals and a delay in a move of apparently his whole army. A request for guides by Jeb Stuart indicated that the movement in preparation was to be around the Federals' right; this corroborated evidence that General Sedgwick had previously reported. Meade, instead of massing his army to engage the outnumbered foe, retreated to save his position from being flanked. The retreat was a long one, all the way to the fortifications on the heights at Centreville — withdrawal from even the most cautious harassment of the enemy movement. Along the way, at Bristoe, a railroad stop just below Manassas, a quarter of Meade's army was attacked by half of Lee's and won a decided victory. But Meade's march did not halt until it reached Centreville. In November it was Meade's army that sought out the enemy and Lee's that avoided being outmaneuvered. The armies then went into winter quarters.

The last days of February 1864 saw the departure of a raid on Richmond by 3500 cavalry under the command of Brigadier General Judson Kilpatrick, who had sold President Lincoln on an attempt to liberate the hundreds of Federals in Richmond prisons. Kilpatrick put a detachment of his troopers under the command of Colonel Ulric Dahlgren, including a group from Sharpe's bureau headed by Captain McEntee. The detachment was ambushed, Dahlgren was killed, and many prisoners were taken, including all but one of McEntee's men; several later escaped and Ebenezer McGee was released, but Martin Hogan was confined in a dungeon and then with two others was sent to the infamous Andersonville prison in Georgia, from which Hogan escaped. McEntee blamed Milton Cline for a disobedience of orders that, he believed, caused the capture of his men. Kilpatrick's regiments, likewise failing to enter Richmond, retreated to the Federal lines at Yorktown. The affair did not end there, however, for on the body of Dahlgren, a firebrand, the Confederates found an order, which he evidently had drafted but never issued, calling for the burning of Richmond and the assassination of Jefferson Davis and his cabinet. In reply to an inquiry from General Lee sent by flag of truce, General Meade denied that Dahlgren had approval from any superior for the actions he contemplated. But an outraged Southern public refused to believe Meade's denial, and one day the Dahlgren papers would be seen as justifying the assassination of Lincoln.

. .   ..   ..

In mid-March the new general-in-chief, Lieutenant General U. S. Grant, paid the Army of the Potomac a visit. He refused a special train and left unexpectedly, upsetting his hosts' plans to fete him. Sharpe was pleased by Grant's unostentatious ways, and also by the fact that he "sent three horses down to this army, . . . a pretty sure indication that he means to move with us. . . . we suppose that after his return the fur will fly in these diggins." By early June Sharpe had seen enough of Grant to rate him "a considerable of a man"; two months later he was spending half or more of his time at Grant's headquarters, consulting with the general almost daily. He figured prominently in the uneasy relationship between Grant and Meade, who resented the general-in-chief's stationing himself with the Army of the Potomac.

Before the spring campaign opened, Sharpe had placed liaison officers with two of the Army of the Potomac's neighbors, the Army of the James, commanded by Major General Benjamin F. Butler, Dix's successor at Fort Monroe, and the Shenandoah Valley army headed by Major

General Franz Sigel. He stationed John McEntee with Sigel; Lieutenant John I. Davenport, a member of the Army of the James staff, took the intelligence job with Butler, soon to be joined by Lieutenant Frederick Manning, a long-time member of Sharpe's bureau. The position entailed managing the army's end of correspondence with a Unionist underground in Richmond; that function was soon taken over by Sharpe.

As in April 1863, the chief intelligence problem was the question of the return to Lee of absent divisions under James Longstreet. His two divisions were now firmly known to have left Tennessee, but were mistakenly believed to have been joined by Pickett, who was actually in the Richmond area. Longstreet's new position was the subject of maddeningly conflicting reports; Sperryville, well to the northwest of Lee's camps, was mentioned much oftener than the more likely Gordonsville-Charlottesville area (Longstreet actually was below Gordonsville). Scouts sent by Sharpe within Confederate lines could not penetrate to the depth of that position; one of them suffered frostbite in an April snowstorm and lost part of one foot. Much of the information on Longstreet came from an improbably located source, John McEntee, at Harper's Ferry.

Longstreet had not yet rejoined the army when Grant on May 3 opened his Richmond campaign by crossing the Rapidan and attacking, with initial success. Again Lee, as in Burnside's campaign, was slow to concentrate his forces. Captured Rebels had warned Sharpe that Longstreet would arrive in time for the second day's fight, and he did, checking the advance that was driving Lee's right. Grant's route of attack, on his left, was chosen in order to cover his communications, and he was committed to it by the time an intercepted message revealed that the Confederates were aware of his concentration on their right. This route required advancing through the formidable Wilderness; the dense woods and undergrowth were a commander's nightmare that seemed to confirm Hooker's decision to end his Chancellorsville battle. The Federals lost their cohesion; the Rebels' knowledge of the terrain was good enough to turn the battle into a bloody draw. Longstreet's welcome upon his return to the army was a wound inflicted, as in Jackson's case, by friendly fire; he was out of action for five months.

Grant, whose army had suffered much the heavier casualties, ended the three-day battle, not by retreating but by swinging around his left to a position ten miles farther south, at Spotsylvania Court House, closer to Richmond than Lee was at the moment. But by the time Meade could organize an attack, the Rebels had constructed breastworks, trenches, and long-log barriers. Atop these works Yanks and Rebels fought face to face for hours, neither side yielding.

At this juncture one of Sharpe's scouting teams captured a member of Stuart's signal party, who revealed that the Rebels had had an observation station on the Potomac, well within the Federal lines, and were "perfectly familiar with everything we have done in that direction."

Grant had repeated Hooker's error in blinding himself by sending Meade's cavalry, now headed by Major General Philip Sheridan, on a raid toward Richmond; thus Spotsylvania was for the Federals a battle of opportunities lost because they were never discovered. Sheridan's object was to wreck Jeb Stuart's cavalry; the only tangible result was the fatal wounding of Stuart.

Meanwhile operations by Butler's and Sigel's armies, intended to act in unison with Meade's (and with Sherman's in Georgia and Banks's in Louisiana), ended in fiascoes. Sigel was defeated by a hastily assembled force that included the cadets of the Virginia Military Institute, and Butler, who could have seized Petersburg early in May, made a blundering attack that ended with his army bottled up on a neck of land on the James River.

By now the only intelligence of any moment was the knowledge that Lee's army lay on the right of the direct path to Richmond. Grant kept pushing southward and on May 23–25 met the enemy at the North Anna River, just north of Hanover Junction. Lee had arrived there in good time and had a well-fortified position on the south bank. Grant decided against attacking and moved on to a crossroads named Cold Harbor; he was now abreast of Richmond, eight miles away on his right. For Lee this was a desperate situation, and it elicited an all-out defense. Again his position was strongly fortified, but Grant attacked with confidence. June 3, 1864, was one of the bloodiest days of the war; the Federals sustained 7000 casualties, five times as many as the defenders. Grant sat the army down at Cold Harbor and pondered his next move.

In this month of marching and fighting, the main producer of intelligence was scouting of enemy moves not only by Sharpe's men but also by Signal Corps parties. Flat and wooded country made the signalmen's flags almost useless, likewise their telescopes; thus they were available for reconnaissance duty. A single opening in the topography, during the operations on the North Anna, enabled a signal station to read for two days messages to Lee's headquarters from one of his outstations.

Grant's next move was a highly successful stolen march. Well before dark on the evening of June 12 the Army of the Potomac began pulling out of its lines on a march of fifty miles, across the Chickahominy to the banks of the James River. A pontoon bridge of record length, two fifths of a mile, took it across to invest Petersburg, where three of the railroads supplying Richmond and Lee's army converged. In three days the bridge carried 115,000 troops, a train of wagons and artillery thirty-five miles long, and 3500 beef cattle. This elaborate and extremely risky operation was assisted by construction of a second fortified line (a backup) at Cold

Harbor, a cavalry feint toward Richmond, and security measures that rivaled Hooker's on his march to Kelly's Ford. Although Lee learned of the enemy's departure by the morning of the 13th, the action he took was a mistaken one, designed to counter a short-range southeastward shift such as the moves Grant had been making ever since the battle of the Wilderness. The Federals' crossing of the James was not completed until the morning of June 17, but no Confederate forces showed up to resist it. Lee had been outgeneraled.

One reason the movement was not discovered promptly on the night of the 12th was that the Army of Northern Virginia was busy that night with its own hidden withdrawal. The Second Corps, now commanded by Jubal Early, was leaving for Lynchburg and the Shenandoah Valley to fight off the incursions of Major General David Hunter, successor to Sigel. Early's position at Cold Harbor was in rear of Hill's; thus his departure easily escaped the Federals' notice. The security of each army's movements was furthered by the tightening of picket lines against desertions and incursions that was a standard accompaniment of such withdrawals. Each army's tightening was a tip to the enemy — who was too occupied with his own getaway to notice the warning. Here we see two stolen marches occurring on the same front on the same night — surely the most remarkable of coincidences in a war replete with them.

General Early enjoyed for a month the fruits of his undiscovered withdrawal. He drove Hunter across the Alleghenies into the new state of West Virginia, proceeded down the Shenandoah Valley, and crossed the Potomac. His departure from Cold Harbor was not noticed until a prisoner informed Sharpe of it a week later, on June 20. The Federals remained unsure of his whereabouts until July 9, when Milton Cline reported having found, and visited, the Confederates' camps on South Mountain, between Frederick and Hagerstown, a position that was a none too distant threat to Washington. Early arrived in the outskirts of the capital on the 12th, there to meet the Sixth Corps, sent by Grant from the lines of the Army of the Potomac. After a short battle witnessed by President Lincoln, Early made good a retreat to the Valley.

·· ·· ··

Even before Cline's confirmation of the enemy's presence on Northern soil, General Grant had set about to reorganize his intelligence service. This action took the form of an order on July 5 giving General Patrick the title Provost Marshal General of the Armies Operating Against Richmond; Sharpe became Deputy P.M.G. of the new command. The reason for elevating Patrick's position was a need for an officer to regulate provost marshal affairs in Butler's army, but Grant's main purpose undoubtedly was to make Sharpe his own intelligence officer and improve the management of intelligence in his two remote armies, Butler's and Hunter's.

The intolerable slowness in discovering Early's move to the Valley and Maryland, the cause of Grant's action, was attributable partly to McEntee's situation. On only a few occasions was he well located to receive prisoners and deserters, and then there were scarcely enough of them to make his mission pay. He was often too far from telegraph offices for efficient communication with Sharpe. General Hunter was an indifferent collaborator, and the scouts he gave McEntee turned out to be "thieves and loafers." The two Bureau scouts who had accompanied McEntee to the Valley were rendered helpless by ever-present bushwhackers; they set out afoot to return to Sharpe, were captured by, and escaped from, Mosby's rangers, then Gilmor's rangers, then a gang of bushwhackers, and finally returned to McEntee tattered and blistered, looking "as bad as any rebels you ever saw." Worst of all, McEntee was now deep in West Virginia, well removed from the area he was supposed to cover.

Grant cured these ills at one stroke by allowing Sharpe to bring McEntee back to headquarters and putting all the Valley problems in the hands of Phil Sheridan, one of the most intelligence-conscious of generals. Sheridan organized a company of fifty soldiers who volunteered for the dangers of scouting duty, headed by a Rhode Island infantryman, Major Henry H. Young. The bushwhackers were no longer a serious threat, nor was the cooperativeness of the commanding general in doubt.

To assuage the displeasure that these changes would inflict on Meade, Grant sought to leave Patrick, and probably Sharpe as well, at Meade's headquarters despite their direct subordination to himself. But the order made General Meade angry enough to confess his displeasure to Patrick. He declared that he wanted "no partnership with Grant" and complained that Sharpe's bureau "was good for nothing — that it furnished no information not already received thro' the cavalry." Since Pleasonton's record as an intelligence source made this comparison ludicrous, it appears that Meade was quite severely agitated.

Patrick attributed Meade's anger to his having "learned that his staff would, all, gladly leave him, on account of his temper." The fur was flying as Sharpe had foreseen. Since Meade shunned "partnership" with Grant, Patrick elected to move to the Armies Operating Against Richmond (Grant's) headquarters. Sharpe's bureau remained at Meade's headquarters; Sharpe had desks both there and at AOAR headquarters at City Point, at the confluence of the James and Appomattox Rivers. In addition to meeting with Grant almost daily, he spent hours there working with Lieutenant Colonel Theodore Bowers, a member of Grant's staff, who by this association would become familiar with the details of the Sharpe-Babcock operation.

Thus there were now two intelligence centers; deserters and other suppliers of information were received at both, reports issued from both, and Sharpe and Babcock spent as much time writing telegrams and notes to each other as they did in face-to-face discussion. At one point when McEntee was substituting for Sharpe at City Point, he and Babcock made estimates of Lee's strength, each unaware of the other's calculation; the two figures differed by only 600. The two totals, about 50,000, were 12 percent below the number of effectives shown on Lee's rolls.

The mollifying of General Meade went to extreme lengths: the heading on some of the reports written at Grant's headquarters and sent to Meade was "Headquarters, Army of the Potomac." Grant placated Meade also by allowing five months to pass, with the new arrangements in effect, before formally issuing the order Patrick had seen on July 5.

By that time the order had a new clause, naming Sharpe's unit the Bureau of Information. This reflected the important fact that Sharpe was now back in the business of all-source intelligence; Meade could not ordain that Sharpe would report to Grant only information from his own sources — spying, scouting, interrogation. Thus the bureau, though it remained at the headquarters of a general to whom it had for a year reported only information of those three classes, had to receive and work into its reports the all-source information Sharpe took to his meetings with Grant.

Meade ignored this new arrangement by continuing for a time to forward to Grant copies of the bureau's reports, thus duplicating information Sharpe would also deliver to Grant. As for Grant, he was showing a capacity similar to Meade's for assimilating large amounts of written information.

Major Young's operations, limited to the Valley, would be of no help in covering the country Early had traveled on his way there. By this time Sharpe had organized a party that filled this void, beginning with Isaac Silver, now living at Belle Plain, near Aquia and the Potomac. Silver again put his Orange County business connections to use as cover for visits to that problem area. He paid special attention to railroad depots, where he questioned railroad employees and travelers, seeking information of movements on the Orange and Alexandria and the Virginia Central, and any other military news they might have. James W. Cammack, who evidently had connections similar to Silver's (and shared with Silver the sobriquet "the old man"), was similarly employed. Their coverage was supplemented by Ebenezer McGee, formerly Silver's messenger, and one or two other members of Sharpe's bureau. On returning from their travels these men were met by one or more members of a four-man team of Sharpe's scouts based at Falmouth. Lacking telegraphic connection from there to Meade's or Grant's headquarters, the scouts took the reports to Babcock, temporarily stationed in the War Department, for

telegraphing to Sharpe. They were provided with tugs, evidently to facilitate their travel to and from Washington. After a few weeks Captain
George K. Leet of Grant's staff relieved Babcock; in ensuing months
McEntee and Babcock in turn joined Leet. It was Leet who wired the
reports to Grant.

This system proved fully effective in preventing movements between
Richmond and the Valley from going unnoticed. It also enabled Sharpe's
bureau to produce reports of goings-on in a considerable section of
country otherwise uncovered. Presumably it was part of an expansion of
operations that Sharpe is known to have proposed and that, according to
Patrick, had been rejected by Meade. Whatever its origin, the system was
a logical part of Grant's intelligence program. It continued operating at
least until mid-January, long after Sheridan had the Valley well under
control. In fact its discontinuance may have been caused only by Silver's
arrest. Thomas Nelson Conrad, a leading Confederate spy, saw through
his thin cover, with the result that Silver spent several weeks or months in
a prisoner-of-war camp at Salisbury, North Carolina. His case was automatically disposed of by Lee's surrender in April.

. .   . .   . .

The profit initially realized from Grant's crossing of the James was unworthy of that masterfully executed maneuver. His subordinates, chiefly
Major General William Smith of the Eighteenth Corps, were intimidated
by elaborate fortifications in front of Petersburg and, not knowing that
the place was held by a force of only 2500, proceeded so cautiously that
Beauregard, the local commander, had time to bring in enough reinforcements to hold the place. By the 18th Lee's First and Third Corps
were present in strength.

The armies settled into a double siege, of Richmond and Petersburg.
The besiegers' attention focused on the railroads supplying the two cities
and Lee's army; especially vulnerable was the line directly south from
Petersburg to Weldon, North Carolina, the northern section of which the
Federals soon demolished, with the result that the freight had to be
hauled to Petersburg on wagons over many miles of roads. After months
of inconclusive fighting, the railroad cut was finally extended to forty
miles. Meanwhile Grant kept advancing his left in an arc around Petersburg, attempting to cut the Southside Railroad, which led west to Lynchburg, an important supply depot. Bloody and costly advances, employing parts of three corps and lasting until February, stretched the army's
lines twelve miles southwestward from Petersburg without reaching the
Southside.

In the Valley Sheridan was given two infantry corps in addition to the
force Hunter had commanded, and two divisions of cavalry. Early was
reinforced by Fitz Lee's cavalry division and Joseph B. Kershaw's division

of Lee's First Corps. Kershaw turned out to be Sheridan's chief intelligence problem; when he left Winchester in September on a summons from Lee, the withdrawal baffled the Federal commander until it was confirmed by Rebecca Wright, a Quaker who kept a small private school in the town. Thus encouraged to attack, Sheridan defeated Early in three consecutive battles. Early then planted on the Federal signalmen a message reporting a huge reinforcement by Longstreet, who actually had not returned from his convalescent leave; Sheridan read it as probably a ruse and went through with a scheduled meeting at the War Department. Returning to find his troops in retreat from a surprise attack at Cedar Creek, he about-faced them and scored his greatest victory.

The Valley was now cleared for Sheridan's devastation of farms and crops, which rivaled the thoroughness of Sherman's concurrent march through Georgia. During the winter Sheridan returned to Grant, and the Rebels' Second Corps to Lee, leaving Early in command of a local force in the Valley.

. .   . .   . .

The siege favored Sharpe's operation by narrowing the spaces between the armies' opposing lines to as little as forty yards; the proximity facilitated desertion. The number of deserters rose to as many as eighty a day as more and more Southern families in the path of Federal armies, especially Sherman's, pleaded with their sons to come home and tend the farms.

Lee constantly changed the positions of regiments and brigades, in full view of Federal signalmen's telescopes. Because of their proximity to the enemy lines, the observation stations' coverage of these movements was virtually complete for moves made in daytime. What was to the Signal Corps an unidentified unit marching within view of their telescopes could sometimes be matched with the move of a unit identified in the report of a deserter or a prisoner. The result of this unique set of circumstances was that Babcock was constantly perfecting his records of the composition and organization of the Army of Northern Virginia.

The siege created a situation that invited the reintroduction of ballooning, but Grant did not seize the opportunity. His reason for disregarding it probably was the near-completeness of his signal stations' coverage of enemy movements, combined with the fact that the Confederate artillerists would now have a better chance than ever before of finally downing a balloon.

One of the observation stations of the Army of the James, atop a 125-foot tower, was so favorably situated that in a single month it produced more than three hundred reports, most of which were important enough to be forwarded to Grant. With seventy signal stations to draw upon in the course of the Richmond campaign, the two armies' chief signal officers, Captains Benjamin Fisher and Lemuel Norton, turned out as many intelligence reports as Sharpe, Babcock, and McEntee combined.

The Confederates' signal stations, like their movements and positions, were within the range of the Federal telescopes. One of them, atop the customhouse in Petersburg, yielded partly readable messages beginning June 21. Federal artillery soon persuaded its operators to withdraw to a less prominent position; the discontinuance of this busy and easily interceptable source would not have pleased Fisher, or Sharpe. The interceptor, Captain Charles L. Davis, found the Rebels' flag alphabet similar to but not identical with the one that had been read in the 1863 campaigns. By the 24th it evidently was fully readable, and the next day it produced several messages showing Confederate signalmen's successful observation of Federal movements. Exploitation of Confederate flag signals continued throughout the siege.

Evidently the Confederates were returning the favor, for in August General Lee sent each of his corps commanders a copy of the Federal flag alphabet. This indicates that at least some of the Yankee messages were being sent in the clear, almost a year after Colonel Myer's issuance of his cipher disks.

.. .. ..

The most productive espionage operation of the Civil War, on either side, that has ever been documented was the service performed by Richmond's Unionist underground. As already seen, Samuel Ruth's slowdown of shipments of Confederate army supplies on the railroad to Fredericksburg began as early as November 1862. By early 1864 General Butler on the Peninsula began hearing from a second Richmond activist, Elizabeth Van Lew, a spinster living in a prominent hilltop mansion. The arrival of Grant's armies in front of Richmond in June stimulated these two leaders to develop overlapping rings of agents. The Van Lew group produced most of the information, and Ruth's agents were its principal conveyors to the army. From the City Point headquarters Colonel Sharpe took over the management of both groups, feeding their reports to Meade or Babcock and to Butler's Army of the James headquarters.

Petersburg was not ignored in these arrangements; early in July a free-Negro agent (whose name did not get into the records) was sent into the town, but he turned up no prospective agents for providing a steady supply of information. Sharpe's earliest (and probably his only) report from "our friends in Petersburg" is dated March 18, when the siege was within two weeks of its end. Petersburg was better positioned than Richmond for information on troop movements, but as already seen, those were well covered by visual observations and interrogation of deserters and prisoners.

Calling on Miss Van Lew after the fall of Richmond, Sharpe considerably expanded his understanding of the success of her operation. Throughout the war she had been perfectly open about her Union sympathies; undisguised affinity for the "other side" had not worked as a cover for Rose Greenhow, but it did for Elizabeth Van Lew. She provided Federals in the Richmond prisons with food, clothing, and bedding until she exhausted her considerable means. With prison administrators she negotiated indulgences of so many kinds for so many sick and needy prisoners that Sharpe declared that she "gained control of the Richmond prisons." She was not the "Crazy Bet" that myth would one day make her; to Sharpe her success was explained by her "attractive manners." "Plain Union people" of Richmond told him that it was the Van Lew family's influence that caused them to maintain their loyalty.

Elizabeth's brother John, a prosperous hardware merchant, was forced into military service in June 1864. He promptly made his way to Meade's headquarters and was sent on to Grant's, where he delivered information that Sharpe found valuable. The main purpose of his visit would have been to inform the Federals of the breadth of information available in his sister's circle of Unionist friends. His store was now closed; it is uncertain whether he returned to militia duty in Richmond or remained with the Federals as a refugee.

Miss Van Lew's and Ruth's reports, averaging perhaps three a week, were carried by couriers who met Sharpe's scouts at five rendezvous points, or "depots," some or all of which were east of the Chickahominy River. The principal courier was Charles M. Carter, an associate of Ruth and his collaborator, F. W. E. Lohman. Some of the other couriers were also spies who assisted Van Lew or Ruth. Carter, whom Sharpe once took pains to meet between the lines, lived in Charles City County, beyond the Chickahominy; that suggests that his cover was supplying farm products to Richmond. The city's impoverishment for food was serious enough to explain the fact that the couriers' travel was seldom officially impeded. When Miss Van Lew pressed one of her servants into courier duty, he would have been ready to explain that he was supplying "Miss Lizzie" with the necessities of her table.

Agents occasionally escorted refugees, in one case as many as eleven, on their trips to the rendezvous. By January, living conditions in Richmond were so grim that such travel did not raise suspicion of Union sympathy; Confederate officialdom was grateful for having even one less mouth to feed.

As the agents' methods and routes of travel became familiar to Sharpe, he began sending a few of his own men into the city, including Sergeant

Judson Knight, successor as chief scout to Milton Cline, who was mustered out in August along with the Third Indiana Cavalry. Evidently these soldier-agents served as their own couriers; it does not appear that they made contact with any of the Van Lew or Ruth operatives. Sharpe's reason for supplementing the citizens' reporting was the fact that he could impress particular intelligence needs on his scouts more effectively than he could on the Richmonders. In the case of certain questions, such as reinforcements to Early, Miss Van Lew and Ruth also received, via the couriers, Sharpe's guidance as to what information was most wanted. The overburdened Elizabeth Van Lew was glad for any feedback; at one point she wrote that her spying "puts me to a great disadvantage and I do not wish to do it unless it is received welcomely."

Probably on the basis of instructions from Sharpe, fortified by their own discretion, the citizen-agents omitted from their reports the identities of the informants. The couriers may often have been able to tell Sharpe who their sources were. However, it probably was only after the war that he learned from Miss Van Lew that she had clerks in the Confederate War and Navy Departments "in her confidence." Thus his security procedure prevented him from drawing from her reports a full sense of the reliability that information from those sources was entitled to. Its extent and value remain uncertain today.

Early in her service she learned to encrypt her reports, using an ancient cipher-square in which each letter was represented by a two-digit number. One of her surviving reports contains 336 words, or approximately 1500 letters, which means that in order to communicate everything on her mind, including such problems as getting cloth for a housedress, she made 3000 laborious strokes of her pencil. Since none of her dispatches is known to have been intercepted, it is fairly safe to assume that her cipher was never read by the enemy. As for Samuel Ruth, he evidently was left to send his reports in the clear, which he did in bold strokes of the pen, in language so firm that if one of his reports on train schedules had been intercepted, his words would have tempted the interceptor to guess that the writer was connected with Richmond's railroads.

Courier travel was not without occasional impedance; for example, on a day when all but one of the roads leading into and out of Richmond were closed to civilian traffic, an agent had to walk thirty-five miles to reach his rendezvous. This duty required a certain brazenness, as when one of the agents encountered, and rode with, the Richmond forces' Officer of the Day as he made his rounds — which were primarily a security check — between the city's inner and outer defense lines. The roads were so lightly patrolled that there is only one recorded instance of a courier having to destroy the report he carried.

Two of the leading agents did not succeed in keeping their activities free of the enemy's suspicion. Lohman was arrested and imprisoned in Castle Thunder from January 20 to the army's departure from Richmond on April 2, and Ruth served a tour in the same prison in January and February.

In the Richmonders' extensive contribution of intelligence, local military movements received less attention than two other topics: the scarcities that plagued the populace even more seriously than they did the army, and the prospect of Lee's evacuation of Richmond and Petersburg. Most of the complaints about life in the economy of shortages dealt with such generalities as how many weeks the food on hand would last. More impressive was the occasional detailed report of a particular shortage, such as one that the army confronted in finding cloth for uniforms. Four or five million dollars of the hopelessly inflated Confederate currency had been appropriated, but there was almost no place to spend it. Quartermasters were "telegraphing everywhere" in search of "every color [on] every shelf of every store and shop." They found only enough cloth to make 1600 pairs of pants, doubtless less than a tenth of Lee's army's need for just that one item.

The fall of Atlanta to Sherman on September 2 planted in Richmond a hope that an army under his late opponent, General Johnston, would be available to join Lee somewhere in the Carolinas, enabling the combined forces to defeat Sherman and then Grant. This talk subsided, but by mid-January it was again "upon everybody's lips." The famed Tredegar iron works, unable to pay its 1500 employees, discharged them and sent its machinery to Salisbury, North Carolina; machinery from at least three other Richmond plants had been moved southward; a laboratory that had employed 2000 girls now had reduced its work force to 50.

And on February 4 Miss Van Lew reported that munitions had been sent south. The army's addition of its existing armament to the southbound shipments was clinching evidence: evacuation was now a certainty. Among all of the Van Lew reports, this one is the likeliest to have come from the source she claimed in the War Department.

Lee sought to prepare for the season of dry roads by attempting a breakout attack that would make captures on such a scale as to cripple Grant's pursuit. The objective was the Federals' heavily manned Fort Stedman, on the left of their line. General John B. Gordon, now commanding the Second Corps, devised a complex breakthrough that was difficult to execute in darkness. Secrecy was a paramount need, but elements of the First and Third Corps were brought in, some of them from north of the James, and the army was canvassed for guides intimately familiar with the terrain. The Federals had warning, according to Ruth and Lohman, who claimed to have discovered these preparations, but they did not know the date of the attack, March 25. The attackers scored an initial penetration and then were overwhelmed; it was Lee who suffered wholesale captures, and total casualties of 5000. Evacuation plans went forward; the army's westward march began at 8 P.M. April 2. As Grant's army was poised to attack in the early morning of the 3rd, his pursuit began immediately.

.. .. ..

One more story of espionage against Richmond remains to be told. Joseph H. Maddox, the smuggler-spy known as "our friend" by Baltimore Provost Marshal James McPhail, was not heard from for some weeks after his timely report during the Chancellorsville battle. He had been "detained" by the Confederates and was now, in August 1863, expecting to come home to Baltimore "very soon," presumably bringing the latest information. He was looking for a messenger who could save him from the Baltimore trips that cost him long absences from Richmond. Then came another interruption of his communication with McPhail; it was not until November 20 that he had what he called his "first opportunity to write you [McPhail] unreservedly since my detention." Until lately he had been closely watched though "permitted to go at large upon parole." Now he believed he had a "safe channel" and was "growing daily in better odour." But with the passage of time he was more and more anxious to be released from a mission "which has kept me in trepidation."

Bradley T. Johnson, colonel of the Confederates' Maryland Line and now a newly appointed brigadier general, proposed to trade tobacco to Maddox in return for cloth for his troops' uniforms. Here was an opening for the kind of business Maddox was hoping his Richmond venture would turn up: investing in tobacco. Within a few months he acquired a huge amount of that commodity, and in April 1864 he started it on its way North, expecting to get it across the Potomac from the Northern Neck to Point Lookout, at the southern tip of Maryland. But the commander of a Federal prisoner-of-war camp at Point Lookout seized the tobacco and Maddox was imprisoned at Fort Monroe on a charge of disloyalty that was not lifted until he had been in prison for three months. The tobacco remained at Machodoc Creek on the Neck until December 1866, by which time it had lost much or most of its value by deterioration. After Maddox filed suit against Secretary Stanton, asking $30,000 for false arrest, the government released the tobacco, Maddox was paid $8100 for damages and depreciation, and he dropped the lawsuit.

Maddox's detention and surveillance by the Confederates and his imprisonment at Fort Monroe severely limited his collection of information and especially its transmission to Baltimore; sometimes several reports arrived together. His most valuable reports were four that included estimates of enemy strength. In December 1863 he gave Lee 40,000 effectives exclusive of cavalry; this was an overestimate of only 10 percent. Two months later he had figures for a considerable area: 19,000 for Beauregard at Charleston, 20,000 for Longstreet in Tennessee (7000 of them lacking shoes), 35,000 for Joseph Johnston's army in northern Georgia, 15,000 for the forces between Weldon and Wilmington, and now 46,000 plus cavalry for Lee. These figures, strongly tending toward overestimates, were difficult for Sharpe and Meade to evaluate since Maddox gave no explanation of how he acquired numbers for armies so distant. The most interesting of the four reports was an insistent item on the defenselessness of Richmond: "1000 or 2000 [cavalry] could land on the Pamunkey at dark and ride in unmolested and take Davis. Only a small picket at Mechanicsville." This piece of intelligence, perhaps with others in the same vein, could have inspired the ill-fated Kilpatrick-Dahlgren raid in February and March, which encountered resistance entirely at variance with Maddox's information. Since he presumably was living in or very close to Richmond, how he could have been so mistaken regarding its defenses is a mystery.

The rest of Maddox's reporting was a wide-ranging miscellany, for which a few examples will suffice. One report gave positions of Confederate batteries on the James and of units as small as the 780-man Maryland Line; such information was valuable if only as corroboration of data Babcock already had. There were details on the Rebels' construction of gunboats on the James, such as the claim of armor five inches thick; that would have raised questions as to Maddox's judgment. John Mosby's whereabouts was a subject that even Richmond sources could not avoid; the report that Maddox picked up placed him in the Valley. A statement that Lee's army had "not had a pound of meat [per man] in ten days" would have been a useful addition to the Van Lew reporting on food scarcity. Maddox discoursed on how Grant should take Richmond, and on "the imbecility of the [Confederate] administration." Sharpe would have preferred that such topics not take up space on a reporting channel as sensitive as Maddox's.

In February 1864 McPhail wrote Sharpe that Maddox "says that if the means were furnished him he could worm the greatest secrets out of the officials of the Government." Maddox believed that the Confederate government was "the most corrupt on the face of the Earth." The "means" he could not supply from his own resources consisted of high-quality clothing and stationery to be given to high-ranking government officials; he looked to Sharpe or the War Department to supply them. Of this proposal McPhail said that if it won approval, "I pledge myself to obtain such information as the government has never had." As disapproval was unlikely but no startlingly valuable information materialized, it appears that the proposed recipients of Maddox's favors were not as corrupt as he thought.

The nonappearance of the information to be "wormed" out of the top levels at Richmond ended the hopes that would have been raised by Maddox's impressive initial report. Even without such information, his reports were very much worth having, but the gaps between reports — the delays in transmission, the interruptions caused by his detention or simply his surveillance — greatly reduced the value of his services. Such drawbacks could be tolerated as inherent in his mission, but only up to a point. Maddox passed that point with his attempt to ship his tobacco North without advance arrangements by McPhail with the commander at Point Lookout and perhaps other officers on the route. In addition to insuring passage of the shipment, that would have averted the charge of disloyalty that put Maddox in prison for three months. When he was operating, his mission was a modest success; when he was out of action or incommunicado it was a serious disappointment to Sharpe and his chiefs. And for almost a year — until the Van Lew–Samuel Ruth ring went into operation in 1864 — Maddox was Federal intelligence's only agent in Richmond.

. .   . .   . .

George Sharpe was promoted to brigadier general in February; his new rank won him the task at Appomattox on April 9–11 of paroling the Army of Northern Virginia, now reduced to 26,000 by the battles that immediately preceded Lee's surrender. Sharpe deliberately refrained from issuing a parole to General Lee, feeling that that act would be presumptuous; but the general's aide, Colonel Charles Marshall, came calling to rectify the omission. General Lee had pointed out that he too was a member of the Army of Northern Virginia. He was wise to the ways of radical Republican politicians; he needed the parole as insurance against the arrest that Lincoln's Jacobins would urge.

Sharpe returned to Kingston in June at the head of his beloved 120th Regiment and resumed the practice of law. In 1867 Secretary Seward sent him to London, Paris, and Rome in a search for John Surratt, suspected of conspiracy in the Lincoln assassination. Surratt's trail was cold wherever his pursuer went; before the end of the year he was back in the United States and had been tried and acquitted. But that errand did not end Sharpe's Federal service; in 1869 President Grant made him U.S. marshal for the Southern District of New York. The appointment was no mere reward for his services to General Grant; it had a special purpose, owing to the prevalence of corruption in New York City elections under Democratic rule. By enforcing, "against violent opposition," an honest 1870 census in the city, Sharpe established that Democratic victories in 1868 had been fraudulent; thus he brought an end to the dominance of the Tweed Ring. Then he served as surveyor of customs at New York until 1878; thereafter he combined the practice of law with public service, mainly in New York State politics. He died in January 1900, thirteen days into the new century.

After Appomattox General Patrick remained briefly in Richmond, then left the army to resume his prewar prominence in scientific farming in upstate New York. In 1880, still remembered as a fair-dealing disciplinarian, he became governor of the national home for disabled veterans at Dayton, Ohio. John McEntee and John Babcock served under Patrick in Richmond and remained there after the general's departure, as heads of the provost marshal system that evidently was called into being by the inadequacy or total absence of a civil police force.

Babcock, though still a civilian, was addressed as "Captain" and functioned in the role of chief of police. His purpose in continuing his government employment probably was to accumulate money with which to go into practice as an architect in New York. He was one of three founders of the New York Athletic Club, in 1868; while a member of the Nassau Boat Club he became known among sportsmen as the inventor of a sliding seat for oarsmen. His design of well-known buildings and monuments and his prominence as a clubman inevitably changed his unofficial title of Captain to Colonel.

In retirement years Babcock began correspondence with William Pinkerton, whom he had known as a teenage boy accompanying Allan Pinkerton's field unit on the Peninsula. He also exchanged letters with Henry G. Sharpe, George Sharpe's younger son, a future quartermaster general of the U.S. Army. This correspondence looked toward the writing of a history of the Bureau of Military Information; it appears that nothing had been written when Babcock suffered a stroke that ended his life in November 1908.

John McEntee remained in military service until April 1866, by then breveted as a full colonel and serving as provost judge of Richmond. After discharge he was employed briefly in New York City and Boston before returning to Kingston to engage in the foundry and machine-shop business. Until his death in 1903 he was one of Kingston's leading citizens, as alderman, library trustee, and officer in local charities.

The intelligence operative most prominent in postwar years was William Palmer. After release from his Richmond imprisonment, upon returning in February 1863 to his western command, now at Nashville, where he found his Anderson Cavalry in a mutinous state. He disbanded the company and turned its successor, the 15th Pennsylvania Cavalry Regiment, into a model regiment that specialized in scouting tasks. He became a brigadier general at the age of twenty-eight and received the

Congressional Medal of Honor for gallantry in action. After the war Palmer, taking his railroading experience West, built the Rio Grande and Western Railroad and the rail system that connected Denver with Mexico City. In 1870–71 he helped found the town of Colorado Springs; when he died in 1909 the press agreed that he was "Colorado's First Citizen."

APPENDIXES

COMMENT ON SOURCES

LIST OF ABBREVIATIONS
AND SHORT TITLES

NOTES

BIBLIOGRAPHY

SOURCES AND
ACKNOWLEDGMENTS

INDEX

APPENDIX 1

· · · · · · · · · · ·

Successes and Failures of
Federal and Confederate Intelligence

The prowess of the Federal and the Confederate intelligence services can be compared by examining the liberal number of clear-cut instances of intelligence success and failure reported in this book. Below are listed performances that are noteworthy for excellence or weakness, or simply for their importance.

Successes

FEDERAL

First Bull Run Campaign: Unionist citizens reported departure of Confederates' Shenandoah Valley army for Manassas (chapter 2).

The "Phony War" of 1861–62: From October 1861 to April 1862, five Pinkerton agents made a total of fourteen visits to Richmond, entering the city easily as smugglers or couriers. Their chief sources of information were medium- and low-level officers (chapters 4, 6).

CONFEDERATE

First Bull Run Campaign: Though lacking information on date of march and attack plans, Rose Greenhow learned of Federal decision to advance on Manassas (chapters 2 and 3, appendix 4).

First Bull Run Battle: The Confederate Signal Corps observed the Federals' turning movement in time for defensive positions to be assumed (chapter 2).

Invasion of Carolina Coast: A Federal expedition assigned to establish a naval base at Port Royal, South Carolina, was under sealed orders, but its destination was discovered at Annapolis or Hampton Roads, its departure points (chapter 3).

Jackson's Valley Campaign: Informed of an exposed flank of the Federals' Valley army, Jackson drove it across the Potomac (chapter 7).

FEDERAL

Peninsula Campaign: Pinkerton identified all of Lee's 178 regiments (chapter 6).

Second Bull Run Campaign: Pope escaped from a surprise attack when warned by a spy who had traveled with Lee's force from Richmond (chapter 8).

Second Bull Run Campaign: Pope's aggressive cavalry reconnaissance baffled Lee's efforts to outflank him along the Rapidan and Rappahannock (chapter 8).

Antietam Campaign: Deviations by Jackson and Longstreet from the terms of Lee's Lost Order were discovered by an itinerant parson who twice mingled with the Confederates in their camps (chapter 9).

Chancellorsville Campaign: A sergeant-spy made an extended visit with Confederate cavalry, twice riding the length of Lee's lines at Fredericksburg (chapter 13).

Chancellorsville Campaign: Federal signalmen, aware of the Rebels' ability to read their flag code, planted a hoax message that caused Lee to send Stuart in pursuit of an imaginary Federal cavalry raid. Through the country vacated by Stuart, Hooker marched three corps to the enemy's rear (chapters 15, 16).

May 27, 1863: Federal intelligence forecast the enemy movement that started the Gettysburg campaign (chapter 18).

CONFEDERATE

Peninsula Campaign: Stuart's cavalry circled McClellan's army, acquiring information on its positions needed by Lee for the attack that opened the Seven Days battles (chapter 6).

Second Bull Run Campaign: In a raid on Pope's rear, Stuart captured telegrams revealing the impending arrival of McClellan's divisions, then leaving the Peninsula (chapter 8).

March 1863: While stopped in Maryland, Burnside's two-division movement from the Peninsula to Ohio was scouted by a spy of Lee's whose report more than doubled the size of the movement (chapter 15).

March 1863: Cross-river movement of a Federal cavalry division was discovered in good time, but Lee acted on the assumption that it was an attack by Hooker's army (chapter 15).

Battle of Chancellorsville: Stuart's cavalry discovered the vulnerable positions of the Federals' right wing, which Jackson's attack then crushed (chapter 17).

Gettysburg Campaign: Under the eyes of Federals camped across the Rappahannock, Lee withdrew westward

FEDERAL

CONFEDERATE

from Fredericksburg without un-masking his purpose. A rumor, prob-ably officially spread, led the Federals to believe that the Confederates' plan was for a huge cavalry raid (chapter 18).

Gettysburg Campaign: A team of soldier-spies learned the positions of most of Lee's main body by spending four days behind enemy lines in the Shen-andoah Valley (chapter 21).

Gettysburg Campaign: Locally organ-ized groups of citizen-scouts blank-eted south-central Pennsylvania, reporting Confederate movements (chapter 22).

Gettysburg Campaign: Lee, belatedly learning from a spy sent out by Long-street that the Federals had crossed the Potomac, began concentrating forces separated by as much as 60 miles (chapter 22).

Gettysburg Campaign: Energetic cavalry scouting led to the capture of couri-ers and detection of the enemy's near-approach to Gettysburg (chap-ters 23, 24).

Battle of Gettysburg: Intelligence officers' knowledge of the composi-tion of Lee's army enabled them to report, after examining hundreds of prisoners, that all but four of the enemy's brigades had been heavily used in two days' fighting. Meade's council of war then unanimously rejected his proposal to move to a supposedly more favorable position in Maryland (chapter 24).

Failures

FEDERAL

CONFEDERATE

First Bull Run Campaign: The Union commander in the Valley rejected the citizens' report of the departure of the enemy's Valley troops, whose arri-val at Manassas turned the battle in the Confederates' favor (chapter 2).

The "Phony War" of 1861–62: Pinker-ton's deliberately exaggerated estimates of enemy numbers were considered too low by McClellan,

FEDERAL

CONFEDERATE

who substituted his own figures. The whole estimating affair was a travesty (chapter 5).

Confederates' Stolen March from Manassas: McClellan ignored balloonists' reports of evidence of evacuation of the Manassas front. The Rebels escaped undamaged (chapter 6).

Peninsula Campaign: Federal units had been landing at the foot of the Peninsula for three weeks before Lee and Johnston recognized that the Peninsula itself was designed as the enemy's route to Richmond (chapter 6).

Jackson's Valley Campaign: The Federals' Valley army failed to detect Jackson's eastward crossing of the Blue Ridge, a temporary move that he expected to attract the enemy's attention while he deceptively moved in the opposite direction (chapter 7).

Second Bull Run Campaign: Jackson, with half of Lee's army, marched undetected around Pope's right flank and destroyed his supply base at Manassas (chapter 8).

Antietam Campaign: McClellan, by rejecting reports of movements that deviated from terms of Lee's Lost Order, made errors in maneuvering his army that erased the tremendous advantage deriving from his acquisition of the order (chapter 9).

Failure to Exploit Leaks of Federal Military Information: Although McClellan's acquisition of the Lost Order was promptly reported in the press, Lee did not learn of it for many months. Information from another leak, on the exact numbers of Hooker's army, was so diluted on its way to Lee that he could not put it to use (chapters 9, 15).

Battle of Fredericksburg: Burnside, neglecting intelligence preparations, designed a battle plan that sent his main attack against the Confederates' strongest defenses; the result was a slaughter (chapter 11).

Fredericksburg Campaign: Burnside's unhidden arrival before Fredericksburg, like McClellan's on the Peninsula, puzzled Lee for some days, seriously delaying his summoning of Jackson from the Valley (chapter 11).

Chancellorsville Campaign: Lee's deception by the Federal signalmen's hoax message was so thorough that he left virtually unpatrolled the

FEDERAL | CONFEDERATE

CONFEDERATE

country vacated by Stuart, thus failing to detect Hooker's march to Chancellorsville until too late to resist it (chapters 15, 16).

Battle of Chancellorsville: Federal pickets and scouts observed an enemy force assembling on the army's right wing; division and corps headquarters believed the Confederates were retreating. The flanking force, led by Jackson, wiped out much of the wing (chapter 17).

June 8, 1863: Like Stuart's troops, Hooker's headquarters accepted as fact the planted rumor of a planned cavalry raid. This erroneous report reached Washington simultaneously with the badly delayed May 27 forecast of Lee's general movement, and diverted attention from that movement. The Federals' Valley army, thus insufficiently warned of the approach of enemy infantry, was wiped out (chapter 20).

Gettysburg Campaign: Lee was blind to enemy movements for a week because of his order that allowed Stuart to march on the enemy's right in the advance to Pennsylvania. Even when nearing Gettysburg, his point of concentration, he did not know that the enemy had preceded him there (chapters 22, 24).

Gettysburg Campaign: Hill's troops' spreading of the misinformation that Longstreet's corps, the army's rear, was marching ahead of them hastened the Federals on their way. Had this blunder not been made, the Confederates would have seized the critical high ground at Gettysburg well in advance of the enemy's arrival (chapter 21).

Not surprisingly, the Federals, having a more extensive intelligence program than the Confederates, acquired a more impressive list of successes. Although their noteworthy feats outnumber the Confederates' only thirteen to eleven, the thirteen include four well-documented cases of Federals' mingling with Rebels in their camps or on the march; of the two Confederate feats of this kind that are known, one produced seriously faulty information. The Confederates' most impressive intelligence feat is their discovery of the destination of the Port Royal expedition; and that is overmatched by the Federals' spying and signal deception that in combination made possible Hooker's unresisted march to Chancellorsville.

That episode shows the Federals' superiority in one intelligence area, flag-signal intercept. In intelligence bookkeeping — tracking changes in the makeup and organization of the opposing army — even Pinkerton's relatively unskilled bureau produced results well beyond the Rebels' known capability. Still another intelligence source, scouting of enemy forces by citizens of invaded country, so effective in the 1863 Pennsylvania campaign, had no Confederate counterpart in Virginia, though the armies spent twenty times as many weeks there as they did north of the Potomac.

Despite Stuart's nonperformance in the Gettysburg campaign, and Buford's excellent work for the Federals, cavalry reconnaissance was an area of unquestioned Confederate superiority. Lee had even greater reliance on scouting by individuals and small parties. Some of his best-known scouts, however, seem to have found fighting and capturing Yankees more interesting than collecting information.

In assessing the performance of an intelligence service, failures are as important as successes; here the Federals' entries in our list of noteworthy deeds again outnumber those of the Rebels, nine to six — and again the Federal record is much more striking. For sheer egregiousness, no Confederate blunders can match the Federals' two rejections of critically important eye-witness information — on the departure of Johnston's army from the Shenandoah Valley and on the formation of Jackson's attack at Chancellorsville; both of these had disastrous results. Another grievous failure was McClellan's ignoring of balloonists' reports of evidence of evacuation of the Manassas front; his neglect gave Johnston another stolen march. On the blundering scale these misdeeds far outrank even Lee's worst error, his acceptance of the Federal signalmen's hoax.

How reliable are these indications of Federal superiority in intelligence? No collection of records of Confederate intelligence operations in the campaigns studied here is known to have survived; thus the Confederates' successes and failures cannot be studied in the same detail as the Federals'. But the extent and correctness of the Confederate commanders' knowledge of the enemy's situation are revealed in their telegrams and letters, especially in General Lee's dispatches to Richmond. There are enough of those to give a clear indication of the quality of his intelligence coverage.

APPENDIX 2

. . . .

A Few Lessons from (and about)
Civil War Intelligence

Three general points can be drawn from the eight campaigns covered in these pages.

"It takes all kinds." Each of the various sources of intelligence, with the sole exception of enemy newspapers, produced at least one windfall.

Espionage had its finest hour in Sergeant Thomas Harter's warning of Lee's imminent surprise attack on Pope. Harter's success in falling in with Lee's movement from Richmond was a piece of extraordinary good luck, and once he escaped the Southern ranks he had the additional good luck to find Pope almost as quickly as if the general had been waiting on the Rapidan bank for him to cross.

Interrogation of deserters, prisoners, and refugees, Sharpe's biggest and most consistent producer, had its greatest success in an unlikely situation, the heat of battle, at Gettysburg. It had served Sharpe and Babcock well as an instrument of strategic intelligence in reconstructing the composition and organization of the Army of Northern Virginia; the huge influx of prisoners on July 1 and 2 transformed it into a source of operational intelligence, a means of determining the enemy's fighting capability in considerable detail.

The chief successes enjoyed by Federal scouting (by individuals and small parties, as distinct from reconnaissance en masse, by cavalry) came in the Confederates' 1862 and 1863 invasions of the North. In 1862 Captain William Palmer's handful of recruits delivered a thorough coverage of the country between the Potomac and Hagerstown, though their findings were largely wasted by the suppression and emasculation of Palmer's reports along the telegraphic route to McClellan. In 1863 the Pennsylvania citizen-scouts covered a much larger area with similar effectiveness; although their operation amounted to espionage when the scouts found themselves in close contact with the invading columns, this was basically a scouting operation.

Cavalry reconnaissance was an effective producer of intelligence in Pope's army until his overuse of it wore out his mounts. It came into its own again with John Buford's vigorous scouting and his captures of enemy couriers in the days immediately preceding the Gettysburg battle. The cavalry's unpro-

ductiveness during most of this campaigning was due partly to its unaggressive leadership but mainly to army commanders' habits in making use of it.
Had they been asked to name their most important intelligence source, the
cavalry would have been their choice; still they found other tasks for it that
displaced information-gathering as its chief function.

The most noteworthy performance by the producers of visual intelligence
— the balloonists and the Signal Corps observation stations — was the discovery by one of Professor Lowe's men of the burnings that foretold the
evacuation of the Confederates' Leesburg-Manassas-Aquia line. Because of
McClellan's distractions, this was another piece of intelligence that went to
waste.

The smallest producer among these sources was the Signal Corps' interception of enemy flag messages, but the signalmen's main contribution was
not an intercept; it was the signal deception that opened General Hooker's
path to the enemy rear, the outstanding intelligence feat in these eight
campaigns, if not in the whole Civil War.

Still another supplier of information was the phenomenon known as ser-
endipity. By putting forth a much more extensive intelligence effort than
their adversary, the Federals gave the serendipitous factor greater scope to
operate. An example of the beneficences this earned them was the discovery
of Charley Wright, the key to their timely pursuit of the northbound enemy.

How a big built-in advantage in intelligence can be overcome. In the contest for
information the Confederates held the upper hand by virtue of operating
on their home ground 95 percent of the time. It seems to have been habitual with Federal commanders, when operating in the Confederacy, to con-
cede the enemy this advantage. It was so evident to Grant and his generals
in the Mississippi theater that their spies were instructed to tell the Confederates the truth about Federal forces, on the assumption that the Rebels
would have correct information anyway, and the spy who made misstate-
ments would only betray himself. (One spy who ventured to interpret this
rule to suit himself wound up having to be reassigned east in 1864.) Pope
resisted this tendency and by force of effort succeeded in getting an even
break or better as long as his cavalry held up. Similarly, Hooker was too
stubborn to be resigned to coming in second in the information contest.
Other Union commanders were liberal in regard to newspaper and flag-of-
truce exchanges, probably because those were situations in which the Northerners for a change seemed to stand a chance of getting a quid pro quo.
Hooker clamped down hard on both. By these and other strong security
measures, and by his insistence on vigorous and competent intelligence
work, he marched to Chancellorsville with well-nigh perfect information,
while Lee, surrounded by a friendly population, had information that was as
bad as Hooker's was good until the armies had been at close grips for two
days. And the advantage Hooker seized early in his command did not prove
transient; Sharpe maintained it, though not without an occasional lapse, all
the way to Appomattox.

A characterization of commanders as getters and users of intelligence. Three rather
sharp classifications emerge from the performances of Hooker, Meade, and

Lee. Hooker, administrator par excellence, saw the value of intelligence and knew how to get the job done right, beginning with his history-making invention of all-source intelligence, which to him was simply the natural way of staying informed about the enemy. Another way in which Hooker did the job right was in selecting Colonel Sharpe, who also recognized competence in Babcock and McEntee. Hooker also did an excellent job of translating his intelligence into a campaign plan, and he devised an excellent solution to the problem of march security. But Hooker did not trust the plan that he admired as much as history does. It is hard to put a finger on his flaw, but this much is clear: he could comprehend the big picture before the battle, and he could create the right plan, but he could not see it through.

Meade's narrowing of the reporting charter Hooker had given Sharpe shows that if he had inherited the army without a going intelligence organ, he would not have set up as good a one as Hooker did. But Meade had one ability in which Hooker did not especially distinguish himself: skill in assimilating and interpreting the intelligence he received. On the morning of June 28, when he left the Fifth Corps and rode over to army headquarters to take command, he was completely uninformed of the enemy's situation (Hooker had carried security too far); by evening he had picked out the correct information from a flood of conflicting reports. Undoubtedly Sharpe aided him in this, but the language of the orders Meade issued and of his dispatches to Washington shows that he played a strong evaluative role. He continued this performance, though not against such great odds as were posed by those conflicting reports. But Meade's performance in applying intelligence was far from ideal. In Maryland he read the evidence correctly and then acted as if the erroneous reports were as sound as the correct ones, and the army therefore would have to go out and look for enemy concentrations all over south-central Pennsylvania. It is reasonable to question whether, if he had not had his generals' views to rely on in his council of war, he would have taken the action his information pointed to.

Lee, as we have repeatedly seen, did not do anything like the job Hooker did in providing himself with intelligence. Evidently he also lacked Meade's flair for interpretation; for example, despite his own use — overuse — of deception, he accepted a planted enemy signal that should have seemed suspicious. But Lee excelled in putting intelligence to use. Given a piece of significant tactical information, he knew what action to take, and he took it, and saw it through.

Thus each of these men seems to have excelled in just one of these skills — getting information, interpreting it, and applying it. Interpretation is a higher skill than acquisition, and application is higher than interpretation, but the higher orders do not seem to require any degree of excellence in the lower ones. This stratification, though it looks over-sharp, may be exactly what a psychologist would expect to find; but it is something that the abundant legacy of Civil War history has not previously been made to demonstrate.[1]

APPENDIX 3

. . . .

Two Strategic Surprises

The battle at Winchester in June 1863, in which General Ewell, on his way to Pennsylvania, captured 4000 of General Milroy's division and drove the remaining 3000 into Maryland, is the first half of a story of history repeating itself. The other half is another disaster suffered by United States forces, the catastrophe known as Pearl Harbor. On six principal points these two histories are remarkably similar.

1. *Well in advance, intelligence delivered a strong warning of an enemy strike, but without identifying the target.* General Hooker knew, from his spies, a deserter, and visible stirrings in the enemy camps, that a general movement by Lee's army was in the offing, but none of this information identified the enemy's objective. In 1941 the government's information came from the army's solution of the Japanese diplomatic service's "Purple" cipher machine; intercepted messages to the two Japanese ambassadors in Washington showed unmistakable preparations for war, but the Pearl Harbor plan was a secret carefully withheld from the Japanese diplomatic service, and thus it was not mentioned in the Purple messages. Washington authorities were left to assume that Japan's objectives lay to the south — as its advance on the Philippines, the East Indies, and southeast Asia was to reveal on that same December weekend.

2. *Delivery of the intelligence to field commanders was delayed and forestalled by bureaucratic bungling.* For reasons unknown, a report by Hooker's intelligence bureau, forecasting a long-range strike by the enemy, was delayed twelve days in reaching Washington. Meanwhile the War Department, which had received notice by telegraph of the dispatch of the report, did nothing to acquire a copy, failing even to inform Hooker of its nonarrival. Equally feckless was Washington's behavior in the 1941 case; a Navy Department admiral who was not even in the intelligence chain of command succeeded in blocking, on security grounds, the transmittal of Purple intelligence to the navy and army commanders in Hawaii.

3. *Warnings sent from Washington to field commanders failed to impress them with the gravity of the situation.* The warnings sent to Milroy at Winchester and Schenck, his superior at Baltimore, were weak — lacking even the all-impor-

tant basic fact that Lee's army might be coming their way. This vagueness resulted from the War Department's having no information except Hooker's too-brief telegram saying a detailed intelligence report was en route. In November 1941 telegrams sent to Hawaii warned against striking the first blow and against alarming the public — cautions stressed so heavily that they dominated the messages at the expense of the need for military preparedness.

4. *The War Department neglected to check on compliance with its warnings.* Milroy and Schenck thought they were being warned about increased activity by the Confederates' small Shenandoah Valley army; the department's supervision was much too loose to uncover this fatal mistake. In Hawaii General Short acknowledged receipt of the warning by reporting that he was acting to prevent sabotage by local Japanese; this mistaken understanding of the warning's intent went uncorrected by the War Department.

5. *The enemy approach was detected but was not recognized for what it was.* Milroy's small cavalry units, probing southward up the Valley, found heavy enemy cavalry forces coming north but did not risk the encounter that would uncover the enemy's strength. Milroy allowed that Jeb Stuart evidently had reinforced the enemy's regular cavalry units, but he remained unaware of the presence of Ewell's full corps of infantry. A parallel slippage took place on the morning of December 7, 1941, when radar operators detected the Japanese bombers flying toward Oahu and were told to "forget it" by an inexperienced lieutenant who assumed that the blips on their screen signified the approach of a U.S. army or navy formation, most probably a flight of new B-17s that was expected from the West Coast.

6. *Communication outage defeated an eleventh-hour effort to avert surprise.* Milroy's telegraph wire, cut or grounded by Confederates, went dead early in the reception of a peremptory order to evacuate Winchester. In Washington at noon on December 7 General Marshall dispatched an urgent message based on an intercept showing that the two Japanese ambassadors had been instructed to call at the State Department at exactly 1 P.M. As a movement southward from Japan's home islands had been confidently expected to begin that weekend, the commanders in Hawaii, the Philippines, and the Panama Canal Zone were expected to infer from Marshall's message that some Japanese action would develop at or about the hour specified for the ambassadors' call. Although the message reached Manila and Panama promptly, the Army's radiotelegraph link with Hawaii was temporarily inoperative, and it arrived at the Honolulu commercial radiotelegraph office so late that the messenger delivering it was delayed by traffic jams caused by the persistent attacks of the Japanese bombers. Before the ambassadors arrived at the State Department, after being delayed by reception of a final set of instructions, Pearl Harbor was under attack and the whole world knew it.[1]

. .   . .   . .

Should the Winchester debacle have served as a warning that might have prevented the Pearl Harbor disaster? The strategic surprise at Winchester has been well hidden, uncovered only by the present study, but even if it had been a well-known part of American military history in 1941, it would not have been likely to influence the government's handling of the troubles raised by Japan's aggressions. For it is only in comparatively recent times that military scholars have studied strategic surprise deeply enough for an 1863 event to be considered relevant to today's military problems.

In lives and materials of war the cost of the Winchester debacle was insignificant compared to Pearl Harbor, but the panic it caused in the North was much like the invasion fears that prevailed on the West Coast after the Pacific Fleet was destroyed at Pearl Harbor. Therefore this comparison of the two disasters is not an invidious one.

APPENDIX 4

· · · · · · · · · · ·

Rose Greenhow's Reports

Reproduced here are copies of nine of Mrs. Greenhow's intelligence reports. The first eight were among the papers confiscated by Allan Pinkerton in Mrs. Greenhow's house at the time of her arrest on August 23, 1861; the ninth was found by the Federals in Confederate archives after the fall of Richmond.[1]

With one exception there is nothing in these reports that is definitely known to have come from "inside" sources claimed by and for Mrs. Greenhow. The exception is information on artillery in the Washington defenses provided by Senator Henry Wilson. Whether the figures he gave were correct is unknown; they occur in an undecipherable (possibly mistakenly enciphered) passage in one of her reports. As pointed out in the text, the figures, if correct, could have been calculated by Wilson to be sufficiently intimidating to persuade Generals Johnston and Beauregard to cancel any attack plans they may have had.

The reports contain numerous other items whose substance and wording can be interpreted as indicating that they might have come from insiders. An example is the story mentioned in chapter 3 of the Federals' fears of attack on Washington via Leesburg and Baltimore. Another is Mrs. Greenhow's report that McClellan "expects to surprise you." But these items and many others fail to qualify as inside information since they were very probably wrong. Therefore all of these suspect items may be classed as reports from unknown sources reaching the ears of Mrs. Greenhow's circle of collaborators. An additional reason for this classification is the probability that Mrs. Greenhow would not have allowed any information traceable to McClellan or any other high authority to appear in one of her reports with its source unnamed.

The ninth report, from a later period when Mrs. Greenhow was under guard in her home, was unlike the earlier ones in that it was confined to a single subject, a forthcoming Federal movement. It was entirely wrong; it was probably founded on mere rumor, though it could have been a plant. But she insisted, "This is positive," a misstatement that indicates that imprisonment was affecting the quality of her reporting more than she suspected.

In the following dispatches, bracketed words or parts of words usually indicate gaps due to incomplete or incorrect assembly of torn-up pages.

31 [July]

All is activity. McClellan is busy night and day but the panick is great and the attack is hourly expected. They believe that the attack will be made simultaneous from Edwards Ferry and Baltimore. Every effort is being made to find out who gave the alarm. A troop of cavalry will start from here this morning to Harpers Ferry. Don't give time for reorganizing.

61.5.8 [Aug. 5, 1861] 9 A.M.

The opinion of A [rest of sentence missing] We are endeavor[ing] to effect an organization here in order to take advantage of emergencies. If possible their telegraph wires will all be simultaneously cut, and their guns spiked along the Va. side. If information of such character reaches you from the proper source we trust immediate reliance will be placed.

[About Aug. 5]

There are 45.000 on Va. side 15.000 around this City[,] to wit[:] Up the river above Chain Bridge[,] at Tennallytown[,] Bladensburg — across Anacostia Branch & commanding every approach to the City. If McClellan's [sic] can be permitted to prepare he expects to surprise you but now [he] is preparing against one. Look out for mas[ked] batteries wherever you go. Their reliance this time is on abundance of artillery — which they have disposed formidably. At proper time an effort will be made here to cut their telegraph wires and if possible to spike their guns wherever they are left unmanned. A line of daily communication is now open through Alexandria. Send couriers [three words unreadable] facilities en-route & where these dispatches enter yr lines below Alex [three or four words unreadable] we will endeavor [word or words unreadable] you.

Friday Aug. 9th 3 P.M.

During the present [week] movements of troops and ordnance [?am]munition has been active. Every approach to the Capitol [has] been and is being fortified. Great reliance is placed in their future or present plan of battle, to wit, plenty of artillery and cavalry. They are not entirely fortified now but add [m]uch to their strength and power of resistance. . . . there are an [sic] 10.000 protecting this city. Every arrival and departure every movement in fact has been noted by eye witnesses placed at the out and inlets for such purpose. . . . the [news]papers do still chronicle the movements correctly as have been verified by means mentioned above. . . . Reconn[aissance of] yr lines may prove much.

The ellipsis points indicate passages, perhaps as long as fifteen or twenty words, where the reassembly of torn pages was too incorrect to make sense. Note that much of the last dispatch is repeated in the following one, written later the same day. Presumably it is a rewrite and the earlier version was not sent.

9-8-61 evening

During present week, movements of troops [and] munitions have been very active. Every approach to the Capitol is being [d]aily strengthened and will soon offer powerful resistance [one word missing] at and above Chain Bridge to the Seneca Dam and [F]erry. The rail-road to Balt. and the other side of Anacostia Branch are being occupied by troops and their [p]roportion of artillery. Masked batteries are commanding [th]e approaches from country. . . . Every reason is had to believe that their [*sic*] are such batteries throughout their whole line of the fortifications from Alexandria to Chain Bridge. It is said also that there are such on 7th St. Road and Bladensburg road leading down to city. In Tennalytown vicinity some heavy guns have been taken since yesterday morning. It is quietly reported that many of their guns are rifled. McClellan is vigilant and [words missing] on a surprise [words missing] among the many p[oin]ts of attack [words missing] There is little or no boasting this time and [l]imited reinforcements.

In the next dispatch Mrs. Greenhow made two drafts and saved the earlier one as her retained copy. She crossed out from the final draft the words "Activity pervades McClellan's forces" and "McClellan's movements indicate apprehension of an attack"; presumably these statements were omitted from the copy sent to Jordan.

10 Aug. 1861

McDowell moved towards Fairfax yesterday at 9 A.M. with 20.000 men. Every order is being executed without attracting attention. Activity pervades McClellan's forces. It is reliably stated that 45.000 occupy the Va. side and 15.000 the approaches from the District side to the city. McClellan's movements indicate apprehension of an attack. Banks has 35,000 men more or less so the reliable rumors tell say [*sic*]. It is doubt[less] [that they] have a combined force of 100.0[oo] [one or two words missing] above mentioned McClellan [one or two words missing].

[no date]

On the 16th an order was given at War Department for the purchase of 80 [one word undecipherable]. A military road is opened from Tenleytown round by Blairs to Bladensburg. Strong works with heavy guns, but they forget the fortifications of Paris. Since sixteenth [five words unreadable] they cant raise them. I am watching the Habeas Corpus Case as they will lose largely by it. Only 50 millions of the loan is available. The plan is now masterly inactivity. I will in a day or so send drawings of the Northern defences of the city. You give me no instructions and not being a military man I can only trust to my untutored judgment as to what is of value. All that I sent is reliable. All efforts are being made to raise an army. Peter [?Jornan] near Laurel Md. General Hiram Walbridge are spies. One regiment with ambulances passed over Long Bridge Saturday night and Battery to-day. Great deal of ordnance stores, some heavy pieces. This goes by safe hands but do not talk with any one about news from here as the birds of the air bring back. But I wish I could see you as I know much that a letter cannot give. Give me some instructions. You know that my soul is in the cause and that I would venture much at the same [*sic*]. An earnest of this discretion but be in the past [*sic*]. Tell Beauregard that in my imagination he takes place of the Cid.

Always yours
R. G.

21st [August]

No more troops have arrived. Great activity and anxiety here, and the whole strength concentrating around Washington, and the cry "the Capital in danger" renewed. I do not give much heed to the rumors of Banks command arriving here, altho he has advanced this way. Troops are thrown into Md. 1400 of Sickles brigade are at Centreville Md., and batteries are being erected all around the city. The chief reliance is now in heavy artillery, of which very large amt. is being accumulated. Wilson told me last night, that they had [number undecipherable] pieces, and over [number undecipherable] and fifty guns of heavy calibre, — confirmed by my scouts. Wilson goes on McClelland's staff to-day as aid and adviser. I regret this, as I know that more vigor and discipline will be infused. He brings unflinching will and determination, and has more practical good sense as to the means of disciplining and satisfying the discontented, than any one, and in my opinion will effect a great deal. The only equivalent to us, is the greater access to the secrets of the Cabinet and War Office. He thinks that there is no present idea of attacking [?Washington], and that it is only a feint to cover movements in W. [?Va.]. In spite, however, troops are moving and ordnance stores also. They feel that something must be done to stem the reaction at the North. As I write, intense [?exertions], in trains in large numbers wind north of the city. Griffin's Battery is ready to start, & officers moving rapidly to & fro. I pray you write and give instructions. On the subject of organization much can be done. Also tell me what to send you, as I know nothing from you of your wishes, and I may be wasting means in sending you what is of no use. 300 cavalry came from Philadelphia Saturday. [?90] on 18th towards Eastern Branch Potomac Bridge. From reliable information received last night at Fort McHenry, [number undecipherable] & sixty [?Lions] are in irons, disaffected. Gen. Porter, the Provos[t] Marshal, to-day sent his wife & child away, in anticipation of attack. Give me instructions.

December 26

In a day or two 1,200 cavalry supported by four batteries of artillery will cross the river above to get behind Manassas and cut off railroad and other communications with our army whilst an attack is made in front. For God's sake heed this. It is positive. They are obliged to move or give up. They find me a hard bargain and I shall be I think released in a few days without condition, but to go South. A confidential member of McClellan's staff came to see me and tell me that my case should form an exception and I only want to gain time. All my plans are nearly completed.

APPENDIX 5

· · · · · · · · · · ·

Strother's Rejected Warning
of the Enemy's Stolen March

How reliable is David Hunter Strother's claim that he provided timely warning that Johnston's army was en route from Winchester to Manassas? He is the only source of the story, and he was not unbiased. Long before writing his 1866 account in *Harper's New Monthly Magazine* he had acquired a strong dislike of Fitz John Porter, the dominant figure in Patterson's headquarters.[1] Another reason for doubt is the fact that the story as Strother published it in 1866 is only partly supported by the version of the incident recorded in his 1861 diary. The diary reports his receiving the information on Johnston's departure, but headquarters' rejection of the report appears only in the published version.

However, those are the only reasons anyone might question Strother's story. And the incompleteness of the diary entry is in keeping with his practice of entering in the diary only as much information as he would need to refresh his recollection on the day when he would be writing about it for publication.[2] Another reason for the difference between the two versions is the "hindsight factor": at the time Strother received the information on Johnston's departure and recorded it in his diary, the Valley brigades' extremely important role in the Bull Run battle was unknowable. But knowing that fact in 1866 would have made the rejection of his information in 1861 more than unfortunate; now it could be seen as the tragic mistake that it actually was.

The story suffers from no improbabilities, large or small. Johnston's march, especially the evacuation of Winchester and the fording of the Shenandoah River, would have been observed by hundreds of citizens, including Union sympathizers, some of whom would have felt impelled to deliver the news to the nearby Federals. Stuart's cavalry screen on the 18th, which would have blocked the roads leading out of Winchester, had been pulled in at dark, and for anyone who knew the local roads, the Federal headquarters at Charlestown even at nighttime was not a hard ride from Winchester and the other Valley points on Johnston's route.

More significant than those points — conclusive, in fact — is the simple fact of Strother's recording in his diary that he received the information on the enemy's departure. No matter how much one may distrust his 1866 expansions on the diary, the diary itself is contemporary evidence. Either it is truthful or Strother deliberately invented the story and placed it in the diary for future use as documentation of a claim he would publish someday — a literary crime that is unthinkable in Strother's case. In order to believe that headquarters' rejection of the information was Strother's 1866 invention, one must also believe that on July 19, 1861, he and Captain Simpson could have kept the information to themselves when it was of such obvious importance to McDowell. And we are not dependent solely on the 1866 account for the fact of the rejection; Patterson did not telegraph the news to Scott until Johnston's troops had been en route to Manassas for two days, and the source he credited for the information was a walk-in civilian, not his cavalry, as one would suppose.

Both the diary and the published version lack an important detail — the identity of the person or persons who supplied the precious information. Strother's omission of that interesting point must have been deliberate; it would protect his informants in case the diary, which was to travel with him for the rest of his military service, fell into Confederate hands. This precaution was still necessary in 1866 and for some years thereafter. Thus we have a spy story without a hero, which may explain why it has remained untold for so long.

APPENDIX 6

. . . .

The McClellan-Pinkerton
Estimates of Confederate Numbers

Although Lincoln and his advisers left little record of their attitude toward McClellan's claims of being outnumbered, there is no doubt that they were properly skeptical. Treasury Secretary Salmon P. Chase, on a visit to the Peninsula in May 1862, wrote, "My conviction is clear . . . that McClellan has a force which, properly handled, is vastly superior to any that can be brought against him." Chase was speaking only for himself, but an indication of the whole cabinet's view appears in Navy Secretary Gideon Welles's diary. Writing late in August 1862, a time when Lee was trouncing Pope a scant thirty miles from Washington, Welles mentioned the possibility "that we overrate our own strength and underestimate the Rebels'" and added, "This has been the talk of McClellan, which none of us have believed."

Lincoln indicated strong skepticism when he told an Illinois friend, Senator Orville H. Browning, that if he sent McClellan 100,000 reinforcements, McClellan would promise to take Richmond the next day, but when that day came he would claim that the Rebels had 400,000 men. And Lincoln certainly had McClellan in mind when he said that the South must have a million men in its army, because he had half a million in his own army and each of his generals claimed to be opposed by twice his own number.[1]

Another doubter would have been Stanton, who had seen, while assisting McClellan in writing his October 1861 situation summary, how irresponsible the general's estimating could be. He saw McClellan report enemy strength at 150,000, a figure that either was invented or was produced by manipulating strength figures for individual components of Johnston's army in such a way as to yield the highest possible sum. Figures of different levels of reliability, none of them very high, were mingled; the resultant sum was even less accurate than the most unreliable one of the group. Stanton was not in the cabinet at that time; whether or not he later told his cabinet fellows about his acquaintance with McClellan's estimating methods, that experience would have influenced his own evaluation of the general's later statements about enemy numbers.[2]

Halleck, despite his experience with McClellan's vacillating statements of enemy strength, apparently supported his views in a limited way. It was Halleck who at the time of Second Bull Run had aroused Welles's fear that Washington might be threatened, and that the Federals might be overrating their own strength and underrating that of the Rebels. During his visit with McClellan on the Peninsula, Halleck evidently had been quite impressed by the confidence that his host's subordinate generals had in the 200,000 total McClellan was giving Lee, though in the report he wrote to Stanton on his return he admitted he had not had time to learn how that estimate had been computed.[3]

Thus McClellan had his doubters, but he does not seem to have ever been asked to defend his claims. Such a request would have quickly exposed the weakness of his evidence, probably its total absence in some cases. He could not even have responded by forwarding one of Pinkerton's estimates, which for almost a year were embarrassingly lower than his own.

The reason there was no official challenge of McClellan's estimates could be partly the fact that in 1861 and 1862 his figures were not entirely outside the bounds of reason. As pointed out in the text, the Confederates were putting a much higher percentage of their men of military age into their army and navy than the Federals were. And their interior lines enabled them to concentrate at endangered points.

Another factor that saved McClellan from having to defend his estimates was his strained relations with his superiors. Evidently they regarded his exaggerations as an effrontery that was easier to live with than to resolve. Whatever they may have believed the comparative strengths of his army and the enemy's to be, they spared for his grand campaign a force averaging only around 100,000. That is a good indicator of how they rated McClellan's claims of being opposed by forces much larger.

Even if the administration leaders had wanted to believe McClellan's jeremiads about enemy numbers, the anti-McClellan and anti-administration newspapers would not have allowed them that comfort. To the reports of Quaker guns left behind in Johnston's lines at Centreville in March, journalists added their own disconcertingly low estimates of the number of troops who had occupied the abandoned huts. Of course the correspondents with the army on the Peninsula had their own ideas about enemy strength; one made the good estimate of 100,000, though some agreed with McClellan that he was outnumbered.[4]

· ·   · ·   · ·

A strong disagreement with McClellan's claims of enemy numbers came from an officer who was extremely well acquainted with troop numbers in the Federal armies — Quartermaster General Montgomery C. Meigs, who accompanied Halleck on his Peninsula visit. Halleck's apparent acquiescence in the 200,000 figure so confidently claimed by McClellan and his generals evidently caused Meigs great anguish, for on returning to Washington he set to work to dispute that estimate. Using reports of the Seven Days battles appearing in just two days' issues of two Southern newspapers, he compiled a list of Confederate regiments showing their brigade assignments.

By extrapolating from some highly doubtful data in one of the papers, Meigs placed Lee's total strength at 105,000, an overestimate only a fifth as great as McClellan's. This lucky near-hit has been admired by some historians as a piece of keen intelligence work; the fact that Meigs's list of regiments and brigade assignments was badly incomplete and laden with error has gone unnoticed. But Meigs's purpose was not to provide his chiefs with operational intelligence; it was merely to show how much could be done with so little source material. Lest they fail to get the point, he wrote, "Permit me to suggest that a careful comparison of the notices which appear in the newspapers, lists of prisoners of war, and deserters, if made by an intelligent, educated man, would soon give us a tolerably correct idea of the force opposing us. If this has ever been done in this part of the country there is, I fear, reason to believe that it has been done by incompetent or unfaithful hands."[5]

Meigs's virulence seems to be directed against Pinkerton rather than McClellan; evidently he did not know that the exaggerations of Confederate numbers that reached the War Department were McClellan's, not Pinkerton's. He had no way of knowing that by midsummer of 1862 Pinkerton had done rather well at the game Meigs was playing, that of listing Confederate regiments and brigades. (It will be recalled that the completeness of Pinkerton's listing of all of the 178 regiments in Lee's army was a fact that Pinkerton himself was unaware of.)

There were disbelievers in McClellan's army, though his chiefs in Washington were not exposed to their heresies. Francis W. Palfrey, a colonel badly wounded at Antietam, wrote home at that time that "we outnumber the enemy" and years later recorded a fully developed skepticism: "it is impossible to believe that McClellan believed . . . the Confederates had the force he attributed to them." General Jacob Cox, who had encountered McClellan's displeasure early in the war, wrote long afterward, "The fiction as to the strength of Lee's forces is the most remarkable in the history of modern wars. Whether McClellan was the victim or the accomplice of the inventions of his 'secret service,' we cannot tell. It is almost incredible that he should be deceived, except willingly."[6]

Meigs suspected "incompetent or unfaithful hands"; Cox saw possible complicity between McClellan and his "secret service"; various historians have found McClellan duplicitous.[7] And Civil War history has its conspiracy-minded school of writers. Thus the ingredients exist for a subgenre of literature on the theme of a McClellan-Pinkerton collusion. This literature would have come into being years ago if Pinkerton's November 1861 reminder to McClellan that enemy estimates were to be "made large" did not escape notice by being buried in one of Pinkerton's wordy, flatulent reports.

.. .. ..

The arguments that would support a theory of estimating aimed at prying more men and more time out of an unsympathetic administration are worth examining. The first one is the possibility of disingenuousness in McClellan's and Pinkerton's understanding that the estimates would be "made large"; perhaps it was with tongue in cheek that they told themselves the overestimating was only for safety's sake. Another reason is the extravagance of the figures, especially those from McClellan's pen. A third reason for suspecting the sincerity of the estimates is Pinkerton's changes in estimating method; by being progressively less scientific, he gives every appearance not of an effort to improve his statistical faculty but of a struggle to produce ever higher figures. Even his basically scientific first method, using the count of regiments as the basis of calculation, had ample room for padding in its generous regimental averages (700 for infantry, 600 for cavalry) and its uncritical acceptance of additional regiments on weak evidence. His next method, more elastic, yielded the highly inflated "medium estimate," which shared attention with a "summary of general estimates"; both were averages of gross figures based on rumor and unofficial guesswork. Next the general estimates elbowed the less bloated medium estimates out of existence. Finally they too failed to satisfy, and a phantom army of unstated numbers was added to the host under Lee's command.

Still another indication that these estimates were a sham is McClellan's willingness to undertake a campaign that would uncover Washington and also maximize the disadvantage that the Confederates' interior lines imposed on him. This incongruity was especially evident when he proposed to Halleck that he resume the Richmond campaign by attacking with 120,000, or even 110,000, an entrenched enemy that he insisted numbered 200,000. But the sharpest indication that he had never believed his own estimates is his sudden desire to attack when the enemy at Richmond was reported to be 36,000, not long after he had declared they numbered 200,000. As he would overstate Confederate numbers in order to gain more men and more time, so he would underestimate them in order to save his grand campaign.

The integrity of Pinkerton's estimates is thrown into question by the performance of Hooker's intelligence bureau. Although that was a much more complete intelligence service than Pinkerton's, its main sources of information on enemy strength were the same — prisoners, deserters, and refugees. And it quickly produced a remarkably accurate estimate of Confederate numbers. Pinkerton's successor achieved accuracy by employing a judicious troops-per-regiment average and greater discrimination in accepting the presence of newly reported regiments and brigades.

Against this evidence of fraud in the McClellan-Pinkerton estimates must be matched a set of indications that the two men really believed their overestimates. Even Pinkerton's written reminder to McClellan about the figure padding can be interpreted as indicating a basic honesty: that he would put such suggestive words in writing indicates that he saw nothing sinister in their understanding about a safety allowance. Neither, apparently, did McClellan, for he allowed that statement to survive in his papers, and also the explanation of the safety allowance that he had considered including in his final report. It is possible, though, that if he had lived to finish his memoirs, he would have destroyed those items, and many others.

The safety allowance was not McClellan's and Pinkerton's only justification for their generous estimates. The inflated figures that Rebel soldiers and officers gave were not always pure fustian; in many if not most cases they represented actual beliefs or sincere "best guesses." But soldiers tended to be misinformed as to the size of their own regiments. The regimental averages of 700 for infantry and 600 for cavalry that Pinkerton used were reasonable ones for the Federals, as no one knew better than Quartermaster General Meigs, who used 700 for the Confederates in making his estimate of 105,000. The Confederates' actual regimental average at this period was about 500, somewhat higher than might be supposed.[8] And the Confederates' mobilization policy may have been a factor in the tendency to overrate their numbers; Northerners and foreign-born Southerners who deserted to the Federals after being forced into the Confederate army, although not very numerous, constituted a sizable fraction of the number of Southern soldiers coming to Pinkerton's attention, and thus would have accounted for some of his generosity with enemy numbers.[9]

McClellan's postwar calculation of Confederate casualties (discussed below) is consistent with his wartime estimates of the enemy's total strength. As this calculation probably was made only for his own enlightenment, it attests that the figures he claimed in wartime represented his actual beliefs.

These persuasive points are merely supplementary to the evidence given in chapter 9 that McClellan really believed he was seriously outnumbered: his self-defeating caution in the Maryland campaign and the whole body of his letters to his wife. Those two points are conclusive: McClellan did not just *believe* he was badly outnumbered; he *knew* it. It was an obsession, a fixation. Its beginning is visible in his first days in Washington, when he adopted the view that the Confederates had 100,000 men poised to strike his hapless regiments. As that figure could not have been supported by any fact-gathering worthy of the credit he attached to it, its basis must have been more emotional than intellectual. The error fed on itself; once he got it into his head that he was heavily outnumbered, the outnumbering force got bigger and bigger. And as it was his soldierly duty not to be surprised by numbers he had failed to count, the inflated figures became solemn truth in his mind.

The strongest reason for suspecting fraud in his estimates is his acceptance of an underestimate, the report in August 1862 that Richmond's defenders had been reduced to 36,000, less than a fifth of the number he had been claiming. However, irrationality is much likelier than duplicity as a cause of so abrupt an about-face.

The depth of Pinkerton's belief in the estimates is harder to gauge. In his case the controlling character trait was not obsessiveness but a personal loyalty for which there is no other name than sycophancy. Pinkerton invited this accusation by declaring in his memoirs his unquestionably sincere admiration and affection for McClellan. He considered himself to be serving McClellan personally rather than the government.[10] The necessity that mothered Pinkerton's statistical inventions was McClellan's conviction of being outnumbered. But sycophancy does not necessarily imply insincerity; evidently Pinkerton honestly absorbed his chief's conviction.

. .   . .   . .

McClellan's views of enemy numbers remained unchanged for some years. This is shown by a set of notes he made after the war in calculating losses on both sides in all the major battles in the eastern theater. His purpose was to establish, at least to his own satisfaction, that his management of the army had produced casualty rates more favorable to the Federals than those suffered under Burnside, Pope, Hooker, Meade, and Grant. For the battles of South Mountain and Antietam he placed Confederate casualties at 30,242; the true count was approximately 12,600.[11] The 30,242 figure is three quarters of the number Lee had on the field; but McClellan's casualty count seemed reasonable enough to him since he had estimated enemy strength at 120,000 during the campaign and 97,445 in his after-action report. For the battles on the Peninsula, however, his estimate of Confederate losses was conservative — 33,045, compared to an actual total of 30,450.[12]

Confederate strength returns in the *Official Records*, which appeared a few years before McClellan's death in 1885, finally shook his belief in the superiority of the enemy's numbers. In his memoirs, after giving his own effective strength as 56,680 on August 31, 1861, he wrote, "This is just about the number reported by the Confederates as composing Johnston's command."[13] The Confederate return for that month, although incomplete, covers enough of Johnston's army to show that McClellan was still overestimating by a considerable amount, but he had come down a long way from the 100,000 and more he had insisted on at the time.

His awareness of his wartime exaggerations is also shown by his omission of the more flagrant of them from his memoirs. Evidently he intended to avoid repeating his old errors without expressly correcting them. But in preparing the book for posthumous publication, his literary executor defeated this attempt at reasonableness by adding wartime documents that included some of McClellan's claims of enemy strength — years after many readers had come to know better.[14]

Pinkerton as a memoirist revealed more faith in those inflated estimates than did his ex-chief. Using his June 26, 1862, estimate as an example, he was "confident" that its 180,000 figure "did not exceed the actual strength of the rebels at that time." He wavered on one point, giving the enemy 50,000 at Antietam — a remarkable drop for September 1862 from the June figure he was still defending.[15] That figure defied history to prove him wrong. Wrong he was, but the very rashness of his declaration shows that he strongly believed it.

.. .. ..

Pinkerton's final success in detailing the composition and organization of the Army of Northern Virginia suggests that if he had had a free hand to get the facts about enemy numbers, independent of his chief's preconceptions, he would be known today as a successful intelligence officer. Instead he presents to history the sorry picture of a famous investigator yielding his judgment to that of his erratic chief, and still not managing to produce estimates the chief would use.

As for McClellan, if his estimates had been completely corrupt — if he had had a fairly correct idea of enemy numbers but concealed it from his superiors — he might have handled his army aggressively enough to score a smashing victory on the Peninsula or, more probably, in Maryland. In the same way that McClellan's obsession made Pinkerton a failure in the eyes of posterity, it ruined his own chance to go down in history as the general who won the war.

Appendix 7

. . . .

Pleasonton's Role in the Intelligence That
Started Hooker in Pursuit of Lee

The story of the intelligence that persuaded Hooker to leave the Rappahannock and pursue the Confederates' northward advance in June 1863 (chapter 19) conflicts at every point with the long accepted version of those
events, which credits General Pleasonton's cavalry with the discovery that
the enemy was assembling at Culpeper for the march that ended at Gettysburg.

The reconnaissance-in-force story. These differences begin with the traditional
view that the battle of Brandy Station resulted from a reconnaissance to
discover what the Rebels were doing out in Culpeper County, where their
cavalry had been based for some time. *The West Point Atlas of American Wars*
says, "Hooker ordered Pleasonton (now commanding the Cavalry Corps)
on a reconnaissance toward Culpeper." Bruce Catton's version is that
"[R]umors of . . . Confederate movement reached camp, and Hooker sent
his cavalry up the Rappahannock under orders to cross over and, if possible,
see what the rebels thought they were up to." Kenneth P. Williams writes,
"Pleasonton had been directed to . . . find out what was going on in the vicinity of Culpeper." These and other authorities have assured the survival of the
story. It was thoroughly refuted in Edwin B. Coddington's 1968 book, *The
Gettysburg Campaign,* but Coddington's correction has not taken root, since
more recent Gettysburg studies have concentrated on the battle proper, to
the exclusion of the armies' movements and other preliminary actions; and
Coddington's treatment of the case lacks the intelligence background of
those preliminaries, to replace the Pleasonton story he refutes.[1]

The most important source for the standard view is the report of the
congressional Joint Committee on the Conduct of the War, which heard
General Pleasonton testify that he had been directed to make a reconnaissance "to see whether General Lee's army was moving in force up the valley."
In *Battles and Leaders of the Civil War* General Henry J. Hunt says that Hooker
"ordered Pleasonton to beat up Stuart's camps at Culpeper, and get information as to the enemy's position and proposed movements." And the *Official*

Records can even be cited if one wishes to stretch a point; two somewhat gratuitous references to Pleasonton's expedition as a reconnaissance appear in a day-by-day summary of the Union army's movements in the Gettysburg campaign, compiled by the *OR* editorial staff.[2] None of these, even the references in the *Official Records,* is contemporary. (Williams does cite a contemporary source, but it is a dispatch that says nothing about information-gathering in connection with the expedition.)

In the records for June 6–9, 1863, are numerous dispatches and orders that show beyond question that Hooker's purpose, and Pleasonton's, was simply to whip Stuart. The letter carrying Hooker's instructions to Pleasonton declared that the object of the expedition would be "to disperse and destroy the rebel force assembled in the vicinity of Culpeper, and to destroy his trains and supplies of all descriptions to the utmost of your ability." Pleasonton was told further, "If you should succeed in routing the enemy, the general [Hooker] desires that you will follow him vigorously as far as it may be to our advantage to do so."[3]

Hooker's dispatches to other correspondents on the subject are scarcely less explicit. To Halleck he wrote, "As the accumulation of the heavy rebel force of cavalry about Culpeper may mean mischief, I am determined, if practicable, to break it up in its incipiency. . . . It is my intention to attack them in their camps." To Meade, whose corps occupied positions that required being ready to cooperate with Pleasonton, Butterfield described the cavalry project as "an attack on Culpeper." Although Hooker often called on Pleasonton to provide information, nowhere in the mass of correspondence relating to preparations for the attack is the procurement of information mentioned as even a secondary purpose. Hooker was confident that he knew what forces were about Culpeper. And Pleasonton's purpose was quite in accord with his chief's; he wrote headquarters that "Culpeper County is the best grazing in Virginia. . . . Its loss will be a great one to rebels."[4] Heading off Stuart's expected raid, the idea that gave rise to Pleasonton's attack, was now superseded by a more ambitious purpose, Federal occupation of Culpeper County.

The reconnaissance-in-force story was roundly attacked by John Mosby. Still driven by the curiosity and persistence that made him an arm of Lee's intelligence "service," Mosby visited the War Department in the 1880s and examined war records, including most of the correspondence relating to Brandy Station that has been used in the present study. Mosby lectured often and wrote copiously in his later years, largely in opposition to prevalent beliefs about various aspects of the war. So strong was his compulsion to be a lone wolf, however, that his views, seemingly warped, fell into disrepute.[5]

What enemy papers did Pleasonton capture, and what did they reveal? His reports immediately after the cavalry battle contained three items of intelligence: Stuart now had 12,000 troops; his grand raid, so long expected by the Federals, had been scheduled to start the day after the Federal cavalry attacked; and the Confederates had an infantry force at Culpeper. There was visual evidence of the presence of infantry; a small, and unidentified, body of enemy foot soldiers had "attacked Gregg's people," on Pleasonton's left wing.[6] It was the other two findings that Pleasonton credited to captured papers. Although he repeatedly referred to these captures, he never admitted that the document revealing the expected raid was not an official one; it was a soldier's letter; thus Pleasonton's readers were left to assume that the captured papers were from Stuart's headquarters records that he falsely claimed he had acquired.

Only five captured papers have turned up, and Pleasonton is known to have seen only three of them. Here is a description of their contents:

1. One gives the order of march for the regiments of Brigadier General W. E. ("Grumble") Jones's Valley brigade in Stuart's review of June 8. Jones had previously been reported joining his force to Stuart's; here was firm evidence that he had arrived — valuable intelligence, but showing nothing about impending movements of Stuart or Lee.

2. Another official item was a June 8 "field return" of Stuart's horse artillery, commanded by Major R. F. Beckham. This was excellent evidence of Beckham's strength (in men and horses, though not in guns), but it too was a nullity as to Confederate plans.

3. A third official paper was a two-sentence order dated June 6 from Stuart's adjutant, Major H. B. McClellan, directing Major Beckham to have his artillerymen strike camp and be "ready to march at 15 minutes notice." This found its way to Sharpe's files without any indication that Pleasonton had seen it. It shows that three days before the cavalry battle Stuart's units, or some of them, had been on the verge of moving. That move could have been a mere shifting about of cavalry units in Culpeper (and possibly adjacent counties), already completed by the time of the capture. If Pleasonton had seen this paper, he would have viewed it as somehow connected with the expected raid, but it did not support his claim of having acquired evidence of a movement by Stuart on June 9.

4. The captures included a letter in which "Bill," an artilleryman, told his father, "I think Stuart is preparing to make a raid into the enemies country, and when it comes, it will be something grand, for he has now about twelve thousand Cavalry at this point where he only had about four thousand before." That Bill was retailing rumors is shown by his next paragraph: "Stuart is to be made Lieut Genl and Hampton & Fitz Hugh Lee are to be made Maj Genls" — promotions that were imaginary. There was no statement of authority for the prediction of a cavalry raid other than the introductory phrase "I think." There also was no mention of a date for the raid to begin; as this is the only captured "document" revealing plans for a cavalry raid that Pleasonton is known to have seen, we are led to infer that he supplied the beginning date himself.

The Federals' original reports of a forthcoming cavalry raid had been based on camp gossip. Now Pleasonton chose to regard those reports as confirmed by Bill's letter — the same camp gossip in written form.

5. A second letter was from another member of Stuart's horse artillery who was looking forward to going on a raid. The basis of his belief was no more "official" than Bill's: "I expect from the preparations that is being made that we are going to make a Grand raid towards the Potomac as soon as the valley

is cleared." He gave the same 12,000 figure for Stuart's total strength — an indication of a common source for the rumors of a raid. From this writer's reference to clearing the Shenandoah Valley it could be concluded that some of Lee's infantry would have a part in the forthcoming raid; he added, almost as an afterthought, "Longstreet's division passed us on Saturday" (June 6). Pleasonton's men had briefly encountered infantry in the cavalry battle; now here was additional evidence of infantry, but it raises a question as to how much reliance could be placed on troop identifications by a soldier who evidently had not caught up with the fact, six months old, that Longstreet now headed a corps. Sharpe's bureau had known for some weeks that Hood's division was in the Gordonsville area; this reference to a Longstreet unit at Culpeper was additional evidence, however slight, of a forthcoming general movement. Among several indications that Pleasonton did not receive this letter is the fact that it was printed in the *New York Times* on June 11 and the *Baltimore Sun* the next day; as McEntee had observed, Pleasonton's officers had no appreciation of the intelligence value of captured papers, and one of them had obligingly given this prize to the press instead of to cavalry headquarters.[7]

How did the story that Pleasonton discovered the movement of Lee's whole army originate? William Swinton, who wrote in 1866 and revised in 1882 a much quoted history of the Army of the Potomac, using many documents before their appearance in the *Official Records,* stated that the fight at Brandy Station uncovered "Lee's presence at Culpepper and his design of invasion, disclosures of both of which facts were found in captured correspondence." Swinton's source for this misstatement probably was the claims Pleasonton made to the Committee on the Conduct of the War. His book, the first comprehensive history of the Army of the Potomac, was widely read; that was enough to launch the story into the Civil War literature.[8]

Although the error originated in Pleasonton's false claims, one quite respectable source tends to confirm his story. General Butterfield many months later told the congressional committee, "On the 11th and 12th of June positive information came of the movement of the head of Lee's column through Sperryville." He said that this information brought about Hooker's decision to move the army, and that its source was General Pleasonton at Rappahannock Station.[9] Since Butterfield was partly mistaken as to the dates, and as Pleasonton's location except during the cavalry battle was at Warrenton Junction, Butterfield's memory may have been faulty also as to the source of the information. Another explanation, however, carries more weight. Butterfield had been intimately associated with Sharpe, not only as his tentmate but as the initial recipient of most of the colonel's reports. When he appeared before the committee, he had long been detached from the Army of the Potomac, but he would have been acutely aware that Sharpe and his men were still engaged with the enemy, some of them perhaps within the Confederate lines. This committee of politicians not entirely sympathetic with the administration was a very risky forum for revealing intelligence secrets. The inference is inescapable that Butterfield, no admirer of Pleasonton, in crediting him with the intelligence that disclosed the Confederates' departure northward, was using the cavalry as a cover to protect the security of Sharpe's operation and his men.

What then was Pleasonton's contribution to the intelligence that started Hooker's army in pursuit? His attack on Stuart yielded the first certain knowledge of the presence of infantry in Culpeper. When he struck, Lee, with all of Ewell's corps and two thirds of Longstreet's to draw upon, moved Rodes's and McLaws's divisions into position to support Stuart if necessary. In the event, less than a brigade of that force was exposed to Federal view. Ewell reported only that he found the enemy retiring; Rodes said his troops "did not get in reach of the enemy." Brigadier General Junius Daniel, commanding Rodes's forward brigade, reported that he threw out skirmishers and the enemy retired before them, and that he kept the rest of his force hidden.

General Gregg, commanding the Federal division on that part of the field, described this non-contact in yet another way: seeing railroad cars loaded with infantry approaching from Culpeper, he sent a party to "obstruct the raid," a move that succeeded brilliantly when his men found a switch and reversed it, diverting the train from a path aimed directly at Gregg's position. Assuredly this was a very limited contact. But Pleasonton would have none of this negative thinking; he wrote that "We [encountered] infantry yesterday, both mounted and on foot. Those mounted are armed with rifles made at Fayetteville [North Carolina], and marked C.S.A. Some were captured. Infantry at Brandy Station jumped from the cars, and attacked Gregg's [division]. . . . I am satisfied the enemy has a strong infantry force at Culpeper." This "eyeball evidence" was unmistakable, though the infantry force, as far as Pleasonton could know, might have been only large enough to serve as support for some cavalry project. And as we have previously seen, Pleasonton's report of the enemy's possession of mounted infantry was a foolish mistake; because of the Confederacy's shortage of horses, any mounts capable of military service would have been turned over to the cavalry.[10]

The remainder of Pleasonton's intelligence contribution consisted of his and his officers' interrogation of prisoners, deserters, and contrabands, which produced on June 10 and 11 a confusing picture of the Army of Northern Virginia's positions at Culpeper and Fredericksburg. This performance improved on the two following days, but the cavalry officers' lack of skill in examining these sources was basically incurable. It was a price Pleasonton paid for allowing his staff to resist McEntee's efforts instead of availing themselves of his knowledge.[11]

In fairness to General Pleasonton it should be noted that he had not joined the army to serve as an intelligence officer, and that it was under his vigorous leadership that the Federal cavalry learned they could match sabers with the proud horsemen of the Confederacy. One of the side effects of his battle with Stuart was the backwash in which Charley Wright and his fellow contraband crossed the Rappahannock. The freeing of these two crucial sources of intelligence is to be credited to the bold cavalry operations of General Pleasonton — one officer of whom it can be said that his sword was mightier than his pen.

APPENDIX 8

· · · · · · · · · · ·

Lee's Crossing of the Potomac
en Route to Pennsylvania

Another "old, gray-headed error," like the acclaim bestowed on General Pleasonton as the discoverer of the Confederates' northward advance in June 1863, afflicts history's treatment of the Confederates' crossing of the Potomac in that same advance. The date usually given for the crossing of Lee's main body, June 24, is an error that historians have borrowed from one another for several generations. The matter is of some importance here because, if that date is accepted, General Hooker's crossing loses the remarkable (though accidental) timeliness with which it is credited in chapter 21.

In giving the 24th as the date of Lee's crossing, historians make the same mistake that Federal intelligence made on the basis of an impressive accumulation of reports. That misinformation led to Hooker's decision to cross.

He put his army over the river on June 25 and 26,[1] the same days Lee's rear element, Longstreet's corps, crossed, and only one day after the June 24–25 crossing of the other half of the Confederate main body, Hill's corps.[2] Thus we see that perhaps as little as one quarter of the combined strength of the two Confederate corps was in Maryland on June 24, the day when most accounts have placed them both there.

The origin of the mistake is obscure. In what may be its earliest occurrence, in William Swinton's *Campaigns of the Army of the Potomac* (1866 and 1882), the date of Lee's crossing was not an unqualified June 24. Swinton wrote, "The corps of Longstreet and Hill made the passage of the Potomac at Williamsport and Shepherdstown on the 24th and 25th." General Henry J. Hunt gave the same dates in *Battles and Leaders of the Civil War* (1884) but accompanied his article with a map showing Longstreet at Hagerstown and Hill a few miles to the south on June 24. Publication of the Gettysburg volume of the *Official Records* in 1889 made the correct dates accessible, but when Matthew F. Steele published his *American Campaigns* under official auspices in 1909 he simply reproduced Hunt's maps without corrections.

The error was carried into the modern era by the usually careful Kenneth P. Williams, who in 1950 included in *Lincoln Finds a General* a map showing

Longstreet near Hagerstown and Hill at Boonsboro on June 24. In *Glory Road* (1952) Bruce Catton avoided exact dates: "Hooker's army had completed its crossing [of the Potomac] only twenty-four hours after the last of Lee's army had crossed"; that would mean that the Confederate crossing was complete on June 25. Glenn Tucker's *High Tide at Gettysburg* (1958) had both Longstreet and Hill at Hagerstown on the night of the 24th; this version also erred by reversing their crossing places, putting Hill over the river at Williamsport and Longstreet at Shepherdstown, twenty miles downriver. The *West Point Atlas of American Wars* (1959) gave roughly the same positions for June 24 as Hunt's and Steele's map and introduced a new error, showing Hill trailing behind Longstreet. In *The War for the Union: The Organized War, 1863–1864*, Allan Nevins wrote (1961): "[O]n June 23–25, the remainder of the Confederate army . . . crossed the Potomac, and moved up toward Chambersburg." Edwin B. Coddington's study *The Gettysburg Campaign* (1968) listed correct crossing dates for Longstreet but gives only June 24 for Hill's crossings, though it is clear that they were not completed until the 25th. Jeffrey D. Wert's 1993 biography of Longstreet, giving more attention to movements previous to the battle than is usual in latter-day Gettysburg studies, avoided the long-standing June 24 error but had Hill's column as well as Longstreet's crossing on both the 25th and 26th.[3]

One account makes the same mistake as to the Confederates' route of crossing that Federal intelligence fell into, putting Hill's and Longstreet's 40,000-plus troops on the same, presumably quite crowded, ford near Shepherdstown. This version is found in *James Longstreet: Soldier* (1952) by Donald B. Sanger and Thomas R. Hay: "[Longstreet's corps] crossed the Potomac on June 24 in the wake of [Hill's corps], which had occupied Shepherdstown a day or so before." Since the fact that General Lee made his own passage of the Potomac at Williamsport has never been challenged, we are left to picture the Confederate commander, astride his horse Traveller, crossing the wide river in majestic solitude twenty miles upstream from his army.[4]

COMMENT ON SOURCES

This book violates one of the canons of modern works on the Civil War: it is not drawn from an enormous list of sources. The bulk of the intelligence story comes from a very small number of documentary collections. The principal ones are described below.

Files of the Bureau of Military Information. This collection, in the National Archives, contains several hundred of the bureau's retained copies of its intelligence reports, in the handwriting of George Sharpe, John Babcock, John McEntee, and their clerk (whose name never appears). The remainder of the collection consists of raw information received in the form of letters, telegrams, and reports (some written in the bureau's tent) from their agents and other sources. In cases where intelligence produced by the bureau appears in the *Official Records* of the Federal and Confederate armies, the compilers of those records would have obtained its reports from the files of the Army of the Potomac, for they did not have access to the bureau's files.

The Bureau's files were raided in 1962 by two professional document thieves. They sold a portion of their haul, 110 items, to a Washington dealer. These were quickly recovered, and another recovery was made in Detroit, where the pair was arrested in 1964. But about 75 inventory items, some of which may be bulky ones, remain unrecovered. The present writer had copied many of those items before the theft; the ones not copied may be counted as lost to history. In more recent years researchers have used the collection so recklessly that it has become thoroughly disarranged, bearing little resemblance to the inventory made at the time of its discovery in 1959. The inventory listed groups of documents (packets of items bound together or envelopes containing items relating to the same subject); many or most of these groupings have been obliterated. It is now impossible to ascertain whether there have been losses in addition to those sustained in the 1962 theft.

The Secret Service Accounts. This is a bulky record (also in the National Archives) of disbursements for "secret service" made by John Potts, chief clerk of the War Department, from the beginning of the war until 1870. Throughout the war Potts's Secret Service Fund was not subject to auditing by the Treasury Department. This was the fund from which Allan Pinkerton's and Lafayette Baker's employees were paid and Sergeant Thomas O. Harter and the Reverend I. J. Stine drew their $500 awards for spying services. But payments directly to spies were rare; nearly all of the money went to provost marshals, quartermasters, or commanding officers in the field armies and geographical departments, to be used for further disbursements that did not get into Potts's records. Some of the money went to a variety of purposes decidedly miscellaneous — and not altogether military; for example, when Secretary Seward in 1863 entertained a party of diplomats on a cruise to Norfolk, his State Department apparently had never heard of "official entertainment" expenses, for the $118.50 worth of liquor and food that the party consumed was by courtesy of John Potts and his unaudited fund. Numerous civilians, notably the governors of Ohio and Indiana, drew on the fund; so did the military governors of occupied states. When General William T. Sherman went reluctantly to Mexico City on a diplomatic errand in 1867, Potts paid his expenses. The postwar continuance of the fund was caused mainly by the investigations of peculations and frauds that the War Department ran into in paying for the war, and by the loose ends of the Lincoln assassination case (John Surratt did not go on trial until 1867).

A few disbursements were "secret" for reasons the government would not have cared to explain. Anti-administration newspapers would have had a field day had they learned of one of Potts's payments — $1342 to the Baltimore and Ohio Railroad in November 1861 for transporting to Baltimore, to vote in a hotly contested state election, 1015 Union-minded Marylanders in the Army of the Potomac or employed in federal departments. This was not simply a Republican scheme; the instigator was General John A. Dix, a Democrat of national prominence, commanding at Baltimore, and the release of the troops was approved by General Randolph B. Marcy, McClellan's father-in-law and chief of staff, whose political sympathies were Democratic.

The Secret Service Accounts have a low yield of spy histories, but by identifying recipients of money paid for intelligence activities, they furnish data leading to those activities in other records. The government got its money's worth for the funds that Potts paid out ($426,869 in the years 1862–1865; the total for other years is not known), and this history is among the beneficiaries.

Other intelligence funding was accomplished through quartermaster channels. Colonel Sharpe's spies, for example, were for record purposes employees of the quartermaster of Provost Marshal General Patrick's brigade, which served as the Army of the Potomac's provost guard. Potts evidently had a hand in keeping that quartermaster supplied with funds through regular military channels, for he became a friend whom Sharpe visited on trips to Washington, and on at least one occasion Potts made Sharpe's tent his base on a visit to the army.

The Scouts, Guides, Spies and Detectives file. Here is another National Archives collection of miscellany. In the years, at least into the 1890s, when the Adjutant General's Office was sorting out mountains of Civil War records, one Captain Kellogg (probably Sanford Cobb Kellogg) had an eye out for the needs of the future historian of Federal intelligence. Undoubtedly he also needed places to put thousands of pieces of hard-to-classify paper. He solved a small part of that problem by creating this file; around the AGO it came to be known as "Captain Kellogg's file." It is the source of most of the 4200 identifications of Federal intelligence operatives in this writer's collection. The bulk of the SGSD file consists of two types of government paper: first, army orders appointing someone to a position as detective, guide, or scout (the avoidance of the word "spy" extended to records such as these); second, vouchers or other records of payment to such employees, or to one-time informants. Again these identifications have been the means of finding records of the activities of these people in other collections.

The Turner-Baker Papers, named for Levi C. Turner, special judge advocate of the War Department, and Lafayette C. Baker, whose official title was special provost marshal of the department. Colonel (later Brigadier General) Baker regularly received his orders and instructions from Major (later Lieutenant Colonel) Turner. As Baker after September 1861 was only peripherally in the business of positive intelligence, and as Turner's concerns were about as broad as the department's own, the great bulk of this collection does not deal with intelligence about Confederate military operations; but where it does it is of considerable value. For example, lawyer Turner, as legal adviser to Secretary Stanton, himself a lawyer, evaluated claims for reimbursement of intelligence operatives on the basis of the elaborate proof of service (successful service at that) that the dollar-conscious secretary insisted upon. Thus we have an evaluation of the accuracy and the usefulness of certain intelligence reports that is both contemporary and stringent — more reliable than the historian could make alone.

But these cases are few; the collection is almost altogether a miscellany deriving from Baker's police activities — jailing peculating quartermasters, tracking smugglers, investigating people observed "hurrahing for Jeff Davis," chasing suspected enemy spies, policing the capital's dens of vice, and doing detective work connected with the Lincoln assassination conspiracy. The Turner-Baker Papers were closed to historians until the 1950s; when opened at the request of the present writer they turned out to be much less "sensitive" than their previous cautious treatment implied.

The Hooker Papers. When General Hooker was relieved of command of the Army of the Potomac, he took with him several cubic feet of headquarters files to use in writing the report of his months in command. He never found the occasion to return those papers to the War Department (or to produce the report). Years later, when the *Official Records* were being compiled, Hooker was among the numerous officers and ex-officers who lent the department wartime papers that were rightfully its own; after copying these, the *OR* editors faithfully returned them to the lenders. Hooker was quite selective in making his loan, withholding numerous items, including most or all of the intelligence reports he had retained.

The present writer had the use of Hooker's papers from the months he commanded the Army of the Potomac, on loan from Joseph Hooker Wood III of Huntsville, Alabama; the papers are now in the Huntington Library at San Marino, California. They are indispensable to the study not only of the Chancellorsville campaign but also of Hooker's long march in June 1863 from the Rappahannock front into Maryland.

The McClellan Papers. This huge collection, in the Manuscripts Division of the Library of Congress, is the principal source for Pinkerton's intelligence reports. Most of Pinkerton's retained copies were lost in the Chicago fire of 1871, and the surviving ones, consisting of one letterbook of carbon copies, are few in number and generally illegible. But the originals in the McClellan collection furnish ample evidence of Pinkerton's celebrated overestimates of Confederate numbers and the limited nature of his intelligence-gathering operation. As noted in the text, Pinkerton's reporting of routine interrogations, tediously detailed while the army was at Washington, ended when the campaign on the Peninsula began. But we have the principal product of those interrogations, a highly detailed "order of battle" on the Army of Northern Virginia — its organization and composition in tabular form. This nineteen-page document, the only fully authentic major item in Pinkerton's thick book of wartime memoirs, was omitted by the university press that republished the book in 1989.

The *Official Records* (full title: *War of the Rebellion: Official Records of the Union and Confederate Armies*), consisting of 139,000 pages in 128 printed books, the most familiar of all Civil War storehouses of fact, has been indispensable in the vital business of relating intelligence to the movements and actions of the armies. It is not, however, a great storehouse of intelligence reports. Incalculable numbers of intelligence documents were lost; some were held back by ex-officers when they lent "their" papers back to the War Department for use in compiling the *Official Records;* some documents were sequestered (the files of the Bureau of Military Information and the Turner-Baker Papers are the only such cases that emerge in the present work); and some intelligence records that reached the *OR* compilers failed to excite their interest. An example is the report seen in chapter 11 in which John Babcock, Burnside's one-man secret service, called the chief of staff's attention to the failure of his immediate superior, General Patrick, to make use of his experience in examining prisoners, deserters, and refugees. This neglect left Burnside with no recognizable positive-intelligence service. Incredibly, the chief editor of the *Official Records* labeled Babcock's indictment of the army's management "unimportant" — unworthy of a place in his publication. This apparent indifference to intelligence matters may have ended with a change of editorial chiefs that took place midway in the twenty years that the work of compilation occupied.

One most desirable source has been scarce — letters and other private papers of the spies and spymasters. When their descendants can be found, which is seldom, they are likely to be innocent of the fact that their ancestor engaged in such activity. The total yield of efforts to locate private papers amounts to a few odds and ends connected with Allan Pinkerton, one document left by Gettysburg's chief spy, David McConaughy, a small collection of papers covering the secret-service experience of Sergeant Mordecai Hunnicutt, twenty wartime letters written by George H. Sharpe, and seven letters by John Babcock.

At last count twenty-three memoirs published by writers who were or at least claimed to have been spies for one side or the other had surfaced. Only three are involved in the campaigns covered in this book; these memoirs are necessarily slighted, for factuality is not one of their characteristics.

The one memoir that finds the most use here is Allan Pinkerton's *Spy of the Rebellion,* first published in 1883. Its use has required great caution, for it contains a high proportion of fiction, typical of this genre. For example, four of the seven agents whose stories Pinkerton tells, crediting them with successful espionage, are complete figments. They are absent from his payrolls, a reliable record, and from his intelligence reports to McClellan. The stories of the seven occupy one third of Pinkerton's book; episodes verifiable in the records add up to only twenty-four pages (all of them, of course, in the sections devoted to the three actual agents). Another example: Pinkerton's account of his arrest of Rose Greenhow contains eight discrepancies with his official report of that incident. As the official version is only fifteen lines long, his invention of as many as eight conflicts took a bit of doing.

Pinkerton did not neglect the clichés that pervade, and cheapen, Civil War spy literature. Example: One of his invented agents meets a Southern belle, as beautiful as she is irrelevant. He saves her virtue from the clutches of a brutish Rebel. Of course this initiates a romance that cannot be consummated until this cruel war is over.

Even in Pinkerton's story of the arrest and hanging of Timothy Webster, his emotional and undoubtedly sincere account of the fate of his favorite agent is marred by manufactured dialogue and other obvious embellishments. But history is dependent on Pinkerton for all but a few details of this story; the best that can be done is to draw cautiously on his version while keeping the reader appropriately warned.

A second espionage memoir is another with the literary merit and the believability of the dime novel, Lafayette Baker's *History of the United States Secret Service* (1867). An indication of the carelessness with which this book was put together is the absence of any mention of Baker's well-documented visit to the Confederate secretary of war in September 1861. Among three copies of the book that the present writer has examined, no two contain exactly the same chapters. This easy interchangeability of contents suggests that Baker did not regard the book as a serious contribution to history — which helps to explain the scores of stretchers and complete fictions; those exposed in chapters 1 and 3 are typical.

In Rose Greenhow's memoir, *My Imprisonment and the First Year of Abolition Rule at Washington* (1863), the tone is set by her boasts of having obtained McClellan's plans and minutes of Lincoln's cabinet meetings, but her other claims of outwitting and outmaneuvering the Yankees, though numerous, are less extravagant. In *The South to Posterity* Douglas Southall Freeman suggests (p. 23) that in writing the book Mrs. Greenhow was motivated by bitterness. He fails to note the wanton damage she did to historical fact, though it is clear that he was aware of the doubtful veracity of the claims made by and for her; he left her unmentioned in his campaign histories, *R. E. Lee* and *Lee's Lieutenants*.

One other espionage "memoir" touching eastern campaigns of this period is entirely ignored here: the memoirist was never a spy. This was Sara Emma Edmonds, a Canadian, author of *Nurse and Spy* (1865). Emma is an interesting study in transvestism; she managed to serve two years as an infantry*man* in a Michigan regiment without being officially discovered. Thus the most interesting part of her spying story is her entering Confederate lines *disguised as a woman*. That fiction and others in Emma's story are exposed in chapter 6, note 44. But the story of Emma Edmonds the Federal spy reappears every few years and by now is one of the established myths of Civil War intelligence.

LIST OF ABBREVIATIONS
AND SHORT TITLES

Sources repeatedly cited are designated by the following short titles or abbreviations.

AP	Army of the Potomac.
B&L	Johnson and Buel, *Battles and Leaders of the Civil War.*
BMI	Files of the Bureau of Military Information (Record Group 393, Part I, Entry 3980, Miscellaneous Letters, Reports, and Lists Received, Division and Department of the Army of the Potomac, 1861–65, National Archives). See "Comment on Sources" regarding possible gaps in these files.
General Telegrams	Collections in Record Group 107, National Archives, consisting of the following microfilm series: M504, Telegrams Collected by the Office of the Secretary of War (unbound), 1860–1870 (454 rolls), and M473, Telegrams Collected by the Office of the Secretary of War (bound), 1861–1882 (282 rolls).
JCCW	Reports of the congressional Joint Committee on the Conduct of the War, published in 1863 and 1865. The entry "JCCW 1863, 1:115–16," for example, means pages 115–16 of the 1863 volume 1; "JCCW 1865, 1:210–11" means pages 210–11 of the 1865 volume 1.
NA	National Archives.
NOR	U.S. Naval War Records Office, *Official Records of the Union and Confederate Navies in the War of the Rebellion.*
OR	U.S. War Department, *The War of the Rebellion: Official Records of the Union and Confederate Armies.* Many volumes are divided into separately bound parts, and the part number is cited after the volume number, thus: 27.3:60 (volume 27, part 3, page 60). All citations refer to Series 1 unless otherwise indicated.

RG   Record Group.

SGSD   "Scouts, Guides, Spies and Detectives" file, Record Group 110, Records of the Provost Marshal General's Office (Civil War), Entry 31 (correspondence, reports, accounts, and related records of two or more scouts, guides, spies, and detectives, 1861–66), and Entry 36 (correspondence, reports, appointments, and other records relating to scouts, guides, spies, and detectives, 1862–66), National Archives.

SHSP   Southern Historical Society Papers.

S. S. Accts.   "Secret Service Accounts" file, Record Group 110, Records of the Provost Marshal General's Office (Civil War), Entry 95, Accounts of Secret Service Agents, 1861–70, National Archives.

Turner-Baker Papers   Record Group 94, Records of the Adjutant General's Office, Entry 179, National Archives. Partially reproduced on National Archives microfilm publication M797, *Case Files of Investigations by Levi C. Turner and Lafayette C. Baker, 1861–66* (137 rolls).

Many of the documents cited here are in unarranged series. The reader who would refer to them will find that locating them is often a matter of blind search despite the identification data (dates, names of sender and addressee, and so on) given in the citation.

NOTES

1. Twenty Thousand Potential Spies

1. The 1857 Army Regulations, the edition in effect during years when an intersectional war was foreseeable, had instructions on reconnaissance, march security, and the like, but that was as close as they came to the subject of intelligence.

2. For information on intelligence in the American Revolution, War of 1812, and the Mexican War, see O'Toole, *Honorable Treachery*, chs. 7 and 9; and the articles on those wars in O'Toole, *Encyclopedia of American Intelligence and Espionage*. The quotations from Frederick the Great, Saxe and Jomini, and others in the same vein are in Wagner, *Service of Security and Information*, 9–10. Jomini seems to have been American officers' favorite military writer (Donald, *Lincoln Reconsidered*, 88–90).

3. Eby, ed., *Virginia Yankee*, 162–63; Nevins, ed., *Diary of George Templeton Strong*, 195; McClellan to H. L. Scott, Jan. 11, 186[7], in Moore, *Rebellion Record*, 10:517; Schuyler Hamilton to McClellan, Oct. 25, 1869, McClellan Papers, no. 18984; Thomas and Hyman, *Stanton*, 111.

4. For an example see chapter 3, notes 9 and 10, and associated text.

5. Jones, *Rebel War Clerk's Diary*, 1:70.

6. Confederate AGO records, in RG 109, ch. 9, 33:1, 8, 18, 22, 68; 36:1, 2, 5, 25, 26, War Dept. Collection of Confederate Records, NA.

7. Freeman, *R. E. Lee*, 1:431–33, 436–38, 633–37.

8. *OR*, 1:252.

9. Thomas and Hyman, *Stanton*, 110–11; Cooling, *Symbol, Sword and Shield*, 16–23; District of Columbia Civil War Centennial Commission, *Symbol and the Sword*, 13; Gen. Scott, "Memorandum of dangers to the Capitol [*sic*]," Jan. 26, 1861, Scott Papers; unaddressed fragment, Jan. 29, 1861, ibid.; Gen. Scott to Secretary of War, Feb. 12, 1861, ibid.; Asst. Secretary of War T. A. Scott to Speaker, House of Representatives, Aug. 5, 1861 (forwarding Holt's report, dated Feb. 18), *OR*, 51.1:435–38; Hendrick, *Lincoln's War Cabinet*, 253–54; Charles P. Stone in the leadoff article of *B&L* 1:7–25. In view of his later troubles, Stone might be suspected of embellishing his deeds narrated in this article, as a way of rehabilitating his reputation. Although evidence corroborating his account is scanty, it is worth remarking that the tone of his article is unpretending and his manner precise. The rather liberal amount of dialogue that he quotes is, however, evidently unsupported by contemporary notes.

10. Pinkerton, *Spy of the Rebellion*, chs. 5–11; Cuthbert, *Lincoln and the Baltimore Plot, passim;* Morn, *"Eye That Never Sleeps,"* 40–41.

11. Cooling, *Symbol, Sword and Shield*, 21–22, citing Charles Winslow Elliott, *Winfield Scott: The Soldier and the Man*, 691.

12. Cooling, *Symbol, Sword and Shield*, 23–27; Scott, *Memoirs*, 611–12; *B&L*, 1:25.

13. *OR*, 1:292–94, 250; Swanberg, *First Blood*, chs. 24–26, particularly pp. 282, 284–85.

14. Wilcox file, S. S. Accts.; *OR*, 1:333–42; *B&L*, 1:26–32. An excellent short history of Confederate designs against Fort Pickens is Grady McWhiney, "The Confederacy's First Shot," in Hubbell, ed., *Battles Lost and Won*, 73–82.

15. *OR*, 1:402–3; 37th Cong., 3rd Sess., Senate Reports, serial 1154, pp. 481–85; Turner-Baker Papers, Turner file 605, roll 19, M797; Kerbey, *Boy Spy*. Kerbey's subtitle is *A substantially true record of secret service during the War of the Rebellion;* the phrase "substantially true" makes this book of fictions and occasional facts unique among Civil War espionage memoirs in its admission that some of its stories might be slightly embellished.

16. *B&L*, 1:32.

17. Plum, *Military Telegraph*, 1:64–65; Mayor G. W. Brown to J. W. Garrett, April 21, 1861, Turner-Baker Papers, Miscellaneous Records (unbound and unmicrofilmed); Manakee, *Maryland in the Civil War*, 38–42; Trefousse, *Ben Butler*, 65–71. Correspondence between the War Dept. and the governors of various states, some of whom were using couriers to communicate with Washington, indicates that the telegraph outage lasted until April 27 or 28 (*OR*, ser. 3, 1:100–166 *passim*).

18. Puleston file, S. S. Accts.; Wilson, *Acts and Actors in the Civil War*, 43–45; Andrews, *The North Reports the Civil War*, 79–80.

19. Committee of Public Safety records, Missouri Historical Society; Monaghan, *Civil War on the Western Border*, 130–31; J. E. D. Couzins file, S. S. Accts.

20. Phillips, Fall Leaf, James Bridger, and Herzinger files, SGSD; *OR*, ser. 2, 3:376.

21. William C. Parsons and Abel H. Lee files, S. S. Accts.; Turner-Baker Papers, file 427B; *OR*, ser. 2, 2:1427, 4:528, 5:483.

22. Howard file, S. S. Accts.; *OR*, ser. 2, 1:691.

23. *OR*, 2:784, 787, 861, 877, 472; Mason file, S. S. Accts. Mason also erred in saying that his arrest at Harper's Ferry was at Gen. Johnston's order; on the date given, Johnston had not yet relieved Jackson. Mason declined to place an exact figure on the value of his services but supposed that "one, two or three (or even more) thousand dollars might not be excessive." Clearly he was out of touch with the going rates.

24. L. C. Baker file, S. S. Accts.; Baker, *History of the United States Secret Service*, 18–20, 45–72; Doster, *Lincoln and Episodes of the Civil War*, 127–28. Baker's expense account for the first Richmond trip (S. S. Accts, unnumbered box) gives July 9 as the beginning of that service. His book (p. 48) gives July 11 as the date of an abortive start on his trip, followed a day later by the second start. Baker's book cited here is an 1867 edition; other editions differ in contents and pagination.

25. Walker wrote, "The bearer of this, Samuel Munson Esq. [Baker's alias] is authorized to purchase supplies for the Southern Confederacy. You will find him a true Southerner in sentiment and feeling. All his interests and future hopes are with us. He takes sterling Bills of Exchange on our friends at the North sufficient to accomplish the object of his undertaking — and may God protect him in his

holy mission." This pass is in the Walter Pforzheimer Collection on Intelligence Service, Washington, D.C. It is dated Sept. 11, 1861, just a few days before Walker's resignation as secretary of war. In *Rebel War Clerk's Diary*, pp. 79–80, Jones recorded that a "man from Washington" whom he did not name called on Sept. 17 but failed to see the new acting secretary, Judah P. Benjamin. As Baker's book does not mention his September visit to Richmond, it does not support the suspicion that Baker was the Sept. 17 caller. Other evidence of Baker's espionage in Richmond is found in Reports of the Committees of the House of Representatives, 40th Cong., 1st Sess.; Report No. 7 (ser. 1314), 110–11.

26. Baker's appointment as "Special Agent of the War Department" was dated March 30, 1862, and the appointment as "special provost-marshal [*sic*] for the War Department" came on Sept. 12, 1862 (Stanton to Baker, Stanton Papers, March 30, 1862; *OR*, ser. 3, 2:539).

27. A study of Baker probably would reveal him to be a competent detective of questionable character; no such study has ever been made. For a short discussion of his service see Fishel, "Myths That Never Die," *International Journal of Intelligence and Counterintelligence* 2, no. 1 (Spring 1988); 30–32, 55–56. An earlier version of this article, under the title "The Mythology of Civil War Intelligence," is in *Civil War History* 10, no. 4 (Dec. 1964), and in Hubbell, ed., *Battles Lost and Won*, 83–106.

2. First Bull Run

1. JCCW 1863, 1:36, 38.

2. *OR*, 2:718–19.

3. McDowell, JCCW 1863, 1:36; Nicolay, *Outbreak of Rebellion*, 173. As late as July 13 Scott repeated this assurance to one of McDowell's division commanders, Brig. Gen. Daniel Tyler (Davis, *Battle at Bull Run*, citing Donald Mitchell, *Daniel Tyler, a Memorial Volume* [New York, 1883]).

4. Davis, *Battle at Bull Run*, 77–78; *OR*, 2:303–4.

5. Although the retirement had been ordered well in advance (*OR*, 2:447), the Federals found a Rebel flag at the courthouse — and, according to a newspaper correspondent, a stock of 50,000 Havana cigars.

6. Hennessy, *First Battle of Manassas*, 9.

7. *OR*, 2:307.

8. Beauregard to Davis, July 11, 1861, quoted in Roman, *Military Operations of General Beauregard*, 82–83; Beauregard, *Campaign and Battle of Manassas*, 39–40; Alexander, *Military Memoirs*, 41.

9. *OR*, 2:439–40.

10. A trenchant but sympathetic analysis of McDowell's delay is in Williams, *Lincoln Finds a General*, 1, ch. 3, esp. p. 89.

11. *OR*, 2:307.

12. *OR*, 2:473; Johnston, *Narrative*, 33.

13. For Beauregard's statements about the effectiveness and usefulness of his spies in Washington, see his book cited in note 8 above, 135–36; his article in *B&L*, 1:197–98, 200; and the book by his literary voice, Col. Alfred Roman, *Military Operations of General Beauregard*, 89. Beauregard's telegram to Richmond asking for reinforcements is at *OR*, 2:439–40. Roman (p. 90) says that it was sent during the night of July 16–17; but as the text begins "The enemy has assailed my outposts in heavy force" and continues with a report of the Confederates' with-

drawal to the Bull Run line, Roman's timing is in error. R. M. Johnston, in *Bull Run,* says, "Davis telegraphed to Johnston the instant word reached him from Beauregard that McDowell was moving" (155). And Johnston says firmly (*OR,* 2:473) that the message from Richmond did not reach him until about 1 A.M. Thursday. Thus the sluggishness in the handling of the alarm was altogether at Beauregard's end.

14. Johnston, *Narrative,* 35; *OR,* 2:473.

15. The movement is described in detail in Davis, *Battle at Bull Run,* 134–43; and Johnston, *Narrative,* 34–38. One of Jackson's companies, the Rockbridge Rifles of the 27th Virginia Regiment, made a delayed start early Friday and boarded a train in the Valley, according to a member of the company who deserted in Jan. 1862 (Pinkerton to McClellan, McClellan Papers, no. 8109). The desertion of Davis's "unsympathetic" trainmen is discussed in chapter 5, note 31 and associated text.

16. *OR,* 2:330–31; JCCW 1863, 1:39. Sudley Ford and a ford downstream were shown on the engineers' advance maps, but "no known road communicated with them" (*OR,* 2:329).

17. *OR,* 2:331, 383, 560; Hennessy, *First Manassas,* 45–46.

18. *OR,* 2:487–88, 317; Beauregard, *Campaign and Battle of Manassas,* 64; Hennessy, *First Manassas,* 43. For the Confederate moves that "temporarily stopped" the Federal push, see Hennessy, ch. 5.

19. Besides the two divisions that McDowell left in reserve (Miles's around Centreville and Runyon's well to the rear) there were two brigades that he did not put into the action or used very lightly: Keyes's (near the field but not in the fight) and Howard's (sent for only very late). Also, Schenck's brigade spent most of the battle trying to make the turnpike bridge passable by searching for mines that were not there. The Confederates' unused or lightly used units were those in the neighborhood of the Federal demonstration at Blackburn's Ford; some did a great deal of marching but little or no shooting. For Beauregard's reinforcements from the Fredericksburg area, see *OR,* 2:565, 980; from Leesburg, ibid., 545; from Richmond, ibid., 566, 980.

20. According to Johnston (*OR,* 2:475), at the height of the battle "a little above nine regiments" and sixteen guns of his army were engaged, as compared to "six guns and less than the strength of three regiments" of Beauregard's army.

21. Parsons file, S. S. Accts; Netherton et al., *Fairfax County,* tells (251–70) of the considerable Yankee migration into northern Virginia in the decades immediately preceding the Civil War, and of the strong Unionist sentiment that persisted there.

22. The poor relations between McDowell and Mansfield are described in McDowell's testimony to the Joint Committee on the Conduct of the War (JCCW 1863,1:38) and in the book by his adjutant, Fry, *McDowell and Tyler in the Campaign of Bull Run,* 9–11.

23. *OR,* 2:680.

24. Davis, *Battle at Bull Run,* 54. The report of "Mr. J———n" is at *OR,* 2:722–23. If "J———n" was not William Johnston, he may have been Thomas T. Johnson, a Fairfax Countian known to have served as a scout and as one of Lafayette Baker's detectives (Hickin et al., *Fairfax County,* 331; L. C. Baker file, S. S. Accts., Jan.–Aug. 1863).

25. Freeman, *Lee's Lieutenants,* 1:48–49.

26. *OR,* 2:304 (McDowell's march order). In his testimony to the Joint Committee (JCCW 1863, 1:39), McDowell said, "At Fairfax Court House was the

South Carolina brigade" — which could mean that before the battle he had actually had some information on Confederate dispositions additional to that appearing in J——n's report.

27. For Baker's Richmond trip, see chapter 1, note 24 and associated text.

28. *OR*, 2:721.

29. *OR*, 2:308, 329.

30. The identity of the guide is uncertain. Barnard named Mathias C. Mitchell as the guide who on the 18th provided information about Blackburn's and Mitchell's Fords, but his report of the campaign does not identify the guide who later located the route to Sudley Ford (*OR*, 2:329, 331).

31. Scheips, *Albert James Myer*, chs. 7–10; Scheips, ed., *Military Signal Communications*, "Introduction" (n.p.); *OR*, ser. 3, 3:256–57; Haydon, *Aeronautics in the Union and Confederate Armies*, 192.

32. Scheips, *Albert James Myer*, 350. The 35,000 figure for overall Confederate strength in March is from Richard N. Current, "Confederates and the First Shot," *Civil War History* 8, no. 4 (Dec. 1961): 360.

33. For example, even as late as Saturday, July 20 — after he had learned he was to make a belated start in command of the Federals' only balloon — Myer took the time to write to the clerk of the Senate's Military Committee (John Callan, mentioned in chapter 1 as having possibly been in complicity with the Confederates) seeking support in what he viewed as a Signal Corps role that had already been legislated (Scheips, *Albert James Myer*, 345–46). If Myer seems to have lacked forehandedness in the preparations for McDowell's campaign, the probable reason is that he had not been summoned to Washington for that purpose; he was a visitor pursuing a long-range problem who happened in on a campaign and a battle.

34. This account of the founding of the Confederate signal service is based on Alexander's account that he provided to the Federal Signal Corps historian, J. Willard Brown. See Brown, *Signal Corps, U.S.A.*, 43–45, and Alexander, *Military Memoirs*, 14.

35. Undated oath signed by Alexander, RG 111, entry 27, Papers Relating to Proposed Plans for Signal Systems, NA.

36. Alexander, *Military Memoirs*, 16. The outstation locations were: (1) "near the house of [Van Pelt], just above the Stone Bridge" (the Warrenton Turnpike bridge over Bull Run); (2) near the McLean house, "opposite our right centre"; (3) toward Centreville, about three miles north of Bull Run; (4) near the headquarters at Centreville.

37. No copy of Alexander's message to Evans is known to survive. Between 1888 and 1907 he wrote at least four accounts of this incident, quoting his words to Evans slightly differently each time. The earliest version, given here, is found in *Southern Historical Society Papers* 16 (1888): 94.

38. Freeman, *Lee's Lieutenants*, 1:64.

39. Alexander did not share Myer's favorable opinion of the topographical advantages of the Bull Run country (*Military Memoirs*, 15). He would have given much weight to the view from the vicinity of Beauregard's headquarters, while Myer probably was influenced by Centreville's clear view all the way to the Blue Ridge. It was only when McClellan's army advanced to Centreville in March 1862 that Myer first saw Alexander's tower at that place. Brown, *Signal Corps, U.S.A.*, 291.

40. *OR*, 2:314–15; Williams, *Lincoln Finds a General*, 1:76.

41. *OR*, 2:393 (report of Maj. I. N. Palmer) and 330.

42. "McDowell not only did not wait for information, he did not even seem to

desire it." The quotation is from an unnamed "military correspondent" in R. M. Johnston, *Bull Run*, 118. An example of the nonuse of cavalry, cited by Johnston, is found in McDowell's orders for Wednesday, the second day of the march, when the advance was to reach the position of a major enemy outpost. Those orders called for no reconnaissance to determine what opposition might be encountered (ibid.).

43. This sampling of newspaper disclosures is drawn from the July 1–18 issues of the Washington *Star, National Republican,* and *National Intelligencer;* New York *Herald, Times,* and *Tribune;* and the *Baltimore American.*

44. Johnston, *Narrative,* 22; *National Intelligencer,* July 16, 1861.

45. Johnston, *Narrative,* 34; Thomas, *General George H. Thomas,* 144.

46. Johnston, *Narrative,* 35. An impenetrable cavalry screen set by Stuart is a standard part of the history of Johnston's movement.

47. [D. H. Strother], "Personal Recollections of the War, by a Virginian," *Harper's New Monthly Magazine* 33 (July 1866):151–52. Although published anonymously, this article, and others in a series under the same title, are clearly from Strother's pen, for they are in the form of a diary that repeats and expands Strother's surviving daily journal kept during the war.

48. *OR,* 2:471–72; 123–24; [Strother], "Personal Recollections," 142–43.

49. [Strother], "Personal Recollections," 151–52, 155.

50. JCCW 1863, 1:5, 96, 100. References to Johnston's supposed numerical advantage are scattered throughout Patterson's testimony (78–114). The only sustained discussion of his information-gathering arrangements is at 94–96. He presented (95, 141) three intelligence reports verbatim, as evidence of the soundness of his information. Although all three were detailed enough to be superficially persuasive, they were all in the past tense — telling, after Johnston left Winchester, what forces he had while there. Brief references to spies and other information-gathering matters that preceded Patterson's advance from Pennsylvania are in *OR,* 2:684, 688, 727.

51. [Strother], "Personal Recollections of the War," 157. The diary entry on which this account is based reads, "Heard . . . the news confirmed of Johnston's having deserted Winchester and passing the Shenandoah at Berry's Ferry with his whole force." The word *confirmed* shows that he had previously received the same information (*i.e.,* on the night of the 18th). This entry is dated July 20, but it obviously was written some days later, for it refers to the Blackburn's Ford battle of July 18 as "the first attack on Manassas," indicating that the entry was made after news of the main attack (the battle of July 21) had reached the Valley, probably no earlier than July 22. In writing his "Recollections" five years later, Strother, by giving July 19 rather than the 20th as the date of arrival of the night-riding "eye-witness," was correcting a dating error in the diary.

52. [Strother], "Personal Recollections of the War," 157; Eby, ed., *Virginia Yankee,* xix–xx. Strother began military service in March 1862 as a captain.

53. *OR,* 2:168, 171.

54. *OR,* 2:172.

55. Ibid.; JCCW 1863, 1:141.

56. *OR,* 2:746.

57. Plum, *Military Telegraph,* 1:75; O'Brien, *Telegraphing in Battle,* 20–21.

58. In *B&L,* 1:182, James B. Fry, McDowell's adjutant, says that the message was not sent until the battle was in progress Sunday. It seems unlikely that Scott would have allowed Patterson's news to remain unsent to McDowell overnight, and Fry gives no indication of having documentary evidence of the time of transmission. In *Military Telegraph,* Plum says (1:75–76) that Scott had Patter-

son's message in time to have stayed the attack but says nothing about the timing of Scott's message to McDowell. McDowell's battle order, dated July 20 (*OR*, 2:326), also bears no time of issue; he said later that it went out immediately after completion of the engineers' reconnaissance around noon (JCCW 1863, 1:39).

59. Gen. Scott to Joint Committee on the Conduct of the War, Mar. 31, 1862. Scott also said that at the time of receipt of Patterson's July 20 telegram reporting Johnston's departure, "It was too late to call off the troops from the attack," adding, "and it is not true that I was urged by anybody in authority to stop the attack."

60. *OR*, 2:325.

61. Patterson first made this claim in an address reported by the *New York Herald*, Nov. 24, 1861 (p. 2, col. 5). The Joint Committee on the Conduct of the War rejected Patterson's claim on the ground that his withdrawal from Bunker Hill to Charlestown on July 17 must have begun earlier than Scott's message of the same date could have been sent.

62. A good analysis of Scott's instructions to Patterson is in Williams, *Lincoln Finds a General*, 1:80–85. Scott even sent, or allowed to be sent, a telegram to Patterson relaying a report that army headquarters had received a report of a Confederate scheme to capture Washington (*OR*, 2:164). Although such fears on the part of even the general-in-chief could be excused in an earlier time, the date of this telegram is July 11, when the Federals were definitely bent on the offensive, seemingly having stopped worrying about Confederate schemes. And the report was forwarded to Patterson with no indication of Scott's or anyone else's views as to its reliability, except for a statement that the source was known. This incident is a clue to the state of affairs, and of mind, at army headquarters at the time Scott was sending instructions to Patterson.

63. JCCW 1863, 1:89, 97; *OR*, 2:175; [Strother], "Personal Recollections," 156.

64. According to Fitz John Porter, Patterson's staff believed from the first that "it was an utter impossibility" for Patterson to hold Johnston in the Valley (JCCW 1863, 1:155). Patterson took a similar view before the Joint Committee while at the same time saying he had believed that as long as he stayed at Charlestown, Johnston would remain in the Valley. These contrary views recur tiresomely in his testimony (JCCW 1863, 1:78–114).

65. *OR*, 2:166–67.

66. *OR*, 2:308.

67. In addition to Jackson's brigade, reinforcements on hand early Saturday included the brigade from Fredericksburg and the regiment stationed at Leesburg. None of Johnston's artillery, five batteries altogether, reached Manassas earlier than midafternoon Saturday; his cavalry, even with hard-riding Jeb Stuart at its head, arrived, escorting the artillery, only Saturday evening, about forty-eight hours after their screening duties at Winchester were over. Among the arrivals on Sunday, after a thirty-hour train ride from Richmond, was a 600-man infantry unit of Col. Wade Hampton's legion, composed of infantry, cavalry, and artillery; this was the one reinforcement not belonging to Johnston that played a prominent role in the battle. (*OR*, 2:473, 565, 545, 566; Davis, *Battle at Bull Run*, 138–43.)

68. *OR*, 2:325, 330.

69. Although on Saturday the troops were cooking rations that had arrived Friday night, they had cooked previous shipments on Friday. McDowell's statement that "a day's delay in getting the provisions forward [made] it necessary to make on Sunday the attack we should have made on Saturday" (*OR*, 2:324) is

disputed by Williams, *Lincoln Finds a General*, 1:88–89 and 1:395, n. 88. Reports of the commissary officers are at *OR*, 2:336–44.

70. JCCW 1863, 1:40; Davis, *Battle at Bull Run*, 155–56. A respected Confederate commentator considered it "strange that all this could go on [*i.e.*, the arrival of reinforcements and their placement in line] in such close proximity to the Federal army without discovery through some negro or deserter" (Alexander, *American Civil War*, 27). Gen. James B. Fry states in *B&L* (1:183), that when McDowell issued his order for Sunday's advance he "did not know . . . that Johnston had joined Beauregard, though he suspected it."

71. *OR*, 2:317, 325 (McDowell's after-action report). McDowell believed after the battle that if he could "have fought a day — yes, a few hours — sooner, there is everything to show that we should have continued successful" in pushing the enemy back on Manassas. That essentially correct view may, however, have been based on partial misunderstanding of the arrival times of Johnston's units. McDowell thought that a larger part of the Valley army arrived during the battle than was actually the case (JCCW 1863, 1:40) — an impression he could have received from Richmond newspapers.

72. Fishel, "Myths That Never Die," *International Journal of Intelligence and Counterintelligence* 2, no. 1 (Spring 1988); 40. The practice of installing intelligence liaison officers at distant headquarters was initiated when Gen. Grant went into the field with the Army of the Potomac in May 1864. Liaison detachments were established then at Federal headquarters in the Shenandoah Valley and at the headquarters of the Army of the James, on the Peninsula.

73. Lincoln to Buell and Halleck, Jan. 13, 1862, in Basler, ed., *Works of Lincoln*, 5:98.

74. McDowell said nothing on these questions either in his report of the campaign or in his appearance before the Joint Committee on the Conduct of the War.

75. Eby, ed., *Virginia Yankee*, 72.

3. "Known in Richmond in Twenty-Four Hours"

1. *OR*, 2:763, 766; Sears, *McClellan*, 51–65, 69.

2. Pinkerton, *Spy of the Rebellion*, 139–40, 152–54, 182–202 (esp. 194); Pinkerton file, S. S. Accts., box 6. The latter source shows Pinkerton spending $13,437.03 in these few months in the Department of the Ohio. Pinkerton's visit to Washington was preceded by a letter to Lincoln in which he offered his services to the government (Mearns, ed., *Lincoln Papers*, 2:576–77).

3. In conversation with a *Chicago Tribune* correspondent Pinkerton was plainspoken about his position as head of McClellan's "secret service" (Andrews, *The North Reports the Civil War*, 153).

4. Pinkerton to Asst. Secretary P. H. Watson, Oct. 7, 1862, and Watson's endorsement thereon, Oct. 8, "by order of the Secretary of War," S. S. Accts.; Pinkerton payrolls, ibid.

5. For this summary of Baker's activities, see Baker file, S. S. Accts. His salary and expenses up to March 9, 1862, had been paid by the War Dept., but with Secretary Seward's approval on each month's statement; the statement for Feb. 9–March 9, 1862, is the first one not bearing Seward's signature (S. S. Accts., unnumbered box).

6. Turner-Baker Papers, files 62-B, 299, 819-B (filed with 1561); Pinkerton and Kerby files, S. S. Accts.; *OR*, ser. 2, 5:889ff. It will be suspected that J. O.

Kerbey in chapter 1 and J. T. Kerby were the same person, especially as J. O. Kerbey used several versions of his name. But J. O.'s handwriting bears no similarity to J. T.'s. Another case of the two bureaus' involvement in the same episode was that of frauds charged against a Baker employee that were investigated by Pinkerton detectives (Turner-Baker Papers, file 323; Pinkerton file, S. S. Accts.).

There was a third investigative activity in Washington, a small force of detectives working for the local provost marshal, a position held for much of the war by Lt. Col. William E. Doster. In *Lincoln and Episodes of the Civil War* Doster describes (93–96) his agents' penetration of several groups of local secession sympathizers who were corresponding with persons in the Confederacy; the account does not mention what valuable intelligence, if any, resulted from the penetration. Presumably Baker was cognizant of this activity; no crossed paths of their agents have come to light in the present study.

7. *National Republican,* July 15, 1861; *Washington Chronicle,* Aug. 25, 1861.

8. Thomas and Hyman, *Stanton,* 147–48; Leech, *Reveille in Washington,* 144–45.

9. *OR,* 2:23–27.

10. *National Republican,* July 13, 1861.

11. Service record of 2nd Lt. George Donnellan, CSA, NA.

12. Callan to Wilson, in RG 107, Personnel Appointments 1846–60 and 1861, A–E, box 1.

13. For Mrs. Greenhow's visitors and other contacts see Ross, *Rebel Rose,* 92–131 *passim.* On p. 136 the Seward assistant whose wife reported Mrs. Greenhow's offer of sending contraband mail is identified as Robert Hunter Morris. Mrs. Greenhow's reference to "who gave the alarm" is in her July 31 report; see Appendix 4. Pinkerton's report of the surveillance and arrest of Mrs. Greenhow is in *OR,* ser. 2, 2:566, 568.

14. For biographical details on Mrs. Greenhow, see Ross, *Rebel Rose,* ch. 1. Pinkerton's characterization of her is in *OR,* ser. 2, 2:567.

15. Ross does not say when Mrs. Greenhow left San Francisco; her only reference to the subject is the statement "By the summer of 1852 Rose was back in the East." District of Columbia records give only the year of the child's birth (1853).

16. Ross, *Rebel Rose,* 104.

17. Beauregard's letter, to Miss Augusta J. Evans of Mobile, is at *OR,* 51.2:688. Bonham's account is in an Aug. 27, 1877, letter to Beauregard, in the Bonham Papers. Beauregard's order of July 11, 1861, in the James L. Kemper Papers at the University of Virginia, is cited by John Hennessy, *First Battle of Manassas,* p. 9. Mrs. Greenhow's book, *My Imprisonment,* says very little about her espionage activities; her July 9 report is among the items left unmentioned.

18. Davis, *Battle at Bull Run,* 68; Beauregard to Evans, *OR,* 51.2:688.

19. The quotation of the text of the message in modern accounts appears to descend from a source of doubtful authenticity, *Recollections Grave and Gay,* by Mrs. Burton [Constance Cary] Harrison (New York, 1911), cited by Louis A. Sigaud in "Mrs. Greenhow and the Rebel Spy Ring," *Maryland Historical Magazine,* Sept. 1946, 173–74.

20. Beauregard to Evans, *OR,* 51.2:688; Greenhow, *My Imprisonment,* 14–15; Tidwell, *April '65,* 64. Tidwell has answered long-standing questions regarding the transmission of this message, but in regard to its contents he was misled by Alfred Roman, Beauregard's personal historian, who blunderingly reported that Mrs. Greenhow had written "McDowell has been ordered to advance tonight" (Roman, *Military Operations of Beauregard,* 89).

21. Beauregard to Evans, *OR*, 51.2:688.

22. Davis, *Battle at Bull Run*, 92–93.

23. Beauregard's account of the event does not advance any explanation of the delay. For details of the Federals' approach to Fairfax, see Bonham's report, *OR*, 2:449–50.

24. Beauregard, *Campaign and Battle of Manassas*, 45. Jordan wrote that Mrs. Greenhow's "one great service" was her message of July 16, but he did not credit it with touching off Beauregard's plea for reinforcements. He said only that it saved Bonham's brigade from "disastrous surprise"; even that credit seems doubtful in view of the warning and retirement orders Bonham already had. (Jordan to Benjamin, *OR*, 5:928.)

25. New York *Herald*, Aug. 23, 1861; Cincinnati *Gazette*, Jan. 13, 1862. Wilson was still commander of the 22nd Massachusetts as late as Oct. 11, 1861 (*OR*, 51.1:496). For details of Mrs. Greenhow's relationship with Wilson see Ross, *Rebel Rose*, 75–81. Love notes presumably from Wilson, some of them on Senate stationery, that were confiscated by Pinkerton are in a handwriting distinctly different from the hand found in many other documents in Wilson's papers that unquestionably were written by him. David Rankin Barbee, author of an unpublished biography of Rose Greenhow, obtained an expert's opinion that Wilson clearly employed two different handwriting styles. (See MS biography in Barbee Papers, p. 454.) Despite Pinkerton's discovery of the love notes and her reference to military information he gave her, Wilson retained his chairmanship of the Military Affairs Committee. Presumably the affair was brought to the attention of Secretary Cameron and possibly Lincoln as well, with the result that the disclosure was regarded as not harmful enough to confront so powerful a Senate figure with it, especially since Mrs. Greenhow's career as a spy was now arrested. Conceivably Cameron or Assistant Secretary Scott took the view that Wilson's disclosure amounted to misinformation, intentional or otherwise. Wilson's loyalty to his wife and his flag remained publicly unquestioned; he was elected Vice President under Grant in 1872.

26. For the location of these reports in the National Archives, see the note to Appendix 4. In his report on the Greenhow case (*OR*, ser. 2, 2:568) Pinkerton said that he found information that "must have been obtained from employees and agents in the various Departments of the Government." Unless he had copies of Greenhow reports that do not survive, which is unlikely, he was overstating the menacing character of her sources. For the reservations of one general, R. E. Lee, about emotionalism in reporting by Confederate women, see his letter to Gen. G. W. Smith, *OR*, 21:1052.

27. Greenhow, *My Imprisonment*, 78.

28. Ibid.; Leech, *Reveille in Washington*, 135. In the Greenhow reports that Pinkerton confiscated the closest she comes to discussing McClellan's planning is this sentence in an Aug. 9 report: "Great reliance is placed in their future or present plan of battle, to wit, plenty of artillery and cavalry." The word *plan* recurs once: "[Their] plan is now masterly inactivity."

29. Baker, *History of the United States Secret Service*, 102.

30. A Pinkerton operative learned in Richmond that an "under-ground railroad" had been getting New York and Philadelphia newspapers to the Confederate capital two days after publication (*OR*, ser. 2, 2:866). As it took a day to get them to Washington, it would appear that a twenty-four-hour delivery time between Washington and Richmond was attained. But the time when the Pinkerton man learned this — about Oct. 1, 1861 — was also the time Pinkerton was closing in on the Marylanders whose ferrying services assisted the couriers. Baker

provides a partial explanation of the speed he claims for this reporting by stating
(Baker, *Secret Service*, 102) that reports were conveyed to disloyal postmasters in
the lower Maryland counties of Prince George's, Charles, and St. Mary's, taken
across the Potomac by blockade-runners, and telegraphed from Fredericksburg
to Richmond. Baker's account of this mode of transmission is plausible, but no
records indicating its use are known.

31. Pinkerton, *Spy of the Rebellion*, 251.

32. House Report No. 7, 40th Cong., 1st Sess. (1867), 111.

33. For details on the low factuality of Pinkerton's *Spy of the Rebellion* see "Comment on Sources" and this writer's review of its 1989 republication (*Civil War
History* 36, no. 4 [Dec. 1990], 352–55). Historians have often treated this book
as a reliable source despite its high incidence of improbabilities. Where used as a
source here, either it is verified by other records or the text warns that this is a
Pinkerton version.

34. Babcock to "Dear Aunt," Dec. 26, 1861, Babcock Papers; *OR*, 5:928–29,
978–79; 51.2:360; ser. 2, 2:565–66, 1354.

35. Dix-Pierrepont Commission report (RG 59, Proceedings of the Commission Relating to State Prisoners, entry 490); Ross, *Rebel Rose*, 180.

36. *OR*, ser. 2, 2:249; Thomas and Hyman, *Stanton*, 158.

37. Dix-Pierrepont Commission report; *OR*, ser. 2, 2:577, 1321; Ross, *Rebel
Rose*, 246–70.

38. Dix-Pierrepont Commission report.

39. *OR*, ser. 2, 2:572, 1308.

40. *OR*, 5:928 (the same letter is in *OR*, ser. 2, 2:564–65). Jordan shows that he
had no illusions about the security of the cipher he gave Mrs. Greenhow. It
consisted of twenty-six hieroglyph-like characters, each substituting for a letter of
the alphabet. It was solvable by the same technique (identifying letters by their
known frequency of occurrence) used to solve the cryptographic puzzles in
today's newspapers. But there also were cipher characters for the ten digits; these
were not susceptible to that technique.

41. Donnellan service record, NA; *OR*, ser. 2, 2:1307–13.

42. *OR*, ser. 2, 2:1354–55.

43. *OR*, 5:928; 51.2:340–41; ser. 2, 2:1346–51.

44. Mrs. Greenhow and later writers (*e.g.*, Sigaud in *Belle Boyd: Confederate Spy*,
183, 186) have intimated that her light treatment was due to her social prominence and the embarrassment she could have brought to people in high places.
But her accomplices received greater leniency.

45. *OR*, 15:510–11.

46. *OR*, ser. 2, 2:237–38, 245, 295, 571, 1320, 1321, 1352, 1356, 1357.

47. *OR*, ser. 2, 2:1357 and 7:849.

48. Adm. Daniel Ammen, *B&L*, 1:671–76; *OR*, 6:3 (Sherman's report).

49. The sealed orders to two of Du Pont's captains, to make for Port Royal in
case of separation, dated at Hampton Roads, Oct. 26, three days before the
expedition sailed, are at *NOR*, ser. 1, 12:229–30. Unlike some or all of the other
subordinate captains, the captain of Du Pont's coaling and powder convoy was
permitted to open his orders upon reaching the open sea.

50. *OR*, 6:306. An earlier message (229) reported promptly the departure of
the expedition from Hampton Roads.

51. *OR*, 6:4 (Sherman's report); Ammen, *B&L*, 682–89; *NOR*, ser. 1, 12:262–
64 (Du Pont's report).

52. Jordan to Benjamin, *OR*, 5:928; see also Jordan to Davis, ibid., 925.

53. *OR*, 5:928. The objective reported by Callan and Van Camp had also been

reported to Benjamin in a letter signed "A. M. H." — initials strikingly similar to those of Augusta Heath Morris.

54. State Dept. Secret Correspondence, 1:434, NA; see Senate payrolls, NA, for Callan's continued employment; Washington City Directories, 1859–1865.

55. Washington *Sunday Chronicle,* June 15, 1862.

56. *OR,* 4:717; *B&L,* 1:632, 661–69.

57. *OR,* ser. 2, 2:857–81, and esp. 861–68; Baker, *History of the United States Secret Service,* 102.

58. Thomas Washington's statement taken by Capt. Patrick Barrett, Nov. 4, 1861, Hooker Papers; *OR,* ser. 2, 2:1027–31; Hebert, *Fighting Joe Hooker,* 63. For the history of the Confederate Signal and Secret Service Bureau and its "Secret Line," the courier route between Washington and Richmond, see Tidwell, Hall, and Gaddy, *Come Retribution,* ch. 3, esp. pp. 87–90, and Gaddy, "William Norris and the Confederate Signal and Secret Service Bureau," *Maryland Historical Magazine,* 70, no. 2 (Summer 1975): 167–88.

59. Dix-Pierrepont Commission report; *OR,* 51.2:340–41; *SHSP,* 16:94–95 (1888); Pinkerton to McClellan, Feb. 25, 1862, McClellan Papers, no. 8838; *OR,* ser. 4, 1:687. In June 1862 Pliny Bryan was under suspicion in Norfolk and Richmond of espionage for the Federals (*OR,* ser. 2, 2:1362, 1490).

60. Turner-Baker Papers, file 710; Dix-Pierrepont Commission report; Pinkerton's receipt for Confederate currency taken from Stewart and Schley, Dec. 15, 1861, in the Hooker Papers. Mrs. Greenhow (*My Imprisonment,* 302–3) says that Stewart, whom she knew in Old Capitol Prison, was shot by a guard he had bribed.

61. Freeman, *R. E. Lee,* vol. 2, ch. 2, esp. p. 12; also see below, chapter 14, p. 332–33, and chapter 18, p. 419.

4. The Phony War of 1861-62

1. Lowe Papers, July 25, 1861.

2. *OR,* 11.3:3–5; 51.1:386–87; 5:639.

3. Circular to division commanders, Aug. 4, 1861, McClellan Papers no. 5234; McClellan to McDowell, McCall to Williams, *OR,* 5:553; McClellan to Welles, McClellan Papers, no. 5313; *OR,* 5:567–68, 579; McClellan to Mrs. McClellan, in Sears, ed., *Civil War Papers of McClellan,* 89.

4. Circular to division commanders, Aug. 27, 1861, McClellan Papers, no. 5522; McClellan to Mrs. McClellan, Aug. 31, 1861, in Sears, ed., *Civil War Papers of McClellan,* 92.

5. For example, on Sept. 6, when the Confederates were reported to have moved off from their base at Manassas, possibly with offensive intent, McClellan simply issued a reminder of the need for vigilance at outposts and on picket lines (McClellan Papers, no. 5727).

6. Smith to Williams, Jan. 8, 1862, and Myer's endorsement, McClellan Papers, no. 7665.

7. *OR,* 5:608–9, 591.

8. McClellan to Cameron, Sept. 13, 1861, Cameron Papers.

9. *OR,* 5:778–79, 881–82.

10. *OR,* 5:884–87, 347.

11. *OR,* 5:167–84 (esp. 168, 182–84), 215–17.

12. Haydon, *Aeronautics in the Union and Confederate Armies,* 116, 123–26. The Richmond newspapers, evidently assuming that the Federals would know about

the withdrawal as soon as it took place, revealed it as early as October 18, describing the new position with Centreville as the apex of an angle pointed at Washington. But this news, even if it reached Federal commanders quickly, would have been received with great skepticism, induced by wildly inaccurate reports from the front that had been appearing in the Southern press ever since the Bull Run battle. Andrews, *The South Reports the Civil War,* 87–99.

13. *OR,* 5:32–34, 288, 290, 294, 295, 299, 308; Copeland to Marcy, Oct. 20, 1861, McClellan Papers, no. 6209.

14. Wills, *Confederate Blockade of Washington,* 63–77 and 89–103 *passim; OR,* 5:384, 410–11, 421–24, 469, 638; Hebert, *Fighting Joe Hooker,* 60–62, 68–70; Haydon, *Aeronautics in the Union and Confederate Armies,* 347–56.

15. *OR,* 5:473–76.

16. Pinkerton file, S. S. Accts.

17. Timothy Webster and Frank M. Ellis each made three round trips to Richmond; E. H. Stein made three, accompanied by his wife on at least one; and C.A.H. one. Reports on seven of these missions are in the McClellan Papers, and two of Ellis's trips are known from other sources; see notes 27 and 28. These trips also are revealed in Pinkerton's payroll records (in S. S. Accts.), though the only details usually appearing there are the dates and the agents' expenses. Three other agents, Pryce Lewis, John Scully, and Hattie Lawton (or Lewis), traveled to Richmond in connection with Webster's last trip but are not known to have performed espionage. All were arrested and none returned to Washington until after Pinkerton had left the service.

18. "E. J. Allen" (Pinkerton) to McClellan, Aug. 31, 1861, McClellan Papers, no. 5593; Pinkerton file, S. S. Accts., unnumbered box. In the latter source Stein is shown to have made two trips to Richmond, both via Memphis and Nashville, between Aug. 2 and Sept. 28, the date of his arrival in Washington.

19. Freeman, *R. E. Lee,* 1:561, gives 15,000 as the number "with Lee" in western Virginia at this time, but they were not the only Confederate forces in that part of the state.

20. Jones, *Rebel War Clerk's Diary,* Aug. 7, 1861. Many other entries show Jones crediting enemy espionage with success in Richmond.

21. Buxton files, S. S. Accts.; Buxton file, SGSD; *OR,* 5:606, 613–14, 339–41; Turner-Baker Papers, file 305 and index; Andrews, *The North Reports the Civil War,* 16–17.

22. This letter, no. 5711 in the McClellan Papers, bears no notations showing how it reached McClellan or what evaluation he placed on it. Lynda L. Crist, editor of the Jefferson Davis Papers at Rice University, points out that (1) no original or other copy of this purported letter has been found; (2) the letter from Harris that Davis purportedly was answering is likewise unknown; (3) several features (the opening "My Dear Friend," the signature "J.D.," and personal subject matter that Davis habitually restricted to members of his family) presume more intimacy between Davis and Harris than actually existed. She also notes that Davis forgeries are not rare.

23. *OR,* 5:778–79.

24. *OR,* 5:937 for Jackson's arrival at Winchester; Jones, *Rebel War Clerk's Diary,* 99.

25. For Federal preparations for moving down the Eastern Shore, see *OR,* 5:424. Pinkerton's reports of Webster's travels and findings, McClellan Papers, nos. 6682 and 6689, are dated Nov. 15, 1861; two summaries of Webster's findings, largely duplicative of each other, are nos. 6678 and 6723. For cavalry regiments the summaries show only as a statewide total, 13 2/3; it is assumed that

11 2/3 of these are to be credited to Johnston's army, as Webster reported Magruder with 1200 cavalrymen, or two regiments, according to Pinkerton's formula (McClellan Papers, no. 6695). Webster grouped the regiments at Leesburg and Winchester into one figure; the Confederate return (*OR*, ser. 4, 1:626–31) includes the Leesburg regiments in the Manassas total and gives a separate figure for Winchester. The figures given in the text are adjusted for these variations.

26. McClellan Papers, no. 6403.

27. Ibid., no. 6830; Dix-Pierrepont Commission report (Ellis), NA; *OR*, ser. 2, 2:271, 278, 1303–06. Ellis's reporting on Confederate forces was at least partly honest: the Rebels' movement from Leesburg toward Dranesville on Oct. 20, which he reported, was also seen by a signal station on Sugar Loaf Mountain (see note 13 above and associated text).

28. Turner-Baker Papers, file 825; Judge Advocate General Records, bk. 2, 143–45, NA.

29. Tyler file, SGSD; Eakin file, S. S. Accts.

30. McClellan Papers, no. 6975.

31. Ibid., nos. 7154, 7456; Pinkerton payrolls, S. S. Accts., entry for July 24, 1862. Maddox will reappear in chapters 14 and 17 and the Epilogue.

32. Pinkerton to McClellan, Dec. 27, 1861, McClellan Papers, nos. 7316, 8153.

33. Pinkerton to McClellan, Jan. 30 and 31, and April 20, 1862, McClellan Papers, nos. 8153, 8187, and 10827; Pinkerton file, S. S. Accts., Jan.–May 1862; *OR*, 5:1029–32 for total Confederate regiments; *OR*, 7:933–36 (Webster's information on Tennessee and Kentucky, sent to Halleck).

34. For example, see Foote, *Civil War*, 1:121.

35. Acquisition of resident spies by the intelligence bureau that succeeded Pinkerton's in the Army of the Potomac is detailed in chapters 12 and 14. Extensive portions of the activities of a ring of Richmond Unionists have been examined by Meriwether Stuart in "Samuel Ruth and General R. E. Lee: Disloyalty and the Line of Supply to Fredericksburg, 1862–63," *Virginia Magazine of History and Biography* 71 (Jan. 1963): 35–109; and "Colonel Ulric Dahlgren and Richmond's Union Underground," ibid. 72 (April 1964): 152–204. Although Ruth is identified as a Unionist in *OR*, and some of the activities of the Richmond ring have long been known, Stuart has used manuscript records to develop a comprehensive and authoritative account of the Richmond Unionists' accomplishments.

5. Mr. Pinkerton's Unique Arithmetic

1. Allan Nevins: McClellan "let himself be deceived by the reports of his friend Allan Pinkerton" (*War for the Union: The Improvised War*, 300). Douglas Southall Freeman: "McClellan was deceived by his incompetent spies" (*Lee's Lieutenants*, 1:236–37). Kenneth P. Williams: ". . . eventually [McClellan] must have realized the fantastic deception that had been perpetrated by his 'better system' for enemy intelligence" (*Lincoln Finds a General*, 1:129). Bruce Catton: "Pinkerton was almost completely incompetent at giving [McClellan] the data he needed about the opposing army." Pinkerton's "intelligence reports were detailed, explicit, incredibly wrong — and believed down to the last digit" by McClellan (*This Hallowed Ground*, 87, 138). Shelby Foote: "Pinkerton, with his tabulated lists compiled by operatives in Richmond, had misled [McClellan]

badly" (*Civil War*, 1:121). Warren W. Hassler, Jr.: McClellan was "placed in a hopeless position . . . in part by the fantastic overestimates of the enemy numbers by Pinkerton's men and others" (*General George B. McClellan*, 171). Numerous other references to McClellan's dependence on and belief in Pinkerton's erroneous estimates are found in the writings of Nevins, Williams, Hassler, and particularly Catton, who devoted considerable attention to Pinkerton in *Mr. Lincoln's Army* (122–23). The view that McClellan's temperament shares, with Pinkerton's estimates, the responsibility for his beliefs about the enemy is occasionally seen; see, for example, Robert Selph Henry, *Story of the Confederacy*, 152. (See also note 10 below.) But the "standard" view of Pinkerton's exaggerated estimates and their effect on McClellan stood basically uncorrected until the 1988 appearance of Stephen W. Sears's biography, *George B. McClellan: The Young Napoleon*, which perceptively examines Pinkerton's operation and McClellan's uncritical acceptance of its product (107–10), and the present writer's "Pinkerton and McClellan: Who Deceived Whom?" *Civil War History* 34, no. 2 (June 1988: 115–42).

2. Pinkerton payrolls, S. S. Accts. Pinkerton's service in Washington began Aug. 1 and detective Kate Warne's the same day. Sam Bridgeman and Pryce Lewis arrived Aug. 3, Timothy Webster and Hattie Lewis (Lawton) on Aug. 8.

3. McMurdy to Halleck, Sept. 26, 1862, RG 94, microfilm roll 121, file 1780-M-1862, NA. En route back to Kentucky (to join his regiment, he claimed), McMurdy was arrested on suspicion of espionage. He spent several weeks in Old Capitol Prison and was released on Pinkerton's recommendation at the suggestion of Asst. Secretary of State F. W. Seward, who sent Pinkerton a collection of McMurdy family letters antedating the arrest and establishing Edward McMurdy's loyalty to Seward's satisfaction. (Pinkerton to Andrew Porter, Oct. 30, 1861, Pinkerton Papers no. 604; *OR*, ser. 2, 2:314–15.) In his letter to Halleck, McMurdy said he left Manassas about ten days after the battle; thus his roundabout trip to Washington probably would have taken place in the early days of August. He said that Adjt. Gen. Lorenzo Thomas and Secretary Stanton had struck him from the army rolls, and the influence of Kentucky congressmen had not sufficed to win him reinstatement.

4. McClellan to Mary Ellen McClellan, Aug. 16, 19, 20, 1861, *Civil War Papers of McClellan*, 85, 87, 89; McClellan to Cameron, Sept. 8, 1861, *OR*, 5:588; and Sept. 13, 1861, Cameron Papers; Livermore, *Numbers and Losses*, 77; Johnston, *Narrative of Military Operations*, 70.

5. The only Pinkerton estimates McClellan is known to have given his superiors were those he forwarded in 1863 as part of the historical report of his period of command. Signed "E. J. Allen," these are in *OR*, 5:736–37, 763–64, and 11.1:264–272.

6. A letter to Johnston from Acting Secretary of War Judah P. Benjamin on Oct. 13 (*OR*, 5:896–97) shows that Benjamin was planning the construction of huts to house about 40,000 men in the Johnston-Beauregard army. Whether this included their force at Aquia on the lower Potomac is unclear. Their return for October (*OR*, 5:932–33) shows 52,435 "aggregate present" and 44,131 "effective total present" in the main force and 5728 "present for duty" in the Aquia district. On Oct. 4, the date of Pinkerton's estimate, these figures probably were somewhat lower.

7. The overage for regiments in Johnston's army was 20 percent, and in numbers of troops present, 23 percent. From the closeness of these two percentages it is tempting to conclude that Pinkerton's "standard" averages of 700 for infantry regiments and 600 for cavalry were fairly accurate. However, the num-

bers of regiments are provided only by a September return and the numbers of troops by an October return; the latter might reflect regiments not present in September. Therefore the two returns cannot serve as a check on the accuracy of Pinkerton's regimental averages.

8. The Oct. 4 estimate is no. 6013 in the McClellan Papers. Three days later Pinkerton reported a "total effective force of 106,405," but because of illegibility of the weak carbon copy in the Pinkerton Papers, it is uncertain whether the figure covered exactly the same Confederate elements as the 98,400 reported on Oct. 4.

9. E. J. Allen to McClellan, Nov. 15, 1861, McClellan Papers, no. 6678, repeated at 6725.

10. One writer who has suggested that Pinkerton may have been delivering strength totals that he believed McClellan wanted is T. Harry Williams. In *Lincoln and His Generals* (50) he notes that Pinkerton may have "sensed that McClellan wanted the enemy magnified as an excuse for inaction." This rare perception, however, does not go so far as to suggest that McClellan was aware of Pinkerton's overestimating, intentional or otherwise; and Williams finds the standard view that Pinkerton was simply incompetent equally as plausible as the possibility of conscious overestimating.

11. Unsigned draft, McClellan Papers, no. 8990. McClellan's "safety first" intelligence policy fits neatly with the overall military policy that, his defenders argue, was the only wise course — a program of thorough preparation and cautious action to preclude another Bull Run disaster.

12. *OR*, 5:9–11; McClellan Papers, nos. 6456–6469, esp. 6463. The intelligence reports that may have yielded this total are Pinkerton to McClellan, Oct. 28, 1861, McClellan Papers, no. 6403, and Hancock to Marcy, Oct. 30, 1861, ibid., no. 6449. Although the time of McClellan's paper is sometimes placed in late November, letters of Oct. 31 from McClellan to his wife and to Lincoln clearly establish that the drafting, at Stanton's home, was going on at that time.

13. McClellan Papers, nos. 6682 and 6689 (reports of Webster's travels and findings), nos. 6678 and 6723 (summaries of the findings), no. 6013 (Pinkerton's Oct. 4 estimate).

14. In order to produce a statewide total incorporating Webster's findings, it was necessary to add in totals from Pinkerton's Oct. 4 estimate for the two areas Webster did not cover, Norfolk-Portsmouth (10,400) and western Virginia (11,000). Then, in order to compare the result with the Oct. 4 grand total, it was necessary to add to the latter figure 21,100, the assumed strength of the Peninsula army (omitted from the Oct. 4 estimate) as reported by Webster (twenty-seven infantry regiments, or 18,900 men, and 1200 cavalry). But instead of using 21,100, Pinkerton substituted 7000, explaining that that was the probable strength of the Peninsula force on Oct. 4, three weeks previous to Webster's visit. Here Pinkerton was guilty of false logic; reports of two troop totals cannot corroborate each other unless they pertain to the same body of troops, and Pinkerton was saying that the Peninsula army had grown from 7000 to over 20,000 in those three weeks. He offered no evidence in support of those reinforcements or of the 7000 figure, and none is found in his other reports to McClellan. As a trebling of that force in so short a time is extremely unlikely, the 7000 figure must be regarded as one of the deliberate artifices mentioned in the text. Its effect was to bring Webster's total, 13,100 (20,100 less 7000), closer to Pinkerton's Oct. 4 grand total than the data in hand justified. Also there were two errors involving the 5 percent safety allowance. As the Oct. 4 total of 126,600 was claimed to have been arrived at by adding in 5 percent of some previously

computed total, the amount deducted from the 126,600 in the reconciling process should have been 5 percent of the earlier total; that total would have been in the neighborhood of 120,600. And the safety-allowance deduction also should have been applied to the 10,400 and 11,000 figures for Norfolk-Portsmouth and western Virginia that were added to Webster's figures. These errors produced another spurious narrowing, amounting to 1320, of the gap between the two grand totals.

15. McClellan Papers, no. 6830; *OR*, ser. 2, 2:1303–6.

16. Sears, ed., *Civil War Papers of McClellan*, 143. This dispatch also appears in *OR*, 11.3:6, without McClellan's emphasis on "nearly."

17. Pinkerton to McClellan, Dec. 4, 1861, McClellan Papers, no. 6925.

18. Pinkerton to McClellan, Dec. 12, 13, 1861, ibid., nos. 7031 and 7043. Only Webster is known to have been in Confederate-held parts of Virginia at the time Pinkerton said that "many" of his operatives were behind enemy lines.

19. McClellan Papers, nos. 7048, 6975; *OR*, 5:52–53.

20. JCCW, 1863, 1:147–49; William W. Pierson, "The Committee on the Conduct of the Civil War," *American Historical Review* 23 (April 1918):552–73 *passim; OR*, 5:1015; Henry G. Pearson, *James S. Wadsworth of Geneseo*, 104–5. In February 1862 McClellan received an order-of-battle compilation on Johnston's army from a source not shown; the timing and the army total, 53,700, suggest that this could have come from Wadsworth. A contrary indication is the fact that its identifications of Confederate units were most numerous (though not necessarily the most correct) for localities distant from Wadsworth's position. This paper draws an accurate general picture of Johnston's command, extending from Aquia to Winchester, and of locations of the major elements. But the writer had record of only fifty-seven regiments, barely half of the total, and only thirty-four of them were fully identified (*i.e.*, both regiment number and state of origin were known). Although the 53,700 total was reasonable, it was rendered meaningless by the incompleteness of the data on the army's composition, on which the total was based. The compiler obviously did not have access to Pinkerton's data; thus it would appear that he was in one of the divisions rather than at army headquarters. McClellan, probably startled by so low a total, wrote marginal notes beside the compiler's data and reworked the total to 68,100; even that figure would have been incompatible with his own views. This compilation, McClellan Papers no. 8266, is mistakenly dated Jan. 1862; it contains information of date as late as Feb. 16.

21. Interrogation reports in the McClellan Papers (the only sizable collection of Pinkerton's positive-intelligence products) are heavily concentrated in the period January–March 1862, February being the busiest month with 301 pages. McClellan's December order on forwarding of prisoners, deserters, and refugees could have contributed to this surge, but its main cause probably was change in reporting practice; during earlier and later periods Pinkerton's staff would merely have added data from ordinary informants to the files rather than making a separate report of each interrogation.

22. Unsigned report to McClellan dated only Feb. 1862, McClellan Papers, no. 8969.

23. Ibid., nos. 8636, 9009.

24. Pinkerton to McClellan, Dec. 20, 1861, ibid., no. 7167. This is the earliest report of interrogation of a deserter in the McClellan Papers.

25. "Statement of 3 Deserters from the rebel forces," dated Lower Potomac, Md., Jan. 3, 1862, Hooker Papers; Pinkerton to McClellan, McClellan Papers, nos. 14704, 7584, 7793, 7826. For examples of escapes from Gen. Hill's drudg-

ery, see ibid., nos. 7300, 7329, 7349, 7478, 7627, 7874; for the Irish escapee, no. 8071; for other escapes with the same woman's aid, nos. 8333, 8476 (her name, when given, was not always spelled Stypes). The Unionist element of Loudoun County, consisting mostly of Quakers and Germans around Lovettsville and Waterford, formed a battalion named the Loudoun Rangers, which provided the rangers under John Mosby and Elijah White with serious resistance. See Richard E. Crouch, *Washington Times,* June 10, 1995, p. B3.

26. McClellan Papers, nos. 8109, 8147, 8247.

27. Ibid., nos. 8275, 8321.

28. Ibid., nos. 8941, 9200.

29. Undated, unsigned memo, ibid., no. 7403. The subject's surname may have been Ring.

30. Ibid., no. 6907. Ringgold also supplied a six-month-old map of the Peninsula battlefield of Great Bethel. (Pinkerton's report observed, "You will see that it is of Southern manufacture and diction.") Having come North on a Confederate pass, Ringgold was a refugee in only a limited sense.

31. McClellan Papers, nos. 9609, 9616, 9688; *OR,* 5:53, 1086. Of the four trainmen interrogated in Pinkerton's bureau, two were Jerseymen and two were Marylanders. The one questioned at Cumberland said his interviewers there were Brig. Gens. Robert C. Schenck and Benjamin F. Kelley.

32. McClellan Papers, no. 8760.

33. See, *e.g.,* the statement of John McChandless and Henry H. Rowlins, ibid., no. 8622.

34. Ibid., nos. 7283, 7204, 8357.

35. Ibid., no. 7100.

36. Ibid., nos. 8180, 8333, 9099.

37. Numerous reports from Pinkerton to McClellan between Dec. 26, 1861 (no. 7283) and Mar. 7, 1862 (no. 9150) are in the McClellan Papers.

38. Ibid., nos. 8670, 8681. According to W. H. Ringgold, Negro servants in regiments on the Peninsula were fully armed, were drilled, and followed their regiments as separate units on the march (ibid., no. 6907).

39. For example, see ibid., no. 9094.

40. Ibid., no. 7951.

41. Ibid., nos. 8690, 9206.

42. Ibid., no. 7944, 8300. Other contacts with Union men in Richmond were made after release from prison by Samuel N. Gosnell, a Fairfax Countian who had been arrested for disloyalty to the South (ibid., no. 8806).

43. Although Butler may not have been the first to apply the word *contraband* to runaway slaves, he is credited as the one responsible for its adoption into the language (Trefousse, *Ben Butler,* 79).

44. McClellan Papers, no. 8494.

45. Ibid., nos. 6863, 7174.

46. Ibid., no. 8502; Pinkerton Papers, no. 778–79.

47. McClellan Papers, no. 8512.

48. Ibid., no. 8883.

49. Ibid., nos. 7064, 7107; *OR,* ser. 2, 2:237, 271. For examples of the release of prisoners of British citizenship, see Neely, *Fate of Liberty,* 25, 110–12.

50. For the assignment and activities of the Orléans brothers see *B&L,* 2:184–85, 338, 342, 429; *OR,* 51.1:723, 5:505, 11.1:426, 534; 11.3:158; *OR,* ser. 3, 1:542, 3:264, 273.

51. Robert d'Orléans to McClellan, [July] 3, 1862, McClellan Papers, no. 12371 (erroneously dated June 3).

52. "Troops and Defences in the vicinity of Aquia Creek/Batteries Along the Potomac," Feb. 1, 1862, McClellan Papers, no. 8295; R. H. Wyman to G. V. Fox, Feb. 1, 1862, ibid., no. 8293; Col. Charles K. Graham, "Statement of two contrabands who escaped from Aquia Creek," Jan. 28, 1862, Hooker Papers; "Statement of 3 Deserters from the rebel forces," dated Lower Potomac, Md., Jan. 3, 1862, Hooker Papers; Pinkerton to McClellan, Jan. 8 and Feb. 25, 1862, McClellan Papers, nos. 14704 and 8838; [L. P. d'Orléans] to McClellan, Feb. 19, 20, 25, 1862, McClellan Papers, nos. 8700, 8737, 8862; OR, 5:1086. For an estimate of the practicality of a "dash" across the Potomac to take the batteries, see Capt. R. S. Williamson to Gen. Williams, Jan. 20, 1862, McClellan Papers, no. 7923.

53. McClellan Papers, no. 8463 (R. d'Orléans report, Feb. 10, 1862, "Troops & defences in the vicinity of Leesburg, Va."), and nos. 8681, 8369, 8357. When Pinkerton reported information from Leesburg contrabands late in February, R. d'Orléans wrote to McClellan that it was mainly only a confirmation of his previous report (ibid., no. 8865).

54. The first of the two Orléans reports on the Shenandoah Valley is no. 8666 in the McClellan Papers; for supporting details see nos. 7321, 7793, 8109, 8439. The Orléans follow-up report is at no. 9070. See also no. 8402 (Jackson-Loring quarrel); no. 7309 (Banks's spy in Virginia); Boatner, Civil War Dictionary, 492; OR, 5:1066–67, 1086; 9:56.

55. OR, 5:1026, 1023, 1028.

56. McClellan Papers, no. 8700, dated Feb. 19, 1862. Slightly higher figures for three brigades are given in a March 5 follow-up (no. 9140), but this covers only half of the Manassas-Centreville army.

57. L. P. d'Orléans's report is no. 8700 in the McClellan Papers; Ringgold's is no. 6907. Orléans's "date of information," Jan. 18, was the day the deserter James H. Maurice escaped from his regiment on the Peninsula; his information is prominent in d'Orléans's summary, but other information there cannot be traced to reports in the McClellan Papers or OR. As Orléans had to repeat his Feb. 19 report the very next day (McClellan Papers, no. 8737), it is not hard to believe that a report as old as Ringgold's was mislaid at the time Orléans wrote his summary. Magruder's troop total is at OR, 11.1:405.

58. This 87,180 total incorporates the lower of the two figures given for the Aquia District (11,700–12,700) and for Manassas-Centreville (50,600–53,100).

59. The Confederate return, at OR, 5:1086, shows another 27,830 troops absent. Although "aggregate present and absent" figures are normally much higher than "aggregate present" all through the returns of both armies, this deviation is an unusually wide one, caused by the large numbers of furloughs the Confederates granted as a re-enlistment inducement.

60. Jan. 30, 1862, entry in L. P. d'Orléans's diary, Fondation Saint-Louis, Amboise, France; translation courtesy of Mark Grimsley. The figures included 13,000 in the Shenandoah Valley.

61. It was during this period that McClellan would have received the order-of-battle summary described in note 20 above from a source, unidentified, in one of his divisions.

62. OR, 5:892, 1086.

63. Pinkerton's Mar. 8 estimate is at OR, 5:736–37; a near-verbatim repeat is at 763–64. The method of computing a "summary of general estimates" is shown in a later report; see chapter 6, note 72 and associated text.

64. In January Johnston's replies to Benjamin's request for a list of brigades and their regiments listed 94 regiments, not including Loring's command, which he believed contained 10 more (OR, 5:1029–32). The 56,392 listed as

"aggregate present" in his February return (ibid., 1086) would translate into 113 regiments at the rate of 500 per regiment, an average based on two Peninsula campaign statistics: the 178 Confederate regiments participating in the battles around Richmond and the 92,400 now calculated as Lee's total in the Seven Days battles before Richmond (see chapter 6, note 66).

65. *OR*, 5:736–37, repeated at 763–64.

66. An 80,000 total would have been composed of 66,500 for the ninety-five infantry regiments he listed, 6000 for the ten cavalry regiments, and 7500 as a rough guess of the numbers in the army's smaller units listed (two battalions, eighteen independent cavalry companies, fifty-seven artillery companies) and militia units, of which he listed two brigades in the Valley and one regiment at Leesburg. Numbers on duty in militia units were much smaller than in regular units.

67. "General M. C. Meigs on the Conduct of the Civil War," a paper written by Meigs for the *Century* War Papers series *(B&L)* but unpublished until printed in *American Historical Review*, Jan. 1921, p. 293. The 50,500 figure is the total of estimates for sixteen different localities between Dumfries and Centreville; see Barnard, *Peninsular Campaign*, 95.

6. "Outnumbered" on the Peninsula

1. *OR*, 51.2:512.

2. Johnston, *Narrative of Military Operations*, 95–97; *OR*, 5:1079, 1083; Thomas Bragg Diary, Feb. 19, 20, 1862.

3. Pinkerton file, S. S. Accts.; Pinkerton, *Spy of the Rebellion*, 485–97. Webster had been gone from Washington less than three weeks; as previous trips South had lasted longer than that, Pinkerton's dispatch of Lewis and Scully to Richmond, in addition to Hattie Lawton's presence there, indicates that he was worried about Webster's health. They left Washington Feb. 18 and according to Pinkerton they reached Richmond without delay.

4. Pinkerton to McClellan, April 20, 1862, McClellan Papers, no. 10827; Pinkerton payrolls, Jan., Feb., and April, 1862, S. S. Accts.

5. Jeffrey N. Lash, "Joseph E. Johnston and the Virginia Railways, 1861–62," *Civil War History* 5, no. 1 (March 1989): 18–21; Johnston, *Narrative*, 96–99, 104.

6. *OR*, 5:49, 526–27, 1083, 1092; McClellan to Halleck, *OR*, 11.3:7; Johnston, *Narrative*, 96–99, 104; Lash, "Joseph E. Johnston and the Virginia Railways, 1861–62"; also Sears, *To the Gates of Richmond*, ch. 1. For details relating to McClellan's preliminary moves see McClellan Papers, nos. 9029, 9180, 9187, 9188, 9225. Johnston was so protective of his withdrawal secret that in writing to Gen. Whiting on March 6 he announced the 8th as the time for the general movement but instructed that no one be told of the planned timing "unless necessary."

7. *OR*, 5:526–27, 1096.

8. After Pinkerton's receipt of fifteen fugitive slaves Feb. 21 and six cavalry prisoners Feb. 22, the file shows no interrogation of anyone from the Aquia-Manassas-Centreville area until the arrival of a contraband on March 9 (McClellan Papers, nos. 8784, 8883, 9282).

9. Ibid., nos. 9021, 9025, 9039, 9159, 9190, 9200, 9206, 9269; *OR*, 5:549.

10. *OR*, 5:736, 763.

11. See chapter 5, note 31 and associated text.

12. Lowe's final report, *OR*, ser. 3, 3:270–71; Haydon, *Aeronautics in the Union*

and Confederate Armies, 369–72; Heintzelman diary, March 5 and 6, 1862. Haydon's statement that previous to the reports of smokes on the Occoquan "rumors and suspicions of the impending Confederate evacuation of Manassas and Centreville had reached the Federal high command" is not supported by the source cited.

13. Sears, *McClellan,* 131, 130; Sears, ed., *Civil War Papers of McClellan,* 170–71; *OR,* 5:42–45; Barnard, *Peninsular Campaign,* 52–54 (same memo is at *OR,* 5:671–73) and 94; Heintzelman diary, March 8, 1862; *OR Atlas,* plates 16, 100.1, 137; undated map by Col. T. C. Cram, "S.E. Portion of Virginia and N.E. Portion of Nth Carolina," Geography and Map Div., Library of Congress. *McClellan's Own Story,* 195, erroneously gives March 8 as the date of his interview with Lincoln and the council of war.

14. Barna d, *Peninsular Campaign,* 94.

15. An example is McDowell's telegram to McClellan, Feb. 1, 1862 (McClellan Papers, no. 8287), which consists of third-hand information that McClellan used to show Lincoln that the Confederates had prepared entrenchments along the Occoquan route proposed by Lincoln (*OR,* 5:43; also in Sears, ed., *Civil War Papers of McClellan,* 164).

16. McClellan Papers, no. 6907.

17. The closest Timothy Webster had come to information on the Urbanna area was his report, at second hand, of very light Confederate forces in the Northern Neck, on the opposite side of the Rappahannock.

18. Sears, *McClellan,* 159–60; Basler, ed., *Works of Lincoln,* 5:149–50. Barnard says (*Peninsular Campaign,* 52) that the generals voted "offhand, without discussion." (Gen. Banks was also appointed a corps commander over the forces he was leading in the Valley; he did not participate in these meetings.)

19. Basler, ed., *Works of Lincoln,* 5:151; *B&L,* 1:698–99; Sears, *McClellan,* 162; Sears, ed., *Civil War Papers of McClellan,* 198; NOR, ser. 1, 7:78.

20. McClellan Papers, nos. 9293, 9282, 9295. Two additional interrogation reports received this date would not have affected McClellan's decision because of late arrival and their concern mainly with the evacuation of Leesburg (ibid., nos. 9269, 9278).

21. Sears, ed., *Civil War Papers of McClellan,* 198, and same dispatch at *OR,* 9:23. Wool replied that his scouts had reported Magruder's troops within five miles of Newport News (McClellan Papers, no. 9369).

22. Sears, ed., *Civil War Papers of McClellan,* 200; McClellan Papers nos. 9298, 9268, 9304, 9296, 9305; *OR,* 5:537, 544–45.

23. In the report on his period in command McClellan presented a quite different version of the discovery of the Confederate evacuation. He omitted the balloon observations reported to his office beginning as early as the morning of March 6 and mentioned only the information received on the 9th, saying that it was "most positive" (*OR,* 5:51). Of course the information on the enemy's evacuation of Leesburg and abandonment of the Potomac batteries, coming from Federals on the scene, was positive, but that was not true of the information on the enemy's main force, at Manassas-Centreville. After the time when McClellan says the "positive" information was received, we find him at Porter's headquarters, telegraphing Marcy and stating his uncertainty as to the enemy's position at Centreville.

24. Averell to F. J. Porter, 7:50 P.M., March 10, 1862, McClellan Papers, no. 9339; *OR,* 5:526–27, 530.

25. Haydon, *Aeronautics in the Union and Confederate Armies,* 148.

26. McClellan Papers, no. 9339; Sears, *McClellan,* 164; *OR,* 5:737.

27. Sears, *McClellan*, 163; *OR*, 5:53 and 1086; Williams, *Lincoln Finds a General*, 1:154, 124. For the Orléans report see chapter 5, note 57 and associated text.

28. *OR*, 5:55, 54, 550; Basler, ed., *Works of Lincoln*, 5:155; Sears, ed., *Civil War Papers of McClellan*, 209–10.

29. JCCW 1863, 1:424, 390; *OR*, 11.1:405, 5:55–56.

30. Prince de Joinville, *Army of the Potomac*, 27; Sears, ed., *Civil War Papers of McClellan*, 210; *OR*, 5:54, 51; Williams, *Lincoln Finds a General*, 1:155; Pinkerton, *Spy of the Rebellion*, 572. A fourth statement is found in McClellan's testimony to the Joint Committee on the Conduct of the War that "my impression has always been that they got wind of our intended movement to the lower Chesapeake" (JCCW 1863, 1:426). The tentativeness conveyed by the word "impression" is of a piece with an indefiniteness in much of McClellan's responses to the committee's questions. A motive for his cautious response in this case could have been a wish to avoid naming suspected sources of leakage — suspicions he scarcely could have supported.

31. Starr, *Bohemian Brigade*, 78–80, 94.

32. *McClellan's Own Story*, 238; *OR*, 11.3:25, 28, 91; Williams, *Lincoln Finds a General*, 1:159; Sears, *McClellan*, 168.

33. *OR*, 11.3:385–434 *passim;* 51.2:512; Johnston, *Narrative of Military Operations*, 109–10.

34. Crouch, *Eagle Aloft*, 383, 388; Williams to Lowe, March 23, 1862, Lowe Papers; Lowe to Macomb, April 2, 1862, ibid.

35. Myer's Peninsula campaign report, *OR*, 11.1:226–64 (the opening of communication with the navy is recounted on 229); Scheips, *Albert James Myer*, ch. 11 *passim;* Plum, *Military Telegraph*, 1:143–44. The Signal Corps later became disenchanted with the performance of the Beardslee wire telegraph equipment; also, its use by the army was opposed by commercial telegraph interests, which had an audience at the War Dept. in the chiefs of the civilian Military Telegraph system, which used many commercial lines.

36. O'Brien, *Telegraphing in Battle*, 71–72, 83–84; Thompson, *Wiring a Continent*, 299–301, 319–20, 323, 433–34.

37. Pinkerton file, S. S. Accts.; Miller, *Photographic History*, 8:263, 264 and frontispiece. Other members of Pinkerton's Peninsula unit were Francis Warner, Seth Paine, D. G. McKelvey, Augustus K. Littlefield, Thaddeus S. Seybold, Sam Bridgman, John C. Babcock, and five men known only by their initials. The number of operatives dropped to eleven in May and remained there throughout the campaign.

38. 45th Cong., Records of the U.S. Senate, "Claim of F. W. E. Lohman, Samuel Ruth, and Charles M. Carter." No clear evidence that the Richmond Unionists had an organized espionage effort at the time of the Peninsula campaign has surfaced. The reports of Pinkerton's agents who visited Richmond reveal no contact with or information on local Unionists. If information from them appears in any of Pinkerton's reports, he concealed the source, a practice he is not known to have used in his reports to McClellan.

39. Webster's report, McClellan Papers, no. 6689. Examples of far-forward reconnoitering by signal officers are in Myer's Peninsula report at *OR*, 11.1:238, 240, 245, 254.

40. George H. Bangs to his mother, June 14, 1863, collection of Michael O. Berry.

41. McClellan Papers, nos. 11455, 11461, 11469, 11522; Myer's endorsement on Hall and Taylor to Cushing, Nov. 28, 1862, RG 111, entry 27 (Records of the Office of the Chief Signal Officer), "Papers Relating to Proposed Signal Sys-

tems," NA; Myer and Howgate, *Report of the Operations and Duties of the Signal Department of the Army,* 87–88 (copy in possession of author); Gaddy, "William Norris and the Confederate Signal and Secret Service," *Maryland Historical Magazine* 70, no. 2 (Summer 1975):171–72. See also chapter 11, note 36 and associated text. From the language used by one of these prisoners, William Hornsby, it is clear that he considered the signaling alphabet a "cipher" (a secret alphabet actually is a very simple cipher). The other prisoners used similar language but with less clarity. Similar loose usage appears among Federal signalmen. Lieut. Camp's ability to read enemy traffic evidently reminded Myer that his own signals were similarly vulnerable, for he attempted to cover a Federal troop movement with a false message. Later, in his report of the Peninsula campaign, he wrote, "It is customary . . . to send with an especial signal messages intended to deceive" (*OR,* 11.1:250). However, such deception, although practiced on some occasions, does not seem to have become "customary."

42. From the Richmond *Examiner*'s report of Webster's hanging, April 30, 1862, p. 3, col. 2. The account of the arrests of Pinkerton's agents and the resultant events is drawn from his book *Spy of the Rebellion,* 486–560. Those pages contain Pinkerton's usual fabricated dialogue and other embellishments, but they appear reliable as to the main facts, and no other source close to these events is known. Lewis, a British subject, had succeeded in appealing to the British consul in Richmond; he and Scully, who claimed Irish birth, were released to Federal prisoner-exchange officers March 18, 1863. Hattie Lawton, still carried on the records as Mrs. Timothy Webster, was one of a party of four Federals exchanged for Belle Boyd Dec. 13, 1862. (Turner-Baker Papers, file 1751 and box 54; also SGS 1865–66/192; Harriet H. Shoen, "Pryce Lewis, Spy for the Union," *Davis and Elkins Historical Magazine* 2, no. 2 [May 1949]:35.) H.J.K. disappears from Pinkerton's payrolls after a May entry that says his account "will be rendered as soon as possible after his being released from the rebel lines."

43. McClellan Papers, no. 10222; diary of James H. McMath, Alabama Dept. of Archives and History, April 5, 1862, entry; letter from Robert H. Miller to his uncle, April 27, 1862, "Letters of Lieutenant Robert H. Miller to His Family," ed. Forrest P. Connor, *Virginia Magazine of History and Biography,* vol. 70, no. 1 (Jan. 1962):82; Dowdey, *Seven Days,* 41; *OR,* 11.3:64.

44. *OR,* 11.3:22, 23; JCCW 1863, 1:393; McClellan Papers, nos. 8275, 8321, 6907, 6689, 11237, 21698; Sears, *To the Gates of Richmond,* 38, 45; Sears, ed., *Civil War Papers of McClellan,* 229, 232–33; McClellan, *Report,* 74. McClellan's defective map is almost certainly the one that appears in the *OR Atlas* at plate 18.1. One fort, a principal part of the Yorktown and Warwick River defenses that were a blank spot in McClellan's advance intelligence, is claimed to have been scouted in great detail by the transvestite spy Emma Edmonds (military alias Franklin Thompson). Her book *Nurse and Spy* (114–15) lists 130 heavy guns of eight different types, a preposterously large number for a single fort. As the diary of the fellow soldier with whom Emma Edmonds had an extended romance shows her to have been present in camp at the time her book says she was on duty as a spy, it is evident that the story is a fabrication. And both Emma's name and alias are missing from Pinkerton's roster of agents; no information attributed to her is found in the thousand pages of Pinkerton reports in the McClellan Papers. In fact she almost certainly was never a spy at all, though her authenticity is unchallenged in popular histories of Civil War espionage (see, for example, Donald E. Markle, *Spies and Spymasters of the Civil War* [New York: Hippocrene Press, 1994], 175–79, and Alan Axelrod, *The War Between the Spies* [New York: Atlantic Monthly

Press, 1992] 97–102, 155). An article by Betty Fladeland, drawn from the diary showing Emma Edmonds's whereabouts at the time of the Peninsula campaign, is in *Michigan History*, vol. 48, no. 4 (Dec. 1963), 357–62.

45. Johnston, *Narrative*, 111–17; Sears, ed., *Civil War Papers of McClellan*, 229; Goldsborough to McClellan, April 6, 1862, and Missroon to Goldsborough, April 23, 1862, *OR*, 11.3:80, 123; Johnston to Hill, May 1, 1862, ibid., 486; *OR*, 11.1:232–33 (Myer's Peninsula campaign report); JCCW 1863, 1:283–84 (Painter's testimony); *OR*, ser. 3, 3:276 (Lowe's report).

46. *OR*, 11.1:232–33 (Myer's report); O'Brien, *Telegraphing in Battle*, 83–84. Lowe claimed (Miller, *Photographic History*, 8:370) that he discovered the evacuation in a middle-of-the-night ascent occasioned by reports of fire in Yorktown; O'Brien states that Lowe reported only that "the fire was either a sloop at the wharf, or a building in town." As Lowe's account in *Photographic History* tends to overstate his successes, O'Brien's is probably the more correct version. By the time Lowe made a second ascent, with Gen. Heintzelman aboard, so much time had elapsed that they observed a Federal skirmish line advancing (*OR*, 11.1:456). O'Brien's impression that McClellan arrived early at "Mc" is refuted in the diary of the comte de Paris, who says he awakened McClellan at 6 A.M. only to hear him refuse to credit the news, whereupon he went back to sleep. (Sears, *To the Gates of Richmond*, 67.)

47. *OR*, 11.3:151; Marcy to Lowe, June 1, 1862, Lowe Papers; Babcock to "Dear Uncle," March 4, 1862, and to "Dear Aunt," June 6, 1862, Babcock Papers; Miller, *Photographic History*, 8:23, 263, 264, and frontispiece; "Record of Service of John C. Babcock during Civil War of 1861–65," Babcock Papers. Babcock's maps are in the collection of the Geography and Map Division, nos. 619.9, 619.95, 620, 620.2, Library of Congress; in vol. 77, nos. 16251 and 16276, Lincoln Papers; in container 1, Heintzelman Papers; in container 82, Lowe Papers. (The Library of Congress cartographic staff recognized the falsity of Pinkerton's claim and named Babcock as the authority for all these maps.) Evidence for the statement that Babcock's was the only scouting ever performed by Pinkerton's organization will be found in chapter 14, note 34 and associated text. Further biographical data on Babcock are in chapter 11, notes 19 and 20 and associated text.

48. *OR*, 11.1:236; 11.3:170, 162, 163–64; McClellan, *Report*, 93.

49. McClellan, *Report*, 94–95; *OR*, 11.3:179–80.

50. *OR*, 11.3:188, 179–80; Sears, *To the Gates of Richmond*, 109–10; McClellan, *Report*, 93–94; McClellan Papers, no. 11884.

51. *OR*, 11.3:191; Sears, *To the Gates of Richmond*, 113–16; Myer, in *OR*, 11.1:240–41.

52. *OR*, 11.3:193; McClellan, *Report*, 105.

53. Sears, *To the Gates of Richmond*, 120–45, esp. 138, 145; *OR*, 11.3:203.

54. Lowe in Miller, *Photographic History*, 8:376, 378. The fact of high winds and Lowe's delay in getting into the air on May 31 is confirmed by an entry in the diary of Louis Philippe d'Orléans. His opinion of Lowe is reflected in a later entry: "I waste my time to [assist] the insouciance of the astronaut who [will be] too late to boast of his exploits" (entry for June 13, 1862).

55. *OR*, ser. 3, 3:280–81; McClellan Papers, no. 12122. The records of ballooning on these two days (May 31 and June 1) are further distorted by errors that occurred when undated dispatches were supplied with estimated dates in the processing of the McClellan Papers many years later. For example, a balloonist's message timed at 10:45 (*sic;* McClellan Papers, no. 12130) reported movement of wagons toward the battlefield. The May 31 date interpolated here would

qualify this as a warning of Confederate attack, but the context of the rest of the message shows that it was written June 1.

56. Sears, *To the Gates of Richmond,* 167–73.

57. *OR,* 11.3:602.

58. *OR,* 11.3:201, 208–9, 240.

59. Andrews, *The North Reports the Civil War,* 688–69; Taylor, *Destruction and Reconstruction,* 83.

60. *OR,* 11.3:602.

61. *OR,* 11.3:232, 234.

62. *OR,* 51.1:693–96; Freeman, *Lee's Lieutenants,* 1:381.

63. Sears, ed., *Civil War Papers of McClellan,* 308; *OR,* 51.1:696; 11.1:49.

64. *OR,* 11.1:49; Douglas, *I Rode with Stonewall,* 98–99.

65. Sears, *To the Gates of Richmond,* 187–89; *OR,* 11.1:51.

66. Pinkerton to McClellan, May 3 and June 26, 1862, *OR,* 11.1:268–69; Fishel, "Pinkerton and McClellan: Who Deceived Whom?" *Civil War History* 34, no. 2 (June 1988): 126–27. The 92,400 figure (Sears, *To the Gates of Richmond,* 156–57) revises various earlier estimates that placed Lee's strength between 80,000 and 90,000.

67. This account of the Seven Days battles after Mechanicsville is drawn from the following: Sears, *To the Gates of Richmond,* 190–345 *passim;* Sears, "McClellan vs. Lee: The Seven-Day Trial," in *MHQ* 1, no. 1 (Autumn 1988): 10–17; Esposito, ed., *West Point Atlas,* 1:39–47. For circumstances of the occupation of Malvern Hill, see Sears, *McClellan,* 218–19. For the Confederate balloon see Sears, *To the Gates of Richmond,* 278, 342; for Lowe's transportation problem, *OR,* ser. 3, 3:291.

68. McClellan to Mrs. McClellan, July 15, 1862, McClellan Papers, C-7:63, D-10:72.

69. *OR,* 11.3:337–38, 333–34. For strength returns of Burnside's command (by this time removed from North Carolina to Newport News, Va.), Foster's in North Carolina, and Hunter's in South Carolina, see *OR,* 51.1:726; 9:414; 14:367.

70. *OR,* 11.3:369, 372–73. Pope's reports of troop departures from Richmond had been relayed to McClellan by Halleck two weeks before McClellan's independent "discovery" of them (*OR,* 11.1:76, 77).

71. *OR,* 11.1:269–70; see Livermore, *Numbers and Losses,* 87, for the strength of the detachment with Jackson.

72. *OR,* 11.1:271–72. The *OR* editors' compilation of Confederate units in the Seven Days battles is at 11.2:483–89.

73. Pinkerton, *Spy of the Rebellion,* 589–607. The authenticity of this list is indicated by the presence of numerous minute errors — in personal names, unit names, etc. — that stamp it as a working document that was subjected to daily correction and addition. As this compilation lists 42 Confederate brigades and 211 regiments, appreciably lower than the 46 brigades and 226 regiments shown in Pinkerton's Aug. 14 report, it appears that updating of the compilation was discontinued some days or weeks before the report was issued.

74. Of the 178 regiments, Pinkerton's tabulators had correctly assigned 126 to fully identified brigades and had correctly assigned 16 others to brigades that were known but incorrectly named. That left 36 correctly identified regiments whose brigade assignments were incorrect or unknown; those flaws were more serious than they might seem, for the identification of a regiment is a tipoff to the presence of the brigade and division to which it belongs. The tendency of artillery units to spawn variant names was another problem; the list omitted 23 of Lee's 73 artillery units, but included 41 others whose names do not appear on

the *OR* list. Correct naming of the 41 probably would have supplied nearly all of the missing 23, and would have eliminated some names that doubtless were alternative names for units already listed. Of Lee's 16 irregular units — the Hampton Legion, Cobb Legion, First Virginia (Irish) Battalion, Palmetto Sharpshooters, etc. — Pinkerton listed only eight, and his information on their brigade assignments was correspondingly spotty.

75. *OR*, 11.1:270.

7. Hard Lessons from Professor Jackson

1. *OR*, 5:557, 559, 623; Boatner, *Civil War Dictionary*, 470 (Lander entry).

2. *OR*, 5:560; McClellan Papers, nos. 5408, 6086, 7076, 8357, 7476, 7391.

3. Lander file, S. S. Accts.; *OR*, 5:702, 1086; McClellan Papers, nos. 7555, 8385.

4. Eby, ed., *Virginia Yankee*, p. xx; *OR*, 12.3:262, 743.

5. McClellan Papers, nos. 8408, 8410, 8432. One other spy known to have been working for Banks at this time was Michael Graham, although no 1862 reports by Graham have come to light (Graham file, S. S. Accts.). A captain in the 12th Virginia Cavalry, Robert W. Baylor, later captured by the Federals, was charged with responsibility for Rohr's murder. He was tried by court-martial and sentenced to be hung, but the proceedings were disapproved in February 1864, and he was included in an exchange of prisoners. See RG 153, case file NN465 (Records of the Judge Advocate General, Court-Martial Case Files, 1809–94), NA, and numerous references to Baylor in *OR*, ser. 2, vols. 5, 6, and 7.

6. Boatner, *Civil War Dictionary*, 470.

7. Richard B. Irwin in *B&L*, 2:123, 132–34; *OR*, 5:341–46; Jacob M. Shorb file, S. S. Accts.; Shorb's statements, McClellan Papers, nos. 8369 and 8384; other statements at nos. 8357, 8427, 8574, 8638, 8711, 8960, 8846, 9190, 9566. Pinkerton's Feb. 24, 1862, report to McClellan (no. 8799) is an example both of the secessionists' good opinion of Gen. Stone and of the reports of Stone's having returned slaves to Virginia owners. Stanton's order for Stone's arrest, Jan. 28, 1862, and McClellan's Feb. 8 order directing Provost Marshal Porter to proceed with the arrest are in McClellan Papers, nos. 8143 and 8426. See also Sears, *McClellan*, 144–46, and Warner, *Generals in Blue*, 480–81.

8. *OR*, 5:1095; Eby, ed., *Virginia Yankee*, 3, 6n, 7, 12.

9. Eby, *Virginia Yankee*, 7, 30–31.

10. *OR*, 12.1:380–84, 385; 12.3:38; Nathan Kimball in *B&L*, 2:302–7; Freeman, *Lee's Lieutenants*, 1:312–13. McClellan's figure for troops with Banks was 23,339 (*OR*, 5:61), but this was part of the force he claimed to have left for the defense of Washington, known to have been seriously overstated.

11. *OR*, 12.3:18, 19–20, 21, 42, 51.

12. *OR*, 12.3:78, 94, 111, 118–19; 12.1:445–46; Eby, ed., *Virginia Yankee*, 31.

13. *OR*, 12.3:106, 122; Freeman, *Lee's Lieutenants*, 1:341.

14. Imboden, "Stonewall Jackson in the Shenandoah," *B&L*, 2:285–87; Henderson, *Stonewall Jackson*, 217–19; Sears, *To the Gates of Richmond*, 97; *OR*, 12.3: 871, 872, 875, 878. Imboden, the source of the statement that Jackson made no effort at concealment, was not in Jackson's movement but had personal contact with him the day after the battle at McDowell.

15. *OR*, 12.3:126–27, 136–37, 132, 135, 140, 152. On May 9, the day Shields reported the probability that Jackson had moved by rail to aid Johnson, Banks, who was with Shields at New Market, placed Jackson at Port Republic (ibid.,

154). Presumably Shields's view was based on information not yet shared with Banks.

16. *OR*, 12.1:462–67 (Schenck's and Milroy's after-action reports); 12.3:137, 147–48, 167–68; Freeman, *Lee's Lieutenants*, 1:354. A report by Milroy's scouts that three trainloads of Jackson's troops arrived at McDowell only after the battle is an obvious error.

17. *OR*, 12.1:523; 12.3:180, 183.

18. *OR*, 12.1:523–24; Eby, ed., *Virginia Yankee*, 38, 47.

19. *OR*, 12.1:701–2.

20. *OR*, 12.1:556, 564.

21. *OR*, 12.1:525–32, 705–6. A somewhat more ominous view of his situation and the enemy's strength was obtained by Banks from a prisoner on May 28, but his report of the interrogation shows a proper skepticism (ibid., 532–33).

22. Taylor, *Destruction and Reconstruction*, 53–54; Douglas, *I Rode with Stonewall*, 51–53.

23. Philadelphia *Inquirer* and New York *Herald*, May 28, 1862; *Washington Star*, May 31, 1862; New York *Tribune*, June 12, 1862.

24. Duffee to Stanton, July 30, 1862, and order signed by Asst. Secretary of War C. P. Wolcott, July 18, 1862, Turner-Baker Papers, file 863; Pinkerton's Washington-unit files for June and July 1862, S. S. Accts.; Davis, ed., *Belle Boyd in Camp and Prison*, 71–72; Sigaud, *Belle Boyd: Confederate Spy*, 63–64. The source of the story of Belle's entrapment is *History of the Fifth West Virginia Cavalry* (Smitley's regiment).

25. These articles, by Curtis Carroll Davis, appeared in *West Virginia History* 27, no. 1 (October 1965), 1–9, and *Maryland Historical Magazine* 78, no. 1 (Spring 1983), 35–53. The 1968 republication of her memoirs, *Belle Boyd in Camp and Prison*, opens with a seventy-two-page biography of Belle written by Davis, who also edited the memoirs.

26. Douglas, *I Rode with Stonewall*, 51; *OR*, 12.3: 878, 882, 888.

27. Douglas, *I Rode with Stonewall*, 52.

28. *OR*, 12.1:643–45; 12.3:219, 228–29; Eby, ed., *Virginia Yankee*, 53–54.

29. McPherson, *Battle Cry of Freedom*, 458; Douglas, *I Rode with Stonewall*, 62–66; *OR*, 12.1:707–8, 682.

30. Jones, *Gray Ghosts and Rebel Raiders*, 81–82.

31. John James Murphy file, S. S. Accts.

32. *OR*, 12.1:12–13.

33. James J. Callahan file, S. S. Accts.

34. *OR*, 12.1:711–16.

35. Stone to Frémont, April 18, 1862, and to Capt. John C. Hopper, Sept. 6, 1863, in the Walter Pforzheimer Collection on Intelligence Service, Washington, D.C.; Louis P. Stone file in SGSD (he is also named there as Henry P. Stone), SGSD file 1861–64/1. Of the numerous scouts for Frémont who served in the Valley campaign, Murphy, Callahan, Stone, and one Ira Cole are the only ones whose names are known. The earlier service of an important spy for Banks, George Howard, is described in chapter 1; see note 22 and associated text. Other Federal spies in this campaign on whom there is no record except the fact of their employment are Pvt. Benjamin V. Hart of the 24th New York Infantry, in King's division, McDowell's corps; and Jack Kade and Benjamin Shaifer of Kimball's brigade, Shields's division (Cole and Hart dossiers, S. S. Accts., and SGSD file 1861–64/92). In 1864 Cole joined L. C. Baker's force of detectives in Washington.

36. *OR*, 12.1:716; 12.3:913.

37. McPherson, *Battle Cry of Freedom,* 460; *OR,* 12.3:122.

38. The two divisions sent to the Peninsula were Franklin's and McCall's, of McDowell's corps. The other seven were the two with Frémont; Saxton's (later Sigel's) division at Harper's Ferry; Banks's division; and Ord's, Shields's, and King's divisions, all of McDowell's corps.

39. *OR,* 12.3:155.

8. Too Little and Too Soon

1. Doster, *Lincoln and Episodes of the Civil War,* 180–81.

2. Halleck's article is a bibliographical curiosity. It was printed in the Feb. 1865 issue of the *United States Service Magazine* (151–61) and there credited to Maj. Gen. George Washington Cullum, a close associate of Halleck's who was then superintendent of the U.S. Military Academy (he later married Halleck's widow). A manuscript version of the same article in Halleck's handwriting was found years later among his papers and in 1911 was published in *American Journal of International Law* 5:590–603. An editor's note shows that the publishers of the *Journal* were unaware of the earlier appearance of the article. Presumably Halleck, because of his prominent position in 1865, felt that his appearance as a contributor to the service magazine was inappropriate and prevailed on Cullum to accept responsibility for the article; perhaps Cullum actually had a hand in the research or the writing. The article quotes liberally from Halleck's book on international law and contains such statements as "We fully concur with these writers [Halleck and others]." There are slight differences between the two published versions, due mainly to a more rigorous pruning of the manuscript at its second publication.

3. *OR,* 10.2:439–42, 618. The pages cited contain both the message as transmitted from Beauregard to Richmond on April 9 and Mitchel's transmission of it to Buell three days later. No copy of a transmission to Halleck appears in the records, probably because Buell and Halleck were together in the field. But it can scarcely be doubted that Halleck received either the message or the gist of it.

4. Among Pope's acts was the issuance of a series of vainglorious orders and pronouncements that assured his unpopularity in the army. The report that he had said his headquarters would be in the saddle is supposed to have evoked from Lee or Jackson the comment that he could "whip any man who didn't know his headquarters from his hind quarters"; it is a disappointment to learn that the story is apocryphal. Pope, observing that "it is even stated that [the story] furnished General Lee with the only joke of his life," wrote after the war that he had first heard the story applied to a general during his cadet days at West Point, and that "as it has perhaps served its time and effected its purpose, it ought to be retired" (Douglas, *I Rode with Stonewall,* 122–23; Pope, *B&L,* 2:493–94).

5. Freeman, *Lee's Lieutenants,* 2:1–3.

6. *OR,* 12.3:463–95.

7. *OR,* 12.3:492.

8. *OR,* 12.3:491, 494, 943; Geary to Gen. H. W. Slocum, June 2, 1863, in BMI.

9. *OR,* 11.3:327–29, 334–36; 12.3:463–500 *passim;* Freeman, *R. E. Lee,* 2:277. Using the same *Official Records* dispatches cited here, Freeman speaks of the "conflicting stories . . . as to Jackson's whereabouts and strength" and of the Federals' "confusion." It is true that Jackson's movement as it proceeded was not followed in detail in the Federal reports and that there was wide variation in the

reports from distant sources. However, the reports from the Federal cavalry and other sources in the same locality as Jackson's force agreed to an extent that made the aberrant details stand out prominently, allowing them to be set aside. Freeman says that Federal estimates of Jackson's strength "ran from 15,000 to 80,000," but he was unaware that the source of the latter figure would have been given little if any credence — Thaddeus Seybold's vanity and cocksureness would have been well known around the high command by this time from his irregular correspondence with Secretary Seward. Seybold was writing from McClellan's headquarters on the Peninsula. The next highest figure reported was Whitlock's 30,000, and, as pointed out in the text, Pope made allowance for the exaggeration it contained. Moreover, Pope was not even on the scene; he was still in Washington, and he developed his understanding of Jackson's movement and strength within about forty-eight hours of Jackson's arrival at Gordonsville.

10. *OR*, 12.3:487, 497, 499–500.

11. Information on Montgomery's employment, etc., is from a dossier in his name in S. S. Accts.; information on his testimony and other data on the assassination trial are from assassination scholar James O. Hall of McLean, Va. It is Montgomery's testimony that identifies him as the courier who stopped at the Federal War Dept. en route to and from Canada. He used the alias Benjamin Courrier in much of his secret-service activity. The incident of the "Longstreet dispatch" he carried is related in Bates, *Lincoln in the Telegraph Office*, 79 and 295. Early's message is in *OR*, 42.2:386; and Sheridan, *Memoirs*, 2:63.

12. Montgomery file, S. S. Accts.; *OR*, 12.3:921, 923; Freeman, *Lee's Lieutenants*, 2:12, n. 54.

13. Steele, *American Campaigns*, 1:242; *OR*, 12.3:525; Freeman, *Lee's Lieutenants*, 2:3, n. 8. The unnamed spy also erred in reporting that traffic on the Virginia Central was interrupted (Freeman, *R. E. Lee*, 2:277).

14. *OR*, 12.3:525.

15. *OR*, 12.3:535.

16. Ibid. Hood headed the division formerly led by Whiting, and Pope's wire referred to it as Whiting's division. As units even as large as corps tended to be known by the names of former commanders long after those men had died or been transferred, the terms used by Pope to designate this division is not necessarily an indication that the Federals were ignorant of Hood's accession to the command.

17. *OR*, 12.3:488.

18. *OR*, 12.3:535, 540.

19. *OR*, 12.2:25–26.

20. *OR*, 12.3:550; 12.2:133.

21. Steele, *American Campaigns*, 1:242–43. Banks's aggressiveness was caused by his misunderstanding of Pope's wishes as conveyed orally by a staff officer (Williams, *Lincoln Finds a General*, 1:267).

22. *OR*, 12.3:571, 575.

23. *OR*, 12.2:5, 9–11; *OR*, 11.3:328, 337–38.

24. See chapter 6, note 70 and associated text.

25. *OR*, 11.1:78–89; *OR*, 12.2:465.

26. *OR*, 11.3; 673–74, 675; 12.2:465; Freeman, ed., *Lee's Dispatches*, 45–49, and *R. E. Lee*, 2:274. Before accepting the deserter's report of McClellan's withdrawal, Lee obtained confirmation the next day (Aug. 14) by having D. H. Hill send out scouts. Hill reported before the close of the day that Fitz John Porter's corps had left; Porter's records show the 14th as the day of his departure. His was

the first sizable movement of usable troops; previous departures had consisted mostly of sick and wounded.

27. *OR*, 11.3, 676–77; Freeman, ed., *Lee's Dispatches*, 45–49. Although in his dispatch to Davis on Aug. 14 Lee indicated that four divisions were to be left behind, Freeman concludes that three is the correct number (*R. E. Lee*, 2:274).

28. *OR*, 12.3:928–31; Freeman, ed., *Lee's Dispatches*, 51.

29. *OR*, 12.2:552; Freeman, *R. E. Lee*, 2:282.

30. *OR*, 12.3:575.

31. *OR*, 12.2:28.

32. One report of this period that must have attracted more than routine attention at headquarters was sent by the Signal Corps party at Raccoon Ford, on the Rapidan, at 4:30 P.M. Aug. 14. It read, "A colored man has just come into camp and reports that the enemy in force reached Clark's Mountain [opposite the ford] yesterday afternoon and are resolved upon an action somewhere in that vicinity." Col. Alfred N. Duffie, who received the refugee, was told to forward him to McDowell's headquarters (RG 393, part 1, entry 4084, Messages Received by Chief Signal Officer, Army of the Potomac Telegrams, 1862–1865). As Lee's concentration was far from complete on the 14th, and as Pope made no move to retire, it is probable that the Negro's information on further questioning turned out to be not especially alarming.

33. *OR*, 12.3:589.

34. *OR*, 12.3:571.

35. *OR*, 12.3:934; Freeman, *R. E. Lee*, 2:283–84.

36. Harter's feat is heavily documented by virtue of two efforts to obtain recompense. The first, which succeeded, led to an examination of the case by Major Levi Turner in the War Department in September 1862. This record (Turner-Baker Papers, file 747 and letterbook "Y," pp. 18–19) includes McDowell's statement; attestations of Harter's reliability by Gen. Sigel and Asst. Secretary of the Interior John P. Usher, who was a director of the Terre Haute, Alton, and St. Louis Railroad and had known Harter in Indiana; and the letter of the general superintendent of the Virginia Central (which supports Harter's story of his experiences inside the Confederate lines). Thirty years later Harter unsuccessfully sought a congressional award. The effort led to a survey of the case by Major F. C. Ainsworth, head of the Record and Pension Office; this file (RG 94, Record and Pension Office, entry 501, Document File, 1889–1904, nos. 313,171 and 323,903) includes two bills, H.R. 3371 and S. 2653, 52nd Cong., 1st sess., and Pope's Jan. 27, 1876, letter to Harter. See also Harter file, S. S. Accts.; Harter service record, NA; *OR*, 12.2:329; McPhail to Sharpe, Aug. 1, 1863, and May 19, 1864, BMI; BMI payrolls, Nov. 1864.

37. That Harter's information was in Pope's hands by 10 A.M. is shown by a message timed at that hour, containing some of the sergeant's information, sent by Gen. Reno (*OR*, 12.3:592).

38. Montgomery file, S. S. Accts. The fact that Montgomery's information placed Lee's threat on Pope's right and had been preceded by Harter's report was possibly a principal reason for McDowell's statement that Montgomery's service was not as valuable as he supposed (see text associated with note 12 above).

39. *OR*, 12.3:940–41.

40. *OR*, 12.2:29. No mention of the loss of Fitzhugh's papers appears in Stuart's report of his capture (ibid., 726).

41. Because his account of the captured letter is so clearly a cover story and no

corroboration is found in Confederate records, it is open to the suspicion that it is a fabrication. But that is ruled out by Pope's report of the capture in an Aug. 22 dispatch to Halleck (*OR*, 12.2:58) and also by a letter that Fitz John Porter, assuredly no friend of Pope, sent on Aug. 27 to Burnside at Fredericksburg-Aquia, mentioning the captured letter (*OR*, 12.3:700).

42. *OR*, 12.2:58. As Fitzhugh was captured on the night of Aug. 17 or early the next day (*OR*, 12.2:726), and the captors were still south of the Rapidan on the 18th and having to find a safe crossing, they could not have delivered the letter to Pope until some hours after Harter's arrival early that day. In any case, both McDowell's statement and Pope's postwar letter to Harter make clear that Harter's report was the only source of Pope's sudden decision to withdraw from the Rapidan.

43. *OR*, 12.3:940–41. Lee also referred to this incident in his after-action report (*OR*, 12.2:552).

44. Freeman, *R. E. Lee*, 2:280.

45. *OR*, 12.3:601.

46. *OR*, 51.2:609.

47. *OR*, 12.2:57.

48. *OR*, 12.2:30.

49. Capt. John McEntee to Col. G. H. Sharpe, June 6, 1863, BMI. Smith later became a principal agent in the Federal secret service; he will be seen again in chapter 19.

50. On Aug. 24 Pope complained to Halleck, "I cannot form an estimate of the forces of the enemy" (*OR*, 12.2:64). Other information on Smith is from Eby, ed., *Virginia Yankee*, 69 (July 21, 1862), and the 1860 census of Culpeper County. Smith was introduced to Strother by W. D. Wallach, another Culpeper resident, whose family included the mayor of Washington and the editor of the Washington *Star*. When not with the army, Smith resided in Washington and was sometimes addressed at the *Star*.

51. Macomb file, S. S. Accts.; *OR*, 12.2:730–32.

52. *OR*, 12.2:553, 730–32; 12.3:941–42.

53. *OR*, 12.3:654–55, 653; 12.2:67.

54. Montgomery file, S. S. Accts.; *OR*, 12.2:65; 12.3:685, 665, 682, 683.

55. *OR*, 12.3:657; 12.2:333, 348, 271, 34–35.

56. *OR*, 12.2:332–35, 359.

57. *OR*, 12.2:351, 334–35; 12.3:672.

58. *OR*, 12.2, 34–35 (Pope's report), 351. Pope indicates that he ordered this expedition on the night of Aug. 25–26, intending for it to set out next morning, but at 7 P.M. on the 26th he informed McDowell of it in language that suggests that the order was then not many hours old.

59. *OR*, 12.2:34, 70.

60. *OR*, 12.3:684.

61. *OR*, 12.3:684; 12.2:14, 72, 35.

62. In *R. E. Lee* (2:298–99) Freeman points out an additional object of Lee's action, namely to provision his army from a region that the enemy would otherwise occupy.

63. Placed with the Federal correspondence of Aug. 26 in *OR*, 12.3:671 is an undated, unsigned note reporting that a movement through Thoroughfare Gap was being observed. The awkward English (*e.g.*, "Some one are still passing through that Gap") and other features give strong indication that it was written by the French colonel Alfred N. Duffie, commanding a Rhode Island

cavalry regiment in McDowell's corps. Duffie, however, was still on the Rappahannock on Aug. 26 and 27 (ibid., 270–71, 688). Thus doubt is cast over the indication that at least one element of Pope's army detected Jackson's march on Manassas. It is suggested by Henderson (*Stonewall Jackson*, 442, n. 17) that the true date of the note is Aug. 28 and that it refers to Longstreet's march rather than Jackson's. Aug. 29 would appear to be a more likely date (see *OR*, 12.2:355).

64. Longstreet's wing bivouacked the night of Aug. 26 near Orlean, midway between Amissville and Salem (*OR*, 12.2:555).

65. *OR*, 12.2:335. Pope's fondness of the idea of "bagging the whole crowd" is shown by his use of the phrase in several other dispatches (*e.g.*, to Reno, *OR*, 12.3:704).

66. Freeman, *Lee's Lieutenants*, 2:104.

67. *OR*, 12.2:670, 735; Taliaferro in *B&L*, 2:508.

68. *OR*, 12.2:354.

69. *OR*, 12.2:37, 74–75, 337, 644–45, 656–57.

70. *OR*, 12.2:14, 37, 74–75.

71. *OR*, 12.2:70, 72.

72. *OR*, 12.3:730. Buford's report was timed at 9:30 A.M. and addressed to Gen. Ricketts, with the request that he forward it.

73. At the Porter trial Pope testified that he had expected a report concerning Longstreet from Buford but that up to 4:30 P.M. none had been received. Later he testified that he had the report by 7 P.M. (*OR*, 12.2, *Supplement:* 851, 853.)

74. *OR*, 12.2:519, 736, and *Supplement*, 903–4; Longstreet, in *B&L*, 2:522–23; Hennessy, *Return to Bull Run*, 227. Hennessy's book, the only in-depth study this campaign has ever received, develops many significant points previously overlooked or unknown. It is especially valuable as a chronicle of Pope's mistakes on the battlefield, hitherto obscure sources of his misinformation, and the almost totally fruitless efforts of his generals to correct his delusion regarding enemy positions and intentions.

75. *OR*, 12.2:571, 607; Hennessy, *Return to Bull Run*, 229.

76. *OR*, 12.2:40; Hennessy, *Return to Bull Run*, 237, 258–59, 291, 312.

77. *OR*, 12.2:519, and *Supplement*, 903; Longstreet, in *B&L*, 2:522–23.

78. The record of the court-martial and of the reexamination of the case in 1878 is in *OR*, 12.2:505–36, *Supplement*, 821–1134.

79. *OR*, 12.2:40.

80. In his *B&L* article on the campaign (2:449–94), Pope again asserted his conviction that Porter could have attacked successfully. He cited the reports of Lee, Jackson, Longstreet, A. P. Hill, and Stuart in support of his contention that Longstreet did not at the time hold the position in enough strength to have withstood an attack by Porter's corps.

81. Hennessy, *Return to Bull Run*, 295.

82. Montgomery file, S. S. Accts. Lee's intention to march into Maryland is first discussed in his correspondence with President Davis on Sept. 3, after his victory over Pope was clear and complete (*OR*, 19.2:590–91).

83. *OR*, 12.3:738. Gen. White's telegram was addressed to Halleck, who had to communicate with Pope by courier and was having difficulty in doing so (ibid., 720, 724, 742). It is likely that Halleck decided that under these circumstances information so completely overtaken by events was not worth sending to Pope.

84. *OR*, 12.2:340; Hennessy, *Return to Bull Run*, 323.

85. *OR,* 12.2:340, 394; 12.3:964; Hennessy, *Return to Bull Run,* 328–30.

86. Eby, ed., *Virginia Yankee,* 94–95; *OR,* 12.2:41, 340, 413; Hennessy, *Return to Bull Run,* 310, 323–24, 328.

87. *OR,* 12.2:557, 565–66.

88. *OR,* 341, 501; Hennessy, *Return to Bull Run,* 393–94.

89. Sears, ed., *Civil War Papers of McClellan,* 397, 416, 390.

90. *OR,* 12.2:83, 16–17; Sears, *McClellan,* 249–56. Pope's report pays tribute, however, to many of McClellan's generals (ibid., 16, 17, 47–49).

91. *OR,* 12.3:807. At this period Pinkerton was back in Washington writing to McClellan to report machinations of the general's enemies there (O'Toole, *Honorable Treachery,* 125).

92. *OR,* 13:617–18.

93. *OR,* 12.3:475. The recipient of this reprimand was Brig. Gen. A. S. Piatt at Winchester. The retreating force was infantry and not cavalry, but the same spirit is shown in Pope's instructions for cavalry reconnaissance.

94. *OR,* 12.2:15.

95. *OR,* 12.2:16.

9. All the Plans of the Rebels

1. *OR,* 19.1:118; 19.2:176–86.

2. RG 98, Office of the Chief Signal Officer, Telegrams of the Army of the Potomac, NA.

3. *OR,* 19.2:184–85, 186; 19.1:118; Brown, *Signal Corps, U.S.A.,* 241–42; *OR,* ser. 3, 3:291–92; Haydon, *Aeronautics in the Union and Confederate Armies,* 294–95. Stuart's report (*OR,* 19.1:815) says that the courier's dispatches were from Davis to Lee and that "by the discreetness of the bearer, had not fallen into the hands of the enemy."

4. Weisberger, *Reporters for the Union,* 289–90.

5. For a fuller discussion of the invasion issue, see Sears, *Landscape Turned Red,* 66–69.

6. *OR,* 19.1:39–40; Freeman, *Lee's Lieutenants,* 2:718, 720.

7. *OR,* 19.2:185–201 *passim,* 238.

8. *OR,* 19.2:200–216 *passim.*

9. Pinkerton file, S. S. Accts. The other five operatives were Seth Paine, Augustus Littlefield, G. H. Thiel, Alfred Cridge, and one other, identified only by the initials O.F.A. A remark by John Babcock indicating that Pinkerton's men did not perform scouting and spying in this campaign will be found in chapter 14, note 34 and associated text.

10. The nine were Samuel Martin, Charles W. Johnson, Reuben Johnson, John Sullivan, James W. Greenwood, David W. Fowler, John Mix, J. A. Blake, and "Sam, Negro of Middletown." (Pinkerton file, S. S. Accts.) Johnson will reappear in chapter 11 and Greenwood in chapter 21.

11. *OR,* 19.1:26; 51.1:839; Pleasonton to Marcy, Sept. 10, 1862, McClellan Papers, 31:A-78. For Lawrence and Meagher, see S.S. Accts. The courier service of Pinkerton's men, unnamed, appears in Sears, ed., *Civil War Papers of McClellan,* 459.

12. Gaines in S. S. Accts; *OR,* 19.2:292.

13. Most accounts credit Lee with about 40,000 men at the battle of Antietam. Straggling was so widespread that he placed his bodyguard at the Potomac to

collect stragglers and send them to Winchester, to be marched into Maryland in large units (Freeman, *Lee's Lieutenants,* 2:152). On Sept. 30, when the army was back in Virginia (presumably with the stragglers back in the ranks), its return showed 53,000 "present for duty" (*OR,* 19.2:639).

14. *OR,* 19.2:219, 221, 222.

15. *OR,* 19.2:233.

16. *OR,* 19.2:247.

17. The operator probably was W. B. Wilson (see p. 219).

18. McClellan Papers, 31:A-78; *OR,* 19.2:249.

19. *OR,* 19.1:42.

20. *OR,* 19.2:254. Delays in the receipt of information, which often explain inconsistencies of this kind, seem to be ruled out not only by McClellan's orders to Burnside but by the fact that McClellan was only twelve miles from the War Dept. The Halleck Telegrams file shows that information from sources other than the Army of the Potomac was routinely forwarded from the department to that army, and many of these telegrams are found in the army's records and its commanders' papers. But *OR,* while showing the receipt of these telegrams in the department, does not routinely show this forwarding.

21. *OR,* 19.2:269.

22. *OR,* 19.2:203, 214, 250–52, 268.

23. *OR,* 19.2:273–74.

24. *OR,* 19.2:277.

25. Alexander K. McClure, "Recollections of Antietam," on file at the Antietam National Battlefield Park.

26. *OR,* 20.2:350–55; 19.2:228; Wm. B. Wilson in Egle, ed., *Andrew Gregg Curtin,* 348–49; personal details about Palmer from his passport and obituary in *Colorado Springs Gazette,* March 14, 1909, Palmer Papers, Colorado State Historical Society; *OR,* 19.2:228, 247; Capt. R. H. Lamborn, Greencastle, to Thomas A. Scott, Harrisburg, Sept. 13, 1862, Palmer Papers, reel 3.

27. Wm. B. Wilson in Egle, ed., *Andrew Gregg Curtin,* 348–49. The discovery of Jackson's turn probably was made on Sept. 11. Wilson gives the messenger's name as Snokes, but it is clearly established that Thomas Noakes of Martinsburg was active as a spy and guide in that locality during the Antietam campaign. He probably was the source of the information reported by Gen. White Sept. 10 (see note 18 and associated text). In February 1864, when Noakes was under arrest at Martinsburg, Brig. Gen. J. C. Sullivan, then commanding at Harper's Ferry, informed the War Dept. that "Thomas Noakes was prior to the war convicted of larceny; a poor man before the war, he is now in comfortable circumstances without any apparent means of livelihood; sells whiskey to soldiers; enters private houses and purloins private property; is a noted horse thief; was arrested, broke jail, was re-arrested and has been sent out of the lines of my division" (Noakes file in SGSD; *OR,* 19.1:558–59).

28. *OR,* 19.2:267; Wm. B. Wilson in Egle, ed., *Andrew Gregg Curtin,* 350–51; McClellan Papers, no. 16088.

29. *OR,* 19.2:267, 277, 287; I. J. Stine file, S. S. Accts.; Fisher, *Builder of the West,* 84–85. The McClellan Papers and all National Archives collections containing telegrams between Harrisburg and its outposts, between Harrisburg and Washington, and between Washington and the Army of the Potomac have been examined without producing any intelligence items attributable to Palmer or Wilson other than those incorporated in this account. As no copies of their reports as transmitted by McClure to Curtin have been found, it is not known how much of

the abbreviating and withholding was done by McClure rather than Curtin. At least some of it almost certainly was Curtin's handiwork, for Wilson is known to have transmitted to Harrisburg one report that met the same fate as the others when relayed beyond that point. In the small book he published on wartime events, Wilson, unaware of the mutilation his and Palmer's reports had undergone, had nothing but praise for Curtin's handling of his situation (Wilson, *Acts and Actors in the Civil War,* 66).

30. *OR,* 19.2:277. Curtin's generosity with telegraphic wordage suggests that the severe condensation of Palmer's and Wilson's reports was less the governor's doing than McClure's. Wilson's messages suffered somewhat less condensing than Palmer's, probably because the captain, observing military propriety, addressed them to his immediate superior, McClure, whereas Wilson, a civilian, did not hesitate to address reports to Thomas A. Scott, a Pennsylvania Central official (and former assistant secretary of war), who was in Harrisburg assisting Curtin.

31. Pleasonton to Marcy, 5 A.M., Sept. 13, 1862, McClellan Papers, A-79.

32. *OR,* 19.2:271, 281.

33. Sears, "The Last Word on the Lost Order," *MHQ,* 66–72. This article corrects various errors and discrepancies that have been part of the Lost Order story; for example, the belief that D. H. Hill's division had bivouacked in the field where the order was found, and Freeman's conclusion (*Lee's Lieutenants,* vol. 2, app. 1) that Lee learned from Stuart late on Sept. 13 that McClellan was in possession of the order.

34. The *Herald*'s version of the story was incomplete and somewhat garbled: "A general order of General Lee was found there [at Frederick], directing that two columns of the rebel army should proceed by way of Middletown, one of them destined for Greencastle, Pa., with all possible expedition, and the other to proceed by way of Williamsport or Shepherdstown, at discretion, to engage the Union force at Harper's Ferry" (p. 1). This was repeated in almost the same words in the editorial columns (p. 4). The flaws in the published version of the Lost Order story probably resulted from changes as it made the rounds of gossiping officers. For the Confederates' "Secret Line" to Washington, see Tidwell, Hall, and Gaddy, *Come Retribution,* esp. pp. 87–90. For Lee's comment, see Murfin, *Gleam of Bayonets,* 337.

35. Sears, "The Last Word on the Lost Order," 70.

36. The full text of the order is at *OR,* 19.2:603–4.

37. *OR,* 19.2:271, 281–82; 19.1:45–46; 51.1:829. That McClellan would send Halleck a message in such sharp conflict with the one to Lincoln indicates that his correspondence with Lincoln, though it passed through the War Department telegraph office, was not routinely accessible to Halleck.

38. *OR,* 51.1:829; Pleasonton to Marcy, 6:15 P.M., Sept. 13, McClellan Papers, reel 31:A-79; Sears, *McClellan,* 284.

39. McClellan's reliance on S.O. 191, in the face of a multiplicity of intelligence reports indicating that some of its terms were no longer in force, is basic to an understanding of the Maryland campaign. It was first noted by Sears, *Landscape Turned Red,* 117–18.

40. *OR,* 19.1:145; Sears, *Landscape Turned Red,* 94.

41. *OR,* 19.2: 247, 248, 249, 256, 257, 266, 267, 268, 269, 270, 277, 286, 287; Curtin to McClellan, Sept. 11, 1862, McClellan Papers, reel 31:A-78; Capt. W. P. Sanders to [Pleasonton], 10 A.M., Sept. 11, 1862, ibid., reel 31:A-79; Pleasonton to Marcy, 6:15 P.M., Sept. 13, 1862, ibid., reel 31:A-79.

42. Palmer to McClure, Sept. [13], 1862, Palmer Papers, reel 3; *OR*, 19.2:287. Palmer's knowledge of the eastern armies was too sketchy for him to catch errors in the deserter's account of the makeup of Longstreet's corps, but this flaw did not reduce the effect of the main point, that Longstreet's "command" was at Hagerstown.

43. *OR*, 51.1:829, 827; 19.1:45; McClellan, *Report*, 195; Sears, *Landscape Turned Red*, 117, 120.

44. The clearest evidence that Boonsboro was McClellan's sole objective is his statement to Franklin on the evening of Sept. 13 that his forces at Frederick would "march this evening & tomorrow morning . . . upon Boonsboro to carry that position." Sears, ed., *Civil War Papers of McClellan*, 454; part of this dispatch is in *OR*, 19.1:45.

45. Sears, *Landscape Turned Red*, 119, 128–43.

46. Ibid., 145–49.

47. I. J. Stine file, S. S. Accts.; Palmer to McClure, Sept. 13, 1862, Palmer Papers, reel 3.

48. I. J. Stine file, S. S. Accts.; Palmer to McClure, Sept. 14, 1862, Palmer Papers, reel 3; *OR*, 19.2:293.

49. *OR*, 19.2:607; 19.1:951; Sears, *Landscape Turned Red*, 125, 150–51.

50. *OR*, 19.2:289, 294, 305; 19.1:53, 539, 951.

51. Palmer to McClure, Sept. 14, 1862, Palmer Papers, reel 3; *OR*, 19.2:270; 51.1:836; McClellan, *Report*, 199.

52. *OR*, 51.1:834–38; 19.2:295, 297, 307, 308; 19.1:54.

53. *OR*, 51.1:837; Sears, *Landscape Turned Red*, 159.

54. Wm. J. Palmer statement, dated Huntsville, Ala., Feb. 12, 1865, in I. J. Stine file, S. S. Accts.; Wm. B. Wilson in Egle, ed., *Andrew Gregg Curtin*, 353; Palmer to Curtin, *OR*, 19.2:311.

55. *OR*, 19.1:955; Sears, *Landscape Turned Red*, 164. Unlike Jackson's march, which occupied parts of two days, A. P. Hill's return was accomplished in less than eight hours. He started early enough to have daylight all the way and covered the seventeen miles without a rest stop. (He left one of his five brigades at Harper's Ferry to complete the paroling of 12,520 prisoners and the handling of captured stores and guns.) For the number of prisoners see *OR*, 19.1:549; for Hill's march see Sears, *Landscape Turned Red*, 197, 276.

56. Sears, "The Last Word on the Lost Order"; *OR*, 19.2:607; 19.1:953–54.

57. Sears, *Landscape Turned Red*, 162–65 and 171–77 *passim*, esp. 174, 176; McClellan, *Report*, 201.

58. This account of the battle of Antietam is drawn from Sears, *Landscape Turned Red*, 176–77 and chs. 6–8; Ezra Carman, "The Maryland Campaign of September 1862," ch. 23, unpublished manuscript, Manuscripts Division, Library of Congress; McClellan's report, *OR*, 19.1:56–65; Burnside's report, ibid., 419–21; Lee's reports, ibid., 141, 149–50; Freeman, *R. E. Lee*, 2:387–402; Steele, *American Campaigns*, 1:269–73.

59. Pinkerton to McClellan, Sept. 22, 1862, quoted in Horan and Swiggett, *Pinkerton Story*, 117.

60. McClellan, *Report*, 213–14 (duplicated in *OR*, 19.1:67); Sears, *Landscape Turned Red*, 366–72; report by Col. John S. Clark, "Return of Forces Under Command of Major [sic] General Robert E. Lee C.S.A. Previous to Battle of Antietam," Oct. 20, 1862, McClellan Papers, no. 16689.

61. Sears, ed., *Civil War Papers of McClellan*, 84, 85, 87, 98, 105, 106, 114, 177, 223–44 *passim*, 315, 399, 477; *McClellan's Own Story*, 150–51, 167, 172.

10. Luck Runs Out for Palmer and Stine

1. One document in the Palmer Papers gives Sept. 17, 1836, as Palmer's date of birth, but Sept. 18 appears in several others.

2. Statement by Palmer, dated at Huntsville, Ala., Feb. 12, 1865, in Stine file, S. S. Accts; A. K. McClure to J. C. Knox, Dec. 5, 1862, ibid.

3. On Hampton, *OR,* 19.1:820 statement by R. M. Evans dated Harrisburg, Sept. 30, 1862, in Stine file, S. S. Accts; Palmer's statement cited in note 2; manuscript article in Palmer Papers, Colorado State Historical Society. This manuscript apparently was prepared for *Harper's New Monthly,* since a parallel account, which appeared in the June 1867 issue, is also in the Palmer Papers. The latter omits the names of Palmer, Stine, Bardwell, and others, and it is more highly embellished than the manuscript version, which bears marks of having been checked by Palmer.

4. Turner-Baker Papers, file 338.

5. Evans statement cited in note 3.

6. Ibid. Evans later served as captain of the Philadelphia City Scouts in the Gettysburg campaign and in Early's 1864 invasion of Maryland (Phila. Scouts file, SGSD; *OR,* 37.1:343).

7. Greencastle *Pilot,* Nov. 4, 1862, in Stine file, S. S. Accts.; L. C. Turner to U.S. Marshal Wm. Millward, Oct. 11 and 14, 1862, ibid.

8. Palmer statement cited in note 2.

9. Stine to the Rev. T. N. Kurtz, dated Ft. Delaware, Oct. 31, 1862, Stine file, S. S. Accts.

10. Greencastle *Pilot,* Nov. 4, 1862.

11. Ibid.

12. Rev. J. George Butler to E. M. Stanton, dated Washington, Nov. 5, 1862; Rev. D. H. Focht and others to Stanton, dated New Bloomfield, Pa., Oct. 27, 1862; A. K. McClure to J. C. Knox, dated Harrisburg, Dec. 5, 1862 — all in Stine file, S. S. Accts.

13. L. C. Turner to Stine, March 3, 1863, in Turner-Baker Papers, letterbook, p. 297.

14. Manuscript article cited in note 3.

15. This quotation is from the version of Gen. Halleck's article on espionage that appeared in the *American Journal of International Law* 5(1911):591.

16. Manuscript article cited in note 3.

17. Ibid.

18. Cowgill to Palmer, Oct. 13, 1862, Palmer Papers.

19. Manuscript article cited in note 3.

20. Hoag to Palmer, April 15, 1881, Palmer Papers.

21. Manuscript article cited in note 3; "W. J. Peters" to unnamed addressee, Nov. 21, 1862, Palmer Papers.

22. *OR,* ser. 2, 5:892, 904, 909, 915, 919; manuscript article cited in note 3. In the *Harper's New Monthly* article, Kerby's name is given as Farin, but Palmer wrote "Kirby" *(sic)* beside it in the margin.

23. Manuscript article cited in note 3.

24. Thomas A. Scott to Stanton. Jan. 10, 1865, Palmer Papers; *OR,* ser. 2, 5:186, 189–90, 199, 208, 806.

25. Palmer to Stine, Jan. 28, 1863 (true copy), Stine file, S. S. Accts.

26. Palmer to Curtin, Jan. 31, 1863, Stine file, S. S. Accts.

27. Stine to Palmer, Dec. 19, 1864, Palmer Papers; Palmer statement cited in note 2.

28. Col. N. P. Chipman to Stanton, n.d., and March 6, 1865, with endorsement by Asst. Secretary C. A. Dana, March 9, 1865, Stine file, S. S. Accts.

29. Manuscript article cited in note 3.

30. *OR*, 20.2:345–80, 505–7.

31. Beyer and Keydel, eds., *Deeds of Valor: How American Heroes Won the Medal of Honor*, 1:478.

32. Brown's case is dealt with at length in Halleck's article on espionage. The Confederates claimed that they executed Brown as a deserter, for he had joined and then deserted their navy in the course of the espionage he performed against them.

11. The Blind Campaign of Fredericksburg

1. *OR*, 51.1:897.

2. *OR*, 19.1:152, 957; 19.2:628–29, 52–55; Freeman, *Lee's Lieutenants*, 2:288.

3. *OR*, 19.1:72.

4. *OR*, 19.2:90–92, 418, 421, 424, 425, 431, 501; 51.1:890–91.

5. *OR*, 19.1:152.

6. *OR*, ser. 3, 3:292.

7. *OR*, 19.2:341, 344–45, 351, 353, 363, 371, 393, 395, 418, 519; Brown, *Signal Corps U.S.A.*, 338.

8. *OR*, 19.2:331, 432, 517; 19.1:152; Pinkerton file, S. S. Accts.

9. *OR*, 19.1:152, 957; 19.2:628–29. Aiken's report is no. 17572 in the McClellan Papers. The other locals on Pinkerton's payroll were Enoch Thompson, Isaac E. Moore, Samuel Martin, L. C. King, and James Riley; individual files for all six men are in S. S. Accts.

10. Eby, ed., *Virginia Yankee*, 126.

11. SGSD file 1865–66/192; Turner-Baker Papers, box 54 and file 1638; S. S. Accts., box 6; RG 153, Abells jacket in Judge Advocate General records relating to the Lincoln assassination. Among Mrs. Abells's aliases were Frank Tuttle and Mrs. Frances Jamieson; it was under the latter name that she was imprisoned in Richmond. "Mrs. Timothy Webster" was Pinkerton's operative Hattie Lawton, Webster's nurse in the Monument Hotel.

12. *OR*, 51.1:897–98; 19.1:6–13, 15–24, 74–82, 97; 19.2:396, 403, 416, 422–24, 492–93, 471–72, 496–98.

13. Rhodes, *History of the Civil War*, 4:188; Dennett, ed., *Lincoln and the Civil War in the Diaries and Letters of John Hay*, diary entry for Sept. 25, 1864; *OR*, 19.2:545. The earliest report of Longstreet's move to Culpeper came from a contraband and was forwarded on Nov. 2 by Gen. Sigel at Fairfax Court House (*OR*, 19.2:534). In his final report McClellan stated, "When I gave up the command to General Burnside the best information in our possession indicated that Longstreet was immediately in our front near Culpeper; Jackson, with one, perhaps both, of the Hills, near Chester and Thornton's Gaps, with the mass of their force west of the Blue Ridge" (*OR*, 19.1:89). McClellan was correct as to Longstreet, but Jackson was twenty-five to fifty miles north of the positions McClellan named; hindsight now gave him more confidence in his information than his telegrams to Washington had conveyed.

14. Bangs to his mother, June 14, 1863, collection of Michael O. Berry; Marcy

to McClellan, Dec. 25, 1863, McClellan Papers, no. 86604 (B-13:49); Pinkerton file, S. S. Accts.; Pinkerton, *Spy of the Rebellion*, 584. The Turner-Baker Papers contain many reports of Pinkerton's claims investigations.

15. Sears, *McClellan*, 58: Boatner, *Civil War Dictionary*, 107–8; *OR*, 19.2:552–54, 583–84, 579.

16. *OR*, 21:84, 86; 19.2:162, 567, 579.

17. Lee's messages to President Davis, Secretary Randolph, Cooper, Jackson, W. H. F. Lee, and the local commander at Fredericksburg are in *OR*, 21:1014–31 *passim*, and in Freeman and McWhiney, eds., *Lee's Dispatches to Jefferson Davis*, 66. See also Longstreet, *From Manassas to Appomattox*, 293. The "equally credible and equally incredible" quotation is from Williams, *Lincoln Finds a General*, 2:512. Lee ordered Jackson to Fredericksburg Nov. 23 but then learned that Jackson had already started. Although Lee foresaw Fredericksburg as a possible destination for Burnside, and although as early as Nov. 20 he was fairly certain that the enemy's whole army was opposite the town, up to the 25th he persistently expressed doubt as to Burnside's purpose. The chief point of uncertainty arose from the reports he received of enemy moves toward Alexandria, which suggested movement by water. On Nov. 19 he wrote Davis that in view of the absence of indications of a water movement, "They must expect, . . . I think, to force their way from Fredericksburg." But four days later he told Jackson, "I am as yet unable to discover what may be the plan of the enemy." Freeman says (*R. E. Lee*, 2:432), "Lee, in fact, had anticipated the movements of his new opponent with a precision that was almost prescience." However, his vacillating views of the enemy's probable intentions, together with his indecision that allowed Jackson to remain so long in the Valley, place his grasp of the situation far short of Freeman's rating.

18. Meriwether Stuart, "Samuel Ruth and General R. E. Lee: Disloyalty and the Line of Supply to Fredericksburg," *Virginia Magazine of History and Biography* 71, no. 1 (Jan. 1963): 35–109. Stuart is an authority on espionage by Richmond's Unionist underground; his other writings on that subject, in the same magazine, relate to activities later than the period covered in this book.

19. The material taken by Pinkerton included not only retained copies of his reports to McClellan but also the raw data that the reports were based on. In a July 1863 letter (McClellan Papers, A90:35) Pinkerton informed McClellan that he had nine clerks at work compiling his final report, which he estimated would total 16,000 pages. As no such report appears in the McClellan Papers, it is probable that Pinkerton never completed the compilation and that, like many or nearly all of the papers in his agency's main office, the incomplete report and the raw data were consumed in the Chicago fire of 1871. The Pinkerton National Detective Agency Papers of the Civil War period in the Library of Congress consist of only a few hundred items — weak, often unreadable carbon copies of letters and reports. The originals of many of them are in the McClellan Papers.

20. Pinkerton and Babcock files, S. S. Accts.; Babcock file, SGSD; Babcock military service record, NA; Mt. Vernon (N.Y.) *Daily Argus*, Nov. 20 and 21, 1908 (Babcock obituaries); "Record of Service of John C. Babcock during Civil War of 1861–65," Babcock Papers; Babcock to "Dear Uncle," March 4, 1862, and to "Dear Aunt," Dec. 26, 1861, Feb. 10, June 6, and Dec. 7, 1862, and Jan. 25, 1863, ibid.; Lt. Henry W. Kingsbury to "Mr. Babcock," June 15, 1862, BMI; Babcock to Wm. A. Pinkerton, April 9, 1908, Babcock Papers; Marcy to Prof. Lowe, June 1, 1862, Lowe Papers. One map drawn by Babcock, showing the defenses of Richmond as reported to Pinkerton in Feb. 1862, escaped the transplantation of Pinkerton's files to Chicago, probably because it found its way into

the files of Provost Marshal General Patrick, where it still remains (Army of the Potomac Miscellaneous Records, Letters Received, box 4002).

21. Babcock to Gen. Parke, Dec. 31, 1862, in Letters Received, Army of the Potomac, NA. The report Babcock copied was the same one Pinkerton had copied from Banks's files (see chapter 9, note 60 and associated text). Pinkerton's copy, now in McClellan Papers, gives unit strengths only down to divisions, thus omitting much of the detailed matter that Babcock copied. Babcock's copy was one of the items stolen in a 1962 theft from the National Archives, many of which have not been recovered.

22. *OR*, 21:84–87, 793–95, 802–3. It appears that no record of the arrivals of pontoons was made by the officers who exchanged telegrams about difficulties and delays in their shipment. On Nov. 24 the officer mainly responsible, Brig. Gen. Daniel Woodbury, reported a pontoon train on hand at Falmouth, its size unstated. A telegram of the 27th shows at least thirty previously ordered pontoons still not received, but includes a request for parts and accessories in amounts indicating that Woodbury now had a considerable number of pontoons.

23. The Skinker farm, Oakley, was on Poplar Road, the present Virginia Route 616, which runs north from the Falmouth–Warrenton road, intersecting the latter six miles from Falmouth. The house was a reference point familiar to Army of the Potomac mapmakers. The 1860 census of Stafford County shows the Skinker family owning $23,000 worth of real and personal property and twenty-three slaves. Living near Howard Skinker (as he was known to the Federals) was his brother Thomas, a Confederate cavalryman, who was well-to-do himself and owned nine slaves. Howard Skinker's farm was in the name of his mother, who was seventy-six years old in 1860. The name is spelled *Schinker* in Gen. Patrick's diary entry for Dec. 30, 1862; although this suggests that it was pronounced *Shinker*, that is not the pronunciation that prevails in Fredericksburg and vicinity today.

24. Skinker file, S. S. Accts. Skinker's claim of services was endorsed by Gens. Reynolds, C. C. Augur, Thomas L. Kane, and Col. Thomas C. Devin of the 6th New York Cavalry.

25. *OR*, ser. 3, 292–94; this is a portion of Lowe's historical report to Stanton at the conclusion of his "operations in the department of aeronautics." Historians are not in agreement that Burnside rejected advance reconnoitering by the balloons. A persistent belief that they were in the air some days in advance of the battle possibly originates with E. P. Alexander. In *Military Memoirs of a Confederate* (p. 288) he states that "the balloons reconnoitering the country about Skinker's Neck, discovered Jackson's camps, and Burnside knew that his designs were disclosed." Alexander then states that this discovery suggested the battle plan that Burnside adopted. Despite Alexander's deservedly high repute as a memoirist, there is no reason to doubt Lowe's statement to Stanton that he was officially grounded until Dec. 13. An item in his papers (Library of Congress) shows that a detail of balloon handlers was not assigned until Dec. 12. They were from the 4th Maine Regiment; the date is corroborated by their colonel (*OR*, 21:371).

26. Babcock to Gen. Parke, Dec. 31, 1862, in Letters Received, Army of the Potomac, NA. Pinkerton had paid Charles W. Johnson fifteen dollars and Reuben Johnson ten dollars for "services within the enemies lines" at the time of the battle of Antietam; no Johnson appears on the payroll after that time (Pinkerton file, S. S. Accts.).

27. Patrick Diary, Dec. 3 and 9, 1862; JCCW 1863, 1:653; *OR*, 21:841.

28. *OR*, 19.2:683–84, 698–99. This order is dated Nov. 6, but Freeman points

out (*Lee's Lieutenants*, 2:269) that Lee's assignment of troops to what became the corps of Longstreet and Jackson had been made by Oct. 27.

29. *OR*, 51.1:928.

30. *OR*, 19.2: 561, 563, 567, 568, 573.

31. *OR*, 19.2:574.

32. *OR*, 19.2:585; 21:766, 771.

33. *OR*, 21:792–93, 797.

34. *OR*, 21:803, 808, 830.

35. *OR*, 21:1021, 1034; Freeman, *R. E. Lee*, 2:438 and n. 25.

36. Hall's report to Cushing, dated Nov. 28, 1862, is in Record Group 111, entry 27 (Records of the Office of the Chief Signal Officer), "Papers Relating to Proposed Plans for Signal Systems," NA. When a copy of Hall's report reached Chief Signal Officer Myer in Washington, he compared the enemy's alphabet that it revealed with the one known on the Peninsula, noting that "the whole style [of the Confederate signal system] was then known." For Myer's instructions regarding secrecy, see Brown, *Signal Corps U.S.A.*, 214. For the Federals' awareness that Longstreet's troops were already at Fredericksburg, see *OR*, 21:103.

37. According to a Nov. 20 return the total present for duty in Longstreet's corps was 37,512 (*OR*, 21:1025). Longstreet's movement to Culpeper was ordered Oct. 28 (*OR*, 19.2:685). Lee's trip to Richmond is recounted in Freeman, *R. E. Lee*, 2:427.

38. Joseph E. Snyder file, SGSD. The same report, omitting Snyder's tabulation of Lee's units and their strength and a long postscript telling of Gen. J. E. Johnston's departure from Richmond following recovery from his Seven Pines wound, is at *OR*, 21:820–25.

39. *OR*, 21:87; Freeman, *R. E. Lee*, 2:449 (prebattle postings of Jackson's divisions).

40. Burnside's statement on this question only deepens the mystery. In the dispatch (*OR*, 21:64) in which he informed Halleck of his decision to attack at Fredericksburg instead of downriver, he said that the Confederates "have been concentrating in large force opposite the point at which we originally intended to cross" (Skinker's Neck), and two sentences later he stated that "a large force of the enemy is now concentrated in the vicinity of Port Royal" — five miles farther downriver. Thus Halleck was left to wonder whether there were concentrations at both places or the statement about Port Royal superseded the preceding one. The nature and source of Burnside's information on enemy at Skinker's Neck are unknown; regarding Port Royal there is a clue, but only a weak one, in Patrick's diary. On the same day as Burnside's communication with Halleck, Dec. 9, Patrick wrote that Burnside's attack would take place within three days, and "the enemy suppose [it] to be at Port Royal and are sending their troops down there. I have had a very intelligent servant of [Confederate] Maj. French here today, who gave me much information." Thus Patrick matches Burnside's careless wording by leaving us wondering whether his interesting Negro examinee was the source of the news about Port Royal. The coincidence of dates induces a suspicion that Burnside's statement about enemy concentration at Port Royal had no more basis than the interrogation of this probably truthful but unauthoritative source.

More definite information about Confederate activity downriver comes from U.S. Navy officers' reports of artillery dueling between their gunboats and a heavy field piece at Port Royal on Dec. 4. Lt. Cmdr. Samuel Magaw observed infantry there; he counted only five regiments, but the appearance of artillery heavy enough to duel with the gunboats suggests the presence of infantry forces of some importance (in fact D. H. Hill was present and watching over these events). A Federal cavalry colonel stationed near Port Conway, across the river from Port Royal, was attracted by the cannonading and discovered Rebels constructing rifle pits on the Federals' side of the river. (*NOR*, 5:182–89; *OR*, 21:826.) These reports, however, do not by any means indicate the concentration of enemy force that Burnside evidently assumed was there.

41. William F. Smith, "Franklin's 'Left Grand Division,'" *B&L*, 3:130. Although Smith was no friend of Burnside (in fact he was one of the officers whose removal from the Army of the Potomac Burnside later sought), this report of Burnside's confidence in his information is consistent with the other findings on that question reported here.

42. Marvel, *Burnside*, 169–70; Burnside's after-action report, 90–91; Greene, "Operations in the South: Meade versus Jackson at Fredericksburg," *Civil War History* 33, no. 4 (Dec. 1987): 299; *OR*, 21:153. Federal strength figures are from Burnside's report; Ted Alexander, National Park Service historian at Antietam, is authority for the 78,000 estimate of Confederate strength.

43. *OR*, 21:89.

44. *OR*, 21:675, 841, 642–43, 663; Freeman, *R. E. Lee*, 2:449.

45. Hooker, in his after-action report (*OR*, 21:356) and his testimony before the Joint Committee (JCCW 1863, 1:667–69), is the only source of information on this prisoner. The fact that Burnside was the recipient of his report allays the inevitable suspicion that Hooker invented the story as part of his effort to discredit Burnside. Of course he may have overplayed it.

46. Greene, "Operations in the South," 297–310.

47. This description of the battle after Meade's repulse follows these accounts: Marvel, *Burnside*, 188–200 (the most thorough analysis of Burnside's two-pronged attack plan known to the present writer); Palfrey, *Antietam and Fredericksburg*, 150–72; Steele, *American Campaigns*, 1:295–300; Burnside's and Hooker's after-action reports, *OR*, 21:82–97 and 354–57. The various orders to Franklin are in *OR*, 21:71, 93–94, 127; to Sumner and Hooker, ibid., 90.

48. *OR*, 21:689–91, 693–97, 705–42 *passim;* Freeman, *Lee's Lieutenants*, 2:405–6. Stuart claimed that from this station he sent messages to Quartermaster General Meigs in Washington, complaining about the poor quality of the mules he was obtaining from the Yankees (*OR*, 21:734).

49. *OR*, 21:924.

50. Bates, *Lincoln in the Telegraph Office*, 58–63. Although the instances of sustained wiretaps are few, there are numerous accounts of taps by operators accompanying cavalry raids, who usually, perhaps invariably, made their presence known to the enemy. The telegraphic pranks of Stuart and his operator were mild compared to those of Brig. Gen. John H. Morgan and operator George A. Elsworth, whose intrusions won him a wide acquaintance among Federal operators at Nashville, Louisville, Cincinnati, and posts in between, many of which were visited by Morgan's raiders. One raid netted Elsworth a twelve-day yield of intercepted telegrams, which would have qualified it as a "serious intelligence project" had Morgan not revealed it in a boastful telegram he addressed to the Federal commander at Louisville. *OR*, 16:774–81; 23.2:517, 668. By far the most productive Civil War wiretap that has come to light took place in the eastern theater in September 1864, when the Confederates intercepted traffic on Gen. Grant's Washington line, including a plain-language message revealing the forthcoming arrival of a huge shipment of beef cattle, which Wade Hampton's cavalry then captured (see Boykin, *Beefsteak Raid*).

51. *OR,* 21:95–96 (a section of Burnside's after-action report); Burnside to Lincoln, Jan. 1, 1863 (ibid., 941–42). At this same time Lincoln wrote instructions to Halleck that the general considered harsh; the note was withdrawn. Halleck made a written request to be relieved of his position; it too was withdrawn (ibid., 940–41).

52. "Excerpts from the Journal of Henry J. Raymond," *Scribner's Monthly* 19, no. 3 (Jan. 1880): 419–24; Patrick Diary, Jan. 13, 1863. Raymond, founder and sometime correspondent of the New York *Times,* learned of McGee's services from contact with Burnside during his planning for what became known as the Mud March. Personal data on McGee are from Harrison, *Chancellorsville Battle Sites,* 46.

53. *OR,* 21:752–55; Babcock to "Dear Aunt," Jan. 25, 1863, Babcock Papers.

54. *OR,* 21:998–99, 1004–5.

55. Babcock to Gen. Parke, Dec. 31, 1862, Letters Received, Army of the Potomac, NA. The only occasion on which records show even a faint possibility that Babcock assisted in interrogations was the army's capture of prisoners in the Dec. 13 battle. In diary entries Dec. 17, 19, 26, and 29, Gen. Patrick reported the examining and forwarding of 674 prisoners; one use of the word *we* shows that he had assistance in this work.

56. Much of this activity was directed by Maj. Gen. George L. Hartsuff, commanding the Twenty-third Corps.

12. A New Client for Attorney Sharpe

1. Gates, *Ulster Guard,* 191–94, is the source of this sketch of Patrick, except for the general's religious habits, which are extensively revealed in his diary.

2. Patrick Diary, Jan. 24, 25, 26, 1863; Patrick to Gen. Parke, Jan. 19, 1863, in Record Group 393, part 1, entry 4029A (Letters and Endorsements Sent, Provost Marshal, Army of the Potomac records, bk. 70, pp. 110–11).

3. Patrick Diary, Jan. 27, 1863.

4. Hebert, *Fighting Joe Hooker,* 167.

5. Bigelow, *Campaign of Chancellorsville,* 5.

6. The letter, often reprinted in its entirety, appears at *OR,* 25.2:4 and *Works of Lincoln,* 6:78–79.

7. Hebert, *Hooker,* 28–34. The generals under whom Hooker served in Mexico were Persifor F. Smith, Thomas Lyon Hamer, William Orlando Butler, George Cadwallader, and Gideon Pillow.

8. Hooker to Bates, May 29, 1878, Bates Collection; Halleck to Sherman, Sept. 16, 1864, in *Memoirs of General William T. Sherman,* 2:117.

9. Hebert, *Hooker,* 47–50; Lincoln to Gen. Mansfield, *Works of Lincoln,* 4:412–13.

10. *OR,* 5:632, 642. The Confederates opposite Hooker's force totaled about 8000 and thus matched Hooker's own strength (ibid., 650, 933). However, the enemy enjoyed the advantage of numerous batteries along the river.

11. A 400-man expedition to the Virginia shore, mentioned in chapter 4, was made early in November without Hooker's knowledge. Although successful in a small way, it encountered his displeasure (*OR,* 5:407–11).

12. *OR,* 5:17, 646, 690. The ownership of horses by enlisted men of the third Indiana is shown in their service records (RG 94, Records of the Adjutant General's Office, NA).

13. *OR,* ser. 3, 3:253, 265, 267, 269.

14. *OR*, 5:653.

15. *OR*, 5:695.

16. Baker to Hooker, Nov. 25 and Dec. 6, 1861, Hooker Papers; Maj. George H. Chapman to Hooker, Nov. 25, 1861, ibid.

17. *OR*, 5:469, 675, 690; Hebert, *Hooker*, 62.

18. Unaddressed statements dated Jan. 3 and 29, 1862, Hooker Papers.

19. On Mar. 12, 1862, Hooker estimated the enemy force facing him at 17,000 (*OR*, 5:744). This was 3500 over the figure in the Confederate return for February (ibid., 1086), but so many new forces had arrived in the area as the result of the Confederates' recent withdrawal from Manassas and Dumfries that Hooker's figure was probably an underestimate.

20. In addition to the sources cited in notes 10–19, this account of Hooker's information service is drawn from *OR*, 5:422, 524, 634, 635, 646, 649, 673, 686, 697, 707, 709–11, 724–25, 735, 743; Hebert, *Hooker*, 60.

21. *OR*, 5:709–11, 731, 735, 743–44, 753–56, 761; 51.1:536, 543, 548; 11.3:16, 19–20; *McClellan's Own Story*, 237.

22. Hebert, *Hooker*, 118.

23. Ibid.

24. *OR*, 11.1:468.

25. Hebert, *Hooker*, 90, citing Kearny, *General Philip Kearny*, 244.

26. *B&L*, 2:465.

27. *OR*, 11.1:461.

28. McClellan to Lincoln, Sept. 6, 1862, in Basler, ed., *Works of Lincoln*, 5:407n; *OR*, 19.2:198.

29. *OR*, 19.1:219; Boatner, *Civil War Dictionary*, 400.

30. *OR*, 19.1:422–23.

31. Except where notes indicate otherwise, this sketch of Hooker is taken from Hebert, *Hooker*, 20–90 *passim*.

32. *Dictionary of American Biography*.

33. Hebert, whose biography of Hooker bears a title *(Fighting Joe Hooker)* reflecting the conventional view of the general, chooses "Administrative Joe" (taken from the *U.S. Army and Navy Journal*, Nov. 8, 1879) as the title for his chapter dealing with this period of Hooker's career.

34. Bigelow, *Chancellorsville*, 36; Williams, *Lincoln Finds a General*, 2:553. Hooker's letter of Feb. 15 to the War Dept. (*OR*, 25.2:77–78) gives a total of absentees, 85,123, that is radically and inexplicably at odds with his tabulation showing about a tenth of the men as deserters or AWOL.

35. *OR*, 25.2:12, 60.

36. Ibid., 2:51, 79. At p. 438 of that volume is a statement by Hooker revealing his preference for operations that could be conducted "within my personal supervision."

37. Gen. Darius N. Couch, *B&L*, 3:154.

38. Hebert, *Hooker*, 172; *Dictionary of American Biography*, entries for both Daniel and Julia Butterfield; Joseph L. Whitney and Stephen W. Sears, "The True Story of Taps," *Blue & Gray* 10, no. 6 (Aug. 1993): 30–33.

39. JCCW 1865, 1:74 (Butterfield's testimony); *OR*, 25.2:10–11, 38, 152, 120–21, 167–69, 43, 78, 119, 161–62, 58, 194–95; Patrick Diary, Feb. 15 and 27, 1863.

40. Patrick Diary, Jan. 27, 1863.

41. *OR*, 25.2:11, 147, 36–37, 86; Capt. Kelton (Halleck's A.A.G.) to Gen. Williams (Hooker's A.A.G.), Feb. 25, 1863, Hooker Papers; Patrick to Supt. John A. Kennedy, New York, Feb. 5, 1863, in AP records, bk. 70, p. 137; Patrick to

Adjutant General's Office, Feb. 9, 1863, ibid., 141; Patrick to Hon. Simeon Draper, War Dept., Feb. 17, 1863, ibid., 156.

42. Patrick to Kennedy, Feb. 5, 1863, in AP records, bk. 70, pp. 73, 84, 121, 137; Patrick Diary, Feb. 17, 1863.

43. Provost Marshal Allen, Aquia, to Capt. Lyttle, PMG Office, AP, April 27, 1863, RG 94, box 54, entry 731, NA.

44. Capt. Lyttle to Capt. Todd, provost marshal, Washington, Mar. 31, 1863, in AP records, bk. 67, p. 53.

45. Patrick's diary entry of Feb. 20, 1863, reports a two-day visit by Gen. Martindale, who came to devise "a plan by which the difficulties of intercourse between Washington & this army may be obviated." For evidence of Patrick's preference for dealing with Martindale's command, see, *e.g.,* his letter to Maj. Wm. E. Doster, provost marshal, Washington, in AP records, bk. 70, p. 135.

46. Letter of Col. D. H. Rucker, depot quartermaster, Washington, Jan. 14, 1863, and Patrick's endorsement thereon, Jan. 16, in AP records, bk. 70, p. 109; Col. Wm. F. Rogers, Aquia Creek, to Capt. Kimball, Patrick's A.A.G., March 5 and 20, 1863, in AP records, Letters Received, box 4002; Capt. Allen, provost marshal, Aquia, to Patrick, April 15, 1863, in AP records, old bk. 180, p. 18.

47. Patrick to Butterfield, Jan. 29, 1863, in AP records, bk. 70, p. 123.

48. Patrick to Asst. Secy. Watson, April 7, 1863, Turner-Baker Papers, file 323-B.

49. Patrick Diary, Feb. 25, 1863. Two months later (diary entry for April 25) Patrick returned to this theme: "These Head Quarters are . . . corrupt. . . . Hooker is mixed in and linked with as big a set of Scoundrels as can be found on this Continent." Patrick's revulsion almost matched the well-known plaint of young Capt. Charles Francis Adams Jr., who wrote years later that during the winter of 1862–63 "the headquarters of the Army of the Potomac was a place to which no self-respecting man liked to go, and no decent woman could go. It was a combination of bar-room and brothel." *C. F. Adams, 1835–1916: An Autobiography* (Boston, 1916), 161. Patrick's remarks, however, are less specific than Adams's; he complained only of corruption and of Hooker's connection with "scoundrels." Although he grumbled about nighttime irregularities in the head-quarters camp, his strictures do not go so far as to support Adams's characterization of the place. Possibly Hooker's officers confined their more ambitious debauches to their visits to Washington; otherwise Patrick's complaints would have been more specific.

50. Patrick Diary, Feb. 27 and 28, 1863; Patrick to Watson, March 7, 1863, in AP records, box 4000.

51. So far as the record reveals, Baker survived this episode without reprimand. Pinkerton's report on this case is in the Turner-Baker Papers, file 2055. The Turner-Baker papers show in detail the nature of Turner's duties and his status as the officer to whom Baker, who for many months outranked him by two grades, reported for orders. Baker's service record (NA) shows that he was commissioned colonel of the 1st District of Columbia Cavalry Regt. May 5, 1863; however, he had been addressed as colonel well before his commissioning (see Heintzelman to Butterfield, Feb. 7, 1863, BMI).

52. *OR,* 25.2:110, 119. Hooker's order respecting flags of truce actually specified that newspapers could be received but not given. The presumed effect would have been to cause the Confederates to reciprocate in the withholding.

53. Lt. Col. J. W. Dickinson, A.A.G., to Patrick, Feb. 4, 1863, in AP records, bk. 24, p. 143.

54. Patrick Diary, Feb. 5, 1863. Babcock's report, which is not in the records,

would surely have included the fact that he had countered Pinkerton's removal of records by making himself a copy of Gen. Banks's compilation of data on the Army of Northern Virginia in the Dept. of Washington files. But Butterfield, testifying a year later to the Joint Committee on the Conduct of the War, declared, "When General Hooker took command of the army there was not a record or document of any kind . . . that gave any information at all in regard to the enemy." Butterfield spoke the truth, however, when he added, "There was no means, no organization, and no apparent effort to obtain such information" (JCCW 1865, 1:74).

55. The 1860 census shows that at that time Morgan owned $38,000 worth of real estate in Spotsylvania County, which lay entirely within Confederate lines. But a detailed map of the locality, made in Dec. 1862 by Army of the Potomac engineers, shows Morgan's residence at a point very near the Eagle Mine in Stafford County (RG 77, map C101–1).

56. Patrick Diary, Jan. 1, 2, 30, Feb. 8, 10, 1863; McKelvey to Sharpe, Feb. 20, 1863, in BMI; Pinkerton file, S. S. Accts.

57. Patrick Diary, Feb. 11, 1863. Sharpe's appointment was announced to the Army of the Potomac by paragraph 9, Special Orders No. 50, AP. Titles such as Chief of Intelligence have been bestowed on Sharpe by historians unaware that the word *intelligence* lay outside the military vocabulary of the 1860s.

58. Another version of Sharpe's selection is that he had come to Hooker's attention at the battle of Fredericksburg when, in addition to leading his own regiment, he placed in line of battle a regiment of French-speaking New Yorkers whose commander did not speak French well enough to direct them on the field. Sharpe, according to this account, was later summoned by Hooker to translate for him a French book on the "secret service." For information on Sharpe's military background see G. B. D. Hasbrouck, "Address on Major General George H. Sharpe," *Proceedings of the Ulster County* (N.Y.) *Historical Society, 1936–37;* Van Santvoord, *The One Hundred and Twentieth Regiment,* 3–5; Gates, *Ulster Guard,* 194; *OR,* 25.1:156; Cullum, *Biographical Register,* entry 833 (on Patrick); JCCW 1865, 1:74 (Butterfield's testimony); Sharpe to Jansen Hasbrouck, Feb. 3, 1863, Sharpe Collection.

59. In the Second World War the Pentagon's top-level intelligence analysis and reporting element was staffed almost entirely by lawyers. Their chief, a New York City lawyer named Alfred McCormack, sought men whose "training teaches them to deal with evidence, to be inquisitive and skeptical, to pursue an investigation through to a conclusion, to meet unfamiliar situations of fact and, most important, to do very detailed work without losing their sense of values" (David Kahn, "Roosevelt, MAGIC, and ULTRA," *Cryptologia* no. 4 [Oct. 1992]: 295). Although McCormack would seem to have found this combination of qualities only among lawyers, other professional types — journalists, historians and academicians in general, scientists, and linguists — were then prominent in intelligence organizations.

60. Sharpe's lineage only partially reflects the mixture of western European nationalities represented in Ulster County and vicinity. The original Dutch settlers were followed by waves of English and Irish. There was also, in adjoining Columbia County, a colony of Germans, refugees from the Palatinate, of whom Sharpe's great-great-grandfather, Jacob Sharp, was one. His maternal ancestors, the Hasbroucks, had a more varied history. Their patriarch, Abraham Hasbrouck, was a Walloon from northern France, the descendant of a noble family, who fled with other Huguenots to the Palatinate in the eighteenth century. Some accounts indicate that he also resided for substantial periods in Holland

and England before coming to America. Many of his male descendants married women of Dutch blood, but there was also a Norwegian strain. Sharpe's wife, Caroline Hone Hasbrouck, was his third cousin. For these and other facts connected with Sharpe and with his history of Kingston and vicinity, I am indebted to Miss Louise Heron of Kingston and to the following particular sources: E. M. Smith, *History of Rhinebeck* (Rhinebeck, N.Y., 1881), 211–13; handwritten notes on Sharpe genealogy (partly attributed to the series "Our Palatine Settlers," Rhinebeck *Gazette*, 1896), in the Sharpe Collection; *Commemorative Biographical Record of Ulster County, New York* (Chicago, 1896); Ralph Le Fevre, *History of New Paltz* (Albany, 1909); 368–69; *Olde Ulster*, 4:186, 217, 249, 252, 315, 432, 376; 5:18, 54; Kingston *Freeman and Journal*, June 3, 1913; Geo. H. Sharpe to Severyn Bruyn, July 7, 1849, Kingston Collection, New York State Library, Albany; and G. B. D. Hasbrouck, "Address on Sharpe," cited in note 58. Despite Sharpe's local prominence in his early years and statewide prominence after the Civil War, nothing concerning his appearance and personality seems to have entered the record; the information on those subjects was obtained by interviews with elderly Kingstonians in 1956.

61. Kingston *Daily Leader*, Jan. 15, 1900 (Sharpe obituary).

62. Van Santvoord, *One Hundred Twentieth Regiment*, 3–4. One searches the 20th Regiment's history in vain for an admission that its legal name after August 1861 was 80th New York Volunteer Infantry.

63. Sharpe to Jansen Hasbrouck, Oct. 29, 1862, Sharpe Collection; Sharpe to John Steele, Dec. 2, 1862, in Sharpe service record, RG 94; Van Santvoord, *One Hundred Twentieth Regiment*, 10–11; Kingston *Daily Leader*, Oct. 19, 1896.

64. *OR*, 21:380, 388–89.

65. Van Santvoord, *One Hundred Twentieth Regiment*, 39.

66. Sharpe to Jansen Hasbrouck, April 28, 1863, Sharpe Collection.

67. This was the Bank of Rondout (*1866 Directory of Kingston and Rondout*).

68. With each transmittal of the soldiers' pay Sharpe customarily wrote his uncle a letter. These letters form the bulk of the Sharpe Collection (in the Senate House Museum, Kingston), the principal basis of this account of Sharpe's personal history.

69. Notes in Sharpe Collection (attributed to Elizabeth Morris Lefferts, *Descendants of Lewis Morris of Morrisania*) show that the three Sharpe children — Severyn Bruyn, Henry Granville, and Katherine — would have been six, four, and three years old, respectively, in the winter of 1862–63.

70. The letterhead of the famous hotel in those years read simply "The Willards." Then as now it was known as "the Willard."

71. Sharpe to Hasbrouck, Feb. 3, 1863, Sharpe Collection; Sharpe to Steele, Dec. 2, 1862, Sharpe service record, RG 94, NA; Seward to Stanton, Dec. 6, 1862, with indorsement Dec. 8 by Asst. Secy. of War C. P. Wolcott, ibid. On at least one occasion — before he left his regiment — Sharpe was permitted to go to Washington for no purpose more official than to deposit $6000 of the regiment's pay (Sharpe to A.A.G., Centre Grand Division, Jan. 27, 1863, Sharpe service record, RG 94, NA). Steele occasionally visited the army to see Sharpe (see, *e.g.*, Sharpe to Steele, Feb. 19 and June 9, 1863, General Telegrams).

72. Kingston *Weekly Freeman and Journal*, July 24, 1890, and Kingston *Argus*, July 26, 1890 (Van Buren obituaries); Marius Schoonmaker, *History of Kingston, New York* (New York, 1888), 490. Col. Van Buren (only distantly related to President Martin Van Buren), an 1838 graduate of West Point, resigned from the army in 1855 and until the Civil War practiced as a lawyer and civil engineer in Kingston. From 1858 to 1861 he was Ulster County's commissioner of common

schools. He was with Gen. Dix as A.A.G. in all of that officer's commands from August 1861 to the end of the war (Cullum, *Biographical Register,* entry 1336).

73. Cuthbert, ed., *Lincoln and the Baltimore Plot,* 7, quoting Pinkerton to W. H. Herndon, Aug. 23, 1866.

74. Van Buren to Sharpe, Feb. 5 and 9, 1863, BMI.

75. See chapter 15, notes 1 and 2 and associated text.

76. Joseph H. Maddox, whose employment by Sharpe will be related in chapter 14, was capable of turning espionage to considerable commercial gain and may have done so, but not, as far as is known, to the detriment of his service to Sharpe.

77. Such cases, although rare among military espionage units, abound in the records of Northern detective organs. For example, one of the agents in Baker's employ at this time was a former Federal army officer who had been court-martialed for cowardice and cashiered, whereupon he opened an agency for obtaining soldiers' discharges, a vocation that led to his being thrown into Old Capitol Prison on charges of fraud and perjury. This record was not enough to put off Baker, who hired the man, put him under charge of one of the regular detectives, and used him "in detecting and exposing frauds &c. upon the government." In less than a year the man was back in Old Capitol. (L. C. Turner to Gen. Joseph Holt, April 14, 1863, in Turner-Baker Papers, Letterbook Y; Baker file for July 1863, S. S. Accts.) For another example, see chapter 4, note 29 and associated text.

78. Dodd belonged to the 1st Ohio Light Artillery, of Brig. Gen. Jacob D. Cox's Kanawha Division, which was part of the Ninth Corps in the Maryland campaign; the Ninth was grouped with Hooker's First Corps under the command of Burnside. Dodd's "scouting" history is detailed in an affidavit of April 4, 1866, supporting the subsistence claim of a colleague, file no. M(D)86, HqA, 1866, NA. Dodd is among a group of spies pictured in Miller, *Photographic History,* 8:281.

79. Patrick Diary, Feb. 11, 1863; Humphreys file, S. S. Accts.; BMI payrolls, Jan–Feb., 1863; Plum, *Military Telegraph,* 1:280, 292.

80. Patrick Diary, March 8, 1863. Brig. Gen. C. C. Augur's statement, Sept. 14, 1862, in Skinker file, S. S. Accts.

81. Other early employees not named in the text are William Littral, William Weaver, E. J. (or E. P.) Smith, William H. Chase, R. Gutheridge, Edward A. Carney and Anson Carney of a New York cavalry regiment, Benjamin F. McCord, Edward (or Edwin) P. Hopkins, Allen Anderson, and John Tyson. Two men named William Littral, one a clerk aged seventeen and the other a cooper aged twenty-eight, lived in Spotsylvania County in 1860. (BMI payrolls and 1860 Census, NA.)

82. This correspondence (all in BMI except where noted otherwise) includes Hancock to Butterfield, Feb. 21, 186[3]; Babcock's map of ford connecting Fredericksburg and Falmouth, Feb. 27, 1863, attributed to "Chidister, Scout" (in AP records, Provost Marshal General, box 4002); Sedgwick to Butterfield, Feb. 17, 1863, and to Sharpe, Feb. 25, 1863; Pleasonton to Butterfield, Feb. 19, 1863, containing also Sharpe's notes of his interview with Reynolds's candidate; Jenkins to Sharpe, Feb. 27, 1863; Heintzelman to Butterfield, Feb. 7, 1863.

83. BMI payrolls. This number included Babcock, who continued to be paid by the War Dept., and Sharpe, whose name does not appear on his own payroll or that of the War Dept.

84. Patrick Diary, March 7, 1863.

85. That McKelvey and Stanley were not hired is indicated by their absence

from the payroll records of Sharpe's bureau. McKelvey asked $7.50 a day, the amount he had received from Pinkerton, and a written request from Patrick to the District of Columbia Commissioners of Police so that he could be employed by the army without having to resign his police job (McKelvey to Sharpe, Feb. 20, 1863, BMI).

86. McEntee genealogical information from Cdr. Girard L. McEntee (USN [Ret.], Alexandria, Va.); service record of Col. John McEntee, NA; Dept. of Interior, Bureau of Pensions, file no. 1299565, NA; Kingston *Daily Leader,* Dec. 21, 1903 (McEntee obituary); letter of Miss Louise Heron of Kingston, Feb. 18, 1963. The description of McEntee was furnished by Mrs. Doris H. Fogg and Mrs. Appleton H. Gregory of Kingston, who had much of his company during their childhood.

87. The Confederates did not apply this distinction so severely, probably because they were less able than the Federals to pass over talent; it would be hard to believe that theirs was the more democratic of the two armies.

88. Bureau of Information and Bureau of Secret Information were other early forms used by Sharpe.

89. One of Potts's visits to the army came on March 28, when he saw Hooker as well as Patrick. Sharpe was absent in Baltimore (Patrick Diary, March 28 and 29, 1863).

90. Pinkerton and Porter files, S. S. Accts.; BMI payroll, Jan. 1863–Sept. 1865. The service of the Negro members of the bureau was short-lived, and their claim was disapproved on the basis of a statement furnished to the War Dept. by Sharpe (RG 393, part 1, entry 4075, NA).

91. Some of the supposedly bona fide names on secret-service rosters were so suggestive as to raise doubts of their authenticity. For example: John W. Willhide, a Federal scout in West Virginia, and David Tory, one of the active Unionists in East Tennessee. Offered as bona fide names for pay purposes were "Doe, John W."; "Roe, Richard"; and "Wash, D. C." For Willhide, see Reader, *History of the Fifth West Virginia Cavalry,* 250–51. For Tory and Roe, see S. S. Accts.; for Doe, Turner-Baker Papers, file 1910; for "Wash," Special Orders 172 and 225, District of Southwest Missouri. None of Sharpe's men bore names more suggestive than his own.

92. See, *e.g.,* Sharpe to Jansen Hasbrouck, Aug. 15, 1864, in Sharpe Collection. An exception to the avoidance of specie, by Sgt. Thomas Harter in the Second Bull Run Campaign, is unexplained.

93. A glaring exception to spies' practice of not carrying memoranda was Joseph E. Snyder, who furnished a long, detailed journal of his travels as a prisoner through Virginia in October and November 1862; see chapter 11.

94. Miller, *Photographic History,* 8:19. The BMI files contain no messages that appear to have been developed from writing in invisible ink.

95. See, for example, the case of a Loyalist mother who gave information from her son in Confederate service (*OR,* 49.1:631), and of a minister of the Gospel who caused the arrest of his father (Turner-Baker Papers, Letterbook Y, p. 237).

96. Turner-Baker Papers, file 295.

97. Several statements to the effect that the Confederates made a practice of using planted deserters are found in the postwar writings of John S. Mosby; see, *e.g.,* his *Memoirs,* 202–3. Stuart's activity in spreading false information — though not necessarily through deserters — was described by Gen. Lee in postwar conversations, of which elaborate memoranda were made by his auditors (see Freeman, *Lee's Lieutenants,* 2:718, 720). These same conclusions can be reached without the direct evidence just cited; instances of deserter information reaching

the Federals that was sharply at odds with the facts are so numerous, and their circumstances so suggestive, that one must conclude that either the deserters were planted (and, more than that, had been carefully chosen and well coached by the Southern generals) or the story they told was in general circulation in the Southern army, perhaps deliberately launched by its commanders, or it was a rumor of more nearly spontaneous origin. In some instances in succeeding chapters one of these alternatives will seem the more likely, but in other instances the choice amounts to guesswork. It will soon develop that Sharpe found an effective countermeasure to untruthful reporting by Confederate deserters.

13. Ten Days of Southern Hospitality

1. For the history of Washington's intelligence operations see O'Toole, *Honorable Treachery*, chs. 2, 4, and 5, which integrate the findings of numerous previous studies.

2. Bidwell, *History of the Military Intelligence Division, Department of the Army General Staff,* notes (p. 31) that Sharpe's "experienced personnel . . . were presumably aware of all available information on the subject at hand." Thus it is seen that Bidwell was aware of Sharpe's all-source reporting mission; he also sensed its historical significance. But the Civil War chapter of his book greatly exaggerates the size and effectiveness of Confederate intelligence organs and repeats several of the intelligence myths refuted in the present study.

3. See the Epilogue for changes that were made in the bureau's reporting function with Gen. Meade's accession to command of the Army of the Potomac and again with Gen. Grant's establishment of the headquarters of the Armies Operating Against Richmond.

4. The originators of this material sent some of it to Hooker via Butterfield, some to Sharpe, and some to both. For examples of these procedures see: Lowe to Butterfield, Feb. 11, 23, March 13, 26, and 9 A.M., April 28, 1863, Hooker Papers; Capt. Samuel T. Cushing to Butterfield, April 13, 20, 1863, Hooker Papers; Cushing to Major Albert Myer, May 23, 1863 (by which date Myer had been promoted to colonel), *OR*, 25.1:217–23; Capt. James S. Hall to Capt. B. F. Fisher, Feb. 19, 1863, BMI; Fisher to Butterfield, April 9, 1863, BMI; packet marked "Balloon and Signal Reports," BMI; Pleasonton to A.A.G., Cavalry Corps, March 17, 1863, BMI; Pleasonton to Butterfield, April 18, 1863, Hooker Papers; Capt. E. J. Farnsworth to C.O., 8th Illinois Cavalry, March 31, 1863, RG 393, part 1, entry 4050 or 3980, NA; Gen. B. S. Roberts to Gen. R. C. Schenck, March 23, 1863, BMI; Gen. J. J. Peck to Hooker, April 12, 1863, BMI. Examples of signal officers' direct correspondence with the Bureau of Military Information are Capt. Wm. L. Candler to Sharpe, March 2, 1863, BMI; Lt. J. B. Brooks to Sharpe, April 8, 1863, in "Balloon and Signal Reports" packet, BMI. Brooks's dispatch answered an inquiry from Sharpe.

5. Patrick Diary, Feb. 7, 8, 1863. Patrick had obtained Hooker's sanction for the pass he issued in this case, for, as will appear later, the practice of exchanging women and other noncombatants had been abolished by the War Department.

6. Patrick Diary, Feb. 15–18, 1863; Sharpe to "General," March 21, 1863, BMI. For identification of the chaplain, whom Patrick referred to only as Landstreet, see *OR*, 43.1:578.

7. This gradual accretion of information is shown in an unaddressed memorandum, "Reb. Regiments from which Prisoners of War have been taken, and deserters come into our lines from the enemy, to April 30, 1863," BMI.

8. Sharpe to Gen. Martindale, military governor of Washington, Dec. 12, 1863, BMI. Sharpe wrote to Martindale to promote the general use of the policy after it had proven successful in the Army of the Potomac.

9. *OR*, 25.2:12, 52–54.

10. Patrick Diary, Feb. 15–20, 1863.

11. Taylor to Capt. Jas. S. Hall, Feb. 19, 1863, endorsed by Capt. B. F. Fisher, chief signal officer, Army of the Potomac, BMI.

12. *OR*, 25.2:93–94.

13. Patrick Diary, Feb. 22, 1863; Kilpatrick to A.A.G. 3rd Cav. Div., Feb. 22, 1863, endorsed by Gen. D. McM. Gregg and Gen. Stoneman, BMI.

14. Memorandum cited in note 7.

15. Kilpatrick letter cited in note 13.

16. Patrick Diary, Feb. 22, 1863.

17. Freeman, *R. E. Lee*, 2:492.

18. Yager's report, Feb. 26, 1863, BMI; *OR*, 25.2:99.

19. Memorandum cited in note 7.

20. *OR*, 25.2:79–81.

21. *OR*, 25.2:99–100.

22. *OR*, 25.2:100, 102.

23. *OR*, 18:818, 872, 876, 883–84; 25.2:624–31, 713, 725; Freeman, *Lee's Lieutenants*, 2:421–22, 427.

24. J. L. Yaryan, chief of scouts, to C. of S. 21st Army Corps, Feb. 23, 1863, in W. C. Nelson file, SGSD.

25. *OR*, 25.2:630–31.

26. Cline service record, NA.

27. Early, *Memoirs*, 184.

28. Another possibility is that Cline accomplished the trickery by means of forged papers. John N. Opie, *A Rebel Cavalryman* (Chicago, 1899), says that it was the Federals' practice to take a Confederate prisoner's pass or furlough paper and find someone in the Union ranks whom the captive's clothing would fit and who also resembled the prisoner in age and general appearance. "The Rebel's uniform, from hat to boots, was put upon this man, who assumed the name of the prisoner, and the Federal left camp, a soldier of the Confederacy." This story does not explain how the pseudo-Rebel could maintain the false identity if he was "returned" to the company where its true owner belonged. It is not corroborated in any records known to this writer.

29. *OR*, 21:1077.

30. Kershaw's position is shown in Bigelow, *Chancellorsville*, map 2.

31. Cline's report, n.d., BMI. There are inconsistencies between this document and Sharpe's notes from his interrogation of Cline (also BMI, n.d.). The most significant of these have to do with the order in which various camps, fortifications, and gun sites were encountered. (Cline's expression "rising the hill" betrays his seafaring background.)

32. The following sources were consulted to identify the units reported by Cline: Bigelow, *Chancellorsville*, map 2; Gen. Anderson's Chancellorsville report, *OR*, 25.1:849; Gen. Barksdale's report, ibid., 839.

33. Bigelow, *Chancellorsville*, map 2. Part of Early's division may have moved from Port Royal to Hamilton's Crossing during Cline's trip. Early, *Memoirs*, 191, gives "about the first of March" as the time of this move.

34. *OR*, 51.1:73.

35. Several maps showing the Fredericksburg area in detail, made by Army of the Potomac engineers in late 1862 and early 1863, are in the Cartographic and

Architectural Division, NA. See particularly maps G101–1, G101–2, Z399–2, and G138, all from RG 77.

36. Memorandum cited in note 7.

37. The actual ration as reported by Lee (*OR*, 25.2:687) was "18 ounces of flour, 4 ounces of bacon of indifferent quality, with occasional supplies of rice, sugar or molasses."

38. Except where otherwise indicated, this account of Cline's expedition is from his report and Sharpe's notes, cited in note 31.

39. Patrick Diary, March 5, 1863; Cole service record and pension record, NA; unaddressed, unsigned report of Cole's expedition, March 22, 1863, BMI. In the fall of 1862 Cole had typhoid fever and upon recovering began to suffer from impaired vision, a condition that may have contributed to his release from regular cavalry duty.

40. Report of Cole's expedition, BMI.

14. Rebel Spies Are Now Second Best

1. Unaddressed memorandum, "Reb. Regiments from which Prisoners of War have been taken and deserters come into our lines from the enemy, to Apr. 30, 1863," BMI.

2. Capt. William L. Candler to Sharpe, March 2, 1863, and Lt. Joseph Gloskoski to Capt. B. F. Fisher, March 14, 1863, BMI; letters with dates between Feb. 14 and 25 (1863) in packet labeled "Captured Rebel Correspondence," BMI.

3. *OR*, 18:549–53, 556, 558.

4. *OR*, 25.2:113–14, 127–28, 132; Freeman, *R. E. Lee*. 2:483.

5. Thomas J. Webb to Walter S. Webb, Jan. 18, 1863, in "Captured Rebel Correspondence" packet, BMI; *OR*, 25.2:189.

6. Service record of T. J. Skinker, 9th Va. Cavalry, NA; 1860 Census of Stafford County.

7. Capt. W. R. Sterling to Butterfield, March 9, 1963, Hooker Papers.

8. Skinker's report, March 11, 1863, BMI. In rewriting the report for Butterfield, Babcock merely polished up the rough spots left by Skinker's hasty composition. He repeated all of Skinker's statements without commenting as to their probable correctness.

9. Sharpe to Butterfield, March 15, 1963, BMI.

10. Patrick Diary, March 10, 1863; *OR*, 25.2, 135–36; Hebert, *Hooker*, 182.

11. Babcock to Butterfield, March 11, 1863, BMI; *OR*, 25.2:135–36. Babcock's obituary (Mount Vernon [N.Y.] *Argus*, Nov. 20, 1908) mentions a Negro woman spy who communicated with Babcock by means of a "clothesline code," but the account gives no time or place.

12. Skinker's report, March 13, 1863, BMI.

13. *OR*, 25.2:136.

14. Army of the Potomac, Letters Received, book 12, entry B178/1863, NA.

15. Unaddressed, undated dispatch from Capt. Henri Dunstetter, Hooker Papers.

16. Kate Ashley to "My Dear Brother," March 11, 1863, BMI. A "Mr. West" was then at the Ashley home; presumably he was the same person identified by Capt. Dunstetter as "Western," but whether the visitor was of such striking appearance Kate Ashley did not indicate.

17. Skinker's report, March 13, 1863; Pleasonton to "General," March 30, 1863; Pleasonton to Hooker, April 1, 1863; all in BMI.

18. Personal information about Silver is from G. H. S. King, a Fredericksburg genealogist, and from interviews conducted for the author by Rev. Robert Shaw, late rector of Trinity Episcopal Church in Fredericksburg. Other details are from the 1880 Census of Stafford County and the Slave Schedules of Spotsylvania County in the 1860 Census. G. H. S. King's personal knowledge tallies with the census data.

19. 1850 Census of Spotsylvania County, plus census data cited in note 18; *OR Atlas*, plate 39, map 3.

20. Because of the absence of signatures, an elaborate chain of evidence has been necessary to identify this spy as Isaac Silver. (1) An envelope in the BMI files labeled "Silver's Communications" contains mainly a group of reports in the same distinctive handwriting as those that began coming via McGee from south of the Rappahannock in March 1863. (2) On the back of an 1864 report (also in BMI) in this same handwriting, a note from McEntee to Sharpe began, "Inclosed I send you the old mans reports." It said that "Old Silver" was now prepared to give full time to "the business" and wanted to be put on the rolls to receive regular pay. In the next month (October 1864) the name Isaac Silver appeared on the bureau's payroll for the first time at three dollars a day. (Two months earlier, one John Silver was on the rolls for a single month at five dollars a day.) (3) The context of the reports from the spy under discussion shows unmistakably that the writer was living within Lee's lines, and very probably on the left wing. That is the position of the house marked "Silver" and "I. Silver" on several maps in *OR Atlas* (plate 91, map 1; plate 39, maps 2 and 3). (Three McGee houses are shown as neighbors of Silver. More precise locations for these houses appear on several of the maps in Bigelow, *Chancellorsville*.) (4) Sharpe and Babcock, evidently for security reasons, usually marked the reports with McGee's name when filing them. The text of one, on April 28, 1863, clearly shows that "Magee" was serving the writer as messenger.

21. The bracketed words "Ewell," "with," "Banks's," and "McLaws'" were obliterated by a hole burned in the sheet Silver had used. They are supplied from a clerk's copy made for Hooker; see note 22.

22. "McGee's Report," n.d., BMI. The date (March 13) was given by Sharpe when he summarized the report for Hooker (Sharpe to Hooker, March 15, 1863, BMI). From the label, "McGee's Report" (in Sharpe's handwriting), and from its heading, "headquarters union army," it might be inferred that the report was written by McGee at headquarters from information he carried in his head or in the form of brief notes. We know that this was not the case because the handwriting in these reports did not change when other messengers were used.

23. Babcock's summary is in BMI; the copy of Silver's report, with Hooker's indorsement, is in the Stanton Papers, reel 13, frames 240–41.

24. *OR*, 25.2, 696; Freeman, *Lee's Lieutenants*, 2:508, 517n. For McLaws's positions see *OR*, 25.1:824, 829–30, 833.

25. Revere to Lt. Col. Joseph Dickinson, A.A.G., in Sharpe service record, NA.

26. Patrick Diary, March 12, 1863.

27. Gen. Pendleton with most of the First Corps artillery was at Chesterfield Depot, between Hanover Junction and Bowling Green; Second Corps artillery was at Bowling Green (*OR*, 25.1:809, 820).

28. See, *e.g.*, Freeman, *Lee's Lieutenants*, 2:xliii, 189–90, 311.

29. Sharpe's figures for the average strengths of regiments and brigades show that prisoners and deserters were being questioned on this matter in detail, probably extending to the strength of individual companies — a practice Pinkerton did not use.

30. *OR*, 25.2:650 (from Lee's return for February). The total shown is 62,600 present for duty in Jackson's corps, McLaws's and Anderson's divisions, Stuart's cavalry, and the artillery in the rear. The 49,000 figure in the text is derived by deducting (from 62,600) the strength of the cavalry, artillery, and Jones's command in the Valley, none of which were included in Sharpe's figures. The 62,600 figure for the entire army is accepted by Freeman (*R. E. Lee,* 2:483–84).

31. *OR*, 25.1:789–93.

32. He placed a "Taylor's Brigade" in Trimble's division, a "Walker's brigade" in Early's division, and a "Featherston's brigade" in Anderson's. Richard Taylor had formerly headed a brigade in Ewell's division but was no longer in the Army of Northern Virginia. Col. James A. Walker had led Early's brigade at the battle of Fredericksburg but appears not to have served in the campaign now getting under way. W. S. Featherston had been succeeded by Carnot Posey, but both those men were shown by Babcock as commanding brigades, and A. R. Wright's brigade was omitted.

33. These positions are either directly stated in or can be inferred from Confederate reports at *OR*, 25.1:907, 939, 950, 966, 977, 1000, 1004. Also see Freeman, *Lee's Lieutenants,* 2:517n.

34. This statement of intelligence failure applied only to the Army of the Potomac. The same indictment could not have been laid to Pope and his Army of Virginia — but Babcock and Sharpe probably would not have known of the several successes of Pope's intelligence service.

35. The report is in the form of a letter from Sharpe to Butterfield, March 15, 1863, BMI. It was accompanied by an annex concerning enemy cavalry, in Sharpe's handwriting.

36. Hooker to Patrick, Jan. 28, 1863, in Letters Sent, AP, bk. 3, p. 10.

37. RG 393, part 1, entry 4029A; Surgeon William H. White to Capt. Doyle, A.A.G., Aquia, April 8, 1863, BMI: *OR*, 25.2:58, 74, 88–89, 142–44; JCCW 1865, 1:203; Patrick Diary, Feb. 13 and 14, 1863.

38. Capt. J. C. Kelton (Halleck's A.A.G.) to Hooker, Feb. 16, 1863, Hooker Papers; Halleck to Hooker, Feb. 3, 1863, ibid.

39. Patrick to Col. William F. Rogers, Aquia, Feb. 1, 1863, RG 393, part 1, entry 4029A; Patrick to Col. William Hoffman, Washington, Feb. 1, 1863, ibid.

40. *OR*, 25.2:119, 217–19; Patrick to Hooker and Hooker to Patrick, March 6, 1863, in RG 393, part 1, entry 3980 (Misc. Letters, Reports, and Lists Received, 1861–65, Army of the Potomac), box 4002, NA.

41. Cavalry Corps circular, Feb. 23, 1863, RG 393, part 2 of entry 3980 cited in note 40.

42. Lt. J. B. Brooks to Capt. B. F. Fisher, March 14, 1863, Hooker Papers.

43. Col. Frank M. Parker to his wife, May 31, 1863, North Carolina State Archives. The Seddon house stood six miles below Fredericksburg on the present Virginia Route 3, which at that point follows the left bank of the river. If there was such a warning, it probably related to the river crossing of Hooker's downriver wing, which did not employ the same stringent security measures as the upriver advance of his right wing. But no indication that Lee received such a warning is found in his reaction to the enemy's crossings, detailed in chapter 16.

44. Strange to Halleck, April 16, 1863, true copy in BMI; *OR*, ser. 2, 5:536–37.

45. Turner to Edwards Pierrepont, Jan. 21, 1863, in Turner-Baker Papers, Letterbook Y, p. 168.

46. William P. Wood, the celebrated keeper of Old Capitol Prison, who sometimes escorted a shipload of civilians going South, once took along a Virginian named James A. "Lucky" Davis, who was secretly in his pay. Turned loose in

Richmond, Davis was promptly arrested by the Confederates and taken to Camp Lee. But he escaped and rejoined Wood in Richmond before the ship returned to Washington. On another occasion Wood and Davis worked the same ruse without interference from their Rebel hosts (Turner-Baker Papers, file 3335). For other examples of the use of this device, see *OR,* ser. 2, 6:40, and SGSD file 1865–1866/192.

47. Patrick Diary, March 16, 1863; Andrews, *The North Reports the Civil War,* 343.

48. Andrews, *The North Reports the Civil War,* 343, 710; Starr, *Bohemian Brigade,* 197.

49. *OR,* 25.2:153–54.

50. *OR,* 25.2:114–15; Plum, *Military Telegraph,* 1:361.

51. De Wardener file, S. S. Accts.; *OR,* ser. 2, 5:847–48; Jones, *Gray Ghosts,* 153–59. De Wardener drew four dollars a day, a high wage for a spy in Heintzelman's command.

52. Col. William Norris, head of the Confederate Signal Corps and Secret Service Bureau, so characterizes the use made of the Northern Neck; see Brown, *Signal Corps,* 210.

53. *OR,* 25.1:2, 12–18, 73–74, 249–50; 51.1:980–87; captured letter of Charles B. Tyson, Halifax C. H., Va., Feb. 5, 1863, and indorsement thereto, Gen. Reynolds to A.A.G., AP, same date, BMI; Col. Lucius Fairchild to Wadsworth's A.A.G., Feb. 16, 1863, Hooker Papers; Col. J. P. Taylor to Gen. S. Williams, April 25 and 28, 1863, ibid.; Bigelow, *Chancellorsville,* 45–47 (citing Lloyd, *History of the First Regiment, Pennsylvania Reserve Cavalry*).

54. *OR,* 25.2:124–27.

55. "Echo" to Maj. J. H. Beveridge and Maj. William H. Medill, n.d., BMI; Lt. Col. D. R. Clendenin (8th Illinois Cavalry) to A.A.A.G., Cavalry Corps, May 28, 1863, BMI.

56. Patrick Diary, March 17, 1863.

57. Sharpe to "General," March 21, 1863; Sharpe to Butterfield, March 22, 1863; notes taken by Sharpe in interrogating Cline, March 20, 1863; all in BMI.

58. Lt. Col. J. A. Kress, A.A.I.G., to Wadsworth, March 29, 1863, with indorsements March 30 by Wadsworth and Reynolds, Hooker Papers.

59. *OR,* 25.2:175.

60. Patrick Diary, March 23, 1863.

61. *OR,* 25.1:22–26; 25.2:100–08, 646, 700; Pleasonton to Butterfield and Butterfield to Stoneman, Feb. 26, 1863, Hooker Papers.

62. Hebert, *Hooker,* 186.

63. *OR,* 25.1:47–50, 58, 60–61; 25.2:672, 675; 51.2:686; Averell to Stoneman, March 18, 1863, Hooker Papers; Bigelow, *Chancellorsville,* 94–100; Brooks to Capt. B. F. Fisher, March 14, 1863, Hooker Papers; Patrick Diary, April 21, 1863. For Lee's references to his "scouting" service, see *OR,* 25.2:622, 642, 646, 664, 691, 700–01, 702–03; 18:906–07, 921–22, 949–50, 954, 966. Also see McLaws to his wife, April 26, 1863, Southern History Collection, University of North Carolina.

64. *OR,* 25.2:700, 691, 622–23.

65. *OR,* 25.2:622, 623, 624, 627, 689, 691, 631, 642, 664, 702–3; 18:921–22.

66. In *R. E. Lee,* 3:24, Freeman says, "For the first time on Virginia soil, thanks to the improvement of the Union cavalry and in the intelligence service of the Army of the Potomac, the Federals knew more of what was happening on the south side of the Rappahannock than Lee knew of what was taking place north of the river." This statement applies to the last weeks of May, but the developments narrated here show that the Federals actually reached that advan-

tage two months earlier. Gen. Charles King's article on the Union "Secret Service" in Miller, *Photographic History* (8:22) — which is an example of the myth that the Confederates always had better information than their adversaries — an improvement in the Federals' information service under Hooker and Meade is acknowledged, but the entire credit for it is given to those generals' intelligent use of cavalry.

67. *OR*, 25.2:139–40.

68. *OR*, 25.2:140.

69. *OR*, 25.2:649.

70. Sharpe to Butterfield, March 15, 1863, BMI; *OR*, 25.1:789–94.

71. *OR*, 18:916. Longstreet also had the North Carolina commands of Whiting and D. H. Hill, totaling 18,900.

72. Dix's summary of this spy's information is at *OR*, 18:563.

73. *OR*, 25.2:190.

74. Unaddressed, unsigned report in Babcock's handwriting March 22, 1863, BMI.

75. Memorandum cited in note 1.

76. Col. William S. Fish, provost marshal, Middle Dept. (Gen. Schenck's command at Baltimore) wrote this description in asking for detective funds (Fish to Schenck, April 9, 1863, in Schenck file, S. S. Accts.).

77. Sharpe to Gen. Williams, Feb. 22, 1863, in Sharpe service record, NA; Patrick Diary, March 27, 1863.

78. See, *e.g.*, *OR*, ser. 2, 2:201; and McPhail to Patrick, with Patrick endorsement, Feb. 16, 1863, in RG 393, part 1, entry 4029A.

79. McCreary, *Ancient and Honorable Mechanics Company of Baltimore*, 106.

80. *OR*, 5:196, 765; *OR*, ser. 2, 3:600.

81. *OR*, ser. 2, 2:1315–18.

82. *OR*, 19.2:304–5; *OR*, 5:765.

83. Fish to Schenck, April 9, 1863, Schenck file, S. S. Accts.

84. In addition to the sources cited above, this sketch of McPhail is taken from the following: Baltimore city directories for 1853–1864; "Memorial of J. L. McPhail, Voltaire Randall and Eaton G. Horner to the Senate and House of Representatives of the U.S., Dec. 2, 1872, Maryland Historical Society, Baltimore" (this document recites the role of McPhail and his colleagues in the capture of Samuel B. Arnold and Michael O'Laughlin, accomplices of John Wilkes Booth); Baltimore *American and Commercial Advertiser, Sun,* and *Gazette,* Oct. 7 and 8, 1874 (McPhail obituaries); McPhail file, S. S. Accts.

85. *OR*, ser. 2, 2:234, 904; Pinkerton payroll, entry for July 24, 1862, S. S. Accts.

86. *McClellan's Own Story*, 535–36. McClellan speaks of having an order for the removal of ordnance stores countermanded. He had, however, written to his wife that if he could "slip" into Washington "I will send your silver off" (Sears, ed., *Civil War Papers of McClellan*, 423–24).

87. McPhail to Sharpe, [Apr.] 10, 1863, in General Telegrams.

88. The history of Maddox's mission to Richmond is based on Maddox-McPhail and McPhail-Sharpe correspondence, some thirty items, in BMI, and from records of postwar litigation involving Maddox. The latter records are part of the War Department evidence that Maddox was the "our friend" of the McPhail-Sharpe correspondence. The litigation was a suit against Secretary Stanton, asking $30,000 for false arrest. In his contraband dealings in Richmond, Maddox in 1864 acquired a large quantity of tobacco, which he attempted to send North by way of lower Maryland. A Federal general stationed there inter-

cepted it and somehow found cause to imprison Maddox on a charge of disloyalty. Intervention by McPhail was required to obtain his release, at the cost of
several months' absence from his espionage activities in Richmond. Maddox
dropped his suit for false arrest but persisted in a claim for damage to the
tobacco; that won him in 1866 an $8108 payment from the Secret Service Fund.
The story of Maddox's tobacco is told at length in the Thomas and Hyman
biography of Stanton (pp. 474–77 and 492–93).

15. The Gray Fox Swallows the Bait

1. Crawford's appearance in Philadelphia followed shortly upon the return
from the Confederacy of the agent whom Dix refers to as "my man" (Franklin
file, S. S. Accts.). Dix's term suggests that he had but a single spy or that this was
his principal spy. In either case Dix's statements to Turner, quoted in the text,
would qualify Crawford as this agent. Further evidence to this effect is a telegram
(*OR*, 18:566) from Peck to Dix: "Is it not time for your peddler to return [from
Richmond]?" Dix replied the next day, March 22: "My man has been here and
has gone to Baltimore." (*OR*, 18:567.)
2. Turner-Baker Papers, Letterbook Y, p. 360; Turner-Baker Papers, file
1465. The latter includes the newspaper account quoted in the text. The newspaper's name does not appear.
3. [Babcock] to Butterfield, April 10, 1863, BMI. For Hood's "false start" see
OR, 25.2:672, 675; see also chapter 14, note 63 and associated text.
4. Pleasonton to Butterfield, April 10, 1863, BMI, and April 11, 1863,
Hooker Papers; Pleasonton to Watson, April 10, 1863, *OR*, 25.2:196–97.
5. Skinker to Sharpe, April 2, 1863, BMI.
6. *OR*, 18:563–64.
7. *OR*, 25.2:691, 702–3; *OR*, 18:953, 959–60; Freeman, *Lee's Dispatches*, 84.
8. *OR*, 14:437; 18:571–628 *passim*; 25.2:190–91; Fisher to Butterfield, April
9, 1863, BMI. Several of these dispatches to Halleck from Dix and his subordinates are in the Hooker Papers (although quoted here from *OR*). As these are
carbon copies of the messages as received at the War Dept., it is evident that they
were forwarded to Hooker by courier. Often, however, such relays were by wire.
9. "McGhee's Statement April 1st 1863," BMI.
10. *OR*, 25.2:700, 713, 725.
11. Forces with Lee increased by 5661, or a little over 10 percent, during
March (*OR*, 25.2:650, 696), but the resultant total, more than 60,000, was,
contrary to Silver's belief, below his strength in December and January. And
Silver's statement about the Confederate artillery's being "quite handy" to Lee
was at best an exaggeration; the huge artillery encampment in Caroline County
was not broken up until Hooker's army appeared on the south side of the
Rappahannock on April 29 (*OR*, 25.1:809).
12. Fisher to Butterfield, April 9, BMI.
13. Patrick Diary, April 6 and 7, 1863; Brooks, *Washington in Lincoln's Time*,
51–60.
14. From planning memoranda in the Hooker Papers: "Information Relating
to the Richmond, Fredericksburg & Potomac & Virginia Central Rail Roads";
"Fords on the Rappahannock & Rapidan Rivers"; "Distances on Roads running
Westerly from Fredericksburg"; "Roads leading Southerly from Fredericksburg."
These are marked (by a hand at work at a later time) "Information received in
preparing for the Chancellorsville Campaign." Only one is dated, the date being

April 22; but as it is a duplicate of another document in the same file, the date does not necessarily indicate the time when these studies were made.

15. Omitted, significantly, from Comstock's study was the crossing directly in front of Fredericksburg where Burnside's pontoons had been laid with such great difficulty.

16. Comstock's memoranda, dated Feb. 3 and April 12, are in Hooker Papers. The *OR* versions (51.1:980–81 and 1003–4) contain a few errors.

17. Hebert, *Hooker*, 187.

18. Basler, ed., *Works of Lincoln*, 6:169.

19. For Ruth's slowdown of rail shipments see chapter 11, note 18 and associated text. The clearest evidence of Hooker's early intention to make his major advance below Fredericksburg is his testimony to the Joint Committee on the Conduct of the War (JCCW 1865, 1:115–16).

20. *OR*, 25.1, 1066–67; 25.2:203–5, 213, 214, 220, 221, and 236–50 *passim;* Patrick Diary, April 15–24 *passim;* JCCW 1865, 1:115–16.

21. *OR*, 25.1:1066–67; 25.2:204, 256–57; Bigelow, *Chancellorsville*, 140, 181.

22. Brown, *Signal Corps, U.S.A.*, 214–15. The near-certainty that Army of the Potomac flag signals had regularly been sent in the clear, with only the secrecy of the flag alphabet for protection, is based mainly on negative evidence, namely the absence, in Myer's well-kept records and lengthy reports, of references to use of cryptography in the Army of the Potomac. Additional evidence, also negative, is the absence of any clear indication of Federal cryptography from the occasional correspondence and reports of signal officers in the field that have come to light in the present study.

23. Myer's selection of the cipher was governed largely by the ease with which signalmen in a field army could put it to use without previous training. Apparently he had it ready for issue at the moment of need. The cipher device he planned to introduce consisted of two concentric disks, each containing an alphabet, that gave a new pairing of letters with each movement of the inner disk. He issued these disks Sept. 10, 1863.

The cipher to be used until then was promulgated in an Office of the Chief Signal Officer Circular dated April 14, 1863; however, twenty-seven Army of the Potomac signal officers indicated that they had received it by signing secrecy oaths on April 9.

Irregular as Myer's issuance of operational instructions to Hooker's signal service may seem, it was in keeping with his usual practice. For example, the reports of the numerous signal officers concerning their operations in the Chancellorsville campaign were submitted to Cushing and forwarded to Myer; Hooker obtained them only by having copies made in Myer's office. (Cushing, chief signal officer, AP, to Myer, dated Washington, May 23, 1863, with forty enclosures, most of which are the reports of Cushing's subordinates. All forty are in the Hooker Papers; Cushing's report with some of the enclosures is in *OR*, 25.1:217–44.)

24. Butterfield's draft, undated and unsigned but unmistakably in his handwriting, is in RG 111, entry 27; the Confederate transmissions of the hoax message, as intercepted by the Federals and sent by Cushing to Butterfield, are in BMI (April 14) and Hooker Papers (April 15). Although Cushing had Myer's order as support for his projected deception, he covered himself further by a notation on Butterfield's draft: "Received from Genl Butterfield with the request that it should be sent at once in the most conspicuous manner. . . . This memorandum is useful if any complaint should ever arise regarding the cypher." The reference to the "cypher" is a puzzle, as the hoax message was ordered to be sent

in the clear. Cushing's concern probably was that the information in Butter-field's draft approximated the truth so closely that it might endanger the Federal cavalry on its projected westward movement.

25. *OR*, 25.2:721.

26. *OR*, 25.2:703, 724–25, 730, 736–37, 749–50; Blackford, *War Years with Jeb Stuart*, 203; McClellan, *Stuart's Campaigns*, 220.

27. *OR*, 25.2:209. The postmaster probably complied with Hooker's request (Bigelow, *Chancellorsville*, 149).

28. *OR*, 25.2:239–41.

29. Lee's dispatches to Richmond on this subject are dated April 27 and May 7 and 10 (*OR*, 25.2:752, 782, 790). Norris's language appears in a relay of the information to Longstreet April 27 (*OR*, 51.2:696). How Lee finally learned that the original source of the information was a medical return is not clear.

30. Skinker to Sharpe, March 21 and 23, April 2, 1863, BMI.

31. Skinker to Sharpe, April 15, 1863, BMI.

32. *OR*, 25.2:213, 220.

33. *OR*, 25.2, 217–19; Patrick Diary, April 21, 1863; Capt. S. T. Cushing to Butterfield, April 13, 1863, Hooker Papers.

34. Bigelow, *Chancellorsville*, 159, citing an April 18 letter of Henry Ropes, a lieutenant in the 20th Massachusetts Infantry.

35. *OR*, 25.2:737–38.

36. Lee reported thus to Stuart April 20 (*OR*, 25.2:738).

37. *OR*, 21:1014.

38. Bigelow, *Chancellorsville*, 179, 187; *OR*, 25.2:267.

39. Patrick Diary, April 21, 1863. That the report of Confederate communication across the river was circulating in the Federal ranks is shown by the letter of Capt. William W. Folwell, 50th New York Engineers, to wife, April 22, 1863 (Folwell Letters, Minnesota Historical Society).

40. Philadelphia *Inquirer*, April 25, 1863, p. 1, col. 1; New York *Times*, April 28, 1863, p. 1, col. 1; Maj. T. T. Eckert to Hooker, April 30, 1863, Hooker Papers; Patrick Diary, April 23, 1863; Andrews, *The North Reports the Civil War*, 358.

41. Folwell letter cited in note 39; diary of John S. Cooper, April 24, 1863; Patrick Diary, April 27, 1863.

42. Patrick Diary, April 29, 1863; *OR*, 25.2:664. Information on the Lacy house is from A. Wilson Greene of the Fredericksburg Battlefield Park staff.

43. The file that ordinarily would contain such a report is vol. 6 in RG 393, part 1, entry 3987, Daily Memoranda for the Information of the Major General Commanding, Jan. 1863–Jan. 1865, NA.

44. It was at this point that Patrick recorded his opinion of corruption at headquarters, detailed in chapter 12, note 49.

45. Patrick Diary, April 23–28, 1863.

46. Capt. Wm. L. Candler, quoted in Bigelow, *Chancellorsville*, 164.

16. Pinpoint Intelligence and Hairline Planning

1. Silver's report, BMI, is marked "McGee — April 15."

2. *OR*, 25.1:833.

3. *OR*, 25.2:703.

4. The three upriver brigades (Mahone's, Posey's, Wilcox's) contained fourteen, or 68 percent, of the twenty and a half regiments in Anderson's division. Silver's estimate of 6000–6200 for those brigades amounts to 73–75 percent of

the 8232 officers and men Anderson reported present for duty at the end of March (*OR*, 25.2:696; 25.1:849, 790).

5. For the information that Chancellorsville was a wintering location of Lee's army the writer is indebted to A. Wilson Greene of the staff of historians at the Fredericksburg battlefield park.

6. Bigelow, *Chancellorsville*, 195.

7. *OR*, 25.2:700, 725.

8. See note 1.

9. Wadsworth to Reynolds's A. A. G., April 15, 1863, with endorsement of same date by Reynolds, filed in BMI as "Wm E Carroll's Statement 47 Va Infty — April 16/63."

10. Cushing to Butterfield, April 14, 1863, BMI.

11. *OR*, 25.2:213, 229.

12. *OR*, 25.2:703. W. H. F. Lee's transfer to the left of the army had been mentioned on April 7 by a deserter from the Army of Northern Virginia who reached Fort Monroe (*OR*, 18:587). But as this report was inexact and was coupled with highly dubious information about Fitz Lee's brigade, it probably was given no credence in Sharpe's bureau.

13. Unaddressed memorandum, "Reb. Regiments from which Prisoners of War have been taken, and deserters come into our lines from the enemy, to April 30th, 1863," BMI; *OR*, 25.2:228.

14. *OR*, 25.2:725; Heintzelman to Butterfield, April 14, 1863, BMI.

15. A. A. Lovett to Maj. T. T. Eckert, April 18, 1863, Hooker Papers. This dispatch quoted the *Enquirer* of April 15 and requested Eckert to clear transmission of the story by the Washington bureau of the Associated Press.

16. Memorandum cited in note 13.

17. Gen. Pleasonton, who served as Otto's amanuensis, made a point of the fact that supply shipments on the Gordonsville-Culpeper line were heavy, whereas none at all were to be seen on the Richmond-Gordonsville leg of the route.

18. Pleasonton to Butterfield, April 18, 1863, Hooker Papers.

19. Certificate of Capt. Robert Randolph, dated Lower Fauquier, March 10, 1863, filed with Pleasonton's letter to Butterfield cited in note 18.

20. *OR*, 25.2:236–37, 238.

21. *OR*, 25.2:244.

22. Cushing to Butterfield, April 22, 1863, BMI.

23. A second possibility is that Lee — persuaded by Federal raids and demonstrations then being made toward Port Royal that a major advance above Fredericksburg was beginning — sent the movement order by signal as a time-saving measure and later canceled it.

24. Gen. E. R. S. Canby, War. Dept., to Hooker, April 23, 1863, Hooker Papers; Turner-Baker Papers, files 1531 and 1873; *OR*, ser. 3, 3:302–17 *passim*.

25. *OR*, 25.2:234; Doubleday to A. A. G., First Corps, April 22, 1863, Hooker Papers; JCCW 1865, 1:16 (Doubleday's testimony); Col. H. A. Morrow to Capt. T. E. Ellsworth (A. A. G. to Gen. Wadsworth), April 25, 1863, BMI; Morrow to Gen. S. Williams, Sept. 28, 1863, Hooker Papers.

26. Col. J. P. Taylor to Butterfield, April 25 (two dispatches) and April 28, 1863, Hooker Papers; *OR*, 25.2:249, 859, 709, 672; Bigelow, *Chancellorsville*, 166. The activity on the Federal right during this period was a movement by Stoneman toward the river to discover whether it was fordable and a demonstration by the two infantry regiments posted below him (*OR*, 25.2:232, 236; Bigelow, *Chancellorsville*, 163).

27. Yager (from Alexandria) to Sharpe, April 24, 1863, BMI; *OR*, 25.2:745.

28. *OR*, 25.2:860, 242; Wert, *Mosby's Rangers*, 57. Stuart's statement of the Federal cavalry's positions was significantly different from those reported by Stoneman April 22.

29. *OR*, 25.2:861–62. That Mosby if permitted could have reached southward far enough to have observed the Federals' march is indicated by the fact that on May 17 he rode with twenty-five men to within a mile of Dumfries, thus penetrating the country occupied by Hooker's infantry. Yager's April 24 telegram to Sharpe (cited in note 27) reporting his arrival inside the lines said that he had learned Mosby's position, but the record gives no details on what he understood it to be.

30. *OR*, 25.2:749–50, 254; 25.1:98–105, 113–21.

31. Bigelow, *Chancellorsville*, 164; *OR*, 25.2:250, 255; JCCW 1865, 1:145. Stoneman replied the next day with a compilation that was ample considering the tight deadline (Stoneman to S. Williams, April 27, 1863, *OR*, 25.2:265; also in Hooker Papers).

32. JCCW 1865, 1:116 (Hooker's testimony). This much of Hooker's change in plans is noted in Bigelow, *Chancellorsville*, 166–67.

33. *OR*, 25.1:195–96. The numerical strength of the pickets and picket supports at Kelly's Ford is not known, but it was clearly insufficient to offer resistance to even a small enemy advance or to observe adequately the extent and movements of a major invading force.

34. Basler, ed., *Works of Lincoln*, 6:189–90.

35. *OR*, 25.1:505, 627, 669; 25.2:255–56, 262, 274.

36. *OR*, 25.1:557; 25.2:268; Bigelow, *Chancellorsville*, 178; JCCW 1:145.

37. Hooker believed that Burnside should have kept a force opposite Culpeper; that removing the whole army and burning bridges behind it entirely exposed the Federal plan. Although Burnside's abrupt and total withdrawal must have speeded Lee's realization that a major movement was afoot, he would not have agreed that it tipped Burnside's entire hand.

38. *OR*, 25.1:305, 306; 25.2:266, 267. The Irish Brigade, which was to be involved in the guarding of houses, marched to Banks's Ford on the 27th but is not known to have shown itself to the enemy that day (*OR*, 25.1:311; Bigelow, *Chancellorsville*, 179).

39. *OR*, 25.1:1065, 774.

40. Patrick, although he was responsible for march security, had on the 26th no more than an expectation of early movement, as has been seen; and when he learned the general plan in his consultation with Hooker the next day, the right wing was already in motion (Patrick Diary, April 25 and 26, 1863). Gen. Gouverneur Warren, chief topographical engineer, said he "did not know any of [Hooker's] plans until I saw them being carried into operation" (JCCW 1865: 1:43).

41. *OR*, 25.2:255–57 and 262–68 *passim*, 274, 291; 25.1:557, 306; 51.1:1014; *B&L*, 3:157; Bigelow, *Chancellorsville*, 174, 179, 184, 187. Lee wrote Davis April 27 that Hooker "may intend to push his cavalry along by [the upper Rappahannock] route while his infantry attempt to seize [the Fredericksburg route]" (*OR*, 25.2:753).

42. Hooker explained later that "the character of the country we were to operate in precluded the uses of a large cavalry force except in raiding." Nevertheless, Stuart used as large a force as he could spare for operating in the same country Hooker was speaking of.

43. Sharpe to J. Hasbrouck, Sharpe Collection.

44. *OR*, 25.2:276; Patrick Diary, April 28, 1863.

45. *OR*, 25.2:276–77; Butterfield to Hooker, 7 A.M., May 1, 1863, Hooker Papers. Capt. McEntee's activities during the march and battle are unknown; he was probably with Sharpe.

46. *OR*, 25.2:276; 51.1, 1015; Sharpe to Butterfield, April 28, 1863, BMI.

47. Silver's report, April 28, 1863 (labeled "McGee's Report"), and Skinker's, of the same date, are in BMI.

48. *OR*, 25.2:267; JCCW 1865, 1:145; Silver's report cited in note 47; Gen. H. J. Hunt to Hooker and Butterfield, 9:50 A.M., May 1, 1863, Hooker Papers. Hunt wrote, "The enemy cannot have more than one or two bridges. To cross only a part of his army would insure his destruction. . . . It would be a desperate resort." Lee had at Gordonsville the materials for a 600-foot pontoon bridge (*OR*, 25.2:715, 735). The fact that his pontoons were sufficient to bridge the Rappahannock had been reported by a deserter from his army who turned up at Fort Monroe April 7 (*OR*, 18:587).

49. "Organization and strength of force comprising the present Army of Northern Virga., Corrected to Apr. 28, 1863." The original is in the Hooker Papers and a press copy in Box 4001, Misc. Records, AP. The report, in tabular form, is unsigned but is in Babcock's hand throughout.

50. Bigelow, *Chancellorsville*, 132–34. Lee did not submit a strength return for April; the return headed "April 30, 1863" in *OR*, ser. 4, 2:530, is actually a repetition of the totals shown in the March return (*OR*, 25.2:696). Bigelow computed Confederate strength by taking the March return as a basis and adding reinforcements numbering 1500 reported as received in April, a figure he divided up into divisional increments and added to the March totals.

51. Although Babcock did not include artillery figures in his estimate, the omission does not invalidate the comparison with Bigelow, who gave separate artillery, infantry, and cavalry figures. This figure is a total for the brigades of Fitz Lee and W. H. F. Lee (which Bigelow did not subdivide into brigade totals). Accordingly, Babcock's parallel figure — composed of 3000 for Fitz Lee, 2500 for W. H. F. Lee — is used here.

52. This narrow difference between Babcock's figure and computation based on postwar study of the returns is supported by Livermore, *Numbers and Losses*, 98–99. In order to make Babcock's and Livermore's sets of figures comparable, one must take account of the absence of a separate figure for artillery in Livermore's computation and also his omission of W. H. F. Lee's brigade, most of which did not get into the battle at Chancellorsville but was fully employed in pursuit of Stoneman. Thus 4400, Bigelow's estimated strength of Lee's artillery, is added to Babcock's total, and Babcock's estimate of W. H. F. Lee's strength, 2500, is subtracted from that total. These adjustments raise Babcock's grand total to 57,200, only 152 short of Livermore's 57,352.

53. During the months when these data were accumulating in Sharpe's files, Fitz Lee's brigade was in Culpeper County and W. H. F. Lee's at Port Royal; Hampton's was south of the James River recruiting and remounting, and Jones's was in the Shenandoah Valley.

54. On May 1, after prisoners had begun arriving in large numbers, especially from Jackson's corps, Babcock produced a revised report covering that corps alone. He dropped the estimated strength of Rodes's division from 8300 to 6700 (thereby increasing his earlier error by 1600), but he improved slightly his picture of the enemy organization. Jackson had 90 regiments; Babcock gave his total as 84; of these, 81 were actually in the corps; of the 81, 76 were placed in the correct brigade. Again all of Jackson's brigades were known. The re-

vised total for Jackson's entire corps, 33,500, was somewhat less accurate than the corresponding figure in the earlier report. ("Organization and estimated strength of Lt. Gen. T. Jackson's Corps, Bureau of Information, May 1st, 1863," BMI.) The 33,500 total in this report happens to be the same as that given by the Confederate writers Jed Hotchkiss and William Allan in *The Battlefields of Virginia — Chancellorsville*, written in 1867, before the returns used by Livermore and Bigelow were available.

55. Basler, ed., *Works of Lincoln*, 6:190; Nevins, *War for the Union: War Becomes Revolution*, 436–37, citing J. E. Hammond to S. L. M. Barlow, April 22, 1863, in the Barlow Papers. As Barlow was an ultraconservative and Hooker a favorite of the Radicals, so favorable a report about Hooker by a correspondent of Barlow's is noteworthy, even though Hooker was a likely source.

56. Stuart's report, *OR*, 25.1:1045; Howard's report, ibid., 627; *OR*, 25.2:202, 212, 214–15; Bigelow, *Chancellorsville*, 148, 163–64; Samuel P. Bates, "Chancellorsville," an essay in the Bates Papers in the Pellettier Library, Allegheny College, Meadville, Pa., esp. p. 14. R. E. Lee's report (*OR*, 25.1:796) states that on April 28 Stuart reported that "a large body of infantry and artillery was passing up the river." No such information from Stuart (or any other Confederate source) has been found by the present writer; Stuart's own after-action report, cited above, indicates that Hooker's turning movement was unknown to him until he received word of the enemy's crossing at Kelly's Ford at "about 9 p.m." If Stuart knew of the huge enemy force heading toward Kelly's Ford, as Freeman implies, he would have resisted the crossing with his entire command.

57. *OR*, 25.2:273–74; 25.1:1045, 627, 505–6, 669, 727–28; Slocum to Hooker, April 28, 1863, Hooker Papers. Sluggishness in the Fifth Corps was so annoying to Meade that he reported one of his brigade commanders to Hooker for reassignment, but the offending officer remained in command (Meade to Hooker, May 1, 1863, Hooker Papers).

58. Bigelow, *Chancellorsville*, 190; Sharpe to Butterfield, April 30, 1863, BMI. This report is mistakenly dated April 29.

59. *OR*, 25.1:1045. The first relay point may have been Gordonsville rather than Staunton.

60. That Lee knew of Sedgwick's crossing before receiving Stuart's report of the crossing at Kelly's Ford is shown by the context of his dispatches quoted by Davis, Secretary James A. Seddon, and General Cooper at *OR*, 25.2:757–59.

61. *OR*, 25.2:757–60. Although Stuart's telegram apparently does not survive, Lee's action based on it shows unmistakably that he confidently believed until Wednesday evening that the Federals were headed for Gordonsville.

62. *OR*, 25.2, 758; 25.1:1045–46. Lee's unfamiliarity with enemy organization and staffing was manifested when, after learning the names of the three corps advancing against his left, he gave the information to Davis in language indicating that the names of the corps commanders were new to him or had previously been known only with uncertainty. Secretary of War Seddon, in relaying some of Lee's dispatches to commanders near and below Richmond, revealed that he had much less familiarity with enemy organization than was consistently shown by Stanton.

63. *OR*, 25.2, 759–60; 25.1:506, 780.

64. *OR*, 25.2:761 (the same telegram, in Freeman and McWhiney, eds., *Lee's Dispatches to Davis*, 85–86, gives 8:30 A.M. April 30 as the time of receipt); 25.1, 849.

65. *OR*, 25.1:1046, 627, 669.

66. Freeman (*R. E. Lee*, 2:509) gives a different timing for this telegram,

stating that it arrived in the afternoon of April 29. His account draws upon Lee's after-action report on the Chancellorsville battle (*OR*, 25.1:796), which was not written until Sept. 21 and contains obvious discrepancies, including conflicts with other dispatches of April 29 (cited above) and with Stuart's after-action report, written May 8, immediately after the battle. The reasons favoring a later time for Lee's receipt of the telegrams are as follows: (1) He received courier reports of the Federals' appearance at Germanna and Ely's fords (originating in the Mahone-Posey command rather than Stuart's) at 6:30 P.M. April 29 and sent them to Davis later that evening. His wording shows that this was the only news from upriver since Stuart's report of the crossing at Kelly's Ford. *OR*, 25.2:759, 756. (2) Lee's relay to Davis of Stuart's information identifying the three Federal corps was not received at Richmond until 8:30 A.M. April 30 (*Lee's Dispatches to Davis*, 85–86). Since Lee's telegraph link with Stuart at Culpeper involved a relay at Richmond, at any time he could receive a telegram from Stuart he could also send one to Davis. Therefore it is reasonable to assume that if he had had Stuart's information on the night of the 29th, he would have sent it to Davis at that time. (In fact the Richmond telegraph office could have sent Davis a copy of Stuart's message while it was still en route to Lee.) (3) It is doubtful whether Stuart could have had the findings of his April 29 assault on the Slocum-Howard column ready to transmit before his telegraph service at Culpeper closed down for the night. The initial news of the column's position did not reach him from his pickets until 1 P.M., and the operation that ensued required time-consuming assemblage and travel (a twenty-mile round trip) besides the piercing of the enemy column and the capturing and interrogation of prisoners. *OR*, 25.1:1046. In fact, Bigelow quotes (*Chancellorsville*, 210n) a statement from the *Southern Historical Society Papers* (8:252): "It was nearly night before the Federal movements became fully enough developed to make it certain that they were directed upon Germanna and Ely's Fords."

67. *OR*, 25.1:849–50, 865.

68. No enemy defensive positions, previously prepared or improvised upon the Federals' appearance, are mentioned in the reports of Slocum, Howard, and Meade (*OR*, 25.1:505–6, 627–28, 669). From enemy parties along the route there was on Wednesday no annoyance more significant than the token resistance by the bridge builders at Germanna Ford. Stuart believed he delayed enemy progress on Thursday (*OR*, 25.1:1047), but Slocum's report indicates that by detaching two regiments to drive off attackers he was able to continue marching.

69. The fact that this series of events began with his receipt of intelligence found its way into Lee's after-action report. He described the intelligence as relating only to the concentration of enemy cavalry on the upper Rappahannock — omitting the fact that it led him to anticipate a threat to the Shenandoah Valley that never materialized. (*OR*, 25.1:795–96.)

70. *OR*, 25.2:759, 760; 25.1:1046. By this time W. H. F. Lee with two regiments had been detached in pursuit of Stoneman, and Fitz Lee's brigade had moved from the upper Rappahannock to join Stuart and two of W. H. F. Lee's regiments in tracking and harassing the enemy's turning movement.

71. Hooker to S. P. Bates, March 21, 1877. This is a retained copy; reproductions are in the author's possession and in a 1990 catalogue of the Abraham Lincoln Book Shop of Chicago; the present owner of the original is unknown. Swinton's reference to this event is in *Campaigns of the Army of the Potomac*, 273–75.

72. Bigelow perceived that Lee was deceived, but his account shows that he

assumed the deception was a lucky byproduct of Hooker's plan rather than a conscious part of it. He writes (*Chancellorsville*, 165), "Stoneman never thought of crossing the Blue Ridge. Lee's deception on this point was . . . a potent and unexpected factor of success in the execution of Hooker's grand maneuver." Bigelow's perception of the deception derived from numerous *OR* references (cited above and in chapter 15), especially Lee's prolonged correspondence with Stuart concerning Stoneman's threat to the Valley.

73. Twenty-six reports of April 29, timed between 5:00 A.M. and 10:35 P.M., are in the Hooker Papers. See also *OR*, 25.2:287–91 *passim;* 25.1:218, 849, 854–55, 874; 51.2:698–99. The telegraphic, signal, and courier dispatches that Butter-field handled each day of the battle numbered well into the hundreds, counting only those in the Hooker Papers that bear marks and notes in his handwriting. On most of them he wrote the time of receipt. When a message was to be relayed, he even took the time to make insertions for better clarity and deletions for better telegraphese.

74. Butterfield to C. O. Sixth Corps, April 29, 1863, Hooker Papers; Sharpe to Butterfield, April 30 (misdated 29th), BMI.

75. *OR*, 25.2:292–93; Peck to Hooker, 7:30 P.M., April 29, 1863, Hooker Papers.

76. *OR*, 25.2:292–93.

77. *OR*, 25.2:306–07, 310; Sedgwick to Butterfield (letter), April 30, 1863, and Hooker's endorsement thereon, Hooker Papers.

78. *OR*, 25.2:309; Reynolds to Sedgwick, Sedgwick to Butterfield, and Butter-field to Sedgwick, all April 30, 1863, Hooker Papers.

79. *OR*, 25.2:301, 303, 304; Reynolds to Sedgwick, April 30, 1863 (four dis-patches, extracted from the report of Capt. C. S. Kendall, acting signal officer), Hooker Papers.

80. *OR*, 25.2:312, 303; Reynolds to Butterfield, 7:30 P.M., April 30, 1863, Hooker Papers.

81. *OR*, 25.1:865.

82. Patrick Diary, April 29, 1863. Patrick noted with disappointment that although the prisoners were yielding "a deal of information, . . . they all want to be exchanged."

17. Paralyzed by a Real Jackson and a Phantom Longstreet

1. Bigelow, *Chancellorsville*, 216, citing *History of the Corn Exchange Regiment*, by the regiment's Survivors' Association, 171, and "Personne," *Marginalia* (no pub-lication data), 53.

2. Bigelow, *Chancellorsville*, 221, citing R. M. Bache, *Life of G. G. Meade*, 260. An abbreviated copy of this order sent to Meade (*OR*, 25.2:304) is timed at 2:15 P.M.; it would not have reached him by the time of his meeting with Slocum, who arrived at Chancellorsville about 2 P.M. (*OR*, 25.1:669).

3. *OR*, 25.1:171.

4. Howard, *Autobiography*, 1:356; Bigelow, *Chancellorsville*, 225.

5. *OR*, 25.1:305, 306, 384.

6. Patrick Diary, April 30, 1863. Patrick recorded that he had as a guest Hooker's nephew, Joseph Hooker Wood, who had come in from the front suffer-ing with diarrhea. Young Wood, a second lieutenant in the 6th U.S. Cavalry, apparently enjoyed almost as much of Patrick's affection as he did of his uncle's,

for Patrick had gone out of his way to visit him in his camp earlier in the month. As the Wood family lived in Watertown, N.Y., Patrick probably had known the young man long before the war (ibid., April 7, 1863; Hebert, *Hooker*, 187).

7. Bigelow, *Chancellorsville*, 233.

8. *OR*, 25.1:797; 25.2:762.

9. *OR*, 25.2:322.

10. As Hooker's order for the May 1 advance specified that his headquarters would be at Tabernacle Church, it would appear that he was unaware that that place was well within the enemy lines. But a Pennsylvania cavalry regiment was picketing within sight of an element of Lee's extreme left (Anderson's division) that spent Thursday digging trenches and constructing breastworks (Gen. Warren, *OR*, 25.1:198). Thus it seems that Hooker expected to brush Anderson aside in short order.

11. *OR*, 25.2:323, 322; 25.1:217–18. For previous mention of the Signal Corps telegraph printer, see chapter 6, note 35 and associated text.

12. *OR*, 25.2:323 (the same Taylor message is in the Hooker Papers, received by Butterfield 11:30 A.M.); *OR*, 25.2:336, 337, 338–39, 325; ser. 3, 3:313.

13. Butterfield to Hooker, *OR*, 25.2:325; Taylor to Butterfield, 10:10 A.M. (also in the Hooker Papers). Copies of the two Taylor messages in *OR*, 25.2:323, show that Butterfield relayed them to Sedgwick as well as to Hooker.

14. This account of the May 1 engagement is drawn from the following sources: after-action reports of the participating generals at *OR*, 25.1:198–99, 670, 677, 728–29, 525, 507, 515, 517, 306–7, 311, 871; Hooker to Slocum and Howard, 4:45 P.M., May 1, 1863, Hooker Papers; JCCW 1865, 1:66 (Hancock's testimony); Bigelow, *Chancellorsville*, 241–50.

15. JCCW 1865, 1:142 (Hooker's testimony); *OR*, 25.1:199 (Warren's after-action report); 25.2:338 (order to Sedgwick); Couch, in *B&L*, 3:159. Hooker's two messages are at *OR*, 25.2:326, 328. It can be concluded, from Gen. Averell's after-action report at *OR*, 25.1:1078, that Hooker's "news from the other side of the river" was a report of 25,000 men under Jackson at Gordonsville, which Averell (on the "other side" of the Rapidan from Hooker) claimed to have sent on the night of April 30. However, Averell's message containing this misinformation, in the Hooker Papers, shows that it was sent on the night of May 1 — several hours after Hooker's withdrawal to Chancellorsville.

16. *OR*, 25.2:764.

17. *OR*, 25.2:327, 332–33.

18. *OR*, 25.2:333–34, 337; Butterfield to Sedgwick, May 1, 1863, Hooker Papers.

19. Peck to Butterfield, 10:30 P.M., May 1, 1863, Hooker Papers; slightly different version at *OR*, 25.2:345.

20. The Confederate picket's remark was reported up the chain of command to Butterfield and repeated by him to Hooker (untimed dispatch, May 2, 1863, Hooker Papers).

21. Capt. Paul Babcock to Capt. Cushing, received 9:05 A.M., May 2, 1863, Hooker Papers; *OR*, 25.2:353.

22. Sharpe to J. C. Babcock, May 2, 1863, Hooker Papers; Sedgwick to Butterfield, 8:55 A.M. and 9:38 A.M., same date, ibid.; Butterfield to Hooker, untimed, same date, and Hooker's 9:00 A.M. endorsement, ibid.; *OR*, 25.2:362; 25.1:257.

23. *OR*, 25.2:354, 355; from the Hooker Papers: Lt. Louis R. Fortescue to Butterfield, 10:45 A.M., May 2, 1863; Sedgwick to Butterfield, 11:50 A.M. and 12

P.M., same date; Capt. James S. Hall to Butterfield, 8:30 P.M., same date; Butterfield to Hooker, 12:20 P.M., same date. Hall's 8:30 P.M. dispatch recapitulated reports he had made during the day.

24. In the Hooker Papers: Gen. Benham to Hooker, untimed, May 2, 1863; Hall to Butterfield, 8:30 P.M., same date; Butterfield to Hooker, 4:27 P.M., same date; Lowe to Butterfield, 5:30 P.M., same date. *OR*, 25.2:354, 355, 367; 51.1:1035.

25. *OR*, 25.2:363. The order began by saying that Sedgwick should first "cross the river," a statement that was repeated in a more detailed order five hours later. Bigelow (*Chancellorsville*, 320) interprets this to mean that Hooker was unaware that Sedgwick was on the south bank of the Rappahannock. It seems, however, that the error could with equal likelihood be that of Brig. Gen. J. H. Van Alen, who wrote both orders. Sedgwick's interpretation (*OR*, 25.1:558) was that Hooker intended for him to cross to the north bank, march to a point opposite Fredericksburg, and recross. Instead he drove directly on the town.

26. *OR*, 25.2:356–57, 367, 368; 25.1:558.

27. Freeman, *Lee's Lieutenants*, 2:606–12; *OR*, 25.2:358, 359; 25.1:558, 1001.

28. Bigelow, *Chancellorsville*, 275.

29. Ibid., 276.

30. Doubleday, *Chancellorsville and Gettysburg*, 16. Although Bigelow says Hooker was unaware of the gap between Howard's farthest right position and the river, Howard says (*B&L*, 3:195) that Hooker's inspection ride took him to the extreme right.

31. This order, bearing the signature of Gen. Van Alen, appears in *OR*, 25.2:360; *B&L*, 3:219; JCCW 1865, 1:126; and in the Hooker Papers. One version has Howard as the only addressee; among the several versions there is variation in the text, but all versions emphasize weakness on the right flank. An analysis of the handling of the order is in Bigelow, *Chancellorsville*, 276–77.

32. Bigelow, *Chancellorsville*, 279–80; *OR*, 25.1, 231.

33. Bigelow, *Chancellorsville*, 280–85; Doubleday, *Chancellorsville and Gettysburg*, 23–26. Some accounts state that a food train followed the marching column by a different route.

34. *OR*, 25.1:231; Bigelow, 287.

35. Hamlin, *Chancellorsville*, 58. The quotation is from Col. Lee's papers, which he furnished to Hamlin.

36. Hamlin, *Chancellorsville*, 55, 145; Hartwell Osborn, "On the Right at Chancellorsville," in *Military Essays and Recollections* (Chicago: Military Order of the Loyal Legion, Illinois Commandery), 4:185–86.

37. Hamlin, *Chancellorsville*, 145; *OR*, 25.1:633–34.

38. This order, timed 2:30 P.M. and signed by Van Alen, is in the Hooker Papers and is also quoted in Bigelow, *Chancellorsville*, 289.

39. Donald C. Pfanz, "Negligence on the Right: The Eleventh Corps at Chancellorsville," *Morningside News*, p. 3.

40. Hamlin, *Chancellorsville*, 56–57.

41. *OR*, 25.1:654 (Schurz's report); Doubleday, *Chancellorsville and Gettysburg*, 31.

42. Hamlin, *Chancellorsville*, 61; and Bigelow, *Chancellorsville*, 288, citing *Publications of the Loyal Legion, Ohio Commandery* (1888), 1:379.

43. Hamlin, *Chancellorsville*, 61; *OR*, 25.1:231.

44. One of the signalmen, Alexander McCollin, Capt. Castle's flagman, paid with his life for his service in transmitting his captain's fruitless warning mes-

sages. An enemy shell exploded at his feet; the injury required amputation of a leg, from which he failed to recover. (*OR*, 25.1:223, 231–32.)

45. An excellent account of these events is given in Pfanz, "Negligence on the Right," 2–6. Other details are from Bigelow, *Chancellorsville*, 289–320.

46. Hooker to S. P. Bates, March 21, 1877 (see chapter 16, note 71 and associated text).

47. Sickles to Hooker, 1:30 P.M., May 2, 1863, Hooker Papers; *OR*, 25.2:358, 367. The movement on the Fredericksburg front included twelve infantry regiments, sixty-eight wagons, and a party of horsemen resembling a general's escort — all heading for the Telegraph Road, one of the two routes south from Fredericksburg. If this information had been received before Jackson's attack struck, it would have given Hooker a false confirmation of his belief that the enemy was retreating. The observation was made by Signal Corps Lt. P. A. Taylor possibly as early as 4:30 P.M. but was not relayed to Butterfield until 8:30.

48. Alexander Webb, an officer in the Fifth Corps staff, to his wife, May 2, 1863; Van Alen to Butterfield, 4:10 P.M., May 2, 1863, *OR*, 25.2:363 (a slightly different version is in the Hooker Papers).

49. Bigelow, *Chancellorsville*, 264; Freeman, *R. E. Lee*, 2:520–21, 585; and *Lee's Lieutenants*, 2:547.

50. Bigelow, *Chancellorsville*, 458.

51. McPhail to Sharpe, May 2, 1863, BMI and Hooker Papers. The same telegram is in *OR*, 25.2:329, misdated May 1.

52. Longstreet's command, the Department of Virginia and North Carolina, had 44,000 troops. The error in allowing him only three divisions, all from Lee's army, may well have resulted from misunderstanding by McPhail of Maddox's findings, delivered orally. Freeman (*R. E. Lee*, 3:5 and 2:499) gives 12,000 as the strength of Lee's two divisions that were with Longstreet.

53. Bigelow (*Chancellorsville*, 460) estimates Imboden's and Jones's combined strength at 6865.

54. McPhail to Sharpe, BMI.

55. *OR*, 25.2:745.

56. For Lincoln's admonition to Hooker, see Couch, in *B&L*, 3:155.

57. Bigelow, *Chancellorsville*, 382–422 *passim*. Midway in Sedgwick's battle for the heights behind the town, the Federals sent forward a flag of truce, which the Confederates "incautiously" received. Observing the weakness of Confederate positions, the bearers of the flag hurried back to their own lines. A successful Federal attack followed immediately (Freeman, *Lee's Lieutenants*, 2:618).

58. *OR*, 25.2:365–66; Bigelow, *Chancellorsville*, 416.

59. *OR*, 25.2:417.

60. *OR*, 25.2:394. Howard informed Hooker early Monday afternoon that a Wisconsin soldier of his corps who had retreated all the way to Fredericksburg in Saturday's rout had just returned, having walked "through the woods between the Plank road and the River road without meeting a man" (Howard to Dickinson, 12:30 P.M., May 4, 1863, Hooker Papers). This suggests that Lee's forces in Hooker's immediate front on Monday were even lighter than is generally supposed.

61. *OR*, 25.1:776, 1076, 1072, 1073, 1079, 1080; 25.2:383; Bigelow, *Chancellorsville*, 418.

62. *OR*, 25.2:401, 413; Comstock to Butterfield, 10:30 A.M., May 4, 1863, Hooker Papers. Although U.S. Ford was Hooker's obvious retirement route and the one he eventually used, he was also concerned, probably on Sedgwick's

account, with the safety of the approaches to Banks's Ford (Hooker to Benham, *OR*, 25.2:404–5).

63. Doubleday, *Chancellorsville and Gettysburg*, 67. Doubleday, who led a division at Chancellorsville, believed that Sedgwick could have held his ground despite the lack of a supporting advance by Hooker.

64. Longstreet's return to Fredericksburg did not begin until four days after Lee summoned him on Wednesday afternoon (April 29), immediately after Sedgwick's crossing of the Rappahannock served notice of the expected Federal attack (and before Lee learned of the turn toward Chancellorsville and Fredericksburg by Hooker's right wing). Lee's summons was not an order sent by him to Longstreet but a request to Gen. Cooper in the War Dept. to round up for him all forces that might be available, evidently for the force to be sent to defend Gordonsville as well as for his own needs. Cooper's dispatch to Longstreet did not reach him until the 30th. (Cormier, *Siege of Suffolk,* 251–53, citing Dowdey, ed., *Wartime Papers of R. E. Lee,* 442–43.) See also *OR,* 18:1038; 25.2:765, 774, 776, 780; 51.2:704; Freeman, ed., *Lee's Dispatches to Jefferson Davis,* 85–86.

65. *OR,* 25.2:370.

66. *OR,* 25.2:381; Butterfield to Hooker, 5 P.M., May 3, 1863, Hooker Papers.

67. Babcock to Butterfield, 3 P.M., May 3, 1863, Hooker Papers, and 7 A.M., May 5, 1863, BMI; *OR,* 25.1:1083–84, 1086, 1066–67; Bigelow, *Chancellorsville,* 447, 448, 458; Hooker to Bates, Aug. 21, 1876, and April 2, 1877, Bates Collection.

68. Babcock to Butterfield, 9 A.M., May 3, 1863, Hooker Papers; Butterfield to Sedgwick, [10:15 A.M.], same date, ibid.; Babcock to Butterfield, May 5, 1863, ibid.; *OR,* 25.2:416, 421.

69. *OR,* 25.2:371, 414–15.

70. *OR,* 25.2:399–400, 414.

71. *OR,* 25.1:560; 25.2:404; Patrick to Sharpe, RG 94, entry 731.

72. Babcock to Sharpe, May 4, 1863, Hooker Papers, and May 5, 1863, *OR,* 25.2:421, 413. Dix's report was received by Halleck at noon and relayed to Hooker via the Falmouth headquarters at 1 P.M. (Halleck to Hooker, May 4, 1863, Hooker Papers). (Dix's announcement of Longstreet's departure evidently was of no influence in Babcock's retraction of his May 4 report of arrival of enemy reinforcements.) Babcock also reported to Sharpe on bureau activities: "Have sent Anderson and Tyson in the direction of Kelly's Ford. Skinker has just returned in a fatigued condition and cannot go out at present. The three Ohio boys are on the way to report to you. I am expecting Chase back tonight. The [$]6000 from the 120th is here all safe. I shall send Skinker out in the morning if he is able to go." (BMI.) Since the "three Ohio boys" were being sent to Sharpe, they may have been intended for service inside enemy lines; but Anderson, Tyson, and Skinker were probably scouting the fringes of the battlefield hoping to encounter well-informed Confederates or even observe enemy movements. (The $6000 Babcock referred to would have been from payday receipts of Sharpe's regiment.) Other known activity of Sharpe's men during the Chancellorsville battle amounts to very little: Chase's mission to Guiney's Station, Manning's messenger duty, and Joseph Humphreys's and George Smith's service with Stoneman and Averell, the products of which are unknown (Humphreys to Sharpe, undated, BMI).

73. JCCW 1865, 1:134–36; Doubleday, *Chancellorsville and Gettysburg,* 67–68; Bigelow, *Chancellorsville,* 419–20; Couch, in *B&L,* 3:171.

74. Van Alen to Butterfield, May 4, 1863, received at 10:45 P.M. and relayed to Potomac Creek for Averell, whom the Military Telegraph operator could not

find (Hooker Papers). As Butterfield had joined Hooker Monday afternoon, his name appearing as addressee is evidently a telegrapher's error. For details regarding Averell's Friday report, see note 15.

75. A large share of the blame for Hooker's loss of confidence has been placed on his abstinence from liquor beginning the day the army marched. Couch, for example, wrote that rather than abstaining from "ardent spirits," Hooker would have been "far better [off] to have continued his usual habit." There was also a widely believed report that Hooker was drunk during the battle; believers and disbelievers got into a public controversy. It suited the soldiers' image of him to picture him as a hard drinker; in one of their marching songs they changed the line "McClellan's our leader, he's gallant and strong" to "Joe Hooker's our leader, he takes his whisky strong." But Hooker's biographer found that "[h]is close followers were ever ready to testify that they had never seen him take a drink." (Couch, in *B&L*, 3:170; Hebert, *Fighting Joe Hooker*, 65 and 225–26, citing esp. the diaries of Gen. Meade and Navy Secretary Welles, a statement by Col. Sharpe, and the testimony in JCCW 1865, vol. 1, of Gens. Sickles, Pleasonton, Birney, and Butterfield.) Both of these opposing points of view were overblown. Hooker probably was more than an occasional drinker, but the explanation of his loss of confidence during the battle does not need the abstinence factor; it lies in the fortunes of battle and his own nature.

76. In *Lincoln Finds a General* (1950), Williams writes, "Hooker had in fact accomplished one of the finest maneuvers in military history" (2:575). Ernest Furgurson, in *Chancellorsville* (1992), rates Hooker's march "one of the most successful opening moves in American military history" (130). If these writers had known that Hooker's feat was in fact an intelligence coup, their appreciation of it would have been even greater. Bates (who also was unaware of the intelligence role) in his 1882 book *The Battle of Chancellorsville* found one writer, a European, who recognized the importance of Hooker's feat. Bates writes (55–56) that "Colonel MacDougal, of the British army, one of the ablest of living military writers" in the book *Modern Warfare and Modern Artillery* (London: John Murray; n.d.) discusses at length the "most celebrated instances of the passage of rivers [and] classes this movement of General Hooker with Hannibal's passage of the Rhone, Alexander's of the Hydaspes, Napoleon's of the Po and the Danube, and Wellington's of the Douro and the Adour."

18. Lee's Army Vanishes

1. Freeman, *R. E. Lee*, 2:557; *OR*, 25.1:802 (Lee's report), 508 (Meade's report), 394 (Sickles's report); 25.2:432.

2. *OR*, 25.2:476; Patrick Diary, May 14, 1863; Kingston (N.Y.) *Daily Leader*, Jan. 15, 1900, Sharpe Collection.

3. *OR*, 25.2:449, 774, 776; *OR*, ser. 2, 5:559. Early in May the Richmond local defense force included two commands whose strength was reported six weeks later as 4140 (*OR*, 25.2:784, 792; 27.3:909). Willich, a brigade commander in the Army of the Cumberland, had been captured in the battle of Stone's River.

4. *OR*, 25.2:417, 421, 439, 473; 25.1:1060–63.

5. *OR*, 25.2:458; Compiled Service Record of James Clifford, in NA; Clifford file, SGSD; *OR Atlas*, plate 8, map l.

6. Trenis file, S. S. Accts.; *OR*, 25.1:1109.

7. The BMI files are very full for this period. Most of the letters received at Army of the Potomac headquarters (which would include communications

to Hooker from Sharpe and other members of the headquarters staff) are missing, but a register of them was kept, and it does not show any reports from Sharpe's bureau that could have contributed to Hooker's statements about enemy strength.

8. *OR*, 25.2:473; Sharpe to Butterfield, May 13, 1863, BMI.

9. Yager file, SGSD; Yager to Sharpe, May 10 and Aug. 17, 1863, BMI; Sharpe to Yager, May 20, 1863, General Telegrams; *OR*, 25.2:479.

10. *OR*, 25.2:792; 18:1058.

11. Special Orders 133, Army of the Potomac, NA.

12. Livermore, *Numbers and Losses*, 86, 92, 99, 103.

13. Statement of S. B. Flandreau, May 22, 1863, BMI.

14. Sharpe to S. Williams, May 22, 1863, and to Butterfield, May 24, 1863, BMI.

15. Sharpe to Hooker and Hooker to Halleck in Letters Received, Headquarters of the Army, 1863, NA. The report and indorsement, with editorial changes made by the compilers of the *Official Records,* are in *OR*, 25.2:528. Hooker's telegram notifying Stanton that the report was en route is at *OR*, 27.2:527.

16. Lt. P. A. Taylor, acting signal officer, to Capt. B. F. Fisher, May 13, 1863, BMI.

17. Lee to Critcher, May 22, 1863, *OR*, 25.2:826.

18. Unaddressed memorandum from Capt. B. F. Fisher, May 28, 1863, BMI; Patrick Diary, May 24, 1863; *OR*, ser. 2, 5:706.

19. *OR*, 25.2:832.

20. *OR*, 25.1:228. The immediate aim of Fisher's complaint, which concluded his report on the Chancellorsville battle, was to induce a change in the army's signaling code — the flag alphabet. But if the Rebels could solve the daily changing cipher, as he implied, a new permanent flag alphabet would not have resisted their cryptanalytic efforts for very many days.

21. This account of Lee's reorganization is based on *OR*, 27.3:919–22, and Freeman, *Lee's Lieutenants*, 3:653 and 688–714 *passim*.

22. Sharpe to Hooker, June 9, 1863, Hooker Papers; Sharpe to Butterfield, June 11, 1863 (two reports), BMI.

23. RG 393, part 1, entry 3964 (vol. 3 of 8), NA.

24. McEntee to Sharpe, May 30 and 31, 1863, BMI; *OR*, 27.3:1065. The reference to secret ink is the only one found in the BMI records for the months covered in this study.

25. *OR*, 25.2:542.

26. A brief, undated report from Silver, received "about June 1," in the Hooker Papers, is the last one he is known to have produced while the army was on the Rappahannock.

27. Col. Byron Laflin to A. A. G. Second Corps, May 29, 1863, in Letters Received, Army of the Potomac, 1863; *OR*, 25.2:595; 27.3:5, 6, 14–15, 24–26, 30, 32–33; 51.1:1044; Sharpe to [Butterfield], June 7, 1863, BMI; and the following items from the Hooker Papers: Stryker to Wiggins, May 27, 1863; Stryker to Butterfield, June 5; Sykes to Meade, Ayres to Meade, and J. Adams to Hq 1st Brigade, June 7; Fisher to Butterfield, June 8.

28. *OR*, 27.3:6; Capt. Wm. H. Hogarth to Hooker, June 2, 1863, BMI.

29. *OR*, 27.3:12–13; 27.1:32–33.

30. Skinker to Sharpe, June 3, 1863, BMI.

31. Buford to Alexander, *OR*, 27.3:8; McEntee to Sharpe, June 6, 1863, BMI.

32. Fisher to Butterfield, June 5, 1863, Hooker Papers. The daily monitoring

of Confederate flag traffic is revealed in numerous intercepts of late May and early June, also in the Hooker Papers.

33. Sharpe to McEntee, June 4, 6, and n.d., 1863, and McEntee to Sharpe, June 6 and n.d., 1863, BMI.

34. Sharpe to Butterfield, June 7, 1863, BMI.

35. McClellan, *Campaigns of Stuart,* 262.

36. *OR,* 27.2:293; 25.2:832, 834, 848, 505.

37. *OR,* 14:923, 933.

38. Hooker to Lincoln, n.d., BMI.

39. *OR,* 27.2:293; 27.3:1090; McEntee to Sharpe, June 6, 1863, BMI.

40. Sharpe to Heintzelman, June 6, 1863, General Telegrams; McEntee to Sharpe, June 6, 7, 8, 13, 1863, BMI; *OR,* 27.3:32; 27.2:785. The Washington cavalry detachment's visit to Winchester reappears in chapter 20 at note 9 and associated text.

41. *OR,* 27.3:27, 28, 42; 27.1:1044; Freeman, *Lee's Lieutenants,* 3:5, 7.

42. *OR,* 27.2:772, 748–49; 27.3:38; New York *Times,* June 8, 1863.

43. *OR,* 27.2:733–36, 683, 722; Mosby, *Stuart's Cavalry,* 33; McClellan, *Campaigns of Stuart,* 271–74; *OR,* 27.1:903, 904, 1045.

44. Richmond *Examiner* and Richmond *Dispatch,* June 12, 1863.

45. Although some mind reading is involved in attributing Stuart's later actions to this one embarrassment, so good an authority as Freeman plainly indicates his acceptance of the theory: "Stuart almost certainly was prompted to undertake a long raid in order to restore the reputation he felt had been impaired in the Battle of Brandy Station" (*Lee's Lieutenants,* 3:xi; see also xxxii, 18–19, 51–52).

46. *OR,* 27.3:876, 890, 896; 27.2:439–40, 546, 564, 295, 313, 315, 348, 357; Freeman, *Lee's Lieutenants,* 3:2, 13.

19. Pursuit

1. *OR,* 27.1:903, 904.

2. *OR,* 27.1:1045; McClellan, *Campaigns of Stuart,* 266, 294–95.

3. Pleasonton's testimony and letter are in JCCW 1865, 1:32–33.

4. *OR,* 27.3:47–49, 62, 875, 882, 888; 27.1:35–36; McEntee to Sharpe, June 12, 1863, BMI. McEntee, allowed to examine one of the Negroes, found that his reason for reporting Ewell's corps at Culpeper was that he had seen General Ewell at Stuart's second review, but as he claimed he had also seen A. P. Hill, whose corps was known to be back at Fredericksburg, and D. H. Hill, who was very unlikely to have left his even more distant command, McEntee discounted the whole story. His denunciation of the reliability of one of the two sources for the mainly correct disposition of Lee's forces probably was overtaken by events, namely, McEntee's own telegrams later that day that led to Hooker's decision to put his army in motion.

5. *OR,* 27.1:34; Fisher to Butterfield, June 10, 1863, Hooker Papers; *Richmond Whig,* June 8, 1863. The War Department supplied a brigade to replace Pickett's at Hanover Junction (*OR,* 27.3:882). A statement by Lee that two of Pickett's brigades were at the Junction and Richmond on June 15 (*OR,* 27.2:295) cannot be reconciled with an item in his Gettysburg campaign report (*OR,* 27.2:315) that places three of Pickett's brigades with him in his departure northward from Culpeper on the same date.

6. The Third and Eleventh Corps were moved upriver (*OR*, 27.3:59, 60, 69), where the First and Fifth Corps were already posted.

7. McEntee to Sharpe, June 11, 1863, BMI; *OR*, 27.1:170.

8. McEntee to Sharpe, June 12 and 13, 1863, BMI; Compiled Service Record of Martin E. Hogan, 1st Indiana Cavalry, NA.

9. Sharpe to Butterfield, June 11, 1863 (two reports), BMI; *OR*, 27.1:35–36; 27.3:67, 70, 72–73; Howard, *Autobiography*, 1:387.

10. McEntee to Sharpe, June 12, 1863, BMI.

11. *OR*, 27.1:37. Hooker was under the impression that Lincoln's proposed visit was two days away; actually the President was planning to join him late on June 13 (ibid.).

12. *OR*, 27.2:184–85.

13. *OR*, 27.3:80. McEntee assured Sharpe by letter on June 19 (BMI) that throughout his tour at cavalry headquarters, any information he reported was also reported by Pleasonton. Obviously this referred only to McEntee's telegraphic reporting.

14. McEntee to Sharpe, June 12, 1863, BMI. This message and the one cited in note 10 are also in Halleck Telegrams (Received), 10:36–37, 41, NA.

15. *OR*, 27.3:80.

16. *OR*, 27.2:295, 313, 440, 357.

17. *OR*, 27.3:80, 81; *OR Atlas*, plate 43, map 7.

18. *OR*, 27.3:70–75, 81–89 *passim*.

19. McEntee to Sharpe, June 13, 1863, BMI.

20. Of 257 names on Sharpe's payroll (the maximum in any one month was 70), 5 are listed as "col'd" (colored) guides. One of them, Louis Battail (or Battle), was employed in June, July, and August 1863 and in May 1864; the others' service was late in the war. Wright's name appears only once in these records, in McEntee's June 13 letter to Sharpe.

21. *OR*, 27.3:84, 88–89.

22. See, for example, T. H. Williams, *Lincoln and His Generals*, 252–54; Tucker, *High Tide at Gettysburg*, 67. K. P. Williams (*Lincoln Finds a General*, 2:624) points out how this belief is unjust to Hooker.

23. Patrick Diary, June 13, 1863.

24. Lowe to Stanton, June 9, 1863, and Lowe to Myer, July 13, Lowe Papers; Haydon, *Aeronautics in the Union and Confederate Armies*, 305–6, 292, 329. Lowe's difficulties with his military supervision are set out at length on pages 302–9 and 316–17 of his historical report, *OR*, ser. 3, 3:252–319.

25. *OR*, ser. 3, 3:317; James Allen and E. S. Allen to Lowe, June 6, 1863, Lowe Papers.

26. Lt. J. C. Kaulbach to Warren, June 12, 1863, Hooker Papers.

20. Lost Intelligence, Lost Battle

1. *OR*, 25,2:567.

2. *Dictionary of American Biography*, 13:20; *OR*, 27.2:157–58, 186–88, 192; 25.2:453–54.

3. *OR*, 25.2:527.

4. *OR*, 25.2:527, 528; Sharpe to Hooker and Hooker to Halleck, Letters Received, Headquarters of the Army, 1863, NA.

5. *OR*, 27.2:92–93. At one point, on May 30, Milroy believed Lee's ac-

tivity consisted of a "tremendous concentration . . . on Gen. Hooker" (*OR*, 25.2:569–70).

6. *OR*, 25.2:567, 570–71, 525–27, 540–42.

7. Schenck, like other commanders, forwarded his more important operational telegrams to Halleck for information. An excellent example of a message that Schenck's headquarters submitted to the general-in-chief's scrutiny was one of June 2 in which he directed Milroy to "act with caution . . . and fall back, when forced, in direction of Harper's Ferry or Martinsburgh, as your better judgment may direct." This message is in Halleck Telegrams (M473), 9:419 and also in *OR*, 25.2:596. But Schenck's message of the same date to Milroy, suggesting that the enemy might merely have his eye on Valley crops (*OR*, 25.2:596), is not in the Halleck Telegrams; thus it probably was not passed to Halleck. If Schenck deliberately chose to avoid having it come under the eye of his chief, his reluctance is understandable, for Halleck would not have been pleased by the reassurance it conveyed.

8. *OR*, 27.3:36; Sharpe to Butterfield, June 7, 1863, MI; *OR*, 25.2:823, 825, 846. See also McClellan, *Life and Campaigns of Stuart*, 293.

9. *OR*, 27.2:785; 27.3:31, 34–37, 75. This detachment's report is also mentioned in chapter 18 in connection with Ernest Yager's report, disbelieved by McEntee, that Confederate infantry was being sent to the Valley (see chapter 18, note 40 and associated text).

10. *OR*, 27.3:35; 27.2:159.

11. *OR*, 27.2:49–50, 124–25, 161–62; Schenck to Halleck, Letters Received, Headquarters of the Army, entry 30, vol. 237, p. 114, NA.

12. *OR*, 27.2: 42–43, 92, 440. Ewell's command also included the brigade of West Virginia cavalry commanded by Albert G. Jenkins.

13. *OR*, 27.2:45, 52, 92, 166, 174. Both Harper's Ferry and Martinsburg were in contact with Winchester later in the day, but the current was apparently too weak for messages to be exchanged. The wire was probably on the ground, unbroken.

14. *OR*, 27.3:86–95, 60; 27.1:38; 27.2: 126, 163; Patrick Diary, June 13, 1863. Although Halleck, when queried by Schenck, did not have copies of McEntee's telegrams, they eventually did find their way into his files (see Halleck Telegrams [M473], 10:36–37, 41). Among the several possible explanations of this anomaly, the likeliest is that Hooker's headquarters was under instructions to send to the War Dept., presumably by courier, copies of its more informative telegrams that did not terminate or pass through the department's telegraph office.

15. *OR*, 27.2:165, 52, 166; *Dictionary of American Biography*, 15:428.

16. *OR*, 27.2:126, 167.

17. *OR*, 27.2:45–52, 166.

18. *OR*, 27.2:166; Compiled Service Record of Capt. Wm. H. Boyd, First New York Cavalry, RG 94, NA.

19. *OR*, 27.2:46–47, 50, 93, 441, 463.

20. *OR*, 27.2:47–49, 53, 58–59, 93–94, 98–99, 110–11, 194, 442, 464, 501, 502, 541.

21. *OR*, 27.3:36, 53, 159, 144.

22. *OR*, 27.3:124.

23. The record of the court of inquiry is in *OR*, 27.2:88–197. Milroy's testimony is at 91–98; Schenck's at 157–68; Judge Advocate General Holt's review, 186–97; Lincoln's endorsement, 197.

24. Schenck, who had represented an Ohio district before the war, was re-

turned to the House in an 1863 election. *Dictionary of American Biography,* 16:427–28; *Twentieth-Century Dictionary of Notable Americans,* vol. 9; *OR,* 31.3:454–55; 38.4:54, 289.

21. Joe Hooker's Magnificent Error

1. *OR,* 27.2:166, 442–43; 27.1:39–40, 41–42; 27.3:101, 114–16.
2. McEntee to Sharpe, June 13, 1863, BMI; *OR,* 27.3:107.
3. *OR,* 27.1:41. Gen. Anderson, whose division was Hill's advance, reported (*OR,* 27.2:613) that his march began on June 14; thus it appears that the movement on the 13th was by some other element of Hill's corps.
4. *OR,* 27.3:88, 175.
5. *OR,* 27.2:315, 348, 442–43; 27.3:890, 144, 161, 36, 53, 159, 173–74, 175.
6. *OR,* 27.1:44, 47–48.
7. *B&L,* 3:241, citing F. A. Walker, *History of the Second Army Corps,* 253–55; *OR,* 27.3:55, 162. For the story of Revolutionary War espionage in Pennsylvania, see Bakeless, *Turncoats, Traitors and Heroes,* 106–21, and O'Toole, *Honorable Treachery,* chs. 14 and 15.
8. David McConaughy file in Military Correspondence, Pennsylvania State Archives; *History of Cumberland and Adams Counties* (Chicago: Warner, Bears, 1886); letter from Adams County (Gettysburg) Historical Society to the author, April 28, 1960; *OR,* 27.3:181, 183, 186.
9. Starr, *Bohemian Brigade,* 203; Patrick Diary, June 17, 1863.
10. *OR,* 27.1:50, 142; 27.3:191, 172–75; Patrick Diary, June 16 and 17, 1863.
11. Patrick Diary, June 17, 1863; McEntee to Sharpe, June 18 (erroneously dated June 19), 1863, BMI; *OR,* 27.1:906–8; 27.3:173, 900. Longstreet's final report of the campaign (*OR,* 27.2:357) gives only June 20 as the date of his move to the Valley; evidently that refers only to his final move.
12. McEntee to Sharpe, June 18 (erroneously dated June 19), 1863, BMI; *OR,* 27.3:266.
13. *OR,* 27.1:50.
14. Patrick Diary, June 17, 1863.
15. *OR,* 27.2:23; 27.3:199–200. As late as 3:30 P.M. on June 18, Hooker's headquarters apparently had not received Tyler's latest information, for at that hour Butterfield wrote Reynolds that the whereabouts of Lee, Longstreet, and Ewell were still unknown (ibid.).
16. *OR,* 27.3:207; M. P. Hunnicutt memorandum, June 22, 1863, BMI; Sharpe to Scammon, June 17 and Aug. 11, 1863, in General Telegrams (M473); Compiled Service Record of Mordecai P. Hunnicutt, NA; undated clipping in Hunnicutt Collection. It is clear that Hunnicutt took the Confederate oath of allegiance. The information on his Confederate enlistment came from his brother.
17. Patrick Diary, June 17, 1863; Babcock to Sharpe, June 19 and 20, 1863, BMI; *OR,* 27.2:503, 550–51, 442–43, 464, 596, 599, 770–71; McPhail to Sharpe, Aug. 1, 1863, BMI.
18. Although at some point in the campaign the Frederick telegraph office was taken over by the Military Telegraph (Plum, *Military Telegraph,* 2:13–14, 17), at this point it would still have been run by commercial operators. Babcock evidently had been instructed to run the risk of reporting his arrival by telegraph. In any case, the purpose of his visit to Frederick would have become clear to the operators whenever he acquired enough information to send a report back to the army. And merely his use of a cipher would have enabled the

Frederick operators to guess the nature of his business. As it was, Hooker's plain-language telegram to Babcock (see text associated with note 19) completely exposed his reason for being in Frederick.

19. Babcock to Sharpe, June 19 and 20, 1863, BMI and Halleck Telegrams (R); Pinkerton file, S. S. Accts.; *OR*, 27.3:225, 226.

20. *OR*, 27.3:209, 210; 27.1:910.

21. Sharpe to Jansen Hasbrouck, June 20, 1863, Sharpe Collection.

22. Patrick Diary, June 17 and 19, 1863.

23. Sharpe to Jansen Hasbrouck, June 20, 1863, Sharpe Collection.

24. *OR*, 27.3:914, 223–24; 27.1:911; 27.2:359.

25. *OR*, 27.3: 227; 27.2: 503, 464; Freeman, *Lee's Lieutenants*, 3:28; Babcock to Sharpe, June 19 and 20, 1863, BMI and Halleck Telegrams (Received), 10:288–89, 301.

26. Babcock to Sharpe, June 21 and 22, 1863, BMI; *OR*, 27.2:290; 27.3:226.

27. *OR*, 27.3:228, 244, 245.

28. *OR*, 27.3:227–28, 255, 914; 27.2:613, 296–97, 315; 27.1:911, 912.

29. *OR*, 27.1:142, 912; 27.3:223. For examples of newspaper reporting of Ewell's operations, see the New York *Herald*, Chicago *Tribune*, and *Alta California* (San Francisco), June 15–19, 1863.

30. *OR*, 27.2:690; 27.3:914.

31. *OR*, 27.3:266, 249; 27.1:913.

32. Babcock to Sharpe, June 22, 1863, BMI; Sharpe to Babcock, June 23, 1863, General Telegrams. Cline's companions are not named in the records.

33. *OR*, 27.1:52; 27.2:22; Headquarters, AP, to Pleasonton, June 23, 1863, RG 393, part 1, entry 3973; *OR*, 27.3:291.

34. *OR*, 27.3:254, 157, 181, 202, 294, 261.

35. *OR*, 27.3:182; L. C. Baker file, S. S. Accts.

36. *Pennsylvania Railroad History*, 1:413–15; *OR*, 27.3:163.

37. *OR*, 27.3:163, 186, 161, 251, 295; McClure to Eli Slifer, June 9, 1863, Slifer Collection; Couch to Schenck, June 21, 1863, General Telegrams; Milroy to Couch, June 20, 1863, Dept. of the Susquehanna Telegrams (RG 393, part 1, entry 4614, NA); Samuel D. Oliphant file, SGSD.

38. *OR*, 27.1:51; 27.3:275, 177–78, 161, 293; 27.2:24.

39. *OR*, 51.1:1059.

40. *OR*, 27.2:296, 442–43, 464, 551, 316; 27.3:914.

41. *OR*, 27.2:24–25; 27.3:249–50, 254, 251.

42. *OR*, 27.3:233, 254, 253; Babcock to Sharpe, June 21, 1863, BMI, and Halleck Telegrams (Received), 10:347; *OR*, 27.3:271; Howard, *Autobiography*, 1:391.

43. *OR*, 27.3: 914; 27.2:316, 443, 464, 551, 613, 677, 428.

44. *OR*, 27.3:275, 923; 27.2:26–27, 297–98, 442, 464, 503.

45. *OR*, 27.3:263, 295; 27.2:551. The Chambersburg citizen-spies were active by this time, but their reports regularly took longer to reach Harrisburg than did those obtained by the Gettysburgers, even when the latter were covering the Chambersburg-Greencastle area.

46. Sharpe to Butterfield, June 24, 1863, RG 107, entry 34 (M473, roll 175), NA; *OR*, 27.3:293, 281; 27.1:56.

47. *OR*, 27.2:28.

48. *OR*, 27.1:55.

49. *OR*, 27.2:29; 27.3:295.

50. *OR*, 27.3:281, 307.

51. *OR*, 27.3:280; 27.2:358.

52. *OR*, 27.3: 294, 920.

53. Babcock to Sharpe, June 24, 1863, General Telegrams. The message also appears, with editorial changes by the *OR* compilers, at *OR*, 27.3: 285–86.

54. *OR*, 27.3:294.

55. *OR*, 27.2.28–29.

56. Babcock to Sharpe, June 24, 1863, RG 107, entry 34 (M473, roll 22).

57. *OR*, 27.3:290; 27.1:143.

58. *OR*, 27.2:358, 428, 366, 613, 677; 27.3:914–15, 1090; 51.2:725–26; *B&L*, 3:249. This account of the intelligence background of Hooker's decision to cross the Potomac is at odds with his own account in his 1865 testimony to the Joint Committee on the Conduct of the War. He stated that as soon as he learned that the enemy's main body was beginning to cross, "I commenced crossing my own army, and by the time that I was over, the whole rebel army was on the north side of the Potomac." (JCCW 1865, 1:169.) Thus he ignored the day-long succession of reports of enemy crossings that preceded his decision to cross. Hooker was telling the inquiring congressmen what he thought they wanted to hear — and at the same time avoiding the story of the intelligence received that day, because of the critical role played by Babcock's telegrams. In 1865 Hooker would have regarded Babcock's mission to Frederick as a secret still worth preserving. Hooker's testimony also ignored the possibility that one of the committeemen would inquire whether his decision to cross took adequate account of the orders to keep his army in position to protect Washington. Hooker in 1865 would still have been unaware that on June 24 Longstreet was well short of the Potomac, and in a position from which he could have begun a march on Washington that would pass around Hooker's army, soon to be across the river.

22. Reaping the Pennsylvania Harvest

1. Sharpe to Babcock, June 25, 1863, *OR*, 27.3:312, and June 27, 1863, General Telegrams; McPhail to Sharpe, June 27, 1863, General Telegrams. Sharpe sent telegrams to Babcock on June 25, 26, and 27, but apparently received no telegrams from him after the 24th. When army headquarters arrived at Frederick June 27, Babcock had left.

2. *OR*, 27.3:927–28, 913, 915, 923; Marshall, *Aide-de-Camp of Lee*, 201; Blackford, *War Years with Jeb Stuart*, 222; Freeman, *R. E. Lee*, 3:60–68, and *Lee's Lieutenants*, 3:54–58.

3. *OR*, 27.2:692–97, 321, 322; 27.3:309, 318; 27.1:62, 63.

4. *OR*, 27.2:321–22, 751; *B&L*, 3:252–53; Freeman, *Lee's Lieutenants*, 3:48 and n. 47. There was more color than accuracy in Mosby's quip about Robertson's route, for Robertson's orders read that he was to "follow the army" and he used the same route as Longstreet.

5. *OR*, 27.2:316, 465; Russell F. Weigley, "Emergency Troops in the Gettysburg Campaign," *Pennsylvania History* 25, no. 1:39–57.

6. Letter to the author from Mrs. James L. McConaughy, Hartford, Conn., May 31, 1960. Mrs. McConaughy credits the account of this incident to three different family sources, including the wife of Samuel McConaughy.

7. *OR*, 27.2:316, 551–52, 566, 596, 613, 358.

8. *OR*, 27.3:289, 295; Babcock to Sharpe, June 20, 1863, BMI. Couch had even picked up the erroneous (planted) report of Longstreet's crossing of the Potomac.

9. *OR*, 27.3:525; Hoke, *Great Invasion*, 157–60; book 1, Letters Sent, Dept. of

the Susquehanna, p. 12, NA; Secretary of War Telegrams (Received), 29:295; *OR*, 27.2:566. Hoke's book, while it contains several episodes connected with the Chambersburg spies and scouts, is mainly a history of the Gettysburg campaign.

10. Operator's note, June 25, 1863, Telegrams, Dept. of the Susquehanna, NA.

11. *OR* and other commonly used sources give conflicting evidence as to whether Lee arrived at Chambersburg on June 26 or 27, and the question has often been sidestepped in secondary accounts. A preponderance of the evidence hitherto available favors the later date, and it is supported by a telegram from Couch to Meade on the 29th (on file in BMI). Two of the Chambersburg spies had left for Harrisburg at a time when Hill's corps, the advance of Lee's main body, was entering the town, Couch said, and he carefully put the hour of the spies' departure at "Saturday [June 27] eleven a.m." For other evidence on this point see *OR*, 27.2:316, 358, 366, 428, 613; 27.3:1090; 51.2:727–28; Sorrel, *Recollections*, 178; Hoke, *Great Invasion*, 160–67; Freeman, *R. E. Lee*, 3:55.

12. Hoke, *Great Invasion*, 162–67. Tucker (*High Tide at Gettysburg*, 49), states, without showing the source, that Huber's report "was the first information reaching the War Department that Lee might be turning toward the South Mountain passes." The records do not support this statement, nor the claim made by Hoke (p. 167) that Washington on June 27 was aware of Lee's eastward turn.

13. Patrick Diary, June 26, 1863; *OR*, 27.1:143; 27.3:336.

14. *OR*, 27.3:334–35, 337–38. Stahel's report, written at Frederick, tallies so closely with Winchester's report of the 24th in several details that there can be little doubt that he received Winchester's aid.

15. *OR*, 27.3:349; Hooker to Bates, Aug. 29, 1876, Bates Papers.

16. *OR*, 27.3:351–52, 335, 350; Provost Marshal, 11th Corps, to Chief of Staff, 11th Corps, June 27, 1863, Letters Received, AP; Howard to S. Williams, June 27, 1863, BMI; Butterfield to Schenck, Halleck, and Secretary Chase, RG 393, part 1, entry 3971 (Telegrams Sent, Division and Department of the Potomac).

17. Capt. J. L. Bodwell, Monocacy Jct., Md., to Gen. Henry S. Briggs, Relay House, Md., June 24, 1863, Halleck Telegrams (R), 11:15.

18. *OR*, 27.1:65; K. P. Williams, *Lincoln Finds a General*, 2:659. This report was not sent to Washington until June 28, but internal evidence shows that it was written on the 27th. From the accuracy of McCammon's figures it would appear that he and his collaborators had information not only on the Confederate units that passed through Hagerstown but also on Early's division, which took a parallel route east of the town.

19. *OR*, 27.1:58–60; T. H. Williams, *Lincoln and His Generals*, 257–59; K. P. Williams, *Lincoln Finds a General*, 2:645–52.

20. *OR*, 27.3,369; 27.1:61; *B&L*, 3:241–43; Hooker to Bates, May 30, 1878, Bates Papers.

21. T. H. Williams, *Lincoln and His Generals*, 260; Meade to Sharpe, June 10, 1863, BMI.

22. Meade, *Life and Letters of George Gordon Meade*, 1:389; *OR*, 27.1:61.

23. Carson (identified as T. J. Carson in *OR*, 27.3:370) was cashier of the Bank of Gettysburg. He and McCreary were closely associated with McConaughy in the recruitment of volunteers. (Letter to author from Adams County Historical Society, Gettysburg, April 28, 1960.)

24. *OR*, 27.3:370, 377.

25. *OR*, 27.3:384, 385, 390.

26. Howard to Butterfield, June 28, 1863, Letters Received, AP; Devin to

Buford, forwarded by Pleasonton to army headquarters, June 28, 1863, ibid.; Secretary of War Telegrams (Received), 29:335.

27. *OR*, 27.1:62, 63; 27.3:372, 379.

28. *OR*, 27.1:64, 66. In disputing Halleck's statement about enemy infantry south of Washington, Meade wrote that the force that had passed through Hagerstown was "Lee's entire army." Presumably this was a slip of the pen, as the presence of enemy cavalry on the right rear of Meade's army was well known.

29. *OR*, 27.1:67.

30. *OR*, 27.3:192; 27.2:689; Mosby, *Stuart's Cavalry*, 65–66. The dispatch captured by Mosby is probably one signed by Butterfield that appears at *OR*, 27.3:176–77.

31. Mosby, *Stuart's Cavalry*, 72–81, 169–70; Mosby, *Memoirs*, 215–16; *B&L*, 3:251; *OR*, 27.2:297, 692–93.

32. *OR*, 27.2:307, 694, 695; Hoke, *Great Invasion*, 205; Tucker, *High Tide at Gettysburg*, 88–89.

33. Longstreet, *From Manassas to Appomattox*, 346–48, 324–25, 333; Sorrel, *Recollections*, 158, 161, 164; *B&L*, 3:244, 249–50; *OR*, 27.2:358; Freeman, *Lee's Lieutenants*, 3:226–27. Harrison's first name and biographical details, long unknown, are as given by James O. Hall, whose article "The Spy Harrison" (*Civil War Times Illustrated*, Feb. 1986, 18–25) put an end to many years of uncertainty as to Harrison's identity and Civil War service.

34. *OR*, 27.2:307, 316–17; 27.3:943–44; Longstreet, *From Manassas to Appomattox*, 347–48; Sorrel, *Recollections*, 164–65. Sorrel says Harrison reported the Federals marching on Gettysburg.

35. *OR*, 27.3:333, 334, 335, 337–38, 351, 372; 27.1:144.

36. *OR*, 27.3:375.

37. Luther A. Rose Diary, June 27, 1863; *OR*, 27.2:695; Plum, *Military Telegraph*, 2:16; Telegrams Received, HqA, entry 30, vol. 347 (see all telegrams for June 28–July 1), NA. Many of these messages appear in *OR* but with incomplete data as to times of origin and receipt. A telegram from Meade to Halleck filed at 7:25 P.M. June 28 (*OR*, 27.1:66), deciphered at the War Department at 9:40 P.M. the same day, was the last one to pass directly over the wires between the army and Washington before the break.

38. *OR*, 27.3:523.

39. *OR*, 27.3:399; Cline to Doubleday, June 29, 1863, BMI.

40. McConaughy to Sharpe, Aug. 4, 1863, BMI; *OR*, 27.3:397.

41. Sharpe's letter is in the McConaughy Collection in the Civil War Institute of Gettysburg College.

42. Ibid.; McConaughy to Sharpe, Aug. 4, 1863, BMI.

43. *OR*, 27.3:162.

44. *OR*, 27.3:370.

45. McConaughy to Sharpe, Aug. 4, 1863, BMI.

46. Ibid.

23. The Thirtieth of June

1. *OR*, 27.1:67–68; 27.2:317, 607, 637; Capt. E. C. Bayard (Reynolds's A.A.G.) to unnamed officer at army headquarters, June 30, BMI; Reynolds to Butterfield, June 30, 1863, enclosing Buford to Reynolds, same date, BMI; Hoke, *Great Invasion*, 199. Hoke says the Southerners' fires appeared on the night of

the 28th, but Hill's and Heth's reports are clear in showing that the movement did not begin until the 29th.

2. *OR*, 27.1:67–68; 27.3:420; 27.2:695, 358; 51.2:729.

3. Tucker, *High Tide at Gettysburg*, 93–94; *OR*, 27.1:922. The information reported by Buford took on added credibility from the fact that earlier reports (*OR*, 27.3:371; Howard to Butterfield, June 28, 1863, in RG 393, part 1, entry 3976, NA) had placed Hill's corps or sizable parts of it at Waynesboro, which would put them on a route leading to Fairfield and Gettysburg. Hill's reserve artillery battalion did march through Waynesboro but proceeded northward from there instead of turning toward Fairfield (*OR*, 27.2:677). Artillery would not have marched without infantry protection, but since most of Hill's units did not report their routes of march, the infantry elements that used the Waynesboro route are not identified.

4. *OR*, 27.3:422, 416–17.

5. *OR*, 27.3:417; Tucker, *High Tide at Gettysburg*, 97–98, citing *SHSP*, 4:157; *OR*, 27.1:923–926, 69; 27.2:607, 613, 637.

6. *OR*, 27.1:926; Sharpe to Butterfield, June 30, 1863, BMI; Buford to [Pleasonton], June 30, 1863, BMI. Gens. Gregg, Hancock, Sykes (commanding the Fifth Corps), and the telegraph operator at Monocacy Junction also contributed details of Stuart's march (*OR*, 27.3:417, 396, 424); 27.1:367; Monocacy operator to Frederick operator, RG 393, part 1, entry 3976 (Letters Received, Division and Department of the Potomac).

7. Couch to Meade, June 29, 1863, BMI; *OR*, 27.2:443; 27.3:407.

8. *OR*, 27.1:69, 61; 27.3:421. For examples of dispatches concerning Lee's advance detachments, see *OR*, 27.3:370, 377; 27.1:67, 68.

9. *OR*, 27.3:416.

10. Williams, *Lincoln Finds a General*, 2:676.

11. Van Santvoord, *The One Hundred Twentieth Regiment*, 223; *OR*, 27.1:62–70; 27.3:416–62 *passim*. Especially indicative of Meade's role are: Williams to Hancock (*OR*, 27.3:423); Butterfield to Maj. T. T. Eckert and Meade to Halleck (*OR*, 27.1:64, 66).

12. *OR*, 27.3:943–44.

13. Howard, *Autobiography*, 1:403–4; Nichols, *Toward Gettysburg*, 198, citing a letter in the Reynolds Papers written Aug. 4, 1863, by his aide, Maj. William Riddle.

14. *OR*, 27.1:923, 924; 27.2:444, 552, 607.

15. *OR*, 27.1:927.

16. McConaughy to Sharpe, Aug. 4, 1863, BMI.

17. *OR*, 27.3:419–20, 415.

18. *OR*, 27.3:943–44; 27.2:443–44, 467–68, 503, 551–52; Freeman, *Lee's Lieutenants*, 3:34–35 and note 93 on p. 35. In this note Freeman says that the two dispatches to Ewell were written on the night of June 27 and the morning of June 28, and that the earlier one reached him on the 29th. The earlier dispatch is not in the records, but the later one, written the next morning, does appear, dated 7:30 A.M. June 28 (and noted as copied from memory). Yet it contains intelligence that numerous authoritative accounts say was not in Lee's possession until the arrival of the spy Harrison on the *night* of the 28th. Moreover, Lee states in his report of the Pennsylvania campaign, "The advance against Harrisburg was arrested by intelligence received from a scout on the night of the 28th" (*OR*, 27.2:316). The conclusion is inescapable that the earlier (missing) dispatch was sent on the night of the 28th and that the second one was written on the

morning of the 29th and misdated. That sequence fits well with the probable time required for Lee's courier to travel from Chambersburg to Ewell at Carlisle; if the date June 27 is accepted for the first message, the courier must have consumed more than twenty-four hours in riding thirty miles.

Mosby (in *Stuart's Cavalry*, 117–27) accepts the June 27 date for the first message and notes that the message dated June 28 appears in correct chronological order in Lee's letterbook. But it is the only dispatch between June 25 and July 1, so it would have been placed at the same position in the book whether it was written on the 28th or 29th.

19. Schenck to [Meade], June 30, 1863, RG 393, part 1, entry 3976. (Another copy of Blair's report is in BMI; as the two copies derive from two different telegraphic transmissions of the same text, it is possible that the BMI copy arrived earlier or later than the other.)

20. Ibid. Early, however, soon turned westward.

21. Wilson, *From the Hudson to the Ohio*, 48–49. Wilson, a busy publicist in his later years, claimed that in the Gettysburg campaign "from the time Lee crossed the Potomac until his advance struck the Susquehanna . . . the enemy was never out of my sight." This statement would put him on the Potomac, but contemporary records fail to place him there. However, this bold claim is supported in a general way by a telegram from his Pennsylvania Central superior, former Assistant Secretary of War Thomas A. Scott, who wrote that Wilson "will always remain until the rebels arrive" and urged the Military Telegraph service to provide him with a cipher. For his work in furnishing intelligence in the Confederate invasions of 1862, 1863, and 1864, Wilson in 1903 received a gold medal and a commission in the Pennsylvania volunteer forces. That the award had political overtones is suggested by the fact that the governor allowed the state legislature's act to become law without his signature. (*Pennsylvania Railroad History*, 415; Scott to Maj. T. T. Eckert, June 22, 1863, book 51, Miscellaneous Telegrams, NA.)

22. Hoke, *Great Invasion*, 105; McClure, *Abraham Lincoln and Men of War-Times*, 410.

23. *OR*, 27.3:433–34 (Couch's telegrams); 27.2:503, 552, 467–68 (reports of Johnson, Rodes, and Early). These Confederate division commanders' reports establish the accuracy of Couch's intelligence. McClure, *Abraham Lincoln and Men of War-Times* (410), says it was Rodes's division on which Seiders reported. The spies' reports as they reached Harrisburg, like most and probably all others from the Pennsylvania citizen organizations, do not survive. (Wilson's unique system of reporting introduces a problem of documentation. It is likely that he transmitted his reports from crude drafts or perhaps none at all — composing his sentences and spelling them out on his telegraph key in a single operation — and that at the receiving end it was given similarly casual treatment.)

24. *OR*, 27.1:22; 27.3:476.

25. *OR*, 27.3:427 (Haupt's telegram forwarded to Meade by Schenck at Baltimore); 27.1:69 (same telegram forwarded by Stanton); Rose Diary, July 1, 1863; *Civil War Times Illustrated*, March-April 1994, p. 24. Printed in *Civil War Times* along with a letter Fonda wrote about his midnight ride is the text of the telegram he said he carried, signed by Stanton rather than Haupt. Its authenticity is questionable for several reasons. First, it was written by someone so misinformed that he thought Early's force constituted the whole of the Confederate advance in Pennsylvania; second, the locale it predicted for Early's rejoining Lee differed from the enemy's possible places of concentration that Meade predicted the next day (this indicates that the telegram was never received by Meade); third, the telegram is not in the *Official Records* or the Army of the Potomac or Secretary

of War files in the National Archives (a strong indication that it is a postwar invention). Its text was given by Fonda to an Omaha newspaperman fifty years after the event — or else the journalist was its inventor. As far as is known, it exists today in no form except as part of a newspaper article.

26. McClure, *Abraham Lincoln and Men of War-Times*, 410–15; Hoke, *Great Invasion*, 217, 222–26. Like Wilson's dispatches, Pomeroy's message to Harrisburg has defied efforts to find it in government archives, at both Harrisburg and Washington. That it furnished the information in Haupt's 12:45 A.M. message is quite clear from these facts: (1) Pomeroy stated that he sent it "about midnight"; (2) he said it stressed the probability that the enemy was concentrating at Gettysburg, a point Haupt emphasized in his message; (3) Pomeroy probably came in contact with (or at least received first-hand information on) the movement of Rodes's division on the "Petersburg pike," another point repeated by Haupt.

27. *OR*, 27.3:474; Stanton to Meade, June 30, 1863 (error for July 1), in Meade Telegrams, NA.

28. *OR*, 27.2:503; *OR Atlas*, plates 43.7 and 116.2.

29. The notation "Sent to General Meade by courier from Frederick at 2 p.m.; copy to General Schenck" apparently was added by the *OR* compilers. Information on operator staffing at Frederick is from Rose Diary, June 27, 1863.

24. Decision and Victory

1. *OR*, 27.3:460. The dispatch was signed by Gen. Williams, Meade's adjutant, but in view of the active hand that Meade was taking in intelligence matters, it must have reflected his own evaluation.

2. *OR*, 27.1:922. This dispatch from Buford to Reynolds is dated June 30, 5:30 A.M., but it reported that the prisoner was captured in a skirmish with a strong enemy picket only three miles north of Gettysburg — a position Rodes could not have reached at any early hour on the 30th. Thus it is clear that Buford's message was written July 1.

3. *OR*, 27.3:414. The addressee was probably Lt. Col. "Lije" White, whose ranger battalion was accompanying Early. On June 30 White had been sent toward Gettysburg to reconnoiter (*OR*, 27.2:468).

4. *OR*, 27.3:460, 476–77. Recent estimates have placed Lee's total strength as low as 75,000 (Pfanz, *Gettysburg: The Second Day*, 8).

5. *OR*, 27.3:460.

6. Doubleday, *Chancellorsville and Gettysburg*, 122.

7. Reynolds had on June 30 recommended to Meade that if "we are to fight a defensive battle in this vicinity, . . . the position to be occupied is just north of the town of Emmitsburg." This recommendation, however, assumed that the enemy would already have seized Gettysburg. (*OR*, 27.3:417–18.)

8. *OR*, 27.3:458; 27.1:70–71. The messages were written at noon and the postscript to Halleck at 1 P.M.

9. *OR*, 27.3:458; Williams, *Lincoln Finds a General*, 2:680–81.

10. *OR*, 27.2:317 (Lee's report); Freeman, *Lee's Lieutenants*, 3:77–78; Tucker, *High Tide at Gettysburg*, 100–101. Heth in his report of the battle said, "I was ignorant of what force was at or near Gettysburg, and supposed it consisted of cavalry, most probably supported by a brigade or two of infantry" (*OR*, 27.2:637).

11. A. L. Long, Lee's "military secretary," in a postwar article said that while army headquarters was at Chambersburg intelligence was received of the enemy's arrival at Emmitsburg, to which place Reynolds had marched on June 29

("Causes of Lee's Defeat at Gettysburg," *SHSP,* 4:122). Other evidence of scouting activities during these days is Hill's statement to Heth showing that the Federals' movement to Middleburg was known.

12. *OR,* 27.2:607; Tucker, *High Tide at Gettysburg,* 101–6.

13. Doubleday, *Chancellorsville and Gettysburg,* 124–25; Tucker, *High Tide at Gettysburg,* 106–7; *OR,* 27.1:927.

14. *OR Atlas,* plate 95, map 1; *OR,* 27.1:140; Doubleday, *Chancellorsville and Gettysburg,* 126–27; Tucker, *High Tide at Gettysburg,* 107, 408. Howard, in his *Autobiography* (1:409–12), asserts that he occupied Cemetery Ridge without orders from anyone, but Doubleday says that Reynolds gave such orders to an aide of Howard's. Doubleday points out that the advantages of holding the height "were obvious enough to any experienced commander."

15. Doubleday, *Chancellorsville and Gettysburg,* 131; Tucker, *High Tide at Gettysburg,* 110, 116; *OR,* 27.1:702–4, 696, 250–52, 728–29.

16. *B&L,* 3:285; *OR,* 27.1:696, 704, 825, 482, 531; 27.2:366, 367, 368–69; 27.3:465–68. The dispatch ordering the Sixth Corps forward was written at 4:30 P.M., and the corresponding order to the Fifth Corps at 7:00 P.M. Until the latter hour Meade expected that the Fifth would have been ordered up by General Slocum. The Second Corps had been sent forward at 12:30 P.M., at a time when Meade did not know of Buford's and Reynolds's battle and thought that Reynolds, possibly through failure to receive the new order for withdrawal in case of enemy advance, might require support (*OR,* 27.3:461).

17. *OR,* 27.1:115; Howard, *Autobiography,* 2:423.

18. *OR,* 27.1:721.

19. *OR,* 27.1:696–97; 27.2:317–19, 321–22.

20. *OR,* 27.1:115–16; 27.3:486; Williams, *Lincoln Finds a General,* 2:694; Meade, *Life and Letters,* 2:380. Lee had learned only that the force engaged by Hill and Ewell consisted of two corps, that another corps was four miles from Gettysburg, and that the rest of Meade's army was approaching, its position undetermined (*OR,* 27.2:317–18).

21. Doubleday, *Chancellorsville and Gettysburg,* 166–84 *passim;* Freeman, *Lee's Lieutenants,* 3:120, n. 62; Pfanz, *Gettysburg: The Second Day,* 117–21; E. P. Alexander, quoted in Brown, *Signal Corps, U.S.A.,* 367–68; *OR,* 27.1:116–17; 27.2:318–20.

22. Babcock (signing Sharpe's name) to Butterfield, 4:30 P.M., July 2, 1863, BMI; *Mount Vernon* (N.Y.) *Daily Argus,* Nov. 21, 1908. In "Organization of the Army of Northern Virginia" for June 22 and July 31 (*OR,* 27.3:919, 1058), Pickett's division is shown as containing four brigades, but one of them, Montgomery Corse's, had been left in Virginia. The Federals took 700 prisoners on July 1 and 660 on the 2nd; the total rose to 3202 by the end of the battle, according to Sharpe's figures (Sharpe to Butterfield, July 3, 1863, in BMI). Sixth Corps casualties in the entire battle totaled only 242; one of the three divisions in the Fifth Corps had but 210 casualties, and two of the six brigades in the Twelfth Corps had a total of 178.

23. Sharpe told this story in an address in Kingston, reported in the Kingston (N.Y.) *Daily Freeman,* Jan. 18, 1899. In his postwar years Babcock gave an account of this event that was strikingly similar (although obviously embellished), doubtless from a different source. It was printed by the Mount Vernon (N.Y.) *Daily Argus,* Nov. 21, 1908, as a follow-up to his obituary of the previous day. The story is consistent with other reports of the council of war except on one minor point: Gen. Gibbon's account (*B&L,* 3:313–14) shows Gibbon accompanying Hancock to the council, presumably arriving at the same time.

The information about Ewell's cavalry (Jenkins's brigade with Rodes, White's battalion and the 17th Virginia Cavalry with Early) is from *OR*, 27.2:443, 468, 697. The reference to the pail of water and tin cup is in Williams, *Lincoln Finds a General*, 2:707.

24. *OR*, 27.1:73–74, 127; Gibbon, in *B&L*, 3:313–14. 27.1:127.

25. Kingston *Daily Freeman*, Jan. 18, 1899; Mount Vernon *Daily Argus*, Nov. 21, 1908.

26. Butterfield to Sharpe, July 3, 1863, BMI. The reply, in Babcock's hand, lists twelve regiments from Ewell's corps from which prisoners had been taken by 8 A.M.; none of Daniel's regiments were included. Sharpe added a note saying that "Ewell's whole corps was on our right yesterday — is now attacking. All prisoners now agree that their whole army is here — that A. P. Hill & Longstreet's forces were badly hurt yesterday." The reference to Longstreet establishes July 3 as the date of this note; Babcock misdated it July 2. The composition of the Army of Northern Virginia is in *OR*, 27.3:919–22 (First and Second Corps only, dated June 22) and 1058–62 (complete army, dated July 31). Daniel's and his regimental commanders' after-action reports are in *OR*, 27.2:566–78. His accession into the Army of Northern Virginia is discussed by Freeman, *Lee's Lieutenants*, 2:710.

27. Babcock and Sharpe wrote the reply to Butterfield on the back of his note (BMI).

28. Examples of history's acceptance of the effect of Dahlgren's capture on Meade's decision to remain at Gettysburg are W. J. Seymour's account, "Some of the Secret History of Gettysburg" in *SHSP* 8:522, and Tucker's statement (*High Tide at Gettysburg*, 392) that the letters were "undoubtedly a strong factor in holding Meade on the battlefield on the night of July 2, when there were valid inducements in his mind to suggest retirement to Pipe Creek." A principal contributor to variations in this story is Jacob Hoke, *Great Invasion* (180–82); still another source is William C. Oates, "The Battle on the Right," *SHSP* 6:172.

29. *OR*, 27.3:5, 25, 28, 30, 86, 172.

30. Hooker to Adm. Dahlgren, July 20, 1863, Letters Sent, AP, book 3, 487–88.

31. This account of Dahlgren's expedition and capture is based on an article by Ted Alexander, Washington *Times*, July 24, 1993, p. B3. His findings, drawn from accounts by participants in the capture and local observers, cut across the long-standing discrepant versions and provide the first reliable treatment of the event. The story also appears in Ted Alexander and W. P. Conrad, *When War Passed This Way*.

32. *OR*, 27.3:924–25.

33. The letters, forwarded by Butterfield to Halleck, are in *OR*, 27.1:75–77. The capture was widely reported in the press; Lee learned of it from a New York *Times* dispatch that he read July 8 when his retreat had reached nearly to Hagerstown (*OR*, 27.2:300).

34. *OR*, 27.3:526.

35. The diary is in *Letters of John A. Dahlgren and His Son Ulric, 1854–1864*, Library of Congress. Information on the time of arrival of Dahlgren at Meade's headquarters is from Coddington, *Gettysburg Campaign*, 773.

36. *OR*, 27.1:761, 775, 780–81, 828–29; 27.2:447, 504–5, 511, 568–69; Tucker, *High Tide at Gettysburg*, 320; Williams, *Lincoln Finds a General*, 2:708.

37. Longstreet, in *B&L*, 3:343.

38. This account of Lee's and Longstreet's discussions follows Freeman, *Lee's Lieutenants*, 3:143–47.

39. Ibid., 146; *OR*, 51.1:1068; Tucker, *High Tide at Gettysburg*, 352. In Sharpe's

files is a tabulation in Babcock's handwriting showing Pickett's total strength as 7020. It is undated; it was probably prepared on the evening of July 2 or the next morning. Babcock had a strength figure for each of the twenty regiments in the division.

40. *OR,* 27.2:360; Freeman, *Lee's Lieutenants,* 3:158–61; Tucker, *High Tide at Gettysburg,* 358–71 *passim;* Edmond Rice and Norman J. Hall in *B&L,* 3:387–91.

41. *OR,* 27.2:360; Longstreet, in *B&L,* 3:347; Doubleday, *Chancellorsville and Gettysburg,* 202–3, 207; Freeman, *Lee's Lieutenants,* 3:162–63.

42. *OR,* 27.3:539.

Epilogue

Grant's reorganization of his intelligence service in July 1864, by dividing the work between his own headquarters and Meade's, greatly enlarged the body of intelligence records available today. Information received at each place was reported to the other; telegrams replaced much of the face-to-face discussion of evidence engaged in by Sharpe and Babcock or McEntee and Babcock. On some days Sharpe divided his time between the two headquarters; at various times McEntee held forth at one or the other for weeks on end; only Babcock was a fixture, at Meade's headquarters. Their Washington visits added substantially to the record. In the months of August and September the three men produced 132 notes and reports that appear in the *Official Records* and an indeterminate number that remained in their files. (See "Comment on Sources," p. 595, for an explanation of the condition of these files that prevents a count of the number of items they originally contained.)

Other manuscript sources used prominently in the epilogue are Sharpe's letters to his uncle, especially informative regarding his association with Grant, and the diary of General Patrick, which provides an excellent view of the key role of intelligence in the uneasy relations between Grant and Meade.

The secondary sources most used here are Freeman, *R. E. Lee* and *Lee's Lieutenants,* and Kenneth P. Williams, *Lincoln Finds a General.* Although these works over the years have been updated and supplemented many times, later writers on the period covered here have not been as intelligence-conscious as Freeman and Williams. An exception is William B. Feis, author of two articles relating to the Shenandoah Valley: "A Union Military Intelligence Failure: Jubal Early's Raid, June 12–July 14, 1864" and "Neutralizing the Valley: The Role of Military Intelligence in the Defeat of Jubal Early's Army of the Valley, 1864–1865." An article by Brian Holden Reid, "Another Look at Grant's Crossing of the James, 1864," is a close study of Grant's preparations for that movement, but beyond attributing his complete success to "systemic" flaws in Confederate warmaking, it does not explain how and why Lee was deceived. *Stanton,* a biography by Benjamin P. Thomas and Harold M. Hyman, is a useful supplement to the government records of Maddox's suit against Stanton and his correspondence on the subject with McPhail.

The arrest and imprisonment of Isaac Silver are known from James O. Hall's unpublished researches into the career of Thomas Nelson Conrad. Samuel Ruth's and F. W. E. Lohman's arrests by the Confederates are recorded in their postwar application, in collaboration with their courier, Charles M. Carter, for congressional approval of reimbursement for their services. Sharpe supported them with a statement that they were entitled to $40,000; their application was disapproved. Elizabeth Van Lew likewise failed to receive congressional reimbursement despite Sharpe's support, but President Grant rewarded her with the postmastership of Richmond. When a later administration replaced her in that position, she faced destitution, which was alleviated with money raised by army veterans, one-time prisoners whom she had assisted.

Appendix 2

1. One commander who may have shown two or all three of these skills is General Grant. He seems to have been well informed from his Vicksburg campaign onward, and his ability to apply intelligence often appears to be in the same class with Lee's. But this study has not touched his history in detail.

Appendix 3

1. Pearl Harbor histories abound, many of them written by conspiracy theorists who argue that President Roosevelt or Prime Minister Churchill deliberately sought or permitted the surprise in order to hasten the United States' entry into the war. Many of these books are out of print; one account that is both available and reliable is Trevor N. Dupuy, "Pearl Harbor: Who Blundered?" in Stephen W. Sears, ed., *World War II: The Best of American Heritage* (Boston: Houghton Mifflin, 1991).

Appendix 4

1. The eight reports confiscated in August are in the National Archives, in (1) the Report of the Dix-Pierrepont Commission, RG 59 (Records of the Department of State), entry 490 (Proceedings Relating to State Prisoners); (2) RG 59, entry 516 (Seized Correspondence of Rose O'Neal Greenhow); (3) RG 107, entry 68 (Secretary of War Records Regarding the Conduct and Loyalty of Army Officers, War Department Employees, and Citizens during the Civil War). Some items are in more than one of these files. The December report is in *OR*, ser. 2, 2:566.

Appendix 5

1. Eby, *Virginia Yankee*, 115, 126, 129, 206.

2. According to Eby, who made a detailed comparison of Strother's diary with the magazine version drawn from it, Strother in his postwar articles frequently embellished the diary's information with colorful items. For example, the diary describes Joe Hooker simply as "a fine-looking man, tall, florid, and beardless." The *Harper's* version preserves that description and adds "altogether very English in appearance." Although the addition was a point Strother had carried in his memory, many another addition was an 1866 invention. However, Eby found no indication of inventions in matters of substantial fact.

Appendix 6

1. Schuckers, *Salmon Portland Chase*, 436; Beale, ed., *Diary of Gideon Welles*, 1:99, entry for Aug. 31, 1862; Pease and Randall, eds., *Diary of Orville Hickman Browning*, 1:563; Wolseley, *American Civil War*, 66.

2. See chapter 5, note 12 and associated text.

3. *OR*, 11.3:337–38.

4. New York *Tribune*, March 13 and 14 and June 10, 1862; *OR*, 5:1086; JCCW 1863, 1:292; New York *World*, June 20, 1862; New York *Times*, June 24, 1862.

5. *OR*, 11.3:340–41. Meigs had identified one tenth of the Confederate regiments, one fifth of the brigades, and four of the ten divisions. He placed three fifths of the identified regiments in their correct brigades and five of the seven identified brigades in the correct divisions. For unexplained reasons he did not consult Northern papers, though the *New York Herald* had listed prisoners from seventy-four Confederate regiments.

6. K. P. Williams, *Lincoln Finds a General*, 1:379; *OR*, 2:288; Cox, *Military Reminiscences*, 1:250.

7. An example of McClellan's duplicity is his statement to the War Dept. on departing for the Peninsula that he was leaving 55,500 of his army for the defense of Washington. After he was out of reach the Department found that the actual number was 26,761. Sears, *To the Gates of Richmond*, 34.

8. An average of 500 is indicated by the known total of 178 regiments in the Seven Days battles and the 92,400 troop strength given by Sears in *To the Gates of Richmond*, 156.

9. For examples of this class of deserter, see McClellan Papers, nos. 8071, 8247, 14704.

10. Pinkerton, *Spy of the Rebellion*, xxxii; Pinkerton to McClellan, March 29, 1863, McClellan Papers, no. 18147.

11. Sears, *Landscape Turned Red*, 143, 296; McClellan Papers, no. 21722.

12. Sears, *To the Gates of Richmond*, 355.

13. McClellan, *McClellan's Own Story*, 76.

14. Sears, "The Curious Case of General McClellan's Memoirs," *Civil War History* 34, no. 2 (June 1988); 109.

15. Pinkerton, *Spy of the Rebellion*, 587, xxx, 567.

Appendix 7

1. *West Point Atlas*, text at plate 1:93; Catton, *Glory Road*, 263; Williams, *Lincoln Finds a General*, 2:623; Coddington, *Gettysburg Campaign*, 60–63. Freeman (*Lee's Lieutenants*, 3:6–7) says the Federal cavalry "had sensed [Lee's] movement and had begun reconnaissance." Thus he indicates that it was Pleasonton's discovery of Lee's general advance that led to the reconnaissance instead of the reverse. Coddington's treatment unfortunately lacks some of the relevant archival material, but in relying mainly on standard sources it shows that a realistic view of Pleasonton's claims need not have awaited discovery of Sharpe's files or canvassing of Hooker's papers.

2. JCCW 1865, 1:32; *B&L*, 3:261; *OR*, 27.1:141.

3. *OR*, 27.3:27–28.

4. *OR*, 27.1:33; 27.3:27–37 *passim*.

5. Mosby's most thorough treatment of this subject is in *Stuart's Cavalry*

(8–13, 16–17, 30–31). This is a 1908 work; an earlier study of the subject is in his *War Reminiscences* (1887).

6. *OR*, 27.3:49.

7. Two of the five captured papers, items 3 and 5, are in Sharpe's files (BMI). Items 1, 2, and 4 were in the Hooker Papers when they were examined by the present writer in 1963, but Coddington later found item 2 missing; thus nos. 1 and 4 were the only captured papers available to him.

8. Swinton, *Campaigns of the Army of the Potomac*, 314; for other examples of the treatment of this story see Dupuy and Dupuy, *Compact History of the Civil War,* 211; Catton, *Never Call Retreat*, 162; Glenn Tucker, "Jeb Stuart Learned on Fleet-wood Hill Federals Could Fight on Horseback Too," *Civil War Times*, Dec. 1960, p. 18; Williams, *Lincoln Finds a General,* 2:623.

9. JCCW 1865, 1:80, 85.

10. *OR*, 27.2:439–40, 546, 564; 27.1:951; 27.3:49.

11. *OR*, 27.3: 47–49, 55–56, 60–62.

Appendix 8

1. OR, 27.1:143.

2. For the movements of Longstreet's and Hill's corps see *OR*, 27.2:358, 613, 677, 366, 428; 27.3:1090; 51.2:725–26. Ewell's corps had been north of the Potomac for some days — Rodes's division since June 15, Johnson's since the 19th, and Early's since the 22nd.

3. For the positions and dates given here see Swinton, *Campaigns,* 320; *B&L,* 3:264, 267; Steele, *American Campaigns,* 1:188; Williams, *Lincoln Finds a General,* 2:640; Catton, *Glory Road,* 243; Tucker, *High Tide at Gettysburg,* 38; *West Point Atlas,* 1:93; Nevins, *Organized War,* 80; Coddington, *Gettysburg Campaign,* 113–14; Wert, *General James Longstreet,* 252.

4. Sanger and Hay, *James Longstreet: Soldier,* 161; Freeman, *R. E. Lee,* 3:50.

BIBLIOGRAPHY

Many archival collections used to only a limited extent that are cited in the Notes are not listed here. This applies also to a small number of books and articles.

Manuscripts

John C. Babcock Papers. Library of Congress.

David Rankin Barbee Collection. Georgetown University Library. Includes an unpublished biography of Rose Greenhow.

Samuel P. Bates Papers. Allegheny College Library, Meadville, Pa., and Pennsylvania Historical and Museum Commission, Harrisburg.

Michael O. Berry Collection. In private hands.

Milledge L. Bonham Papers. South Caroliniana Library, University of South Carolina.

Thomas Bragg diary. Southern Historical Collection, University of North Carolina, Chapel Hill.

Bureau of Military Information files. Record Group 393, entry 3980, National Archives.

Simon Cameron Papers. Library of Congress.

Ezra Carman manuscript, an unpublished history of the Antietam campaign. Manuscript Division, Library of Congress.

Comte de Paris journal. Fondation Saint-Louis, Amboise, France.

John S. Cooper diary. Duke University Library.

John A. Dahlgren and his son Ulric, letters, 1854–1864. Manuscript Division, Library of Congress.

William W. Folwell letters. Minnesota Historical Society, St. Paul.

Gibbon, John. An Address on the Unveiling of the Statue of Major-General George G. Meade, in Philadelphia, October 18th, 1887.

Samuel P. Heintzelman diary. Manuscript Division, Library of Congress.

Joseph Hooker Papers. Huntington Library, San Marino, Calif.

Mordecai Hunnicutt Collection. In private hands.

Kingston Collection. New York State Library, Albany.

Abraham Lincoln Papers. Manuscript Division, Library of Congress.

Thaddeus S. C. Lowe Papers. Manuscript Division, Library of Congress.

George B. McClellan Papers. Manuscript Division, Library of Congress.

David McConaughy Collection. Gettysburg College.

David McConaughy file. Military Correspondence Section, Pennsylvania State Archives, Harrisburg.

James H. McMath diary. Alabama Department of Archives and History, Montgomery.

Albert J. Myer and Henry W. Howgate. *Report of the Operations and Duties of the Signal Department of the Army, 1861–1865.* Copy on deposit, New York Public Library.

William J. Palmer Papers. Colorado State Historical Society, Denver.

Marsena Patrick Diary. Manuscript Division, Library of Congress.

Walter Pforzheimer Collection on Intelligence Service. Washington, D.C.

Luther A. Rose diary. Manuscript Division, Library of Congress.

Winfield Scott Papers. Manuscript Division, Library of Congress.

Scouts, Guides, Spies and Detectives file. Record Group 110, entry 31, Records of the Provost Marshal General's Office, National Archives.

Secret Service Accounts file. Record Group 110, entry 95, National Archives.

George Sharpe Collection. Senate House Museum, Kingston, N.Y.

Slifer-Dill Papers. Dickinson Collection, Dickinson College, Carlisle, Pa.; microfilm copy, Pennsylvania Historical and Museum Commission, Harrisburg.

Southern Historical Society Papers, 1876–1959, 52 vols. Richmond.

Edwin M. Stanton Papers. Manuscript Division, Library of Congress.

Turner-Baker Papers. Record Group 94, especially entry 179 (28 vols.) and microfilm publication m797, National Archives.

Alexander Webb letters. Yale University Library.

Books and Articles

Adams, Charles Francis. *C. F. Adams, 1835–1916: An Autobiography.* Boston, 1916.

Adams, Michael C. C. *Our Masters the Rebels: A Speculation on Union Military Failure in the East, 1861–1865.* Cambridge, Mass.: Harvard University Press, 1978.

Alexander, Edward Porter. *Fighting for the Confederacy: The Personal Recollections of General Edward Porter Alexander.* Ed. Gary W. Gallagher. Chapel Hill: University of North Carolina Press, 1989.

———. *The American Civil War.* London: Siegle, Hill, 1908. Published in the United States as *Military Memoirs of a Confederate.* New York: Scribner's, 1907.

Alexander, Ted, and W. P. Conrad. *When War Passed This Way: A Greencastle Bicentennial Publication.* Greencastle, Pa., n.p., 1982.

Andrews, J. Cutler. *The North Reports the Civil War.* Pittsburgh: University of Pittsburgh Press, 1955.

———. *The South Reports the Civil War.* Princeton: Princeton University Press, 1970. Reprint, Pittsburgh: University of Pittsburgh Press, 1985.

Bakeless, John. *Turncoats, Traitors and Heroes.* Philadelphia: Lippincott, 1959.

Baker, Lafayette C. *History of the United States Secret Service.* Philadelphia: published by author, 1867. Reprint, Philadelphia: John E. Potter and Company, 1874.

Bancroft, Frederic. *The Life of William H. Seward.* 2 vols. New York: Harper & Brothers, 1900.

Barnard, John G. *The Peninsular Campaign and Its Antecedents.* New York: Van Nostrand, 1864.

Bates, David Homer. *Lincoln in the Telegraph Office.* New York: Century, 1907.

Bates, Samuel P. *The Battle of Chancellorsville.* Meadville, Pa.: E. T. Bates, 1882.

Battles and Leaders of the Civil War. Ed. Robert U. Johnson and Clarence C. Buel. 4 vols. New York: Century, 1887–1888.

Beauregard, G. T. *A Commentary on the Campaign and Battle of Manassas of July, 1861. Together with a Summary of the Art of War.* New York: Putnam's, 1891.

Beymer, William G. *On Hazardous Service: Scouts and Spies of the North and South.* New York: Harper & Brothers, 1912.

Bidwell, Bruce W. *History of the Military Intelligence Division, Department of the Army General Staff: 1775–1941.* Frederick, Md.: University Publications of America, 1986.

Bigelow, John, Jr. *The Campaign of Chancellorsville.* New Haven: Yale University Press, 1910.

Blackford, W. W. *War Years with Jeb Stuart.* New York: Scribner's, 1945.

Blakey, Arch Fredric. *General John H. Winder C.S.A.* Gainesville: University of Florida Press, 1990.

Boatner, Mark M. *Civil War Dictionary.* New York: D. McKay, 1959.

Boyd, Belle. *Belle Boyd in Camp and Prison.* Ed. Curtis Carroll Davis. New York: Thomas Yoseloff, 1968.

Brooks, Noah. *Washington in Lincoln's Time.* New York: Century, 1895.

Brown, J. Willard. *The Signal Corps, U.S.A. in the War of the Rebellion.* Boston: U.S. Veteran Signal Corps Association, 1896.

Browning, Orville H. *The Diary of Orville Hickman Browning.* Ed. Theodore C. Pease and James G. Randall. 2 vols. Springfield: Illinois State Historical Library, 1925, 1933.

Carpenter, John A. *An Account of the Civil War Career of Oliver Otis Howard Based on His Private Letters.* Ann Arbor, Mich.: University Microfilms, 1954.

Catton, Bruce. *Glory Road.* Garden City, N.Y.: Doubleday, 1952.

———. *Mr. Lincoln's Army.* Garden City, N.Y.: Doubleday, 1951.

———. *Never Call Retreat.* New York: Doubleday, 1965.

———. *This Hallowed Ground.* New York: Doubleday, 1955.

Chase, Salmon P. *Inside Lincoln's Cabinet: The Civil War Diaries of Salmon P. Chase.* Ed. David Donald. New York: Longmans, Green, 1954.

Cleaves, Freeman. *Meade of Gettysburg.* Norman: University of Oklahoma Press, 1960.

Coddington, Edwin B. *The Gettysburg Campaign: A Study in Command.* New York: Scribner's, 1968.

Connelly, Thomas L. *The Marble Man: Robert E. Lee and His Image in American Society.* Baton Rouge: Louisiana State University Press, 1977.

Cooling, B. Franklin. *Symbol, Sword and Shield.* Hamden, Conn.: Archon Books, 1975.

Cormier, Steven A. *The Siege of Suffolk: The Forgotten Campaign, April 11–May 4, 1863.* Lynchburg, Va.: H. E. Howard, 1989.

Cox, Jacob D. *Military Reminiscences of the Civil War.* New York: Scribner's, 1900.

Crouch, Tom D. *The Eagle Aloft: Two Centuries of the Balloon in America.* Washington: Smithsonian Institution Press, 1983.

Cullum, George W. *Biographical Register of the Officers and Graduates of the USMA at West Point, New York, from Its Establishment in 1802, to 1890 with the Early History of the USMA.* 3rd Ed. New York: Houghton Mifflin, 1891.

Current, Richard N. *Lincoln's Loyalists: Union Soldiers from the Confederacy.* Boston: Northeastern University Press, 1992.

Cuthbert, Norma, ed. *Lincoln and the Baltimore Plot, 1861.* San Marino, California: Huntington Library, 1949.

Davis, William C. *Battle at Bull Run.* Baton Rouge: Louisiana State University Press, 1977.

District of Columbia Civil War Centennial Commission. *The Symbol and the Sword.* Washington, 1962.

Dix, Morgan. *Memoirs of John Adams Dix.* New York: Harper & Brothers, 1883.

Donald, David H. *Lincoln Reconsidered: Essays on the Civil War Era.* New York: Knopf, 1956.

Doster, William E. *Lincoln and Episodes of the Civil War.* New York: G. P. Putnam's Sons, 1915.

Doubleday, Abner. *The Army in the Civil War.* Vol. 6. *Chancellorsville and Gettysburg.* New York: Scribner's, 1882.

Douglas, Henry Kyd. *I Rode with Stonewall.* Chapel Hill: University of North Carolina Press, 1940.

Dowdey, Clifford, ed. *Wartime Papers of R. E. Lee.* New York: Bramhall House, 1961.

———. *The Seven Days: The Emergence of Lee.* Boston: Little, Brown, 1964.

Early, Jubal A. *War Memoirs: Autobiographical Sketch and Narrative of the War Between the States.* Ed. Frank E. Vandiver. Bloomington: Indiana University Press, 1960.

Egle, William H., ed. *Andrew Gregg Curtin.* Philadelphia: Avil Printing, 1895.

Elliott, Charles Winslow. *Winfield Scott: The Soldier and the Man.* New York: Macmillan, 1937.

Evans, Eli N. *Judah P. Benjamin.* New York: Free Press, 1988.

Feis, William B. "A Union Military Intelligence Failure: Jubal Early's Raid, June 12–July 14, 1864." *Civil War History* 36, no. 3 (Sept. 1990).

———. "Neutralizing the Valley: The Role of Military Intelligence in the Defeat of Jubal Early's Army of the Valley, 1864–1865." *Civil War History* 39, no. 4 (Dec. 1993).

Fishel, Edwin C. "Myths That Never Die." *International Journal of Intelligence and Counterintelligence* 2, no. 1 (Spring 1988).

———. "Pinkerton and McClellan: Who Deceived Whom?" *Civil War History* 34, no. 2 (June 1988).

Fisher, John Sterling. *A Builder of the West: The Life of General William Jackson Palmer.* Caldwell, Idaho: Caxton Printers, 1939.

Fladeland, Betty. "New Light on Sara Emma Edmonds, Alias Franklin Thompson." *Michigan History* 48, no. 4 (Dec. 1963).

Foote, Shelby. *The Civil War: A Narrative.* 3 vols. New York: Random House, 1958–1974.

Freeman, Douglas Southall. *Lee's Lieutenants: A Study in Command.* 3 vols. New York: Scribner's, 1942–1944.

———. *R. E. Lee: A Biography.* 4 vols. New York: Scribner's, 1934–1935.

———. *The South to Posterity: An Introduction to the Writing of Confederate History.* New York: Scribner's, 1939.

Freeman, Douglas Southall, and Grady McWhiney, eds. *Lee's Dispatches to Jefferson Davis.* New York: Putnam's Sons, 1957.

French, Steve. "Wagoners' Fight Opened Way for Retreat." *Washington Times,* Nov. 11, 1995, p. B3.

Fry, James B. *McDowell and Tyler in the Campaign of Bull Run, 1861.* New York: Van Nostrand, 1884.

Gaddy, David W. "William Norris and the Confederate Signal and Secret Service Bureau." *Maryland Historical Magazine* 70, no. 2 (summer 1975).

Gallagher, Gary, et al. *Third Day at Gettysburg and Beyond.* Chapel Hill: University of North Carolina Press, 1994.

Gates, Theodore B. *The Ulster Guard (20th N.Y. State Militia) and the War of the Rebellion.* New York: B. Tyrrel, 1879.

George, Joseph, Jr. "'Black Flag Warfare': Lincoln and the Raids Against Richmond and Jefferson Davis." *Pennsylvania Magazine of History and Biography,* July 1991, 291–318.

Gibbon, John. *Personal Recollections of the Civil War.* New York: Putnam's, 1928.

Gordon, George H. *History of the Campaign of the Army of Virginia under John Pope.* Boston: Houghton, Osgood, 1880.

Grant, Ulysses S. *The Papers of Ulysses S. Grant.* Ed. John Y. Simon. 20 vols. to date. Carbondale: Southern Illinois University Press, 1967–.

Greene, A. Wilson. "Opportunity to the South: Meade versus Jackson at Fredericksburg." *Civil War History* 33, no. 4 (December 1987).

Greenhow, Rose. *My Imprisonment and the First Year of Abolition Rule at Washington.* London: Richard Bentley, 1863.

Hall, James O. "The Spy Harrison." *Civil War Times Illustrated,* Feb. 1986.

Hamlin, Augustus C. *The Battle of Chancellorsville.* Bangor, Me.: published by author, 1896.

Harrison, Constance Cary. *Recollections Grave and Gay.* New York: Scribner's, 1911.

Harrison, Noel G. *Chancellorsville Battle Sites.* Lynchburg, Va.: H. E. Howard, 1990.

Hassler, Warren W., Jr. *General George B. McClellan: Shield of the Union.* Baton Rouge: Louisiana State University Press, 1957.

Hay, John. *Lincoln and the Civil War in the Diaries and Letters of John Hay.* Tyler Dennett, ed. New York: Dodd, Mead, 1939.

Haydon, F. Stansbury. *Aeronautics in the Union and Confederate Armies.* Baltimore: Johns Hopkins Press, 1941.

Hebert, Walter H. *Fighting Joe Hooker.* Indianapolis: Bobbs-Merrill, 1944.

Henderson, G. F. R. *Stonewall Jackson and the American Civil War.* New York: Longmans, Green, 1898.

Hendrick, Burton J. *Lincoln's War Cabinet.* Boston: Little, Brown, 1946.

Hennessy, John. *The First Battle of Manassas: An End to Innocence.* Lynchburg, Va.: H. E. Howard, 1989.

———. *Return to Bull Run: The Campaign and Battle of Second Manassas.* New York: Simon & Schuster, 1993.

Henry, Robert S. *The Story of the Confederacy.* New York: Grosset & Dunlap, 1931.

Hesseltine, William B. *Civil War Prisons: A Study in War Psychology.* Columbus: Ohio State University Press, 1930.

History of Cumberland and Adams Counties [Pennsylvania]. Chicago: Warner, Beers, 1886.

Hoke, Jacob. *The Great Invasion of 1863.* Dayton: W. J. Shuey, 1887.

Hood, John B. *Advance and Retreat: Personal Experiences in the United States & Confederate States Armies.* Ed. Richard N. Current. Bloomington: Indiana University Press, 1959.

Horan, James D., and Howard Swiggett. *The Pinkerton Story.* New York: Putnam's, 1951.

Hotchkiss, Jed, and William Allan. *The Battlefields of Virginia — Chancellorsville.* New York: D. Van Nostrand, 1867.

Howard, Oliver Otis. *Autobiography.* 2 vols. New York: Baker & Taylor, 1907.

Hubbell, John T., ed. *Battles Lost and Won.* Westport, Conn.: Greenwood Press, 1975.

Humphreys, Andrew A. *From Gettysburg to the Rapidan: The Army of the Potomac, July, 1863, to April, 1864.* New York: Scribner's, 1883.

———. *The Virginia Campaign of '64 and '65.* New York: Scribner's, 1883.

Johnston, Joseph E. *Narrative of Military Operations.* New York: D. Appleton, 1874.

Johnston, Robert M. *Bull Run: Its Strategy and Tactics.* Boston: Houghton Mifflin, 1913.

Joinville, Prince de. *The Army of the Potomac: Its Organization, Its Commander, Its Campaign.* New York: Anson D. Randolph, 1862.

Jones, John B. *A Rebel War Clerk's Diary.* 2 vols. Philadelphia: J. B. Lippincott, 1866.

Jones, Virgil. *Eight Hours Before Richmond.* New York: Henry Holt, 1957.

———. *Gray Ghosts and Rebel Raiders.* New York: Henry Holt, 1956.

———. *Ranger Mosby.* Chapel Hill: University of North Carolina Press, 1944.

Kamm, Samuel R. *The Civil War Career of Thomas A. Scott.* Philadelphia: University of Pennsylvania, 1940.

Kearny, Philip. *General Philip Kearny, Battle Soldier of Five Wars.* New York: Putnam's, 1937.

Kerbey, J. O. *The Boy Spy.* Chicago: Donohue, Henneberry, 1892.

———. *Further Adventures of the Boy Spy in Dixie.* Washington: National Tribune, 1898.

Keyes, Erasmus D. *Fifty Years' Observation of Men and Events, Civil and Military.* New York: Scribner's, 1884.

Leech, Margaret. *Reveille in Washington: 1860–1865.* New York: Harper & Brothers, 1941.

Lincoln, Abraham. *The Collected Works of Abraham Lincoln.* Roy P. Basler, ed. 9 vols. New Brunswick, N.J.: Rutgers University Press, 1953–1955.

Livermore, Thomas L. *Days and Events, 1860–1866.* Boston: Houghton Mifflin, 1920.

———. *Numbers & Losses in the Civil War.* Boston: Houghton Mifflin, 1901. Reprint, Bloomington: Indiana University Press, 1957.

Longstreet, James. *From Manassas to Appomattox: Memoirs of the Civil War in America.* Philadelphia: Lippincott, 1896.

Manakee, Harold R. *Maryland in the Civil War.* Baltimore: Maryland Historical Society, 1961.

Marshall, Charles. *An Aide-de-Camp of Lee.* Frederick Maurice, ed. Boston: Little, Brown, 1927.

Marvel, William. *Burnside.* Chapel Hill: University of North Carolina Press, 1991.

Maslowski, Peter. "Military Intelligence Services in the American Civil War: A Case Study." *The Intelligence Revolution: A Historical Perspective.* Proceedings of the Thirteenth Military History Symposium, U.S. Air Force Academy, 1988.

McClellan, George B. *The Civil War Papers of George B. McClellan: Selected Correspondence, 1860–1865.* Ed. Stephen W. Sears. New York: Ticknor & Fields, 1989.

———. *McClellan's Own Story.* New York: Charles L. Webster, 1887.

———. *Report on the Organization of the Army of the Potomac, and of Its Campaigns in Virginia and Maryland.* Washington: Government Printing Office, 1864.

McClellan, Henry B. *The Life and Campaigns of Major General J. E. B. Stuart.* Boston: Houghton Mifflin, 1885.

McClure, Alexander K., ed. *Annals of the War, Written by Leading Participants, North and South.* Philadelphia: Times Publishing, 1879.

———. *Abraham Lincoln and Men of War-Times.* Philadelphia: Times Publishing, 1892.

———. "Recollections of Antietam." On file at Antietam National Battlefield Park.

McPherson, James. *Battle Cry of Freedom.* New York: Oxford University Press, 1988.

Meade, George G. *The Life and Letters of George Gordon Meade.* 2 vols. New York: Scribner's, 1913.

Meigs, Montgomery C. "General M. C. Meigs on the Conduct of the Civil War." *American Historical Review* 26, no. 2 (Jan. 1921).

Military Signal Communications. Ed. Paul J. Scheips. 2 vols. New York: Arno Press, 1980.

Miller, Francis Trevelyan. *The Photographic History of the Civil War.* New York: Review of Reviews, 1911.

Miller, Robert H. "Letters of Lieutenant Robert H. Miller to His Family, 1861–1862." Ed. Forrest P. Connor. *Virginia Magazine of History and Biography* 70, no. 1 (Jan. 1962).

Mogelever, Jacob. *Death to Traitors: The Story of Lafayette C. Baker.* New York: Doubleday, 1960.

Moore, Frank, ed. *Rebellion Record: A Diary of American Events.* New York: Putnam's, 1861–1863; Van Nostrand, 1864–1868.

Morn, Frank. *The Eye That Never Sleeps: A History of the Pinkerton National Detective Agency.* Bloomington: Indiana University Press, 1982.

Mosby, John S. *Mosby's War Reminiscences and Stuart's Cavalry Campaigns.* New York: Dodd, Mead, 1887.

———. *The Memoirs of John S. Mosby.* Ed. Charles W. Russell. Boston: Little, Brown, 1917. Reprint, Gaithersburg, Md.: Olde Soldier Books, 1987.

Murfin, James V. *The Gleam of Bayonets: The Battle of Antietam and the Maryland Campaign of 1862.* Baton Rouge: Louisiana State University Press, 1965.

Neely, Mark E., Jr. *The Fate of Liberty: Abraham Lincoln and Civil Liberties.* New York: Oxford University Press, 1991.

Netherton, Nan, et al. *Fairfax County: A History.* Fairfax County (Va.) Board of Supervisors, 1978.

Nevins, Allan. *The War for the Union.* Vol. 1. *The Improvised War, 1861–1862.* Vol. 2. *War Becomes Revolution, 1862–1863.* Vol. 3. *The Organized War, 1863–1864.* New York: Scribner's, 1959–1961.

Nichols, Edward Jay. *Toward Gettysburg: A Biography of General John F. Reynolds.* University Park: Pennsylvania State University Press, 1958.

Nicolay, John G. *The Army in the Civil War.* Vol. 1. *The Outbreak of Rebellion.* New York: Scribner's, 1882.

Nolan, Alan T. *Lee Considered: General Robert E. Lee and Civil War History.* Chapel Hill: University of North Carolina Press, 1991.

Oates, William C. "The Battle on the Right." *Southern Historical Society Papers* 6, no. 102.

O'Brien, John E. *Telegraphing in Battle.* Scranton, Pa.: n.p., 1910.

Osborn, Hartwell, "On the Right at Chancellorsville," *Military Essays and Recollections.* Chicago: Military Order of the Loyal Legion, 1927.

O'Toole, G. J. A. *Honorable Treachery: A History of U.S. Intelligence, Espionage, and Covert Action from the American Revolution to the CIA.* New York: Atlantic Monthly Press, 1991.

O'Toole, G. J. A. *The Encyclopedia of American Intelligence and Espionage.* New York: Facts on File, 1988.

Palfrey, Francis W. *The Army in the Civil War.* Vol. 5. *The Antietam and Fredericksburg.* New York: Scribner's, 1882.

Paris, Comte de. *History of the Civil War in America.* 4 vols. Philadelphia: Porter & Coates, 1875–88.

———. "We Prepare to Receive the Enemy Where We Stand." Ed. Mark Grimsley. *Civil War Times Illustrated,* May 1985.

Patrick, Marsena R. *Inside Lincoln's Army: The Diary of Marsena Rudolph Patrick.* Ed. David Sparks. New York: Thomas Yoseloff, 1964.

Patterson, Robert. *A Narrative of the Campaign in the Valley of the Shenandoah in 1861.* Philadelphia: John Campbell, 1865.

Pearson, Henry G. *James S. Wadsworth of Geneseo.* New York: Scribner's, 1913.

Pfanz, Donald C. "Negligence on the Right: The Eleventh Corps at Chancellorsville." *Morningside News* (Dayton), 1984.

Pfanz, Harry W. *Gettysburg: The Second Day.* Chapel Hill: University of North Carolina Press, 1987.

Pierson, William W. "The Committee on the Conduct of the Civil War." *American Historical Review* 23, no.4 (April 1918).

Pinkerton, Allan. *The Spy of the Rebellion.* Chicago: A. G. Nettleton, 1883. Reprint, Lincoln: University of Nebraska Press, 1989.

Plum, William R. *The Military Telegraph During the Civil War.* 2 vols. Chicago: Jansen, McClurg, 1882. Reprint, New York: Arno Press, 1974.

Raab, Stephen S. "A Midnight Ride." *Civil War Times Illustrated,* March–April 1994.

Reader, Frank S. *History of the First West Va. Cavalry, Formerly the Second Virginia Infantry, and of Battery G, First West Va. Light Artillery.* New Brighton, Pa.: F. S. Reader, 1890.

Reid, Brian Holden. "Another Look at Grant's Crossing of the James, 1864." *Civil War History* 39, no. 4 (Dec. 1993).

Richardson, Albert D. *The Secret Service, the Field, the Dungeon, and the Escape.* Hartford, Conn.: American Publishing, 1865.

Roman, Alfred. *The Military Operations of General Beauregard.* 2 vols. New York: Harper & Brothers, 1884.

Ross, Ishbel. *Rebel Rose: Life of Rose O'Neal Greenhow.* New York: Harper & Brothers, 1954.

Rowan, Richard W. *The Story of Secret Service.* New York: Literary Guild of America, 1937.

Sanger, Donald B., and Thomas R. Hay. *James Longstreet: I. Soldier. II. Politician, Officeholder, and Writer.* Baton Rouge: Louisiana State University Press, 1952.

Scharf, J. Thomas. *History of Baltimore City and County from the Earliest Period to the Present Day.* Philadelphia: Louis H. Everts, 1881.

Scheips, Paul J. *Albert James Myer, Founder of the Army Signal Corps: A Biographical Study.* 2 vols. Ann Arbor, Mich.: University Microfilms, 1966.

Schmidt, C. T. "G-2, Army of the Potomac." *Military Review,* July 1948.

Schoonmaker, Marius. *History of Kingston, New York.* New York: Burr Printing, 1888.

Schuckers, *The Life and Public Services of Salmon Portland Chase.* New York: D. Appleton, 1874.

Scott, Winfield. *Memoirs of Lieut.-General Scott.* New York: Sheldon, 1864.

Sears, Stephen W. "The Curious Case of General McClellan's Memoirs." *Civil War History* 34, no. 2 (June 1988).

———. *George B. McClellan: The Young Napoleon.* New York: Ticknor & Fields, 1988.

———. *Landscape Turned Red: The Battle of Antietam.* New York: Ticknor & Fields, 1983.

———. "The Last Word on the Lost Order." *MHQ* 4, no. 3 (Spring 1992).

———. *To the Gates of Richmond: The Peninsula Campaign.* New York: Ticknor & Fields, 1992.

Seymour, W. J. "Some of the Secret History of Gettysburg," *Southern Historical Society Papers* 8.

Sigaud, Louis A. *Belle Boyd: Confederate Spy.* Richmond: Dietz Press, 1944.

———. "Mrs. Greenhow and the Rebel Spy Ring." *Maryland Historical Magazine* 41, no. 3 (Sept. 1946).

Smith, Gustavius W. *Generals J. E. Johnston and G. T. Beauregard at the Battle of Manassas July, 1861.* New York: G. C. Crawford, 1892.

Smith, Henry Bascomb. *Between the Lines: Secret Service Stories Told Fifty Years After.* New York: Booz Brothers, 1911.

Smith, Lamar W. "Rose O'Neale Greenhow: The Spy of the Confederacy." Thesis, University of Alabama, 1948.

Sorrell, G. Moxley. *Recollections of a Confederate Staff Officer.* New York: Neale, 1905.

Starr, Louis M. *Bohemian Brigade: Civil Newsmen in Action.* New York: Knopf, 1954.

Steele, Matthew. *American Campaigns.* 2 vols. Washington: War Department, 1909.

Strong, George Templeton. *Diary.* Ed. Allan Nevins and Milton H. Thomas. Seattle: University of Washington Press, 1988.

Strother, David H. *A Virginia Yankee in the Civil War: The Diaries of David Hunter Strother.* Ed. Cecil D. Eby, Jr. Chapel Hill: University of North Carolina Press, 1961.

[Strother, David H.] "Personal Recollections of the War, by a Virginian." *Harper's New Monthly Magazine,* June–Nov. 1866.

Swanberg, W. A. *First Blood: The Story of Fort Sumter.* New York: Scribner's, 1957.

Swinton, William. *Campaigns of the Army of the Potomac.* New York: Charles B. Richardson, 1866.

Tatum, Georgia Lee. *Disloyalty in the Confederacy.* Chapel Hill: University of North Carolina Press, 1934.

Taylor, Richard. *Destruction and Reconstruction: Personal Experiences of the Late War.* New York: D. Appleton, 1879.

Thomas, Benjamin P. *Abraham Lincoln: A Biography.* New York: Knopf, 1952.

Thomas, Benjamin P., and Harold M. Hyman. *Stanton: The Life and Times of Lincoln's Secretary of War.* New York: Knopf, 1962.

Thompson, Luther. *Wiring a Continent: The History of the Telegraph Industry in the United States, 1832–1866.* Princeton: Princeton University Press, 1947.

Tidwell, William A. *April '65: Confederate Covert Action in the American Civil War.* Kent, Ohio: Kent State University Press, 1995.

Tidwell, William A., James O. Hall, and David Winfred Gaddy. *Come Retribution: The Confederate Secret Service and the Assassination of Lincoln.* Jackson: University Press of Mississippi, 1988.

Trefousse, Hans L. *Ben Butler: The South Called Him Beast.* New York: Twayne Publishers, 1957.

Trudeau, Noah André. *The Last Citadel: Petersburg, Virginia, June 1864–April 1865.* Boston: Little, Brown, 1991.

Tucker, Glenn. *High Tide at Gettysburg.* Indianapolis and New York: Bobbs-Merrill, 1958.

———. "Jeb Stuart Learned on Fleetwood Hill Federals Could Fight on Horseback Too." *Civil War Times,* Dec. 1960.

U.S. Congress. *Reports of the Joint Committee on the Conduct of the War.* Washington, 1863, 1865.

U.S. Naval War Records Office. *Official Records of the Union and Confederate Navies in the War of the Rebellion.* 30 vols. Washington: Government Printing Office, 1894–1927.

U.S. War Department. *The War of the Rebellion: A Compilation of the Official Records of the Union and Confederate Armies.* 128 parts in 70 vols. and atlas. Washington: Government Printing Office, 1880–1901.

Van Santvoord, Cornelius. *The One Hundred and Twentieth Regiment, New York State Volunteers.* New York: 120th N.Y. Regimental Union, 1894.

Wagner, Arthur L. *The Service of Security and Information.* 11th ed. Kansas City: Hudson-Kimberly, 1903.

Warner, Ezra J. *Generals in Blue.* Baton Rouge: Louisiana State University Press, 1964.

Webb, Alexander S. *The Peninsula: McClellan's Campaign of 1862.* New York: Scribner's, 1881.

Weisberger, Bernard A. *Reporters for the Union.* Boston: Little, Brown, 1953.

Welles, Gideon. *Diary of Gideon Welles.* Ed. Howard K. Beale. 3 vols. New York: Norton, 1960.

Wert, Jeffrey D. *Mosby's Rangers.* New York: Simon & Schuster, 1990.

Whan, Vorin E. *Fiasco at Fredericksburg.* University Park: Pennsylvania State University Press, 1961.

West Point Atlas of American Wars. Ed. Vincent J. Esposito. New York: F. A. Praeger, 1959.

Williams, Kenneth P. *Lincoln Finds a General.* 5 vols. New York: Macmillan, 1950–1959.

Williams, T. Harry. *Lincoln and His Generals.* New York: Knopf, 1952.

Wills, Mary Alice. *The Confederate Blockade of Washington, D.C. 1861–62.* Parsons, W. Va.: McClain, 1975.

Wilson, James Harrison. "A Staff Officer's Journal on the Vicksburg Campaign." *Journal of the Military Service Institution of the United States* 43 (1908): 93–109, 261–75.

Wilson, William Bender. *A Few Acts and Actors in the Tragedy of the Civil War in the United States.* Philadelphia: published by author, 1892.

———. *From the Hudson to the Ohio.* Philadelphia: Kensington Press, 1902.

———. *History of the Pennsylvania Railroad Company.* 2 vols. Philadelphia: Henry T. Coates, 1899.

Wolseley, Garnet. *The American Civil War: An English View.* Charlottesville: University Press of Virginia, 1964.

Newspapers

Baltimore: *American and Commercial Advertiser, Gazette, Sun*
Chicago: *Tribune*
Cincinnati: *Gazette, American, Enquirer*
Greencastle, Pa.: *Pilot*
Kingston, N.Y.: *Argus, Freeman and Journal, Daily Freeman, Daily Leader*
Mount Vernon, N.Y.: *Daily Argus*
New York: *Herald, Times, Tribune, World*
Philadelphia: *Inquirer*
Richmond: *Dispatch, Examiner, Whig*
Washington: *Star, National Republican, National Intelligencer, Chronicle*

SOURCES AND ACKNOWLEDGMENTS

During years when no collection of Civil War intelligence records was known to exist in the National Archives, my Archives research leading to this book consisted of examining payrolls and other administrative records to identify scouts, spies, and detectives. By 1959, when the files of the intelligence bureau established by General Hooker were found, I had identified 4200 Union and 600 Confederate intelligence agents. The archivist who supplied me with the records that yielded this mass of data was the late Sara Dunlap Jackson. She was to have had a role in the next phase, which would consist of searching for those 4800 names in the indexes to records of army commands. Some of the records thus located would provide entry to the elusive intelligence story.

That exhaustive search, which would have occupied a number of man-years exceeding a lifetime, thus forcing me to hire assistants, was obviated by the discovery of the records of Hooker's bureau, which covered enough of the war to form the basis of a sizable book. Archivist Francis Heppner ran across these papers (while browsing, as he says) in an assemblage of unorganized records of the Army of the Potomac. He immediately called them to my attention; the first glance told me that this was a discovery of the first importance.

It was apparent that these papers at some early point had been sequestered, for they all lacked the stamped legend "Examined for War Records," used by compilers of the *Official Records of the War of the Rebellion*. Its absence indicated that these envelopes and bundles had never been opened since the war.

Many of the National Archives collections to which I would have been led by pursuit of the 4800 identified agents have in recent years been tapped with little effort on my part, through the present Archives staff's familiarity with their holdings. Archivist Michael Musick has been indispensable in locating documents vital to the intelligence story. Other chief sources of manuscript material have been the McClellan Papers, in the Library of Congress, which contain Allan Pinkerton's intelligence reports, and the Hooker Papers, now the property of the Huntington Library of San Marino, California.

Of much help to me has been the generosity of James O. Hall, of McLean, Virginia, well known as the leading expert in Lincoln assassination history, who has also investigated the careers of a number of leading spies, both Northern and Southern. I have enjoyed collaborating with Peter Maslowski of the University of Nebraska faculty, author of a 1988 paper that covers Federal and Confederate intelligence in all theaters—a uniquely broad study; with William B. Feis of Ohio State University, whose forthcoming doctoral dissertation, "The Role of Military Intelligence in the Campaigns of U. S. Grant," will be a valuable complement to my study of the eastern campaigns; and with Curtis Carroll Davis of Baltimore, the expert on Belle Boyd.

The resources of the extensive collection of intelligence-related manuscripts owned by Walter Pforzheimer of Washington have been continuously available to me. I have also had the benefit of a close association with George O'Toole of Mount Vernon, New York, the highly informed author of *The Encyclopedia of American Intelligence and Espionage*. My concern with Civil War signaling and cryptography has been aided by Paul Scheips of Silver Spring, Maryland, Albert Myer's biographer, and William Price of Vienna, Virginia, a keen student of U.S. Signal Corps history. On occasions early in my researches when I needed to know the contents of messages preserved only in enciphered form and the cipher overmatched my own cryptanalytic skill (not a difficult feat), it was readily solved by Rosemary Youmans, of Alexandria, Virginia.

The manuscript was read by two intelligence professionals—the late Louis Tordella, who served as a sounding board in many face-to-face discussions, and Henry Knoche, my colleague in Korean War days, who critiqued my interpretations and perceived the larger implications of many of my findings. A third reader was Stephen Sears, the most intelligence-conscious historian Civil War literature has ever had; he made direct contributions to the manuscript by catching errors, by providing obscure source material that helped me over many a rough spot, and by identifying passages where a point needed sharpening.

Old friends and new acquaintances who made one-time contributions to my research are too numerous to recall, with these outstanding exceptions: Joseph L. Harsh of George Mason University, a McClellan specialist, who introduced me to that general's papers by the extended loan of his copies of them; Cecil D. Eby of the University of Michigan, who sent me the section of David Hunter Strother's journal that established Strother's role in reporting the Confederates' departure from Winchester for Manassas in July 1861, and the rejection of his report at the Federals' Shenandoah Valley headquarters; William Marvel, Burnside's biographer, and battlefield park historian Wilson Greene, who clarified for me the long misunderstood malfunctioning of Burnside's plan for his Fredericksburg battle; and Mark Grimsley of Ohio State University, for his translation of the Comte de Paris journal.

Assistance in the preparation of photographs was provided by Tony Clements of Fairfax, Virginia, and August Scheele of Arlington, Virginia, both of whom were familiar with modern techniques for restoring the readability of faded pencil handwriting, which they applied to documents connected with the Federals' signal deception of Lee in the Chancellorsville campaign. Especially gratifying has been the renewing after many years of my association with Robert Benjamin of Shepherdstown, West Virginia, who translated my vaguely expressed cartographic ideas into a set of handsome maps.

This book has been a family project. The earliest draft, 180,000 words, was typed errorlessly by my wife, Gladys, and her mother, the late Lou Ellen Leech. Eventually typewriter gave way to computer, thanks to the persuasiveness of our daughter, Katie Horan. Our son, Reverdy Fishel, an intelligence historian in his own right, worked through tangles of source material to clarify my treatment of two troublesome episodes, Pope's battlefield errors and Lee's unimpeded departure from Fredericksburg, the first move in his Pennsylvania campaign.

Considerable benefit has accrued to this book from the suggestions of my editors, Harry Foster and Peg Anderson, whose patience was never exhausted by my proclivity for making revisions.

INDEX

Page numbers in italics refer to maps.

Abells, Frankie, 253–54
Adams Express Company, 283
Aiken, John, 252–53, 255
Aldie, battle of, 457–58,*476, 482,* 498
Alexander, Capt. E. Porter, 39–40,
    148, 161
Allen, A. R., 111
"Allen, E. J." *See* Pinkerton, Allan
Allen, Ezra, 443
Allen, James, 443
all-source intelligence,3–4; Hooker's
    "invention" and use of, 298–99,
    300, 321; abolished by Meade, 540–
    41; revived by Grant, 548
American Revolution: espionage in,
    8, 9, 298, 496, 541
Anderson, Gen. Richard H., 197,
    223, 227, 228, 234, 303, 318, 342,
    364; Bureau's report on, 319; and
    Chancellorsville campaign,
    376,377, 381, 389; and battle of
    Chancellorsville, 389, 393, 404;
    situation after Chancellorsville,
    416, *418;* new command, 420; and
    Gettysburg campaign, 492, 507,
    512; and battle of Gettysburg, 525,
    533
Anderson, Gen. Robert, 12, 16, 218
Anderson Cavalry, 218–19, 233, 558
Andersonville prison, 543
Annapolis, 70, *539*
Antietam, battle of, 235–40, 275,

289, 586; R. E. Lee and, 235–37,
    239, 240; casualties of, 237
Antietam campaign, 211–40, *212,*
    293; R. E. Lee and, 211, 212, 213,
    215, 217, 221, 222–35, 238–40;
    Gen. McClellan and, 212, 213–17,
    222–23, 224, 226, 227–28, 229–30,
    232, 233–35, 236–40; Pinkerton
    and, 213, 215; Gen. Pleasonton
    and, 213–14, 216, 221–22, 224,
    227, 228; estimate of Confederate
    forces, 214; Gen. Halleck and, 214,
    215, 216, 217, 224, 235; Harper's
    Ferry in, 214, 215, 217, 219, 220,
    221, 223, 224, 227, 232–35, 240;
    Pennsylvania as false objective of,
    214, 217–21; Stonewall Jackson
    and, 214, 216, 218, 220, 221, 223,
    224, 225, 231, 232, 234–35, 238,
    239, 242, 248; Gen. A. P. Hill and,
    215, 235, 236, 237; Gen. Long-
    street and, 215, 220, 225, 228, 229,
    231, 232, 239, 248; scouting and,
    215, 218–22; estimate of Confeder-
    ate numbers, 216, 217; Gen. Stuart
    and, 216, 224; Gen. Burnside and,
    217, 222, 228, 236; Gen. Hooker
    and, 218, 228, 236, 238, 280; Gen.
    Porter and, 218, 237, 241, 243;
    Lee's Special Orders No. 191, 222–
    28, 229, 230–33, 234, 235, 238–40,
    530; Gen. D. H. Hill and, 223, 224,
    225, 228–29, 239; battle of South
    Mountain, 228–29, 230, 232–33,

238, 248, 275, 289, 586; fall of Harper's Ferry, 232–35; analysis of, 237–40; signalmen in, 265; intelligence successes, 564; intelligence failures, 566

Appomattox, 535, 557, 558

Aquia, 79, 183, 252, 299, 371, 418

Armies Operating Against Richmond, 546–47

Armistead, Gen. Lewis, 534

Army of the James, 543–44, 550–51

Army of the Potomac (Confederate): Pinkerton and McClellan's estimates of, 2, 86, 92, 95, 102–29, 141–42, 581–87; intelligence on components of, 6, 164; estimates at First Bull Run, 44–46, 47; Buxton on, 86–87; reports on size of Johnston's forces, 86–87, 91, 93, 95, 96, 99, 107, 109, 110, 118, 127, 160, 581, 582, 586; Webster's reports on, 89–91, 97–101; report on size of Magruder's forces, 91, 126, 142; Ellis on, 91–94; estimate of Rodes's forces, 124, 376; estimates of Early's forces, 124, 319, 321, 376; estimate of forces for Peninsula campaign, 126–27, 141–42; estimates of Lee's strength, 160, 162, 163, 164, 319–20, 375–77, 376, 402–3, 462, 492–93, 494, 581–87; Lee reorganizes, 263; Sharpe's report on, 319–22; Silver's report on, 320, 361; Babcock on strength of, 375–77, 392, 393; composition and strength revealed in Chancellorsville campaign, 375–77; estimates of Longstreet's strength, 376, 402–3; estimates of Stuart's forces, 376, 425–26, 428, 433, 591; Maddox's report on, 402–3, 555–56; strength for Pennsylvania campaign, 415–17, 418; Lee reorganizes, 420–21; Pleasonton tracking, 421, 425, 431, 435–36, 437, 438, 441, 447, 454, 588–92, 593; Capt. McEntee tracking, 421–23, 422, 425, 426–28, 430–31, 434, 435–40; estimates of A. P.

Hill's strength, 455; Meigs's estimates of, 582–83, 585; Official Records on forces of, 586

Army of the Potomac (Federal; see also individual campaigns): under McClellan, 80; Lincoln divides, 137; withdrawn from the Peninsula, 162–63; returns to Virginia after Antietam, 250–54; Burnside assumes command and reorganizes, 255, 256; Hooker assumes command, 273, 276; Hooker reorganizes, 281–82; Hooker demands reinforcements after Chancellorsville, 414; Stuart rides on right of, 486–88; Meade assumes command, 495

Army of Virginia (Federal): creation of, 162, 182; and Second Bull Run, 182–210; Pope commands, 184–85

Ashby, Col. Turner, 170, 171, 172, 174, 177

Atlanta, fall of, 554

Averell, Gen. William W., 139, 310, 314, 330, 350; and Manassas evacuation, 141; and battle of Kelly's Ford, 330–31, 341, 357–58, 368; and Chancellorsville, 402, 405, 410

Babcock, John C., 153–54, 155, 215, 257–59, 262, 290, 292, 297, 300, 314, 423, 540, 548, 550, 551, 556, 557, 598; hired by Burnside, 257–59, 266, 272, 273; on McClellan and Burnside, 259; interrogations by, 262, 300–302; Hooker and, 286–87, 300; salary of, 294; and report on Bureau's findings, 319, 321, 322; on Pinkerton's work, 322; and Chancellorsville campaign, 341, 374, 375–77, 382, 383, 392, 401, 404, 405, 409, 410, 413, 414; accurate estimate of Confederate strength, 375–77, 392, 393; and Lee's reorganization, 420; and Gettysburg campaign, 457, 460, 461, 463–64, 466, 467, 471, 473, 478, 479, 480, 481, 486, 489; and battle of Gettysburg, 526–27, 528,

Babcock, John C. (*cont.*)
529, 530, 536, 537, 569; and intelligence after Gettysburg, 540, 541; postwar career, 558
Baker, Col. Edward, 168
Baker, Lafayette C., 24–28, 36, 54, 55, 73, 75, 85 95, 130, 242, 247, 254, 279, 292, 359, 471, 595; contemporaneous with Pinkerton, 55–56, 255; and Greenhow, 64, 65, 66; memoirs of, 65, 599; as special provost marshal of the War Department, 284; rivalry with Patrick, 284–85, 292; hold on Burnside, 285; as source, 596–97, 599
balloon surveillance (Confederate), 161
balloon surveillance (Federal), 3, 5, 6, 10, 55, 81, 83, 84, 212, 365, 570; Myer and, 38, 81, 443; and evacuation of Manassas, 132, 135, 138, 139, 140–41, 298; and Peninsula campaign, 146, 154, 156, 161; in Shenandoah Valley, 166–67; after Antietam, 251, 261; Burnside's failure to use, 261, 267; Hooker and, 278; Sharpe and, 298, 300; and Chancellorsville campaign, 344, 384, 389–90, 394, 395; after Chancellorsville, 418, 423; end of use of, 442–43; Lowe's history of, 442–43
Ball's Bluff, 79, *183*
Ball's Bluff, battle of, 83, 87, 91, 168–69, 282, 400
Baltimore, 18; Webster's correspondents in, 89
Baltimore American, 355
Baltimore and Ohio Railroad, *166, 212, 441,* 444, *445,* 448, *469,* 471, *482, 485,* 486
Baltimore Sun, 111, 591
Bangs, George H., 72, 113, 215, 255; and Peninsula campaign, 147
Banks, Gen. Nathaniel Prentiss, 22–23, 87, 118, 124–25, 134, 139, 143, 182, 545; and Peninsula campaign, 158, 162; and Shenandoah Valley campaign, 165, 168, 169–75, 181; and Kernstown, 170–71; intelligence collecting, 171–72, 211,

251, 259; and Second Bull Run, 185, 186, 188, 197, 200; tracking Lee after Antietam, 251–52, 253–54; Rose Greenhow's reports on, 577, 578
Banks's Ford, *299, 398, 418;* and Chancellorsville campaign, 369, 372, 373, 388, 394, 395
Bardwell (scout), 241, 242
Barksdale, Gen. William, 308, 388, 393
Barnard, Gen. John G., 33; and McClellan's Urbanna plan, 136, 137; and Peninsula campaign, 142, 150
Barnum's Hotel, Baltimore, 291
Bartow, Francis, 34
Bates, Edward, 20
Bates, Samuel P., 382
Battail, Louis, 295
Battle of Chancellorsville, The (Bates), 382
Baxley, Catherine V., 335
Bayard, Gen. George, 197, 209, 251, 253
Beardsley, Col. John, 197
Beaufort: siege of, 73
Beauregard, Gen. P. G. T., 16, 25, 81–82, 85, 110, 133, 157, 415, 531, 549, 556, 575; at First Bull Run, 29, 31, 32, 33, 35, 36, 41, 43, 48, 58, 96; Rose Greenhow's information to, 58, 59, 60, 61, 62, 575–78; reports on size of his forces, 86–87, 99; telegram on his army's weakness, 184
Beckham, Maj. R. F., 431, 590
Bee, Gen. Barnard, 34, 40
Bell (Federal informant), 407–8, 409
Benjamin, Judah P., 71, 72, 89, 92, 93, 98–99, 119, 125, 337
Benning, Henry, 407
Benson, Joseph, 125
Berry, Col. Hiram G., 135
Berryville, *212, 441, 445, 469, 476, 482, 485;* Lee at, 468
Bigelow, John, 375
Birney, Gen. David, 269, 528; and battle of Chancellorsville, 396, 398

Blackburn's Ford, battle of, 31–32, 33–34

Black Horse Cavalry, 351–52, 363, 364

blacks: runaway slaves (*see* contrabands); Pinkerton and, 110–11; free refugees, 117–18, 119

Blair, Francis P., Jr., 19, 20

Blair, S. S., 513–14

Blenker, Gen. Louis, 83, 171

Blockley, Eugene, 176

Bonham, Gen. Milledge L., 59, 60

Booth, John Wilkes, 187

Bouvier, Lt. John V., 314

Bowers, Col. Theodore, 547

Body, Belle, 26, 175–77, 254

Body, Capt. William H., S., 450–51, 454

Brag, Gen. Braxton, 214, 531, 542

Brandy Station, battle of, *422, 431–32, 433, 434, 435, 436, 437, 442, 463, 476,* 588–92

Breckinridge, John C., 15

Brewer, Maj. Melvin, 448

Briscoe, Fred, 170

Bristoe campaign, 542–43

Bristoe Station: encounter at, *183,* 199

Brooks, Lt. J. B., 364

Brooks, Gen. W. T. H., 472

Brown, Spencer Kellogg, 249

Browne, William H., 92

Browning, Orville H., 581

Bryan, Capt. E. Pliny, 74, 124, 331

Bryan, William P., 74

Buchanan, James, 11, 12, 13, 14, 16, 58

Buell, Gen. Don Carlos, 184, 218

Buford, Gen. John, 195, 197, 198, 199, 201, 202, 209, 425, 426, 435, 569; and cavalry reconnaissance, 195, 197, 198, 199, 201, 202, 209, 425, 426, 435, 569; and Gettysburg campaign, 502, 506, 507, 510–11, *512,* 513, 515, 518; and battle of Gettysburg, 511, 519, 520, 521, 522, 523, 536

Bull Run, *30, 79, 183*

Bull Run, first battle of, 46–49, 53, 62, 63, 77, 82, 96, 277, 288, 536

Bull Run, first campaign, 3, 10, 25, 27, 29–52, 134–35, 579–80; Gen. McDowell and, 29, 31–43, 47–52, 59, 60, 580; inadequacy of intelligence in, 29, 37–41, 51–52; Gen. Johnston and, 31, 32, 33, 37, 40, 43, 44, 45, 46, 47, 49, 50, 61, 579–80; Gen. Patterson and, 31, 35, 42, 43, 45, 47–48, 49; Gen. Stuart and, 32, 43–44, 579; Stonewall Jackson and, 32–33, 34, 40; Confederate battlefield signaling in, 37–40, 265; Federal cavalry reconnaissance at, 40–41, 43–44; Northern newspapers and, 41–42; estimates of Confederate forces at, 44–46, 47; topography and, 44–46; Johnston's forces join, 46–50, 51, 579–80; Rose Greenhow's espionage and, 58–61, 62–63; intelligence successes, 563; intelligence failures, 565

Bull Run, second campaign and battle of, 52, 182–210, *183,* 237, 260, 275, 280, 293, 337, 382, 407, 569, 582; Gen. Pope and, 182, 184, 186, 187–91, 192, 193–96, 197, 198, 199, 200–210, 212, 280; Gen. Sigel and, 182, 188, 190, 191, 192, 197, 198, 199, 200, 205; R. E. Lee and, 182, 190, 191, 192, 193–94, 195, 196, 197, 198, 199, 201, 204, 207; Gen. Banks and, 185, 186, 188, 197, 200; Confederates occupy rail junction at Gordonsville, 185–86, 187; Stonewall Jackson and, 185–86, 187, 189, 194, 199, 200–202, 205, 207, 210; Gen. Longstreet and, 187, 188, 189, 195, 201, 202, 203, 204–6, 209; Gen. Stuart and, 190, 192, 193, 196, 199, 200; Gen. McDowell and, 191–92, 200, 201, 202, 204, 205; Harter's espionage in, 191–94; capture of Lee's letter to Stuart, 192–94; Fitz John Porter and, 195, 199, 202, 203, 205, 206; Gen. McClellan and, 195, 196, 199, 206, 207; Gen. Halleck and, 198, 206, 207; cavalry reconnaissance and, 208,

Bull Run (*cont.*)
  209; intelligence successes, 564; intelligence failures, 566
Bunnell, Jesse, 153
Bureau of Military Information, 3–4,
  294, 318–22; staffing of, 293–94;
  pay rates in, 294–95, 595–96; and
  all-source intelligence, 298–99,
  548; role of, 298–300; report on
  first month's findings, 318–19,
  320, 321–22; and Lee's reorganization of army, 421; name dropped,
  540; files as source, 595
Burnside, Gen. Ambrose Everts, 2,
  206, 302, 315, 325, 332, 342, 354,
  370, 373, 529, 586, 598; and Cape
  Hatteras expedition, 72; at
  Fredericksburg in second Bull Run
  campaign, 189; and Antietam campaign, 217, 222, 228, 236; assumes
  command of Army of the Potomac,
  255–56; at First Bull Run, 256;
  background of, 256; reorganizes
  corps, 256; and Fredericksburg
  campaign, 256–62, 264, 266–74;
  and intelligence activity, 257–59,
  260–62, 266–67, 272, 273, 300; request for pontoons, 259–60; failure
  to use cavalry reconnaissance, 261–
  62; complaints against, 271–72;
  and Mud March, 272–73, 290, 346;
  relieved of command, 273, 276; on
  Hooker, 280–81; Hooker disbands
  Grand Divisions of, 281; and aker,
  285
Buschbeck, Adolphus, 377–78
Butler, Gen. Benjamin F., 18, 72, 120,
  545, 547, 551; and Army of the
  James, 543, 551
Butterfield, Gen. Daniel, 282–83,
  288, 300, 312, 314, 330, 342, 352,
  359, 416, 426, 439, 440, 542, 589,
  591; chief of staff to Hooker, 282–
  83; and circulation of intelligence
  reports, 300, 323; and military security, 325; and writing of planted
  message, 348, 349; and Chancellorsville campaign, 362, 364, 370,
  374, 382, 383, 385, 386; and battle
  of Chancellorsville, 388, 389, 390,

  391, 392, 394, 401, 405–6, 407,
  408; and fears of Confederate invasion, 456; and Gettysburg campaign, 457, 460–61, 468, 477, 509;
  and battle of Gettysburg, 526–27,
  529, 530
Buxton, Frank Lacy, 86–88, 89, 94,
  97, 336; on Confederate forces, 86–
  87

"C.A.H." (Pinkerton agent), 95–97,
  111
Callahan, James J., 179, 180, 363
Callan, John F., 11–12, 57, 71, 72
Cameron, Simon, 19, 20, 57, 78, 80,
  81, 103; and McClellan's estimates
  of enemy forces, 103, 107, 109
Cammack, James W., 548
Camp, Lt. Henry, 148, 538
Campaigns of the Army of the Potomac
  (Swinton), 382–83, 593
Camp and Outpost Duty for Infantry
  (Butterfield), 282
Campbell, William, 90
Cape Hatteras, 72–73
Carney, Anson, 421, 422–23, 430
Carney, Edward A., 421, 430
Carney, Yaller, 455
Carr, Lt. J. H., 496
Carson, T. D., 457, 495
Carter, Charles M., 552
Casey, Gen. Silas, 155
Cashtown Pass, 505
Castle, Capt. Davis E., 396, 399, 542
Castle Thunder, 246, 249, 553–54
Cavalry Corps (*see also* cavalry recon-
  naissance *and individual command-
  ers*): Hooker organizes as corps,
  281–82
cavalry reconnaissance, 3, 5, 10, 77,
  569–70 (*see also individual leaders*);
  Confederate advantages in, 5, 6; at
  First Bull Run, 40–41, 43–44;
  McClellan and, 55; during Phony
  War, 82–83; Buford and, 195, 197,
  198, 199, 201, 202, 209, 425, 426,
  435, 569 (*see also* Buford); and Second Bull Run, 208, 09; after Antietam, 253; Burnside's failure to use,
  261–62; Hooker and, 278, 279,

281–82, 300; Sharpe and, 298, 300; in Chancellorsville campaign, 389; in battle of Chancellorsville, 398–99, 405; tracking Lee after Chancellorsville, 421–32; at battle of Brandy Station, 431–32, 433, 434, 435, 436, 437, 442, 487; major successes, 569–70

Cedar Creek, *539;* battle of, 550

Cedar Mountain, battle of, 163, 188–89

Cemetery Hill, 523, 525

Cemetery Ridge, 523, 524, 525

Central Intelligence Agency, 299

Centreville, *30, 79, 183, 539;* Federal espionage in, 35, 36, 90, 91–92, 95–96, 97; estimates of Confederate forces, 82–83, 128, 92, 95–96, 99, 107, 109, 112, 118, 122–23, 125–26, 127, 142–43; Johnston's evacuation from Manassas and, 131–43; rail line to Manassas, 132; Meade reaches in October 1863, 543

Chain Bridge: Confederates at, 81

Chambersburg, Pa., *472, 474, 482, 485, 500, 512, 539;* Confederates at, *485,* 489–90, 498, 499, *500,* 505, 507, 513, 516–17

Chancellorsville, *252, 299, 317, 371, 398, 539*

Chancellorsville, battle of, 83, *317,* 365, 387–411, *398, 408,* 412, 483, 537, 570; Gen. Couch and, 387, 391, *398,* 409; Gen. Meade and, 387, 390, 391, *398,* 409, 412; Gen. Sickles and, 387, 388, 391, *398,* 409; Gen. Slocum and, 387, 390, 391, 395, 396, *398,* 404, 409, 413; Gen. Hooker and, 387–91, 404, 393, 395, 399, 400, 401–2, 405, 406, 407, *408,* 408, 409–11, 412, 529; Gen. Butterfield and, 388, 389, 390, 391, 392, 394, 401, 405–6, 407, 408; Gen. Sedgwick and, 388, 390, 391, 392, 393, 394, 395, 404, 405, *408,* 408, 409, 410; Gen. Anderson and, 389, 393, 404; Lt. Taylor and, 389, 391, 395; Stonewall Jackson and, 389, 390, 392,

393, *398,* 399, 400, 401, 403, 410; Gen. Stoneman and, 391, 402, 407; Hooker suspends attack, 391; R. E. Lee and, 391, 394, 401, 402, 403, 404–5, 407, *408,* 412, 413, 415; Gen. Pickett and, 392, 406, 407, 409, 412, 415; Gen. Stuart and, 392, 404, *408;* Gen. Early and, 393, 394–95, 404, 406; Gen. Howard and, 395–96, 397, *398,* 398, 399, 400–401, 409; Gen. Devens and, 396, 397, 400, 401; cavalry reconnaissance in, 398–99, 405; scouting and, 398–99; analysis of Hooker's failure in, 400–402, 404–5; Gen. Hood and, 407, 409, 410, 412, 413, 415; caring for casualties of, 412–13; Federal retreat, 412–13

Chancellorsville campaign, *299,* 307–411, *371,* 570; R. E. Lee and, 4, 341, 343–44, 345, 348–49, 353, 355, 356, 366, 367, 369, 370, 372, 373, 375, 376, 379–80, 381, 382, 390; intelligence and, 1–2, 382–84, 389–90, 400–402; Babcock and, 341, 374, 375–77, 382, 383, 392, 401, 404, 405, 409, 410, 413, 414; Gen. Hooker and, 341, 355, 373–77, 342, 344–46, 349, 350, 351, 352, 358–59, 361, 363, 365–67, 368–70, *371,* 379, 381, 382–83, 385–86; balloon surveillance at, 344, 384, 389–90, 394, 395; Federal Signal Corps and, 344, 347–48, 355–57, 374, 384, 385, 389, 393, 396; Provost Marshal Patrick and, 344, 351, 352, 353, 355–56, 357, 358–59, 374, 386, 388, 408; scouting and, 344, 350–51; U.S. Mine Ford and, 344–45, 361, 364, 366, 369, 370, 371, 373, 375, 381; Confederate Signal Corps and, 347–48, 355–57; Confederates solve or obtain enemy's flag code, 347–48; Federals use hoax messages, 348–49; Col. Sharpe and, 349, 351, 352, 373–74, 377, 379, 382, 383, 404, 406, 410, 413; size of Federal forces disclosed in press,

Chancellorsville campaign (*cont.*)
349–50; Gen. Sedgwick and, 352–
53, 359, 369–71, *371*, 372, 373,
377, 379, 380, 383, 384, 385, 386,
387; Gen. Stuart and, 353, 356,
363, 367, 369, 373, 376, 378, 379,
380, 381, 382; picket duty in, 355–
56; Gen. Stoneman and, 360, 362,
364, 366–67, 368, 369, 370, 372,
373, 375, 378; Isaac Silver and,
360–62, 369, 370, 374–75, 383,
389; estimates of Confederate numbers, 361; W. H. F. Lee and, 361,
362–63, 364, 366, 368, 379; deserter informants in, 362, 374,
406; flag messages and, 362; Gen.
Butterfield and, 362, 364, 370,
374, 382, 383, 385, 386; Gen.
Longstreet and, 362, 364, 376,
379, 384, 392, 402, 405, 408, 409,
410; prisoner informants and, 362,
386, 406; Stonewall Jackson and,
362, 365, 366, 375, 376, 383–84;
Fitzhugh Lee and, 362–63, 368,
369, 383; pontoons and, 366, 372,
377–82; Federal Twelfth Corps
and, 368, 370, 380, 388, 395;
Kelly's Ford crossing, 368–70, 372,
374–75, 377–82; Gen. Howard
and, 370, *371*, 378, 380, 387; Gen.
Couch and, *371*, 372, 373, 385;
Gen. Meade and, *371*, 372, 378;
Gen. Sickles and, *371*, 385; Gen.
Slocum and, *371*, 372, 378, 379,
384, 387, 390, 391; Gen. Pleasonton and, 372, 373, 399, 405; Gen.
A. P. Hill and, 374, 376, 377, 384,
393; Gen. Rodes and, 374, 384;
Gen. Trimble and, 374, 376, 377,
384; Prof. Lowe and, 374, 384,
386, 389, 393, 394; Confederate
strength estimated, 375–77; Gen.
Anderson and, 376, 377, 381, 389;
Gen. Early and, 376, 377, 388;
Gen. McLaws and, 376, 383, 388,
389, 393, 404; cavalry reconnaissance in, 389; telegraph lines and,
389–90; intelligence successes,
564; intelligence failures, 566–67
Charleston: siege of, 343–44

Chase, Salmon P., 581
Chase, William, 406, 407
Chesapeake and Ohio Canal, 461
Chester Gap (Blue Ridge), *441*, *476*;
Confederates move through, 432
Chicago Tribune, 111
Chickahominy River, *145*, 155, *539*
Chickamauga, battle of, 542
Chilton, Col. R. H., 394
Chinn Ridge encounter, 34
ciphers, 4, 59, 61, 62, 184, 347–48,
402, 551. *See also* cryptography
City Point, *539*; intelligence head-
quarters at, 547
Clark, Henry T., 72, 73
Clark, Col. John, 174, 196–97, 237
Clay Guard, 282
Clifford, James, 413
Cline, Sgt. Milton W., 292, 306–10,
317, 327, 332, 361, 440, 501, 543,
546, 552; and the Neck, 327–28;
and Gettysburg campaign, 459,
460, 463, 470, 471, 477, 501, 502–
3, 531, 536; in 1864, 546, 552
Clinton, Capt. Henry P., 272, 294,
295
Clinton, Sir Henry, 456
"clothesline code," 314, 324
codes, 4 (*See also* ciphers; cryptogra-
phy); newsmen's use of, 325
Cold Harbor, *539*; battle of, 545
Cole, Sgt. Daniel, 292, 310, 321, 333–
35, 363, 423
Committee of Safety, St. Louis, 20
Committee on the Conduct of the
War, 112; Hooker and, 368;
Pleasonton and, 433, 588, 591
compensation: for spies, 21, 595–96
Comstock, Capt. Cyrus B., 344–45,
346, 365, 368, 442
Confederate bureaucracy, 11
Confederate currency: devaluation,
110; Sharpe's use of,
295–96
Confederate forces. *See* Army of
Northern Virginia
Confederate intelligence, successes
and failures of, summarized, 563–
68
Conrad, Thomas Nelson, 549

Constitution (steamer), 144
contraband informants, 5, 73, 152, 185, 278, 592; Pinkerton and, 111, 114, 115, 120–21; and Manassas withdrawal, 139; Hooker and, 278, 279; Lee's concern over, 419; and Lee's move on Pennsylvania, 424, 437–38, 439, 440, 442; Charley Wright, 437–38, 439, 440, 442, 535, 592
contraband mail and materials, 56, 69, 73, 75, 311, 313; Maryland to Virginia, 73–75, 95; spies' cover as smugglers, 291–92, 296, 327–29, 555–59; on Northern Neck, 326, 327–28, 334, 338
Cook, A. H., 211
Cooper, Gen. Samuel, 10, 530, 531, 532
Copperheads, 27
Corps of Observation, 166–67
Couch, Gen. Darius N., 220–21, 302; commands Second Corps, 282; and Chancellorsville campaign, *371,* 372, 373, 385; and battle of Chancellorsville, 387, 391, *398,* 409; and Gettysburg campaign, 456, 457, 472, 473, 475, 477–78, 484, 489, 490, 491, 496, 502, 505, 508, *512,* 513, 514, 515, 516, 518; and battle of Gettysburg, 521, 522
couriers, 18–19; and Gettysburg campaign, 489–90, 491; and Richmond campaign, 552–53
Cowgill, L. P., 246, 247
Cox, Gen. Jacob, 228, 583
Craige, James, 341–42
Crampton's Gap, *212;* in Antietam campaign, 229
Crawford, William, 333, 340–41, 403
Cridge, Alfred, 176
Critcher, Col. John, 418–19
Cross, George, 119
Cross Keys, *166*
Cross Keys, battle of, 179, 180
cryptography, 184, 265, 347–48, 553. *See also* ciphers
Culpeper, 79, *183, 252, 299, 418, 422, 441, 469, 476, 539;* Confederates at, 423, 424, 427, 428, 430,

431, 434, 435, 438, 440, *441,* 442, 455, 588–92; Lee departs, 455–56; Lee's retreat to, 540
Culp's Hill, 523
Curtin, Andrew G., 19, 214, 216, 218, 219, 220, 221, 227, 230, 232, 241, 243, 244, 248, 489, 491, 517
Cushing, Capt. Samuel T., 265, 348, 419; and signal deception, 348

Dahlgren, Adm. John A., 531
Dahlgren, Capt. Ulric, 256, 261–62, 543, 556
Dana, William, 176
Daniel, Gen. Junius, 462, 530, 592
Daniels, Capt. Nahum, 475
Davenport, Lt. John I., 544
Davis, Benjamin F., 436
Davis, Capt. Charles L., 551
Davis, Jefferson, 11, 12, 25, 39, 69, 71, 75, 82, 88, 92, 96, 107, 126, 194, 211, 331, 337, 338, 413, 419, 530, 531, 532, 557; forged letter of, 88–89; and Johnston's evacuation from Manassas, 131, 132, 133; and Peninsula campaign, 144; and suspected double agent, 186–87; alleged plan to assassinate, 543
Dawson, George W., 215
decoding and deciphering, 264–66
deserter informants, 3, 5, 10, 125, 158–59, 167, 215, 334–35, 569; pseudo-deserters, 5, 117, 150, 291, 297, 462; at First Bull Run, 45; Pinkerton and, 55, 103, 111, 113–14, 115–17, 167; in Peninsula campaign, 158–59; Hooker and, 279; Federals transfer north for security, 323; in Chancellorsville campaign, 362, 374, 406; after battle of Chancellorsville, 416, 417–18, 435; Lee's concern over, 419; on Confederates at Culpeper, 435; on Confederate move north, 437
desertions: Federal efforts to manage, 283–84
Devens, Gen. Charles, Jr., at Ball's Bluff, 83; and battle of Chancellorsville, 396, 397, 400, 401
Dilger, Capt. Hubert, 397–98

Dix, Gen. John A., 67, 69, 74, 75, 94, 291, 304, 312, 313, 332, 342, 343, 424, 437, 531, 543, 596; commanding on the Peninsula, 291–92, 302; "plan by smuggling," 333, 335, 340, 403; during battle of Chancellorsville, 409, 410
Dodd, Henry W., 292, 421, 422
Donellan, George, 57, 61, 68–69
double agents, 87–88, 94, 186–87, 336–38, 555–57
Doubleday, Gen. Abner, 269, 366, 405, 502, 521, 523
Douglas, Maj. Henry Kyd, 176
Dranesville, 79, 183; reconnaissance around, 83–84
Duffee, Dr. Washington, 176
Dulaney, G. L., 116
Du Pont, Adm. Samuel F., 70, 343
Duval, Bettie, 59

Eagle (balloon), 390
Eakin, Samuel, 95
Early, Gen. Jubal, 187, 303, 306, 309, 318, 319, 546, 547, 548, 549–50; at First Bull Run, 34; estimate of forces of, 376; and Fredericksburg campaign, 269; and Chancellorsville campaign, 376, 377, 388; and battle of Chancellorsville, 393, 394–95, 404, 406; situation after Chancellorsville, 416, 418; new command, 420; and Gettysburg campaign, 467, 473, 474, 475, 482, 488, 489, 492, 495, 501, 507, 510, 512, 513, 515; and battle of Gettysburg, 520, 524, 525, 526, 530, 533; in Valley and attack on Washington, 546, 549–50
Edmonds, Emma, 599
Edwards Ferry, 212, 482, 498
18th Georgia Infantry (see also McLaws): and Gettysburg campaign, 478, 480
Eisenhower, Gen. Dwight, 239
Electoral College: election of Lincoln, 14–15
Eleventh Corps (Army of the Potomac), 256, 261, 346, 542 (see also Howard); and Chancellorsville cam-

paign, 368, 370; and battle of Chancellorsville, 380, 388, 395, 398, 400, 402, 403; and Gettysburg campaign, 509; and battle of Gettysburg, 524, 525, 535; transfer to Sherman's army, 542
Ellis, Frank M., 74–75, 91–94, 100, 101, 292, 338; reports on Confederate forces, 107, 109, 126; arrest of, 109
Ely's Ford, 299, 371, 398; and Chancellorsville campaign, 370, 380, 405
Elzey, Gen. Arnold, 417
Emancipation Proclamation, 255
Emmett, Nugent T., 116, 121
Emmitsburg, Md., 485, 497, 500, 505, 512
espionage, 3, 5, 569 (see also spies); pre-Civil War American, 8–9; Pinkerton and, 55; Halleck on, 184, 245; Harter and, 191–92, 193–94, 208, 248, 382, 463, 470, 537, 569; and Antietam campaign, 215–16
European authorities' references to intelligence, 9
Evans, Gen. Nathan G., 40, 91
Evans, Robert M., 242
Ewell, Gen. Richard L., 60, 172, 173, 174, 185, 187, 199, 309, 312, 318, 393, 592; commands Second Corps, 420; situation after Chancellorsville, 423, 424, 429–30, 432, 439, 441; and capture of Winchester, 445, 448, 449, 451, 454, 460, 468, 572; and Gettysburg campaign, 455, 456, 461, 463, 465, 466–67, 468, 469, 471, 472, 473, 474, 477, 482, 485, 486–87, 488, 489, 491, 493, 498, 500, 505, 506, 507, 508, 509, 511, 512, 513, 514, 515, 516, 517–18; and battle of Gettysburg, 519, 520, 521, 525, 526, 528, 529–30, 533, 535; retreat after Gettysburg, 540

Fairfax Court House, 30, 79, 183, 445, 469, 476, 482, 539; Federal espionage in, 35, 36; Confederates at, 82

Fair Oaks (Seven Pines), battle of, 156–57

Fall Leaf, Captain, 20

Falmouth, *79, 183, 252, 299, 371, 398, 476, 539;* rumored underwater telegraph connection to Fredericksburg, 354–58; in Chancellorsville campaign, 389

Fayetteville, N.C.: ordnance works at, 96

Federal intelligence, successes and failures of, summarized 563–68

Fields, William, 122–23

Fifth Corps (Federal; *see also* Meade): at Hanover Court House, 155; and Chancellorsville campaign, 370, 380, 388, 401, 404; and Gettysburg campaign, 509, 524, 526, 527, 571

Fifth Virginia Cavalry, 458

15th Pennsylvania Cavalry, 219

First Arkansas Regiment, 99

First Corps (Confederate), 549–50 (*see also* Longstreet); at Chancellorsville, 370, 393, 404

First Corps (Federal; *see also individual commanders*): and Gettysburg campaign, 509, 524

First Maryland Regiment (Confederate), 99

First Maryland Regiment (Federal), 174

First North Carolina Cavalry, 122

First Virginia Cavalry, 122

First (West) Virginia Regiment, 185

Fisher, Capt. Benjamin F., 321, 344, 419, 424, 435, 551; chief signal officer, Army of the Potomac, 540–41

Fisher, William, 120–21

Fitzhugh, Maj. Norman R., 192–93

flag signals. *See* interception of enemy signals; Signal Corps (Confederate); Signal Corps (Federal)

flags of truce: Hooker restricts, 322, 324

Flat Foot, 20

Florida: secession of, 16–17

Floyd, Gen. John B., 12, 179

Flying Dutchmen. *See* Eleventh Corps

Fonda, Ten Eyck H., 516

Fort Devens, 400

"Fort Greenhow," 66–68, 258

Fort Monroe, 126, 138, 142, *145, 539;* signal training at, 38, 39; and Peninsula campaign, 142, 143, 144, 145, 150

Fort Pickens, 16–17

Fort Stedman engagement, 554–55

Fort Sumter, 12, 16, 41

Franklin, Benjamin, 88, 340

Franklin, William B., 154, 174, 206, 224, 229, 233, 236, 302; and Fredericksburg campaign, 268, 269, 270, 272, 273, 289

Franklin's Crossing, battle at, 425

Fraser, Capt. (signal officer), 426

Frederick, *166, 212, 441, 469, 476, 500, 512, 539;* in Antietam campaign, 214, 216, 217, 222, 223; Federal headquarters (in Gettysburg campaign), 494–95, 498, 499, 500, 501, 502; telegraph connection lost, 502

Fredericksburg, *30, 79, 166, 183, 252, 299, 371, 398, 418, 441, 445, 476, 539;* McDowell occupies, 172; in Chancellorsville campaign, 389, 393

Fredericksburg campaign and battle, 250–74, *252,* 289, 293; Gen. Sigel and, 256, 261, 262, 263, 264, 266; R. E. Lee and, 256–57, 267, 269; casualties, 270; Gen. Burnside and, 256–62, 264, 266–74; Gen. Longstreet and, 257, 263, 264, 267; Burnside's intelligence in, 257–59, 260–62, 263, 273–74; Gen. Halleck and, 259–60, 267, 272, 273; Stonewall Jackson and, 263, 264, 267; Confederate Signal Corps and, 264–66; Federal Signal Corps and, 264–66; Gen. A. P. Hill and, 267, 268; Gen. Hooker and, 268, 269, 270, 272; Gen. Smith and, 268, 269, 272; Gen. Franklin and, 268, 269, 270, 272, 273, 289; Gen. Meade and, 269, 270; intelligence failures, 566

Fredericksburg, second battle. *See* Chancellorsville campaign
Frederick the Great, 9
Frémont, Gen. John Charles, 81, 182, 266, 334; and Peninsula campaign, 158, 162; and Shenandoah Valley campaign, 171, 172, 177–78, 179, 180, 181
French, Gen. William Henry, 270, 494, *512*
Friend, Col., 397
Frietschie, Barbara, 216
Front Royal, *79, 166, 183, 469, 476, 539;* battle of, 174–75, 176, 177

Gaines, W. J., 215
Gaines's Mill, *145;* battle of, 160–61
Galena (ship), 162
Gamble, William, 523
Gardner, Alexander, 154
Garnett, Gen. Richard, 464, 534
Gates, Maj. Theodore B., 288
Geary, Gen. John, 185
General Jackson (Indian scout), 20
Germanna Ford, *299, 371;* in Chancellorsville campaign, 378–79, 380–81
Getty, Gen. G. W., 270
Gettysburg, *474, 482, 485, 512, 539*
Gettysburg, battle of, 443, 519–37; Gen. Buford and, 511, 519, 520, 521, 522, 523, 536; Gen. Ewell and, 519, 520, 521, 525, 526, 528, 529–30, 533, 535; Gen. Meade and, 519, 520, 521, 522, 523, 524–25, 526, 527–28, 529, 530, 532, 533, 534–35; July 1, 519–25; Gen. Early and, 520, 524, 525, 526, 530, 533; Gen. Longstreet and, 520, 521, 525, 526, 527, 533, 535; R. E. Lee and, 520, 522, 523, 525–26, 527, 529, 530, 531–32, 533, 534, 535, 536; Gen. A. P. Hill and, 521, 522, 524, 525, 533; Gen. Couch and, 521, 522; Gen. Howard and, 523, 524, 525, 528; Gen. Rodes and, 524, 525, 526, 533; Gen. Slocum and, 524, 528, 529, 530, 533; Gen. Anderson and, 525, 533; Gen. Hood and, 525, 533; Gen.

Pickett and, 525, 527, 529, 533–35; July 2, 525–33; Capt. McEntee and, 526, 535; Col. Sharpe and, 526–30, 532–33, 536, 569; Gen. Johnson and, 526, 530, 531, 533; Babcock and, 526–27, 528, 529, 530, 536, 537, 569; Gen. Butterfield and, 526–27, 529, 530; Capt. Dahlgren and, 530–31, 532; Pickett's charge, 533–35; July 3, 533–37; summary of effect of Federal intelligence, 535–37
Gettysburg campaign, 3, 4, 5, 444–537, *469, 474, 476, 482,* 569–70; Gen. Johnson and, 461, 466, 473, 489, 490, 495, 507, *512,* 513, 515, 517; intelligence and, 1, 3, 456–57, 459–60, 470–71, 480–83, 486, 535–37; battle of Brandy Station, 431–32, 433, 434, 435, 436, 437, 442; battle of Winchester, 444–53, 454, 455, 456, 468, 572–74; fall of Martinsburg, 452, 454, 455, 456; Gen. Halleck and, 454, 459, 460, 472, 477, 489, 494–95, 496, 497, 508, 521; Gen. Longstreet and, 454, 455, 457, 458, 459, 463, 464–65, 466, 468, *469,* 470, 471, 473, 477, 478, 479, 480, 481, *482, 485,* 486, 489, 492, 493, 496, 498, 499, *500,* 501, 507–8, *512;* Gen. Stuart and, 454, 458, 459, 460, 465, 466, 468, *469,* 470, 481, *482,* 483, *485,* 486–88, 489, 508, *512,* 515, 535; prisoner informants and, 454, 477; R. E. Lee and, 454, 455, 457, 458, 459, 460, 461, 465, 467, 473, 475, 478, 479; Capt. McEntee and, 454–55, 457, 458, 460, 464, 467, 480, 486, 503, 531; Col. Sharpe and, 455, 456, 457, 458, 460, 461, 462, 463, 465, 466, 467, 470–71, 473, 475, 477, 480, 484, 486, 491, 493, 494, 495, 496, 497, 502, 503, 504, 508, 510, 511, 569; Federal Signal Corps and, 455, 471, 483; Gen. A. P. Hill and, 455, 457, 459, 461, 462, 464–65, 468, *469,* 470, 473, 478, 479, 480, 481, *482,* 483, *485,* 490, 492, 493, 498, *500,* 501, 505,

507–8, 511, *512*, 593; Gen. Ewell and, 455, 456, 461, 463, 465, 466–67, 468, *469*, 471, 472, 473, *474*, 477, *482*, *485*, 486–87, 488, 489, 491, 493, 498, *500*, 505, 506, 507, 508, 509, 511, *512*, 513, 514, 515, 516, 517–18; Gen. Sedgwick and, 455, *512*, 528; Gen. Jenkins and, 455–56, 457, 463, 466, 473, *474*, 486, 488, 490, 493, 496, 514–15; determining Confederate objective, 456; Gen. Couch and, 456, 457, 472, 473, 475, 477–78, 484, 489, 490, 491, 496, 502, 505, 508, *512*, 513, 514, 515, 516, 518; Gen. Hooker and, 456, 457, 459, 460, 463, 465, 466, 468, 473, 477, 479, 480–81, 483, 484, 491, 494–95, 536, 593; scouting and, 456–57, 471–72; Babcock and, 457, 460, 461, 463–64, 466, 467, 471, 473, 478, 479, 480, 481, 486; battle of Aldie, 457, 458, 498; Fitzhugh Lee and, 457, 486, 496, 508; Gen. Butterfield and, 457, 460–61, 468, 477, 509; Gen. Pleasonton and, 457, 458, 468, 470, 483, 486, 487, 492, 498, 502, 508, 531, 588–92; Gen. Schenck and, 457, 460, 471, 479, 496, 516, 518; Provost Marshal Patrick and, 457, 460, 464, 465, 466, 491; Gen. Hampton and, 459, 486; R. E. Lee and, 459, 480, 508, 510, 513, 517; Sgt. Cline and, 459, 460, 463, 470, 471, 477, 501, 502–3, 531, 536; Gen. Tyler and, 460, 461, 463, *469*, 472, 473, 475, 477, 478, 480, *482;* Gen. Rodes and, 461, 466, 473, *474*, 475, 489, 490, 493, 495–96, 507; Sgt. Hunnicutt and, 461–63, 493, 532; McPhail and, 463, 471, 472, 473; Gen. Pickett and, 464–65, 470; Gen. Early and, 467, 473, *474*, 475, *482*, 488, 489, 492, 495, 501, 507; Gen. Slocum and, 468, 478, 481, *512;* situation on June 20, *469;* Gen. McLaws and, 470, 478, *512*, 525, 533; Gen. Milroy and, 472, 473, *482*, 490; Confederate Signal Corps and, 473, 475; Gen. Howard and, 473, 480, 491, 492, 510; Gen. Early and, *474*, 510, *512*, 513, 515; Gen. Gordon and, *474*, 488, 495, 513; Gen. Rodes and, *474*, *512*, 513, 515, 517, 519; Lee's advance into Maryland (June 3–28), *476;* situation on June 24, *482;* Stuart's ride around Federals, 486–88, 489, 496–97, 498, 501; telegraph lines and, 489, 490, 492, 496, 497, 502, 516; couriers and, 489–90, 491; Gen. Anderson and, 492, 507, *512;* refugee informants and, 493; Meade assumes command, 495, 501; Gen. Meade and, 495–97, 501, 502, 503–4, 505–11, 513, 515, 516, 518; Federal Sixth Corps and, *500*, 501, 508–9, 524, 525–26, 527; Federal Twelfth Corps and, 501, 502, 509, 524, 526, 527, 533; Gen. Buford and, 502, 506, 507, 510–11, *512*, 513, 515, 518; on June 30, 505–18, *512;* Gen. Sickles and, *512*, 524; intelligence successes, 564–65; intelligence failures, 567

Gettysburg Pike: Confederates on, 490–91

Gettysburg citizen-spies, 456–57, 471–72, 488, 502, 503–4

Gibbon, Gen. John, 269, 385, 386, 528, 529

Gilmor, Maj. Harry, 467, 473, 486, 547

Gloskoski, Capt. Joseph, 383

Gloucester Point, *145*, 151

Gooch, Daniel, 46

Gordon, Gen. John B., 554; and Gettysburg campaign, *474*, 488, 495, 513

Gordonsville, 79, *166*, *183*, 299, *418*, *476*, *539;* Confederates at, 185–86, 187, 189–90; and Chancellorsville campaign, 379, 408, 410

Grace, Rose, 75

Graham, Michael, 447

Graham, Mrs. Michael, 304

Grant, Gen. Ulysses S., 2, 184, 278, 285, 416, 443, 449, 531, 570, 586;

Grant, Gen. Ulysses S. (*cont.*)
    general-in-chief, 543; relations with
    Meade, 543, 547–48; use of intelli-
    gence, 543, 545, 546–47, 552, 570;
    Sharpe and, 543–44, 546–47, 548–
    49, 556; and 1864 campaigns, 543–
    45, 546–47, 549; stolen march
    across James River, 545–46, 549;
    and 1865 campaigns, 549, 550,
    555; as president, 557
Great Britain: running Federal block-
    ade, 90; Confederate hope for sup-
    port from, 110
Greencastle Pilot, 244
Greenhow, Robert, 59
Greenhow, Rose O'Neal, 32, 57, 58–
    68, 69, 70, 73, 75, 84, 130, 552; ar-
    rested, 58, 61, 598; background of,
    58–59; and First Bull Run, 58–61,
    62–63; memoirs of, 60, 64–65,
    599; her sources of information,
    62, 63–65; imprisonment of, 66–
    68; deported, 68, 69–70; reports
    of, 575–78
Greenwood, James W., 464, 467, 468,
    471
Gregg, Gen. David, 430, 459, 470,
    512, 589, 592
Griffin, Gen. Charles, 390, 391
Groveton, *30, 183;* battle of, 200–201
guerrillas (Confederate), 204
guides: Sharpe's use of, 294; National
    Archives records on, 596
Guinea's Station, *299;* and battle of
    Chancellorsville, 406–7

Hagerstown, *212, 469, 474, 476, 482,
    485, 500, 512, 539;* intelligence on
    Lee from, 492–94, 497
Hall, Lt. James S., 265, 266; and
    Chancellorsville campaign, 390
Halleck, Gen. Henry W., 157, 251,
    302, 304, 311, 313, 324, 325, 333,
    417, 542, 589; general-in-chief of
    army, 162, 182; and McClellan's es-
    timates of enemy forces, 162–63,
    581–82; and intelligence work,
    182–84, 186; writings of, 182–84;
    on definition of a spy, 184, 245; di-
    rects McClellan to join Pope, 189;

and Second Bull Run, 198, 206,
    207; and Antietam campaign, 214,
    215, 216, 217, 224, 235; and
    Fredericksburg campaign, 259–60,
    267, 272, 273; relations with
    Hooker, 277; and management of
    desertions, 283; and battle of Win-
    chester, 444–50, 452, 453; and Get-
    tysburg campaign, 454, 459, 460,
    472, 477, 489, 494–95, 496, 497,
    508, 521; relieves Hooker of com-
    mand, 494–95
Hamer, Gen. Thomas, 277
Hamilton, Gen. Charles S., 144
Hampton, Gen. Wade, 40, 241, 303,
    319, 417, *418,* 422; and Gettysburg
    campaign, 459, 486
Hampton Legion, 34, 124
Hampton Roads, 70–71, *145*
Hancock, Gen. Winfield Scott, 151,
    270, 400, *441,* 498, *512,* 527, 528,
    529, 533
Hanover Court House, battle of, 155
Hardie, Gen. James, 270
Harding, Jackson, 272, 273, 294
Harding, William W., 355
Harney, Gen. William S., 19, 20
Harper's Ferry, *30, 79, 166, 212,
    441, 445, 469, 482, 485, 500, 512,
    539;* Confederates at, 23–24, 29,
    35; in Antietam campaign, 214,
    215, 217, 219, 220, 221, 223, 224,
    227, 232–35, 240; balloon surveil-
    lance at, 251; Hooker reorganizes
    command, 281; and battle of Win-
    chester, *445,* 451–52; garrison in
    Gettysburg campaign, 460, *469*
Harris, Isham G., 88, 99
Harris, Spencer, 117
Harrisburg Telegraph, 244
Harrison, Henry T., 499, 501, 505,
    510, 513
Harter, Sgt. Thomas O., 191–92, 193–
    94, 208, 248, 382, 463, 470, 537,
    569, 595
Hasbrouck, Jansen, 289, 290
Hasbrouck family, 288
Hatch, Gen. John P., 171, 172, 203
Haupt, Gen. Herman, 325, 516, 517,
    520

Hay, John, 143, 255
Hays, Gen. Alexander, 326
Hazel Grove, *299, 371, 398;* and battle of Chancellorsville, 395–96, 403, 404
Heintzelman, Gen. Samuel P., 135, 137, 199, 205, 206, 292, 303, 326, 330, 419, 471; and Peninsula campaign, 144, 155, 156, 161; and Department of Washington, 281
Henry House Hill encounter, 34
Herr, A. H., 93, 94
Herzinger, J. L., 21
Herzog, Charles, 152
Heth, Gen. Henry, 420, 505, 506, 511, *512*, 524, 525, 533
Hicks, Thomas H., 18, 22
Hill, Gen. A. P., 187, 195, 199, 200, 201, 253, 263, 264, 308, 374; and Antietam campaign, 215, 235, 236, 237; and Fredericksburg campaign, 267, 268; Federal report on, 319, 321; and Chancellorsville campaign, 374, 376, 377, 384, 393; and battle of Chancellorsville, 392; situation after Chancellorsville, 416–17, *418*, 424, 429, 431, 434, 437, *441*, 442; commands new Third Corps, 420; and Gettysburg campaign, 455, 457, 459, 461, 462, 464–65, 468, *469*, 470, 473, 478, 479, 480, 481, *482*, 483, *485*, 490, 492, 493, 498, *500*, 501, 505, 507–8, 511, *512*, 593; estimates of strength, 455; circulation of misinformation on Potomac crossings, 480–83; and battle of Gettysburg, 521, 522, 524, 525, 533
Hill, Gen. D. H., 116, 130, 151–52, 253, 263, 305, 318, 402, 407, 508; withdrawal from Leesburg, 134; at Leesburg, 167; and Antietam campaign, 223, 224, 225, 228–29, 239; and Lee's Lost Order, 223; and Fredericksburg campaign, 267, 269; Sharpe's report on, 319, 321
H.J.K. (Pinkerton agent), 100, 148
Hoag, Lt. Izrael V., Jr., 247
hoax message. *See* signal deception
Hogan, Martin E., 436–38, 455, 543

Hogg, Capt. Robert, 148
Hoke, Jacob, 489, 490, 491, 515, 516
Hollar, Anthony, 490
Holmes, Gen. Theophilus H., 90, 92, 95, 100, 115, 146; estimates of forces, 95, 100, 124, 125–26
Holt, Joseph, 12, 13
Hood, Gen. John B., 188, 392, 229, 305, 312, 319, 331, 341, 343, 361, 416; and battle of Chancellorsville, 407, 409, 410, 412, 413, 415; situation after Chancellorsville, 417, *418*, 425, 429–30, 437; and Gettysburg campaign, *512;* and battle of Gettysburg, 525, 533
Hooker, Gen. Joseph, 1–2, 573, 586, 591; and establishment of intelligence bureau, 2, 3–4, 238; misuse of intelligence, 4; order-of-battle records, 6; and Maryland contraband traffic, 73, 278; and Potomac blockade, 83–84, 138, 300; and Antietam campaign, 218, 228, 236, 238, 280; and Fredericksburg campaign, 268, 269, 270, 272; Burnside recommends cashiering, 272; assumes command of Army of the Potomac, 273, 276; Lincoln's letter to, 276; comments on First Bull Run, 277; in Mexican War, 277; 1861–62 command experience, 277–81; and balloon surveillance, 278; and cavalry reconnaissance, 279, 589; under McClellan, 278, 279, 280; and intelligence problems and activities, 278–79, 286–87, 298–300, 312, 317–18, 324, 325; and Negro informants, 279; and Confederate Potomac batteries, 279; on Confederate numbers, 279; and Peninsula campaign, 280, 300; and Second Bull Run, 280; at Williamsburg, 280; reputation for leadership, 280, 281; administrative genius of, 281, 282–83; reorganizes army, 281–82; appoints Butterfield chief of staff, 282–83; and newspaper exchanges with enemy, 286–87; originates all-source intelligence, 298–99, 300, 321; tracking

Hooker, Gen. Joseph (*cont.*)
enemy movement, 302–3, 304–5,
311–13; Sharpe-Babcock report on
Bureau's findings, 318–19, 320,
321–22; and army information security, 322–24, 325–26; statement
on cavalry failures, 330; intelligence advantage over Lee, 332–33;
receives reports on Confederate
numbers, 333; and Chancellorsville
campaign, 341, 355, 373–77, 385–
86, 342, 344–46, 349, 350, 351,
352, 358–59, 361, 363, 365–67,
368–70, *371*, 379, 381, 382–83,
385–86; discusses campaign plans
with Lincoln, 344; and underwater
telegraph story, 355; Kelly's Ford
route, 368–70; advance to Chancellorsville, *371;* and contributions of
intelligence to Chancellorsville
campaign, 382–83; battle of Chancellorsville, 387–91, 404, 393, 395,
399, 400, 401–2, 405, 406, 407,
408, 408, 409–11, 412, 529; orders
delaying of advance, 388, 389; suspends attack, 391; analysis of failure at Chancellorsville, 400–402,
404–5; orders withdrawal, 409–11;
retreat after Chancellorsville, 412–
13; Sharpe's forecast of enemy campaign of long marches, 416–18;
and reports of enemy's move
north, 423–24, 428, 429, 431, 435,
449; and pursuit of Lee, 433, 440–
43; and Gettysburg campaign, 456,
457, 459, 460, 463, 465, 466, 468,
473, 477, 479, 480–81, 483, 484,
491, 494–95, 536, 593; delays advance awaiting indications of Lee's
objective, 457; crosses Potomac,
481–83, 484; relieved of command, 494–95; Pleasonton's role in
pursuit of Lee, 588–92, 593; orders
attack on Stuart, 589; as source, 597
Hooker's Horse Marines, 84, 292
Hopkins, Ed, 421, 427, 503
Hopper, Capt. John C., 178, 180
Houston, Sam, 166
Howard, George W., Jr., 22–23
Howard, Gen. Oliver O., 270, 351;

commands Eleventh Corps, 282,
346, 368; and Chancellorsville campaign, 370, *371*, 378, 380, 387;
struck by Jackson's flank attack,
395–400; and move north, *441;*
and Gettysburg campaign, 473,
480, 491, 492, 510; and battle of
Gettysburg, 523, 524, 525, 528
Howe, Sir William, 456
Huber, Benjamin S., 491, 508
Huger, Gen. Benjamin, 125, 146, 160
Humphreys, Gen. Andrew A., 154,
258, 270; as Meade's chief of staff,
541
Humphreys, Joseph M., 292
Hungerford, Capt. John W., 306,
307, 308, 309
Hunnicutt, Sgt. Mordecai P., 292,
598; and Gettysburg campaign,
461–63, 493, 532
Hunter, Gen. David, 41, 343, 546,
547, 549
Hutton, J. D., 57

Imboden, Gen. J. D., 367, 402, 403,
420, 486, 488, 525
Indian scouts, 20–21
Ingalls, Gen. Rufus, 284
intelligence (*see also* balloon surveillance; cavalry reconnaissance; espionage; interrogations; newspapers; scouting; Signal Corps):
Lincoln's view of importance of, 1;
and Gettysburg campaign, 1, 3,
456–57, 459–60, 470–71, 480–83,
486, 535–37, 564–67; George
Washington and, 8, 9, 298, 496,
541; use of term, 8, 294; inadequacies at First Bull Run, 29, 37–41,
51–52; McClellan's organization
and reporting of, 54–55; counterintelligence, 76; "positive," 102, 294;
McClellan and Pinkerton overestimate enemy, 102–13, 581–87;
McClellan on leakages, 111–12,
130; Confederate, in Peninsula
campaign, 144–46; Federal, in Peninsula campaign, 146–49, 155–57;
McClellan's in Peninsula campaign, 146–49, 300; Gen. Banks

and, 171–72, 211, 251, 259; Halleck and, 182–84, 186; Gen. Pope and, 186, 207–10, 569, 570; in Antietam campaign, 238–40; Burnside's in Fredericksburg campaign, 257–59, 260–62, 263, 273–74; Hooker's all-source, 298–99, 300, 321; and Chancellorsville campaign, 1–2, 382–84, 389–90, 400–402; Butterfield's circulation of memos on, 300, 323; Gen. Meade and, 495–97, 503–4, 505–7, 509, 510, 540–41, 547–48, 552, 570–71; and battle of Gettysburg, 535–37; Grant and, 543, 545, 546–47, 552, 570; Meade and Grant divide reporting activities, 547–48; successes (summary), 563–65; failures (summary), 565–67; lessons from Civil War, 569–71

interception of enemy signals, 419, 426, 542, 544, 545

International Law and the Laws of War (Halleck), 183–84

interrogations, 3, 5 (*see also* contraband informants; deserter informants; prisoner informants; refugee informants); Pinkerton and, 55, 84–85, 111, 113–14, 298; systematized routine by Pinkerton, 113–14; disposition of informants, 114–15; Burnside's failures at, 262; Sharpe and, 301

invisible ink, 296, 423

Irish Brigade, 327

ironclads, 3, 96, 97, 137–38, 155

Jackson, Frank H., 246

Jackson, Gen. Thomas J. (Stonewall), 22–23, 115, 116, 134, 289, 304, 305, 307, 308, 312, 334, 420; and First Bull Run, 32–33, 34, 40; at Winchester, 87; assumes Shenandoah command, 90, 92–93, 165; estimates of Shenandoah forces of, 124–25, 160, 162; feud with Loring, 125; and Peninsula campaign, 156, 157, 159, 160, 162; and Shenandoah Valley campaign, 156, 165, 169, 170–81, 563, 566;

at Cedar Mountain, 163; defeated at Kernstown, 170–71; at Rude's Hill, 171; at Front Royal, 174–75; and Second Bull Run, 185–86, 187, 189, 194, 199, 200–202, 205, 207, 210; estimates of strength of, 185–86; takes Manassas station, 199–200; and Antietam campaign, 214, 216, 218, 220, 221, 223, 224, 225, 231, 232, 234–35, 238, 239, 242, 248; returns to Virginia, 252–53; and Fredericksburg campaign, 263, 264, 267; Second Corps under, 263; use of pseudo-deserters, 297; Federals tracking, 312; and Chancellorsville campaign, 362, 365, 366, 375, 376, 383–84; strength of Second Corps, 376; and battle of Chancellorsville, 389, 390, 392, 393, *398*, 399, 400, 401, 403, 410; rout of Federals' right wing, 399–400; fatal wounding, 400

James River, *145, 539;* Federal crossing of, 546, 549

Jenkins, Gen. Albert, 420, 425–26, 436; and Gettysburg campaign, 455–56, 457, 463, 466, 473, *474,* 486, 488, 490, 493, 496, *512,* 514–15

Jenkins, Gen. Micah, 420, 422–23

Jermantown, *30;* Federal espionage at, 35

Jerome, Lt. A. B., 152

Jessie Scouts, 178

"Johnson" (Confederate agent), 262, 273

Johnson, Andrew, 27, 65

Johnson, Gen. Bradley T., 172, 555

Johnson, Gen. Edward, 172, 420, 451, 575; and Gettysburg campaign, 461, 466, 473, 489, 490, 495, 507, *512,* 513, 515, 517; and battle of Gettysburg, 526, 530, 531, 533

Johnson, Nicholas, 285–86

Johnson, Reverdy, 97, 336

Johnston, Gen. Albert Sidney, 96

Johnston, Gen. Joseph E., 6, 10, 82, 86, 110, 221–22, 531, 554, 556; at First Bull Run, 31, 32, 3, 37, 40,

Johnston, Gen. Joseph E. (*cont.*)
43, 44, 45, 46, 47, 49, 50, 61, 579–
80; evacuation of Manassas, 131–
43, 151, 152, 423; size of his forces,
86–87, 91, 93, 95, 96, 99, 107, 109,
110, 118, 127, 160, 581, 582, 586;
estimate of own forces, 125;nd Peninsula campaign, 130–31, 142–46,
151–52, 154, 155, 156, 160, 172,
178; withdrawal to Richmond, 153,
154–55, 174; wounding at Seven
Pines, 156, 221; Strother's report
on, 579–80
Johnston, William, 35–36, 41
Joinville, prince de, 123, 143
Jones, David R., 229
Jones, John B., 11, 86, 90, 98, 100,
130
Jones, Gen. John M., 420, 461
Jones, Gen. John R., 420, 461
Jones, Gen. William E. ("Grumble"),
313, 319, 332, 333, 348, 367, 417,
420, 425–26, 486, 590; reinforces
Stuart, 425–26, 428
Jordan, Thomas, 59, 62, 63–64, 68,
69, 71

Kearny, Gen. Philip, 138; on Hooker,
280
Kelley, Gen. Benjamin, 472
Kellogg, Capt. Sanford Cobb, 596
Kelly's Ford, *183, 299, 371, 418, 422;*
in Chancellorsville campaign, 368–
70, 372, 374–75, 377–82, 386,
546
Kelly's Ford, battle of, 330–31, 341,
350, 357, 358
Kemper, James, 407
Kenly, Col. John R., 174, 177
Kentucky: Pinkerton intelligence
from, 114
Kerbey, Joseph O., 17
Kerby, J. T., 56, 85, 247
Kernstown, battle of, 170–71
Kershaw, Joseph B., 549–50
Key, Col. Thomas M., 149
Keyes, Gen. Erasmus, 137; and Penin-
sula campaign, 155, 156, 161
Kilpatrick, Col. Judson, 303, 407,
508; raid on Richmond, 543, 556

Kimmel, Judge Francis M., 489, 490,
491, 508, 516
Kincheloe, Daniel B., 120
King, Jackson, 117
King, Gen. Rufus, 187, 200–201, 203
Kinney, J. R., 490
Knight, John A., 215
Knight, Sgt. Judson, 552
Kress, Lt. Col. John A., 329

Lackland, Mr., 47
Lacy house, 356–57, 358
Lamon, Ward Hill, 489
La Mountain, John, 83, 140
Lander, Gen. Frederick W.: and intelli-
gence, 168–69
Landstreet, Rev. John, 301
Lawrence, Atkins S., 215
Lawton, Hattie, 131, 148
Lee, Abel Huntingdon, 22
Lee, Gen. Fitzhugh, 190, 192–93,
303–4, 313, 314, 318, 330, 333,
348, 350, 362, 549; and battle of
Kelly's Ford, 330–31, 357, 358; and
Chancellorsville campaign, 362–
63, 368, 369, 383; situation after
Chancellorsville, 417, 423; and Gettysburg campaign, 457, 486, 496,
508; and battle of Aldie, 457–58
Lee, Col. John C.: and battle of Chancellorsville, 396–97, 400
Lee, Gen. Robert E.: and Chancellorsville campaign, 4, 341, 343–44,
345, 348–49, 353, 355, 356, 366,
367, 369, 370, 372, 373, 375, 376,
379–80, 381, 382, 390; Special Orders No. 191, 4, 222–28, 229, 230–
33, 234, 235, 238–40, 530, 532;
and intelligence, 5–6, 571; in Mexican War, 9; sides with Confederacy,
12; on lack of spies in Washington,
75, 419; and Peninsula campaign,
145–46, 152, 156, 157–59, 161–64;
replaces Johnston, 156; estimate of
opposing forces, 160; and Second
Bull Run, 182, 190, 191, 192, 193–
94, 195, 196, 197, 198, 199, 201,
204, 207, 208, 209, 280, 569;
Pope's capture of letter of, 192–93;
and Antietam campaign, 211, 212,

213, 215, 217, 221, 222–35, 238–40; hope for European support by invasion of North, 213; and battle of Antietam, 235–37, 239, 240; tracked by Pleasonton after Antietam, 251, 253; Banks's tracking after Antietam, 251–52, 253–54; and Fredericksburg campaign, 256–57, 267, 269; reorganizes Army of North Virginia, 263; use of pseudo-deserters, 297; relations with Longstreet, 311; shortage of intelligence, 331–33; pickets' knowledge of Federal moves, 353; and battle of Chancellorsville, 391, 394, 401, 402, 403, 404–5, 407, *408*, 412, 413, 415; his forces for Pennsylvania campaign, 415–16, 417, *418*; Sharpe's forecast of his advance north, 416–18, 421–22, 423, 424, 425, 426, 427, 428–29, 431, 434, 435, 437, 439, 447; concern for security and need for intelligence, 418–19; reorganizes Army of Northern Virginia, 420–21; and battle of Brandy Station, 432; and Gettysburg campaign, 454, 455, 457, 458, 459, 460, 461, 465, 467, 473, 475, 478, 479, 480, 508, 510, 513, 517; secrecy of moves, 460; estimate of forces, 462; advance into Pennsylvania, 484, *485*, 486–92, 494, 497–99, 501–2, 588–92, 593–94; lack of intelligence, 486–88, 489, 497–98, 501; size of forces, 492–93, 494; and spy Harrison's information, 499, 501; misplacement of Federals, 501–2; and battle of Gettysburg, 520, 522, 523, 525–26, 527, 529, 530, 531–32, 533, 534, 535, 536; retreat from Gettysburg, 538–40, *539*, 541, 542, 546; surrender of, 549, 557; and 1865 campaigns, 554; Sharpe refuses to parole, 557; Pleasonton's role in Hooker's pursuit of, 588–92, 593

Lee, Gen. W. H. F., 306, 310, 314, 328, 349, 361, 362; and Chancellorsville campaign, 361, 362–63,

364, 366, 368, 379; and Gettysburg campaign, 486

Leesburg, Va., *30, 79, 166, 183, 212, 441, 469, 476, 482, 500, 539;* reports on Confederate forces at, 86–87, 89–90, 107, 124, 127, 128; Confederate withdrawal from, 134; and Valley campaign, 165, 167; Slocum at, 468

Leet, Capt. George K., 549

Leib, Charles, 18

Letcher, John, 120

Lewinsville, Stuart's and W. F. Smith's contest for, 82

Lewis, Pryce, 131, 148; arrest, 148–49

Library of Congress: intelligence records in, 2, 595–98

Lincoln, Abraham, 27, 187, 214, 543, 546; and importance of intelligence, 1, 183; first inauguration, 13–15, 53; call for recruits for Washington, 17–18; fear of Confederate invasion, 45; response to First Bull Run, 51–52, 53; myth of Greenhow's penetration of cabinet, 64–65; and McClellan's estimates of enemy forces, 103, 106–7, 109–10; suggests attack plan to McClellan, 109–10; and McClellan's Urbanna plan, 135, 136, 137, 141; divides Army of the Potomac, 137; and Peninsula campaign, 139, 142, 144, 151, 153–54, 155, 182; retains McDowell's First Corps to defend Washington, 144, 151, 155, 171; replaces general-in-chief during 1862 Valley campaign, 172, 177, 178; and Second Bull Run, 207; and Antietam campaign, 216, 218, 224, 227, 232–33; urges action by McClellan after Antietam, 250–51, 254; appoints Burnside commander of Army of Potomac, 255; issues Emancipation Proclamation, 255; and Fredericksburg campaign, 256, 272; letter to Hooker, 276; and army information security, 323; and Chancellorsville campaign, 344, 345, 352, 364, 368, 370, 377, 388, 404, 414; on vulner-

Lincoln, Abraham (*cont.*)
  ability of Richmond, 413; and loss
  at Winchester, 452; and Gettysburg
  campaign, 456, 460, 472, 494; and
  Meade's assumption of command,
  494, 495
Little Round Top, 523, 526
Lloyd, Alexander, 472
Lockwood, Gen. H. H., 327
Logan, William, 493
Lohman, F. W. E., 147, 552, 553,
  554
Longstreet, Gen. James, 301, 304,
  305, 309, 332, 335, 358, 402, 429,
  542, 544, 556, 591, 593; and Second Bull Run, 187, 188, 189, 195,
  201, 202, 203, 204–6, 209; and Antietam campaign, 215, 220, 225,
  228, 229, 231, 232, 239, 248; returns to Virginia, 253, 255; and
  Fredericksburg campaign, 257,
  263, 264, 267; Suffolk campaign,
  311–13, 333, 341–43, 384, 402,
  409, 413; and Chancellorsville campaign, 362, 364, 376, 379, 384,
  392, 402, 405, 408, 409, 410; estimates of strength, 376, 402–3;
  tracking of moves after Chancellorsville, 432, 434, 439, 440, *441*, 442;
  and Gettysburg campaign, 454,
  455, 457, 458, 459, 463, 464–65,
  466, 468, *469*, 470, 471, 473, 477,
  478, 479, 480, 481, *482*, *485*, 486,
  489, 492, 493, 496, 498, 499, *500*,
  501, 507–8, *512*; and spy Harrison,
  499, 501; and battle of Gettysburg,
  520, 521, 525, 526, 527, 533, 535;
  and Richmond campaign, 544
Loring, Gen. W. W., 125, 365
Lost Order (Special Orders No. 191),
  222–24
Louisa Court House, *183*, 187–88,
  418
Lovett, A. A., 355
Lowe, Thaddeus, 38, 77, 81, 84, 135,
  141, 167, 212, 251, 261, 267, 278,
  279, 442–43; and Peninsula campaign, 146, 152, 154, 156, 161;
  financial problems of, 365; and
  Chancellorsville campaign, 374,

384, 386, 389, 393, 394; writes his-
  torical report, 442–43
Lucretia (schooner), 69
Lumpkins, Dr., 158
Lyon, Capt. Nathaniel, 19, 20
Lyons, Lord, 88, 93

MacArthur, Gen. Douglas, 239
Macomb, Col. John N., 196
Maddox, Joseph H., 97, 336–39, 341,
  402–3, 407, 555–57; report on Confederate forces, 402–3, 555–56
Magruder, Gen. John B. ("Prince
  John"), 89, 104; report on size of
  forces, 91, 126, 142; and Peninsula
  campaign, 142, 146, 149–50, 160;
  magnifies numbers of his troops,
  149–50
Mahone, Gen. William, 308, 318; and
  Chancellorsville campaign, 380,
  381
Mallory, Stephen R., 93
Malvern Hill, *145*; battle of, 161–62
Manassas, *30*, *79*, *166*, *183*, *441*, *469*,
  476, *482*, *539*; Confederate forces
  at, 26–27, 29–31; Beauregard's
  forces at (First Bull Run), 29, 31,
  32, 33, 35, 36, 41, 42, 43, 48;
  Johnston's evacuation of, 131–43,
  151–52, 420; Webster's visit to, 90;
  Pinkerton-McClellan estimates of
  forces at, 92, 103, 107, 109, 110,
  112, 118, 122, 125–26, 127–29,
  141–42; balloon surveillance in
  evacuation, 132, 135, 138, 139,
  140–41, 298; rail line to Centreville, 132
Manassas campaign. *See* Bull Run
Manassas Gap Railroad, *30*, *32*, 118,
  134, *166*, 171, *441*, *469*, *482*
Manning, Lt. Frederick, 544
Mansfied, Gen. Joseph K. F., 21, 22,
  91, 236; relations with McDowell,
  35; mortally wounded at Antietam,
  236
mapmaking: in Peninsula campaign,
  153–54, 155
Marcy, Gen. Randolph B., 115, 139,
  596; and Peninsula campaign, 152,
  154

Marshall, Col. Charles, 557
Marshall, George, 119–20
Martindale, Gen. John H., 284
Martinsburg, *30, 166, 212, 445, 469, 476, 485, 500, 512, 539;* fall of, 452, 454, 455, 456
Marye's Heights: in Fredericksburg campaign, 268, 269, 270, 300; in Chancellorsville campaign, 391, 394, 404, 406, 533
Maryland: at outbreak of war, 18; Confederate sympathizers in, 56; contraband traffic to Virginia, 73–75, 95; Lee's advance into (June 1863), *476*
Maryland Line, 313
Mason, Ebenezer, Jr., 365
Mason, John Francis, 69
Mason, Kirk R., 23–24
Maurice, James H., 116–17, 151
Maury, Matthew F., 96
McCall, Gen. George A., 80, 83
McCammon, Thomas, 493–94, 520
McClellan, Gen. George B., 11, 22, 75, 322, 325, 336, 337, 423; and estimates of Confederate numbers, 2, 63, 86–87, 92, 96, 99–100, 102–29, 140, 141–42, 155, 160, 162–64, 216, 217, 237, 238–39, 581–87; and Pinkerton, 2, 3, 53, 54–55, 209; and Lee's Special Orders No. 191, 4, 222–28, 229, 230–33, 234, 235, 238–40; in Mexican War, 9; and intelligence organization and reporting, 54–55; myth of Greenhow's procurement of his plans, 64–65; and defense of Washington, 77–82; difficult relations with Scott, 78; becomes general-in-chief, 80; and "Phony War," 82, 84, 85, 87, 88, 89; and blockade of Washington, 84; and Pinkerton's reports during Phony War, 84–85, 87, 91–96, 99–100; and forged letter of Davis, 88–89; plans against Richmond, 99–100; using intelligence sources other than Pinkerton, 104; collusion with Pinkerton, 106–9; and disposition of informants, 114–15; uses d'Orléans brothers as intelligence analysts, 123–27; and Peninsula campaign, 130–31, 142–64, 178, 184, 300; and Johnston's withdrawal from Manassas, 132–41; and Urbanna plan, 135–37, 141, 142; mishandling of intelligence about Confederate evacuation of Manassas, 135, 138–40; failure to intercept Johnston's withdrawal, 139–40; relieved of general-in-chief post, 142; overestimates enemy intelligence, 143, 144–45; intelligence for Peninsula campaign, 146–49, 300; battle of Williamsburg, 153, 155; and mapmaking, 153–54; and trial of Gen. Stone, 169; battle of Seven Pines, 156; Seven Days battles, 160–62; takes Yorktown, 174; withdrawal from Peninsula, 189, 190; and Second Bull Run, 195, 196, 199, 206, 207; and Antietam campaign, 212, 213–17, 222–23, 224, 226, 227–28, 229–30, 232, 233–35, 236–40; acquires Lost Order, 222; rejects reports concerning Lost Order, 225–26; use of intelligence in Antietam campaign, 238–40; Stuart's ride around Army of Potomac, 243; confusion about enemy movements after Antietam, 250–51, 253, 254–55; removed from command of Army of the Potomac, 255; relations with Hooker, 278, 280–81
McClellan, Maj. H. B., 590
McClure, Alexander K., 218, 219, 220, 227, 230, 232, 245, 472, 515
McConaughy, David, 456–57, 471, 472, 488, 495, 503–4, 506, 511, 598
McCord, Benjamin F., 421, 422
McCreary, R. G., 457, 495
McCubbin, Samuel, 149
McDowell, Gen. Irvin, 25, 162, 252, 358, 529; at First Bull Run, 29, 31–43, 47–52, 59, 60, 580; and Urbanna plan, 137; First Corps defending Washington, 144, 151, 155, 171, 174; and Shenandoah Valley campaign, 177; and Second

McDowell, Gen. Irvin (*cont.*)
  Bull Run, 191–92, 200, 201, 202, 204, 205; Rose Greenhow's reports on, 577
McDowell, Va., *166;* battle of, 173–74, 181
McEntee, Capt. John, 293–94, 377, 414, 543, 544, 547, 548, 591; tracking moves of Lee's forces, 421–23, *422,* 425, 426–28, 430–31, 434, 435–40; relations with Pleasonton, 435, 438–39, 440, 454–55; discovers Charley Wright, 436–38; and Gettysburg campaign, 454–55, 457, 458, 460, 464, 467, 480, 486, 503, 531; and battle of Gettysburg, 526, 535; in Grant's Richmond campaign, 544–51; postwar career, 558
McGee, Ebenezer, 272, 273, 292, 315–16, 343, 423, 548; and Chancellorsville campaign, 374, 389
McGee, Richard, 316
McGee farm, *316*
McKelvey, D. G., 293
McLaws, Gen. Lafayette, 223, 224, 227, 228, 229, 232, 233, 234, 301, 303, 305, 307, 308, 318, 416, 592; Federal report on, 319, 321; and Chancellorsville campaign, 376, 383, 388, 389, 393, 404; situation after Chancellorsville, 423, 424, 429–30, 437; and Gettysburg campaign, 470, 478, *512,* 525, 533
McLean, Nathaniel, 396
McMund, Ocque, 20
McMurdy, Edward B., 103
McPhail, James L., 192, 335–39, 341, 403, 415, 555, 556; and Gettysburg campaign, 463, 471, 472, 473
McPherson's Heights, 524
McVicar (Jackson's spy), 176
Meade, Gen. George G., 1, 2, 345, 346, *441,* 551, 586; and Fredericksburg campaign, 269, 270; commands Fifth Corps, 282, 346, 495; and Chancellorsville campaign, *371,* 372, 378; and battle of Chancellorsville, 387, 390, 391, *398,* 409, 412; and picket information, 424, 429–30; assumes command of Army of the Potomac, 495, 501; and Gettysburg campaign, 495–97, 501, 502, 503–4, 505–11, 513, 515, 516, 518; use of intelligence, 495–97, 503–4, 505–7, 509, 510, 540–41, 547–48, 552, 570–71; and battle of Gettysburg, 519, 520, 521, 522, 523, 524–25, 526, 527–28, 529, 530, 532, 533, 534–35; remains at Gettysburg, 529; abolishes all-source intelligence, 540–41; relations with Grant, 543, 547–48
Meagher, Edward, 215
Mechanicsville, *145;* battle of, 160
Medicine Armstrong (Indian scout), 21
Meigs, M. C., 129, 496; and estimates of Confederate forces, 582–83, 585
Memminger, Christopher G., 92
Merrimack, U.S.S. (ship), 96, 97, 137–38
Mexican War, 277; espionage and scouting in, 9
Miles, Col. Dixon S., 217, 219
Miller, Francis Trevelyan, 154
Milroy, Gen. Robert, 172, 173, 304, 313, 333, 343, *441;* and battle of Winchester, 444–53, 454, 460, 572–74; and Gettysburg campaign, 472, 473, *482,* 490
Miner, Lt. Brinkerhoff N., 211, 213
Mitchel, Gen. Ormsby M., 184
Mitchell, Corp. Barton W., 222
Monitor (ironclad), 138
Monroe, James F., 115
Montgomery, Richard, 186–87, 188, 192, 197, 204, 205–6, 208, 407
Moore, Isaac E., 464, 468, 471
Morgan, Edwin, 289
Morgan, Col. John, 287, 316
Morris, Augusta Heath, 69, 70, 71, 74
Morton, Oliver, 178
Mosby, John S., 306, 326, 367, 378, 381, 547, 556, 589; situation after Chancellorsville, 417, *418,* 421, 422, 432; and Gettysburg campaign, 497–98
Mountain Department, 178

Mud March, Burnside's, 272–73, 290, 346
Munson's Hill: Confederates at, 81
Murphy, John James, 178–79, 180, 363
Myer, Albert, 10, 251, 348, 443, 542, 551; and flag signaling, 37–39, 266; and ballooning, 38, 81, 443; and Peninsula campaign, 146, 147, 148, 155, 156; originates hoax message to deceive Lee, 348–49
My Imprisonment and the First Year of Abolition Rule in Washington (Greenhow), 60, 64–65, 599

Nashville: Confederate defenses at, 98
National Detective Police, Baker's, 27
National Republican (Washington), 41–42
National Security Act of 1947, 299
naval expeditions: Port Royal, 70–72; Cape Hatteras, 72–73
Neel, W. H. R., 152
New Orleans Crescent, 336
newspaper correspondents, 18–19, 86 (*see also individual newspapers*); expose Pinkerton, 110–11; and Manassas evacuation, 141; and Front Royal battle, 175–76; and Antietam campaign, 212–13, 222–23; Hooker and, 286, 322, 324–25; expose Dix's smuggling plan, 340–41, 403; deceived by underwater telegraph story, 354–55, 357
newspapers (Confederate), 55; Sharpe's examination of, 298
newspapers (Federal), 75; and First Bull Run, 41–42; and leakage of military information, 324–25
Newton, Gen. John, 44–45, 528, 529
New York City: Sharpe's postwar career in, 557–58
New York Herald, 41, 144, 175, 184, 222–23, 325
New York Journal of Commerce, 223
New York Times, 431, 591; and underwater telegraph story, 355, 357
New York Tribune, 86, 176, 325, 457
New York World, 144
Nicolay, John, 143

Ninth Corps: transferred to Peninsula, 302
9th Virginia Cavalry, 351
Noakes, Thomas, 219
Norfolk, Va., *539;* Confederate defenses at, 97; Peninsula campaign and, 146; Confederates evacuate, 155
Norris, Maj. William, 148, 337, 350
Northam, Rev. George, 327
North Anna River, *539;* Grant withholds attack, 545
Northern Central Railroad, 471–72
Northern Neck, *79, 299;* scouting and smuggling in, 326, 327–28, 334, 338; and Chancellorsville campaign, 366
Northwest, Department of the, 207
Norton, Lemuel, 551
Noyes, Charles, 20

Oak Grove, battle of, 159–60, 161
Occoquan River, *30, 79,* 109–10, *183*
Ocean Queen (steamer), 144
Ohio: fear of Confederate invasion, 452, 456
Ohio, Department of the, 218; McClellan and, 114
Old Capitol Prison, 67, 87, 109, 340
Oliphant, Samuel P., 472
Operative P.H.D., 72
Orange and Alexandria Railroad, *30, 79, 183, 252, 299, 418, 422, 441, 469,* 548
Orléans, Louis Philippe d', 123–27, 141–42, 231
Orléans, Robert d', 123–27, 141–42, 231
Otto, D. G., 292, 315, 363

Painter, Uriah H., 152, 212–13, 355
Palfrey, Francis W., 583
Palmer, Capt. William J., 218–22, 225, 226, 227, 230, 231, 233, 234, 240, 294, 321, 341, 363, 472, 514, 569; capture of, 241–42, 243, 245–49; awarded Medal of Honor, 249, 558; promoted to brigadier general, 558; postwar career, 558–59

Parke, Gen. John G., 259, 261, 273, 276
Parker, Charles, 120
Parsons, William C., 21, 22, 24, 34–35, 102
Patrick, Marsena R., 262–63, 272, 273, 275–76, 282, 283, 287, 290, 293, 295, 300, 308, 310, 314, 318, 322, 324, 425, 442, 596, 598; replaces Porter, 259, 275–76; and Army Regulations, 275; background, 275–76; and desertions, 283–84; difficult relations with Baker, 284–85, 292; and Sharpe, 287–88; increasing role in intelligence, 301; and army information security, 323, 325, 331; and Chancellorsville campaign, 344, 351, 352, 353, 355–56, 357, 358–59, 374, 386, 388, 408; and Lincoln's visit to army, 344; and Gettysburg campaign, 457, 460, 464, 465, 466, 491; as Grant's provost marshal general, 546, 547, 548, 549; postwar career, 558
Patterson, Gen. Robert, 165, 168, 170, 579, 580; and First Bull Run, 31, 35, 42, 43, 45, 47–48, 49
Paullin, William, 84
Pearl Harbor, 572–74
Pech, Herman, 116–17, 121
Peck, Gen. John J., 312, 313, 384, 392, 406, 407
Pender, Gen. Dorsey, 420, 505, 511, 512, 525, 533
Pendleton, Gen. William N., 245–46
Peninsula campaign, 75, 123, 130–31, 142–64, 145, 174, 182, 582, 586, 587; estimate of Confederate forces for, 126–27, 141–42; Gen. Johnston and, 130–31, 142–46, 151–52, 154, 155, 156, 160, 172, 178; Gen. McClellan and, 130–31, 142–64, 178, 184, 300; Fort Monroe and, 142, 143, 144, 145, 150; supplants Urbanna plan, 142–44; Gen. Porter and, 144, 155, 158, 159, 160; Gen. Heintzelman and, 144, 155, 156, 161; Gen. Stuart and, 144, 157; Confederate intelligence on, 144–46, 157–58; R. E. Lee and, 145–46, 152, 156, 157–59, 161–64; balloon reconnaissance, 146, 154, 156, 161; Lowe and, 146, 152, 154, 156, 161; Myer and, 146, 147, 148, 155, 156; Federal Signal Corps, 146–47, 152; telegraph lines, 146–47, 152–53; Federal intelligence in, 146–49, 155–57; Pinkerton and, 146–49, 154, 161, 376; Webster and, 147, 151; Confederate Signal Corps, 148, 265; prisoner informants, 148; Magruder magnifies numbers of his troops, 149–50; Gen. Wool and, 150–51, 153; Warwick River, 150–51; Johnston's evacuation of Yorktown, 151–53; battle of Williamsburg, 153, 155; mapmaking, 153–54, 155; topography, 153–54; scouting, 154–55, 156, 300; Chickahominy River, 155; Hanover Court House, 155; Norfolk evacuated, 155; Stonewall Jackson and, 156, 157, 159, 160, 162; Seven Pines, 156–57; Gen. Banks and, 158, 162; deserter informants, 158–59; Oak Grove, 159–60, 161; Seven Days battles, 159–62; casualties of, 160, 162; battle of Mechanicsville, 160; Gaines's Mill, 160–61; Harrison's Landing base, 161; Savage's Station, 161; Malvern Hill, 161–62; intelligence successes, 564; intelligence failures, 566
Pennsylvania: as Lee's possible objective (Antietam campaign), 217, 221; Lee's 1863 campaign into, 415–32 (see also Gettysburg campaign); Lee's forces for, 415–17, 418; tracking Lee's movements, 421–32; pursuit of Lee into, 433–43; panic at Confederate invasion, 452, 456–57; use of Gettysburg spies, 456–57; Lee's advance into, 484, 485, 486–92, 494, 497–99, 501–2, 588–92
Pennsylvania Central Railroad, 471–72; spies of, 514

Perry, Edward, 308, 361
Peters, W. J. (W. J. Palmer), 245, 246, 247
Petersburg, Va., *145, 539*, 549–59; Grant's investment of, 545; campaign against, 549–52
Pettigrew, Gen. Johnston J., 506, 522
Philadelphia: fear of Confederate invasion, 452, 456
Philadelphia Inquirer, 152, 175, 212; and underwater telegraph story, 354–55, 357
Philadelphia newspapers: compromise of Dix's espionage plan, 340–41, 403
Phillips, John G., 20
Phony War of 1861–62, 82–101, 563, 565–66; cavalry activity in, 82–83; Pinkerton's agents' reports during, 84–85, 87, 91, 92, 93, 94, 95, 96, 98, 99–100
Photographic History (Miller), 154
Piatt, Col. Donn, 446, 448–49, 496
Pickens, Francis, 16
picket duty, 324; interrogations, 10, 167; and Chancellorsville campaign, 355–56; and Confederate moves after Chancellorsville, 423, 424; Gen. Meade and information from, 424, 429–30
Pickett, Gen. George, 305, 312, 319, 331, 335, 341, 343, 361, 542, 544; during battle of Chancellorsville, 392, 406, 407, 409, 412, 415; situation after Chancellorsville, 417, *418*, 429, 435; and Gettysburg campaign, 464–65, 470; and battle of Gettysburg, 525, 527, 529; leads July 3 charge, 532–35
Piedmont: intelligence gathering in the, 542
Pierrepont, Judge Edwards, 67, 69, 74, 75, 94
Pillow, Gideon, 277
Pinkerton, Allan, 27, 241, 260, 286, 291, 298, 300, 311, 321, 335, 537, 558, 595; on Confederate numbers, 2, 86, 92, 95, 102–29, 140, 141–42, 160, 163–64, 238, 376, 581–87; memoirs of, 3, 54, 65, 66,

94, 163–64, 586, 598–99; record-keeping by, 6, 298; and Lincoln's inauguration, 14, 53; McClellan and, 53, 54–55, 298; early career of, 53–54; limited scope of intelligence bureau, 53–55; agents of, 54, 84–101, 113, 131 (*see also individual agents*); deserter interrogations, 55, 103, 111, 113–14, 115–17, 167; prisoner interrogations, 55, 111, 113–15, 121–23, 167; and refugee interrogations, 55, 111, 113–15, 117–20, 167; coverage overlaps Baker's, 55–56; Confederate sympathizers and spies in Washington, 56–70, 75–76; and Rose Greenhow, 58, 61, 64–66, 73, 130, 575, 598; and Greenhow's collaborators, 68–70; Maryland-Virginia contraband trade and communication, 73–75; agents' reports during Phony War period, 84–85, 87, 91, 92, 93, 94, 95, 96, 98, 99–100; activities during Phony War, 84–101; use of intercepted letters, 110; loses "E.J. Allen" cover, 110–11; interrogations of runaway slaves, 120–21; salary and payroll of, 113, 295, 595–96; interrogation routines, 113–14; concentration on Virginia theater, 114; disposition of interrogated informants, 114–15; and Peninsula campaign, 147–49, 153–54, 158–61, 376; and Antietam campaign, 213, 215; intelligence after Antietam, 251–54, 255; departs with McClellan, 255, 257; on Burnside, 255; remainder of wartime career, 255; Babcock replaces, 258–59; avoidance of other services, 260
Pinkerton, William, 558
Pipe Creek, 521–22, 528, 532, 536; Order, 521–22
Pittsburgh: fear of Confederate invasion, 452, 456
Pleasonton, Gen. Alfred, 162–63, 264, 287, 293, 342, 351, 588–92; and Antietam campaign, 213–14, 216, 221–22, 224, 227, 228; track-

Pleasonton, Gen. Alfred (*cont.*)
   ing Lee after Antietam, 251, 253;
   and Chancellorsville campaign,
   372, 373, 399, 405; tracking Confederates, 421, 425, 431, 435–36,
   437, 438, *441*, 447, 454, 588–92,
   593; and battle of Brandy Station,
   431–32, 433–35, 442, 588–92;
   claims discovery of Lee's invasion
   movements, 433–35, 588–92; relations with McEntee, 435, 438–39,
   440, 454–55; Gettysburg campaign, 457, 458, 468, 470, 483,
   486, 487, 492, 498, 502, 508, 531,
   588–92; and battle at Aldie, 457–
   58; June 21 assault on Stuart, 470;
   role in Hooker's pursuit of Lee,
   588–92
Plew, Daniel, 292
Pollock, Dr., 155
Pomeroy, Stephen W., 517
pontoons: mishandling of Burnside's
   request for, 259–60; failure to use,
   264; Confederate, 302–3; and
   Chancellorsville campaign, 366,
   372, 377–82
Poolesville, *166, 212, 482, 500;*
   Hooker's headquarters at, 491–92
Pope, Gen. John, 3, 52, 213, 215,
   248, 260, 290, 292, 404, 415, 529,
   569, 586; and Army of Virginia,
   162, 182, 194; at Cedar Mountain,
   163; and Second Bull Run, 182,
   184, 186, 187–91, 192, 193–96,
   197, 198, 199, 200–210, 212, 280;
   use of spies and cavalry, 186, 207–
   10; reputation of, 194, 200; responsibility for loss at Bull Run, 207–10;
   Burnside compared with, 273–74;
   admires Hooker, 280; and intelligence, 569, 570
Porter, Gen. Andrew, 258, 295; as
   Pinkerton's superior, 114; and Antietam campaign, 218, 237, 241, 243
Porter, Gen. Fitz John, 19, 44, 45, 95,
   139, 168, 282, 579; and Peninsula
   campaign, 144, 155, 158, 159, 160;
   and Second Bull Run, 195, 199,
   205, 206; cashiering and exoneration, 202–3

Port Republic, *166,* battle of, 179
Port Royal, S.C., 70–72, 89, 563
Port Royal, Va., *252, 299;* and Chancellorsville campaign, 345, 366
Posey, Carnot, 308, 318, 381
Posey family, 73
positive intelligence, 102; defined,
   294
Potomac River: Maryland-Virginia
   crossings in contraband trade, 73–
   75, 95; Confederates close to commercial traffic, 83–84; McClellan re-
   sponds to blockade, 132;
   Confederate batteries abandoned,
   133, 135; Confederates cross to
   Maryland after Second Bull Run,
   212–13; Federals cross to Maryland
   after Antietam, 250–54; Hooker
   and Confederate batteries, 279;
   Patrick's closing as escape route,
   283; Hooker crosses, 481–83, 484,
   498; Lee crosses into Pennsylvania,
   593–94
Potter, John F., 56–57
Potts, John, 295, 595–96
prisoner informants, 3, 10, 111, 167,
   215, 334, 569; Pinkerton and, 55,
   111, 113–15, 121–23, 322; as spies,
   122–23; and Manassas withdrawal,
   139; in Peninsula campaign, 148;
   Sharpe and, 301–2; and Chancellorsville campaign, 362, 386, 406;
   Lee's concern over, 419; from
   Brandy Station, 437; and Gettysburg campaign, 454, 477
Protzman, William H., 493
provost marshals: Patrick's relations
   with, 284
Puleston, J. Henry, 18

Quincy, Capt., 93, 109

Randolph, George W., 130, 337
Ransom, Robert, 305, 319
Rapidan River, 79, *183, 252, 299,
   418, 441, 476, 539;* front in Second Bull Run, 189–94, 208, 210;
   and Chancellorsville campaign,
   370, 380, 382–83, 391
Rappahannock River, 79, *145, 183,*

299, 317, 371, 398, 418, 422, 441, 445, 469, 476, 539; and Chancellorsville campaign, 344–45, 409; Kelly's Ford crossing, 368–70, 372, 374–75, 377–82; Federal recross after battle, 412–13

Rean, Charles, 158–59

Rebel War Clerk's Diary (Jones), 11

Rebough, Rev., 242

reconnaissance. *See* cavalry reconnaissance

refugee informants, 3, 5, 10, 111, 167, 569; cover as spies, 55, 111, 113–15, 117–20; Pinkerton and, 55, 111, 113–15, 117–20; and Gettysburg campaign, 493

Reno, Gen. Jesse L., 191, 197, 280; and Antietam campaign, 228; killed, 229

Republican Radicals: and arrest of Gen. Stone, 168–69

Revere, Gen. Joseph W., 318

Rex, Dr., 176

Reynolds, Gen. John F., 202, 205, 206, 218, 232, 260, 329, 359, 439; and Fredericksburg campaign, 269, 270; commands First Corps, 282; and Chancellorsville campaign, 371, 384, 385, 386, 388; and battle of Chancellorsville, 388, 392, 393, 409; and Gettysburg campaign, 441, 480, 486, 491, 492, 495, 502–3, 504–5, 507, 508, 510, 511, 512; and battle of Gettysburg, 519, 520–21, 522–23; killed, 524

Rice, Maj. Owen, 399

Richardson, Gen. Israel, 236

Richardson, Col. William H., 309

Richardson, Col. William P., 397

Richmond, 26, 27, 79, 145, 539; telegraph lines, 18; Federal espionage in, 55, 85, 89–91, 95–96, 133, 147, 148–49, 336, 551–57; supposed access to Washington secrets, 64–66, 130; "Secret Line" to, 75; Tredegar iron works, 85, 554; estimates of Confederate defenses at, 97, 100, 104; McClellan's preparation against, 100–101, 135; leakage of plan to evacuate Manassas, 131; report on fortifications, 334; Maddox on fortifications of, 402; Grant's siege of, 549; Dix's threat to, 531; Kilpatrick's raid on, 543; 1865 campaign against, 549–59; Unionist underground in, 551–57

Richmond, Enos, 252–53, 255

Richmond, Fredericksburg and Potomac Railroad, 145, 252, 257, 299, 345, 398, 418

Richmond campaign (1865), 549–59; couriers and, 552–53

Richmond Enquirer, 363

Richmond Examiner, 184, 413, 416, 432

Ricketts, Gen. James, 188, 205

Ringgold, W. H., 117–18, 126, 151; and Urbanna plan, 136–37

Roanoke Island: Confederate defenses at, 97

Robertson, Gen. Beverly H., 420, 425–26, 485, 486, 488, 512, 525

Robinson, J., 425–26, 434

Rodes, Gen. Robert E., 308, 374, 592; estimate of forces of, 124, 376; and Chancellorsville campaign, 374, 384; situation after Chancellorsville, 416, 418; new command, 420; and Gettysburg campaign, 461, 466, 473, 474, 475, 489, 490, 493, 495–96, 507, 512, 513, 515, 517, 519; and battle of Gettysburg, 524, 525, 526, 533

Rose, Luther A., 516, 517

Rosecrans, Gen. William S., 179, 542

Round Top, 523

Rowe, John, 230, 248

runaway slaves. *See* contraband informants

Rush's Lancers, 329

Ruth, Samuel, 257, 345, 551–52, 553–54, 557

St. Louis, Mo.: intelligence in, 19–20

Salem Church, 299, 398, 404, 405

Saunders, William. *See* Buxton, Frank Lacy

Savage's Station: encounter at, 161

Saxe, Marshal, 9

Scammon, Gen. E. P., 461

Scanlon (telegraph operator), 490
Schenck, Gen. Robert C., 173, 281,
    313, 323, 327, 336, 340, 402, 419;
    and battle of Winchester, 444–45,
    446, 447, 448, 450, 451, 452, 572–
    73; and Gettysburg campaign, 457,
    460, 471, 479, 496, 516, 518
Schurz, Gen. Carl, 379–80; and battle
    of Chancellorsville, 397, 400; and
    battle of Gettysburg, 525
Scott, F. T., 514, 515
Scott, Col. Henry L., 10–11
Scott, Thomas A., 58, 242–43, 247,
    516
Scott, William H., 147, 176
Scott, Gen. Winfield: as general-in-
    chief of U.S. Army, 9, 10–11, 12,
    13, 15, 18, 19, 25, 26, 27, 35, 47,
    48, 77, 78, 80; in Mexican War, 9;
    and First Bull Run, 47, 48, 49, 50,
    580; relations with McClellan, 78;
    retirement of, 78, 80; and McClel-
    lan's estimates of enemy forces,
    103; relations with Hooker, 277
scouting, 3, 55, 569; and security of
    intelligence, 112; and Peninsula
    campaign, 154–55, 156; Shenan-
    doah Valley campaign, 178–79; An-
    tietam campaign, 215, 218–22; Pal-
    mer and, 218–22, 218–22 (see also
    Palmer), 225, 226, 227, 230, 231,
    233, 234, 240, 294, 321, 341, 363,
    472, 514, 569; Hooker and, 278;
    Sharpe and, 294, 298; Babcock on,
    322; on Northern Neck, 326, 327–
    28, 334, 338; Chancellorsville cam-
    paign, 344, 350–51; battle of Chan-
    cellorsville, 398–99; Gettysburg
    campaign, 456–57, 471–72; after
    Gettysburg, 541–42, 596
Scully, John, 131, 148, 363; arrest of,
    148–49
secession, 11, 12, 15–16
"secession clerks," 11, 57–58
Second Corps (Confederate), 550
    (see also Early; Ewell; Jackson); reor-
    ganized, 420–21; in Pennsylvania,
    485, 546
Second Corps (Federal; see also indi-
    vidual commanders): at Chancellors-

ville, 371; in Gettysburg campaign,
    509, 526
Second World War: intelligence in,
    239–40, 299
secret ink, 296, 423
secret service: use of term in 1860s,
    8; Hooker and, 287; Sharpe and,
    287–97 (see also Bureau of Military
    Information)
Secret Service Accounts, 595–96
Secret Service Bureau (Confederate),
    74, 75
Secret Service Fund, 294, 295, 595–
    96
Seddon, James, 499
Seddon, Maj. John, 324
Seddon, Mrs. John, 354
Sedgwick, Gen. John, 292, 542; com-
    mands Sixth Corps, 282; in Chan-
    cellorsville campaign, 352–53, 359,
    369–71, 371, 372, 373, 377, 379,
    380, 383, 384, 385, 386, 387; and
    battle of Chancellorsville, 388, 390,
    391, 392, 393, 394, 395, 404, 405,
    408, 408, 409, 410; seeking infor-
    mation on enemy moves, 425;
    moves after Chancellorsville, 441;
    and Gettysburg campaign, 455,
    512, 528
Seiders, John A., 515
Seminary Ridge, 525
Semmes, Gen. Paul J., 308, 361
Seven Days battles, 123, 159–62, 163,
    164, 280, 322, 415, 582
Seven Pines, 145; battle of, 156–57,
    160, 178, 221, 322
Seward, William H., 13, 26, 67, 71,
    88, 103, 285, 289, 291, 336, 557
Sharpe, Col. George Henry, 3–4, 5,
    113, 287–97, 318, 327, 328, 402,
    571, 591, 595, 596, 598; and secret
    service organization, 287, 291–97;
    and Patrick, 287–88, 546; back-
    ground of, 288–91; plan to use mili-
    tary spies, 291–92, 295–97; use of
    civilian agents, 292–93; selects
    McEntee as assistant, 293; and bal-
    loon surveillance, 298, 300; and
    cavalry reconnaissance, 298, 300;
    and flag-signal intercepts, 298; and

all-source intelligence, 298–99,
300; and interrogations, 301; inter-
rogates Cline, 308; tracking Longstreet, 311–13; reports to Hooker
on Bureau's findings, 318–22; and
McPhail, 335–36, 341; and Chancellorsville campaign, 349, 351,
352, 373–74, 377, 379, 382, 383,
404, 406, 410, 413; and care for
casualties after battle, 412–13; and
tracking of Lee's movements, 416–
18, 421–22, 423, 424, 425, 426,
427, 428–29, 431, 434, 435, 437,
439, 447; and battle of Winchester,
447–48; and Gettysburg campaign,
455, 456, 457, 458, 460, 461, 462,
463, 465, 466, 467, 470–71, 473,
475, 477, 480, 484, 486, 491, 493,
494, 495, 496, 497, 502, 503, 504,
508, 510, 511, 569; size of Bureau,
460; and battle of Gettysburg, 526,
527, 528, 529, 530, 532–33, 536,
569; report to Meade at council of
war, 527–28; intelligence gathering
after Gettysburg, 540–42, 543, 544–
45; intelligence reporting to Grant,
543–44, 546–47, 548–49,6; and
Richmond/Petersburg campaigns,
550–51, 552, 553; and Richmond
underground, 551, 552, 553; issues
Lee parole, 557; postwar career,
557–58
Sharpe, Henry G., 558
Shenandoah, Confederate Army of
the, 165; at First Bull Run, 29–30,
31, 32, 33, 37, 40, 43, 45, 46, 47,
49, 50; estimates of strength, 45–
46; McClellan estimates of
strength, 124–25, 128; in Peninsula campaign, 157–58
Shenandoah, Department of: Hooker
reorganizes, 281
Shenandoah, Union Army of the,
165, 543–44
Shenandoah Valley campaign of
1862, 87, 165–81, 166, 182; Gen.
Banks and, 165, 168, 169–75, 181;
balloon surveillance of Leesburg,
166–67; battle of Kernstown, 170–
71; Gen. Frémont, 171, 172, 177–

78, 179, 180, 181; Gen. Shields,
171, 172, 173, 174, 177, 180; Gen.
McDowell, 173–74; battle at Front
Royal, 174–75, 176, 177; Federal
scouting, 178–79; battles at Cross
Keys and Port Republic, 179, 180;
Confederate intelligence successes,
563; Federal intelligence failures,
566
Sheridan, Gen. Philip, 187, 545, 547,
549–50
Sherman, R. A., 94
Sherman, Gen. Thomas W., 70, 71
Sherman, Gen. William T., 433, 545,
596
Shields, Gen. James: and Shenandoah Valley campaign, 171, 172,
173, 174, 177, 180
Shiloh, battle of, 184
Shorb, Jacob M., 167, 169
Sickles, Gen. Daniel, 269, 346–47,
578; commands Third Corps, 281–
82, 289, 346; and Chancellorsville
campaign, 371, 385; and battle of
Chancellorsville, 387, 388, 391,
398, 409; moves after Chancellorsville, 441; and Gettysburg campaign, 512, 524; and battle of Gettysburg, 526
Sigel, Gen. Franz, 176, 413, 423, 436,
545; and Second Bull Run, 182,
188, 190, 191, 192, 197, 198, 199,
200, 205; and Fredericksburg campaign, 256, 261, 262, 263, 264, 266;
commands Eleventh Corps, 282;
and Shenandoah army, 543–44
Sigfouse, John, 507
Signal Corps (Confederate), 337 (see
also Secret Service Bureau); at First
Bull Run, 39–40, 265; and Maryland espionage, 74; and Peninsula
campaign, 148, 265; and
Fredericksburg campaign, 264–66;
and Chancellorsville campaign,
347–48, 355–57; gains possession
of Federals' code, 347–48; and Gettysburg campaign, 473, 475; and
Petersburg campaign, 551
Signal Corps (Federal), 4, 5, 6, 37–
38, 39, 55, 74, 336, 570; at Sugar

Signal Corps (Federal) (*cont.*)
Loaf Mountain, 83, 211, *212;* and
Peninsula campaign, 146–47, 152;
party attached to Pleasonton, 251;
and Fredericksburg campaign,
264–66; Sharpe and, 298, 300; and
Chancellorsville campaign, 344,
347–48, 355–57, 374, 384, 385,
389, 393, 396; after Chancellorsville, 418, 419, 423, 435; loss of
confidence in, 419–20; ballooning
and, 443; and Gettysburg campaign, 455, 471, 483; after Gettysburg, 540–41; and Peters-
burg/Richmond campaign,
540–41, 542–43, 545–46, 550
signal deception, 344, 347–49, 426
Signal Hill, Manassas, 39–40
Silver, Catherine, 315
Silver, Isaac, 272, 273, 292, 315–18,
332, 343, 358, 361, 423, 541–42,
548, 549; report on Confederate
forces, 320, 361; and Chancellorsville campaign, 360–62, 369, 370,
374–75, 383, 389; 1864–65 service, 542, 548; arrest by Confederates, 549
Silver farm, *316*
Simpson, Capt. Thomas H., 44, 45, 46
Sixth Corps, 546 (*see also* Sedgwick);
and Chancellorsville, 370; and Gettysburg campaign, *500,* 501, 508–
9, 524, 525–26, 527
Skinker, John Howard, 260–61, 267,
292, 294, 296, 297, 312, 313–15,
342, 350; report on Confederate
forces, 320; and Chancellorsville
campaign, 350–52, 364, 368, 374,
375; tracking Confederates after
Chancellorsville, 425, 434
Skinker, Thomas, 314
Skinker's Neck, *252;* in
Fredericksburg campaign, 267,
268–69
slaves, runaway. *See*
contraband informants
Slemmer, Lt. Adam J., 16–17
Slocum, Gen. Henry W., 229, 271,
313, 346–47; commands Twelfth
Corps, 282, 346; and Chancellors-

ville campaign, *371,* 372, 378, 379,
384, 387, 390, 391; and battle of
Chancellorsville, 387, 390, 391,
395, 396, *398,* 404, 409, 413;
moves after Chancellorsville, *441;*
and Gettysburg campaign, 468,
478, 481, *512;* and battle of Gettysburg, 524, 528, 529, 530, 533
Smith, Gen. Edmund Kirby, 34
Smith, George S., 195, 292, 294, 296,
297, 342, 343, 363, 427–28, 430,
438–39, 440, 455
Smith, Gen. Gustavus W., 156, 167,
313
Smith, Henry M., 111
Smith, Gen. William F., 81, 82; and
Fredericksburg campaign, 268,
269, 272; commands Ninth Corps,
302; and Petersburg campaign, 549
Smithson, William T., 69, 70
Smitley, C. W. D., 176
smugglers. *See also* contraband mail
and materials: spies as, 291–92,
296, 333, 335, 340–41, 403, 557;
on Northern Neck, 326, 327–28,
334, 338
Snyder, Joseph E., 266–67, 334, 363,
423
Sorrel, Maj. G. Moxley, 265–66, 499
South: Union sympathizers in, 55; rumors of Federal naval expeditions,
70–73
South Carolina: secession of, 12, 15–
16
South Mountain, *212, 474, 476, 485;*
battle of, 228–29, 230, 232–33,
238, 248, 275, 289, 586
Special Orders No. 191, 222–24
spies (*see also individual spies and campaigns*): memoirs of, 2–3, 25–26,
54, 60, 64–66, 94, 163–64, 586,
598–99; in Washington, D.C., 11–
12, 13, 14, 56–70, 75–76; compensation for, 21, 595–96; in Richmond, 55, 85, 89–91, 95–96, 133,
147, 148–49, 336, 551–57; refugee
informants as, 55, 111, 113–15,
117–20; prisoner informants as,
122–23; Halleck defines, 184, 245;
Hooker and, 278, 279, 286;

Sharpe's use of military men as, 291–92, 295–97, 303–10; in Gettysburg campaign, 456–57, 471–72, 488, 502, 503–4; provided by Pennsylvania Central Railroad, 514; letters and papers as sources, 598

Spotsylvania Court House, 252, 299, *371, 539;* battle, 544–45

Sprague, William, 259

Spy of the Rebellion (Pinkerton), 3, 54, 65, 66, 94, 163–64, 586, 598–99

Stahel, Gen. Julius, 448, 492, 508

Stanley, Marcus Aurelius Cicero, 358

Stanton, Edwin M., 17, 27, 57, 70, 143, 172, 182, 183, 243, 255, 272, 285, 318, 345, 350, 365, 428, 442–43, 555; as attorney general, 11, 12, 15; as secretary of war, 54; and Pinkerton, 54; and McClellan's estimates of enemy forces, 106, 107, 113, 581; and Peninsula campaign, 151, 155, 159; and arrest of Gen. Stone, 169; and Shenandoah Valley campaign, 172, 174, 178; and Stine case, 245; and battle of Winchester, 445, 446, 449; and Gettysburg campaign, 456, 472, 484, 494, 532

Staub, Dick, 170

Steele, John, 291

Stein, E. H., 56, 85–86, 100, 131, 148; on Confederate forces, 86

Stein, Mrs. E. H., 85

Steinwehr, Gen. Adolph von, 400, 525

Steuart, Gen. George H. ("Maryland"), 99; and Gettysburg campaign, *474,* 490

Stevens, Gen. Isaac, 205

Stevens, Thaddeus, 218

Stewart, Henry A., 74–75, 91, 94

Stine, Rev. I. J., 230, 231, 341, 471; arrest of, 241–45, 248–49; compensation of, 248–49, 595

Stone, Gen. Charles P., 13–14, 15, 19, 24, 80, 81, 83, 165, 166; and Corps of Observation, 166–67; arrest of, 168–69, 203, 282; services sought by Hooker, 282

Stone, Louis P., 179, 180, 363

Stoneman, Gen. George, 142, 330, 346, 352, 413, 427; commands Cavalry Corps, 281–82; in Chancellorsville campaign, 360, 362, 364, 366–67, 368, 369, 370, 372, 373, 375, 378, 391, 402, 407

Stone's River, battle of, 249

Stoughton, Gen. Edwin H., 326

Strange, E. M., 324

Strother, David Hunter, 44–47, 50, 51, 52, 168, 169–70, 174, 195, 205, 253, 579–80

Stuart, Gen. James E. B. (Jeb), 6, 84, 211, 213, 243, 261, 262, 264, 273, 304, 305, 311, 326, 330, 331, 333, 353, 436, 542, 544, 592; and First Bull Run, 32, 43–44, 579; in Peninsula campaign, 157; rides around McClellan's army, 157; in Second Bull Run campaign, 190, 192, 193, 199, 200; captures Pope's files, 196; and Antietam campaign, 216, 224; again rides around McClellan's army, 243, 250; and Fredericksburg campaign, 271; Sharpe's report on, 319, 320; moves headquarters to Culpeper, 349; and Chancellorsville campaign, 353, 356, 363, 367, 369, 373, 376, 378, 379, 380, 381, 382; estimate of forces, 376, 591; in battle of Chancellorsville, 392, 404, *408;* discovers Federals' exposed wing, 392, 399; moves after Chancellorsville, 415, *418,* 424, 425, 428, 429, 430, 431, 432, 433–34, 439, *441,* 446, 447–48, 454; and reorganization of forces, 420, 421; reports on enlarged forces of, 425–26, 428, 433; and battle of Brandy Station, 431–32, 463, 589, 590, 591; and Gettysburg campaign, 454, 458, 459, 460, 465, 466, 468, *469,* 470, 481, *482,* 483, *485,* 486–88, 489, 508, *512,* 515, 535; Pleasonton's June 21 assault on, 470; marches to Pennsylvania on right of Federals, 486–88, 489, 496–97, 498, 501, 505, 508; raid through Maryland, 498–99, *500,* 505, 508; destroys telegraph lines, 502; fatal wounding of, 545

Sturges Rifles, 257, 258

Stypes, Margaret, 116

Sugar Loaf Mountain, 79, 166, 183, 212; Signal Corps at, 83, 211, 212

Sumner, Edwin V., 137, 156, 161, 206, 214, 236; and Fredericksburg campaign, 268, 273

sutlers, 322–23, 358

Swinton, William, Campaigns of the Army of the Potomac, 382–83, 591, 593

Sykes, Gen. George, 390, 512, 528

Sypher, J. R., 325

Taliaferro, James, 57, 268

Taylor, Lt. Peter A., 265, 266, 302; and battle of Chancellorsville, 389, 391, 395

Taylor, Gen. Richard, 175

Taylor, Gen. Zachary, 277

telegraph lines, 4–5, 11–12, 18–19, 326, 569; military use of, 37–38; and Peninsula campaign, 146–47, 152–53; Sharpe and, 298; in Chancellorsville campaign, 389–90; and Gettysburg campaign, 489, 490, 492, 496, 497, 502, 516

telescope observation, 4, 211. See also Signal Corps

Third Corps (Confederate), 549 (see also Hill, A. P.); organized, 420; in Pennsylvania, 485

Third Corps (Federal; see also Sickles): and Chancellorsville campaign, 371, 395, 396; and Gettysburg campaign, 509, 524, 526

Third Indiana Cavalry, 73, 84, 279, 292, 552

Thom, William N., 351

Thomas, Col. George H., 43, 249, 558–59

Thompson, Gen. Michael, 68, 69, 70

Thoroughfare Gap, 79, 183, 476; and Gettysburg campaign, 458

Tod, David, 456

Toombs, Robert, 232

Topographical Engineers, 153

topography: and First Bull Run, 44–46; and Peninsula campaign, 153–54

trading post, front-line: restriction of, 323

Tredegar iron works, Richmond, 85, 554

Trenis, Bertram E., 414

Trimble, Gen. Isaac R., 308, 312, 319, 321, 374, 420, 454; in Chancellorsville campaign, 374, 376, 377, 384; situation after Chancellorsville, 416, 418

Tull, Charles, 168

Turner, Lt. Col. Levi C., 27, 192, 245, 285–86, 324, 340, 341, 365; as source, 596–97

Tweed ring, 557–58

Twelfth Corps (Army of the Potomac), 256, 542 (see also Slocum); in Chancellorsville campaign, 368, 370, 380, 388, 395; in Gettysburg campaign, 501, 502, 509, 524, 526, 527, 533

Tyler, Gen. Daniel, 38, 50; in Gettysburg campaign, 460, 461, 463, 469, 472, 473, 475, 477, 478, 480, 482, 494

Tyler, George E., 95

Ulster Guard, 288

United States Military Telegraph, 38, 326

United States Mine Ford, 299, 317, 371; and Chancellorsville campaign, 344–45, 361, 364, 366, 369, 370, 371, 373, 375, 381, 389, 405, 412

United States Secret Service, establishment of, 294

United States Secret Service, History of the (Baker), 65, 599

Urbanna plan: of McClellan, 135–37, 141, 142–43, 145

U.S. Army: at beginning of Civil War, 8, 9, 10, 13; headquarters relocated to Washington, 13

U.S. Military Telegraph: and Peninsula campaign, 146–47, 152–53

Van Buren, Col. Daniel T., 291, 300, 301, 335, 338

Van Camp, Dr. Aaron, 68, 69, 70, 71

Van Lew, Elizabeth, 551–53, 554, 557
Van Lew, John, 552
Vicksburg, siege of, 416, 449, 531, 535
Vienna-Dranesville: reconnaissance around, 83, 84
Virginia: Maryland contraband trade, 73–75, 95
Virginia (ironclad), 96, 137–38; destroyed, 155
Virginia Central Railroad, *79, 145, 166, 183, 418,* 548
visitor passes: military countersigning of, 323
visual observation, 3, 570. *See also* balloon surveillance; Signal Corps
visual signaling. *See* Signal Corps
von Gilsa, Col. Leopold, 396, 398, 399

Wadsworth, Gen. James S., 112–13, 329, 366, 523, 524
Walker, Dabney, 295
Walker, Gen. Francis, 400
Walker, Gen. John G., 220–21, 223, 224, 234, 239
Walker, Leroy P., 26, 42–43
Walker, William, 462
Wardener, Rudolph E. de, 326
War of 1812: espionage in, 8–9
War of Independence: intelligence in, 8, 298–99, 496, 541
War of the Rebellion: Official Records. See Official Records
Warren, Gen. Gouverneur K., 443
Warwick River, 150–51
Washington, George: intelligence operations, 8, 9, 298, 496, 541
Washington, Thomas, 73
Washington: Confederate sympathizers and spies in, 11–12, 13, 14, 56–70, 75–76; fear of plots against Lincoln's inauguration, 13–15; defenses at outbreak of war, 17–19; telegraph lines, 18–19, 146–47; secret service in, 21–23, 27; Greeenhow's espionage in, 58–68, 130, 575–78; fear of Confederate attack after First Bull Run, 77, 80–82;

McClellan and defense of, 77–82; blockade of, 83–84; fear of espionage in, 130; Pope and defense of, 184; fears after Second Bull Run, 212–13, 214; Clay Guard, 282
Washington, Department of, 21, 77; Hooker reorganizes, 281
Washington Morning Chronicle, 349–50
Washington Star, 110–11, 176
Watson, Peter H., 255; Patrick and, 284, 285
Webster, Timothy, 55, 89–91, 92, 95, 97–101, 107, 108, 109, 110, 131, 133, 147, 151, 296, 336, 363, 557; intelligence from Kentucky, 114; arrest and execution, 148–49, 598–99
Welles, Gideon, 80, 581
Westminster, Md., *476, 485, 497, 500, 512, 539*
West Point, Va., *79, 145, 539;* and Urbanna plan, 135, 136, 142; and Peninsula campaign, 154–55
Wheeling Intelligencer, 178
White, A. M., 144
White, Capt. (guerrilla), 216
White, Elijah, 144, 463
White, Gen. Julius, 204, 217, 219
Whiting, W. H. C.: estimate of forces of, 124; and advance of Federals on Potomac, 132, 139; joins Jackson's army, 157–58
Whitlock, Charles, 185, 252, 253, 255, 263, 313
Wigfall, Louis T., 12, 96
Wiggins, Lt. John, 538
Wilcox, Cadmus, 308, 318, 361
Wilcox, Richard, 17
Wilderness, battle of the, 544, 546
Wilderness, the, 307; in battle of Chancellorsville, 401
Williams, Gen. Alpheus, 222
Williams, D. F., 18
Williams, Hosea H. H., 122
Williams, Gen. Seth, 509–10
Williamsburg, *145*
Williamsburg, battle of, 174
Willich, Gen. August, 413
Wilson, Henry, 57, 63–64, 110, 575
Wilson, William Bender, 219, 220, 221, 222, 226, 227, 233–34, 240,

Wilson, William Bender (*cont.*)
242, 472; and Gettysburg campaign, 514
Winchester, *30, 79, 166, 183, 212,
441, 459, 482, 485, 539;* Confeder-
ate forces at, 35, 43, 44, 47, 48, 90,
151; McClellan's estimate of forces
at, 125
Winchester, E., 464, 489
Winchester, first battle of, 87
Winchester, second battle of, 444–53,
454, 455, 460, 468, 572–74; Col.
Sharpe and, 447–48; Federals' mis-
takes compared to Pearl Harbor,
572–74
Winchester Rifles, 115
Winder, Gen. John H., 89, 90, 93, 97–
98, 100, 119, 149, 191, 247, 363
Winder, Capt. William, 97–98
Wise, Gen. H. A., 402
Wise, John, 38
Wofford, Gen. W. T., 308
Wood, William P., 247

Wool, Gen. John E., 9, 138,
149, 214, 323, 335–36; and
Peninsula campaign, 150–51, 153
Worth, William, 277
Wright, Gen. A. R., 380–81
Wright, Charley, 437–38, 439, 440,
442, 535, 592
Wright, Rebecca, 550

Yager, Ernest, 292, 297, 303–4, 305,
306, 309, 367; and enemy activities
after Chancellorsville, 414–15, 430–
31
York, *485, 500, 512, 539;* surrender
of, 496
York River Railroad, 136–37, 154–55
Yorktown, *145,* 146, 148; and Peninsula campaign, 150–51, 160, 300;
Johnston's evacuation of, 151–53,
160
Youmeycake, Charles, 21
Young, Maj. Henry H., 547